Life's hidden Meaning

dedicated to the advancement of consciousness in humanity

Ageless Wisdom Publishers, Book One LLC; Tempe, AZ USA

Acknowledgements

For the use of Synthetic Yoga™ and the Synthetic Yoga Lotus™ ©1989 and for all art in the book, excepting that listed below, Ageless Wisdom Distributors and Publishers LLC

For clipart on the front and back cover and some of the illustrations within the book, Canvas by Deneba Systems Inc. with some additional clipart from CorelDRAW by Corel Corporation

For some additional clipart used in some of the illustrations within the book, Art Today by Zedcor, Inc. and Arts and Letters Editor by Computer Support Corporation

Special Thanks

Hart Graphics of Austin, Texas, for very helpful and courteous service and the highest quality of professional printing work

First Edition and Printing
Ageless Wisdom Publishers, Book One LLC; Tempe, AZ USA
Published and Printed in the United States of America, 1999

ISBN (pbk.): 0-9648483-0-9

About the Author...To assist the readers of *Life's Hidden Meaning* and of other material created by the author, only a very general series of statements is being conveyed with regard to the author's life. It is hoped that this brevity will assist readers by not encouraging either an enamoured and possibly glamoured response, or a potential and more specific emotional reaction to information that might be included in a detailed biography. The author has chosen to write under a pseudonym, mostly to support the just-mentioned reasons concerning those who might meet him and know him outside of his role as author and teacher. For quite a number of years, the author has disciplined himself for spiritual improvement in order to serve others. His life has been completely dedicated in this way, quite consistently, for a long time. He and Ageless Wisdom Distributors have a certain mission of service to the world; *Life's Hidden Meaning* is a relatively important part of that service, but only a small part. The author asserts that this and his other spiritual creations are to stand on their own merit relative to their value in assisting others; the more that this merit is evaluated on its own—without evaluating its creator—the greater its importance and its help to others who are in need of what is offered. The author is attempting to truly love those whom he can be of assistance to, and is aware of nothing that he has received or will receive for himself personally in return. He has, for many years, consistently done what he could to create into service for others what most likely would otherwise have been personal gains. He attempts to create truth in the minds of others as much as he possibly can. To his students within the group that they, together, comprise, he may be an example of a certain result of all of that is stated above about him, yet he is mostly invisible to most others who are members of humanity. Over time, the author's role may change, and some of these statements may no longer be valid; thus that which is stated herein is accurate as of the publishing date of this first edition of *Life's Hidden Meaning*.

About the Group...Ageless Wisdom Distributors has been in continuous existence since the mid-1980's. Several of its present-day members have been a part of this group since its inception. Ageless Wisdom Distributors is a spiritual group that has a second ray focus and has accepted a very large mission of service to the world. Those who have become a part of this service are nearly continuously giving as wisely as possible, and create significant amounts of virtue. As a second ray spiritual group, one of the many functions that each member has is to become a teacher of everything contained within this volume and, in addition, of a great deal more information as well. The members of this group have been and still are creative experimenters in developing a new mental yoga that includes the first scientific view and explanations of the mental energies within the causal body, or the spiritual lotus. These new views and explanations are an integral part of Synthetic Yoga, as another part of the creative mission of Ageless Wisdom Distributors.

About the Construction of This Book...*Life's Hidden Meaning* was created to serve several categories of potential readers. In order to meet the different requirements for each category, the book has been produced as economically as possible while still being of exceptionally high quality so that it will last through numerous readings and general use as a reference source. A "paper" back was chosen for its first edition in order to keep costs low; however, for durability the cover stock that was chosen is over forty percent heavier than what is industry standard. Also, the cover is coated on both sides to reduce soiling on the inside of it. The binding is a more durable and easier to use "lay-flat" design that reduces stress on the binding as the book is read, while significantly increasing its strength in holding together its pages—without moving up to the very costly sewn binding. The highest quality of vellum paper was chosen, to provide a very bright white background for easier reading and a higher resistance to tears and fraying. The text printing was done on a heated press for very crisp and fine letters and illustrations. The cover was printed on a very high quality, higher-resolution sheet fed four-color press. It is hoped that the balance of cost versus quality, readability, and lasting value can be seen and appreciated by those who will avail themselves of *Life's Hidden Meaning*.

The magnitude of the subject matter of this book has made its creation a particularly arduous task because human and financial resources were very limited, and the book's size and complexity of information pushed these resources to tenuous levels. The great difficulty in understanding the material caused its editing to be fifty to sixty times slower than was the writing, even though the editing was done by co-members of Ageless Wisdom Distributors. Illustrations were done by different group members at different times. All of these factors contributed to a work of unusual construction, which in many ways did not adhere to one or more conventions of "proper" professional book publishing. Some criticism is likely to arise relative to these issues. However, despite the rough edges and notwithstanding any small inaccuracies in a few of the vast number of "how's" presented, if the opinion of most of those who have read *Life's Hidden Meaning* prior to its publication is to be accepted, the content of the book and its method of conceptual explanation carry it to a very high level of credibility. Still, it is the intention of this author and of Ageless Wisdom Distributors that future editions will be improvements over the original.

There are very likely to be some factual errors in the book. The area most vulnerable to being inaccurate concerns the "exact" dates of prehistoric events of hidden civilizations. The reason is that the source of information for some of these dates is the mental plane akashic record, which can be inaccurate; in addition, some of the circumstances recounted may be in error for the same reason. The author is aware that some other spiritual books and articles offer information about dates and circumstances that differs from what is presented in *Life's Hidden Meaning*. He poses the suggestion that any esoteric prehistoric date be interpreted with a ten percent margin of error. Individual incidents as described can be somewhat integrated allegorically into their underlying concepts until greater levels of evidence support or disprove the author's awareness of them. None of the major concepts presented, as far as the author is aware, contradict any other ones when all of their given explanations are considered. Because some concepts are so difficult for many readers to understand, the reader is encouraged to first try reading additional related sections of the book in order to improve his or her comprehension before assuming that the material is in error. The author and Ageless Wisdom Distributors are very concerned about errors in any concepts, especially spiritual concepts, and are available for communication regarding any potential corrections.

The emphasis of this book is not on the complete accuracy of all of its information, although accuracy certainly is important; rather, the emphasis is on raising the understanding, or consciousness, of its readers so that the *hidden* meaning of life can be revealed to them. Because of this emphasis, over ninety-five percent on average of the information known to the author regarding each area of information covered has not been included in the book. Some of this unincluded information has been previously written about and taught by the author, in over three hundred written articles and more than one thousand lecture tapes of one to two hours each. This much information in book form would exceed the average encyclopedia set, and would hinder a reader's development of understanding life's hidden meaning because the major concepts would be likely to become obscured in many readers' minds. There is no question that the accuracy of the information would be greater with a more exhaustive inclusion of factors and the many exceptions, as well, that contribute to each concept. However, as stated above, one of the book's major purposes is to raise consciousness, and information is being used as a tool, or a means of raising consciousness and is balanced with a number of other factors. Too much information causes an imbalance among all the necessary conditions for raising consciousness, and can ruin the desired effect.

The author makes no claims with regard to his level of consciousness, education, recognition by others concerning his competency on the subject matter, or any factors at all to convince the readers that they should, without further proof, *believe* what he has written. The author and Ageless Wisdom Distributors do want as many people who can understand *Life's Hidden Meaning* to find it and have the opportunity to read it. This book has been written to include many whole concepts, or "why's," behind what is stated. These concepts give the readers a method of verifying the information's accuracy by being able to test the concepts' effects concerning both past incidents in the reader's memory and future experimentation. The author does not want, and deliberately has made it difficult for, readers to *believe* the truth of this work without applying significant amounts of analytical thought, which leads to whole mental thought. The author is attempting to teach—and not preach—various spiritual understandings. Some readers may miss having a preaching element in the text, but for consciousness to become more permanently raised, and more unconditionally so, each reader needs to individually convince himself or herself of this book's validity (or lack thereof, where and if possible) using wisdom to create the truth in her or his own mind.

To assist some readers of this book and others who might not read it, the author and Ageless Wisdom Distributors are (slowly, at present) developing an interactive compact digital disc and also an animated video that more visually and entertainingly explain some of the concepts. As additional potential assistance becomes available, these learning tools could become offered at some (not-too-distant) point in time. Resources for these endeavors have had to be prioritized secondary to the publishing of this book, and possibly even to the publishing of some subsequent ones.

At the end of *Life's Hidden Meaning* is information about how to contact the author and Ageless Wisdom Distributors, who together produced the book. Not everyone who contacts them with questions will receive detailed answers, because of time constraints; sometimes all that will be conveyed will be a simple reference to a page that may need to be read (or reread). The glossary may be of particular assistance to some readers who may lack an understanding of certain words that are used. Readers of *Life's Hidden Meaning* who seek to co-serve in some way with the spiritual group known as Ageless Wisdom Distributors would facilitate that communication by stating that as their reason for contacting the group. Also, this group is interested in knowing about the work of other groups who are functioning spiritually, or who are creating more virtue. Finally, constructive criticism and/or comments by those who find this material helpful or by those who do not are welcome, in that they might provide perspective about the book's effects on its readers and where and how it can be improved.

The reading guide that follows the introduction may assist the readers in individually determining the most helpful order for each of them to read the chapters. In addition, this reading guide may assist some readers in better understanding the rays of their personalities and mental bodies (or both), or the ways in which their personalities and minds tend to function.

What follows in this paragraph is technical and will probably be difficult for some readers to understand without first having read the book. However, this information needs to be included in the preface because it applies to the entirety of the book and is relevant prior to the book being read. Much of the information contained in *Life's Hidden Meaning* is likely to produce some amount of controversy because it provides new, unhidden concepts that expose a different side—often a third one—to issues that are controversial. The cause of this effect is that lower, less unified concepts that are more separative and selfish, and are heavily plagued by higher mental pairs of opposites in their construction of relatively less truth, are sometimes raised in this book into the spiritual mind—or to a higher position in the spiritual mind, if already there—wherein more truth is created and the lower pairs of opposites become unified. Those readers who have egotism blocking these higher spiritual parts of their minds may tend to react emotionally, by having some emotions connected to the lower, more separative concepts and these concepts' mental effects, or their thoughtforms. Thus some readers of *Life's Hidden Meaning* may become offended by some of the concepts that it offers. Others of its readers, even those who find the book's concepts to be largely correct, may hesitate to openly support these concepts because of feared reprisals from other people.

By promoting sharing and cooperation, unconditional love, truth, and beauty, the information in this book was written and is presented in ways that attempt to increase inclusiveness in its readers, as well as in those who do not read the book but have contact with some of the people who do. This attempt involves a process of having an effect on the readers' consciousness, rather than just providing information. Also, the book is designed to attract people to it who will read most of it and who, as they do, will gain more understanding of the meaning in life. Many of the readers of this work may have somewhat different to very different theories and beliefs concerning its content. The author and Ageless Wisdom Distributors do their best to think inclusively and are attempting to convey that the similarities between, potentially, the thought of most of its readers and the book's concepts will be found in the seeking of truth with understanding. It is suggested that those who are seekers of both truth and understanding are usually also attempting to create more wisdom and love, or the giving of wisdom. Having these qualities in common will be likely to create a consensus that bridges the differences between many readers' differing theories and beliefs and the concepts contained within *Life's Hidden Meaning*. It is important to the author and to Ageless Wisdom Distributors to convey that while this work is offered with the motive and labor to make its information as accurate as possible, they do assume it to contain some errors and, further, it is possible that some of these errors could be serious ones that would affect the information's overall accuracy. This book was created as a tool to help teach those seeking to understand its information. The book is not offered as a proof that its contents are right—which would emphasize its information as being its most important attribute—but as an attempt to share understanding to help people become more one with all. To some people, the information in *Life's Hidden Meaning* may be "politically incorrect," or not within the current policymaking of society, while its purpose and the overall effects on its readers—and on others—may to these same people or others be quite "politically correct." The author chose information that he concluded would create the greatest effect of helping the largest number of readers to achieve the highest level of understanding the hidden meaning of life.

Certain subject areas were chosen to exemplify the basic concepts regarding life's hidden meaning. These areas are the ones in which many people already focus considerable time and energy in deriving unhidden meaning from life, and were chosen for this reason. Included within these subjects are human sexual activities; relationships with pets; communication with and interaction with other people; various living conditions that encompass health, welfare, and family life, including children; and the ways in which people may respond to their and others' control of some material objects. Each of these areas holds significant hidden meaning in life that most people can relate to in their own lives.

How God is or, by some, is not seen is another consistent area of focus in general; however, *specific* ways of experiencing and/or relating to God, which would constitute more of religious conviction, are not addressed. Therefore, this text attempts to avoid being a religious doctrine, although some readers may find otherwise. That perception may occur because the book's concepts assert both the existence of God and what God generally is, along with some of God's purposes and methods of attaining greater levels of them—but certainly not all of either. If the reader can accept that there are elements of every religion that are conflictive with other religions (because religions are created by humans, who are imperfect), then this book's concepts are not likely to be found contradictory to the fundamental concepts of most religions. Some of the information in *Life's Hidden Meaning* may contradict numerous doctrines in each specific religion—still without attempting to be a religion itself, but to augment existing ones. Those who find their religions to be perfect are much more likely to find *Life's Hidden Meaning* to be a repudiation of their convictions. The *rejection* of this book by anyone in that group of people who read it may still unhide some meaning in that person's life, through the paradox of the inclusiveness of God—no matter how one does or does not relate to God.

Life's hidden meaning is the meaning in life that many people cannot find. It is hidden, or esoteric, to these people because they lack understanding, or a high enough consciousness, to create it. Those who seek life's hidden meaning, while many others do not, do so because they already understand and have created in their lives most of the meaning in life that is not hidden. This unhidden meaning involves many ways of increasing a person's self, or who a person has created herself or himself into and understands herself or himself to be. The hidden meaning of life comes from creating one's self into more than what a self is, and into something much greater than a self. This creation is accomplished through a remarkable journey and transformation that does not involve a certain prescription that can be universally applied by all people. Rather, it is a process of raising consciousness and of choosing to dramatically improve, over time, one's senses and the synthesis of the information that the senses supply, which becomes knowledge. This book explains the process of improving one's consciousness and senses, and, much more importantly, *why* such a process increases the unhiding of life's meaning.

Those who are seeking more meaning in their lives and who have developed most of themselves are likely to be the readers of this book. Most of these people are likely to fall into three general groups. The vastly largest of these groups will be made up of people who have significantly developed most of themselves and who are finding life to be lacking in meaning, but who have never yet chosen to improve their senses, nor to consistently raise their consciousnesses. These people are in the greatest turmoil concerning the lack of meaning in their lives because they have the least understanding of life's *hidden* meaning. For many of these people, this book will be a tremendous relief in, at a minimum, increasing their understanding of what it is that is missing from what they have created in their lives. On average, in the more developed societies where a majority of these people live and where self development has progressed to very high levels, *Life's Hidden Meaning* could be of great help to this first and largest group. In those societies this group may comprise as much as twenty-five percent of the adult population (in spiritual terms, those over age twenty-eight). This book can help to improve the lives of many members of this very large group of people, whether they are living in a more advanced society or not.

The second group of people comprises those who seek *to create* more meaning in their lives and in a prior life have done so. These people have, at some point (most often prior to the present lifetime), chosen to improve their senses and to raise their consciousnesses because they had started to create *some* of the *hidden* meaning into their lives. However, these people have ceased to create this meaning and thus no longer understand life's *hidden* meaning. Some of them have gone backwards and have attempted to increase their selves, finding virtually no meaning in so doing as they age past twenty-eight years; many reach a crisis soon after reaching thirty-five years of age, but do not understand why. By age forty-two, the crisis can become a progressive and permanent reduction in meaning for the remainder of that lifetime. In the more advanced societies, these people may be about two percent of the total population. While the information in this book may seem factually new to these people, the underlying concepts will be readily understood, especially by those regarding the need to improve senses and consciousness. These people need to be "awakened" (to their souls) back to their prior, more enlightened positions.

The third, and much smaller group of readers will be those who have probably read some other esoteric and spiritual material prior to reading this book. The people who compose this group are already consistently trying to raise their consciousnesses and are increasing their senses, or their awareness. They already know *some* of life's hidden meaning, but because of a lack of structured instruction and teaching, are finding it difficult to fully understand the process they are already functioning within. They greatly need the more-difficult to understand sections of *Life's Hidden Meaning*, in order to continue to increase their functioning in the process of creating more meaning in their lives. This group, today, represents a fraction of one percent of the total population in the more advanced societies, and about seven percent of the second group. One purpose of Life's Hidden Meaning is to, as much as possible, increase the population of the third group by "awakening" those in the second group and educating them to function spiritually.

The main purpose of *Life's Hidden Meaning* is to help as many of its readers as is possible to understand the *hidden* meaning of life. Although several other purposes do exist for this book, if its main purpose is accomplished at the level of the first (and largest) group understanding about half of the larger, basic concepts, and comprehending these specific concepts at about a fifty percent level, then the book will have achieved the level planned for. For those in the second group to become members of the third group will require that they understand more of the concepts, including many more of the relatively smaller ones at the same time as, and held together with, the larger basic ones—and all of these comprehended at a somewhat higher level than fifty percent.

In the third group, an understanding of most of the concepts in the book is needed (perhaps ninety percent or more of them), at a similar level of comprehension. These more difficult concepts, mostly because of the sheer volume of them as well as their intricacy, will most likely be meaningful to the lives of those who will be able to use them to both further unhide and then create the meaning in their lives.

As will be explained again, later in this book, a concept is first understood by re-creating it within one's conceptual mental mind. This usually occurs by either reading the concept or having it explained in the context of other previously understood concepts. Someone comprehends a concept by how much he or she can use that concept to build and understand other concepts; also, when a person comprehends a concept, she or he can then create forms of thoughts, as words, to explain the concept correctly. Thus comprehension is the ability to use concepts that one can create or re-create, depending on that person's ability to do so. When thinking conceptually, the vast majority of people mostly only re-create concepts because the creation of a new concept, at the present time (and increasingly more so in the future), requires very whole and well developed mental thought.

The quite large physical size of *Life's Hidden Meaning* may intimidate some readers. Not all of the book needs to be read during a single period of time within a person's life. By reading only half (or less) of the book, some people will gain most of what they would have gained by reading it in its entirety—provided that these people select the portions of the book that are the best parts for them to read. In order to assist these and other readers, a reading guide has been provided. Many readers may read what at first is all that they think they need to or want to read in order to achieve their anticipated improvement in understanding; then, as their consciousnesses (understandings) grow, they may elect to continue reading, with a return to those sections they had previously avoided. Although *Life's Hidden Meaning* was not written to primarily supply information, it is likely to be used as a reference book by some readers. The reason is that almost all of the structured information that it contains is not available from any other written source.

The body of prior knowledge to which much of the information in *Life's Hidden Meaning* is connected is referred to by some as Ageless Wisdom. The word ageless is used to describe the wisdom because it is knowledge that is created at the level of truth (mostly for the benefit of humanity), and truth changes when time and space do. Truth creates a structure, or a balancing of all the forces against its type of thought. This thought consists of concepts and thoughtforms used together that are balanced only at a particular point in time and space. New structures need to be constantly created as more knowledge is added that imbalances the forces and leads to a lack of wholeness in the mental thought as it is communicated to others. Today's truth was not yesterday's, and will need a rebalancing of its concepts and thoughtforms if it is to become tomorrow's. Also, a change in location, or the space between events, can alter truth.

Ageless Wisdom is whole mental thought, or wisdom, that is continuously changing as it grows. Ageless Wisdom needs to be adjusted in order to remain correct as it is communicated to meet the needs of others to understand it and use it as truth. In some books the words *Ancient* Wisdom are used to define this body of knowledge; that name indicates a lack of change and would indicate a truth for an earlier time and another place. That name is not used by this author.

Life's Hidden Meaning is divided into three broadly generalized methods of conceptually understanding the information within it. Each method is used primarily in four chapters, of the total twelve. All three methods are used throughout the book, but in each group of chapters one method is primary, and the other two are secondary. The first method involves understanding the information through descriptive and analogous explanations. These include historical accounts, narratives of general living circumstances, and practical suggestions that address common areas of concern. Chapters One, Eight, Nine, and Twelve are the four chapters that fall under this first method of conceptually-written emphasis. Of the four, Chapter One has the greatest level of representation of the other two methods—but they are much simplified. Reading the chapters first that use this first method is likely to be generally the easiest way for most readers to initially understand the concepts in this book.

The second method of gaining understanding that is generally used in *Life's Hidden Meaning* is an analytical and conceptually comparative one. These methods use inductive thinking. The four chapters that use more of this method are Chapters Five, Six, Seven, and Eleven. These chapters include the development of larger concepts from beginning smaller ones and then a comparison of the large ones to each other. This process shows how these concepts support one another as a whole and help the reader to create more whole structured thought. The later explanations further analyze the information to ensure that whole concepts are being created to reveal whether most or all of the concepts, together, support a much larger general one. For many readers, this method will be second in difficulty of gaining initial understanding.

The last method generally employed to create concepts in *Life's Hidden Meaning* does so through scientific explanations that follow logical deductions from one (usually large) concept to the next (usually smaller) one. The structure of this method challenges the accuracy of each statement of fact to be deducible from all prior ones made. Chapters Two, Three, Four, and Ten use this general method of explaining the information. Many people will find these chapters to be the most difficult to initially understand. The reading guide that follows should further help the reader to use the above information in a practical manner.

Life's Hidden Meaning helps to join together the areas that are hidden from many of its readers' understandings of science and theology. The intention is that as the readers explore the various subjects in which they may gain more meaning in their lives, they will simultaneously raise their consciousnesses. What many readers are about to enter is a journey that offers the possibility of gaining a reasonable understanding of the basic concepts concerning *why* our universe and the life within it exist, and exist as they do. The entire book may represent a completed cosmology and ontology of our universe by unifying its physics while bringing God back into science, and bringing logic into theology. Perhaps the most important contribution to the readers' understanding of *Life's Hidden Meaning* is the answering of many questions that are, by what is likely to be the majority of people, believed to be unanswerable. A large number of these questions are answered in ways that make them potentially testable, scientifically, by many of the readers. Those who are ready are now invited and challenged to determine for themselves the validity of the explanations found within this book.

Life's Hidden Meaning comprises twelve chapters of text with illustrations, a preface, an introduction, a summary, a glossary, this reading guide, and separate indices to the tables and illustrations and the text. In addition, information is given about the group known as Ageless Wisdom Distributors, the author, and the construction of this book. The twelve chapters and related text are grouped into three levels of difficulty, as follows:

1. The first level comprises the Introduction and Chapters One, Eight, Nine, and Twelve. The average reader is likely to find the range of this material to be fairly easy to moderately difficult to understand.

2. The second level comprises the Summary and Chapters Five, Six, Seven, and Eleven. The average reader is likely to find the range of this material to be moderately difficult to difficult to understand.

3. The third level comprises Chapters Two, Three, Four, and Ten, plus the Glossary. The average reader is likely to find the range of this material to be difficult to very difficult to understand.

THE ANTICIPATED DIFFICULTY IN UNDERSTANDING THE BOOK

ANTICIPATED LEVEL OF DIFFICULTY IN UNDERSTANDING	SECTIONS OF *LIFE'S HIDDEN MEANING*
FAIRLY EASY TO MODERATELY DIFFICULT	INTRODUCTION; CHAPTERS 1, 8, 9, 12
MODERATELY DIFFICULT TO DIFFICULT	SUMMARY; CHAPTERS 5, 6, 7, 11
DIFFICULT TO VERY DIFFICULT	GLOSSARY; CHAPTERS 2, 3, 4, 10

Table R.1

In the above-listed three groups, the designated levels of difficulty are based on only the more basic concepts in each section, and do not include those parts of them that are filled with many smaller concepts that are technical or detailed. Many readers could skip over these smaller concepts and still gain an overall understanding of the book.

The ability for each reader to understand any particular section of *Life's Hidden Meaning* will be dependent on a number of conditions, such as the reader's prior levels of understanding similar concepts and, most importantly, his or her overall level of consciousness. An important factor that this guide tries to address is the probable inclination of the individual readers' personalities and minds, as determined by their "rays"—which are explained later in the book. Even without understanding rays at this point, their principles can still be used to assist many readers.

Some people might find that reading the chapters of *Life's Hidden Meaning* in a certain order based upon their personality characteristics and mental inclinations will produce greater ease in understanding the more basic concepts in the book. The following information is provided so that each reader might encounter the least amount of difficulty in understanding the more basic concepts; each description corresponds to a "ray" focus of the energies within either the personality or mental body. The reader, at this point, does not need an understanding of the rays; however, the information about types of personalities and mental mind inclinations that follows may augment any such (present or future) understanding that he or she might have, which could come from already having read or, in the future, reading about the rays in various parts of this book or in other books. Note that the various reading orders suggested below apply only to the chapters and not to the rest of the book, whose comprehension, unlike that of the chapters, is unaffected by ray issues. Thus—regardless of one's ray structure—it will probably be the most helpful to read "About the Author, the Group known as Ageless Wisdom Distributors, and the Construction of *Life's Hidden Meaning*," the "Preface," the "Table of Contents," the "List of Questions," the "Introduction," the "Summary," and the "Glossary," as well as this "Reading Guide" in the order in which they are presented. The readers who most strongly recognize themselves to be in one of the following seven groups may find the basic concepts in *Life's Hidden Meaning* easier to understand if its chapters are read in the order that is suggested for that group. The way to know whether to use the personality or mental body ray (if they are not the same), in determining which order to read the book in, is to choose the group of characteristics that most strongly apply to one's life.

THE FIRST RAY

1st Ray Personality—Those who are actively involved in politics as policymakers, especially as a vocation; many lawyers, especially adept litigators; land developers; promoters; surgeons; those who in life have nearly always been leaders; demolition *experts*, or those who regularly plan the destruction of some things.

1st Ray Mental Mind—Creative writers; some judges (especially those who write opinions); people who think creatively in their structured thoughts when faced with a problem (they tend to create new structures in their own mental solutions); those who can strongly limit their thoughts to exactly the area of structured thought they want to think about; those who tend to lead others through their structured thoughts.

Recommended first ray reading order:
Chapters 1; 2; 10; 3; 4; 8; 9; 5; 6; 7; 11; 12.

THE SECOND RAY

2nd Ray Personality—Those who are teachers; those who are practicing a spiritual discipline and who are seeking more understanding of it; those who are students of a spiritual, educational, or teaching profession.

2nd Ray Mind—Those who like to study certain subjects, especially spiritual or educational ones; those who enjoy learning more than they enjoy other parts of life; those who find it very helpful to be taught concepts rather than to only read them (these people often find it necessary to have someone teach them, besides only reading or learning in some other way); those who structure their mental thoughts to include the thoughts of others whom they communicate with. Also, those who always need to understand completely what they learn—when they are thinking unselfishly; the reverse is true when they think selfishly.

Without consideration of the personality or mental ray, those who want to gain the highest level of understanding *regardless* of the difficulty in doing so also fall into this group.

Recommended second ray reading order
(or for those who want to achieve maximum understanding):
Chapters 1; 2; 3; 4; 5; 6; 7; 8; 9; 10; 11; 12.

THE THIRD RAY

3rd Ray Personality—This is a large category. Many who are involved in police work; the career military; banking (especially bank officers); the communications industry, including radio and television but not on the entertainer or "talent" side; many psychologists and some psychotherapists; land developers; contractors; those who work in certain applications of technologies; accountants who are more involved in some regulatory function; tax regulators and tax collectors; many other government regulators—but not makers of broad policy, because these are politicians and fall into the first ray category.

3rd Ray Mental Mind—Those who prefer thinking structurally of ways of growing more of anything materially—these could be bankers or accountants, but the structured thought is the focus rather than merely the chosen professions (which could be indicated more by a third personality ray, as described above); those who tend to want to mentally communicate in ways that clearly define their thoughts to others; those who nearly always seek to define the subject that they are thinking of.

Recommended third ray reading order:
Chapters 1; 7; 8; 9; 2; 3; 4; 5; 6; 10; 11; 12

THE FOURTH RAY

4th Ray Personality—Those who are involved in creating more beauty in the arts; many types of entertainers including but not limited to musicians, actors, and actresses; artists; arbitrators; decorators; designers (including those in architecture who are more design-oriented); and certain—usually non-medical—healers.

4th Ray Mental Mind—Those who usually structure their thoughts to include the spiritual (and often hidden) parts of what they are thinking of. These people tend to want to find a balance between the spiritual part of a thought and its more material part—they often accentuate the spiritual side in order to achieve this (beautiful) balance. Their thoughts are more non-verbal and they often see spiritual patterns, but sometimes miss some (of the more obvious to most others) material patterns; when recognizing spiritual patterns, or patterns of light (or lack thereof) in others and their own thoughts, they create structured mental material effects that represent one-half of the amount and patterns of light that they mentally are aware of; they balance the light that presently exists.

Recommended fourth ray reading order:
Chapters: 1; 8; 9; 2; 5; 6; 11; 7; 3; 4; 10; 12

THE FIFTH RAY

5th Ray Personality—Those who are scientists; medical doctors (excluding most surgeons) and nurses; engineers; mathematicians; inventors of more technical things (some inventors, however, may fall under the first ray); and technical technicians (some less technical technicians fall under the third ray).

5th Ray Mental Mind—Those who are highly structured in their thinking (those who seek to create or find formulas for what they think); those who prefer to balance the reasons for, or causes within, their mental thought and the outcome, or the effects of their thoughts (for each cause, the effects seem to be complete, or whole—or they will think of a way of making the effects complete); those who seek the causes for effects they are mentally aware of, and often will use logic and analytical thinking to determine the causes.

Recommended fifth ray reading order:
Chapters 1; 2; 10; 3; 4; 5; 6; 7; 11; 8; 9; 12

THE SIXTH RAY

6th Ray Personality—Those in the clergy; those devoted vocationally to an ideology or a person (or more than one), philosophy, religion, or group (this can include some housewives or househusbands—especially those who have children that they are devoted to raising); historians; archivists; some librarians, usually those who are involved with the protection and restoration of existing information; and caregivers.

6th Ray Mental Mind—Those who focus on one activity at a time when they structure their thought; those who tend to (first) think of those thoughts that they like or love more than other thoughts—this liking or loving is often based upon how easily a structure can be created with the mental thought; those who first think of the more obvious and singular solution—but may ignore contradictions in their thought by being overly focused on the (wrong, or incorrect) singular solution; those who limit the structured thought that they sense from others, so that it will *correctly* fit into their own thinking (this is *not* always egotism; it may be a way of thinking). Thinking in this way may cause them to at times misunderstand the full or complete thoughts of others. These people tend to think that the structured thought of others is just like their own because they limit how they choose to understand others' thinking so that it appears to be giving, or loving towards their thought; also, they will tend to modify both their own and others' thoughts together in order to establish a relative truth among all these thoughts that is more loving.

Recommended sixth ray reading order:
Chapters 1; 2; 3; 5; 6; 8; 9; 11; 4; 7; 10; 12

THE SEVENTH RAY

7th Ray Personality—Those who are in business; those employed and who plan to be or already are long-term employees of a business; farmers and ranchers; librarians involved with mostly the organization of information; some chefs; cooks; domestic workers and housekeepers; recreation workers; laborers; equipment operators; organizers; and managers.

7th Ray Mental Mind—Those who tend to synthesize the structured mental information that they think about—they join together structured information in new ways to solve problems or to increase activity; these people tend to think more deliberately, taking a bit more time to deliberate over the best means of synthesizing a solution. The structured thought of these people attempts to organize information in order to economize the time that it will take to think about the same or similar thoughts in the future.

Recommended seventh ray reading order:
Chapters: 1; 8; 9; 5; 6; 7; 11; 2; 3; 4; 10; 12

The use of vocation and mental structure of thoughts to determine personality and mental mind rays is a fairly accurate one for the purposes in this reading guide; one's vocation and mental structure of thought are based upon the effects of the rays on human civilization. This method is, however, too inaccurate to determine one's rays with any certainty regarding spiritual discipline or service. To gain the level of accuracy needed for these purposes, one needs to understand how the senses in the mental body are being used, in determining the mental body's ray. The personality ray can be ascertained by understanding how the information provided by the senses in the three lower bodies is being synthesized into knowledge. These levels of awareness are likely to be too difficult to achieve by the reader who is just beginning to read this book, and for many readers after having read it as well. For most, the less accurate method employed in this reading guide should suffice. One or more future books to be published by this author and the group known as Ageless Wisdom Distributors will help those who need further information on the much more accurate ways of determining the ray focus of the senses of all of the bodies and the personality.

The author suggests that the "Glossary Help Guide" be consulted before each chapter is read. In order to gain clarity in understanding certain words *as the author uses them*, the reader can choose from among those definitions that he or she had not yet read. By centralizing most of the definitions into the glossary rather than redefining each glossary word in each chapter when the word is first used in that chapter a significant amount of space was saved for new information. Also, using the glossary as recommended has been found by sample readers to increase the overall ease of reading *Life's Hidden Meaning*. Nearly all of the available space in the book has been used as carefully and intelligently as possible in order to enhance the book's value to the reader. Most readers who follow the author's suggestion regarding the use of the glossary are likely to receive more benefit in their comprehension of the information in *Life's Hidden Meaning* than will the readers who do not.

QUESTIONS AND
BRIEF, INCOMPLETE ANSWERS

Illustration 1.1

Author's Suggestion: First turn to the "Glossary Help Guide" and read the definitions for this chapter.

Welcome to a journey of gaining an understanding of life's hidden meaning. This first chapter is the only one in the book to be written in a question-and-answer format. The intention in using this format is to provide the reader with a survey of the entire book that is as easy as possible to understand. Although the concepts used in the answers are incomplete, only rudimentary understanding of these concepts is required. For this reason and for some other ones as well, the first chapter will only slightly raise the reader's understanding of life's hidden meaning, but it will increase the knowledge level that most readers are likely to want concerning what the book is about in general. This first chapter, through what is missing from it, challenges many readers to expand their understanding by reading further into the book.

Each answer to a question includes a reference to one or more subsequent chapters where a much more complete answer is explained. Such a system of organization facilitates the process of reading certain sections of the book before certain other sections, for those readers who decide that doing so would help them to better understand the material, and for those who have more of an interest in certain areas of explanation than in other areas. The questions and their brief answers are grouped, starting with those that are more abstract and somewhat more difficult for many people to fully understand, and ending with the more specific and sometimes practical questions and answers about life and its meaning. Readers are encouraged to use the reading guide at the beginning of this book, immediately following the introduction. Some readers might find it easier to continue reading the questions and answers in Chapter One instead of switching after each question to a later, referenced, chapter in the attempt to develop a more complete understanding—particularly of the earlier, more abstract answers. Some of these people might, at first, become overwhelmed by the information in these corresponding chapters of this book that are the most difficult to read; those who experience this problem are encouraged to read the easier chapters, or those chapters that seem easier to them depending upon how their minds function. Each chapter is designed to raise the reader's understanding, and certain chapters will seem easier to understand than will others, based upon more than the information's inherent difficulty. By reading a later chapter that was found to be easier than an earlier one, the reader's understanding may increase, enabling him or her to then more easily understand the earlier chapter that was originally harder to understand.

In the chapters subsequent to Chapter One, concepts are often repcated several times, from varying perspectives of being understood. These concepts are often further increased in scope with each presentation of them. Although such an approach can, admittedly, sometimes be confusing, it is likely to provide assistance to many readers in gaining greater understanding than they otherwise would. Thus the writing style is altered based upon the amount of repetition in each of the chapters, in order to compensate for the varying levels of difficulty in understanding the information in each chapter. This approach is also used within Chapter One, although in a much more limited—and less potentially confusing—manner.

Question #1: Where did everything come from?

Brief, Incomplete, Answer: There is but one life that created a means of self-expression and growth. This one life is the source and cause for diversity, change and growth, and free will. The one life can be referred to as "God" for ease in explaining this process by which a living, growing universe can be created from a single unified one. God created a process by which its own self-sacrifice generated more new life that would be free to choose to do the same.

To begin with, imagine being God and wanting to create a system in which more of yourself is being continually created. In this system, the growth of yourself needs to be endless and along a general plan, but it is important that you allow each new part of yourself the freedom to choose within the parts' own abilities to do so, and to be unique and different from everything else. Otherwise, all growth would be identical to you (a cloning of you) and would be boring repetition. Since God (and you, in your imagination) begins as being everything—as one, as all-knowing, all-powerful, and all-present—in order to allow there to be more that is free in its choices, God chooses to limit itself. God chooses to reduce its knowingness, powerfulness, consciousness, and presence. The more God sacrifices these parts of itself, the more its sacrifices create its new and diverse parts. The process is a sort of birthing by self-limitation, or by sacrifice. This all occurs because God *willed* it (consistently chose it) to be, since God begins by being the All.

The Creator of our universe was created from a state of timeless unlimited potential before its choice to create our universe. It then chose to limit its mind, or its collective thoughts, into three enormous parts that were extremely limited in comparison to its beginning unlimited potential. The first part became manifested in our universe as choice, or will, or purpose; the second, as consciousness, or the ability to understand each separated thing as a part of the whole, or to understand giving that helps others to give comes from recognizing that each is a part of the One—the Creator. The third part of the Creator's mind became created in our universe as the ability to intelligently interact so that the first two parts can increase; this third part is the container for the first two, when it is manifested as energy. Throughout our universe, the Creator, now as God, chose to create more of itself by increasing purpose/will/sacrifice/ choice, and consciousness/love/giving–to-help-others-do-the-same, or increasing the recognition of the oneness of all by expressing these two parts through a third part, of manifested energy. The energy creates the forms that can then intelligently interact to create new and more growth to life.

Life is the result of these three parts of God's mind being separated and extremely limited, as a great sacrifice, by God. Yet these three parts of God remain within our universe and within all life, producing growth to life and to God simultaneously, because each part of life is a part of all of life and of God. Life, and God, is self-created from the unlimited potential to create in comparison to the extreme sacrifice and limitations that were required to create new life and any growth within it. [For a much more complete answer and for greater potential understanding, see Chapter Two: "The Creator and The Big Picture."]

Question #2: **If God limits itself to create a diverse universe, which includes people, then does God no longer exist?**

Brief, Incomplete, Answer: Included within God's creation of the universe is a plan for the universe to be a loving (giving) expression of life, or an expression of God itself. This plan is not dictated nor forced upon the new diverse parts of God, because doing that would not allow for free choice. Instead, God chose to leave a clue (a remembrance) of itself and its plan (the giving of its thought process, or consciousness). This clue is constant and is found throughout the universe as God's thought, or light. As each part of the diverse new life self-discovers some part of the light by its own creations, it discovers that it is a part of God and that God is everywhere with a plan. This plan includes each of God's parts giving of itself. [For a much more complete answer and for greater potential understanding, see Chapter Three: "Cosmic Virtues, Parts of God's Light in Form."]

Question #3: **What do you mean by light? Is this the light that shines from the sun and other luminous sources?**

Brief, Incomplete, Answer: Light is the first two parts of God's thought process, of will/purpose and giving/consciousness, joined together by the thought of some part of life. Light is both creative and directive; it creates through choices and directs through givingness. It includes the idea of life giving of itself and making sacrifices in order to create. This thought process, when energized by the third part of God's mind (the energizing is what gives God's thought a form and its activity in relation to other form in our universe), can be physical light. Physical light allows everything that is physically alive to physically respond to its environment and to coordinate itself so that it can *share* and *cooperate* with everything else around it. Light can also provide everything emotionally alive with a means of emotionally responding to everything else. When it can respond in this way, the emotional light (God's thought process) becomes a limited form of *love* (givingness of its motion, or movements that are added to coordinated responses). A third way that light can be energized (formed) and also can be made more intelligent in its activity is mentally, through structured (in logical time) thinking. When added to the emotional giving and intelligent physical responses (love, plus the coordinated responses), this third way of energizing and intelligently activating light allows everything mentally alive to conceive of whole and complete concepts and well-connected examples of these concepts that help others to think better. These are called *truths*. All of these ways that God's thought process and plan are energized can also be named *virtues*. Virtues are the light of God in some part of form, or the thought of God that is energized and is returning to intelligent activities. [For a much more complete answer and for greater potential understanding, see Chapter Three: "Cosmic Virtues, Parts of God's Light in Form."]

Question #4: **What do you mean by the word energized, when you say that light—God's thought—is energized?**

Brief, Incomplete, Answer: Everything started as the One. Energy is less than perfect in its activity and is a separated part of the One, and this separation is what leads to the creation of form. Seen another way, God's thought takes on characteristics of the form it is within. The more that energy is confined or limited from the other parts of God's mind, the more the energy densifies in its form. As a form becomes enlightened, the light is energized by the nature of the density of the energy that makes up the form. The lower the density of a form's energy, the easier it is to see the light (God's thought). An example of this concept can be found in picturing a colored balloon, perhaps a blue one, inside which there is a lit light bulb. As the balloon becomes inflated, the outer skin is stretched and becomes less dense because energy is being added into the balloon by the injected air, and some of this energy is transferred into the skin. The light becomes easier to see because the density of the skin has been reduced by the increased activity in the state of energy within it. In this example, it could be stated that the light is energized by the nature of the form it is contained within. It could also be said that if the form were somewhat changed by changing its density, one's ability to see the light would change. With higher energy and less density, the light becomes less blue in color and more white; it lightens because the skin is stretched. If the air (the energy) is let out of the balloon, the light becomes darker and more blue. [For a much more complete answer and for greater potential understanding, see Chapter Four: "Understanding Spirit and Energy."]

Example of Energy's Density Affecting Light

As this example illustrates, the light in the balloon on the left is less visible than the light in the balloon on the right. The reason is that the skin (or the energy that the light must travel through and become formed by) of the balloon on the left is more dense than is the skin (energy) of the balloon on the right. Adding energy into the balloon on the right causes the skin (as energy, or form) to be stretched and to become less dense by exciting the state of its energy by the added energy as air pressure. The light is able to move more easily through the energy, or to be formed by it. This makes the light brighter and much easier to see. In these examples the light represents God's thought, which becomes easier to see in the parts of our universe where form is less dense than it is here in the physical realm.

Illustration 1.2

Question #5: **If light is God's thought contained in form, then what is thought?**

Brief, Incomplete, Answer: A very limited and basic way of explaining thought is that it is *the self-created awareness that "I am."* A more complete definition is that thought is also two or more choices in a similar direction, or similarly connected, that can limit the field (can cause other choices to become similarly connected) that these choices exist within. Anytime anything thinks, it is creating more of itself if its choices create limitation by connecting more future choices. Everything lives within God's original thought, even though everything might be adding to it. Therefore, everything is a part of God and helps to further create more of God as it creates more of itself through its thought that is in the direction of God's thought. Something *can* create more of itself that is not in the manner of God's thought. However, when it does this it does not increase God's thought, it only increases itself—temporarily. [For a much more complete answer and for greater potential understanding, see Chapter Five: "Giving Thought—the Mode of Self Creation."]

Question #6: **What about those things that do not think, like a rock or a dandelion? What creates them, and are they a part of God?**

Brief, Incomplete, Answer: There is a part of these forms that is thinking, or informing them, or creating them. This thinking part is unseen by most people; it is called the soul part. This soul part does the thinking while the energy part is in the process of learning to think. When very dense, the energy part becomes the matter of, for example, a rock or dandelion. The energy follows the thought because both the soul and the energy came from the One (the three parts of God's mind), and the energy has a very strong affinity for rejoining with the soul (which came in part from spirit) that is producing the thought. This rejoining affinity is the love, or givingness, within the original thought of God and its plan. The givingness with purpose is represented by light, which is in everything to some degree.

The givingness is also responsible for creating consciousness, because in order to choose to give there has to be a giver, a receiver, and an understanding of what is being given. What underlies this understanding is the *choice* concerning what to give. Something becomes conscious when it understands its choice to give, and the more it chooses to give and the more it understands its choices, the more conscious it must be. As something increases its giving in ways that acknowledge the oneness between itself and who or what it is giving to, then it must, necessarily, have greater understanding.

Seen another way, each act of giving inherently causes us to recognize that we exist and that others do, too. If we take from others and we benefit at their cost, we lose consciousness because we have not gained understanding as a result of our choice to take. Instead, our selfishness has denied us the affirmation of existence that would have come from increased understanding of who we are. Selfishness denies that we all come from One, and that we are all a part of the One. The penalty for selfishness is a diminishing in the creation of who we are, and the creation of who we are is what we call *consciousness* of ourselves. The sensation and awareness of losing (or having lost) consciousness is *suffering*, because the loss of affirmation of our own existence is the ultimate source of suffering. [For a much more complete answer and for greater potential understanding, see Chapter Three: "Cosmic Virtues, Parts of God's Light in Form" and Chapter Five: "Giving Thought—the Mode of Self Creation."]

Question #7: **Then does a single rock have a soul?**

Brief, Incomplete, Answer: Each type of mineral as an element or compound (inorganic or organic) has a single group soul that intelligently determines the minerals' nearly constant means of interacting. The thought process of minerals is chemical and is difficult for many people to see as thought because it was developed such a very long time ago. Once established, the process changes very little over time until a higher thought source, from a human soul, for example, decides to intervene and create new chemical reactions. The higher the level of thought that is used to create the form, the easier it is for people to recognize it as thought, up to their own level of thinking. Some people might be able to more easily recognize the group soul part (the "thinking" part) behind a dandelion and many other plants by observing the interactions among different parts of nature. It is important to note that the first kind of life on a planet to have an individual soul is human life; what this means is that each human thinks for herself or himself, and is no longer part of a group soul. It also means that humans have individual, integrated bodies (as their form nature), and that their bodies are connected to their individual soul nature. In other words, the energy that forms the bodies of humans closely follows the individual thought and soul of each particular human. [For a much more complete answer and for greater potential understanding, see Chapter Six: "About Souls" and Chapter Nine: "The Kingdoms and their Purpose."]

The Collective Thought of Involutionary Energy Creating Gravity

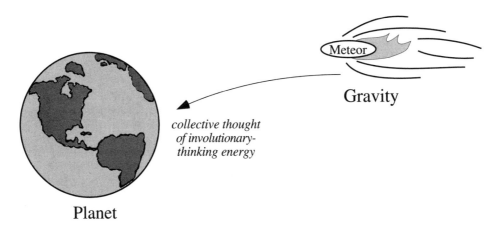

collective thought of involutionary-thinking energy

Gravity

Planet

The collective thought of involutionary energy attracts other energy. The attracted energy does not have informing spiritual thought that is greater than the thought of the involutionary energy.

Energy that is not being attracted by the informing thought of a soul or other spirit responds to itself because it is attracted to its own very low levels of thought. The levels of thought that allow energy to be self-attracted are so slight as to be almost imperceptible unless the amount of energy (or mass) creating its own thought is very large. Such a great amount of the added together slight thought of energy is what is referred to as *gravity*.

Illustration 1.3

> *Question #8:* **Since humans have individual souls and can think for themselves as individuals, what about pets (like dogs and cats) and those apes that have learned sign language?**

> *Brief, Incomplete, Answer:* The more closely an animal physically, emotionally, and mentally resembles a human, and, further, the more contact it has with humans, the more it thinks as an individual. Even though animals do not have individual souls, some of their instinctual behaviors (which come from the thoughts of their respective group souls) are over-ridden by their own thoughts that are examples, or forms, of partial concepts. The concepts themselves are mostly unrecognized by the animals and either come from humans or are represented in nature by the collective group souls. For example, if you were to say to your pet dog, "Let's go for a walk," and this phrase has been used many times before going for a walk, the dog would most likely become excited. It would have this reaction because it would be using its creative imagination to see itself going out and experiencing some new smells and enjoying itself. This use of imagination occurs because the dog has associated its emotional nature with the form of thought that represents going for a walk. What the dog does *not* have is the concept of the walk, or *why* it is being walked; humans may have this concept in their thought processes. You may think to yourself, "My dog 'Squirt' needs some exercise, some fresh air, camaraderie with me, vicarious communication with other dogs through smell, and some fun. I will take him for a

walk." Notice that the concepts (answering the question "why") come first, *before* the example, or the form of the concept, or the thoughtform. The thoughtform explains the "how" and the "what." The dog understands the form (the "how" or "what"). Humans have the ability to understand the "why," as well. By understanding the "why's," humans can be mentally creative. Animals nearly completely lack this capability on an individual level. Concepts are abstract and are moving pictures of the structure of mental thought, while thoughtforms are like snapshot pictures of a concept in example form. When connected to their concepts, thoughtforms become structured in their movements within time, or logically moving in relation to each other. The concepts represent the relationship of the thoughtforms in structured, or logical, time. Animals (and people, too) can bring these thoughtforms into their emotional systems and then create moving pictures of them without time structure, in what is referred to as the capability of *creative imagination*. [For a much more complete answer and for greater potential understanding, see Chapter Five: "Giving Thought—The Mode of Self Creation."]

Question #9: **Then is the main difference between people and animals that people can think in concepts?**

Brief, Incomplete, Answer: People are able to think in concepts because they have individual souls that can create whole thoughts both of concepts and the examples (or forms) of the thought, connected together. The individual souls allow people to be mentally creative through concepts. Having this type of creativity enables people to find the light of God, or virtues, through the use of their mental minds, if they create enough whole concepts and thoughtforms that are connected together. Mentally virtuous thought is whole structured thought that is creatively given for the benefit of others, or truth. When people choose to think along the direction of this thought (which is also God's thought within them) and to create more of it they then see and experience more of the mental light within themselves and others. [For a much more complete answer and for greater potential understanding, see Chapter Three: "Cosmic Virtues, Parts of God's Light in Form" and Chapter Six: "About Souls."]

Thinking for and Giving to Others

Illustration 1.4

Question #10: **Can the light of God be found within us by learning about it, like in school—or through this book?**

Brief, Incomplete, Answer: To experience and to understand virtue, people need to create it according to the needs that others have for what they can give. To *fully* understand virtue, people need to create it and give it to and as souls. What this means is giving in a way that requires one to be creative in order to meet the needs that others have *to creatively give.* The reason is that souls only give as a group, i.e., together. They give to meet the needs that others have to give. For humans, virtuous creation involves mental sense and thought and is further developed through both emotional and sensual (using the five physical senses) thought and awareness. This process can be read about, and the concepts that are written about it can be re-created by the reader in order to help himself or herself prepare to create the virtue. By preparing in this way, it is possible to change the focus of the mind to create concepts that are more whole. In other words, the reader creates "why's" that are more complete. Assisting in this process is a part of the purpose of this book. [For a much more complete answer and for greater potential understanding, see Chapter Five: "Giving Thought—the Mode of Self Creation" and the Summary.]

Question #11: **For what reason are there people? What is the purpose of human life?**

Brief, Incomplete, Answer: All life is interconnected, and the purpose of any part of it is best understood by seeing the purpose of the whole. However, to develop a partial under-standing would be helpful at this early stage in the exploration of "life's hidden meaning." For humans the partial purpose of life is first to create more of themselves and to eventually create more of God's thought, which people both live within and are a part of. Therefore, the partial purpose is to be *self*-creative, and eventually to be so within the direction of God's thought (virtue), because each person is a part of God. As each person creates more virtue, her or his life becomes more purposeful.

Members of the human kingdom are far more self-creative than members of the lower king-doms are. The reason is that in the lower kingdoms the thinking part of an organism (its group soul) is not connected to a single body, but to many bodies that are similar to each other. Even though each of these animal, plant, and mineral bodies has many different experiences, since each is connected to a group soul and not an individual soul, the *individual* self creation of any one organism is minimal. What has just been described is a spiritual process of evolution—whereby the group souls (as spirit) are gradually teaching the energy in their bodies (in the organisms), through the energy following spirit's thought, to become more and better aware of other energy, or other matter when in dense form. In this process, the energy learns to think for itself. The thought of the spirit of the group soul needs to be an average of meeting the needs for all of its bodies, and this is what is referred to as "instinctual" thought. Because of this aver-aging of thinking for so many bodies, evolution is very slow and organisms going through it mostly lack self-thought and self creation. In the human kingdom the soul, or the thinking part, is directly connected to an individual body. Humans are the joining together of spirit with the best results of the evolutionary process in producing bodies. Humans eventually improve upon their planet's evolutionary process so that as life improves, the future for all improves. [For a much more complete answer and for greater potential understanding, see Chapter Six: "About Souls" and Chapter Nine: "The Kingdoms and Their Purpose."]

Spirit Informing Form

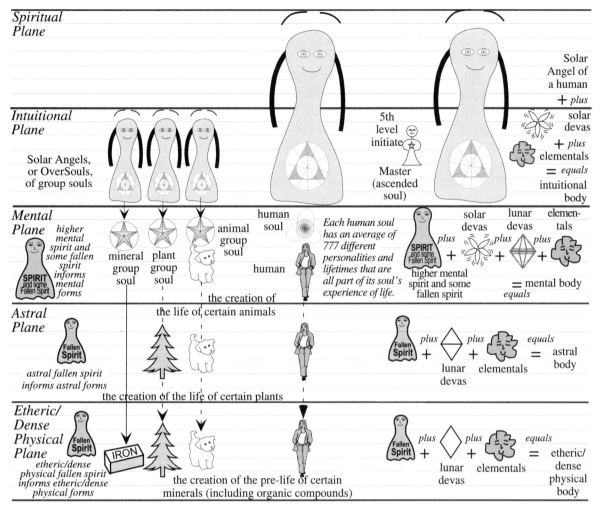

Group souls think for many of the same types of lifeforms. They each have an Oversoul that assists them in this process. Group souls inform "fallen" spirit on the planes that their lifeforms have bodies on, so that the fallen spirit can directly inform the energy within the bodies of the lifeforms. The Solar Angel's higher mental Self is shared by the group soul, so that the group soul can better think about the needs of its pre-life forms or lifeforms. Each group soul and its individual Solar Angel, or OverSoul, overcome some of the limitations caused by their pre-life forms or lifeforms not providing a completed sense of time of the dimension these forms exist within. With the help of its Solar Angel, a human soul creates and informs an individual lifeform of a human being. The human lives with senses on all three of the lower dimensions of the universe. Through its connected self, each soul gives thought to spirit that is "fallen" and that cannot think well enough to get surrounding energies of lunar devas and elementals to follow its thought. With the informing thought of the soul and its self, the fallen spirit can integrate the forms in the lower dimensions, creating the senses and bodies of pre-life forms and lifeforms. Eventually a human soul becomes a Master of the three lower worlds, or dimensions of time and space, by enlightening all of the energies within his or her three lower bodies through serving others. Then the fully enlightened (and ascended) Soul begins to join with the OverSoul, or Solar Angel, that has been helping that human soul—often for millions of years.

Illustration 1.5

***Question #12:* Do people become happy when they create virtue?**

Brief, Incomplete, Answer: When people create virtue, the internal response may be joy or bliss, or both. The reason is that by creating virtue, people create more consciousness of themselves by giving to others, which affirms the oneness of all and of their being a part of this oneness (a part of God). Happiness is transient and is based mostly on the satiation of desire— for a limited period of time. Happiness occurs within each person emotionally. Desires are located in people's emotional systems and are related to taking and self-centered focus, while creation of virtue is the directing of their focus towards giving to meet the needs of others. Giving on a soul level is giving to others to meet the needs that the others have to be able to better give. As people creatively give to meet others' needs they use energy that travels through their physical, emotional, mental, and spiritual systems. As long as this energy is freely given to others, it travels unimpeded through the person who is giving it. These parts of a person that the energy travels through are becoming more enlightened because that person's creative thoughts are focused on others, and the energy follows her or his thoughts. The light comes from people's choices to focus on giving their thoughts, feelings, and physical actions to others. It becomes energized by the energy that is attracted by their thoughts moving outward, travel-ling through them, as they act as directing consciousnesses. When people act in this way, the energy is not retained selfishly within them. The free flowing of this energy combined with the light (which then *is* virtue) enlightens them and produces the effect that is referred to as *joy*, on mental, emotional, and physical levels. When a person uses all of her or his energy in this way and helps others to sense at a particular time, the effect becomes consistently spiritual. This is because she or he is constantly joining the first two parts of God's mind and is constantly producing light, and the joy becomes bliss. Joy and bliss are self-sustaining and last forever as a part of memory because what creates this effect (the virtue) lasts forever in its effect. [For a much more complete answer and for greater potential understanding, see Chapter Four: "Understanding Spirit and Energy" and Chapter Twelve: "How to Increase Consciousness."]

***Question #13:* Why does virtue last forever?**

Brief, Incomplete, Answer: Virtue is light in form, or the thought of God (as light), which is then immersed in energy (is energized, or made into form). All form is composed of some level of density of energy. The type and levels of energy may change, but the light remains as a constant, as God's thought (purpose and plan). A part of this plan is that everything that follows the direction of God's plan is immortal and will last forever because it grows God and becomes a part of its Creator. This factor allows for a universe with free choice, but ultimately guarantees that the universe will grow more virtuous—more like God's thought as it exists in form. The products of our universe grow endlessly forever, with cycles of growth and rest, and all that has become more of God by its own creation remains immortally. [For a much more complete answer and for greater potential understanding, see Chapter Two: "The Creator and the Big Picture."]

***Question #14:* Do people last forever?**

Brief, Incomplete, Answer: Those parts of a person that she or he has enlightened by choosing to use them for the purpose of creating virtue are immortal and do last forever. The reason is that the energy itself, which makes up the form, has developed some levels of self-awareness by becoming enlightened through the informing soul's givingness. Once enlightened by having been used to create virtue, the form part can remain intact on its own, keeping an imprint of its nature for future use. The effect is one of having physical *and* emotional, mental, and spiritual "genes" that remain for as long as they need to. [For a much more complete answer and for greater potential understanding, see Chapter Seven: "The Bodies and the Senses" and Chapter Eight: "The Three Subtle Dimensions that Humans Live In."]

Question #15: **But people are far from perfect, and most create virtue only infrequently. Almost no one uses all of her or his energy and thoughts all the time for creating virtue; are we all, then, doomed to oblivion?**

Brief, Incomplete, Answer: Each person is a part of an individual soul, and souls are completely unselfish because they are enlightened enough to recognize when they are ignorant. They can also recognize what has been thus far presented in this book. Souls only give, and they restrict themselves to giving only when they can sense in a manner that is responsive to the needs that others have to give. In other words, they have a spiritual sense of responsibility. Souls, in part, create people in order to learn ways of giving that they are ignorant about and for which they lack ways of sensing. They learn these ways so they can better respond to others in need. A soul creates a person in order to gain these very important aspects so that the soul can continue to create more of itself and of God. Souls know that all are one because all are a part of the one life, and they know that as they give they are also being self-creating. What remains immortally of each person is whatever that person chooses to create virtuously—and this is added to the soul. Only that which is dark and away from God's light is eventually discarded. [For a much more complete answer and for greater potential understanding, see Chapter Six: "About Souls" and Chapter Eleven: "Reincarnation."]

Question #16: **Then when a person dies, does she or he stop existing?**

Brief, Incomplete, Answer: When people die from the physical world they continue to live in consciousness in a subtle dimension and a world of emotion and then, later, in a world of mental thought. These dimensions seem, to the people existing within them, somewhat similar to the physical world. It is much easier to live in the subtle dimensions, though, because there are no dense physical problems to contend with. The lower-density energy of these other dimensions more easily follows the thought of the people within them. People in these other dimensions have bodies that somewhat resemble the physical bodies they had when they were physically alive, although these bodies are made up of energy that is less dense. In these subtle worlds, people continue to have both emotional and mental senses, but the only parts of their five sensual senses from the dense world that remain during astral life are those that were fused to a person's emotional senses through light. Whatever amount of fused emotional and sensual sense a person has remaining at the end of astral life can be used by that person during his or her mental life; the amount of fused sensual and emotional senses that were destroyed during a person's astral life is gone and, of course, is not available to him or her during mental life. These people can use their emotions and mental minds in ways that simulate the five sensual senses, but that are necessarily different—because physical matter does not exist in these dimensions.

As time goes by, people slowly "die" from their emotional senses and the emotional body and then, later, from their remaining purely mental senses and the mental body. They awaken to being their souls by gradually becoming their souls through only giving and by often realizing some of what is written in this book and possibly more. The consciousness of a person never ceases. It grows as each inner dimension is traversed and "died" from, until it grows back into the soul. There is no oblivion for souls, and all people who choose to go back to being their souls achieve that state. [For a much more complete answer and for greater potential understanding, see Chapter Eight: "The Three Subtle Dimensions That Humans Live In."]

Scenes of Various Astral Sub-planes

The above scenes from top left to bottom right depict the following sub-planes of the astral plane: first or second sub-plane; third sub-plane; fourth sub-plane; fifth sub-plane; sixth sub-plane; and seventh sub-plane. These illustrations also appear in Chapter Eight, in larger size and with text that explains them.

Illustration 1.6

Question #17: **What happens after a person "dies" all the way back to being a soul?**

Brief, Incomplete, Answer: As a person dies from each body, she or he is in the process of becoming her or his soul. A person's consciousness increases after her or his death from each body, when she or he leaves a more dense dimension and enters into a less dense one.

The reason is that the energy that creates the forms of the thought is less dense and is, therefore, easier to change. Because the energy is less dense, it is easier for a person to think. Once a person has died from her or his three lower bodies and their senses (the physical, emotional, and then the part of the mental body that thinks separately), she or he then awakens to being her or his soul. At this point the person experiences great joy and is not only still aware and alive in consciousness, but is much more so than at any time during which she or he had lower bodies and senses.

After having reached the awakening of being one's soul, a person then freely chooses to reincarnate again, to return to physical earth as a new person—and to limit himself or herself in the process. People do not lose consciousness as they die from their dense bodies; rather, they gain in it. People sacrificially limit themselves within the process of incarnation so that they can each both create a new personality and learn to give in these very dense realms that personalities inhabit. Then, as they reincarnate, they bring with them as subconscious memory in their spiritual "genes" that which they have already created in virtue, or, more rarely, incomplete memory of some very selfish creations from past lives.

Because people tend to become more selfish as they incarnate into the denser dimensions, they lose consciousness. If they remembered that they really are souls, they might just selfishly choose to not continue the incarnation process and to instead return to the state of being their souls, in which state, interestingly, they would still want to incarnate. In other words, without this system of limitation people could become a sort of consciousness yo-yo. They could get stuck in a loop of wanting to give while they were clear in their thinking as souls, and then losing that level of clarity of thought as they become illusioned during the process of incarnating and increasing their suffering, which would then cause them to selfishly resist the process. Consciousness is created from giving and is lost as people take and become selfish. The loss of consciousness is actually a very helpful condition in this circumstance, as people incarnate, to avoid the otherwise possible yo-yo effect.

Each soul has the collective large purpose that was stated earlier. This purpose is in overcoming its ignorance within the denser dimensions, gaining senses and bodies that it helps to develop, and gaining a sense of responsibility in giving to meet the needs that others have to give. Within this large purpose, souls have much smaller missions that they take on in the self-development of virtue for each lifetime that they choose to incarnate into. Eventually the soul, in concert with many other souls, chooses to create a new person (with a new personality). This new personality will have all the love and wisdom from the prior lifetimes incorporated within its nature because these characteristics are in its physical, emotional, mental, and intuitional bodies' "genes." This love and wisdom re-appear as the new personality creates more virtue in his or her life.

If all people did in all of their lifetimes was create virtue, then they would remember everything about their prior lives. They would also have perfected senses in their bodies as a result of the enlightenment that was produced by their constant creation of virtue. Much of what people create in their lives is selfish and lacks light (Godliness). Because of this, most of these creations are abandoned through the loss of these bodies and senses during the dying process from the physical, emotional, and mental bodies and senses. The loss is a result of misuse by selfishly retaining the energy that needs to be given in order for it to both grow in consciousness in its own right and to be used to energize the light that is used with which to create virtue. Retained energy, which is always the result of selfishness, creates forces inside people's bodies by one energy pushing against another. This causes the senses, capabilities of thought, and other parts of the bodies to become damaged. A relatively small amount of the selfishly retained energy can be retained in the "genes" of a person's body if he or she is unusually selfish in the use of that particular body and its senses by continual, focused, selfish thought, even while on the inner dimensions after physical death. This retained energy can stay in the "genes" of that body and then remanifest in the next personality, producing a tendency towards selfishness in the previously mentioned ways and/or tendency for diseases. Fortunately, most of the selfishness does *not* remain because many people in the inner dimensions after physical death are thinking much more clearly, and so they often decide to be more virtuous. Then they create more virtue and give it to others. Having given in this way allows many people to start each new life mostly without the selfishness they had while physically alive in the last one. A person's after-death experiences are of tremendous value because they reduce his or her tendencies to retain energy in the "genes." [For a much more complete answer and for greater potential understanding, see Chapter Seven: "The Bodies and the Senses" and Chapter Eight: "The Three Subtle Dimensions That Humans Live In."]

Question #18: **Is it possible to remember prior lives?**

Brief, Incomplete, Answer: As explained in the answer to question #17, what most adult people might remember, if indeed true memories of their own prior lives, would be only those experiences in which they either created virtue or, in the case of evil people, were quite unusually selfish. In order to have past-life memory, most people need to have connected together in their minds about sixty percent of any group of events, which is the minimum level required for a person to be able to accurately remember that group of events. This sixty percent level of connectivity would come from creating significant amounts of virtue during that period of time—which few people actually do. People would remember the virtuous experiences only as they created more virtue within their present lifetimes because the energy (in the "genes") follows the same thought that first created it. The type of thought that is lower in light will not get virtuous memories (from the energy in the "genes") to follow it—nor be *re-membered* (to it).

The very selfish deeds that were not resolved during the prior lifetime or after death from that lifetime may be remembered as fears and unusual responses in the present life, but usually not as direct memories. The prior life "memories" that most people have are more along the lines of emotional creative imaginings that could stem from what is described above, but without factual foundations. Children have the highest likelihood of having a direct memory from a prior life because they are able to focus on the one body and sense that is growing the most. The order of development of the bodies and senses in children is as follows:

ORDER OF DEVELOPMENT OF THE BODIES AND SENSES IN CHILDREN	
AGE RANGE	BODY AND SENSES DEVELOPED
0–7 years	the physical body and physical senses
7–14 years	the emotional body and emotional senses
14–21 years	the mental body and mental senses

Table 1.1

During these periods of growth, virtuous memories as well as those related to a focused self-centeredness may suddenly become realized as a result of the focus. Rarely, a few very young children (below the age of seven) may quite vividly recall their own previous physical deaths. This potential ability exists because children are so focused on the development of the physical body and senses before the age of seven, and because the corresponding "genes" are so strongly used in the creation of the etheric/dense physical form. [For a much more complete answer and for greater potential understanding, see Chapter Seven: "The Bodies and the Senses" and Chapter Eleven: "Reincarnation."]

Question #19: **After death, then, does everyone go back to being his or her soul, and does everyone experience increasing levels of consciousness (as well as great joy) in the process?**

Brief, Incomplete, Answer: Nearly everyone eventually does, yet there are some people (though very few) who make a concerted effort to take and to avoid giving while physically alive as well as while they live on the inner planes after death. These people choose to disconnect first from all giving and then from their souls, and they eventually succeed in doing so. As a person takes, his or her consciousness keeps decreasing because consciousness comes from giving. Thus people who are consistently very selfish eventually lose their individual self-awareness, which was what made them distinctly human in the first place. In many ways, these people are more animal-like than human because of their very low consciousnesses. Instead of becoming more conscious as they die from each of their bodies, they become less so because they are not moving closer to being their (more giving) souls. They are subconsciously aware of this condition, which terrifies them while they live. People who are consistently selfish suffer immensely from these fears.

Most people, while alive physically and then on the inner planes (prior to death from a body), can either increase or decrease their consciousness of themselves. This comes from a person's level of consciousness, or giving. If a person chooses to be selfish and to regularly take but remains connected to his or her soul, he or she will lose consciousness while he or she lives. However, at the death of a body, a person's consciousness will naturally increase as he or she moves closer to being his or her soul. After shedding the personality's lower bodies and senses that have been caught in illusions and used selfishly, most people do eventually experience the great joy and the increased consciousness of being their souls. [For a much more complete answer and for greater potential understanding, see Chapter Five: "Giving Thought—The Mode of Self Creation" and Chapter Eight: "The Three Subtle Dimensions That Humans Live In."]

Question #20: **What happens to those few people who choose to disconnect from their souls, and how does anyone live without a soul in the first place?**

Brief, Incomplete, Answer: There is a collective group soul that replaces the individual human soul when a person consciously chooses to live a nearly totally selfish and dark life (away from God's thought, or light). This collective soul is called cosmic evil. When people connect to the group soul of evil they lose most of their consciousness of themselves, because this group soul does much of their thinking for them. All of this thought has a common theme, which is the attempt to reverse anything that is light in form, or is virtue. Sometimes in this theme is the chosen attempt to be destructive towards virtue, and to change it into darkness (selfishness). The group soul of evil is not very creative, because it mostly tries to destroy that which others have created. It wants to destroy the light of God's mind. When people become possessed by this soul of cosmic evil they seek to destroy because, in their illusion, they think that being destructive will help them to be powerful and important. They desperately seek this illusion of power and importance in compensation for their tremendous and terrible feelings of loss of both their self-awareness and their own souls. Once a person heads down this dark road, it is very difficult for her or him to change towards becoming giving. [For a much more complete answer and for greater potential understanding, see Chapter Six: "About Souls" and Chapter Eight: "The Three Subtle Dimensions That Humans Live In."]

Question #21: **What happens to those who become possessed by evil?**

Brief, Incomplete, Answer: Souls are immortal, and while a personality can become possessed by cosmic evil and can eventually disconnect itself from its own soul, that soul continues on and has several options to compensate for its loss of a particular lifetime and its associated personality. The evil personality can continue on without its own soul for a number of lifetimes because it takes with itself the "genes" of its physical and emotional nature and mostly the form part of its mental mind. These "genes" then become its physical, emotional, and lower mental natures in each life—but without the improvements that would have resulted from the creation of virtue. The consciousness of evil personalities remains very low (actually, sub-human) because of their extreme greed. They suffer from excessive fears and a lack of consciousness, which result directly from their own choices to be selfish. Eventually these people lose nearly all consciousness of themselves and cannot even choose to be selfish, because they ultimately destroy all parts of their consciousness except the small part of God that still integrates them (givingly) as lifeforms. This is what frees them to begin a very long path back into redeveloping themselves into giving beings and to becoming individually ensouled again. The punishment these people receive is self-inflicted, based upon a system that scientifically rewards giving and causes those who are selfish to suffer. Very few people ever choose to become evil, although most people do suffer somewhat from their own levels of being selfish and from taking rather than giving. [For a much more complete answer and for greater potential understanding, see Chapter Eight: "The Three Subtle Dimensions That Humans Live In."]

Question #22: **How does the system that you mentioned work scientifically to reward those who are giving and cause those who are selfish to suffer?**

Brief, Incomplete, Answer: We all live within one Great Being, and whatever we do to (or for) others is eventually done to (or for) us. It is our limited concept of time that causes us to not be aware of this effect. As our consciousness grows from giving, we become more aware of the truth about how the system works. Some people may refer to this system as karma, with some long-term type of banking system of credits and debits of good and bad deeds. Actually, it is in some ways much more simple and straightforward than that. As we give we become more conscious and as we take we lose our self-awareness, causing an immediate effect on us for those "bad" (and "good") deeds. The longer-term effects are, like those mentioned above, also causal. This means that everything is connected. If we do something (as a cause) to someone else, the effect will eventually work its way back to us. Any time someone does something to (or for) someone else, the effect will eventually work its way back to that person. The concept of karma can be illustrated by a gigantic network of interconnected ropes, with each rope tied to another rope at some point, and with every person tied to one of those ropes. Any time a person pulls on his or her rope, the tug will eventually be felt in that person's rope as well as in the other ropes that are being pulled on by that person's tug. Actually, it may take lifetimes for that person's tugs on the other ropes to work their way back to him or her. The reason for the delay is that other people are connected to these ropes, which diverts those tugs for a while. Selfish tugs receive, eventually, selfish tugs in return, from those whose ropes that were selfishly tugged. Likewise, giving tugs cause giving tugs to be returned. In both cases, energy is following thought that is greater than its own.

Karma is based upon creation in the right (or, in reverse, wrong) direction. Creation in the right direction is creation along the line of God's thought (light in form); this is what we call virtue. When we are virtuous, the direction of our creation enlightens others and brings *their* creation of virtue towards us because the energy that makes up the form of their creation follows their virtuous thought and ours. But if we create darkness (away from God's thought in form— non-virtue) we bring towards us the dark creations of others…again, because energy follows thought that is greater than its own. Note, as a reminder, that energy follows thought because at one time energy and thought were joined together as one, but a Great Being (whom we call God) decided to separate parts of its thought from energy in order to create our form universe.

So now the energy follows the thought in order to learn to think, as well as to recombine and to virtuously become one again. [For a much more complete answer and for greater potential understanding, see Chapter Ten: "Time and Space" and Chapter Eleven: "Reincarnation."]

Example of How "Good," or Positive, Karma Functions

Each person is giving "rope" to each other person. No one experiences forces on his or her "rope" from those who are also giving. The type of 'rope' is either that which is given or that which is taken. The type of "rope" follows the thought of those connected to it. Those who are giving "rope" continuously attract "rope" that was given by others.

Illustration 1.7

Example of How "Bad," or Negative, Karma Functions

Each person is taking "rope" from each other person. Everyone experiences forces on her or his "rope" as others pull in differing directions. Each only experiences "rope" that is being taken by others because her or his thought is attracting only the type of "rope" that is taken (and not given). "Rope," or energy, follows thought that is greater than its own. Taken "rope" is a type that is selfish, and it follows selfish thought. Given "rope" follows the thought of givers, who are more loving.

Illustration 1.8

Question #23: **If karma exists, then why is it that people who are criminals sometimes do not get caught, and what about when something very bad happens to a large group of people—like in the case of an airplane crash, or when thousands of civilians die in a war?**

Brief, Incomplete, Answer: Those who die in a group, or, probably worse, those who *suffer* as a group, often do so because they, as a group, have some common karma. In the case of wars, the karma of the whole nation to which the affected group belongs is frequently involved. The laws established by humanity are not the only means by which karma works itself out with criminals. In some cases, criminals' karma may not come back to them for many years (or even lifetimes) because karma is a balancing of causes and their effects and is not a vindictive tool for punishment. The selfishness that people act out can be offset and balanced by their creation of virtue. By becoming more giving and/or virtuous in other ways, people can reduce or eliminate any consequences of their previous selfishness. In the case of disasters, such as airplane crashes, group karma can play a role. However, sometimes there is a common thread in the individual karma of the people who suffer and/or die, which could be as simple as a common time of death so that the entire group can be reborn together at a certain time. Souls sometimes need to leave the physical plane within a certain time period in order to be better prepared to serve in a future one during which their service will be more important. It is important to realize that death is not an end, but a change in the way in which people live. Death is sometimes an improvement to people's lives and can increase the levels at which they live virtuously if they, through increased consciousness, choose to create a great deal more virtue. [For a much more complete answer and for greater potential understanding, see Chapter Eight: "The Three Subtle Dimensions That Humans Live In" and Chapter Eleven: "Reincarnation."]

Question #24: **Does God or any "Great Being" watch over us and help us, if maybe we deserve it?**

Brief, Incomplete, Answer: Being a human is quite difficult because humans have individual souls and must learn nearly everything on their own, rather than relying on the instincts of a group soul. This condition makes humans much more independent and creative, but it also causes them to have some problems that the lower kingdoms (such as animals) mostly do not have. Humans need input about how to recognize virtue and how to be aware of any time when they are not creating it. This input is supplied by a person's conscience, which is really the meditative thoughts of a Great Being who is referred to by a number of different names, one of which is the "Inner Guide." Some people may prefer the name "OverSoul," or "Guardian Angel," or, perhaps, "Solar Angel." Each person, as a soul, has his or her own Great Being, or Inner Guide, who helps his or her soul's incarnations through all of their lifetimes. The part of a person's mind that can think creatively of virtue is a part of this Great Being's mind as well, so a person is joined with her or his Inner Guide on a soul level, or from the higher mind. A person can hear the meditative thoughts of his or her Inner Guide, or Solar Angel, only when he or she chooses to allow these thoughts into his or her self-awareness by having chosen to be more giving at that moment. People who are nearly always selfish, or are indeed always selfish, may have turned off the Inner Guide to their hearing.

Solar Angels are Beings who are enlightened energy that is conscious of its Self. They are not humans and do not incarnate on earth. They are not dead people talking to us from other dimensions, although they are on other dimensions. A person's Inner Guide speaks to her or him only from the higher part of her or his mental mind—the higher, spiritual part of the mental plane—and above. Again, a person can hear his or her Solar Angel because of the energy that the person and his or her Solar Angel share in the person's mental mind.

Others who can help us include members of the entire next kingdom beyond the human, that of (liberated) Souls. This kingdom works very hard to help humanity collectively, as a group. The help comes in the form of unusually high levels of giving and in extraordinary hidden effects. A very few individual members of humanity who are themselves approaching becoming members of the Kingdom of Souls also provide assistance. One way in which the Soul kingdom helps is through the teaching and elevating of consciousness of the few members of humanity who are making the change from the human kingdom to the next. These few individuals then help some other members of humanity in somewhat similar ways.

Even further away from the human kingdom, the remaining higher kingdoms have less to do with individual members of humanity and concern themselves more with larger groups. This does not rule out a "personal" relationship with God, though, because as people create virtue they raise their *awareness* of God within themselves (through enlightened thought) to a higher level. Those who consistently create virtue realize that they and God are *mutually* conscious of and concerned for (at their different levels) one another. [For a much more complete answer and for greater potential understanding, see Chapter Five: "Giving Thought—The Mode of Self Creation," and Chapter Nine: "The Kingdoms and Their Purpose."]

Question #25: **If a part of the purpose of life is to learn to give as well as to become more giving, then does that mean that we should not do things for ourselves, like earning money and owning things?**

Brief, Incomplete, Answer: People are here to become creative in their giving and not just to give, but to give in terms of others' needs, especially in ways that help the *others* to better

One Man Using His Material Possessions Virtuously and Another Using Them Selfishly

Using material things in a shared way can cause the material parts of life to become a part of the creation of virtue. Types of virtue are helping others to become more cooperative and sharing, more loving, more truthful, and beautiful in their balance of spirit to form. The more a person gives, the more that he or she experiences life as One.

Accumulating material things for personal use that does not include some means of cooperating and sharing, loving, and creating more truth or beauty in others separates the material parts of life from the growth of more of life. People who use material things in such a way decrease their growth and understanding of life that can come from including the material parts of life. The decrease causes people to lose meaning in life as they lose understanding of life (because they understand less of something—material or otherwise—as they give less of it to others). As less growth occurs in a person's life because he or she retains so much material (energy), he or she increases his or her aging and moves closer towards death.

Illustration 1.9

give. Their creations include those things that help others to be sharing and cooperative, to be empathic and loving, and to experience more wholeness, or truthfulness, in their thoughts. These things can include material goods plus families, friends, and some reserves of money because each person needs to serve his or her own bodies (physical, emotional, and mental) as well as the bodies and spirits of others. If people give to themselves so that they can better give to others in order that *the others* can better give, then one's self-interest is really interest in all others and is, therefore, not selfish at all. For example, there might be two men who both have very expensive and elaborate hi-fidelity stereo systems. The first listens to his music because it makes him happy and he likes having such a fine-sounding system—it makes him feel special, as well. The second has the same system and enjoys the music because he invites many different people in to listen and to learn to appreciate music so that they might help even more people to be interested in music. The quality of the sound helps to improve the effect of the appreciation of music as well as the emotional nature of people, provided that the music has beauty in it.

People who share their material things and treat them as vehicles for serving others are not being selfish when they have nice things because these nice things are for others as well. The same applies to that which people feel and think. People need to use their emotions and thoughts in a giving manner, for others, yet they also can improve upon and have better quality of emotions and thoughts without being selfish, if their motive is ultimately to creatively give. [For a much more complete answer and for greater potential understanding, see Chapter Twelve: "How to Increase Consciousness."]

Question #26: **How can we improve ourselves in our giving?**

Brief, Incomplete, Answer: People can choose to focus on certain parts of their physical, emotional, and/or mental natures in order to improve their senses and the use of these senses in giving. When people focus their senses to ultimately be able to better give, they are making a sacrifice of their senses to their spirit, or soul, who *wants* to give. People are actually limiting themselves when they focus. Self-imposed limitation and sacrifice are much the same thing; when people enact either or both for the purpose of giving, they are becoming more their souls. Some people may call this *spiritual discipline*. It is all self-chosen and is not done to them by others—as many people might consider the word *discipline* to mean. [For a much more complete answer and for greater potential understanding, see Chapter Seven: "The Bodies and the Senses" and Chapter Twelve: "How to Increase Consciousness."]

Question #27: **Does joy or bliss come from spiritual discipline?**

Brief, Incomplete, Answer: Until people actually are giving or creating other virtue, even though their motive is to *eventually* give, self-limitation (or spiritual sacrifice, which can be called spiritual discipline as well) is not joyful or blissful because joy and bliss occur only as the giving takes place and helps others. There is a disparity in the time that it takes to improve oneself and the amount of giving that one can do to meet the needs of others—especially the needs that others have to become more giving. Because of this time lag, changing oneself into a soul (a person who only appropriately gives) can be a rather long and difficult process because the "rewards" must be within one's plans for each new element of future spiritual self-limitation. The seeking of joy or bliss without commensurate levels of discipline is selfish, and will not realize the intended goal because the seeking lacks the creation of virtue.

There is a side to spiritual sacrifice that is somewhat more immediately gratifying. It is true that the first move in this direction can be the most difficult step and can take the longest time to reach, and each new discipline may be difficult because it provides no immediate reward. However, once a person has made the first move in this direction, the earlier disciplines that were enacted may provide him or her with the ability to begin to give wisely to others because of the improvements in himself or herself. This does produce joy, as others create more virtue. [For a much more complete answer and for greater potential understanding, see Chapter Twelve: "How to Increase Consciousness."]

***Question #28:* I am not sure that I want to change myself to become more giving or to create more virtue. How could this book be of any value to me?**

Brief, Incomplete, Answer: Something can be of value to a person even when she or he chooses not to use it. Since you are asking this question, or reading the question and re-creating its meaning in your mind, it is very likely that some information in this book will be of help to you. Most people are afraid to give and to create other types of virtue, and are self-ish out of both fear and ignorance. Reading this book can help to change the ignorance. But the fear of giving that comes from the false belief that one will lose something in the process is ultimately a fear of loss of life, or a fear of death. This fear needs to be overcome by actual self-experimentation, possibly by using some of the concepts in this book as a basis for exper-imentation and testing in one's daily life. [For a much more complete answer and for greater potential understanding, see Chapter Seven: "The Bodies and the Senses" and Chapter Twelve: "How to Increase Consciousness."]

***Question #29:* What kind of fears do you mean we have when you say the fear of dying prevents us from giving?**

Brief, Incomplete, Answer: Most people have a fear of death, even if they are reli-gious. Many people think that they might lose their conscious lives. The loss is, to them, at least a possibility. This fear of death then becomes part of the fear of not having enough of everything while they live. The reason is that having more seems to ensure prolongation of, at least, phys-ical life. Then people respond selfishly to have and keep all they can get, in order to alleviate this fear, of death in disguise. [For a much more complete answer and for greater potential understanding, see Chapter Eight: "The Three Subtle Dimensions That Humans Live In" and Chapter Eleven: "Reincarnation."]

***Question #30:* Can you explain exactly what death is like, so that maybe this fear could be alleviated?**

Brief, Incomplete, Answer: The exact experience of death is somewhat variable, because of differences in the ways that people have lived. A close but general explanation that would fit most people's experience of death is as follows:

A person stays alive in a body for as long as her or his soul focuses its thought on that body and keeps the energy (and coalesced energy, as matter in the physical world) together as form, because the energy follows the thought of the soul. At some point, staying in that body will no longer be helpful towards a person's mission of learning to create virtue. In addition, the energy/matter of a person's body may need a rest from following the thought of her or his soul and personality. When these conditions occur, a person's soul decides to remove its thought-ful attention from the body, and then the body ceases to remain integrated. It begins to disin-tegrate into its constituent parts. This is the point at which a person dies from that body; the process can be extended over a long period of time (inviting disease) or physical death can be imposed suddenly.

Experientially, for most people, the process of death begins with the leaving of the dense physical body. The person will generally stay for anywhere from a few seconds to several days or more in a much less dense (but still physical) form, which is sometimes referred to as the etheric body. A person who has left his or her dense physical body can move simply by his or her thought alone. This happens because the energy in the etheric body is so much less dense that it moves much more easily, and can actually move by following *that person's* thoughts. In their etheric bodies, many people float to a level near the ceiling of the rooms they are in, or float to some height above their dead dense physical bodies if they are not in a room. All sensation of physical pain that came from the dense physical body ceases as a person leaves this body, because physical pain is caused by the disintegration of the form, which, at this stage, is mainly occurring in the dense body. The etheric part of the physical body also begins to disintegrate at death, but because it is so much less dense it stays together longer, usually for a few seconds to several days, but sometimes much longer.

Some people, particularly if they become fearful, might "see" their Inner Guides through their mental minds. These people might believe that their Inner Guides, or Solar Angels, are directly with them after they have died and while they are in their etheric bodies on the etheric sub-plane. This thought projection of the Inner Guide can look like and might take the shape of whatever would be comforting to the person; the image may even be of a deceased relative, several people, or perhaps of a religious figure. At that point most people experience a profound sense of peace. They also experience great relief upon discovering that they have not ceased to exist. Most others who are still physically alive cannot see the physically dead but etherically alive person. While the etheric plane is still a part of our world, because of its higher frequencies it is too subtle in its effect on the senses of those who are physically alive to receive them. Radio and television waves are, as is all higher electromagnetic radiation, a part of the etheric sub-planes, but these waves cannot be directly seen by most people. It might be said that our etheric bodies are composed of a sort of "radio waves" that have both a much higher frequency than that which is known to modern science, and an unusual and presently unknown phase, or a direction of *organic* etheric energy, that is not measurable by modern science. Today's science can measure the phase of inorganic matter only, and does not understand phase concerning etheric organic matter.

The length of time that a person spends on the etheric plane after death greatly depends upon that person's own desires. The next dimension to which people travel is the astral (emotional) plane, which is a totally different dimension from the etheric dimension and is composed of energy that is either emotional or loving in nature. Humanity has not yet discovered this energy, which is a separate energy from that which is already known about. This astral, or emotional/loving, energy evokes a sense of desire, or the energy's movement that a person wants towards himself or herself, in those who retain it in their emotional senses and bodies (a person's emotional senses are a part of her or his emotional body). The retention of this emotional energy is caused by the choices (in thought) of a person to be selfish with his or her emotions rather than to give of his or her emotional energy by changing it into love. If a person focuses his or her thought on himself or herself emotionally, some part of the emotional energy becomes retained in that person's emotional senses and body because the energy follows the thought and then causes him or her to sense (to feel) desire. If a person desires to remain on the etheric plane and to observe what is happening in the dense physical world, he or she will remain for a while in the etheric body, at least until it so disintegrates as to leave that person senseless. Usually before that point is reached, most people let go of any desires regarding the physical plane and go on to the astral world. Within a fairly short time, most people find themselves fairly uninterested in observing physical plane life because the most they could do would be to observe. They are much more interested in what lies ahead of them even though they are leaving loved ones behind. Part of the reason for this interest is that some people do not realize that once they leave their etheric bodies they will no longer be able to return to them, nor, with little exception, will they be able to use their sensual senses to even observe anything happening on the physical earth.

Many people find themselves on the astral plane almost immediately following physical death because what they desire is to know the future, much more than to grieve the past. Whatever their desires, it is the individual people who are in control of the events immediately after death and then for as long as they live on the astral plane. Once arriving on the astral plane, people will experience what they desire, either in a constructed fantasy that seems very real to them, or in concert with others who inhabit this world with them. People can live in their astral bodies for up to fifty of dense earth years, with the average length of time closer to thirty-five to forty dense earth years. By many people's standards, astral life is quite wonderful, if not heaven-like, because whatever they desire they receive nearly instantly. Only those who desire violence, suffering, or some other disquieting condition could be considered to have less than a "heavenly" life upon first arriving on the astral plane. For nearly all people, life after death is happier and far less stressful than physical life was. [For a much more complete answer and for greater potential understanding, see Chapter Eight: "The Three Subtle Dimensions That Humans Live In."]

Question #31: **It sounds like death, or at least life after death, is better than life. Why should we toil and suffer so much in this world if the next one is so much nicer?**

Brief, Incomplete, Answer: Despite the "rosy" picture of the astral world, people still suffer when they function selfishly in this world of emotion. The suffering is much more emotional, and with little or no sensual senses (the five physical ones) the emotional suffering is greatly emphasized. The main cause of emotional suffering becomes the eventual boredom that results from all desires being nearly immediately met. After a while, unless a person is creative of virtue, there is nothing new. Retained energy destroys the senses of astral energy much more quickly than those of physical energy because the astral energy is so much less dense. As a person's emotional senses diminish from the retained energy of her or his accumulative selfishness, she or he is rendered numb—and bored, which is a very unpleasant state. Eventually the astral body does die, and those who are suffering from the boredom and numbness are released from this body and go on to the next dimension.

The place and time within which people can be most creative and virtuous is when they have the most senses to do so—when they are physically alive. Those people who create virtue experience great joy, and either less boredom or none at all. In addition, their physical senses that remain fused with their astral senses stay more intact. Their astral senses may remain mostly intact as well, until nearly the end of astral plane life because so little of the emotional energy gets retained within their senses, and so there is very little damage to the senses from retained energy. Interestingly, the very same principles apply to people while they are physically alive, mostly about their etheric/dense physical senses. Those who are physically alive may choose to ignore these principles or they may never even notice that they exist, because the process is so very slow as a result of the much greater density of matter in the etheric/dense physical senses. [For a much more complete answer and for greater potential understanding, see Chapter Eight: "The Three Subtle Dimensions That Humans Live In" and Chapter Twelve: "How to Increase Consciousness."]

Question #32: **Why isn't the meaning of life just to experience things and to have fun wherever we are?**

Brief, Incomplete, Answer: If people make their purpose for living different from the purpose of God—the Being they live within—they make their lives stressful and difficult because many of the principles that are incorporated within God's thought will be in contradiction to their choices. Most people experience fun as a very limited period of time during which one or more of their desires are satiated enough so that they temporarily do not experience their other desires. Within some relatively short period of time, new desires will surface and the "fun" and apparent happiness will end. This can lead to a compulsive series of life actions that are in endless pursuit of desires, but with no permanent, long-lasting, or even meaningful effect. The result can be despair and depression—and is certainly not long-term "fun." To simply experience life without being a creator within it is also an incredibly boring thing to do; eventually, even emotional excitement becomes boring if one is not being creative. Creation without God's direction (having no virtue) leads to incompleteness and, eventually, to chaotic conditions. Ultimately, the only thing that leads to a meaningful and enjoyable life is the creation of virtue. [For a much more complete answer and for greater potential understanding, see Chapter Three: "Cosmic Virtues, Parts of God's Light in Form."]

Question #33: **When does a person's growth end?**

Brief, Incomplete, Answer: The universe grows as each of its parts grows; the universe, while being cyclical in nature, is also infinite as far as creation is concerned. The more that people contribute to the growth of God by creating more virtue, the more that God grows, as do all of the relationships between the parts of God. A person can never catch up to the end of such a system because it grows both from that person's growth and from the growth of all others, without end. [For a much more complete answer and for greater potential understanding, see Chapter Two: "The Creator and the Big Picture" and the Summary.]

Question #34: **What do you mean when you say that the universe is cyclical in nature?**

Brief, Incomplete, Answer: One of the ways in which people can create growth is through focus and sacrificial limitation; when one part is focused on, the others are not. Focus and sacrificial limitation produce a cyclical effect in the universe, sort of like breathing in and out. Sacrificial choices lead to cyclical effects, but they do not cause a universe to be finite. For

Seven-Day Watering Cycle

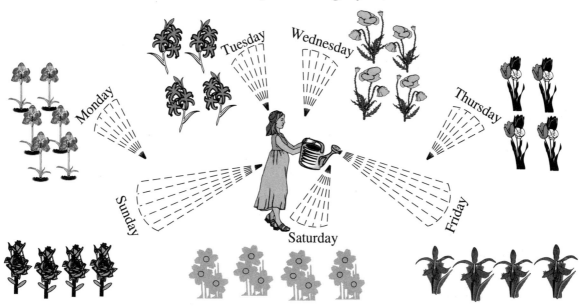

This woman waters one of seven different types of plants, in differing amounts, per day. The activity of watering, while different for each one of the seven days, establishes a cycle of time. This cycle is caused by the connection of her choices in thought affecting the activities she is doing. Cycles in time are evidence of some type of thought changing time and space. The larger the thought, the greater the amount of time and space affected in the cycle and the more activities that occur within each cycle.

Illustration 1.10

example, imagine that you had a garden in which there were seven different types of flowers that you focused on in terms of watering them, and that you watered one type of flower per day. Once you had watered all seven types of flowers, you would have created a watering cycle of one week for each of the flowers. Your focused attention created the cycle. [For a much more complete answer and for greater potential understanding, see Chapter Ten: "Time and Space."]

> ### *Question #35:* **You mentioned that people live, on average, the equivalent of an average of about thirty-five physical earth years on the astral plane; is time there different from the way we experience it here?**

> *Brief, Incomplete, Answer:* The experience of time does change quite a lot on the different inner planes. The reason has to do with the great differences in the density of energy on each plane and the speed of light, or of the thought of the great creative Being of the entire dimension. With the energy of each less dense-in-energy plane following the thought that is present, a great deal more energy surrounds each being who is thinking. Modern physics has proved that when a lot of energy or mass (which is coalesced energy) is present, the intense concentration of energy creates a condition known as time dilation. The time and space surrounded by the concentrated energy moves much slower than the time outside it does.

As an example of this principle of modern physics, time dilation would be caused by a very powerful spaceship that left earth at close to the speed of light. The energy produced by the engines of the spaceship (creating "speed") would create a difference in time. When the spaceship returned to earth, one day might have elapsed for those in the ship, while centuries could have passed here on earth.

There is not only less density of energy on all of the inner planes, but the energy is also of a higher frequency. According to modern physics, energy causes time and space to change. What happens is that the more energy (or matter) that is concentrated in one place, the more the time and space curve and change for those beings who occupy it. As the energy/matter that is used to create the form of the thought itself becomes less dense, it is easier to think and create thoughtforms, just as it is easier to move styrofoam balls together than to move steel ones. The space (and time) *inside* each dimension that is higher in its frequency of energy but lower in density becomes more curved from the intense thought of each being. This causes the space and time between the beings in the same dimension to shorten, allowing them to communicate more easily and to function together more as a group unit, or to become more group conscious. The intensity of the thought is greater because the less dense energy is more easily attracted around each thinking being, and the concentrations of the energy then cause the space to curve around the beings. Less time is required for these beings to communicate with one another. It should be noted that the real cause of some of this effect is time separating from space.

Again, this is the principle known as *time dilation,* and it occurs wherever energy or matter exists in space—which is everywhere that we know of in our world. The greater the concentration of energy or matter (remember, matter is densely coalesced energy), the more the space becomes curved from the energy's presence and the greater the dilation of time within that space, as compared to other places. The dimensions of our universe are created by the thought of beings who occupy the space of these dimensions; as these beings create with their thought they change the relationship of energy to the space, which then affects the time. Each dimension is a field of expression of creative thought that has its own specific and unique dilation of time as compared to other fields of creative expression. This effect is due to the differences in the quality of the energy in each dimension and how the thought affects it.

For example, on the astral plane (where the energy is higher in frequency and much less dense than the energy generally found on the dense earth) people find it easier to create from their thought because less effort is required for people to get the energy to move together around themselves. Even though the astral plane is less dense in energy overall, it is much easier to concentrate the energy in this dimension around the thought of people. The result is that the inside space of the plane becomes more curved, and shortens the time and space between people. The outside dimension of the astral plane is much larger and less curved than is the space on the dense earth because the energy is both higher in frequency and less dense (like the skin of the balloon in the answer to Question #4). The result is a time dilation between the planes, with more time available—or less time being separated from space—for those who are alive astrally. These people live in greatly dilated time.

Time and Space between Beings on Various Dimensions

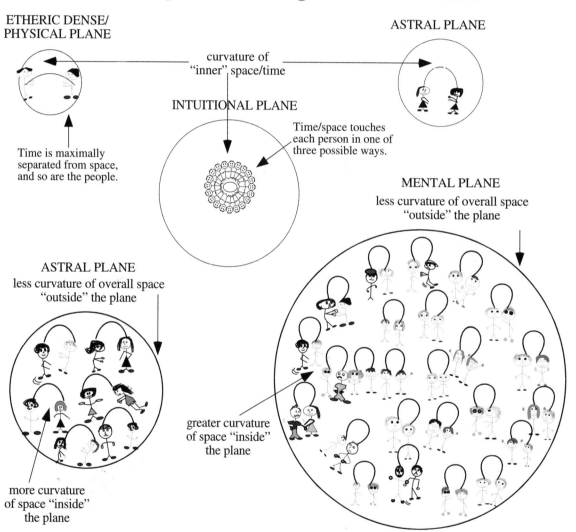

The greater the levels of thought between people, up to the speed of light (thought) of the corresponding Ray Lord of the dimension the people are on, the more that time joins with space. As time joins with space on a dimension, less space exists between people there because the curvature of space around each time vortex is greater. When the space completely curves around at least one time vortex of a Now's three vortices, space becomes completely curved and people who are all at the same level of consciousness are in contact with one another. Note that space completely curving around a vortex of time in a Now for more than one person at a time occurs from the intuitional plane, up.

Illustration 1.11

The time dilation caused by the above-described conditions causes those on the higher planes, or dimensions, to experience the passage of time at increasingly slower rates. For example, a person on the astral plane might experience time to be twelve times slower than would someone on dense earth. When people sleep they sometimes go to the astral plane in consciousness; for each minute that a person is sleeping in bed, she or he might experience perhaps twelve actual minutes of activity in the astral world. Most people have had this experience, of dreaming while asleep for just a few minutes yet having had experiences that they were certain had lasted for over half an hour. This is an example of time dilation. Some scientists have determined that nearly *all* dreams take place within about two to nine minutes of time on physical earth. Most people experience some of these dreams as lasting for much longer periods of time.

When people die and go to the astral plane, the average of thirty-five dense earth years or so that they spend on the astral plane may seem like and may actually be hundreds of years of time to them because their time is dilated, as compared to the way that people on dense earth experience time. [For a much more complete answer and for greater potential understanding, see Chapter Ten: "Time and Space."]

Question #36: **My dreams seldom make much sense. Are thought and life on the astral plane (or in other dimensions after death) like my dreams?**

Brief, Incomplete, Answer: While people sleep, the senses of their bodies become isolated both within each body and between the bodies. The integrating element, the personality, is mostly lacking because it needs for all the parts of itself that are alive to be active, if it is to maintain its focus. One of these parts at a time is under repair by the body itself, which requires that the personality relinquish its focused thought on that body if it is to be free to repair itself. The reason is that bodies are energy, and need to be free of informing thought in order to think for themselves and to perform their tasks. Since bodies are the energy, and the personality somewhat represents the soul (for most people, in absentia) as the thinking, informing, aspect, the energy in the bodies follows the personality's thought. The problem is that in order for each of the three human bodies (the physical, emotional, and mental) to repair themselves, they need to have no other thought from the integrating personality to follow. Sleep furnishes these conditions for repair or growth and also leaves people in a condition in which there is a lack of personal integration of both their senses and bodies, and of their identity, which the personality and its self provide for a person.

When a person dreams on the astral plane, often either the etheric/dense physical body or the mental body is being repaired. The dream both helps to identify retained energy in the body *and* to release some of it by using that amount of it to construct the dream, often before the body is further repaired. If it is the etheric/dense physical body that is being repaired and the person is therefore likely to be dreaming either astrally or mentally, a person's dreams will be more lucid and will make better sense. She or he may not remember these dreams, though, because the etheric/dense physical brain may be unable to record them if it is under repair by the etheric/dense physical body at that time. Dreaming etherically or sometimes astrally while a person's mental body is not under the personality's focus (and is, therefore, under repair) causes him or her to have very disjointed dreams that cannot have logical, structured sequence because logical structure and sequence are what the mental body and senses provide. However, dreams of this nature are often recorded in the etheric/physical brain because it sometimes *is* available for the personality's use, and so the person more often remembers them.

When people are alive and awake astrally, just as when they are alive after physical death, they are fully conscious and, on average, and especially when they first arrive there, can think better than they did while they were physically alive. As people live in awake consciousness on higher dimensions, it is easier to think because the energy in which they create the forms of thought is less dense. [For a much more complete answer and for greater potential understanding, see Chapter Seven: "The Bodies and the Senses."]

Question #37: **Do people who live on the higher planes sleep and dream, and is the lack of personality integration that you described the reason why I can't seem to fully remember who I am when I dream?**

Brief, Incomplete, Answer: The second part of your question is the simplest to answer; the lack of personality integration while people sleep prevents them from both knowing fully who they are and from remembering what happened yesterday in their lives, as well as what plans they may have for the future. While a person may know her or his name and some qualities about himself or herself, depending upon where the dream is taking place and which one of the other bodies is under repair, that person's self-concept is quite limited. The sleeping person's self-concept is at the level of a not-too-smart animal, in many cases.

On each higher plane that humans inhabit, the need for sleep greatly diminishes because there are fewer bodies to repair. When a person has died from her or his astral body and has only the mental body remaining, the mental body still needs repair, even though it is far less stressed in total than the amount of stress in all the bodies when they exist. Therefore, some amount of sleep is still necessary. While the mental body is being repaired, the personality disappears and the person experiences the concepts of being her or his soul on the *higher* mental plane and, as in the other scenarios, does not fully know who she or he is. Only after complete death of all the human bodies does the personality awaken to being its soul in full self-consciousness. [For a much more complete answer and for greater potential understanding, see Chapter Seven: "The Bodies and the Senses" and Chapter Eight: "The Three Subtle Dimensions That Humans Live In."]

Question #38: **Can people who are dead contact those who are alive here on earth?**

Brief, Incomplete, Answer: Very infrequently, people who have died from physical life may not want to go on to live in other dimensions. They may have committed suicide, or they may be particularly interested in and/or concerned with certain aspects of the physical world more than anything else, even their future lives as they might be on the astral plane. Because of their very focused thought, these people can maintain life in their etheric bodies for up to a hundred or so dense earth years, remaining on the etheric plane for this long a time. Even though the etheric body is still composed of energy from the etheric/dense physical dimension, it is energy that is disconnected from its denser constituents that make it into matter. The etheric body fully disintegrates more slowly (although it initially disintegrates much more quickly) than the physical body does. This condition results from changes in time caused by dilation and from the lower density of the etheric body, as compared to the change, over time, in the person's ability to think. The reason that the presence of a person in etheric form is very difficult to sense by those in dense form is that the senses of people in dense form are tuned to frequencies that are lower than those of the energy in these etheric bodies. An etheric person can still see physically alive people through the use of his or her higher-frequency senses, but he or she loses, for the most part, the ability to touch them or dense physical things. In reverse, for example, people physically alive can see physical fire but can only feel and not see its heat; the heat exists at a frequency that is too low for their senses to detect. A change in dimension causes a change in the ability to sense.

If the etheric people stay in one place for too long a time, they cause problems in the space and time around them because of their disconnected matter. Modern physicists might refer to this effect as a shift in the quantum constant, but the easiest way to understand it is that the atoms of these people's bodies are in two places at the same time; the first is where the physical body is (even if it was cremated and dispersed, although this greatly limits the effect), and the second is where the etheric body is. For this reason, a "ghost" is specific to a single location. If this condition lasts more than several weeks, it may become possible for dense physical people to begin to see the etheric person as a "ghost" because the space that the physically alive people share with the "ghost" has changed enough for *their* senses to begin to become more etheric in nature.

Related Senses and Energies

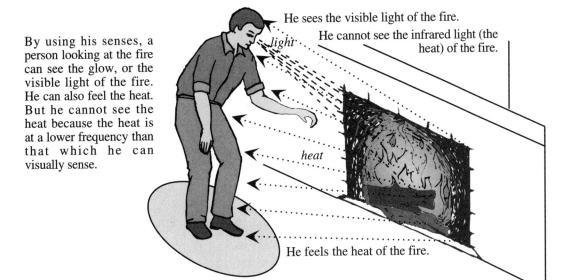

By using his senses, a person looking at the fire can see the glow, or the visible light of the fire. He can also feel the heat. But he cannot see the heat because the heat is at a lower frequency than that which he can visually sense.

He sees the visible light of the fire.

He cannot see the infrared light (the heat) of the fire.

light

heat

He feels the heat of the fire.

Illustration 1.12

Upon moving on to live on the astral plane, people who are physically dead and astrally alive lose most of the ability to have contact with those who are physically alive because they mostly lose the five sensual senses of their physical bodies. A physically dead person living on the astral plane *can* tune in on those who are physically alive and can empathically sense their feelings. Then, if that person so chooses, he or she can reconstruct the physically alive person's environment using astral senses and can then imagine what these feelings indicate in actions. However, this is a quite limited means of communication that works only in one direction.

Some people who are living in the astral world do want to communicate with those who are still physically alive, and some of those who are physically alive also want to communicate with those on the astral (or any other) plane. Such contact can be accomplished sometimes by the dense physical person splitting his or her whole emotional sense of empathy into its five distinct constituent parts and then focusing on just one of these senses (which allows the astral sense to be increased). Oddly, these senses are called soul, or psychic, senses. The main reason is that they are not the personal senses, which are the ones that are normally used. Note, however, that these psychic senses are usually lowered, or split, soul senses and not the whole sense that a soul would use for only giving. These split senses are often used for self-serving reasons, even when used to somewhat benefit others, because much emotion and egotism, or self-importance, typically surrounds their use.

Some people on the astral plane can communicate with a very few people in dense physical form who have lowered psychic senses, and vice versa. When this communication takes place, the senses that are used become damaged to the degree that the person is using them selfishly. The damage comes from the retention of energy and the self-inflicted separation of a more whole sense. The few people who are channels and other types of psychic readers and who are not fakes or self-deluded imaginers use these lowered psychic, or lowered soul, senses. The real question is whether people who have died and have gone on to the astral world and *desire* to be generally recognized and to express themselves in the physical realm are, from the vantage point of those physically alive, any wiser than those who are physically alive or can function as good advisors to them. For the most part, the astral world is filled with selfish emotional desire and is far from where human souls and the Kingdom of Souls exist in consciousness. [For a much more complete answer and for greater potential understanding, see Chapter Seven: "The Bodies and the Senses" and Chapter Eight: "The Three Subtle Dimensions That Humans Live In."]

Related Senses and Energies of Beings on Different Sub-Planes

She sees the trees and cow, but cannot see nor feel the ghost. Her senses would be unable to receive the frequencies of the ghost unless those senses have been changed by the ghost's continual presence.

The ghost can see people and things, but cannot physically touch them. Some of the ghost's senses lack the ability to sense lower frequency energies from the dense world.

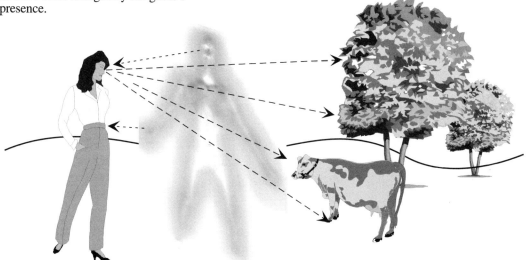

Sometimes some people may be able to see ghosts if the ghost stays in an area for a long enough time, and if the ghost is not in direct physical contact with the earth.

Illustration 1.13

Question #39: **Is it possible to visit these other dimensions while we are awake and thus fully integrated in our personalities—and still be physically alive?**

Brief, Incomplete, Answer: Nearly all people leave their physical bodies each night while they sleep and find no difficulty in doing so. To leave the dense physical body in full consciousness requires that the personality stay focused on all three of the human vehicles and that it not fall asleep while it leaves the physical body. Leaving the dense body in full consciousness is something that the personality is not accustomed to doing, but in many people can be trained to do. Younger children have more of a "natural" ability to do this because they have not yet trained their personalities to stop focusing in this way, and they do not have as much personality development in the first place.

For many diligent and willful adults, consciously getting out of the physical body can be accomplished within weeks to a couple of months, through daily practice. For someone to have any control over where she or he goes and what is experienced, though, can take much longer. And, unfortunately, such people would end up damaging their senses to the level that they selfishly used them, as is the case with the other forms of lowered psychic sense use. Few people who consciously leave their physical bodies do any significant creation of virtue, so consciously leaving the body is mostly a selfish, self-centered adventure that can cause them some harm. The single best reason to have *one* fully conscious out-of-body experience is to break through the illusions that all that exists is what people can physically sense here on dense physical earth. [For a much more complete answer and for greater potential understanding, see Chapter Seven: "The Bodies and the Senses," and Chapter Eight: "The Three Subtle Dimensions That Humans Live In."]

Question #40: **Why should I believe what you are saying in this book?**

Brief, Incomplete, Answer: This book attempts to present concepts, or the "why's," behind much of the information so that the reader can use the concepts to construct experiments in his or her own life through both observation and actions in order to determine the validity of the information. The more creative each reader is in his or her thinking, the more he or she will be able to prove or disprove what has been written. It is hoped that the reader will not strictly "believe" what is presented, but will test it out in his or her own mind and in action.

The author of this book is a physically alive person, like most of the readers, who has experienced and experimented with the information written in this book. *No* part of this book is borrowed information from another written source. It is not channeled from some source, nor has it been recorded without direct experience and experimentation in order to verify its validity. Any information that may have originated from a source whom the author believes to be a consciousness higher than himself is still experienced and experimented with to determine its validity and to conceptualize it in a way that helps others to understand this information as best as possible. This author is fully responsible for all the information contained within this volume as it is presented. The readers are invited to create with it themselves and to determine its validity for themselves. The author makes absolutely no claims with respect to his consciousness, credentials, or abilities. The best way to know a tree is by its fruit, and the best way to know the fruit is to plant it and to grow a new tree. [For a much more complete answer and for greater potential understanding, see the Preface, Introduction, and Summary.]

Question #41: **Is it possible to meet someone on the higher inner planes who is much higher in consciousness than most humans are?**

Brief, Incomplete, Answer: (Liberated) Souls, who are members of the next kingdom, have liberated themselves from thinking with a time lag in-between first the concepts and then the thoughtforms. These liberated souls think intuitively. Their concepts are all whole and joined to completed thoughtforms without a time lag. The ability to think intuitively allows these members of the next kingdom to develop an omniscience, or all-knowingness, by being interconnected in the giving use of their minds, as a collective group. Because (liberated) Souls focus only on giving and serving others to help *these others* to be better at creating virtue, they are fully group conscious. They function, at a minimum, as one in their use of knowledge. Only those who can think at or near their level of givingness and group consciousness could expect to meet one of these beings. Usually those who do are actively leaving the human kingdom and are in one of the four levels of self-created initiation prior to joining the Kingdom of Souls. A (liberated) Soul is a great loving and wise super-human, sometimes called a Master of the Ageless Wisdom and the three lower worlds. [For a much more complete answer and for greater potential understanding, see Chapter Six: "About Souls."]

Question #42: **If these liberated souls, or Souls, of the next kingdom are super-humans, do they look like people, and are there any who are physically alive?**

Brief, Incomplete, Answer: At present, most liberated souls exist in a higher dimension and are not dense physically alive, but it is important to distinguish the consciousness of the Soul from the body(-ies) that it may serve from. It is possible for many of these Souls, at present, to take dense physical human form. And it does happen that a Soul still inhabits the physical human form that he or she was born into, in his or her final lifetime as a human prior to joining this next kingdom, although there are only a very few Souls in this situation. In neither case is it likely for most people to meet them because the purpose of these super-humans is to create virtue in order to help others do the same; unless a person is doing what the super-humans are doing, he or she would not have contact with them. [For a much more complete answer and for greater potential understanding, see Chapter Six: "About Souls" and Chapter Nine: "The Kingdoms and Their Purpose."]

Question #43: **Can the use of drugs transport, or help to transport, someone to the higher inner dimensions?**

Brief, Incomplete, Answer: Before a person can leave one of her or his bodies, she or he must first traverse an energy field that surrounds the portal (which is a major center in that body) connecting her or him to another plane, or dimension. Since these portals themselves are made of specialized energy and are a part of the person and the other dimensions can be reached only through them, the other dimensions are referred to as inner dimensions. People travel through a part of themselves to reach them. The energy fields, or centers, referred to here are sometimes called *chakras*. They are usually spinning spheres that can create vortices of energies, and each sphere and its vortex connects to one of the inner dimensions. Those who leave their bodies while somewhat or fully conscious can sometimes "feel" themselves moving through one or another of these centers. Surrounding each center is another energy field that is composed of retained energies from all of the selfish focused thought of the personality that has moved energy into that center and has not given this energy to others. It composes a web of energy that separates the centers from each other, and separates a person's consciousness from the other higher dimensions and her or his other bodies, centers, and brains within those dimensions. Groups of two or more centers in two or more different bodies share parts of the same web, but are still separated from each other by this web. These webs then isolate the centers, bodies, and brains along with their senses, to the dimension they exist within.

A web is composed of the selfishly retained energies from two bodies that are dimensionally adjacent to each other. For example, the retained energy from both the etheric and astral bodies, when integrated by the focused thought of the personality, joins together between the two dimensions and bodies to create the etheric/astral web. There is also a web between the astral body and the mental body. The webs separate the centers and brain in one body from the centers and brains in the adjacent one. Furthermore, the illusion (retained energy) in the centers of each body functions as a web to keep the centers of that body separate. When two bodies that are dimensionally adjacent are integrated through the focus of the personality, a web is created. The web dissolves when the personality loses focus—through sleep or sometimes through the use of drugs. Note that drugs used non-medicinally also *add* into the centers' energies that damage the webs with the remaining level of selfish personality thought that is involved in such very emotional use of a drug. From another perspective, a web is retained energy in two centers or two brains in dimensionally adjacent bodies that are linked together by the integrating thought of the personality. Once a center becomes fully enlightened, no part of the web can exist between it and its corresponding center in the dimensionally adjacent body. When both corresponding centers in two dimensionally adjacent bodies (such as the etheric/dense physical sexual center and the astral sexual center) are fully enlightened, it would be possible to both travel inter-dimensionally between those two dimensions using the centers, and to join these two parts of the bodies. The two centers become joined through the intelligent activity and light, thus making this inter-dimensional travel possible.

When a person falls asleep, he or she can leave the body that is being repaired. When a person is physically alive, this process always starts with the etheric/dense physical body because this is the first body that the personality has stopped focusing its attention on. The focus of attention on the part of the personality is what integrates the bodies. The lack of focus causes the webs that surround the etheric centers to loosen and to somewhat disintegrate, temporarily, because the personality provides no thought for this energy to follow. Because the personality has been unfocused, when a person returns to his or her etheric/dense physical body he or she can re-enter it. This is the reason that most people leave their bodies only while their personalities are not focused on them and while they are asleep. Since energy follows thought that is greater than its own, a person can get the energy fields to temporarily loosen if his or her willpower and thought are great enough and the person wants them to loosen. However, it is easiest to do so by people who are relatively virtuous and therefore have less energy in their webs to either separate or rejoin with. Over a period of time, practice and applied motive can achieve this effect. Then a person can leave the physical body while fully conscious of the self, and any amount of harm that might befall him or her as a result will be determined by his or her motives in leaving and the amount of helpful creation of virtue that he or she did while gone. Unless a person repeatedly leaves the body selfishly, the webs remain mostly intact upon his or her return. If done frequently and with selfish motive, however, out-of-body journeys while fully conscious of the self can harm the webs by leaving permanent holes in them or by leaving them imbalanced, with parts of them having too much energy and other parts not having enough. Although the etheric/dense physical body has been mostly referred to here because it is always the first body that people leave when they are physically alive, similar conditions apply to the other bodies and dimensions when people leave or enter them.

While actually formed by a person's own selfishness, the webs are very helpful because they prevent a person's centers from coming into direct contact with each other. They also prevent a person's consciousness from contacting other dimensions while the person is awake. If people did have such contact while they were fully conscious, the compounded selfishness within them would cause their consciousnesses to be reduced. This is because consciousness comes from giving and is reduced by taking, or selfishness. The increased levels of sense would allow them to be selfish in more ways. Therefore, *greater awareness of other dimensions while people remain selfish reduces their consciousnesses* and is not helpful to them. Consequently, the energy fields (webs) that separate people's centers from each other and separate the other dimensions besides the physical from people do serve them in a very helpful way.

Using drugs that affect consciousness *can* get a person through the energy fields and into other dimensions, but great hazards and problems lie in wait for those who selfishly do this. Nearly all of these drugs work by forcing the personality to not focus on some or all of the bodies and their senses, to varying degrees. The de-focusing allows the drug user to then sometimes leave through one of the disintegrated webs and, usually, to return in similar manner. Some drugs can actually indirectly affect certain aspects of the webs. The drugs change the chemistry of the brain, nervous system, and endocrine system in the etheric/dense physical body to produce the forced effect on the personality. Since in most cases very little thought is used in the process, the energy fields may not reintegrate properly after their use. Drugs also change the way someone re-enters through the webs.

When drugs are used selflessly, with a purpose (motive) that is giving and spiritual, the retention of energy is low, the webs reintegrate without much change, and the personality can fully regain its use of the bodies and senses when it refocuses itself on them. An example of selfless use of drugs is their use by some earlier mystical societies of people, in religious and spiritual ceremonies. However, nearly all people today who either experiment with drugs or use them regularly do so for mostly self-centered, selfish reasons. In these cases, the drugs de-focus the personality and, if used regularly, destroy it—particularly the personality that is not yet fully formed, like that of a teenager. What happens is that the personality loses control over the webs, the webs become damaged by repeated and forced movement through them, and consciousness becomes *lowered* by the selfishness. This all leads to poor judgment, irresponsibility, and, possibly, possession and criminality.

Webs Separating One Body's Centers and Brains from Those of an Adjacent Body

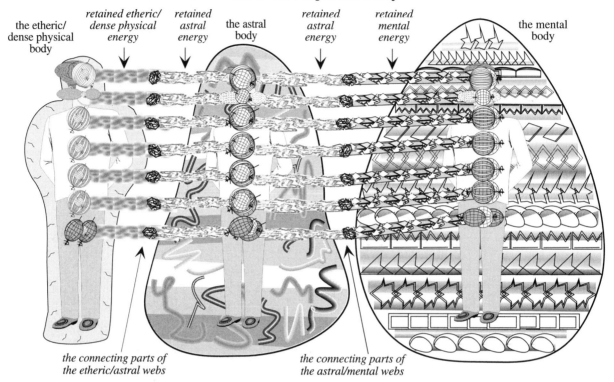

Note that although the three lower bodies are shown side-by-side, for the sake of illustration, in actuality a higher body interpenetrates a lower one.

The structure of a web is created by the unenlightened deva energy in a permanent atom. The webs are filled in and held together by darker elemental energy. This darker energy is attracted to unenlightened deva energy that is replicated from the permanent atom's structure. The darker energy creates a barrier that prevents the brain or center in one body from being in contact with the brain or center in another.

Even though the webs are created and maintained by selfishness, they protect people by keeping the brains, centers, and associated bodies separated while a person is conscious and within the control of her or his personality. If not for the webs, the energy within one body would not only follow the thought of the brains and centers in that body, but it would follow the thought of the brains and centers of other bodies, as well.

Illustration 1.14

The most important point here is that the use of drugs, for nearly everyone, *lowers* consciousness and does not raise it. Once the webs of energy surrounding the centers have been damaged or, worse, destroyed, a person can end up being in a "free fall" of lowered consciousness and increased selfishness (the two are the same). This can and often does lead to a quick trip into darkness from which the person may not return in that lifetime. These statements are not made in moral judgment. There is a science to these effects, and what has been described are the effects of self-induced causes. Cigarettes and other tobacco products, as well as alcoholic beverages and even caffeinated drinks, are included within the category of drugs in their effects on the lowering of consciousness, as explained above. The ill effects depend upon the quantity, type of drug, and length of use. These drugs do affect people, but in different ways and not nearly as severely as might mescaline, peyote, or LSD. The ways that the drugs affect the centers and webs are unique to their chemistry and interactions, which are too complex to further explain within the context of this book. [For a much more complete answer and for greater potential understanding, see Chapter Seven: "The Bodies and the Senses" and Chapter Twelve: "How to Increase Consciousness."]

 Question #44: **What do you mean by becoming possessed?**

Brief, Incomplete, Answer: Whenever a person (usually) selfishly, willfully chooses to de-focus his or her personality from a body and its senses while fully conscious, another entity from the same dimension that the body is in could influence the energy in what is that body, and get it to respond to its level of thought. The body from which a person has chosen to remove his or her focus designates the dimension from which that person may become possessed. The energy of a person's bodies follows thought, and if the person is not willing to think enough to even maintain integration, someone—something—else might. Possessing entities can be people or even animal-like creatures from either the etheric or the astral plane. They are themselves very selfish and seek to express themselves through people's either etheric/dense physical or emotional (astral) bodies.

Since possession is done by very selfish beings, people can become possessed when they are also being very selfish. People's bodies would generally not otherwise follow that line of (selfish) thought. Also, because sleep is a way that personalities give to bodies so that they can repair themselves and become rejuvenated, people are naturally protected from possession while they sleep. The rare exception is in those who are unusually selfish and/or are already possessed when they go to sleep—although since their possessing entities are so selfish, possessed people usually have trouble sleeping, and typically sleep less than people who are not possessed.

Most of the time, possession is transient and can be overcome by the personality refocusing itself on the possessed body, which will drive out those entities who are in use of it. Drugs can lead to more permanent possession, particularly in young people or if used for protracted periods of time and with any regularity. The time period for more permanent possession to take place varies greatly, depending upon the type of drug used; addiction is a sign of possession. Possession is also quite prominent among children who have been abused. Most possessions are only partial possessions, but nearly all possessing entities are ultimately, over time, destructive to the host as well as to others whom the host interacts with. The reason for the destructiveness is the extremely low consciousness of these possessing entities, which is the same as their extremely high levels of selfishness and their overall darkness. The level of darkness relates to the levels of selfishness and lowered consciousness. [For a much more complete answer and for greater potential understanding, see Chapter Seven: "The Bodies and the Senses" and Chapter Eight: "The Three Subtle Dimensions That Humans Live In."]

Question #45: **So far you have only mentioned earth in your answers; are there other planets or solar systems with life on them, and do they involve other dimensions as well?**

Brief, Incomplete, Answer: Stars have three general categories, and they are:

1. Those stars that are in the process of developing the conditions that will support lower forms of pre-life, and then develop the form parts of life through the creation of a type of intelligence in the chemistry of their planets. The planetary system is developed first, then the conditions that will support life, and then the forms of lower life are created.

2. Those stars that are focused on developing consciousness of the beginning life that has already been developed within their planetary systems. Earth is presently in a star system that is working on this second category—of developing love and givingness, or consciousness.

3. Those stars that have very advanced planetary systems in which the Beings have developed into very virtuous (liberated) Souls who are learning to create new life themselves.

Life is abundant and is nearly everywhere. Not only are there other planets that have life on them, nearly all planets are involved with creating life. Unlike earth, most planets do not have dense physical life on them because to support this form of life requires a very specific and narrow range of proximity and angle to a sun, proximity to a certain type of sun, etc. Dense physical form is necessary if the focus of consciousness is under development in a solar system, and only some solar systems are in that stage of developing life. The other planets in our solar system as well as planets in many other solar systems do have life on them. This life exists in some of the other dimensions that have been referred to in this book. There are people on some of these planets who have already lived in dense form on a dense planet. Sometimes a planet can support dense forms of life during one part of its existence and then, later in its existence, its lifeforms will exist in the etheric, astral, or mental (or another, different) dimension. A planet can remain in dense physical form while its lifeforms move on to other dimensions that it also exists within, while some other planets may exist outside dense form altogether. At present, most people would be unable to see these planets that are outside dense form.

With all of the above possible conditions, it is easy to get confused about which planets have life on them, and where these planets are. The safest assumption is that *all* planets support life, and that many have human or beyond-human life on them. While a planet is developing consciousness in dense physical form, more conscious (giving) life on other planets remains hidden from it by the choice of those higher in consciousness. The reason is that direct interaction with the much higher givingness (consciousness) of the more advanced worlds would *lower* the consciousness (givingness) of those on the dense planet and would actually hinder their development. Many of those who are intellectually centered might argue that people could learn from those more advanced than they are. But consciousness, while sometimes helped by learning and knowledge, can be raised only by giving and not by receiving, no matter how good the motives might be of both those who are higher and those who are lower in consciousness. Consciousness is the ability to wisely give, or understand, the oneness of life. Many planets and solar systems have determined that wise giving, or love/wisdom, is the correct method of interaction between those learning to give and those much more advanced in their giving to the point of always giving, as Souls. [For a much more complete answer and for greater potential understanding, see Chapter Nine: "The Kingdoms and Their Purpose."]

Question #46: **Then what about all those outer-space vehicles being spotted by some people, and the claimed abductions?**

Brief, Incomplete, Answer: Those more advanced than us in consciousness (love/givingness) seek only to help us to become more wisely giving ourselves. The carrying out of this task is left mostly to those super-humans, or (liberated) Souls in consciousness, who are indigenous to this planet. The reason is that the Souls from earth are the ones who are most aware of the needs of this world. Those who have a higher consciousness have higher senses of responsibility and would not be malevolent, nor would they intervene without beneficent purpose for those on earth. For various reasons, a *few* visitors from other worlds may be on earth from time to time, but most people would neither be aware of what they are doing nor of their presence. These helpful visitors do not involve themselves directly with humanity, and they certainly are not abducting people. Those who might visit earth are far ahead of people of earth in their development, and it is a mistake for anyone to attribute human motives and any emotional quality to these visitors' actions, unless that quality is pure unconditional love.

Some of the phenomena that people claim to have experienced come from their imagination and desires. Some are fraudulent stories to gain personal attention. Some are real! By *real* is meant that these people actually see and experience most of what they claim to. The experiences these people are having are of travelling to other dimensions because of a de-focusing effect from the personality. This effect can be caused by a number of possible conditions, such as sleep disturbances, high selfishness in one or more specific personal ways, emotional disturbances, overuse of the senses of one or more bodies (extreme fatigue), some drug combinations in which neither one of the drugs alone would have much of this effect, and a lack of a sense of self-importance. These are only some of the conditions that can cause people to travel to other dimensions; there are quite a few more. The commonality of the experiences is produced by the common thoughtforms and creative imagery that exists on the astral plane, peculiar to the last fifty or so years of the twentieth century, of focused attention on the topic of outer space and possible visitors from outer space. As is common knowledge, during the twentieth century much was written about outer space, there were numerous movies and television shows devoted to this topic, and, of course, many people used their imaginations to picture what outer space and "aliens" might be like.

Prior to the twentieth century, much of people's imagery was more religious in nature. Under the same circumstances people met angels or devils—and some still do. Once in another dimension, such as the astral world, people are unaware that conditions around them have changed because what they experience is what they desire, even if it happens to be nightmarish in nature. The more negative and frightening experiences are produced by the only *semi*-integration of the personality and the inherent struggle that ensues between the personality and its bodies/senses that are not fully responsive. This struggle is projected, astrally, into a fantasy about bodies, struggles, and all the other elements that are a part of the imagination. It is important to remember that these events *are* really happening to the person, even if they are self-induced and are not what he or she thinks they are.

Some experiences come from *etheric* plane phenomena (sometimes caused by a physics effect referred to as quantum constant anomalies), and are in some ways even stranger than astral ones. Etheric experiences can be witnessed by several people at the same time and may lead to astral experiences. Those involved interpret the etheric plane phenomena that they see as if it were really dense physically there, and they then give their own further creative imaginings to these events.

Finally, under the rarest of circumstances, it is possible to meet Souls (super-humans) from earth or from other worlds, but only if one is consistently *serving* others and wisely *giving* to them, and in great amounts throughout each day of his or her life. Such experiences would most likely go unreported and would not be on the front pages of the weekly tabloids, nor would there be one-hour or longer television specials to sensationalize such events. [For a much more complete answer and for greater potential understanding, see Chapter Eight: "The Three Subtle Dimensions That Humans Live In" and Chapter Nine: "The Kingdoms and Their Purpose."]

Question #47: **Besides the astral plane, can we be somewhere else on the higher dimensions either when we are asleep or when we are out of our physical bodies?**

Brief, Incomplete, Answer: Many people dream while on the mental plane, particularly while their astral bodies are being repaired. The plane and corresponding body that a person had used the most to sense from while awake during the previous day's activities is where most of her or his dreams tend to take place. The reason is that dreams are a means of releasing some of the retained energies in the etheric body, the astral body, and in the mental body. As people dream, they work off this energy through their dream activities. Retained energy results from a person's own selfishness, and can be etheric, emotional (astral), or mental. Dreaming reduces some of the stress on people's bodies and both keeps people healthier and keeps their senses clearer than they otherwise would be. Dreams also locate the areas of a body that, because of remaining retained energies, are in most need of repair by that body's elemental energy. When most people awaken in the morning, the senses of their three bodies are as clear as they will be for that day, and by late evening their senses have become diminished from the energies they have retained throughout that day. This can be tested by, first, at night, reading part of a book such as this one and then, early the next morning, either rereading the same section or reading a different one and comparing the levels of concept comprehension.

When out of the physical body and awake, a person can travel to any dimension that he or she is capable of remaining conscious in. For most people who can achieve this travel, this consists of the etheric, astral, and lower mental planes. [For a much more complete answer and for greater potential understanding, see Chapter Eight: "The Three Subtle Dimensions That Humans Live In."]

> ***Question #48:*** **Do liberated souls, or the Masters of the Ageless Wisdom, never dream because they are always giving and thus have no retained energy to work off?**

> ***Brief, Incomplete, Answer:*** Liberated souls, or Souls, stay awake and conscious while their bodies rest and repair themselves from the effects of the energies that *other* people retain. As long as a Soul, even a liberated one, is serving a planet, that Soul is karmically connected to it. Certain energies are received for use in service that will unavoidably be thwarted, which causes part of this energy to become retained. These Masters then use this energy consciously on the lower inner planes rather than through dreams because they are conscious enough to be aware of and to plan out the best uses for these energies. Advanced humans who are almost out of the human kingdom can do some of the same during a part of the time that their physical bodies sleep, while they are awake on the inner planes. Masters dream on higher planes than the three lowest. [For a much more complete answer and for greater potential understanding, see Chapter Eight: "The Three Subtle Dimensions That Humans Live In" and Chapter Nine: "The Kingdoms and Their Purpose."]

> ***Question #49:*** **Can dreams be significant towards teaching us something, or might they even be prophetic?**

> ***Brief, Incomplete, Answer:*** Some dreams, particularly those on the mental plane, can reveal areas in which people are selfish, or are likely to become selfish. Sometimes these dreams are even tests that let people gauge how selfish they actually are in certain situations. This is particularly true for spiritual disciples, or people who are trying to discipline themselves so that they can create more virtue. Most of the dreams that most people have are of little significance, and the important thing about their dreams is that they do take place. Dreaming allows the retained energies to be released, whether the dreams are remembered or not.

Although rare, prophetic dreams do sometimes occur. They usually take place on the mental plane through images projected by each person's Inner Guide, or OverSoul, in order to help him or her to understand an imminent danger or problem that would affect others and that he or she might face. This type of dream functions as a service to others and not as a direct benefit to the person dreaming, because the Solar Angel, or Inner Guide, functions as a soul and only gives, to help its human better give. Much of dream analysis that is done in spiritual circles and some that is done in psychology is of some value by helping people to recognize thoughts and feelings that are selfish. Any dream analysis that does not help people to recognize their own selfishness is counterproductive to the development of their consciousness. If used as selfish "prophetic" information or some other self-centered activity, dreams reveal nothing of value, and the study of them as an activity only lowers consciousness because of the selfish motive behind the actions. [For a much more complete answer and for greater potential understanding, see Chapter Seven: "The Bodies and the Senses."]

Question #50: **Why do people get sick? Does disease result from us being selfish?**

Brief, Incomplete, Answer: Disease is the result of all the less-than-perfected consciousness within this world, not all of which comes from humanity. Before there were humans, disease existed because one part of energy was attacking and taking from another. This condition initially occurred and still remains because the planet itself and all of nature have not yet been perfected in the physical world. Energy follows thought greater than its own, and the thought that energy follows, worldwide and in all of nature, is not perfected in this dimension. The lack of perfection is what allows disease to continue.

Humans do add a great deal of selfishness into the existing system. Because of their relatively low consciousness they tend, at present, to affect the rest of the lower kingdoms rather negatively. Humans are also beginning to control the planet, and all of the lower kingdoms are thus dependent upon humans' giving, or their lack thereof. As humans become more capable of behaving responsibly towards this planet and do not do so, their selfishness then results in more disease than it did before. Since humans are the most important kingdom on earth at this time, once they become less selfish as an entire kingdom most disease will disappear. This will occur because of humans' interventions through intelligent actions *and* through their overall creation of virtue.

On an individual basis, as a person increases her or his consciousness she or he generally becomes healthier. However, increased consciousness causes karma to become accelerated. In those people who are just beginning to increase their giving by self-chosen methods of focus (discipline), some disease may increase. What happens is that past selfishness can manifest itself as disease. It is possible to avoid this effect, provided that one "sees" the karma coming and becomes even more virtuous before it creates a crisis of disease within one or more of her or his bodies.

Once people lose their health, healing becomes difficult. This happens because the reason they became ill is that they were too selfish to not stay well and offset the karma in the first place. It *is* possible for people to heal themselves, but only through increasing their creation of virtue and becoming more soul-like. "Positive thinking" or emotional affirmations are of no value when they are selfish and self-centered. The concept behind them fails to recognize that the cure is to focus on others and to give rather than to seek a cure by being self-focused on the illness.

People should not reject modern disciplines of medicine. These disciplines do provide at least treatment for the effects of disease and, in some cases, can cure or prevent certain diseases. Those who are functioning within modern types of medicine and modern science can be just as spiritual as those who may study spiritual material. Those in the former group are sometimes even more spiritual than those in the latter might be, because the measure of a person's spirituality is the amount that he or she freely, wisely, and creatively gives. There are many people in the medical fields today who truly seek to create virtue in that way. The selfishness that exists in types of the healing arts and sciences can be avoided by those who are wise enough to recognize it. Sometimes the help offered through the various treatments by the practitioners who are the wise creative givers can be of real value. These wise creators of virtue are spiritual and are creating virtue, even if they do not recognize it. [For a much more complete answer and for greater potential understanding, see Chapter Seven: "The Bodies and the Senses" and Chapter Nine: "The Kingdoms and Their Purpose."]

Question #51: **How many times have we reincarnated, and how often do we come back?**

Brief, Incomplete, Answer: Almost all people have been born before, and some people have been born hundreds of times. Souls choose to incarnate based upon the needs that others have so that they can become better givers, and recognition of these needs requires group consciousness. Most souls are assisted by their mentally and spiritually connected alter egos—

their OverSouls, or Solar Angels—who are more advanced in consciousness than is any non-liberated soul. These wise beings are made up of energy that is in its last stages before recombining with additional spirit and becoming the One again. The energy in these Beings has become fully conscious of the self at a very high level and has become a Great Thinker, on its own, that helps us to think. At this stage the roles of spirit and energy actually become reversed and are about to come full circle. The spirit and energy then reach the point at which they become equals and are joined as a One. This One is sometimes referred to as a Monad in spiritual terminology.

The OverSoul, or Inner Guide, plays a crucial role in helping the soul under its care through Its decisions about when to incarnate. A factor in these decisions is, among other things, the need for suitable bodies that meet the new person's soul mission to both learn to better create virtue and to give more wisely while learning. Enormous thought is required to correctly balance all the variables that go into an incarnation. The older and more advanced the human soul is, the greater its mission in general, and the more complicated the thought required to correctly balance the variables. As human souls become increasingly advanced they can contribute more to the process of their own incarnations, assisting their Solar Angels with this intricate thinking.

Young human souls generally incarnate more frequently, but have very small missions of both learning and giving during each lifetime. The process is quite slow, but picks up momentum from the cumulative virtue that is created in each lifetime. These young souls may, for example, presently incarnate in average cycles of about seven lifetimes upon certain focused cosmic potentials for growth, with about fifty years between each incarnation; there will often be a long period of rest on the higher mental plane in-between each cycle of seven lifetimes. Seven lifetimes is an average for the focus of the growth of a stimulating factor, or "cosmic ray," of the energy of, or the form part of, the soul. Older souls usually end up having more advanced personalities that accomplish much more in each lifetime. They do not necessarily, however, create proportionately more virtue, and so they may need much more time on the inner planes in order to expend their selfishly retained energies. These souls may incarnate less within a particular period of time, but more frequently overall because they incarnate at times when their respective rays are not in focus. There can be nearly seventy years between incarnations. People who have decided to embark upon a spiritual path and to change themselves to become more giving through self discipline, i.e., people who have decided to become spiritual disciples, generally have well-developed souls that often choose to incarnate quite frequently. The reason is that after physical death they need relatively little time on the inner planes to overcome their selfishly retained energies. In addition, these people often incarnate when there is no corresponding growth stimulation "ray" focus on earth that reaches the energy part of their respective souls.

The general principles mentioned above have to be mitigated by both the needs of others and the opportunities to be of service to others. For example, if an advanced soul had the opportunity to incarnate because the right bodies and conditions for birth and life would be present (in a certain family, country, etc.), but its mission would be compromised by wrong timing relative to the needs of others, then that soul might not incarnate at that time. Sometimes souls will choose to incarnate because the need is great, even if appropriate bodies and conditions for incarnation are far from ideal. These sacrifices may lead to a strife-filled life, particularly during the younger years, but as long as the soul and OverSoul determine that there is a reasonable opportunity to meet certain needs, the soul still incarnates. This most often occurs with those souls who are advanced, because their service is so frequently needed. [For a much more complete answer and for greater potential understanding, see Chapter Eleven: "Reincarnation."]

Question #52: **Are there new human souls in our world today, who have never incarnated before?**

Brief, Incomplete, Answer: There are some human souls who are at present incarnating on earth for the first time. A few of these souls *have incarnated* on what was a predecessor to earth's development. There is also a small number of souls who have incarnated on different, unassociated planets, and who would be considered new *young* souls because of their lack of familiarity with this world. The majority of souls have been incarnating on earth for hundreds of thousands of years, though some began to incarnate here just tens of thousands of years ago. Some others began incarnating here millions of years ago. The differences have to do with how advanced the souls were when they first started to incarnate on earth. Generally, the more advanced souls from other worlds tend to wait to incarnate until a relatively later period in the planet's development. [For a much more complete answer and for greater potential understanding, see Chapter Nine: "The Kingdoms and Their Purpose" and Chapter Eleven: "Reincarnation."]

Question #53: **When did humans first incarnate on earth?**

Brief, Incomplete, Answer: The bodies of ape-like animals had to be adapted for use by a human soul, using methods that seem to be evolutionary. Behind the scenes, however, the group soul of this species of animal, which was the most advanced of the group souls on earth at the time, was involved in the thought process. Other group souls and the consciousness that oversees and *created* the life on this planet were involved, as well.

The very first attempts at human incarnation on earth began about twenty-one million years ago and showed promise. They were not completed, though, because the animal bodies needed to be further developed. The next attempts took place about eighteen million years ago, with incarnation into the level of etheric form only. While carried out to completion etherically, these attempts at physical incarnation failed overall because of both the inexperience of the young new souls and the primitive nature of the etheric animal-like bodies. About sixteen and a half million years ago, the first fully successful human incarnations on earth took place *on the etheric level* with much less of a physically manifested body in proportion to the etheric body. Over millions of years, these excessively etheric humans gradually developed into a race of humans who inhabited dense bodies that were correctly proportioned to their etheric bodies. About eight and a half million years ago, virtually all humans incarnated into normal dense physical bodies. After the first early generations were etherically created, humans have since been created by two other humans through the process of sexual procreation. [For a much more complete answer and for greater potential understanding, see Chapter Nine: "The Kingdoms and Their Purpose."]

Question #54: **Modern science states that humans did not exist before two to three million years ago, but you state something different. Why is there no fossil evidence of humans from eight million (or more) years ago?**

Brief, Incomplete, Answer: The race of humans that existed eight million years ago lived primarily on a continent that existed in the South Pacific, where only islands remain today. Some people have referred to this landmass as Lemuria, and believe that it sank back into the sea. It actually sank partially *below* the sea floor, into the earth's crust and possibly somewhat even into the mantle. This major race of people, who are referred to as the Lemurians, were the first dense physical humans on earth. They were quite primitive by today's standards. What little would have endured of their primitive culture, including their fossilized remains, was mostly inundated by land and sea.

The more primitive fossil remains that have been found of pre-humans and some human types are mostly the degenerated after-effects of the Lemurian race. In a few cases, they are the evolved forms of the animals that were used for the original human incarnations, but these were the ones who did not receive human ensouling and thus remained animals. The evolutionary model is partially correct as a means of form development for life. But because modern science wants so much to believe in evolution based on only an energy model, it ignores certain inconsistencies and seeks to structure its knowledge based on energy and matter only—omitting spirit and souls from the structures. [For a much more complete answer and for greater potential understanding, see Chapter Nine: "The Kingdoms and Their Purpose" and the Summary.]

Question #55: **Are there any other landmasses and races of people that have appeared and then vanished from record?**

Brief, Incomplete, Answer: At the same time that Lemuria was being inundated in stages, a much larger landmass was rising from the Atlantic Ocean along the Atlantic ridge. This landmass lay between some parts of North America and Europe, and the northern-most parts of South America and Africa. Some of the water that was ultimately displaced by this continent became a part of the ice caps. As this new continent arose, it blocked the Gulf Stream and brought on some of the ice ages that are widely known about (although earlier ice ages were related to the rise of Lemuria, and especially its fall about two and a half million years ago, and to other factors). The continent was called Atlantis, and its eventual inhabitants were the Atlanteans. These people were a new major race of human types because their focus of development was predominantly on the emotional body and senses, while the Lemurians were predominantly focused on the etheric/dense physical body and the five sensual senses. Most of the people on earth today are members of a different major race, which is predominantly developing the mental body and its sense of thought.

About a million years ago Atlantis began to be inundated, in stages, beginning with its islands. The last remnant of it is a section that now comprises the four islands of the Azores, off the coast of Portugal. Stories about a great flood can be found in many of the holy writings from various cultures. These stories are descriptions of the last and final inundation of the continent of Atlantis. The Atlanteans colonized many areas and left more artifacts of their civilization than the Lemurians did. Someday in the not-too-distant future, more direct evidence of their existence is likely to become revealed, stemming from such places as Egypt, South America, Asia Minor and Greece, and India. [For a much more complete answer and for greater potential understanding, see Chapter Nine: "The Kingdoms and Their Purpose."]

Question #56: **Why does there seem to be so much hidden information about these topics that you have addressed?**

Brief, Incomplete, Answer: Not all of what has been answered had been hidden, but it takes an open mind to look for and find that which can be found. Some of what your question refers to is, however, true. Much of the information was *deliberately* hidden immediately following the final inundation of the Atlantean continent. During the later period of the Atlantean civilization's development, nearly all of the information regarding spiritual principles and facts was disseminated by the Kingdom of Souls through their students' (who were spiritual disciples) own choices, to most humans who wanted to know it. This information was, therefore, widely known. The Atlanteans were *very* emotionally centered in their consciousness and lived almost exclusively according to their desires. They were selfish to levels that most societies today would severely censure in order to ensure common good. Some of the later-period Atlanteans used the information they were given in order to satiate their desires and to gain control and power over others. In other words, they used this information to pursue a course of darkness. The problem of selfish and dark use of the information reached, towards the end of their development, such epidemic levels that only the eventual total inundation of these people's civilization could, at that time, arrest the growth of evil on earth. It was then decided that for a long time, until virtually the present day, most of this information would be available only to those who first create certain levels of virtue within themselves. Then these people could learn more through mystical meditations in what were called esoteric mystery schools. This process of veiling the information was called mystification. As a result of the mystification process, only myths remained of what once were commonly known, completely formulated axioms and principles. [For a much more complete answer and for greater potential understanding, see Chapter Nine: "The Kingdoms and Their Purpose" and the Summary.]

Question #57: **Then why is it that you and perhaps some others are writing books to tell about these myths and this mystified knowledge in more modern scientific ways, possibly revealing once again what had been hidden?**

Brief, Incomplete, Answer: This author can speak only for himself and the books that he writes. All that is written in this volume and in others that he may write is done within a larger plan that may fit the needs of the next kingdom concerning the revelation of the Ageless Wisdom, which is the name in general for what *Life's Hidden Meaning* explains. While taking full responsibility for the material, it is not being presented in a vacuum, away from the Great Teaching Body of the planet (the Kingdom of Souls). Paradoxically, to say any more about this would be to reveal more than is prudent at this time.

Humans in the present major race have developed themselves in consciousness and in mental abilities to much higher levels than the Atlanteans did. Many who are alive today once were Atlanteans. People today are much more capable of creating virtuously through an understanding of the concepts being presented, and of using them to become more giving. Most of what is presented to the reader is in conceptual form, which would not be very well-understood by selfishly motivated people who follow darkness; this material would, therefore, be of little value towards their destructive goals. About the worst that would be expected from such types of people would be to confuse, reverse and/or to slanderously discredit this volume, if they could possibly do so. This in no way means that those who disagree with what is presented in this book have the same motives. People who follow darkness will find the information presented to be of virtually no use, and that is the intention of this author. Because humanity today can conceptually understand Ageless Wisdom, it is safer now to disseminate the information—in a conceptual format. The Atlanteans understood mostly the thoughtforms, which were given out to them without making them think first conceptually, because they were for the most part incapable of so doing. [For a much more complete answer and for greater potential understanding, see Chapter Nine: "The Kingdoms and Their Purpose," the Introduction, and the Summary.]

Question #58: **What determines which country and locale, racial group, and social stratum a person is born into?**

Brief, Incomplete, Answer: People are here to learn ways to better create virtue and then to use those ways to create virtue. They need, ever increasingly, tremendous variety in their life experiences if they are to continue to create virtue and to expand their consciousnesses. These experiences are the fuel for creation. The soul, with the OverSoul, needs to search for and creatively think of the best birth circumstance that is possible within the soul's capabilities to develop a personality. Souls are often faced with trying to overcome impending karmic crises caused from prior selfishness, including prejudice and greed of previous personality incarnations. Sometimes the solution is simple and direct, such as a soul choosing to be born as a black person in a region prejudiced against black people and possibly against other people of color. A good reason for this might be that in its last incarnation its personality was a white person who was prejudiced against people of color. At other times the circumstances may be more circuitous because multiple types of selfishness are dealt with at the same time, such as a genius in one incarnation being born deaf in the next and to ignorant parents who scorn education and intelligence. In this case, the purpose may be for the person to learn to appreciate and *give* his or her great intelligence rather than to use it for self-aggrandizement. The struggles inherent in the circumstances can lead to the future creation of virtue by a personality who, in its last one or more lifetimes, may have selfishly misused its abilities.

The general principles applied by souls in creatively selecting the conditions of birth are *that which is abused in one lifetime is limited and/or reduced in the next one*, and *that which is given wisely is further developed and improved upon.* This may be seen as a form of karma, but it is also a very effective tool for the soul to use. [For a much more complete answer and for greater potential understanding, see Chapter Eleven: "Reincarnation."]

Question #59: How does a soul control the factors you mentioned—does it have some kind of direct control over us once we are born?

Brief, Incomplete, Answer: There are seven basic types of energy that correspond to and come from God having sacrificially divided itself into seven interpenetrating, growth-stimulating parts, which are sometimes called the seven "rays." Each of these types of energy vibrates to a distinctly different quality that can be conceptualized into modes of action. The seven types of energy are as follows.

THE SEVEN TYPES OF ENERGY, OR THE SEVEN RAYS AS THEY AFFECT ENERGY, IN OUR UNIVERSE	
TYPE	DESCRIPTION
Type 1	Energy that creates and/or destroys in order to develop purpose, and through limitation, is a means of creation.
Type 2	Energy that brings together and joins back into wholeness, or oneness (through love, or giving).
Type 3	Energy that intelligently creates interaction between two or more things.
Type 4	Energy that balances itself in relation to spirit, or to informing thought.
Type 5	Energy that structures itself and other energy into a balance of forces and of logical sequences.
Type 6	Energy that focuses itself into singular discreet movements to increase the bringing together of one type or one other energy with it.
Type 7	Energy that organizes itself and other energy so that a synthesis can be achieved and inertia can be overcome.

Table 1.2

These seven types of energies correspond to and come from the seven types of "rays," or growth-stimulating parts of God, in the corresponding numbered order. They are selected by a person's soul and OverSoul to represent each one of her or his bodies as well as the collective unit that people refer to as the personality. For example, with the help of its OverSoul, or Solar Angel, a soul may decide that its next personality should have an etheric and dense physical body that is composed of energy of the seventh type. Energy of type number six may be chosen for the emotional body. The mental body might have energy of type number four, and the collective unit of all three bodies, represented by the personality, could have energy of type number three. Any one of these bodies could be made up of energy of any one of the seven types. Even the soul itself inhabits a form that has an energy type of one of the seven rays. However, this ray type stays the same throughout all of the personality lifetimes, while the rays of the other bodies and the personality are changed from lifetime to lifetime by the soul and OverSoul.

As the combinations of these energy types are changed, the bodies and senses that come from the coalesced energy also change in quality according to the way that these senses and abilities function. This concept allows the soul to have an indirect influence over the personality, starting at birth, but one that the personality can choose to work either with or against in its application. These energy types can be used to help create either virtue or darkness, or they also can be ignored entirely in any conscious use by the personality. [For a much more complete answer and for greater potential understanding, see Chapter Three: "Cosmic Virtues, Parts of God's Light in Form," Chapter Four: "Understanding Spirit and Energy," and Chapter Eleven: "Reincarnation."]

Question #60: **How much are we affected by these different types of bodies and the differing influences of the rays?**

Brief, Incomplete, Answer: The more creatively that people give wisely, the less these energies affect them because then their thought overpowers the nature of the energy. If a person's thought is weak and/or if she or he is less virtuously creative, then the energies have a much greater effect on that person because they do not follow her or his thought as well. The more selflessly creative that people are, the more that their senses and bodies become all-inclusive and able to sense and create in all ways. [For a much more complete answer and for greater potential understanding, see Chapter Three: "Cosmic Virtues, Parts of God's Light in Form" and Chapter Seven: "The Bodies and the Senses."]

Question #61: **Why does the "ray," or energy type, of the soul stay the same?**

Brief, Incomplete, Answer: Souls (even un-liberated ones) are all-giving, all the time, at their respective levels of responsibility. Because of this, they can use all the energy types equally well as long as they can sense responsibly. When their ignorance prevents them from sensing responsibly, they are aware of this condition of ignorance, and they do no harm because they then choose to not think at all. Souls do not need to change their "rays," or energy types, in order to correctly give because they rely upon group consciousness. They share each other's strengths in wisely giving. However, for a soul to be creative through its specialized energy functioning as a sense, it must *create* along its ray focus of its energy part, or body. Because liberated souls (Souls) have no ignorance in any of the three human worlds and bodies, they can use *all* types of energy *all* the time in these three bodies and worlds, whether these Souls are creating or are wisely giving. The three human worlds and bodies are the physical, emotional, and mental, and include the higher part of the mental body that a (non-liberated) soul exists within. A (non-liberated) soul has one of seven ray types, in order to specialize more so that as a group these souls can better serve each other through the *creation* of more virtue. Because (liberated) Souls are so much better at creatively giving than souls are, the Souls are specialized according to only the first three rays, or energy types. Even though the original soul ray type is maintained within a Soul, if this ray type is one of the lower four, it becomes fused to one of the first three types. The three types still allow the Souls, or who are Masters, to specialize. However, this specialization is along broader lines that lead to more wholeness, or oneness, among themselves than that which is produced by the highest levels that non-liberated souls can achieve. This oneness is sometimes referred to as monadic awareness (awareness of "The One"). [For a much more complete answer and for greater potential understanding, see Chapter Four: "Understanding Spirit and Energy" and Chapter Six: "About Souls."]

Question #62: **Does astrology have anything to do with the process of the soul incarnating?**

Brief, Incomplete, Answer: Astrology is mostly misunderstood by those who believe in and follow it, because it has been used almost entirely to forecast and/or explain *personal* information, which is self-centered in nature. The more hidden soul, or esoteric, astrology, which is used by and affects the soul, is very useful and is a necessary part of the process of incarnation. The seven rays and the corresponding seven types of energy are an integral part of understanding and using astrology. From its history of selfish use, personal astrology has lost a great deal of credibility because this type of use concerns more generalizations and incorrect determinism than it does truth.

A combined field of ray energies comes from certain star systems that are known as constellations. These constellations interact with the energy types within the bodies and then affect the person. Once the related ray information is understood and correlated with this combined field of ray energies, people can use astrology as souls do—to become more virtuous. Two people born at the same time and place will not be identically affected, although there may be a number of similarities, especially if their bodies share one or more of the same types of energy. The reason is the compounding of the rays of the constellations on the energy types of the bodies, and each person's level of consciousness. Overall, the system is too complicated for a book of this nature to completely describe. [For a much more complete answer and for greater potential understanding, see Chapter Eleven: "Reincarnation."]

Question #63: **What is the general purpose of this book?**

Brief, Incomplete, Answer: This book presents conceptual material in completed form, while what was formerly available of these concepts was incomplete. Some entirely new completed concepts have been included as well. All these concepts, while simplified, are written for three general categories of readers. The first is the largest group, of intellectually curious and thoughtful people who want a better, more complete, and truthful understanding of the "why's" (the concepts) behind that which they have experienced as meaning in their lives—revealing a hidden meaning. In addition, they are likely to be open to finding out more about that which they have not yet experienced, and which is also hidden from them in meaning.

The second group of readers, which is considerably smaller than the first, is made up of people who aspire to live as more virtuous people overall. They share some qualities in common with or similar to the members of the first group, but in a prior life had committed themselves to becoming more virtuous through spiritual self discipline. Now they are deliberating about whether to make significant and what they perceive will be difficult changes to their lives, to become much more creatively virtuous and to (again) spiritually discipline themselves.

The third group, which is much smaller than either of the preceding two groups, is made up of people who have committed themselves to change. They have previously in this lifetime chosen to become more creatively virtuous through spiritual self discipline and are functioning at least somewhat more virtuously than are those who are not disciplining themselves for spiritual purpose.

It is hoped that all three of these groups of readers will find this book interesting and—helpful. This author makes no qualitative judgment about anyone who seeks any of the numerous means of enlightenment and sees us all as one, and sees each one of the all…as unique, irreplaceable, and self-created parts of God.

THE CREATOR AND THE BIG PICTURE

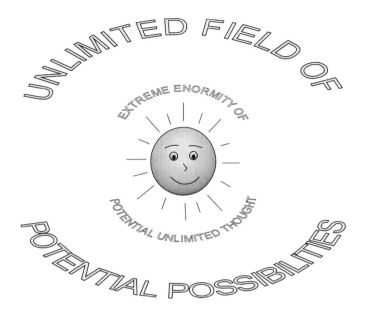

Illustration 2.1

Author's Suggestion: First turn to the "Glossary Help Guide" and read the definitions for this chapter.

We will begin our journey into gaining a further understanding of the hidden meaning of life by exploring the creation of both a Creator and our universe. The answers to some basic questions that many readers might have will be covered. However, for the sake of maintaining a level of understanding that the majority of readers will need, the answers will be less comprehensive than what would provide complete accuracy. To thoroughly cover just this one topic would require an entire volume, and many reading it would be simply overwhelmed by the sheer number of complex concepts. Still, it is likely that this second chapter, and probably the third as well, will be found to be the most difficult of all in this book because the number and size of the concepts somewhat match the enormity of the subject. That should not be a discouragement, for part of the purpose of this book is to help the reader raise his or her understanding as more of it is read. Therefore, it is likely that what may not be immediately fully grasped will fall into place and become better understood with further thoughtful reading. Throughout this chapter and throughout the entire book, concepts are repeated several times in somewhat different ways to assist with this process. In these circumstances, additional concepts are often included. Although this approach of repetition may be found by some readers to be somewhat awkward, it was chosen for several reasons—all to assist the reader in his or her understanding. Some of the reasons for the use of this approach are as follows. Because people's minds work in different ways, this approach reaches as many people as possible and, by repeating concepts from different perspectives, it may be conducive towards elevating the reader's overall comprehension. People generally learn best when the information is layered with new material that is presented in relation to what has already been presented, because the new information holds their interest. Comprehension of a concept is the level to which that concept can be used by the reader to create additional concepts and to also put the concept into his or her own words—or thoughtforms. Also, presenting the information in a variety of ways will, it is hoped, broaden its meaning for many. The potential difficulty is for confusion to arise when the reader comes upon information that is assumed to be new, but then is recognized to be material that has already been covered. It is important to keep in mind that, in these cases, the material will not be *identical*, and that there is something more to be gained by continuing to read it. Also, whatever difficulty may be encountered as a result of this method of repetition should be more than offset by the gained higher levels of understanding—which is also higher consciousness—and which is one major purpose of this book. Chapters Two through Twelve are likely to be found more difficult to understand than Chapter One will be because these topics are so vast that the more that each is explained, the greater the potential difficulty. Although the offering of anything near complete understanding is outside of the scope of a book such as this one (*complete* understanding is something no *book* in itself could provide, in any case), each chapter after the first does explain in considerably more depth the material that is very briefly, and less accurately, explained in the first chapter. The book is *designed* to raise understanding, or consciousness, by increasing the understanding of the oneness of life—and of God…and this concept will be further explained in the current and subsequent chapters.

Another concern of this author is that this second chapter and its treatment of the subject of the Creator, or God of our universe, may be offensive to some people who have deep religious convictions. While the information as it is presented in this chapter has not been found by some readers to be in significant contradiction to most major religions as they are understood by these readers, it would not be unusual for a very focused view of some religious doctrines to produce an emotional response to the material, in some people. Perhaps the following state-ment will be of reasonable assistance to those who experience such responses. It is the author's intention for this chapter—and indeed the entire book—to completely support the concepts that the God of our universe is the original sole Creator with great purpose(s); has the greatest of all love for its creations—beyond any human understanding, including that as presented in this book; and is the ultimate source of all life in our universe, and of all power towards and within everything in it. Now, perhaps, it is possible that offense might be taken by some atheists who are reading this(!); if so, the suggestion is to read further because there are likely to be enough purely scientific explanations to satisfy many in this group, as well.

 ## SOME IMPORTANT ANSWERS TO QUESTIONS ABOUT THE CREATION OF OUR UNIVERSE

Where did God come from? What existed before our universe? How does something come from nothing? First, the attempt will be made to answer these and many other questions through suggesting ways for the reader to use her or his imagination to make it easier to see part of the concepts that are more fully covered later. The reader is asked to picture the following scenario in her or his mind, keeping as much of an open mind as possible until the concepts behind the scenario can be more completely explored. Imagine an unlimited field of possibilities; any and all things possible are present in this field, including the possibility of the existence of choices, or that some possibilities are much more likely to occur than are some others. Since there is the possibility that other fields also exist, in this particular field of possi-bilities choices of some possibilities become more likely to occur than do others. As two or more of these choices reach a similar probability of occurrence, or are in a similar direction, or are developing a oneness in relation to one another, with this similar probability of occur-rence going on to affect other choices, a thought is created—the first creation in this field of possibilities. Within our field of possibilities, a vast many choices have a similar probability of occurrence, or of being in a similar direction, or are similar to each other in the ways their choices connect to each other and therefore greatly affect many other choices. This similarity produces a unity to the choices and creates an enormous thought that is large enough to affect a majority of the entire new limited field by directing many more choices of the potential possibilities, turning them into probabilities. At this point in our scenario much of the unlimited field is now being both limited (and has created its own new field) and directed by the enormous collective thought—as a great potential mind, which is a Director of the field. The Director can become the Creator of a future field. The Director has become self-created into a mind when the thought itself becomes large enough to limit the majority of the limited field to become more probabilistic than just possible. A mind is the potential part of a field that can grow to become a creator of other fields of thought, from a collection of thought in which thought has already limited the majority of choices in a similar direction. All Directors that are or could be Creators have minds; later in this book how all selves do, as well, will be explored.

Illustration 2.2

Now imagine yourself as this great Creator who just became self-created. This Creator is (you are) capable through its directed choices, or thought, of limiting the field of possibilities it is in, into more of a field of probabilities and then creating a new field of thought. You have just created yourself, through thought, but now you think, "I want there to be more than *I Am*, I want there to be growth to all that I Am and immediate growth to some parts of me. But I Am all that there presently is." Now you decide to do a remarkable thing—you choose to greatly limit and sacrifice a part of yourself. You create a universe as a new field in which the greatly limited *part* of your mind that you just sacrificed becomes the first creation within this new universe, and is further separated into three parts. You then equally disperse these three parts. Doing so further separates the three parts of your mind. You do this so that the extremely limited part of yourself can grow by remaining independent from both your mind outside the universe *and* from the focused and very limited three parts of your mind inside the universe. The complete separation and equal dispersion of the three parts of your mind forces the remaining thought in each part to think in new ways that grow more of you inside the new universe. So much of you in this universe is limited that something new has been created. This new creation is life.

Part of the purpose of life is to grow more of the Creator, which becomes God in the universe it has created; the three parts of God's mind exist to some degree in all life. These three parts of God's mind are kept separate by God's will (will is the consistency of the choices) until the life itself creates enough thought, a mind, and a self—to bring these three parts of God's mind together itself. As God, to imagine its perspective, you have created a situation in which you can grow, amazingly, by great self-sacrifice and limitation. You have given a freedom of will, or of choices, to your creations of life. Doing so is a necessity; otherwise, instead of growing, you would be redundantly controlling the thought of life, making life and the universe only a copy of your own thoughts, and a puppet show. It is by your choice that life contains the three parts of your sacrificed and limited mind in the universe. The first part is that life is free to choose—its own thoughts, its own understanding, and its own actions. The second is that life can understand, or be conscious of, itself and others in some way(s). You have created these ways based upon giving, or love, as you already have given, or loved. And the third is for all life in this universe to have activity with other life either through perfect communication or through form (energy) when communication is imperfect. When perfected, this activity with other life can accurately communicate change from one part of life to another—this is called intelligence. Intelligence occurs as life reduces the separation of the three parts of your (God's) mind.

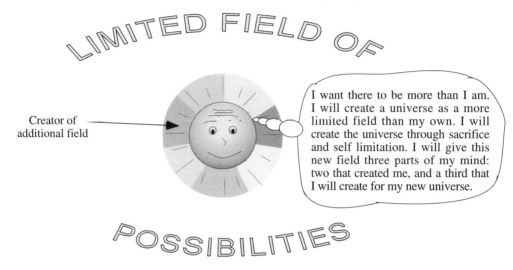

Illustration 2.3

Let us now more thoroughly examine the concepts in your imagined scenario, taking them further in explanation as well.

 ### UNDERSTANDING FIELDS OF POSSIBILITIES

What existed before God, and how does something create itself? How can something come from nothing? The answers to these questions involve an understanding of what a field of possibilities is and how that field interacts with fields of manifested creations. To begin with, in any place at any time there virtually never is "nothing," because a field of possibilities nearly always exists, and the less that is actualized or created from this field, the greater the field is. A Director that can become a universe can think and thus creates itself within a field of unlimited *potential* possibilities by developing thought that is large enough to create limitations within such an infinite field, which creates a new limited field. This means that its thoughts can encompass enough of the field to create a series of choices within a direction, or unity in similarity, of choice. These thoughts can then further alter the field of possibilities by making certain possibilities much more likely to occur, or by creating probabilities—just as you may have done when you imagined the earlier-described scenario. Thought itself, when great enough, is the limiting factor on a field of potential possibilities because thought is the result of the potential before it becomes realized. Nearly every field of possibilities creates some level of thought—the probable first thought of a Director of a field is "I am"; an unlimited field of potential possibilities may create enough thought to become a mind of a Creator. The Creator actualizes itself when it thinks and limits the field of possibilities to certain likely probabilities, which begins the process of the creation of something other than just itself. Creation is the result of thought that is great enough to limit a field of possibilities into a field of probabilities in order to create a new, more limited field. Note that some fields of unlimited possibilities may not have the potential to create a Director or a Creator because, amazingly, all of the possibilities therein have the same or a similar likelihood of becoming manifested. Under these circumstances, no choices could be created (at least none that could limit or affect the field as thought), and thus there could be no thought. Also, the possibility that *no* field exists becomes nullified as soon as one field does—which is the paradox of non-existence. Further, *our* existence, or the existence of anything at all, is proof of the nullification. An unlimited field can become limited, with a majority of the limited field then eventually becoming limited when it is dynamically changing from an unlimited state (before enough thought, or choices with oneness that could limit the field, was present) into a limited state. As thought is created in the unlimited field, its quality of being unlimited changes by the mere presence of the thought within it. An unlimited field that did not dynamically change through the presence of thought would in all likelihood prevent the creation of thought within it; attempting to create from this antithesis seems impossible (!) (and is another paradox).

Various Choices in a Creative Limited Field

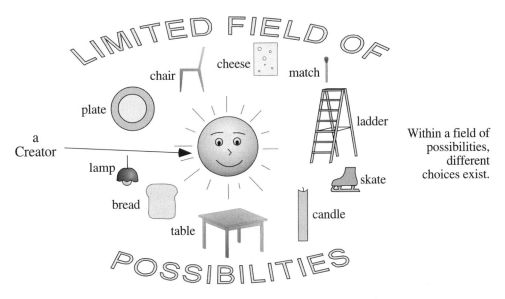

A limited field has possibilities that are limited by thought.

Illustration 2.4

A choice is created in a field of possibilities each time one possibility is more likely to occur than another is. The creation of choice is nearly inevitable in large fields because it is so unlikely that all possibilities will be equal in their ability (or lack thereof) to manifest into a creation. Thought is a series of two or more choices in a similar direction, which creates unity in the choices, and which affects the other choices, or limits the field it is in. To use a much less accurate description, thought occurs in humans when their concepts both fit together and support each other, and thus create more unity to the concepts. Within nearly every field of possibilities, thought, like choice, becomes inevitable because at least some of the possibilities will be chosen, and further, two or more of these choices will be directed, such as sharing concepts that support each other, which provides a oneness to the concepts. The larger the field, the more likely the number of directed choices, and hence the larger the levels of thought. When unlimited thought is directed, as a possibility, a Director becomes created as a probability. The Director then limits the field of possibilities into probabilities as it directs many additional choices. The Director may be creating more of itself in the process and making itself into a mind and a Creator. In Chapter Five the reader will have the opportunity to examine much more about thought, minds, and their creations, but for now it is hoped that this basic explanation will suffice.

Some Choices Creating Similar Thoughts Within a Creative Limited Field

Thought is two or more choices in a similar direction, which creates a unity to the remaining field of possibilities by creating a greater likelihood that more possibilities will connect into additional thought.

The different choices that are in a similar direction are attracted to each other and come together to produce thought.

Illustration 2.5

Thoughts Coming Together from the Prior Creative Limited Field to Create a New, More Limited Field

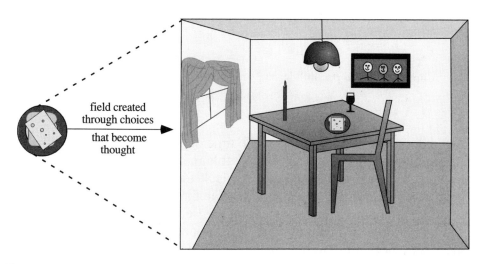

field created through choices that become thought

Thought is two or more choices in a similar direction, which creates a unity to the choices and the field they are in. The existing thought of bread, cheese, plate, table, chair, lit candle, and lamp create the probability and then, from their connectiveness, the thought of a dining room (a limited field).

Illustration 2.6

ELECTRICAL ATTRACTION BETWEEN THE CREATING AND CREATED FIELDS

The less thought that has been created in a limited potential field, the more there is of a field of possibilities within the unlimited field. This occurs because creation comes from choices that are in a similar direction that limits the field, and the two are connected to each other through both limiting and creative thought. The relationship between the two parts of the field is creation of thought, which can be measured by the relative amount of potential possibilities versus the amount that thought has limited those possibilities into a creation. This difference produces an electrical effect when a second field is created from the thought of the first and the first field does not sacrificially prevent the electrical field from occurring through will; the effect is of the creations in the second field being attracted to the thought of the creator in the larger field. In these cases the creations themselves contain thought within a much smaller field of possibilities, and this thought limits this much smaller field. The remaining possibilities of the smaller field that cannot be limited, because the thought within the smaller field is not great enough to do so, are instantly converted back into the larger field of possibilities. Thus, as it thinks, that which is created becomes attracted to its creator by the remaining possibilities that it cannot limit being potentially limited by its creator. The primary means of this attraction is a purely electrical potential (causing positive to attract negative) of lesser thought seeking to be more from the creating

A Small Field of Thought
Being Electrically Attracted to Its Larger Field

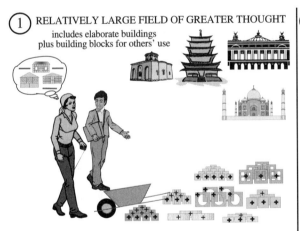

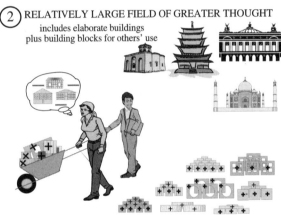

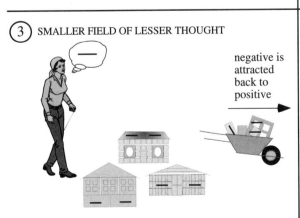

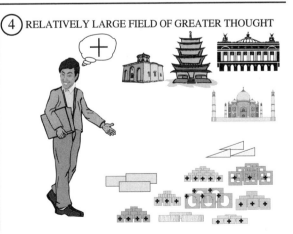

Illustration 2.7

thought between the two fields of possibilities. Both of the fields have been limited by thought, but the field that created the smaller one is much larger. The remaining possibilities of the smaller field after the creations within it have limited it into probabilities through their thought instantly become a part of the larger field, creating an electrical attraction between the creator's thought and that which is created in the smaller field through its own thought.

For example, imagine that a friend (a creator) gave you a group of differently shaped blocks with which to build some models of houses. You then choose which of these blocks to use for each of your houses; however, a number of blocks in various shapes and sizes are left over. The blocks left over are returned to your friend and put back into his very large collection, which he created for his very elaborate buildings and which he makes available to his friends when needed. Every time you want to build a different model of a house, you go back to your friend to get more blocks because he is the originating source of them (and of thought). An attraction is established in your need to further think and to create more, to go to the larger source of thought and blocks. The attraction exists because your friend thinks and creates better than you do and you rely upon him. You may also choose to have more blocks given to you, and if your friend also chooses this, your field of blocks and the potential to use your thought to create with them then grows.

 ## SUMMARY OF UNDERSTANDING FIELDS

What follows is a summation of what has been explained thus far in "The Creator and the Big Picture." Within an unlimited field of possibilities that can create, some of the possibilities are more likely to occur than others are. The possibilities that do occur, or become manifested, are called choices. Some of the choices in the field share a similarity concerning both the likelihood of their existence and the ways in which they limit one another and other choices. These similar choices create a unity, or oneness, among themselves and they create a similarity among the limitations that they place on other choices, giving, then, a direction to their collective limitation within the field. Once the choices have unity, or oneness, *and* can limit the field by affecting other choices, or by creating a direction, they become a thought. Once thought exists within an unlimited field of possibilities, the field is changed to a part of it becoming a limited field. When thought can limit the majority of the field that it exists within, it becomes a Director of that field. When the field has the potential to grow based upon its own collection of thought that also has the potential to create enough limitations to create a new field of thought, it becomes a mind. When the mind actualizes any of its potential to grow more within its field, it becomes a Being who is the Creator of a new field. Thus if the Director decides to create more than the entirety of what it is within its field, it becomes a Creator. A Creator creates a second field wherein it limits itself through great sacrifice. The Creator's first field is a field of potential, and the second field, which is the one it creates, is its field of actualization, or of manifestation. There is an electrical attraction of negative to positive between a creating field (that allows the attraction to occur through its will) and its field of manifested creation.

 # THE CREATION OF OUR UNIVERSE

Our universe is its Creator's second, or smaller, field of manifestation, or actualization. The Creator of our universe gave to our universe a replication of a majority of the mind part of Its field of potential. This part of mind contains the majority of Its thought, or Its choices with direction that can limit a part of what was originally the unlimited field. The Creator further created a third part of its mind from its thought, of intelligent activity, and gave that to our universe, as well. The Creator willed to *not* give any further parts of its field to our universe. As these three parts that were given to our universe by the Creator thought together, they created themselves into God within our universe. God then decided to grow more of itself by separating its mind into its three constituent parts, or aspects, and for this purpose as well as other ones, created the potential for life. All life has the three separated parts of God's mind within it. Life is a new, smaller field within God's, or our, universe. God's *thought* is the same as the Creator's original thought, which is the first two parts of God's mind joined together. Life is attracted to God's thought as it uses the first two parts of God's mind within its own thought. The reason is that the thought of God is so much greater within God's field as compared to life's field. Within our universe, God is functioning as a field of potential, and life is a field of actualization, or of manifestation. A powerful electrical attraction exists between these fields of potential and actualization.

Like God and the Creator, life has a mind within its field. This mind uses a part of all three of the parts of God's mind. This mind creates life as it further thinks and grows more of its mind, and therefore grows a greater part of God's mind. When the third part of God's mind thinks intelligently within life by life joining together the first two parts of God's mind, and by thinking in God's thought (which is light), all three parts then become closer together and grow more of God's mind. Life is created from this thought within itself, and, similarly to God and the Creator, life creates itself. God creates the *potential* for life, but through great sacrifice also creates *freedom* of choice and of the direction, or oneness, to the choice. The oneness can be measured by the amount of love, or givingness, in the thought. These freedoms created and given by God permit life to create itself through its own thought—rather than through God's—thus creating growth instead of duplication. These new concepts of life and God are further explained within the next several pages.

For some physicists, the entire explanation of the Creator and the Big Picture thus far presented may be labeled as a quantum field theory. In spiritual explanations where Ageless Wisdom is understood, it is likely to be labeled as the concept behind the first cosmic fire of creation. For most of those who read this book, the important concept is that God is self-created. The reason is that a field of unlimited probabilities creates thought that is great enough to limit a field as large as our universe. Since life is the growth of God in our universe, life, as a much lower correspondence, is also self-created at some level; as our exploration of life's meaning continues, this concept will become clearer.

Explained another way, the Creator of our universe chose to grow and to become more than It was, although It existed as a self-created Being with enormous potential within Its thought. Time and space and our universe as we know it did not yet exist—only the enormous potential and thought of the Creator, or the Creator of God in our universe, to limit it. This Great Being, because it chose to create more of itself, decided that in order to become more it needed to greatly sacrifice and limit itself, through its will. The Creator created more of itself within a field of potential so small in comparison to its original state that an entire universe of growth to Itself would be created. The growth needed to be new and different. This growth could be achieved only if the Creator's less limited state were changed to a very limited one in which the growth of God would be contingent upon choices made by something other than itself. This new something that God created within our universe was life. Life is God's means of self-growth in our universe. Life is able to think for itself because God chose to limit its own thoughts and to further separate them within our universe. God gave free choice, or free will, to life so that both It and life could grow. For clarity in understanding, note that the word *Creator* is used to denote the majority of thought in unity, or in a similar direction, that limits an enormous field of possibilities and makes it into a potential of creation of a new, smaller, more limited field—of our universe; the name *God* is used to describe the limited state of the three parts of the Creator's mind that are sacrificially given to create our universe.

The Creator of our universe is a self-created Being who was originally capable of thinking within a field of infinite possibilities (and as soon as thought existed dynamically, that field became limited) without becoming lost or overwhelmed by the field. The Creator can thus maintain its ability to think in oneness, or unity. The Creator can therefore be conscious of a majority of the more likely possibilities, or choices, within this field as a part of this unlimited field dynamically becomes a new, limited field. This capability permits the Creator to be able to create an entire universe because It first must be totally unlimited within the type of universe It is going to create. Before It can choose to create a universe through a process of self-sacrifice, or self-limitation and will, the Creator will need to keep the two fields separate. The Creator of our universe chose to grow by being separate from it until the universe's very end. God grows by life's continuous growth, and is therefore more limited and *less* sacrificial than was the Creator. By sacrifice is meant the choice to give up, or relinquish, one or more choices that interfere with one's growth, or, put another way, sacrifice is creation that will at a later time increase creation or growth. A spiritual sacrifice is not masochistic or harmful or a lessening of self, as some other ways of defining it might imply. Even as some self is sacrificed, more has the potential to grow—which ultimately neither lessens nor harms the self. (Note that the word self has not yet been defined herein, and is being used in a more general way than it will be used later in this book.) What creates our universe is the huge potential in difference between the Creator's enormous thoughts in its original field of possibilities and its extreme limitation, or sacrifice, of willing to be no longer connected to the field of thought and of itself contained within the three parts of God's mind. On a much smaller level, anything in our universe relies upon the same process of choosing to limit itself, which then in all spiritually sacrificed creation creates a potential difference between the self and that which is to be created, with the creation free to create something new.

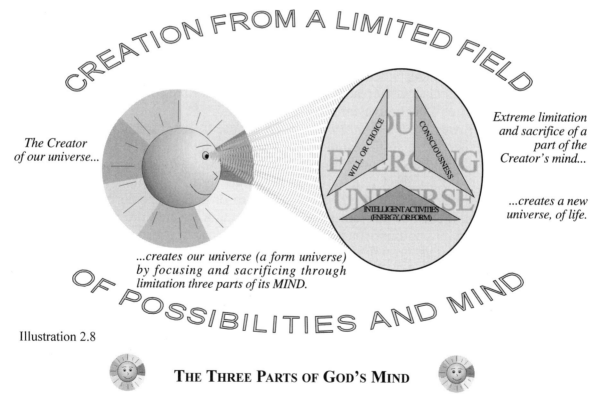

CREATION FROM A LIMITED FIELD OF POSSIBILITIES AND MIND

The Creator of our universe...

...creates our universe (a form universe) by focusing and sacrificing through limitation three parts of its MIND.

WILL, OR CHOICE

CONSCIOUSNESS

INTELLIGENT ACTIVITIES (ENERGY, OR FORM)

Extreme limitation and sacrifice of a part of the Creator's mind...

...creates a new universe, of life.

Illustration 2.8

THE THREE PARTS OF GOD'S MIND

The enormous thought of the Creator is limited into three parts, or aspects, which while extremely limited in comparison to its thought within its enormous field of possibilities, are ubiquitous within our universe since they are the foundation of the creation of our universe. These three parts, or aspects, of God's mind are as follows.

THE THREE PARTS, OR ASPECTS, OF GOD'S MIND	
ASPECT OF GOD'S MIND	DESCRIPTION
1st	Choice, or will (a series of choices in a similar direction)—which further leads to *purpose* and self-sacrifice (to be more, or to grow)
2nd	A Plan of giving both oneness to others, or the direction of choices to grow more like God, and unconditional (on the part of the giver) love—which leads to growth in *consciousness*, or the ability to recognize oneness and God's thought
3rd	Intelligent interaction among the parts of life (which brings the three parts of God's mind more together), or of God's growth—which can also lead to interactions that are not perfectly intelligent, and to the manifestation of *energy/form* as a container for life and the mover of the container in life's imperfect actions

Table 2.1

Notice that the first two parts are, to begin with, what created the Creator from the unlimited field of possibilities. The third part when added to the first two, but kept separate extremely limits all three parts. Through its own sacrifice and self-limitation, the Creator gives two parts of its original mind and adds the third part, or intelligent activity. Its purpose is to create a universe of manifested energy, or form—all to create life, or growth of God.

These three aspects of God's mind exist everywhere in our universe; however, they are separated because God chose separation as the means of Its self-limitation and sacrifice so that life could exist in relative freedom from Its thought. God's sacrifice is less than the Creator's because God chooses to grow more as its parts of itself, or as life, grows. The three aspects exist in all life, but by being either separate or creatively joined together, the life can think for itself. If the life brings together the three parts of God's mind in a newly created way, it then grows God's mind. It shares in that growth and remains an individual Being who, through its own creation, has become a functional part of God.

God's Mind Separating

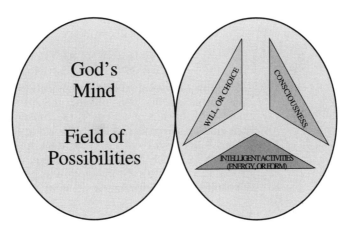

At the beginning of our universe the three parts of God's mind became separated and created the entire space of our universe.

Illustration 2.9

The first aspect of God's mind is choice, or will, and when thought of by life as God thought of it, the will, or choices, are to create more growth in all life—which then grows more of God.

Will is the consistent repetition of the same choice. Will can be identified in thought by the reflection of the choice in the mind of another, thereby unifying choice with the chooser. Most of life at its present stage in our universe does not use *all* of its will in this way. Instead, most life chooses to create, or grow, more of only its kind of life, some of the time. The procreation process of life growing more life comes from growing mostly more of form, or more of a manifestation of the third aspect of God's mind. The process of life growth is the part of its will, or consistent choices, which do grow life and God, but for the much more limited purpose of growing only life that is like itself. Most of the will, or consistent choices, of life fall into this category. They do, therefore, help to grow God, but they do so with a lack of choosing to use the complete purpose of God. The process of life creation, while diverse, is nonetheless a lower correspondence of, yet is somewhat similar to the way in which the Creator originally created our universe—through will and self-sacrifice.

The second part, or aspect, of God's mind in our universe is to plan as God did. This planning is to connect the choices into a thought that recognizes the oneness of all life, with this oneness leading to God's growth. Planning in this way produces a direction of thought to give others more thought of the oneness of all life. The giving of this thought of oneness to others creates consciousness. This occurs because in order to have the thought of oneness, the giver needs to both recognize with purpose and understand not only itself, but also that which is given and the one being given to. Consciousness is fostered by the procreation process, though it diminishes the consciousness and giving from that of creating more of the One to creating more of life that is the same as or very similar to that which is procreating. The consciousness of this second aspect can be increased as more of life is included outside of just that which is similar to the giver, as someone gives to this other life the thought to do the same.

The Three Limited and Sacrificial Parts
of the Creator's Mind That Create Our Universe

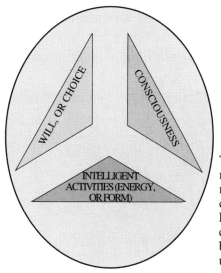

Illustration 2.10

WILL (CHOICE)

Creation through consistent self-sacrifice and choosing one possibility over others.

CONSCIOUSNESS

The understanding that we are all one, that life is all one—the level of givingness of oneself to others. The level of connectedness of the choices that is producing thought.

INTELLIGENT ACTIVITY AND/OR
REPRESENTED BY ENERGY, OR FORM

The activity that communicates to other activity or to energy all of its movements and that joins together the space between them, creating more light. Intelligent activity is the container that both the will and consciousness need in order to have interactions with energy, or form. Forms help consciousness to grow in the small field of life so that will can sacrifice to either create more of life or interfere with life's growth, based upon the life's own choices. Energies are the manifestation of unintelligence, by separating light into space and time.

The third aspect of God's mind is for there to be diversity to life. The diversity is based upon life's separated interactions that, if intelligent, create more of all of life and of God's growth in our universe. This third aspect also makes up the container, or form, of life so that it becomes further diversified. The manifested imperfect third aspect of God's mind is a result of the effect caused by there being some *lack* in intelligence within activity of this third aspect, as energy. Energy enables life to have forms and for these forms to learn to become more intelligent forms that communicate with one another and move. These capabilities produce diversity and the ability to improve forms in intelligence, and grows more of God in the process. When unintelligent in communications and movements, lifeforms relatively decrease the growth of God by decreasing the growth of life through increased separation.

The mind of God is composed of these three enormous series of thoughts. These three are the aggregate of what the Creator chose to think within our universe. These thoughts exist everywhere, in everything, to some degree. God chose to separate them so that its thought would not control the thought by the parts of life; thus free choice is created. However, the ubiquitous presence of the three separated parts of the Creator's mind still creates a probability at any particular time that a significant proportion of life will choose, through its own thought, to join the three parts back together. The separation of these three parts is a further sacrifice of the already immense (and greater) one of the Creator limiting its mind in our universe to merely the below-described three aspects.

The complete separation of these aspects of God's mind creates our universe through the separation of the first two aspects (creating space), and the third, which when separated from the first two, creates energy. The entire space of our universe was created at the universe's inception. This creation was accomplished through the separation of choices/will/purpose/sacrifice from oneness/planning/consciousness/love (giving), or through the separation of *God's thought*. What happens is that when the two parts of God's mind (which are the first and second parts of thought) are not joined, then life (God's growth) is separated by the limitation of not thinking as God does. When these two parts of God's thought are mostly separated, not only is God limited, but all else is as well. The reason is that God's thought is enlightening, or brings one part of life together with another, reducing the space between these parts of life. Although limited, God's thought remains *at least* a fraction of the part of all else in our universe. Space is the limitation caused by not being fully enlightened. The third aspect of God's mind is intelligent activities, which when separated from God's thought that is also separated become manifested as energy. God's thought is the joined first two parts of God's mind. Our entire *manifested* (in energy) universe has some type of energy within it, because the third aspect of God's mind (in a separated state) exists throughout every part of our manifested universe. When intelligent activity, or the third aspect of God's mind, exists in the presence of the first two parts of God's mind joined together, as

The Three Parts of God's Mind
Became Equally Dispersed as They Separated

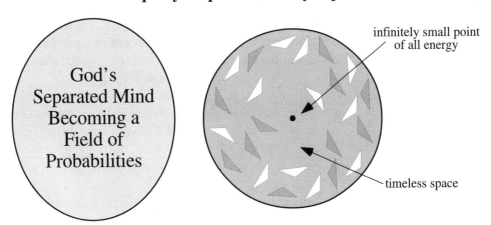

When the point of maximum separation within this universe was reached, the first two parts of God's mind created the space of our universe, and a portion of the third part created an infinitely small point of all energy. The remainder of the third aspect of God's mind was dispersed throughout the manifested universe in ratios based upon how much this third aspect had become manifested into energy.

Illustration 2.11

God's thought, then the third aspect remains as completely intelligent in all of its activities and does not create a more limited field of manifested energy. The state of maximum separation of energy from space (again, space is the first two aspects of God's mind when separated) is an infinitely small point first outside space and time and then within the very center of the most separated space of our universe. That point is where beginning, or primordial energy, begins. The reason is that this is the most separated from space this energy can become, since initially no space exists within this point of energy. Note, however, that the unmanifested third aspect is found everywhere as a potential for activity. Intelligent activity begins in an unmanifested state of the third aspect of God's mind, and is gradually reconstituted as the energy moves outward from the infinitely small point and rejoins with some space, and also creates the manifested universe. When energy, as a part of life using intelligent actions, joins equal amounts of itself with consciousness/planning/love/givingness and choices/will/purpose/sacrifice, light is created in form as space becomes joined together with the energy, thereby reducing and eventually removing separation from life.

 ## GOD'S THOUGHT AS LIGHT

Light is the joined first two parts of God's mind, or is God's *thought* when it is whole, in our universe. When a part of life brings these two together within itself, it, to some extent, thinks as God does. That part of life then becomes less separated from other life and reduces the space between itself and other life, converting this space into light. The light allows some parts of life that brings these first two parts of God's mind mostly together through its own thinking to eventually recognize that God exists in both itself and in others. When the third part of God's mind, or intelligent activity, is mostly added to the first two parts, some parts of life not only can recognize God in itself and others but can also create more of God, by creating more light in *both* itself and in others. Note that intelligent activity does not exist in an equally dispersed condition within the unmanifested-in-energy parts of our universe. It exists only in either a separated state from light or in union with only the second and the first parts of God's mind under unique circumstances as described in Chapters Three and Four. In our universe, time began when energy began to rejoin with space (or from another perspective, when it was first manifested from intelligent activity); when space itself also rejoins, the three together create light in form and time stops. Time is relative to the quantity of energy present and the degree to which energy is rejoining with the two parts of space, or of God's mind. Thus time varies based upon three factors: what part of space it exists within; the quality of the thought of those who are thinking within the space; and the amount of energy present. Put another way, time varies based upon the relative degree of intelligence (or lack thereof) to energy's activities. Much more about time and space will be covered in Chapter Ten.

The following exercise may be of benefit at this point: Think to yourself what it is like to be selfish. Notice that your selfish choices are choices to create more separation between yourself and most others. If you do become closer to some others through selfishness, then you and they become separate from even greater numbers of others. Also notice that instead of giving and helping others to be more giving, when you are selfish you are taking and in numerous ways are increasing the likelihood that others will become more selfish. Every time you make a choice that does not in some way eventually create enlightened growth in at least some life besides that what you perceive to be "your own," your and others' lives become more separated, and your thought and that of God are being separated. Notice how your life is created from the way in which you think. God's choice is to make sacrifices for its creations of life so that more life can grow; when we think only of ourselves we go against this thought, and we create from choices that are not for the benefit of others. The second part of God's thought is to plan in ways that help others to recognize and understand, or be conscious of, the oneness of life. When we plan in ways that help others to plan, by us giving to them in ways that improve their understanding and their ability to plan and give, as well, we are understanding that we are all a part of one life. We are then helping others to do the same and to thus gain the same understanding. This one life is God's growth. Each of us participates within that growth as we join together the first two parts of God's mind (light) and use them to create intelligent actions within and through our bodies. When all three are brought together we are creating virtue, or more light in form.

Life can create itself more into a functional part of God as it brings the mind of God together within itself. When the first two aspects of God's mind in our universe are joined together by the thought of anything within our universe, light is created. Part of light is God's choices and these are a part of its *purpose*, to grow itself by sacrificing/self-limiting itself in order to create life that is free to choose to do the same (or not to). This first part of light is joined with God's plan to give this thought to all life. Included in God's plan of growth through free-thinking life is the ability for a part of life to eventually recognize the plan. This occurs when the life has made enough choices and sacrifices that grow life while recognizing the oneness of life and helping other parts of life to also recognize this oneness. Life can bring together the first two aspects of God's mind that are inside itself but separated (inside the third, manifested, aspect of God's mind, or inside the form of God's mind). When it does, it can then give this, or God's thought, to the form part of itself in order to grow its bodies (as a part of life). A part of life can also give light to some other part of life that it still may somewhat recognize to be separate but also sharing some sameness. When life is successful in this endeavor, then both it and other parts of life become enlightened. This process of enlightening joins the first two aspects of God's mind, or thought, into light and then further joins this light with the form, or energy (the third aspect of God's mind in a manifested state), creating intelligent activity out of the energy. The three aspects of God's mind all together create a virtue, or a certain type of light within that

The Mind of God in Different Lifeforms

Because God chose to grow in our universe as a result of life's actions and interactions, which must come from either energy or intelligent activity, the first two parts of God's mind must be represented at all times through the third part—of either energy or intelligent activity.

Energy provides will and consciousness in lower types of life with a means through which to function in our universe. Energy enables the growth of consciousness in smaller fields of life. It creates the ability for life to relatively recognize the oneness of itself with all other life. Consciousness is measured by the amount that life is willing to give of itself to other parts of life. The relative amounts, closeness, and balance of the three parts of God's mind in life determine life's ability to think *and* to be conscious.

Illustration 2.12

type of energy, or form. This leads to actions that are exclusively intelligent because all space is then eliminated within and between one part of life and another.

THE CREATION OF THREE GREAT BEINGS
FROM THE SEPARATED THREE PARTS OF GOD'S MIND

Continuing now with our earlier scenario, imagine again that you are God, the Creator within our universe. At the point where the scenario stopped, you had limited your mind to three relatively very limited parts, of choice/will/purpose/sacrifice, planning/giving-love/consciousness-understanding, and intelligent-activity/perfect-communication, or interactions that exclusively enlighten forms of life and bring them closer together. You choose to separate these three parts, and, as they separate, each part becomes its own field of limited possibilities. The limitations from the three separated parts result in the high likelihood of the thought that this creates producing a new Being who is connected to the larger joined thought of yourself— God—because your field of potential is so much larger than the other, limited fields. One of these Beings is produced by each of the three separated parts of your mind in our universe; one Being is created for each field. Each of these Beings now creates from more limited choices/will/sacrifice and a plan, or consciousness, that has a somewhat different direction than, but is not against, your plan's direction. Each Being attracts to itself through its great thought some intelligent activity that is related to its choices and its plan that have become joined, or to its light. These Beings each have a different light that is lesser in choices/will/purpose/ sacrifice (as a much more limited concept, these can also be referred to as vibration) and is of a different direction and complexity in its planning/consciousness/love (again, in a much more limited concept, the phase, or angle to God's—your—original thought is different). The light within the form that these Beings attract, or their created virtue, is only a part of your—God's— original thought for our universe. Because their thought is more limited, their type of light is as well; it has a lower speed, which is really a measure of this Being's thought within the form it attracts. The light also has a different color because of the differences in both its vibration and its phase, or its angle in relation to your/God's light/thought.

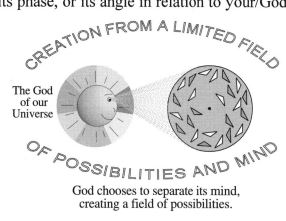

God chooses to separate its mind,
creating a field of possibilities.

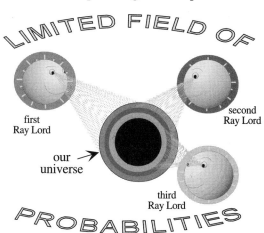

Each of the three Beings' fields of mind are joined,
and are creators producing a field of probabilities.

Illustration 2.13

The purpose of these three originating Beings is for them to be the foundation of life creation. They accomplish this feat by stimulating the most receptive of the energies that are attracted to them through their thought. The receptive energies become organized as a sensing part of form, of each Being's type of light in form, or its creation of virtue. You have chosen this indirect means of creating life in our universe. You have done so because each of the three Beings is somewhat different from yourself, diversifying and further freeing life from your—God's— thought. Life can then grow as a unique and inter-dependent, yet independent part of yourself.

Stated in a somewhat different way, each one of the three aspects of God's mind becomes a new field of possibilities because these aspects are separated. Each of these fields of possibilities then creates thought and self-limitation. There is a new realized potential for a new life of a Great Being who is less in thought than God is, but who is the Lord of Life Creation within the field of possibilities created by the separated aspects of God's mind. God chose that its growth would occur through all three aspects of its mind joining together. To accomplish this growth, space has to be joined into light through the first two aspects. This light has to become a part of the third aspect, or intelligent activity, which only enlightens energy. Each of the three Great Beings can join some of the space within the field of possibilities for the aspect of God's mind that it represents through its thought. As each does so, it creates the light that is characteristic of the corresponding aspect of God's mind at a focal point of its thought. These Great Beings choose to not join their created light with all the energy in their respective dimensions. They make this choice because if they did not, then the created life would think only like themselves, and would lose its free will. Instead, these Lords of Life Creation choose to allow energy that is attracted to their respective limited field of probabilities (which were created by their thought) to become enhanced in its propensity to rejoin with space. They accomplish this feat by increasing the probabilities of such an occurrence for certain energies while decreasing it for others, creating specialization of and diversity of life—and a new way for God to grow.

The Three Fields of the
Three Lower Correspondences of God's Mind

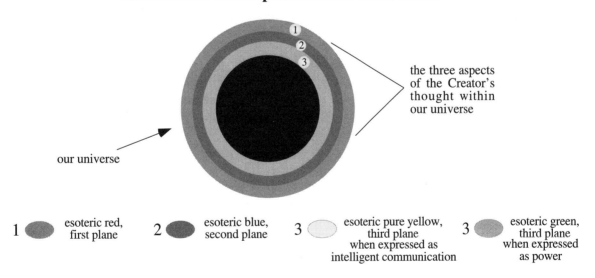

the three aspects of the Creator's thought within our universe

our universe

| 1 | esoteric red, first plane | 2 | esoteric blue, second plane | 3 | esoteric pure yellow, third plane when expressed as intelligent communication | 3 | esoteric green, third plane when expressed as power |

Colors are the separated and lower frequencies of a lower level of choices with somewhat changed direction as compared to God's field within these Beings' fields.

Illustration 2.14

The Great Being who is Lord over Creation of Life within one of the three aspects of God's mind thinks and limits the field of possibilities of the aspect to certain probabilities. These probabilities attract some energies more than other energies. The reason is that some of the energy, as a manifestation of the third aspect, tends to itself very slightly "think" more similarly to the way one of these Great Beings does. At the beginning of our universe, which energy is attracted to which probabilities is based mainly upon the density of the various energies that exist. The very limited thought of the energy within its relatively very small field of possibilities slightly limits the field. As a result, most of the possibilities that remain instantly rejoin with the Great Being's field; they create a large potential difference of electrical attraction between the energy (and its very slight thought) and the Great Being and Its much greater thought, causing the energy to follow this much greater thought. The better the energy is at thinking at least somewhat similarly to the Great Being, the more it is affected by this Being's thought and the Being's created field of possibilities for creating new life. This condition exists because the energy's limited field that is produced by its own thought is more similar to its Creator's field. The interaction between the better-thinking energy at any particular time (which still has only a very small amount of thought) and the Great Being's thought of more life creation produces a ray of focused probabilistic life creation. The ray is a field of probability that connects two fields of possibilities, with the lesser one being a field of energy. A cosmic ray in spiritual terms should not be confused with the fairly recent use of the words "cosmic rays" to define high speed sub-atomic particles originating from outer space. Each of the three Great Beings creates one of these rays of focused probabilistic life creation that affects our entire universe, or is cosmic. We can name these three Great Beings "Cosmic Ray Lords of Focused Probabilistic Life Creation," but the shorter name "cosmic Ray Lords" is easier and has been in use in spiritual language for many thousands of years.

CONCLUSIONS FROM CHAPTER TWO

Conclusions can now be drawn about some of the hidden meaning of life, from the information within this chapter. Life was created by a Creator who became the God of our universe by extreme sacrifice and by willing itself to remain separate from God. Life possesses the two parts that created that same Creator's mind. They are choice/will/purpose/sacrifice, and planning/consciousness/direction/love (givingness). The Creator chose to add into our universe a third part that it created of its mind: intelligent activity. When not perfectly intelligent, activity manifests as energy/form, which greatly limits a creator within a field of life. Then God (as a limited part of the Creator) further separated all three parts of its mind, but ensured that the parts, or aspects of mind, would be present everywhere throughout the manifested-in-energy universe. Life is created by having the separated mind of God (or at some point, the mind of God that has been joined by a highly advanced lifeform) limited within a form so that the life can think for itself. God grows as life does by unifying God's mind within itself. From what has been presented in this chapter, the following partial meanings of life can be revealed:

1. The partial meaning of life is to grow into becoming more and more like the Creator and God, while adding uniqueness and diversity to God. God sacrificed part of itself to make room for this growth and for the creation of life as being the vehicle for the growth.

2. As more freedom of choices are joined with life (as light), or through the giving of oneness to the thought of others, God is revealed to life; as the communication and interrelation of activity are intelligently brought together with this revelation of God (as light in form, or virtue), life gains in meaning through participating as God has in its (God's) growth.

This second partial hidden meaning to life is covered in significantly more detail in the next chapter, where it is more fully developed as a concept.

COSMIC VIRTUES, PARTS OF GOD'S LIGHT IN FORM

Illustration 3.1

Author's Suggestion: First turn to the "Glossary Help Guide" and read the definitions for this chapter.

 SUMMARY OF INFORMATION FROM CHAPTER TWO

In the previous chapter, information was presented that explained how our universe was created, along with some of the large constructs of its beginnings. The way in which a field of possibilities creates thought from two or more choices was described. Choices were defined as those effects that are more likely to occur than some other effects are, from within the field's possibilities. Choices that have a similar level of probability of existing and of eventually limiting the field in certain ways share a oneness. This also gives them a direction towards joining with additional choices. The more choices that share a oneness, or a common direction, the greater the probability that more will continue to. The reason is that these choices are altering, or limiting, the field of possibilities every time they further connect. Once the choices reach a level at which they are limiting the field that they exist within, through enough connection, or oneness/direction, they become a thought within that field. As a series of connected thoughts exists within an unlimited field of potential, a part of the field becomes limited. When enough thoughts can limit the majority of this field by sharing the same direction that joins them with each other, the collection of thought within the field becomes a Director of the field. When the Director of the field chooses to create a new, or second, field from itself, it changes its field of possibilities into a field of probabilities, or becomes a creative field. At this point the Director also changes itself into a Creator, and its mind has become actualized.

Starting with an unlimited field of possibilities, the thought that is created into a Director and that chooses to create concomitantly more than itself and of itself, and then creates a new limited field of possibilities becomes a Creator of a universe. Because a Director started in an unlimited field with its types of probabilities reaching the level of choosing to create more than and of itself, the limited field that comes from the unlimited field is large enough to allow its

Director to become a Creator of a universe. Choice and its direction were given to our universe, as a probable part of all thought within it. The first two parts of God's mind joined together, or choices that are in the direction of growing additional, similar choices, share a similar direction to and create more of God's thought. The first two parts of God's mind joined together are, in our universe, always light. Light is the thought of God; light can be created through choices that are in a *similar* direction to God's thought. Note that the level of oneness, or givingness, shared by the choices establishes their direction. When the first two parts of God's mind are separated, the same thought in which they were joined becomes space and is dark, or lacks light. However, a part of light's thought is to sacrifice itself through separation so that there can be growth. The choice to sacrifice through separation initially causes the thought that was given to our universe to separate and to create enormous space—the space of our universe.

In addition to the choices and direction, an added part of thought—the third aspect of God's mind—is given to our universe by the Creator. A mind is the potential part of a field that can grow from a collection of thought that exists within a field in which thought has already limited or has the potential to limit the majority of choices in a similar direction and can create a new, more limited field. All Creators have minds; later it shall be explored how all selves do as well. A lifeform that can grow from thought can also have a mind. However, the majority of lifeforms on earth do not have their own minds because there is not enough thought contained within their forms to limit their respective fields of life. The third part of the Creator's thought that is given to our universe is activity that is intelligent, or whose function is to bring space back together and create light by rejoining the first two parts of the Creator's thought. If activity exists without being perfectly intelligent and thus does not perfectly enlighten space, then energy manifests as a more limited field of possibilities that contains certain probabilities for creation. The manifestation of energy, or form ("matter" when the energy is dense, in the physical dimension), creates the probability that some of the first two parts of God's thought will rejoin within some of the manifested energy, while the remainder will not. When this process takes place at a level that is sufficient to limit the field of manifested energy within a given period of time, life is created through the slight thought of the energy within the field following a greater thought.

The entire three parts, or aspects, of the Creator's thoughts that are given to our universe become the mind of God, with God representing the part of the Creator that God chose to grow more of within our universe. When the thought from the first and second parts of God's mind are reasonably balanced to the third, the result is life. Life is the method of growth chosen by God, and was the probable means of growth given to our universe by the Creator in its thought. Freedom of choice is a critical element to the Creator's plan; freedom of choice is a part of the Creator's direction that is common to its direction and thus connects its choices. Freedom makes life possible because it allows a created field to function somewhat autonomously relative to its creator. Freedom of choice is given to life by the Creator and by God through the choice by both to be sacrificial and to separate themselves—an extreme limitation. The Creator's sacrifice is replicated by God, who is the part of the Creator that is *choosing to grow* within our universe. The amount of freedom that any part of life has is determined by the amount of sacrifice it is willing to make that helps others to create more light. For example, if everything in the universe sacrificed at the same level to help others to create more light, all would have the same amount of freedom. Freedom is lost by those parts of life that choose to sacrifice less and not help to create more light in others.

The limitation chosen by God on the three aspects of its mind creates space and intelligent activity in three separated and further-limited fields; each of these large fields is represented by a probability that is caused by the nature of the thought within it, from one of the three parts of God's mind. Each field creates one of three distinct sub-lights of God's thought (of light) by reducing the number of choices and by changing the direction of the choices, or the ways of connecting them. From these three sub-lights, or separated parts, of God's mind are created a total of seven sub-lights and corresponding Great Beings. Within these seven new, more limited, fields the choices that created the sub-lights of God's thought and the fields' Beings, or Directors, are a lower correspondence to the choices made by God in its sacrifice to create its space, its light, and the intelligent activities. Each of the seven Beings creates a new way of growing life, or of growing God. They do so by both further limitation (sacrifice) and the connection of choices of thought that are large enough to limit a very large part of the space created by the separation of God's mind. Within a small part of this space, the third and lower Great Beings create light. They use the remaining space to attract energy that has been manifested from activity that is not yet perfectly intelligent because it could not rejoin space nor thus create light from thought. Energy that (very slightly) thinks as these Beings do in the connection of their choices, using similar choices, is greatly attracted to the space and field of the much greater thought. Each of the Great Beings creates a field that affects the thought of the energy by greatly increasing the number of choices that the energy might be able to use in its very slight thought. The Great Being creates this field so that it can join with energy through light, or through the thought given to the energy within this field. These fields are rays because each, as a field, is focused and directed exclusively on energy that is responsive to it. A ray is a field that is focused exclusively on energy. The energy that is responsive to the ray grows with other energy through light, or the thought of the cosmic Ray Lord who is focused on it in order to create life. Eventually enough enlightened energy joins together, reducing space between itself and other energy so that it (the enlightened energy) can become more intelligently informed through its attracting thought. This energy is then able to provide life with sense, by attracting a very small amount of other energy similar to itself, or intelligent information regarding other energy and its activity. The cosmic Ray Lords of life creation create life through their individual and limited versions of God's thought, or light, in form—which is focused thought, as a field, on the (very slight) thought of energy. Enlightenment of energy is referred to as virtue, and when effected cosmically, or focused throughout our universe on all the energy therein that has similar thought (that is responsive), the enlightenment becomes a cosmic virtue.

Before continuing into this third chapter, mention is made again that groups of concepts are explained in several different ways throughout the chapter. As was previously explained, this practice is common to all of the chapters after the first one. It is important for the reader to keep this in mind in order to avoid confusion when coming across information that has seemingly already been covered. Additional aspects of a subject are often included most of the times that it is explained, and for this reason the reader is encouraged to continue reading through any sections of information that he or she believes to be already understood.

At this point the focus will be more on what cosmic virtue is and how it is created. Later in the chapter how the creation of virtue is a part of the hidden meaning of life will be covered. Also in this chapter what life is can be more completely defined, though still only partially. For those who would prefer not to wait until later in the book to read what life is, later in this chapter a relatively brief but limited description is offered.

 ## THE CREATION OF THE THREE RAY LORDS OF ASPECT

The complexity of how cosmic Ray Lords create their own dimensions and the life or pre-life and virtue (light in form) within these dimensions may at the outset seem daunting as these thoughts are attempted to be held together in conceptual understanding. Let us imagine that we are watching these Ray Lords create life. In our visualization we initially observe the first cosmic Ray Lord, and we notice that its thought is focused on creating new types of life that can grow by sensing, or by being aware of, choices, or purpose, or will. Will is the consistency to choices within a field. The apparent amount of will is the level of consistency to the choices that an observer can be aware of. As we watch, this Ray Lord limits the very large field it is created from and creating within—the first aspect of God's mind—by sacrificing some of this field into a much smaller one. God's purpose for our universe includes the part for God to grow more of itself through life and its growth, and, as a part of this growth, also includes God's choices. These two parts of God's purpose (to *sacrifice* to *grow* more of life) are contained within the larger field. God's choices for accomplishing its purpose are included within this larger field. The larger field also includes parts of its means of initially doing so, through the self-limitation and sacrifice that created the three parts of its mind within our universe. The first Ray Lord now sacrifices some of this very large yet limited field of probable creation. The Ray Lord limits the field much further into just the choices and amount of purpose that some energy can use to first create sense, and then enable life to grow. This includes the energy that will eventually become parts of lifeforms. This new and relatively very limited field of probable life creation is the cosmic ray of the first Ray Lord. We watch this cosmic ray of probable life creation affect certain energies. We notice that those energies that very slightly think with a focus of their thought on distinguishing choices, will, purpose, and sacrifice in themselves and in others and that are in the direction of the first Ray Lord's thought, or its light, become affected by the cosmic ray of this first Ray Lord. The process takes place because some of the choices within the ray add to and are in a similar direction to the choices that the energy is very slightly thinking of. Of the energy that has thought that is in the direction of the first Ray Lord's thought, we notice that its remaining choices that are not being used to distinguish choices within itself and other energies instantly return to the larger field of the Ray Lord each time the energy thinks and somewhat limits the ray itself. When the energy uses the new choices from the cosmic ray to think by distinguishing, or directing, them so that it can better *understand* choices in itself and in some other energies, it then seeks even more choices from this, the first cosmic ray. The cosmic ray then instantly (initially, at the speed of the first Ray Lord's thought—or the speed of light for Its plane) becomes available to supply these new choices. Again, it does so as a sacrifice and limitation coming from the much larger field of the first part of God's mind, which the first Ray Lord exists within. Notice that when understanding is part of the function of energy that is developing a first ray sense, the first two parts of God's mind are invariably present—choices and understanding. Together, these two create light; the emphasis of first ray energy is on creating a sense of choices in others, and if the sense has light in it, the energy will gain some understanding as well. Note that energy can choose to think along the choices of the first ray, while choosing to not think in the same connectedness, or direction. Under such circumstances, the first ray will not help the energy to better think because although the energy is sensing, it is not doing so in light. When not stimulated by a ray, a sense can grow from the existing very slight thought of energy. However, without the help of a ray, energy and eventually the sense it creates grow much more slowly.

The dependence of the first ray type of energy, which has very slight thought about choices, or seeks more choices from the first Ray Lord's larger field, directs the first cosmic ray to the energy's very slight thought. It can be stated that we are observing this type of energy that thinks (such as it does) along the first ray invoking the first cosmic ray from the first Ray Lord, who in a much larger field and through great sacrifice is evoking this ray. There is a great electrical attraction between the first Ray Lord and the energy's thought and use of the first cosmic ray to grow in its thought about choices. Attraction exists because every time the energy seeks to think more about choices that are in the first Ray Lord's direction, it becomes greatly attracted to the vast number of remaining choices created by the first Ray Lord. Each thought within the same or a similar direction tends to create a momentum towards future thought being in a similar direction because it is easier to think in the same direction that one's last thought or thoughts were in. Life creations of the first Ray Lord are focused on will (choices, or purpose), but when enlightened, they always also create some—albeit a lesser amount of—awareness of understanding within themselves and about other energy. Once created, life can, as it chooses to, gain in consciousness. It can also gain the ability to recognize and plan the rejoining of the oneness of life through its increased focus on choices and God's purpose—which comes from its increased understanding about choices. The first cosmic Ray Lord attracts energies to its thought that tend to (slightly) think and grow in their thought as a sense of the activities of other energies *based upon* those other energies' choices (will, or purpose) and sacrifices. The effect of somewhat enlightened first ray energy gaining some amount of understanding, although usually less than the amount gained of choices, causes this energy to have a great affinity not only with other first ray energy, but also with second ray energy that, like it, is somewhat enlightened. The first Ray Lord is specializing the way it creates life or pre-life, through increasing the probable awareness of energy that very slightly thinks more along the Ray Lord's choices (or vibration, as a more limited human concept). When added together with Its direction of thought (with commonality, or oneness, to the choices), energy is thinking in that Ray Lord's type of light. Energy attracted to the first cosmic Ray Lord's thought then further stimulates the energy's awareness of other energies that are similar to itself, helping to develop it into a first ray type of sense concerning the activity of other energies. If enlightened to some level, the energy can also sense second ray energy, although to a somewhat lesser degree, because it can sense the components of light. Energy develops itself into a sense of other energies when it has the highest level of its type of thought that is corresponding to the thought of one of the seven Ray Lords within a body and when the energy attracts some other energies to it. One energy can attract a small amount of another energy to itself when the attracting energy's thought is greater than (or equal to) the other energy's very slight thought.

The more that the energy is attracted to our observed first ray and accurately follows the first Ray Lord's type of thought, or light, the more the energy itself becomes enlightened. Then it can more accurately sense the activity of other energies that are similar to itself, or are aware of choices/will/purpose/sacrifice in other energy. These energies can also discriminate those other energies that are different from themselves, but they cannot sense enough about different energies to understand very much about them unless the energies that are sensing are fully enlightened. Energy functions as a sense by attracting a small amount of similar-thinking energy (usually of the same ray type) towards itself by its thought being greater than the thought of the energy that it is sensing; a sense can function because energy follows thought that is greater than its own. Fully enlightened energy can sense all types of energy through the other energies' strong attraction to it because regardless of its ray type, all energy is at least somewhat attracted to light. Also, enlightened energy is the easiest type of energy to sense because it is continually being given to others.

As we conclude our observation of the first cosmic Ray Lord, we can recognize that it is creating and using a part of God's thought, or light. It is using the first part of God's thought to create its ray of probable life creation in order to attract and enlighten energy to become a sense of other energy—or become more aware—in just one of seven specialized ways. We can realize that the method of more life creation through specialization of the first ray is to increase the very slight thought of energy, with the focus of the ray on sensing choices/will/purpose/sacrifice in other energies. The name for the entire process is the creation of a cosmic virtue. Therefore, a virtue is a creation that results in the growth of life. The growth comes from creating more light into a form of pre-life or life to develop its senses, using the light that is a part of God's thought. These partial-, or sub-lights, or thoughts of God, are created by Great Beings who are referred to as cosmic Ray Lords. When performed on a cosmic scale as a cosmic Ray

Lord does, the creation of virtue becomes cosmic and establishes a type, or specialization, of God's thought to grow itself through growing more life. Specialization of light to create life is established either for the entire dimension to which energy is attracted and in which it becomes a part of a Ray Lord or for the first two, or highest, dimensions that the energy is fully sacrificed from. We can even say that the energy (or intelligent activity, in some cases) and the entire dimension that it becomes a part of are like the Ray Lord's body—on an enormous scale. All other parts of life that the Ray Lord creates are a part of its body and its life. Thus the cosmic virtue is enlightening energies that are being created into new types of life or pre-life. These energies are a part of the life of the cosmic Ray Lord who is effecting the creation.

The virtue that is created by the first cosmic Ray Lord, or its light in form that grows life, is the will (consistent choices) to grow more life through self-sacrifice and using a part of God's purpose, which will be a part of the life. The more that life is choosing to grow additional life through some sacrifice(s) of itself, the more it is creating of this first virtue, or light in form. The first ray helps energy that is receptive to it to develop a sense of this virtue by providing the energy with more choices as the sense grows. Energy that chooses to think but does not use its corresponding ray does grow in its very slight thought, but it grows into darkness. It does so by reducing the space between itself and similarly thinking energies, through carrying out activities that are non-intelligent. This process, which results in the effect referred to as gravity, will be explained in upcoming chapters.

In continuing our visualization and hence our observation of the second Ray Lord in its probabilistic life creation, we see that its thought is focused on developing life that is aware of planning, consciousness, and understanding. This Ray Lord's thought is focused on the creation of life through the increase in thought about the oneness of life, through its givingness (its love), and through its planning, or understanding (its consciousness). All of these are part of the second aspect of God's mind in our universe. We can also see that the second Ray Lord is using *some* of the choices and purpose of the first part of God's mind in addition to the emphasis in its thought on the second part, or ray. Because the second Ray Lord is more limited in its thought than the first is, a reduction occurs in the number of choices (and the frequency) of its thought. While this first aspect of God's mind is used with which to create thought (and light) by joining with the second aspect in the thought of the second Ray Lord, it is not used by this Ray Lord as the emphasis on the creation of sense in energies that are responsive to it. The reason is that the second Ray Lord, like the first, is considerably more limited than God is. This occurs because the total amount of sacrifices within its thought and the amount of choices that each of these Ray Lords has made, while enormous, do not have the immenseness of God's.

The second Ray Lord has chosen to create life through a light that, although limited, still gives diversity and freedom of thought to its creation. We can see that this Ray Lord is using will and choices to have a part of God's purpose, but one that is more limited because it chooses to grow life from the angle, or direction, of increasing the recognition and understanding of the oneness of all life. Eventually, the life will develop understanding that this one life is a part of God and is its growth in our universe. The second Ray Lord attracts energy that (very slightly) thinks along this line of thought and is more easily enlightened into an increasingly better sense of the activities and quality of other energy that is similar to itself. When enlightened, this energy can also be aware of and can attract first ray energy. However, in most cases, without added thought from another source the second ray energy will still be more aware of and more attracted to other second ray energy than to energy of the first ray. The second cosmic Ray Lord assists by increasing the proclivity of the more advanced very slightly-thinking energies to grow more as a sense of other energies that are similar to those that make up the sense, based upon how much these other energies are giving/loving/conscious. The increased sense is accomplished by the second cosmic ray focusing the direction of choices on the quality of choice. The amount of oneness that is created between or among two or more thoughts is a measurement of the quality of the choices within each thought. As the collective energy that makes up the sense gains more direction in its thought towards identifying oneness in the thought of other energy, it itself learns to give more, which allows it to become more one with other life. The second cosmic Ray Lord is creating life with an emphasis on consciousness and understanding. Even though it is still using light as its thought, the light is a sub-light of God's light. The light in form, or the cosmic virtue, that the second Ray Lord is creating as it creates life along the second cosmic ray is energy's giving of unconditional love, or of givingness, to other energy. The enhanced energy eventually becomes a part of life and senses with other life to give to this other life so that it might choose to do the same. The Ray Lord gives this thought of oneness as life or pre-life is attracted to the Ray Lord's thought and then uses some of Its ray from which to grow in sense.

Creation of the First and Second Ray Primordial Energy

The first and second rays focus on responsive energy from the big bang, and attract this energy into the five densest dimensions of form.

Illustration 3.2

The sense of unconditional love, or giving, is created when one energy that has developed as a second ray sense of a part of life understands its oneness in relation to another energy and perhaps even as a part of all life; as this sense is created, consciousness increases. The increase is in direct correlation to the level of understanding oneness between the light in one form and another, and possibly to the level of recognizing the oneness of all life. Thus consciousness is understanding the oneness between two or more parts of life or pre-life, and the more this oneness is understood, the higher the consciousness. Because a sense is needed before there can be understanding, the greater the sense of *and* the understanding of the oneness, the more conscious a lifeform is of others. The same is true in reverse: the less a lifeform is aware, or the less it senses oneness with other lifeforms, the less it develops an understanding within its thought about others. Consciousness is lost when one cannot understand others. The loss occurs because one's thoughts are *reduced* in their connectedness concerning the others; since the amount of connectedness of thought *is* consciousness, the greater the increases in consciousness, the more the others are understood as one. The less conscious that life or pre-life is, the less it can understand thought that is like the Ray Lord's—like God's—in light concerning what has been sensed. A loss of light causes separation between oneself and others, by increasing space, which reduces the sense and understanding of oneness and of consciousness. Since forms are a part of the second cosmic virtue, the amount of giving of this understanding of oneness to others who are in need of it in order to increase their sense of giving is what ultimately controls the growth of consciousness or, conversely, the loss of it. The giving to other parts of life so that these other parts might better give is unconditional love. The love is unconditional because the giving is done in the best way possible in order to help the part of life that is given to, to give in the same unconditional way without qualifications from the giver that can limit consciousness, with the receiver free to do with this love whatever it will; it can give more of itself from what was given to it as it chooses, or it can choose to not give and be selfish. The second ray creates the light in form, or virtue, of unconditional love of one part of life for another, by being conscious of the oneness of life; the degree of consciousness (understanding), which comes from giving awareness/sense *and* thought, matches the level at which the giving part of life unconditionally gives in the best way possible to some other part of life so that it might do the same. In our imaginations, we now have observed the creation of the two great, or cosmic, virtues as created by the first two Ray Lords.

The third cosmic Ray Lord focuses its probabilistic creation on intelligent activities of forms. We can observe that this Ray Lord creates life in two distinct ways. First, it attracts energies to its thought that are focused on better communication and movement relative to the energy's surrounding energies. The better communication and movement lead to intelligence between and among lifeforms or pre-life forms, which causes the space between them to become reduced and replaced by light. The third Ray Lord's thought (choices and direction), or type of light, is increasing the probability that the energy that is attracted to Its thought will develop a sense of the activity of other energy that is similar to itself. This activity includes the other energy's intelligence, or its ability to communicate its choices or its direction, or both. The third cosmic Ray Lord is also capable of focusing on the attribute of the energy itself, or its relative level of density. This density is mostly responsible for how the energy tends to (originally, very slightly) think. The Ray Lord can, at will, change the density of the energy that is attracted to its thought, or its light. In so doing the Ray Lord creates enormous power because when energy changes density, its potential for creation changes in ratio to its density—creating power. Power comes from intelligent activity and remains after an intelligent activity is partly manifested as energy. Power is the potential for energy to return to intelligent activity (by usually further *decreasing* its density it becomes more enlightened), and this potential is present whenever energy is manifested. Power can usually become increased by reducing the energy's density and moving it closer to becoming intelligent in its activity. Therefore, power is the ability to create using form, or energy, as an expression of the creation. Some of the life that we observe this Ray Lord creating is brought into being through power, because in these circumstances the attribute of the form is being changed, enhancing the most responsive energy to increase its sense of other energies' density and power. Note that power is related to the ability to alter the density of energy, and that power is always connected to activity. As an example, a cup of alcohol can be used to create power. For this to take place, the density of the energy in the alcohol must be altered. As the alcohol is ignited, it changes from a liquid state to a gaseous one, and, in the process, power is produced. The change in the energy's (the alcohol's) state of density creates movement, and the measure of that movement is the measure of the power. The power itself is the "left-over" potential in the field of intelligent activity that was not manifested as energy. See Chapter Four and Chapter Ten for further explanation of this concept.

The light that the third cosmic Ray Lord is creating in form in order to create more life or pre-life is the cosmic virtue of *both* intelligent activity *and* power, *used together*. We can see that as this third ray stimulates responsive energy to become an improved sense of other energies' activities and communication, it also enhances the ability of these energies to determine the relative density of other energies as well as their own. Intelligent interaction and its communication must be joined with the creation and use of power if there is to be increased light in form. Interactions and communication that are *relatively* intelligent create some level of knowledge. How this occurs will be covered later in this book. When communication and potential intelligent activity exist either without enough or with too much power, light (and inclusiveness) is lost and darkness and separation increase, in one of two ways. Either the intelligence is not converted into form because of a lack of power, or there is too much power and too little intelligence…which does further create the form, but into a darker one that has less light. If the power to create forms exists with little or no intelligent activity in its communication, as darkness increases under certain circumstances, the power can lead to evil. The third ray is by nature (as a result of the separation of spirit and energy, which will be further explained later) more separative than the first and second are, which makes it more difficult for this ray to consistently enlighten energy and create its cosmic virtue. The virtue of the third cosmic ray is to grow all new life or pre-life within a duration of time and space—all together at the same time and space. These new types of life are intelligent in their activity with other energy, and they also use the power to create forms to only support this intelligence by making it manifested as a part of the newly created forms. The word intelligence means, in this case, the relative ability for energy to join with other energy as the two are *simultaneously* rejoining with space, or creating light. These conditions can occur only as the joining energies communicate with each other in ways that support their joining *both* with each other and with space. Therefore, the third cosmic virtue is the creation of new types of life that help to grow all other life within the third Ray Lord's duration of time and space, through intelligence and power.

Another way of explaining the third cosmic virtue is that it is the joining of energy with other energy while the space around them becomes lessened and light becomes increased. This creates new life or pre-life for *all* of the third Ray Lord's dimension and below—or for its *duration* of life creation. As the space between the energies decreases as a result of their enlightenment, the amount of movement necessary in order to stay intelligent decreases. What this means is that the *relative* level of potential power increases (while the absolute manifested, or used, levels decrease). Space is light that is separated into its two component parts. When space is joined (which enlightens it), light is created, and the need for energy to move is decreased because the space between the energies is lessened as they are moving closer together.

 ## CONCLUSIONS REGARDING THE FIRST THREE RAYS

In examining the first three rays of the aspects of God's mind and the virtues, or the light in form, that they create, several conclusions can be reached:

1. Because the three parts of God's mind created our universe, no one part exists without some amount of the other two present within the same dimension. The only exception to this principle is the third part of God that is manifested as energy at the very first instant of the beginning of time at our universe's inception—when energy was maximally separated from space on the seventh plane. Note that potential intelligent activity,

or the third aspect of God's mind, still existed even when all of the energy that was on the seventh plane was fully separated.

2. Each of the three cosmic virtues of the aspects of God's mind contains some amount of the other two, since for a cosmic virtue to exist, all three parts of God's mind must be present.

3. To create more virtue within a type of cosmic virtue corresponding to one of the three aspects of God's mind requires creative thought that is similar to and within the dimension of the Ray Lord who initially created the cosmic virtue. This means, for example, that a lifeform creating virtue on the third, or spiritual, plane would need to be able to exist within the time and space of that dimension; such a being would need to think similarly to the third Ray Lord *and* it would need to think within the type of form of the Ray Lord's dimension and thought. In other words, in order to be aware in a dimension, a being would need to share with the Ray Lord of that dimension a body that has adequate sense in that dimension. This same concept holds true for the four remaining lower dimensions, which concern attributes of energies rather than aspects of God's mind. Those who are creating virtue within these dimensions will also have to share similar thought and form with the Ray Lord of the dimension they exist within; each must have a body with developed sense that corresponds to that dimension.

THE CREATION OF THE RAY LORDS OF ATTRIBUTE

Before we observe the remaining four Ray Lords, of attribute, each creating new types of pre-life and life through their respective probabilistic rays that stimulate certain responsive energies to grow into a sense, it might be helpful to have a brief explanation, using a simplified example, of how these Ray Lords' bodies (their forms, or dimensions) are created. Imagine that you want to create some new people as friends, using for each of them parts of either two or three people who already exist. We will name these existing people friends numbers one, two, and three. You would like your new creations of people to be somewhat like the existing ones, but also largely self-created and therefore self-thinking (using a new limited type of God's thought, or light). You decide that for this reason what you will use from the existing friends are the most obvious qualities that are mostly attributes (densities, amounts, and types of movement) of *form* rather than aspects of God's mind. You decide to create new friends numbers four, five, six, and seven, using copies of the obvious features of the attributes of the *forms* of the existing friends' bodies. You utilize mostly their attributes of energy (when lacking intelligent activity), without a focus on making them think in any certain way. These new friends will use the system of thought created by the first three friends, but within their respective systems they are free to think as they choose to. To create new friend number four, you use the potential that existing friends numbers two and three have for the creation of differing densities of energy amounts and their movement, which are their attributes. You use these two friends because friend number two has a created life and qualities of thought that created the form, or attribute of energy, that you are borrowing from her. These qualities are associated with the even, or feminine, number to her name, like friend number four will have. Friend number three is unique in that one part of him is distinctly entirely focused on creating his life from form, or energy; the focus on form lends itself quite naturally to be used as one of the borrowed qualities for friend number four, whose body will be focused on the attribute of form. You now take a partial clone of the left side of friend number two's body and join it to a partial clone of the right side of friend number three's body, using parts of certain components from both—such as the eyes, ears, arms, and legs—while using some elements exclusively from each, so that there will be differences in each side as well as between the original friends and the new ones. Only about half of half (one-fourth) of each of the two existing friends' bodies are used for cloning, leaving about half of friend number four's body, or form, to still be created from newly attracted energies. The thought, or light, of each new friend, who represents a Ray Lord, must be great enough to convert the energy within its most focused thought within its dimension, or within its form, into intelligent activity. Less thought, however, or a lower type of light, is required to alter each lower Ray Lord's energy at the focus point of that Ray Lord's thought. The reason is that each lower Ray Lord's field of energy and the energy's collective thought *at the focus point*, while much more dense and diverse, come from a smaller field of choices whose total percentage of change in direction and creativity as compared to the preceding (higher) Ray Lord diminishes on each lower sub-plane. In addition, this condition also leads to a much smaller focus point, or atomic level of completely enlightened energy, or intelligent activity, for each lower Ray Lord. The diversity is caused by the thought of the energies being more separated when not affected by their own gravity.

Atomic Levels of the Five Lower Planes

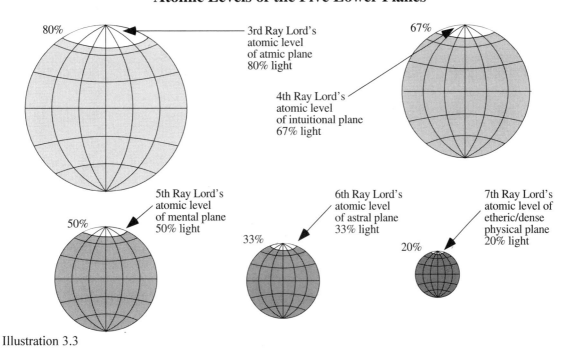

Illustration 3.3

The general process of creating the fourth and lower Ray Lords is as follows: Ray Lords four through seven are created using a combination of parts of Ray Lords three and either one or two (and sometimes an additional Ray Lord of attribute, as explained later in this section of the chapter). Ray Lord three is used because it represents the form side of God's third aspect of mind. Ray Lords four through seven represent the attributes of form. Ray Lords one or two are used with Ray Lord three because the first three Ray Lords represent the three parts of God's mind and the way the consciousness of the form is expressed. For Ray Lord number four, we have decided to use parts of the bodies of Ray Lords two and three. We will use one-fourth of each of these two Ray Lords' bodies, which will make up half of Ray Lord four's body, or dimension. The other half of Ray Lord four will come from the two types of energy that the combination of what the thought of Ray Lord four attracts to itself—primordial energy (attracted to the dimension during the big bang) and elemental energy (attracted by spirit's thought). Note that these concepts are more fully explained in the next chapter. The attracted both primordial and elemental energy will follow the pattern that we made for it by using parts of Ray Lords two and three. We have chosen Ray Lord two to be a part of Ray Lord four because the number two is a feminine number, like the number four is, and Ray Lord two has connectedness/direction/consciousness/love that Ray Lords one and three lack. (The concept of masculine and feminine numbers is further explained later in this book.) However, the love that Ray Lord two will contribute will be changed, or shifted, from the unconditional love that is found in the second Ray Lord's dimension, to conditional love that will exist only when there is twice as much spiritual thought than the amount of energy's thought within a body. In the fourth Ray Lord's dimension, energy will respond completely lovingly, or givingly, only when this condition exists. The third Ray Lord contributes the exact density of energy needed for the form of Ray Lord number four, but only half of one-half of the total amount.

The Creation of Friend Four

Friend 3

Friend 2

To make a new friend, join parts of the forms of Friend 2 and Friend 3.

Illustration 3.4a

The Creation of Friend Four

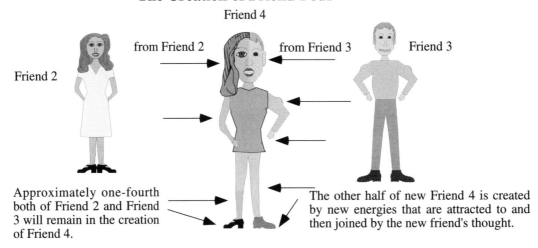

Friend 4

from Friend 2   from Friend 3   Friend 3

Friend 2

Approximately one-fourth both of Friend 2 and Friend 3 will remain in the creation of Friend 4.

The other half of new Friend 4 is created by new energies that are attracted to and then joined by the new friend's thought.

Illustration 3.4b

Next, for the creation of new friend number five you decide to use existing friends numbers one and three. Again, only parts of their form are used, and will make up only half of the total energy of friend number five because the other half will be attracted by his own thought as he creates himself. You use existing friend number one because this friend has a created life and the qualities that created his form that are associated with his odd-numbered, or masculine, name—like number five will have. Again, number three is used because he is so good at his powerful creativity, utilizing form to create precisely the correct density of the energy.

The Creation of Friend Five

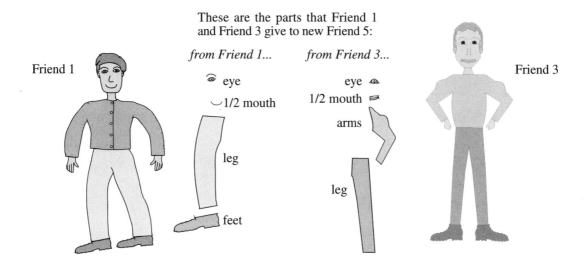

These are the parts that Friend 1 and Friend 3 give to new Friend 5:

from Friend 1...   *from Friend 3...*

eye   eye

1/2 mouth   1/2 mouth

arms

leg   leg

feet

Friend 1

Friend 3

Illustration 3.5a

The Creation of Friend Five

Friend 5 is made of parts from Friend 1 and Friend 3.

Friend 5

Illustration 3.5b

For new friend number six you decide to again use existing friends numbers two and three, but you use less of them and then add some of the form of newly created friend number four, so that new friend number six will have the two even-numbered parts. You use less of the left and right sides of friends number two and three, and from friend number four you copy some middle parts—the nose, mouth, and stomach—which you divide and use sections of. Friends number two, three, and four each contribute about one-sixth of their own form and one-sixth of the total amount of energy cloned for friend number six; together, they provide one-half of her form. The other half is made up of energy that is attracted to her by her thought.

The Creation of Friend Six

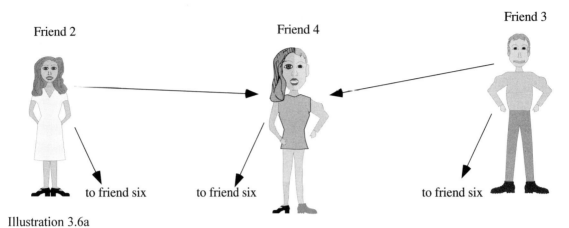

Illustration 3.6a

The Creation of Friend Six

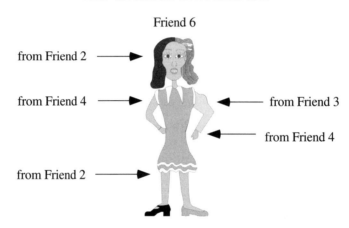

Illustration 3.6b

Finally, you create new friend number seven from existing friends numbers one, three, and five similarly to how friend number six was created, using about one-sixth (one-third of about half) of the form qualities of each of the three existing friends. Again, at this point only a total of one-half of the form that friend number seven will have exists, because his thought has not yet attracted to himself the remainder of the energy that he will need.

The Creation of Friend Seven

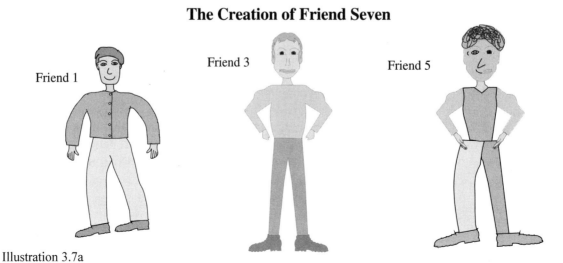

Illustration 3.7a

The Creation of Friend Seven

These are the parts that Friends 1, 3 and 5 give to the new Friend 7.

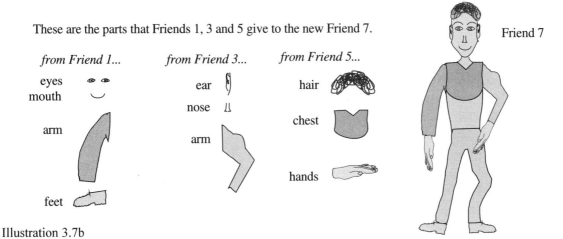

from Friend 1...   *from Friend 3...*   *from Friend 5...*   Friend 7

eyes   ear   hair

mouth   nose

arm   chest

arm

feet   hands

Illustration 3.7b

Notice that in the above examples, all of the newly created friends of form attribute came, in part, from the existing third friend because he has one part that is distinctively focused on form creation, and he is very good at using energy with power to create new density of forms. Also notice that the energy that is first cloned from the qualities (the types of consciousness that come from the form being given) of the higher Ray Lord (represented by friend number three) is manifested from the intelligent activity, or the third part of God's mind; this energy is then changed in density by the power of the third Ray Lord. The Ray Lords of attribute are created in similar manner, as follows:

1. Some of the form parts as well as their qualities included in and given from the intelligent activity of Ray Lords two and three partially create the fourth Ray Lord.

$\frac{1}{4}$ of the second Ray Lord's body + $\frac{1}{4}$ of the third Ray Lord's body =
$\frac{1}{2}$ of the fourth Ray Lord's body

The remaining $\frac{1}{2}$ of the Ray Lord's body is attracted to it through Its light, or thought.

2. Some of the form parts as well as their qualities included in and given from the intelligent activity of Ray Lords one and three partially create the fifth Ray Lord.

$\frac{1}{4}$ of the first Ray Lord's body + $\frac{1}{4}$ of the third Ray Lord's body =
$\frac{1}{2}$ of the fifth Ray Lord's body

The remaining $\frac{1}{2}$ of the Ray Lord's body is attracted to it through Its light, or thought.

3. Some of the form parts as well as their qualities included in and given from the intelligent activity of Ray Lords two, three, and four partially create the sixth Ray Lord

$\frac{1}{6}$ of the second Ray Lord's body + $\frac{1}{6}$ of the third Ray Lord's body +
$\frac{1}{6}$ of the fourth Ray Lord's body = $\frac{1}{2}$ of the sixth Ray Lord's body

The remaining $\frac{1}{2}$ of the Ray Lord's body is attracted to it through Its light, or thought.

4. Some of the form parts as well as their qualities included in and given from the intelligent activity of Ray Lords one, three, and five, partially create the seventh Ray Lord.

$\frac{1}{6}$ of the first Ray Lord's body + $\frac{1}{6}$ of the third Ray Lord's body +
$\frac{1}{6}$ of the fifth Ray Lord's body = $\frac{1}{2}$ of the seventh Ray Lord's body

The remaining $\frac{1}{2}$ of the Ray Lord's body is attracted to it through Its light, or thought.

The body, or form, of a Ray Lord is the entire dimension of time/space that is either created from energies that are attracted to Its probabilistic ray of life creation or, in the case of the first two Ray Lords, are created from intelligent activity. Nearly everywhere within each dimension of space/time, the Ray Lord's light, or joined thought, is deliberately kept separate by will and sacrifice. The exception is the part of a dimension in which energy has completely joined with the Ray Lord's thought as if energy never existed (or is completely separated from light, as is the case on the first two planes), and has become intelligent activity, or has joined with its choices and God's direction of these choices. The part that is joined is initially that which was created from the above-described partial cloning of borrowed energies and that also can be limited in thought by the newly formed Ray Lord, and is the atomic part. The atomic part of a dimension is always enlightened because it originated from the enlightened parts of either other Ray Lords (for Ray Lords four through seven) or from God's mind (for the first three cosmic Ray Lords) and still can be limited by the new Ray Lord's thought, or light. This enlightened part can be completely sacrificially given by the new Ray Lord. This part is referred to as the *atomic* part because it is the beginning and most basic part. Thus some of Ray Lords four through seven are partly created from the atomic, or the most basic and fully enlightened, parts of the dimensions of the Ray Lords that helped to create them. Through the thought of each newly created Ray Lord, part of that Ray Lord is connected with those dimensional parts that always contain only intelligent activity.

    ## HOW THE RAYS OF ATTRIBUTE CREATE VIRTUE

We now look at the fourth cosmic Ray Lord and notice that this Ray Lord is changing the probability for life by affecting only the attribute, or *density*, and relative enlightenment of form (energy) and its quantity in relation to outside enlightening thought. This Ray Lord is adding qualities of the third Ray Lord's creation through attributes of only form, or energy, with the second Ray Lord's focus on oneness and consciousness of the form it creates, in order to perfect a balance between the two. However, the fourth Ray Lord is also dividing the thought, or light, of these two Ray Lords by two, as it adds the two thoughts', or lights', angles (and vibrations) of the form they create together, simultaneously creating a new light that is more limited. We observe this cosmic Ray Lord creating a ray of probabilistic life creation that stimulates energy that is attracted to it. The energy's slight thought is to grow more in sense by sensing the amount of *outside* thought, from spirit, that is affecting the sensed energy. Briefly explained, spirit comes from the first two parts of God's mind interacting with the third part. Spirit is separated from the thought of other parts of spirit at increasing amounts from the third dimension and Ray Lord's thought, down, through the seventh dimension. Spirit is the part of form that primarily thinks and is learning to sense and act from the energy as it informs and directs energy through its (spirit's) thought. The reason is that energy follows thought that is greater than its own. Energy that is affected by spirit is manifested from the third part of God's mind, and when energy is separated from intelligent activity (intelligent activity only enlightens other energy) it follows the thought of spirit, because spirit, through its additional thought, creates some increased level of probability of enlightenment within each corresponding ray. Energy can take action and communicate, and is learning to think. The fourth ray grows sense in energy that indicates the amount of energy and spirit that are needed to either increase or decrease the amount of energy to the perfect level, at which the spirit's thought can completely think for the energy as well as for itself. The amount of thought needed for this perfection is always twice the amount needed to enlighten the energy, or to perfectly think through and with the energy. (It is necessary herein to use the concept of spirit, which has not yet been fully explained—but will be in the next chapter.) Whenever there is a perfection of balance in the level to which spirit can think completely for both itself and energy, the energy, or the form, perfectly expresses the spirit within it and becomes perfectly enlightened. The perfect expression of spirit by energy (or form) and the resultant perfect enlightenment is referred to as beauty. Thus beauty is the cosmic virtue, or the light in form, of the fourth cosmic Ray Lord. The remaining Ray Lords continue the process of changing the probability for the creation of more and different life.

The fifth Ray Lord affects the probability for life creation by changing the structured attribute of energy, or how well the energy can replicate its prior designs of forms. As we observe this Ray Lord creating new types of life, we can see it *structuring* energy in ways that allow the energies to replicate other forms more easily, through formulas of balancing energies to reduce forces so that the forms stay together longer in whole time. This structured approach relies on a mathematical creative application to form/matter and intelligent activities. When used to excess, it tends to ignore the consciousness aspect, or the second ray aspect, of God's mind, because the approach comes from adding together some (but not all) of the form elements that come from the intelligent activity of the first and third Ray Lords. Also, the balancing of forces can last for only a limited period of time, which eventually causes separation within the form and of time from space; this separation counters the second ray effect of inclusiveness and keeping things together. The energy that we can observe being attracted to this fifth Ray Lord's thought tends to sense other energy by how the other energy is itself structured and is formulating still other energies. Again, the (relatively) best-thinking of this attracted energy becomes a sense along the fifth ray within a lifeform because this energy follows the thought and the ray of the fifth Ray Lord better than other energies do.

The light of the fifth cosmic Ray Lord in its attracted form (energies) is created as a sense, or a collection of the type of energies that think best along the fifth ray and that can perfectly replicate the forms of other energies that they can sense. The energy that is sensing along the fifth ray can sense other fifth ray energy, which it attracts to itself and then replicates through structure and can remain so for long periods of time by balancing forces, thus making it identical, or true. When the replicated structure of a fifth ray sense has balanced the forces within the structure and is identical, or true, to the energy it has sensed, the sense becomes enlightened. The fifth cosmic virtue is truth, or a whole, exactly replicated structure that has been perfectly balanced in its forces in whole time—which is what makes a part of it identical to the original. The balanced, structured parts need to be adjusted for changes in time and space that cause changes in the forces, and, therefore, truth needs to be adjusted as well.

The sixth Ray Lord affects the probability for life creation through Its thought causing a change in the attribute of energy that is attracted to It, to become very focused and devoted to joining together with one other part of, or sometimes one specific group of, energy. The joining is done by completely focusing on the direction of movement of one energy towards that of another, so that the first energy, or form, can become one with the second. The very focused and limited type of giving of one form, or energy, to another is also a focused and limited type of (a conditional) love and a limited type of consciousness, or quality of the second ray. As we observe the sixth Ray Lord, we see that it is consistently stimulating the growth of the sense of the most advanced energies that are attracted to its thought, to then be able to sense the movement and likely ability to join with certain other energies. As the sense of energy grows along the sixth ray, it can predict the probable movements of certain other energies based upon those energies' relative ability, through directed choices, to give. In human terms, we refer to this ability as empathy. The virtue of the sixth Ray Lord is devoted (conditional) love, or love/giving-ness that is focused on or devoted to one energy or group of energies at a time.

Our observance of the seventh Ray Lord shows us a probabilistic ray of life creation that stimulates the energies that are most attracted to It that can sense either intelligent coordinated response or inertia (resistance to movements in differing directions) in other energies. This sense, when grown, allows one energy, or form, to recognize the relative position of other form, or energies, based upon their resistance to movement (and communication) towards and away from each other. Life reaches its maximal levels of separation in this Ray Lord's dimension, because, as we can see, inertia is producing great forces between lifeforms whenever their senses are less than perfect, or are unenlightened. Generally, we observe that one part of life created by this Ray Lord has great trouble in coordinating its quite limited movement with the life of other forms, and also in even reasonably intelligently communicating its actions. This all occurs because inertia (the effects of gravity, coupled with density) and friction are overwhelming the limited sense that is developed by somewhat enlightened energy and the energy's stimulation of growth, through the seventh ray. Gravity and friction are the effects of the density and thought of unenlightened energy, and will be further explained later in this book. When enlightened seventh ray energy overcomes inertia and creates intelligent coordinated response to other energies, it then produces cooperation and sharing, or the virtue of the seventh Ray Lord's light in its dimension.

The Seven Dimensions of the
Cosmic Ray Lords and Their Virtue

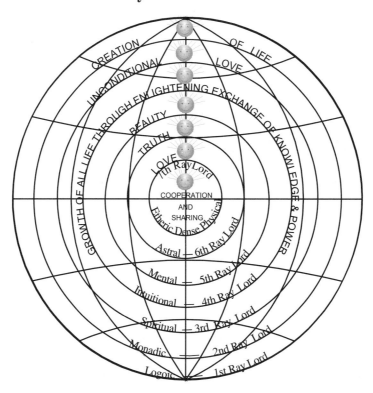

Illustration 3.8

CONSTRUCTION OF THE RAY LORDS' DIMENSIONS

The remaining possibilities of the limited field that energy very slightly thinks within and that it cannot limit with its existing thought are rejoined to the Ray Lord's field. In order for the energy to think more and differently than it has and still remain in light, it (the energy) must move towards the source of the increased possibilities that are similar to its own thought. This causes the somewhat enlightened energy to follow the thought of the Ray Lord. In most cases the energy, as part of life creation, seeks to think more and differently than it has, but still within the general direction of its preceding thought. Since thought is two or more choices in a similar direction that can limit the field it exists within, thought is much easier to create in similar directions to that which has been previously created and has limited its field. Because of the above-described factors, a momentum of energy movement and life creation is established within the Ray Lord's focused thought.

Some energy may choose to not follow the thought of the Ray Lord because the energy's thought is too obtuse to the Ray Lord's. When a large amount of such energy is part of a lifeform that has a self-structure, it can become a part of evil—which is that part of thought that is the antithesis of God's mind. Evil eventually establishes a direction of choices *nearly* completely away from God's. This direction of choices serves as a attracting field to some dark energy having consciousness that is high enough to be attracted to it, but too low to be able to recognize God's mind. Evil eventually fails in its will to destroy God and to be all that God is not, because each thought creating itself away from its Creator reduces its consciousness until its own levels of thought destroy itself. We will cover much more of this process in later chapters. For now it can be stated that the major concepts concerning evil are that evil exists in our universe within certain conditions during the growth of consciousness, and, that God chose that evil would be self-destructive and self-limiting—rendering evil able to slow the growth of life and God, but not able to destroy either (although evil frequently believes that it can). Evil is free to think however it chooses to; however, evil's thought is self-limiting because creation against and away from the Creator (God) usually gradually in time un-creates, or nullifies, one's self.

A Ray Lord's thought is in a different direction than are the three aspects of God's mind when joined, because the Ray Lord's thought comes from a separated aspect of God's mind. Although in a different direction, the Ray Lord's thought is still an uncompleted part of God's plan and therefore is still a part of what God chose to be, and is thus in accord with its plan. The Ray Lord's thought, though different from God's consciousness, remains a part of it. The reason is that all of the Ray Lord's creations are brought about by joining together some of the first two parts of God's mind, which always creates light within the Ray Lord. Each Ray Lord can create intelligent activity at the atomic level of its dimension and can therefore join time and space for that dimension, thus creating its own type of light. The first two cosmic Ray Lords create the first two cosmic rays of growth of life potential by their effects of growing the thought of the most responsive energies to these ray types in the five lowest dimensions. The cosmic ray of the third cosmic Ray Lord also stimulates the growth of life potential by helping energies that are responsive to this ray to better think. This Ray Lord and aspect of God's mind also creates energy that is separated from space, as a manifestation of intelligent activity that is separated from both consciousness (the second aspect and ray) and will (the first aspect and ray). Energy becomes manifested from the intelligent activity and eventually becomes attracted to its own plane—the third. Technically, the potential for energy does exist in some way when intelligent activity is joined with either consciousness or will and is separated from the other. This creates space between intelligent activity and light. This condition occurs on the first two dimensions of our universe except at their atomic levels and will be explained later in this book. It should be noted that when intelligent activity is manifested in the first two dimensions and is separated from light by space, this intelligent activity is an abstract of pure power and the potential to create new types of life, rather than the creation of some type of form, within that dimension. The third cosmic Ray Lord can create the potential growth for all of life within its duration (which encompasses everywhere from the spiritual plane through the etheric/dense physical) by altering energies of life and creating many lifeforms. As it uses lifeforms and their created diversity as a means of increased growth in all life, the Ray Lord is creating this potential from the *attribute* of the form rather than from the amount of intelligent activities between that part of life and other parts. When this Ray Lord creates its growth in all life potential within its duration through intelligent interaction, it is doing so through the *aspect* of God's mind.

Example of the Creation of a Cosmic Ray—The Third

Part 1

primordial energy outside the Ray Lord's plane

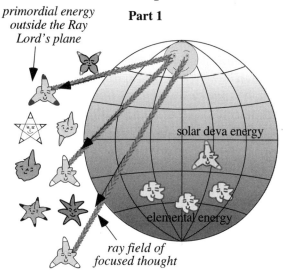

solar deva energy

elemental energy

ray field of focused thought

The third Ray Lord focuses its thought (its light) on all types of primordial energy. However, only energy along the third ray responds to this energy that this Ray Lord is focusing on. The reason for the responsiveness is that the primordial energies think in one or both of two ways. The first way of thought is the ability for energy to sense other energy's density and power. Power is the ability to change the density of energy. The second part is the ability to think and sense intelligently about how to communicate with other similar-thinking energy.

Part 2

primordial energy not responding

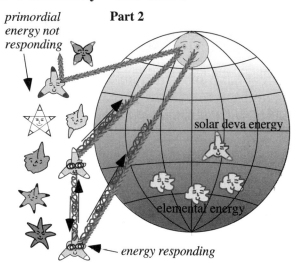

solar deva energy

elemental energy

energy responding

The Ray Lord creates a field that helps the energy to think better and to develop better senses if the energy responds to the energy within Its field. A field is created by the focused thought of the Ray Lord on the extremely small field of the thought of energy that is helped to think better if it chooses to think in the Ray Lord's direction. (Rays affect only energy.) Similar-thinking energy joins together and responds to the energy focused on by the Ray Lord. Energy that does not respond is not assisted in its ability to think and sense.

Part 3

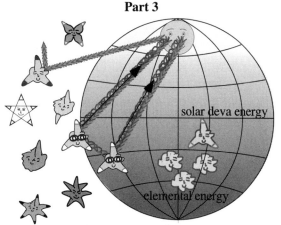

solar deva energy

elemental energy

Some primordial energy responds and some does not.

Through its very slight thought, primordial energy is attracted into the plane that it responds to with its very slight thought. Other similar-thinking energy is also attracted into the plane by the Ray Lord's thought. Elemental energy and solar deva energy that think similarly to the Ray Lord increase Its body with their very slight thought. All of these energies together form the Ray Lord's body.

Part 4

primordial energy that did not respond to the thought of this Ray Lord

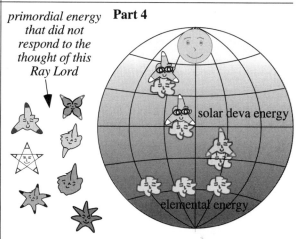

solar deva energy

elemental energy

In a majority of cases, primordial energy becomes deva energy. However, some primordial energy chooses to not think in the direction of the Ray Lord that it was initially attracted to. This energy then responds involutionarily, or more like elemental energy—becoming attracted to the thought of other involutionarily energies, and falls to a lower part of the plane. As energies are attracted to the Ray Lord's thought, they think better and develop better senses. Note that primordial energy that did not respond to the thought of this Ray Lord may be attracted to the thought of another Ray Lord.

Illustration 3.9

The third cosmic Ray Lord is unique in its ability to create new potential growth in all life within its duration through either an attribute of form or an aspect of God's mind, or from both at the same time. The direction of the third Ray Lord's thought remains the same, regardless of its method. However, when it creates its potential for all life growth within its duration using the attribute of the form, it is changing the density of the energies that make up the lifeforms. When it creates its potential for the growth of all life within its duration through its aspect of God's mind of intelligent activity, it alters the energy's intelligence *between* and *among* lifeforms, affecting their communication and movements, and when the lifeforms sense communication and movements, they can then synthesize knowledge.

 ## FURTHER EXPLANATION OF THE RAY LORDS' CONSTRUCTIONS

To again explain the method of structures that create forms of the Ray Lords of attribute, the directions of thought and the choices, or vibration, of the first three cosmic Ray Lords (sometimes with Ray Lords four and five added) can be added together and then divided by the number of directions that were used (either two or three), resulting in new, lesser, fields of possibilities and correspondingly more limited cosmic Ray Lords. The number of combinations reaches a total of seven, with the created potentials for life growth manifesting as new cosmic Ray Lords and cosmic rays four, five, six, and seven. Each of these fields of possibilities must be a sub-field of the third Ray Lord's field because the fields' first condition of creation—as the lower part of our universe is constructed—is of *separated*, or *manifested*, energy. Thus the third ray's direction as it affects form is added to the direction of another one or two rays as they affect form, and then is divided by either two or three. The result is the new directions and vibrations or choices/will/sacrifice of rays four through seven—and as growth acceleration of the thought within energies, or as they affect *only* form. Each of these new, and lesser, Ray Lords can, within its field of possible life creation, create the potential growth in life only through changing the attribute (the density, amounts, and type of movement) of the form. These Ray Lords can no longer directly completely use one of the aspects of God's mind, since it has been decreased in vibration and direction as well as hampered by less intelligent activity and more and denser energies. By being able to create potential for new types of life diversity through only the attribute of a lifeform, these Ray Lords and the life within their dimensions cannot always create diversity in life that is God-like, or that has incorporated the three parts of God's mind as a reasonably closely joined unity. Much more of this effect and the way it affects life's hidden meaning will be covered later in this book.

From a different perspective, each of the seven Beings who are creating the seven cosmic rays of probabilistic life creation (each of the seven cosmic Ray Lords) creates the potential for new types of life. Each does so from its thoughts limiting its field of possibilities, by choosing a new direction to its thought—but one that is still in accord with God's plan, or is still within the consciousness of God. The space created is an alteration of that space that God originally created for the entire universe. The reason is that the direction of thought is different (and less inclusive of all of God's direction) and the aspect of sacrifice is less. The changed direction modifies the second aspect of God's mind, but it remains within its plan, while the lower level of sacrifice reduces the amount that is used of the first aspect of God's mind. By using less of the first aspect of God's mind and by altering the second, but by still joining these two together, the cosmic Ray Lords create new types of light that each travels at a different, successively lower, speed (because of each one's successively lesser thought) and has a unique color. Each Ray Lord can completely enlighten the space at the atomic level of its dimension, or this part of its body of energy, into intelligent activity, by having enough thought (light) to convert the atomic level energy into only intelligent activities. At the atomic level of each lower Ray Lord's plane, or dimension, there is less intelligent activity than at the atomic level of the Ray Lord's dimension above it. These Ray Lords also create new types of space in the areas where the two aspects of light are separated because of the presence of either attracted energy or separated intelligent activity, as on the first two dimensions of our universe. This new light and space create a new dimension for each cosmic Ray Lord and its created ray to grow more life within. Since seven cosmic Ray Lords function within our universe, there exist seven major dimensions of light (God's thought) and space. As energy is used with which to create from all dimensions including energy that is manifested from the first two dimensions, and as it moves and interacts within the remaining five dimensions, seven major divisions to time are created. Note, however, that time becomes relatively changed even within these dimensions, through the amount of energy that is present (or absent) and the thought that affects both the energy and the surrounding space. Time and space, and their effect on life and its meaning, will be covered throughout the remainder of *Life's Hidden Meaning* and extensively in Chapter Ten.

The Seven Planes, or Dimensions, of Our Universe and the Colors of Their Light

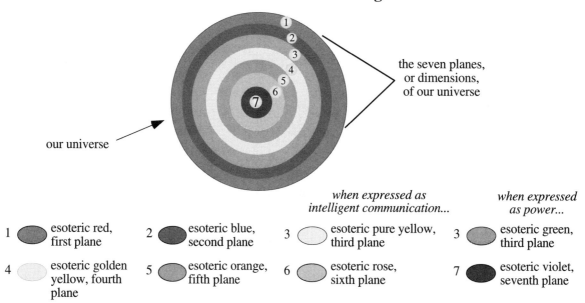

Note that esoteric colors emit light, while mundane colors absorb and reflect light.

Illustration 3.10

Each of the seven Ray Lords is creating its own dimension, or plane, of time and space because its thought, or light, is in accord with God's thought but is also more limited in choices and has a somewhat different direction or connectivity (oneness) to these choices. When a Ray Lord's thought attracts energy that all very slightly thinks in a certain similar way, the energy shares a part of the Ray Lord's field of created probabilities that are produced by its limiting thought, or by light and its effect on the energy in that field. The energy and its very small field of possibilities are connected to the Ray Lord's field of possibilities by the Ray Lord's ray of probable life creation. This ray stimulates the responsive, or higher-thinking, of the similar-thinking (in ray type) energies to help them grow in their thought towards the choice and direction, or vibration and phase (to use terms that are less accurate but more familiar to some people), of the Ray Lord's thought, or light. The growth stimulation comes from an increase in choices and correct direction given to the responsive energy's field through the connecting field of the cosmic ray. The more that the responsive energy brings the choices within the ray field together in a similar direction to the Ray Lord's thought, the more that the energy becomes enlightened, and the closer is its sense of other energies to the Ray Lord's sense. Life uses these senses of the most responsive energies in order to sense other energy and the accumulated energies that have become other parts of life within other lifeforms, as well as to sense energy that is not part of a lifeform (and is pre-life).

 ## A PARTIAL EXPLANATION AND DEFINITION OF LIFE

The previously mentioned partial explanation and definition of life can now be given. Within a Ray Lord's dimension or sometimes within only its ray field, some energies that best follow the Ray Lord's thought, as a part of life or light, follow only the Ray Lord's thought and become enlightened. Then the light of the Ray Lord exists within these forms, or energies. When this occurs, the light is referred to as virtue because it has been replicated into form by the growth of pre-life or life. Energy that has not yet become alive cannot create virtue using *only* its own thought and not relying on the thought of spirit because, as pre-life, it has not yet brought all three parts of God's mind into itself within the same time and space. These three parts are choices, direction of the choices, and intelligent activities. The Ray Lord's cosmic ray of probabilistic life creation causes energy to gradually bring together the three parts of God's mind to a level that is sufficient for the creation of life when spirit helps the energy to think. Energy reaches the level of being alive when within the same time and space, or within what most humans recognize as a lifeform, the energy can make choices and direct them while simultaneously sensing and creating actions that support its direction of choices. If the direction of the choices is similar to a Ray Lord's (the direction of its light) and if the actions support, or further develop, more of a similar direction of choices, then the actions are intelligent. They then convey the thought of God that is within them to the lifeform and to other parts of life.

As energy is stimulated to grow in its very slight thought in a specialized way, the energy becomes sensitive to other energy that very slightly thinks similarly to the way that it does. The energy is becoming a sense. When two or more of these advanced groups of energies, as senses, that are dissimilar exist within an organism, or within a different focused and limited field of time and space for each sense, then the two or more dissimilar senses are forced to expand their awareness. They need to cooperate within and share the time and space and they need to expand their sense beyond only other energies that within the same time and space are similar to themselves, in order to maintain their existing levels of awareness and to grow. This struggle, to *give* to dissimilar energy (within the same field of two or more bodies) rather than just to receive sense from only similar energies, causes these senses to start to develop consciousness, because the process creates more oneness in the thought of the energies within the senses. At this point, energy—as pre-life—is starting to become alive. The quality of the consciousness, when developed by awareness of movement of energy that is dissimilar to one of two or more senses in that which has this awareness, is referred to as sentiency. Thus all life must have or use two or more senses and centers of energies of specialization in two or more different times and spaces that create their senses and therefore have sentiency. Life must bring together the three parts of God's mind enough so that a reasonable balance is established between its choices and a similar direction of them (its thought) and the awareness of the energy that this thought is contained within. This balance is the special type of consciousness described above, and is called sentiency.

The Development of Sentiency in Plants

To create life there must be, at a minimum, two centers on one plane and one center on the plane above it. To create pre-life, there must be at least one center on one plane. Spirit gives the lifeform a higher sense of thought that raises its level of consciousness. The senses of the lifeform or pre-lifeform give spirit the ability to sense other spirit and energy, and to learn about the lower dimensions so that spirit itself can grow.

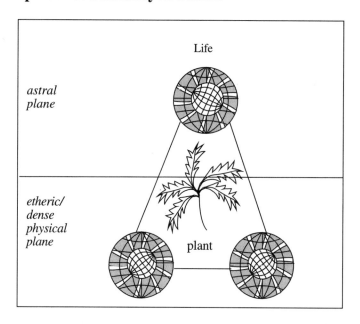

Illustration 3.11

 EVIL AS PART OF LIFE

The growth of life is contingent upon greater amounts of energy that is guided by spirit, with spirit's much greater thought, bringing together the three parts of God's mind within the same time and space, or within a lifeform. Since life is God's growth within our universe, God's mind must be rejoined to some extent through the thought of a lifeform if more life is to be created. Evil is an aberrant *form* quality of consciousness because it reduces the growth of life through separating light and densifying energy, thus keeping a part of God's mind separate within a lifeform. Evil attempts to separate the second part of God's mind from the other two. This second part is the part that plans, has consciousness, and sees oneness to life through giving, or love, and eventually recognizes and understands God in all of life. Evil does not try to reduce life's consciousness—only to keep it separated. However, evil's consciousness does become reduced because taking, or selfishness, replaces giving, or love, when consciousness is separated from choices, or purpose, and intelligent activity. When life is selfish, or focused on the self, it loses consciousness because with each selfish action *and thought* it ceases to understand others, since it is no longer giving to them. Evil attempts to maintain its consciousness by attempting to "understand" others by taking from them instead of giving—which it falsely believes will at least keep its consciousness at the same level. Every time evil uses its thought in this way, it "understands" more of how to take, but much less of what the other lifeform is like in total. The net loss of understanding lowers the consciousness of evil, despite its delusion to the contrary. An increase in space between a part of life and other parts, as well as between life and God, causes the effect of losing consciousness. Space is increased as light is separated, or as consciousness becomes separated from choices (from purpose). Space is dark because all the light in it is separated. Evil is very dark, because it uses its consciousness to create separation and space—and darkness...all to negate God's thought, or light.

THE SEVEN COSMIC VIRTUES
AS THEY HELP TO GROW LIFE

Virtue is God's and the Ray Lord's thought within form, while evil is the opposite of virtue and is the negation of light—through the separation of light—within form. There exist seven very large virtues, or one light in form for each of the seven Ray Lords. These virtues give a unique set of choices and a specific direction, or quality, or consciousness to these choices, for each of the seven dimensions. The first Ray Lord has the largest amount of and size of choices when they are joined together through being directed in a similar direction. Its thought (light) in form, or its virtue, is to increase the creation of God's growth, or of life. This virtue in human understanding is to become a functional part of the Creator, or of God in our universe, by *both* recognizing and understanding God *and* creating more growth to God through more bringing together of God's mind within life, or through creating more virtue.

The first and second Ray Lords have no manifested energies within their dimensions (their bodies). These Ray Lords' cosmic rays are focused on the collective five lowest dimensions instead of their own, through the participation of the lifeforms (the Monads) on their planes. The Ray Lords do this in order to grow more enlightened energies that will become senses of life in these lower dimensions. The Ray Lords of these two highest planes achieve this effect by separating all intelligent activity through their thought, or light, or the use of sacrificial thought, hence altering their rays to be focused on the five lower planes. The energies that become the most responsive to the corresponding rays of these two Ray Lords often are attracted to each other through their mutual enlightenment at the atomic levels of each of the five lower planes, and create fusion. These energies are sub-rays of the corresponding Ray Lord and its plane—the one of the lower five that each energy is attracted to. Often, when all five dimensions are created from a large collection of these energies being present and balanced, these fused energies create first-stage stars. A star is the unifying agent, or unifying entity, for our universe; it joins all five of the energy dimensions of our universe, beginning with the fusion of the first and second rays and their responding energies. The elemental and darker energies that gravitate together are a part of these stars. These energies are gradually enlightened by the fusion of the first and second sub-ray energies under the direction of a Great Being from outside our universe. This Being exists in consciousness in the (a) Cosmic *Mental* Universe. Some of these first and second sub-ray energies are not so enlightened, and are used as senses and bodies of lifeforms below the atomic levels of these five lower planes. Evil people use some of the darkest first sub-ray energies to create more of their sense of darkness by keeping this energy nearly completely separated from all second sub-ray energy. Additionally, sub-rays of ray energies also exist that are attracted to one of each of the five lower Ray Lords' dimensions or are created there by spirit; these sub-rays include first and second sub-rays of each corresponding ray energy. The first and second sub-ray energies originally attracted by the rays into a dimension can join with these first and second sub-ray energies created by spirit below the atomic level of the plane they are attracted to. In order to be alive, every lifeform needs at least a small amount of first (sub-) ray energy within it, to connect a life "thread" from an informing Monad; for a lifeform to be conscious, some second sub-ray energy is necessary for connection to a Monad through a consciousness "thread." A thread is a ray that semi-permanently connects the thought of a Monad to a life's form (to energy). Even the life in the lowest of plants has some consciousness, although, at present, most humans would refute this concept. All life is alive and has some consciousness, and so all life contains some of the energies within it that create stars. These concepts will be further explained in the next chapter.

How the First and Second Rays Function

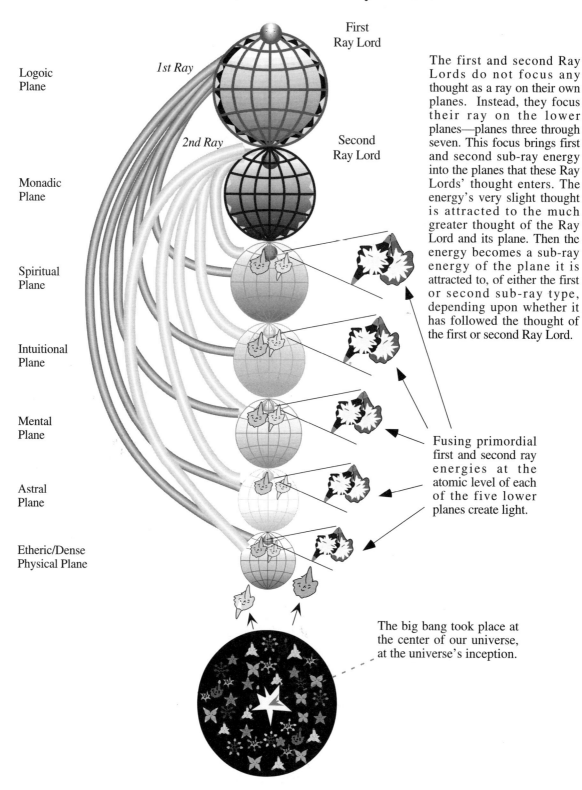

Logoic
Plane

1st Ray

First
Ray Lord

2nd Ray

Monadic
Plane

Second
Ray Lord

Spiritual
Plane

Intuitional
Plane

Mental
Plane

Astral
Plane

Etheric/Dense
Physical Plane

The first and second Ray Lords do not focus any thought as a ray on their own planes. Instead, they focus their ray on the lower planes—planes three through seven. This focus brings first and second sub-ray energy into the planes that these Ray Lords' thought enters. The energy's very slight thought is attracted to the much greater thought of the Ray Lord and its plane. Then the energy becomes a sub-ray energy of the plane it is attracted to, of either the first or second sub-ray type, depending upon whether it has followed the thought of the first or second Ray Lord.

Fusing primordial first and second ray energies at the atomic level of each of the five lower planes create light.

The big bang took place at the center of our universe, at the universe's inception.

Illustration 3.12

The second Ray Lord's thought (light) in form is to recognize and understand the oneness of life, or of God's growth. This Ray Lord's thought still uses part of the purpose of the first Ray Lord's thought to create more growth to God in our universe, or more life, because its thought is always light and must join these two parts together. However, its focus on enlightening form, or creating virtue, is on increasing the consciousness of life by life recognizing and understanding the oneness of itself with all other life—creating unconditional love. Thus the second Ray Lord creates an understanding of God and more love, while the first Ray Lord creates more growth of God by becoming a functional part of the Creator. Both are connected to one another, because both are a part of thought and, in these cases, are a part of God's thought, or light. Within these two Ray Lords' thought, there is a significant emphasis on one part over another—causing the distinguishing differences in probable life creation, through their cosmic rays.

The third Ray Lord creates virtue in two distinct ways based upon its focus of thought, which can shift from the more-thinking part to the more-energy part of a lifeform. The more-thinking part of a lifeform is referred to as spirit; the concept of spirit is somewhat discussed in this chapter, and a more complete explanation will be provided in the next. Most of the life creation that this Ray Lord encourages for higher levels of lifeforms comes from the part of its virtue that increases the intelligent communication between lifeforms and increases their interactions. In mostly lower levels of lifeforms, this Ray Lord's cosmic ray and thought affect the density of energies and their effect through their power to change life. When power is used to change life, the manifested energy that is contained in life is limited, and forces (which are one energy in movement against another within the same time and space) are created as a conflictive and imbalanced use of directed energy, in order to grow life. This process is continually occurring on earth; for example, one animal attempts to kill and often to eat another, with either the animal that kills or the one that survives the other's attempt to kill it having the better senses and awareness. Power is utilized in attempt to transmute energy, or, put another way, in the process of transferring one animal's type of energy into another animal, the transferred energy is *changed* within the receiving animal. Life develops through this conflictive process, which is based so heavily on changing the form of energy. Changing the form of energy is the foundation for the evolution of life and is the focus of what humans refer to as evolution. Thus increases in evolutionary life are developed at the cost of increased forces and conflict, all through the use of the third Ray Lord's thought of power. Intelligent communication can grow life in higher-level lifeforms, through a focus on the spiritual, or more thinking, part of the lifeform—provided that the thinking, or spiritual, part of the lifeform is the dominant element in its growth. Then intelligent activity takes place because knowledge and the exchange of knowledge replace force. The virtue of the third cosmic Ray Lord is the growth of *all*-life (all together, as each part of life affects the other parts) in and below its dimension, or within its duration of life, through the enlightening exchange of knowledge and the use of power. Thus when spiritual plane virtue is created *all of life (or pre-life) grows at once (!)* within the spiritual duration of time and space for the one creating.

Humans today tend to use the method of intelligent communication, which leads to intelligent activity, much more often than they use force. They do so particularly as they develop more in consciousness (givingness), and gradually recognize both spirit and life to be one. The next kingdom beyond the human, or the spiritual kingdom, uses intelligent activity at all times among and between its own members as well as in its interactions with members of the next higher kingdom. This constant use of intelligent activity is achieved throughout the kingdom by each member maintaining a very high level of consciousness, which permits him or her to be completely humble and to function in a hierarchy of consciousness. No forces are created in this hierarchy because each member of the kingdom is focused on serving the others and is therefore conscious enough to recognize and gain understanding of others who are more conscious than he or she (or it) is at any moment. In human terms, the virtue of the third Ray Lord is the increase in the growth of life through one or both of two ways. The first is intelligent communication, which includes the intelligent exchange of knowledge. The second is the changing of the density of energies of a lifeform—thus changing types of forms of life— through the use of power. For this virtue to exist, *both* ways of creating it must be used together as is needed. If only the first, or the spiritual, side is used, the growth of lower-level life is reduced at a cost of increasing only higher-level life. If only the second side, or energy, is used, then lower-level life grows at a cost to higher-level, more spiritual life. Note that evil uses exclusively power to "grow" life, which eventually causes higher-level life (which, paradoxically, evil is a part of) to decline in its growth.

The Two Ways that the Third Ray Lord Expresses Its Thought

Illustration 3.13

The third cosmic Ray Lord is attracting energies to its thought and stimulating their growth along its cosmic ray of probable life creation. The energies that can slightly think more towards sensing the intelligent communication (of knowledge) of and with other energies, along with sensing the relative density of other energies, are attracted to this ray and the ray is attracted to them. The third ray supplies more ability to create a sense of *knowledge* to the responsive energies and their informing spirit, to be used to gain more knowledge with other energies and their informing spirit. With the third ray focus helping to build the *sense*, or the collective higher thought of the energies that are most responsive to the third ray, information derived from the sense is synthesized with prior information, which is what is creating the knowledge that is developing. Some of the information from the third ray sense is brought together with existing information, or becomes synthesized, concerning other energy's density as it affects movement and communication of information. Some information is also directly communicated about the relative density of other energies and the amount that they and the sensing energy can change this density, or how much power is present or has the potential to be present. The third cosmic ray is stimulated by increasing the choices and their direction in the thought of the third ray energies towards more thought, and their sense of the above-mentioned two ways of being informed. This part is similar to the ways that the first and second rays helped to stimulate sense development in the energies that are attracted to them. However, a new element—knowledge— is added to the third ray's stimulation and to the way that the third ray type of energy responds. The third ray energy is much more separated from the thought of the third Ray Lord than are the second and first ray energies from their respective Ray Lords, and so it has a much lower propensity to become enlightened; knowledge is used to assist this energy. As this energy is stimulated to grow as a sense, through increasing choices and their direction (their thought) about communication and density/power of other energies, the sensing energy functions much more separately than did the first and second ray energies. The third ray energy no longer has as a condition of its nature a focus on either of the first two parts of God's mind, even though they exist within it as it (slightly) thinks in light. The focus of life creation of the first ray is on increasing choices/will so that more life will grow. The focus of life creation of the second ray is on oneness/direction/understanding/consciousness, in order to grow more life. The third ray's focus (which all the lower rays share) is to grow more responsive life through the use of knowledge, or the synthesis of information, i.e., new information that is compared with and joined with existing information about other energy, with this information supplied by a sense and synthesized by informing spirit.

The remaining four Ray Lords create growth in life through their respective cosmic rays and virtue, or light in form, by making changes only to the energies within life, or to the form side of life. These changes are to improve the senses by altering their densities, or increasing the highest level of thought within the energies of a lifeform. As the senses improve, then the more-thinking part of the lifeform can use the three parts of God's mind, to understand and create more of life, or God's growth. This more-thinking part is spirit, or the part of life that is emphasized by its components being the first two parts of God's mind, or *thought*. The third part of God's mind when emphasized and separated from light is form, or separated energy, and it mostly, but not entirely, lacks the first two parts. Therefore, separated energy is mostly lacking in thought, but not completely because all energy is at least somewhat joining with space. The space has these first two parts of thought within it, but separated. The rays of attribute of form, or rays four through seven, grow only the sense of energy's density in form (including the amount of energy present in the sense itself). Because each of these Ray Lords of attribute, or of densities of form, cannot fully use *power* on all life (or pre-life) in their respective durations to create intelligent activity, these lower Ray Lords are very limited; further, only the fourth Ray Lord can fully use *all-knowledge* to create intelligent activity for all life within its duration of life, or for all life on and below its plane. The third ray can grow either the sense of energy or the sense of spirit as spirit synthesizes knowledge within form (but still must rely on the *form's* senses); this synthesis is the intelligent exchange of knowledge. The two senses of spirit use the first and second ray energy centers in a lifeform when all of the senses are somewhat fused to them within that body. The first sense of spirit that is grown is the sense of understanding God, and this first spiritual sense leads to the second one, of creating more of God. When the third Ray Lord's thought is used in total (as virtue), as the spirit side of life becomes enlightened so does the energy side. With the thought in form, or the virtue, of the second and first Ray Lords, the energy is always automatically enlightened as the thought is, creating a fusion of light. These concepts will be further explained in the next chapter.

The fourth Ray Lord's thought in form is to increase the senses of the form to *perfectly* equal, or balance, the needs that spirit has to think through the form. In human understanding, this virtue creates and is beauty. Beauty occurs as a result of the perfection of the senses and then the giving of the information taken in by the senses to a lifeform (or the form of pre-life) according to what that lifeform (or pre-life form) needs in order for its informing spirit to recognize and understand in thought, and to then create more of life, or of God's growth (its thought). Thus beauty is the perfected, or enlightened, use of the senses and their corresponding energies to correctly inform a lifeform or pre-life enough so that its most thinking part, or spirit, can perfectly recognize, understand, and create more of God and its growth, or can create life or the potential for life at the level at which the spirit can think. The ratio of perfected thought to create beauty is twice as much of spirit's thought to that of the energy within the energy's body. Note that on the intuitional plane, the thought of the energy in any one lifeform's body exceeds the thought of all of the unenlightened and darkened gravitating energy on the entire plane. Also note that every intuitional plane lifeform has more thought within the senses of its body than the combined thought of all the unenlightened energy on the entire plane. Beauty is conditional love because it exists only when spirit can think perfectly for both itself and energy. This gives the spirit perfect sense and information.

The fifth Ray Lord's thought in form, or virtue, is to formulate a structure in the growth of sense of energy so that it can eventually perfectly balance its forces and exactly replicate one energy to another in whole time, or can make it true. The energy can then be balanced with other, differing, energies through the use of formulated structures to create a wholeness, or completeness, to all of the energies within the structure by reducing force because each energy is then supported in whole time by the other existing energies. The completion of the trueness, or the fully supporting structure of each energy to another without producing forces, creates truth—the fifth Ray Lord's cosmic virtue. Note that force is one or more energies that do not support one another's movement, and instead go against other energies within the same time and space. With truth, all of the energy equals all of the existing thought of spirit through the use of formula and structure. However, this balance is in a one-to-one ratio, and unlike the fourth ray and beauty, which has twice the amount of spirit's thought than energy's, both the beauty in the form and the complete self-awareness in spirit of itself and any other spirit (in at least one of three possibility ways) become lost. Complete self-awareness is perfect information provided by the senses in the form and given to spirit for its use. Except at the mental atomic level, spirit can think perfectly only for itself or for energy but not both at the same time in the mental Ray Lord's dimension. At no level on the mental plane can spirit think perfectly for itself and other spirit while it thinks perfectly for energy.

The sixth Ray Lord's thought in form is to increase the sense of energy that is devoted to giving all of itself to as much of another energy as is possible. This creates a limited and conditional form of love, as the virtue of the sixth Ray Lord, and is a lower correspondence of the fully unconditional love of the second ray. The devotion of the sixth ray to giving of itself comes from using the sacrifice of the first part of God's mind, which is a very limited and *single* direction—at a time—applied to a lower correspondence of the second ray. The sixth ray's sacrifice applied to only one direction of thought at a time results, in human terms, in motive because motive is limitation applied in a single direction of consistent thought, or will. The motivation to give all to one then results in devotion to what the one represents in the thought of the giver. Love becomes conditional upon the direction (the associated oneness with the giver) of movement of the one given to, and is thus no longer unconditional.

The seventh Ray Lord's thought in form is to increase the sense of energy in order to overcome force created through gravity, inertia, and friction. The overcoming of these three limitations on form is accomplished through the creation of intelligent coordinated responses of one energy towards another. The result of overcoming inertia is cooperation and sharing, or the virtue of the seventh Ray Lord.

Notice that each numerically lower Ray Lord is more limited in its thought and ability to create life than is the Ray Lord above it because less of God's original angle of thought, or direction, is present, and less of God's sacrifice is used with which to create life. The sense that is developed in energy that is stimulated to grow from its ray of probable life creation is less developed and so, therefore, are the lifeforms that exist focused within the Ray Lord's dimension.

There are seven dimensions of space, time, and life that are created by the joining of energy and some amount of intelligent activity with the space of a Ray Lord; the energy and intelligent activity become part of that Ray Lord's space by being attracted to Its thought. Some of the names of these seven dimensions, as found in many spiritual teachings, are as follows:

THE SEVEN DIMENSIONS OF TIME, SPACE, AND LIFE IN OUR UNIVERSE	
CREATOR	DIMENSION, OR PLANE
1st Ray Lord	Logoic, or Divine Dimension (the plane of Adi, or All)
2nd Ray Lord	Oneness, or Monadic Dimension
3rd Ray Lord	Spiritual, or Atmic Dimension
4th Ray Lord	Intuitional, or Buddhic Dimension
5th Ray Lord	Mental, or Manasic Dimension
6th Ray Lord	Emotional, or Astral Dimension
7th Ray Lord	Physical, or Etheric/Dense Physical Dimension

Table 3.1

THE REJOINING OF GOD'S MIND
AND ITS CREATION OF LIFE

God's mind is found on each of the seven dimensions; from the physical to the logoic, increasing amounts of it exist within each lifeform, it is increasingly better balanced, and its three parts are larger and are brought closer together. The collection of energies that make up each sense and that slightly think along one of the seven ray lines, or in the direction of a specific Ray Lord, supplies awareness and information to the lifeform. These energies are the manifested part of the third aspect of God's mind. Within each of these energies, on a subatomic scale, there is relatively more space than energy, and on the seventh plane (the etheric/dense physical dimension) there is more space than there is energy and matter; matter is extremely densified energy and is found only on the lower part of this lowest dimension, or plane. On the seventh plane there is great space between atoms, as well. The totality of all of this space within a sense of a lifeform is the amount of the separated first and second aspects of God's mind. When not yet alive, energy is developing a single sense, and once that sense is developed it becomes pre-life and it (the sense) can take in other energy and, in its givingness, can emit energy. In order to create life, the energy needs to join with other energies that have at least one sense that is different from its sense and is located in a different space and time, so that both types of energy can give to each other. Then both energies develop consciousness through their giving—they develop sentiency. Energy cannot achieve these results on its own because it contains far too much space within the forms that it creates, including senses. The separation of the first two parts of God's mind prevents energy from having more than just slight thought, even with the help of the cosmic ray. For energy to gain sense of energies that are different from it, the form that it creates needs to be informed by spirit. Spirit is only the first two aspects of God's mind and, depending on the level to which spirit both thinks and gives thought to energy, it can join these two aspects into light. The addition by spirit of the at least somewhat joined first and second aspects of God's mind into the form that energy is creating is what allows energy to increase its consciousness and to give to differing ray types of energies in different space and time, thereby producing life.

In the seventh Ray Lord's dimension, the life created is done so through an emphasis on the third aspect of God's mind, with all three aspects remaining separated within the lifeforms. Spirit can join the three aspects together at the atomic level of the plane by connecting all of them together through light. In order to accomplish this, the spirit at this level must be completely virtuous in accord with the Ray Lord's light. This virtue for the seventh plane is cooperation and sharing of energy and movement. On the seventh plane a fully enlightened lifeform and the Ray Lord's atomic focus equal one-fifth, or twenty percent of God's mind. Four-fifths, or eighty percent, of all the intelligent activity on the first sub-plane is manifested as energies.

The Mind of God on the Etheric/Dense Physical Plane

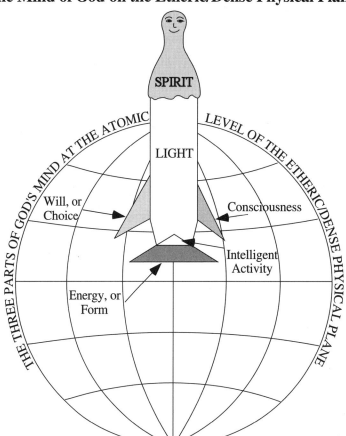

Illustration 3.14

Within the sixth Ray Lord's dimension, life is emphasized through the second aspect of God's mind, with the three aspects still kept isolated within the lifeforms. A limited type of directional love, or love that is focused on only one other, is created as a virtue. The motion of *other* form is the overriding characteristic of the senses and their corresponding and constituent energies. The part of a lifeform that is focused in life astrally, or the part of a lifeform that corresponds to the sixth, or astral plane, has within it the three aspects of God's mind growing closer together. On average, the three parts of God's mind are in better balance and in greater amounts than within the part of a lifeform that is focused on and exists on the seventh plane. The closer proximity and better balance of the aspects of God's mind allows spirit, through the thought that it adds, to more easily connect these three aspects together. Note that in order to create life, spirit must bring the three aspects into balance. On the sixth plane there exists a somewhat greater amount of intelligent activity, on average, in the third aspect of God's mind than on the seventh plane; however, on the sixth plane there is still considerably more energy than there is intelligent activity. On the first sub-plane of the astral plane there is twice as much energy as the amount of intelligent activity. On the first sub-plane of the seventh (the etheric/dense physical) plane, there is five times as much energy as there is intelligent activity. At the atomic levels of these two planes, the Ray Lord's thought, or light, can focus on only either one-third or one-fifth, respectively, of the energy on the first sub-plane at a time, to change it into intelligent activity. Technically, the atomic focus point of these planes is two-thirds to two-fifths of the size that the atomic focus of light is on the mental plane.

The Mind of God on the Astral Plane

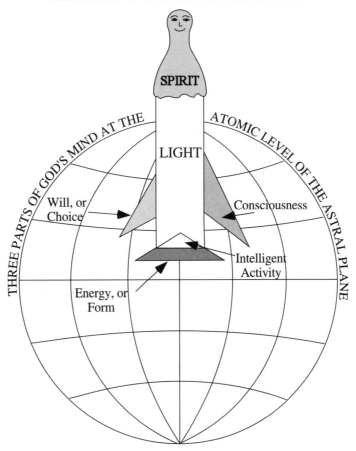

Illustration 3.15

In the fifth Ray Lord's dimension, the three aspects of God's mind are much closer together and are in relatively better balance within the lifeforms that are focused in life there. Souls are the most abundant form of life that is focused mentally. Next to souls in the number of mentally focused forms of life are humans. It is considerably easier for spirit to join the three aspects of God's mind within a lifeform on the mental plane than on the lower two because the mental plane contains much less manifested energy. On the first sub-plane of the mental plane there is an even ratio, with one part energy to one of intelligent activity; at the atomic level there are equal amounts of spirit's thought to energy, creating an equal balance between the two and in forces that could otherwise disrupt a form. This equalization in force allows the creation of structures, or a formulated design to forms, that permits all three parts of time and space to come together at the atomic level of this plane. Lifeforms that are focused in life mentally, and that are therefore creating themselves mostly through mental thought, are still unable to connect any part of the three parts of God's mind within them to any other lifeform on the mental plane or below. Similarly to life focused on either the astral or etheric/dense physical planes, lifeforms on the mental plane are greatly limited in their creation of more growth in life. The effects of God's mind still being separated between lifeforms causes each lifeform to perfectly experience only itself. This is true even though within each lifeform, spirit at the atomic level can mentally fairly easily bridge the three aspects through the light, or the thought of the Ray Lord. The fifth cosmic Ray Lord can enlighten one-half of all the energy that is present on the first sub-plane of its plane. On the atomic level there is a unification of time and space because the spirit within one lifeform there can join enough of God's mind. At any one time, the mental Ray Lord can focus its thought on only one-half of the energy present on the first sub-plane of its plane. All of the energy that the Ray Lord does focus its thought on becomes enlightened and becomes that dimension's atomic level of intelligent activity.

The Mind of God on the Mental Plane

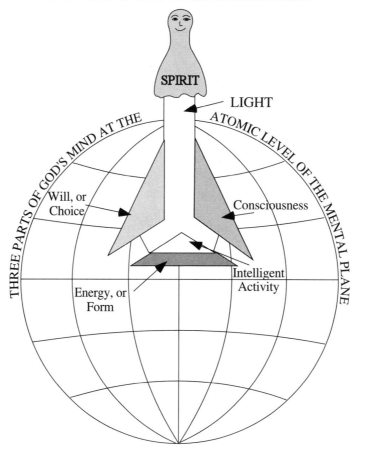

Illustration 3.16

The lowest three cosmic Ray Lords' dimensions of our universe are sometimes referred to in spiritual language as the Cosmic Solid dimensions. This name is given to the dimensions because no part of God's mind is joined between any two lifeforms on these lowest three dimensions, which contain more energy than intelligent activity. These two conditions prevent life from *fully* consciously being its own creator; while life's thought on these lower dimensions does create itself, it cannot *fully* understand why it is doing so. Mental plane souls and human beings are among the life that is functioning under these conditions. In Chapter Six the development of souls, and their life while they are focused mentally will be explored. Full consciousness, or full understanding, in at least one of three possible ways is needed in order to become the *fully conscious cause* of one's creations—beginning with oneself, then others, and, eventually, a shared creation of the entire universe. Above the three lowest dimensions there are four more, which, in spiritual language, are often referred to as Cosmic Etheric dimensions because the lifeforms there are fully consciously the *cause* of what they create.

The fourth Ray Lord is found on the intuitional plane, or dimension; the life created on the first sub-plane of this dimension has twice as much intelligent activity as it does energy. All of the energy on this Ray Lord's first sub-plane is fully enlightened in one of three ways when focused on by spirit, or any intuitional plane being. The Ray Lord can fully enlighten two-thirds of the energy on the first sub-plane at the atomic level with Its thought. There is also twice as much thought of informing spirit in a lifeform as there is of all the energy on this plane that thinks in one particular selfish gravitational way (creating gravity). Because of this ratio, spirit can finally join two-thirds of the third part of God's mind (in the form of intelligent activity) to two-thirds of the light, which it created by joining two-thirds of each of the first two aspects of God's mind within each lifeform. The remaining one-third of the third aspect of God's mind (in the form of manifested energy) is perfectly balanced in a two-to-one ratio in the light of the fourth Ray Lord through spirit thinking for both itself and all other spirit in all-knowledge and this remaining energy. At the atomic level of the intuitional plane, the two-thirds of intelligent activity become connected from each intuitional plane lifeform to every other one because there is no longer any energy creating forces between the lifeforms. All of the energy is used to create only enlightened, or beautiful, fourth-dimension form. Everywhere on the intuitional plane below the atomic level, the lifeforms are still connected even though there is less intelligent activity. The energy remains perfectly enlightened by spirit at the level to which the spirit is serving with the all-knowledge, or omniscience. Omniscience is what intelligent activity on the intuitional plane becomes when given in service to others. Spirit on each lower intuitional sub-plane perfectly balances a *lesser* amount of energy (as knowledge), thereby creating light and intelligent activity at these lesser levels. Spirit must choose to humbly and sacrificially think and create from its thought only when all of the energy it is creating with is completely given to others according to what the others are in need to give. Spirit thinks and creates in this way only when it is more capable of doing so than is any other spirit on each of the intuitional sub-planes—creating a hierarchy of consciousness and thought. The top of the intuitional plane is the only place in our universe, before reaching the first sub-plane of the logoic plane, where all three parts of God's mind are perfectly balanced in amount and in closeness. Perfect balance in *closeness* refers to the three parts of God's mind being equidistant from each other, and perfect balance in *amounts* refers to the three parts of God's mind being present in equal amounts within every lifeform. To achieve this balance at the atomic level of the logoic plane, a Being—an ascended Monad—has unified and grown God's mind, and has left our universe. Note that on the logoic plane accomplishing this task is increasingly difficult for each Being who subsequently does so because each time one Being accomplishes this task, more of God's mind must be grown and kept perfectly balanced by the next one who does.

The Mind of God on the Intuitional Plane

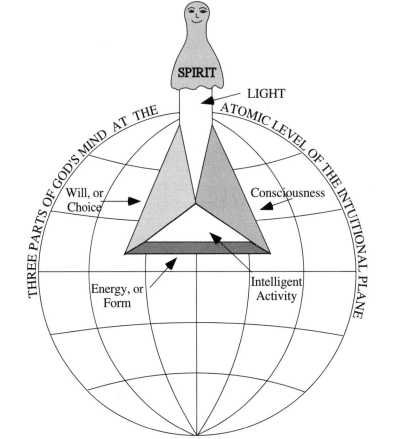

Illustration 3.17

Within the third dimension, or plane, the three aspects of God's mind are further grown in a lifeform, and they are closer together; although their amounts are greater, their perfect balance in closeness, or proximity, is maintained, but they are less balanced in their amounts. Below the atomic level of the spiritual plane there is less balance to the three aspects of God's mind in both proximity and amount than on the intuitional plane, but these three parts exist in much greater amounts and they are closer together than on the intuitional plane. The perfected balance in amount and equal distance apart, or proximity, on the intuitional plane is sacrificed first on the spiritual plane in order for greater amounts of God's mind to be grown in a spiritual plane lifeform, while being closer together but not as balanced in their distance apart. On the first sub-plane of the spiritual plane, there is five times as much intelligent activity as there is energy, and five times the thought of spirit within one lifeform as all of the thought of the remaining not fully enlightened energies on the entire plane. This creates an imbalance in the amount of spiritual thought compared to the amount of energy. The third and second aspects of God's mind are joined with other spiritual plane lifeforms (these are Great Beings who exist two kingdoms above the human); four-fifths of the third and second aspects of God's mind are joined among spiritual plane lifeforms at the atomic level of this plane. The Great Beings who exist here can use all-power and all-knowledge joined together to make themselves omniscient and omnipotent in sense in the dimensions, or worlds of life, on and below their own.

The Mind of God on the Spiritual Plane

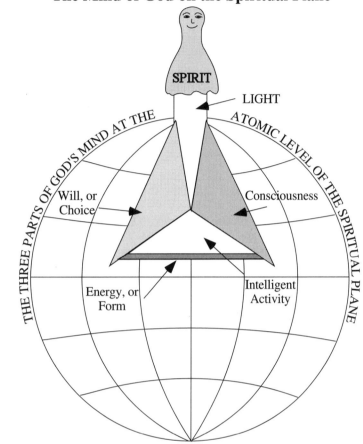

Illustration 3.18

Life on the monadic plane changes with the mind of God being used as a great progenitor of life creation for the lower dimensions. The first and second aspects of God's mind are fully joined together, creating a life "form" of pure light, with *no* darkness, or separation, anywhere within it. The monadic plane is truly a plane of One. However, the One still consists of many individuals because the third part of God's mind, or intelligent activity, is sacrificially kept separated from the light by a sphere except at the atomic level and that surrounds the light sphere with darkness, or space—nothing can live within it. There is no separated, or manifested, energy anywhere on the monadic plane; only light and the barrier of space exist, with all of the intelligent activity kept outside light and separated from it. The intelligent activity is kept separate because it is to be used to create additional energies *only* on the planes *lower* than the monadic. Monads on the monadic plane share the first two aspects of God's mind, but not the third. They sacrifice the third aspect so that a collective part of them (spirit) will use it later to create life in the lower planes. Monads use the increased consciousness part of their thought to create the spirit that exists on all the planes lower than the monadic. (See illustration 4.3.)

The first Ray Lord's plane, or dimension, is inhabited only by ascended Monads, whose spirit has created life on all of the lower planes and has successfully brought the life into complete intelligent activity. All three aspects of God's mind are joined back together on the logoic plane after having been grown beyond the level at which they began as separate parts. From their perspective of all-presence, or omnipresence, these ascended Monads experience our universe in its entirety—its past, present, and future; they can both sense and think as One with everything. By being present everywhere in our universe in the present, and by already having developed all-knowingness (omniscience), as well as all-power (omnipotence), they can remember *and experience* all of our universe's past, from memory of life and pre-life (group souls). Ascended Monads can know and experience all of the universe's present, and they can extrapolate and experience from created thought all of its future. These Monads create their experiences from one of the seven ways (or nine, if the Monad came from a sacred planet) that each decided upon while still on the monadic plane and changing energy into intelligent activity in advanced lifeforms. Finally, an ascended Monad leaves our universe, having created more of God and having become a functional part of God in omnipresence. Truly, the Creator and the created have become as One. The ascended Monad then goes on initially to one of three greater universes to create in new ways, with the process continuing ad infinitum.

THE AMOUNT OF GOD'S MIND JOINED AND THE AMOUNT OF ENERGY ON EACH PLANE			
PLANE	NUMBER	AMOUNT OF GOD'S MIND JOINED WITH A FULLY ENLIGHTENED LIFEFORM / THE AMOUNT OF INTELLIGENT ACTIVITY AT THE ATOMIC LEVEL OF THE PLANE	AMOUNT OF ENERGY ON THE FIRST SUB-PLANE
Etheric/Dense Physical	7th	1/5 – 20%	4/5 – 80%
Astral	6th	1/3 – 33.3%	2/3 – 66.7%
Mental	5th	1/2 – 50%	1/2 – 50%
Intuitional	4th	2/3 – 66.7%	1/3 – 33.3%
Spiritual	3rd	4/5 – 80%	1/5 – 20%
Monadic	2nd	100% of the first two parts of God's mind	None
Logoic	1st	100% of all three parts of God's mind	None

Table 3.2

 ### THE SENSES CREATED BY THE RAYS AND ENERGIES OF THE RAY LORD ON EACH DIMENSION

The Ray Lord of each of these lower dimensions helps to create a unified sense, or awareness, in life. These senses will be more fully examined in subsequent chapters, but for now the following description of the sense for each dimension of life creation may be helpful. Humans who are physically alive (and all that most people reading this know of humanity concerns those who are physically alive) live on the dense part of the physical dimension, or within the seventh Ray Lord's creation of pre-life and life physically. The whole sense that is created in life physically is intelligent coordinated response to other physical pre-life and life. The sixth Ray Lord helps to create the whole sense of empathy; humans also have this sense within their emotional bodies, which correspond to the sixth plane, or dimension. The fifth Ray Lord helps to create a limited sense when only the lower part of wisdom, or whole structured thought, is being used. This sense can be made whole only through helping others to create it, or through giving wisdom to others by helping them to think more wholly through structure. Sometimes the giving of wisdom is referred to as love/wisdom. Most humans today are gradually developing love/wisdom as a whole mental sense if they are creating more of the mental cosmic virtue, or truth, while they think and give this thought to others so that the others might choose to do the same. The whole sense that the fourth Ray Lord helps to create in life is controlled intuition in completed service to others; this sense is also sometimes referred to as buddhi. The sense of buddhi is mostly beyond human ability and comes from the ability to hold as many concepts together within the intuitional mind (which is within the intuitional body) as is needed to completely serve whomever/whatever is one's service at the time. As one uses the sense of buddhi, one becomes omniscient, or all-knowing (which is another part of the whole sense of buddhi). The sense that the third Ray Lord helps to develop in form and life is the whole awareness of spirit—found in anything. This whole sense comes from being aware of all the intelligent actions of a form while helping it to increase in intelligence through exercising power, which changes the form's relative density and also then affects the form's ability to communicate and sense. The entire thought within and controlling the form is understood. This then reveals all of the spirit of the form and all of this spirit's ways of attracting energy, along with the ability to create new types of life—making one omnipotent, or all-*power*ful. The whole sense created by the second Ray Lord is that of recognizing and understanding the oneness, or God, in everything. The whole sense created by the first Ray Lord is the sense of *being* God, or of being omnipresent—in both thought and sense with everything—throughout our universe, for all of time and space. Whole senses of a lifeform are created by the lifeform as it creates in its thought and adds to the cosmic virtue in the dimension of the corresponding Ray Lord. Humans on earth at this time mostly neither think nor sense in the cosmic virtue of the Ray Lords above the fifth, or mental dimension, nor do they add to these virtues.

 ## PRELIMINARY CONCLUSIONS FROM CHAPTER THREE

The following can now be added to developing more meaning of life. Part of life's hidden meaning is to create more of cosmic virtue, or more of God's thought in form, through sensing and living in ways that correspond to the direction of the Ray Lord's thought within a dimension in which a lifeform has a body, senses, and thought. This creation of virtue then enlightens both the lifeform's form as well as the forms of others with whom or with which it interacts, and it does so in the direction of that Ray Lord's light. Humans on earth today are capable of creating three types of cosmic virtue and meaning in their lives. These virtues are created through cooperation and sharing; devoted giving to others, or love that is conditional in one or more ways; and the giving of whole structured thought, which is also known as love/wisdom, to others in order to create truth. Some humans are beginning to develop controlled intuitive senses to create beauty, but for most, the meaning in life from this creation of virtue is not yet possible.

Three distinct events occur as life increases in meaning. These events correspond to the three parts of God's mind coming more closely together within a lifeform. First, the awareness is increased as the senses become refined by improvements in the ways that the energy of the sense is thinking. This first way is affected by the third part of God's mind and the corresponding Ray Lords' rays three through seven. The second way is by increasing consciousness (understanding) through the second part of God's mind coming more closely together with the other two parts. Then the recognition and understanding of God in life and the oneness of life become realized. Finally, the greatest meaning in life is unhidden as one creates oneself into more of a part of God while fully aware and conscious of what is being created and why this creation is being effected. The creation of cosmic virtue follows these steps, as some of life's hidden meaning then becomes revealed.

UNDERSTANDING SPIRIT AND ENERGY

Illustration 4.1

Author's Suggestion: First turn to the "Glossary Help Guide" and read the definitions for this chapter.

 SUMMARY OF INFORMATION FROM CHAPTER THREE

As Chapter Four begins, the reader is again reminded that groups of concepts will be repeated several different times and in differing ways. The purpose for this approach is to build understanding of the concepts from various mental angles, or views. Additional information will frequently be included each time the concepts are expressed, in part to hold the interest of those readers who understood the information as it was previously presented, while helping them to develop a deeper understanding. Although potentially awkward and perhaps even confusing at times, understanding will most likely be improved enough to offset this risk.

In the last chapter, information was presented that describes how seven rays of probabilistic life creation are developed through the sacrificial thought of seven cosmic Beings. Each of these seven cosmic Beings, or cosmic Ray Lords, also creates a dimension of time and space. To each Ray Lord, its dimension is like an enormous body that the life the Ray Lord helps to create is also a part of—sharing the form of the dimension and body. Each of the seven Ray Lords creates its own type of light by joining the first and second parts of God's thought in its own unique ways. Space is created when the first two parts of God's mind are separated from each other when manifested energy is present. This condition, of space, occurs anywhere in our universe that separated energy could be present *and* where form, or energy, is manifesting itself in some part of that dimension or in another one.

The first two cosmic Ray Lords and their respective dimensions of life creation do not contain separated manifested energy. The reason is that the third cosmic ray exists within these two greater fields as a potential only. This is because within their dimensions the first two cosmic Ray Lords choose to not focus their thought on the third part of God's mind, which would actualize it. The first cosmic Ray Lord's lack of focus in its dimension on the third part of God's mind is a temporary condition, and for the second cosmic Ray Lord it is always the case. In the above-described way, the first two cosmic Ray Lords always defer the actualization of this potential; the second Ray Lord defers the actualization and manifestation of the third part of God's mind to the third and lower cosmic Ray Lords for use in their dimensions. The first cosmic Ray Lord defers some of the actualization of its unmanifested third part of God's mind to ascended Monads. Thus the part of God's mind that is intelligent activity, along with its manifestation of energy (form separated from light), exists at the inception of our universe as only a potential of great power in the first two dimensions of our universe.

  ## THE CREATION OF SPACE, TIME, ENERGY, AND SPIRIT

An interesting paradox now arises in the way that space is created in the first and second Ray Lords' dimensions of *space*. There is no manifested energy in these dimensions, *and*, the first two parts of God's mind (choice/will/purpose/sacrifice and love/givingness/consciousness/oneness) are joined, creating light—everywhere in these dimensions that life exists. Space in these two dimensions is created not by how much energy is separated from and manifested from non-intelligent actions, but by how much intelligent activity is *sacrificially kept separate* from choice/will/purpose/sacrifice and love/givingness/consciousness/oneness by the thought of the corresponding Ray Lords and their life creation. The reason this occurs in the second Ray Lord's case has to do with the existence of two fields of possibilities, each acting upon the other; whenever thought limits one field it decreases limitation on the other by the same amount. The first field is light, or the first two parts of God's mind joined together; the second field is what is created from the sacrifice of intelligent activity, or from the potential from the third part of God's mind. The first field is much larger than the second, and so because of the limitation of this larger field, there is a field of probable life creation (the light of the second Ray Lord) interacting with a field of possible life creation (the sacrifice of potential intelligent activity). The two fields create space, not by separating light from (within) God's thought, but by separating intelligent activity and its potential to create new life, from light. Spirit is created in this way by separating the non-actualized third part of God's mind from the joined and actualized first two parts.

Spheres of Light and Potential Intelligent Activity Separated by Sphere of Darkness on the Monadic Plane

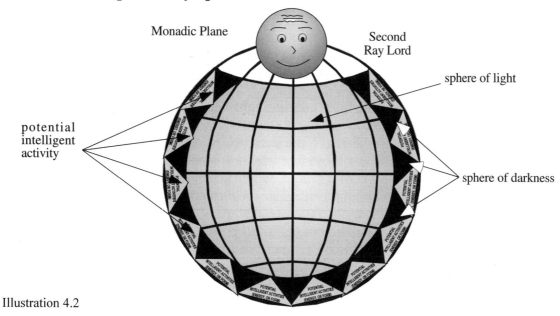

Illustration 4.2

THE LIFE IN THE FIRST TWO DIMENSIONS

Because the nature, or quality, of the space and time is different in the first two dimensions of our universe, so is the life that is created there. Life in these dimensions is created by the first and second Ray Lords' sacrifice of keeping intelligent activity separate from light in order to eventually grow life in the lower dimensions. The only type of life that can exist in the space of the second dimension, or plane, is a life that lives as one Being in thought, of constant givingness. The reason is that the Being needs to, by constantly giving, keep all intelligent activity sacrificially separated in order to grow more of God. The life that is created at the level of the second plane is a Being called a Monad. There are many Monads, yet all think as one with all others at and below their level of consciousness. Thinking in this way is accomplished by the space having light everywhere within it except at its periphery, or at the very edges of where the sphere begins. This is where all of the intelligent activity is kept separate from both the light and the life of the sphere that is created. Because there is so much light on their (the monadic) plane, Monads have the ability to think and eventually to sense in omnipresence (*all*-presence). They have this ability because the minds of all of the Monads that have the same or lower consciousness are in complete contact with each other. As one Monad experiences thought on one of seven monadic sub-planes and all the sub-planes below it, all others at and above that level do, too. Yet each is still a separate Being because all intelligent activities are kept separate. This system allows Monads to be individual and to grow more of God in the lower parts of our universe, as co-participants within this process while parts of themselves exist in different dimensions of time and space.

A part of the thought of each Monad on the monadic plane is focused on separating intelligent activity. Intelligent activity is the third part of God's mind. It is separated from light, which is the first two parts of God's mind that together are God's thought. This focused sacrificial thought to separate God's mind *for the purpose of creating more life within God's plan* creates a new part of life. It does so because it alters the two fields of potential, of light and of sacrificed intelligent activities. The first two parts of God's mind are composed of parts of pure thought, and when they are joined they become light; the first part is choice/will/purpose/sacrifice, and the second is unconditional-love/unconditional-givingness/consciousness/oneness. The new life created by the Monad is imbued with a highly thinking nature because it is made up of the first two parts of God's mind, creating God's thought. The second part is further emphasized from the second Ray Lord's ray interacting between it and the intelligent activity that is kept separate from it. The Monads give to this new part of life the use of all of the intelligent activity, or their third part of God's mind, that exists on the monadic plane and additional amounts on lower planes as well. The first two parts of God's mind create immense thought. This part of life—the immense thought when it is *focused* on intelligent activity in dimensions lower than the monadic—is referred to as spirit.

All spirit contains some amount of God's thought—and light—within it. Spirit *contains* neither intelligent activity nor manifested energy because it chooses to sacrifice these in order to grow more of life. All spirit comes from the sacrifice of Monads (and *all* life must contain spirit, or this part of the Monad). God chose that life, or its growth, needs to have *three* parts of Its mind within it: the first two parts of Its mind, which when joined create light, plus the third part, which when not in fully enlightened space becomes manifested as energy, or form. Initially, Monads who have not developed themselves are unique in our universe because they have great potential to create life, but are not yet a full part of life. This is because they, at first, sacrifice the third part of God's mind in order to create life. Thus the Monad—this Great Being who thinks as one with others of its kind—lives at first, oddly, separated from all other parts of life as a result of its sacrifice of intelligent activities.

Spirit Created from the Monadic Plane

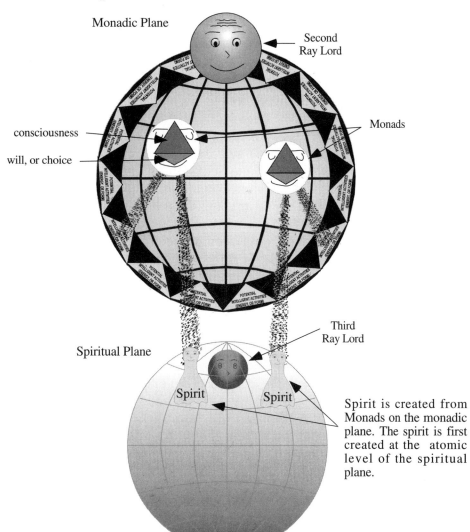

Illustration 4.3

 THE CREATION OF MONADS

Monads are created by a "cloning," or mirroring, effect that is first begun by a Great Being from outside our universe who informs a star. Monads are additionally created by the second cosmic Ray Lord's type of thought focusing on replicating God's thought and the first two parts of God's mind, with an added emphasis on love (giving, or oneness). The emphasis on love is created by the second Ray Lord's ray being directed in its dimension *at first* on intelligent activity in order to sacrifice and give it to the Monads, but instantaneously reflected to and further creating the Monads who are also focusing to separate *all* intelligent activity from themselves on the Monadic plane. This process prevents the growth of the third part of God's mind as life on this plane, in order to achieve the growing of more of life in the lower dimensions. The second ray then stimulates the growth of consciousness by giving its thought exactly, as a reflection of choices to sacrifice its unification with intelligent activity. The second ray does this because consciousness is stimulated to grow from the giving to spirit's immense thought. The Monads are also sacrificing all use of the third part of God's mind on their dimension. The sacrifice is used to separate the third part of God's mind from consciousness on the monadic plane so that the intelligent activity can later manifest as energy on the lower planes. The third part of God's mind cannot manifest as energy on the monadic plane because if it did, the energy would instantly become enlightened. This means that there would be none of the separated energy that is needed with which to create a diversity and growth of life, and thus the life of Monads would be rendered superfluous. *Qualities* of choices are the second part of God's mind applied to the first part, which gives *consistency of direction* to the choices (by comparison, *consistency of choices* is *will*). When these qualities are emphasized within God's mind, they produce a consciousness and new life of Monads who think in and eventually sense in oneness. The reason is that although there is no separated, manifested energy in this dimension, the field of potential probabilities (the second ray) stimulates the *potential* for energy to grow in oneness. Energy's potential to grow oneness grows more of consciousness. This occurs because the oneness that is created by the Monads' collective consciousness is being used to keep intelligent activity separate. Then this thought is further given to spirit—which then increasingly reflects the second ray back to the Monads. Their consciousness becomes raised through their sacrifice and giving to spirit of *potential* energy that the second ray will help to grow. The mirroring effect is further produced by all-presence, or omnipresence, since each Monad experiences in its thought the thought of other Monads at or below its level of consciousness.

As each Monad experiences in its thought the entire first two parts of God's mind, the mirroring effect begins with the second part emphasized as a manner of creating new life. This new life is Monads that have a *grown consciousness* beyond that of God's mind as it was at the inception of our universe. The growth is caused by the second Ray Lord's ray being reflected off the intelligent activity that the Monads are also sacrificing and giving. The Monads' consciousness then further grows through their giving their thought of sacrifice and the intelligent activity to spirit. All-presence with God's light, or the first two parts of Its thought joined, makes each Monad a mirror of this thought and one with each other. *Initially* Monads *think* in all-presence but cannot *sense* in all-presence. The reason is that a sense is an advanced type of energy that originally comes from the unmanifested third part of God's mind becoming somewhat manifested; when unmanifested, this part is intelligent activity. Monads on the monadic plane choose to sacrifice this third part of God's mind in order to create new life within the lower dimensions of our universe. They can gain a sense of omnipresence only when they choose to grow themselves and then do so through a journey using a part of themselves to join with the manifested third part (the energy part) of God's mind in the dimensions lower than the second (the monadic) plane. The part of themselves that Monads sacrifice to experience and grow in the journey of life is spirit.

Another way to understand spirit is that spirit is the Monad's thought of its *potential* Self-sacrifice to have intelligent activity remain as a separated part of God until life can be created in regions lower than where Monads exist, without, or separated from, the Monad's life of thought in all-presence with all other Monads. Thus spirit becomes isolated from being one with all others in thought as a result of the Monad's sacrifice of its potential Self through its complete, or total, love/givingness/consciousness/oneness. Monads neither have nor need a Self; the solution to the seeming paradox of sacrificing that which one does not have or need is that the Monads sacrifice the *potential* to have a Self. Spirit does need a Self because it cannot think in all-presence. A more accurate description of what a Self is and what it does will be covered in thorough detail in the next chapter.

Spirit Informs Energy to Create a Lifeform

Spirit no longer can think in omnipresence, as one with all other spirit since it is not on the monadic plane. Spirit cannot sense other spirit or energy because it does not have any sense to do so. Therefore, it must think using an isolated body and one or more senses, which it needs to help to create by bringing together energies with its informing thought.

Spirit has a high level of thought. Energy is attracted to the higher thought of spirit, following the spiritual principle that energy follows thought that is greater than its own. Energy is attracted to spirit's thought that it has some commonality with.

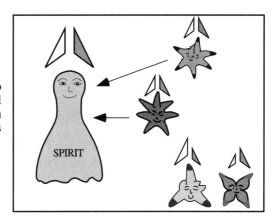

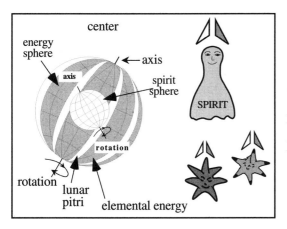

As energy is attracted to spirit, energy creates a center, or sphere. Spirit enters the center as a spiritual sphere, and both energy and spirit function together. The spirit sphere is much smaller than the energy sphere on the astral and etheric/dense physical planes. It is the same size on the mental plane, and larger than the energy spheres on the intuitional and spiritual planes. The reason is that on the lower planes there is much more energy in comparison to the amount of spirit, and on the higher planes there is more spirit to energy.

To create life there needs to be, at a minimum, two centers on one plane and one center on the plane above it. To create pre-life, there needs to be at least one center on one plane. Pre-life is a condition in which enough spirit informs a form to create a spirit sphere within at least one energy sphere within a form. Spirit gives the lifeform a higher sense of thought that raises its level of consciousness. The senses of the lifeform or pre-lifeform give spirit the ability to sense other spirit and energy, and to learn about the lower dimensions so that spirit itself can grow.

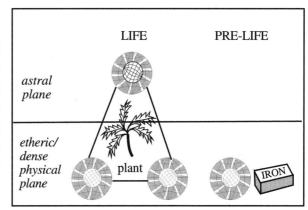

Illustration 4.4

Because spirit loses its ability to think in all-presence, or as one with all other life, it must think using an isolated body and one or more senses. The joining of spirit with manifested energy on any of the dimensions, or planes, lower than the monadic is what creates a lifeform; the thought of spirit causes the energy to come together into a lifeform because energy is attracted to thought that is greater than its own. Spirit is pure thought with at least some light, or some amount of God's thought, within it. Spirit needs to join with energy, which has at first in comparison to spirit very little thought, and a significant amount of the energy that spirit initially informs is completely devoid of God's thought. As was explained in the previous chapter, the highest energies, or those that think the best (though only slightly in comparison to spirit) eventually become a sense along a ray focus. When joined with spirit, these energies give to spirit sense about the form within the rest of the dimension(s) where the life of the spirit exists. Spirit, in symbiosis, gives the energy a great potential for improvement in its slight thought. Thus spirit uses form with which to sense and become informed about the dimension as well as the energy and other spirit in lifeforms within the dimension that the sense is aware of. At the same time, energy is helped in its ability to think by becoming spiritualized. Energy becomes joined with the great thought of spirit that converts energy and the information that is supplied by a sense into knowledge. Spirit achieves this conversion by synthesizing one part of information and/or a particular sense with another sense and part of information.

Notice that in this system of life development there need to be at least either two centers of sense or one sense and a storage center of information (a brain, e.g.) so that knowledge can be

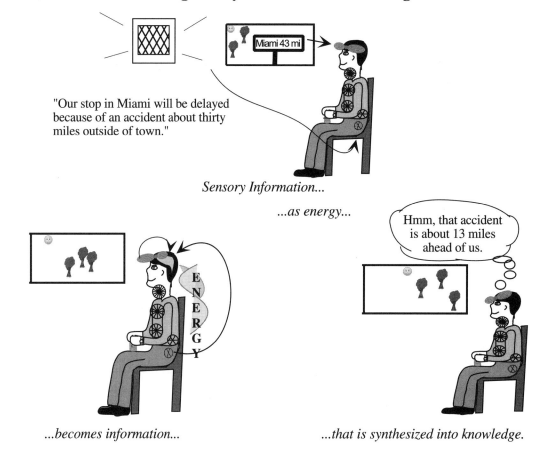

**Information Joining Together
as Thought Is Synthesized into Knowledge**

"Our stop in Miami will be delayed because of an accident about thirty miles outside of town."

Sensory Information...

...as energy...

Hmm, that accident is about 13 miles ahead of us.

...becomes information...   *...that is synthesized into knowledge.*

Illustration 4.5

synthesized through the spiritualization of the energy that makes up the sense(s), which affects the capacity of spirit to think within the form. Enlightening thought is what spiritualizes the energy, causing a reduction in the space (which changes, in part, into light) between different parts of energy. Knowledge is the conversion of two or more parts of information, from one or more senses, into a thought. Thought is two or more choices that, through the connectedness of the choices, have a similar direction and that can limit a field of possibilities in some way. In this process of creating knowledge, spirit enlightens form if the knowledge is given back to its form and to forms of other life in order to improve the forms' ability to better sense through developing better thought themselves. The enlightening is accomplished through the reduction of space (darkness) between any two or more parts of energy that think anywhere from slightly differently to very differently from each other.

   ## ENERGY AS THE MANIFESTATION OF INTELLIGENT ACTIVITY

Energy becomes manifested from a field of potential intelligent activities by thought that is less than perfectly enlightened and that comes from another field of probabilities, or a field of likely outcomes that is the result of the presence of thought. The field of intelligent activity is developing thought because God, Ray Lords, and Monads all sacrificially chose to separate the intelligent activity from their thought—which is also fully enlightened. Spirit's thought, or its light, is always lacking some quality, or some type of consciousness, or giving-ness. As spirit focuses on intelligent activity, it *reduces* the part of the field that it focuses on concerning its number of choices (its frequency). Spirit also *restricts* the number of directions in thought as well as, if below the atomic level of the plane, alters the direction of the choices to some degree away from God's direction. Since God's direction is ways of connecting Its choices within Its thought (within light), spirit's focus on intelligent activity causes its (spirit's) choices to connect in a direction that to some degree moves away from light. When intelligent activity is lowered in choices, or frequency, the levels of activity likewise become lowered. The results then are for "density" to occur within activities of the same type and for space to become created between different types of activity while light becomes commensurately decreased between those *different* types of activities. As the direction (consciousness/givingness) of the choices moves away from God's direction *and* also connects choices in fewer ways, intelligence, or communication between two *different activities*, simultaneously becomes reduced.

Lowered consciousness (less givingness) within each activity causes the activity to join with activity that is also low in consciousness, but causes it to not join with activity that is more intelligent. The reason is that the more intelligent activity has *more space* between itself and the activity that is of lower consciousness. The activity that has lowered consciousness continues to densify as it loses the ways in which it connects its choices (its ways of directed choices), and as the overall direction of those choices moves away from God's direction. Note that densification is a loss of space between two or more like-thinking energies, but with no increase in God's thought and, therefore, no added light. In addition, the densification is increased by the decrease in choices. These *powerful* components to the field of potential intelligent activity change parts of the field from intelligent activity into energy that is manifested at the focal point (which can create an event) of the direction chosen by the thought that is altering the field of intelligent activity. Thus as intelligent activity becomes less intelligent because of a drop in its consciousness, and has fewer choices (which decreases its overall levels of activity), it becomes transmuted into energy, with great power being either released or stored. Power is the remainder of the activity that is not used and was not lowered in frequency from the original intelligent activity. As the remainder of the intelligence that is left after some of it has been decreased from the original intelligent activity and then as energy is manifested, this remaining intelligence becomes *knowledge* and *knowledge's ability to be communicated*. Thus when spirit creates any activity that is less than fully connected to light and is less than fully intelligent, the result is that power and knowledge are "left over." This power and knowledge can be used by any being who can create more light within the activity by creating more intelligence in the (energy) activity.

 ## SPIRIT AS THE INFORMING THOUGHT OF LIFEFORMS

All spirit comes from the fields of potential that are created by the sacrificial thought of Monads on the second (the monadic) plane. The reason is that the fields themselves are in a symbiotic relationship of one growing in potential as the other sacrifices some of its potential. One field is the potential to create life from enlightened consciousness (of Monads). The other is the potential to create life through enlightening both intelligent activity and its manifestation of energy in the dimensions lower than the monadic. In order for the second field to exist, the Monads must sacrifice the use of intelligent activity while they live on the monadic plane. On lower planes, Monads can use intelligent activity through partially joining with it, by focusing the spirit-created part of themselves into intelligent activity and its manifested energy. When a Monad has spiritualized and enlightened energy/form on every dimension lower than the monadic, and has joined the senses of these forms eventually into one *spiritual* sense of being a functional part of God, it ascends to the first (the logoic, or divine) plane, or dimension. There it becomes *fully joined with intelligent activity* and then joins a growing all three parts of God's mind. At this point, such Monads can not only think as one in all-presence (omnipresence), but can also, for the first time, sense as one. This perpetuates and grows the experience of being God in our universe and permits a Monad to leave. The Monad can leave because as a lifeform it has gained all that is possible to be in growing God in our universe and has become God here, as God is at that time. The Monad is now ready for a new life in another type of universe.

There is a technical concept concerning how spirit becomes directed to its plane by its corresponding Monad. Each Monad *first* directs its thought onto the *spiritual* plane, and most of the spirit then cannot use its own thought (which is a limited part of its creating type of Monads' thought) to access any location beyond the limited field of intelligent activities that its creating type of Monad has created for it. However, spirit is given freedom by first being created at the atomic level of the spiritual plane, and if it can think well enough and remain conscious enough to access more than the limited field of its creating type of Monad, it can become located on the dimension where the majority of the field of intelligent activity can be limited by its (spirit's) own thought. The vast amount of spirit does descend to the lowest plane that its corresponding creating type of Monad is creating life on.

 ## MORE ADVANCED INFORMATION ABOUT MONADS

The following section explains more about Monads, and includes some concepts that are based upon information that is presented later in this book. Some readers who are reading this chapter out of numerical sequence and other readers who have knowledge from other sources might have a clearer understanding of this particular section of this chapter. Parts of this section will also be repeated in later sections of *Life's Hidden Meaning*....There are three classes of Monads who are creating more of their sense of life in the three lower worlds and are found on the monadic plane. Those that are least able to sense lower life are found, in consciousness, on the sixth and seventh monadic sub-planes. These Monads create the life of a class of Solar Angels and the Solar Angels' corresponding group souls. (Much more about this will be explained in Chapter Six.) The next class of Monads who create the life of a more advanced class of Solar Angels and their corresponding human souls are gaining the sense of the Monads' lifeforms, including their associated souls. These Monads come from the advancement of the first, lower class of Monads who create, from their spirit part, the life of group souls. This human class of Monads is found on the fifth monadic sub-plane. On the fourth and third monadic sub-planes are found a class of Monads that focus on the creation of triadal life of a whole Solar Angel and that of its liberated soul, or a Master of the three lower worlds—and in some cases, of some of the higher dimensions as well. These Masters are fifth and sixth level initiates. The spirit part of these Monads is found on either the intuitional or the spiritual plane. This part has advanced its Self beyond the mental plane and the human class of Monads. The most advanced Monads on the monadic plane are found on the first sub-plane and are seventh level initiates; their spirit part is found at the atomic level of the spiritual plane. Monads found on the second monadic sub-plane have not yet begun to gain sense of life that is lower than themselves, but still can think in omnipresence with all Monads at and below the second monadic sub-plane. These Monads are waiting to create more spirit and life based upon the plan of their life-creating Solar Logos. They are usually awaiting a certain time in the development of a particular planet upon which they will gain senses of certain parts of that planet's life. Each Monad can think as one with all other Monads at and below its level of monadic sub-plane consciousness. Although they can think as one, at varying levels, Monads on the monadic plane cannot *sense* as one. Monads develop a sense of oneness as they develop on the logoic plane.

Monads who advance to the logoic dimension develop omnipresence in both thought *and sense*. Monads on the seventh logoic sub-plane can think and sense as one in universal (in all of time) omnipresence for all minerals and some plants throughout our universe (the Cosmic Physical). Monads on the sixth logoic sub-plane are advanced beyond seventh logoic sub-plane Monads, and can think and sense all that the seventh logoic sub-plane Monads can; they can think and sense for *all* minerals, plants, and, in addition, for animals found everywhere, and at all times (in omnipresence) throughout our entire universe. Fifth sub-plane logoic Monads can think and sense in all time omnipresently for all humans and all minerals, plants, and animals. Fourth sub-plane logoic Monads can think and sense in omnipresence for all time—past, present, and future—for all intuitional plane and lower levels of life. These four classes of Monads who are focused in consciousness from the seventh through the fourth logoic sub-planes are all eighth level initiates at various stages of that initiation. They create additional virtue as they are omnipresent in accord with their prior choices and decisions made while on the monadic plane. Each has decided upon one of seven ways (or nine, on sacred planets) to leave our universe. Each of these ways leads to one of several greater universes. Third logoic sub-plane Monads can think and sense omnipresently for all life on the spiritual plane and below, in all of time. The Monads on the second logoic sub-plane can think and sense in omnipresence, for all of time for all Monads that are not unified with God. The Monads whose consciousness is focused on these sub-planes are in various stages of the ninth initiation. These Monads are referred to as "Silent Watchers" because they do not change any part of the universe as they experience it. First logoic sub-plane Monads think as God by unifying the three previously separated parts (aspects) of God's mind. These Monads, as they reach the atomic level, have transcended themselves into God as a point in our universe, by becoming one in thought and sense with everything, including God for (and from) that point in universal time and space. They are completing the ninth initiation. They then leave our universe (the, or a, Cosmic Physical one) for the (a) Cosmic Astral, Mental, or Intuitional Universe.

As an example of many of these concepts presented above regarding Monads on the monadic plane, Monads who are creating life from the sixth monadic sub-plane are doing so by first sacrificially focusing their thought on the corresponding responsive intelligent activity that surrounds the monadic plane. These Monads' thought is to *not* use this intelligent activity, which is the third part of God's mind and is responsive to the sixth ray when it manifests as energy; they will not use this intelligent activity anywhere that they can think on the monadic plane, which, for sixth sub-plane Monads, encompasses the sixth and seventh sub-planes. The sacrificial thought of these Monads is shared with all other Monads, in omnipresence, from the sixth monadic sub-plane, *up*. At the same time these Monads focus their thought onto both the mental and the astral planes because those are the planes upon which they will create *lower* life. On the spiritual and intuitional planes, these Monads simultaneously create more of the higher life of Solar Angels that were previously created by the Monads on the seventh monadic sub-plane. As the sixth sub-plane Monads focus their thought onto the astral plane, they direct intelligent activity from their plane that will manifest as sixth-ray, or astral, elemental energy into a new field of potential probabilities *that is created by the fallen spirit*. The potential of this new field, along with the Monads' sacrifice of creating new life on the monadic plane, causes a part of these Monads to separate from them. These separated parts resemble their parent Monads because the parts are limited replications of the Monads' thought as it can eventually exist while, in this case, on the astral plane. The separated part is limited because it can think using only the light of the astral Ray Lord; further, the field of potential intelligent activity from which it can create is much smaller than the entire third part of God's mind. This new limited part of the Monad below its own level and duration of life creation is destined to become fallen astral spirit. The spirit on each sub-plane is then pooled together and collectively energized because it is coming from Monads who, at their level of thought, all think together. Certain amounts of spirit from this pool join with corresponding energies according to the spirit's ability to think on a specific sub-plane and plane. Until spirit is joining with a form, as energy or when fully enlightened with intelligent activity (at the atomic level of a plane), it is incapable of sensing and creating thought regarding its plane. These same Monads are simultaneously creating group souls as new life on the mental plane. The spiritual part of these group souls comes from spirit that has descended from the spiritual plane and from the focused monadic thought. This spirit manifests elemental energy from the corresponding intelligent activity on the monadic plane by incompletely giving, or being incompletely conscious mentally. One Monad becomes connected to a single group soul through the life thread that connects to a part of the soul's and OverSoul's form, which is referred to as a permanent atom. The Solar Angel, as an OverSoul, ensouls (thinks for) the either group soul or human soul. Then that soul ensouls (thinks for) the lower fallen spirit that informs the body(-ies) of the lifeform(s) it helps to create. The first OverSouls, or Solar Angels, begin their existence as the spirit that remains fully enlightened at the atomic levels of the spiritual, intuitional, and mental planes that, through this spirit's thought, is eventually joined with other spirit from the first and second sub-planes on each of these planes. The spirit from the next lower sub-plane along with the atomic level spirit bring together relatively enlightened energies from the second and first sub-planes and some fully intelligent activity, to create a permanent atom at the atomic level of the plane. The lower energies are fused to some degree by the spirit, creating a "mini-star"–like body of the permanent atom, which on the mental plane and higher always has a fully enlightened top. The Solar Angel's spirit surrounds the enlightened parts of the permanent atom on each of the planes. This spirit begins as three separate parts that are each referred to as a Self. These parts are found on the mental, intuitional, and spiritual planes, respectively, and are eventually shared with the soul, as are the permanent atoms.

Monads Creating Life from the Sixth Monadic Sub-Plane

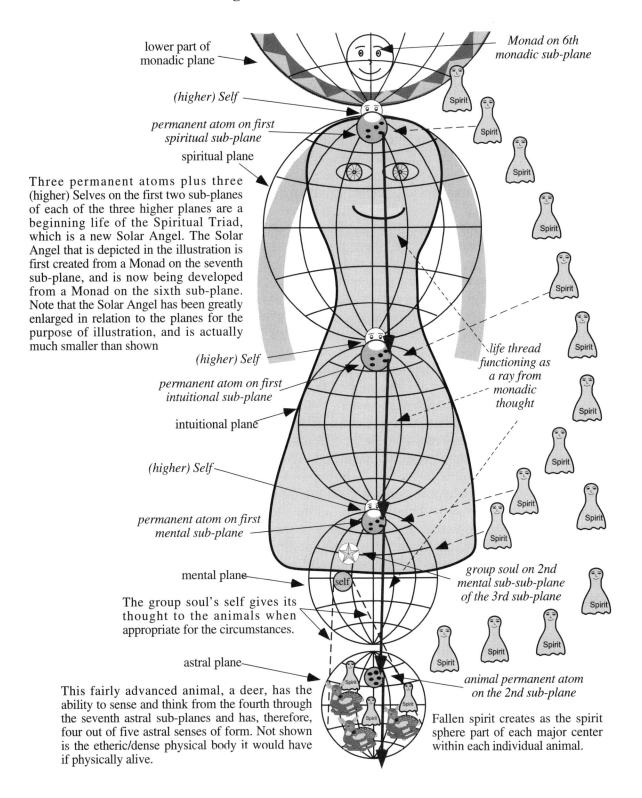

lower part of monadic plane

Monad on 6th monadic sub-plane

(higher) Self

permanent atom on first spiritual sub-plane

spiritual plane

Three permanent atoms plus three (higher) Selves on the first two sub-planes of each of the three higher planes are a beginning life of the Spiritual Triad, which is a new Solar Angel. The Solar Angel that is depicted in the illustration is first created from a Monad on the seventh sub-plane, and is now being developed from a Monad on the sixth sub-plane. Note that the Solar Angel has been greatly enlarged in relation to the planes for the purpose of illustration, and is actually much smaller than shown

(higher) Self

permanent atom on first intuitional sub-plane

intuitional plane

(higher) Self

permanent atom on first mental sub-plane

life thread functioning as a ray from monadic thought

mental plane

The group soul's self gives its thought to the animals when appropriate for the circumstances.

astral plane

This fairly advanced animal, a deer, has the ability to sense and think from the fourth through the seventh astral sub-planes and has, therefore, four out of five astral senses of form. Not shown is the etheric/dense physical body it would have if physically alive.

group soul on 2nd mental sub-sub-plane of the 3rd sub-plane

animal permanent atom on the 2nd sub-plane

Fallen spirit creates as the spirit sphere part of each major center within each individual animal.

Illustration 4.6

MORE ADVANCED INFORMATION ABOUT SPIRIT

Spirit contains the first and second parts of God's mind, similar to the way its parent and creator, the Monad, does; however, spirit's level of enlightenment on any lower plane is no higher than the light of that plane, or the thought by the Ray Lord of that plane. For example, as long as the astral spirit that was created by sixth sub-plane Monads remains on the astral plane, it can only think as well as the thought of the astral Ray Lord. Once spirit becomes located in its thought on a plane that its parent (creating) type of Monad has directed it to (but still with the choice of spirit to be there), this spirit immediately accesses the associated limited potential field of potential probabilities that the Monads have created for it. As soon as the spirit focuses its thought onto this field, some of the intelligent probabilities that have already been designated for spirit's corresponding plane become manifested as energy. Since the spirit on any plane is limited in its thought by the maximum speed of the Ray Lord's thought on that plane, some of the thought that spirit is giving to the third part of God's mind (spirit's field of limited intelligent activity) is incomplete, or is less than perfect in its consciousness. In addition, below the intuitional plane, on the mental, astral, and etheric/dense physical planes, spirit cannot perfectly give, using any one of the three parts of God's mind in its thought. The reason is that none of the lower three Ray Lords' thought, as light, is fast enough to join all three parts of time (past, present, and future) for more than one lifeform at a single point, or location, in space. Below the atomic level of the mental plane, the three parts of time cannot be joined to *any* even *single* location in space. At the atomic level of the astral plane, only two parts of time (the past and the present) can be perfectly joined to a location in space, and at the atomic level of the etheric/dense physical plane, only one part of time (the past) can be perfectly joined to only a single location in space. (See illustration 4.14.)

The above-described effects severely limit spirit on each of the lower three planes. In addition, spirit creates more limitation by further separating time from space and, also, by fracturing and mixing up the parts of time. Spirit does this by mistakenly identifying itself with energy rather than with God's thought—which is light—or the corresponding light of the Ray Lord's thought on the plane whereupon spirit exists. Once spirit mis-identifies itself with energy, it is no longer creating virtue, or more of its enlightened thought, within the energy (or form) that it has informed. The energy that spirit separates from its limited field of intelligent activity becomes a type of energy that replicates spirit's loss in consciousness. This energy comes from thought that is not as enlightened as the corresponding Ray Lord's thought in the dimension that spirit exists on. Only spirit's thought *at the level* of the corresponding Ray Lord's thought, or at the atomic level of the plane that it (spirit) exists on, can create intelligent activity from its limited field of probabilities without first manifesting as the less conscious energy.

In the example of sixth sub-plane monadic life, most of the spirit of sixth sub-plane Monads descends from the atomic level of the spiritual plane to the astral plane; however, increasing amounts of spirit (as spiritual thought) may be found entirely on the *atomic* levels of the mental, intuitional, and spiritual planes. When spirit does not descend onto the plane that corresponds to the monadic sub-plane from which its type of Monad is creating life, it *begins* but may not remain in its creation of lifeforms at the *atomic* level of the plane it has been able to adequately think from. This spirit may limit the majority of the corresponding field of intelligent activity, to create a somewhat enlightened lifeform from somewhere below the atomic level of its plane. As spirit attempts and succeeds in the creation of lifeforms within which there is a majority of intelligent activity, or the creation of lifeforms that are more enlightened than not, it can remain on the higher mental plane (or higher) regardless of whether the rest of the spirit has descended below this level, even onto a lower plane. This spirit on the mental plane that can enlighten both itself and the energy in its form to a level of at least fifty percent becomes, at the atomic level of the mental plane, a part of a Solar Angel and, additionally, on the second or third sub-plane of the mental plane, a soul—which we will cover much more about in Chapter Six.

The thought that the Monads are using on their sub-plane in order to separate intelligent activity from their thought, which is exclusively light, is added to the thought that these Monads use to create life on the lower dimensions that correspond to their sub-plane and level of life creation. This thought is then given and shared among themselves and all other Monads at and above their level of sub-plane consciousness and life creation. This omnipresence is part of the "mirror" effect, through which each Monad creating new life, or more of God's growth, shares this growth in *thought* with all other Monads at and above its level of consciousness. Every time a Monad gives this thought to so many other Monads, it increases its own consciousness. Thus as Monads create life, they simultaneously raise their consciousness by giving, in thought, what their and the informing spirit's thoughts are that are given to the lifeforms. While Monads on the monadic plane do give and share their thoughts, in omnipresence, they cannot give and share their *sense* and the *direct experiences* from their created Solar Angels, souls, and then life-forms. These Monads do not use any part of the third part of God's mind, which can create a sense, while they are on the monadic plane. Only ascended Monads, on the logoic plane, have such capability. To further exemplify this concept of sharing thought versus sharing sense, imagine that a friend tells you all about his great vacation to the mountains, in elaborate detail. This is similar to sharing his thoughts about his vacation; however, it is not the same as having been there yourself. Now imagine that you can become a part of all of your friend's senses and can experience the vacation exactly as he experienced it. These two scenarios are the differences in realities between Monads on the monadic plane, who share thought, and those on the logoic, who share sense in addition to thought.

The Ascending Monad

Divine Plane

1 Will, or Purpose

2 Consciousness

3 Intelligent Action

The ascending Monad fully joins the three parts of God's mind upon reaching the atomic level of the logoic, or divine, plane.

Illustration 4.7

The long journey by the Monad to become its Creator (and to grow more of its Creator in the process) is accomplished through spirit. The process begins on the first plane, or dimension, below the monadic. This third plane of our universe is the body and thought of the third cosmic Ray Lord. The very top of this plane (sphere) is the point at which all the energy within the atomic space in the sphere is enlightened from the focal point of the third Ray Lord's thought. A great deal of spirit exists there because all of the spirit that was separated from all of the Monads first exists as separated monadic thought at this point. One of the names for this plane is the spiritual plane because, to begin with, it contains all of the initially separated monadic thought. The third Ray Lord is better able to unify the first two parts of God's mind than are the Ray Lords of lower dimensions. This means that the third Ray Lord's light is more effective in enlightening energy than is the light of any of the lower Ray Lords. When energy is fully enlightened it becomes completely intelligent in its activity, and is no longer manifested as separate from the third part of God's mind. Because of this effect, the third, or spiritual, plane has mostly intelligent activity within it and relatively little manifested (and therefore separated) energy. There exists on this plane a great deal of spirit to a relatively small amount of separated (manifested) energy.

The much larger amount of spirit than energy causes the spirit to join with energy and create lifeforms that are relatively similar and not diverse as compared to lifeforms on lower dimensions. Initially, these lifeforms are part of a Spiritual Triad of Selves and permanent atoms that create a beginning Solar Angel. Diversity is the result of many ray types of energies that have differing levels of thought and enlightenment, coming together in different ways of developing senses and bodies. A greater quantity of manifested energies strongly affects the ability to create differences because of a higher likelihood of differing thought and ray focus, and this affects diversity of lifeforms. Newly created Solar Angels lack diversity as lifeforms. As more energy becomes present on a plane, there is more of each sub-ray type of energy of any one ray type of energy (the one that corresponds to the Ray Lord's ray and plane). Because there is so much spirit in comparison to energy, it is relatively easy for spirit to think within the lifeforms on the spiritual plane—causing nearly instant and complete enlightenment of these lifeforms' energy. Because the energy becomes as enlightened as the spirit, these Beings, as new Solar Angels, are considered energy Beings. Their energy (mostly as intelligent activity) thinks as well as their spirit does, and their spirit thinks as a Self. (Self is explained in detail in Chapter Five.) The greater the amount of spirit (with its great capacity to think) in comparison to the amount of energy needed to completely sense, the easier it is for spirit to create knowledge from the senses within its form. Also, the faster the lifeform can become enlightened if the spirit is choosing to think in light, or in God's thought.

The enlightening thought of spirit on the third plane can nearly instantly change manifested energy from one state of density to another, if separated and not yet enlightened—creating great power. Alternatively, energy can be converted into completed intelligent activity, where all action *only* further enlightens energy, joining energy with light and illuminating (joining) space between itself and other energy that is different in its slight thought. The result is the thought creating a new *sense* of intelligent activity at the same time. In either case, spirit functions on the spiritual plane all-powerfully (omnipotently) as well as all-knowingly (omnisciently) in its thought because there it can use its thought to alter all energy, whether separated from light (and space) or not. This capacity of spirit's thought as represented in the spiritual body of a beginning Solar Angel and the sense spirit eventually develops at the atomic level, of omnipotence, is lost in the lower dimensions because the lower cosmic Ray Lords cannot enlighten energy nearly as well. Also, since spirit on each plane must think in the light of that plane, and a large amount of spirit on this plane can think omnipotently, some of spirit remains on the spiritual plane. This leaves less of the Monads' separated thought (less spirit) available for the lower planes. As each lower Ray Lord enlightens energy at a lesser amount in time and space, more and more energy becomes manifested (separated from intelligent activity). This causes larger amounts of manifested energy to become available, with smaller amounts of spirit on each lower dimension of our universe. In addition, what is occurring is that the two fields of potential that have a symbiotic relationship on the monadic plane are now actualizing a part of this effect on the lower planes. It would be correct then to state that as a hidden cause, spirit's sacrifice of itSelf on the monadic plane is resulting in increases in manifested energies on the lower planes, because the two monadic fields are responding to each other in an inverse manner.

The two fields that respond to each other inversely on the monadic plane, of light and of sacrificed potential intelligent activity, become a part of the thought of spirit, creating a third field—of spirit and life—on each plane below the monadic. When a potential field manifests something because of its limiting thought, which it creates from choices in a similar direction that are great enough to limit the field, the similar direction of the choices causes the manifesting probable field to rotate and to eventually create a sphere. The rotation is at an angle relative to the original field, before it was limited by thought, and is determined by direction of the choices in the limited field. The third field, of spirit and life creation, manifests from the spiritual, or third, plane and in all the planes below it. From the third plane, down, each cosmic Ray Lord's plane, or body, is itself a sphere of both potential intelligent activities and some level of manifested energies, and rotates at a fixed angle to the limited field of potential in our universe that represents all of God's mind. A field of spirit eventually exists within (and on some planes, surrounding) each plane from the third, down; this field of spirit is also a sphere that rotates at an angle to God's mind. As would be expected, these two spheres—on the lower planes, the larger (of the Ray Lord of intelligent activities and some amount of manifested energies) and the smaller (of spirit)—interact because the manifested energies are changed by the thought of the spirit. This situation reverses on the planes above the mental, where the spirit spheres are larger than the energy spheres. The energy on the higher planes follows the thought of spirit because the spirit's thought is so much greater. At the beginning of our universe each spirit sphere was elongated vertically, creating a slightly more elliptical than perfectly round shape. The elliptical formation is a result of spirit's lack of perfection in both thought and in its ability to give its thought to energy (to think for energy). Though only very slight on the spiritual plane, the elongation becomes slightly more prominent on each lower plane as a result of the increasing losses in spirit's thought. The bodies of most of the lifeforms take on more of an elongated shape than the shape of a true sphere because the form, or energy, of these lifeforms is attracted to spirit's thought, which the elongated spheres represent.

To briefly exemplify the preceding concepts, the spiritual plane has one part of energy's thought to five parts of spirit's thought; the etheric/dense physical plane has five parts energy's thought to one part spirit (spirit is only thought). Also, the corresponding angles, or phases, of the consciousness at the atomic levels of these two planes are opposite in relation to the absolute, or the 0°, angle of God's thought at the atomic level of the first (the logoic) plane. The logoic Ray Lord's thought is 360° in relation to God's. This angle is the same as 0° from one perspective, in the simplified explanation using just two dimensions. The corresponding angles are as follows: On the spiritual plane there is 150° of spirit's phase change of consciousness to 30° of energy's. This is the reverse of the angles of each of the two spheres on the etheric/dense physical plane. On the etheric/dense physical plane these angles reverse to the energy sphere having a 150° angle to God's thought. This creates five times the amount of collective thought of energy as compared to the spirit sphere having only a 30° angle and one-fifth the amount of phase shift of spirit's consciousness on the spiritual plane. Note that the factor of five regarding energy's collective thought must be multiplied by the frequency differences—which are enormous. The more that spirit is similar to God's consciousness and still is fully enlightening (at the atomic level of a plane), the more of God's thought it creates. As it descends into lower dimensions of time and space, spirit loses its ability to create God's thought. The more energy that thinks as one and is very slightly "conscious," or giving in diminishing amounts, in a direction that is away from God's thought and towards itself, the greater is its gravity and the less it creates of God; in the process, spirit becomes increasingly hampered in its ability to use a body and senses to become a functional part of God through enlightening the energy. At the atomic level of the monadic plane, "spirit" and "energy" are both at 180° (opposite each other) because there is no energy or spirit—only their potential—and both "spirit" and "energy" have equal potential to create light, or more of God's thought. At the atomic level of the logoic plane, "spirit" and "energy" are at 360° to God (or 0°, depending upon one's point of view if only two

Relative Size and Phase of the Spirit and Energy Spheres on the Masculine Dimensions

The plane angles as shown are perfected ones; the actual angles will vary according to the selfish thought on a plane of a particular planet.

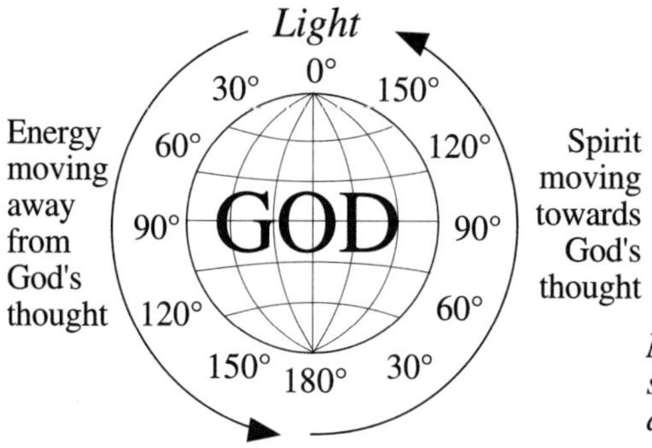

Masculine Planes
(as determined by the energy sphere's spin)

Logoic Plane

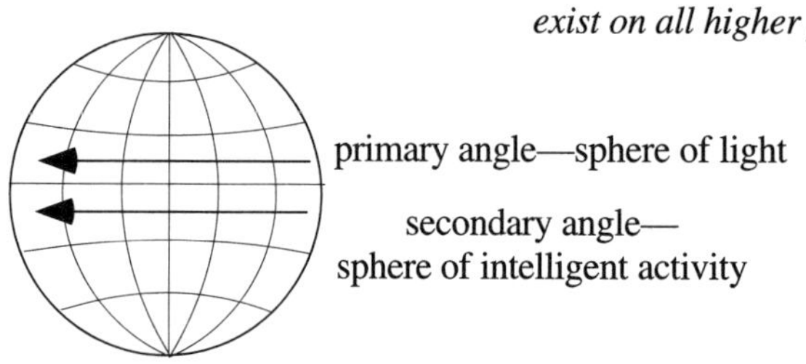

Spiritual Plane

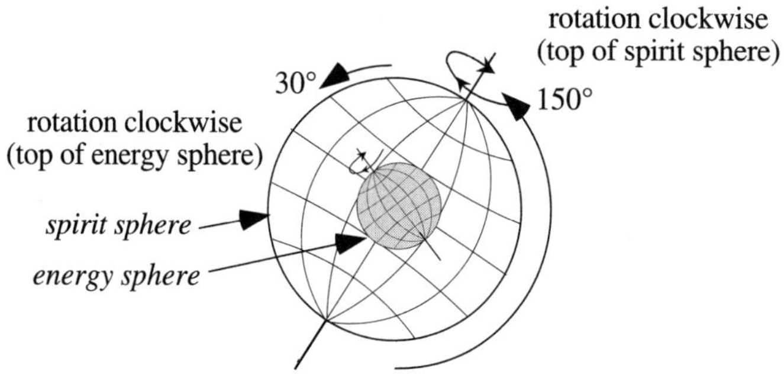

Mental Plane

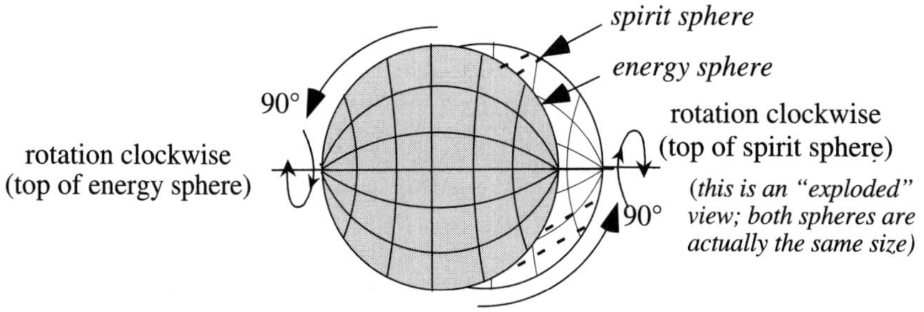

Etheric/Dense Physical Plane

Light

Energy moving away from God's thought

Spirit moving towards God's thought

GOD

Note that only two of the three split dimensions of the etheric dense/physical plane are shown. Additional dimensions exist on all higher planes.

primary angle—sphere of light

secondary angle—sphere of intelligent activity

rotation clockwise (top of spirit sphere)

rotation clockwise (top of energy sphere)

spirit sphere

energy sphere

spirit sphere

energy sphere

rotation clockwise (top of spirit sphere)

rotation clockwise (top of energy sphere)

(this is an "exploded" view; both spheres are actually the same size)

energy sphere

spirit sphere

rotation clockwise (top of spirit sphere)

rotation clockwise (top of energy sphere)

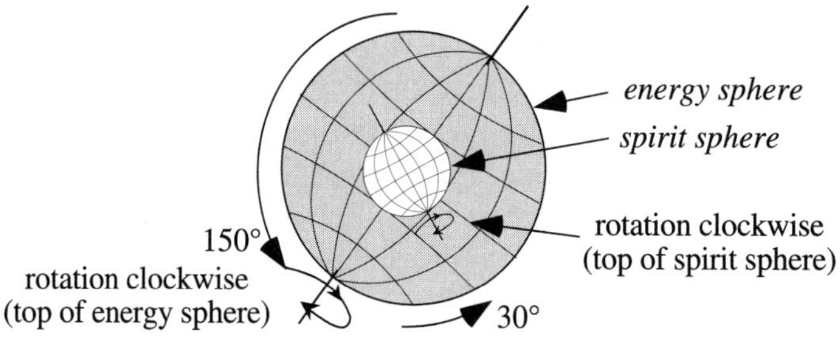

Illustration 4.8

Relative Size and Phase of the Spirit and Energy Spheres on the Feminine Dimensions

The plane angles as shown are perfected ones; the actual angles will vary according to the selfish thought on a plane of a particular planet.

Feminine Planes
(as determined by the energy sphere's spin)

Monadic Plane

Intuitional Plane

Astral Plane

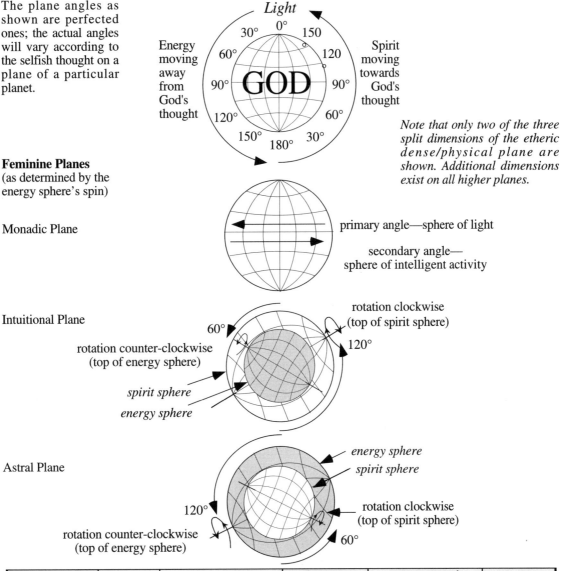

Note that only two of the three split dimensions of the etheric dense/physical plane are shown. Additional dimensions exist on all higher planes.

PLANES	PRIMARY SPHERE	SPIRIT SPHERE'S DIRECTION OF ROTATION	SECONDARY SPHERE	ENERGY SPHERE'S DIRECTION OF ROTATION	RELATIVE SIZE (SPIRIT TO ENERGY)
	LIGHT		*INTELLIGENT ACTIVITY*		
Logoic	0°		0°		Same
Monadic	180°		180°		Same
	SPIRIT		*ENERGY*		
Spiritual	150°	Clockwise	30°	Clockwise	5 to 1
Intuitional	120°	Clockwise	60°	Counter-clockwise	2 to 1
Mental	90°	Clockwise	90°	Clockwise	1 to 1
Astral	60°	Clockwise	120°	Counter-clockwise	1 to 2
Etheric/Dense Physical	30°	Clockwise	150°	Clockwise	1 to 5

Illustration 4.9

dimensions of the physical plane are considered), and their joined sphere becomes fully a functional part of God while they have grown more of God. All of these angles are added to a third physical dimension plus additional dimension for each higher Ray Lord; in order to establish the time differences in gravity between planes, these angles must be multiplied by the frequency differences (see Chapter Ten for further explanation). For simplicity, these additional dimensions have been omitted from the explanations and drawings.

 BASIC TYPES OF ENERGY

ELEMENTAL ENERGY

The presence of a spirit sphere on each dimension below the monadic alters the amount of intelligent activity relative to the amount of manifested energies. This change occurs because the two originating monadic fields are altering the probability of life creation, making it much more probable that certain life will be created. The spirit sphere on each dimension, or plane, lower than the monadic is no longer able to create thought that is in all-presence, which is the way Monads think. Instead, spirit must think in isolation through a form (through separated energy) and must use the senses of that form. Some of spirit's thought is unable to create intelligence, or perfection in knowledge that is created and given perfectly, in all of the activities it directs within its form and that of others. The reason is that spirit within a lifeform must think for itself separately from other spirit. Spirit within a lifeform must rely upon the form it is using to think through, in order to become informed about other form—using the best-developed energies of the form, or the sense(s) of form. As a result of these difficulties, some amount of intelligent activity on each plane below the monadic is further converted into (more) energy, which is caused by separation and manifestation. In certain spiritual language, the name of this additional manifested energy is elemental energy. Elemental energy is created from the inability of spirit to think and sense perfectly from the spiritual plane, down. This energy comes from existing intelligent activity on both the monadic plane and the plane the spirit is focused on, with the intelligent activity not potentialized in enlightened thought. Because of this, instead of being created through fully enlightened thought, the elemental energy is created from the less than perfect thought of spirit. Because all of the intelligent activity is not focused on by the second Ray Lord within its dimension, the intelligent activity present on the plane can create all seven ray types of elemental energies. The type of energy is determined by the spirit's thought and corresponding plane and sub-plane. In some cases of first and second ray elemental energies, spirit first attempts but fails to enlighten first or second sub-ray *primordial* energies. These energies may become elemental-like.

Similar to elemental energy in some respects is primordial energy. Primordial energy is the spiritual name for energies that are created from the separation of the third part of God's mind and that are not a potential for perfect intelligent activity within a specific Ray Lord's body. The primordial energy first becomes manifested at the center of our universe at the universe's inception, and creates the big bang. All of these energies are attracted into the dimension of one of the lower five cosmic Ray Lords and become the manifested primordial energy of that plane. Six-sevenths of the intelligent activity that was originally in each field of cosmic Ray Lords three through seven is *not* a potential for activity for that Ray Lord, and therefore manifests as separated energy in the center of our universe at its beginnings. This six-sevenths of energy from each of the lower five dimensions creates an enormous amount of initially manifested energies that are concentrated into a point with no space or time between them (as was described in Chapter Two).

Elemental energy can join with some primordial energy and the two can, to humans, become indistinguishably one, but elemental energy has an overriding quality—a primitive consciousness—that also affects primordial energies that join with it. Either at the atomic level or below that level on the plane where spirit is focused through its own thought, spirit focuses on intelligent activity or on energies on a lower plane that its corresponding type of Monad is creating life on. In the second case, spirit uses some intelligent activity from the monadic plane that its corresponding type Monad there is sacrificially not using with which to think. Spirit's ability to think for, or give its thought to, energy (which determines spirit's consciousness) is dependent upon its level of perfection, or completeness of the above-mentioned three types of thoughts of purpose, love, and applied intelligence, for both itself and energy. Spirit can think for itself one level (usually a plane) higher than it can think for energy, and it can think perfectly for just itself only on the spiritual plane. On the spiritual plane and, increasingly, below it, spirit's thought for energy (its ability to give its thought to energy) is increasingly flawed, or incomplete. Because the elemental energy's consciousness is created by following thought that is given to it and is less than complete in the way it is given, in at least one of the three ways (purpose, love, knowledge), the energy has a propensity in the slight amount that it does think to do so with one or more of these qualities of consciousness, or givingness, missing.

The first quality that is always missing from elemental energy to some degree is the consciousness (givingness) of creation and energy's purpose. This quality is missing because spirit became less than perfect in its ability to give this quality in its thought upon its separation from its Monad. Also, because spirit was created from the first two parts of God's mind with an accentuation on the second, when both parts become lessened by equal amounts (which is what occurs progressively as spirit descends into lower and lower planes), spirit contains relatively less of the first part of God's mind than the second—so less can be given. This first quality of consciousness, of the *giving* in thought of creation and purpose, is lost on the first plane whereupon spirit exists as a separate part of life—the third, or spiritual, plane. In addition to this first quality, the second quality of consciousness that is lost from elemental energy is love (the giving in thought of givingness), and this loss occurs on the next lower plane (the fourth plane, of intuition). Finally, on the mental (the fifth) plane, all three qualities of consciousness are lost from elemental energy, when applied intelligence (the giving in thought of the ability to perfectly communicate completely synthesized correct information, or knowledge) is no longer a part of elemental energy's consciousness. The progressive losses occur at increasing amounts as spirit descends lower on each plane and everywhere below the atomic level of each corresponding plane. Only at the atomic level does the Ray Lord's thought completely enlighten all the spirit and energy of that plane with its light, keeping the energy in intelligent activity *at the Ray Lord's* level of thought.

The more of these qualities of consciousness that are missing in elemental energy, the denser it becomes. With less consciousness (givingness) in the energy that is attracted to the thought of spirit, energy's own very slight thought causes it to become attracted to other energy that is similar to itself in consciousness (or, actually, lack of consciousness!). The elemental energy densifies by its slight thought attracting other energy, *and*, on each lower plane, by its thought becoming increasingly less receptive to the thought of spirit. The effect of elemental energy (or *any* energy) being decreasingly attracted to spirit's thought and being attracted through its own (slight) thought to other energy that thinks the way it does is what is referred to as gravity. Gravity significantly increases on each lower sub-plane within the Ray Lord's body, or sphere, that it corresponds to, because the elemental energy on each lower sub-plane is increasingly densifying.

Some primordial energy also develops gravity and becomes denser on each lower plane, but, unlike elemental energy, it is sometimes not created from the lack of perfection in thought by spirit. The Ray Lord's thought on each plane, while diminished from the thought and light of the Ray Lord on the plane above it, is still perfect in its light and thus in its thought at its atomic level. Spirit, however, is not perfect, and this lack of perfection causes it to be unable to perfectly give in its thought at its atomic level. Then the elemental energy follows the spirit's thought, which causes it to also be less than perfect, to become uncooperative with spirit, and to even *seek* a development of form that is *more dense*. Unlike elemental energy, the majority of primordial energy thinks in deference to the Ray Lord and seeks to join with It and become more developed through stimulation by the Ray Lord's cosmic ray. Its ability to actually do so, however, is quite minimal—which causes some of the primordial energy, when not enlightened by spirit, to gravitate to the lower parts of each plane, where the light of the Ray Lord affects it the least. This primordial energy was attracted to the Ray Lord's ray and dimension, but then chose not to grow as much from the ray in thought because it (the energy) thought too differently from the Ray Lord. Therefore, some of the primordial energy on the lower part of the plane chooses very differently, and does not follow most of the Ray Lord's thought after having been attracted into its dimension; this primordial energy then responds more in the way that elemental energy does. It is the responsibility of spirit to change the elemental energy (and the primordial energy that behaves as such) into a cooperative, loving, actively intelligent, and eventually self-creative and purposeful consciousness by, usually gradually, enlightening the quite resistant elemental (and elemental-like) energy. Elemental energy is termed *involutionary* because it seeks to be separate from spirit and to become more dense, and it increasingly lacks "consciousness" (relative to the level that any energy *is* conscious) on each lower dimension of our universe. Interestingly, elemental energy behaves in these ways because spirit does not think perfectly—it lacks some amount of light. Therefore, it is spirit's responsibility (and a part of its purpose) to rectify the situation by learning to think perfectly—as God—through enlightening the energies in the lower dimensions of our universe (from the spiritual plane, down).

Spirit on the higher planes needs to help lower plane spirit to accomplish this task. The methods spirit uses rely on self-limitation and sacrifice to better develop its enlightened thought. Using its slight thought, primordial energy mostly seeks to join with the cosmic Ray Lord that it corresponds to in thought, through the attractive stimulation of its ray. To the primordial energy, the Ray Lord's thought represents God's thought. That part of primordial energy that seeks more to join with a Ray Lord (through choosing to be stimulated in its thought and growth by its ray) is *evolutionary* in its development. By evolutionary is meant that responsive primordial energy cooperates with and gives to spirit (by helping to develop better senses and bodies) in order to help develop more of God's growth, or more of life. Elemental energy (and elemental-like primordial energy) densifies on the lower planes as it increasingly lacks responses while thinking of only "itself" and other energy that resembles it. This involutionary-thinking energy seeks to join with other energy unconsciously in opposition to the enlightened thought of spirit (and the corresponding Ray Lord). In contrast, the evolutionary type of primordial energy seeks to respond more to spirit, decreasing its density and its almost exclusive focus of thought on energy that is, in its somewhat enlightened thought, mostly similar to itself. Responsive primordial energy seeks to help spirit create life because it has some of the Ray Lord's enlightened thought within it, since it was stimulated to grow from the cosmic Ray Lord's ray. This responsive energy contains some of the virtue of its corresponding Ray Lord's light. Most elemental energy on the three lower planes (and primordial energy that is thinking separatively, as elemental energy does) that has not yet become informed by the enlightened thought of spirit is primarily missing the virtue of its corresponding Ray Lord's light. When spirit has adequately enlightened elemental energy (and primordial energy that thinks like elemental energy), the energy can change from involutionary to evolutionary.

DEVONIC ENERGY

Energy that seeks to become more enlightened in its growth and is therefore evolutionary has long ago been termed *devonic*, from the ancient Sanskrit language. The word *deva* in this ancient language means God-*like* in qualities, or consciousness (giving/understanding). The English equivalent (but not exactly so) of the word deva is *angel*. Thus these evolutionary energies are called devonic, or angelic, energies because they tend to think like God, or more in light. These lesser energies on the three lowest planes when a part of a spiritually informed form are often referred to as *pitris*, or "partially devonic," or "partially angelic" energies. Elemental energy tends to think in darkness and generally will not grow more of God, or life, on its own. It thinks away from God, unless directed by overriding thought of the spirit that is joined with it. Also, elemental energy can be enlightened only very slightly, by joining with ray-responsive devonic, or somewhat enlightened, energies. However, this enlightenment usually requires that spiritual thought still direct the joining as well as the maintaining of the elemental energy within the form. Without the help of informing spirit, the deva, or pitri, energy usually does not have enough enlightened thought to direct the elemental energy that it joins with. This is nearly always the case on both the etheric/dense physical and astral planes.

On the third, or spiritual, plane the amount of elemental energy is relatively small and is less involutionary as compared to elemental energies on the planes lower than the spiritual. The reason is that most of spirit on this plane is capable, through its thought, of enlightening elemental energy and its consciousness in two of the three ways of God's thought. The first of these two is through active, or applied, intelligence, which causes the energies to much more effectively communicate—as a sense—accurate information with each other and with spirit. The second is through love, or the giving of consciousness as a part of its information to other energies and to spirit. While elemental energy on the spiritual plane is more conscious and less involuting in its thought, it also, overall, *thinks* the least of any elemental energies. The reason is that this energy so lacks the first part of God's mind (of choices/will).

Spirit is initially unable to completely enlighten energy either through creation and purpose or through the energies becoming able to create a sense of purpose through giving their thought of creating new types of energy on their own; spirit and energy need to learn this process together by creating more of life on the lower planes and ultimately by joining the senses of all life together. Thus for spirit to completely enlighten all of energy, or form, requires that it do so in all the ways that form can sense, from the lowest (the seventh) plane, up. To accomplish this task requires that some spirit (with the assistance of higher dimensional spirit) descend to the lowest levels and fully sense other forms as well as other spirit. Eventually, the spirit needs to fully sense God. The spirit uses, together with its thought, the fully enlightened senses of the forms that it has helped to create. Only when the senses of form become enlightened can spirit itself become fully enlightened and gain in its consciousness, or its understanding of, the part of God's purpose that extends beyond growing more of God. The only way that spirit can fully reveal this to itself is to completely enlighten the senses of the form it is a part of on all the planes from the third, down. In order for spirit to completely enlighten energy in the ways it was initially unable to, manifested energy must return to its unmanifested state because such enlightenment (creation) requires development of and access to a higher field of possibilities. By definition, such a field is missing from manifested energy, since manifested energy comes into existence by *the loss of the possibilities to be intelligent in all activity by itself and its own very slight thought.*

On the spiritual plane most elemental energy is enlightened, in two of the three possible ways. There is much more spirit than manifested energy as well, since some of spirit is, most of the time, capable of still completely creating intelligent activity in these two of three possible ways, from its joined choices/will/purpose/sacrifice and love/givingness/consciousness/oneness, which together are the light within it. Some spirit makes choices in its thought that reduce its abilities to enlighten energy in these two (of three) ways (love and intelligence). The reason is that such spirit chooses with its creating corresponding type of Monad to create new life that increases in diversity, or in the amount and types of separated energies. This spirit is usually less able to think in the light of the spiritual plane Ray Lord. As some spirit chooses, with its Monad that is of a corresponding type, this spirit descends from the very top, or atomic level, of the spiritual plane. This is where the Ray Lord's thought is focused and fully enlightens, with its light, all that can exist there.

 ## THE DESCENT OF SPIRIT AND THE ASCENT OF MONADS

The process of spirit descending further into lower dimensions is based upon, at first, the originating choice of the spirit's "parent," or creating, type of Monad to sense, experience, and grow (create) more of life (of God) in the lower dimensions of our universe. The Monad's type of thought and creation of life correspond to those of its responding spirit. However, spirit is free to think as it chooses to; spirit's choices are determined by its own thought, and not by where it came from. Spirit may be able to think better than the thought that its parent Monad chooses for it. For example, spirit that came from a sixth dimensional class of Monads of life creation of animals may be able to respond to Monads creating human life and located on the fifth monadic sub-plane. In these cases, spirit is choosing to respond to the higher-level Monads. Each Monad focuses on a specific planet or series of planets upon which to create spirit and life, with its creation taking place on a plane that corresponds to the monadic sub-plane where it is located in consciousness. The process is, in addition, based upon the choices of separated spirit within the lower dimensions to continue to do the same. The final factor is the capability of the spirit to inform a lifeform and think for it, which is determined by the spirit's ability to think. In each case, spirit is free to determine (to the level that it is capable of so doing) its rate of descent and/or ascent, its creation of light in form (of virtue), and how much of God's mind it unifies in life—as well as how much of life it creates. Spirit has freedom because Monads on the monadic plane *always* choose to not focus on intelligent actions, and spirit must always think through intelligent actions (and the actions' manifestations of energy when they are less than perfectly intelligent) in an opposite manner and in equal amounts, separating its thought from the Monads who are its creator on the monadic plane. The opposite manner and equal amounts in which spirit must think through form are the result of the two fields, of light and of separated intelligent activity, on the monadic plane being inversely related. When spirit ascends back to the monadic plane after its very long journey in the lower dimensions of creating life, it creates a new Monad (the first two parts of God's mind, joined) that can fully join with the third part of God's mind. This new Monad (which is a fusion with the previously created Monad) then ascends onto the logoic, or divine, plane (the first plane, or dimension, of our universe) as it begins to fully join with the third part of God's mind. When the three parts of God's mind have been rejoined by the enlightenment of spirit and energy, life has come full circle and the ascended Monad has grown and fully become a part of God because it has *grown and joined* its part of the three parts of God's mind.

Monads who exist on the monadic plane are referred to as sparks, or lights, of God because they contain only God's thought (light), or only the first two parts of God's mind—making them brilliant points of light. Ascended Monads on the first plane add to their brilliant points of light a shared body of pre-life and life in our entire universe, which is sometimes referred to in some spiritual language as the Cosmic Physical Universe. These Monads sense and experience everything within our universe—past, present, and future—and as One, or as God, and they also

Classes of Monads on the Monadic Plane

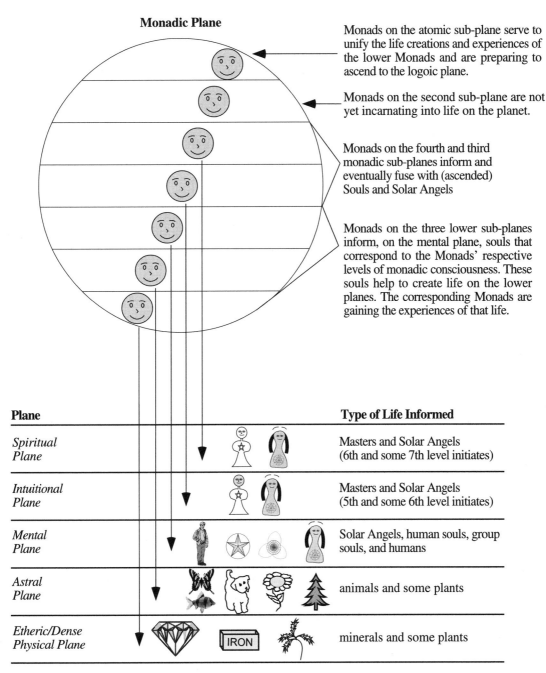

Monadic Plane

Monads on the atomic sub-plane serve to unify the life creations and experiences of the lower Monads and are preparing to ascend to the logoic plane.

Monads on the second sub-plane are not yet incarnating into life on the planet.

Monads on the fourth and third monadic sub-planes inform and eventually fuse with (ascended) Souls and Solar Angels

Monads on the three lower sub-planes inform, on the mental plane, souls that correspond to the Monads' respective levels of monadic consciousness. These souls help to create life on the lower planes. The corresponding Monads are gaining the experiences of that life.

Plane		Type of Life Informed
Spiritual Plane		Masters and Solar Angels (6th and some 7th level initiates)
Intuitional Plane		Masters and Solar Angels (5th and some 6th level initiates)
Mental Plane		Solar Angels, human souls, group souls, and humans
Astral Plane		animals and some plants
Etheric/Dense Physical Plane		minerals and some plants

Illustration 4.10

share their thoughts about this sense. They *become* God as God has grown until the point of their departure, but they experience God as it was, is, and will be. *Beingness* for an ascended Monad is an existence of God only as God *is*. The sense and experience of God traverse time and space for ascended Monads because they can both think *and* sense in omnipresence. This provides them with the ability to extrapolate *and to sense* from the thought and senses of *everything* in our universe how everything will eventually think and sense, and how it formerly thought and sensed; the ascended Monad during this extrapolation process is sometimes referred to as the Silent Watcher. What the ascended Monad creates (as an eighth level initiate) and experiences (as a ninth level initiate) on the logoic plane is based upon which path of service that particular Being chose as a sixth level initiate. There are seven paths out of our universe (or nine, for Monads on a planet that is without evil, or is sacred), or "Paths of Decision," and the ascended Monads apply their creation and experience on the logoic plane to their further creation in other universes. Several of these paths deal with stars, and those Beings who choose these paths bypass the, or a, Cosmic Astral Universe and move straight to the, or a, Cosmic Mental Universe when they leave this one, the, or a, Cosmic Physical Universe. After exceeding this level, there is nothing further to think about or sense within our universe, which allows this Great Being to move on into universes beyond the, or a, Cosmic Physical one.

The Silent Watcher on the Logoic, or Divine, Plane

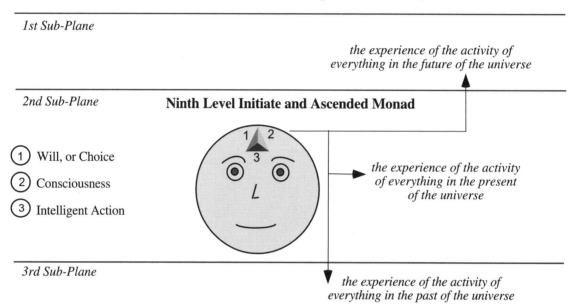

A Silent Watcher is a ninth level initiate and an ascended Monad who has given up all of its permanent atoms except its logoic one. The Silent Watcher experiences the activity of everything in the universe in the past, present, and future, and has joined together the three parts of God's mind in a new way. During its existence as a Silent Watcher, this Great Being exists as God does at that time.

Illustration 4.11

Monads on the monadic plane are creators of pre-life and life within planets of a specific star. Monads on the logoic plane are creators of all within our universe in the present, and are extrapolating the past and future creation of pre-life and life. Spirit is pure thought, and all parts of spirit at the atomic level *on any particular plane* contain the same level of consciousness within their fields of life; stated another way, at the atomic level of any plane each part of spirit is able to give its field of life equally to all other parts of spirit at this level. The measure of spirit's consciousness at the atomic level of a plane is in its ability to give to *all* of its field of life with its type of thought (exactly) as the Ray Lord of that plane's light (thought) is given within its duration of life. The reason is that spirit at this level thinks in the exact direction that the Ray Lord does. Energy mostly lacks thought, and elemental energy's slight thought is, much of the time, not God's thought. A significant amount of the time when it is not joined with elemental energy, primordial energy's slight thought is attracted by a ray, and a small amount of the primordial energy's thought becomes a part of its corresponding Ray Lord's thought. Then the deva energy's (the pitri's) slight thought becomes to some degree light, or God's thought. To determine the amount of energy's thought *that is not enlightened* requires that it be calculated for the entire plane because each part of unenlightened energy's thought, which is very slight, is identical in one of the ways in which it thinks (completely selfishly, or self-focused) with the thought of other unenlightened energy on that plane (to become more dense and of greater amounts). All of this unenlightened energy, including the unenlightened energies within life-forms, is thus attracted to each other by its slight thought added together. Every lifeform on the intuitional plane and higher planes has more thought in its senses than the totality of thought in all of the unenlightened energy on the entire plane. Great space is hence created between the life-forms on the three lowest planes because the thought in the spirit and senses of these lifeforms often cannot overcome the collective thought of the unenlightened energies. The space prevents one energy from joining its thought with other energy except when the thought in all of the energy is identical and focused on "itself" and similar-thinking energies—which is referred to as gravity.

 ## SPIRIT'S INVOLVEMENT WITH ENERGY

It is gravity and what gravity is manifested from (dark, "selfish" thought) as a condition of energy that interferes with all of the following: energy's sense, spirit's use of form, and, eventually, spirit's capacity of thought in form to synthesize knowledge into information. What spirit loses first is its ability to think in omnipresence—as a Monad can. This leads to spirit progressively losing its ability to enlighten form. The only way that spirit is measured is by its thought within the lifeform(s) it informs because it must use its informed lifeform(s) through which to communicate with other spirit and its energy. On the first sub-plane of the intuitional (the fourth) plane, there is twice as much of spirit (its thought) than the collective thought to join together, or to form gravity, of unenlightened energy on the entire plane within any one life-form on that plane, which allows spirit at this level to think perfectly for both itself and the energy it informs, in one of three ways (in all-knowledge). As a result, spirit's thought that is given is able to completely enlighten the elemental fourth ray energy there (in one of three ways). Spirit is usually limited, however, because its information comes exclusively from the senses of the form(s) it informs. Spirit must use the senses of the form(s) in order to contact other spirit on the dimension where it exists; the only exception to this condition occurs when the energy of the form becomes completely enlightened, which enables spirit to then directly communicate with all other spirit through intelligent activity. This occurs at the atomic level of the intuitional plane, and anywhere on the spiritual plane.

On the first sub-plane of the spiritual plane, spirit is in a five-to-one ratio in its ability to think in comparison to the amount of manifested energy's thought. Because of the inverse proportions created by the two inverse monadic fields that create spiritual thought and the thought of manifested elemental energy, the amount of spiritual thought in comparison to the amount of thought by manifested elemental energy changes quite dramatically from one plane to the next. On the intuitional plane spirit can enlighten energy in only *one* of the three ways that correspond to the three parts of God's mind. This one way is through applied intelligence, or the giving and sharing of all-knowledge. What this means is that the elemental energies and the life they are a part of that are manifested on the intuitional plane, or are created from the third part of God's mind, contain a consciousness (givingness/oneness) that is solely giving/sharing all-knowledge. What it also means is that these energies can (eventually) build a sense that is exclusively all-knowledge, or omniscience, since this is the maximum level of their givingness/consciousness, as determined by the level of the parts of God's mind with which they are joined and give.

The ratios of spiritual thought to the thought of manifested elemental energies are inversely proportionate. On the first sub-plane of the spiritual plane, spiritual thought when given to energy, or *when in form*, is two-thirds of God's thought, i.e., contains intelligent activity and love/consciousness/givingness, but lacks will/choices/creativeness/purpose. The spirit there has the *potential* to *think* in all three parts of God's mind if it perfects all types of energy, but it can *sense* only from the manifested energy that, in its givingness as a sense to spirit, it has joined with and become a part of the lower two parts of God's mind. This condition of spirit remains true everywhere that spirit exists separate from Monads, i.e., it can always think or is capable of thinking in at least one more way than it can sense, or than it can think while using energy to inform it. The reason is that within a lifeform spirit needs to think for itself *and for energy*, which it is a part of, and which it needs in order to be able to sense other form. On the spiritual, or third, plane, the combination of the two ways that spirit thinks for itself, using God's first two parts of its mind (or light) with the two ways that spirit thinks through form—applied intelligence and love—totals four ways, or amounts, of spiritual thought. A fifth way, or amount, occurs because spirit can use its two ways of *thought* as they apply to either manifested energy or intelligent activity. Spirit thinks either using all-power as a single capacity of its thought, or using power together with omniscience (all-communication/all-knowledge). Omnipotence in thought develops all-power as a *sense*, and each of these two become a sense and thought at the atomic level. The *total* amount of *all* the thought by energy on the spiritual plane that is manifested from intelligent activity and, therefore, is not perfectly enlightened is equal to one-fifth of the total of spiritual thought within a lifeform. This means that the total of all of the thought of all the unenlightened relatively dark spiritual plane energy, or all of this energy's choices that share similar direction with other choices and can limit a field of potential, is one-fifth of the amount of thought in *one part of spirit that informs any lifeform* at the atomic level. Note that the capacity of spirit's thought is *not* additive between lifeforms, since spirit has lost the omnipresence that the Monad has in Its thought.

The elemental energies informed by spirit at the atomic level of the spiritual plane contain two-thirds of the consciousness of spirit and can eventually create two senses that correspond to them. These senses are all-knowingness (all-knowledge, or omniscience) and all-power (omnipotence). Notice that the elemental energies on this plane gain the fifth, or synthesized, sense of all-power from spirit rather than the more basic sense of all-love because all elemental energy is missing the consciousness of purpose, or creativity; the elemental energy can give creatively only when spirit's thought has assisted the elemental energy by completely informing it *and* has created new life. From another perspective, spirit has five capacities of thought, but can enlighten energy through only two of them because there is too *little* of manifested energy available, reducing the sense of life from being all-loving (as a Monad is) to just all-powerful, since there is not enough life to be all-giving to another part of life. Thus one part of life (all of spirit) has more to give than the remaining parts of life (all of energy) are in need of. This is an anomaly created by so much spirit and so little manifested elemental energy on the spiritual plane. Note that much more of spirit is creating only intelligent activity, and is therefore not causing elemental energy to manifest. Both of the above-mentioned conditions limit spirit's sense through form at the atomic level of the spiritual plane to that of omnipotence rather than all-love. The second sense, of omniscience, is also present.

 ## GRAVITY AND ITS EFFECTS ON SPIRIT

Gravity is the effect of energy all thinking exactly the same in one particular way and seeking to join with one another, rather than to join with and be affected by the thought of spirit (or of God—when spirit's thought is enlightened). Gravity increases in direct proportion to the loss of enlightened spirit and spirit's enlightened thought in affecting the energy of a particular plane, or dimension of time and space. Since spirit's ability to affect energy through its thought on each lower plane of our universe dramatically and increasingly decreases, gravity equally dramatically and progressively increases. As was previously explained, energy follows thought that is greater than its own. However, unenlightened energy's very slight thought is *additive* for the entire plane because the gravity of the plane affects all spirit everywhere on the plane. Spirit's thought may sometimes not be greater than or may be even less than the collective of unenlightened energy's thought, depending upon the amount that spirit is thinking in light. Below the atomic level of the mental, astral, or etheric/dense physical planes, respectively, no part of spirit's thought is perfect, or *completely* in light, unless joined with some higher and enlightened spirit. Below the mid-point of the mental plane (on earth at this time), gravity, or the collective of a certain selfish type of thought by darkened energy, is *greater* than the thought of at least one-half of the spirit (and of all spirit that is not connected to higher spirit on at least the middle part of the mental plane). The reason is that most spirit, which already has a diminished capability of thought, chooses to not think in enough light; spirit and life then become controlled by gravity and by the space, or separation, of energy that is not joined to spirit. If spirit is capable of thinking above the middle of the mental plane, but does not think as virtuously as it could on any of the three lowest planes (the mental, astral, etheric/dense physical) for other parts of spirit that it affects, the lower spirit then becomes engulfed by the dark thought of energy on that lower plane. Without the connected higher spiritual thought, the lower spirit thinks less than the surrounding energies do.

Involutionary Energies Producing Gravity

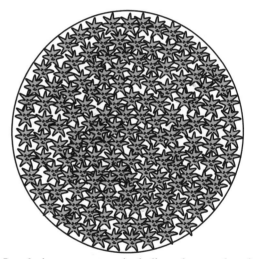

The most frequent and consistent thought of involutionary energy, including elemental and darkened energy, is to be attracted to other energy that thinks similarly to the way that it (slightly) does, because it is seeking to join with other energy.

Involutionary energy, including elemental and darkened-in-thought energy, focuses on its thought of seeking to join with other energy that has similar thought. This focus is what creates gravity.

Much more so on the three lowest planes than anywhere else, energy joins together because most of its (slight) thought is similar to the (slight) thought of other energy on its plane. The energy on those lowest planes is attracted to other energy that thinks similarly to the way that it (slightly) does. This similarly-thinking energy all seeks to join together to be more of "itself."

Illustration 4.12

On the first sub-plane of the fifth, or manasic, plane there is a measure of one part of the totality of energy's thought to one part of the amount of spirit's thought in a lifeform (an even ratio). Below the atomic level and on the first sub-plane, spirit can think completely for either itself or for energy—one at a time, and not both at the same time. Below the atomic sub-plane of the mental plane, since spirit needs to think for both itself and the energy that is its body, or

Darkened Spirit Is Lost from Its Self

The group soul's self is located on the 5th, 6th, and 7th sub-sub-planes of the third mental sub-plane, blurred in time.

Human crises and catastrophes can cause damage to the ability of group soul and its self to communicate with the fallen spirit that controls the energies in their lifeforms. An example of what happens is that the group soul and self of an affected animal do not understand what an oil spill is, and so they have no helpful information to offer the fallen spirit that informs the animal and others of its kind....

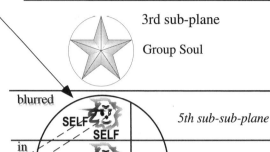

Higher Mental Plane

3rd sub-plane

Group Soul

blurred — SELF — *5th sub-sub-plane*

in — SELF — *6th sub-sub-plane*

time — SELF — *7th sub-sub-plane*

...In such cases, when the fallen spirit recognizes that its lifeforms are dying and that the thought of the group soul and self are not providing solutions, it begins to ignore their thought, and instead follows the thought of the energies that surround it.

Lower Mental Plane

4th sub-plane

The human self is located within the mental unit on the fourth sub-sub-plane of the fourth sub-plane. The personality's location spans the first through third sub-planes of the fourth sub-plane.

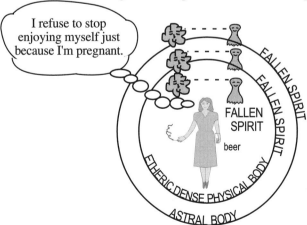

I refuse to stop enjoying myself just because I'm pregnant.

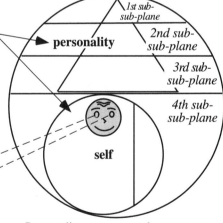

1st sub-sub-plane

personality

2nd sub-sub-plane

3rd sub-sub-plane

4th sub-sub-plane

self

Personality over-control can cause the human self to become self-focused. When the fallen spirit recognizes that the personality's informing thought is not helpful, the fallen spirit begins to follow the thought of its surrounding energies.

Illustration 4.13

form, spirit cannot *perfectly* do so for either itself or for the energy that it informs; moreover, none of the elemental energy has consciousness, or givingness, as a part of its nature. These factors cause spirit to have to struggle in its ability to think within its lifeforms; its thought at the atomic level and on higher planes is effortless. Below the atomic level of the fifth plane and everywhere on lower planes, spirit's thought is frequently unable to remain in light, and sometimes spirit loses its thought completely…in which case the effect is as though spirit is not even present. Everywhere below the atomic level of the fifth plane, spirit is in a contest not only to enlighten energy, but to enlighten itself as well. The reason is that spirit loses much of its enlightened thought during its descent onto the fifth plane. The lower it descends, the more of enlightened thought it loses and the more choices it tends to make that are in a direction away from light. This decline causes it to fall into a downward spiral of diminished capability of thought, choices away from light, and loss of the enlightened thought that it once had. One of the results of spirit losing control over its ability to think perfectly with others is that time becomes fractured and space becomes separated enough so that no two lifeforms are ever completely together in consciousness (givingness—understanding), as one. The last way this was possible, in all-knowledge, or omniscience, was lost after spirit descended from the intuitional plane.

TIME AND ITS RELATIONSHIP WITH
THE THOUGHT OF SPIRIT, AND WITH GRAVITY

Time on the first through fourth dimensions, or planes, of our universe is sensed and thought through in past, present, and future all at the same time (in one or more of three possible ways), which enables two or more lifeforms to *understand* (or *be conscious of*) what is referred to as effects that are always connected to their causes. There are three ways (of sensing) in which an effect can be connected to its cause for more than one lifeform at a time. One is through intelligence, or correctly and completely communicated knowledge; the second is through love, or consciousness, or the giving of oneness to others. The third way of joining an effect to a cause is through choices and will that create God's purpose. Note that these three ways correspond to the three parts of God's mind, and that each is a means of experiencing time as a Now. The more of these three *ways* that are used to connect an effect to its cause, the greater the size, or unity, of experiencing time and the more complete the perspective. When one or more of these three ways connects an effect to a cause, the whole ("complete") time is called a Now because past, present, and future are experienced—Now. This occurs experientially, all together, for either just one lifeform that is separated from others or for lifeforms that have no time delay between or among them. The more thoroughly that effects are connected to causes, the greater the size of the Now. A completed Now of time (a completed Now exists for more than one lifeform at a time) in one or more of the above-described three ways exists from the intuitional plane, up; a Now exists on the atomic mental plane for individual lifeforms, but cannot be shared between or among lifeforms. Everywhere below the intuitional plane, however, time is too fractured to *completely* join an effect to a cause (for more than one lifeform at a time), even in just one of the three ways. This problem occurs because spirit can no longer perfectly think for others, itself, and energy. Below the atomic level of the mental plane, spirit becomes increasingly overwhelmed by the collective thought of unenlightened mental energy. This causes it to even sometimes think more like and to identify itself with the (dark elemental) energy than in light and as a spiritualizing part of life. Another way to understand this effect is that spirit anywhere below the atomic level of the mental plane cannot both think and sense in the same time. This condition exists because spirit can think only for energy and then for itself, or the reverse—it must think and sense in sequence. Thus spirit can lose itself as it causes time to fracture, in the process of descending into the mental and lower planes. As a result, spirit is no longer able to think in whole time, or to understand the cause of each effect, without a delay, or split, in time. Time is actually a dimensional part of space, caused by one of two conditions. The first is the separation of intelligent activity from light, and the second is energy being separated from the first two parts of God's mind, which are also in a state of separation—and which compose space.

Time as a dimensional part of space becomes unstable and mostly unrecognizable to life-forms below the atomic level of the mental plane because the experience, or sense, of whole time is lost as the Now becomes lost. The mental plane is the lowest plane whereupon cause and effect can even be fully recognized to exist; below the mental plane only partial—at best—effects can be related to causes. More about this fascinating subject of time and space will be covered later in this book, in Chapter Ten.

The Three Parts of Time—Creating a Mental Now and Disconnected

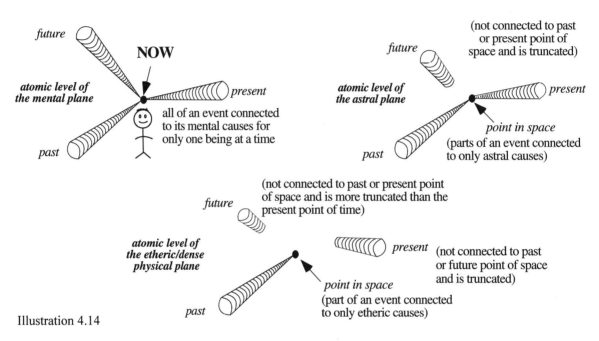

Illustration 4.14

Below the atomic level of the mental plane, spirit begins to lose its whole *individual* sense of time (its Now) and can lose significant parts of itself, which is tied closely to its whole sense of time. In the next chapter, what a self is will be thoroughly covered, along with how one is created from thought. For now, it is important to understand that spirit creates a self by maintaining a level of thought that can join an effect to a cause reasonably closely together in time *and* by giving this thought at least fifty percent of the time. This level of thought and the amount of it that is given enable spirit to know who it is relative to the enormous amounts of energy and other parts of spirit that it comes into contact with. It also enables spirit to know who others are. This state of closely, but not all at the same time, joining effects to causes in parts of fractured time (past, present, and future) is lost at about the mid-point of the mental plane. Once the loss occurs, spirit can no longer create a self from its thought because one or more parts of its time are either missing or imbalanced or both, and it loses itself in a sea of involutionary energy. Spirit that can *maintain* a connected self *on the mental* plane is referred to as a soul; spirit that maintains a self through creating a Now and is connected to a soul in order to gain sense of form is referred to as a (higher) Self—spelled with an uppercase "s." Spirit that loses its self because it descends below the approximate mid-point of the mental plane is sometimes referred to as fallen spirit (or lower spirit, entrapped spirit, or "darkened" spirit).

Spirit's Thought on the Mental Plane

The ratio of spirit to energy at the atomic level of the 1st sub-plane is 1:1.
Spirit can think for both itself and energy, but for only one lifeform at a time.

The Mental Plane

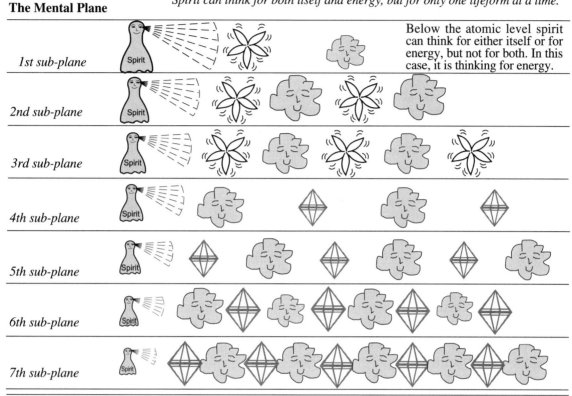

Spirit and energy are in a less than even ratio on the first sub-plane, but below the atomic level. Thus spirit can think for either itself or for energy, but not for both, because its thought is only sufficient for one or the other at any one time. As spirit becomes less enlightened it has less thought for either itself or to give to energy. At the same time, energy is becoming denser, and more thought is needed to enlighten it. Without spirit's enlightening thought, energy joins with other energy and begins to gravitate more and more, from its own selfish thought.

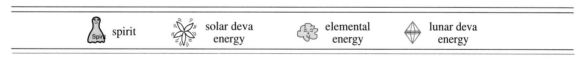

Illustration 4.15

INTERACTION OF THE DIFFERENT TYPES OF ENERGIES

There are three types of energy that have thus far been somewhat examined herein—primordial, deva, and elemental. Primordial energy is manifested from the separated (from light) third part of God's mind, or the part that is separated from God's thought of creating life to grow more of itself through choice/will/purpose/sacrifice joined with love/giving-ness/consciousness/oneness. *All* energy is manifested from the third part of God's mind, or intelligent activity; however, based upon differences in how this manifestation is achieved, the types of energy have different qualities, or rudimentary consciousness of their own. Primordial energy, or the energy manifested at the inception of our universe, comes into existence because when the Creator and the God chose that its mind be separated, its third part, or intelligent activity, was equally distributed throughout our entire universe (see Chapter Two for more details on this effect). Some primordial energy becomes relatively enlightened and is referred to as the pitris, or a lower class of deva energy when part of a spirit-informed form. Pitris are not fully self-aware, and the lowest ones (lunar pitris) have no individuality, and respond as a group.

Each of the seven cosmic Ray Lords begins with one-seventh of all of the intelligent activity in our universe (the third part of God's mind) within its dimension, or body. However, six-sevenths of each one-seventh of intelligent activities does not match the limitations of the particular Ray Lord (from the third through the seventh dimensions) whose thought is creating and developing its ray and plane. The reason is that God chose to *equally* distribute its mind throughout all parts of the universe, ignoring (wisely) the special ways that a cosmic Ray Lord may choose to focus, or not, on the third part of its (God's) mind. God's sacrifice to not focus on any intelligent activity left to the Ray Lords this choice of focus and ways of focusing. From the third cosmic Ray Lord, down, each focuses on only one-seventh of the original intelligent activities (the third part of God's mind) within its dimension. The remaining six-sevenths is then instantly manifested as separated energy, collectively into a point at the center of but at a point lower than the lowest, or seventh, sub-plane in the lowest dimension of our universe (but actually outside time and space). This point is created by the expelling forces of the Ray Lords not focusing their light, or thought, upon the six-sevenths of the intelligent activities within their respective dimensions, but still focusing on one-seventh. These forces are enormous and are instantly released. Then each of the energies that corresponds in its potential thought to the thought of one of the Ray Lords becomes instantly *attracted*, with great impetus, to become a part of its *corresponding* Ray Lord's dimension. These corresponding attracted primordial energies are attracted as sub-ray energies to each one of the seven sub-planes of the Ray Lord's dimensions that these energies are attracted to. First and second ray energies become sub-rays of the five lower Ray Lords as a result of the focused thought of the first and second Ray Lords *equally* on the five lower Ray Lords. Each lower cosmic Ray Lord can respond to the first and second Ray Lords progressively less because each one's light (thought) is progressively more limited. The result is that increasingly lesser levels of first and second sub-ray energies are attracted to the lower five planes.

The second cosmic Ray Lord chooses to mirror God's sacrifice, and to not focus on *any* of its intelligent activity, or the third part of God's mind, within its plane. This limitation permits this Ray Lord to create a dimension that has light everywhere there is life, and for its creation of life—the Monads—to think in only light. Much of its manifested energy becomes the elemental energies that are created by the Monads' sacrifice of their potential Selves. The Monads on the highest dimensions keep the intelligent activity separate from light in order to grow life in lower dimensions by interacting with a part of themSelves, which is this sacrificial thought on the lower planes, or is spirit. Some of the first and the second Ray Lords' energy becomes manifested as primordial energy; this energy is attracted to and distributed among all five of the lower Ray Lords' dimensions during the big bang because the first and second Ray Lords focus their respective rays into them. Because each of these two Ray Lords' rays compose one-half of light, their rays do not conflict with the lower five Ray Lords' rays whose thought always contains—albeit a more limited—light. Each dimension contains seven sub-rays, and the amount of the dimension's first and second sub-rays of energies determine the amount of first and second sub-ray energies that are attracted into that dimension. Stated another way, the amount of first and second ray energy that is attracted into a dimension during the big bang is determined by how well the Ray Lord of each dimension is able to think. This thought of the Ray Lords attracts a certain amount of first and second sub-ray energies of a Ray Lord's ray. These energies then affect both the rays of the first and second Ray Lords and how much of first- and second-rayed energies are initially attracted into the lower five Ray Lords' planes.

STARS, PLANETS, AND FIRST AND SECOND RAY ENERGIES

The first cosmic Ray Lord chooses to focus only on intelligent activities within its dimension that have been first fully joined with light. Thus no separated, or manifested, energy exists within its dimension, just as none exists on the second dimension, or the monadic plane. Intelligent activity exists on the enlightened part of the first plane, exclusively through the (eventual) complete perfection of spirit to energy, or through virtue having been completed on every plane. This perfection is accomplished by the ascended Monad. The first cosmic Ray Lord does manifest primordial energy, as does the second. In both cases, the amount and type of primordial energy are altered from that found in lower dimensions because at the inception of our universe the first two Ray Lords completely sacrifice their focus on intelligent activities within their dimensions. The second cosmic ray and the life it creates sacrifice their intelligent activities to create life (God's growth) in the lower dimensions that has increasingly greater diversity. The first cosmic Ray Lord's intelligent activities *within its dimension* creates life that is greater than its dimension and that leaves our universe, eventually having become its Creator within our universe. The primordial energy of these two Ray Lords does not return as energies to their respective dimensions because neither of these Ray Lords focuses on intelligent activities that are separated from light within their own dimensions; they focus on energy only outside their dimensions, through the sacrificial thought of the Monads within their dimensions. Much of this primordial energy joins together in the lower dimensions of our universe to create the first bodies of light. Collections of these initial energies as seen by humans in the etheric/dense physical dimension when *first* joined together are referred to as first-type, or first-stage, stars. The rays of the first two Ray Lords stimulate the responsive energies to create stars. Stars are the bodies, or forms, of the thought that is *beyond* our universe and is connected to it through the thought of Monads (which are a mirror of God's thought). Thus stars and the thought of Monads connect the God of our universe to other universes and the Creators of them. In brief, Monads connect our universe to other universes by becoming a field of potential for another universe while still in this one. There is a corresponding larger field of potential within the other universe, as well. Thus Monads act as the connecting life between our and another (greater) universe, allowing these universes to interact and grow together in various ways, but also greatly isolating them except within conditions that grow more of their Creators. The complexity of the interaction and connection of other universes to our own is too vast a subject to more comprehensively cover within this book, and would not significantly add to human understanding of life's hidden meaning. Further study in this area is being deferred until another time. For a listing of these other universes and connections without additional explanation, see Table 9.2.

The rays of the first two cosmic Ray Lords stimulate manifested energies that slightly think towards either of them, respectively, to grow *and* to further join together through creating light (they fuse) to create stars. These rays accomplish this by first balancing gravity on each of five planes and then transmuting the densities of the gravities and their creating energies into light. These energies that create stars are enlightened, and when they join together through the process of fusion, their collective light, which they give, becomes much greater than the sum of their individual amounts of light. Stars are the physical manifestation of God's light, or thought, and as such give off light. Stars create and stimulate the creation of life, and Monads are connected to stars because both are the beginnings of life (God's growth), or the joining of spirit with energy, and use the second ray approach of fusion. Fusion is the result of intense thought from the second part of God's mind (or from unconditional love, consciousness, and understanding—

The First and Second Rays Creating First and Second Sub-Ray Energy That Produces Fusion and Stars

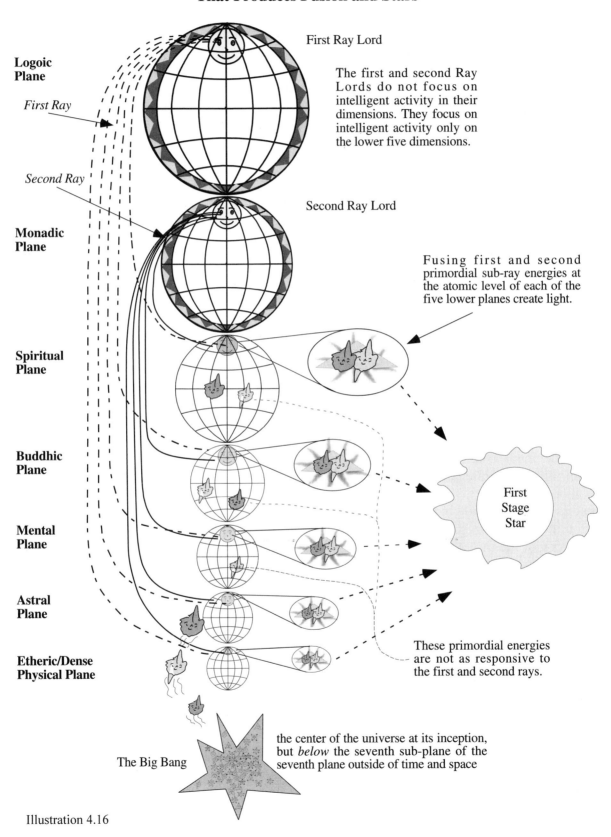

Logoic Plane

First Ray

Second Ray

Monadic Plane

Spiritual Plane

Buddhic Plane

Mental Plane

Astral Plane

Etheric/Dense Physical Plane

First Ray Lord

The first and second Ray Lords do not focus on intelligent activity in their dimensions. They focus on intelligent activity only on the lower five dimensions.

Second Ray Lord

Fusing first and second primordial sub-ray energies at the atomic level of each of the five lower planes create light.

First Stage Star

These primordial energies are not as responsive to the first and second rays.

The Big Bang

the center of the universe at its inception, but *below* the seventh sub-plane of the seventh plane outside of time and space

Illustration 4.16

which all lead to oneness), and is referred to as the second cosmic fire of creation. Through inclusiveness, fusion directs and brings together parts of spirit and energy that have previously been enlightened. The bringing together of these enlightened parts creates a light that is larger than the sum of the parts—through fusion. Stars provide diversity in the primordial energy created by the Ray Lords through fusing energies together. Stars are the bodies and the expression of thought of the God of our universe, of Monads, and of Beings outside our universe—joining our universe with other universes as a means of growing Creators of universes. Stars transmute certain types of hydrogen (a first ray element) into helium (a second ray element). Eventually helium and other transmuted elements are transmuted into oxygen (a third ray element). Then oxygen becomes transmuted into all the elements—up to iron—in the periodic table. These elements are along any one of the seven ray types. Then fission is added to fusion, for the creation of the remaining elements. The fission usually takes place either within a star or within the inside of some planets.

The Monads connected to a star progress through a development of growing life on planets in amounts that are consistent with the amounts of life that exist within some of the lower five Ray Lords' dimensions that surround those planets. Eventually each Monad experiences the dimensions by growing life in them on a planet of its associated star. Some of these planets do *not* exist in the etheric/dense physical plane at all, which means that none of the energy of which they are composed is from the dimension where physically alive humans live. In our universe, all the planets exist on several (usually three, juxtaposed) of the five lower dimensions at any one time. The Monads who are developing life on these planets then experience growing life (more of God) that develops both sense and thought connected to a sense (to form) within these dimensions that are lower than their own (the monadic). The Monads exist in a higher dimension than do the life and the spirit that, as a part of them, are separated from them by a different time and space. Ascended Monads exist on "planets" within our universe (though not what humans would recognize to be planets) wherein form exists on only the spiritual (the third) plane, and only light exists on the two highest planes. These planets of creative light, are, as is any planet not manifested in etheric/dense physical energy (energy of the seventh plane), invisible to physically alive humans—who lack the senses that are necessary to see these other dimensions.

Planets are the places where spirit and energy can interact to create life, or God's growth. They exist as a part of a star's system of life creation, and both a planet and a star are a part of God's plan to create life in seven dimensions of time and space. The spirit, or the sacrificially limited and focused thought of Monads, joins with energy and attempts to increase the very slight thought of energy. The spirit does this while the energy that can think the best and at a sufficient level supplies to itself and to spirit a sense of other energy. The thought of spirit supplies energy with a sense of spirit and eventually a sense of God. Because there are five manifested forms of energy that are *separated* from both intelligent activity and any completed part of light, there are five types of sense composed of a sub-ray type of energy that can sense other energies. Each developed sense of a ray type of energy mostly recognizes energies of like kind. Life that contains all five senses on each plane where it exists can be fully aware of the forms of other life on that dimension. The more senses a lifeform has and the more dimensions these senses exist on, the greater its awareness of other lifeforms. Spirit gives life the sense of other spirit and eventually of God through its capacity of thought used through first and second (sub-) ray senses on each of the dimensions where the lifeform lives. The more dimensions within which a lifeform can think through its spirit's thought, the better it can recognize and understand the thought of other spirit. Eventually, when spirit can recognize and understand enough of other spirit's thought, it can recognize and understand the thought of God, or light, because all spirit has some light within it. Then the spirit can choose to participate within the creation of more of God's thought in form, or of creating more virtue.

Humans are the first and lowest type of life that has all five senses of energy (form) on the three lowest dimensions of our universe (the etheric/dense physical, the astral, and the mental—both lower and higher). Also, within their individual lifeforms, humans have *both* capacities of spirit's thought on each of these dimensions. These two capacities are understanding the thought and sense of other spirit and of God, and the creation of more of God. The lower capacity is the recognition and understanding of other spirit and, eventually, of God. The higher capacity is the creation of more of spirit's thought of light in form, and therefore more of God, by *creating* more virtue within its life (within the human's own life as well as within other life it comes into contact with). First and second ray energies create in a human only the senses that direct the thought of and sense of spirit in each body towards other bodies that have spirit informing them. Thus humans have a total of seven senses (five of form and two of spirit), which allows them to eventually *fully* sense both the form of the three worlds, or dimensions, they can live within *and* the thought and sense of other spirit as well as the thought of God. The full sense of spirit and of God can be realized only as a human creates *more* of spiritual thought and of God by creating more virtue in herself or himself *and* in others. This spiritual thought then further develops the two spiritual senses in each body. The meaning of life for a human grows as more senses of energy are used to increase awareness, and as the two capacities of spiritual thought are used to sense more of spiritual thought and of God's thought, or light. This is accomplished by the human creating and giving more light in her or his form and the forms of others—simultaneously. When the spiritual senses are used through corresponding first or second ray energies, fusion is created—as it is in stars—that unifies the senses while it creates more light than the sum of the light that was originally within them. As the spiritual capacities of thought are *used*, they create more of the spiritual senses—the use of which grows consciousness. What happens is that with the use of these senses, the sense of oneness between one part of life and another continually increases. Thus as consciousness (the ability to recognize, understand, and participate in the oneness of life) grows, so does the sense and then the meaning of life.

 ## FURTHER EXPLANATION OF PRIMORDIAL ENERGY

There exist increasingly greater amounts of primordial energy from the third plane, down, because each lower cosmic Ray Lord is less capable of completely focusing its God-like thought on all of the third part of God's mind, or all of the intelligent activity, that is present. Whatever part of God-like thought the cosmic Ray Lord can focus on completely without additional focus from spirit and the life created on Its plane is usually at the atomic level, or the very top, of its sphere because this is the point at which its thought is the most focused. Starting with the seventh plane, each higher Ray Lord has an added element, or dimension, to its time and space. The added dimensions are created from each Ray Lord's thought of growing more of God (of life) through virtue (the Ray Lord's particular light in form). A higher Ray Lord's better capacity to think creates a larger and more complex dimension of time and space—and a larger part of life. The atomic level, or very top, of a Ray Lord's sphere is the most representative of that particular dimensional light, or that Ray Lord's thought. It is also the point in thought, or light, that is the most like the *next higher* Ray Lord's dimension, or plane, even though it is considerably different. The lower parts of a dimension are different from its higher parts. The differences exist because the further away from the atomic level, the less intelligent activity, or the third part of God's mind, that is focused on (fully enlightened). The lack of focus causes the primordial energy to remain manifested and to not return to the state of intelligent activity, or to activity that enlightens itself and other energy, completely joining the space between them into light. Increasing amounts of primordial energy are manifested as this energy moves lower *within* each dimension, and more primordial energy is present on each lower dimension, as well.

What follows is a further examination of how primordial energy is created in different dimensions, or planes, of life creation. At the beginning of our universe God chose to separate the three parts of its mind, equally dispersing them throughout the universe. Each Ray Lord from the third, down, eventually had one-seventh of the third part of God's mind—of intelligent activity, or activity that produced only more light within whatever action took place. Also as part of God's plan, which the Ray Lords chose to cooperate with, six-sevenths of the potential intelligent activity was not focused on at all. The one–forty-ninth of intelligent activity (one-seventh of one-seventh) that stayed in each of the five lower Ray Lords' dimensions remained initially as intelligent activity at the atomic level of that plane. Depending upon the dimension, even some of the beginning intelligent activity eventually manifests as energy within the lower parts of a Ray Lord's plane because of the Ray Lords' differing abilities to think. In the case of the first two Ray Lords, one-half of one-seventh of intelligent activity was expelled and converted into primordial energies, and some of it, as it returned as deva, or evolutionary, energy, was eventually fused into stars at the atomic levels of the five lower dimensions. Most of the potential intelligent activity in each dimension was not focused on by the Ray Lord of that dimension, and therefore did not stay enlightened. In each dimension, this intelligent activity converted into six ray types of energy that the Ray Lord of that dimension did not focus on. The lack of focus caused the expulsion of the six-sevenths of the potential intelligent activity from each of the five Ray Lords, which resulted in the immediate and *total* separation of this six-sevenths of it from their thought, light, and dimensions. Then, instantly, because this potential intelligent activity was no longer part of a field (of light, which would have kept it intelligent), it converted into manifested energy. The energy had no space between any parts of itself, at a concentrated point "below" the lowest plane outside of time and space until it rejoined the etheric/dense physical dimension in the center of the lowest sub-plane of our universe. This point is the place of energy's maximum separation from space, or from the two (separated) parts of God's thought.

The Big Bang

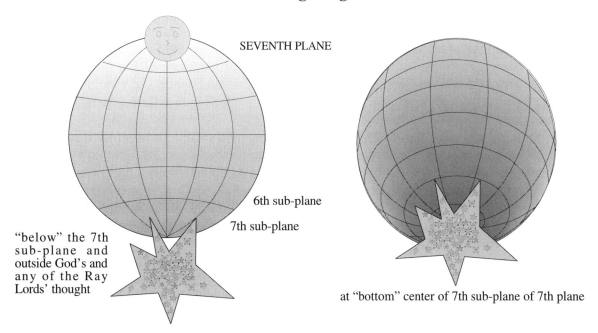

The big bang occurred outside time and space, which is the same as stating that it occurred outside God's and the Ray Lords' thought, "below" the seventh sub-plane.

Illustration 4.17

The second Ray Lord chooses to focus its light on *no* intelligent activity within its own dimension of time and space; the life it creates, of Monads, makes the same choice on this plane. Technically, the second Ray Lord does focus its *split* thought, or space, on intelligent activity, which both reflects thought *through light* and separates the intelligent activity *by space*. Below the second (the monadic) plane, the second Ray Lord through the thought of the Monads present in its dimension does focus on energy that is responsive to its ray, and spirit focuses on amounts of intelligent activity that correspond to its thought. The first Ray Lord focuses its thought (light) in its dimension on intelligent activity only if it is perfectly fused with its light. This perfect fusion is an ascended Monad, which is the only part of life that can exist within this dimension. Like the second Ray Lord, the first separates intelligent activity from its light, or whole thought, with the separation of this thought into space. Below the first plane the first Ray Lord's cosmic ray is focused on energy that is responsive to its ray; it does so through the thought of the Monads that are present in its dimension. When these two Ray Lords' rays help to grow energies that think along their respective rays, the energies sometimes fuse together. They do so because of the similarity of what they do *not* focus on within their Ray Lords' dimensions. Another reason is that they are both one-half of light, and they often eventually create a first-type, or beginning star. These "young" stars comprise energies that are responsive to the first and second rays (i.e., types of hydrogen, and then helium as a transmuted result), and come from all of the dimensions in our universe below the monadic (from the third through the seventh), connected together through one enormous consciousness that exists outside our universe.

When the fusion of energy takes place on the fifth, or mental, plane these energies become restructured, or transfigured, back into intelligent activity as the space between them is converted back into light. They then give light and energy to other energy and its forms that surround them (certain planets, for example). When one type of energy is changed into another it becomes *transmuted* because of changes in density (the measure of space between one part of energy and another); when the changes in density within a lifeform cause a change in the quality, or consciousness, of the life, then the lifeform becomes *transformed*. When all of the amount of one or more types of energy is converted by light into only intelligent activity (and some of this occurs on the mental plane through structure), thus *eliminating* the space (darkness) within, then the energy and the form it inhabits become *transfigured* (by the light). This is caused by time becoming fully connected to space in at least one of the three ways for one individual lifeform at a time—creating a Now. When time and space and God's mind are fully joined and grown, with all energy converted back into intelligent activity, then the completed Being has *transcended* our universe.

After the big bang, the manifested energies created by the first and second Ray Lords non-focusing on intelligent activity at first manifested on the first and second sub-planes of the space of each corresponding dimension. A significant portion of these first and second ray primordial energies eventually become stars. On the first and second planes is a reversal of what occurs on the third through seventh in the creation of primordial energy. Because neither the first nor second Ray Lord focuses its light on any intelligent activity within its dimension after the beginning of our universe, only the intelligent activities that are both responsive to and are correspondences of the first and second rays are expelled from the first two dimensions (these equal about half of either type per plane), respectively. This happened because the Ray Lords there are focusing their rays into the five lowest dimensions through the Monads that are present in their respective dimensions. These expelled intelligent activities become primordial energies after the big bang. The *remaining* five-sevenths of intelligent activity plus about one-half of the first or second ray type of intelligent activity remain on the first two planes. On the first, or logoic, plane this remaining intelligent activity eventually becomes a part of ascended Monads who have completed their journey of life in the lower parts of our universe. On the second, or monadic, plane the remaining intelligent activity is eventually used to create elemental energy on the lower planes; this elemental energy becomes informed by spirit. Some transmutation of primordial energies (before and outside of stars) occurred at the beginning of our universe, changing the density and ray focus of some energies as a result of the altering effects of the third ray having two expressions. Its first expression is through communication and intelligent activity, and its second is through power, or transmutation of energy. The majority of transmutation of energy in our universe still occurs within stars through the concurrent thought of the Monads, or spirit, expressing themselves through a particular star. Our Cosmic Physical Universe may go through one hundred cycles of the entire above-described process, if certain spiritual texts are correct. Whether there is one cycle or more than one does not alter the eventual outcome. At the "end" of our universe, God's mind has grown by the sum of all of its lifeforms' growth, and each fully enlightened lifeform has eventually become a transcended Monad. The God of our universe then can create a Cosmic Astral Universe. (See Chapter Nine for further explanation of this process.) *All* life would have transcended into the next or a higher universe.

The spirit of the Monads that is expressing (focusing) its thought through some stars creates elemental energy within the center of the star by not being able to create *only* intelligent activity, or light, within the star. Instead of only light, the star creates manifested energies (and heat) that come from some of the intelligent activities that are not being focused on by the second Ray Lord on the monadic plane. These energies are transmuted into various types of *elements*, or diversified and basic energies. Beginning, or first-stage, stars are originally created from primordial energy. However, because the Monad's thought as spirit is imperfect in creating light, as this spirit expresses its thought through a star and in some cases, on that star's developing planets, the star manifests elemental energies that are transmuted (changed in densities) into a large number of elements to be used in the future creation of lifeforms. Spirit will then attempt to enlighten these elements.

EFFECTS OF SPIRIT'S THOUGHT ON
TIME AND SPACE IN THE LOWER DIMENSIONS

On the seventh plane, or the etheric/dense physical dimension, elemental energy reaches its densest state; in the dense physical part of the dimension, the energy changes into matter. The energy on the seventh plane is also at its highest resistance to change because of its resistance to following the thought of spirit, as a result of gravity and its effect on density, or inertia. The seventh plane on earth is the dimension where humans live while physically alive, and its sub-parts are split into two sections. The first section comprises four etheric, or causative, sub-parts (sub-planes), and the second is made up of three dense physical sub-planes, where the effects from the etheric sub-planes manifest in matter. The reason for the split in the space is a result of the previously explained split, or fracture, in time. Because time is a dimensional part of space, as time splits—so does space. Note that all seven planes, whether split or not, contain seven sub-planes, in correspondence to the seven cosmic Ray Lords' rays. The other, and highest, dimension on earth where space splits is the mental, or manasic (the fifth), plane, where spirit can no longer connect most effects to causes. On this plane the split occurs at the third sub-plane (from the top, or atomic level, of the sphere) because at this point there are somewhat more effects than causes. The greater levels of effects as compared to causes are a result of the lower levels of illusion within spirit and the much lower density and amounts of mental elemental energy, as compared to the spirit and energy that exist on the seventh plane. On the etheric and dense physical sub-planes, there are somewhat more causes than effects because of the increased levels of illusion within spirit, and the very high densities of corresponding elemental energy and its resistance against creating effects. This resistance is what is a part of inertia. Mentally, spirit experiences time (and space) as an effect of thought because it senses time as more effects than causes. But on the etheric/dense physical plane, when spirit physically focuses on effects from this dimension—and especially when spirit is within physically alive humans—it senses time (and space) as *a cause of thought*...a great illusion. Spirit on the seventh plane senses time (and space) more as the cause of everything. Neither the mental nor etheric/dense physical senses of time are correct, but the etheric/dense physical sense of time and space distorts reality considerably more, creating even greater levels of illusion.

Illusion is the condition of spirit being unable to control energy enough through its thought to accurately sense through its body, or form; it also is caused by spirit losing its sense of other spirit and of God. Illusion is caused by spirit having too little light, or God's thought, within its thought, as a result of choices that it has made to be selfish. *Self*-ishness is a condition in which the spirit within a self (or something connected to a self) thinks for itself rather than for other spirit and/or energy. Being selfish causes the self to shrink, because a self is created through its giving instead of taking. Selfishness is caused by the spirit in the self mistakenly identifying itself with darker form, or with involutionary types of energy. The less light (God's thought) that is within spirit, the less that the energy is attracted to and will follow spirit's thought because spirit's dark thought in its field of potential (which is attracting the energies to become a sense) is so small that it fails to attract the better-thinking energies. Also, when spirit's thought becomes dark, even the better-thinking energies that formerly made up a sense will no longer be attracted to this thought. As a result, those energies that think higher than the dark spirit will leave, causing the sense to decline because the highest-thinking energies that are then attracted to become the sense are, themselves, dark. At this point, all that exists within a sense is that which is most inaccurate, from the darker of energies. The sense itself becomes less capable of informing spirit because it becomes increasingly composed of lower types of and darker-thinking energies. These darker energies can still think and give whatever information they attract, but in diminished amounts and with less accuracy. More will be covered about sense and bodies later in this book, in Chapter Seven.

If spirit thinks with enough light it can join effects to causes, reducing the splits in the planes that are a result of fractured and confused time on those planes. Thinking in this much light can eventually unify spirit's corresponding body, and as many humans unify their bodies, they can eventually unify the plane. Such unification does exist on one plane, the astral—where it was completed a very long time ago. The knowledge of this occurrence and of the people or civilization who accomplished it are hidden. Modern science has yet to realize the existence of these people. The reason is that its evolutionary model thus far usually includes neither spirit nor the *degeneration* of species, particularly humans, as a result of spiritual losses of light in thought. Since senses and bodies can decline when selfish thought replaces light, if this occurs on a broad scale among an entire civilization of people, the people also can decline. They then become what appears to the less enlightened to be beginnings of (!) rather than degenerations of humanity. This type of confusion can lead to grossly inaccurate conclusions about human origins.

Energy follows thought, provided that the thought is greater than the collective thought of unenlightened energy within that plane and is along the energy's ray type, or its general way of very slightly thinking as the energy is found within the body of the spirit's lifeform. When spirit's thought falls below this level, gravity controls and some spirit becomes a puppet of energy. Time fractures and further separates (from) space, producing more illusion. All of this is caused by spirit's inability to accurately think through inaccurate sense(s). Eventually spirit needs to think in enough light to change the very resistant elemental energy into enlightened energy. This process can be started by spirit choosing to limit itself so that it can think better, with more light; the self-limitation is referred to as spiritual discipline. In the process, spirit uses its thought to regulate the sense to focus on energy (or bring in energy that becomes information) that is

A Comparison of Virtuous and Non-Virtuous Use of Energy in the Centers

I refuse to quit enjoying myself just because I'm pregnant

Etheric/Dense Physical Centers

inner stationary spirit sphere

etheric/dense physical solar plexus center
top of energy sphere = 170°
top of spirit sphere = 20°

energy sphere is rotating clockwise

energy sphere is rotating clockwise

beer

It's more important for my baby to have a healthy chance in life than it is for me to consume whatever I want.

inner rotating spirit sphere

etheric/dense physical heart center
top of energy sphere = 153°
top of spirit sphere = 28°

Selfishness causes darker energy to enter the energy sphere of a center. The reason is that spiritual thought in the center is less than the consciousness of the energy itself. The center retains the energy (the body ages), and the person's sense associated with that center diminishes.

When someone is virtuous, enlightened energy moves into the spiritual sphere of a center and then into the energy sphere.

The elementals, the lunar pitris, and the energy sphere all become more enlightened because they are following the thought of the previously fallen spirit within the spirit sphere that is following the thought of the virtuous self.

◇ *Lunar pitri* ◊ *enlightened lunar pitri* *elemental energy*

The solar plexus center of the fetus is damaged when the mother is selfish from her solar plexus center. Not only do the etheric/dense physical centers of both the mother and the fetus become damaged, but their astral and mental solar plexus centers may be damaged as well.

The heart center of the fetus grows when the mother is giving from her heart center. The fetus then grows a greater sense of love and of understanding God's thought, or virtue.

Illustration 4.18

enlightening. Then spirit uses its thought to change the enlightened information into enlightened knowledge. When the enlightened knowledge is given to its senses and those of others, it creates more light, or virtue within the senses. It does so because the first two parts of God's mind are being further joined with the third part; the *choice* to *give* the *knowledge* (all three parts of God's mind represented) creates virtue. The etheric/dense physical dimension is where this battle for God (light) is mostly fought, with, on earth today, spirit losing much more often than winning. To a much lesser extent the battle is also fought on the astral and mental planes, because although less dense, the elemental energy still overwhelms spirit's thought there, which remains illusioned (lacking in light).

Spirit does manage to enlighten some amount of etheric/dense physical elemental energy; these affected energies become evolutionary, or devonic, and reverse their direction from seeking increased density and no cooperation and sharing with spirit, to seeking to join with, to cooperate with, and to share themselves with spirit. As the elemental energy is enlightened it becomes deva, or angelic, energy (becomes God-like in thought—which is light). It then reverses its direction, or focus, changing itself into evolutionary energy. There are two types of deva energy as parts of the pitri class of energy. Any deva energy that needs the informing thought of spirit to keep it thinking in light is referred to as *lunar* deva energy. The word lunar is used because it means moon-like, or has the quality of a moon, which only *reflects* light— the light of spirit—rather than creating any of God's thought, or light, itself. Eventually lunar deva, or lunar pitri, energy becomes enlightened enough to *create* some light on its own, and no longer completely needs informing spirit to help it totally do so through reflection of spirit's thought. These deva energies that create some of their own light are referred to as *solar* devas and comprise the solar pitris, named after our sun (Sol)—a star—which creates its own light.

Of the two types, *only lunar* pitri energy exists on earth's etheric/dense physical, astral, and four lowest mental sub-planes. The reason is that spirit at these levels on earth at present has too little light to consistently enlighten energy enough so that it can create God's thought on its own. On the higher mental sub-planes (the third, second, and first), a higher spirit can and an OverSoul does think in enough light to somewhat enlighten the devas, or pitris, there. Many humans on earth sometimes further enlighten them because these energies are more advanced and are thus the easiest to enlighten; once these solar pitris are enlightened, they can eventually become radiant, or creators of light completely on their own. Notice that not only is spirit better at enlightening energy above the fourth mental sub-plane, but other conditions such as closer proximity to the mental Ray Lord's thought on the mental atomic level, as well as the deva energies themselves advancing progressively, all lead to the solar effect. No lunar pitri energy exists from the third mental sub-plane, up. The solar pitri energies dominate the elemental energies that also exist on these higher dimensions, helping spirit to better control them, and building much better senses and forms (of concepts).

The bodies and senses of lifeforms are composed of both elemental energy and deva energy (lunar or solar, or both). Lunar deva energy, or lunar pitris, can be overwhelmed by the denser elemental energies from the lower mental plane, down, similar to the way spirit is and in part resultant of the failure of spirit to think in light. Solar deva energies, or solar pitris, are generally in control of elemental energy, except when they (the solar deva energies) are separated and damaged by spirit's overly selfish thought. Anywhere below the atomic level of the mental plane, solar deva energy can control elemental energy only if they both exist on the same plane, sub-plane, and sub-sub-plane. The reason is that below the atomic level, the time is fractured (and space is separated)—increasingly so, into very small and discrete parts. On the intuitional, or buddhic, plane, spirit in cooperation with solar deva energy can collectively affect all elemental energy on the plane at once, in only one of the three possible ways that the energy can be enlightened in givingness, or consciousness. This one way is through applied intelligence for all of the energy, or through all-knowledge (omniscience), in a lifeform. From the elemental and controlling solar deva energy, this builds the sense of omniscience in intuitional plane lifeforms. On the intuitional and spiritual planes, solar devas go on collectively to become a part of the great spiritual Beings of completely spiritualized and enlightened energies. The various names of these types of Beings are the Spirits of or Angels of the Presence, the OverSouls, or the Solar Angels, and they are sometimes thought of in some religions as the Guardian Angels.

SUMMARY OF INFORMATION
IN CHAPTER FOUR

What follows is a summary of the information presented herein about spirit and energy and how they affect the hidden meaning of life, with these two parts of life in a continual interplay together of wonderful and complex ways of growing God. Every Monad experiences the lower realms through its spirit at a duration of life creation that varies according to the thought of the Ray Lord of each plane lower than its own (the monadic). This system provides the Monad with a unique experience in becoming immersed in the manifestation of the third part of God's mind, or the manifestation of energy from a pre-enlightened state—before the energy's return to fully intelligent activities. Each Monad eventually contributes all that it has created in intelligent activities, as these become fused in light and it ascends to and through the logoic, or divine, plane (the first, or uppermost, of our universe). The spirit of Monads is the great traveler, or pilgrim, on a journey that in human terms and for the spirit that informs humans spans many hundreds of lifetimes. God is grown by spirit enlightening energy, with the elemental energy in the lower realms providing the greatest challenge for spirit to enlighten and, concurrently, to grow the most that it can of God. As God's growth increases, so does the meaning to its growth, or to life. Spirit has the capability of growing the most of God by choosing to think in light instead of becoming overwhelmed by energy. This energy's dark thought of gravitating towards more of energy that is like "itself" in the thought to become bigger causes the spirit that follows its thought to become "selfish." Because more of God is grown as more energy is converted back into intelligent activity, the meaning of life is increased the most for spirit that can remain enlightened and enlightening while focused in thought on the seventh plane (the etheric/dense physical). It is while humans are physically alive that the greatest amount of meaning can be created in their lives, by growing more of God, or of life, through the highest amount of senses, or energies, by creating more virtue, or light in form (in themselves and in others), while alive in this most difficult dimension.

Unfortunately, for too many people an understanding of the principles explained above is often not developed until after death from the seventh plane, and while focused in life on the sixth plane (the astral), or even later, on the fifth plane (the mental). Once on these higher planes, where it is much less difficult to think and live, much less of God can be created and some of life's meaning is thus lost. The next chapter holds an explanation of how a self is created and what a self does for spirit—it helps spirit to overcome its problems of enlightening energy—and how a self relates to the creation of souls. Then much more will be explained about souls in Chapter Six. Souls' critical function as the last vestiges of a part of spirit that contains enough light to consistently enlighten all of energy within itself to the same level the spirit is enlightened will be somewhat explained. How souls unify God's mind while growing more of God will more fully reveal the role of spirit and energy. It is in these and later chapters that many readers will gain a significant increase in their understanding of the hidden meaning of life.

GIVING THOUGHT—THE MODE OF SELF CREATION

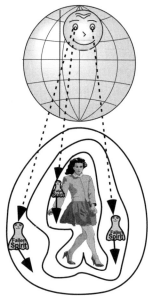
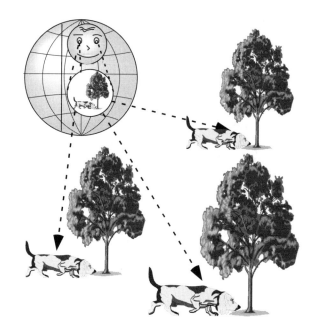

Illustration 5.1

Author's Suggestion: First turn to the "Glossary Help Guide" and read the definitions for this chapter.

 ## BASIC INFORMATION ABOUT THOUGHT AND SELVES

The way that life is created by spirit informing form, or energy, to grow more of God in our universe was described in the previous chapter. The fourth chapter examined how spirit is created, along with the several ways of creating different types of energy. These energies are created based upon both ray focus and the energy's consciousness and amount of enlightenment. A great saga was recounted about how spirit helps to create elemental energy. Spirit uses elemental energy and other types of energy in order to become informed about other energy through senses and awareness, while synthesizing this information into knowledge. If spirit then intelligently gives the knowledge to both its form and other form, as well as to other spirit, all of the forms involved gain in light. As spirit enlightens forms, or energy, it also enlightens itself and moves closer to becoming its Creator, or God. The entire process of spirit descending into increasingly dense form in our universe in order to create more intelligent knowledge, consciousness/love/understanding, and choices with God's purpose takes place in order to grow more of life, or more of God. A part of life's meaning is for humans to be able to fully consciously help spirit to enlighten form, and for humans to then grow more of themselves into a functional part of God through this process.

In the previous chapter the concept of illusion was also briefly touched upon. One particular way in which illusion is created is through time first becoming separated from space, and then becoming further fractured. Possibly the greatest illusion of time and the greatest difficulty for spirit to correctly sense time occur on the etheric/dense physical plane, where humans live while physically alive. On this plane, instead of understanding that thought is a series of (at least two) choices that are connected by their similar direction and can limit the field they exist within, nearly everyone experiences thought as a product of time versus choices (or the results of choices that concern movement). Sometimes people experience time as a product of "decisions," because gravity and inertia so greatly overpower thought. From this faulty perspective, thought becomes indefinable, since it appears to "take" time to think. This perspective lacks the truth that the separating of God's thought *creates* a loss of time (and produces space). Thought is hampered by, or "uses," time when it (time) is separated from space by the manifestation of energy that is not rejoining into intelligent activity. In order to experience time correctly and then to correctly understand thought, time needs to be joined into a Now as a part of God's thought (the experience of past, present, and future together at the same time)—in at least one of three ways. A being who is thinking in this way is provided with an opportunity to fully join effects to causes. When effects are joined to causes, it no longer takes time to think. The illusion that it does take time to think becomes eliminated as spirit joins first with energy and eventually with other spirit, starting at the atomic level of the mental plane. Time is completed into a Now for more than one being at a time in one way, from the bottom of the intuitional plane, up.

Another illusion is that a self is necessary in order for thought to be created, i.e., that there must be a thinker of the thought. This illusion seems perfectly reasonable to humans, and particularly to those who are physically alive. "Thoughts 'must' come from someone thinking" is the generally accepted belief. The idea that thoughts can be created by some possibilities becoming more probable than other possibilities seems, perhaps, too mechanical and lacking in the specialness that life has. The reason for these assumptions is that they are, in our universe, for the most part accurate! Since God chose that life would have all three parts of Its mind within it, thought and life are intimately tied together. Thus, in our universe, thought and the creation and growth of life are a part of the whole, or of God. But outside our universe thought is different because it exists before life, or God's growth, does. Thought in its most basic and definable condition is two or more choices that are connected in a similar direction that can further limit the field they occur within—by causing additional choices to be similarly connected into thoughts.

The question arises as to whether anyone could create a random generator of choices, *within our universe*, that could produce fields of probability that generate thought that is great enough to either destroy or create life. The answer is no. The reason this cannot be done has to do with the condition that everyone already exists within such a very large field of life (of God, Ray Lords, Monads, spirit, etc.), which was created in accord with God's thought. Therefore, any new method of creating a field of life, or a way of creating life other than spirit informing energy, would necessarily be created in a direction that is in opposition to God's thought. No thought within God's field is great enough to alter God's thought of how life is to be created through spirit informing energy and then creating a lifeform. Any thought that might attempt to circumvent God's system, or plan, for life creation would create a field of potential life creation that would collapse as soon as the thought within it was created. The reason this new field would collapse is that it would have no connection to the *larger field of life* that it was already a part of and would be in opposition to. The new field would therefore be unable to limit its existing field of life. As an example of this concept, evil cannot create new types of fields of life, but can only limit and/or slow the growth of life by changing both the relationship, or ratio, of spirit to energy and the energy's density (however, to do so, evil still must use spirit and energy). In order to become thought, the two or more choices that are connected in a similar direction *must* have the capability of eventually limiting the field it is focused in, which alters the probability of the field. In our universe, only life can generate thought *within a field of life*, because God already chose (thought) this to be the case in its direction, or plan, for that field. People are not capable of limiting God's thought and field of life on their own, which leaves them unable to generate thought that does so through their own inventions. As an example, for computers to actually think as a living being does—and not mimic the programmers' preconceived thought (their programs)—the computers would need to become spiritualized (joined with spirit and become a lifeform), and therefore become alive. Notice that random "thoughts" of a computer that do not limit the field of thought, are not, by definition, thought, but are only non-directed choices *without purpose*. An example of a living computer that would exist in contradistinction to the above-described concepts would be a computer that both started and ran with *no* programs—or "operating system." This computer would think for itself; however, without being informed by spirit, such a computer cannot exist in our universe.

The next section that covers what a self is holds the key to understanding this entire chapter. Before progressively more intricate understandings about the self can be realized, it is necessary to have, as a foundation, a clear grasp of what a self is and how one is created. The abstract nature of concepts regarding a self is likely to be difficult for many people to understand. For this reason, a relatively slower pace shall be maintained in the building of these concepts, and there will be repetition, from different viewpoints, of each constructed concept.

 ## THE HUMAN LOWER SELF AND HIGHER SELF

In the second chapter of *Life's Hidden Meaning* it was explained that when the thought within what began as an unlimited field of possibilities was in a similar direction and was great enough to dynamically create a new limited field and to potentially limit at least half of that field, a Director of the field was created. The ability to choose and direct over half of such an enormous field established a high probability that a Creator would emerge of one or more new fields, or would enter a state of Creative Beingness. This creation existed outside, and even before, our universe did. As was discussed in the previous two chapters, *limited* fields of life within our universe are being created by God, by the cosmic Ray Lords, by Monads, and by spirit and energy; note that spirit and energy must cooperate together in order to create their field of life. Each succeeding field of life created by any of these four creators is more limited than is the preceding creator's field. Each one of these four creators, in order to create a new (smaller) field of life, needs to create enough choices that are connected in a similar direction. Also, the connected choices need to in some way limit the prior creator's limited field of life as well as the new field that is created. The point in this explanation has now been reached at which what a self is needs to be addressed.

A (lower) self (spelled with a lowercase "s") is, in some lesser ways, somewhat like the Creator of our universe, though a much lower correspondence. The very significant and main difference between a self and the Creator is the size and type of the field of possibilities that each is created from. The Creator originally comes from an enormous unlimited field of possibilities (which is then created into the *potential* for a new universe—ours). The self is created from a relatively small and limited field of life. This field of life is a probability, or likelihood, of development of a different part of life from the existing thought within the field. The probability is that this thought will become part of one or more specific kinds of lifeforms. As was described in the previous chapter, a self develops from the field of life created by spirit and energy. This field is already quite limited by the limitations of the collective thought of spirit and energy that makes up the field. When the thought within the limited field of life as created by spirit and energy is adequate to limit at least half of the entire field through giving this thought to the lifeforms it is helping to create, a self is created. A part of the direction of the self's field comes from the field all *being given* to an individual lifeform or to one group of lifeforms. In addition, thought that is all in a similar direction and is large enough to eventually in some ways limit the entire field of life created by spirit and energy does so by increasing the probability that one or more certain types of lifeforms will develop therein. As one or more lifeforms are created, the thought within the new field (which makes up, at a minimum, over half of the field) is given to the new lifeform(s). The giving of this much thought to the same one or more lifeforms within the same field creates a new consciousness. The new consciousness, or oneness, is a part of the lifeform(s) and connects the new consciousness to its higher, larger field of life that it is a part of. The first new part of these new one or more lifeforms is a self. What will be explained next is what a self does, what is special about a self, and why and how a self is different from the limited field of life previously created by spirit and energy.

Individual and Group Soul Selves and Their Not-Selves

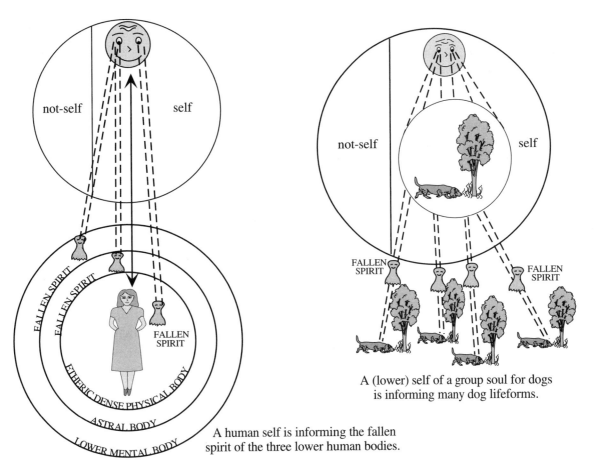

A human self is informing the fallen spirit of the three lower human bodies.

A (lower) self of a group soul for dogs is informing many dog lifeforms.

Illustration 5.2

Once at least half of the thought within the limited field of probable outcomes could eventually limit the *entire* field in certain ways and creates a certain type of lifeform (of its choosing), the thought can identify with the entire field. Put another way, the thought knows that it can eventually limit the *entire* field through choices, will, or purpose, so the thought and the field are connected together in the way(s) that the thought that is thinking in the field can eventually limit the field completely. The identity of the thought with the *entire* field that has certain probable outcomes for the life can occur only where there is a majority of thought in a similar direction, or more consciousness/understanding than not. The reason is that as the choices and similar direction build a larger and larger thought, the probability for certain outcomes from activities of life continually increases (and then further limits the eventual possibilities of the field). The common direction of the choices builds consciousness by creating more oneness to the choices and their increasing probabilities of some action of life over other actions. Action is the result of the direction of choices manifesting in form as an activity in the separated thought of God, or in space. When the oneness of the choices from their similar direction is equal to over half of the random possibilities within the field of life and when this new consciousness changes the actions of the lifeform(s) it is connected to, a new consciousness of self is created— which is also a new part of life. The critical point of exceeding more than half of the field of life whose choices are connected by their similar direction, or by similar thought, results in the *entire* field then having a probability rather than just a possibility that a specific type of life will be created *based upon the unified but limited consciousness within the field*. The unified consciousness is the self. Note that the definition of a self contains within it the definition of a mind; therefore, every self has a mind, or is a mind. A mind is defined as a field of possibilities in which at least one-half of the field has chosen the same direction for its choices, with these choices having the potential to further limit a smaller field that the larger could be a creator of and is therefore potentially connected to.

A self has enough consciousness to its thought to help create one or more types of lifeforms that are unique. These new lifeforms are directly related to the self's own (two or more) choices and the common direction to them that had limited spirit and energy's field of life. Depending upon its level of consciousness (givingness, or love), a self can help to create either an individual lifeform or a group of lifeforms from the field of life. The creation of an individual lifeform connected to a single self requires greater consciousness, or givingness to the individual lifeform. This consciousness comes from a larger field, rather than from just the more connectedness in choices that is required for creation of groups of lifeforms connected to one self. The larger field of the human self is needed because the self of a human has the opportunity to *give* to only one lifeform. The lifeforms provide the senses of form that the self uses as its source of information; the human self needs to think very accurately because only one lifeform is supplying its senses. Selves have certain qualities of consciousness that function like a sense when these qualities are expressed through their creation of new, specialized types of life. As a self limits its field of life to create certain probable outcomes to the lifeform(s) that it is affecting through its thought and the giving of its thought to the lifeform, or through the self's consciousness, it compares the majority of the field of life that it is conscious of with the smaller part that it is not. A self cannot *through its consciousness* (givingness, or love) limit for its lifeform(s) all of the smaller part of the field of possibilities that it exists within; it cannot give, or understand, whatever is the smaller part of its field in thought to its lifeforms, and therefore it is not conscious of this smaller part of the field. Neither can the self *initially* identify with this smaller part of the limited field of life when it is separated from the whole, or entire, field; this part is its not-self, even though the self's choices, or purpose, do affect the entire field and the self can eventually identify with the entire field within certain probabilities of purpose that it eventually *creates* in this field. When the self compares the majority of the field that it can limit by giving, can identify with, and is conscious of, with the smaller part that it cannot limit by giving, cannot *initially* identify with, and cannot understand, it develops a *sense* of (its) self. The sense of (its) self allows the self to first recognize what it is by comparing itself to what it is not. Humans refer to the thought behind the recognition as discriminative thought, or thought that sees differences between two or more things.

The self can expand its sense of (its) self by eventually detecting how it is still similar to the parts of the field that it cannot limit through being conscious of them, *but can* in some ways (other than through giving, or consciousness) identify with. It creates this second part of the sense of self by pondering the purpose of its life; sometimes it ponders the purpose of other parts of life. The self can ponder the likelihood and ways of joining with (giving from) its not-self by giving energy and knowledge, from the parts of its self it is conscious of to both its and some other lifeforms *at some future time*. To complete this process the self must, at some future time, give in the ways it has *characterized* itself so doing. Humans sometimes refer to the thought that creates this type of recognition and sense of self as discerning thought, or thought that sees similarities between two or more things—that at first seemed different.

How a (Lower) Self Develops

The Self's Sense of Itself

A self initially develops its sense of self as a result of unsuccessfully limiting its entire field of probability through thought that is focusing on its purpose. Since the self cannot give a part of its field of thought to the lifeform, it develops a sense of its self and its not-self, or of discriminative thought.

Discriminative Thought

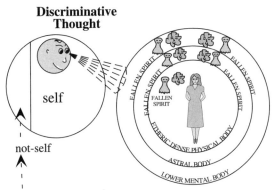

This not-self contains the self's full purpose when added to its self, which the self wants to know and is motivated to find out. The self understands what it is, or becomes conscious, through what it gives in thought to fallen spirit.

The Self's Sense of Good Character

The self first contemplates giving to others by comparing its known self to parts of itself that it does not yet understand. By using its not-self in this way it builds good character—if it later gives parts of its known self to others when they need them. The self realizes that some of its not-self is parts of others' selves but does not yet give its not-self to them.

Discerning Thought

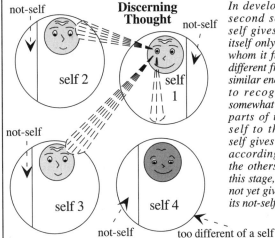

too different of a self

In developing this second sense, the self gives parts of itself only to others whom it finds to be different from it, but similar enough for it to recognize and somewhat later give parts of its known self to them. The self gives to others according to what the others need. At this stage, the self is not yet giving any of its not-self.

The Self's Sense of Group Consciousness

The third sense of self is created when the self is better able to identify with other lifeforms, and then gives some of its thought from its limited field of not-self to these others. The self then becomes group conscious, or conscious that *all* selves are part of this oneness. The not-self becomes a part of the self as the self becomes a part of other selves through its consciousness, or giving (of its not-self). The self then understands its not-self by understanding the others whom it helps to create more of and gives its not-self to.

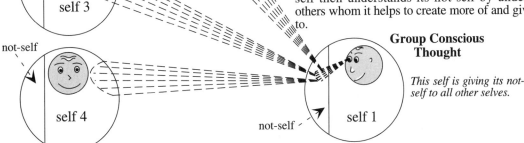

Group Conscious Thought

This self is giving its not-self to all other selves.

Illustration 5.3

A third sense of self can be created as the self further improves its thought within the limited field of life that it is a part of but is not fully conscious of, by being able to both identify with and *give* some of its thought from this not-self limited field. Doing so is possible only if the self creates more of and gives some of its not-self to other lifeforms and not to its own informing fallen spirit, to improve its own senses. Giving some of its not-self to other lifeforms then makes the self conscious of *some* of that which it is not and changes this part into the larger part, or majority, of the field. Note, however, that the self is still not able to completely limit the remainder of the field of possibilities through consciousness, or givingness/love. When this third part of the sense of self is developed, the not-self part that the self becomes conscious of, through creating more of and giving this part of the sense to other lifeforms, creates a unity in thought between it and the other lifeform(s). If the self attempts to give part of its not-self to only its created lifeform(s), it will fail because the field of life of these lifeforms is too small. Only through the creative process of giving of its not-self to the larger field of life (of spirit and energy) that the self is connected to can the self become conscious of parts of its not-self. The type of thought that is behind the sense is referred to as group conscious thought, or thought that understands that life (or at least some parts of it) has oneness and that other *selves* are a part of the oneness.

All selves must have the first sense of self, of discriminating thought, in order to maintain their existence because otherwise they cannot recognize their *own* selves. Also, the more of the second sense of (its) self that is created, the more the self can recognize some other selves and the more it identifies them as being like it is (a self). The second sense of self develops good character in humans; good character is the self-created ability to give to others in thought according to what they need, with the thought containing knowledge as applied to the three lower bodies that has been synthesized from information. Stated another way, the more a self has of additional senses of self, including its second sense (of discernment in its thought processes), the more of a self it is. Upon developing its third sense, a self can recognize some parts, but not all, of spirit and energy and how they, in ways that create selves, create life. This third sense of self is of the self creating more of itself by then giving to spirit and form what it has created of its not-self in order to help create more of other selves. A self understands other selves in some ways by creatively giving of some parts of its not-self; when giving these parts to others, the self gains some limited consciousness of what was its not-self. When added to the first two senses of (its) self, the third sense allows the self to become more spiritual, or to consciously increase its thought of the oneness of life through being group conscious in its thoughts. The self then recognizes that the smaller part of its field of life is a part of the fields of life of some other selves, because it created more of itself from this field by increasing its thought and then giving this thought to others. Then the self becomes aware that others are like the part of itself that it formerly did not understand, and mistakenly perceived to be its not-self.

Stated another way, the self grows, or creates more of itself, as it develops its three particular senses. To develop the first sense, it senses simply itself and what it is not. To develop the second sense, it grows more self from its larger field that it is conscious of. It may identify more and more of its not-self as some *eventual* part of itself—but a part that it is not yet ready to completely give to others. It does this by planning to give and then giving some part of its (*known* and *conscious*) self to others; this process eventually develops good character. Then the self develops more character, or a specialized part of itself that grows exclusively through discerning thought that recognizes other parts of other selves. Eventually, if the character is good (God-like), the self recognizes these other parts to be parts of itself. The self gives its knowledge (created from information given to it by its senses) to others in order to help their selves better inform the spirit in one of their three lower bodies. This creates an understanding of these others as selves. The self enables itself to do this by contemplating ways that it can give in the future. Thus a part of good character must be created *first*, before it can be used with which to give. Bad character is created by the self using its larger field to take from others; taking reduces the size of the larger field, causing the self to lose consciousness. Finally, in developing the third sense, a self further grows by creating more parts of its *not-self* and then giving these parts to other selves *for their use*. These parts then become new parts of the self in its consciousness. The result in growing consciousness is that a group of selves is created in the perspective of the self, from the self giving to others that part of its form that it further created. The way in which a self creates more of its not-self into itself is through improving its senses of form through the motive to give—*for the benefit of other selves*—the eventual increases in its knowledge to the fallen spirit that is informing the lower bodies. Again, this giving creates group consciousness.

Bad Character and Good Character of the Self

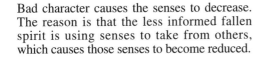

Bad Character

Good Character

When it's time to hire someone at my company, it would be good to call the homeless shelter. We'll have to pay taxes on those people, but their taxes help everyone. The taxes may even help some illegal aliens when our country shares some of its taxes, as aid to theirs. Then as their country improves its economy, some of their citizens will not decide that they need to illegally work in, and often be displaced culturally in our country.

Tomorrow I'll hire some illegal aliens because those guys will work for almost nothing, and no taxes have to be paid. Those illegals like the pay, and who does it hurt?

Bad character causes the senses to decrease. The reason is that the less informed fallen spirit is using senses to take from others, which causes those senses to become reduced.

Good character causes the senses to grow. The reason is that the consciousness of both the self and fallen spirit grow as thought is used with which to give.

Illustration 5.4

Eventually a self will recognize that its entire field of life is a part of *all other* fields of life. This is the point at which the self becomes *transformed* in consciousness into what is referred to as a (higher) Self (spelled with an uppercase "s"). (Higher) Selves are always group conscious and are always spiritual because they think only in the direction of the Ray Lord's thought, or light. They are aware of spirit and energy and are increasing their givingness, or consciousness. They recognize all parts of life that are within their dimension and lower dimensions as being one—as growing some part of God in our universe. A Self can limit (or give) the *entire* field of life that it exists within as a sub-field in the Ray Lord's field of life, in one or more of three ways, or types of *consciousness*; it therefore shares some of the *consciousness* of that Ray Lord's thought. The Self can limit, through its *choices*, or creativity, only a majority of the Ray Lord's field, but *not* the entire field of life as the Ray Lord can in its thought. As was explained in the previous chapter, all three of these ways of giving consciousness involve giving in thought. The first is the giving in thought that helps others to give applied intelligence. The second is the giving in thought that helps others to give unconditional love, as consciousness, and the third is the giving in thought that helps others to give choices and purpose to others.

To restate some of the previous explanations, with new concepts added, when thought within a field has altered enough of the possibilities in that field to create a majority of *probabilities* that can eventually affect the *entire* field, then the field itself becomes a thinker and, when given to one or more lifeforms, becomes a self. In these cases over half of the thoughts within the entire field are directed in a similar direction (by giving), which limits the field overall and mostly towards a single direction, of giving to one or more specific lifeforms. The majority of this direction of thought within the field can now compare its *self* to the rest of the field (the minority) that is not (yet) its self. Being a self is a state of recognizing that the self is a part of a collection of thought in comparison to that which it is not a part of. A self is created within a field by the existence of a majority of thought that is in a particular direction (and is given to the same one or more lifeforms) and thus limits the field, while some of the field still has thought in other directions. (Lower) selves in a physical universe, such as ours—where intelligent activity when not perfectly enlightened manifests as energy, or form—create forces within the energy (the form). The reason is that by definition each self and its field (of its life) are somewhat conflictive to the self's thought within the larger field of life (of other selves' lives) of spirit and energy that both of them exist within and that is different from its own. These differences in thought result in some energy in the larger field of life of spirit and energy following the thought of other selves that is different from any particular self's thought, imposing forces upon each self that is different in thought. Thus two or more selves within the same larger field of life might limit the majority of their smaller fields in different ways, thereby producing these forces that come from the larger field of spirit and energy and that are imposed upon each of the smaller fields. These selves are giving to their one or more lifeforms in different ways, which creates the different directions to their thought. The forces can also transfer down to the level of the lifeforms, which then results in conflicting activity.

Two (Lower) Selves Creating Forces

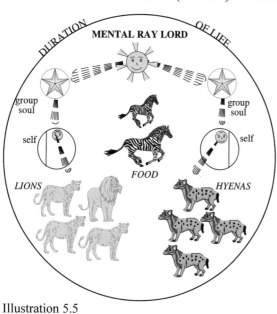

Illustration 5.5

(Lower) selves think within the duration of their respective Ray Lords and the Ray Lords' fields of life, of spirit and energy. Each self creates different types of life because it is informed by a different group soul. The self and its informed lifeforms create a new field of life from the shared field of life with other selves of spirit and energy, from making different choices within the Ray Lord's thought. The opposing fields created by the selves creates force in opposition to the other selves. For example, lions prefer fresh meat, hunting for food, and having a male leader. Hyenas prefer to not hunt if they can scavenge food, even though they are capable of hunting. Hyenas are also a more feminine and nurturing species towards their packs than lions are. When hyenas and lions are both present in the same territory, forces are created in their lives. These forces are due to differences in the informing thought by the self of the lions and the self of the hyenas. Note that this informing thought is what is known as instincts.

To become a self, spirit needs to limit to some extent the field of its life (or pre-life) within the Ray Lord's thought (light) and the dimension of time and space where the Ray Lord's focus of thought and life are directed. This field includes time and space within our universe and corresponds to the Ray Lord and its creation of life. If a lifeform who attempts to focus in thought away from the light, or thought, of a Ray Lord had a self, it could lose some part of its self and possibly all of itself. As explained above, that self would lose the ability to give to its lifeform(s) during the majority of the time, and thus it could no longer limit its smaller field of life. In addition, that self would also be unable to maintain its connection to the larger field of light that it is a part of. The resultant lessening of consciousness would reduce its self.

As previously described, there are two types of self in our universe: the self and the Self. The first type, the self, is developed by spirit informing energy and using the sense(s) of the form(s) to create enough knowledge so that the consciousness limits the majority of the field of both its life and the lives of its lifeforms. This field of life of spirit and energy is originally created by each Ray Lord's thought, or light, as well as by its ray. A smaller field is then created from spirit informing energy in order to create life. The self can limit the majority of a field of life through consciousness using the senses of form. Thus in some ways the self limits the prior field of life of spirit and *energy*. This is why a self is created from and is associated with limiting a field that includes senses of form, or of energy. This self is referred to as a lower, or smaller, self—which for clarity in differentiation is spelled with a lowercase "s." The second type of self, or the (higher) Self, spelled with an uppercase "s," is developed by spirit consistently thinking in the direction of light, with its thought limiting the majority of the Ray Lord's field in one or more of three ways through *both* its consciousness *and its choices*. It can limit the *entire* field through consciousness alone, in one or more of three ways. The direction of light comes from the thought of the Ray Lord of the particular plane that spirit is focused on. Thus because Selves all give (givingness) in the same direction using the light of their respective Ray Lords to guide them, the consciousness of the Self is unified with all other Selves. The consciousness of the Self is great enough to give the entirety of its existing thought in one or more of three ways (in cooperation with other Selves) to all of the life within the Ray Lord's dimension and below. However, because Selves do not make identical choices, they can limit only a majority and not all of the Ray Lord's dimension of life (and below) through their completed thought (*choices* with direction, combined with limitation—which creates greater probability in their fields of life).

Human Selves Creating Different Choices Within the Same Larger Field of Creating Life

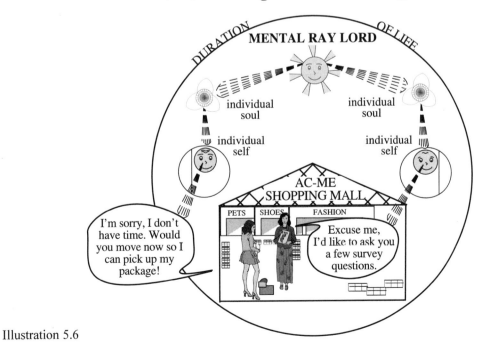

Illustration 5.6

THE (HIGHER) SELF

There are two types of spirit's thought that create a Self and that correspond to spirit also sensing at the same time; more about these types of thought will be explained after the next paragraph. The sense and thought in a Self occur at the speed of light for whatever dimension the spirit within the Self is thinking on; its sensing and thinking both occur at the same time—in a Now and at the atomic part of the space of that dimension. All of the Self thinks only in the direction of light and only while it is in the Ray Lord's focus of thought, or light. Note that a Self can exist only within a Now. Thus to distinguish between any spirit's higher senses and thought when they are enlightened is more semantic than observable to most humans. Thinking in light is a process of giving after having made choices with consciousness; thinking *and sensing* in light is a process of Self-creatively understanding. Spirit's higher senses and thoughts (its ability to create a Self) concern only the light in other spirit. When enough of the light in other spirit is sensed and thought about, spirit's senses and thoughts become about God. This shift in focus of sense and thought occurs because the created Self thinks only while in the Ray Lord's light. As it senses the light of other spirit, the Self is sensing increasingly greater amounts of God's thought. The amount that spirit needs to sense and think about the light in other spirit in order to sense and think about giving to God is the amount of thought needed to limit the majority of the field of God's growth (the majority of the life that spirit is a part of), as this field is connected to either a single lifeform a group of lifeforms. For a Self, this amount is the majority of the Ray Lord's thought that creates life in its dimension and below, or within its *duration* of life. This, of course, is a part of the same definition as what a self is, but applied to sensing and thinking about God using God's or the Ray Lord's thought that limits a much larger field of life rather than a body of energy (the information supplied by senses of one or more lifeforms). The sense(s) and thoughts of the Self need to be at the speed of light of the dimension that the sense/thought is on because they must join time and space rather than separate them. Thus the Self is created by spirit sensing God in one of two ways, and simultaneously thinking about giving to God in one of two ways, as described below. Notice that a Self can sense only light and can also think only in light because the Self exists only at the atomic level of the dimension it exists within.

The Self has two means by which it can sense and think about giving to God or all of life so life and thus God can grow. The first is sometimes referred to as the lower sense of and lower thought about God. This sense and thought are the recognition of God in one or more of three ways regarding giving consciousness in life and within the Self who is doing the recognizing. The three ways are through giving the thought of intelligence in activity, consciousness, and/or purpose to help to enlighten another's giving in order to increase life. Each of these three ways is developed progressively on the atomic (highest) level of the mental plane, then on the atomic level of the intuitional plane, and, finally, eventually on the spiritual plane. There is a growing understanding of how life is God's growth. Notice that as God is recognized and understood in life, the (lower) self grows as well if it is choosing to give some of this thought because it is beginning to understand that the form of "other" life and selves are a part of itself. The recognition and understanding of part of God through the understanding of oneness in life also reduces some of the forces that spirit experiences against itself that are caused by other selves limiting the larger field of life differently from its self's field. The forces are reduced because the self is beginning to include some of these other selves' thought as its own. The Self grows as it gains an understanding of God through giving *all* of its thought in one or more of the three ways of being conscious at the Ray Lord's level. This thought becomes a part of its Self and of other Selves—all being part of the One. Each Self is conscious that all life in its dimension and lower is a part of its entire field, even the part it is not yet fully conscious of in all three of the ways that it could be. This awareness causes a Self to think in unison with other Selves by each choosing to *wisely give* in their sense/thought (of giving to God) whatever the others may not have, but need in order to *wisely give*. (Higher) Selves create a hierarchy of thought based upon their always giving wisdom, or wholeness in thought, and each giving according to what the other Selves need in order to better wisely, or wholly, give. By hierarchy of love/wisdom, or giving wisdom, is meant that each Self thinks and gives based upon its *capability* to think, and only as is helpful and needed by others.

There is a second, or higher sense and thought of a Self. This higher sense and thought can be developed only as the lower sense and thought are used to create a hierarchy of wise giving thought, or understanding/consciousness of the group of Selves giving to God as described in the preceding paragraph. The higher sense and thought both come from creating more of God— at the speed of light—in a hierarchy of thought in cooperative wise giving with other Selves. The higher sense and thought are more of a state of "beingness" than the one of consciousness that occurs when a Self uses its lower sense and thought, of understanding its and other selves' oneness with God through giving wisely whatever thought it already has. By beingness is meant that as a Self creates more of God by creating more virtue (light in form) in itself and with other Selves on three or more planes at one time in order to unify time and space, the Self is *being* more of God, whom it is helping to create more of. The lower sense and thought of Self creates more consciousness, or understanding of what God is, by recognizing and understanding its oneness with God (through giving what it is or is capable of being). The higher sense and thought of Self creates more virtue, or light (God's thought) in form on at least the three lowest planes at the same time. This produces more growth of God, or of life (by growing more Self in itself and other Selves). The increased virtue comes from the Self increasing its choices and creativity of light in the lifeform(s) that it is connected to as well as in the lifeform(s) of other Selves. The lower and higher spiritual senses are a correspondence of the second and first parts of God's mind, respectively. As a Self in concert with other Selves creates virtue, it is *being* a functional part of its Creator.

THE HIGHER SELF AND THE LOWER SELF		
SENSES OF THE HIGHER SELF	WAYS IN WHICH THE HIGHER SELF GIVES, AND PLANE WHERE DEVELOPED	SENSES OF THE LOWER SELF
Understanding God	Purpose—spiritual plane	Discriminative Thought—creates a sense of itself
Creating more of God	Consciousness—intuitional plane	Discerning Thought—creates a sense of some other selves
	Intelligent Activity—mental plane	Group Conscious Thought—creates a sense of all others' selves being the same as itself

Table 5.1

The Lower Sense of Higher Selves

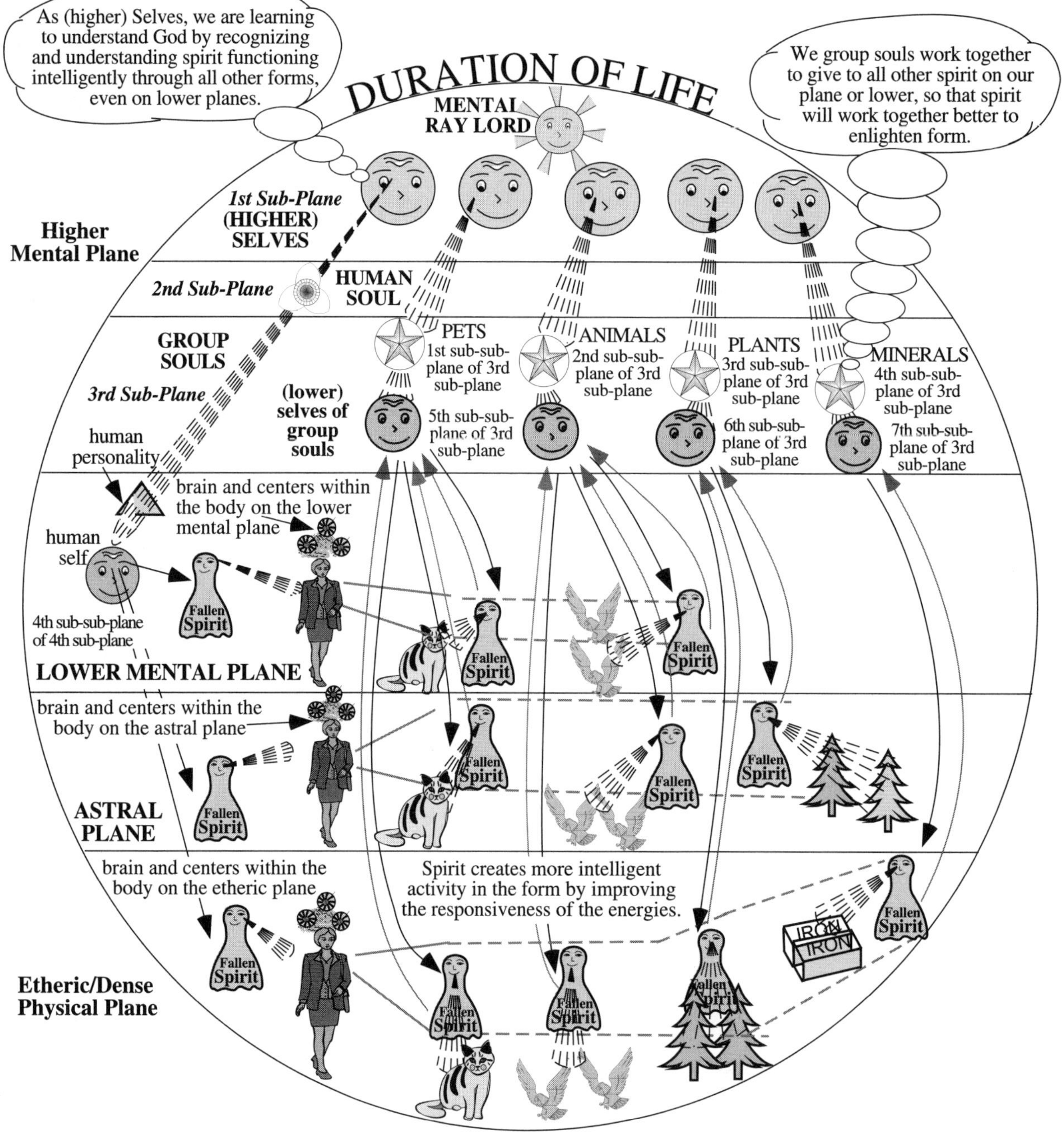

DURATION OF LIFE

MENTAL RAY LORD

As (higher) Selves, we are learning to understand God by recognizing and understanding spirit functioning intelligently through all other forms, even on lower planes.

We group souls work together to give to all other spirit on our plane or lower, so that spirit will work together better to enlighten form.

Higher Mental Plane

1st Sub-Plane (HIGHER) SELVES

2nd Sub-Plane HUMAN SOUL

GROUP SOULS

3rd Sub-Plane

(lower) selves of group souls

human personality

human self

4th sub-sub-plane of 4th sub-plane

PETS 1st sub-plane of 3rd sub-plane

5th sub-plane of 3rd sub-plane

ANIMALS 2nd sub-sub-plane of 3rd sub-plane

PLANTS 3rd sub-sub-plane of 3rd sub-plane

6th sub-sub-plane of 3rd sub-plane

MINERALS 4th sub-sub-plane of 3rd sub-plane

7th sub-sub-plane of 3rd sub-plane

brain and centers within the body on the lower mental plane

Fallen Spirit

LOWER MENTAL PLANE

brain and centers within the body on the astral plane

ASTRAL PLANE

Fallen Spirit

brain and centers within the body on the etheric plane

Spirit creates more intelligent activity in the form by improving the responsiveness of the energies.

IRON IRON

Etheric/Dense Physical Plane

Fallen Spirit

The lower sense of the (higher) Self is understanding God by reaching the consciousness level of the Ray Lord. The Self reaches this level by giving to all the spirit, on its plane and lower, virtuous thought that was created by itself and other beings in the past. More of the lower sense of Self develops from the (lower) self giving, which then affects and causes growth of, or enlightens, the mind of the Self. The lower sense of Self develops from the Self learning that spirit is collectively a part of God and then by the Self affecting and causing growth of the fallen spirit on all the planes and sub-planes below It. Humans, unlike lower life forms, can choose to help the Self of other fallen spirit of other forms to develop the lower sense, of understanding God. This assistance is given through communication and applied knowledge with other spirit, and helping all spirit in all form to grow, to better sense, and to give.

Illustration 5.7

The Higher Sense of Higher Selves, or the Higher Spiritual Sense

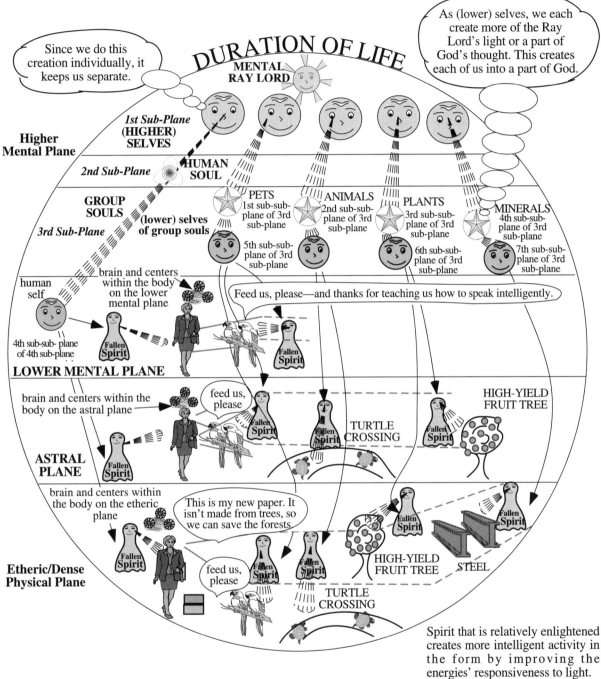

The higher sense of the (higher) Self is the creation of being more a part of God by creating more virtue within a Ray Lord's duration—in this case, the mental plane Ray Lord. When the Self is successful in this endeavor, it starts becoming more of a part of God. Then the Self helps other spirit to better join with form/energy through light. The Self thus creates the virtue that causes it to develop the second, or higher, spiritual sense. Each (lower) self is giving to the higher Self information about the fallen spirit. Humans are able to create virtue in all kingdoms lower than their own kingdom. However, group souls and their lower selves except when radiant usually can create virtue only within their own respective kingdoms, and then usually with outside assistance.

Illustration 5.8

THE LOWER SELF AND HIGHER SELF FROM ANOTHER PERSPECTIVE

From another perspective, a (lower) self is created by the existence of enough thought in a similar direction (a similar way of connecting, or giving, choices) that is given to lifeforms and can limit more than half of the field the thought exists in. The self creates the sense that it, or the majority of the field that is limited, is something different from the remainder of the field and the thought contained therein. Within a large field, such as a duration of life (of God's growth as it exists in each cosmic Ray Lord's dimension) as compared to a much smaller field (of life of the individual lifeforms), there can be many selves. While the selves can all limit over half of the smaller field, each can do so in a different way by having different choices and/or a fixed direction to its thoughts, which makes each self unique. A self also limits the larger field of higher spirit and energy in some way(s), but often differently than other selves do and sometimes in ways in which other selves are incapable of giving—with both factors then creating forces within the selves' smaller field of life. A self can eventually realize that other selves are similar to its self even though they think using different choices or in a different direction, or both. (Lower) selves can eventually recognize their similarity because they all can limit the majority of their smaller fields through their own thought and thus give what they have learned, even if the giving is done uniquely. If the self chooses to give in ways that are needed by others, it develops understanding, or consciousness, of the others in the process (of recognizing and helping to create more of oneness). A self's full sense of itself and of other selves is achieved through the following three steps. In the first step, the self recognizes who/what it is in its form and its senses in comparison to who/what it is not in form and sense—it develops discrimination. In the second, it recognizes who some others are in their form and senses by increasing its consciousness, or its understanding of them. The self prepares in advance and then later gives to these others the use of some of its senses' information that has been synthesized into knowledge and its understanding of the knowledge. Because the self increases its understanding and prepares to give, it sees some shared oneness, or similarity, between itself and the others—it develops discernment and good character. Finally, in the third step, it realizes that all selves are a part of One, by creating more of itself from its not-self and then giving to the others *all* of its sense, form, knowledge, and its consciousness that it has created. By creating more of itself and then giving this creation to all other selves that it could give to, the self develops a group consciousness, or the beginning of God consciousness. As the (lower) self builds this third part of the sense of self, it eventually reaches (transforms itself into) the beginning of the development of the lower sense/thought of (higher) Self. In the Christian faith, the developed third part of the sense of the self is referred to as Christ consciousness. Through a group of selves all creating more of themselves and then giving to each other and to others, a commonality of direction to their thought develops as their choices are synergistically supportive of each other. The result is that the collective selves eventually limit over half of the larger field they think within, in similar or sometimes even the same ways, and thus use the senses of their lifeforms in similar ways to create knowledge and consciousness that is common to all of them. This is the use of the lower sense of (higher) Self.

Notice how developing a full sense of self necessarily grows consciousness because in order for the self to create the direction of its choices, towards oneness, it must also recognize the similar direction in the choices of other selves by giving to them. Thus a self's consciousness has to be focused on creating understanding larger than its own choices that lead to more oneness; as it makes more choices in that direction and also recognizes and gives them, its consciousness grows and it can become aware of this growth. Conversely, in theory it would seem as though a self could also completely recognize the shrinking of its consciousness.

However, this is usually not the case because spirit often loses some awareness, which comes from the information supplied by its senses, faster than it loses consciousness. The reason is that spirit's loss of consciousness is the result of its selfishness, which means it is thinking only for itself and not for the energy of its lifeform's senses. Since this energy needs the thought of spirit in order to function properly and develop, when spirit removes the focus of its thought, the senses diminish. This means that the information and *awareness* provided to spirit decreases and becomes less accurate. Spirit's consciousness lessens because it has been selfish; however, because its senses have been damaged in the process, what it loses fastest is its ability to be completely aware of the loss of its consciousness, or its complete awareness of its loss of under-standing. The remaining sense, which is much less than full awareness of itself because the senses have been lessened, is not registered as the sense of a loss in consciousness; instead, it is experienced within the personality as *suffering,* which will be further explained later in this chapter.

Lower Sense of a Human Higher Self

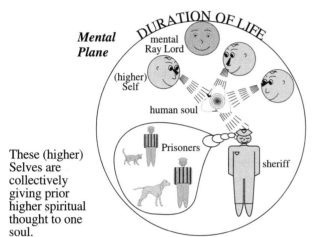

The (higher) Self can give its newly created thought to its human soul. If the personality and self are in contact with the soul and Self, then all four of them together inform the human to create a soul conscious solution to a circumstance. The solution will be either a previously thought-of conceptual solution or a newly created one (as in the second example, shown below).

This first illustration exemplifies how the (higher) Self can help the human (the sheriff) to think of virtuous, previously thought-of ways by other Selves for prisoners to rescue dogs and cats from animal shelters and love these animals as pets. In the process, the prisoners are helped to become more loving, and the animals are saved from being killed.

A human (higher) Self limits the entire field of the Ray Lord's duration of life, through consciousness.

Higher Sense of a Human Higher Self

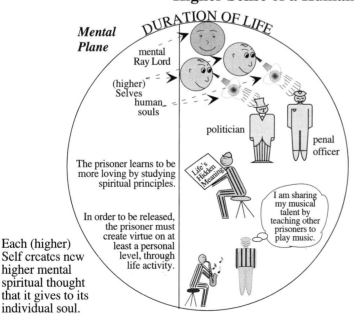

The (higher) Self is creating new mental thought in its giving, and can create with half or more of the field. The Self creates beyond what is already there.

This exemplifies how the Selves share this concept with the souls of a politician and a penal officer: to help prisoners improve their understanding of spiritual principles before they can be released back into society. If the prisoners can prove that they have learned these principles conceptually, then their consciousness has grown beyond the level of their personality disorder and lack of self. The level of their improvement would need to be commensurate with the prisoner's prior level of criminality.

Note that the ways in which a prisoner exhibits giving need to be related to the crime and the prisoner's type of personality disorder, to ensure change from his or her criminal thought processes.

A human (higher) Self limits the majority of but less than the entire Ray Lord's field, through creation.

Illustration 5.9

The sense of (higher) Self has two parts to it, and to those who are not enlightened to at least the same level of the Self, this sense is indistinguishable from the thought of Self. The reason is that the Self's sense and thought both happen at the speed of light for the dimension that they occur within—taking no time, in a Now. The first part, or the lower sense of Self is to recognize and be conscious of, or to understand, God on the particular dimension where the Self is, and below. This sense is developed as the Self gives its thought wisely, or in wholeness, in cooperation with other Selves according to their need for its thought. This takes place in a hierarchy of group thought and consciousness (givingness/love/understanding). (Higher) Selves can develop this sense because they have mostly eliminated the forces created by (lower) selves, who each limit in a different way the larger field that their thought exists within. The varying limitations are a result of the choices by the selves to use different connections from the larger field that they are all a part of. These dissimilar connections create different directions in the majority of the thought that is creating each self in the smaller field. The Selves on any one plane all use the direction of that cosmic Ray Lord's thought, or its light, to guide and unify their thought even though the choices within their thoughts may be somewhat different. This common direction of giving thought (and, therefore, of consciousness) to God's growth, or life, greatly reduces the forces. The forces are reduced because the forms that the Selves inform are all being enlightened—to some extent—by the light that is produced by the Selves' thought. The direction, or consciousness, or givingness, is one or more of three possibilities, depending upon the dimension in which it occurs (the mental, intuitional, or spiritual). Another interesting point about Selves is that because they at times think in light and therefore sense in light, they not only share thought, they also sometimes share senses.

The higher sense of Self is created as the Self both recognizes and understands God in its lower sense and then chooses through its thought to create more of God's thought, or light, in the form that it is using and the form used by other spirit. In each dimension wherein spirit can sense and think, God's thought is represented by the corresponding Ray Lord's thought, or specialized light in form (the virtue of that Ray Lord's plane). As spirit thinks and creates more of God's thought (as represented by the Ray Lord's thought), spirit is becoming more a functional part of God and is growing life, or more of God, in the process. Developing a higher sense of Self on each dimension below the monadic is the enlightened goal of spirit and is a part of the purpose and plan for spirit that comes from the Monads on the monadic plane. The higher sense of Self is one of being a functional part of God and being able to sense life as it needs to be further created in order to create more of God. Even though created individually, the creation is still given in a hierarchy of thought with all other Selves within the particular dimension and lower.

The Self of spirit continues to grow by unifying the thought of spirit on each dimension below the second, or monadic plane—the plane of One. The Self is sacrificially given up on the monadic and logoic planes because all Monads think as one, with no Monad limiting the field of possibilities of the monadic sub-plane and above "differently" from any other. The sacrifice of Self is (as all spiritual sacrifice is), for the Monad, the removal of that which is an obstacle to its growth. Monads all have the same direction to their thought, as do Selves, and, in addition, Monads all have the same shared choices. Further, because Monads think in *only* light *as One*, they limit their *entire* field of possibilities on the monadic plane through their consciousness and *choices*. Through their thought they eliminate the condition that creates both a self and a Self. Eventually, they *share* their *sense*. The condition that creates a self is that a majority but less than all of the field of possibilities is limited by the self's consciousness, or givingness, or love, which allows the self to compare its differences to that which it is not. The condition that creates a Self is that the entire field of the Ray Lord's dimension is limited through consciousness (in one or more of three ways), but not through choices because the Self is limited in its thought by its choices not being all the same. The limitation through creative choices occurs by

Communication Between the Human (Higher) Self and the (Lower) Self in the Mental Unit, and Fallen Spirit

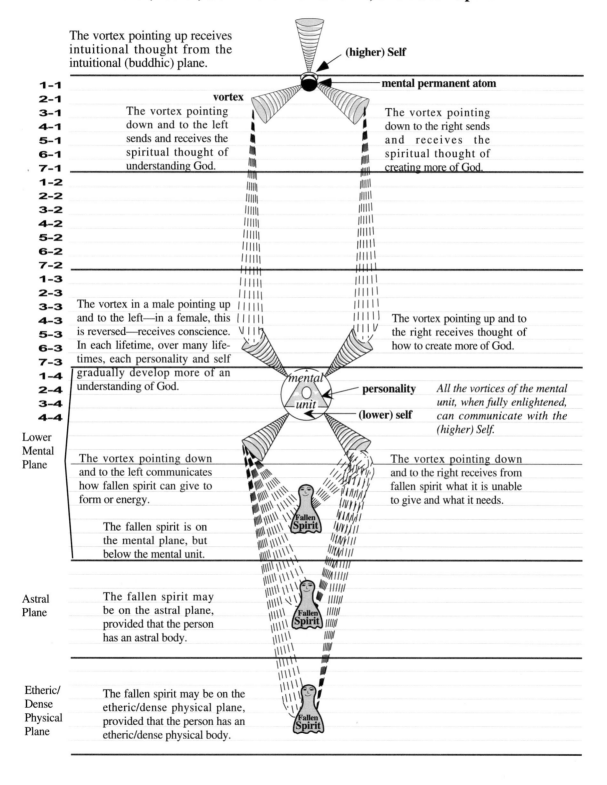

The vortex pointing up receives intuitional thought from the intuitional (buddhic) plane.

(higher) Self

1-1
2-1
mental permanent atom

vortex

3-1
4-1
5-1
6-1
7-1

The vortex pointing down and to the left sends and receives the spiritual thought of understanding God.

The vortex pointing down to the right sends and receives the spiritual thought of creating more of God.

1-2
2-2
3-2
4-2
5-2
6-2
7-2
1-3
2-3
3-3
4-3
5-3
6-3
7-3

The vortex in a male pointing up and to the left—in a female, this is reversed—receives conscience. In each lifetime, over many lifetimes, each personality and self gradually develop more of an understanding of God.

The vortex pointing up and to the right receives thought of how to create more of God.

1-4
2-4
3-4
4-4

mental unit

personality

(lower) self

All the vortices of the mental unit, when fully enlightened, can communicate with the (higher) Self.

Lower Mental Plane

The vortex pointing down and to the left communicates how fallen spirit can give to form or energy.

The vortex pointing down and to the right receives from fallen spirit what it is unable to give and what it needs.

The fallen spirit is on the mental plane, but below the mental unit.

Fallen Spirit

Astral Plane

The fallen spirit may be on the astral plane, provided that the person has an astral body.

Fallen Spirit

Etheric/ Dense Physical Plane

The fallen spirit may be on the etheric/dense physical plane, provided that the person has an etheric/dense physical body.

Fallen Spirit

Illustration 5.10

the Self giving all of its field of life as is needed to understand God, but only a part of it to both understand and grow more of God. At least half but not all of the Self's field can be limited by its *choices* because the Self is not of one mind with all other Selves in all of its thought; in addition, it lacks the single complete sense for *all* dimensions, which an ascended Monad has (Selves do share *some* senses). Each Self thinks using the same direction, or consciousness, of light of the plane its thought is focused on. Each Self does not use the same *choices* in its thought that other Selves do; therefore, only half of what makes up Selves' thought is the same. This half is the *connectedness* of their choices, or their thoughts' shared consciousness/understanding/love/direction. The possibility of this condition that is created by spirit separating from the thought of the Monad and having less ability to perfectly think and be conscious takes place on the planes below the monadic. No such condition exists on the two highest dimensions of our universe, so no selves/Selves exist there.

 ## MONADS AND (HIGHER) AND (LOWER) SELVES

Monads live beyond selves, but are still individuals. This occurs because the Monads on the monadic plane create a spiritual part and an energy part of their existence that does have a self/Self, on the planes lower than the monadic. The parts, as spirit and energy, develop uniqueness by creating more of God's mind in all of the lower dimensions. They do so either through intelligent activity or through energy that when less than perfectly enlightened causes form and senses to be created. Thus a Monad on the monadic plane has a part that develops a self/Self on the lower planes, while it continues to exist as an omnipresent Being in its thought on the second, or monadic, dimension.

Monads on the first, or logoic, plane are ascended in Beingness from the monadic plane. This occurs after they have created intelligent activity in all activities and form that they were (the spirit that they created life through and the energy that this spirit informed was) part of on every plane below the logoic. These Monads are Great Beings who have completely and perfectly rejoined the three parts of God's mind into One. These Monads think and *sense* as one together and with their Creator. However, they remain as individuals because each one leaves our universe based upon its *unique creation* of more of God through its incredible journey of creating more life, and by part of it (spirit) becoming a part of this creation. Amazingly, ascended Monads are the most unified that any life can be in our universe, while at the same time they are also the most unique, and therefore the most individual of all beings. A confusion has sometimes arisen in the minds of some students of spirituality (usually beginning students, but sometimes even those who are somewhat more advanced) and perhaps in the minds of some readers of this book, regarding the concept of individuality within oneness (unity of consciousness and/or of beingness). At first, individuality and oneness may seem to be antithetical to each other. For those with that perspective, it is hoped that light is being shed on this illusionary pair of opposites—of individuality versus oneness. A self/Self is not needed for the maintenance or existence of individuality *if* enough thought that is part of the Being is enlightened, or is unified in the thought of God. Individuality *is lost* in those who choose to think in separation and away from God's thought. The reason is that in these cases the self is lessened, and God's thought, or light, is not *replacing* it inside the being. Thus a Self is given up by spirit in form that is becoming fully enlightened as all three parts of God's mind join or, as light, perfectly joins with the form. These three parts replace the Self within a greater Being who no longer needs to be *separate* to be *individual*.

An important lesson to learn *experientially* for many humans who are advancing in consciousness is that individuality does not have to be lost when separateness is given up. The development of group consciousness is in the beginning often intertwined with the personality's fears of losing individuality. While much of this will be covered in Chapter Twelve, for now the

Monads Create Life, Making Them Individual
while They Become One with All

A MONAD IS AN INDIVIDUAL BUT IS NOT SEPARATE

A Monad is an individual because it has created life, as follows...

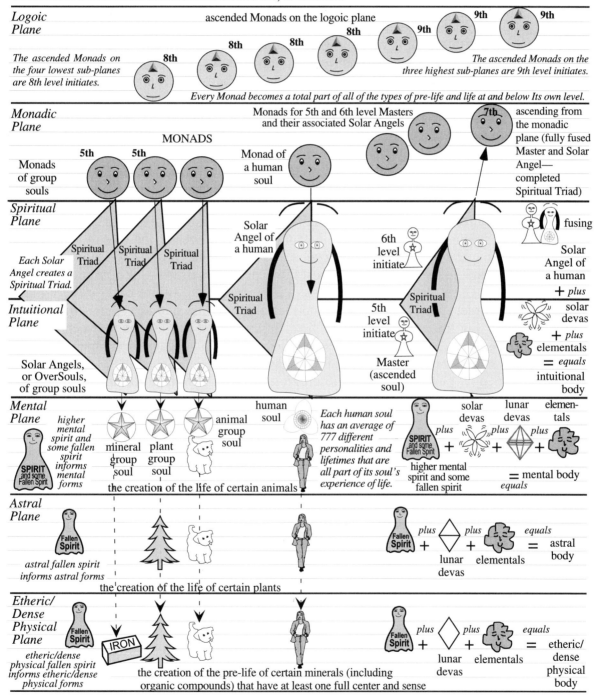

Illustration 5.11

explanation is that a self and especially its counterpart in a human—the personality—are very concerned with controlling the personality's senses and its thought that allow it to think enough (a majority of the time) to sufficiently limit its field of possibilities (its life) to be able to maintain and perpetuate its self. The fear of loss of self is the ultimate of all fears, and for humans is the real fear of death. This fear of losing one's self, which plagues humanity in the physical world, becomes layered with the fear of losing individuality. While illusion is producing many falsehoods regarding these concepts, the desire to be separate and to remain so produces more illusion and then more fear...and more desire to be separate. The process feeds on itself and leads to significant losses in meaning to life.

The *less* separate that people are, the greater the meaning to their lives because then the more they can sense, think, create of their selves/Selves and eventually create more of life, or of God's growth. As people are selfish they lose some of their selves, and increase their fear of death (which a loss of self triggers in the emotional, or astral, body and the personality). Meaning to life is increased as the self/Self is increased. When the Self is sacrificed (at an advanced stage of Beingness), God's growth—life—replaces the "loss of Self," and God's mind becomes the mind and thought of what used to be the thought of the Self.

        SPIRIT AND SELVES

Time is fractured, or split within the etheric/dense physical, astral, and mental planes, which constitute the three lowest dimensions of our universe; the reason for the split is the incomplete thought of spirit, which contains a lack of light, or of God's thought. In order for a self to limit its field of life in these lowest dimensions, a self must be able to join together the time/space enough so that time includes the past, present, and future fairly closely together and in the correct order (past, then present, and then future relative to activities—movement of energy—in space). For the self to recognize the differences and similarities between its thought and that of others, time needs to be complete and logical, and the space (and time) that its field of thought has created needs to be dimensionally correct. A self loses itself as it loses its ability to logically identify past, present, and future; logic gives these three the correctness of order in relation to the space that the time is a part of. Thought that includes only one or two of the three time zones cannot recognize itself in comparison to other thought because this limited thought loses its ability to discriminate within its field of possibilities. Also, even if all three zones of time are able to be thought of, if the three parts are not in correct order (are not logical), discrimination is lost because, again, w*ho is doing what, and where, and when?* cannot be understood, i.e., time and space cannot be correctly held together in the thought of the "self"— who then loses some of itself. It is much more difficult for spirit to think in these three lowest dimensions, where the gravity (the collective thought that unenlightened energy has towards other energy) is relatively strong and the dense elemental energy is so resistant to the thought of spirit. These conditions cause difficulty in sensing, and sensing is required for spirit to be able to think. A majority of the time, spirit finds itself unable to think enough to limit the field of its life. In these cases the spirit cannot create a self because it cannot adequately join time and space together. Furthermore, at times the amount of time and space that spirit can join cannot be maintained in a logical order or closely enough in the correct time sequence.

The spirit contained *in* pre-life and *in* the individual lifeforms of plants and most animals on the lower planes where these lifeforms live cannot think well enough to create a self at these levels. The reason is that the spirit in *individual* plants is found mostly on the etheric part of the etheric/dense physical plane. For many plants, only a very slight amount of some plant spirit along with informed energy exists on the lowest part of the astral plane. Spirit in *individual* animals mostly exists on the astral plane, with some on the etheric plane when the animal is physically alive. In some more advanced animals, a range of very small to moderate amounts of spirit is found on the lowest parts of the mental plane. The spirit within all of these individual lifeforms is located below the middle of the mental plane, and cannot recognize itself. This spirit lacks self either because time and space are too fractured or because some time zones, or parts of fractured time, are actually missing from its thought, or both conditions may apply. Left on its own, this spirit is too overwhelmed by thought of the surrounding sea of relatively dark elemental energies to hold the energies and spirit together, even with the assistance of lunar deva energies, and keep a lifeform alive. This spirit (as was mentioned in the previous chapter) is sometimes referred to as fallen, or "dark," spirit because it contains *less* light, though it still contains some light. Fallen spirit cannot raise itself on its own because its thought is overridden by gravity, or the thought of the unenlightened energy that surrounds it.

The thought of spirit that is higher than the fallen spirit comes to its rescue. The spirit that is located from the middle of the mental plane, up, is capable of joining all three parts of time together and based upon actions in space, and it often does so in logical order. In the cases of the life of animals and plants and the pre-life of minerals, the higher mental plane spirit does most of the thinking for the fallen spirit within the individual lifeforms. The higher spirit, which exists above the middle of the mental plane, creates a (lower) self who then thinks for lower spirit and individual lifeforms (or the pre-life of minerals). Because this spirit is *always* thinking for—and *giving* to—either one lifeform or a number of them that contain fallen spirit, it is also creating some additional amount of a (higher) Self because it is *raising* its consciousness by consistently giving some of its thought. This higher spirit creates (manifests) a new lifeform because it is interacting between two fields of life. The higher/larger field is life as a Self; the lower/smaller field is its self and its self's thought for the individual lifeforms (or the pre-life), and for the more advanced animals, a slight sense of self. The Self and self are helping to create these lower lifeforms and helping them to think (and eventually, for the more advanced animal lifeforms, to develop a slight sense of self). Helping the lower lifeforms to think occurs after a new lifeform is created and, in the process, the self is created—sometimes including the creative giving of the Self; all three (the self, the Self, and the new lifeform) are created from the thought of higher mental plane spirit. The new lifeform that is created is a soul. The soul is the higher spirit and energy field of life that a self is connected to and originally came from. The soul is the new field of life created from higher mental plane spirit; it is located between the Self and the self, which the Self creates through sacrifice and the soul through giving. Eventually, the Self becomes a connected spiritual part of the soul. The soul's body and senses allow the soul to sense both the self and the Self. The self and Self are connected to the new field of life (the soul) through consciousness, or givingness. Note that a more thorough explanation of what a soul is will be provided both later in this chapter and in the next. The Self is the potential to always create more light. The self is the potential for some new *forms* of life to gain an understanding of themselves, of other selves, and of the entire group of selves. This understanding is accomplished through the synthesis of information from senses within the lifeform(s), as well as eventually comparing the information to the light of the Self. All three of these fields of life (the self, the Self, and the soul) initially develop together, but the soul's further development is contingent upon the thought of its self and Self.

 ## GROUP SOULS AND (LOWER) AND (HIGHER) SELVES

In the cases of pre-life creation of minerals and life creation of plants and animals, the higher helping spirit, which creates part of the soul along with its (lower) self and developing (higher) Self, all think for a large number of the lower lifeforms. The souls of the higher helping spirit are called *group* souls because they think for large numbers of lifeforms that have fallen spirit within them and that do not have individual selves. The thought that group souls use (which is given to the lifeforms by each group soul's self) does not connect to individual effects, but only to the average of a group of effects. The thought used is preconceptual. This thought is easier to create logic out of because all that is needed to do so is the joining of a concept to only an average or typical group of effects (referred to as thoughtforms on the lower mental plane), rather than to a specific effect that is correctly defined in time and space. For example, let's say that we wanted to tell some people when it would be appropriate for them to eat, instead of simply relying upon them to eat when they feel hungry. If we used conceptual thought we would need to know a great deal about when they each last ate, their individual metabolisms, weight, activity, types of food each person eats, etc. Then we would need to evaluate these factors for each person, and decide when each should eat. This is conceptual thought, and is the way humans mostly think. Now let's use preconceptual thought instead. We would first gain information about a group of people similar to the people whom we are helping to determine when to eat. The information would come from a collection of many other people and would then be synthesized into knowledge. The information would contain averages about metabolism, weights, activities, types of foods they eat, and how often they eat. We could then preconceive how often other similar people should eat. We then would (through our selves) convey this information to the group of people whom we are presently thinking for—but only as a group. The individual effects for each person are ignored, and are actually unknowable because, in this example, we think *only* in preconception. Note that in the above example, the behavior (timing of eating from one moment to another) that was chosen to illustrate preconceived thought is, in actuality, seldom controlled by such thought in more advanced lifeforms; this specific example was chosen in order to isolate and better define the concept. Preconceived thought of souls generally creates *complex* patterns of behaviors, and would be superfluous for such a simple activity as when to eat on a moment-to-moment basis, which the organism itself can usually (but not always) sense without using thought.

Preconceptual thought in group souls is referred to as instincts when it is given to fallen spirit in individual animals and plants, and is termed pre-instinctual for the pre-life of minerals and its fallen spiritual thought. Instinctual thought helps the lower lifeforms to think as a group, but cannot address individual differences in time and space. The preconceived concepts are connected only to averages of effects. Group souls usually cannot develop a concept or thought that is joined closely enough together in past, present, and future (i.e., with thought in these three time zones at near the same time) to create a concept that is also connected to a specific effect in time and space. The reason is that the higher spirit of most group souls and their selves/Selves have not developed enough of the experience in creating and giving the thought on the upper half of the mental plane that would enable them to think using the majority of this half of the plane at any one time. Instead, the group soul more slowly in time pieces together a concept, but then the concept is "blurred" in time and space and can be applied only to an average of effects, rather than to any one effect. This blurring in time is also an effect of a group soul's inability to record from the senses of its lifeform any event in the event's exact time and space; when put together, these effects are much like a too-slow camera shutter trying to take a picture of a moving object.

Because group souls "blur" time and space as they more slowly build preconceptual thought that is connected to the average of effects, they also "blur" their spirit's creation of a self, which is trying to give the thought to the lifeforms it is connected to, and to create a sense of self for the soul (and a slight sense of self for some advanced animals). The self of a group soul is relatively weak in its ability to recognize itself, and even weaker in its ability to recognize other selves and their thought and especially the selves of human life, which is usually too advanced. While group souls can recognize and somewhat understand some other group souls and their thought (usually those most similar to themselves), their ability to do so is somewhat tenuous

Blurring of Time on the Mental Plane

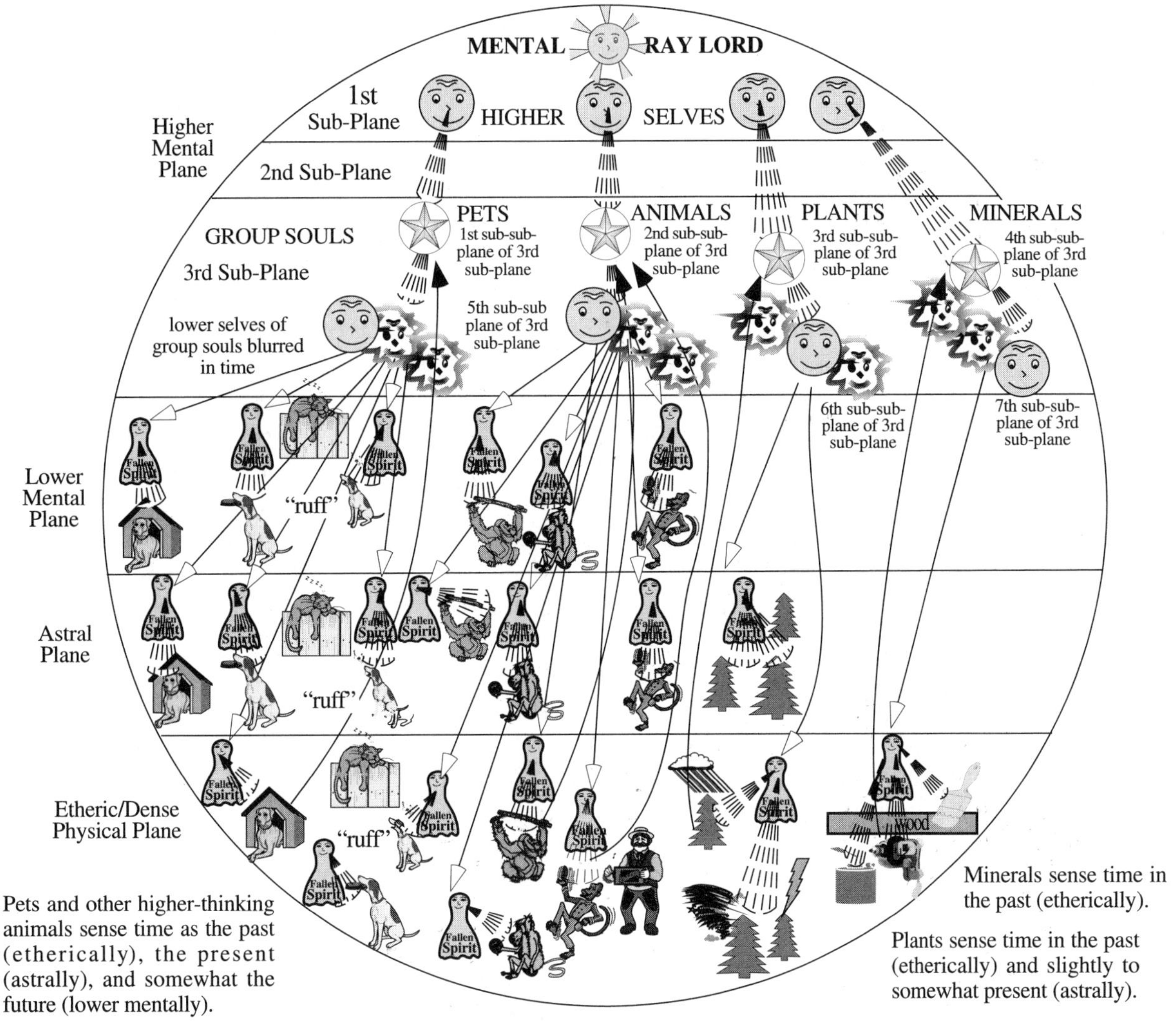

MENTAL — RAY LORD

Higher Mental Plane

1st Sub-Plane   HIGHER   SELVES

2nd Sub-Plane

GROUP SOULS

PETS 1st sub-sub-plane of 3rd sub-plane

ANIMALS 2nd sub-sub-plane of 3rd sub-plane

PLANTS 3rd sub-sub-plane of 3rd sub-plane

MINERALS 4th sub-sub-plane of 3rd sub-plane

3rd Sub-Plane

lower selves of group souls blurred in time

5th sub-sub plane of 3rd sub-plane

6th sub-sub-plane of 3rd sub-plane

7th sub-sub-plane of 3rd sub-plane

Lower Mental Plane

"ruff"

Astral Plane

"ruff"

Etheric/Dense Physical Plane

"ruff"

Pets and other higher-thinking animals sense time as the past (etherically), the present (astrally), and somewhat the future (lower mentally).

Minerals sense time in the past (etherically).

Plants sense time in the past (etherically) and slightly to somewhat present (astrally).

Because group souls obtain incomplete and relatively inaccurate sensory information from more than one lifeform (perhaps thousands or millions of lifeforms at a time), the group souls must average the information they receive from their lifeforms. This averaging helps group souls to compensate for the lack of accuracy in the information they receive, which is inaccurate because it does not contain all three time zones. Time is separated between each sub-plane of the mental plane, and the group souls are not able to think strongly enough to overcome this split mental plane time. Humans are supposed to unify the mental plane, and if they do they vastly improve the group souls' thought and selves in the process (which also builds the humans' civilization). Group souls as well as their (lower) selves are too inexperienced at thinking and too weak in thought to unify their thought on the mental plane. They cannot unify time, nor can they create completed concepts. An additional effect is caused by human souls thinking since souls do most of the thinking and thoughtform creation on the mental plane. However, humans thinking selfishly further splits the mental plane. The group souls collect and unify the information from the senses of their specific lifeforms. Information provided by minerals (pre-life) to their respective group souls comes from the minerals' one or two etheric senses, and focuses on the past. Information that plants provide to their respective group souls concerns the present and the past. And the information that animals provide to their respective group souls concerns the past, present, and, somewhat, the future. Some animals think on the lower mental plane.

Illustration 5.12

because of the slowness of preconceptual thought. Fortunately for group souls, the much higher Self of a Master and/or an energy Being (a Solar Angel) associated with the group souls' kingdom (and thought) assists them in their thought. This higher Self and thought come from the next group, or kingdom, of life *beyond* the human—sometimes referred to as either the spiritual kingdom or the Kingdom of Souls. Notice that within the scenario of self and Self helping lower spirit, what is required is a self that is higher to help spirit that is lower to think. This system of the higher helping the lower is common to how spirit functions, because all spirit contains some light, or God's thought (of light), of *choosing* to *give* to others in order to grow more of life.

Group souls usually inform a large group of individual lifeforms, keeping their elemental and lunar deva energies together and providing these lifeforms the benefit of preconceived thought in order to help them develop. When the preconceived thought is given to the individual lifeforms through the self of the group soul, it becomes what is referred to as instinctual thought. In return, the collective individual lifeforms contribute their senses of form and their information for the concurrent use by the lifeforms and their group soul, to synthesize into knowledge. While the lifeforms have the senses of form, group souls have the (two) spiritual senses of Self. The lower spiritual sense, of being able to recognize and understand other spirit and God, is the more developed of the two. The reason for the lower spiritual sense being better developed than the higher is that since its split from the Monad, spirit—together with other spirit and energy—always has had less of its ability to think in creative choices. This occurs because when spirit loses some of its ability to think, the more difficult to develop higher spiritual sense is what is lost first. Group souls derive their sense of form, or of energy, from the collective sense of the lifeforms on the dimensions where their lifeforms are alive. The group soul's collective and then synthesized information from the senses of forms is used by the group soul's self to inform it about other forms and other spirit as represented by other selves. A group soul cannot think conceptually by joining the higher mental sub-planes together at the same time. It cannot join at near the same time the lower mental sub-planes with the higher after the higher have become joined as much as the group soul can join them. Therefore, it can neither recognize nor think for an individual lifeform. Its self is not well enough developed through its mental thought to limit its field of life to the level in consciousness of an individual, which needs more thought given to it by its self. What it can do is limit the field to an average of the senses of all the lifeforms. Then it can use its self to discriminate, discern for its group of lifeforms, and somewhat group consciously give to other group souls and selves whose thought it can recognize concerning the *averages* of the activities of different groups of lifeforms.

Nearly none of the individual lifeforms of virtually any group souls have any significant sense of self. There are a few advanced animals, which through contact with the next higher kingdom (the human), gain a small amount of sense of individual self. This occurs by the humans loving the animals and thus thinking for them more, beyond the animals' level of thought, and helping them to better think and love more at times. These animals are usually pets of humans, and not just working animals. Working animals gain some help in thought through humans, but because they are generally not loved as much (if at all), their consciousness is less affected. The group soul and its self of some advanced pets sometimes becomes capable of isolating and then will isolate an animal from its preconceived thought. This reduces the instincts of the animal because the human thought is more advanced and substitutes for the self structure of the group soul. The structure of a self includes the self, its soul or group soul level of synthesizing thought, and its connections in thought to its one or more lifeforms. It is under the circumstances of isolation as described above that an individual animal is most likely to develop some significant level of self, which generally occurs because of a great deal of love exchanged between the animal and the human(s). Notice that what makes an animal a pet is the amounts of love it receives from human(s), and not who owns it or even whom it may live with.

Animals that have some significant sense of individual self are capable, at times, of recognizing who they are. They can make rudimentary plans in their thought *based upon one or more concepts.* These animals have at least a small conceptual sense of past, present, and future—although, again, only at certain times. Such an animal's developing individual self is fragile, and any type of threat or even excitement in its astral body can cause it to think instinctually again and lose its budding self. The human masters of these pets must be very loving or the pet will not be able to develop an emerging individual self or to maintain one that was previously developed. The reason why loving the pet is so important is that love builds consciousness, and it also calms the pet's astral body by changing emotion(s) into giving, or love, through the pet following the more advanced thought and consciousness of the human(s). One of the easiest tests in identifying an animal's sense of individual self at a particular time is whether the animal looks at itself in a mirror *and* demonstrates that it recognizes who it is through behaviors that react to the image in the mirror as being its self (and not as just another of its kind looking back at it). Any of such recognition and behavior is a signal of the presence of the sense of individual self in the animal.

An Animal That Has a Sense of Self Recognizes Itself

An animal that has no sense of self does not recognize itself or know who it is. In these circumstances, an animal looking into a mirror would think that it was looking at an animal other than itself.

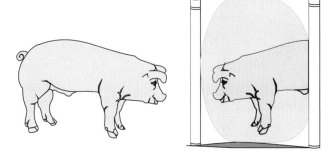

An animal that has a sense of self recognizes its image in the mirror, and responds accordingly. It responds to its own image because it knows who it is. Such an animal might observe something about its own body and know that it is observing itself. In this example, the dog is exhibiting this behavior by wagging its tail and observing the wagging as it changes it, while looking at its reflection in the mirror.

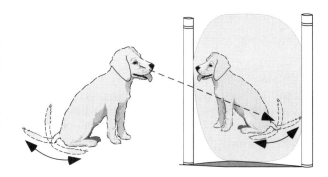

Illustration 5.13

In wild animals some exceptions to the above explanation exist. Chimpanzees have some sense of individual self even *without human contact*; at times other apes (including the gorilla species), as well, may come close to developing an individual self. The explanation is that these few species of animals today (and even more species that have become extinct) were altered in their DNA and its astral equivalent, or their genetics, a very long time ago through inappropriate human contact. One result was that these animals' DNA became more similar to human DNA; actually, the animals' permanent atoms were altered. What happened will be covered in more detail in Chapters Seven and Nine. Amazingly, some spiritual books have mentioned this condition since long before the genes of apes or the study of their self structure was known and, in fact, long before the concepts of genes or DNA even existed within human understanding. Certain ape species were "experimented on" and, in even earlier times, were used for sexual exploitation; sometimes, as a part of this process, modified types of human procreation with these apes were attempted—with some "success." These gruesome experiments and other immoral acts and purposes (immoral because they were for purely exploitive purposes—and harmed the animals, human civilization, and the lower kingdoms) occurred in times and within civilizations that are mostly unknown today by those who do not study certain types of spiritual material. Within some existing spiritual material, a significant amount has been written about some of these ancient and hidden civilizations. Their mention in this book before Chapter Nine is more anecdotal and explanatory of certain exceptional circumstances that are an effect of these prior civilizations' existence. A fairly thorough explanation and study of these civilizations will be presented in Chapter Nine. Note that in all of the above-described cases of experimentation and exploitation, some effect did occur, and it often involved damage to the self of the group souls of these apes, as humans selfishly interfered with this part of life. Sometimes the lower spirit, a fallen spirit, within the animals became dominant and no longer connected to its group soul, but instead connected to evil. When not fatal to the life of the animal, this fallen spirit created some types of monsters. These were usually in etheric and astral form, and mostly not in dense physical form.

Centers of DNA and Pre-Life

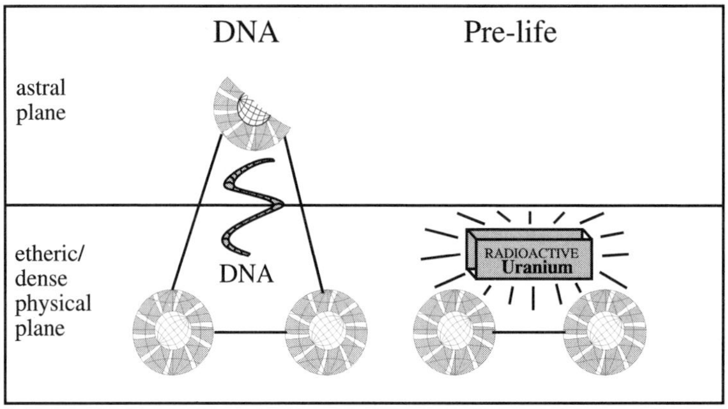

DNA is not life. DNA makes up life, but is itself not yet alive. It has two centers on the etheric/dense physical plane and only an incomplete astral center on the astral plane. In order to be alive, or have sentiency, complete centers on at least two planes are required. An advanced mineral such as radioactive uranium has two etheric/dense physical centers and no astral plane center. Because the uranium lacks an astral center, it lacks sentiency as well.

Illustration 5.14

A self needs to be able to sense the three fractured parts of time (past, present, and future) logically together and at close to the same time in order to recognize who it is in comparison to others. Some group souls have a great deal of difficulty in achieving this in their thought. The group souls of pre-life minerals gain only a single sense, and in only one dimension: the lowest; what limits minerals to being pre-life is that they have only this one sense. A second mineral sense, and an additional one on a second dimension as well (which would be indicative of life), is not yet developed. This second sense, and an additional one on a second dimension, would allow energy to transfer from one center to another and between dimensions, creating conscious, or sentient, movement within the form. Sentiency is the ability for an individual life-form to move in time and space by its own thought and awareness. This attracts energy from one sense and dimension to another. The ability for a lifeform to move on its own thought (of the fallen spirit that informs it) requires that it have one or more senses in two or more dimensions of time and space. For example, a plant can slightly (and sentiently) move because etheric energy focused in the past is transferring (and transforming consciousness at the same time) into lower astral energy in the present. Most botanists today would not recognize plants as being sentient because botany defines the term by only certain effects (which are very difficult for humans to detect), rather than causes. The one sense that many minerals have is of the energy itself—and usually takes the form of heat, pressure, or molecular interactions. Some minerals have two senses on the etheric/dense physical plane, but none on the astral. These minerals are either radioactive or are complex organic compounds. DNA is the transitional mineral of a very complex organic compound that has two etheric/dense physical centers and one *nearly* complete astral center. The astral center of DNA cannot stay completely together without the informing additional thought of spirit to assist the astral lunar pitris, or lunar devas, in the center.

The "thought" of minerals is extremely small, even within whatever amount of single or multiple senses they do have. Most chemists and physicists today would not recognize the thought that is in energy, because they do not understand spirit and they mostly observe effects without understanding the causes behind these effects. The mineral group soul develops a very rudimentary self by using the collective sense of its minerals to build mostly a sense of time in the past; this is in correspondence to the etheric/dense physical plane, where minerals are most focused in their pre-life. The part of fractured time that is most represented, that remains somewhat whole after spirit fractures time, and that is emphasized on this (the seventh) dimension, or plane, is the past. When humans who are physically alive are focused on physical effects in their thought, they can mostly sense time only after it has occurred, or can mostly sense time only as the past. Because the emphasis in time on the seventh plane is mostly on the past, the self of mineral group souls is likewise mostly focused on this part of time, because that is what is provided by the mineral's slight sense. The slight sense of minerals is transmitted to the mineral group soul, which synthesizes it with preconceived thought using the three parts of time and then gives this thought to its connected self (which gives the thought to the fallen spirit that is informing the pre-life form). To develop its self, the mineral group soul must be able to additionally focus somewhat on the present and future, and to bring these together on the higher mental plane enough to create preconceived thought. The mineral group souls achieve the difficult feat of linking time together by using for some of their thought the light (of the mental plane Ray Lord) that is given to them by their Self and then remains inside their spirit and their mental form, to guide them according to the plan for their development. When this light is inside their spirit and their mental form, it (the light) becomes virtue. Mental virtue is whole *structured* thought (wisdom) that is a part of form and is given. The mineral group souls borrow some of the Ray Lord's thought that is given to them through their respective Selves to create structures that are a part of the Ray Lord's plan for minerals. These structures are then, through the informing thought of fallen spirit, given to minerals by the group soul and its self. Thought towards these minerals interacting with other minerals is needed in order to create chemical compounds for future life. As the spirit within a group soul gives, through its self, the structure from the light of the Ray Lord to minerals, this spirit gains a sense of time in the present, from what the structure does, and in the future, from what the structure will do for minerals and developing future life. The more enlightened that the mineral group soul is, the better it can give structure to the minerals that it informs as pre-life, and the better its self structure is built. When minerals are selfishly used to "destroy" the growth of life by humans (which really only slows it down or just ignores such growth), the corresponding group souls can lose some of all of their selves…leading to far-reaching and unexpected—deadly—either new compounds or new effects on life from existing compounds, or both. The less light that is in a mineral group soul, the less the group soul can synthesize all three parts of time together.

Time on the Three Lower Planes

Each plane has a zone of time that energy can become a sense of. The time on the etheric/dense physical plane is the past, the time of the astral plane is the past and present, and the time of the mental plane is the past, present, and future. If the centers and senses of a lifeform or pre-life form exist only on a particular plane, then only the corresponding time zone can be sensed by that form. Group souls use the light of the Ray Lords to extrapolate whatever senses of time are missing, so that all three times zones are included. However, since the extrapolated missing sense or senses of time are based on thought, and not based on direct sensation and experience, they are less accurate.

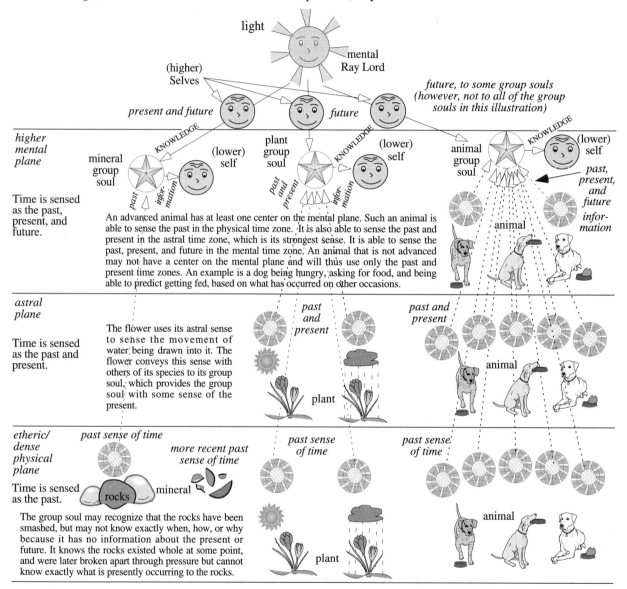

higher mental plane

Time is sensed as the past, present, and future.

An advanced animal has at least one center on the mental plane. Such an animal is able to sense the past in the physical time zone. It is also able to sense the past and present in the astral time zone, which is its strongest sense. It is able to sense the past, present, and future in the mental time zone. An animal that is not advanced may not have a center on the mental plane and will thus use only the past and present time zones. An example is a dog being hungry, asking for food, and being able to predict getting fed, based on what has occurred on other occasions.

astral plane

Time is sensed as the past and present.

The flower uses its astral sense to sense the movement of water being drawn into it. The flower conveys this sense with others of its species to its group soul, which provides the group soul with some sense of the present.

etheric/ dense physical plane

Time is sensed as the past.

The group soul may recognize that the rocks have been smashed, but may not know exactly when, how, or why because it has no information about the present or future. It knows the rocks existed whole at some point, and were later broken apart through pressure but cannot know exactly what is presently occurring to the rocks.

As pre-life, a mineral has only one or two centers, only on the etheric/dense physical plane. Minerals with less than the one full sense are still developing themselves into pre-life. Thus the mineral can sense only what has already occurred (the past). This sense conveys information to the group soul about pressure, heat, and electro-chemical reactions. The group soul takes this information and converts it into knowledge that it gives to the self. The self uses this knowledge to inform fallen spirit that is helping each center to have better sense and to better respond to the environment.

A plant has at least two centers on the etheric/dense physical plane and up to two centers on the astral plane. A plant can sense what has occurred in the past and somewhat what is occurring in the present. In order to sense the present, at least one sense on the astral plane is needed.

An animal has a minimum of three centers on the etheric/dense physical plane and at least three centers on the astral plane. An advanced animal may have one or more centers on the mental plane. These centers allow the animal to sense the past, present, and, for some animals, somewhat the future. The animal conveys this information as senses of these three time zones to its group soul.

Illustration 5.15

The group souls of plants have much better-formed self structures because the lifeforms they inform are alive, or have at least two senses on the etheric/dense physical plane and one on the astral (some have up to three etheric/dense physical and two astral) or a sense or senses and a brain (however, plants on earth do not yet have brains). The two senses of plants (with at least one sense on the astral plane as well) allow energy to move from one part of the same life-form to another, producing some movement within plants based upon the thought and needs of the *individual* lifeform to grow. Plants exist as life on the etheric/dense physical plane, and much less so on the lower astral plane. Their group souls have two senses of time, the past and present, from the senses of the plants that are their informed lifeforms. The senses exist on only two planes (the etheric/dense physical and the astral). These two planes give to the plant group souls and their development of self the sense of past and present in time, as well as etheric senses and a very slight to moderate astral, or emotional, sense. Animal group souls need only to construct the future sense of time to create a self from the light (of the mental plane Ray Lord, given to them by their respective Selves) within their spirit and form. Again, the mental plane is where the life of souls is focused, since the spirit of a soul must be at or above the middle of the mental plane in order to stay enlightened and not lose its ability to create a self.

Animal group souls gain at least three senses and sometimes up to five on at least two planes, from their lifeforms that they inform. For some animal species, senses are developed on the etheric/dense physical, astral, and mental planes, allowing the group soul to sense and think directly in all three parts of time. These group souls have the added benefit of fully developing a self from both their informed lifeforms and from the structure of the virtue of the mental plane Ray Lord, given to them by their respective Selves. These group souls are the most advanced and, because of the benefits of improved self structure, can change and improve their species more rapidly on average. However, a group soul of an advanced plant, such as some trees or flowers (which have three senses of form on the etheric plane, and at least one but usually two on the astral plane), might be able to improve its species of lifeforms better and even faster than the group soul of a primitive animal species of, e.g., microscopic amoebas (which have three senses of form on both the etheric and astral planes). The reason is that the spirit of the plant group soul is likely to be more enlightened (and therefore relatively advanced), which makes up for the lack of sense it gains from its plant lifeforms. At equal levels of enlightenment (advancement) within such types of group souls, animal group souls have the most developed self and minerals have the least, with plants in-between. This order exists because the development of self depends upon the quality and number of senses within the self's lifeforms, if other conditions of their souls are equal.

The selves of many group souls are helped, as is needed, in their development of self and their enlightenment. They are sometimes helped in their creation of virtue (which is a part of their creation of Self) by the spiritual kingdom, or by Beings who are advanced beyond the human stage of life. Without such help, what many humans refer to as evolution in its later stage would be unable to maintain the growth of life. The reason is that the selves of many group souls would too often fail to stay sufficiently integrated in time and space to inform their pre-life or life with adequate instincts, or enough thought. Then the lifeform would fail to overcome the resistance of some of the more dense elemental energies on the astral plane and especially the etheric plane to keep a lifeform alive or to keep pre-life progressing towards life. Although they occur infrequently, too many life-stressing factors do occur in weather, geology, and outside of terrestrial (extraterrestrial) conditions for more advanced evolutionary life to sustain itself. Particularly troublesome are the problems caused by the human kingdom, once it has developed. These problems over-tax many group souls and their selves. Because of their capricious and selfish nature, humans introduce so many problems that prior to the emergence of the human kingdom on this planet there was much less need for direct intervention by any higher

Beings to assist group souls. With humans sharing the planet (or not sharing, as is mostly the case at present), unless higher spiritual thought is provided to the group souls, many simply would not be able to think fast enough and then communicate their preconceived thought into the instincts that keep their lifeforms alive. While humans are ultimately responsible for the kingdoms lower than their own, unless the group souls were otherwise assisted, humans would be likely to destroy these kingdoms (and these kingdoms' selves) before ever reaching the point of extending any loving help towards them.

Evolution is *not* simply a mechanical process of complex chemicals (genes) responding to stress, or forces, by changing the direction and amounts of the energies within them, with the surviving ("the fittest") chemicals being the ones that respond best to stress (which is "heat," or forces, or opposing energies). Note that at their *core*, strictly non-spiritual theories of evolution do espouse this concept. Such a process (even if possible) would be far too slow—especially for more advanced forms of life. The reason is that as the lifeforms advance they become more complex in their structures and they suffer greater stresses from other life, particularly from human selfishness. These advanced lifeforms have more advanced souls (either group souls or, in the case of humans, individual souls) *that think* and have better self structures. Their self structures do change life much more quickly and complexly at times in order to overcome the above-mentioned forces. In mechanical evolution, the model that is based on forces of energies becomes progressively *slower* in its ability to change a lifeform as more complexity is added into the energies. The preceding concepts expose some inconsistencies in purely mechanical evolutionary models. Evolution as an all-mechanical model would lead to eventual failure of advanced life, as the result of an inability to adapt quickly enough to environmental problems (many of which are caused by humans, when they are present). Life would succumb to the various forces, which allow the success of evolution, as an energy model of life development, but which would destroy higher life and eventually all of life. A completely mechanical evolutionary model, or one without spirit, also fails to explain what life and thought are and where they come from. Evolution when joined with spiritual causes is the method of life development, with theories of evolution primarily explaining the development of energy; group souls and their selves (and *creative thought*) explain mostly how spirit develops life. The two parts—spirit and thought, and evolution and energy—need to be considered together in order to gain a clear understanding of life, or God's growth. Evolution mostly affects lower forms of life wherein energy tends to overcome the thought of spirit; spirit, group souls, and their selves (and the selves' giving of *thought*) have more of an effect on higher forms of life because energy follows thought that is greater than its own. Both methods are a part of each Ray Lord's plan for creating life in its corresponding plane, or dimension of time and space.

Group souls are developed in a hierarchy of consciousness based upon self development, from differing levels of development of the spirit that composes them. Their development in hierarchy spans from the mineral level to the animal. (Much more will be covered about group souls in the next chapter and in Chapter Nine.) Eventually spirit reaches the level of being able to create a self that can think conceptually and that is also enlightened enough to use both of its spiritual senses (of Self) equally *in capability* (based upon its choices to do so). The most advanced spirit, which comes from a collection, or pool, of the very best spirit in all of the most advanced and enlightened of the (animal) group souls that are capable of advancing when the time is right, creates a self that can focus on all three parts of fractured time *equally* well, creating very good logic in its thought. This collection of the very best spirit from animal group souls divides itself into a hierarchy of parts based upon its ability to think, which then creates a structural replication of a much higher source of spirit and energy that is referred to as an OverSoul, or Solar Angel (some people use the more general names of Inner Guide or Guardian Angel). On earth today billions of parts of the most advanced spirit from group souls are *each* structured from their "own" Solar Angel, or OverSoul, and become a spark of light on the higher mental plane. Every one of these sparks is caused by a fusion, or fusing together, of all the different parts of higher spirit through the very high directive, or conscious, thought of the OverSoul; each spark is, at first, protected from selfish thought of darker spirit and elemental energy by an energy field of solar devas on the higher mental plane. The innermost part of these solar pitris come from the best-thinking ones that are indigenous to the planet the spirit is created on. The remainder of the protective energy field is given from the lowest part of the OverSoul's body to the spark of highest spirit from the most advanced group souls. These same solar devas, as an enlightened energy field, guide the elemental energies of the higher mental plane to better hold together the conceptual thought that is created by the self and possibly the Self of the spirit that is this spark.

Creating a Human Soul's Spirit and Energy

The best-thinking spirit and energy from the most advanced animal group souls progresses out of the animal kingdom and goes on to become part of new human souls.

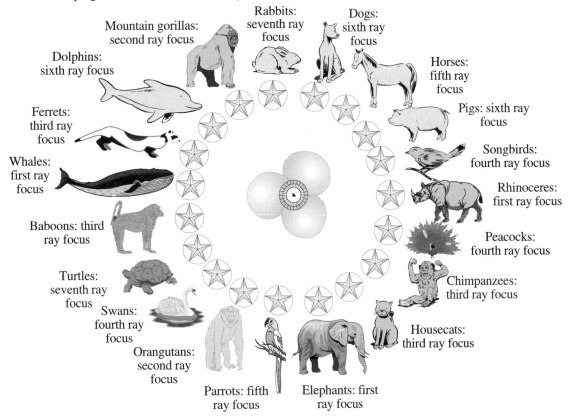

Illustration 5.16

 HUMAN SOULS AND SELVES

The spark of the spirit that comes from the most advanced group souls and that structures itself in light according to the structure of the OverSoul, or Solar Angel, is the spiritual part of a new human soul. The energy part of the best-thinking energies of group souls that are indigenous to the planet form a collection of solar pitris. These solar pitris form the three inner sacrifice petals of the human soul. The spirit and the surrounding energies compose the human soul. (Solar Angels will be more fully explained in the next chapter.) Each human soul is connected to a human Monad that exists on the monadic plane. Each human soul is focused on two areas of development. The first is the development of the fourth, or human, kingdom, which is guided by the fourth ray towards increasing senses and life development. The second is the eventual development of consciousness in individual lifeforms, or of givingness and oneness to this part of life. The qualities, or consciousness and oneness, in human life also make it an expression of the second Ray Lord, and, of course, the life that it helps to create—the Monads. Thus humans are a much lower correspondence of the life of Monads, but are more affected by the fourth ray and are working towards making life more beautiful, rather than perfectly conscious, as the Monads are—who are much higher in consciousness. As humans perfect their selves they advance to the next kingdom and make human and lower levels of life more beautiful. As Monads perfect their Beingness, they move on to the next kingdom and make all life more conscious. This process of moving ahead to the next kingdom through focus of a specific ray is referred to as a ray line.

Human Soul Connected to the Monad

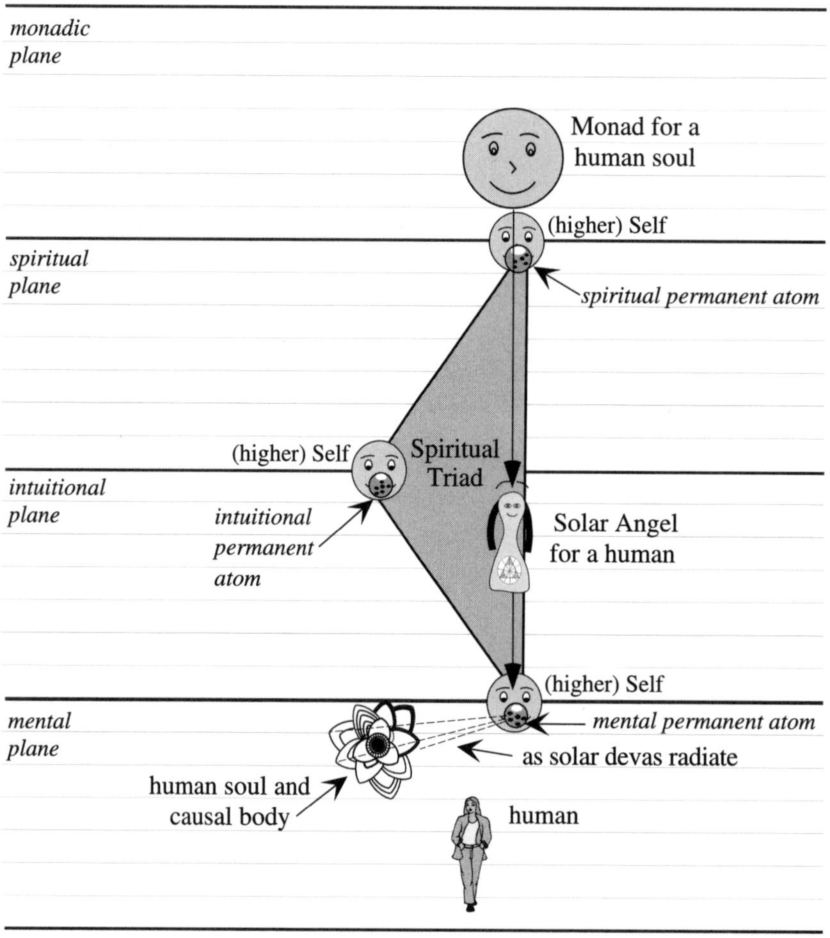

monadic plane

Monad for a human soul

(higher) Self

spiritual plane

spiritual permanent atom

(higher) Self Spiritual Triad

intuitional plane

intuitional permanent atom

Solar Angel for a human

(higher) Self

mental plane

mental permanent atom

as solar devas radiate

human soul and causal body

human

The human soul connects to the human Monad as the human's causal body solar devas radiate light between the human soul and its (higher) Self. This radiation begins at the accepted stage of the first initiation and progresses through the entire second initiation and beyond.

Illustration 5.17

Because of their combination fourth and second ray nature and because they function mentally, human souls are found in the very middle of the higher mental plane, or the *fourth* sub-*sub*-plane of the *second* sub-plane. This precise location is determined by the ray focus of the human soul, as mentioned above, and the ray structure of the form, or body—including the soul's body, of the inner sacrifice solar devas, which surrounds and protects each soul. These protective solar pitris are also a part of the causal body because they eventually help to create concepts, or causes of thought mentally. It is this form (the solar pitris) that is responsive to the fourth and second rays. Rays affect only form directly, and they affect spirit indirectly through its use of form with which to sense; this gives spirit more freedom to make choices and to think on its own. The location of a human soul is determined by its need to be assisted in its conceptual thought (mentally) and initially to be protected from the selfish thought of darker spirit and from mental elemental energy's gravitational thought. In a way, a human soul is entrapped in its location on the higher mental plane because of these inadequacies in developing thought. The soul can leave this position only as more of its thought and body together become enlightened—and thus no longer in need of an additional energy field (of both the outer and the inner solar pitris), or a causal body, to surround it.

The (lower) self of group souls is sacrificed *by each group soul* as it *chooses* to give its spirit that has the highest level of thought. This spirit is to be joined with other spirit that has the highest level of thought of other group souls. As long as spirit is not created into a self, it can, collectively in a pool, join with other spirit. The sacrifice is that the self of the group soul does not move on to become a part of the collection of highest spirit because the highest level of group soul spirit is above the group soul's self, on the higher mental plane. The spirit that has the highest level of thought of animal group souls is joined together to become a pool of the highest spiritual thought that will become, but is not yet, a human soul. The pool then divides itself into a hierarchy of thought that contains enough thought to limit the field of energies that will compose a human soul. Human souls are created from this hierarchial pool of highest spiritual thought; in most cases the self must be sacrificed because it holds the preconceptual thought, instincts, and memories that did serve its animals, but would interfere with the new humans' growth. The (higher) Self is joined with the very highest spiritual thought of group souls and their selves that reached a level of mental enlightenment; the Self of each group soul is further grown as it sacrifices its self. Some of the self remains as an individual part of the light that is transferred and fused with the group soul's Self, which is a shared part of the advancing Solar Angel (who often leaves for another planet). The process is called transfiguration because the light and consciousness are *not* destroyed, but are changed and fused through light, or transfigured, in structure from one type of life to another. Figuration is a method of determining the structure of a lifeform through the use of light, which means that at least some processes of any transfiguration occur on the mental plane because the mental plane is where structure exists.

Once the self that is connected to the highest level of spirit is sacrificed by the group soul, most memory of the knowledge that had been created through the collective synthesis of its individual lifeforms' senses is lost. The reason is that most of this knowledge, which was created from instincts, was not *perfectly* created or used. In God's plan, *only perfection remains immortally*. Instincts coming from the group souls and given by their selves are likewise destroyed by the sacrifice and do not transfer into the human soul. Knowledge that was given wisely *remains* as a part of each group soul's shared Self (with its Solar Angel) because this knowledge became a part of light, or a part of God (the Ray Lord) as its thought. In other words, some of the energy of the form became enlightened and returned to intelligent activity, or to knowledge that was perfectly communicated and that exclusively enlightened other form as it was given. In most circumstances, group souls cannot detect any of the experiences of their individual lifeforms because the group souls cannot think conceptually, and preconceptual thought cannot sense or think in a specific effect—only in averages. Thus the knowledge that group souls sacrifice is based upon the *collective* information of their individual lifeforms' senses. Most of the relatively small amounts of enlightened knowledge that become a part of the group soul's shared Self comes from the same *collective* senses of its lifeforms. But there is an exception to this, and for the most advanced spiritual thought of some group souls, it is of significant importance and effect. The experiences of pets that are isolated from much of the instinctual thought of the group souls can be experienced by the group soul as individual sense. The group soul is able to sense individually when its instinctual thought is replaced by human conceptual thought that is given (in love) to the pet. These enlightened senses are synthesized by the group soul into knowledge within its Self. It is at this point that one of the most wonderfully poetic parts of life occurs in the transfiguration process of the group soul's shared (with its OverSoul, or Solar Angel) Self.

The self of each advanced animal group soul gives its advanced spirit to make up a specific human soul. A significant portion of the enlightened knowledge within the shared Self of the group soul and OverSoul came from previous humans and their souls loving and creating more virtue in their pets. Some of the *individual* thought of these pets becomes a part of the thought of the Selves of new human souls and their OverSouls, usually while on a different planet. Only a human soul—and usually not a human being—eventually has direct contact with this thought of its Self because the soul chooses to only give whole structured knowledge, or love/wisdom; the eventual giving of love/wisdom connects the soul with its Self, which thinks only in light. Individual humans usually cannot access the memory of their soul's Self, unless they are mostly fused in thought with their souls by creating enough virtue in their lives. The Self helps the human self to develop. The human soul gains its highest levels of thought from its collective group souls' thought and the *loving* experiences of hundreds to thousands of pets of prior humans (often from a different planet), from different animal group souls, of different ray focuses, as it gains contact with its Self. If pets are treated generally cruelly, then the human Self is lessened and the selves of the new human souls will be much more selfish and will therefore have much lower consciousness than if they had had the benefit of loving experiences as a part of each one's soul and Self. It is stated in a number of spiritual books that the ways in which humans treat their pets is *more* important than the ways in which humans treat each other; this statement is based upon an understanding of the above-described concepts.

Most of the advanced and enlightened spiritual thought of group souls is transfigured in cycles of life creation. These cycles help to maintain the integrity of life, and protect one part of life from the selfishness, or darkness, of another. This issue will be further studied in Chapter Nine. Most new human souls are created in the process of transfiguration of group souls' Selves during these same cycles, when the majority of and the highest part of each kingdom is advanced. The highest spirit of these group souls is joined into a greater Self of an OverSoul that has been transfigured into a human OverSoul. The "door" of advancement from one kingdom to the next, however, is never completely closed during the off-periods of life advancement. Those individuals within the most advanced species (including humans) that are the most developed and are ready can advance if their bodies, senses, and spirit are enlightened enough to become transfigured into the next kingdom. When this occurs for an animal group soul, the *one individual* pet of the specific group soul develops enough capabilities of giving, or consciousness, to equal that of *the average* of consciousness, or givingness, of the human kingdom (on the *same* planet) *at that time*. This is a formidable task and rarely takes place, but when it does, the group soul advances tremendously from the growth of its self and gives this amount (and more) of this growth, in concert with other group souls who can appropriately give some of their selves, to create a new human soul. The new human soul then is ensouled by a Solar Angel and its Self from the same planet; this will be further explained in the next chapter. Note that in these circumstances the advancing pet's group soul must sacrifice that part of the senses and its self that the pet was contributing to the group soul. As this rare exception to the more normal course of events takes place, the new *human* is likely to retain some memory of its last life (or lives) as an animal. The reason is that the new human retains some of the self of the primary contributing group soul, which informed it as an animal lifeform. This self did not dissolve into fallen spirit and at least somewhat fused with its Self during transfiguration and that part of it transfigures into the shared Self of the new human OverSoul.

In the above-described system (as in all of Ageless Wisdom), anything that becomes enlightened, and therefore perfected, becomes immortal. All enlightened parts of the self, which is spirit, become (transformed into) a part of the Self, and no part of the Self is ever lost in transfiguration—it is only added to. Also, (enlightened) individuality is not lost because a greater individual is created, with no parts lost from any of the (smaller) parts of selves from the group souls. All enlightened parts of every self from each of the group souls are *added* together but not *averaged* together within the Solar Angel. In transfiguration each *gains* from the other parts and still remains. As can be seen, consciousness is both shared and individual.

The shared Self of a human soul and its OverSoul have a shared consciousness of spirit from the selves of a number of animal group souls. This shared nature gives human souls and their Selves great diversity and subsequent creativity in their thought; these qualities also come from all seven rays of life focus through all seven different types of animal group souls' energies and their lifeforms. As a result of the probability factors of joining together seven different fields of life under *one* larger Self with its human soul and Solar Angel and the soul's senses, each human soul when functioning with its Self has *one* ray that is more capable of limiting its corresponding field than the other six ray fields. The reason is that the thought by a human soul still limits the field of energy in a specific way. Because the Self contains only spirit, it has no ray focus without its soul—which does contain an energy part. Note that this one ray will be better developed in the human soul than will the other six rays of contributing group soul energy. Yet because the individual highest spirit of each of the group soul's ray focus of thought remain within a human Self, and soul, human Selves and souls can think equally well along any of the seven rays of focus *when they give together* with other souls and their Selves. Individually, a Self cannot *create equally well* when joined with its soul along each ray focus because although each Self only gives and creates consciousness as one with other Selves, it only some of the time chooses, or makes choices, that are in unison with other Selves. Each Self is most creative of life and its Self along a particular ray focus when It is focused through the soul's senses. All of the seven rays of focus, of ways that group souls sense and help to create more of a Self from the soul's sense, become a part of a human Self, and eventually part of a human soul. This provides humans with huge amounts of diversity in thought, givingness (love), and creativity, as compared to any animal.

Humans are, in addition, able to think conceptually because they have the best of the spiritual thought available from the group souls that gave each human its soul, and each personality and self that the human soul creates receives this thought as it chooses to. This self is structured based upon the very advanced thought of the OverSoul. Collective high levels of spiritual thought give humans the ability to think using the entire mental plane. The human Self (which is shared with its OverSoul) can limit the majority of the mental plane Ray Lord's field of life by being connected to the lifeforms of humans it is helping to create. This Self is so creative of virtue that it is consistently giving with other Selves, in kingdoms from the mineral to the human. A Self can give its field of life (in one or more of three ways) perfectly at the atomic level of the mental plane and above, but must learn to do so below this level; it, like all other parts of life, is on a journey to improve itself by giving whatever it can give wisely, while further developing its ability to do so—and growing more of God in the process. Because a Self is synonymous with enlightenment and because humans are focused on mental development, the human Self is located at the atomic level of the mental plane, or where the mental plane Ray Lord focuses its thought. A new human soul has initially almost no contact with its shared Self because the energy field of solar devas that surrounds it acts as a barrier to the Self's thought. This barrier causes the new human soul to fall asleep (because it chooses either to think only in light, or not at all) and causes the OverSoul to temporarily communicate through the shared Self and carry out the human soul's function. Note that the shared Self is the lowest part of the OverSoul sacrificed for use by the soul. Each OverSoul has developed part of its shared Self through, first, functioning as an OverSoul to a group soul—usually on another planet. Its Self that will be used as part of the Self for a human being is created through the process that has just been described. This process joins the highest (the enlightened) part of the selves, as spirit that is not self conscious—in the progressive transfiguration of several, usually seven, animal group souls, and often takes place before the leaving of that planet for a developing sister planet. The OverSoul continues in its aforementioned role until the human soul has become developed enough in light to do these things in concert with the Solar Angel and eventually on its own. The Self relies on the sense of the human soul to inform it; this sense comprises three groups of solar pitris that create three inner petal-like formations and surround the soul. The sense must become developed and used by the soul through its self, or the devas that compose it interfere with the contact between the soul and its Self. The devas and thus the sense are developed by becoming enlightened and radiating mental light into the Self and soul and/or self. As this development occurs, the soul becomes transfigured and connected with its Self through structured (radiating) light. The Self then also becomes informed of what the personality has created in enlightened knowledge. This knowledge is synthesized and enlightened information coming from the senses of the three bodies—the etheric/dense physical, the astral, and the mental. The personality is described and defined in the paragraphs that immediately follow.

The first major function of the human soul, which in the beginning of its existence is carried out by the OverSoul, is to create bodies and their senses in the three worlds where humans can live, or the mental, astral, and etheric/dense physical dimensions. Except for the upper half of the mental body, these bodies and senses are composed of the thought of the highest levels, or best-thinking, of the fallen spirit of these worlds that attracts, as a lower correspondence, energies that are similar in quality, or consciousness, but that only very slightly think. The upper one-half of the mental body is composed of three parts. The first part is spirit that is more enlightened than not and the better-thinking lunar devas. The second part is the solar devas, and the third part is the higher and lower mental plane elemental energy. All of these components have been developed by the most advanced animal group souls, similar to the way the human soul was developed (from a pool of spirit and energy that is the best-thinking of its kind). Human bodies are brought together by the thought of the higher spirit of the OverSoul and/or in the case of a more advanced human soul, additionally through that human soul's thought. The thought of the human Self—working in concert with the needs of other human Selves and souls—creates a unit of matching thought as an effect on the lower mental plane. When humans are created, the effects of certain concepts' structures from the mental permanent atom are focused on as thoughtforms on the fourth mental sub-plane. The personality is inherently selfish because these concepts, while not the very most selfish ones in the permanent atom, concern the areas that are not fully enlightened and that the personality will have the opportunity to improve upon in that life. The Self reconstructs these structures based on what is missing from the light within the permanent atom.

The effect on the lower mental plane of creating concepts of bodies and senses on the higher mental plane is that there must be enough thought as an effect to limit, or control, the new life-form of a human being. It is important to remember that the causes in thought are on the higher mental plane, and that the effects from these causes are on the lower…all a result of the split in

Recipe for a Human Being

Part 1

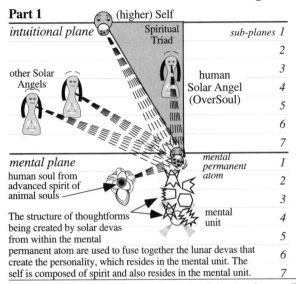

intuitional plane

other Solar Angels

(higher) Self

Spiritual Triad

human Solar Angel (OverSoul)

sub-planes	1
	2
	3
	4
	5
	6
	7

mental plane

human soul from advanced spirit of animal souls

The structure of thoughtforms being created by solar devas from within the mental permanent atom are used to fuse together the lunar devas that create the personality, which resides in the mental unit. The self is composed of spirit and also resides in the mental unit.

mental permanent atom

mental unit

	1
	2
	3
	4
	5
	6
	7

The human Solar Angel and sometimes other Solar Angels, as well as the (higher) Selves and human soul focus their energy on the mental permanent atom. In so doing they re-create the structure of the solar deva energies from the permanent atom. The solar deva energies become the structure, and the lunar deva energies (when fused together) become thoughtforms. These thoughtforms replicate the solar deva structure, producing effects that form the personality in the mental unit. The thoughtforms represent an area of creating more virtue in life that the personality needs to further develop in itself. The intensity of the thought that these energies follow causes the thoughtforms to last for up to 150 years.

Part 2

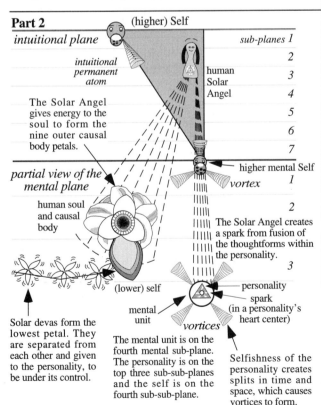

intuitional plane

intuitional permanent atom

The Solar Angel gives energy to the soul to form the nine outer causal body petals.

(higher) Self

human Solar Angel

sub-planes	1
	2
	3
	4
	5
	6
	7

partial view of the mental plane

human soul and causal body

higher mental Self

vortex

	1
	2
	3

The Solar Angel creates a spark from fusion of the thoughtforms within the personality.

(lower) self

personality spark (in a personality's heart center)

mental unit

vortices

Solar devas form the lowest petal. They are separated from each other and given to the personality, to be under its control.

The mental unit is on the fourth mental sub-plane. The personality is on the top three sub-sub-planes and the self is on the fourth sub-sub-plane.

Selfishness of the personality creates splits in time and space, which causes vortices to form.

Illustration 5.18

Part 3

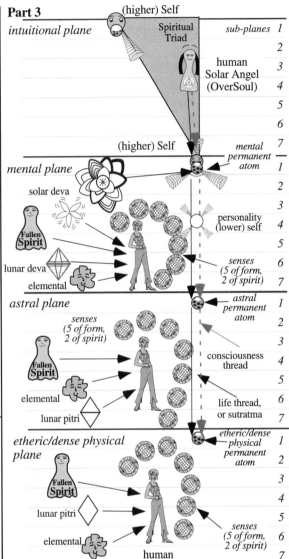

intuitional plane

(higher) Self

Spiritual Triad

human Solar Angel (OverSoul)

sub-planes	1
	2
	3
	4
	5
	6
	7

(higher) Self

mental plane

solar deva

Fallen Spirit

lunar deva

elemental

mental permanent atom

personality (lower) self

senses (5 of form, 2 of spirit)

	1
	2
	3
	4
	5
	6
	7

astral plane

senses (5 of form, 2 of spirit)

Fallen Spirit

elemental

lunar pitri

astral permanent atom

consciousness thread

life thread, or sutratma

	1
	2
	3
	4
	5
	6
	7

etheric/dense physical plane

Fallen Spirit

lunar pitri

elemental

human

etheric/dense physical permanent atom

senses (5 of form, 2 of spirit)

	1
	2
	3
	4
	5
	6
	7

A life thread is focused through the permanent atoms on all of the planes from the monadic, down. Through the Monad's will and with the informing thought from the Solar Angel, Self, and soul, the life thread connects these permanent atoms and uses the information in them to create the body of a new human on those planes. Each major center in each body has a spirit sphere that is made up of fallen spirit, and all of the spirit spheres are connected together through the (lower) self and (higher) Self, via the consciousness thread.

The self controls how the energy will be used. Energy composed of solar devas, lunar pitris, and elementals of a similar quality of consciousness are drawn to the structure of the permanent atoms and form the bodies. The Self directs fallen spirit contained in each spirit sphere of all the major centers to inform energy that creates senses and that the personality uses to synthesize and organize knowledge with. Each body also has five senses of form that are under the control of the personality and two senses of spirit that are under the control of the self, if the personality permits this control. All the senses give back information to the personality; the personality can give synthesized information as knowledge to the self, soul, Self, and Solar Angel, if it decides to.

time and space. The new lifeform has three bodies, each with five senses of form and two senses/means-of-thought of spirit. It has an individual soul and Self, as well as an OverSoul. The matching effect of thought on the lower mental plane is the amount of thought necessary to limit and control the senses of the three bodies a majority of the time. The effect is created and given to the new human being, or lifeform, by the human-soul/OverSoul and the human Self. The unit of lower mental thoughtforms is structured in exact measure to the type and structure of the three bodies and their senses added together. The type and structure are related to ray types and levels of advancement of the energies, with a specific ray type and level of consciousness for the energy within each of the three bodies. The forms of the thoughts that are used are unique for each human being, for two reasons. The first is that they come from the past lives' creation of virtue and selfishness of that soul's prior incarnations. The second reason is that the bodies and senses are also uniquely formed, based upon the needs of all the incarnating souls, or souls creating life at around the same time in the three lowest worlds—the worlds that humans live in. The collection of the mental forms of thought on the lower mental plane that control the three human bodies and senses is called the mental unit. Within each mental unit, or unit of controlling thoughtforms, exists the self of a particular human being. Each human being has its own individual self that is separated (by most or all of the higher mental plane) from both its soul (and OverSoul) and its Self. The name given to the controlling part of the three bodies and senses along with its sense of the self—all of which are part of the mental unit—is the personality.

 ## THE PERSONALITY AND SELVES

A personality is a collection of thoughtforms that are held together by stronger thought than that of the joined spirit that surrounds it, on the first through third sub-sub-planes of the fourth mental sub-plane, where it resides. These thoughtforms are the effects of a human-soul/OverSoul and the human Self, all thinking in concert with other souls, OverSouls, and Selves. The collective great causal thought, or conceptual higher mental plane thought, creates a very powerful group, or unit, of effects in the split time and space continuum of the mental plane. The causal thought is so strong that it fuses the unit of thoughtforms on the lower mental plane together for a relatively very long time as compared to any other thoughtforms. A typical thoughtform on the mental plane lasts only a few seconds to minutes, while the thoughtforms in a mental unit can last for one hundred fifty years (measured in dense physical time)—and even longer. The fusion of the thoughtforms that creates the mental unit produces a spark of light, as a lesser reflection of the human soul's spark and the much greater OverSoul's brilliant light. The personality receives all of the information that comes from the senses and brains of the three human bodies. Then the personality organizes, integrates, and synthesizes the information by comparing it structurally to the thoughtforms the personality is composed of, and at that point creates logic. The OverSoul gives to each personality that it creates the exclusive use of its three lowest-in-thought mental solar devas, or solar pitris, which are located on the three lowest sub-*sub*-planes of the higher mental plane. These three solar pitris are separated from each other and from other solar pitris because they cannot think well enough to keep the elemental energy of their respective higher mental sub-sub-planes connected to any other solar pitri or to the elemental energy that the solar pitri is helping. Each of these three limited and separated solar devas joins together with higher mental plane elemental energies on its specific sub-sub-plane to create limited and separated concepts. It is these concepts that personalities use to understand the knowledge that they derive through synthesis of the information that they organize and integrate when it is provided by their bodies/senses and brains. Personalities also use these concepts in thought that is created by their selves, sometimes joining together the separated concepts from the three lowest solar devas, through higher spiritual concepts. As the personality develops (as part of a child's growth process), it can also, first, use the solar devas to create concepts and then create thoughtforms and language that represent these thoughtforms in communication with others.

The human self is closely associated with the personality, and in many circumstances these two terms might be used interchangeably in explaining either's function; however, the self is different from the personality. Unlike the personality, the human self does not think simply by organizing, integrating, and gathering information that it can understand by conceptualizing and giving the knowledge. The human self, like the selves of group souls, develops the same three senses—of understanding itself, understanding the selves of others, and eventually understanding groups of selves as all being part of one, through increasing its consciousness, or understanding, of each self. The thoughts of the self are conscious because the self consistently gives its thoughts to fallen spirit in the three lower bodies; the thoughts of the personality are subconscious because the personality mostly uses its thoughts in order to control. Thus the subconscious part of a human is the thought of the personality, and its conscious part comes from the thought of its self. The personality is selfish because it usually takes more from its self in consciousness than what it gives to its self in knowledge; what the personality gives, when it does give, is knowledge. It sometimes gives knowledge to its self, but seldom a greater amount than it (the personality) is using; later, as it fuses with its soul, the personality (eventually) does give all of its knowledge to its soul, and ultimately this knowledge is also given to the Self by the soul. The self of the human is typically very well developed in comparison to the selves of group souls because it has all three time zones as represented by the addition of all three bodies and complete sets of senses as well as each body's different sense of time. Also, the self has the entire mental plane and body available to it as it recognizes and cooperates with its soul, OverSoul, and Self, since their light enlightens the self as it shares thought with them. The human self is created using a similar method to the way the selves of group souls are, but a human self uses the senses from only one lifeform, which first must be organized, integrated, and synthesized by the personality. Thus the personality controls the self subconsciously where basic issues of thought are concerned because it controls the use of the senses and brains of the bodies. The self affects the personality through its senses of self and the choices and directions within its thought, including the joining of separated concepts to build larger ones that also, through comparison to each other, further develop the self. A human self is created because it can limit the majority of the field of knowledge that a personality can create and that the self can then give as thought to lower spirit. The more knowledge that the personality synthesizes, including its conceptual understandings, the more the self must grow in its thought to be able to limit the field of knowledge created by the personality and thus remain a self. It does so by creating concepts that are larger than the personality is capable of creating through using the three lowest separated solar pitris. These concepts are more inclusive and they integrate the self with other selves, in order to help it to develop its three senses of self. These concepts are spiritual, or enlightening, and are created with solar pitris from the higher mental spiritual mind.

The personality also has a sense of its self. This sense is developed by the personality comparing its level of knowledge against the amount of this knowledge that is given by its self to the fallen spirit within each of the three lower bodies and then used by this lower spirit to help the senses within the three lower bodies to better think. The personality receives its knowledge through information that is taken in by its senses and synthesized in its brains; the personality only somewhat and sometimes gives its knowledge to its self. A personality limits the field of the thought of the energies that it controls, by using the strong thought in its thoughtforms added to the surrounding weaker thought of its joined spirit. The personality will compare its synthesized information with its own semi-permanent thoughtforms to then conceptualize with the three separated and lowest solar pitris the meaning of its synthesized knowledge. The energies that supply information to the personality include, from each body, the best-thinking lunar devas and elemental energies that comprise the personality's senses and brain in each dimension it is alive on. In addition are the energies of the three lowest solar pitris, or devas (and their separated concepts), which control the personality's conceptual thought and its understanding, or the level to which it gives its synthesized knowledge back to its senses through its self. The self also greatly affects this giving by the personality, through the extent to which it creates larger concepts from the separated ones. Personality is more a function of the energy side of a human being, while self, because it is constructed only from spirit, is more a function of a human being's spirit side.

The human self gives thought to the fallen spirit in each of the three bodies by directing the spirit of these bodies and bringing this thought together (directing the thought) within the mental unit. However, instead of comparing its and the lower spirit's thought to *thoughtforms*, the self compares the lower spiritual thought to either the personality's concepts created by the three lowest solar devas (and how easily the self can join these separated concepts) or the spiritual concepts created by the OverSoul (and soul, if awake), along with the thought of the Self. The self communicates with these higher spiritual sources of thought through four vortices that function by focusing light and that are connected to the outer edge of the spherical mental unit. The two vortices that face upward, or towards the higher mental plane, predominately receive thought (light) from the OverSoul, soul, and Self, but have the capability of transmitting thoughts (light) to the soul and Self as well. The first of this thought that is received is what is referred to as the conscience, which the OverSoul sends to the self as flashes of light through the vortex. The lower two vortices of thought (with, predominantly, the one vortex on the lower right in a male person, when seen from the view that is depicted in *Life's Hidden Meaning*) only slightly receive whatever the enlightened thought of lower spirit thinks, and mostly help the self to become aware of how much lower spirit has of light. In people who are not spiritually disciplined, these two vortices mostly send thought (as light only, in those who are not evil), and predominately to lower spirit to help this spirit better function. Within the mental unit, the self, when enlightened enough in its thought, follows the thought of the OverSoul, soul, and Self and then thinks and gives this thought to the lower spirit within the lower bodies, and also to the personality. The self also shares with its Self the increased understanding that it receives from its three lower bodies. The self can (when the personality permits it to) use and further develop some of the higher solar pitris that make up the causal body that surrounds the soul and that are used by the OverSoul, soul, and Self when each new personality is created. The self can use these higher solar pitris to create much larger concepts that are also much better joined together, but only as it thinks more in the light that the OverSoul, soul, and Self are thinking within. Then the OverSoul, soul, and Self benefit from the more developed sense of the soul, which allows them to become aware of, or to sense, the lower worlds. The sense comprises the three inner petals of solar devas that surround the soul and that compose the inner sacrifice petals of the causal body, and that are the energy part of the human soul while it is on the mental plane.

The self gains more access to higher mental plane spiritual thought from spiritual concepts being held together by developing the cooperating solar pitris from enlightened thought. It can then share these much larger and more whole spiritual concepts with the personality, which is within the mental unit. The personality, being more like the energy that it controls, is very attracted to this higher mental plane spiritual thought—in part, because it begins to explain the origin of the personality (which is the loving creative thought of the OverSoul, soul, and the Self all thinking in light). Throughout most of their existence, personalities seek to know where they come from. Likewise, personalities seek to know where they are going, since they exist to control and without such knowledge feel at least somewhat if not very much out of control. The self and personality have a symbiotic relationship, and neither can successfully function without the other. The level of light in each the self and personality and that which they control or influence is the determining factor in how well they work together.

When the personality has too much darkness and then chooses more separation from its creators and higher sources of life, it will cause destruction of the senses, bodies, and brains—thereby reducing the levels of knowledge that it synthesizes. The self then shrinks because its level of thought needs to be supported by accurate senses that create accurate information and knowledge. Even with relatively good spiritual thought in a body, without accurate senses the self will be lessened. For example, when the five senses of astral form are used together, or are somewhat enlightened, they comprise the sense of empathy. The thought of spirit in the astral body when directed by the self is creative imagination. Without empathy, creative imagination becomes dark or lacking because then the self is inaccurately informed of *what* to think about in its use of creative imagination. Faulty and/or incomplete knowledge reduces the ability to think accurately—and lack of accurate thought reduces the self. Lack of empathy, which results in less or wrong use of creative imagination, is one way in which a selfish personality ends up reducing its self.

In reverse, a selfish self can lessen its development by the self making too few choices to follow the thought of its OverSoul, soul, and Self. This process usually takes place by the personality first over-controlling the self and making it selfish; as a result, the higher thought from these higher beings becomes blocked and either ignored at times or not heard at all. The first spiritual thought is the conscience—the *con*-nected *science*, or the whole structure of the mental mind. When blocked or ignored, the self will fail to think as well. It will not have as much ability to join larger concepts from the spiritual part of the higher mental body that are held together by the solar pitris or to communicate directing thought to the lower spirit that it is informing in the lower bodies. The reason is that the vortices transmit only light, or thought that is in God's direction. This light is missing from the self's thought when it ignores the thought of the OverSoul, soul, and Self. Sometimes, without enlightened higher spiritual thought from the self, thought in these lower bodies becomes selfish; for example, the nature of the astral creative imagination would become self-focused, or selfish (resembling the darker thought of the selfish self). The fallen spirit would then become overly influenced by the dark thought of the surrounding involutionary energies. Further, the personality would not receive the higher spiritual concepts from the self about where it came from and where it is going. Then the "missing" thought is, at a minimum, the conscience and can reach to the thought of its creator, or of God in more developed selves. The (self's chosen) lack of informing thought by higher spirit causes the personality to become very fearful because it is losing its self, which is lessened each time the self becomes selfish. Then the personality's fears and lack of ordered creation of synthesized knowledge cause it to lose some of its control over its bodies, which brings in a sense of inadequacy to replace its lost sense of self.

As can be deduced, both of the above-described conditions feed on each other and one leads to the other. Both can produce a personality that cannot even order its information, much less synthesize knowledge, and therefore becomes disordered. Both lead to a reduction in self, although the second much more quickly causes a loss of self because the self is so intimately tied to its connection, or lack thereof, to spiritualized (larger and more whole) conceptual thought—and to the light it creates in forms, or to creating virtue. When the self decides to not create virtue, it quickly loses its sense of itself in the following three stages. First, it loses both its thought that other selves and it are all a part of oneness, and the ability to create more of itself from its not-self and to give this thought to other selves. Next, the self loses both the thought that some others are like itself and the ability to give to them; the associated good character that this thought produces is lost as well. Finally, it loses the thought of who it is and the ability to give who it is to its personality. By the time the self reaches this last stage, the personality has also reached its stage of becoming disordered because of these two factors' symbiotic interconnectivity. When the human self loses its second, or middle, sense, it fails to recognize correctly and to give, or to understand, who others are (they are like its self), and then it starts to develop bad character. Good character is the ability to correctly recognize and understand who others are, by giving knowledge and some consciousness and its effects to them in some way, using its senses and thought about the information they supply to help others. The self that has good character realizes that others are like, or similar to, its self. Bad character is evidenced when knowledge, including the effects of knowledge such as other types of forms, is taken from others, and others are recognized as being different from the self and, as a result, are misunderstood. Also, the self that has bad character uses the existing knowledge of the self to construct ways of taking. Acts of bad character often result in the lowering of consciousness of others, depending upon how the others choose to react. Criminals choose to carry out acts of crime on their victims in order to lower these people's selves by taking from them in numerous ways even to the point of murder and hoping to entrap them in selfishness. The diminishing of another person's self causes the criminal, who almost always has a disordered personality and a reduced self, to "feel" better because then other selves are lessened in relation to his or her own self. This is the fundamental *hidden* cause of crime.

A person is the joining of the personality and the self and includes the three lower bodies, and the bodies' senses and brains, and also the personality's and self's senses of self. What a person fears the most, usually unknowingly, is the loss of his or her ability to create and sense from his or her self; the second greatest fear is usually the loss of control by the personality (including the loss of its sense of self), which leads to a loss of awareness and knowledge. Both of these fears are caused by a reduction in light within the human. Notice that the addition of a personality into a human lifeform changes the role of the self from its former role as part of a group soul. In the animal kingdom and below, it is the group soul that controls the synthesis of information provided by the *collective* senses of the lifeforms that are informed by the self; in a human, the personality controls the synthesis of information brought in by the much greater senses and brains of the individual human's three lower bodies. The human is more specialized because of the sheer volume of senses and brains, and the synthesized knowledge to be created from them. It becomes necessary to have a personality to deal with all of these elements that are related to form, and still have control over the lifeform. The personality also can create rudimentary conceptual thought about such information if it chooses to. In addition, each individual human lifeform has its own self, which creates higher levels of thought that it gives to fallen spirit, enabling full integration of the three bodies into one consciousness.

As a human self thinks more spiritually and uses more of the causal body of solar pitris to create larger and more whole spiritual concepts, it begins to join with the soul, Self, and OverSoul because the thought and developing higher sense of the four are becoming one. The self (and the other three) needs the personality to first create knowledge, then to give it for their virtuous use, as well. They also need the personality to increase and improve the levels and qualities of the senses and brains of these three bodies so that a greater quantity and accuracy of information is brought into each body. If the personality decides to cooperate, it can achieve the improvement if its motive is to join with the other four and create more virtue. The personality can achieve the effect of improvement by limiting each brain and group of senses by focusing on only energies and information that increase virtue. These limitations are referred to as spiritual discipline, and the people who choose to carry them out are referred to as spiritual disciples (note that the term *disciple* is derived from the word *discipline*).

Even when four parts (the self, OverSoul, soul, and the Self) of the five mental parts of a human are thinking in light together and seek to spiritually discipline the personality, mostly in the beginning of such efforts the personality usually undermines the process because it fears that it is losing control. Spiritual discipline is a very difficult and long-term (lifelong) enterprise, which can sometimes lead to a disastrous loss of self and even to a personality disorder, or at least increases in bad character, in those who are reckless in their spiritual discipline and/or motives. Spiritual discipline is usually attempted only after the soul and each different self it has helped to create have developed through dealing with many different types of bodies, senses, brains, and personalities in control of them, over many lifetimes. As the human soul grows from the virtue that each personality and self creates in each lifetime, the soul tips the balance—upward towards light—between the personality and self versus the OverSoul and the Self. The OverSoul is a higher correspondence of the personality and is a very advanced Being of energy, and the Self is the lowest part of the OverSoul's spirit, which is gradually over time sacrificially given to the soul. The human soul (composed of equally conscious levels of spirit and energy) is the middle point and as it grows, slowly, it increases the levels of light given to the self. Then each personality gives more of its knowledge to create virtue and becomes less afraid of losing its control. Note that the Solar Angel gives up its lowest body and a part of its Self to help create a human soul.

It takes many hundreds of different personality and self lifetimes for one of these personalities with its self to reach a level at which it is ready to *begin* the process of spiritual discipline. Each personality generally improves because the thoughtforms that construct it have greater levels of light in them from the virtue that was created in the last lifetime and stored within the mental permanent atom. Then it takes many dozens of lifetimes to complete the process and for the personality to fuse in connectedness with the soul, for the self to fuse with the Self, and then for these four fused together to begin to fuse with the OverSoul, or Solar Angel. Fusion is the result of intense thought from the second part of God's mind (or from unconditional love, consciousness, and understanding—which all lead to oneness). Through inclusiveness, fusion directs and brings together parts of spirit and energy that have previously been enlightened. The bringing together of these enlightened parts creates a light that is *larger* than the sum of the parts—and creates fusion. The average number of lifetimes before one of the personalities decides to begin spiritual discipline is seven hundred. The average number of lifetimes that it takes for the personality, self, soul, and Self to then fuse together is seventy, and the average number of lifetimes before the four together begin to fuse with the Solar Angel is seven. These averages can vary considerably for individual humans, and are listed here just for perspective. There is no prescribed number of lifetimes, *only these averages*, because the process is one of choices by each individual. At the end of the process the human moves on to become a member of the next kingdom of life focus. This kingdom is sometimes referred to as the Kingdom of Souls because the fused human soul is liberated from its single sub-sub-plane on the mental plane to a position of much more flexibility and freedom, starting at the middle of the intuitional plane. Here the (liberated) Soul (spelled with an uppercase "s") still contains its last, fully enlightened, human personality as a rejoined part of the Solar Angel, which is fused with it, as well as the fused and transfigured self and Self, but it sacrifices its causal body and thus frees itself from mental form. All of these fused parts are sharing the consciousness with the Soul and have perfect mastery of the three lower worlds that humans still live in, because their spiritual thought and their senses in these worlds have become fully enlightened and *masterful* in producing only intelligent activity.

CONCLUSIONS AND SUMMARY ABOUT SELVES

In conclusion of our discussion of the self and its creation from thought that is given, it can be stated that when thought can limit the majority of a field of life that it exists within and can be given to one or more lifeforms, a new part of life is created that, by definition, is a mind and is referred to as a self. If the field of life that is limited by a self is focused on the creation of form through gradually enlightening fallen spirit—including senses and sometimes brains, and also, in some circumstances, synthesizing knowledge with them—then the self that is created is a smaller (lower) self that is spelled with a lowercase "s." When the self that is created by thought can limit all of a Ray Lord's field of life through consciousness as it affects its lifeform and other Selves and their lifeforms, and can create choices to limit the majority of this field, the Self that is created is a larger (higher) Self that is spelled with an uppercase "s." Under such circumstances of creation, a Ray Lord's field of life comprises the part of the duration of life created up to that time by the Ray Lord in its thought, or light. The higher Self participates in some of the creation of all the life that is affected by its field of life within that dimension. Because in order to limit its field a Self must think only in the direction of thought of the Ray Lord, or its light's direction, a Self is always an enlightened part of spirit and is thus always found at the atomic level of the plane it can limit. A self does not always choose to think in light. However, as it chooses not to, it diminishes itself as a result of the forces that it creates in energies moving against one another within its field of life. These forces are the result of and come from within the larger fields of spirit and energy and of the Ray Lord that the self's own field is a part of. A self must have the three parts of the fractured time present within its field of thought at near to the same time and in correct, or logical order. This condition can exist only on the upper half of the mental plane because below the center of this plane, gravity (or the collective thought of unenlightened energy) overpowers the thought of spirit. Then gravity prevents spirit from joining all three parts of time together, which actually causes time and space to further fracture, or separate.

Depending upon the type of lifeform the self is part of, a self is found in one of two places. For animals, plants, and minerals, the self is found as part of a group soul, on the lower part of the third mental sub-plane ("blurred" in time and space between the fifth and seventh sub-*sub*-planes), and the group soul is found on the higher part of the third sub-plane. This placement of the self allows the self to think more easily, but less accurately, when it is giving its thought. The human self is part of the mental unit of a human being and is intimately tied to the personality; it is created by the OverSoul and the Self, as well as the human soul once the soul has become more fully developed. The self of a human being is found on the fourth sub-sub-plane of the fourth sub-plane, which is the exact mid-point of the mental plane. This position of the self is the lowest and most difficult place for spirit to attempt to give its thought from. However, successful giving by the self from this position develops much higher consciousness. The personality is found from the first through the third sub-sub-planes of the fourth mental sub-plane. The self exists within the mental unit on the fourth sub-sub-plane of the same plane— one sub-sub-plane lower. The human self is found at the exact middle of the mental plane because this is the lowest point to which higher spirit can descend and still maintain a self, without becoming overwhelmed by gravity. The human self descends to this most difficult level in order to unify its mental body and part of the mental plane, through eventually creating enough mental virtue in its life. Since the human self is wholly spirit, in the lower worlds on all planes (dimensions) humans live within, it must be connected to its personality in order to have senses of form. Likewise, a group soul's self must be connected to its group soul and its lifeforms if it is to be able to sense form, for the same reason.

A Self can exist at the atomic levels of the mental, intuitional, and spiritual planes only, because a Self needs to limit the field of life for each of these planes by thinking exclusively in the direction of light and perfectly in consciousness in at least one or more of three ways. No Self can exist below the atomic level of the mental plane because no Now in time exists below this level. Although the atomic level of the astral plane is completely enlightened by the thought of the astral Ray Lord, only two of the three parts of time exist fully joined to each other on this plane—the past and present; the future part fully joined with the past and present for any event, and all accurate structure of time and space are missing. This gap prevents the existence of a Self at any level of the astral plane or lower, including the (enlightened) atomic levels. When a Self exists for a Being on the atomic level of more than one of the planes it can exist on (the atomic levels of the mental, intuitional, and spiritual), more than one part of the Now is that Being's senses of time—and space. Then more than one way of being perfectly conscious exists within its spirit. The entire time and space, or completed three Nows, of a Self are referred to as the life of the Spiritual Triad because the three ways in which spirit as a part of a lifeform can express itself maximally in life through its thought and in consciousness (love) are all present.

The purpose for a self (or God's purpose for creating the part of life that is selves) is to give life the ability to sense, or recognize through the use of form, and then understand through giving knowledge that came from the information provided by the senses, as follows: first—itself, next—other selves, and finally—that all selves are a part of one life. For Selves the purpose in the beginning is to sense (recognize) and understand lower spirit, including spirit in lower life-forms and the lifeforms' lower selves. As a Self develops this lower sense, its purpose is in recognizing higher spirit, including souls and other (higher) Selves. The Self thinks only in the light of the Ray Lord. This light is at least part of the thought of all spirit on that plane because all spirit has at least some light in it; by recognizing all the states of spirit within the plane and those that are lower (the duration of life) that the Ray Lord is on, the Self can clearly understand the differences between the spirit and energy parts of lifeforms. Such understanding leads to a recognition and understanding of God's growth, or to life with clarity and consciousness (with love/understanding). The Self can always understand the difference between spirit and energy, and does not believe, in illusion, that it is form (energy). A self, however, falls victim many times to that illusion and thus often does identify with its form. The misidentification occurs because the self has not enlightened the senses of form that it is using; this misidentification precludes the self from accurately sensing itself as spirit. The use of the second, or higher, sense developed by the Self is a state of being a functional part of God by creating more of the Creator of life, or of God. For a spiritual being, such as a Self, this state of creation of more of life always involves the creation of virtue, or more of light in form, because all spiritual beings must think and live through form, or through some type of energy.

The meaning for life that has a self is to increase the self by increasing its sense of itself. As the self is able to further limit its field of life in differing ways of thought, it increases its sense. There are three major ways in which a self increases its meaning through its three major ways of sensing. Each of these ways can grow in a particular lifetime for a human, based upon how much the personality fears a loss of self and how much it additionally fears a loss of its senses; all of these fears comprise the fear of death, and may cause the personality to overly control and limit the self in creating larger and more whole spiritual concepts in the higher mental body. The more fear a personality has, the more it seeks to control, and the less chance the self will have to grow in its senses. However, the self can choose to listen to the OverSoul and (if awake) the soul through the vortices of the mental unit, first by hearing the thought that is referred to as conscience. Perhaps it is obvious that the less self a person has, the less higher spiritual thought she/he will hear, or the less conscience she/he will have. The more that the self listens to and joins its thought with its conscience and, later, with other more spiritual thought, the more it can affect the personality and lessen its fears. The fears of the personality are lessened by the spiritual thought of the OverSoul/soul. The reason is that these fears lead to the personality gaining first more knowledge, and then an understanding of why it exists—if it gives to its self by helping it to grow more of the self's three senses. When enlightened, the three senses of self then tell the personality where it came from and where it is going. Eventually the personality realizes that it can be a part of the life that is its self, soul, and Self, and that participating in this life makes the personality immortal. At this point the personality also realizes that death is actually a state that it brings onto itself, by reducing its senses and its self, and thus disconnects itself from its soul and Self—all through persistent selfishness.

The more the sense of self grows, the greater its meaning to life. The first meaning that a self attains from its life is to recognize and develop who it is in comparison to everything (and everyone) else; this initial meaning may persist as the sole meaning for a human over many lifetimes of selves. The next stage for developing more meaning in life comes from recognizing and helping to develop the selves of others using the areas of itself it already understands, or in developing good character. The last stage of developing meaning in life for a self is to understand and help to develop a oneness among all selves—as being a part of God by increasing itself from its not-self and giving all of its increased self to other selves. After this third sense of self is developed, a self can gain more meaning from life by joining in enlightened thought, or fusing, with its Self. Then the human being can create more meaning from recognizing and understanding more light in all of spirit and life for the three lower worlds it lives within, by giving all parts of itself. Instead of simply focusing on the oneness of selves, the human focuses on the oneness of all life and of God's growth.

The light that is brought into life comes from *giving* that which can be given, which creates more consciousness with the lower sense of Self. A great deal more meaning can be then *created* in life by creating more to give. A human who has begun to join its five connected mental parts—the personality, self, soul, Self, and OverSoul—through the thought of the Self can choose to create more of the light that is needed by life. Then the human can give this light using *both* of the senses of the Self and its thought, combined. This giving produces the largest amount of meaning to and for human life because it creates more *of* life in addition to more of love, or consciousness (oneness), *for* life. Actually, using the higher sense of Self surpasses having meaning to life, because the higher sense of Self *creates* the very life that meaning is derived from. This chapter now comes to a close, having largely unhidden the self and Self as created from the giving of thought…and having simultaneously revealed more of life's hidden meaning.

ABOUT SOULS

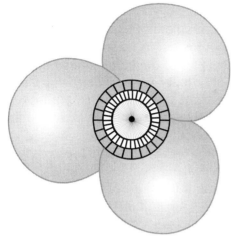

Illustration 6.1

Author's Suggestion: First turn to the "Glossary Help Guide" and read the definitions for this chapter.

THE BASICS ABOUT SOULS—
A SUMMARY FROM CHAPTER FIVE

In the last chapter an explanation was given of how selves are created by thought that is able to limit the majority of a field of life. This thought creates either many lifeforms or an individual one. The self is a new part of life that has the senses of recognizing and understanding who it is, who others are, and, ultimately, who all are, which is a part of all other selves. When a (lower) self has all three of these senses, it can think enough like its (higher) Self to begin to fuse with, or become one with, its Self in givingness (consciousness). Then the self participates in developing the lower sense of Self, which concerns increasing the Self's consciousness. This lower sense of Self, on the mental plane, is the recognition and understanding of God's thought in all of life through an understanding of spirit and form (energy) in souls and lifeforms. Finally, in their fusion of consciousness the self and Self develop the higher sense of Self, which is the recognition of, the understanding of, and the actual beingness of a functional part of God through the creation of more of God's thought, or light, in form—which is the creation of virtue. The more the combined self/Self is developed, the greater the meaning to its life that is based upon the amount of sense of self/Self that a being has.

A rudimentary explanation of what a soul is was presented in the last chapter. A soul in its beginning as a part of life is spirit that is enlightened to at least half of its level of mental thought and is joined with form (energy), with both components having *similar ability to think*. This means that the energy (form) of a soul is, initially, at about the same level of enlightenment as the thought of spirit that is in the soul. Stated another way, the spirit in souls is initially enlightened enough to fuse with, or become one in givingness (consciousness) with, the energy and sensing part of a soul; the energy part (body) of a soul is about as enlightened as the informing spirit's thought of the soul. Each soul is between the self and Self in its creation of time and space regarding its ability to join these two parts of the mental plane, or dimension, through its thoughts. A soul can think within the time and space where a self is (and when), and where a Self is (and when), provided that the self who is connected to the soul is thinking in the light of the soul's thought. The soul thinks in the selective light of the mental plane Ray Lord as this light applies to creating virtue through the lifeform(s) informed by the soul. Thus the thought of the lower self controls the ability of the soul to think beyond the time and space of its specific mental plane location. Souls need the connection with their selves in order to also connect with their Selves. For a soul to become wise (it is already always giving), it needs the wholeness provided by the bridge of thought that spans the mental plane between its self and Self. Thought that takes place between a self and a Self and that is connected to its soul is, for a being, what unifies that part of the mental plane's upper half that is a part of the being's mental body. Within a human being's mental body, what unifies the lower and upper parts of the mental plane is the addition of the personality and its use of the self's conscious thought, joined with the personality's synthesis of the knowledge that it derives from the senses of its three lower bodies.

A soul is the lowest part of life that can join enlightened spirit with enlightened energy, or form, and keep them together. The first type of soul is a group soul that is created by the spirit on the upper half of the mental plane. In the lesser ways that are possible for souls, a group soul can join together some parts of the mental plane at a time but not all of them at the same time, no matter how well developed the group soul might be. As a result, effects on the lower part of the mental plane are almost never fully joined to causes, or to the upper part of the mental plane. The thought of the group soul is consequently forced to be limited, nearly exclusively, to preconceptual thought. The reason is that the limited ability of the group soul to think causes a great deal of time to be separated from space. As more time is "used" (separated from space) in order to produce a thought, the thought becomes spread out, or "blurred" in time (and space), which causes the thought to become preconceptual. A pre-concept cannot accurately represent a specific form and its action within time and space. The pre-concept represents only the averages of many forms, and their actions can be derived from the collective information provided by those forms.

A mineral group soul is formed through its preconceptual thoughts. Its actual form is constructed from solar deva and elemental energy that is semi-enlightened. A mineral group soul is found in the upper part of the mental plane, on the fourth sub-sub-plane of the third sub-plane, and initially surrounds its spirit in a spherical shape. For most of its existence, the mineral group souls' self structure is blurred between the fifth and seventh sub-sub-planes of the third mental sub-plane. The seventh sub-sub-plane is where the self of mineral group souls is mostly emphasized. The reason is that the seventh ray focus of this part of the sub-plane matches the focus of the pre-life of the mineral kingdom, which is on the seventh plane. All souls' Selves, including those of mineral group souls, are created at the atomic level of the mental plane. (Higher) Selves of mineral group souls are created and further developed as each group soul, with help from the additional Selves of members of the spiritual, or Soul, kingdom (energy Beings, or Solar Angels, and Masters), creates pre-life compounds for later use by lifeforms. These compounds are mostly what humans refer to as (ending up to be) organic and used by lifeforms. As the mineral group souls focus their selves on the "fallen" spirit of the etheric plane, and think and give pre-instinctual thought to elements or simple compounds, or both, they develop a sense of time by creating it mostly from the fractured part of time that concerns the past. In fact, the only whole part of time that even exists on the seventh, or etheric/dense physical, plane of our universe is the fractured segment of the past. The collective thought of the fallen spirit that is not helped by the thought of spirit within a self actually has no self in this very low dimension. The quite high levels of gravity and lack of spiritual thought fracture time and space because the spirit identifies more with energy than it does with "itself." All that is left here of whole parts of time from spirit's thought and creation of separated time and space is the past. Energy is maximally manifested from spirit's very weak and incomplete thought. Space is maximally separating one form, or group of energies, from another. Gravity and inertia, or the resistance of movement of energy as it interacts with other energy, controls both spirit and the energy it informs.

The mineral group soul needs to gain a completed sense of time in order to have a self. The reason is that only logical and complete mental thought, which therefore has past, present, and future represented within it, can limit the majority of the pre-life field of possibilities. When limited, this pre-life field of thought creates probabilities that certain compounds necessary for life creation on a particular planet at a particular time will be developed. In order to gain this needed complete sense of time that enables the creation of a self, the group soul of minerals relies upon the enlightened structure, or mental light, within its spirit and form on the mental plane. This light comes from the group soul's Solar Angel, or OverSoul, directing the mental plane Ray Lord's thought (light) and plan for structuring minerals into compounds that will create life on a dense planet, such as earth. Notice that in order for life to be created on them, all dense planets need to have a part of themselves located within the mental Ray Lord's dimension, so that all three parts of time exist. The group souls are aided in their thought to create and maintain a self by the thought coming from the mental plane Selves, which are parts of members of the spiritual kingdom. Mineral group souls develop a completed sense of time from the light brought into themselves, coming from the Selves. This completed sense of time reveals some of the mental Ray Lord's plan for the minerals that will be used at some later point in creating life. The sense of time that concerns the future is constructed from the mineral group soul making changes in its thought, in order to coincide with "the Plan," or the plan for the planet, it functions on. The sense of time that concerns the present develops as the mineral group soul gains understanding through giving its changes in thought in order to create compounds for new life (as best as it can) at exact times and places in accord with the plan on a planet. These two senses of time are constructed purely from thought of the mineral group soul, rather than from the (etheric) sense and thought of the minerals it informs. The sense of whole time is considerably weakened when two-thirds of it is constructed without including the sense (thought) of energy, or form, from the dimension the thought is about. When the thought of energy is not present within the sense of time, the result is an inability for the group soul to perfectly determine its pre-life or life forms' exact locations of space within time (and time within space). The mineral group soul is left with the least-developed self and the most difficulty in creating preconceptual thought because it lacks sense that more enlightened etheric/dense physical energy would be able to provide. Most of the mineral pre-life has only one center (the most advanced may have two), and all of it on only one dimension (the lowest). The reason is that the centers need to be created and held together by the mineral group souls' thought—which is missing the needed sense from the form it is informing. To begin with, the spirit of the mineral group soul is very weak in its thought (the weakest of all group souls). Then this spirit fails to be able to get the highly resistant etheric/dense physical elemental energies to follow the weakest of the evoluting (etheric) lunar devas' thought. This thought usually creates no more than one or two senses and centers. These are only on the etheric/dense physical plane, since lunar deva and elemental energies have difficulty following the thought of the mineral soul's fallen spirit. Note that some less developed mineral group souls may be unable to create even pre-life, or minerals that have one whole center. These group souls are much more common in first-incarnation solar systems.

The group souls of minerals cannot inform energy to the level of creating life. The reason is that their thought and the thought of the self that is part of them are too weak in creating and joining together the needed time and space. Without this thought being strong enough to create the two centers necessary on one dimension and at least one center on the next higher dimension, there is no space created for energy to move within time. In order to grow, life requires movement in space and time—and this movement creates sentiency. The potential for growth is always a part of life because life is God's growth, and God's thought is for life to grow more of Itself. Movement of energy *from the informing thought of spirit within the same part of the life-form* creates direction, or consciousness, within a form. Humans refer to this as sentiency.

Mineral Group Soul Creating All Three Parts of Time

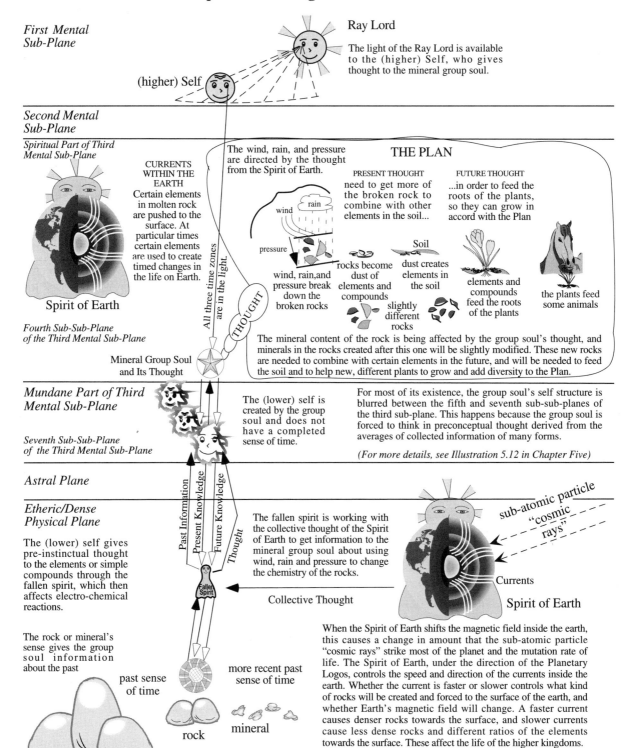

First Mental Sub-Plane

Ray Lord

The light of the Ray Lord is available to the (higher) Self, who gives thought to the mineral group soul.

(higher) Self

Second Mental Sub-Plane

Spiritual Part of Third Mental Sub-Plane

CURRENTS WITHIN THE EARTH
Certain elements in molten rock are pushed to the surface. At particular times certain elements are used to create timed changes in the life on Earth.

Spirit of Earth

The wind, rain, and pressure are directed by the thought from the Spirit of Earth.

THE PLAN

PRESENT THOUGHT
need to get more of the broken rock to combine with other elements in the soil...

FUTURE THOUGHT
...in order to feed the roots of the plants, so they can grow in accord with the Plan

wind
rain
pressure

Soil

wind, rain, and pressure break down the broken rocks

rocks become dust of elements and compounds

dust creates elements in the soil

elements and compounds feed the roots of the plants

the plants feed some animals

slightly different rocks

All three time zones are in the light.

THOUGHT

Fourth Sub-Sub-Plane of the Third Mental Sub-Plane

Mineral Group Soul and Its Thought

The mineral content of the rock is being affected by the group soul's thought, and minerals in the rocks created after this one will be slightly modified. These new rocks are needed to combine with certain elements in the future, and will be needed to feed the soil and to help new, different plants to grow and add diversity to the Plan.

Mundane Part of Third Mental Sub-Plane

The (lower) self is created by the group soul and does not have a completed sense of time.

For most of its existence, the group soul's self structure is blurred between the fifth and seventh sub-sub-planes of the third sub-plane. This happens because the group soul is forced to think in preconceptual thought derived from the averages of collected information of many forms.

Seventh Sub-Sub-Plane of the Third Mental Sub-Plane

(For more details, see Illustration 5.12 in Chapter Five)

Astral Plane

Etheric/Dense Physical Plane

The (lower) self gives pre-instinctual thought to the elements or simple compounds through the fallen spirit, which then affects electro-chemical reactions.

The rock or mineral's sense gives the group soul information about the past

Past Information
Present Knowledge
Future Knowledge
Thought

Fallen Spirit

The fallen spirit is working with the collective thought of the Spirit of Earth to get information to the mineral group soul about using wind, rain and pressure to change the chemistry of the rocks.

Collective Thought

sub-atomic particle "cosmic rays"

Currents

Spirit of Earth

When the Spirit of Earth shifts the magnetic field inside the earth, this causes a change in amount that the sub-atomic particle "cosmic rays" strike most of the planet and the mutation rate of life. The Spirit of Earth, under the direction of the Planetary Logos, controls the speed and direction of the currents inside the earth. Whether the current is faster or slower controls what kind of rocks will be created and forced to the surface of the earth, and whether Earth's magnetic field will change. A faster current causes denser rocks towards the surface, and slower currents cause less dense rocks and different ratios of the elements towards the surface. These affect the life of the higher kingdoms.

past sense of time

more recent past sense of time

rock

mineral

When the past information is given back to the group soul, the group soul may recognize that the rocks have been smashed, but it may not know exactly when, how, or why because it has no information about the present or future. It knows the rocks existed intact at some point, and were at a later time broken up through pressure.

Illustration 6.2

Minerals lack sentiency because the informing thought of fallen spirit that is informed by higher spirit and is contained within any amount of mineral form on the etheric/dense physical plane is insufficient to direct the movement of energy within the form both in space (from one plane to another) and from past to present in time (within and from the etheric/dense physical to the astral plane). As was stated above, the thought of the group soul needs to be strong enough to create the centers and senses in order to provide both places, or the space, for energy to move to and from in time. The thought of mineral group souls is too weak to accomplish this effect.

Plant group souls contain spirit and energy that have existed on the mental plane for much longer periods of time than have the spirit and energy of mineral group souls. The reason is that before becoming a part of the plant group soul, the plant spirit and energy were both a part of increasingly better-thinking levels of different mineral group souls. At the beginning of our universe and at the beginning of each star system's life cycle and development of planets, mineral group souls are developed first, then the highest-thinking spirit and energy of the mineral group souls become part of plant group souls. Plant group souls likewise provide their highest-thinking spirit and energy to animal group souls. Because of their much greater familiarity with and experience with the informing of life from the mental plane, plant group souls can create at least two centers of a sense etherically for each lifeform, and one center of sense astrally. This takes place more often very low on the seventh astral sub-plane. The thought of the informing spirit in the individual plants is stronger than the thought of most informing spirit in minerals; the two etheric senses and the at least one astral sense give energy space, or places to enter into and exit from within the lifeform. These senses give plants the ability to think both in the past and (somewhat) in the present parts of time. The astral elemental energy in the plant's sense is less dense and less involutionary than its etheric elemental energy is, and is thus more responsive to the informing thought of spirit; the astral lunar deva energy in the plants' sense is more evolutionary and is better at helping to direct the elemental energy, as well. All of these factors join together, enabling the plant group soul to create life. Plants have a quite limited type of sentiency, which in the very long (separated) past to present parts of time that it takes them to move, and the minimal amount of space that they move within, can be missed by humans' senses. As humans become more aware, or sense more reliably, they can sense the slight sentiency of plants. Sentiency is the ability of plants to respond and move in response to the informing spirit's thought on the plane that a plant's body is in, with this movement taking place as a result of the plant's own (slight) thought.

 ## RADIANCE

The greater the levels of light within the group soul, the better it informs and creates life that is within God's plan. The better are the instincts, or pre-instincts, given to the individual forms, as well. When a group soul increases its light to the point at which its Self uses greater amounts of thought to inform its lifeforms (or pre-life forms) than its self does, then the lifeforms (or pre-life forms) begin to *radiate* some of the light within the group soul. The Self gives the thought to *other* forms of life, for them to grow or for new forms of life to be created, or both. When this radiance of light is absorbed by other lifeforms that are not fully enlightened, it increases the light within the lifeforms and helps them to create more light along their ray line of life development. For example, a human is along the fourth ray line of life development because humans are advancing their kingdom of life onto the fourth plane and into the fifth kingdom while they advance all of the lower kingdoms. If a human receives the radiance of light from a mineral or a plant (or an animal or another human), the center and sense of energy of the human receiving the radiance become slightly enlightened. As the human senses the radiance from its fourth ray focus, he or she experiences beauty. Beauty is the virtue, or the light in form, of the fourth ray and plane; upon being received within the center of the human sensing it, the radiance instantly becomes converted into virtue. The radiance is also causing a slight transfiguration in the mental sense(s) that the human is using to perceive the radiance within the senses of its astral and etheric/dense physical bodies. Because animals are along the sixth ray line focus in their kingdom of life, some advanced animals would experience from the same radiance the virtue of love, or givingness, within one or more of their centers and corresponding senses.

The ray line focus of a kingdom indicates how that kingdom is designed to create more virtue on a planet *as it (that kingdom) advances into the next kingdom*. As the following table exemplifies, ray lines of focus for kingdoms do not follow the order of the kingdoms. The ray line of each kingdom eventually causes that kingdom to create a certain type of virtue, as follows.

RAY LINE FOCUS OF AND VIRTUE CREATED BY EACH KINGDOM*		
KINGDOM	RAY LINE	VIRTUE EVENTUALLY CREATED BY THAT KINGDOM AS IT ADVANCES INTO THE NEXT
Mineral Kingdom (creates dense physical energy from transmutation of prana and minerals)	7th Ray	Cooperation and sharing to create complex compounds necessary for the creation of life
Vegetable, or Plant, Kingdom	3rd Ray	Creation of all life—through supporting all life etheric/dense physically by providing food and oxygen on the dense physical plane
Animal Kingdom	6th Ray	Conditional love based upon movement
Human Kingdom	4th Ray	Beauty
Spiritual, or Soul, Kingdom	2nd Ray	Unconditional love/consciousness/oneness
Planetary Kingdom (of dense physical planets that are not yet rid of evil, or are not yet sacred)	5th Ray	Creation of whole given planetary structures and formulae (because for non-sacred planets the causes of all life in dense worlds of life are on the mental plane)
Solar Kingdom	1st Ray	Further creation of the three parts of God's mind on a solar scale

*See Chapter Nine for further explanation.
Table 6. 1

Radiance occurs when, within any integral period of time (in which time is consistently rejoining with space), the amount of energy that a pre-life form or lifeform takes into itself constantly equals the amount of energy it gives out. Radiance also requires that the energy taken in be in some ways transmuted into different energies. The last condition of radiance is that the speed of the transmutation of the energies involved in the radiance must be at the speed of light for the plane on which the radiance occurs. Energies that meet the first two conditions but fail to be transmuted at the speed of light create some level of radiation and become heat. Note that some forms have both radiation and radiance occurring within them at the same time.

The radiance caused by the most advanced non-organic minerals takes on one of two qualities, depending upon how the mineral is advancing its consciousness. The first way the non-organic mineral could be advancing its consciousness is from dense physical causes (e.g., extremely high levels of heat and/or pressure, and/or electro-chemical structuring) that result in an internal unity of direction (consciousness) of the mineral's molecular structure, or, in human terms, crystallization of its form. The other way is from etheric causes such as the inner heat and light that develop from (pre-) fission, with the affected mineral sacrificing some of its atoms in the transmuting of its energy while it (the mineral) transforms its consciousness, and eventually, transfigures its group soul. Dense physical radiance of minerals refracts the light from other sources of the etheric/dense physical Ray Lord and changes it into radiance. Note that refraction comes from inside the crystal and is not the same as reflection; refraction shows the crystal's internal physical structure and its complex wholeness within the light, whereas reflection merely bounces light off the surface. The minerals achieve the effect of refraction at greatly improved levels as they are structured, or faceted, along the outside surface in various ways so that the light is held within the form and magnified "before" radiance takes place, or—to be more accurate—*as* the effect takes place. Minerals that radiate etherically give off light that they create themselves, and that humans refer to as radioactivity. Until very recently in human development, nearly all of this radioactive transmutation took place deep within the earth. At present, most still does take place in these deep-earth regions. This transmutation adds much internal heat to earth that creates additional internal *movement* to large amounts of molten metals and rock; much of the original and some of the continuing movement within the earth is created by gravity and earth's spin. The above-described source of heat and some radioactive transmutation effects that occurred near to or on earth's surface and that affected organic compounds was a part of the beginning of life on earth (as on other dense planets). Today the internal movement within the earth is used by the Being who expresses its thought and life through earth mostly to alter large groups of existing lifeforms in numerous ways.

Each of the two types of non-organic minerals that radiate affect different types of group souls that are the most advanced in consciousness of all the non-organic mineral group souls. They are more advanced because they contain considerably more enlightened spirit and form

The Two Methods by Which
Non-Organic Minerals Become Radiant

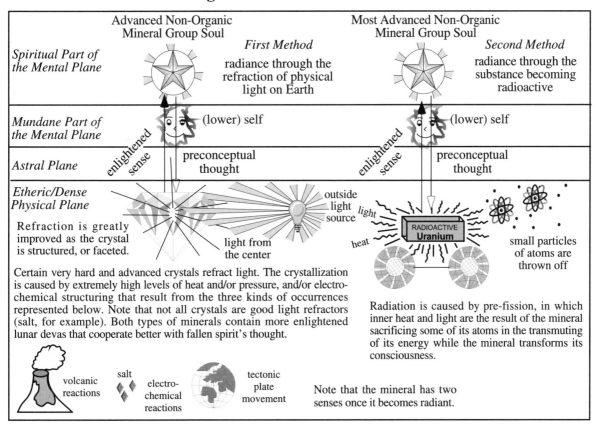

Illustration 6.3

than do the other non-organic group souls on the mental plane, where they exist. These mineral group souls give more thought to their pre-life forms that is more whole. The group souls that create organic compounds do so by dividing compounds that they can take in, somewhat transmute, and then they expel various types of energy. When these compounds are part of plants, most of the group souls use these compounds in more advanced and complex systems. They do so to transmute etheric light and a gas, usually carbon dioxide, along with a dense physical compound in correspondence to their astral part represented in its etheric/dense physical form, or water, with small amounts of electro-conductive and synthesizing minerals to produce a relatively dense (organic) substance, of mostly various types of sugar. The organic mineral group souls create the compounds that are the building blocks of taking in energy and somewhat transmuting it while also redirecting it. This is the process of building a sense of life and becoming a part of life.

All life that is physically alive must have at least two centers and corresponding senses on the etheric/dense physical plane and one center on the astral plane. The reason is so that energy can move both within one dimension and between two dimensions, thereby creating sentiency, or movement in time and space that results from the individual thought of the lifeform's fallen spirit on the planes where the lifeform is alive. The thought that produces the sentiency also connects with the much greater thought and spirit of the lifeform's self and group soul. The first astral sense is developed to distinguish the quality of the substance that is required to be both etherically and astrally present in order for organic life to exist in either of these two dimensions. This substance is water. Water is composed of the lightest and most basic first-ray element, or hydrogen, which is ubiquitous in the creation of most lifeforms. Water's second component, oxygen, when not joined to hydrogen provides a transmuting quality through heat to burn fuel along the third ray. The two elements joined together create a compound that is transformed in quality by the second ray (which replaces the first and third rays of the elements) focusing on the forms of life in the lower three worlds. The molecular compound of water then changes into

The Method by Which Organic Minerals Become Radiant

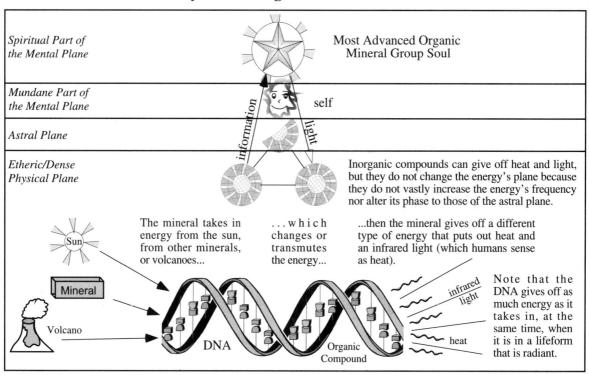

Illustration 6.4

a sixth ray focus. This is because water opposes the heat of its component element of oxygen while simultaneously altering the ubiquitous creation of hydrogen into a very focused and singular method of life creation. Purpose and action, which are effects of the first and third rays, respectively, are changed into a vehicle that connects and allows focused movement, which is a sixth ray effect. All the group souls involved with creating pre-life organic compounds use water because it joins the etheric/dense physical plane to the astral plane. Water is *devoted and focused* as a basic compound to create physical and astral plane life by initially providing the method of energy transfer within an organic form from one center and sense to another. Later, water is used as a medium that transfers energies from all parts of the body. This basic method of organic life creation is mostly but not exclusively relied upon in the three lowest worlds of our universe.

At both ends of the spectrum of the three lowest worlds of our universe, there exist some seeming exceptions to the rule of water being the basic factor of life, yet because those lifeforms are not organic, there is no inconsistency. Humans are unaware of these lifeforms because lifeforms that basically use water in their senses (as part of the cell structure) are generally unaware of those lifeforms, which are at the extremes of the life spectrum in the lower three worlds, that do not. The group souls of these non-water lifeforms do not function within the evolutionary side of the planet. They are themselves dealt with differently in their advancement through the kingdoms. These group souls for most of a planet's development remain as part of the sub-kingdom of the fifth, or spiritual, kingdom. This sub-kingdom is referred to as the energy kingdom because the life within it is composed more of higher-frequency energy than of densified form. Some of the more unusual lifeforms of this energy sub-kingdom that is hidden from humans live within the molten earth. Note that this last statement's incredibility to most who read it shows how atypical and hidden this part of life is. There are other strange forms of life that shall be briefly described in later chapters, with fuller explanations to be left for another time.

Another critical element used by most organic life is carbon, which is a fifth-ray focusing element that structures heat in organic lifeforms—keeping heat, or energy, stable and in the right amount in the correct places. Carbon controls combustion by balancing oxygen when the oxygen is not joined with hydrogen and thus creating water. Carbon interacts between pure hydrogen and oxygen, holding a balance on energy until energy is either added or removed in relatively large amounts or in amounts that suddenly change the structure of the compound it is in. Carbon's structuring quality is used by most group souls of organic lifeforms. Carbon-based lifeforms have trouble sensing other lifeforms that do not use carbon because the senses of a carbon-based lifeform use carbon as a part of themselves. Another element, nitrogen, can help to release energy, thereby making movement within carbon compounds easier. Nitrogen is used with carbon in many lifeforms in order to create cycles of growth of energy movement and then containment.

Organic mineral group souls generally develop pre-life forms that contain all of the above-mentioned elements. Without these pre-life compounds, most life could not progress on a planet that includes as part of itself the relatively dense worlds (the etheric/dense physical, astral, and mental). When the group souls of organic minerals can use these compounds to create centers and senses beyond just the etheric/dense physical, the spirit and energy within them advance to the plant kingdom as group souls of that kingdom, and then they focus on creating life rather than just pre-life. The group souls of organic minerals create radiation through transmuting energy in carbon, hydrogen, and nitrogen—usually in the presence of oxygen and with these elements using water in order to move within the lifeform. The radiation is most often in a type of light that humans cannot see unaided, but can feel as heat. Within kingdoms, it is generally true that the more a lifeform radiates heat, the more advanced the group soul is that informs it. A lifeform's relative size compared to the amount of its radiation is also a significant factor. However, the ultimate measure of radiation in organic lifeforms is the amount of "food," or stored energy, the lifeform consumes from life as compared to the amount of energy it gives to other parts of life. This last statement is "food" for thought for this book's readers, and so further explanation will not be included herein.

Radiance is a means of enlightening lifeforms through their centers and senses, while it advances the group souls of the lifeforms that are radiating. There are three ways in which minerals radiate light. The first method of radiance for minerals is through visible light that is etheric/dense physical. Note that radiance, which is the emission of pure light, becomes radiation when some of the radiated light also becomes heat. Radiance is sometimes referred to as "cold light" in some spiritual sources. Crystallization is the method employed by the group souls of these minerals, with high levels of energy brought into and then kept within the form dense physically. Then the structure is used as the refracting mechanism to create this lowest type of radiance of light. In more advanced types of crystallized minerals, additional energy can be temporarily and intelligently added to or used on the form through physical faceting. Then the added energy can enhance the light refraction and radiance if proper structure is used. The second and more advanced method of radiation is created by the group souls of minerals producing internal light that is created by etheric fission, or by giving off (sacrificing) parts of atoms. This method of radiation creates heat and light to affect lifeforms mostly through changes within the inside of the earth (most other dense planets also function in this way). These movements within the earth create tectonic plate movement, vulcanization, earthquakes, tidal waves, and changes to earth's magnetic field, as well as other major changes that affect large groups of lifeforms. The first pre-life compounds were also originally affected by the addition of heat and, rarely, direct radioactive transmutative effects that helped to produce life. The third method of radiation is utilized by minerals' creation of organic compounds that are pre-life. Most of these group souls use a method of bringing in energy either from the sun, or, less often today, from another non-life energy source such as a volcano, and then transmuting the energy

How the Lower Types of Radiance
are Converted and Used by DNA

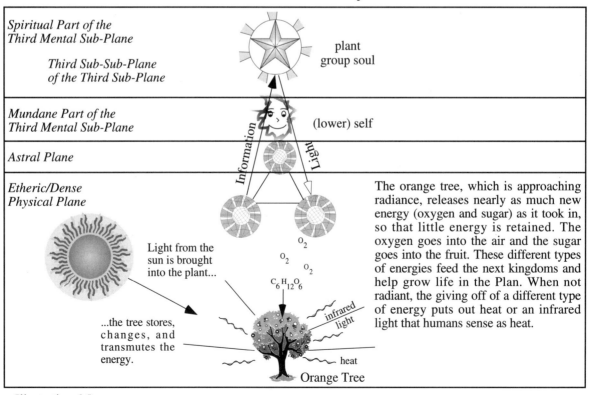

*Spiritual Part of the
Third Mental Sub-Plane*

    *Third Sub-Sub-Plane
of the Third Sub-Plane*

plant
group soul

*Mundane Part of the
Third Mental Sub-Plane*

(lower) self

Astral Plane

Information

Light

*Etheric/Dense
Physical Plane*

Light from the
sun is brought
into the plant...

O_2

O_2

O_2

$C_6H_{12}O_6$

...the tree stores,
changes, and
transmutes the
energy.

infrared
light

heat

Orange Tree

The orange tree, which is approaching radiance, releases nearly as much new energy (oxygen and sugar) as it took in, so that little energy is retained. The oxygen goes into the air and the sugar goes into the fruit. These different types of energies feed the next kingdoms and help grow life in the Plan. When not radiant, the giving off of a different type of energy puts out heat or an infrared light that humans sense as heat.

Illustration 6.5

while creating movement. Alternatively, energy is brought in from either other pre-life or from life that previously used the two dense methods, as food to then be transmuted into energy.

Organic pre-life compounds must be able to take in, store, and release energy; they use some of the methods of radiance and radiation that the first two less-advanced types of non-organic group souls use in creating modifications of crystallization and radioactive fission. The structuring of form from crystallization is modified to allow elements and compounds to be *exchanged into* and out of the structure. The effect is the changing of the crystallization and fixed storing of energy into an organized and structured storing of energy that can move, grow, and replicate by exact mirroring as it divides itself. From radioactive fission of elements comes the fission of very complex compounds along with the internal creation of heat through transmutation of compounds rather than just elements. Then the two simpler methods of radiance and radiation become the complex biochemical means of creation of life, beginning with organic pre-life. Ultimately, the third and most complex means of radiation for mineral group souls ends in the creation of DNA or DNA-like substances, which represents the culmination of radiation for pre-life.

Some group souls are unable to completely function within their respective kingdoms because they are somewhat in-between kingdoms in their ability to think preconceptually. These group souls sometimes create parasitic forms that use a part of or all of a center and sense plus other parts of the bodies of other forms, in order to create and maintain themselves. Sometimes they serve and help the forms they inhabit, while some parasites injure and even destroy the forms they infect. Some of the spirit within these group souls was caught between kingdoms when the "door" for advancement closed. This left them stranded and needing to develop parasitic lifeforms in order to gain sense and create life. The reason is that in God's plan for life, nothing can (spiritually) move backwards. The largest group of parasitic lifeforms is that of bacteria. Note that many types of bacteria are not parasitic of lifeforms, and feed on (use the energy and one or more disintegrating centers from) only energy that comes from organic compounds that are no longer informed by a lifeform's spirit, or that are "dead." Other bacteria can feed on certain chemical

Fungi Using Centers of Dead and Living Forms

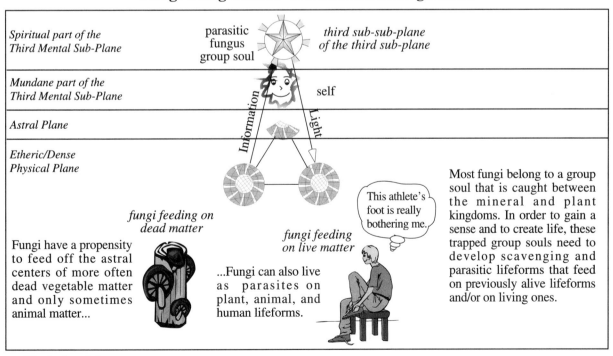

Illustration 6.6

reactions from the heat of volcanoes, and while parasitic to the mineral kingdom, they use only the single sense either of pre-life or of lower animal forms that have less than one complete center. Sometimes bacteria use the two centers of the organic minerals. A large group of bacteria are parasitic, and all bacteria, whether, parasitic or not, are in-between either the mineral and plant kingdoms or the plant and animal; the vast majority are situated between the plant and animal kingdoms. Many molds and fungi are similar to bacteria, but most of them are between the mineral and plant kingdoms. Viruses are nearly all located between the mineral and plant kingdoms in their consciousness and life development. Bacteria make up the largest group of life-forms on earth. There are so many bacteria because they (along with molds and fungi) are needed to break down the remaining complex compounds of energies that informing spirit higher than their own has ceased to inform. Once these complex compounds have disintegrated, their component energies reconstitute themselves into less complicated types of elemental and lunar deva energies. These can then recombine into even more advanced compounds in the future, in even higher lifeforms than those they "died" from. A bacterium will usually accomplish this feat by using more of the lunar deva (evolutionary) part of the energy than the energy's elemental (involutionary) part of its host within the bacterium's own lifeform. The process tends to free more of the elemental energy—at least at first, until the bacteria die—giving this relatively primitive-in-thought energy more time to develop with freedom from informing thought.

Time is fractured on all of the three lowest planes, where the lower the plane, and the lower on the plane, the more difficult it is to think. As a result, the thought that is found on the lowest (the seventh) plane concerns the past, because the past is the easiest part of time to think within. However, thinking in the past takes the most amount of time, or causes the greatest separation of time from space—all a result of thought. To think in the past, all that is required is thought about something that has already taken place, which uses up more time in the slower thought process than does thinking additionally of the present and/or future. Thought in the present involves what is occurring at the moment and requires faster thinking. Thinking in the future is more difficult and requires faster thought than does thinking in the past or present because thought about the future contains at least some of all three parts of time. If whole, thought in the future also contains enough planning, or thought that is better at givingness (love, or consciousness), as part of the thought that is used together with the past and present. Thought that is about the future but that does not sufficiently plan causes time to separate from space, and for many "mistakes" to take place since time and space together regarding any activity can no longer be accurately determined.

The development of group souls and life on a dense planet such as earth goes through a progression, or develops a hierarchy of thought, of more spirit and energy increasing the light in their thought while on the mental plane. Using their preconceived thought, the group souls are then better able to inform their connected lifeforms through the lifeforms' self structures. These selves are connected to their group souls and higher Selves by the fallen spirit of the lifeforms being given to by them. The group souls with the lowest level of thought, along with their selves, create minerals. The first minerals created are the simplest inorganic compounds that have, usually, less than one completed center. These compounds come from various elements on a planet whose star is in its earliest incarnation (its first stage). Such a star has not yet created all of the elements needed for advanced life, through transmutation and fusion within its core. Earth's star, the sun, is in its second incarnation; a second-incarnation star is much longer-lived etheric/dense physically than is one in its first incarnation, and it uses materials in its solar system that were produced by first-incarnation stars. The corresponding mineral group souls of earth are also more advanced as an effect of being a part of a second incarnating solar system. Mineral group souls on earth have all of the elements available to them that a second-stage star, or one in its second incarnation, has. As a result, earth's mineral group souls were able to develop more complex inorganic (and eventually, organic) compounds from the time of the planet's inception.

How Viruses Infect Living Centers

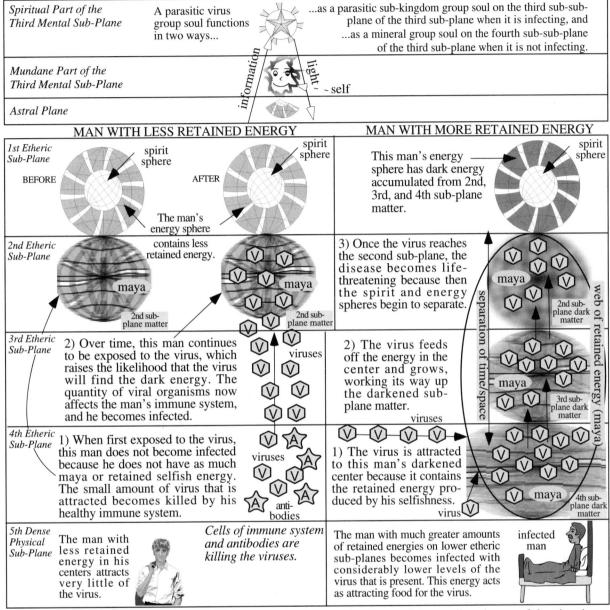

Spiritual Part of the Third Mental Sub-Plane	A parasitic virus group soul functions in two ways...	...as a parasitic sub-kingdom group soul on the third sub-sub-plane of the third sub-plane when it is infecting, and ...as a mineral group soul on the fourth sub-sub-plane of the third sub-plane when it is not infecting.
Mundane Part of the Third Mental Sub-Plane	information light - self	
Astral Plane		

MAN WITH LESS RETAINED ENERGY   **MAN WITH MORE RETAINED ENERGY**

1st Etheric Sub-Plane

BEFORE   spirit sphere   AFTER   spirit sphere

The man's energy sphere

This man's energy sphere has dark energy accumulated from 2nd, 3rd, and 4th sub-plane matter.

spirit sphere

2nd Etheric Sub-Plane

contains less retained energy.

maya

2nd sub-plane matter

3) Once the virus reaches the second sub-plane, the disease becomes life-threatening because then the spirit and energy spheres begin to separate.

maya

2nd sub-plane dark matter

3rd Etheric Sub-Plane

2) Over time, this man continues to be exposed to the virus, which raises the likelihood that the virus will find the dark energy. The quantity of viral organisms now affects the man's immune system, and he becomes infected.

viruses

2) The virus feeds off the energy in the center and grows, working its way up the darkened sub-plane matter.

viruses

maya

3rd sub-plane dark matter

4th Etheric Sub-Plane

1) When first exposed to the virus, this man does not become infected because he does not have as much maya or retained selfish energy. The small amount of virus that is attracted becomes killed by his healthy immune system.

viruses   anti-bodies

1) The virus is attracted to this man's darkened center because it contains the retained energy produced by his selfishness.

virus

maya

4th sub-plane dark matter

5th Dense Physical Sub-Plane

The man with less retained energy in his centers attracts very little of the virus.

Cells of immune system and antibodies are killing the viruses.

The man with much greater amounts of retained energies on lower etheric sub-planes becomes infected with considerably lower levels of the virus that is present. This energy acts as attracting food for the virus.

infected man

Both men are exposed to the same virus. The man on the left has been less selfish overall, and most of the virus is not attracted to him because his center is more enlightened and resilient. Notice that for him there is very little retained energy or dark matter on the second sub-plane to attract the virus. However, if this relatively unselfish person is continually exposed to a large quantity of viral organisms, there is a higher chance that the virus will find the dark energy and that he will become infected.

On the right, the center of spirit and energy located on the first etheric sub-plane is being separated through time and space by the selfish use of senses. The blurring is the maya, as a part of the webs of retained energy that cause the loss of sense and diminished immunity of the body. The virus is attracted to and infects this man's center because years of selfishness have produced a large amount of maya, or retained energy, on the lower etheric sub-planes, where the virus more easily infects from. When the virus works its way up to the second sub-plane matter, it becomes life-threatening. Not only has it infected all the lower sub-plane parts of this man's etheric/dense physical body, but it adds more dark energy into the afore-mentioned center by unifying it with the lower etheric sub-plane parts of the body the virus exists in, and causes that center to wobble. Once the spirit and energy spheres completely separate, the person dies. Note that some viruses and bacteria may first infect only the second sub-plane energy in a person's body; these organisms usually become life-threatening when and if all the sub-plane parts below the second sub-plane in a person's body also become infected. These infections are often very fast growing.

Illustration 6.7

MINERAL GROUP SOULS

The mineral group souls and their selves/Selves that think relatively well within light (but not the very best) can somewhat enlighten the densest part of their minerals. They do so by incorporating some of the structure from the thought, given to the group soul by its OverSoul, of the mental plane Ray Lord and its plan for creating life. This structure is then given by the self to the fallen spirit of the minerals that are most responsive in their slight thought and sense of structure. First, the group soul receives from the Self of the Solar Angel the structure of the mental plane Ray Lord's thought at the atomic level. Then the group soul synthesizes the Self's thought with the collective sense and information of the past from the minerals it informs. Its self then appropriately gives the needed knowledge to the spirit and the energy it informs on the etheric/dense physical (the seventh) plane. The fallen spirit on the seventh plane is greatly helped in its thought by the group soul and the enlightened structured thought that the Self and self together give. As a result, both the etheric elemental and lunar deva energies that create and improve the sense follow much better the structured thought of what was fallen spirit, which is helping them to become a better sense.

The form, or mineral, that is created becomes highly structured on the dense part of the seventh plane, emphasizing the effect of the structure; energy is still retained within the mineral, but some light is also present within its structure. Some minerals contain mixed amounts of retained energies and some amount of light within the form of certain crystals. These minerals can then refract some level of physical light from within their structures. Actually, most things that have substance on the dense parts of the seventh plane are made up of some retained energy, but only certain crystals that are more enlightened than not can refract light; when the form has no light within its structure, it can only reflect light off its surface. The first and lowest type of radiance is created by these more advanced-thinking mineral group souls of certain crystals. The longer-lasting the crystal (the harder and more resistant to heat and pressure it is) and the more light that it refracts, the more advanced the mineral group soul is in its thought. This thought mostly comes from the mineral's group soul and its shared—with its OverSoul—Self receiving mental light from the Ray Lord. Certain crystallized forms of minerals are more advanced than their non-crystallized counterparts are, although the chemistry of their elements may be the same.

Only one-third of the mineral group souls' thought is from the form that its connected lower spirit is informing. This one-third of its thought is created by the best-thinking energy in the sole (exclusively etheric) sense or two senses of minerals. This sense is focused on by the inform-ing (fallen) spirit and transmitted back to the group soul as sense of other energy and, via its self, as a sense of time. Then each group soul's thought synthesizes this one-third of thought that is provided by the minerals it informs, with the thought of its Self and of the mental plane Ray Lord. The only part of fractured time that the mineral group soul receives from its less than one, one, or two senses and focused thought of previously "fallen" informing spirit on the seventh plane is that of the past. The past is the easiest part of fractured time for energy and/or spirit to think within. The remaining two parts of time need to be synthesized with the past part by using the enlightened thought of the mental plane Ray Lord; this thought is transmitted to the mineral group soul through its Self that it shares with its Solar Angel.

The most advanced mineral group souls can equally enlighten both the etheric and dense physical parts of a form. When the group soul of non-organic minerals enlightens form in this way, it creates controlled fission as a part of the plan of the seventh plane Ray Lord; controlled fission is an advanced third ray method of energy creation. Until about the middle of the twen-tieth century, controlled fission on earth took place only within the earth and was unknown to humans. Since about A.D. 1940, humans have been attempting to direct the development of controlled fission, but still are creating more dense physical energy (as radioactive waste, or pollution) than perfect balance with etheric energy. The result is an imbalance created on the entire plane, causing some additional separation of the plane. Humans are responsible for this condition and, at present, think too selfishly to unify the plane and create perfect controlled fission. When humans create non-organic fission, the mineral group souls are following the humans' thought—and so are the minerals and their informing spirit. Humans, through civilization, can and most likely will eventually take over most of the choices and direction of thought of the lower kingdoms. Civilization is the extension and use of the three lower kingdoms by humans as a part of humans' senses and form. It is the taking over of the choices and direction of thought of the lower kingdoms. As humans civilize using light, God grows as life increases. If civilization takes place through darkness, the growth of life and of God diminish.

It is possible for the selfishness of humans to completely destroy an entire planet; the informing focus of life of that planet, or its Logos, would be required for that planet to begin again. The Logos of a planet is a Being who has ascended as a Monad in a cosmic universe that exists in form (a Cosmic Physical one, such as ours) and who has left that universe and lives in a more advanced one while it helps to create life within either the same or another Cosmic Physical Universe. We, of course, know of only one Cosmic Physical Universe—the one we live in—which may be the only one, but is very likely not to be. The Logos of a star exists in (has consciousness within) an even more advanced universe, and some Solar Logoi develop through each having been a Planetary Logos who successfully developed seven different planetary chains of life, with the focus of life creation on each of these planets along one of the seven rays. Some Solar Logoi develop ten planetary schemes. These schemes each have the development of one Planetary Logos focusing on each one of the seven rays for each chain of a planet's life creation. Thus in a Solar Logos's ten planetary schemes, ten Planetary Logoi will each develop a scheme of seven chains of planets, each with seven planetary incarnations, with each planetary chain having one of seven ray life focuses on it. Our earth and its informing Planetary Logos are along the third ray in planetary life development (which is why oxygen, a third ray element, is the most abundant one). The Planetary Logos is along the *fifth* ray line in its own development, eventually into the Solar Kingdom. The focus of earth's Planetary Logos on the third ray type of life development is to produce the acceleration of life on earth through advancement of the thought and sense of energy by use of the third ray as a primary focus. The third ray is used more often to accelerate the growth of life on a dense physical planet than are any of the other six rays.

THE SPIRIT OF EARTH
AND THE CREATION OF PRANA

Mineral group souls on earth today that develop radiance on the highest levels etherically, and are not affected by human thought, greatly affect the life of earth in very broad ways. These group souls are affecting the rate of movement of the inner parts of the earth. They do so by creating fission that releases light and heat into the inner earth. The result is a broad effect on tectonic plate movement, which then creates vulcanism, earthquakes, the building of mountains, the creation of seas, and changes to earth's magnetic field. All of these tremendously affect large groups of, if not sometimes all of life on earth. The collective enlightened spirit on the seventh plane connected to the most advanced mineral group souls is sometimes referred to as the Spirit of Earth. This spirit is cooperating with the mental plane Ray Lord and Its structured plan for minerals as represented within the thoughts of the mineral group souls' Selves and as they are transferred and given in light through the group souls' selves to their informing fallen spirit and forms on the seventh plane. The Spirit of Earth in part includes the collective enlightened thought of the most advanced and enlightened previously fallen spirit concerning water and air, in addition to that part that uses fission to control radiance inside the earth. Liquid water becomes radiant when it moves in ways that grow more life nearly perfectly in relation to the land that confines it and the air that surrounds it. Water's quality of movement is also represented in either its frozen form (as ice) or in its gaseous form (as vapor), but then its radiance changes to either solid or gaseous structures. Etheric air becomes radiant as it absorbs sunlight, and becomes changed in structure by the sunlight so that it (the air) can support life. One of these structured changes uses non-nuclear (electro-chemical) fusion, or a second ray method of the third cosmic fire, of friction (using the ultraviolet part of sunlight) to create ozone. This simultaneously changes the etheric *ultra*violet light into a part of our etheric atmosphere, or creating more light into the form of (creating virtue in) our etheric atmosphere so that life can grow. Life that is not joined etherically and dense physically cannot effectively use ultra-violet light.

There are six other methods through which sunlight is etherically created into form within our atmosphere. However, these etheric conditions are mostly still unrecognized, as are their effects on the dense form of air. All seven of the methods come from the seven sub-types of etheric light

The Creation of Third Ray Prana

The Etheric Sun and Sunlight

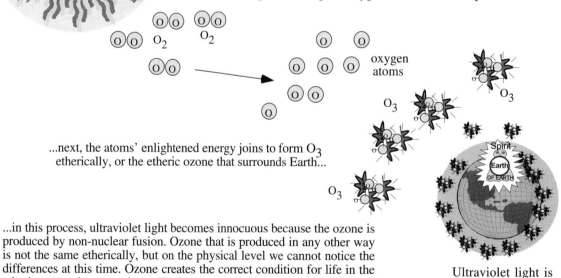

Etheric sunlight affects the atomic level of the etheric part of the earth. The etheric (ultra-violet) sunlight breaks the oxygen molecules into individual etheric atoms that re-join with the enlightened energy during chemical (non-nuclear) fusion, and the third ray prana, or etheric ozone, is created.

The etheric sunlight breaks up the oxygen molecules into separate atoms...

O_2 O_2 oxygen atoms O_3 O_3

...next, the atoms' enlightened energy joins to form O_3 etherically, or the etheric ozone that surrounds Earth...

O_3

...in this process, ultraviolet light becomes innocuous because the ozone is produced by non-nuclear fusion. Ozone that is produced in any other way is not the same etherically, but on the physical level we cannot notice the differences at this time. Ozone creates the correct condition for life in the etheric atmosphere—and can do the reverse in the more dense parts of Earth's atmosphere.

Ultraviolet light is converted into O_3, or etheric ozone, surrounding Earth.

There are seven ray types of etheric pranic energy that can be absorbed by a living being. Each of these energies is helping to grow life. In the above example, fission occurs when the third etheric sub-ray of the seventh etheric ray energy around Earth is enlightened by the sun, which splits the oxygen molecules. Fusion occurs when the enlightened oxygen molecules join with the enlightened energy. The more that the energy is enlightened, the more conducive the energy is to life. The enlightened light is transformed to make it life-giving instead of harmful to the growth of life.

Illustration 6.8

from the etheric/dense physical part of our sun. Each of the seven parts of etheric energy (and also of the more subtle energy from the higher planes) in our atmosphere, or structured changes to our atmosphere through sunlight, is frequently referred to in spiritual language as a *prana*.

Each prana comes from the highest thought of one of seven types of mineral group souls as this thought is affected by the etheric (and astral and mental) light of the sun; these seven mineral group souls, collectively, are a part of the Spirit of Earth and help to create our atmosphere. The Spirit of Earth functions as a regulator of the atmosphere by optimizing it for the sustaining of life. The thought of the mineral group souls then induces the etheric sub-plane's spirit and energy to join with the seven types of sunlight, each in a way that is specific to that corresponding sub-light and its ray. The new pranic energies are then used by any lifeform that uses one or more parts of air to create heat within itself, because all are a part of the third cosmic fire, of friction. Each one of the seven pranas helps to release energy from one of the seven different ray types of centers. This process is a critical element for most lifeforms in their use of energy from the "food" they consume. Pranic energies are also found in dense form in food, and when eaten, release energies similar to the ways in which they do so when used directly from the air. There are differences, however, since the prana in the food is in dense form rather than etheric, with the density greatly slowing both the prana's movement within the body and the rate at which it moves other energy through a corresponding center. Without additional atmospheric etheric prana, the center retains excessive amounts of energy and may become diseased.

 ## OTHER PRANIC AND KUNDALINI ENERGIES

There are also astral and mental pranas, which directly energize the astral and mental bodies, respectively, through each corresponding center. These pranic energies come from the astral and mental sub-planes, and affect the astral and mental plane atmospheres. The enlightened spirit on those two planes helps to fuse these energies and light together on each of them through its focused thought. Astral and mental pranas do *not* function by releasing the energies in denser etheric or dense physical form because no such energy exists on these subtle planes. Instead, these pranas are used to directly build the corresponding ray parts and full bodies by being distributed through the matching, according to ray focus, centers. Much less heat is created from the metabolism of either the astral or mental bodies. The reason is that in these bodies no dense prana (food) is joined with atmospheric pranas as on the etheric/dense physical plane. *Some* heat is still produced and continues to be until kundalini replaces the use of astral and mental pranas. This heat is created by frictional forces that are created as the elemental energy in the body is continually replaced with new elemental energy from within the pranic energies. The lunar devas in the pranic energies create frictional heat only if lower consciousness devas are replacing higher consciousness—and thinking—ones in the same centers or body. The cause for such a replacement would invariably be selfishness. The enlightened spirit of *plants* and *animals* is what mostly composes the astral Spirit of Earth; mental plane pranas come mostly from enlightened (lower) mental plane fallen spirit of advanced animals and from humans. Enlightened fallen spirit especially comes from the collective enlightened thought of, usually, humans who are mentally alive (and who are etheric/dense physically and astrally dead).

The Spirit of Earth includes the spirit from all of the sources of enlightened seventh plane spirit within the mineral kingdom. Because it is so strongly affected by its enlightenment of elemental energies that are all *involuting*, the greater proportion of the Spirit of the Earth is focused on the etheric/dense physical plane, which is where the most advanced involutionary energies are found. It is also affected by any other enlightened spirit on the seventh plane, including that which is in plant and animal life and alive etheric/dense physically. The collective enlightened thought of the Spirit of Earth is mostly on the etheric plane. It also joins with equally

Kundalini Energy

Less enlightened spiritual elemental energy from the seventh, sixth, and fifth sub-planes of the spiritual plane is attracted to the collective and enlightened thought of the Spirit of Earth...

...kundalini is the name of this energy that is transmuted from less enlightened spiritual elemental energy from the spiritual plane to fully enlightened etheric elemental energy. This enlightened elemental energy can then be used by some kinds of energy beings, Masters, and only those humans who are very advanced.

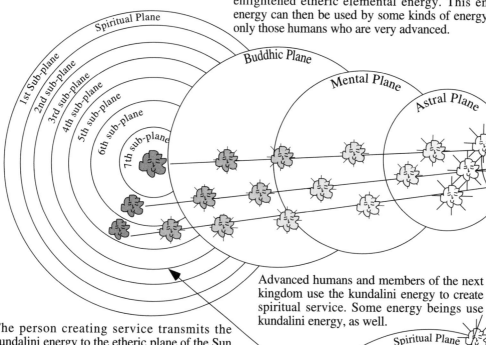

Advanced humans and members of the next kingdom use the kundalini energy to create spiritual service. Some energy beings use kundalini energy, as well.

The person creating service transmits the kundalini energy to the etheric plane of the Sun through her or his intuitional body, freeing the energy from Earth's higher mental ring-pass-not between Earth and Venus. This energy helps to further create elements through fusion in the center of the Sun. The kundalini energy becomes deva, or evolutionary, energy before it reaches the Sun and is transmitted back to the etheric sub-planes.

Through the giving of kundalini energy in service on Earth, Earth is connected to the Sun. The being transmitting the kundalini energy becomes connected to the etheric plane of the Sun.

An advanced intitiate who can further enlighten kundalini energy must do so as is needed in his or her service. Spiritual service causes less need for prana or for food. As a result of this service, all the centers in the body gradually become fused through the three kundalini energies of pingala, ida, and sushumna.

An advanced initiate is sometimes unable to completely use the kundalini energy because of the selfishness of his or her students. In these cases, the initiate will retain the kundalini in his or her bodies. This energy will slowly destroy his or her bodies because retained kundalini becomes radiation. Retained kundalini appears green to someone who has super-etheric or higher than super-etheric sight.

Illustration 6.9

enlightened fallen spirit on the astral and mental planes. The entire collective thought of this enlightened spirit is strong enough to attract some transmuted elemental energy from the spiritual plane because this thought is strong enough to attract some of this energy inter-dimensionally. Energy from the spiritual plane is connected to our sun, since stars' highest levels of energy are from the third, or spiritual, plane. After the Spirit of Earth attracts the spiritual elemental energy, if the energy is further enlightened through spiritual service it either becomes attracted back to the *etheric* energy part of the sun (and some slightly to the sun's astral and lower mental parts) and helps to further create elements in the center of the sun through fission and fusion or becomes a part of other planets in the solar system (through solar flares, for example). A person or being who is alive dense physically or etherically and can further enlighten some amount of the attracted third plane, or spiritual, energy needs to do so as is needed in his or her service. These people or beings include very advanced humans and members of the next kingdom beyond the human, or the spiritual kingdom. The name for the spiritual plane elemental energy attracted to the etheric plane, astral, and lower mental planes—and connected in some ways to these dimensions—is kundalini. When kundalini is used *in service* it further enlightens and replaces the need for a person or a being to use prana as a means of animating energy through any of the centers used for service. The use of kundalini in service also reduces and sometimes eliminates the need to consume food; it also connects the person or being to the spiritual (and spiritual plane) part of our sun, as well as to the spiritual plane itself. It eventually connects all the centers in the bodies to the highest center and body in a lifeform. Kundalini that is the most advanced type and that is used in service becomes fully enlightened etheric energy, or etheric elemental energy that is about to become spiritualized and to enter the deva kingdom—which is the evolutionary part of the energy kingdom. As etheric kundalini passes through the etheric/dense physical form, if it is not completely enlightened through service it creates a radioactivity as it is retained within the much denser etheric form. The radioactive etheric part of the dense form will glow a shade of green corresponding to the spiritual, or third, plane and the color of the energy there. Most humans cannot see retained kundalini because it manifests as a green radioactive glow only on the third (mostly) through first etheric sub-planes (the super-etheric, sub-atomic, and atomic) of the etheric plane. While alive dense physically, a human needs considerable amounts of enlightened etheric sense in order to see these sub-planes. Kundalini is another way in which organic minerals can become radioactive. It is the chief way in which the previously mentioned non-organic energy beings receive energy through their centers, and it therefore intimately connects them to the Spirit of Earth (and to spirit enlightening earth). All of the mineral group souls are either indirectly or directly affected by energy beings, by the Spirit of Earth, and by the development and use of kundalini. (See Chapter Seven for further explanation of kundalini energies.)

 PLANT GROUP SOULS

Plant group souls are considerably more advanced in their ability to think mentally than are mineral group souls. This is because the spirit and energy within these souls has existed for much longer periods of time on the mental plane and has thus learned better ways in which to think in structured thought. Their improved structured, or mental, thought allows them to better join together mental plane time with space. When this joining occurs it allows the plant group souls to better inform their groups of lifeforms through the self structure of the souls. The lifeforms are alive because the plant group soul can create enough preconceived thought to think in the *two* dimensions (the etheric/dense physical and the astral) at close to the same time. The plant group soul is creating two parts of time that are logically connected to space, in its preconceived thought that it gives to its group of lifeforms. These two parts of time are the past, for the part of the plant that is alive etheric/dense physically, and the present, for the part that is alive astrally. The preconceived thought of the plant group soul and its self attracts energies that move through at least *two* different etheric centers. This allows for movement etheric/dense physically, and at nearly the same time. For the plants, however, it can actually take minutes to hours in human terms for the corresponding astral part of *some* of the etheric/dense physical energy to move through at least one astral center. This movement creates the consciousness of sentiency, or the ability to sense astral movement *and* to create some etheric/dense physical movement from astral and etheric thought of previously "fallen" spirit *within a plant*. As a result of the very slow connection of the two parts of time, many types of plants require minutes or even hours to create movement from sentiency. This makes it very difficult for most humans to sense that plants are sentient. All plants can grow and can also respond to their environments using the preconceived thought of their respective group souls (e.g., responding to light or water in certain prescribed ways), which also results in etheric/dense physical movement. The movement, however, is based upon average responses to outside stimuli for growth (or its lack thereof). It is not based upon the slight astral and etheric/dense physical thought of the fallen spirit within the individual plant, nor, therefore, upon plant sentiency. In discovering sentiency in advanced plants, humans are most likely to find response to sound and touch because these are the two senses that most *advanced* plants have some consciousness of. These two senses are the first to be developed on the etheric/dense physical and astral planes, respectively.

Many plants use a combined group conscious, or joined astral, sense to develop their slight sentiency. Plant colonies from mosses to grasses rely upon such methods. These group-sentient plants usually have just one astral center that is used as long as they are etheric/dense physically and astrally touching, with this astral center only slightly developed. Plants that have a sole astral center can live only on the etheric/dense physical plane. The reason is that when they die from this plane, they cannot continue to live on the astral plane—which would necessitate a second astral center. The astral plane is distinctly missing these plant forms, unless they are created by the

Plant Colonies Sharing an Astral Center

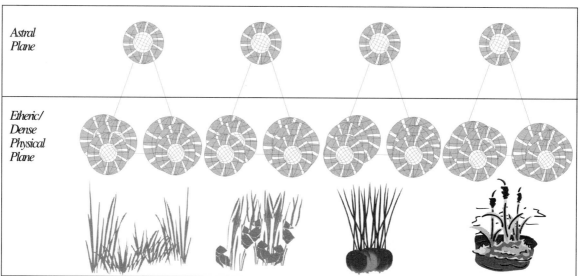

Some plants, such as grasses, use a combined group conscious, or joined astral, sense to develop their slight sentiency. Each colony of a type of grass shares its own astral center. The members of each colony share a common astral sense. In order to share this sense, the members need to be in close proximity to each other. Averages, and not individual events, are relied upon for the plants' responses.

Illustration 6.10

thought of advanced animal and human life through creative imagination, or the creative thought on the astral plane. Plants that have more than one astral sense and corresponding center can remain alive astrally provided that some advanced animals and humans are also present who can think and who have bodies that are on the mental plane. Some parts of the senses and centers of the animals and humans who think mentally are then borrowed by the plants. For a plant to remain alive astrally, it must borrow the partial use of at least one mental center; one advanced animal or human can enliven thousands or more plants. The plant group souls become greatly helped in their mental development as their astrally alive plants borrow some of a mental center and sense from an advanced animal or human who is focused in life (or is alive) while on the astral plane. Notice that when no advanced animals or humans have been present on a part of the astral plane, no plants are, either. The above holds true for the astral construction of minerals from the use of astral centers of humans and animals, and also from the use of one of the two or more astral centers of plants—which puts even greater demands on the higher lifeforms' astral sense as compared to its mental sense. Thus without the thought of humans, of advanced animals, or of plants (which are informed by the humans or advanced animals), the astral plane just seems to disappear.

To restate the above-described concepts from a different angle of thought, in order for a mineral to exist on the astral plane requires that it have a minimum of one center on that plane. As pre-life, minerals need only one center because they are not alive and hence do not grow as life. For plants to be alive on the astral plane requires that they have a minimum of two astral centers and one mental center, and the minimum for animals is three astral centers and one completed mental. The reason for these minimums is that existence on a plane requires having a center there, and without having two centers on one plane and at least one other center on another plane, the astral energy cannot connect with time and space, and the growth of life cannot take place. However, because the group souls of minerals, plants, and all but the most advanced animals lack adequate preconceptual thought to create these minimums—in particular, the mental center—the missing center or centers are provided by members of a higher kingdom. In the creation of life on the astral plane, any animal can create minerals in its (astral) imagination (even an amoebae can create water), but an advanced animal or a human is required to create a living plant or an animal that is relatively less advanced. In the case of all of these scenarios, when the animal or human whose thought (and one or more centers) has created pre-life or life and has animated that life leaves the vicinity of the astral plane where this pre-life or life exists, that part of the plane remains exactly as it was left, for a fairly long period of astral time. Even if the plant that created a mineral on the astral plane remains in the vicinity, if the advanced animal or human that created that plant leaves, then the plant will not be able to sustain its created mineral's existence. However, minerals created by advanced animals and humans will remain for a period of time. The plant's own existence is dependent upon the thought (and center or centers) of the advanced animal or human who created it. The reason is that on the astral plane, non-advanced animals and plants can neither grow nor change without a mental center, and minerals cannot change, or even exist, without an astral one, which none of these pre-life or lifeforms has on its own on the astral plane. What fosters the change and growth is the mental or astral center (or both) of the astral animal or human that created the plant or mineral. When this creator (the advanced animal or the human) is no longer present, the creation becomes torpid and appears to be in suspended animation for a fairly long period of time, and then disintegrates. Differences in time and space on the etheric/dense physical plane as compared to the astral mean that the physics of the two planes are different, and a suspended state of life growth does not occur etheric/dense physically as it does astrally. Thus "if a tree falls" in an etheric/dense physical forest with no one present, it does make a sound, but in an astral forest, when no one is present the trees never fall at all! The reader is referred to Chapter Eight for a much fuller explanation of what the astral plane is like.

The Requisite Centers for Astral Existence

A mineral cannot exist on the astral plane without having at least one astral center. A plant's life (focused in astral life) on the astral plane requires that the plant have at least two astral centers and a part of one mental center that is supplemental and is completed by an even higher animal or human. An animal can be alive (focused in life) on the astral plane only if that animal has at least three astral centers and one complete mental center. Minerals, plants, and animals each begin existence with a certain number of centers, but the remaining centers that are needed for life focused astrally on the astral or mental plane (or both) come from beings that are more advanced. For example, a plant can share its astral center with a mineral, and an advanced animal can share its mental centers with plants. An animal that is relatively less developed may have no mental center or one that is only a partially developed and needs to be completed. For members of the three lowest kingdoms, missing centers (or parts of them) come from either an animal that has a somewhat developed mental body or from a human. These advanced animals and humans can supply the missing center or centers that the mineral, plant, or less advanced animal needs so that astral energy in the lower lifeforms can connect with time and space, which enables astral life and its growth to take place.

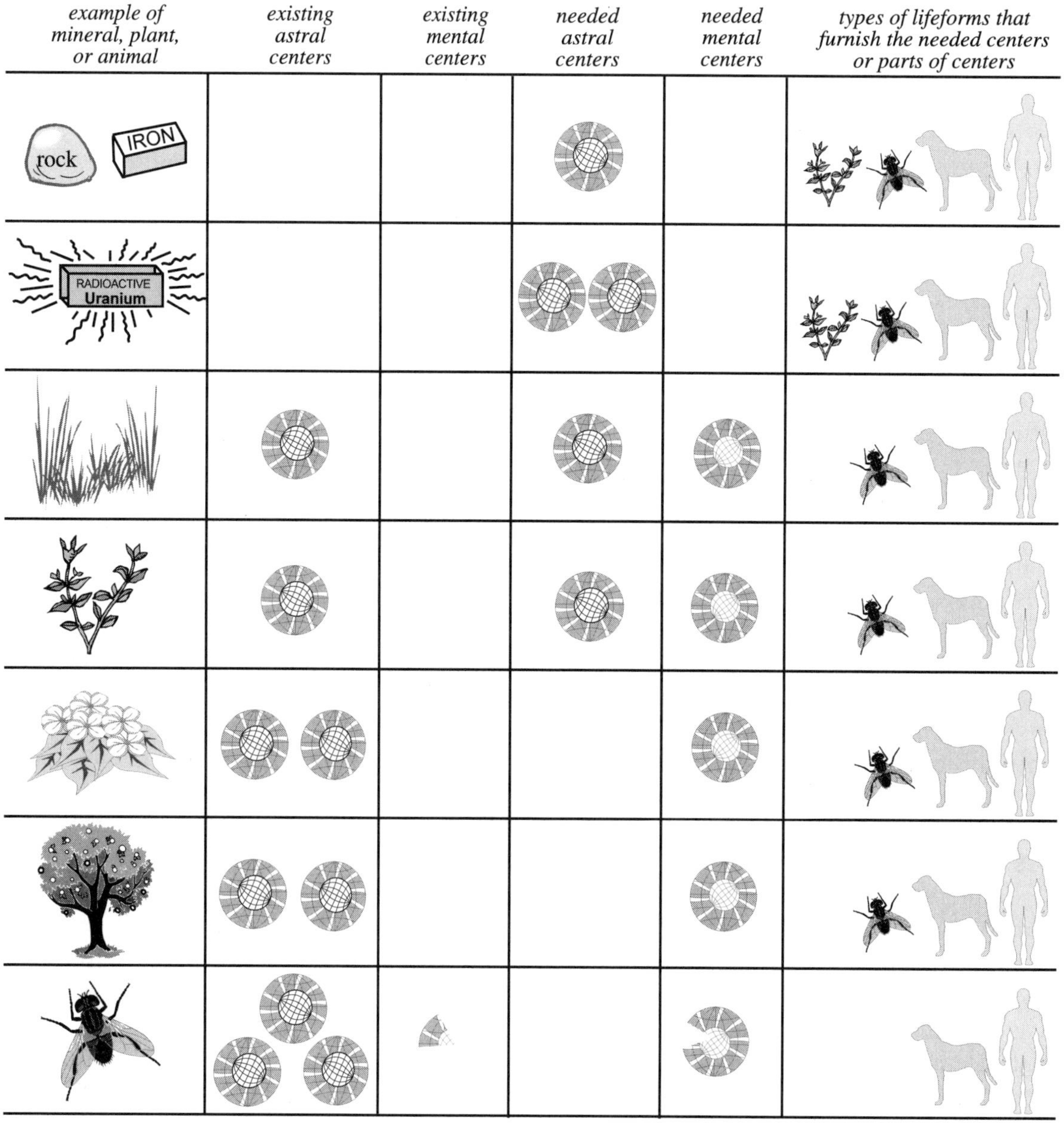

example of mineral, plant, or animal	existing astral centers	existing mental centers	needed astral centers	needed mental centers	types of lifeforms that furnish the needed centers or parts of centers
rock / IRON			⦿		plant, fly, dog, human
RADIOACTIVE Uranium			⦿⦿		plant, fly, dog, human
grass	⦿		⦿	⦿	fly, dog, human
plant	⦿		⦿	⦿	fly, dog, human
flowers	⦿⦿			⦿	fly, dog, human
tree	⦿⦿			⦿	fly, dog, human
fly	⦿⦿⦿	◗		◖	dog, human

Illustration 6.11

ADVANCEMENT OF GROUP SOULS

The energy and informing spirit components of the most advanced plant group souls—those that think the best—eventually collectively join together in a pool of spirit and energy, based upon a hierarchy of ability to think. The spirit and energy that thinks the best within each of the most advanced plant group souls joins with other best-thinking parts from other plant group souls, to become new, animal group souls. The remaining, less advanced, spirit and energy that is not used to create new group souls in the next higher (the animal) kingdom stays at its location on the mental plane (on the third sub-sub-plane of the third higher sub-plane) and forms new plant group souls. This spirit and energy cannot remain together as an existing group soul in the same kingdom when a kingdom advances. Mineral group souls undergo a corresponding transformation to create new plant and mineral group souls. The (higher) Selves of all group souls that a Solar Angel helped to develop remain immortally and as a shared part of that Solar Angel throughout its development. Because group souls and their selves have direct contact with their Selves, they do not suffer from a fear of annihilation of the self. Energy from plant or mineral group souls that joins together in the above-described way almost always shares the same ray type, which could be any one of seven. There are seven ray types of mental plane energy; each is a sub-ray of the mental ray (the fifth) and corresponds to one of the seven rays of the Ray Lords. These seven mental sub-rays create seven distinctly different types of plant group souls as they affect the growth of the energy in its thought and its developing sense and awareness within each soul. Based upon these differences, the plant group souls create distinct self structures (the way their selves are connected on the mental plane to the soul and to the fallen spirit they inform), which then informs their plant lifeforms differently, producing greater diversity to life. A similar process occurs in mineral group souls as they create pre-life. Based upon how they sense and what they are aware of (as a result of differences in their ray types), there are seven categories of plants as sub-parts, or that represent sub-rays, of the plant kingdom. Most humans on earth do not yet fully recognize the slight awareness that plants have nor the limited senses that provide this awareness. Consequently, most humans do not notice the seven sub-rays of plants that help to develop the plants' senses. There are also seven sub-rays of minerals, which may be even more obscure. The previously mentioned plant sub-kingdom, of molds and fungi, is also grouped into seven categories of plants, and it is further classified into seven sub-ray parts. The plant sub-kingdom is below the plant kingdom in its ability to think, and is thus not able to progress into the plant kingdom in the way that has been described. Some of the life in this sub-kingdom is parasitic because of its lack of one or more needed centers and senses, which then causes it to use one or more centers and senses of its host—or its victim!

Most plant group souls (as well as group souls in the other kingdoms) collectively join parts of their best-thinking spirit and energy during designated periods, or when "the door is open" for them to advance into the next kingdom. The Planetary Logos of a planet is ultimately in control of when these periods for en masse advancement can occur for the most advanced part of each kingdom of life on that planet. Assisting the Planetary Logos of earth are certain advanced Beings who have mastered the lower three worlds *and* the intuitional plane as well. These super-human Beings have advanced beyond the fifth kingdom, of Souls (the spiritual kingdom), and while still members of the fifth kingdom have become junior members of the sixth kingdom, of Planetary Logoi; this kingdom is also referred to as the planetary kingdom. *Manu* is the spiritual name given to an advanced Master, or a Chohan, who, in addition to other duties, helps to determine when the advancement of life on his or her planet should begin and end. This name is a title such as would accompany an office holder, and is not the actual name of any particular Chohan, or sixth level initiate. There are various offices held by advanced Masters, and, sometimes, by other Great Beings who help the Planetary Logos, including the Bodhisattva who functions along the second ray and is both the World Teacher and the head of the spiritual hierarchy of the fifth kingdom. Because any additional information on this matter would be extraneous to the purpose of this book, further discussion of this topic shall be reserved for another time.

Parts of the better-thinking spirit and energy in plant group souls join together when deemed appropriate by the Manu, and move into the animal kingdom. Each collection of spirit and energy that joins together is usually along one of the seven ray types, and all of the energy within each joined collection generally shares the same sub-ray of mental energy. Based upon a hierarchy of thought, the somewhat advanced parts of spirit and energy form the somewhat more advanced of the new animal group souls. The collections of spirit and energy that join together and become new *advanced* group souls in the next higher kingdom are able to do so because they became fully enlightened, or radiant, by giving perfectly to the lifeforms they informed in their respective *former kingdoms*. They did so by consistently mentally creating and giving to the lifeforms they informed—unconditionally creatively loving them *mentally*—while on the mental plane as members of that lower kingdom. However, in the next higher kingdom, the combined advanced spirit and energy must begin anew as group souls in that kingdom, which is a far more complicated endeavor. Therefore, this combined advanced spirit and energy usually does not immediately create an advanced group soul and lifeform in the next kingdom, and may wait until a later a period of time in the round of life development to do so. The new, higher-level lifeforms are also given time to develop on the etheric/dense physical and the astral planes, and sometimes on the lower mental plane as well.

The process by which the spirit and energy within a group soul advance within a kingdom and from one kingdom to the next is explained as follows. Within a kingdom, the spirit and energy of a group soul is in a state of either being enlightened or not. The spirit that is fully enlightened is the group souls' (higher) Self that it shares with its OverSoul. This Self surrounds the energy that has become enlightened. Both are found on the first sub-plane of the mental plane. All of the Self and some part of the energy (that which is enlightened) are located at the atomic level of that plane. The combined enlightened energy (or that which is becoming enlightened) and surrounding Self of the group soul produce the single mental permanent atom for the one—or, in rare cases, the more than one—species that a group soul informs. However, when a group soul informs more than one species, a different astral and etheric/dense physical permanent atom is used for each family, genus, and species of lifeform. Note that mental permanent atoms are the structural blueprints of the forms and are like "mental genes." A few group souls inform at the same time two or more types of species that are different but that share some similarity in the way they use their senses. Whether a group soul informs one or more than one type of species is dependent upon the degrees of difference in levels of the various species' enlightenment and their growth in the same sense or senses that the lifeforms and soul are mutually developing. Sometimes even families of species are too different, or too specialized, to be informed by a single group soul. The reason is that the ways in which the one or more senses are being developed need different supporting informing thought from the (lower) self and mental permanent atom. A very few advanced group souls may inform more than one type of species that use some of their senses differently. This usually occurs when the species have very close symbiotic relationships to one another and use their sense or senses in symbiotic ways that grow the different sense or senses in an interrelated manner. Some advanced group souls work together under these same circumstances, where each soul has a symbiotic relationship of growth of senses with the other.

The spirit within the group soul that is not enlightened is still very giving, or has half of the quality of light. This spirit does not yet give wisely, nor can it create what it gives; it is helped

How a Group Soul Advances

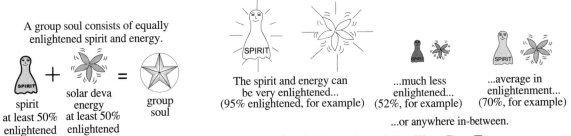

A group soul consists of equally enlightened spirit and energy.

spirit at least 50% enlightened + solar deva energy at least 50% enlightened = group soul

The spirit and energy can be very enlightened... (95% enlightened, for example)

...much less enlightened... (52%, for example)

...average in enlightenment... (70%, for example)

...or anywhere in-between.

Three Different Mineral Group Souls That Are of the First Ray Type

Notice that some group souls have more enlightened spirit and energy than others do.

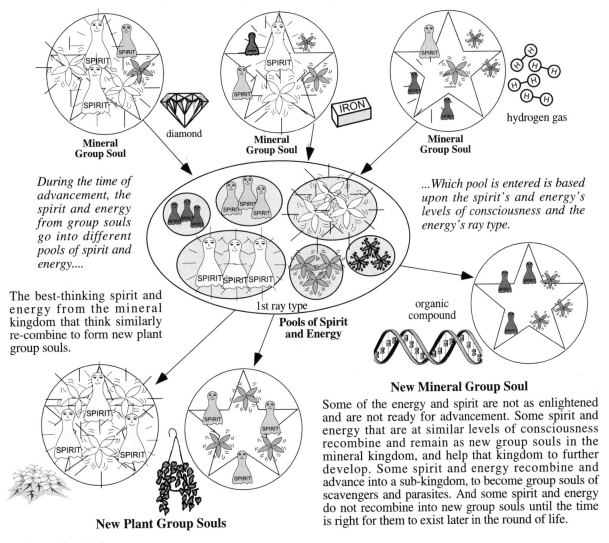

During the time of advancement, the spirit and energy from group souls go into different pools of spirit and energy....

The best-thinking spirit and energy from the mineral kingdom that think similarly re-combine to form new plant group souls.

Mineral Group Soul — diamond

Mineral Group Soul — IRON

Mineral Group Soul — hydrogen gas

...Which pool is entered is based upon the spirit's and energy's levels of consciousness and the energy's ray type.

Pools of Spirit and Energy

1st ray type

organic compound

New Mineral Group Soul

Some of the energy and spirit are not as enlightened and are not ready for advancement. Some spirit and energy that are at similar levels of consciousness recombine and remain as new group souls in the mineral kingdom, and help that kingdom to further develop. Some spirit and energy recombine and advance into a sub-kingdom, to become group souls of scavengers and parasites. And some spirit and energy do not recombine into new group souls until the time is right for them to exist later in the round of life.

New Plant Group Souls

Illustration 6.12

with both of these qualities by the thought of its Self. Higher Selves think group consciously together about how to best give, but they think individually as they create within their thought (see Chapter Five for further explanation of this concept). The unenlightened energy within the group soul is not yet ready to become enlightened. The reason is that the lifeforms that the particular group soul is informing have yet to develop enough centers and senses that are capable of providing the information to be converted into knowledge that would be enlightening.

The energy in the permanent atom for each group of informed lifeforms is capable of being enlightened or has already become enlightened by the senses of the corresponding and connected type of lifeform.

When all of the energy within the mental permanent atom concerning one or more specific senses has become enlightened (the energy has become intelligent activity and is within the surrounding Self of a group soul), then the spirit and energy within the group soul may separate. The lower energy that was least responsive to light is given to less advanced group souls. In these less advanced souls, this energy is relatively more responsive than is the energy that is already within them. The energy within the group soul that was more responsive is then joined by advanced energy from another advanced group soul, usually along the same ray line. Because similar energies grow best in new group souls, this energy often comes from more advanced group souls. These group souls generally have similar senses and therefore similar types of energy and have informed lifeforms of a similar ray type of species or family of species. A ray type of species is a species in which one of its centers and senses or a certain combination of them is oriented in growth along a particular ray focus, according to the thought of the group soul of that species. If that ray is in focus on the planet, the effect is greatly enhanced.

Sometimes some group souls perfect one or more of the senses of the lifeforms they inform, in relation to the overall level of development in life of that type of lifeform. Such group souls do not significantly develop any other of the lifeform's senses. In these cases a group soul may progress through its kingdom, growing itself and keeping the same energy, spirit, and self for very long periods of time. Then it does not change the one or more types of lifeforms that are perfected in the way they use their sense(s) in relation to the respective levels at which they live. These conditions occur because of directions from the Planetary Logos, which are then followed as a plan for the planet by Its helpers; the conditions are eventually structured within the plan by the mental plane Ray Lord of the planet. Note that planetary Ray Lords are lesser Beings than, and a sub-category of, cosmic Ray Lords. The group soul follows the structured light of the mental plane as best as it can, depending upon its own levels of light in its spirit and form. The group souls that have one or more relatively enlightened lifeforms, as needed for them to function perfectly while using at least one sense at their level of life development, are often the rare group souls that inform more than one species of life. The species with at least one perfected sense, based upon the various species' levels of advancement in life, are often eventually relatively primitive as compared to the species that such a group soul is further developing. Close symbiotic relationships are necessary among the group souls' non-changing species as well as the ones that do change. The reason is that the self and its mental plane structure that connect it to the group soul remain the same for prolonged periods of time. These group souls are extremely slow to advance into the next kingdom. Sometimes they may even remain in the same kingdom for a majority of that planet's focused round of etheric/dense physical life development. The whole concept behind these group souls is to keep certain lifeforms that have one or more relatively enlightened senses in existence for protracted periods of time, while other somewhat enlightened lifeforms advance and change. As part of the Plan, the Planetary Logos needs some forms to remain the same for these extended periods. Those forms, as examples of relatively perfected sense at their level of life development, can be used to challenge the senses of other lifeforms that are affected by the forms' one or more relatively perfected senses, and that are often in symbiotic relationships with them. Also, these unchanging lifeforms constitute the life that will remain on dense physical earth as this round of life shifts to the next round wherein senses will develop at an increased speed. A relatively perfected lifeform at its level of life development is one that has become relatively enlightened through the perfection of its sense(s). This perfection is defined by the lifeform's correct use (in accord with the Plan) of one or more of its senses; such use makes the lifeform very successful in living through its sense(s). Examples of these lifeforms include

Enlightened Sense of a Primitive Lifeform

One does not normally think of a cockroach as having enlightened senses; however, a cockroach has become relatively enlightened through the perfection of some of its etheric/dense physical senses. Its etheric/dense physical senses are highly developed, and some are separated. Notice that some senses are joined better than a human's whose are used selfishly and are separated. A cockroach has three astral centers, but little astral sense—which its group soul did not focus on to develop, in a sacrifice to perfect some of its etheric sense in relation to its life. It has no mental senses and only a sliver of a mental center. A cockroach's senses allow it to be extremely adaptable, which ensures its survivability, but not its overall enlightenment as a species for its advancement into the next higher kingdom. The group soul of the cockroach is, at this time, sacrificing its development of astral senses in order to better develop its etheric/dense physical ones.

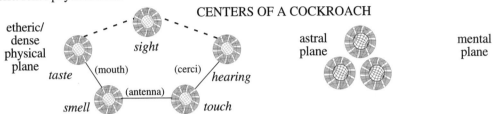

CENTERS OF A COCKROACH

These centers are fusing together, which causes this group soul to develop some radiance. However, it cannot become completely radiant because of its greatly imbalanced lack of astral senses.

Antennae—Antennae, or feelers, provide cockroaches with a sense of smell and the ability to detect vibrations in the air.

Eyes—Each eye is made up of 2,000 individual lenses so that cockroaches can see movement and especially differences between light and dark. This gives them a sense of sight. Humans have only one lens per eye. Cockroaches cannot see in red light, but they can see in green light.

Food—The cockroach eats almost anything, including injured or dead cockroaches. It has two sets of teeth. One set is in its digestive tract so that it can survive on any diet. The cockroach can carry diseases such as salmonella, and not be affected by them.

Heart—The cockroach's heart is shaped like a tube and can even stop without the cockroach dying.

Body—There is a waxy coating on its body to prevent moisture loss. The cockroach can survive on only one drop of water per day.

Fat—The cockroach stores fat, as energy, in its body. The fat breaks down nutrients to get energy, and helps to treat, or detoxify, insecticides that are sprayed on it.

Legs—The cockroach's legs are covered with hair, to provide a sense of touch.

Reproduction—A male will give a female a package of sperm that may continually keep her pregnant for most of her life. This system ensures survival of the species in case a male is not around.

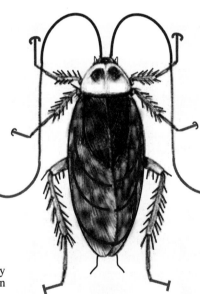

American Cockroach

Mouth—A cockroach uses its mouth to both smell and taste, which means that its mouth has two senses at the same time. This produces greater versatility with one organ and the ability to detect poisonous food before swallowing it.

Brain—A cockroach does not have a concentrated brain. Instead, it has a rudimentary nervous system throughout its body. A cockroach can survive with its head cut off for as long as a week, until dying of thirst or starvation.

Lungs—The cockroach breathes through a series of holes in the sides of its body. Thin branching tubes carry oxygen to all parts of the body. This system allows the cockroach to remain alive when parts of its body are damaged.

Cerci—Cerci are two little hairs on the rear end of the cockroach. They act as a motion detector, alerting the cockroach to any movement so it can run in the opposite direction. Cerci are connected to the cockroach's legs so that it will start running even before its brain receives the signal to. This sense is similar to a sense of hearing and/or touch.

Exoskeleton—Having its skeleton on the outside of its body greatly protects the cockroach from harm. The exoskeleton is shed and regenerated as the roach grows.

Temperatures—A cockroach can survive in a temperature range of 45° to 115° Farenheit.

Existence—Cockroaches have been in existence on Earth since the Earth's second round of life development, or for about 300 million years. They predate the dinosaur, and emerged during the Carboniferous Period. They have few natural enemies.

Illustration 6.13

certain species of sea urchins, ferns, frogs, and cockroaches; to the typical person these lifeforms may not represent "enlightenment" as this word is more commonly used.

The spirit and energy in group souls are ready to move into the next kingdom of life development when they can perfect the one or more senses of the highest type of lifeform (or of pre-life form, for minerals) for that life (or pre-life) kingdom they are in. The perfected sense or senses along one of the seven ray lines of development sometimes causes the lifeforms to become radiant in their specific ray-focused sense or senses. Most spirit and energy from the group souls move on when the "door" to the next kingdom opens. The timing is based upon the plan for that planet. When they advance in this way, the best, or most enlightened, spirit and energy join with similarly enlightened spirit and energy along the same ray line of life development, in order to create a new (larger and more advanced) group soul in the next kingdom. These group souls still focus on the giving part, or consciousness side, of light (the second part of God's thought) more than the creative, purposeful, and willful side of light (the first part of God's thought) in their development. Souls are always giving, or loving, but group souls in particular lack some level of creating virtue. The level that they lack equals the disparity between one hundred percent enlightenment and their at least fifty percent enlightenment that comes from them always being giving. The original helping Self, which is from the fifth kingdom and is the mental spirit part of a Solar Angel, remains and shares its Self to an even greater degree. The total number of Solar Angels must increase to eventually reach a count of sixty billion human Solar Angels. There will eventually need to be billions of Solar Angels that are fusing with Masters. This greater Self attracts enlightened and somewhat enlightened energies on the first and second sub-planes of the mental plane. Those energies then become the form for the new permanent atoms that are created for the next species that will be created as lifeforms that the emerging group soul will inform. Notice how Selves focus on developing more of the creative and purposeful side of light as they help to create new life. The amount that each Self attracts fully enlightened energies into itself in order to create new permanent atoms for the lifeforms that will be created is determined by the collective levels of creativity, sacrifice, will, and purpose that each contributing Self had developed while connected to its group soul, while it was a member of the previous kingdom of life. This amount is what determines the level of advancement of lifeforms that each new Self and its group soul will create and develop in the next kingdom of life.

The selves of group souls are sacrificed as the group souls' spirit and energy advance into the next kingdom during the "open door" period of advancement. The group souls themselves also are sacrificed as their spirit and energy are joined together in hierarchial thought and varying levels of ability to think in light. On each plane, only the atomic levels of spirit and of energy that will make up the most advanced new groups of lifeforms (the enlightened parts of the permanent atoms for the groups of all new lifeforms) remain as parts of a group soul while in a lower kingdom, and move on to become a new group soul within a higher kingdom. The spirit that is in the Self at the atomic level of the mental plane always remains intact, as well. In God's plan, all that becomes perfected in its thought, or in light, remains immortally, while everything that is imperfect in form is eventually sacrificed and destroyed. Life is to eventually add to its Creator; since its Creator, or God, is perfect, only those parts of life that reach perfection in having complete light (of a particular Ray Lord) in their form (those that become completely virtuous) become a created part of God.

 ANIMAL GROUP SOULS

Beginning, or young, animal group souls need to create a self structure that can help to create a minimum of three centers on the etheric/dense physical *and* three on the astral plane, for energy to pass through. These animal group souls generally need to think better on each plane than plant group souls can. The reason is that there are numerically more centers with geometrically greater levels of complex information that is supplied by the senses of these centers. In some animal species, up to five major centers may be created on each of the two planes. In the more advanced animal species, mental plane centers and senses are also developed by the animal group soul and its self for its lifeforms. As animal group souls become more advanced, they also create brains in their animal species to integrate and hold information coming from the senses within each body. Beginning animal group souls that have a lower level of thought usually have great difficulty in thinking enough on their own, in preconceived thought, to completely inform an animal species…which has such increased sense over that of a plant. To compensate, they often create colonies of primitive animals, unifying most of the collective senses of the individual animals. This copies a method used by lower-thinking plant group souls, in creating collections of plant lifeforms.

Animal group souls are the most advanced group souls, on average, in their thought. The reason is that their spirit and energy have remained on the mental plane, helping to create and to inform lifeforms for a longer period of time than have the spirit and energy of group souls in the kingdoms below. First, the spirit and energy informed through its self and the thought of minerals develops increasing levels of complexity and enlightenment; next comes increasingly better levels of slight sentiency within plants. Finally, animals are created and informed, which allows the energy within the form to become fully animated. The slight sentiency of plants is greatly enhanced in animals because the animals have more centers and senses within each body. These centers and senses are connected together through a system in which the energy that is associated with the plane of the body that the centers are in can freely move from one center to another. When in dense physical form, the system is referred to as a nervous system. Plants lack a nervous system because their group souls cannot consciously (givingly) think through their selves enough to inform two or more centers closely enough in time to create a permanent connection between or among them in the lifeforms that they inform. The animal lifeforms with the lowest level of thought and consciousness usually develop communication by sharing centers. They do so through very close proximity to each other in time and space. These colonies of life are found most often in the seas because water has as one of its qualities the ability to transfer energy. For this reason, it is easier for lifeforms living within water to create and maintain sentiency, or movement that results from their own thoughts, than for lifeforms living within air to do so.

Animals are more than simply plants with additional centers and senses; animals have much better communication between and among their centers because they have nervous systems. There is a synergistic effect that results from the animals' ability to synthesize information while "using" much less time, or separating much less time from the space created by their thought, than plants do. It can be difficult for humans to distinguish a nervous system in some of the lowest forms of animals that are dense physically alive. The reason for the difficulty is that the etheric system of these animals—which is sometimes referred to as a nadis system— never fully becomes a completed dense physical effect. The lack of dense physical effect is due to inertia, or the energy tending to remain in the same motion or at rest without motion, based upon how energized and dense it is coupled with the relatively short lifespan of each of these animals. Some animals have and use both of the methods of connecting centers to each animal lifeform. These animals use a nervous system to connect centers within individual lifeforms, *and* they live part of their lives in very close proximity to each other, and frequently touching…further communicating and sharing their centers. Bees and ants are included among the species of animals that use both methods and that live in air. There are advantages to using both methods, such as much better levels of organization and, therefore, greater stability of etheric/dense physical form. However, these advantages become a trade-off in reduced evolutionary development, because the forms are so resistant to change.

Bees Have Individual Etheric/Dense Physical Senses and a Shared Astral Sense

Bees have individual etheric/dense physical senses, and each bee has its own nervous system to connect these senses. Because the bees are frequently touching each other physically, this provides an exchange of chemicals that have etheric parts that join the bees' etheric centers.

Bees share a single astral center with other bees that they live in close proximity with. They share one of their astral centers by frequently touching each other astrally. Note that because the bees' astral bodies extend further than their physical bodies do, the bees can be touching each other astrally when they are not physically touching.

Sharing an astral center allows bees to give as a unit and to respond emotionally as a unit—which explains at least some of their responses. An example is a beehive being disturbed, and all the bees swarming to attack the intruder. What happens is that *all* the bees become angry and attack because each bee, itself, experiences having been intruded upon, and not just the bee or bees that were directly affected. The bees' communication using their shared astral sense informs all of them of the intrusion in a faster and more accurate way than the communication that could occur with chemical reactions or a "dancing" movement used to communicate information about food sources. Note that colonies of ants have very similar responses. For example, numerous fire ants on a person's or animal's body all bite at exactly the same time. The reason is that these ants are all sharing the astral aura of the person or animal they are attacking, which joins the ants' astral auras, and so they respond emotionally with a single—shared—response.

THE CENTERS OF A BEE

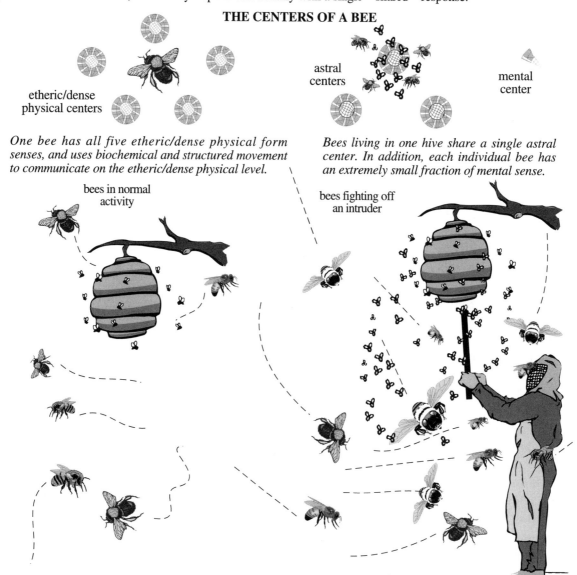

etheric/dense
physical centers

astral
centers

mental
center

One bee has all five etheric/dense physical form senses, and uses biochemical and structured movement to communicate on the etheric/dense physical level.

Bees living in one hive share a single astral center. In addition, each individual bee has an extremely small fraction of mental sense.

bees in normal
activity

bees fighting off
an intruder

Bees that live together use their etheric/dense physical senses individually, but function as one emotionally.

Illustration 6.14

As animal group souls become increasingly developed, they can eventually develop fairly large amounts of information from the connection and synthesizing of information that takes place within each individual animal's etheric/dense physical and astral body. This information cannot be used by the individual animal's (previously "fallen") spirit in each of the two bodies unless it can be stored. The reason is that time and space are separated, and in the case of lower-in-thought animals—which are the majority of animals on earth—the future, or mental, sense of time is missing. The spirit in each body needs considerable time to think when using the information supplied to it by its body's senses (the slight thought of the energy within the centers). To facilitate this individual thought in those animal species that take in greater amounts of information, a brain is created in each of the two or three bodies in order to integrate and store the sensory information from the centers and through the nervous system. Without brains in the lifeforms, the group souls could still receive information from the individual lifeforms (through each soul's self), but the individual lifeforms would be overwhelmed with so much information in each body that the previously "fallen" spirit would be unable to use it to think. When this overload of information occurs in a lifeform that has a damaged brain, the spirit in that body shuts down. It creates a state of either being comatose (in the case of damage to the etheric/dense physical brain) or of autism (if the astral brain is damaged). In autistic humans, the mental brain and the personality usually cannot connect to the etheric/dense physical brain because of damage, often to the astral brain.

In addition to etheric/dense physical and astral brains, advanced animals (and humans, of course) have mental brains as well. The mental brain is found only on the lower mental plane; in animals it is found at the highest point on the highest sub-plane whereupon the animal has mental sense and thought. In nearly all of the advanced animals that have mental brains, these brains are only partially developed because of limited mental senses. The mental sense and brain provide these advanced animals with the ability to hold and then to better understand the mental thoughts of other advanced animals, and sometimes of humans. A human's mental brain is the semi-permanent thoughtforms of its mental unit, *including the connections* to the rest of the lower mental body and to whatever part of the causal body that is functional on the higher mental plane. Animal mental brains, when present, are relatively small and incomplete. Even the most advanced animals use their astral and etheric/dense physical senses and connecting brains far more than they use their mental ones. In humans, the reverse is true; humans use their mental brains an overwhelming amount of the time. The reason is that the human personality is a part of the mental brain, and is what collects information from the senses in all three bodies at nearly the same time. The human personality is, along with its connected self, located within the mental unit. When humans think primarily focused mentally, they mostly can think in all three parts of time—the past, present, and future. For example, if a person (selfishly) focuses on her etheric/dense physical body and its senses of time, while focused selfishly in this way she loses the present and future senses of time. This loss is the result of the person mostly using only her etheric/dense physical senses to receive information. In illusion she will also often convert her selfish past focus of time into a very incomplete future time perspective. People who are greedy and non-cooperative through the withholding of their physical energies from others frequently have only this incomplete and inaccurate future sense of time. The reason why this illusion occurs is that the personality becomes more fearful (of death) when it senses only its past; to compensate, it will partially invent, or confabulate by filling in, a future that is based not upon reason and truth, but on the selfishness of greed and avarice, and on acquiring whatever it deems important for "its future."

As a specific example of the concepts in the preceding paragraph, imagine a man named John who believes that the nature of his existence is to have as many material possessions of his choosing as he can. John derives meaning in his life from his personality exercising physical control over all material things, including some people's physical bodies and what these people do with their bodies. John is a businessman because the seventh ray focus of business helps him to achieve his goals in making his life meaningful. John is greedy and very controlling of others. He uses his etheric/dense physical senses to excess and nearly always in a self-focused way, which causes them to remain separated. His personality tends to ignore how others feel or mentally think because the feelings and thoughts of others do not advance his goal in life, of gaining materially. As John's personality ignores the astral and loving parts of others and the structured thinking and truthful parts of others, he is simultaneously blocking the information that his astral and mental senses are trying to supply. The more that the personality refuses to accept information from a sense, the less able the sense is to attract other information in the future. What occurs is that the unaccepted information becomes retained energy within the sense, which damages the sense and diminishes its functionality. Refusing information from the astral and mental senses, plus only partially sensing physical information causes the personality to synthesize much less knowledge. Less knowledge synthesized by the personality means less knowledge that the personality can share with its self. This is especially the case concerning the related informing fallen spirit and senses in the astral and mental bodies. Then the self has less knowledge to give to the fallen spirit that would help this informing spirit in each body to attract better energies into the senses, which would then receive more and better information.

John's senses are being damaged every time he is selfish. His consciousness is being lowered by his self having less to give to the fallen spirit in his bodies, which causes the self to diminish. Also, John's personality becomes over-controlling of his self because his loss of self triggers his personality's fear of death. When the personality is over-controlling, it often blocks the self's communication with its Self and Solar Angel. These two are sending messages of conscience to the (in this case, John's) self to stop being selfish in specific ways and circumstances. Without a higher source of spirit helping him to realize God and to overcome his increasing loss of consciousness, John is becoming more and more fearful of life. As John's sense of the past is used exaggeratedly from his overuse of his etheric/dense physical senses and lack of virtuous use of his astral and mental ones, in order to help lessen his fear of further meaninglessness he chooses to invent a false and quite illogical future. This future is still applied to the area where John's life is focused, or the materiality of the dense physical world. John has converted the real time of the past into a confabulation of the future, with the missing time zones filled in, but he ignores the present most of the time. He lives for what he can accumulate in material wealth that he anticipates using *at some future time*. The illusion is that John can save time by accumulating more things—but the opposite is what is actually occurring. The meaning of John's life is not in what he has had or in what he presently controls, but in what he will acquire. He may rationalize that his life has meaning from the material things that he has and controls. However, his behaviors reveal that he continues to *create* in his life through what more he can acquire either in material items or the control of them. John lives in his world of illusion, unaware that he is making himself miserable and is creating his own suffering. He also creates enormous forces of conflict in this life, on a daily basis, because his self and personality are creating mostly against the Ray Lord's duration of life, or against God's thought (of cooperation and sharing, in the case of the seventh Ray Lord). John's self and personality are making choices from their larger field that go against the vast majority of choices by other people and other kinds of life.

John can change the focus of his life to either the astral or mental body and can thus significantly alter his means of sensing and of time focus. If he chooses to become astrally focused but remains selfish, his time focus will be past and present with an exaggeration of the past at times. He would then live for how he feels, including the need to have his desires met and to experience excitement and pleasure. John may vacillate between etheric/dense physical and astral focus, which is a common approach to selfish living. If John focuses mentally but still selfishly,

Developing an Exceptional Group Soul That Advances Before the End of the Round

In order to advance into the next kingdom before the end of a round, a group soul must become radiant. This means that the group soul's lifeform transmutes all the energy that comes into it, such as minerals or sunlight, and gives it to other lifeforms. Radiant group souls have lifeforms that give out whatever amounts of energy they take in (and sometimes more), at the speed of light for the planes they are alive on, after adding their own (the group souls') slight thought.

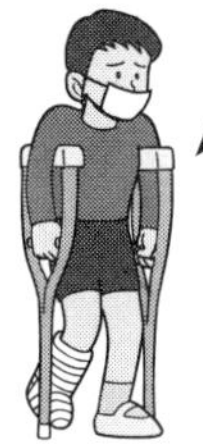

group soul for a member of the plant kingdom that creates radiance in all the senses provided by its lifeforms

The tree gives all the nutrients that are needed by many other plants.

healthy

not healthy

ticks

roots moving towards water

The tree can move its branches to face the sun, to get the optimal amount of sunlight it needs.

The tree provides shade at all times of the year at an angle opposite to the sun's angle—providing a micro-environment for new types of life.

The tree gives off a greater amount of moisture than most other plants do, which produces a greater cooling effect when the air temperature is hot.

The fruit is delicious and sweet.

Fruit is continually developing so there is always fresh, ripe fruit to eat.

The fruit is balanced nutritionally and has more than just a predominance of carbohydrates.

The fruit contains a natural antibiotic and anti-fungal substance that keeps people and animals healthy.

The tree has roots that can move several inches an hour, to reach water and other nutrients.

The tree has a green glow that provides light at night.

This tree blooms all year around, so it has a nice fragrance all the time.

People can rub the leaves on their skin to keep insects away, and also to protect themselves from sunburning.

The same fragrance attracts beneficial insects and repels those that attack plants and animals.

The tree and its leaves have a natural resistance to insects, so severely infectious insects do not eat it.

Fallen leaves can be used to feed animals. These leaves provide nutrients that the animals have difficulty finding elsewhere.

The fallen leaves disintegrate quickly, leaving trace minerals for surrounding plants and trees.

Note that such a tree does not yet exist. Its description, however, provides an example of what a lifeform of a very advanced group soul could be like before the group soul advances on to the next kingdom prior to the end of the round.

Illustration 6.15

he will experience all three parts of time. However, John will have little balance in time as he exaggerates parts of it to (egotistically) make it seem as though he is always mentally right in his thinking. Should he create himself into a condition of arrogance, then he would tend to be selfish in all three of the above-listed ways—physically, emotionally, and mentally—focusing on first one and then another. He would, in general, be uncooperative, unloving, and untruthful. Each focus of a body that is added in selfishness causes John's life to lose meaning while time for him becomes more distorted, and his suffering increases.

Rarely, a group soul that is very advanced within the mineral or plant kingdom and that informs only one most advanced type of pre-life or species of life may perfect the sense(s) of that part of life for *all* of the life within that kingdom. When this occurs, even if the "door" for advancement is closed, all of the spirit and energy of that one group soul moves into the next kingdom, to create and inform one or more new lifeforms. In these rare cases, the group soul *and* its self and connecting structure remain intact. Spirit and energy from the very advanced group soul are thus not pooled together with other spirit and energy from other group souls that have similar ability to think. Instead, the very advanced and quite unusual group soul has created so much light and radiance inside itself and has grown itself to such an extent that it does not need additional advanced spirit and energy collectively from other group souls in order to create (with its Self) and inform one or more new lifeforms in the next higher kingdom. These rare very advanced group souls use their "own" selves along with the helping shared Self of the Solar Angel from the fifth kingdom to create life in the next kingdom. They do so without the normal process of using additional enlightened spirit along the same ray line joined and structured in mental light, or transfigured.

The more advanced animals have one or more centers and senses on the mental plane. These animals are capable of structured thought and can individually learn; they can formulate solutions to problems because they can somewhat use the three parts of time in their thinking. All birds and mammals have some mental sense and can use the future (mental) sense of time in their thought. Some advanced types of other animal species also have some levels of mental sense and thought. However, only some birds and mammals can reach the higher sub-planes of the lower mental plane. The number of lower mental senses *and* the level to which these senses are developed on each lower mental sub-plane determines how well an animal can sense the mental thought of other animals and sometimes even of humans. These factors also determine how well the lower mental plane spirit can become aware. In addition, they determine how well this spirit can think and inform the lower mental lunar deva and elemental energies within the animal's one or more centers. When challenged with unique circumstances in its surroundings, if the animal can create structured thought, or can formulate individual solutions that are not instinctual (that do not come from its group soul's preconceptual thought), then that animal has some mental sense and thought. Most animals do not have full conceptual thought. This type of thought would enable them to understand *why* they are structuring their lower mental thought in certain ways. They use only a part of a concept, connected to an incomplete but useful thoughtform—mostly of simple problem solving. This leads to trial and error thinking, because not enough of the future part of time (which is the mental component) is incorporated into these animals' thought. There is still too much of an emphasis on the past and present parts of time, from their much stronger astral thought. Note that humans may also think in this way when they think too selfishly astrally, or think emotionally, and not enough conceptually (from the higher mental plane). As was previously mentioned, advanced apes, including gorillas, are the only wild animals that can sometimes think using a full concept.

Some advanced pets may at times use a full concept, especially if their human masters have loved them *and* helped the pets to think in their higher minds. These pets are the unusual ones, and a few of them might individualize into the human kingdom at some point prior to the

Trial and Error Thinking Focused Mostly on the Past and Present Time Zones

past thought
I found food in this kind of tree before.

present thought
I am hungry.

AN ANIMAL'S TRIAL AND ERROR THOUGHT PROCESS

1) The monkey tries to find food by climbing the tree, but there are no bananas in the tree.

2) The monkey goes to a different tree and simply looks up to see if there is any food. The bananas are hidden from view, so the monkey does not find them.

3) The monkey then tries to shake the tree, but the bananas will not drop.

4) The monkey then decides to pull a branch down, which bends the tree and put the bananas within reach.

past thought
When I hooked up my printer, the operating system used plug and pray to do everything for me.

present thought
I need to get this scanner hooked up to my computer.

A HUMAN'S TRIAL AND ERROR THOUGHT PROCESS REPLICATING A MONKEY'S (AN ADVANCED ANIMAL'S)

no device found

scanner

1) The man tries to hook up the scanner, but it does not work using plug and pray.

2) Next, he tries loading the scanner driver from a floppy disk, but the scanner still does not work.

no device found

scanner

Scanner found and is ready to use

scanner

3) He then thinks that it must be a defective cable, so he tries another cable.

4) The man finally tries a different adapter card, which solves the problem. The problem was that he was using an incompatible adapter card. There was much time lost because there was no future thought, which would have helped him to plan. Whole structured thought contains all three time zones and gives a person wholeness in his or her thought process.

Illustration 6.16

"door" for advancement opening again. Animal group souls are limited in their ability to adequately inform a lifeform with enough structured higher mental plane concepts that would enable them to develop this type of thought within their lifeforms. The limitation comes from specialization of center and sense development within life. It is a condition forced upon life and that relies more upon evolution (of energy) than spiritual development. Spirit within group souls needs to advance itself in order to achieve some conceptual, rather than all preconceptual, mental thought. When a group soul develops conceptual thought, it does so in accord with the light of the mental plane and the Ray Lord of that plane; then the group soul's concepts are partially whole from its position on the higher mental plane and below. This is not true for the group soul's individual lifeforms that, at best, create incomplete concepts. Unlike the few individual lifeforms that think conceptually, advanced group souls of animals create more concepts that contain some level of wholeness and light because these group souls do so by following light more consistently. However, they also are quite slow in this development, and seldom create very many concepts or any large ones. The main limitation of group souls is their single focus on creating life within one specific ray focus, which is the result of the way they think along a single ray. This thought includes, eventually, the creation of narrow concepts that are created mostly on corresponding single ray sub-sub-planes of the higher mental plane. If humans choose to, they can think equally well in the thoughts given to them by their respective souls. They have this ability because each soul can completely give what it thinks to its personality and self. The self with the Self's and soul's assistance can think on all of the mental sub-sub-planes. All human souls are initially equal in their ability to give their thought, which is always designed to help the personality become more giving. All human souls can think of concepts along all seven rays, and can use the entire spiritual part of the higher mental plane. The soul, personality, and self can use the entire mental plane. They can accomplish thought along all seven soul rays of focus by using the soul's causal body as a higher mental sense of all seven rays. Note that a soul chooses to think only when it can give what it thinks, in a way that will help the personality and its self (which the personality controls) to become more giving.

HUMAN SOULS

In comparison to the most advanced animal group soul, the human soul has many advantages in its capacity to think mentally. Each human soul informs only one lifeform per lifetime—a human being. The human soul's only source of sense of the lower worlds comes from the three bodies of its human: the lower mental, astral, and etheric/dense physical bodies. The quality of the spirit and energy within these three bodies is the highest on average that had been developed within the animal kingdom within a prior round of life creation on the (a) planet; note that some of the best-thinking of the mental energy, as the lowest body of the human's Solar Angel, often comes from another planet. The senses within each human's bodies provide the best *unified* sense (when the senses are joined together) of any lifeform below a human being. When the senses are separated, which is the result of selfish thinking by the informing personality, self, and fallen spirit, individual human senses are *not* as good—not as accurate and sensitive—as are the individual senses of many types of animal species. The reason is that animal group souls develop specialized sense because of the single ray focus in their thought, and they generally follow some of the light of the mental plane Ray Lord. Human souls at equal levels of development can think equally well along all seven rays when they give thought that is used for the purpose of further giving. A personality that is giving and using the soul's light, or thought, can unify the five senses of form and two of spirit in each human body and then can unify the three bodies together, as well. When selfish, the personality separates its senses, its bodies, its self from both its soul and its personality, time from space, and itself from God. Then the individual, separated senses of the human do *not* function in thought and sense as well as the senses of even some primitive forms of animals can.

The human soul receives the very best spirit and energy from seven animal group souls, each along a different ray. This energy surrounds the spirit of the human soul, which is located on the fourth sub-sub-plane of the second mental sub-plane. As a lower correspondence of the three parts of God's mind, the energy is separated into three sections. The first section comes from the energy of the most advanced group souls of first ray animals; the second comes from the most advanced group souls of second ray animals; and the third comes from the most advanced animal group souls along the third through seventh rays. Once opened, these three sections resemble petals of a flower, although, in the beginning of a human soul's existence, the sections, or "petals," are completely closed into a mostly spherical shape. The petals comprise the inner solar deva, or pitri, energies. When the petals are open and used, their energies control the higher mental elemental energies sacrificed by the animal group souls that were the most advanced and could thus mentally think the best. Because of their origins and the ways in which they become opened, the three petals are referred to as inner sacrifice petals. The human soul also receives energies from its OverSoul, or Solar Angel. These energies are another group of solar devas, or pitris, that then control higher mental and elemental energies that also form lotus-like petals. They do so because of the ways in which two or more of these solar deva energies interact together and further affect the space between themselves. The energies come from the lowest part of the Solar Angel's body, which is found on the higher mental plane. The Solar Angel of a human usually has come from another planet that had a prior development of group souls. Together, all of the energies given by the Solar Angel make up what is referred to as the causal body of the human soul.

Construction of the Three Inner Sacrifice Petals of the Human Soul and Their Order of Opening

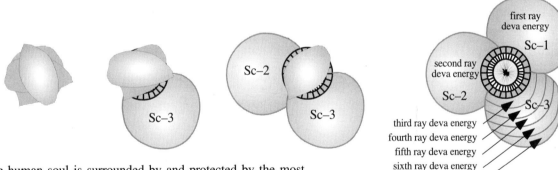

The human soul is surrounded by and protected by the most advanced energies from the group souls of animals. These energies come from pools of energy that advance into the human kingdom in ways similar to those of group souls when group souls are advancing. The difference is that the best-thinking energies from one each of seven ray types of advanced animal group souls are contributed by those group souls. These energies resemble petals of a flower.

The first petal that opens is the Sc–3 petal. "Sc" stands for sacrificial center, and each of these inner sacrifice petals is assigned a number to denote its location.

The next petal to open is the Sc–2 petal, and the last to open is the Sc–1 petal. The human soul can be partially seen as the petals unfold. When all three inner sacrifice petals have fully opened, the soul is completely uncovered, or exposed.

Illustration 6.17

A causal body holds the shape of concepts by its solar deva energy creating the shape of the concept, and then higher mental elemental energy filling in the shape. A full concept is a moving picture of the structure, or formula, of the thought, and includes the past, present, and future. The higher mental elemental energy is involutionary and is thus affected by its own thought to

Concept Construction Missing from the Trial and Error Thought

Concept
It looks as though there might be some problems getting this scanner hooked up and working because of some issues with the way that plug and pray works.

1) According to the manual, the plug and pray system uses certain memory addresses. My past experience tells me that these are the same addresses that my controller for the cd rom burner uses and that will probably cause a conflict. Also, the jumpers on this older adapter card in the computer can only be set to higher addresses than plug and pray can recognize. In order to get the scanner to work, I will need a different adapter card.

2) The driver should be fine because it is current and, according to the manual, all drivers written after 1996 should be plug and pray compliant.

3) The last thing that could cause a problem is the cable that is not IEEE compliant, as in the manual recommends it to be, but maybe that is not necessary. This kind of problem is most likely to be in the plug and pray setup. Once I get another adapter card, everything should work fine.

Structured thought ensures that there is no time wasted on trial and error.

This programmer who creates plug and pray parts of an operating system fails to plan for the enormous amounts of conflicts that the program needs to resolve for this system to be helpful. He works with other programmers who also think separately. Together they create an operating system that does not even cooperate with parts of itself, much less with other programs.

selfish programmer

There is a conflict with your new scanner device and the CD ROM burner at address FD6FF000.

The following are available alternatives in order to resolve the conflict. Please choose the one you prefer, and hit enter.

a) Switch CD ROM burner to FC000000 and leave the scanner at FD6FF000.
b) Assign any available address to the new device.
c) If you prefer to change the address manually, simply type in the device ID next to the address, and changes will take effect

unselfish programmer who writes code to get programs to work together.

One-Light Programming "No more conflicts, no more aqua screens of death!"

Now that I have taken the time to figure out how to get past all these possible problems, it is clear to me how easy it would be to solve these for everyone. First of all, we could get the programmers and manufacturers of devices to quit being selfish and to instead create devices that would communicate properly and cooperate together. Second, it would be fairly straight-forward for someone to create code allowing the operating system to identify the conflicts, communicate them to the user, and then offer the user choices to resolve the problem. If these two reasonable changes would occur in the computer industry, problems like these would disappear.

Illustration 6.18

join and stay together. The concept therefore remains together for a much longer period of time than the solar deva energy itself could keep it together. The solar deva energy is first prompted to form the shape of a concept by outside thought. Without the addition of higher (spiritual) thought, the personality and its self can use the three separated solar pitris that are located on the fifth, sixth, and seventh sub-sub-planes of the third mental sub-plane. These three solar pitris are the very lowest of the solar devas given to the human by its Solar Angel, and have the least ability to think and hold together a concept. First the personality and self think of relatively small and incomplete concepts on their own. The personality and self hold together the higher mental elemental energies that make up the concept, for anywhere from less than a second to about two seconds. Then, depending upon the type of thought, one of these three solar devas uses its more durable mental energies, with their superior sense and thought, to nearly immediately hold the structure of the concept in higher mental elemental energy for several seconds to minutes, and sometimes longer. The solar devas contained within the outer causal body are more advanced in mental thought and sense than are other mental plane energies within a human's mental body or within even its soul for most of the soul's existence. The reason is that the Solar Angel has spent a much greater part of its life creating light on the higher mental plane and the dimension above it. This usually took place on another planet while last serving animal group souls that were most advanced (this process will be explained in further detail later in this chapter). After the partial and incomplete concept is created from one of the three lowest solar devas and its associated higher mental elemental energy that the solar pitri is controlling, incomplete thoughtforms are created. These thoughtforms are incomplete because less (sometimes much less) than the entire lower mental plane is used in their formulation. As a result, less mental time and space are joined and less wisdom is created than from thoughtforms that are completed, or that use all of the lower mental plane. Thoughtforms are created through the attraction of the lower mental elemental energies (in the lower mental body) to the lunar devas (also in the lower mental body). These elemental energies were previously attracted either to the causal thought of solar devas in the higher mental body or to the focus of the personality and self onto just the lower mental spirit and thought. The thoughtforms create mental words that explain the mentally structured "moving pictures" that the concepts produce. Thoughtforms are necessary for the accurate communication of concepts to others. In addition, thoughtforms help the person thinking with them to establish the correct time sequence of events within a concept because thoughtforms at least somewhat unify the lower mental plane to the higher. This above-mentioned process of correctly establishing a time sequence is referred to as the creation of logical thought.

In order to create and wisely give thought that is more whole and thus includes more time and space of the mental plane, or that creates more wisdom in the structure of the concepts and their thoughtforms, a personality and its self needs to use some of the thought created by the Self and correctly given by the human soul. Sometimes the help of the OverSoul is needed to give the thought, besides helping to create it from its shared Self. The reason is that the human soul might not yet be developed enough to understand the concept completely, and is therefore unable to give the concept completely itself. The process of creating and wisely giving whole thought is referred to as the capacity of love/wisdom. The Self mostly creates the potential complete mental thought while its human soul most *appropriately* gives it through its thought. When a human has become so advanced that he or she is becoming a member of the next kingdom, the capacity of love/wisdom becomes a sense (that is used as a partial sense of buddhi on the intuitional plane) that is used effortlessly in a Now. At that point, functioning with love/wisdom no longer requires the (relatively slow) process of thinking through several steps, or with separated bodies and spirit both creating and giving as best as they can together.

When the causal body is first formed and used, it takes the shape of a partially opened flower bud and has a somewhat uneven surface; the larger part of the "bud" comprises the lowest parts of this body. The bud shape is a result of all of the solar deva "petals" being closed except the lowest one. The lowest petal starts out being about one-third open and contains the three lowest solar devas. This petal can be used by a new human's personality and self that the Self, OverSoul, and human soul initially create in the human's potential for existence. As each personality with its self creates concepts in its life that are selfish, causing the concepts to be incomplete and non-spiritual, it further unfolds the lowest petal (which contains the three lowest solar pitris) to some degree, though less than completely.

The very lowest solar pitri holds together concepts that contain the non-spiritual causes regarding the material nature of the human being's life, with disregard for nearly all spiritual (structural) causes. This lowest solar pitri is located on the seventh sub-sub-plane of the third mental sub-plane. The next higher solar pitri, on the sixth sub-sub-plane, can hold together concepts concerning ideals, which when incompletely formed by this deva energy become a concept about an ideology. The incompleteness and separation in form from other energy and from spirit change the ideal into a mental idol, or just the mental form of the ideal. When complete, or mentally whole, the ideal is the whole structure of the mental concept and is a representation of a much greater idea from a dimension higher than the mental plane.

Closed Spiritual Lotus

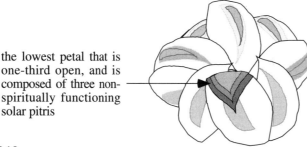

the lowest petal that is one-third open, and is composed of three non-spiritually functioning solar pitris

Illustration 6.19

Ideas need to be represented in dimensional aspects beyond just structure because more time and space must be incorporated within ideas in order to create their effects. It is common for people to refer to an idea as any thought that seems to solve a problem and that they cannot recollect ever having been thought of before in a certain circumstance. Spiritually, an idea is original thought. An idea is something that had never before been thought by anyone. It joins the entire dimension in the time and space of that type of thought—within that or any lower dimension of time and space. Ideas require thought within a Now, because by definition they must completely join time with space in at least one of the three ways that are possible in a Now. Partial ideas, in spiritual terms, contain only one or two of the three ways in which a Now is created. A full, or complete, idea is created within a Now in which time and space are joined in all three ways. Complete ideas exist only at and above the atomic level of the spiritual plane.

The remaining isolated solar pitri of the causal body is located one sub-sub-plane higher on the higher mental plane than the last solar pitri mentioned; this one is on the fifth sub-sub-plane. Selfish use of these three solar devas by the personality and its self cause the pitris' isolation; their sub-sub-plane locations are the seventh, sixth, and fifth sub-sub-planes, respectively. These numerical sub-sub-planes correspond to sub-categories of the mental, or fifth, ray and include all seven sub-rays. Because of their locations, these devas are affected by the seventh, sixth, and fifth rays, respectively. The solar deva *energy* is assisted in thought by its corresponding ray as a sub-ray of the fifth ray. When the solar pitri located on the fifth sub-sub-plane is used by a selfish personality, this deva is kept isolated in its holding of incomplete mental concepts regarding cause and effect. These include selfishly, or non-spiritually, created concepts that include, but are not limited to, the following three types. The first of these types of concepts are those that narrowly construct scientific thought and knowledge based exclusively upon form, or energy, without spirit included (missing some of the second aspect of God's mind). The second are those that concern legal constructs of laws that either do not include love (that lack inclusiveness), do not include the purpose of the Creator, or that include neither of these two (missing some of the second and/or the first aspect of God's mind). And the third are those that concern causal elements of philosophies (without their ideals) that do not include a spiritually integrated component as their rationale for existence (missing some of the first and/or second aspect of God's mind). When any of these three isolated solar pitris are used in the general self-ish ways described in this paragraph, all three of these devas remain separate; however, they still can be somewhat unfolded to build larger (and more selfish) incomplete concepts. Most human concepts heretofore and today created on earth have been and continue to be created using these three solar devas in an isolated and selfish manner, without a spiritual component. A spiritual concept is a concept that contains light, or God's thought, within it. Since a concept is mental form, spiritual concepts create virtue, or light in (mental) form.

Mental Plane Thoughtforms as Effects of Causes

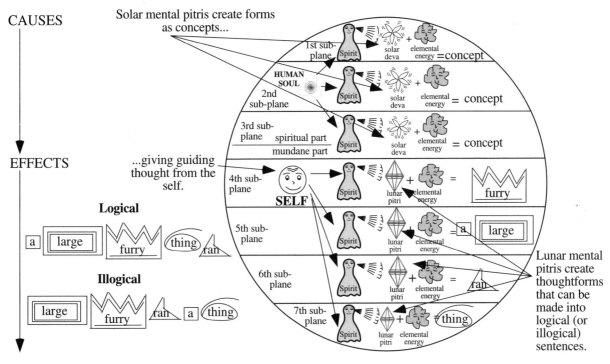

Illustration 6.20

 TECHNICALLY COMPLEX INFORMATION REGARDING THE HUMAN SOUL

The following section of this chapter contains a greater degree of technically complex information regarding the human soul, its inner sacrifice petals, and its use of the causal body. Most of the explanations in *Life's Hidden Meaning* have not included the more technical information because the first goal of the book is to raise understanding, or consciousness, with informing as a secondary goal. Still, most of its readers are likely to find the book in its entirety to be highly informative. Some of the readers will be people who have chosen to discipline themselves spiritually to become better creators of virtue in their lives. For these readers, the next section, which is about one-fourth of the entire chapter, will provide more technically complex information that they might seek and are not likely to find written elsewhere. For the rest, and probably greater number of readers, the reading of the material will still provide additional concepts that bring understanding about the unity of life, and of the human soul's part in this unity. Most of the information in this upcoming section will be presented in its technically complex form just this once within this book, in order to not unnecessarily burden those readers who lack interest in that material.

Spiritual concepts have inherent within them the cause that produces the non-spiritual effect. It is necessary that a person who is exercising spiritual discipline understand that spirit is what creates the cause part of a spiritual concept (the first two parts of God's mind joined together in a part of life that is creating the concept). It is also important to understand what produces the light needed by the personality in order for the personality to grow so it can conceive the concept. Spirit, or God's thought in life, is the *cause* of form, and form's activity is an effect—in terms of mental plane time and space, or causal structure. The lowest part of a human's spiritual mind is the entire third mental sub-plane. This part incorporates the solar devas within the causal body on this sub-plane and includes the three lowest of them. However, the three lowest solar pitris *are not isolated* when one or more higher solar pitris are utilized to hold together a spiritual concept. The spiritual concept expands upon and grows the non-spiritual concept. The spiritual concept is still using some of the previously isolated parts of the lowest solar devas. Spiritual concepts created by using the solar pitris above the fifth sub-sub-plane and that are part of the third sub-plane are more focused on personal gain and development of the personality than on the soul. These concepts still develop the soul because they are, in part, giving, but to a much smaller level as compared to concepts from the second sub-plane. While somewhat giving on a personal level to others, third sub-plane spiritual concepts fail to give to others in order to help the others wisely give (they fail to give in the way that souls give). These concepts are spiritual because they increase some understanding of light, or a part of God's thought. God's thought is to give to others, even if this giving at this level is personal in nature and lacks wisdom. On the next higher sub-plane (the second) the focus reverses, and shifts to more emphasis on the soul than on the personality. The concepts created by the personality and held at this second level, or the soul level, by the causal body produce the balanced and completed understanding that God's thought, or light, is to only give to others in ways that help them to wisely give to still others. These concepts are balanced between the spiritual focus and the energy, or the form part, of what the concept is about. Such giving is wise because it has wisdom and completeness. It also has appropriateness in helping others to be more giving, or has relative wholeness in structured mental thought. The first and greater motivation in creating thought at this level is to grow the soul, with the growth of the personality secondary to that of the soul. Finally, concepts created on the first sub-plane involve only growing the souls of everyone and everything, while fusing together the personality as one with the soul. They also include concepts that extend beyond the growth of the soul all the way to the growth of the Monad, to become a fully participating part of God.

The three petals of solar devas that surround the human soul—the inner sacrifice petals—when used *together* can replace the thought of all of the solar devas within the causal body, which hold together concepts for the human. Until this point is reached, the spiritual concepts for all of the higher mental body tend to "blur" together across it in the higher mental time and space. This happens because the concepts are formed by adding together the thought of more than one solar pitri from more than one sub-sub-plane. All three unfolded inner petals of solar devas are located in a single time and space that they share with the spirit that is within the human soul. As a result, these devas can create very clear spiritual concepts that include the entire higher mental body up to their location on it, and that then create whole thoughtforms on the lower mental plane. The creation of whole structured, or wise, concepts with the added assistance of the human soul's Self, and then the creation of the thoughtforms that accurately represent these concepts unifies the mental body of a human as well as a part of the mental plane, which each human's mental body is a part of. (See Appendix, part B.)

The solar devas that make up the causal body create groupings of petals that correspond to one of three aspects of God's mind and the first three rays. The personality can use the three lowest solar devas of the lowest petal without added thought from either the OverSoul, Self, or human soul. All of the other petals in the causal body are the ones that create the *spiritual* petals, which collectively comprise the remaining solar deva energy. These petals unfold as they are used in each lifetime of a human being. They unfold as each personality and self share and help give thought from themselves, the OverSoul, the Self, and the human soul. Between each lifetime of each human being that the OverSoul and human soul are informing, the petals remain in their state last used and at the last stage of development and unfoldment. As each human being who is connected to its OverSoul, Self, and soul uses her or his thought to create larger and more whole *spiritual* concepts, the petals unfold more and take on the appearance, somewhat, of a

Solar Deva Energy of the Lower Lotus Petal, Shown with and without Retained Energy

The causal body, or lotus, comprises solar deva energy that resembles petals that progressively unfold as they are used in each lifetime of a human being. The personality is given the use of the three lowest solar pitries, independent of the thought of the OverSoul, the (higher) Self, and the human soul. These solar devas are found on the lowest petal, on 5–3, 6–3, and 7–3 as illustrated below. This lowest petal (also known as K–3) unfolds to some degree because higher elemental energy directed by the thought of the personality forces the solar deva energy in the petal to open. Once the highest relatively selfish concept has been formed by the personality, the highest amount of higher mental elemental energy that can enter this petal through that type of thought has entered the petal and has opened it as much as that type of thought can. Further opening of the petal can take place only through different selfish concepts or spiritual thought. When a solar deva on this lowest petal is used, but not in spiritual thought, or not in conjunction with a higher level deva on 1–3, 2–3, 3–3, 4–3 (or higher), that solar deva begins to retain energy. The retained energy creates forces that cause damage to that solar deva, and to higher ones as well. Higher solar devas can be harmed because the three lowest solar devas are needed for the higher devas' construction of spiritual concepts. The damage affects the solar devas' ability to hold together concepts—even of the mundane kind—and can harm the entire higher mental mind for that lifetime and possibly future ones.

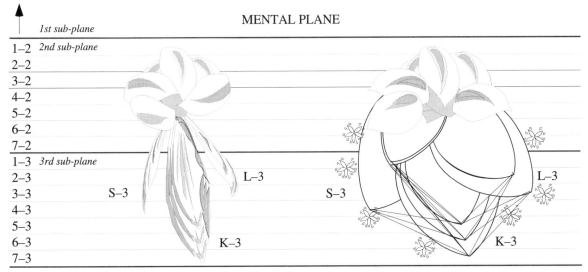

MENTAL PLANE

1st sub-plane

1–2	*2nd sub-plane*
2–2	
3–2	
4–2	
5–2	
6–2	
7–2	
1–3	*3rd sub-plane*
2–3	
3–3	
4–3	
5–3	
6–3	
7–3	

L–3

S–3

K–3

There is no connection between the spiritual mind and the mundane mind, so there is no spiritual thought. Forces are created from the energy that is being retained in the petal. Notice the darkness and ugliness of the K–3 petal. The S–3 and L–3 petals are also affected because they are not able to develop.

The spiritual concepts from S–3, L–3, and higher allow the solar devas in K–3 to grow. Retained energy of the K–3 petal is reduced, giving the solar devas the ability to think better and to further unfold.

Illustration 6.21

lotus flower. The word "lotus" is frequently used in place of "causal body" in spiritual language. Each spiritual petal contains three or more solar pitris that already contain thought from their development while part of the Solar Angel, or OverSoul. They can sense and re-create the spiritual concept at the level of the mental sub- (and sub-sub-) plane they exist on. This unfoldment is based first upon *use* and later upon increased ability created in the solar pitri and by the personality and self in each lifetime, and increased ability created within the human soul. A similar condition is true for the lowest isolated solar devas. However, when used selfishly and not being interpenetrated by the higher spiritual conceptual thought and solar devas, their rate of unfoldment is dependent upon to what degree the personality's thought is selfish—and not upon the OverSoul's or human soul's thought. In the beginning use of a solar pitri within the lowest petal, the petal will unfold to some degree. It does so because higher mental elemental energy is *forcing* the petal open as this mental energy is held together by the solar deva energy as a concept. Once the largest *relatively* selfish type of concept that can be formed by the one or more solar pitris of a petal has been created (the forces prevent any further opening), the greatest amount of higher mental elemental energy has entered the petal and opened it to its maximum level attainable through the *relatively* selfish and similar thought. Subsequent to this point, only additional created concepts that are different or ones that are more spiritual can further open the petal. The three lowest solar devas of the causal body are the isolated ones that make up its lowest petal. If mostly (or, worse, exclusively) selfish concepts are used to partially open, or unfold, this petal, then higher mental elemental energy becomes retained and creates forces on the corresponding one or more isolated solar devas. These forces can damage these solar pitris' future ability to hold together concepts (even spiritual ones), harming the entire spiritual (as well as the mundane) mental mind in an effect that can persist for lifetimes.

THE MENTAL STRUCTURE
OF THE HUMAN INITIATIONS

The first inner sacrifice petal that surrounds the human soul opens partially and gradually as some of the causal body petals of the third sub-plane are fully opened and used to create spiritual service. This service involves the use of the relatively whole third sub-plane spiritual concepts that are created from the comparatively small fusion between the personality and its soul. Note that when the term "service" is used in a spiritual context, it refers to the use of all the available energy, which is then given to and enlightens someone or something other than the self; the subsequent enlightenment occurs because there is no self focus when virtue is created. As concepts from the third sub-plane are used in spiritual service, the petals that have fully opened and their constituent solar devas begin to *radiate* mental plane light with colors that correspond to their ray focus and sub-sub-plane position. This radiance takes place as the petals and their devas fuse both together and with the lowest of the three separated solar devas, or pitris, on the lowest petal. This light connects from the human soul to the personality and forms a "rainbow bridge" of semi-permanent enlightened spiritual concepts, keeping each new personality connected to its informing human soul from one lifetime to the next. The bridge functions somewhat like a communications device that connects human lifetimes and begins to build continuity of *spiritual thought*, which eventually includes *spiritual memory*. What happens is that when the human, first, has thought somewhat spiritually, its soul can then directly inform the human being of spiritual thought that is related and that a prior personality and self had thought during a former incarnation. Humans on earth who are thinking spiritually still usually do not unfold all of the causal petals on each higher mental sub-plane within a reasonable number of lifetimes, nor do they typically use all of the solar energy on a petal at one time to create concepts that are used in spiritual service. For this reason, it has been and remains too difficult for humans to completely unfold an inner sacrifice petal and then complete its development without outside assistance. Given enough time, a human on earth could achieve these results; however, thus far the excessive amount of time required for such a mentally arduous task would prevent the Plan (for spiritual development of the planet) from being correctly developed. (See Appendix, part A.)

The spiritually developing human being and its soul are given assistance by some of the members of the next (the fifth) kingdom, of fully functional and mentally liberated souls (Souls), i.e., Masters of the three lowest dimensions and of the Ageless Wisdom. This kingdom consists of Beings who think *only* spiritually, or virtuously—using God's thought in form. Since they think only spiritually, the kingdom is referred to as both the spiritual kingdom and the Kingdom of Souls. Its members are Souls who have become joined together with their Selves, and are free to create and give their thought in a Now—in time and space that are joined. Several of these Beings choose to focus their spiritual thought using a part of either the Planetary Logos' or the Solar Logos' (or both of their) thought in the Plan, onto a person's partially opened inner sacrifice petal, instantly completing the opening of that petal. When they do so, it is at the completion of the person's *initiation*. The entire process of gradually and partially opening the inner sacrifice petal is referred to as the process of initiation. This process usually requires a number of lifetimes, while what is referred to as the completion of an initiation—as described above—takes place in only a few seconds. The entire process of initiation in which the first inner sacrifice petal becomes opened is referred to as the first initiation.

The second inner sacrifice "petal" of solar deva energy that partially surrounds the human soul gradually opens as some of the causal body petals of the second sub-plane become fully opened and are used in the creation of spiritual service. As this occurs, much greater levels of fusion take place between the personality and soul. The reason is that the spiritual concepts created and used in service are more focused on the development of the soul in those being served than on their personalities. The petals and their component solar devas on the second sub-plane (which is sometimes referred to as the second *tier* of petals) that are fully open radiate a light that corresponds to each pitri's sub-sub-plane as the deva is used in service; the above-described process also occurs for the third sub-plane. The process further fuses the second tier devas to the separated two lowest solar devas, or pitris, in the lowest petal in the causal body. Use of second tier, or second sub-plane, solar devas constructs the second part of the "rainbow bridge" from each enlightened concept, or from the *radiance* of joined solar deva and higher mental elemental energy that is repeatedly used in service. This radiance connects the spiritual thought within the human soul to both the Self and the mental permanent atom that is surrounded by the Self. The Self at first surrounds only the atomic enlightened part of the permanent atom, and eventually surrounds the entire atom as the atom becomes fully enlightened. As more strands of radiant light connect from the solar devas of the second mental sub-plane petals, further enlightenment of the mental "genes" (the mental permanent atom) takes place. The effect on each subsequent human being created in potential by the human soul (and its Self and OverSoul) is that the human's prior spiritual thought is not only communicated to him or her as he or she lives and creates virtuous thought in service to others—this began to take place when the first part of the bridge became functional. What also happens is that when virtue from the second tier has first been created at some earlier time in that lifetime, the spiritual thought that is in the Self is then communicated to the personality, which is fusing with the soul simply by *thinking* from the second tier (*prior* to creating additional virtue as service to others). As the personality integrates itself in each subsequent lifetime, the spiritual concepts can be constructed from the added thought of the Self and soul, as the personality fuses with the soul by *thinking* from the level where the soul abides (the second sub-plane, or tier). Under these circumstances, when the second "leg," or part, of the of the triangle of light, or the "rainbow bridge" of radiance, has been built in a prior life, spiritual service is more likely to occur earlier in life and at a greater level. The reason is that a more creative part of the service that comes from the added thought of the Self is added every time a person thinks spiritually from the second tier. Note that the first part of the bridge remains and it continues to be further developed, adding spiritual thought to the disciple as she or he creates virtue using her or his personality and self to create all of the thought. Also note that this first part can be augmented as more solar devas radiate from fully opened petals on the third mental sub-plane because these concepts are being interpenetrated and joined as they are used in service with the larger concepts from the second mental sub-plane. A synergistic and geometric effect takes place as more strands of radiant light and more "legs" of the "rainbow bridge" triangle are built from spiritual concepts that are used in service for others.

When an inner sacrifice petal has become opened to a certain level, initiation is completed with the assistance of Masters, or Souls (ascended souls), who are members of the next kingdom. This includes the one or more fused Selves of each Master's Solar Angel. The minimum necessary level of openness increases as humans on earth develop in consciousness. As a result, the initiatory process becomes perpetually increasingly difficult in absolute terms. However, the human disciples are commensurately more capable of spiritual thought and thus find this raised level relatively and subjectively no more difficult. Each new generation of humans slightly increases the minimum level of service that the human initiates need to provide, which thus continually elevates the standard for initiation. The process of opening the second inner sacrifice petal is the process of the second initiation. Note that any one of the three petals may slightly open during any one of the initiations, depending upon one's creation of service. The second initiation often takes more lifetimes to complete, on average, than does the first. Part of the difficulty is that the second initiation corresponds to some mastery in service from spiritually disciplining and using the astral body. The human needs to overcome some of the relatively more difficult astral selfishness, or glamours (which are fixed selfish desires), within his or her astral body. The measure of relative difficulty is based upon a spiritual disciple's (the human's) ability to change. The astral selfishness is considered relatively more difficult to overcome than is the inertia of the etheric/dense physical body, which causes that body's tendency to continue in the same direction it has been in. Inertia is caused by a lack of cooperation and sharing, and is the way in which selfishness in the etheric/dense physical body manifests; note that the etheric/dense physical body is the focus of the first initiation. The growth in mastery over the etheric/dense physical body continues throughout the later initiations at an accelerated pace, but because the first inner petal is now fully open, this discipline is less difficult. The next chapter will cover, in more depth, factors of spiritual growth within the human bodies. At this point it can be stated that at present, and for about the last eleven thousand or so years, the lower part of the astral body has been connected in a dark and selfish way to the lowest part of the lower mental body of most humans. This has left them the legacy of a somewhat inherent selfish nature—from birth. The name in spiritual terms for this dark link is the *kama-manasic connection*. This problem of the astral body being linked through darkness to the lower mental body is mostly overcome at the completion of the second initiation. However, in the meantime, the process of that initiation is made more difficult—sometimes precariously so, often leading to failure in some lifetimes. More often than not, humans in the second initiation fail to progress and may actually become *more* selfish and possibly personality-disordered as a result of their selfish frustration and egotism, and even arrogance. The growth of the human soul is then slowed, and further fusion of the personality with the soul is prevented until the circumstances are remedied—usually in a future lifetime—after considerable amounts of added suffering that is resultant of the spiritual disciple's prior selfish acts.

As the first inner sacrifice petal (Sc–3) begins to open, the spirit that is inside the human soul becomes further exposed. This spirit becomes more conscious of the higher mental plane and becomes exposed to, first, the personality and its self, along with the radiance from the "rainbow bridge." This radiance then connects the personality to the energized human soul's spirit. Next, as the second inner sacrifice petal (Sc–2) opens, the human soul's spirit becomes exposed, fully conscious of, and connected to the higher Self and the mental permanent atom that this Self is surrounding on the atomic level of the mental plane's first sub-plane. The higher Self is the Solar Angel's lowest part, which it shares with the human. With the opening of each of these petals, the human soul becomes much more sensitive to any selfishness that a personality creates in its life; note that this holds true for selfishness within its own personality and self *and* the selfishness within others. The soul also becomes progressively *much* more conscious of the Self and of its own need to give to the self and for the self to give to it rather than to the personality. Because the soul does not directly experience the self before the inner petals begin to open, the soul with fused parts of the personality can (and so can the self) become either quite self-conscious or overly sensitive to selfishness in others concerning any selfishly created imperfection within its or someone else's personality. These conditions are even further exacerbated following an initiation, after a petal has suddenly become fully opened. As an example, a spiritual disciple sometimes, in her or his personality, might become shy, withdrawn, and self-critical or critical of other selves because of her or his selfish failings to create enough virtue. This can occur especially in the beginning of the disciple's initiation process subsequent to the completion of the preceding initiation and the full opening of a petal. A person who has practiced spiritual discipline in a prior incarnation but who has not yet begun to in the current one, may *sub*-consciously (to the self) exhibit the same traits relatively early in life. Such difficulties are overcome as the spiritual disciple becomes more involved with creating virtue *together with* the group of souls whom she or he came into incarnation with. It is through this group process of creating more light that the soul finds relief from its abrupt exposure, which is caused by the accelerated process of human initiation. This process of initiation, however, is what helps to keep the human kingdom in step with the plan for earth.

The third inner sacrifice petal (Sc–1) begins to open as one or more solar devas of the causal body radiate light through their creation of concepts that were first thought of by the *fused* personality and soul, and to some small extent, with these two fused with their Monad—which includes their Solar Angel. The solar devas reach this level by holding higher mental elemental energy together on the first mental sub-plane, in concepts that are used to create service. The three lowest and previously separated solar pitris, or devas, on the lowest causal petal now are all fused together and connected to all three of the higher spiritual tiers in the causal body. As the third inner sacrifice petal opens, the radiant third "leg" of the "rainbow bridge" is built. The third "leg" of the triangle of radiance is created from the mental permanent atom and its Self (at

Open Inner Petals of Lotus

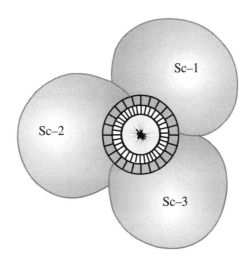

Illustration 6.22

the top of the higher mental body) and connects to the mental unit (at the top of the lower mental body) on the fourth sub-plane. The third part of the bridge connects the Self with the self, and the mental permanent atom with the lifelong thoughtforms (lunar devas alone and when used in thought with lower elemental energies' thoughtforms) that create the personality in the mental unit. The mental permanent atom and its surrounding Self are also a shared part of the lowest part of the Solar Angel. From this point forward the personality and its self, which are within the mental unit, can receive *complete* whole mental spiritual thought directly from the Self and the Solar Angel, while using some of the whole awareness, or complete sense, of the mental body (both lower and higher together), which the direct connection with the mental permanent atom provides. In addition, with each strand of radiant light that is added into the third leg of the triangle of the rainbow bridge, the personality becomes integrated earlier in the next new human life. The earlier integration is resultant of the *spiritually* continuous memories within the mental permanent atom that are from prior virtuous lifetimes, and most often from the more recent ones.

An *average* person today on earth can become fully integrated in her or his personality in a mundane, or non-spiritual, capacity at about twenty-one years of age; an additional seven years are needed for the personality to integrate and control the development of whatever level of spiritual integration and control an average person will exercise in that life. Thus, on average, seven years are needed for the personality to gain full control of the etheric/dense physical body and its senses in a way that allows the self to communicate with this body and receive communication from it. Between the ages of seven and fourteen, the personality usually gains control over the astral body and its senses, and then can achieve integration of the etheric/dense physical body with the astral. By age fourteen, the personality often gains full use of its etheric/dense physical senses, and the self is in full communication with the astral body.

PROGRESSION OF DEVELOPMENT AND USE OF SENSES IN EACH OF THE FOUR LOWER BODIES				
BODY	ENTITY IN CONTROL	AVERAGE AGE FOR CONTROL OF SENSES AND FULL INTEGRATION	AVERAGE AGE FOR FULL USE	COMPLETED WHOLE SENSE IN ABLILTY TO SERVE
Etheric/Dense Physical	The personality through the self	7 years	14 years	Intelligent Coordinated Response
Astral	The personality through the self	14 years	21 years	Super-Empathy
Lower Mental and the three lowest solar devas	The personality through the self	21 years	28 years	Limited Wisdom
Mental, including the Spiritual/ Higher Mental	The personality fused with the soul	28 years	35 years	Love/Wisdom
Intuitional	The self fused with the mental Self plus the other intuitional parts of the OverSoul and slightly with the Monad	35 years	42 years	Controlled Intuition, leading eventually to Buddhi*

*Each sub-sense of the intuitional body is still considered whole in its own ability to create spiritual service because each sub-sense always functions within a Now.

Table 6. 2

Between ages fourteen and twenty-one, the personality usually gains control over the mental body and its integration with the astral and etheric/dense physical. By an average age of twenty-eight, the personality can fully *use* the lower mental body and the three isolated solar devas of the causal body, on the higher mental plane. Finally, when the personality in non-spiritually disciplined people is functioning with its Self, OverSoul, and soul, by age twenty-eight it gains control over the *previously* developed parts of the spiritual mind, or those parts that are higher than the lowest three solar devas of the causal body. For a spiritually disciplined person, the inner sacrifice petals are also within the personality's control by age twenty-eight, provided that she or he continues to create virtue. In addition, some relatively small amounts of the intuitional body and senses may have been developed; if so, then they are also integrated into the *fused* personality and soul, for communication with the self *and* Self together. When the intuitional body is being integrated and controlled, developing some level of controlled intuition in the process, another seven years are added to the fused personality *and* soul's development of control. Note that full *use* of a body requires an average of seven years after full *control* has taken place. For further clarification, the reader is referred to table 6.2. Note that the next chapter will examine much more how this information relates to sense development and how each human becomes a unique individual.

The human soul develops fusion with its personality and self by the lower two of them (the personality and self) becoming more wisely loving. This is accomplished through the use of the highest body and sense available, in the creation of the most virtue possible at any particular time within the human's life. When a person who is not a spiritual disciple uses a body and sense at the highest levels of virtue created in his or her prior lives, in order to further develop the body for the creation of more virtue the person, with her or his personality's permission, may choose to think in the following way. If thinking mentally, he or she would choose to think from the spiritual mind, and create larger spiritual concepts using either more solar devas or higher-level solar devas (or both), to hold the concepts together in the causal body. In a spiritual disciple, or someone who is fusing her or his personality and self with her or his soul and Self, the process is similar—but with some important differences at certain critical points in time. A spiritual disciple is unfolding the petals of his or her causal body *and* is unfolding the inner sacrifice petals that surround the spirit in his or her soul. Disciples create virtue somewhat as souls, giving wisely in cooperation and empathy with other souls who are creating similar virtue. They accomplish this together in group consciousness, and, today, within a group structure that is also spiritually hierarchial in thought; however, many of these groups do not identify themselves as being spiritual. Each disciple gives wisely and helps to create more virtue based upon her or his relative ability at any particular time, as is needed and can best be done in comparison to the other members of the group. When functioning as souls, these group conscious spiritual disciples are humble, and through their humility—as functional souls only—can then create hierarchial spiritual thought and consciousness. To create hierarchial spiritual thought within the spiritual group, a disciple needs to, through proper use of humility, defer to the thought of the person who is creating the highest thought and is thus creating the most virtue at any one moment (unless she or he is the one who is thinking the highest spiritual thought at that moment—and, of course, the others in the group concur). To accomplish this difficult feat requires *both* humility and relatively high levels of consciousness, or givingness that is wise. Humility is developed as mental thought becomes more whole, because humility is the ability to understand—through the *process* of loving, or giving—the thought of others, often as completely as the person who is thinking the thought does (and sometimes better than that person understands his or her own thought); if in a spiritual group, this understanding grows in a hierarchy of thought. Mental thought becomes whole through wise giving, and so does the development of understanding, or of consciousness. The human soul chooses to think only when its thought is giving to others (so that they can best, or most appropriately, give); thus souls are always humble. If a soul cannot think with humility and wise giving, it chooses to not think at all. This is a great sacrifice for the soul because thought is what creates the soul and its life (and the souls and lives of everything else that has sufficient thought).

When a petal in the causal body that is used unselfishly begins to open, it also begins to rotate, or spin around the causal body on its sub-plane (tier). The spin is caused by the large amounts of completely unimpeded energy moving through it at the speed of the mental plane light. Petals that are partially open frequently wobble in their spin because they cannot freely move energy through themselves, without retaining some of it through self-focus, or selfishness. Note that the energy is following the thought of the personality and the self. All causal bodies have some spin to them because the lowest petal, at a minimum, is partly open from the thought of the Solar Angel. The direction of the spin of the third sub-plane, or tier, of solar devas and their petals determines the gender of the etheric/dense physical body. It does so through interpenetration of the higher body into the lower, and structures the permanent atoms for that lifetime. The spin affects the etheric/dense physical sexual center, which the lowest solar deva on the lowest petal corresponds to). Also, as the personality begins to develop control over the bodies, through the integration of the personality and self in that lifetime (beginning before birth), the effects of the sexual spin become more prominent. The direction of the spin is chosen by the consciousness of the OverSoul and human soul, as is needed for the best possible wise giving in conjunction with other souls; this also includes choosing which gender the personality will need to be in order to best help it and its self to become more virtuous. As the causal petals fully open, their rotation becomes faster and more stable. The "rainbow bridge" of radiant solar deva strands of light usually, in the beginning, appear as the inner spokes of a wheel that is turning slowly enough for each spoke to be barely distinguished. The opened petals on the second mental sub-plane, or tier, also rotate, but in the opposite direction of the third tier petals. Any opened petals on the first sub-plane, or tier, rotate in the same direction as those on the third tier; when this rotation becomes stable at about the same speed as the rotation of the third tier, the gender becomes fixed for all subsequent humans created through that causal body.

A more complete way to describe the appearance of a "leg" of several or more strands of a rotating rainbow bridge is as the outside of a cylinder of light that is turning at such a speed that each strand of colored light can barely be distinguished. The rotation of each leg of the triangular bridge is caused by the rotation of the tier of petals and their component solar devas. The rotation of the rainbow bridge alters the radiance of the solar devas by increasing the effectiveness of the radiance on the centers of others by *adding* rotation to the already existing rotation of others' centers. If stable, and not wobbly, the rotation can also stabilize the mental body and corresponding brain, and centers of other people. Conversely, in correspondence, a person's wobbling causal body spin can *adversely* affect other people who are weaker in thought and who associate with that person, through the addition of (selfish) wobble to the centers in these people's mental and corresponding lower bodies. Notice that the lower corresponding body is affected because the mental body, which is higher in thought, interpenetrates the lower and is also integrated with the lower, through the control and functioning of the personality. Thus those who have less developed mental bodies may become victimized by those whose mental bodies are more developed but are more selfish (and darker). The correspondences of the parts of the human causal body and its lower bodies are as follows. The part of the causal body on the third mental sub-plane corresponds to the etheric/dense physical body, the part of the causal body on the second sub-plane corresponds to the astral body, and the part of the causal body on the first sub-plane corresponds to the lower mental body. As the parts of the higher mental become perfected, so do the corresponding lower body's centers and associated senses. The same is true as the higher mental body is joined together and unified with the lower mental body. The lower bodies then eventually become correspondingly unified with the mental body, creating, effectively, a single unified body from three.

All of the factors that develop the higher mental body through light in form, or virtue, develop the human soul as well. The human soul is creating its inner sacrifice petals, which are composed of solar devas, into thinking energies so that it will no longer have to rely upon the causal body that surrounds it and limits it in thought, to the overall abilities in thought of its combined causal solar devas. The causal solar devas are limited in new creative thought (but are also helped to think) both by their experiences while they were a part of the Solar Angel from which they came. Solar devas are also helped by, but are limited by, the thought of all other causal bodies on the mental plane. The causal bodies were created from the thought of Solar Angels and with their development added to by human souls. This arrangement gives the causal solar devas considerable ability to think and contain higher mental elemental energies in order to hold together concepts that were first thought of by another source (they nearly always *follow* greater thought from a spiritual source because they are not fully individualized energy beings). However, it prevents the human soul from creating new, or original, mental thought that has *never* been thought of before on the section of the mental plane that surrounds earth. To create original mental structure, or new mental thought, requires the use of one or more inner sacrifice petals; for an inner sacrifice petal to fully replace the causal body's helpful control in *service* of holding together a concept, the petal must be *fully* open. Full opening of a petal occurs only after a person has spiritually disciplined himself or herself and has completed a spiritual initiation.

As can be inferred from the preceding paragraph, all *human* thought that has served others and has been original and structured (all mental thought) has been created by humans who are the most advanced thinkers and who are spiritual initiates. Those spiritual disciples who are in the last stage, or the accepted stage, of the initiation process that is needed to completely unfold an inner sacrifice petal begin to create some levels of *original* mental thought. They can complete this original thought in their service only when they complete the initiation. The reason is that additional thought and higher mental energy are needed in order to fully open the corresponding inner petal surrounding the soul. This thought and energy are provided by some members of the next kingdom. Each initiation involves four stages: the probationary, the accepting, the pledged, and the accepted. Prior to beginning the initiation process, a person aspires to create her/himself into a greater contribution in service to others. However, that person has yet to take the actions of further spiritual discipline that are required for the aspiration to become realized. In this pre-stage of initiation, a person is an aspirant, or is aspiring to discipline himself or herself, or limit the use of certain senses for spiritual information that is consequently more complete, as is needed in order to serve at his or her level of consciousness. Those who are spiritually disciplining themselves and who are in the accepted stage of the first initiation create a focus of spiritual discipline on their own etheric/dense physical bodies and senses, and often on those of others. Disciples at this stage, or level, begin to create *original* mental thought that serves in some important way the etheric centers and senses of lifeforms, including humans, and the dense physical parts of civilization. This original thought also makes them into leaders of whatever group or groups of people are following the thought. These disciples complete this service as they complete the initiation, first by fully opening the first inner petal, and soon afterwards (which in human time, may still be several years) completing the communication of their original thought in some appropriate vehicle of communication, e.g., writing, speech, teaching, and sometimes bold action. In today's world, accepted disciples create their service in unison and hierarchial thought with others within their respective spiritual groups (which they may not initially recognize to be spiritual groups). Before A.D. 1925, it was possible to complete service and initiation in less group conscious ways, using groups of other souls in more distant and far less spiritually disciplined ways. Because members of the next kingdom (the Masters) would help to unify the original mental thought with that of other souls, humans could continue to think more separatively and less group consciously, or less soul consciously, with less humility. Their devotion, astrally, to a Master replaced some of the humility they would otherwise have needed. In A.D. 1925, Masters decided to no longer add to the higher mental plane their helpful thought that would assist human spiritual disciples in the completion of their service. Since then, Masters have had very little and sometimes no contact with humans prior to the human's completion of each lower initiation. One result of this change was the *requirement* that original mental thought be *of service to others*, and that it usually occur group consciously within a group that is functioning *spiritually* and in the same dimensions that the disciple is alive on. This group needs to be contributing more of God's thought, or light, into life (its form) and creating more virtue.

As the causal body's petals open, along with one or more of the inner sacrifice petals, its appearance changes from bud-shaped to, increasingly, spherical. This change is the result of higher petals and their solar pitris being used in service, and the interpenetrating use of the lower solar devas that are within lower petals. A result of the process is a more uniform use of the entire body because more solar devas are working together to hold the higher mental elemental energies into large spiritual concepts. On each tier, or sub-plane, there is a total of three "petals"; each of the petals represents one of the three aspects of God's mind. One petal on each tier represents God's first aspect of mind, of choice/will/purpose/sacrifice, and these are referred to as the (outer) sacrifice petals; the solar pitris that compose them are known as the sacrificial solar devas. A second petal on each tier is referred to as the love petal because it represents God's second aspect of mind, or direction/givingness/oneness/love. The third petal on each tier represents intelligence/activity/communication/knowledge, or the third part of God's mind, and is referred to as the knowledge petal. When all three petals of one type fully open on each of the three tiers, or higher mental sub-planes, all three of the petals begin to spin in an additional direction to the direction of the spin associated with the tier (the first spin). Thus the petals are spinning in *two* directions at once, and as members of two different groups; this is possible only in five-dimensional, or mental plane, space. The second spin and group unifies the higher mental body; the unification begins with the spin of the first group of three petals of the same type on all three tiers. As all three groups of these petals (nine petals, in total) begin to rotate like three concentric pinwheels, the higher mental body unifies with the lower—unifying the mental body and mind of the very advanced human initiate. The second spin also greatly increases the integrated radiance of each leg of the rainbow bridge. As the petals spin in their second direction, more light and energy are "pumped" into the personality and self from this new spin of the first leg. The second leg's second spin is established between the soul and the Self, and the third leg's second spin is established between the Self and the personality and self. The first leg is "pumped," or intensified in directed radiance, from the soul to the personality by the spin of the three knowledge petals rotating together. The second leg is intensified in directed radiance from the soul towards the Self by the three love petals rotating together. And the third leg is intensified in directed radiance from the Self and the mental permanent atom towards the personality and its self by the three sacrifice petals rotating together. (See Appendix, part C.)

The first group of petals to develop a second spin is usually the three knowledge petals. The second spin generally occurs after completion of the second initiation and while creating service during the third, using the three spinning love petals. The Solar Angel begins a fusion process with the spirit part of the human soul when the three inner sacrifice petals have somewhat opened. It also, in conjunction with the first direction of spin of the first (the highest) tier, fixes the gender of the soul and fused personality until the soul returns to being a Monad. A Monad who is ascended still has a gender, but the gender is based upon the decision of service that he or she made during the sixth initiation. Depending upon which type of service was chosen, the ascended Monad's gender may change at the eighth initiation. The chosen service also indirectly

The Rotation of Petals and the Rainbow Bridge

When the energy composing them is fully enlightened, all the petals and legs of the antahkarana that form a person's rainbow bridge rotate. The direction of rotation of petals and legs is determined by the person's gender, the sub-plane (tier), and the type of petal. All the petals on each tier spin in the same direction. When rotation is clockwise on the third tier, the person is male, and when counter-clockwise, the person is female. The rotation illustrated is that of a male. The first leg of the antahkarana, which comprises solar pitri energy, rotates in the same direction as do the petals on the third tier. The second tier spin is opposite to the third, and the first tier spins in the same direction as the third. The antahkarana strands from the second tier form the second leg of the antahkarana. The third leg is formed from the solar pitri energy from the first tier connected to the mental permanent atom, down to the mental unit. With the first spin, all the petals on each tier spin in the same direction. The second spin occurs when the petals are fully enlightened and petals of the same type spin in a big circle through the tiers, creating a pinwheel effect. All the K (knowledge) petals and S (sacrifice) petals spin in the same direction as the first and third tiers do. The L (love) petals spin in the opposite direction. The second spin causes the radiances from the petals to move in two different ways and in two dimensions—movement and time—around the legs of the triangle.

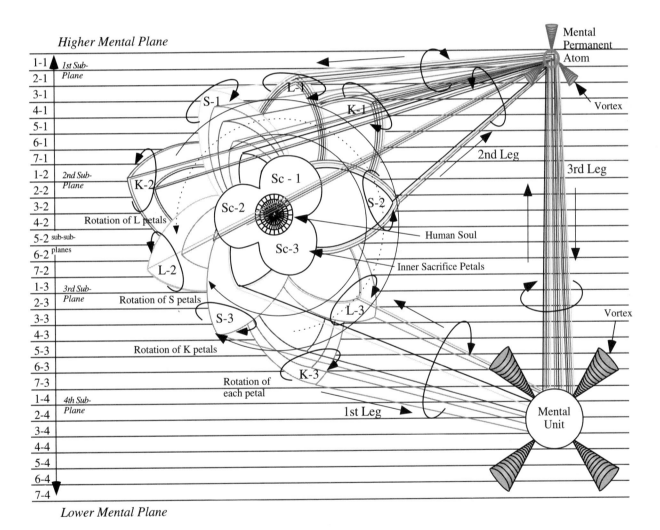

Solid line indicates clockwise movement for K and S petals ⟶
Dotted line indicates counter-clockwise movement for L petals ⋯⋯⋯▶

Illustration 6.23

determines which universe the Monad is likely to serve in, in the future. Because the third initiation is focused on developing the mental senses and body for service, this is the appropriate initiation to begin the unification of the mental body. As the third initiation is completed and the fourth is taken, or begun, the three inner sacrifice petals become fully open and then they begin to spin around the spirit that is within the human soul. This spin causes the solar devas within the petals of the causal body to begin to individualize by allowing them to think on their own; since they are now completely relieved of the responsibility of creating concepts by following thought, they are *creatively* giving their thought *first,* rather than following thought from another source. The solar devas in the causal body are becoming creators of thought, or are becoming spiritualized. The light within them is becoming balanced between the first and second parts of God's mind. One or more of these solar devas chooses on its own to fuse with a less developed solar pitri (of the same type and sub-sub-plane position) within the causal body of one of the students of the *Teacher,* who is a fourth level initiate. For a period of time, the individualizing solar devas exist as a part of both causal bodies. There is a total of thirty-six solar pitris within the causal body, and after all of them have begun to fuse with the causal bodies of the *Teacher's* students, the fourth level initiate can suddenly release them through a sort of initiation of these solar devas. These devas will serve for a period of time functioning in the causal body of the student(s), and will be receptive only to the Monad of the student, rather than to his or her Self, soul, personality, or self. Until the fourth initiation, the receptivity to the Monad's thought occurs only during the accepted stage of each initiation the student goes through. The addition of one or more creatively thinking spiritualized and individualizing solar devas to the causal body of a student allows the monadic thought to become sensed through her or his causal body. As a result, the accepted disciple can become more creative of virtuous thought prior to completing her or his thought in service, through completion of the initiation process for that initiation. Note that in some circumstances a *Teacher,* as a fourth level initiate, is available to teach a student only from a Master's inner ashram, or group; these *Teachers* are between lifetimes and incarnations. Such a spiritual group, or inner ashram, is found in consciousness on the intuitional plane, where the student in the lower initiations has very limited development of sense and body. Consequently, much less transference of the *Teacher's* solar devas occurs within a period of time—slowing the process.

The causal body of the fourth level initiate is released during the fourth initiation, with this very advanced human initiate then relying upon only the inner sacrifice petals to hold together higher mental elemental energies into concepts. Each of the solar devas of these inner petals has individualized, has monadic sense, and can construct original thought. Just prior to the release of the causal body, the advanced initiate's mental body becomes unified through the completed (second) spins added to the three spins of the tiers. At this point, the spins of the causal body's three series of three outside petals and the spin of the three inner sacrifice petals inside it are together creating enormous amounts of radiance and of completely unimpeded energies that have become fully enlightened at their particular levels of time and space. Once the fourth level initiate, or arhat, releases his or her causal body and uses only the inner sacrifice petals of his or her soul to hold concepts together, he or she becomes what is known as *adept*. A person who is adept is one who has fully perfected and unified at least one but not yet all of the three human bodies and their senses through light, or by creating virtue. In the past, a Master needed to unify only one body; in those times, all who were adept were Masters. A person who is adept today has attained the highest level of enlightenment available to a human; further enlightenment occurs only when a person moves on to the next kingdom by mastering the three lowest bodies and planes, or the three lower worlds.

In order to enter the next kingdom, a person who is adept must release—with sudden power—all three of the inner sacrifice petals of solar deva energies that surround his/her spirit within the soul. The release takes place in an instant, when the adept person has perfected all

The Transfiguration of a Human into a Master, and the Gradual Fusion with the Solar Angel

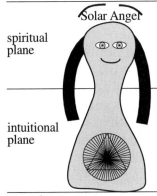

The Arhat becomes Adept

During the third initiation, the human begins to slightly fuse with his or her Solar Angel. The Arhat, who is a fourth level initiate, increases the amount of fusion as a result of the high levels of virtue that he or she creates in accord with the Plan.

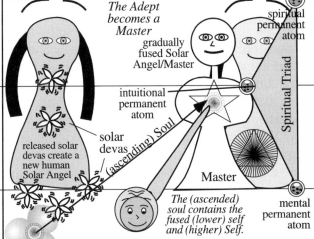

The Adept becomes a Master

The (ascended) soul contains the fused (lower) self and (higher) Self.

spiritual plane

intuitional plane

mental plane

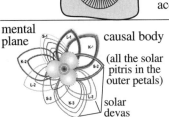

causal body

(all the solar pitris in the outer petals)

solar devas

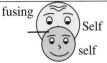

fusing

Self

self

The (lower) self is fusing with the (higher) Self.

The Arhat sacrifices the use of her or his causal body of solar devas, which have been assisting with the process of conceptual thought. For the first time, the Arhat begins to think and create virtue without the assistance of the solar pitris in the outside causal body. This allows the Arhat to create new (never before thought of on the mental plane) thought. The Arhat must hold these concepts together herself or himself without the assistance of the outer energy devas, but with some assistance from the solar devas within the inner sacrifice petals. These pitris assist the Arhat only when she or he is serving. Since the concepts are no longer being held together by the outer solar pitris, these pitris can be distributed among and given to one or more—up to 12—of the Arhat's students.

the world of humanity

solar devas

Arhat

The Arhat creates new knowledge and gives it to the world of humanity, through the service of his or her group, which is serving along one of the seven rays of focus.

the arhat's group

causal body of student

The solar devas of the causal body begin to be released during the fourth initiation. When fully released, the Arhat becomes Adept. As the solar pitris are released, they are shared with and eventually given to the students of the Arhat, who is a *Teacher*. While the pitris are being shared, the Arhat shares his or her mental mind with his or her students.

released solar devas create a new human Solar Angel

solar devas

inner sacrifice petals

The more that the Arhat sacrifices the outer solar devas originally given to him or her by the Solar Angel, the more that he or she is sacrificing as the Solar Angel has. The Arhat's sacrifice causes him or her to fuse with his or her Solar Angel. The concept is that the more one functions as a higher being, the more one becomes that higher being. The Adept uses only the inner sacrifice petals of his or her soul to hold concepts together, and only when those concepts are being used in service.

The Adept becomes a leader in the world among humans, and now changes the world by teaching humanity how and when to use the new knowledge that she or he has created along one of the seven rays.

Adept

An Arhat creates himself or herself into an Adept by creating new knowledge within the mental body in service, which unifies that entire body. The unification causes the higher mental body, in unison (in a "Now"), to join with the lower mental body. The union of the mental body is what creates the Arhat into an Adept.

In order for the Adept to enter the next (the spiritual) kingdom, he or she must release the inner sacrifice petals of solar deva energy. When this happens, the Adept becomes a Master. The human soul is freed from the fourth sub-sub-plane of the second mental sub-plane and ascends to the fourth sub-plane of the intuitional plane. The soul becomes the (liberated) Soul of the Master. The freed inner sacrifice solar devas create a new human Solar Angel.

The last personality of thoughtforms changes from lunar devas to solar devas and becomes a part of the mental permanent atom. The Master retains his/her permanent atoms from the lower three bodies for a while, in order to serve in the three lower worlds, along with his or her Solar Angel, which he or she has partially fused with.

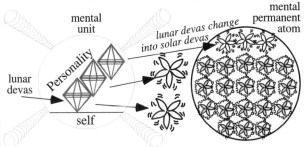

mental unit

lunar devas

Personality

self

lunar devas change into solar devas

mental permanent atom

Illustration 6.24

three human bodies through her or his service. As the adept's three inner sacrifice petals are released, the three perfected bodies become unified and then function as one in time and space. The human soul is freed from the fourth sub-sub-plane of the second mental sub-plane and ascends to the fourth sub-plane of the intuitional plane. This is where it contains the fused spirit of the last self that has fused with the Self—all fused with the liberated soul of the Master. The last personality of thoughtforms becomes changed from lunar devas to solar devas and a part of the mental permanent atom. The Master retains this permanent atom for a period of time for future service in the lower worlds, as is needed, with his or her partially fused Solar Angel. The intuitional, or buddhic, part of the Solar Angel begins to fuse with the Master's soul. This creates buddhic form and sense to the controlled intuitional thought that the Master thinks in—within a Now. When used (in service), the buddhic form of a liberated soul contains five centers of completed service, with each center having a part of the fifth sense, of buddhi. These five centers take the shape of a five-pointed star with the spirit of the Soul within its center. The two additional spiritual centers are also a part of the intuitional body, and manifest as two lights above the head in the form of somewhat flattened concentric spheres and unify part of the Master with his or her Solar Angel when the completed sense (and body) of buddhi is developed.

     ## SOLAR ANGELS

To resume now the somewhat less technically complex explanation, the soul is continuously balancing its form, or its energy part (the solar devas), to its spirit. In a human soul, the balance is nearly always kept equal but is never perfect because the spirit is unable to think for both itself and the solar devas within the surrounding inner sacrifice petals at the same time. The human soul is a lifeform with a fourth ray focus, attempting to create perfection between its spirit and form, or energy, and striving to create beauty. It achieves the state of perfection when it ascends to the intuitional plane and has twice as much spiritual thought than that of its form. However, once achieved, the perfection is sacrificed to create more of God. The perfection of form and spirit is only a stepping stone to perfecting God's mind. This is a perfection of God's thought (light) and the unification of it to intelligent activity rather than energy, or less than fully intelligent activity. This is why the fourth ray is only an attribute of the third aspect of God's mind and of the third ray as a mechanism of growing this aspect. Souls are the "foot soldiers" for God's thought (light) in life, or enlightened spirit, to join with enlightened energy and create lower lifeforms in the realms where spirit is overwhelmed by relatively dark-thinking energies.

Solar Angels are fully spiritualized, and are therefore individualized energy beings. They are composed of energy that has completely joined with the spirit and energy on their mutual plane of existence. A Solar Angel is also the OverSoul of a human soul; there are three parts to Its *body*, as follows. The mental (plane) energy part is composed of higher mental solar devas and a mental permanent atom. The intuitional (plane) energy part is composed of intuitional plane solar deva energies and an intuitional permanent atom, and the spiritual (plane) energy part is composed of spiritual plane solar deva energies and a spiritual permanent atom. The Solar Angel shares its mental Self, first, with group souls; then it shares its growing mental plane Self with a human. Finally, the Solar Angel shares all three of its Selves with a fusing Master. The permanent atoms of a Solar Angel always comprise solar deva energies from the corresponding plane where the atoms are found. Elemental energies, from the corresponding planes, are used along with deva energies to create bodies. The entire three parts of the body of the Solar Angel with their corresponding spirit, or three Selves, are referred to as the Spiritual Triad. The Spiritual Triad eventually encompasses the following: (a) a Solar Angel, (b) a Master, and (c) a Monad. A Solar Angel lends the use of its permanent atoms and its spirit, or Self, on the sub- or sub-sub-plane where the soul is, whom it helps to create and then informs. The first souls that Solar Angels help to create and inform are group souls that are located on the higher mental plane. Progressing through the lower kingdoms of group souls, a Solar Angel provides not only helpful spiritual thought in guidance through its mental Self to a group soul, but also some of the energy parts that the group soul needs. These include permanent atoms for the group soul's use on and above the mental plane. Note that the Solar Angel's mental plane Self is further grown through the thought of the group soul's self. The OverSoul, sometimes with help from its group soul, creates the permanent atoms

The Transfiguration of a Group Soul's Spirit into a New Human Solar Angel

The Solar Angel informs, at differing periods of time, at least one of each ray focus type of each level of group soul.

EXAMPLES OF SUB-RAYS OF ANIMAL GROUP SOULS

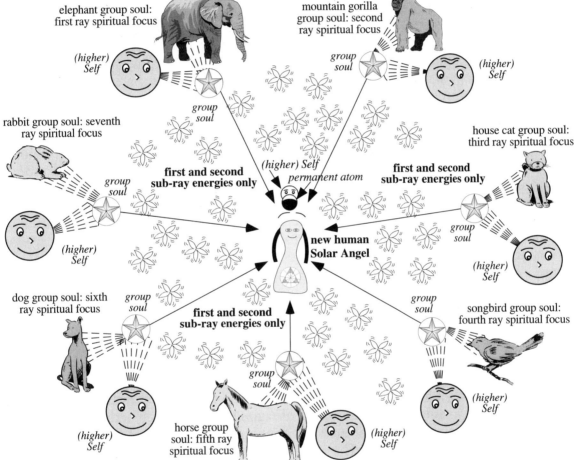

The Solar Angel in the later part of the first triadal stage informs advanced animals along seven different ray focuses, with perhaps some of these animals having been pets of humans. Its shared (higher) Self transfigures through its *creative* thought the virtue that each group soul created into the Solar Angel. When all seven sub-rayed lights have been transfigured, the Solar Angel advances from the collective increased spirit (of collective enlightened thought) into becoming a human Solar Angel of the second triadal stage. The enlightened spirit from each group soul remains intact because it is transfigured in light rather than averaged from friction and forces. Only first and second sub-rayed solar deva energy can enter and fuse into the mental permanent atom from the Solar Angel's vast fusing thought. The new permanent atom will be for a human souls's use in creating incarnating human beings.

Many of the above-represented species of animals have members that are already advanced enough to function as pets. By the end of Earth's fourth round (the present one), it is likely that all of these species will be able to do so.

Illustration 6.25

for their group of lifeforms to use on the astral and etheric/dense physical planes. These permanent atoms are created from energies that exist below the first sub-plane of their respective planes;
which sub-plane energies are used is dependent upon how well the self of the group soul can
think, because the self must be able to give thought to the informing fallen spirit on that sub-plane.

Solar Angels are members of the energy sub-kingdom of the fifth, or spiritual, kingdom.
Those Solar Angels who inform group souls are in the first stage of Spiritual Triadal growth of
their Selves. These Solar Angels first come from intelligent activity combined with light within
spirit that remained on the atomic level of each of the three planes where parts of the Spiritual
Triad are found: the atomic parts of the mental, intuitional, and spiritual planes. The combined
solar deva and elemental energies on the atomic levels are created from intelligent activity as
this activity is sacrificed and initially used by these Solar Angels to partially create the permanent atoms for the souls they inform. Some of the fully enlightened energies remained on the
respective planes and were not a part of the big bang. Four-fifths of the first and second sub-ray
energies that originally focused into the lower five dimensions are a part of the big bang and
some of these energies, as the first and second sub-rays of each of the three planes that the Solar
Angel exists on, become fused by the Angel's thought to initially create some additional parts
of its permanent atom. Its Self is the attracting thinker that surrounds the enlightened part of the
permanent atom on each of these planes. Notice that a Solar Angel is created from the same
energies as first stage stars are, and in a similar way—through fusion. However, the fusion that
creates a Solar Angel comes from the highest-thinking spirit on each of the three triadal planes,
whereas the thought of a Being in the Cosmic Mental Universe causes the fusion that creates a
Star. As a human on a planet creates himself or herself into a member of the next kingdom
(becomes a Master), his or her inner sacrifice petals are released and given to a newly created
Solar Angel for a human soul, to create the Solar Angel's mental, intuitional, and spiritual
permanent atoms. The release of the inner sacrifice petals is a second way of creating a Solar
Angel that begins its life at the second triadal level. These petals often replace the primordial
use of intelligent activity and manifested energy on the mental, intuitional, and spiritual planes,
where intelligent activity and manifested energy are in relatively short supply. They also help
the newly created Solar Angel to be millions of years ahead of where it would otherwise be in
its helping to create and then its informing of a new human soul. These Solar Angels begin their
triadal lives as Solar Angels of humans. This advancement takes place because the energy
within the inner sacrifice petals is fully Self conscious and can co-create and give so much
better than the solar devas in the causal body can with the Selves of the new (human level) Solar
Angel and of its created human soul. As a planet progresses in spiritual development from the
thought and service of humans, a proportionately greater number of the human Monads create
more spirit that also manifests more elemental energies that are used in additional human souls.
Some of this spirit remains at the spiritual, intuitional, and mental atomic levels, creating new
triadal Selves for new Solar Angels. The third-through-seventh ray inner sacrifice petal, which
is the first to open in a human initiate, spends more time being developed on the higher mental
plane than do the other two inner sacrifice petals. This petal contributes third through seventh
ray energies. When the energies from this first petal are released, they ascend to the atomic level
of the mental plane and become a part of the permanent atom of a new (human) Solar Angel.
This Solar Angel may eventually leave for another planet, depending upon the advancement of
the rounds. Many of the Solar Angels that were created from humans who advanced themselves
before the end of the round will remain on their original planet. The reason is that these Solar
Angels have already increased enough in consciousness from having been created from such an
advanced human soul's highest energies relative to the other humans on that planet. The second
ray inner sacrifice petal is the next to open, and when its second ray energies are released they
become a part of the intuitional permanent atom for the same new Solar Angel. The third inner

sacrifice petal's energies, when released, become a part of the spiritual plane permanent atom for this new Solar Angel and contribute first ray energies. Notice that the ray energies do not correspond to the planes; e.g., the first ray enlightened energy goes to the third plane. Further explanation of this process will be provided in upcoming chapters.

The spirit part of the first stage of triadal development of Solar Angels comes from the remaining part of spirit that is found exclusively at the atomic level of each plane and creates the Self. The Self surrounds the enlightened part of the permanent atom of that plane. These great Energy Beings begin their existence at the same level of consciousness (givingness, or love) as that of a new Master of the Ageless Wisdom (in the fifth level of initiation) today on earth. Note that Ageless Wisdom is a growing *structured* knowledge—one that is based upon *mental* wisdom— of how God, through life, creates our universe. Ageless Wisdom is a living and growing cosmology because it is knowledge based upon God's growth, or life. One masters Ageless Wisdom when one has mastered the three lower worlds in life- (God-) creation as they exist *at that time*.

When a Solar Angel has completed the first stage (the higher mental) of the development of the Spiritual Triad of Selves, it usually leaves the planet whereupon it had been helping to create group souls and their life. It does so, in part, to add to the diversity of life between planets while, paradoxically, joining parts of the planets together. At this point, the Solar Angel has completed the development of the solar devas in the lowest part of its body—the higher mental part—which will later be sacrificed and given to a human as that human's causal body. The accomplishment of such a task requires *millions* of (earth) years of helping to develop group souls on the higher mental plane of the planet where it had been living. When Solar Angels leave a planet, they usually do so en masse as the planet changes its focus of creation of new life on a plane from one lower plane to a higher one (such as the etheric to the astral). The effect of such an exodus is that the growth of life nearly ends on the lower plane that the Planetary Logos has removed from its focus. When Solar Angels leave a planet, the life development on the new sister planet they travel

The Higher Mental Planes of Venus, Earth, and Mars

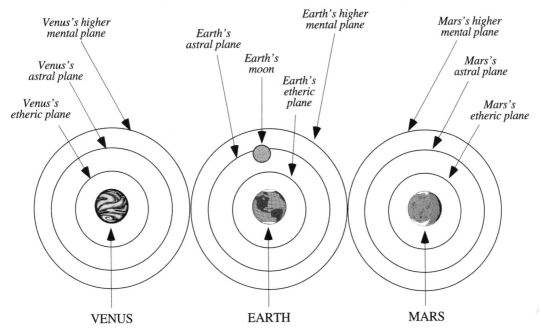

The higher mental planes of Venus and Earth touch at the mid-points of the three dimension etheric/dense physical space between these two planets. Likewise, Earth's and Mars's higher mental planes touch at a point that is equidistant between those two planets.

Illustration 6.26

to is in sync with the planet they left; both planets, and usually a third, are being developed within the Solar Logos' plan to create life etheric/dense physically on all three planets, but the development of etheric/dense physical life on each of these planets will occur at a different time in the cycle of life creation on each planet's etheric/dense physical plane. The development of new life on each planet is staggered among the three planes. In addition, each planet's *focus* of new life development will be on a specific and different plane in the three lowest worlds, i.e., the majority of the life that is developed on each of the three planets will be on either the etheric/dense physical, the astral, or the mental. Each planet's major development of life occurs on a different one of these planes. The Solar Angels travel through the higher parts of the mental plane, which connects the planets that are participating together in etheric/dense physical life development. The higher mental plane surrounding each of these planets touches the other at the mid-points of the three-dimensional etheric/dense physical space between them. Upon their en masse arrival on the new planet, the Solar Angels begin the second, or intuitional, stage of development of the Spiritual Triad of their Selves and the permanent atoms they surround. This stage includes the development of a human soul that eventually fuses with its self, the parts of its personality that are enlightened, its Self, and its Solar Angel, as was described earlier in this chapter.

Once the Master and his/her Solar Angel fuse, they enter the third stage of the Spiritual Triad development. This stage involves fusion and, eventually, completely electrical (pure) creation into an ascended Monad. In this stage no energy is used, only intelligent activity, or "pure" power, is used to change all energy into intelligent activity. When accomplished individually, as on earth today, the above-described process requires the completion of a total of seven levels of initiation. These levels include the first four human ones, although a slight amount of this pure electrical creation through completed power is first used by an adept initiate when creating herself or himself into a Master. At some point in the future of earth's development, some Masters and their fused Solar Angels will help to create new life etheric/dense physically on a third planet in our solar system. Solar Angels on earth mostly came from our sister planet, Venus. Millions of years ago (the last time was over 220 million years ago) Venus supported life etheric/dense physically, although nearly all of its life was etheric because Venus is one round ahead of earth and is a sacred planet (one where there is no evil). About 21 million years ago, in a mass exodus from Venus, the first of the Solar Angels for humans came to earth. Today all of the life on Venus is etheric (not dense physical), astral, and mostly mental. Mars will be the planet whereupon some Masters (or advanced super-humans) who have fused with their Solar Angels will eventually create new life. Tens of millions of years to a hundred million years ago (after Venus, in this last cycle), Mars supported etheric/dense physical life, and was focused upon the development of *animal* life on the etheric/dense physical plane. Mars is one round *behind* Earth in its development, i.e., Mars has completed its third round, wherein animals are the focus of life development.

Most of the information in the above paragraph was written about long ago, sometimes from oral accounts, and survives today from over five thousand years ago. This is long before humans had scientifically discovered the nature of these planets. When the majority of the total sixty billion human souls that are attached to earth have become liberated into Masters, our sun and its Solar Logos will enter into the third stage of solar system development. At this point, there will be advanced third-stage development of Spiritual Triad life on Venus, on Earth, and it will be under development on Mars. This advanced triadal life of fused Masters and Solar Angels who will arrive en masse will function as intelligent builders of planets under the direction of each planet's Logos. The focus of mental development will be on Venus, Mars will focus on astral development, and Earth will focus on the etheric/dense physical. The completion of the plan for life on the planets will unify the three lower worlds and dimensions of the solar system as the triadal life that arrived in large groups ascends into completed Monads on the first, or logoic, dimension.

Solar Angels develop through three stages of Spiritual Triad unification of their Selves and permanent atoms. The first stage of this unification is mental (on the mental, or manasic, plane), and results from service to group souls. The second is intuitional, or buddhic (on the intuitional plane), and results from service to a human soul. The third is spiritual (on the atmic, or spiritual, plane), which results from service that is combined with that of a Master—with the Solar Angel and Master together serving a Planetary Logos, and creating themselves into an ascended Monad. When a Solar Angel comes to a new planet to serve a human soul and to develop a Master of the three lower worlds in life (God) creation and of the Ageless Wisdom, it completes the fifth initiation and becomes a sixth level initiate (as the initiations are on earth at this time). A Master and Solar Angel who are beginning the third stage of the spiritual Triad fusion (which begins at the bottom, or seventh, sub-plane of the spiritual plane) are both sixth level initiates; because of their equality in consciousness and in their creation of virtue, they can complete their fusion together (their "Cosmic Marriage"). When the two together complete the unification of their shared bodies and spirit as the completed third stage of the unification of the Spiritual Triad, they complete the seventh initiation and become an ascended Monad. Prior to (such as on earth, at present) the exodus en masse of fused Solar Angels and Masters on a planet (after the planet has become sacred), Spiritual Triadal development into an ascended Monad takes place through service to the planet whereupon the Master and Solar Angel have fused, rather than the next planet in the cycle for life development. This condition limits the ascended Monads' options for leaving our universe, from nine to only seven "paths of decision"; the chosen path is, at present on earth, *decided upon* during the sixth initiation.

The human soul develops itself over millions of years from the collection of the best animal consciousness from the very last cycle of animal group soul development. Eventually the human soul becomes a super human co-creator and developer of new life, including new human life, on planets that create life in the three lower worlds. After their ascension onto the logoic plane as Monads, the focus of life creation for these Great Beings *starts* with planets that are typically the outer ones of a solar system, but specifically planets that support life on the mental plane and *above*. Through co-creating life on these planets that are usually very large, gaseous, and relatively cold etheric/dense physically, ascended Monads begin to learn about the creation of stars from the spiritual plane level as well as, to some extent, the life creation of systems of stars. These ascended Monads are also experiencing all life within our universe, beginning with pre-life minerals and plant life.

Within its inner sacrifice petals, the human soul comprises energies along all seven rays. In nearly all human souls, one of these seven energies is more dominant than the other six because of probability factors in joining together the seven of the best-thinking energies from animal group souls. The one dominant ray energy in the inner sacrifice petals is most often found in the third petal (and the first) to open, which contains ray energies three through seven. The majority of human souls each exhibits its soul ray type through *creating* virtue during and after the first initiation. The reason is that the third inner sacrifice petal usually begins to open during the first initiation. A second or first ray soul type often exhibits its type of soul ray as it creates virtue during the second and third initiations, respectively, when the associated two inner petals usually begin to open.

The ray type of a human soul is important only concerning how that soul further develops an individual Self, and in how it will eventually fuse with its OverSoul, Self, and personality/ self. Human souls can create virtue through love/wisdom equally well along all seven rays of using senses and energies. As it co-creates and participates with its Self (which is the mental spirit part that it shares with its Solar Angel) in creating *new* knowledge as a part of the Plan, the human soul further develops from its ray, and exhibits qualities of that ray. When a human soul has not yet created a human being who has chosen to spiritually discipline himself or herself and who thus has not begun to fuse with his or her soul, it will usually (in cooperation with its OverSoul) create the potential for a new human being who will incarnate with a soul ray type that corresponds to one of the ray types of energy that is in focus on that planet. These human souls are often the younger ones, who need the added ray focus in order to develop enough sense from the energy within their closed inner "petals" to appropriately (wisely) give the slight thought that they do have to the personality and self, through the Self and the vortices of the mental permanent atom and the mental unit.

Each planet receives a focus of cosmic rays that are directed by the Ray Lords who surround that planet and who make up a sub-category of the cosmic Ray Lords. Each planetary Ray Lord is an ascended Monad who has chosen, as its path of development, service through giving one of its bodies for use as a dimensional space within which a planet can develop. These advanced Beings work in conjunction with other advanced Beings (from the Cosmic Intuitional Universe) who inform groups of constellations that are focusing the cosmic rays onto our solar system. At present, at any one time, earth receives from the above-listed sources a directed focus of four of the seven cosmic rays. One of these rays changes focus, on average today, about every hundred to several hundred years and will continue to do so with increasing frequency until a fifth focused ray becomes added. Then the cycle continues, with one additional ray being focused on at a time in each subsequent round. The next change in the number of rays to be focused on at one time will occur sooner than the period of time that it took for the fifth one to be newly added, and subsequent changes, in which one of the five rays are focused on will, come at an increasing rate until a sixth one is added. Note that the seventh focused ray is added in a corresponding manner. Each time the total number of rays that will be focused on at one time is increased, the entire process is accelerated—the first change in ray focus occurs more quickly, *and* the ray focus then changes more frequently. The focus of the cosmic rays increases the type of senses in a lifeform that then become accelerated in their development. As more rays change more often, life diversifies and changes more often; as more rays are added, life grows faster. Without intelligent activity replacing forces that are produced by energy, or without more light created in the senses of lifeforms (without spirit creating enough virtue), too-rapid changes of focused rays or too many rays focused on a planet (or both) can destroy lifeforms and the growth of life. The reason is that many forces are created within and among the lifeforms. These forces further separate the lifeforms' senses and the lifeforms from each other in space (and time).

Many more relatively younger human souls incarnate on a planet when rays change. The reason is that the younger souls whose ray focus and sense focus of energy in their closed inner petals corresponds to the new incoming ray tend to incarnate human beings at the same time. A more advanced human soul (and especially one that has helped to create, in potential, a human who had begun to fuse with it through spiritual discipline) incarnates a new human more often and with less or no regard for the ray focus. These souls each create the potential for a human to incarnate based upon *the needs of other souls* and what service the human can contribute to the plan for the planet to grow more enlightened life.

 SUMMARY OF CHAPTER SIX

In summation of Chapter Six, souls are critical in the development of life within the lowest three dimensions, or worlds, of our universe. They function using a fifth ray method of life creation within their mental form and the spirit it surrounds, by balancing (through structure) the spirit and the mental energies within themselves. Group souls balance their spirit to only one ray type of energy—limiting the creativity and diversity of their lifeform creations. Human souls go on to create using all seven ray types of energy, mentally balanced in structure to their spirit. These souls create human lifeforms who are immensely more creative than the most advanced lifeforms that any group soul (of animals or the lower kingdoms) can create. Eventually human souls increase the light within their spirit and energy (form) to create a perfection between their spirit and energy; the perfection is full enlightenment of the spirit and energy, with twice as much spiritual thought within the soul as the amount of sense, or than just the thought of the human soul's surrounding energies. As a result, through the fourth ray line the human soul has made itself beautiful through its creation of beauty in some of its service to others. When this level of service is consistently achieved, the human soul frees itself from mental, or structured, thought and raises itself into controlled intuitive thought on the next higher (the intuitional) plane. The human soul then consistently uses intuitive thought that always creates beauty in its service. At this point, the human soul has become a part of a super-human with shared thought from the same Self as its fusing Solar Angel, whose shared new focus is to create an ascended Monad.

Human souls begin their existence by receiving the highest level of enlightened spirit and solar pitri energy that comes from the most advanced animal group souls, and each group soul is along one of seven rays; the human soul receives all seven rays of solar deva energy from this animal group soul collection from the planet it is created on. The solar deva energy surrounds the spirit within the human soul in three formations of "petals." What is usually the first petal to open comprises third through seventh ray solar deva energy; the second petal, second ray solar deva energy; and usually the last petal to open, first ray solar deva energies. These inner sacrifice petals are closed around the spirit that is within the human soul for most of the soul's existence. The spirit of the human soul is composed of the highest spirit of the prior collections of animal group souls *and* a "spark," or fusion, created by the new Solar Angel's mental plane Self intensely focused on the spirit. Surrounding the entire human higher mental body is the collection of solar devas, in "lotus petal" formations, that make up the lowest part of the OverSoul's mental body. These are sacrificially given to the human soul at the beginning of its life. The lowest three of these solar devas, which form the lowest petal of the causal body, are sacrificed by the human soul for use by each new personality and self that the soul helps to create in potential. The solar pitris of the causal body have been developed into superior higher mental senses of higher mental plane thought and this thought's effect on higher mental plane elemental energies. The three lowest solar pitris of the causal body can sense thought coming from the personality and self alone; the solar pitris on the third sub-plane, or tier, that are above these three need to, in addition, sense thought that is emphasized by the personality, the self, and (to a lesser amount) the soul, because the thought is somewhat giving. The solar pitris of the causal body on the second sub-plane, or tier, can still sense the thought coming from the personality and self, and the human soul; however, to do so, the soul's thought on the second tier must have greater emphasis than the thought of the personality and its self, and needs to be used in relatively greater amounts than the (lower) thought of these two. First tier solar devas, on the first sub-plane, can sense the fused thought of the personality to the human soul, that of the self to the Self, and that of the human soul slightly fused with the Monad and its Solar Angel through their shared mental Self.

The fusing of the human soul to the Self as a shared part of the Solar Angel is sometimes referred to in spiritual terms as the Cosmic Marriage. The consummation of this Cosmic Marriage occurs when the Master and Solar Angel fuse and become a Monad on the first sub-plane of the monadic plane just prior to their ascending to the logoic plane. Once the solar pitris of the causal body can sense a thought, they also can sense the higher mental elemental energies that the thought is affecting and getting these energies to follow. This elemental energy then creates an abstract higher mental moving picture of the *structure* in the thought, at the picture's corresponding position in the higher mental body and the mental mind. The structured moving abstraction can be held for only a split second to up to possibly two, by just the initial outside thought from either the personality and self, or from both these two and a less advanced human soul's thought. The appropriately sensing solar devas within the causal body immediately re-create the outside informing thought (as the elemental energy is forming the concept on the inside) and take over the creation of the structure for the holding together of the higher mental elemental energy into a moving picture of the structure in the thought, or into a concept. A moving picture without the structure of thought is creative imagination, or thought created by spirit within the astral body. This thought is missing the third part of time—the future. The thought can create neither structure within nor the structure of the picture, nor can it complete causal time, of cause (concepts) and effects (thoughtforms), which would indicate the causes of the movement. Sometimes, depending on how much they have been used and developed, the causal solar devas can hold the outside structure of a concept together from their re-created mental thought for several minutes or longer. The longer they can hold the outside structure of the one or more concepts (or moving picture of the structure) together, the better, or the more completely, the personality and self will be able to construct the thoughtforms (with each thoughtform being a non-moving structured picture). The personality and self create the forms of words on the lower mental plane in order to represent the one or more concepts. For example, while the reader was reading this paragraph of thoughtforms (and the other paragraphs in *Life's Hidden Meaning*, as well), it is hoped that he or she created the originally structured non-moving pictures of the words into structured moving pictures of the thoughtforms that came together as sentences (the better readers *re*construct whole—containing all three time zones—moving pictures of just the structure of each sentence). These sentences are re-created moving pictures that are constructed from the effects of the concepts on the lower mental mind. Each re-creation can then be put into a structured motion within the lower mental mind as a picture example of one or more of the three parts of time of the conceptual moving picture *of the structure* within the higher mental mind. The structure is re-created in the higher mental mind from the example of effects in the lower. Then the reader understands the structure rather than merely the moving picture and a single example as an effect. Alternately, a person may first think conceptually of a structure as a moving picture that represents it, and then create the thoughtforms to represent the effects of the structure in movement, or concept. The latter method creates a moving picture of forms of a specific example in time in space, or as events taking place. The result is one or more whole sentences if, in their structure, they correctly represent the concept and contain all three parts of time in logical order. The building of the concept with the effects in thoughtforms and sentences reduces forces and produces wisdom. (See illustrations 12.3 and 12.7.)

The personality and its self create thoughtforms that attempt to be whole, or that correctly describe the time and space within which a concept is taking place. They also can be used to determine the accuracy of the concept by checking its potential for creating accurate movement in time or space. Doing so employs the use of logic, or wholeness in time, in the lower mind. Logic then provides the concept with a means of being communicated to others that includes the level of intelligent activity both within the concept and within the thoughtforms conveying it. When thoughtforms are whole in relation to the concept they describe, they join with the concept to create some level of wisdom, or relatively whole structured thought. When some of the human soul's thought is included in the concept and the subsequently created thoughtform, intelligent activity can be created. This is accomplished by enlightening the energies in the minds of both the one communicating and in those being communicated to or with. The thought of the human soul is spiritual because it both contains *and* gives light to others. A personality who is thinking with its soul is thinking in light, and then fuses with its soul. The fusion process is one of the personality joining with its soul through the second means of electrical attraction to, or invoking, a higher source (field) of thought—through radiated light. The personality then connects with the soul's field of thought (the fusion occurs in the larger field). The process takes place because the personality first chooses to think in light within its own, the smaller, field of life. As the personality fuses with its soul, it uses less of its prior electrical method of movement through energy that is unenlightened. This method, which is also known as the third cosmic fire, produced friction, or heat that was wasted energy and was retained because of a lack of light; note that fusion is the second cosmic fire. In the friction process, the retention of energy would then separate the personality and isolate it from other spirit and energy, and, to some degree, from the thought of its own spirit.

Each personality and self whom the human soul creates in potential, with the help of its OverSoul and Self, is constructed to improve upon the last created personality and self through a variety of methods, as follows. Sometimes greater wisdom was developed during the person's last lifetime; any wisdom that is created and given to others as service remains immortally in the soul. Different ray bodies and corresponding emphasized ray centers and their senses may be chosen, thereby creating a unique person in each incarnation (more about this will be covered in the next several chapters). If virtue was created by the former incarnation of a person's soul, the thoughtforms in the mental unit will be better-constructed and there will be improved structure to the mental permanent atom—from which the new personality is, in part, created. In addition, when the self creates virtue in any one incarnation, it (the self) develops and somewhat fuses with the Self. This then adds virtuous parts to each new self and its structure (from the improved spirit on the lower mental plane). Further, there may be an increase in the spins of the vortices on the mental unit, caused by the increased spins of the vortices on the mental permanent atom, with both of these increases resulting in the later fusion of the Self and human soul. The increase in spins that resulted from the prior personality allowing spiritual thought to reach its self leads to a stronger conscience. It also leads to better receptivity to potential structured thought from the Self to the self. Both occur as the result of virtuous messages coming through more clearly as the personality controls the self less. Finally, help is available from other advancing souls and their Selves. The collection of these developments that occurred in one or more prior incarnations improves the quality, or consciousness, of each new personality and its self. In addition, this collection develops the human soul and brings it closer to fusing with its Self. The Self is more creative in its thought than is the soul because the first part of God's mind is emphasized in the Self's growth; the soul's creation of thought is more focused on giving its growth, thus emphasizing more of the second part of God's mind. When the Self and soul fuse, they double the thought of spirit and simultaneously balance God's thought, or the light, within them. The Self and soul accomplish this by creating virtue in service to others in the three lower worlds through the use of each personality and its self. The human soul is also enlightening the solar energies in the three inner sacrifice petals while it fuses with its Self. It is creating twice as much thought than the amount of energy, or form, which makes up its body by fusing with its Self. Further, the soul is balancing its thought completely to the thought of the mental plane Ray Lord while it fully enlightens its causal body of solar devas through creating more service with its virtue. When completed, the human soul, its fused Self, and its fully enlightened solar deva body are beautified, or perfectly balanced between fully mentally enlightened spirit and energy.

The liberated human soul, or the Soul, is returning to full enlightenment and eventually to a state of fully intelligent activity. Then the soul and Solar Angel will together become a Monad who will ascend itself through fully joining together the three parts of God's mind into One. All of the energy, as solar devas, within the fused Solar Angel and liberated super-human soul (the Soul—either of the two together are spelled with an uppercase "s") become fully intelligent activity as the shared Triad of Selves are joined into a newly fused Monad at the top of the monadic plane and are sacrificed on the logoic plane. The pilgrim has returned as a self-created and grown part of its Creator. The Soul and Solar Angel and then the "Father" are "One."

Souls are the most significant element in creating meaning to life. The reason is that they help to create more of life, and its diversity, than any other part of life in the lower worlds. The human soul is the instrument used to create immortality in all life that is part of the soul, and it creates meaning to a human being's life. More advanced humans who are not creating virtue and are thus separated from the time that their souls live within, have lifetimes that span, on average, the equivalent in total time of about one hundred fifty etheric/dense physical earth years. This time includes pre-birth as well as physical life, and, after physical death, life on the astral and mental planes. To the human alive on the astral or mental plane after physical death, the experiential time is much longer. Up to thousands of years of time can be experienced, with an average of about one thousand. However, the parts of the personality and self that are not fused to their soul eventually disintegrate. They do so because only God's thought, or light in spirit, survives along with God's activity, which is always intelligent, and which survives as form (and which must be joined with enlightened spirit). The soul is the "glue" of life that joins together the enlightened parts of life through its own *selfless* giving. Human souls alone on the second mental sub-plane have neither selves nor Selves; instead, in humans, the soul fuses with the advanced self of each personality and with the Self or, later, its intuitional and spiritual plane Selves of its Solar Angel. Souls can accomplish this only as each personality permits its self to fuse with its Self. A personality chooses to allow such fusing as it fuses with and becomes its soul through mutual wise giving to others in service. The personality is overcoming its fears of losing its self (as its self further develops and fuses with the Self). In group souls, fusion with the self occurs directly, as both the self and fusing group soul fuse with the Self to some small degree. A human soul eventually, when it becomes an ascended Soul, fully fuses with its Selves and its Solar Angel, who shares the three Selves of the Spiritual Triad.

The original primary and most important concept to the meaning for the life of group souls is to diversify lifeforms through averaging of individuality of the best mental plane spirit and energy that they can affect. The thought of each group soul is averaged in pre-concepts that it creates and forms, with the averaging creating forces in order to keep one energy balanced with others that are either similar or dissimilar. This process is the engine of evolution and is amazingly effective for the lower levels of lifeforms in the kingdoms below the human. Diversity of life through averaging produces great forces in the life. A group soul somewhat offsets these forces through the assistance from and fusion with its Self—from its informing Solar Angel, or OverSoul. Group souls eventually create light in some of their lifeforms and the lifeforms' centers and senses. As they become individuals, these somewhat enlightened lifeforms wisely give more energy than the amounts of force they produce, with force being the amount that one energy is against another. As this wise giving occurs, meaning increases in the group soul's life.

A human being can choose, by being selfish and unwise, to live by creating more forces in life. These created forces prevent a person from fusing with her or his soul, which has learned to create either *no* forces in its thought and created life, or not to think until it can, but to consequently live less. Without their souls, humans are so selfish that they destroy them*selves*—they create the very thing that each human fears the most, which is the destruction of one's self. They *lose* their individuality as they create the forces that the lower kingdoms and their group souls develop growth from. As a human fuses with his or her soul, he or she stops thinking and living like lower-level animals might, who create force in their lives in order to diversify. The human can, through its fused soul, become individual by creating its self into its Self and a part of God. Instead of life's meaning becoming increasingly diminished, from forces created by selfishness that destroy a person, life's meaning can become a *permanently* and *continuously* growing part of virtue and of God. The *clear* choice is for either suffering and death, or for immortality, love, and life—which is the gift of the light of the soul.

THE BODIES AND THE SENSES

Illustration 7.1

Author's Suggestion: First turn to the "Glossary Help Guide" and read the definitions for this chapter.

 SUMMARY OF INFORMATION FROM CHAPTER SIX

In the last chapter, souls were described as the lowest part of God's growth, or life, that can maintain a balance in the light, or in God's thought, within their form and spirit. Souls contain enough light to recognize and understand the second part of God's mind from the higher mental plane, down, as this part of God's mind functions within life. Souls on the mental plane have and further develop the lower spiritual sense of God because of the enlightened balance that they maintain between their spirit and energy. They do not, however, have the higher spiritual sense of—the awareness of—God that comes from creating new (mental) thought and from *being* a functional part of God, which is the result of creating more virtue through *new* thought. To obtain this higher spiritual sense requires that the soul fuse with its (higher) Self, which is also the lowest part of its Solar Angel's Self structure. Fusion with the (mental plane) Self can occur only as the soul's (lower) self creates more of the (higher) Self by being conscious for the one or more lifeforms that the soul and self inform in the three lower worlds. In a human being, the personality is the controlling entity of a person and her or his three lower bodies and senses. It is up to the personality to choose to give the consciousness of its self to its Self, for the Self's further creation of virtue within the human lifeform that it (the Self) and its soul informs. The personality's greatest fear is the loss of its self and the corresponding consciousness that the self creates. To the personality, this loss is *real* death, so it attempts to avoid such a possibility at nearly any cost. Through the vortices of the mental unit and then under the control of the personality, the self receives the transmitted enlightened thought from the Self; the thought is transmitted from the mental permanent atom's vortices. This thought is given to the personality, who controls whether the self will be given to its Self; when the self gives itself the personality *gains* in consciousness. However, until the personality allows itself to receive enough of the Self's enlightened thought—and to not ignore this thought or block it from being transmitted through the mental unit's vortices—it will not permit this giving to occur. When the personality eventually allows the giving of thought and consciousness of its self to the Self, it begins to function in the way that its soul does because then the personality with its self is giving wisely. As it shares wise giving as part of its thought, the personality begins to fuse with its soul. It begins to give the use of the information and knowledge from its lower bodies and senses to its soul, with which to create more virtue.

Soul infusion with the personality leads to spiritual discipline. It leads to establishing a commonality of spiritual concepts in the higher mind. These are created and given in spiritual service by the personality and soul who have fused together. A bridge of rainbow-colored light is formed from the radiance of solar pitris that are used to create and give these shared spiritual concepts that are used for service. The first part of the bridge produces additional consciousness in the personality and self after they have created some spiritual thought and service. The second part of the bridge, from the human soul to its Self, *adds* spiritual thought as the lower two (the personality and self) create their spiritual thought—before they complete it and before they serve with it, but as they are about to do so—making them much more spiritually creative in their thinking. Finally, the third leg of this triangular-shaped bridge is built by additional radiance from higher solar devas, which adds increasing *memory* (which is present from birth) of past spiritual thought and service. This part of the bridge spans from the mental permanent atom and its surrounding Self to the personality and its self, which are contained within the mental unit. This third leg, which completes the triangle of radiance, substantially joins the higher mental plane permanent atom with the mental unit. It joins higher mental time and space to part of the lower mental plane. This effectuates a continuity in thought from one lifetime to another of spiritual memories. When the third leg has been built, the personality overcomes most of its fears. The reason is that its fear of loss of self is replaced by its (the personality's) identification with its immortal Self. The personality's fears have become abolished by the creations of virtue by its soul's prior personalities as well as its current one. The personality has created continuity of consciousness between lifetimes within its self by fusing with its soul and its light and thus creating immortality.

Souls always give, and human souls are the wisest givers of all souls who are found exclusively on the mental plane. Unlike group souls, human souls can use all of the mental plane at the same time in order to create whole thought. They do this in conjunction with a fusing personality because the personality controls the three lowest solar pitris of the causal body and the construction of thoughtforms in the lower mental body. When a relatively whole, or spiritual, concept is connected to relatively whole thoughtforms, then wisdom is created; as this wisdom is given in service to others, the soul and its fusing personality develop the capacity of love/wisdom, or whole thought on the mental plane. Human souls focus on creating love/wisdom, while group souls focus on the development of either love or wisdom, but not both together because they are so limited by their preconceptual thought. Love/wisdom is what allows the human soul to participate in consciously understanding God. It then allows the human soul to be able to communicate this understanding to a cooperative personality and self. Life in the kingdoms lower than the human cannot understand God because the souls in these kingdoms cannot think in love/wisdom. One proof of this concept is that even advanced apes—the highest form of wild animals on earth, or of any wild life that is lower than human—have no spiritual creations. Although some animals sometimes express love through individual acts, animals have no religion for communing with God, no expressions in behavior that suggest an understanding of a God, and no known behavior that manifests consciousness of the oneness of all life. One example of this lack is that even though some animals do sometimes give to other animals that are similar to themselves, no animal—no matter how advanced—has ever been known to be out doing charity work for life that is different from itself. This point is further emphasized when acts of charity are included towards lifeforms that are quite different from those that are doing the giving, i.e., apes have yet to be observed working to save the whales. The reason is that animals cannot understand the oneness of life; they can experience only the life that they are aware of being a part of and sometimes interacting with. Animals certainly can love, which is mostly an expression from their respective very loving group souls and each group soul's self. But humans can love *God*, which means that humans sometimes *understand* both love *and* God, and when they do, this understanding causes them to want to create love/wisdom in others so that love (one-third of God's mind) can further grow.

At this point, some readers may experience a revelation regarding God's purpose. It has thus far been stated in *Life's Hidden Meaning* that one part of God's purpose for creating all things in our universe and life is for life to create more of God by eventually becoming a part of God. Souls, and particularly the human soul when it is understood well enough, reveal another purpose of God. This purpose is to create life—especially the human part of life—for God to love, *and as the most important part of this concept*, the creations of life are free to choose to love God (life), as they create themselves into a functional part of God. Since God is everything within our universe, loving God (or all of life as God's growth, as a lower correspondence) is the same as receiving love from everything else that loves. It also means that love (giving) causes one to, at the same time, receive it. "Love is its own reward" is a great self-evident truth. God's love/wisdom is perfect, and the human soul is striving to create perfect love/wisdom in all it encounters, including itself. This second revelation is supplied by understanding that the human soul is the second part of God's mind actualized into spirit and form. Humans are so fortunate that they have the opportunity to become a part of this amazing gift of love of life—which God created and the human soul supplies.

The capability to love life is a gift to the human from its soul; loving life increases a human being's ability to receive meaning from life through loving others. Life becomes increasingly meaningful for a younger soul and its created personality as each of these personalities grows more of his or her self. After a certain developmental point in a soul's and a human's life, meaning can be further created *only* through growth of the self by giving more to other parts of life, as God's growth—which is also the growth of the Self. Advanced wild animals receive the astral sensation of love as they love others, but they cannot understand the love and cannot, therefore, derive meaning in their lives through their love. Some pets manifest an exception to this concept because a small amount of an understanding of love may be transferred between the human master(s) and the pet. With this gift of receiving meaning to life when one loves, and increasingly more meaning as the love is *wisely* given, comes an immense responsibility to love and a dire consequence in suffering should a person, through his or her own choices, fail to meet this responsibility. The responsibility is for a person to love, at a minimum, to the level that he or she can understand the love. This includes an understanding of the one(s) being loved and his or her (or its or their) needs to receive this love.

If one loves either irresponsibly, too little, or not at all, then meaning to life diminishes for that person. The loss in meaning occurs because her or his personality suffers from a substantially increased fear of death, which often translates into many and varied superficial fears for the purpose of masking this deeper fear. The intensified fear of death comes from a loss of self, which is resultant of the personality not using the self to give its (the self's) consciousness, or understanding, to the Self. The Self needs more understanding from the self regarding the person's experiences in life so that as the self and Self fuse, they can improve the person's life by helping to increase his or her creation of virtue in it. The less virtue created, the greater the selfishness, and the more suffering and fear of death a person creates for him or herself. The "rainbow bridge" gradually fuses the self to the Self by creating more virtue in life in the lower three worlds. It accomplishes this feat by connecting the self and the Self through radiance. Radiance is the completely enlightened energy of solar devas (solar pitris) and the associated mental elemental energies when concepts are formed while these energies are controlled by the solar pitris. (See Chapter Six for more information on the rainbow bridge.) The structure of the completed connection of light (the rainbow bridge) also transfigures the human soul. The reason is that the structured light perfectly balances the energy within the human soul to its spirit, through the use of mental plane light. When a human soul has become completely transfigured, it ascends into the intuitional body on the intuitional plane. It can then use its three lower bodies completely as vehicles of spiritual service, as is needed in the Plan.

THE MAJOR CENTERS' CONSTRUCTION

THE PERMANENT ATOMS

If the three lower bodies and their senses are to be of use to spirit in spiritual service, they need to become gradually enlightened from one lifetime of a personality and self to the next, or by each incarnated person of a human soul. The prior levels of overall light, or lack thereof, in each body and its senses need to be stored so that each subsequent life can be built upon the preceding one. The bodies require a memory that is created from the thought of energies. They do so because the thought of lower spirit within any personality and self that was used selfishly enough to create a lack of light, or darkness, does not become a part of either the human soul or its Self. As a result of lower spirit's own thought of identifying itself with form rather than with God's thought, or light, it increasingly forgets who it is as the three lower bodies and their senses lose integration during its process of dying from each of them. The lower spirit does remain, but without a self. This is because the self disintegrates as the three lower bodies and senses, along with the controlling personality, fail to supply adequate sense and knowledge that would allow the self to give at least half of its field of thought. (See Chapter Five for further explanation.) The self then becomes simply more of the darker, or fallen, human spirit on the lower mental plane.

The permanent atoms are the energies that contain the memory information relinquished from within the three lower bodies between lifetimes. They are called atoms because they reside at the highest level of time and space for a dimension that a lifeform can exist within while being informed by its self. For humans, this level is the atomic level of each plane they are alive on. A permanent atom is the most basic, or a fundamental, "blueprint" or design for each entire body. In mundane terms only, permanent atoms are conceptually resemblant of genes. Each permanent atom is composed of the highest level of relatively enlightened *deva* energies that are in that lifeform on the corresponding plane. For example, somewhat enlightened lunar deva energies create a permanent atom for humans at the atom's highest point at which these devas can be conscious of the human self's and its Self's informing thought (they are group conscious), through connection with their respective selves. This location is the first sub-plane of both the etheric and astral planes. Without the group consciousness of these lunar devas, selves would be unable to keep permanent atoms together, and the permanent atoms would fall apart. Solar deva energies on the first sub-plane and on the atomic level of the mental plane are used to create the mental permanent atom there. The devas on the first sub-plane that do not have enough consciousness to be there unaided can be sustained in their position by the balancing of forces within the permanent atoms' structures. The very highest point in the structure of each human permanent atom is fully enlightened intelligent activity because it reaches into the atomic level of its plane. The remaining parts of each human permanent atom are located on the first sub-plane of its plane. All mental permanent atoms for all lifeforms are found on the first sub-plane and, to the level that they are fully enlightened, at the atomic level of the mental plane; however, the etheric and astral permanent atoms of lifeforms lower than human are found at the highest

The Creation of the Bodies from the Three Lowest Permanent Atoms

The soul and the self attract and direct from their thought both fully enlightened and somewhat unenlightened pitris from the three lower permanent atoms, to re-create certain parts of each permanent atom's structure. These pitris on each of these planes attract and direct, from their slight thought, other lunar pitris that then attract elemental energies from the lower parts of that plane, to form the body on that plane.

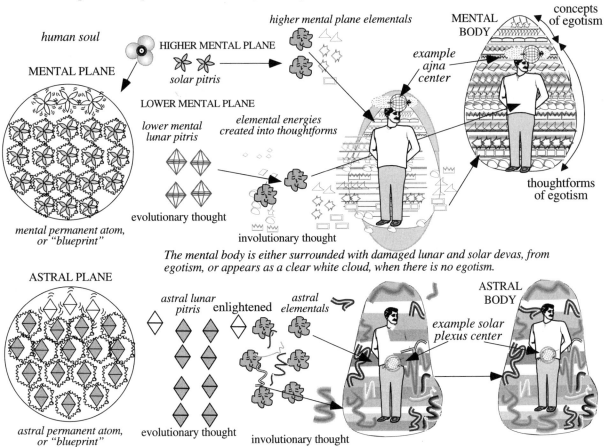

The mental body is either surrounded with damaged lunar and solar devas, from egotism, or appears as a clear white cloud, when there is no egotism.

The astral body either contains selfishness as emotions and glamours, or appears as a clear rose cloud when there is no selfishness.

The lunar and solar pitris follow the blueprint, or the structure of the permanent atom, to re-create the design for that body on that specific plane. Next, the elemental energies "pour" into the blueprint, and the pitris continue to provide structural containment in order for the energies to provide a body.

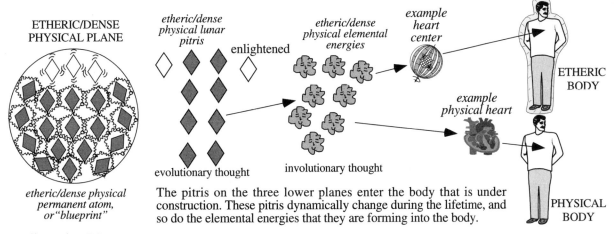

The pitris on the three lower planes enter the body that is under construction. These pitris dynamically change during the lifetime, and so do the elemental energies that they are forming into the body.

Illustration 7.2

level of the etheric and astral planes whereupon the self of the group soul can be conscious to any extent. For more advanced animals in general, this location is the second sub-plane of both the astral and etheric planes. For the most advanced plants in general, it is the third sub-plane of the astral and etheric planes, and for many bacteria and some molds and viruses (when they are not infecting a higher lifeform), it is the fourth etheric and the seventh astral sub-planes. The permanent atoms for group souls' lifeforms are used as a pattern for its collective group of lifeforms.

The way in which a permanent atom operates is that the relatively enlightened devas (the highest levels of light among *all* the energy within a body), in humans, for example, contain all of the information from one of the bodies that was used by a person in his or her most recent incarnation, along with information from earlier lifetimes that was not changed in the most recent one. This information, as energy, is that which was taken in through the senses of the body and either given to another, possibly in service, or retained in selfishness, in which case it eventually produced disease and death. The information in a permanent atom is *not* memory of knowledge that had been synthesized by the spirit. This sensory information (as energy) in the permanent atom is stored in time-sensitive form that is crystallized; it is structured in a way that prevents atrophy of the energy by balancing one energy with another, thus equalizing the forces in those parts of the atom that are *not* enlightened. In the enlightened parts of the atom's form, no forces are created because those devas, or pitris, are either semi-individualized (the astral and etheric lunar devas) or fully individualized (the mental solar devas). The light replaces the need for balancing and holding energies, because light is God's thought and can attract new energies to itself according to the energies' need for the light, so that they can give it. The mental solar pitris can become fully individualized when they are enlightened because they exist within all three parts of time, or within whole time. The etheric and astral lunar pitris within the permanent atoms can reach only partial individualization because they experience and think only within one or two parts of the three that whole time contains. When devas somewhat or completely individualize they can think for themselves at a level that matches their amount of individualization. Thus all the fully enlightened deva energies, including those of the etheric and astral permanent atoms that are not completely individualized, can maintain the memory of the most recent personality's corresponding body within their *thought*, whereas the less enlightened devas must preserve a record of that body through crystallized structure, or a design that contains energies whose forces are balanced.

In both of the above-described cases, the permanent atoms construct the bodies incrementally through the following process. The deva energy is called upon by the higher spirit's thought within the soul and the soul's Self, both of which are following the will of their Monad to create life; this energy follows the additional thought of surrounding spirit and re-creates certain parts of a permanent atom's structure using surrounding and responsive elemental energies. Deva energies at lower levels than those that are not enlightened in the permanent atom are brought into the body being constructed through the crystallized structure of energies. The enlightened parts of the permanent atom bring in only the enlightened and at least somewhat individualized devas into the bodies. The enlightened and lower deva energy then helps to contain the elemental energies, which then remain intact for fairly long periods of time. However, the entire body and the permanent atom that is creating it—the either lunar or solar deva, and the elemental energies—are in a dynamic and mostly continual exchange of slightly better- or worse-thinking energies of all the types of energies present, unless they are fully enlightened.

The relatively more enlightened deva energy (either solar or lunar, depending upon the body) within each permanent atom controls some of the lower devas on each corresponding plane. The level of enlightenment of these lower deva energies is determined by the level of force being balanced within the structure between the less than fully enlightened devas within the permanent atom. This control comes from the greater thought of the relatively more enlightened deva

The Etheric Centers

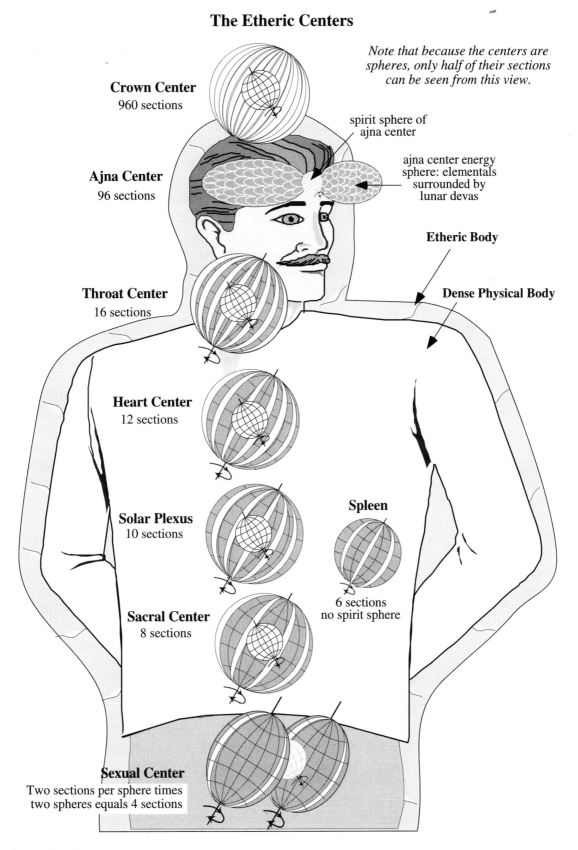

Crown Center
960 sections

Ajna Center
96 sections

Throat Center
16 sections

Heart Center
12 sections

Solar Plexus
10 sections

Sacral Center
8 sections

Spleen

6 sections
no spirit sphere

Sexual Center
Two sections per sphere times
two spheres equals 4 sections

*Note that because the centers are
spheres, only half of their sections
can be seen from this view.*

spirit sphere of
ajna center

ajna center energy
sphere: elementals
surrounded by
lunar devas

Etheric Body

Dense Physical Body

Illustration 7.3

energy, which attracts the lesser thought of the lower devas. The lower devas follow the thought of the higher devas to create structures, and then use elemental energy to fill in these structures. The structures are like molds, or forms, and are constructed directly from the deva energy. Once a form is constructed, the elemental energy "pours" into and around it; the elemental energy is attracted to and directed by the thought of the devas, which is slight, but still stronger than its own thought. This energy then stays together without constant thought from the informing devas until a change is directed by informing spirit and the permanent atom or until degradation occurs from frictional forces by retained energies. Elemental energy is lower in thought and follows the higher thought of the deva energy. What causes the elemental energy to maintain its shape is the involutionary nature of this energy. It seeks to join together with other energy that is similar to it, and then it is resistant against movement (other than its gravitation from and towards itself). Every day, small amounts of the elemental energies of humans' bodies are changed from their original structure, as a result of the forces created by selfish informing thought of spirit. This selfish thought comes from the self and is directed by the personality. This change in the energy is corrected mainly at night while (or any time when) a person is sleeping. During those times the personality and its self are mostly dissolved, which allows the solar and lunar devas to be fully in control. The primitive consciousness of elemental energy is what keeps bodies intact, but is also what makes elemental energy so difficult to change. The first forms, or structures, created are those that will control the body's functioning. These structures are the major centers, with the informing fallen spirit becoming a sphere as a part of them.

Some of the structures within the permanent atoms of a person who is about to incarnate need to match the genetic information within the soul and Solar Angel's chosen fetus's etheric/dense physical body. The permanent atoms define the new human's forms, or bodies, and therefore—acting karmically—control which fetus would provide an appropriate etheric/dense physical body. Human souls are limited (karmically) to incarnating only into bodies that have some (usually over one-half) matching structure in their genes that correspond to the permanent atoms. More than one fetus may match enough structures in the permanent atoms to be a suitable match for a particular human to incarnate into. However, if no fetus's genes adequately match the permanent atoms' structures, a soul is prevented from incarnating. Some souls are too advanced to incarnate at a relatively early period of human development on a planet, and must wait for the availability of more advanced bodies. The souls who fall behind in their development on a planet may reach a point at which *no* fetuses have a genetic structure that is at a low enough level to match the structure of the soul's mental permanent atom. In such a case, that soul will need to leave the planet for a more primitive one, and possibly permanently (see Chapter Nine for more information about this process). Notice that the choice of parents for a newly incarnating human is somewhat controlled by the need for genetic matching to her or his permanent atoms, *plus* there are likely additionally karmic connections, as described in Chapter Eleven.

Every lifeform has at least two major centers in one body on that body's corresponding plane, and at least one in the next higher body and plane. All plants have at least this total of three centers on two planes (see illustration 7.9). An animal that is physically alive (and not parasitic) has at least three major centers on the etheric/dense physical plane and in its etheric body, and three on the astral plane and in its astral body. Each major center is a sphere of rotating energies, both deva and elemental. The rotation is at first established by the relative direction, or consciousness, of the controlling thought of the devas within the permanent atom for that body. In the case of group souls of large numbers of either animals, plants, or minerals that have little differentiation among them, one permanent atom per plane (etheric and astral) may be used for the group of evolving pre-life or lifeforms. The more advanced the lifeform and the more virtuous its life, the more closely the center's angle of rotation matches that of the Ray Lord of the corresponding plane. For all lifeforms, the controlling thought of higher spirit (from the human

The Consciousness and Life (Sutratma) Threads

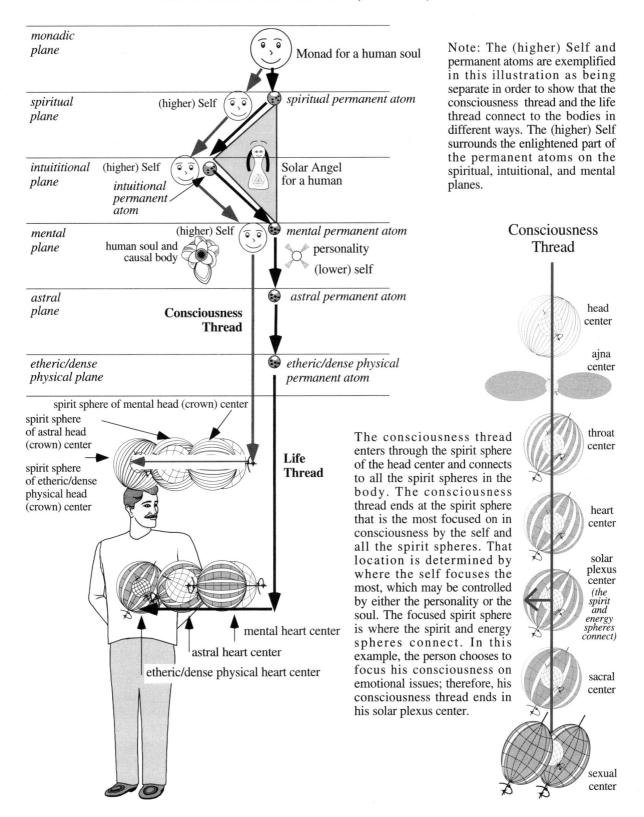

Note: The (higher) Self and permanent atoms are exemplified in this illustration as being separate in order to show that the consciousness thread and the life thread connect to the bodies in different ways. The (higher) Self surrounds the enlightened part of the permanent atoms on the spiritual, intuitional, and mental planes.

Consciousness Thread

The consciousness thread enters through the spirit sphere of the head center and connects to all the spirit spheres in the body. The consciousness thread ends at the spirit sphere that is the most focused on in consciousness by the self and all the spirit spheres. That location is determined by where the self focuses the most, which may be controlled by either the personality or the soul. The focused spirit sphere is where the spirit and energy spheres connect. In this example, the person chooses to focus his consciousness on emotional issues; therefore, his consciousness thread ends in his solar plexus center.

Illustration 7.4

soul and its Solar Angel and Self along with the will of the Monad) must activate and direct the permanent atoms (one per plane per lifeform), with the major centers of the lower bodies informed by the spirit on the plane where they are located. These lower major centers are the lower mental, the astral, the etheric/dense physical. There are higher mental centers as well, which function somewhat differently. Because the centers of the higher mental body use solar devas as well as higher mental plane spirit, these centers are somewhat different from those in the lower bodies and will be explained later in this chapter. The, initially, "fallen" spirit that is attracted into the major centers is actually *lower* in consciousness than is much of the energy that surrounds it. This spirit is closer to the average level of consciousness of all energy for the level of plane whereupon it is found, while the energy in each major center is the best-thinking energy that can be attracted into the center by the current level of development of the controlling permanent atom. The spirit forms a sphere that is inside of and on the etheric/dense physical plane and is much smaller than is the energy sphere of every major center in the etheric/dense physical body because of the outside forces produced by the rotating energy sphere and the relative amount of thought of spirit to that of the energy in the energy sphere. There are progressively *much* less forces on the astral and mental planes and consequently, the spirit spheres are larger—as are the levels of spiritual thought within them. The "fallen" spirit within each sphere is, at first, able to think only when it does so at or above the level of the surrounding energy sphere (unless it is within a body of a person who has chosen to be evil and who has actualized this choice). All of the spirit connected to the permanent atoms and in all of the spheres in all of the major centers in each body of a lifeform are connected to each other and to the soul and Solar Angel through a thread, or beam of thought (light) that functions as a ray when it, eventually, controls the energy within the center. This thought comes from a Monad who created the type of soul and spirit that is informing the lifeform. For a human being, the spirit is at the human, or advanced, level of development. This spirit has an individual soul and an advanced Solar Angel who is in the second major triadal stage of development. A developing human Monad consistently focuses its thought as will on a portion of the human spirit that is informing each body below the monadic. The thought, as will, is to create new life; the beam of light that the thought creates is called the life beam, or the life thread of light. Its name in some spiritual language is *sutratma*. In the higher bodies (above the mental body) that a human, technically, has, there exist un-developed permanent atoms surrounded by the spirit, or Self, of the higher triadal parts of the human's Solar Angel. The life thread of light extends through each of these, even though there are no centers nor, therefore, bodies yet developed by the human on (as part of) these higher planes.

Each major center—its outside energy sphere and inner developed or undeveloped spirit sphere—is referred to in spiritual terms as a chakra. Humans have seven major chakras, or centers. A major center always contains the two spheres of informing fallen spirit and of energy. A primary purpose of each center includes creating a sense that is specific to that center. Because each center needs to sense with other centers in each body, the informing thought of spirit and the permanent atom's structure connects each specific sense with other senses from other centers. This purpose also includes the balancing of the information supplied by these senses in ways that maximally contribute to increasing life within that body. The centers and their senses need to cooperate and balance information between the bodies, as well. In lifeforms lower than human, this last function of the senses is accomplished under the control of the self of the group soul, with some assistance coming from its Self. In human beings, the personality controls the integration of the centers and their senses *between* bodies. The control is generally subconscious to its self because the personality usually takes more than it gives, which causes it to not be conscious of itself. The development within each body still generally takes place subconsciously to both the personality and its self, and is regulated by the centers and, when change is needed, is directed by the permanent atom of that body. For short periods of time the personality can, as an unusual occurrence, use force to control individual centers and their respective senses in a body (such as breathing or heart rate, for example), but usually without the self being aware of the personality's control. Note, however, that in the case of controlling breath, the self often would be aware of the control.

As the major centers and their senses are developed and connected together, a second thread of light is connected into the spirit sphere of each of these centers. This second thread of light is created by the spirit in each sphere being integrated and affected by the giving of *all* of the differing energies that surround it, and by the giving on the part of the spirit that is helping to create life within the lifeform. All of this giving, including that of the self, causes the previously "fallen" spirit to become slightly conscious of itself and of its body. At this point the consciousness, or givingness, is being done on a consistent basis and forms a thin thread of the corresponding Ray Lord's virtue, or of light, in each corresponding body. The connected second thread of light allows the personality in humans to supercede and, when it chooses to, take control over some of the functions of the centers. When the personality fuses with its soul, the fused two can fully control all of the centers and their functions within the three human bodies because all of the spirit in these centers has become fully conscious. The second thread of light connects the spirit in the centers to one another and, if in a group soul, to the self, or, if in a human being, to the personality, its self, and its soul; this second thread is referred to as the consciousness thread of light.

The major centers not only create senses in a body, they also create organs and glands. The major centers control entire areas of the body, including many subsidiary minor centers that manage much smaller specialized body functions. A minor center has an energy sphere only, and not a spirit sphere. This holds true whether the body is etheric/dense physical and composed of etheric energies and matter, or is made from the subtle energies of the higher dimensions. Within a body an organ is created and controlled from a center and may organize, transmute, synthesize, and store energies. Each organ might have more than just one part, and, if so, each part will usually focus on one ray type of energy. The main part of an organ (which is sometimes its only part) is focused on the energy that is along the specific ray type of the center that created it. Each major center has an initial focus of one particular ray type of energy. Glands (which are, in a broad, general way, a third ray correspondence in their function) mostly transmute but may also store energy that they then send to organs in order to help the organs in their functions in the body. Glands are also internal timers and messengers for the entire body's growth, and are governed by the permanent atom in most circumstances of growth. Regardless of whether the energy is of matter or of more subtle form, it still requires direction from organs and glands if it is to be properly used, regulated, and replenished within a body. The brain is an extremely important organ in a human because it helps to store and organize information from all of the centers; the human brain's main part stores information from the center that the personality and self within the mental unit use to synthesize the information that they choose from among the other centers in each body. The center that corresponds to the brain is one of the major ones; it is along the fifth ray focus, and is referred to in some spiritual language as the ajna center. Humans have an ajna center in the lower mental, the astral, and the etheric bodies (the ajna center in the higher mental body functions only in a fused state). Most lifeforms do not process enough information from their centers to need brains. The remaining six (of the total seven) major centers of a human are also found in these three bodies. In the etheric/dense physical body, the centers are found only in the etheric, or the causative, part of this divided body that exists on a divided plane. The effect, or the dense physical, part is where the organs and glands are, since the time and space of the etheric plane, as well as the bodies that are constructed from energies within it, are separated because of the selfish thought of spirit and the high density of energy there.

THE CROWN AND HEART CENTERS

Consistent with the purposes of this book, whose primary purpose is to raise the consciousness, or the understanding, of the reader, in this chapter the focus will be mostly on the human bodies and their senses. The reason is that in the three lower worlds, human bodies are the most complete and advanced, and expose how all life is connected and is one, much more so than do bodies in lower kingdoms. The etheric/dense physical, the astral, and the lower mental bodies of a human plus the lowest three solar devas of the causal body are a microcosm of our universe. They reveal, through correspondences to the universe and its planes, and to the ways in which life is created, some of the hidden meaning of life. The crown center in a human is the major center that is along the first ray. It uses first (sub-) ray energies of the body's ray type to create its sense from its energy sphere. This center is found just above the crown of the head in all three bodies, and in the mental body it is found on the higher mental plane. The center becomes functional when a human has become spiritually disciplined and has started serving others; it nourishes the spiritual part of the brain, which synthesizes only spiritual thoughts and related information. Advanced *whole* psychic, or soul, senses are sometimes referred to in spiritual terms as higher psychic senses. As these senses are created from joining together the lower centers and bodies, as well, *through service*, the crown center and three associated minor centers stimulate the growth of esoteric spiritual glands, and, especially, stimulate the growth of the *spiritual* parts of the brain. These esoteric spiritual glands, which have the same names as their corresponding minor centers, are the pineal and the pituitary, and one that is presently unrecognized by modern science—the "carotid." The crown center is referred to in some spiritual language as the crown chakra. For spiritually advanced humans, the consciousness thread from all of the spirit spheres in the centers in each body is focused and connected to the spirit sphere of the crown center. For all humans, the consciousness thread enters into the etheric, astral, and *higher* mental body of each human being through the crown center, which is found in each of these three bodies. Until a lifetime in which a

The Crown Center and Its Associated Major Glands

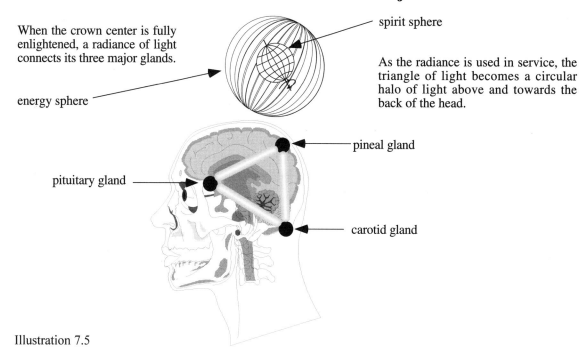

When the crown center is fully enlightened, a radiance of light connects its three major glands.

energy sphere

spirit sphere

As the radiance is used in service, the triangle of light becomes a circular halo of light above and towards the back of the head.

pineal gland

pituitary gland

carotid gland

Illustration 7.5

human creates spiritual service (which excludes most of the human lifetimes created by the soul), this center is only minimally used. The sense created by the crown center is the highest one in the human body. It is the higher *spiritual* sense of being a functional part of God. This sense is used only infrequently until a human develops it by creating herself or himself into a consistent advanced level of service.

The major center with a second ray focus is the one that creates the heart and the thymus gland in a human being, and is referred to as the heart chakra, or heart center. A heart center exists in each of the three lowest human bodies. The life thread enters into each body through the energy sphere of this center, which is also where the end of the life thread is found once the center has become fully developed through virtue created by a human and its soul. Note that in each person, the two threads of light—the life thread and the consciousness thread—end in the center where that person is focused the most during that lifetime in the thought that applies to each of the two threads. The sense developed by the heart center is the awareness of God in life, which leads to the understanding of God—and life. The heart center can be developed to a level of about a third of its full potential to create its corresponding sense, when done so by giving love that is less than fully wise; giving love that *is* fully wise develops the center completely. The more a person can understand the oneness of life (and helping to create this understanding is a major purpose of this book), the more his or her heart center develops. As a person lives her or his life from a recognition and understanding that life is God's growth, the heart and crown centers begin to fuse, and the crown center rapidly develops.

Lunar Deva and Elemental Energy Placement within a Sphere

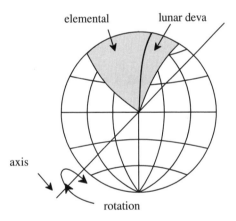

Illustration 7.6

When a center is undeveloped, it inefficiently retains energies within it. This is a result of too much selfish thought created by the person in the use of that center's sense and information. What happens is that the energy is following thought that is greater than its own. Information from each sense is the actual energy that becomes retained. These retained energies tend to move towards the outside of each energy sphere. The forces produced then flatten the energy sphere into a doughnut shape, moving the retained energies more towards its middle part of the outside of the "doughnut," with the spirit sphere occupying the center "hole." The devas in each sphere, when it is round, resemble sections of a peeled orange. The energy sphere comprises a series of a relatively thin section of deva energy that alternates with a more plump section of elemental energy. The attraction of elemental energy to the deva energy's better thought causes the energy sphere of the center to spin. The direction of each center's spin is established in part by the spin of the sexual center, which will be covered later in this chapter. Until a person has used a center and its corresponding sense to create significant amounts of virtue, the center remains flattened, with the sections of energies sometimes giving it a flower-like appearance (usually upside-down on the etheric and astral planes), and with "petals" surrounding a center. Most spiritual writers who have described a center's, or chakra's, appearance have done so similarly to the preceding description because of the relative rarity for a chakra to appear spherical.

View of Etheric Centers:
One with Retained Energy and Illusion, the Other Without

ETHERIC SOLAR PLEXUS CENTER

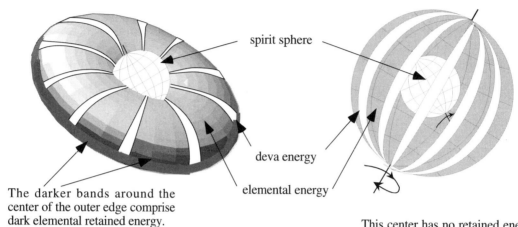

spirit sphere

deva energy

elemental energy

The darker bands around the center of the outer edge comprise dark elemental retained energy.

This center has retained energy and is seen with levels of distortion from illusion of the observer.

This center has no retained energy and is seen from the atomic level.

Illustration 7.7

   THE THROAT CENTERS

In humans the major etheric center that is *initially* of a third ray focus is located around the area of speech, or around the throat. The throat center initially connects regions of the etheric brain that affect the vocal cords, tongue, and neck. The throat center also relates to hearing as a sub-sense because communication through speech requires either physical hearing or its corresponding symbolism as created in the brain. The "sub-" sense of hearing associated with the etheric throat center relates it to the sexual center because that center develops the full sense of hearing, which, again, will be covered herein. The main sense of the throat center in the etheric body is taste, which is actually a sense developed from touch and smell when in a liquid medium that usually contains water. Beyond just supplying a sense of physical taste, this center provides information to the person regarding the speech of others. It conveys, first through hearing, the inflection and tone of other speech, and then through taste as a sense, any gestures, which all greatly color the meaning of the speech. The throat center also provides information that helps a person to communicate with others through her or his speech and its inflection, tone, and gestures. One of the first elements, and an important one, to a person's inflection, tone, and gesturing is his or her gender. Notice how the initial third ray focus of this center causes it to be involved both in communication and the communication's relative levels of intelligence. As the throat center is used more in an intellectually developed and somewhat creative person, its ray focus changes from just the third to the fifth ray added from the ajna center, as well, which helps the person to think before speaking. The throat center eventually fuses with the sexual center as a person begins to spiritually discipline herself or himself in ways that affect these two centers. This adds the fused seventh ray to the third ray of the throat center. As the recognition and creation of speech becomes much more conscious (rather than subconscious, as in most people), the speech part of the *mental* mind in humans becomes joined together with the part that thinks causatively; then the structure of sentences, and their logic and truthfulness become paramount. The etheric throat center also creates and regulates the thyroid and parathyroid glands, which greatly affect metabolism and the rate of oxygen consumption. Oxygen is taken in through the throat area and then becomes absorbed through the lungs and burned in the body. The speed of the heart in its pumping of oxygen and other components of energy, or fuel, is also affected by the throat center and its glands. Oxygen is a third ray element, and in the human body it is mostly controlled by this major third ray center. Oxygen focuses mostly on the transmutative side of the third ray, which is the changing of the density of energies through the use of power. The throat center adds this power aspect to its third ray function through its glands and their relationship to oxygen.

Like its etheric counterpart, the astral throat center initially has a third ray focus in its use of energies. The sense it creates is different from that of the etheric/dense physical body because the energy and the space and time are different; in addition, the speed of the astral Ray Lord's thought (the speed of light on the astral plane) is greater. Unlike the etheric/dense physical senses of a human, all five of the astral senses of form in most humans today are at least somewhat joined together into the single sense of empathy. These five senses of form are controlled by the five rays that are focused on form, or rays three through seven. However, more than one and a half million years ago the astral senses were separated much as the etheric ones still are today, in most people. Senses within a body are either joined through their spirit spheres or are separated, based both upon the level to which the soul over many co-created lifetimes has used them (or not) to create virtue in that body. Over one and a half million years ago, a whole civilization of people who were focused in the development of their astral bodies and senses joined together the five astral senses of form by creating love (the astral virtue) throughout their society in general. This left the two astral senses of spirit, which come from the astral heart and crown centers, still to be fused to each other and then, further, with the already fused five senses of form. When used separately today, the five astral senses of form are known in spiritual terms as *lower* psychic (psychic means soul) senses because these separated senses are somewhat unreliable and are not unified in their sensing of astral energy. When used separately to much of an extent, astral senses quickly diminish and become very unreliable. The reason is that their separation reduces empathy, which, as a unified sense, is a higher sense overall than any of its separated components. Also, the astral energies and physics cause much faster diminishing of these more fragile senses when separated. If used infrequently *in service to others*, these lower psychic senses today seem super-human to some people. These senses are extra-sensory as compared to present-day use of the astral body and its unified sense of empathy. The reason is that when focused on individually they can become as effective as the etheric/dense physical senses, which usually overwhelm the more subtle separated astral senses in people who are physically alive.

The *separated* sense created by the astral throat center is astral telepathy and is sometimes referred to as clairimagination, although more often as astral telepathy. Astral telepathy is the ability to both communicate through astral thought how one "feels" emotionally about his or her creative imagination, as well as to determine, from the communication of others' astral thought, how these others feel emotionally about their creative imagination. Astral feeling is the subjective inner sense that is supplied by the astral nervous system and brain as a response to information, which contains the energy from others that is supplied by a sense. Astral hearing is still used as a "sub-" sense in the development of this *astral sense of taste*. Unlike on the etheric/dense physical plane, where the movement of physical matter is necessary in order for the sense of hearing to work, on the astral plane the astral thought of imagination can be used to *convey* and receive the speech. Such speech is then sometimes "heard" and "tasted" directly in one's astral mind as a "picture" of the other person's imaginative thought with their associated feelings about it. Thus a picture (imaginative thought) is sent and received in the same way in the other person's astral mind. This form of telepathy is accurate, provided that the past and present are fully represented in the picture that represents each person's feelings. Because each picture is fixed in time for the past and present (at that moment), astral telepathy fails to accurately convey future feelings (beyond that moment). The entire astral plane is deficient in telepathic communication concerning future events, feelings, and relationships between and among forms because the future part of time connected to the past and present is mostly lacking there. Humans overcome this problem by thinking primarily from the mental body and mind. If, however, a person relies upon a lower astral psychic sense—whether that person is alive etheric/dense physically, or if after etheric/dense physical death while focused in life astrally— she or he will greatly lose mental focus, and, therefore an accurate sense of the future.

Astral speech using mental thoughtforms is still commonly used as a means of communication between and among people who are alive astrally and are, in most cases, etheric/dense physically dead. In those who have died from the etheric/dense physical plane, the etheric/dense physical throat sense remains only to the level at which it was used in the creation of virtue; as light in etheric/dense physical form, whatever of this sense does remain can fuse through the two astral spiritual senses and with the astral throat sense and thus still be used, though only virtuously. All selfish use of etheric/dense physical speech and its associated communication, as well as the sub-sense of hearing, become lost when a person is focused in life astrally. The retained selfish energy from the prior etheric/dense physical life then becomes crystallized in the etheric permanent atom and will affect that person's next etheric/dense physical incarnation. Thus unless a person who is astrally alive and etheric/dense physically dead was extremely virtuous in the etheric/dense physical life he or she has died from (and most likely other prior lives, as well), his or her ability to etheric/dense physically hear and/or communicate with those who are alive etheric/dense physically is lost. The astral throat sense of telepathy in either its higher (whole) or lower (separated) form can be used by astrally alive people to understand imagination-pictures in the astral minds of people who are physically alive. The etheric/dense physical and astral bodies are nearly unified in a person who is physically alive only if he or she is a very advanced human initiate—nearly a Master. With the exception of these rare cases, only those physically alive humans who have separated, or split, astral senses can consciously communicate with and receive communication from someone who is astrally focused and alive on the astral plane. This communication can be accomplished because the (usually single) split astral sense can be more easily focused on and increased beyond the quite frequently overwhelming etheric/dense physical senses of an etheric/dense physical alive person.

These physically alive people are the legitimate psychics (albeit lower psychics), and some of them use the separated astral throat sense, of astral telepathy. Others might use one of the remaining four separated astral senses, which will be described later in this chapter. Lower psychics who are alive etheric/dense physically can communicate with people who are alive on the astral plane, who are focused astrally, and who seek this communication. A separated astral sense is often the result of *astral* injury that was, most often, incurred during a person's prior lifetime (including astral life after etheric/dense physical death). Frequently, the astral injury that split the sense was caused by extreme emotional strain concerning love versus emotionalism. Sometimes, but less frequently, the astral injury is a result of such strain during the person's current lifetime. If it occurred in a prior lifetime, this strain often ended the person's *astral* life; it is possible, though rare, for the strain to have occurred during and have contributed to the causes that ended her or his last physical life. The most common example of love versus emotionalism that can damage the astral body and its senses, causing a lasting split in them, is

Separated Astral Senses

Each separated astral sense is associated with a center that gives the person the ability to sense astrally.

Astral Telepathy (Clairimagination)

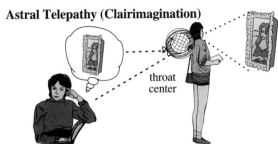

The first woman imagines what a picture that she could paint would look like. The second woman sees in her creative imagination some time later (seconds or longer) that picture using her split astral sense of telepathy, or clairimagination. She uses her astral throat center and the split astral sense of taste. The second woman may hear (as a sub-sense of hearing of the throat center) the astral thoughts and her feelings about them that the first woman had about the painting.

Astral Sight (Astral Vision)

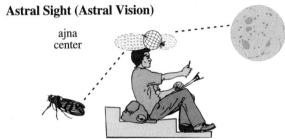

Astral sight uses the split astral sense of sight from the ajna center to see astrally telescopically, microscopically, and/or 360° in any direction. This person uses his astral sight to see the detail of the moon or the detail of a fly, even if it is behind him. He does this by projecting his sense outside himself and/or bringing a small amount of the energy closer to him so he can sense it better. He can attract a small portion of the object's energy towards him through his thought, and/or he can send some of the energy in his sense closer to the object—depending on the size, distance, and amount of his thought.

Astral Hearing (Clairaudience)

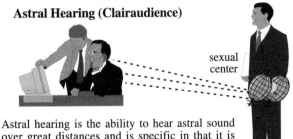

Astral hearing is the ability to hear astral sound over great distances and is specific in that it is focused between two people or groups of people. This man can hear the conversation of two people who are on the other side of the building by using his separated astral sense of astral hearing through his sexual center. Other people with astral hearing would not hear the conversation unless they were focused in the same specific direction to the same source.

Astral Smell (Clairtelemetry)

Astral smell, or clairtelemetry, is the split astral sense of awareness of movement of an animate object, even when outside the line of physical sight, when there is a focus of thought or attention from one to another. This sense explains a person's awareness of someone behind him or her, someone watching him or her, or knowing that a person one is focused on is some distance away. This split astral sense is felt primarily in the abdomen (sacral center), or sometimes in the area of the nose.

Astral Touch (Clairtouch)

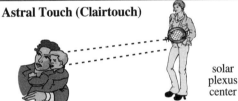

Astral touch is the split astral sense that enables one to experience what others are feeling emotionally. The woman on the right is using her split astral sense of touch coming from her solar plexus center to sense the affection that the woman holding the child is feeling towards that child.

Astral Clairvoyance

Astral clairvoyance is the ability to sense future events based upon a sense of past and present activities. This sense is produced by astral telepathy and astral sight together, at a minimum, which provide the senses of past and present that are needed before the future sense of time can emerge. Astral clairvoyance can be accurately used only for an average of different people's astral thought as applied to an event, or one or more person's thought as it affects an average of events. A person can use her creative imagination to see that four of her friends are each separately thinking about things that have to do with a party, such as missing friends, showing off a new outfit, meeting new people, and wanting something to do next weekend. If she perceives a connection between the people, her astral clairvoyance would predict that there will be a party.

planning what to say to an old friend

unpacking new purchases

writing a list of friends to see soon

talking to people about the weekend

The clairvoyant sees a party in her creative imagination. Note: the physical actions are shown for clarity, and do not have to be taking place. With astral clairvoyancy, all that is needed is creative imagination.

Illustration 7.8

an inability to give enough to (to adequately love) someone who is in genuine need of being given to (being loved) and who is very important in some, often personal, ways to the person who cannot adequately love and whose astral senses consequently become split. In these cases, *prior* selfishness has limited the ability to wisely give on the part of the person with the split sense, which is what was likely to have initially caused some split in the first place; in addition, the retained energies from the selfishness have created forces within that person's senses and astral brain. As a result, the appropriate and wise love is not available when it is needed. Remorse exacerbates the problem, and splits or separates the sense from the other split senses even further because it increases astral self-focus. When reincarnated in the next life, these people so affected often serve in ways that use their split sense to overcome their prior lack of empathy and wise loving. They help and sometimes somewhat, on a subconscious level, teach others the lessons they are also learning. Some of the true psychics who are lower psychics use their split sense selfishly; however, the sense will usually fail within a relatively short period of such use, leaving such lower psychics astrally senseless in at least some ways. They might then, at times, compensate for the loss by faking the sense. Of course, there are many people who fake having psychic senses, who never had them to begin with.

Someone who is focused in life astrally can be physically dead and alive astrally, or, although relatively rare, can be alive physically and "astral-travelling," i.e., fully conscious astrally while out of the etheric/dense physical body. In any case, a person who is astrally focused on herself or himself is selfish and is therefore emotional rather than loving. Note that people who are physically alive can be just as selfish astrally as people who are physically dead and alive on the astral plane can be. Astral energy is in much more motion than etheric/dense physical energy is, and moves in one of two directions. It can move towards the self of a person, creating an *e*-motion—which is self-focus in astral thought (note that astral thought is creative imagination), or it can move outward towards others, as love (or, at times, it can move in some combination of both of these). Thus the same astral energy can be either an emotion or love (or a mixture of both, at times), depending upon the focus of the person whose thought is directing the energy. Those who remain emotional rather than being loving split their senses by retaining astral energies within their bodies, as well as within their centers, as fixed desires that their emotions built. These fixed desires are referred to in spiritual terms as glamours. Energy follows thought, and it does so to an immensely greater extent on the astral plane than on the etheric/dense physical— where inertia rules and keeps energy in the motion it was previously in, most of the time. As a result, the more a person selfishly, or emotionally, uses her or his astral thought of *creative* imagination, thus focusing the energy on himself or herself, the greater the *creation* of desires that are selfish and retained as fixed energies. The astral thought is using the self-focused astral energies to reconstruct the astral body—creating glamours. Glamours exist in their astral form because there is enough highly focused movement on the astral plane to create them; on the etheric/dense physical and the mental planes, this condition does not exist. A glamour is a picture created by imagination and crystallized both in astral lunar deva energy and in lower elemental energy that is denser (darker) than average; it is built through a number of emotional, or astrally selfish, responses to certain circumstances when love would have been the virtuous response. The picture becomes active any time any one of the emotions that helped to create it stimulates further creative imagination, thereby enacting the glamour. If a person chooses to creatively imagine the same or a similar picture within a glamour, the glamour can be activated, as can its associated emotion. Once active, a glamour can also stimulate other similar glamours in the astral body, creating a sympathetic response and causing all of the responding glamours to function as a single large one. Glamours, as fixed desires, create an astral "itch," which when extreme can lead to anxiety. "Scratching" a glamour's "itch" causes the glamour to become activated, temporarily relieved, and then to grow further—making it "itch" more the next time.

Glamours are destructive to the astral whole sense of empathy because they interfere with the union of the astral centers and their associated senses. This union requires free communication, through enlightened energies, between and among astral centers and their senses. Glamours are retained pockets of the darker (denser) energies in the astral body that, through their gravitation and discordant vibrations, block enlightened energies in their movement from one center to another and thereby prevent the creation of empathy. For empathy to exist requires that the five senses of astral form be joined together. A greater empathic sense becomes created as the two astral senses of spirit and of God are added to empathy, creating a super-empathy in a human being as all seven of the astral senses are used in the creation of service to others. Super-empathy as a whole sense that is used subconsciously from the astral body requires a complete, or whole, sense of time. This super-sense must be *consciously* connected to the higher mental capacity of thought, or love/wisdom, through thought that is used in service by the fused personality and soul on the (corresponding) second sub-plane of the mental plane. Glamours prevent the use of both empathy and super-empathy because they cause the astral senses to split, or separate from each other. A person's glamours can join together and become quite large; when they do, their collective discordant vibrations create a sensation of anxiety within the person. Note that anxiety is the fear of loss of control by the personality over a body and sense, which leads to mistakes and pain. If glamours are held and frequently activated within the astral body, they can fill the body and seriously disease it; the overwhelming anxieties and high levels of emotionalism can create emotional diseases. These diseases include manias and depressions, and in some other forms of connected glamours create neuroses, including obsessive and compulsive disorders. Neuroses and obsessive-compulsive disorders are created particularly where fears are focused and surround a large part of the astral body that is separated from other parts of it.

In addition to the etheric/dense physical and astral bodies, the throat center and its lower mental sense are found in the mental body, on the lower mental plane part of this body. The sense of lower mental taste has become mostly fused with lower mental hearing in most human beings on earth today when they are not focused in their mental thought. These two together create the semi-fused sense of lower mental telepathy. The joining of these two separated senses comes from the mental joining of the thoughtforms of materiality, emotions, sex and love, and the structure of these mental thoughtforms of communication in general. The astral throat center in most people became fused with the sexual center over one and a half million years ago; very few people, however, have fused these two centers and senses etheric/dense physically. The precipitating factor behind much of the mental semi-fusion was the creation of the ideology from the religion of Christianity and most religions created subsequent to Christianity or that were modified based upon its ideology. The ideology of Christianity, in part, connected sex and love in thought *mentally*, and it connected materiality with giving, or love. The two separate mental senses of mental taste and mental hearing join as two of the four lower mental sub-planes are used together to create more whole thoughtforms. These two senses joined create mental telepathy. What these two senses do is create the ability to mentally hear and understand the mental thinking of others through etheric/dense physical written, oral, or pictorial words, or, additionally, through astral imaginative pictures and *directly* through mental thoughtforms (mentally). When people *hear* thoughtforms mentally, they hear the words; when thoughtforms are *tasted* mentally, a person can experience all the words put into a sentence that has meaning. Since these two senses are mostly fused within most non-egotistically thinking people today, both mental hearing and mental taste are sensed simultaneously. These senses also provide a person with the ability to adjust her or his communication with others by mentally sensing how the others are receiving what is being communicated. Without mental telepathy or both of its component senses, which are mental hearing and mental taste, a person can hear or read what others are saying but cannot understand their thought. Also, a person could communicate with others, but would be less successful at accurate communication because he or she would not perceive (be aware of, or mentally sense) how well the others are understanding his or her communicated mental thought.

The mental sense of telepathy, which corresponds to the mental fused throat and sexual centers, is imbalanced in its sense of time because it is still a split sense. All three parts of time are to some degree a part of each split mental sense because the mental plane itself contains some amount of all three time zones on all parts of it. Even so, each somewhat fused split sense contains more of one part of time than do the other two (remaining) senses. Also, lower mental senses can sense only *effects* of causes in thought, because of the split in time and space of the mental body and plane. Lower mental telepathy is primarily focused as a sense of the past part of time, since when another person receives the telepathic thoughtforms and/or sentences in full meaning, they have already taken place in time and space within the first person's mental mind. The three lower (split) psychic mental senses can fully fuse together only when the higher mental senses become fused, because these lower senses are the effects that are caused by the higher mental thoughts.

 ## THE SACRAL CENTERS

The next focus of study will be on the major center that is initially in the focus of the fourth ray and is located at the base of the spine. For most of the human lifetimes that are co-created by a soul, this center balances as best as possible the thought of the energies in its own center and all of the other centers in the body with the thought within the spirit sphere of each major center. The base of spine center attempts to create beauty in the body, which would require that the spirit sphere have twice the thought of the energy sphere; this center seldom succeeds in the attempt, though, because it is, most of the time in all of a person's earlier lifetimes, overridden by the overwhelmingly selfish thought from each personality and its over-controlled self. These thoughts create selfish spirit spheres that cannot even think as well as the energy spheres can, and they certainly cannot think in light. During each lifetime, a human, on average, gradually manifests less selfishness. However, even while spiritually disciplining themselves in the first two human initiations, people are more selfish than not during most of every day that they live. Also, people at these levels and below have less than twice the thought in their spirit spheres as compared to the collective thought in their respective energy spheres. Thus the base of spine center primarily does the remedial job of attempting to mediate in the distribution of high levels of retained energies in centers and thus attempts to prevent disease in each center and in the body as a whole. This center and its associated organs of the small and large intestines transmit energies while maintaining balances in the body. The base of spine center also, at times, enlists the aid of the spleen center. The greater the levels of retained energy within a center, particularly a major one, the greater the likelihood of disease because disease is a result of too many forces within a center. Disease uses one type of energy as a lower level of life growth, which actually reduces some of the forces, but it also reduces the growth of the higher (in this case, human) life. Forces are caused by one energy moving in a different direction as another energy is within the same time and space. Energies that are retained within a center create numerous forces. This occurs because the energies share a similar space and time that are in a direction away from those of the Ray Lords, and then become retained because they are *not* given, or do not share a similar direction focused from a virtuous self. Note that evil people attempt to have all of the energy moving towards their respective selves, in an attempt to eliminate force; however, even evil people must *give* some energy to other centers besides the base of spine center…which makes these people's attempts always less than successful. As can be seen from the above explanation, selfishness creates force.

The amount of force that the base of spine center can relieve when this center is under the control of the personality and sometimes its self is related to the selfishness of these two. Generally, the personality (which is in control, with the self often unaware) attempts to keep the energy and spirit spheres of the base of spine center as balanced as possible through its (the personality's) thought, because without the balance, the personality loses considerable control over the other centers. This preferential treatment of the base of spine center can lead to relatively more disease in the other centers. This is done for purely selfish reasons of control, rather than to create better balance throughout the body and to create beauty within it. The result can be considerable increases in ugliness as a person ages, since ugliness is what results when beauty is compromised by selfishness. The sacredness of the base of spine center's responsibility to attempt to create beauty in a human body can be reduced to that of a mundane, self-serving traffic-control device that transfers energies from one center to another when doing so does not interfere with the personality's sense of control. Another name for the base of spine center is the sacral center, because of its associated eventual sacred responsibility within the body. Note that some spiritual sources mistakenly refer to the sexual center as the sacral center. Among the seven cosmic virtues previously described, the three lowest are considered virtues of the lower kingdoms and are a part of life's growth on the three lowest planes, or the *solid* cosmic planes of our universe. The remaining four higher virtues are part of the growth of life on the *etheric* cosmic planes. These four are considered sacred because they represent the causes for the lower three virtues. A cause is the part of something that creates it, and corresponds to the more God-*Creator* part of our universe, which is also the sacred part that *lasts forever*. The base of spine center is the one that is intended to create sacredness within the body it is in (making part of it immortal as a functional part of God). This center is supposed to create beauty, or one of the cosmic etheric (causative) virtues, and for this reason it is referred to in some spiritual language as the sacral center.

The base of spine center becomes used as a spiritual center when its spirit sphere has developed, is spinning evenly, and is where energy *first* enters the center (as a cause rather than an effect); when this takes place, the base of spine center synthesizes the energies *and spirit* (and thought) of the other major centers, in each one of the bodies the centers are in. During the beginning of spiritual discipline in the first two initiations, the seventh ray and its center, the

How Plants Develop Senses

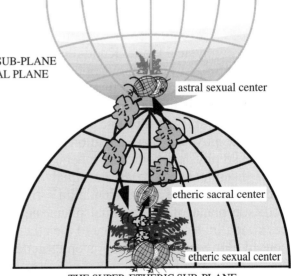

THE SEVENTH SUB-PLANE
OF THE ASTRAL PLANE

astral sexual center

etheric sacral center

etheric sexual center

When this plant takes in water and minerals it is also taking in fourth ray prana into its sacral center and seventh ray prana into its sexual center, which are located on the super-etheric sub-plane. The seventh ray prana is transmuted into seventh sub-plane astral prana for the astral sexual center. The plant is further developing its astral sexual center and senses and has begun to develop its astral body. In this example, prana is energy that is enlightened by the sun and gives life to the plant.

THE SUPER-ETHERIC SUB-PLANE
OF THE ETHERIC/DENSE PHYSICAL PLANE

Illustration 7.9

sexual, is added for use in service to the fourth ray and its center by the focused thought of the soul and Self. The somewhat fused personality and self, using the seventh ray energy with the fourth, give the sacral center better organizing and synthesizing abilities, besides just its capacity to balance energies. The spirit sphere and the soul-infused personality are required to change the focus of each major center from mundane to spiritual. This change in focus occurs when spiritual discipline is employed by the soul-infused personality (with the soul infusion usually occurring later in the stages of each initiation), allowing the personality to "see" its own self-ishness usually for the first time and creating a spiritual fifth ray focus from the ajna center. In mundane use, every center is taking in prana—either etheric or other more subtle pranas (astral or mental)—through the center itself, depending upon which body the center is in; the more dense energies are transferred into and out of parts of the body through each center's corresponding organ(s) and gland(s) and the nervous system. When the somewhat fused etheric sacral and ajna centers are spiritually focused, some of this etheric pranic energy, which is both fourth and fifth ray in focus, is replaced by one of three types of kundalini energy.

 ## KUNDALINI ENERGY

Kundalini energy is elemental energy that is attracted from and transmuted from the spiritual plane by the collective and enlightened thought of the Spirit of Earth. The Spirit of Earth is mostly focused in its thought from the etheric plane, and only to a small extent on the astral and mental planes. The thought connects this spirit mostly to both the spiritual plane and etheric plane energy parts of the sun, and also, in much smaller amounts, to the sun's astral and mental plane energy parts. The sun is the living Being whose dense physical body is the physical sun of our universe. Kundalini that is used in service becomes fully enlightened mostly etheric energy (transmuted from unenlightened spiritual plane elemental energy). The kundalini etheric elemental energy is about to become spiritualized and to enter the deva part of the energy sub-kingdom—which is the evolutionary (life-producing) part of the energy sub-kingdom. The spiritual plane energy part of the sun is its heart center and uses fusion, or central spiritual creation of energy, as a part of its body. Earth's etheric/dense physical plane is the effect of this fusion, which also causes the etheric/dense physical plane to be the etheric/dense physical heart center of the sun; the sun's effect is earth's cause for life creation. In our universe, the sun is the body of our Solar Logos—just as the earth is the body of the Planetary Logos. The sun's body extends from the spiritual plane all the way down to the etheric/dense physical plane and includes the entire solar system. Earth's body extends from the mental plane to the etheric/dense physical plane. Kundalini helps to connect the earth to the sun, and the Planetary Logos to the Solar Logos in our universe.

The first part of kundalini that is used by the sacral center in a spiritually disciplined human being replaces a small amount of etheric prana in the major centers, depending on which ones are used in the spiritual disciple's *service*. This service begins in the first initiation mostly as etheric/dense physical plane creations of virtue that help to enlighten, or create virtue in, the etheric/dense physical bodies of others. Before serving (helping to create virtue in) others, the spiritual disciple needs to create equal or greater amounts of virtue within her or his own etheric/dense physical body. Kundalini's first part originates from and is transmuted from the seventh sub-plane of the spiritual plane, and its seventh sub-ray (of the third ray) of energy makes kundalini a correspondence of the etheric (the seventh) plane. When elemental energy that is focused along the seventh ray is enlightened, it organizes and synthesizes other energy; thus when the first part of kundalini is used in service (which makes it enlightened), it organizes and synthesizes the centers that it flows through and connects. The second part of kundalini that is used by the sacral center causes the further and increased replacement of etheric prana in some centers, and causes astral pranas to become replaced in the astral body because this kundalini also rises into the astral sacral center. With this second kundalini added, the centers are also brought more closely together through bridges of light. The second kundalini, which has a sixth sub-ray focus and thus corresponds to the astral plane, originates from and is transmuted spiritual elemental energy from the sixth spiritual sub-plane. It usually first becomes raised during the second initiation, when a spiritual disciple is focused more on creating astral virtue, or love, in his or her own body and within the bodies of those whom she or he serves. Energy that is enlightened and focused along the sixth ray devotes itself to improving the movement of other energies from one location to another, helping the other energy to be more giving, or creating a oneness of enlightened motive in its and the other energy's co-creation of form. Use of the second part of kundalini in service is what causes the enlightenment of this energy; this enlightenment connects the centers and their associated senses, and motivates them to function as one—giving maximally to those capabilities of the body that are used for service. The third kundalini comes from elemental energies transmuted from the fifth spiritual sub-plane and corresponds in its sub-ray type (the fifth) to the mental plane. When this energy is added to the first two, it creates fusion of the centers, using some small part of the central spiritual sun's means of creating light from energy from the spiritual plane. The mental sacral center is the focus of the third kundalini, with the mental centers using much less mental pranas, and the lower bodies increasingly using less of the prana of their planes, as well. Fifth ray enlightened and focused energy creates a balance of structure, which includes a balance to the past, present, and future use of the energy within a form, creating a perfection in balance between cause and effect. This fifth ray focus usually brings each sacral center into full spiritual sphere rotation and use, causing the entire center to be focused more spiritually. Forces become equalized, preventing retained energy from increasing in a form (but not removing all of the energy that was previously retained).

When the enlightened third part of kundalini (this third part has a fifth ray focus) is added to and perfectly balanced with the other two parts, fusion then becomes possible because *all* forces and consequently all frictional components of heat are eliminated, which then enables this more advanced union of elemental energy. Fusion is focused from God's second aspect of mind onto its whole third aspect, and is referred to in some spiritual writing as the second cosmic fire of creation. Friction and its resultant forces are focused from the third aspect of God's mind, when that aspect is not fully enlightened and therefore manifests as energy. Thus friction, or heat, is the result of the manifested field of potential energy being electrically attracted to the greater field of intelligent activity from which it was created. In some spiritual writing, friction and force are referred to as the third cosmic fire of creation. Fusion is created by the electrical attraction of intelligent activity towards the second aspect of God's mind, or unconditional love and wise-love/consciousness/oneness, as this second aspect is fusing with God's first aspect of mind and is creating light. The emphasis of fusion is on the second aspect, the second joining with the first in order to create the light notwithstanding. The fusion that three parts of kundalini creates in the centers allows advanced initiates some of the time and always allows Masters to sense with their three lower bodies, in wholeness, all of the understanding of God in the three lower worlds, and some of the creation of being a functional part of God. Together, the three kundalinis also fuse the three bodies and their fused centers with each other, creating singularity in sense for all three bodies at the final initiation for a human, who has been an adept initiate. At this point, the human body has become an enlightened part of earth *and* the sun. The sacral center eventually lives up to its name, because it has made the human, earth, and the sun more enlightened and has truly become sacred through its completion of the joining and use of the three kundalini energies. These three energies together are sometimes referred to in spiritual language as the serpent fire because they twist around each other and rise up the etheric spine, crossing into other centers and resembling a snake of brilliant radiant elemental energy. The names of the three kundalini energies in ancient Sanskrit, and also found in some spiritual writings, are, for the first part of kundalini—pingala; for the second part—ida; and for the third—sushumna. Some people refer to the first kundalini, or pingala, as the elemental energy of "chi," or the "unifier of life" energy when used in ways other than just through the sacral center.

The sacral center, which is a major center, affects the spleen center, which is a minor center. The sacral center has its effect through the spleen center's functionality as a less than major center as well as in the spleen's gland-like qualities of affecting the immune system. The spleen takes in all seven pranas and converts them into an immune system response by balancing the pranas through the use of the sacral center. Then, when there is too much or too little prana in one center as compared to another—this imbalance is what leads to disease—the spleen center uses its prana to balance the other pranas and eliminate the need for disease. Like the spleen center, disease attempts to balance the centers, but disease does so at the cost of reducing the host's growth of life. In some spiritual material, the spleen center is sometimes mistakenly represented as one of the seven major centers in a human body, with the ajna usually, erroneously, then not considered to be a major center. The spleen center does have a major role to play in each body, since it also stores pranic energies and can, for several months, keep pranic levels up when they are environmentally reduced, or even missing. This center does not have a spirit sphere, which is the distinguishing quality of a major center. Instead, the spleen center sometimes uses the spirit sphere of the base of spine center, or even more frequently of the solar plexus center, depending upon the spleen center's function. The reason is that all of the *minor* centers share one or more (at a time) of the seven major center's spirit spheres. There are hundreds of minor centers within the human body, and the spleen center is one of the most important of them.

The sacral center creates the sense of smell in the etheric body and creates a correspondence to this sense in the astral and lower mental bodies. The nose, which contains the sensory organs of smell, is connected to the base of spine through the fourth ray focus of balancing energies with thought. The sense of smell functions similarly, since it *accurately* registers a scent only when other energies are isolated from it by being balanced in order to negate their effect. The sacral center balances extraneous energies so that a single odor, or scent, can be focused upon. In reverse, when used spiritually in cooperation with the sexual center, the sacral center uses the seventh ray from the sexual center to synthesize smell and scents into a complexity of more subtle understanding, usually of esoteric (hidden) information. In these cases, the crown chakra, or center, is also used rather than the more mundane olfactory organs in the nose. An added first ray element then becomes part of the sacral center's function as it begins to fuse with the crown center in a spiritual disciple. The full spiritual sense of the sacral center is to give the personality the sight of itself and its self for people during the stages of the initiation process. As it fuses with its soul, the personality gains a revelation of its previous selfishness in spiritual sight, which the sacral center provides by comparing (through meditation) its prior selfish self-focused use of balance with its use in service as it fuses with the (fifth ray) ajna center.

In the astral body, the sacral center creates the astral equivalent of smell as a sense, which is clairtelemetry, or the ability to sense the movement of something that one is neither in direct contact with nor in direct line of sight of. When used as a split, or lower, astral psychic sense, the "feeling" of the movement of objects, including people's bodies other than one's own, is felt in the lower back or sometimes the mid-to-lower abdomen (in line with the location of the sacral center) when the one sensing is focused on the sense and the one being sensed. Sometimes a simultaneous sense is recorded in the astral nose (or above the astral nose at the center between the eyebrows—the astral ajna center), and usually "feels" like a sense, or awareness, concerning the proximity of another object or person to the one sensing. Then the astrally sensing person

Separated Mental Senses

The mental body has three separated senses, two of which are partially fused. Because people on the etheric/dense physical and astral planes are overwhelmed by their physical and astral senses, respectively, these people are frequently unaware of their mental senses.

Mental Telepathy

The sense of mental telepathy comes from the fusion of the lower mental sexual (hearing) and throat (taste) centers. This sense is to understand thoughtforms (words) that others have previously thought of, and to experience those words in a sentence that has meaning. A person who has mental telepathy understands another's thoughts and knows what he or she is thinking. This sense concerns the past sense of time because the person who has mental telepathy sees in his or her mental mind the thoughts of the other person *after* (a second or more) that person thought them.

Mental Vision

Mental vision is the sense from the ajna center of sight. Mental vision is the ability to see the thoughtforms and structured meaningful sentences in another person's mind at the same time he or she is creating them and to visualize what is being created in real time. It uses the present sense of time because seeing what is in the other person's mind occurs at the time that person is creating it.

He sees the thoughtforms and sentences at the time they are being created. He reads her mind and then responds to her thoughts. He has mental vision.

Mental Clairvoyance

Mental clairvoyance comes from the fusion of a minimum of two centers, the solar plexus (touch) and sacral (smell) centers and increases as more centers are fused with the first two. It focuses on the future sense of time because it approximates, like statistical sampling, what people in the future will be thinking in whole structured thought based on the thoughtforms and sentences they created in the past and present. It is not accurate for one person in a single circumstance, but may be for averages of people's thought for a general circumstance and for larger numbers of situations. In this example, seeing these people's thoughts can lead to predicting they will form a group to help each other to become more virtuous.

Non-Wisdom vs. Wisdom

When a person uses all five mental senses of form together, that person is wise because he or she is able to see other people's minds and help them to think in whole structured thought. A person who does not have whole mental thought or lacks mental senses because of egotism and arrogance puts information together incompletely so that it is not truthful, not in whole structured thought, and creates darkness in other people's minds. That person is not wise. When the two spiritual senses are added to the five of form, a person develops love/wisdom.

Illustration 7.10

might exclaim that she or he can "feel," or sense, the other person's presence and/or movement. Clairtelemetry can work over relatively quite large distances, just as smell can etheric/dense physically; generally, the greater the distance, the less accurate the sense of position and movement of the object or person being sensed because time and space are so separated when a split sense is being used.

The sacral center's sense of smell in the lower mental body has been mostly fused with the sense of touch in most modern-day humans who are not thinking egotistically. These two senses used together provide mental clairvoyance, or a sense of what others will be mentally thinking in thoughtforms (and sentences made from them) in the future. The time zone that is emphasized in this semi-fused mental sense is the future. In most people today, this sense is less developed than are the other two mental senses because it requires more balanced development of the two mental centers—the base of spine and solar plexus—than most people have created in their lower minds, on the fourth and sixth sub-planes. For many people, the kama-manasic connection of the sixth mental sub-plane to the sixth astral sub-plane has interfered with further development of this fused sense. The word kama in more modern history refers to the Hindu God of love; however, in antiquity kama has meant selfish—*emotional*—love. The original meaning of this word meant *any* self-focused astral energy. Evil has in more modern times changed the word association to "love." In esoteric spiritual writing, kama is synonymous with emotion. The kama-manasic connection causes people to think emotionally *first*, before thinking mentally. Then they, consequently, frequently rationalize their mental thoughtforms relative to how they feel and what they imagine—often in fantasy. When used as a fused sense, mental clairvoyance is more accurate than the other two split mental senses are because it focuses on the future (effects) part of time, which tends to unify the past and present when accurately depicted.

THE AJNA CENTERS

The next major ray center (in numerical order) is the ajna center, which is initially focused along the fifth ray. This center initially uses fifth ray pranic energy to create its energy sphere and sense. Unlike most of the other major centers, the ajna center in all but the most advanced humans is much more distorted from the way most of the other centers appear (each as a squashed sphere). Rather than resembling a flower that is sort of upside down when viewed from one angle, or a doughnut that has sections when seen more completely, in most humans the ajna center resembles an airplane propeller, from a single and limited viewing position. The cause of this appearance is that all of the lunar deva energies have been forced to either side of the spirit sphere, creating two elongated and elliptical, egg-shaped forms. These two egg-shaped forms revolve around the spirit sphere that is between them. They also develop a second spin, in opposite directions to each other, along their elongated center axis. The forces that create this unusually-shaped center are produced by the personality and its unequal selfish use of the three brains. The three brains' structured and synthesized information is then sensed through the sense that is created by the ajna center in each one of the three bodies. The personalities in the human beings of younger souls use the information from the brains and the sense of the ajna center predominately selfishly, almost all the time. The fifth ray creates balanced structure when creating light, but when this ray is selfishly used, much of the balance to the structure is lost...as in a mundanely used ajna center.

The ajna center in the etheric/dense physical body creates the sense of sight. It is located between the eyes, centered above them at the brow line. In some spiritual writing the ajna center is often referred to as the brow chakra because of its location. Without unification with the other etheric/dense physical senses, the sense of sight (or any of the other four separated senses in this body) cannot create intelligent coordinated response, which is the whole, exclusively virtuously used sense of the etheric/dense physical body. Since this body was not unified by the first major race of humans to use it, because its members did not collectively through their civilizations create enough virtue to do so, all of the etheric/dense physical body's senses and centers of both form and spirit remained (and still remain) mostly split.

Although much more will be covered in Chapter Nine about this area of information, it can be explained at this point that there is only one way in which a body and its center and senses can be unified for all future humans. This sole method involves an entire major race. A major race comprises seven sub-races based upon the rays in development. The unification occurs as a group of humans collectively focuses on attempting to create virtue through developing their civilizations. The race of people as a whole need to create enough virtue to unify the senses of the body wherein their development is focused. This creation of virtue must occur while these people's civilizations (extensions of their senses through use of the lower kingdoms) are developing, and not disintegrating. Each sub-race needs to integrate a particular, usually corresponding, one of the seven senses. As long as the sub-race is functioning with a high level of civilization, its members can continue to work in their focused sense's integration even if a more advanced sub-race is also in existence. Once a sub-race's civilization in a major human race has mostly disintegrated, its members cannot integrate the particular sense that they were here, on the physical earth, to unify through the creation of virtue in themselves and in the lower kingdoms. If a civilization disintegrates without having integrated its focused sense, then only the individual members of each race and sub-race who create great amounts of virtue with each body can unify the five senses of form and two senses of spirit in their respective bodies.

The first two major human races never reached physical form. The first major *physical* human race (which was the third actual major human race) was the Lemurian, and it had seven sub-races, each corresponding to one of the rays. These seven sub-races of people mostly failed to integrate the etheric/dense physical body's senses because its members collectively failed to create enough virtue in themselves and the lower kingdoms that they used with which to create their civilizations. The second major *physical* race (and its seven sub-races, which also each corresponded to one of the seven rays) was the Atlantean. The first five sub-races of this race created civilizations that were virtuous enough to unify all five of the astral body's senses of form, thus creating empathy for all future humans. However, the last two Atlantean sub-races did not create enough virtue to either adequately develop their two astral spiritual senses or to unify these two senses to the five of form; the unification of all seven astral senses would have eventually created super-empathy in the astral body. The first spiritual astral sense, or the lower spiritual sense, is the ability to sense God, or to sense all life as One, and the second, or the higher spiritual sense, is the sense of being a functional part of God through the consistent creation of virtue. The third major *physical* race (the fifth major human race in total), which far prior to the twentieth century was (in some spiritual material) referred to as the Aryan race, has as its focus the creation of civilizations based upon the mental body and its senses. However, the name Aryan was misappropriated by the Nazis to refer to their relatively small group of people—small, considering that the majority of people on earth at the time were members of the real Aryan race (which is still the case today). Because of the confusion created by the Nazis concerning the meaning of the term "Aryan," a new name may need to be coined to represent this planet's third major *physical* race of humans, which is currently under development. Note that one of evil's tricks is the use of spiritual names and language in very dark and atrocious and/or confusing contexts in order to destroy the ability to virtuously and clearly communicate. The first four of seven sub-races of the mental (the Aryan), or the third major, *physical* race of humans on earth has already unified the five mental senses of form into three, in the mental bodies of nearly all people who are members of that race. The process began about 7000 years ago, with the first of the three having been unified about 4000 years ago.

Sight that is joined with the other etheric/dense physical senses creates the single whole etheric/dense physical sense of intelligent coordinated response. This sense that is created from virtue, or light in the body, allows the person to correctly be aware of everything around him or her in the dense physical world when the five senses of form are unified, and in the etheric and dense physical worlds when all seven senses are unified. Once someone is accurately aware in the etheric/dense physical body of everything around himself or herself—including all of the inertia, or the resistance to changes in movement of energy, with the resistance caused by less than intelligent activity—then intelligent responses can be coordinated with everything else in order to reduce inertia. When responses are intelligently coordinated, then cooperation and sharing of energy and thought takes place. Cooperation and sharing of energy and thought is the virtue that is created in etheric/dense physical form.

The etheric/dense physical ajna center fuses first with the sacral center and eventually with the etheric/dense physical crown center as the ajna center is used virtuously in spiritual *service*. In these circumstances of use in service, the personality, which relies so heavily on all of the ajna center's sense, is fusing with the soul. The crown center is the center that corresponds to the soul, as the seat of higher consciousness, or the focal point of the consciousness thread. Accordingly, the human soul is the focal point of higher consciousness in a human being. Note that the soul is focused on the development of the lower spiritual sense. This sense is the understanding of God through the creation of beauty along the fourth ray, or creating consciousness from love, or giving, or understanding the direction of a Ray Lord's thought. The spiritual focus of the fourth ray is added to an ajna center that is being used with which to create virtue when fused with the sacral center; then the ajna center is used to balance the personality with the soul in both sense and thought as they fuse together.

When the astral ajna center is used selfishly, it provides the split sense of astral sight, or astral vision. This sense provides a person with awareness of an object that is within a line of sight as illuminated by astral light, much as etheric/dense physical vision does. However, astral vision additionally provides awareness by magnifying small or distant objects, through the movement of some of the observer's energies (and some of the energy being observed is also moved with greater ease much closer to the sense) within his or her sense closer to the object and *outside* his or her astral body! This amazing condition is possible on the astral plane and not on the etheric/dense physical. As a result of astral energy's lower density and the astral plane's higher frequency of light, astral energy follows astral thought much more readily than etheric/dense physical energy follows etheric/dense physical thought. Thus most thought by spirit on the astral plane has overall increased strength over spirit's thought on the etheric/dense physical because the speed of light (and the Ray Lord's thought) on the astral plane is much faster than on the etheric/dense physical. By the same effects as described above, astral vision works in all directions outward from the head of a person; thus from within an astral body, vision from the back of the head is as good as from the front of the head where the eyes appear in the manifestation of the person. Note that the way in which a person on the astral plane appears to others who are astrally aware is as whatever he or she is capable of creatively imagining, or astrally thinking, of himself or herself.

Most astral people's appearance from within the astral body is as a somewhat improved image of the best that they thought of themselves on the etheric/dense physical plane. In addition, surrounding this image of a person is a large, somewhat egg-shaped, often jagged-edged and multi-colored astral body, which is visible when focused on astrally. In a person who is physically dead and astrally alive, there is no boundary between his or her physical appearance and astral body proper. In a physically alive person on the astral plane, a boundary of the densest astral elemental energy from the specific astral sub-plane that the astral body is on surrounds and separates the physical appearance from the astral body. The astral body contains whatever glamours are present—which may be many—as well as all of the astral centers. Surrounding the astral body is a much larger mental body; compared to the astral, the mental body in most people has a more even outer edge and is formed more clearly in the shape of an egg, with the larger part at the bottom. The mental body is not visible to most people on the astral plane, just as neither it nor the astral body is visible to most people on the etheric/dense physical plane. The most incredible part of the astral ajna sense of vision is its ability to join with clairtelemetry and clairimagination, which then enables an astrally sensing person to sense what any other sentient lifeform is sensing in its *related* astral centers and senses. It is from this foundation of three astral senses becoming partially joined that empathy is built up to, eventually, the five astral form senses fused together. The five astral senses become three, and then the three become the one sense of empathy. Note that technically, all lifeforms are sentient; however, on the astral plane some lifeforms are kept alive by the astral thought from other, more advanced lifeforms. The lifeforms that are sentient on their own can be sensed from very far away. As long as these lifeforms can be accurately depicted in creative imagination, what these lifeforms sense in one or more of the five astral senses can also be sensed by the distant observer. Other people's creations that spring from their astral imaginations and that were created by those people using some or all of their astral centers *cannot* be directly sensed as *alive* (but can be sensed as inanimate form) because these creations are not fully sentient. Astral creations that are created by others' imaginations can be sensed as alive only by focusing on the person who is helping to create them, while that person is sensing her or his creations. In these cases, the person who is creating would most likely become immediately aware through either empathy or the use of the split astral sense of clairtelemetry that someone is focusing astral senses on her or him.

Additional split senses, such as astral hearing, can be added to those senses that have already become joined; the addition of astral hearing would enable a person to hear what other sentient lifeforms are hearing from very far away. If all five senses of astral form within a person are joined together and used, then the full sense of empathy is available to that person when she or he is sensing astrally. Then, regardless of the observer's distance from and obscurity to other sentient lifeforms, all that they are sensing astrally in all of their form-based centers can be sensed by the observer if he or she is empathically sensing. Empathy is considerably restricted in its abilities while a person is physically alive and focused physically in sensing, because the physical senses in most people overwhelm the more subtle astral ones. Also, the space and time on the physical plane restrict a person's sense of empathy because this astral sense generally cannot be extended outside a person's astral body. The reason is that the overriding gravity and inertia and lessened physical *thought* on the physical plane reduces most people's sense of empathy there to a much lower level than when this sense is focused on the astral plane. Those who astral-travel may temporarily and briefly overcome this restriction. Such people's physical senses are actually lessened, while their astral senses are heightened—for a brief and temporary period—upon their physical return. Also overcoming the restriction, but in a more lasting manner, are a rare few (lower) psychics who occasionally use their split astral senses without *any* self focus, in consistent selfless service, choosing to receive nothing for themselves at these times. In so doing, they can unify their five astral senses of form with light (the two senses that come from spirit's thought of God), thus creating within themselves the temporary fused astral sense of super-empathy. All Masters focused on life in the three lower worlds have super-empathy. In the next chapter more will be explored about how senses affect life on the subtle planes of reality.

When the astral ajna center's sense of vision is joined with astral telemetry (or if other astral split senses are added), the two or more senses together start to become astral clairvoyance. Astral clairvoyance is a sense of future events based upon a sense of past and present activities. The cause of astral clairvoyance is that a future sense of time starts to emerge when comparisons are made between the time and space of one location (where the observer is) and another (where the other sentient lifeform that is being observed is). Some mental thought must also be used in the comparison, so only a partial future sense of time is ever astrally realized. Also, the process of astral clairvoyance is very slow and resembles a higher mental preconceptual type thought in its accuracy (or lack thereof) in use as applied to individual circumstances. (See Chapter Five for more information about thought and the way that group souls think.) Thus astral clairvoyance, which includes astral vision, is always somewhat inaccurate as a sense. This is because within the thought of the person who is sensing and thinking astrally, the future part of time is still quite separated from time's past and present parts. The more that the astral clairvoyance applies to averages of circumstances, the greater its level of accuracy, while the more specifically it is used, the less accurate it is. With astral clairvoyance, time is not closely joined together with either itself (in its three parts) or with space.

Those people who are astrally and not etheric/dense physically alive and those etheric/dense physically alive astral travelers who selfishly use their astral senses emphasize the use of one or more astral split senses over the other ones. Which sense or senses are emphasized depends upon which astral sub-plane the person is on. Those on the seventh astral sub-plane use the seventh, or sexual, astral center the most, and they rely more on the single split astral sense of astral hearing, or clairaudience, when they are selfish in their astral sensing. People on the sixth astral sub-plane tend to emphasize the use of the astral solar plexus center and its associated sense of clairtouch; often the seventh astral sub-plane partial sense of clairaudience is used together with clairtouch. The reason is that the consciousness levels of those on the sixth astral sub-plane interpenetrate the consciousness levels on both their own sub-plane and any lower ones (in this case, the seventh). Those people splitting their empathic sense on the fifth astral sub-plane use mostly the split sense of astral vision, or astral sight, joined with the sixth and seventh astral sub-plane emphasized and split senses of clairtouch and clairaudience, respectively. On the fourth astral sub-plane those who use selfishly their astral senses emphasize clairtelemetry joined with astral sight, clairtouch, and clairaudience from the fifth, sixth, and seventh astral sub-planes. Selfish astral people on the third sub-plane emphasize astral telemetry, which is sometimes referred to in spiritual writings as clairimagination. The inclusion of the word imagination in the name of this split lower psychic astral sense should not be confused with creative imagination, which is the thought on the astral plane. Each higher sub-plane and its added time and space, with increased sense, is additive to and interpenetrates the sub-planes below it. Even when selfishly used, the split astral senses are still geometrically more whole and greater on each higher sub-plane. On the second and first astral sub-planes, super-empathy is being created first from the lower sense of the (higher) Self and then, on the first astral sub-plane, from the added higher sense of its (higher) Self—added to empathy. The process joins the second and first astral centers of the heart and crown centers with the lower five centers and their senses. (See Chapter Eight's section entitled "Life on the Astral Sub-Planes" for more about the use of centers on astral sub-planes.)

The lower mental split sense of the ajna center is mental vision. Mental vision, which is created from the fifth ray focus of the ajna center, corresponds to the fifth, or mental, plane. The commonality of fifth ray focus for both this split sense and its plane strengthens the functioning of the sense; as a result, mental vision is the most used of the lower mental split senses, on average. The (split) sense of mental vision allows a person to see what is in another's lower mental body and mind exactly as the other person can see it, in real time, or in the present—while the mental activity is taking place. One of the things someone using mental vision might see is another person's completed thoughtforms as a structured moving picture of them, while the other person is thinking them, in a meaningful sentence that is structured in time and space. Unlike mental telepathy, which is delayed from the time a person thinks of a thoughtform (or a

The Astral Centers

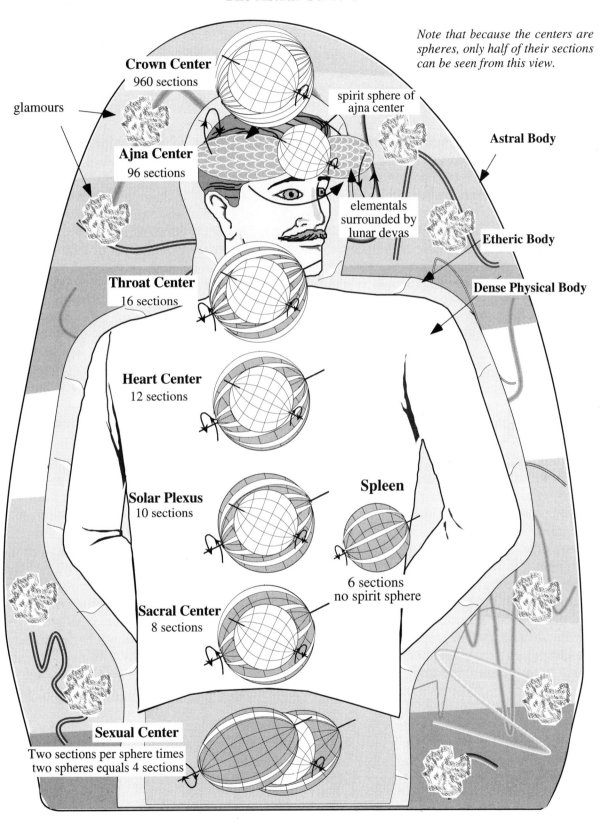

Note that because the centers are spheres, only half of their sections can be seen from this view.

Crown Center
960 sections

glamours

Ajna Center
96 sections

spirit sphere of
ajna center

Astral Body

elementals
surrounded by
lunar devas

Etheric Body

Dense Physical Body

Throat Center
16 sections

Heart Center
12 sections

Solar Plexus
10 sections

Spleen

6 sections
no spirit sphere

Sacral Center
8 sections

Sexual Center
Two sections per sphere times
two spheres equals 4 sections

Illustration 7.11

group of thoughtforms in a sentence) until the point at which another person receives the thoughtform(s), mental vision takes place as if one were directly within the other person's lower mental mind, seeing his or her thoughts. Mental vision enables people on the lower mental plane to "see" another person, lower mentally, from the inside out if the observer so chooses. This can occur if the observed does not resist such awareness of himself or herself on the part of the observer. Today on earth, mental vision is still a *single* split sense, which means that it has not, as yet, joined with any other split lower mental sense. However, it is still a more accurate sense, in its singular use in *selfishly* used lower mental bodies, than are the other two mental senses that have become semi-fused and then are used selfishly (which tends to then split these partially fused senses apart). Mental clairvoyance, for example, is more accurate if it is used relatively unselfishly. The increased accuracy is usually a result of the sense being associated with concepts from the spiritual part of the third mental sub-sub-plane of the higher mental body. The personality's reliance on each ajna center and its sense is greatly exaggerated because of its (the personality's) need to control the bodies through the brains, which the ajna center helps to create. As a result, when added to the previously mentioned fifth ray strengthening of the sense of mental vision, the personalities of people who are focused from and sensing from the lower mind use this sense more than they do any of the other mental senses.

There are only very few people who are physically alive and can remain conscious while out of their physical bodies and travelling to the mental dimension. The reason is that the high speed of mental plane thought and the use of the split lower mental senses require very high levels of giving, or consciousness. This high level of consciousness is needed in order to connect the mental sense to the mental brain and thought in a personality that is still processing synthesized information from the astral and etheric/dense physical brains. In most people, so much time is separated from space, or is used up, in trying to connect the brains of the three bodies from a focus in *consciousness* mentally that it is not possible for them to remain conscious from the self. The self of a person needs to be nearly completely focused on giving all of itself to the Self for service that the Self and soul will give, if it (the self) is to remain conscious while physically alive and on the mental plane. Such a complete level of service, or givingness, is found only in very advanced human initiates because they have disciplined their bodies—and particularly the mental body—in order to be able to serve others at this high level. Of those people who are alive on the astral plane, an initiate of any level can usually remain fully conscious, or conscious from his or her self, while mental travelling for the purpose of serving others. This happens because the self needs to give to only the remaining alive bodies, which requires less giving, or less consciousness, in someone who has no etheric/dense physical body. Note that the more advanced the initiate, the longer she or he can remain conscious. As an example, the lower-level human initiates can sometimes remain fully conscious for only brief periods on the lower mental plane. The reason is that mental senses quickly tire as a result of levels of energy that are retained through relative selfishness and not enough givingness, or consciousness, from their selves. In all human initiates, the personality has fused to some degree with the soul, reducing the personality's need to control. This allows the soul and Self to use higher psychic sense, or to unify all seven senses within the body that is being served from, at some periods of time.

The added focus of the fourth ray to the ajna center that is fusing with the sacral center is used to balance the personality's use of the bodies and senses with the soul's, as the two fuse together through spiritual service. Spiritual service, which is the only context within which the word "service" is used in this book, means the complete giving of all of the energy that is focused on one or more others for his, her, its, or their benefit, to help the other(s) become more virtuous. Thus when any sense is used in service, all of the energy that enters the sense must go outwards towards one or more others who or that are being served, to help to create virtue within them. The only way that this energy can be completely given is for spirit's thought within the body that the sense is a part of to become completely, one hundred percent, focused on creating more light, or virtue, in others, thereby enlightening the energy. During the gradual process of spiritual discipline, disciples who are less advanced will choose to create a few periods of service. Then, much more time is spent in less than service but with some levels of created virtue—cooperation and sharing, giving, and creation of truth—and, for lower-level disciples, long periods of selfishness. The fourth ray focus that is added to each of the three ajna centers in the corresponding bodies balances the personality's selfish use of all the senses of form in each body (every use of the senses for self-focus) to the periods of creation of both some virtue and service. The method of balance comes from the spiritual disciple contemplating future use of the ajna center. The disciple uses this center's sense of future vision and the sacral center's sense of inner vision in order to determine more virtuously appropriate use of that body's sense(s), brain, and capacity of (spirit's) thought in certain anticipated situations. Then, later, the ajna and sacral center "tell" the personality about this contemplation, through the fourth ray sense of creating an inner vision picture in the brains. They do this so that the personality can see what it had previously chosen to change concerning its selfish use of the senses. This picture illustrates the spiritual disciple's prior spiritual thought, balanced to the amount of information, or energy, that is available at that time within each sense for the creation of virtue. These pictures are generated through the brains of each body in which the ajna center and sense were used in the discipline. Note that this process is very much the reverse of how the sacral center initially informs the personality (through its *reflection*) of its *prior* selfishness and need to change to become more its soul; together, the sacral and ajna centers create a focus of past (reflection) and future (contemplation) to help develop virtuous change. Much more about this meditative process will be discussed in Chapter Twelve.

As can be deduced, sometimes people who have not yet, consciously, chosen to consistently spiritually discipline themselves use the added fourth ray spiritual focus of the ajna center. Spiritual meditation is focus on the self to become *less* selfish. When people meditate in reflection on selfish parts of their personalities that they want to change, they are using the spiritual sense of the sacral and ajna centers in the body or bodies and senses they are concerned about changing the use of. If not for the gradual increase in the ajna centers' spiritual sense, humans would be apt to fail to grow spiritually. Those who damage one or more of their three ajna centers through excessive selfishness can, for protracted periods of time, lose the ability to spiritually grow. In addition, with the close connection of the personality to the ajna centers, the personality with ajna center damage will frequently become disordered; a disordered personality loses control over not only its bodies and their senses, but some of its self as well. Then the self is no longer capable of giving enough to the bodies to maintain its prior level of consciousness.

THE SOLAR PLEXUS CENTERS

The major center that is focused along the sixth ray is the solar plexus center; this etheric center creates the split sense of etheric/dense physical touch, which is the ability to perceive pressure, texture, and movement to something etheric/dense physically that is in very close proximity. The use of this sense requires close proximity to an object that is outside the body, since the etheric/dense physical senses, which are split, are so affected by gravity and friction. Physical touch can convey more subtle information to a human than the other (split) physical senses can, especially when empathy, from the astral body, is used in conjunction with it. Because of its sixth ray focused nature, physical touch can accurately discern very slight qualities in movement of the touch, making it an effective communicator between two people (only two at a time) or between a person and one other object of any type.

When used virtuously etheric/dense physically, the solar plexus center fuses with the etheric/dense physical heart center and provides a sense of love, or "touching," for up to large numbers of others (people, animals, plants, even certain material non-living forms). The heart center adds a second ray quality, which expands upon the more limited sixth ray type of love given by one person to one other. This sense of love is to give, using physical touch in some ways within the giving for the purpose of increasing the light within the others. While the fused center that comprises the solar plexus and heart centers can be used to give to one other, if the giving is done for groups of others then this center tends to grow as it fuses. This occurs because more unity, or oneness, is then experienced in life, or in God's growth. Whether used selfishly or virtuously, the solar plexus center remains focused along the sixth ray exclusively, with no added focus for the center prior to fusing. The center's astral, and main, corresponding sense (of empathy) from its sixth ray focus was unified in humans long ago. The heart center has a second ray focus, which also does not change because it is a center in which the spirit sphere is the primary functional sphere from the beginning, since the heart center in humans is connected to the Monad through the life thread; this connection allows for the creation of a spiritual sense of God in humans. Before it fuses with the solar plexus center, the heart center is focused on the creation of astral virtue, or limited love, and its energy sphere sends energy into the solar plexus center instead of processing the energy through its own energy sphere. After fusion begins, the heart center's focus changes to the creation of monadic virtue, or unlimited—unconditional—love for the oneness of life. The solar plexus center then sends its energy directly into the heart center's *spirit* sphere. Notice that when energy is used to create virtue, thereby returning it to intelligent activity, the energy first enters a center through its *spirit* sphere. Next, the energy leaves through that center's energy sphere, since the energy is then following the virtuous thought of informing spirit. The Monad is connected to the human through the sutratma, or life thread, which is seated in the energy sphere of the heart center, and gives this center when functional its unconditionally loving sense of understanding God. When fusion between the solar plexus and heart center takes place, the person has chosen to transform his or her personal and conditional loves into universal (God-level) and unconditional love through spiritual discipline. Note that the solar plexus center can still sense individually focused love, and that this quality is *not* lost as the two centers fuse through spiritual discipline. A common mistake is to conclude that individual love and the sense of it are lost as humans become spiritually advanced—the sense of individual love is only added to.

Because of the astral solar plexus center's corresponding and shared sixth ray focus with the astral plane, it is the astral center that is used the most, on average, when isolated through selfishness, in all animals but the very lowest animal lifeforms on earth. On all three planes, the solar plexus center is the second-most used center in humans on earth today (only the ajna center is used more). The solar plexus center creates the split sense of astral touch, or clairtouch, which is the ability to sense, as a feeling or sensation within one's own body, what others are sensing emotionally outside of their own astral thought. Unlike etheric/dense physical touch, astral touch can be used across great distances because the sense can be projected outside the astral body with ease, using only slight astral thought to direct it. Astral touch is not empathy because this split sense cannot accurately sense love, only emotions. This includes the feeling within the astral body of being loved or of giving love. Love is the movement of all the focused and given energy in a direction away from oneself towards another; sensing the energy's movement, amount, and direction of love requires empathy. Clairtouch is the ability to sense any one or two of the three parts of love (movement, amount, and direction of the energy), but not all three; for example, one could, paradoxically, sense all three only if the direction towards the self who is sensing it was sensed, as one or more emotions of the self, and this cannot, by definition, be love. The sense of unconditional love further requires a part of super-empathy and not just the five astral senses of form joined together. The sense of unconditional love requires at least six of the seven astral senses of form and spirit joined together with some amount of the seventh included. The heart center's sense is a *spiritual* sense, which requires some amount of super-empathy.

When two people on the astral plane touch each other, they are not touching physical matter, but only astral form of either emotional or loving energy. The astral touch senses the emotions or love, or both, of the other person relative to each of the two people and gives the subjective sensation of a sense's information, or energy from another. Thus clairtouch is the experience of others' feelings, created by associating with others whether those involved are "touching" each other or not. Certain activities, such as sexual relations, are significantly different astrally than etheric/dense physically. The reason is that whether used as a split sense or as a part of the whole sense of empathy, clairtouch experientially elevates the physical touch to a much closer astral contact. As a result, people (and all sentient beings) are much closer in life experience to one another on the astral plane than on the etheric/dense physical. All of this is controlled by the changes in astral time and space (and the astral plane's physics), along with the increased ability for spirit to think on the astral plane as compared to the etheric/dense physical dimension. In Chapter Ten, which is about time and space, this effect and its causes will be more fully examined.

The mental solar plexus center creates the split lower mental sense of touch, which was fused with smell and the lower mental sacral center in humans who do not think egotistically using the sense, several thousand years ago. These two fused split lower mental senses create mental clairvoyance, which has been previously mentioned herein. Mental clairvoyance for those alive mentally uses its component of lower mental touch to locate the thoughtforms within the minds of others and to sense the following about the thoughtforms: their connectedness together in direction, or oneness; their focus towards others in communication as mental movement; and their strength of thought in how wholly they describe a concept and as a balance in the three parts of time, which determines their logic in a sentence. When joined with mental smell, the split sense of mental clairvoyance can somewhat accurately depict a logical, structured mental image of a future event in mental time and space regarding a group, or average number, of similar circumstances (or one circumstance coming from a group of people) that are likely to occur. Mental clairvoyance can provide this sense by sensing how thoughtforms of others are creating mental movement, strength in communication or motivation mentally, and connectedness, in order to determine their likely direction in thought together. It also determines the combined logic of others' thought, determining whether or not a collective result will become actualized by being logical together in time and space. Mental clairvoyance cannot, however, be used to accurately predict with any amount of certainty the outcome of a specific event from any one person's thought because the whole sense, of wisdom, is missing. Wisdom is all of the five lower mental senses of thought in form (thoughtforms), joined to the higher mental senses in form (a part of concepts that also contain higher mental thought). Love/wisdom as thought can be *created in the one who is giving wisdom to others*, when the others receiving the wisdom use it *personally* to improve their own thought—making their thought structurally more whole. To *use* love/wisdom, as service, in creating virtue in others, the giver must give both love and wisdom. This then results in the receiver not only becoming wiser, but also becoming more loving and choosing to wisely give the wisdom that he or she has had improved in his or her mind. Thus lower mental clairvoyance lacks wisdom, and is therefore inaccurate in use as a split sense to determine effects of individual future events. The reason is that when one is still somewhat mentally selfish and using a split mental sense, she or he does not receive as accurate an understanding of the other who is being mentally sensed.

THE SPLEEN CENTERS

The previously and partially described (minor) spleen center, which, at times, uses the spirit sphere of the sacral, or base of spine, center, also uses and is even more frequently affected by the spirit sphere of the solar plexus center. This duality gives the spleen center two ray focuses. First, the spleen center uses fourth ray pranic energy to construct its energy sphere when it is focused through and affected by the thought of the spirit sphere within the sacral center. Then its function is to bring into the body, to store, and to transmit all seven pranic energies *through* its energy sphere, to supply a balance in energies to all of the other centers in the body. However, only the fourth and sixth ray pranic energies can become a part of the sphere, which contains mostly sixth ray energy. These energies, as directed by the sacral center, are then used to compensate for a lack in a ray energy within other centers, in order to either reduce disease or increase the body's immunity. Note that each center initially focuses on one of the seven ray types of energy at a time. When functioning through the solar plexus center, the spleen center uses sixth ray energy to construct its energy center. Under these circumstances the spleen center organizes and distributes most of the non-dense in form pranic energies that enter the etheric, astral, or mental body—which each has a spleen center. In the dense physical body, when food is eaten (which contains very dense pranic energies in the form of matter) the etheric spleen center needs to digest the rate of etheric pranic energy released to match that of the dense food. Until fully fused, when the spleen is carrying out this function it cannot simultaneously function in its immune system activities. This is why many plants (while they take in minerals), animals, and some people choose to not eat much of the time while they are ill. When improperly functioning because of selfishness, the spleen center can lead to different types of indigestion from the effects on the pancreas and the adrenal glands (when the adrenals are not directly controlled by the pituitary gland), which the center also controls. This usually occurs while the solar plexus and heart centers are controlling the liver, which they are interpenetrating. Indigestion is also affected by the spleen's and pancreas's functioning because dense prana can be properly absorbed from food only as it is matched by etheric prana from the spleen center. Improper digestion also occurs as a result of energy that is retained within the solar plexus center because of selfishness. This also creates additional problems in the spleen center (including its immune system functions), since it relies so heavily on the solar plexus center's spirit sphere. The spleen center is the central "clearing house" for most of the pranic energies that are not in dense or relatively dense form within each body.

The spleen center uses its two rays of focus, the fourth and sixth, to allow it to transfer all seven pranas through it. When focused on the spirit sphere of the sacral center, the spleen center brings all pranas except the sixth directly through its one sphere in amounts that are balanced to the overall needs of the body. Then, when the spleen center is focused through the solar plexus center and the sixth ray, it is highly selective in giving the specific prana needed in other parts of the body for nourishment. In addition, it receives its sixth ray pranic energy from the solar plexus center that nourishes it and that it gives out to other minor centers. By sacrificing its ability to receive sixth ray pranic energy directly in order to build its own energy sphere, the spleen center gains the ability to receive the other six pranas directly, etherically, from the etheric atmosphere. The reason is that very little or no force is created from its mostly sixth ray energy center. Other centers usually receive only one ray type of pranic energy unless fused— then they may receive two or more.

The Spleen Center Distributing and Balancing Prana

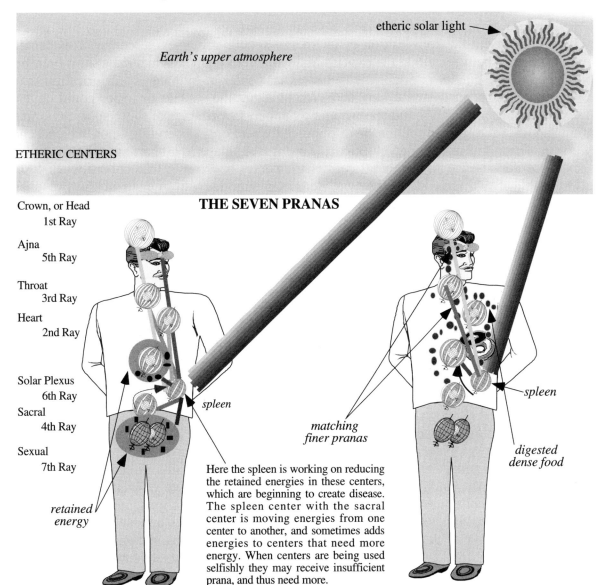

Earth's upper atmosphere

etheric solar light

ETHERIC CENTERS

THE SEVEN PRANAS

Crown, or Head
        1st Ray

Ajna
        5th Ray

Throat
        3rd Ray

Heart
        2nd Ray

Solar Plexus
        6th Ray

Sacral
        4th Ray

Sexual
        7th Ray

retained energy

spleen

matching finer pranas

spleen

digested dense food

Here the spleen is working on reducing the retained energies in these centers, which are beginning to create disease. The spleen center with the sacral center is moving energies from one center to another, and sometimes adds energies to centers that need more energy. When centers are being used selfishly they may receive insufficient prana, and thus need more.

The spleen center in each of the three lower bodies organizes and distributes the seven pranas to that body. The spleen center of each of the three lower bodies uses sixth ray pranic energy to build its energy sphere when it is focused on the spirit sphere of the solar plexus center.

The *etheric* spleen center functions differently from the astral and mental spleen centers as a result of the process of digestion. This center matches its release of etheric prana to that of the dense food. The center's function at that time is to compare the dense prana in the form of food and provide at a matching rate an appropriate finer prana to the corresponding center, organ, or gland so that digestion can ensue, and disease, possibly leading to death, does not result from failing to add the proper finer pranas. When the spleen centers focus on the solar plexus centers' sixth ray energy, they make sure that each center is receiving the proper amount of sixth ray prana it needs at that time. These centers distribute the non-dense sixth ray pranic energies in their corresponding bodies.

When the spleen centers focus on the spirit sphere of the sacral centers, all seven of the finer pranas are used to reduce the amounts of retained energies in each of them. As the centers are balanced in their energy amounts they communicate better together, improving sense and reducing the potential for disease.

Illustration 7.12

THE SEXUAL CENTERS

The major center that initially uses seventh ray energy in its function and that uses the seventh ray in the composition of its energy sphere is the sexual center. This center is ultimately located between either the ovaries in a woman or the testes in a male; however, prior to birth, before the gender is established, the sexual center in humans is in a location that is between and equidistant from the two areas where either the ovaries or testes could develop. The sexual center in humans contains *two* energy spheres, with each of these spheres normally rotating in either the same direction or in opposing directions, depending upon which gender they create. These spheres have an elliptical, or elongated, shape in all humans who do not have the sexual center fused with the throat center (the center becomes a true sphere when fused). The "wedges" of two lunar deva and two elemental energies within each of the two energy spheres are layered in the elongated direction, from the top to the bottom of the center (with the top of the etheric and astral centers pointed away from a person's head or more towards a person's feet). The elemental energy in each of the three sexual centers of the lower bodies is the most dense and is of the highest total volume of any elemental energy within any of the energy spheres of that body. This density is the result of the presence of only two lunar devas in each energy sphere—with the remainder of the space containing quite dense elemental energy, of the seventh ray type. The force that the spinning of these very dense elementals imposes on all of the other elemental energies in the spheres in the body keeps the direction of and regularity of spin for each center. The energy centers are interconnected through the synthesizing thought of the personality. Note that the ray focus of the centers for each body is either feminine (two, four, and six) or masculine (one, three, five, and seven). A center's energy spheres for that body usually spin in the same direction as the sexual center (either clockwise or counter-clockwise as viewed from the top of each sphere of the center); the sexual center and the other centers in an opposite-spinning body usually spin in the opposite direction. Thus the sexual center's energy spheres usually control the regularity of spin of the centers in each body.

All the centers besides the sexual in each body become additionally directed in their spin by the lowest (the sexual) center, which overpowers them with its relatively dense elemental energy when this energy is not cancelled out. Between the two elongated energy spheres and inside both of them is a single spirit sphere. When the elongated energy spheres oppose each other in spin and eliminate the force of the elemental energy in the energy spheres, the gender of a person is determined by the permanent atom and is always female. The permanent atoms represent form, or a female quality, while spirit represents thought, or a masculine quality. In females, the effect is the creation of a counter-clockwise rotation in the etheric and lower mental bodies' energy spheres, as observed from the top of the center. The energy spheres in the centers in the astral body rotate clockwise in females. The etheric and lower mental sexual center is rotating counter-clockwise in the female's left-side energy sphere and opposes the other sexual energy sphere; the left side is the dominant, or controlling, sphere of opposition because its rotation is the same as determined by the permanent atom in that body. When the two elongated sexual energy spheres are rotating together in the same direction, additional seventh ray energy is needed in order to produce this effect. This direction is, in humans, most of the time, clockwise for both of the sexual energy spheres on the etheric and lower mental bodies, in observing them from the top of the center (which on the etheric and astral bodies is towards the feet and away from the head). The human will become formed as a male when the spins are the same, countering through force of the dense elemental energies the permanent atom's direction of spin, but also in accord with the soul, Solar Angel, and their shared Self's higher mental thought of which gender will be more conducive towards the human creating the most amount of virtue in that

The Sexual Centers

Etheric/Dense Physical Sexual Centers

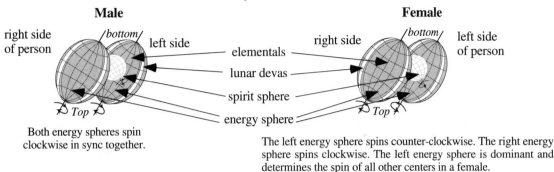

Male

right side of person /bottom/ left side

elementals
lunar devas
spirit sphere
energy sphere

Both energy spheres spin clockwise in sync together.

Female

right side /bottom/ left side of person

The left energy sphere spins counter-clockwise. The right energy sphere spins clockwise. The left energy sphere is dominant and determines the spin of all other centers in a female.

The Exchange of Sexual Energy on the Etheric/Dense Physical Plane

The phase, or degree, of the Ray Lord of the etheric/dense physical plane is 150° for the energy spheres and 30° for the spirit sphere. There is a range of +/- 29° from 150° in phase for each center on each plane for each person.

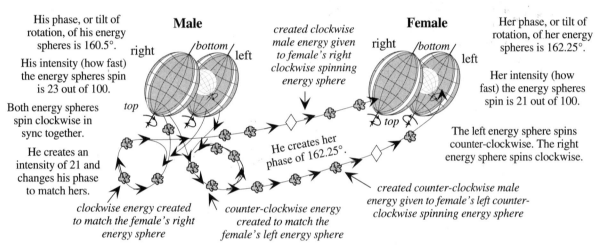

His phase, or tilt of rotation, of his energy spheres is 160.5°.

His intensity (how fast) the energy spheres spin is 23 out of 100.

Both energy spheres spin clockwise in sync together.

He creates an intensity of 21 and changes his phase to match hers.

Male

right /bottom/ left

top

created clockwise male energy given to female's right clockwise spinning energy sphere

He creates her phase of 162.25°.

clockwise energy created to match the female's right energy sphere

counter-clockwise energy created to match the female's left energy sphere

Female

right /bottom/ left

top

Her phase, or tilt of rotation, of her energy spheres is 162.25°.

Her intensity (how fast) the energy spheres spin is 21 out of 100.

The left energy sphere spins counter-clockwise. The right energy sphere spins clockwise.

created counter-clockwise male energy given to female's left counter-clockwise spinning energy sphere

Seventh ray etheric sexual energy is created by each person so it can be given to the other person. Both partners must be close in degree of phase and intensity or there will not be sexual attraction between them (which does not entirely prevent them from exchanging sexual energy—but usually results in fewer sexual interactions). In the exchange of sexual energy the male gives energy to the female's spins. Both the phase and intensity of the partners have to be similar for there to be the creation of love.

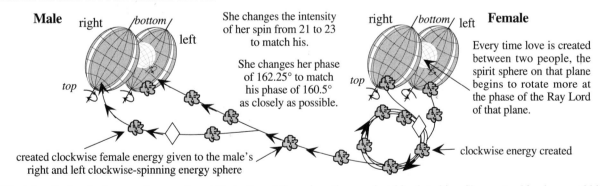

Male

right /bottom/ left

top

created clockwise female energy given to the male's right and left clockwise-spinning energy sphere

She changes the intensity of her spin from 21 to 23 to match his.

She changes her phase of 162.25° to match his phase of 160.5° as closely as possible.

Female

right /bottom/ left

top

Every time love is created between two people, the spirit sphere on that plane begins to rotate more at the phase of the Ray Lord of that plane.

clockwise energy created

She takes the level of energy he gave her, adds to it, and then gives the new level back to him. She creates his phase and his level of intensity in the energy she gives to him. This exchange continues to go back and forth between the two people. Note that the numeric value of 100 used in the intensity of the spin is arbitrary and was chosen to illustrate the concept. Also note that the angles, or phases, are shown in only two dimensions in these examples, and actually contain three to five dimensions.

Illustration 7.13

The Exchange of Sexual Energy When Love Is Not Created

When the phase and intensity of both partners are not close in both degree and intensity of spin, or if the degrees or the intensity of spins are close but either person does not choose to give the other all of the energy, the created energy is not fully given to one another and then becomes retained energy. Some energy becomes retained in the person who created it because the energy is not fully given. That person may also not be giving the other person energy that she or he can use. Then the reasons for giving what was given are selfish. Some energy becomes retained in the person receiving the energy because it does not add to his or her spins and the person cannot use it, but accepts it because it is stimulating. The result is emotion (not love) in one or both. There are different levels of giving and selfishness, so the amount that energy may be retained varies by circumstance and person.

Male Giving Sexual Energy to the Female

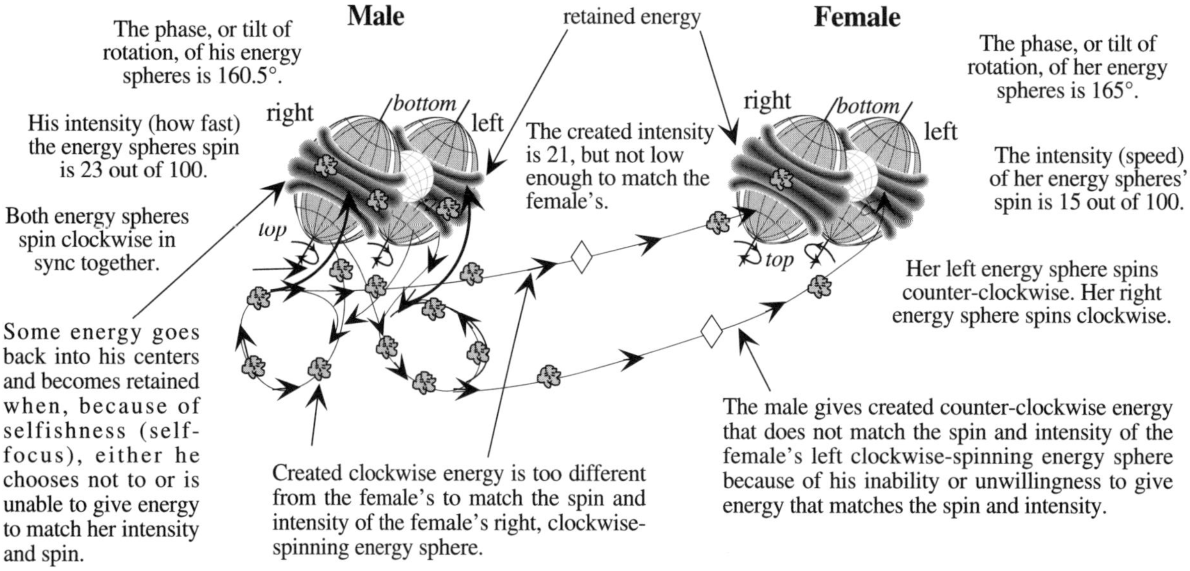

Male

retained energy

Female

The phase, or tilt of rotation, of his energy spheres is 160.5°.

His intensity (how fast) the energy spheres spin is 23 out of 100.

Both energy spheres spin clockwise in sync together.

Some energy goes back into his centers and becomes retained when, because of selfishness (self-focus), either he chooses not to or is unable to give energy to match her intensity and spin.

right */bottom/* *left* *top*

The created intensity is 21, but not low enough to match the female's.

right */bottom/* *left* *top*

The phase, or tilt of rotation, of her energy spheres is 165°.

The intensity (speed) of her energy spheres' spin is 15 out of 100.

Her left energy sphere spins counter-clockwise. Her right energy sphere spins clockwise.

Created clockwise energy is too different from the female's to match the spin and intensity of the female's right, clockwise-spinning energy sphere.

The male gives created counter-clockwise energy that does not match the spin and intensity of the female's left clockwise-spinning energy sphere because of his inability or unwillingness to give energy that matches the spin and intensity.

Female Giving Sexual Energy to the Male

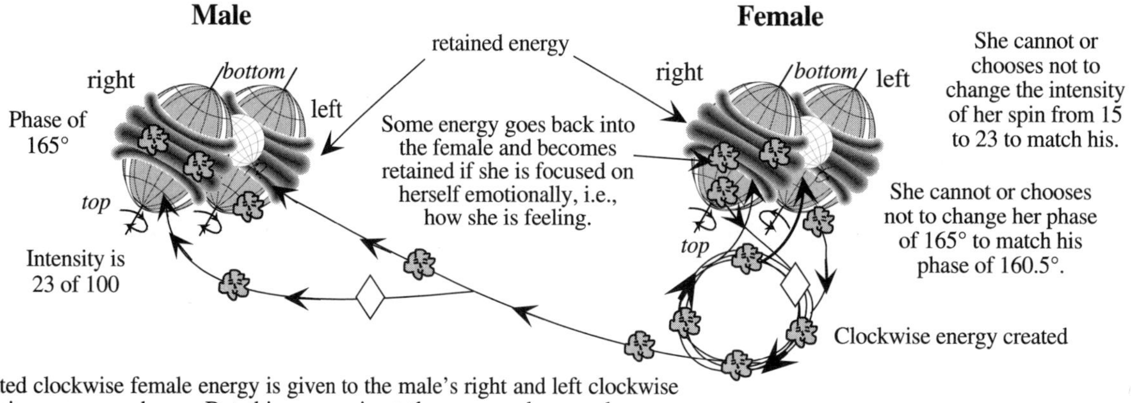

Male

retained energy

Female

Phase of 165°

right */bottom/* *left* *top*

Intensity is 23 of 100

Some energy goes back into the female and becomes retained if she is focused on herself emotionally, i.e., how she is feeling.

right */bottom/* *left* *top*

She cannot or chooses not to change the intensity of her spin from 15 to 23 to match his.

She cannot or chooses not to change her phase of 165° to match his phase of 160.5°.

Clockwise energy created

Created clockwise female energy is given to the male's right and left clockwise spinning energy spheres. But this energy is at the wrong phase and wrong intensity, so it does not add to his spin and he cannot use it to give. Energy that is not used to give becomes retained. He still accepts her energy since it stimulates him because of his self-focused position.

Retained energy in the sexual center causes the center to wobble and slow down. This, in turn, has an adverse effect on all the other centers since the sexual center has the most dense energy and affects the rate and spin of the other centers. Note the numeric value of 100 used in the intensity of the spin is arbitrary and was chosen only to illustrate the concept. Also note that the angles, or phases, are shown in only two dimensions in these examples, and actually contain three to five dimensions.

Illustration 7.14

The Astral and Mental Sexual Centers

The Astral Sexual Centers

The direction of spin is opposite to that of etheric/dense physical plane centers.

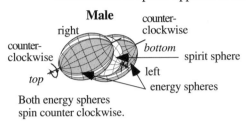

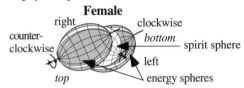

Both energy spheres
spin counter clockwise.

The left energy sphere spins clockwise. The
right energy sphere spins counter-clockwise.

The male creates counter-clockwise energy to match the female's right energy sphere and clockwise energy to match the female's left energy sphere.

The female creates counter-clockwise energy to give to the male. The spirit sphere is larger than in the etheric/dense physical center.

The Mental Sexual Centers

The direction of spin is similar to but not necessarily the same as that of etheric/dense physical plane center.

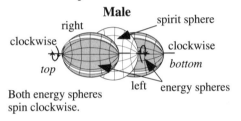

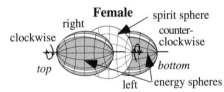

Both energy spheres
spin clockwise.

The left energy sphere spins counter-clockwise.
The right energy sphere spins clockwise.

The male creates counter-clockwise energy to match the female's left energy sphere and clockwise energy to match the female's right energy sphere.

The female creates clockwise energy to give to the male. The spirit sphere is the same size as the energy sphere.

The phase, or degree, of the Ray Lord of the astral plane is 120° for the energy spheres and 60° for the spirit sphere. The phase, or degree, of the Ray Lord of the mental plane is 90° for the energy spheres and 90° for the spirit sphere. There is a range of +/- 29° from the Ray Lord's phase for each center on each plane for each person. The spirit sphere (the white sphere between the energy spheres) is larger in size on each higher plane. In both males and females, the spirit sphere rotates in a clockwise direction on all planes.

Illustration 7.15

life. This combined thought is recorded in the spins of the tiers in the causal body for each incarnation of a human. Then the sexual center causes the spins of the masculine-rayed centers to spin in a clockwise rotation on the etheric and lower mental planes, as observed from the top.

When the sexual center's elongated energy spheres are rotating against, or opposed to, each other, they cancel out each other's energies, allowing the female spin imposed by the permanent atom to be created in each center of the body. In the astral body, all of the spins are reversed under all of the varying conditions. In the etheric and lower mental bodies, the opposing spins (of a woman) of the elongated sexual energy spheres are controlled by the left-side spin (when observed from the top), which moves counter-clockwise and is the controlling spin in women who are heterosexual; note that the spin on the right side moves clockwise. These directions are reversed in a woman's sexual center in her astral body. In a male's astral body, both of the sexual center's elongated energy spheres rotate counter-clockwise (or are reversed from one of the female's), when observed from the top.

On average, a Solar Angel, soul, and Self (which is also a part of the Angel) change a human's gender after every three lifetimes, although there are many exceptions to this average.

Comparison of Sexual Energy in the Three Lower Bodies of Two People

Everyone has sexual centers in all three (etheric/dense physical, astral, and mental) bodies. Each center has a different intensity of spins and a degree of rotation depending on the selfishness in that body and center. Compatibility between two people is based upon the similarity in phase and spin of each of one person's centers compared with those of the other person, for each body and center. Complete compatibility of the lower three bodies between two people is very difficult to achieve between two people who are selfish because of the variability in the above two conditions in the sexual center within each of the three bodies. Differences in the phases can be +/- 29° from the Ray Lord's phase of that plane for each center.

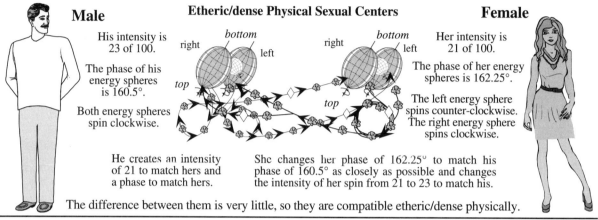

Male

His intensity is 23 of 100.

The phase of his energy spheres is 160.5°.

Both energy spheres spin clockwise.

Etheric/dense Physical Sexual Centers

Female

Her intensity is 21 of 100.

The phase of her energy spheres is 162.25°.

The left energy sphere spins counter-clockwise. The right energy sphere spins clockwise.

He creates an intensity of 21 to match hers and a phase to match hers.

She changes her phase of 162.25° to match his phase of 160.5° as closely as possible and changes the intensity of her spin from 21 to 23 to match his.

The difference between them is very little, so they are compatible etheric/dense physically.

His intensity is 25 of 100 and the phase of his energy spheres is 130.5°.

Astral Sexual Centers

Her intensity is 40 of 100 and the phase of her energy spheres is 142.75°.

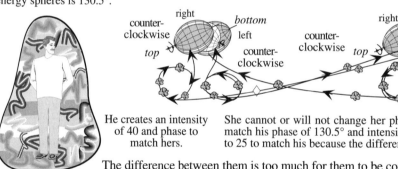

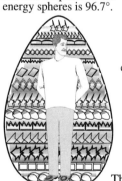

He creates an intensity of 40 and phase to match hers.

She cannot or will not change her phase of 142.75° to match his phase of 130.5° and intensity of spin from 40 to 25 to match his because the difference is too great.

The difference between them is too much for them to be compatible astrally.

His intensity is 50 of 100 and the phase of his energy spheres is 96.7°.

Mental Sexual Centers

Her intensity is 30 of 100 and the phase of her energy spheres is 114.75°.

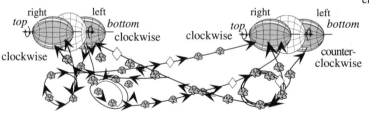

He creates an intensity of 30 and phase to match hers.

She cannot or will not change her phase of 114.75° to match his phase of 96.7° and intensity of spin from 30 to 50 because the difference is too great.

The difference between them is too much for them to be compatible mentally.

People who are not compatible can have sex together, because it is stimulating and emotional to them. Having sex with large numbers of people—especially if the other people are not compatible to the person—causes large amounts of retained energy in the sexual centers. In these cases, the sexual center wobbles or slows, affects other centers, and can cause the retained energy to attract disease. However, every time love is created, the spirit sphere begins to rotate more at the phase of the Ray Lord of that plane, and all of the centers improve in their spins and senses.

Illustration 7.16

Some personalities become disordered through being selfish in various ways in a lifetime, but often reach this state as a result of added retained energies from the previous lifetime or even lifetimes. As one of the effects of being disordered, these personalities lose consciousness because their selves cannot give as much to bodies and senses that are not being properly controlled and if the self is not being given sufficient knowledge to by the (disordered) personality. Loss of consciousness results in suffering because much less meaning comes from a personal life with less self (to understand the life). Under such circumstances, sometimes a personality will rebel against her or his soul, Solar Angel, and their shared Self. The personality rebels because it is suffering and in many cases feels unloved; by rebelling it gains a (false) sense of being in more control, i.e., the personality seems to be more in control if its soul, Solar Angel, and Self are not. One such rebellion is to choose to be the opposite gender in sexual expression and lifestyle. This rebellion is most likely to occur when the soul, Solar Angel, and Self have decided to change their created human's gender from one lifetime to the next, creating the new person in the opposite gender of the last person they created. As an example, the soul, Solar Angel, and Self might create three consecutive personality incarnations as females, and then create the next personality incarnation as a male. Then the male rebels against the change and lives his life as a homosexual. The rebellion is usually subconscious to the self, and often leaves the person with a feeling that she or he was born, or created, as the wrong gender in her or his body. Note that such a personality, especially when it is disordered, lacks consciousness because it takes more than it gives. Then the person "feels" that he or she does not understand, or is not conscious of, the thoughts and actions of the personality. Because energy follows thought, if this rebellion is carried out for very long periods of a person's life or possibly even during several lives, the spin of the sexual center in each body can gradually be reversed. This can occur if high enough levels of consistency of choices, or will, were employed in the thought that created one or more types of the homosexual thoughts and especially behaviors. For a person who is rebelling against being born as a woman, the direction of the sexual center's elongated energy spheres opposing spins is usually first reversed, causing an attraction towards and from some other women; however, in this first stage, the rebelling woman will be less inclined towards other masculine traits. With greater levels of rebellion and will (consistency of thought), the opposing spheres can change to move in the same direction as each other, but most often will still be opposite per body to that of a heterosexual man. Men experience a more radical effect from homosexual rebellion that results from personality disorder than women initially do. This more radical effect occurs because although homosexual men can reverse their spins, they almost never create opposing spins, as a woman can, in the sexual center's elongated energy spheres. The reason is that the men's spheres were created from the added seventh ray energy—initially of a sperm. Note that a woman who has altered her opposing spins to the reverse of male sexual center's spin has the same spin as a man who has reversed his sexual center's spin. Thus two homosexuals of different gender, when the woman has rebelled long enough and with considerable will, will have much more in common with each other concerning the oddity of their gender resemblance than they have with those of the other gender who have normal sexual centers (because both of these homosexuals have a reversed male spin of the sexual center).

The rebellion of the personality to the soul, Solar Angel, and mental plane Self leads to further loss of consciousness and suffering from a loss of meaning in life as the self also becomes diminished. One loses meaning in life when one loses *consciousness* because then the person can no longer *understand* parts of his or her life. Lost contact with the Solar Angel, soul, and their shared Self is a seriously deficient condition for growing life, and goes against God's plan for humans. Homosexuality is *not a moral issue* because of one's individual sexual expression, unless it is accepted as, or, worse, promoted to others as a virtuous means of living, in and

Sexual Energy of Homosexuals on the Etheric/Dense Physical Plane in the Physical Act of Sexual Activity

First-Stage Homosexual Female

The rotation of both energy spheres is reversed from those of a heterosexual female.

A significant amount of energy is retained in the centers of both female homosexuals because the energy created increases the spin of the energy spheres in the opposite direction of their natural spin. A person can reverse his or her sexual centers, but not any of the others. Since all the centers are connected, putting reversed sexual energy into the sexual center causes it and all other centers to become imbalanced and wobbly, which can lead to loss of senses, aging, and disease. It is not loving to give homosexual energy since it hurts the other person by increasing that person's spin of the energy spheres in the wrong direction. This makes the other person more homosexual, likely to be more emotional, less loving, less in contact with her soul, and damages all of her other centers and their senses.

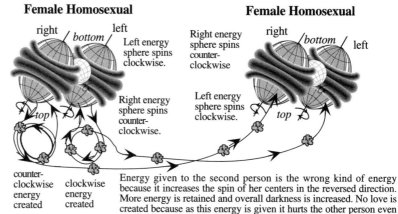

Energy given to the second person is the wrong kind of energy because it increases the spin of her centers in the reversed direction. More energy is retained and overall darkness is increased. No love is created because as this energy is given it hurts the other person even though the energy can be experienced as emotionally stimulating.

Second-Stage Homosexual Female

Both energy centers spin in the same direction, and are the same (counter-clockwise) as those of a homosexual male. This explains why second-stage homosexual females and homosexual males may appear similar in the way they express their sexual identity.

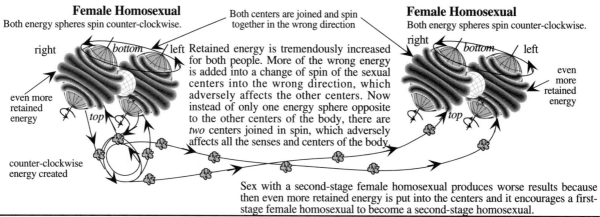

Retained energy is tremendously increased for both people. More of the wrong energy is added into a change of spin of the sexual centers into the wrong direction, which adversely affects the other centers. Now instead of only one energy sphere opposite to the other centers of the body, there are *two* centers joined in spin, which adversely affects all the senses and centers of the body.

Sex with a second-stage female homosexual produces worse results because then even more retained energy is put into the centers and it encourages a first-stage female homosexual to become a second-stage homosexual.

Homosexual Male

A high amount of force is needed to change the direction of the spins of the energy spheres from the clockwise spin of a heterosexual male to the opposite, counter-clockwise direction, of a homosexual male. The type of spin of a second stage homosexual female and homosexual male are the same.

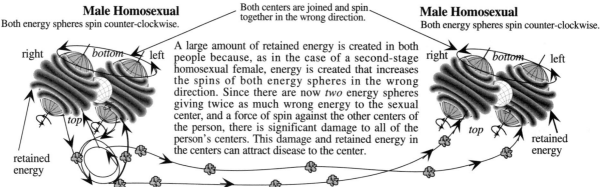

A large amount of retained energy is created in both people because, as in the case of a second-stage homosexual female, energy is created that increases the spins of both energy spheres in the wrong direction. Since there are now *two* energy spheres giving twice as much wrong energy to the sexual center, and a force of spin against the other centers of the person, there is significant damage to all of the person's centers. This damage and retained energy in the centers can attract disease to the center.

Sexually expressed male homosexuality increases darkness in others by encouraging others who are sexually involved to be less loving, more likely emotional, more focused on themselves, and less in contact with their souls. Furthermore, such activity damages all the centers and senses of both partners.

Illustration 7.17

of itself. Morality comprises the effects that human consciousness and behaviors have on virtue in a civilization as a whole. Consciousness and behaviors that lower virtue in civilization as a whole are immoral, just as consciousness (givingness) and behaviors that increase virtue in civilization are considered to be morally upstanding. Consciousness and behavior that neither raise nor lower virtue in a civilization as a whole are amoral. People who are homosexual can create virtue, and many spiritual disciples have been homosexual for some or all of a lifetime. They have not, however, created virtue for themselves and their partners while behaving homosexually. The reason is that in those circumstances they were decreasing their own as well as their sexual partners' ability to be more virtuous in some ways. This harm to each other occurs because during homosexual activities, both partners are increasing the incorrect spins of the centers in themselves and in the other person. Humans are complex beings, and can create virtue in some ways while being destructive to its creation in other ways. Something to ponder is the following statement (which will be further explained later in this and other chapters): It is not possible for two homosexual people to love each other through the involvement in some form of sexual expression (whether physical or not), because in the attempt to give to the other, each is harming the other through the reversal of their centers' spins; furthermore, both parties are reducing the contact between their personalities and their souls, through their mutually supported rebellion. For anyone who has an issue of homosexual rebellion and who wants to increase her or his consciousness and become—in thought, love, and behaviors—the gender that her or his soul, Solar Angel, and Self intended, Chapter Twelve should provide adequate information with which to start the process.

Not all people who have sexual spin problems develop them from personality rebellion; however, at least ninety-nine percent of these problems today are a result of such rebellion that is subconscious to the self. The remaining one percent or less of these problems are caused by other effects of retained energies within the permanent atoms. One of these effects is that the sexual center does not move from its original location, because of forces in the permanent atoms that are imbalanced as a result of excessively retained energies; these retained energies originate from high levels of selfishness in one or more prior lives, and keep the center in its central position in the lower body. This condition then creates, to varying levels, both types of (but usually not well developed) sexual organs and supporting glands. Such a person will have outward indications of being both genders, with the actual gender unable to be determined accurately until his or her personality is mostly developed, sometime around age twenty-one; however, if someone who is afflicted in this way becomes very virtuous earlier in life, the increased soul contact will enable that person to determine his or her true (soul-chosen) gender at an earlier age. There are many other conditions and even more uncommon ones that can result from problems in the sexual center's spin. Some of these conditions will be more fully explained at a different time, since such explanations fall outside of this book's purpose.

The etheric/dense physical sexual center creates the split sense of hearing. It is a sense that, when used selfishly, leads to incorrect selectivity in what will be heard—especially in communication (verbal as well as non-verbal) from others. This selectivity in hearing is most restrictive of accuracy when humans selfishly relate to each other and *attempt* to communicate with each other when sexual emotions are involved. The cause of this problem is that the seventh ray, which helps to build the sense of this center, is strongly affected by both gravity and inertia; in addition, the condition is the worst for those who are alive etheric/dense physically, on the *seventh* plane. The reason is that the seventh plane corresponds to the seventh ray and center and the center's split sense of hearing.

To improve the difficult condition of human hearing not being very accurate, which is a condition created by the separated sexual center, this center needs the third ray added by more giving, or by using the center and its sense of hearing in a more loving manner. When the third ray is spiritually added to the seventh (through the thought of the higher spirit of the human soul, directed through and added to the spirit sphere of the throat center), hearing is improved to include more of all of the other senses in the etheric body, and is used objectively and completely rather than selectively and selfishly. The more that this takes place, the greater the level of fusion between the sexual center, starting from its spirit sphere, and the throat center, starting from its spirit sphere, which provides the added third ray focus. Then the person uses his or her etheric/dense physical sexual center to not just procreate and/or receive pleasure through exchanging sexual energies with another, but to give to another, clearly communicating that this other person is loved by him or her. Communicating love in this way then becomes one of the spiritual purposes of exchanging sexual energy. Spiritual discipline leads to fused hearing, which allows a person to hear those who are more conscious than himself or herself; someone who can hear in this way is practicing at least some amount of spiritual discipline, which begins at the start of the first initiation.

Because of imposed forces, it is impossible for the sexual centers to fuse with the throat (or any other) center in people who are homosexual. The energy spheres can reverse spin, but the spirit spheres never do, which prevents fusion of centers whose energy spheres are reversed. Note that homosexual people, *through* their sexual actions, will have much difficulty in communicating with each other, especially that they clearly love each other. The spirit sphere cannot gain control over a center that is reversed in spin, which means that in homosexuals fusion cannot occur and the *completion* of an initiation is impossible.

The sexual center can receive seventh ray energy and possibly third ray energies, as well, depending upon whether this center is used selfishly or virtuously. The sexual center's first function is to receive the seventh ray pranic energy that it uses to create substances in the body,

SEPARATED ETHERIC/DENSE PHYSICAL SENSES OF FORM AND COMPLETED SENSES OF SPIRIT, THEIR CORRELATING CENTERS, AND THEIR RAY CORRESPONDENCES			
SEPARATED ETHERIC/DENSE PHYSICAL SENSE	ASSOCIATED CENTER	RAY CORRESPONDENCE	CENTER FIRST COMPLETELY FUSED WITH
Hearing	Sexual	Seventh ray	Throat
Touch	Solar Plexus	Sixth ray	Heart
Sight	Ajna	Fifth ray	Sacral
Smell	Sacral	Fourth ray	(after Ajna) Crown & Heart
Taste	Throat	Third ray	Crown, Heart, & Sacral
JOINED ETHERIC/DENSE PHYSICAL SENSE	ASSOCIATED CENTER	RAY CORRESPONDENCE	CENTER FIRST COMPLETELY FUSED WITH
Lower spiritual sense, of understanding God	Heart	Second ray	Solar Plexus
			Eventually all other centers
Higher spiritual sense, of being a functional part of God	Crown	First ray	Ajna (first fused with the sacral)

Table 7. 1

which allows each of the three bodies when physically alive to procreate. The etheric sexual center also provides seventh ray energies to grow the etheric/dense physical body more than the other centers do on this plane because the etheric/dense physical body requires mostly seventh ray prana (which produces the gender and some of the growth hormones) to develop its dense form. Unlike the other etheric centers in the body, the sexual can exchange energies with other people, permitting one person to give seventh or seventh and third ray pranas to another (the added third ray prana can be given when the sexual and throat centers are, at least, somewhat fused). If only seventh ray prana is given sexually etherically, then communication between the sexual partners decreases and their relationship diminishes over time. When the third ray prana is added spiritually (through higher spiritual thought), then the partners become closer and more loving within themselves and towards each other.

On the astral plane and within one's astral body, the sexual center provides the split sense of clairaudience. The sense of hearing is extended outward towards one or more others within the same location together, whom one is focused on emotionally. Astral sound is transmitted through emotional energy by vibrating the astral molecules of a medium (astral air, water, or other substances). The atomic structure of astral form is much larger, and the energy inside each atom is *less* dense (there is no matter) and more energetic, and the atoms are closer together than in physical form and matter. (See Chapter Ten for a much more complete explanation.) When a sound vibrates astral form, since there is relatively little inertia in the medium that the waves travel through, the sound moves freely; however, if directed by thought, it will move almost exclusively towards the direction of the thought—quite differently than the way sound responds on the etheric/dense physical plane. A fairly large change has occurred on the astral plane in the

SEPARATED ASTRAL SENSES OF FORM AND COMPLETED SENSES OF SPIRIT, THEIR CORRELATING CENTERS, AND THEIR RAY CORRESPONDENCES			
SEPARATED ASTRAL SENSE	ASSOCIATED CENTER	RAY CORRESPONDENCE	PARTIALLY FUSED ASTRAL SENSE
Astral Telepathy (clairimagination, or astral taste)	Throat	Third ray	Astral telepathy and astral sight together provide the minimum combination that can produce astral clairvoyance.
Astral Smell (clairtelemetry)	Sacral	Fourth ray	
Astral Sight (astral vision)	Ajna	Fifth ray	
Astral Touch (clairtouch)	Solar Plexus	Sixth ray	
Astral Hearing (clairaudience)	Sexual	Seventh ray	
JOINED ASTRAL SENSE	ASSOCIATED CENTER	RAY CORRESPONDENCE	PARTIALLY FUSED ASTRAL SENSE
Lower spiritual sense, of Partial Super-Empathy	Heart	Second ray	Understanding God
Higher spiritual sense, of Completed Super-Empathy	Crown	First ray	Being a functional part of God

Table 7. 2

LOWER MENTAL CENTERS AND THEIR CORRELATING SENSES, AND THEIR RAY CORRESPONDENCES			
SEPARATED LOWER MENTAL SENSE	LOWER MENTAL CENTER AND ITS LOCATION	RAY CORRES-PONDENCE	PARTIALLY FUSED LOWER MENTAL SENSES
Lower mental hearing	Sexual—seventh sub-plane	Seventh ray	
Lower mental touch	Solar Plexus—sixth sub-plane	Sixth ray	Lower mental hearing (seventh ray) and lower mental taste (third ray) are partially fused and produce lower mental telepathy
Lower mental vision	Ajna[1]—fifth sub-plane	Fifth ray	
Lower mental smell	Sacral—the throat, 4th sub-sub-plane of the 4th sub-plane	Fourth ray	
Lower mental taste	Throat—the mental unit, throat, third sub-sub-plane of the 4th sub-plane	Third ray	
Lower mental sense of the personality understanding its self	"Heart"—the personality part of the mental unit on the second sub-sub-plane of the fourth mental sub-plane; the personality's sense of self stands in for the real heart center, which is on the higher mental plane until it becomes developed through spiritual service.[2]	Second ray	Lower mental touch (sixth ray) and lower mental smell (fourth ray) are partially fused and produce lower mental clairvoyance
Lower mental sense of the personality creating more of its self	"Crown"—the personality part of the mental unit on the first sub-plane of the 4th sub-plane; the self on the fourth sub-sub-plane and the personality's sense of it is connected to on the first sub-sub-plane of the fourth sub-plane—the personality's sense of control stands in for the real crown, or head, center on the higher mental plane until it becomes developed through spiritual service.[3]	First ray	

1. The lower mental ajna center creates the ability to speak using language—through mental symbols, or thought-forms that are formulated into sentences. In humans, the fifth mental center is used the most.

2. The personality's sense of its self, which is to understand the self more is a much lower correspondence of the higher mental heart center's sense of God in life and to understand God and life more.

3. The personality's higher sense of its self, which allows the personality and the self to become more creative, is a much lower correspondence of the higher mental crown center's sense of being a functional part of God as it helps to create more mental virtue, or truth.

Table 7.3

THE MAJOR CENTERS IN HUMANS, AND THEIR RELATIONSHIPS TO THE BODIES AND TO EACH OTHER						
CENTER—IN ANY ONE OF THE THREE HUMAN BODIES	SELFISH SENSE WHEN USED SEPARATELY	RAY FOCUS IN HUMANS (MUNDANE / SPIRITUAL)	SENSE USED TO CREATE VIRTUE, AS THE SENSES BECOME ENLIGHTENED	PLANE CONNECTED TO[1]	INITIATIONS DURING WHICH FUSION OCCURS WITH HIGHER CENTERS	
					Initiations	*Center(s) Fused With*
Sexual	Hearing	7 / 3	Hearing others to better interact through using discrimination (fuses with the throat center)	Etheric/ Dense Physical	1, 2, 3	Throat
Base of Spine	Smell	4 / 5 (and 1 in those who are being transfigured)[2]	Sight—coming from both a synthesis and new mental structure as truth, as in a revelation (fuses with the two highest centers)	Buddhic	1, 2	(partially with lower centers) and Heart
					1, 2, 3	Ajna and then Throat
					4	Crown, Heart and Throat, all fused
Solar Plexus	Touch	6 / 6	Touch as needed in love (fuses with the heart center)	Astral	2, 3, 4	Heart
Heart	Touch when emotionally loving	2 / 2	Understanding God (fuses with the base of spine and crown centers)	Monadic	4	Crown (with Ajna) and Throat
Throat	Taste[3]	3 / 7	Taste to discern one's service (fuses with the sexual center)	Atmic	1, 2, 3	Ajna
					2	Heart
					3, 4	Crown and Heart
Ajna	Sight	5 / 4	Smell to discern and discriminate the service of others (fuses with the sacral and crown centers)	Mental	3, 4	Crown
Crown	Inner Vision when used to create some virtue in a limited way	1 / 1	Creatively *being* a part of God (fuses with and through the base of spine, and with the ajna, heart, and throat centers)	Divine	5	The Spiritual Triad[4]

1. Each sense corresponds to a ray quality and to senses developed on one of the seven planes.
2. The base of spine center, in addition, uses the first ray during the following times:
   a. The accepted stage of initiation during spiritual discipleship, when monadic will is infused during service
   b. After the third initiation, because some monadic will is permanently present while serving
3. The selfish sense of the throat center has a sub-sense of hearing because people can hear only themselves— their own speech—when they are selfish.
4. The Spiritual Triad is a combination of centers at the atomic levels of the mental, intuitional, and spiritual planes.

Table 7.4

constant that controls the amount of energy in its field of potential that is attracted to the thought of spirit in *its* field of potential. The constant is established by the two different Ray Lords' thought, or speeds of light, between the etheric/dense physical and astral planes. In modern-day physics, this constant on each plane is referred to as the quantum constant. The much larger constant established by the astral Ray Lord's thought causes astral energy to follow the thought of astral spirit to a much greater extent. This relative ease in following thought allows some of the astral energy that makes up an astral sense to become temporarily projected outside the astral center and its body. It also allows spirit's thought to direct and accelerate the movement of astral energies, such as sounds, towards the astral sexual center's sense, again, enhancing the ability to hear.

 ## ESOTERIC EFFECTS IN THE SUBTLE SENSES AND BODIES

Another, seemingly amazing, change in the ability of spirit to affect energy occurs on the astral plane and is directly related to the increase in the quantum constant. Spirit can move many objects of astral form through thought. This capability of spirit's thought is referred to as telekinesis, and is the primary means of all movement created on the astral plane. The astral body does not oxidize or transmute dense physical energy, or matter, into etheric energies in order to produce movement, as the etheric/dense physical body does. Instead, it transmutes astral energies either into just a more energetic state or further into light (when the movement created is loving). This method of movement (when light is not completely created) is still based upon the third cosmic fire, which produces some friction and heat as a by-product and waste in the creation of the movement, because it is not fully intelligent in its activity. When super-empathy is used, or when all seven astral senses are joined, then fusion occurs between astral energy and the next dimension's (the mental) energy. This fusion then joins the two dimensions, their senses, and bodies to some degree. As is explained in Chapter Nine, the most advanced members of each civilization from each sub-race of people are the ones who can join the spiritual senses to those of form and can fuse adjacent bodies to each other through the two spiritual senses. Thus it is the most advanced spiritual disciples and initiates who fuse one dimension to another and use the second cosmic fire of creation in the lower worlds. Telekinesis, as well as any movement created by spirit's thought controlling energy, is also caused to a slight degree by one of the lower uses of the first cosmic fire (but not of creation)—of pure electrical (potential) attraction between two fields of thought. When used as a split sense, the cosmic fire is not used as a creator of life, which is its full potential in use; instead, it may slightly increase intelligent activity when love is created in some energy for a short time. This slight use of pure electricity, while very useful for lifeforms, astrally has little lasting effect on creating more of God. The more loving someone is, the better his or her telekinetic abilities because then greater amounts of intelligent activity are temporarily created. Those on the astral plane who have little love are likely to have little or no telekinetic ability. Evil, in its own astral realm, uses the first cosmic fire to destroy form and, in illusion, believes that it can also destroy spirit. The faster that evil destroys the form and then chaotically densifies its remaining energy, the more the evil person can move through telekinesis! This reversal of the use of the first cosmic fire requires that the power (the ability to change the density of energy) that evil has can be maintained only by continually destroying form—and lifeforms.

Those people who can use their etheric senses separate from their dense physical ones by "etherically leaving" their dense physical bodies can use these separated etheric senses somewhat similarly to the way in which astral senses are used on the astral plane. Because of the quantum constant increase from the dense physical to the etheric plane, one "travelling" etherically (this can be just a few inches outside the dense physical body, in focused consciousness) can project her or his etheric senses *somewhat* outside the etheric body. This etheric projection is usually not nearly as far or as accurate as someone can who is using astral sense on the astral plane. The use of the etheric senses in this way can allow someone to see and hear, and, much more rarely, to electrically touch, something that may be miles away (but usually is closer). Also, telescopic and microscopic vision as well as *slight* vision from the back of the head is possible; the latter is experienced much in the way that normal peripheral vision is. These extended etheric senses are greatest on the first etheric sub-plane and are progressively some-what reduced on each lower sub-plane. With great practice, a person can etherically *project* herself or himself great distances from *exclusively* the first etheric, or atomic etheric, sub-plane. Note that most people without either spiritual discipline or certain other types of training cannot maintain consciousness on this sub-plane. Only spiritual disciples can maintain consciousness at the atomic level.

The most spiritually advanced people (spiritual disciples and initiates) of the third major human race, the Lemurian, were members of the sixth sub-race and were able to unify the spir-itual senses of the etheric/dense physical body to the astral body through the use of fusion, or the full use of the second cosmic fire of creation. As a result of their creation of virtue, these people created new *astral* life for all humans. The Atlantean spiritually advanced people of the fourth major human race (disciples and initiates) were unsuccessful in creating enough virtue through fusion to join their spiritual astral senses and astral bodies with their mental senses and mental bodies to join these two planes together enough to create new mental life for humans. Thus members of humanity today both on average and as a whole still live their lives mostly gaining meaning in life astrally rather than mentally. They do so because they understand too little of their lives mentally, as a result of their lack of unified and connected spiritual sense. It is up to the most spiritually developed people in the third major *physical* race (the Aryan, or the fifth major race), who have a mental focus on their development of sense, to create new life for humans through fusion of the mental spiritual senses to the intuitional spiritual senses, on the intuitional plane. Note that while the Aryans are the third major *physical* race, they are actually the fifth major human race in total to develop on earth, if the races that developed on the subtle planes are counted. The success of this labor would create great beauty on earth and would transform earth into a sacred planet. The next thousand years are likely to reveal the eventual outcome, with the next seventy-five years playing a significant role in how the third millennium turns out.

The astral body was fused to the etheric/dense physical body by spiritual disciples millions of years ago (about four or so million), towards the end of the Lemurian race. This fusion created a new kind of life of astral focus for humanity. It meant that the astral senses and either emotions or love would greatly affect the etheric/dense physical body: emotions would reduce the senses of the etheric/dense physical body, and love would improve them. The failures of the Atlantean spiritual disciples means, today, that most people (except those who are more spiri-tually advanced) do not live mentally, and receive little meaning from their lives through mental thought. The resultant lack of truth in people's lives does not significantly negatively affect their astral bodies, just as truth does not make this body more loving. Even if people today use their mental minds to a large extent vocationally, unless quite virtuous in their creations, people are deriving most of their life's meaning astrally through either emotions or love; they cannot receive much meaning by creating wisdom, unless it produces truth in their own *and others'* mental minds. If the Atlantean spiritual disciples had been better at fusing the spiritual centers of their astral bodies to the senses of their mental bodies, as humans became wiser they would—on a daily basis—experience significant amounts of meaning in their (mental) lives. Currently, only love/wisdom can create such meaning. This is a much more difficult creation. When some-one today does create wisdom, or more wholeness in the structure of her or his mental body and mind, she or he usually experiences it astrally as either a (selfish) exciting emotion or as more ability to give and as love. To experience mental life, the fifth major race has to create love/wisdom in others, or truth; as the others do the same (create more truth in still others), *then* the person experiences mental plane life—as *joy*. Joy, or something like it, could have been the experience of creating wisdom alone *for everyone*, which is missing except in someone who has fused the astral body to the mental. This loss cannot be recovered because, similar to the fusion of senses within a body for each sub-race and race, the opportunity to fuse one body to the next for all future humans as a whole is lost by spiritual disciples living within one of the remaining civilizations when that civilization becomes no longer spiritually viable. Note that spiritually viable civilizations are the collection of one or more of the seven sub-races that are still capable of further spiritual development within that major race.

Thoughts in the mental body do not affect the astral body nearly as much as if these two bodies were fused in light; however, a dark—even evil—fusion did occur between the two lowest astral sub-planes (the seventh and the sixth) and the two lowest lower mental plane sub-planes and their senses (also the seventh and the sixth). This fusion is the previously mentioned kama-manasic connection, which instead of creating joy produces loneliness and suffering. It is not natural for people today to be able to easily change their emotions to love through their mental thought—unless they are creating truth mentally, or mental virtue, which then creates fusion between these two bodies and corrects the situation. It was necessary that a mental yoga be created that would do this very thing, so that the mental body could assume its superior position in the mental race, and especially in spiritual disciples.

There have been three major yogas invented to unify the etheric/dense physical body and three to unify the astral body. There were two yogas invented prior to A.D. 1989 to unify the mental body—Raja Yoga and Samadhi Yoga. With both of these yogas it is significantly difficult to unify the astral body through and with the mental body at the same time. The reason is that both yogas still rely on the astral body in some of their methodology, to create devotion, spiritual aspiration, and, especially, uncontrolled intuitive responses mentally. This author, with assistance from the spiritual group known as Ageless Wisdom Distributors, has invented a third mental yoga that is free of the astral limitation, and much better structured than the two previous mental yogas were. This third major mental yoga has proven successful at unifying the mental body while simultaneously and remedially fusing the astral body and its super-sense of super-empathy with the mental capacity of thought of love/wisdom. The speed of mental unification along with the astral body becoming further unified can be accomplished in a matter of years instead of the lifetimes that were often required using the prior mental yogas. Also, complete unification of the mental body itself is greatly accelerated. This has created the potential dramatic savings in the time needed for group level initiation. The name chosen for the third major mental yoga is Synthetic Yoga, a name first chosen in the 1930's by a Master of the Ageless Wisdom, who is sometimes referred to as the Tibetan, or just D.K.—short for one of his names. This Master suggested that Synthetic Yoga would be first developed in the 1990's to accomplish what has been described immediately above, and so the name has been applied accordingly.

The preceding paragraph is likely to have greater meaning to those readers who are spiritually disciplining themselves than to those who are not; however, the effect that spiritual disciples have on their civilizations and on the fusing of bodies through the spiritual senses is extremely important to all people. While most readers of this book and most people in general will not be spiritually disciplining themselves at this time, they will greatly benefit from any improvements that can be made to help those who are. Further, the meaning that is hidden in life is also significantly revealed through an understanding of how life's meaning for nearly everyone is so related to the fused bodies of such a relative few, but more advanced-in-consciousness, humans.

The Mental Centers

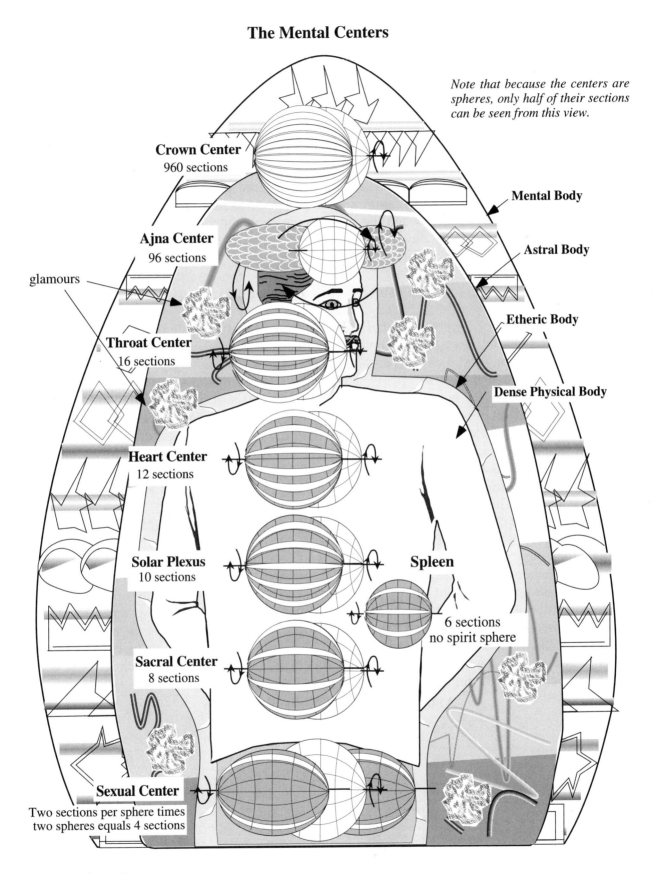

Note that because the centers are spheres, only half of their sections can be seen from this view.

Crown Center
960 sections

Mental Body

Ajna Center
96 sections

Astral Body

glamours

Etheric Body

Throat Center
16 sections

Dense Physical Body

Heart Center
12 sections

Solar Plexus
10 sections

Spleen

6 sections
no spirit sphere

Sacral Center
8 sections

Sexual Center
Two sections per sphere times
two spheres equals 4 sections

Illustration 7.18

The ability for the fused personality and soul along with the self fused with the Self to control, integrate with other senses, and create virtue within a center and its sense within a body is determined by how much the spirit sphere within the major center is controlling the center. In the three lower bodies, the spirit spheres are composed of "fallen" spirit, which initially tends to identify more with form and its thought, or with the energy in the energy sphere, than with its own thought. This misidentification creates the condition of illusion, or a lack of light, in thought, within the spirit to direct the thought of energy. Illusion reduces the self because it prevents the self from being able to give as much to the lower bodies, the centers, and their senses—which reduces its consciousness. Illusion causes the personality to lose some control over the centers and senses, which can lead to a disordered personality; it causes the control problem because the energy in the center and sense becomes more resistant to the controlling thoughtforms of the personality when the spirit in the center identifies its thought with that of energy rather than helping to direct the energy's thought. Then the senses fail to correctly inform the personality, and a multitude of mistakes are made.

 ## ILLUSION WITHIN THE BODIES

The five senses of form of the etheric/dense physical body are often referred to as sensual senses because they seem to have a tangible, or material, connection to the physical body—making them "real," or sensual—of sense, senses. Interestingly, these five separated senses are most often the *most illusioned* in comparison with the other bodies' senses, and seldom are "real," or very accurate, in their sense. The inertia of the most involutionary of the elemental energies on the etheric/dense physical plane and the increased gravity, along with the lowered thought of "fallen" spirit on this plane (and the lack in development of the evolutionary lunar devas), causes the senses to become very congested with retained energy along their ray focus (the ray focus of each one's energy sphere). A sense works by attracting a small amount of energy from outside itself that is some amount less in (or sometimes equal to) thought than *it* is. Then the energy in the sense gives this attracted energy to spirit as information. Each instance of giving the information slightly raises the consciousness of the energy that the sense is composed of. When the sense does not give all of its energy, as information, to spirit that is informing it, then the energy that is not given becomes retained in the sense. The amount of this retained energy is a measure of the level to which the spirit is in illusion relative to its senses. The amount of retained energy is also a measure of how much a center and its sense will fail to accurately function, and, eventually, how long the body will survive as a part of the life-form. Retained energies also attract disease entities that feed on the energy ray type in the particular center. Thus disease is related to the amount of total illusion in each body, and specific diseases are caused by the varying levels of retained energies in each specific center and its associated sense, organ(s) and gland(s).

Another Illusioned View of a Center

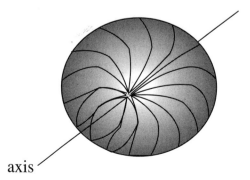

Illustration 7.19   axis

The etheric/dense physical body, with its average of having the highest levels of illusion of any of the lower three bodies, tends to consequently have the highest levels of disease and the least accuracy in sense. The illusion in the etheric/dense physical body is referred to in most spiritual language as "maya." As retained energy etherically, maya affects the nadis system, which physically becomes the nervous system, and also affects each center, which physically become all the organs and glands in the body. To those who have etheric sight, maya appears as a dark gray to black shadow—depending on the maya's severity and the amount of illusion, or lack of light—obscuring the outside of the etheric body. The etheric body normally appears to be electrically radiating the Ray Lord's light in that body, with this radiation sometimes referred to as an aura. Through the effects of greater density of etheric energy and its increased inertia, maya reduces or completely obscures this radiation (or radiance, in those fully etherically enlightened) of light. Maya increases, on average, with age, and is what actually causes aging, or the degradation of a previously more accurately created form; it also reduces growth of a life-form. In both cases, the illusioned (with maya) etheric/dense physical brain and the centers prevents the balanced and growing interaction and communication between spirit (the first two parts of God's mind) and form, or energy (the third part of God's mind in manifestation). It is this balance and communication that creates life when they are brought together within the same time and space, or within a lifeform.

Maya in the Body and Seven Centers

ETHERIC CENTERS

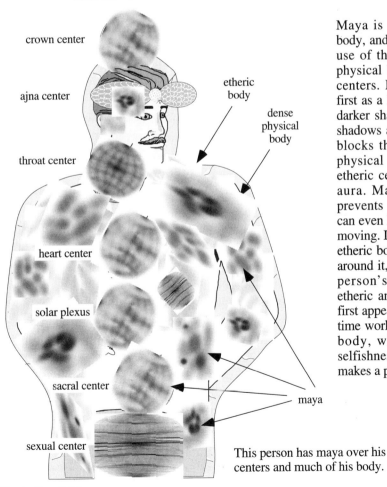

crown center

ajna center

etheric body

throat center

dense physical body

heart center

solar plexus

sacral center

maya

sexual center

This person has maya over his centers and much of his body.

Maya is illusion in the etheric/dense body, and is caused by selfishness in the use of the senses in the etheric/dense physical body and their corresponding centers. Maya, when seen, appears at first as a light gray shadow. It turns into darker shades of gray and then to black shadows as illusion increases. The maya blocks the light of the etheric/ dense physical Ray Lord radiating from the etheric centers and body, or its etheric aura. Maya densifies over time and prevents a sense from functioning and can even keep the body part it is on from moving. It is a barrier between a person's etheric body and the energy in the world around it, and reduces the amount of the person's etheric sense. Between the etheric and dense physical body, illness first appears in the etheric body and over time works its way down to the physical body, where it manifests. Years of selfishness in the etheric body is what makes a person age and look old.

Illustration 7.20

Astral illusion, or glamours, are fixed desires in the astral body, and are caused by a willful, or consistent, astral thought (creative imagination) that is used in self-focus, or selfishly, on one or more specific emotions. Glamours vibrate discordantly to astral light, accentuating fears (ultimately of death) and anxiety. Anxiety is fear of the inner astral feeling, or sensation, of pain and of being out of control. Note that pain comes from mistakes, which themselves originate from loss of control (because of selfishly retained energies) by the personality. The fear of death and of pain—which registers astrally as anxiety—is caused by the discordance of vibration within glamours. What happens is that the personality loses some control over the astral body as a glamour takes control, even when the personality still desires the selfishness within the glamour or glamours. Glamour reduces light in the astral body by changing some of this body's choices and their direction, or vibration and phase, away from the Ray Lord's thought. With less light within it and less control of the personality over it, the astral body cannot be given to in ways that will produce more light and consciousness by and within the self. The self is reduced, which then leads to a loss of meaning in its life because it has lost understanding of its life. The fear of death (of one's self) and then subsequent anxieties concerning many prior painful experiences (that were caused by mistakes) as well as fear of the pain of the death itself can lead to repression, as a defense method of controlling perceived anxiety. What is repressed are feelings of fear and anxiety, which causes further loss of control by the personality, which sets up a spiral of self destruction.

A Glamour

Being Stimulated   **Not Being Stimulated**

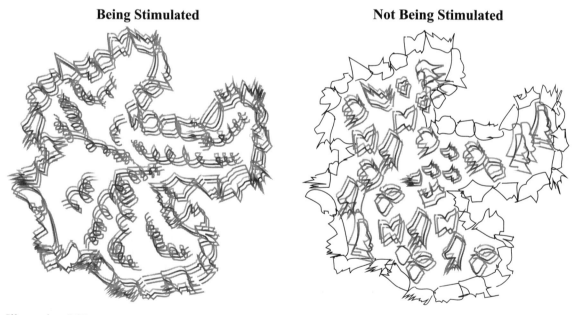

Illustration 7.21

The personality initially loses control of the astral body because of the interference from glamours concerning the joining of the astral senses in communication from one center to another. The glamours' interference keeps the senses separated, which greatly reduces empathy (the whole astral sense of all five senses combined); it then causes many mistakes in sense because of the separation of time and space and the information that is resultant of separated senses, and, of course, causes the pain that ensues from the mistakes. Mistakes in sense become mistakes in synthesized information that is created by the personality within the astral brain.

How a Glamour Is Created

This woman has an emotional need or desire to feel special. In order to meet this desire, each time she gets involved in a relationship, she chooses to use her imagination to selfishly create an unreal scenario, or fantasies. She imagines herself getting married in order to always have someone around to pay special attention to her, and spend all his time with her. Every time the woman does this, she creates more retained selfish energy that becomes bound to her emotional body because the emotion becomes tied to the astral thought. On the astral (emotional) plane, what a person thinks in creative imagination can become a part of him or her if it is connected to a strong enough energy that is attracted back to the self. After a period of time, every time this woman has either the desire or the unreal thought, each will trigger the other because they have become a connected part of her glamour. If the woman does get married, it will most likely not work out because there is no way the man could meet all of her unreal expectations and desires. The glamour, which she created over time, becomes illusion, which she is trapped within. The only way to get rid of a glamour is to give the same type of emotion to others as love.

How a Glamour Is Destroyed

On a spiritual/ personal level...

On a group level...

On a world level...

The woman frequently chooses to help someone else become more loving, so that person does not need to feel special or important. After a period of time, she converts her glamour about her thought and need to feel important into love for others in order to help meet their needs to be loving.

The previously homeless woman chooses to work through a group of people in order to help teach homeless people a trade, help them with their emotional/mental problems, and get them to be more loving and giving back to society. This helps the homeless people to develop self worth and to become more loving. The glamour is destroyed much faster because she is choosing to give on a much higher level than just personally.

The way that an adept might destroy this type of world glamour (needing to be important on a national level) is by helping nations, or the world, to realize that sometimes it is better not to give in some ways to another country. Although this might have made the US appear less important and not having control, it would have been more appropriate to help the people of Iraq through education and basic needs that would help them to overcome their evil, dictatorial government. Had this taken place, rather than selling arms to the Iraqi government (mostly to kill Iranians) and supporting other governments that did, perhaps Iraq would have become more loving. Instead, the karma came back when Iraq eventually used the arms purchased from the US and a number of other countries to fight some of these same countries.

The overall concept is that once a person has glamours, the only way to destroy them is to give to others, in a way that is loving, all the energy from the retained emotions that are tied to specific thoughts. To be successful, this giving needs to take place at the giver's level of responsibility.

Illustration 7.22

Then these mistakes are compounded when they are joined and synthesized within all three brains by the personality. Finally, the thought and subsequent judgment of informing spirit within the self becomes mistaken. Each mistake leads to pain and potential further anxiety, or fear of the pain.

Only light, or virtue, within the personality and the light in the self can stop the spiral into darkness that what is described above leads to. This light is *continually* offered by the (mental) Self, as a part of the Solar Angel, and by a human soul who is conscious (awake and aware) enough to give the appropriate thought, or light. Thus the light of the soul or the OverSoul, or both, can save a cooperative and loving-enough personality and self from fear and anxiety. The personality, through its self, needs to learn to adequately discipline itself so as to not misuse its astral body's thought to create imagination that is selfish and dark. For the majority of a human soul's existence on the mental plane, most of that soul's personalities fail to regulate their use of creative imagination towards creating more love. Instead, they mostly use the self's astral thought (creative imagination) to create emotions from self focus onto desires that are perceived as pleasurable—if they are met. Every "pleasurable" desire that is met leads to even more glamour. Every self-focused desire also has the potential for not being met, which then produces a fear of pain, or anxiety. When emotions are transmuted into love through the light of the soul and the OverSoul, then anxiety is transformed into tranquility and glamours are broken apart, creating more harmonious vibration within the astral body. Glamours will shrink, or lessen, from not being activated by the self's thought, but they can be destroyed only when the emotion *that created them* is transmuted into love. This occurs as the thought of the self is transformed into more givingness.

Glamours in the Astral Body

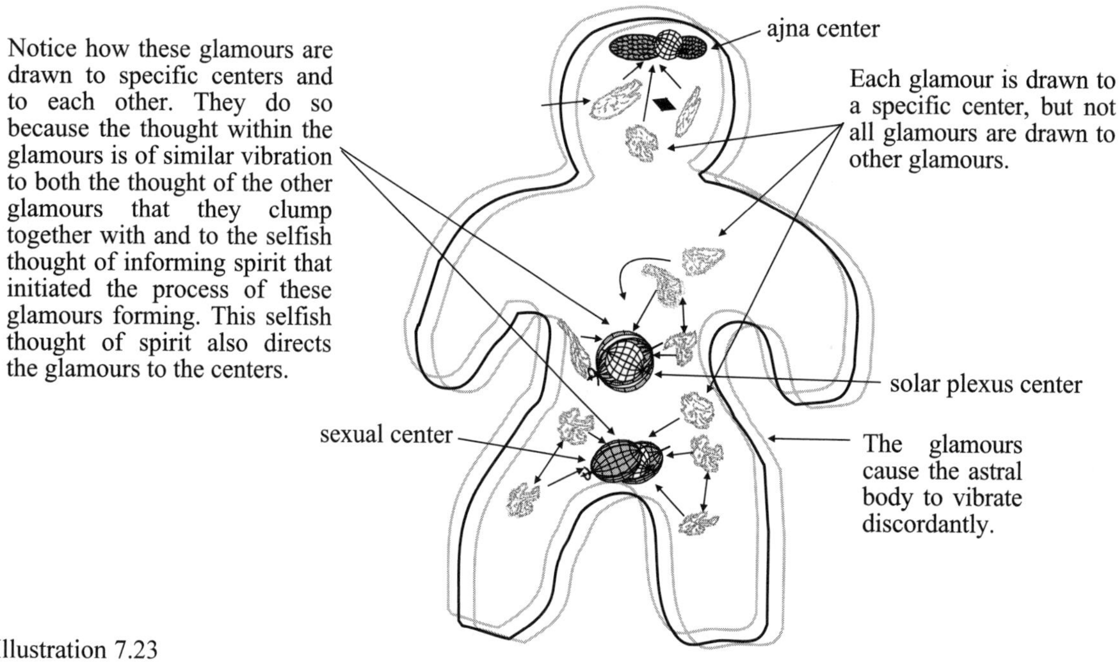

Notice how these glamours are drawn to specific centers and to each other. They do so because the thought within the glamours is of similar vibration to both the thought of the other glamours that they clump together with and to the selfish thought of informing spirit that initiated the process of these glamours forming. This selfish thought of spirit also directs the glamours to the centers.

ajna center

Each glamour is drawn to a specific center, but not all glamours are drawn to other glamours.

solar plexus center

sexual center

The glamours cause the astral body to vibrate discordantly.

Illustration 7.23

It is appropriate at this point to further explain pain, and then suffering. Pain is a response of the energy, or form, side of a lifeform to a loss of energy that is needed to maintain the form. It can be caused by a simple cut on a finger, with the slight loss of energy caused by the force of a sharp object against the skin. The body usually can restore the energy (and form) to nearly its original state, relieving the pain when it does. Pain that is caused by disease is a bit more complex because the disease is initially consuming retained energies, and therefore may not be detected until it begins to consume energies that are needed by the lifeform to maintain its form (or contaminates and poisons the lifeform with its waste products). Some people can perceive pain from injury or disease that is consuming only retained energy in a center because they have adjusted their other centers to the levels of selfishness and retention of energy. However, these people often feel the pain in the *other* centers, rather than in the one that is injured or diseased. Too much energy in a center can cause pain, because then the excess energy is not being used to maintain other parts of the body by being given to them as needed, and then the senses, organ(s) and gland(s) of that center may fail to properly function.

Pain is a message, as a third ray communication that is usually sent through the nervous system or its equivalent, by the evolutionary energies (deva energy) to the spirit informing the body. Pain is created by the deva energy creating a sudden discordant vibration as compared to its normal vibration, which is used to control the elemental energies. The greater the pain created by the devas, the less control they can exercise over the elemental energy; as a result, pain causes a further degradation of the body (form) if it continues for very long or is intense, or both. As a warning signal, pain is invaluable—but if chronic or intense (or both), it is quite harmful to a lifeform.

Most plants cannot *experience* pain because they have no nervous system to communicate it. Pain is registered by the deva energy in plants, and if chronic or intense (or both), the plant will experience a loss of life capability and will eventually die of stress, or the forces imposed by its elemental energies not responding to the lunar deva energies. While most individual plants cannot experience pain, a group soul's self can experience suffering from the death of large numbers of the plant lifeforms it informs; this loss of life causes the self to be able to give less, and to lose some consciousness as well as meaning to its life because it then understands less of its life.

In humans, pain can have a similar effect on the self. As the self loses consciousness, the personality experiences *suffering*. Suffering is markedly different from pain. Suffering is the "pain" experienced by spirit, but it is not a mechanical response to loss of needed energy. Suffering is the loss of consciousness that is recognized through the senses and fed back to spirit as such awareness. Spirit suffers when it is aware that it formerly had a higher level of consciousness than it does at present, because it loses some meaning in its life as it loses its understanding of it. The personality therefore suffers when it and its self have chosen to be selfish. This suffering ensues because selfishness lowers its self's consciousness and reduces its understanding of its life, which reduces its meaning from its life. Suffering is *chosen* rather than mechanically imposed. Pain is somewhat preventable through the reduction of karma, by making fewer mistakes and increasing the creation of virtue; however, pain cannot be eliminated for an individual human because all humans are connected together as a group at some level, and experience the mistakes of others. Thus to eliminate pain for each member of a kingdom requires that mistakes be eliminated throughout the entire kingdom as a group. Some Masters, or members of the Kingdom of Souls, no longer experience any pain in their three lowest bodies (corresponding to the three lower worlds) when they function within them. The reason is that they do not make any mistakes in their use of these bodies. A Master might, infrequently, choose a sacrificial role in one or more of these three bodies in order to absorb some karma from the human kingdom. Then some pain in the body(-ies) will ensue because at those moments the Master has lowered himself or herself, through great sacrifice, into the human kingdom.

Plants cannot suffer individually because they have no self to lose. Most animals do not, on their own, have an individual self, and therefore cannot suffer; however, a human can transfer or impose some amount of his or her self onto an animal in either an enlightened or an evil way. When humans transfer some self to an animal by loving the animal, that animal may suffer when it loses some of its self through either its own selfish acts or those of humans. Humans can also "give" (actually, force) a part of their dark or selfish selves onto animals that they have close contact with. This dark imposition of self even can occur if an animal is tortured for protracted periods of time. An animal so affected can develop a consciousness of the self that is of darkness or even evil, from the human. It can then suffer as it loses some of this selfish self from further selfishness that it (the animal) creates in its own thought. Mostly only animals that are advanced (in mental thought) are susceptible to such selfish transfer of self from a human. Without the presence of humans, most individual animals do not suffer because these animals have no individual self. Animals can experience pain and considerable levels of discomfort through mistakes and through the actions of other animals and forces of nature. Very advanced animals, and especially some primates, have some individual self structure and therefore can suffer to whatever level they become aware of having lost some amount of self.

Egotism

Egotism is illusion in the mental body caused by a person not thinking in whole structured thought and, instead, thinking in incomplete, self-focused thought. Thought is composed of elementals and solar devas in the higher mind, and lunar devas and elementals in the lower mind. When a person thinks in incomplete thought, forces build up in the solar and lunar devas (pitris) that make up the incomplete concepts and thoughtforms. This causes the devas to become damaged and fractured. Continued force pushes the damaged solar and lunar deva energy into the mental body, where they become a rigid part of that body. The person identifies with them, and the damaged energy becomes rigid and does not allow any thought that is different from it to enter the mental body on that specific sub-sub-plane. This process reduces the amount of others' thought that is in some way contradictory to the egotism, and keeps the contradictory thought from being allowed into the sub-sub-plane the egotism is on. An egotistical person then believes that his or her egotistical thoughts are correct, while he or she does not sense others' thought, and rationalizes that his or her own thought is correct. Then he or she uses that rationalization to "prove" the correctness of his or her thought. Such a person frequently will not even physically hear what others are saying relative to that egotistical area of her or his mind.

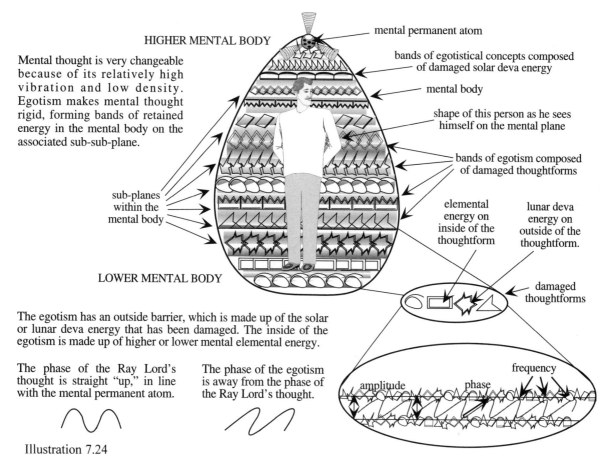

HIGHER MENTAL BODY

mental permanent atom

bands of egotistical concepts composed of damaged solar deva energy

mental body

Mental thought is very changeable because of its relatively high vibration and low density. Egotism makes mental thought rigid, forming bands of retained energy in the mental body on the associated sub-sub-plane.

shape of this person as he sees himself on the mental plane

bands of egotism composed of damaged thoughtforms

sub-planes within the mental body

elemental energy on inside of the thoughtform

lunar deva energy on outside of the thoughtform.

LOWER MENTAL BODY

damaged thoughtforms

The egotism has an outside barrier, which is made up of the solar or lunar deva energy that has been damaged. The inside of the egotism is made up of higher or lower mental elemental energy.

The phase of the Ray Lord's thought is straight "up," in line with the mental permanent atom.

The phase of the egotism is away from the phase of the Ray Lord's thought.

amplitude   phase   frequency

Illustration 7.24

Humans are particularly sensitive to loss of self because each human has a personality that, in part, exists in order to be aware of its self. Thus humans in particular suffer to a much greater extent than do members of any other kingdom. Humans are "designed" to suffer by their very place in life. But each human is given an individual soul and Solar Angel to foster the choice to choose to give, which can stop the person's suffering. This peculiar circumstance means that humans create their own meaning in life, or lack of meaning, and consequently create their own suffering. Also, less advanced humans, who have senses and personalities that are not as developed, therefore suffer *less* from the same levels of selfishness than those who are more aware do. The disparity exists because suffering is not simply selfishness and a loss of self; the human needs to become *aware* of the loss in order for suffering to take place. Thus karma and responsibility both increase as a human develops himself or herself through improving his or her senses. Note that understanding this concept is of particular importance to spiritual disciples. The importance is because those who chose to discipline themselves and raise their awareness, but then, later, choose to be selfish, will suffer much more than if they had committed the same act(s) of selfishness but had not raised their awareness through discipline.

Mental illusion occurs in two stages, and the second is a much more severe condition than the first is. The first stage of mental illusion is egotism. When the personality and its self identify with either the thought of the three lowest and separated solar pitris of the causal body (located on the fifth, sixth, and seventh mental sub-sub-planes), respectively, or some of the lunar mental pitris' thoughtforms—or both—then what the person mentally thinks (albeit slightly) becomes who she or he is. The partial and untrue concepts from the three lowest sub-sub-planes of the higher mind and their incomplete thoughtforms in the lower mental body are repeatedly used to create the person's own pseudo-truth, which he or she rigidly believes to be correct. The continuous thinking with these same mental deva and elemental energies causes some parts of them to become semi-permanently affixed in bands of energy that surround the mental body in the location that corresponds to their position on the mental plane. These bands then become retained mental energy, which can also work its way into the corresponding ray centers after a period of time.

Prior to moving into a mental center, the bands of mental illusion (the egotism) restrict other, different, mental energies' entrance into the mental body and their being sensed through a center; the illusion causes this effect by creating forces along the outside of the mental body that repel dissimilar energies and prevent them from entering and being sensed. The result is a reduction in the mental sense, to a level that corresponds to the amount of egotism associated

Examples of Normal and Illusioned Mental Centers

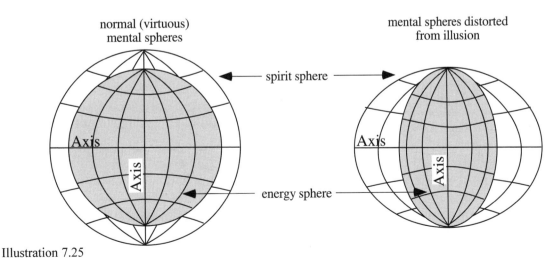

Illustration 7.25

with that sense within the (mental) thought of the person. The person who is egotistical in certain areas of thought cannot accurately understand other people's mental thoughts. Such a person often creates, in place of others' thought, a different type of sensory information that rationalizes and "proves" his or her own mental egotistical thought to be right, or correct. Egotism is insidious because it removes outside checks and balances to one's own selfish thought by reducing accurate sensory input of others' thought. Egotism is very difficult to change because of this mental defense mechanism.

As one egotism is surrounded by another in the form of a redundant, unwhole either concept or thoughtform, bands upon bands of retained mental energies become stacked on top of each other, causing the mental body to become inflexible. The mental thought of the personality and its self then rigidly resist any type of thinking other than its own in that area of thought. Eventually the mental energy, which by nature is very changeable because of its relatively high vibration and low density, changes form and becomes damaged regarding the flexibility, or changeability, of the dense energies. Then the elemental component, or the incomplete replication of the concept or thoughtform, becomes affected by a gravitational effect of much more elemental energy being attracted to the thought. As this takes place, the egotism in the bands on the outside of the body sink inside it and gravitate towards the center that corresponds in ray energy, and into the center's energy sphere. Once affixed to the energy sphere, the associated sense is separated and eventually becomes more permanently damaged by the retained mental energy. The spirit spheres are controlled by the energy spheres and their selfish thought as this condition grows beyond more than one center and sense. The selfish thought from one energy

Arrogance

Arrogance occurs when there is so much hardened egotism throughout a person's mental body that the damaged energy, or incomplete thought, becomes affected by the gravity of more and more elemental energy attracted to the thought. Gravity forces the egotism on the outside of the body to sink inside the mental body and to gravitate towards the center that corresponds to it in ray energy, and into that center's energy sphere. This process damages the mental sense associated with that center. Arrogance can connect the spheres to each other, producing a darker completely mentally self-focused sense. Arrogance is a condition in which a person believes he or she is right and others are *always* wrong. It destroys truth in a person as well as his or her ability to be wise, and blocks that person's ability to give mental thought to others. It leads to a severe lack of compassion and love because as it joins the lower centers of the mental body in dark energies, it increases the kama-manasic connection.

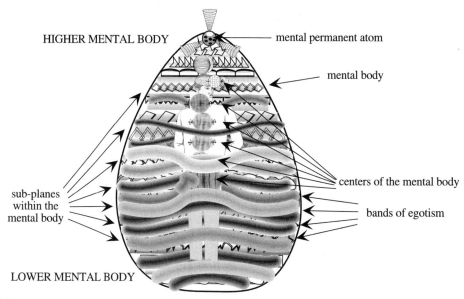

Illustration 7.26

sphere then connects to another. It does so because mental energy, even when densified with excessive elemental energy, still seeks to connect with other similar selfishly thinking mental senses much more than energies do in the bodies lower than the mental. As these centers connect, the senses form a unity in dark sense; because the self is identifying with this dark sense, it thinks more in darkness. The egotism then has changed into arrogance, which marks the beginning of the second, more severe stage of mental illusion.

Once the personality and its self have become arrogant, then not only are certain, specific, areas of thought that are untrue rigidly believed to be correct, but all areas of thought are then so affected. The person thinks exclusively egotistically about everything. Egotism is a condition in which a person rigidly believes that certain areas of his or her thought is right, or correct, and further ignores others' thought relative to those subject areas. Egotism replaces truth, or mental virtue (light in mental form), with intractable and unwhole, or unwise, mental thought. This causes the egotistical person to lack wisdom. The second stage, arrogance, is much worse. Arrogance isolates and destroys the mental body's ability to connect with the astral body in light, or through virtue. With arrogance all concepts and thoughtforms become self-focused. Arrogance not only destroys truth in a person as well as her or his ability to be wise in nearly all thought, as egotism does about certain thoughts, but it also blocks the ability to give mental thought to others (even egotistical thought). It does this by increasing astral selfishness by blocking the connection of the more enlightened parts of the astral and mental bodies. The arrogant person is not only not wise, but is also unloving, and destroys her or his higher mental capacity of thought, or love/wisdom. Thus egotism is a stage in mental illusion of identifying with some untruths and holding onto them as correct, while reducing the mental sense that would otherwise be able to recognize the fallacies. Egotism creates a lack of wisdom in the areas of thought that it is contained in. Arrogance is an advanced stage of mental illusion, wherein egotism has become generalized to all mental thought, and has become a part of the entire personality. This second, more serious stage of illusion leads to a severe lack of both compassion and love, in an unwillingness to give to others in any way mentally (by helping them to think). It disassociates the mental and astral bodies from connections with light, and further encourages a dark connection between them (increasing the kama-manasic connection substantially). Arrogant people render themselves lonely, uncompassionate, and so self-righteous that they often believe that others do not deserve the benefit of their selfish (and incorrect) mental thought.

Mental illusion can lead to the mental diseases of mental thought disorders. However, not all egotistical or arrogant people move towards mental disease. The reason is that mental disease requires not just high amounts of retained energies, but also a severe imbalance, with usually one (or at most, usually two) major mental centers becoming overwhelmed with elemental and deva energies that are severely out of balance with each other and with the other major centers. A severe wobble in the energy sphere, resultant of all the retained energy in the mental center(s), begins to cause some separation between the energy sphere and the spirit sphere. This condition usually does not create complete separation, which in a major center would lead to death of the body. This separation prevents almost *any* use of the corresponding mental sense, and leads to mental diseases, such as the schizophrenias. Although they often contain an astral component, mental diseases are diagnosable by a person's lack of one or more of the mental senses and, therefore, her or his real inability to understand some types of mental thought by other people. When this mental thought of others that would ordinarily be mentally sensed, but is not, is missing, then the personality, because of its severe fear of losing control when it cannot sense and its subsequent fear of losing its self, confabulates, or fills in, the lost sensory information with self-created thought. Excessive confabulation can lead to creations of alternate realities. The fears and frustration that the personality experiences in losing some mental sense and self frequently add an active dimension of paranoia. Note that paranoia is a mixture of anger and fear concerning the same or similar thought, and concurrently creates both an approach and an avoidance response to the thought. This leaves the person experiencing the paranoia as having no adequate response to circumstances—other than exaggerated angers or fears, or both.

Mental disease is most often caused by damage to the mental sacral center, and sometimes to the mental spleen center, as well. This damage, which is the result of egotism relative to the fourth ray energy, translates into an over-concern and unwhole redundant thought regarding how others think about oneself, and leads to improper balance of retained mental energy in the centers. Mental disease is most likely to occur in people who imbalance the same centers in both the higher and lower mental bodies at the same time. There is a higher likelihood, therefore, for mental disease to occur in those who think more in unwhole concepts and use the higher mind more, or, in mundane terms, are more intelligent, and, unfortunately, often are those who are relatively more advanced in soul development.

 ## THE ENERGY WEBS

Chemicals that are ingested into the etheric/dense physical body can dramatically affect all three lower bodies because the astral and mental bodies are connected via their brains and the personality's integration of the senses and information in the brains. Some chemicals, or drugs, disrupt the etheric centers, which alters the centers' ability to correctly communicate with one another and to therefore accurately sense; the etheric brain is often simultaneously disrupted in its ability to retrieve and/or receive sensory information. In addition, a web of darker and lower-in-dimension energy surrounds each of the three bodies' brains as well as the centers, keeping the bodies separated from one another until they can be joined by light, through the person's creation of virtue in each lifetime. The web of darker energy around each brain and center is created by structuring from the corresponding permanent atom. These structures are based on the amount of forces versus the amount of light created in a prior lifetime and stored in the permanent atom.

A web is composed of the selfishly retained energies from two bodies that are dimensionally adjacent to each other. For example, the retained energy from both the etheric and astral bodies, when integrated by the focused thought of the personality, joins together between the two dimensions and bodies to create the etheric/astral web. There is also an energy web between the astral body and the mental body. The energy webs separate the centers and brain in one body from the centers and brains in the adjacent one. Furthermore, the illusion (retained energy) in the centers of each body function as a web to keep the centers of that body separate. When two bodies that are dimensionally adjacent are integrated through the focus of the personality, a web is created. The web dissolves when the personality loses focus, through sleep or sometimes through the use of drugs. Note that drugs used non-medicinally also *add* into the centers' energies that damage the webs with the remaining level of selfish personality thought that is involved in such very emotional use of a drug. From another perspective, a web is retained energy in two centers or two brains in dimensionally adjacent bodies that are linked together by the integrating thought of the personality. Once a center becomes fully enlightened, no part of the web can exist between it and its corresponding center in the dimensionally adjacent body. When both corresponding centers in two dimensionally adjacent bodies (such as the etheric/dense physical sexual center and the astral sexual center) are fully enlightened, it would be possible to consciously both travel inter-dimensionally between those two dimensions using the centers, and to join these two parts of the bodies. The two centers become joined through the intelligent activity and light, thus making this inter-dimensional travel possible.

The forces in each body's permanent atom are the result of a prior lifetime's personality having not given information within the brain or center to others, appropriately for the others' use—which means not loving them. The structure of the web is created by the unenlightened deva energy in the permanent atom. It is filled in and held together by the darker elemental energy that is attracted to unenlightened deva energy that is replicated from the permanent atom's structure; it then creates a barrier that prevents the brain or center in one body from being in contact with the brain or center in another body. When a person is asleep or unconscious, the webs naturally dissolve because no selfish thought is holding them together. Although created by selfishness, the webs protect the person by keeping the brains, centers, and associated bodies separated while the person is conscious and within the control of the personality. Without the webs, the energy within one body would also follow the thought in the brains and centers of other bodies. If the bodies and brains become joined together prematurely, through selfishness, then the personality loses control over them when the soul is not controlling them by their being joined through light.

The Webs between the Centers in the Three Lower Bodies

Illusion is the retained energy in a center that comes from a person using the senses of that center selfishly. The retained energy comes out of the center and then surrounds it. When illusion from corresponding centers from two adjacent bodies interconnect and join together from the synthesizing and interpenetrating thought of the personality, they form a web. The thought from the integrated personality then keeps the webs in place. When asleep or at other times when the personality is not fully integrated, the webs do not exist between the bodies, but the retained energy in each of the centers remains. While asleep or when the personality is not fully integrated, a person is able to travel through the centers to different dimensions because there is no web there to stop him or her; however, since the self is mostly missing, so is the consciousness of the person doing the traveling. When the bodies become enlightened and webs no longer exist between the bodies, a person can fully consciously leave each body for another in a different dimension. Some people can train their personalities to stay conscious through the self—while keeping the personality not focused on any thoughts that integrate the centers and brains between the bodies. Then these people can consciously travel from one body and dimension to another because the webs are kept mostly disintegrated by the meditative state.

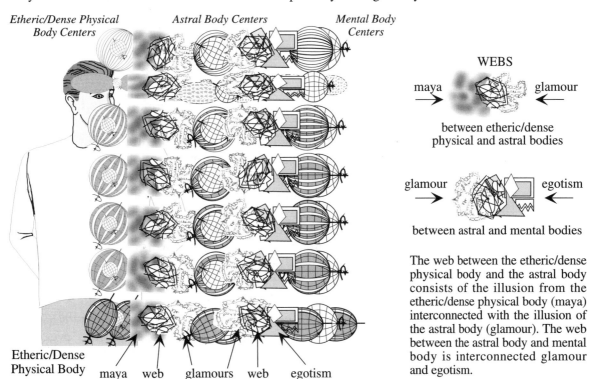

Etheric/Dense Physical Body Centers *Astral Body Centers* *Mental Body Centers*

WEBS

maya → ← glamour

between etheric/dense physical and astral bodies

glamour → ← egotism

between astral and mental bodies

The web between the etheric/dense physical body and the astral body consists of the illusion from the etheric/dense physical body (maya) interconnected with the illusion of the astral body (glamour). The web between the astral body and mental body is interconnected glamour and egotism.

Etheric/Dense Physical Body   maya   web   glamours   web   egotism

Illustration 7.27

The information concerning how much of a darkened energy web is to be built around each brain and center is stored between and during lifetimes in the permanent atom for the corresponding body. When the brain is being created in that body for a personality lifetime, the web is also constructed. Drugs, including alcohol and nicotine, create forces against the etheric web that surrounds the etheric brain and certain centers. These forces can destroy parts of the web for that lifetime. Some drugs can also affect the web between the astral brain (and body) and the lower mental brain (and body) by transferring and transmuting the etheric forces into the astral energy (or astral energy into lower mental). The personality is an unwitting partner in this destruction of the astral and lower mental webs, by synthesizing the etheric forces with the astral and lower mental web energies in an attempt to synthesize the misinformation that the drug is bringing into the centers and brains. These very discordant energies of misinformation can usually enter the astral and lower mental bodies only with the added focus of the personality.

An example of the effect of the webs is in playing with a pet dog, trying to catch it or take a toy away from it, the dog usually wins as long as it wants to. Not only might the dog have better senses that permit it to move faster than the human can, but it also makes faster decisions about which way to move and how to coordinate its movements. The reason is that the etheric/dense physical and astral bodies of most animals are joined by their respective group souls, and so—unlike a human—the dog can almost simultaneously sense astrally and respond etheric/dense physically. A human's selfishness creates webs that surround the brain in each of the three lower bodies, which prevents the thoughts in one brain from directly inter-mingling with thoughts in another. Ordinarily, thoughts in different brains must be integrated by the personality. Animals do not have such selfishness, and they do not have personalities. Because most animals' etheric and astral brains are joined, there is a natural connection of these bodies and thus an immediate transfer of information between the etheric/dense physical and astral brains in most animals' bodies. In addition, not only does the animal have less information to process than that which a human's senses provide, the animal's information is clearer because most animals do not have the illusion in these two bodies that humans do…as a result, most animals typically have better senses than humans do.

Psychologically, the same drugs usually affect animals and humans differently because the animals are missing a personality. Advanced animals, however, and especially pets may be starting to develop a very small amount of self that substitutes for personality within them. Some people observe in an animal's behavior indications of what connotes, to these observers, the presence of a personality in the animal. These observations are, in *effect*, often correct. In nearly all animals, the group soul and its self function as the personality and integrate most of their (the group soul's and self's) knowledge using sensory information. This causes drugs to have much less of a lasting effect on the small amount of the webs created by the group soul's self and on the astral brain and whatever amount of lower mental brain that the animals have. Humans are quite different from animals in this respect. Any damage to the webs, which occurs almost exclusively to humans, remains for an entire lifetime. The damage remains until its repair within a newly incarnated person from the re-created structuring in the permanent atoms. Note that although the permanent atoms can be changed within a lifetime, the restructuring of the webs cannot. The reason is that the *entire* structuring of the bodies and webs must occur all at the same time. This happens because each web's structure is part of the centers of that body and the web and centers of the adjacent body. Because the bodies are so tied together, at no time other than prior to one's incarnation are all of the bodies dissolved to such a level, with the complete structure of the atoms available with which to create, that would permit this level of restructuring to take place. Once a web is damaged, direct contact between one body's brain and center and another can occur without control by the personality. Then, without adequate control from higher thought, the selfish person becomes animal-like in some thoughts and behaviors, because the personality (and its control) has been circumvented. Because of selfishness, the thoughts in one brain are not the same as in another, which causes erratic behavior. However, the behavior of people who have one or more damaged webs is much more erratic than animal behavior typically is. The reason is that animals are guided by the instincts that their respective group souls provide. What happens with humans who have damaged webs is that dark, or selfish, astral and/or lower mental thoughts can directly be connected to the etheric/dense physical brain without control from the personality and its self, nor, of course, from the soul or OverSoul and Self. Functioning in this way can quickly lead to a human life becoming lost and spiraling downward into the path of darkness, and possibly to possession. All of these effects can be caused by the premature destruction of the webs.

Under certain circumstances, which would occur only rarely today (and most often in primitive societies), a personality that is somewhat fused to its soul may choose to ingest or otherwise introduce into its etheric/dense physical body chemicals, or drugs. The purpose of doing this is to dissolve the webs in order to become more virtuous, or thinking more spiritually in form (spirit's thought is composed of light, or the first two aspects of God's mind). These practices are usually regulated by societal restrictions concerning which people can follow the practice and when. The practices usually involve some level of supervision, at least in the beginning. Since the motive in these cases of drug use is to become more spiritual, and the personality is choosing to use the drug in order to become more giving, the results are approximately the opposite of what happens to those who ingest drugs for selfish reasons. In modern societies, nearly everyone who uses drugs for either curiosity or "pleasure" is doing so for selfish reasons. Pleasure is the (temporary) meeting of a desire, which also causes that desire to be more easily created next time because thought in one direction is more easily grown in the same direction than in other directions. The webs can also be disrupted by having energies forced into them by certain yogas; this practice, if not done for spiritual growth, can lead to problems that are similar to the ones created by inappropriate use of drugs.

A Cancerous Glamour

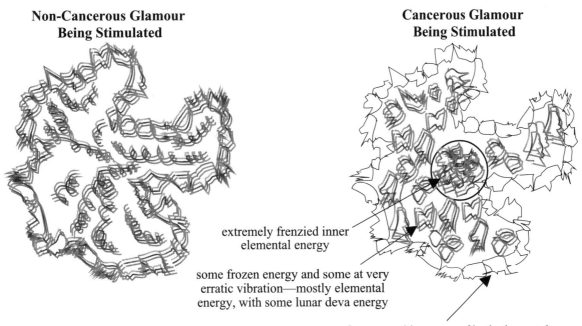

**Non-Cancerous Glamour
Being Stimulated**

**Cancerous Glamour
Being Stimulated**

extremely frenzied inner
elemental energy

some frozen energy and some at very
erratic vibration—mostly elemental
energy, with some lunar deva energy

frozen outside energy of both elemental
and damaged lunar deva energies

Illustration 7.28

Although all three types of illusion (in the three lower bodies of humans) can cause disease, the deadliest etheric/dense physical diseases are mostly fostered by astral illusion, or glamours. Included in this category are cancers that do not have etheric causes (such as etheric irradiation or toxic chemicals). Those cancers whose causes are astral begin with the repression of the *effects* that certain glamours are having on a person. Glamours are astral selfishness expressed in form, and their effects on the person within him or her *and on others*, if repressed, exaggerates the loss of control that the personality has over the glamour(s). The more that the glamour gains control without personality intervention, the less that the astral body functions as a part of the whole organism. In animals, a similar condition can occur when the group soul loses control over the astral body of, most often, its older animal lifeforms. Note, however, that in order to exist, most cancers do require the previously mentioned component of large amounts of retained energy in a center's energy sphere. As greater amounts of astral elemental energy gravitate through the astral energy sphere, the spirit sphere begins to separate from the energy sphere, with change resulting in the corresponding astral sense, organ, and gland. The sense, organ, and gland then become the focus of the energy within the glamour to uncontrollably further build up elemental energies in the center. Weeks to months (or even more time) might

Retained Energy Separating a Center

The Etheric Solar Plexus Center

This is a normal, healthy, and giving solar plexus center on the etheric/dense physical plane. The rotation and spin are steady and there is no or little retained energy. The energy sphere has a phase of 150° and the spirit sphere has a phase of 30°. The spirit sphere is able to give directing thought to the energy sphere or the outer sphere of the center. There is a single consciousness thread that connects the spirit center with all the other spirit spheres.

This center has retained energy in it, which causes it to flatten and have a pronounced wobble in its rotation. The spirit sphere has difficulty in giving to the energy sphere.

When the amount of retained energy in the energy sphere becomes so great that it works its way to the spirit sphere, a separation, or space, is caused between the two spheres. When the spirit and energy spheres become completely disconnected, the spirit sphere is unable to give to, or focus thought onto, the energy sphere. At that point the consciousness thread cannot connect with the spirit sphere of that center, and breaks. There is only *one* consciousness thread in a human body, and it must connect with all the seven major centers of that body for consciousness to be maintained. The life thread, which connects to the energy sphere, may not be further directed into the center because of the lack of informing thought of spirit. (A major center is one that contains both a spirit sphere and an energy sphere.) When the life thread breaks in any one of the seven centers, the person dies.

Illustration 7.29

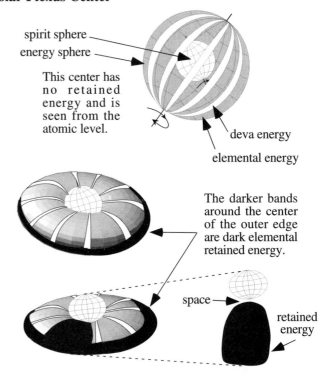

spirit sphere
energy sphere

This center has no retained energy and is seen from the atomic level.

deva energy
elemental energy

The darker bands around the center of the outer edge are dark elemental retained energy.

space
retained energy

This center has a lot of retained energy, which at first causes it to become flattened by the pull of gravity. Then the retained energy eats its way to the spirit sphere and creates a space between the two spheres. The space disconnects the energy sphere from the spirit sphere, which causes the consciousness thread to break. When the center can no longer be communicated with by higher informing spiritual thought, the center may fail to maintain life—causing the life thread to be removed.

pass before astral effects become manifested etherically as diseases, which have energies that are denser than average and are thus more affected by inertia. Normally, however, most astral energy somewhat manifests etherically within several weeks; the overall time delay is caused by time dilation, which will be explained more thoroughly in Chapter Ten. Illusion in any higher body will eventually result in a corresponding illusion in a lower body within a lifeform. It does so because thought of spirit is integrating the bodies into a lifeform, and the energy in the illusion will follow the spirit's integrating thought. Illusion in a lower body might not become a part of illusion in a higher body. The reason is that the higher body's senses are often considerably clearer, since both spirit and energy function in a relatively more enlightened manner in the higher bodies. The amount of illusion in a lower body as compared to the amount of enlightenment in the senses and spirit's thought in a higher one regulates the level to which the lower body's illusion affects the higher body.

 ## THE HIGHER MENTAL CENTERS

The centers and senses of the higher mental body are constructed of *solar* deva energy. Solar devas, or solar pitris when integrated into a form by spirit, are individualizing energies, which are slowly developing their own self structure. The solar pitris in the causal body also work together, mostly from group thought and following the thought of informing spirit, which is the soul and its personality. However, these solar pitris were given to the soul and personality for their use to help think in concepts by the OverSoul, or Solar Angel. Note that a Solar Angel is initially constructed from its highest spirit and energy within each of its bodies, down. This causes its youngest, last-developed, solar devas to be at the lowest part of its body. With the exception of the three lowest (and youngest) of them, which are given for the exclusive control by the personality, these solar pitris are very advanced in their co-creation of concepts with each other. They are so advanced because they functioned together as the lowest (mental) part of the Solar Angel's body while being used by the Solar Angel for millions of years in service to group souls. The human being greatly benefits by this gift from its Angel.

Only when the personality is using some of the soul's and OverSoul's thought can it create concepts by using the solar devas within the spiritual mind part of the causal body. These thirty-three higher solar pitris are individualized enough to *respond* only to thought that contains various levels of light. Each pitri's response is dependent upon its individual level of light. All of the connected solar pitris are impervious to the outside selfish thought of spirit. They choose, as a great sacrifice, to not use a relatively selfish spirit's help to think creatively; each of them chooses to not think creatively until being led by spiritual thought that is equal to or greater than

Bud Lotus

This bud lotus is completely closed; the lowest petal opens about one-third when
the first personality is created by a new human soul. (See illustration 6.19.)

Illustration 7.30

its own. In the beginning of a human soul's existence, all of the solar devas in the causal body except the three separated and lowest ones are closed in on each other. They can communicate only amongst themselves and can understand the thought only of other solar devas that are at corresponding levels on the mental plane. They create an energy field that surrounds the soul and its inner sacrifice solar devas. The causal body structure is then referred to as a "bud" lotus, because all of the "petals" of the lotus, except the lowest one (which is still only partly opened), are closed together around the soul.

The three lowest solar pitris that make up the lowest petal of the causal body create the lowest, or the seventh ray, center and sense within the higher mental body. They correspond to and eventually fuse with the lower mental body's sexual center (which is also today, in most people, fused with the lower mental throat center). The three petals that are the third tier of petals, which includes the lowest petal, create the next (the solar plexus) center and sense, along the sixth ray, in the higher mental body. Moving upward from the lowest part of the higher mental body, the three petals of the second tier create and are the fifth ray, or the ajna, higher mental center and sense. The human soul creates the fourth ray center and sense, which fuses with the fourth through seventh sub-sub-planes on the fourth (lower) mental sub-plane; this higher fourth ray center is the higher mental sacral center. The first tier of petals constructs the third ray center and sense in this body. This center fuses with the lower mental throat center, which is found on the third sub-sub-plane of the fourth sub-plane, as the lowest center within the personality. The inner sacrifice petals surrounding the soul constitute the second ray (the heart) center and sense of the higher mental body; this center fuses with the personality's heart center, which is located on the second sub-sub-plane on the fourth mental sub-plane. Also in the higher mental body is the first (ray) center from the top of the body, which is also the highest center—the head center, or crown chakra. The head center's sense is made up of the Self and mental permanent atom. This highest center in the higher mental body eventually fuses with its corresponding center in the lower mental body *and* with the fusing self. That center is the lower mental head center (the lower mental brain center). It is found where part of the personality is found, on the first sub-sub-plane of the fourth mental sub-plane, and is connected to where the self is found, on the fourth sub-sub-plane of that same sub-plane. The ray focus for the energies of each higher mental center and sense is as follows: seventh and lowest center and sense, seventh ray; sixth center and sense, sixth ray; fifth center and sense, fifth ray; fourth center and sense, fourth ray; third center and sense, third ray; second center and sense, second ray; and the first, or highest, center and sense, first ray.

Each higher mental plane center's spirit sphere becomes active in spiritual thought as it either develops a spin or as its energy sphere (if in a minor center) becomes fused with a center that is already spinning. The lowest center of the lowest petal is always active in a normal human being. The lowest, seventh ray, center can sense *and help to create* concepts about non-spiritual, or non-enlightened form; these concepts are divided into three types. They are in structured concepts either material, ideological, or causative (revealing cause and effect). Each type corresponds to one of the three lowest separated solar pitris within the petal. The next, or sixth ray, center and sense are aware of *and can help to create* concepts about spiritual, or enlightened, form that is a part of the personality and self, i.e., focused and limited love personally, which is what defines this petal in its sixth ray focus. The fifth ray center and sense are aware of *and can help to create* concepts about spiritual, or enlightened form that is part of a soul's structure, whether a group soul or an individual human soul. This center gives awareness of how souls are connected to one another, or their mental structure, through giving. It also *helps to create* such concepts. The fourth ray center, of the human soul, senses other souls and creates concepts about giving what is needed by the other souls so they can give more virtue, creating a balance, humility, and hierarchy of thought and need in giving virtue. The third ray center and sense create a spiritual awareness of the Planetary Logos, the plan of the next (the spiritual) king-dom, and the limited role that the human initiate who has this sense can create, as virtue that is needed within the entire world. This virtue concerns the advancement of *new* knowledge that is communicated to humanity in accord with the Plan. The plan of the Spiritual Hierarchy usually needs to be communicated from the Planetary Logos's initial purpose through the consciousness of the Spiritual Hierarchy, or the next kingdom (beyond the human). The information about the Plan is then transmitted to the initiate, who recommunicates it in a new (mental) way—which he or she creates—and contributes to other humans' development of civilization, worldwide, to assist in creating beauty as virtue, on earth. Note that while serving in present-day spiritual groups, initiates may sometimes have direct contact with the Plan, by-passing the Spiritual Hierarchy by understanding the purpose of the Planetary Logos through using hierarchial group consciousness. The greater focus of the entire third tier is on the third ray, communication, civi-lization, and right use of knowledge; the initiate actually needs to *create* the knowledge as *new* (never before mentally thought of). The second ray center and sense to develop and be used increase the initiate's spiritual awareness, in understanding that he or she is a part of God. This awareness comes through creating virtue. This often involves teaching in some capacity within the spiritual group and, as an accepted disciple through each of the first three initiations. The initiate becomes a leader as the inner sacrifice petals are opened and used—one added per initi-ation. Finally, the last, or highest higher mental center and sense are developed, of the Self and mental permanent atom, which then provides the fourth level initiate with the awareness of being a functional part of God, through creating more of God in a *fully* aware and conscious method.

All-Knowledge Is Created as a Sense on the Intuitional Plane

Intuitional (Buddhic) Plane

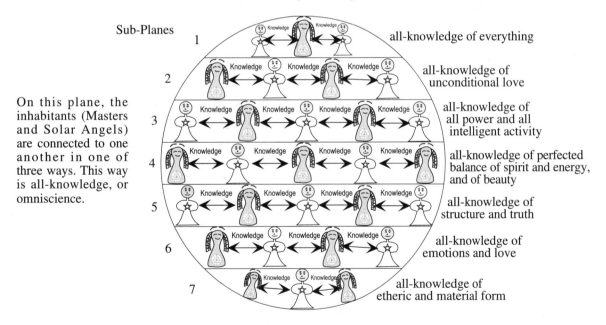

On this plane, the inhabitants (Masters and Solar Angels) are connected to one another in one of three ways. This way is all-knowledge, or omniscience.

all-knowledge of everything

all-knowledge of unconditional love

all-knowledge of all power and all intelligent activity

all-knowledge of perfected balance of spirit and energy, and of beauty

all-knowledge of structure and truth

all-knowledge of emotions and love

all-knowledge of etheric and material form

All-knowledge is developed by sharing the sense of the intuitional sub-plane's focus, including the focus of the beings on all the sub-planes below it, because all Beings on each intuitional sub-plane touch one another through the sense of omniscience.

Illustration 7.31

With the higher mental senses, awareness is accompanied by increasingly greater levels of creation as the senses are developed. Also, these senses *develop* only as they are fused with the *fused* senses in the lower mental body. When joined together, the higher and lower senses of the mental body create controlled intuition, which is the lowest sense that can be used on the intuitional plane (as a part of the whole sense of buddhi). Controlled intuition is what gives a human, as a fourth level initiate (sometimes referred to in spiritual language as an arhat) the ability to sense what is needed to create, as both a sense and thought process, new mental knowledge for the entire world.

 ## MEDICINE AND HEALING DISEASE IN THE CENTERS

While etheric/dense physical chemicals that enter the etheric/dense physical body can affect all three bodies through dissolution of one or both webs of energies that separate the brains, most medicines used by modern medical science affect only the etheric/dense physical body when used correctly, or when the appropriate medicine is used to treat an illness. When an appropriate medical-science medicine is used to treat illness, it mostly redistributes energies among centers. It uses some levels of force, often creating a structural balance among major centers. Even some antibiotics, which seem to "kill" hostile microbes, usually do so by removing some of the excess energy within a center, effectively starving the disease-causing entity of some needed energy. Less often, a force is created directly against the disease-causing microbe, disrupting its form through underlying frictional, or heat, factors. Surgery and other mechanical methods used on the matter component of the dense physical body use such frictional methods, as well—but only on the dense physical part, or the *physical effect*, of the disease.

Because energy follows thought (that is higher than its own very slight thought), when medicine is used to *appropriately* treat disease, the medicine affects the centers in the etheric body without disrupting the webs of energy. The personality is directing the energy (usually subconsciously to the self) to help to heal the body. The medicine will cause "side effects" if (as most medical-science medicine does) it transfers excess energies to other centers. The reason is that these other centers may become dysfunctional or diseased, from the addition of the energy. Disease in these other centers can ensue if the excess energy is retained in one or more of these centers, through selfishness. Since the personality is often not equally selfish in the use of its senses, medicine can be effective in shifting excess energy from one center that selfishly retains energy to another center in which the sense is used less selfishly and releases some of the excess energy. Also, some medicine increases appropriate energies in centers that have a lack of energy because of selfish imbalances in the personality's control of them. The "side effect" that a medicine produces is somewhat determined by these factors. The more directly that a medicine causes a force against a disease through frictional heat, the more likely a side effect is to occur within the same center for which a medicine is used against a disease. Killing microbes creates both heat and waste products of dissolved energies.

Medicine used inappropriately, including for pleasure or experimentation and emotional excitement, can disrupt the energy webs exactly as illicit drugs can. Thus motive determines the effects, through the thought of the informing spirit controlling the effect of the energy within the medicine. Most herbal medicines use less force and more methods of attraction of certain energies in order to balance the centers. While usually slower in their effect, their more fourth ray process than the fifth ray methods of patent medicine can often more completely heal a diseased etheric body. The fifth ray method is most often markedly stronger in its effect and more appropriate in treating severe diseases, at least initially. The herbal fourth ray method is often slower, is sometimes ineffective with severe disease, and usually cannot directly disrupt the form of disease entities. A fourth ray attractive and balancing herbal medicine can be converted into a structured, more forceful fifth ray patent medicine through transmutation, or (in these cases) densification of the medicine. This causes extreme concentration of some parts of the herbal components, but often removing important attractive energies that reduce side effects and produce long term healing. The fourth ray attractive and balancing components of an herbal medicine, in part, causes the disease to feed on the herb and to reduce its feeding on the infected center. Without these components the disease may return when a concentrated structured medicine is withdrawn; the disease could recur if the body's defenses have not been improved.

Homeopathic medicines use only the second ray method of attraction with no rebalancing of energies among centers. These medicines give the infecting source more of the energy they are feeding on within the center, and as the disease feeds on the homeopathic remedy, the center is given a chance to recover. The body's immune system needs to then take over to rid the body of the disease. In people whose immune systems are significantly compromised, homeopathic medicine will fail when used exclusively, because then the disease is not eliminated from the center(s) it is infecting. As can be surmised, all three medicinal types need to be available for use, if *proper* healing is to be consistently expected; unfortunately, most Western scientific medicine rejects herbal and homeopathic components of healing. By using no force, the homeopathic method is the safest form of medicine, but also is the slowest, and its appropriate use requires a very intuitive mind that can correctly discern its potential effectiveness.

 ## THE RAYS OF THE BODIES

The personality is initially created by the OverSoul (sometimes with the assistance of the evolved human soul) focusing tremendous levels of thought and love, or consciousness, from certain energies in the mental permanent atom as a conceptual structure. These energies came from thoughtforms that were lived by former incarnations. The structure is focused onto certain mental lunar devas on the three highest sub-sub-planes of the fourth mental sub-plane. The loving thought of the Angel and, when available, of the soul, creates light within the lunar devas that resembles a semi-permanent spark within the energy. This light allows the collection of thoughtforms that these lunar pitris create to last for an entire human lifetime; note that most thoughtforms last only a few seconds to minutes! The personality is affected by one of the seven rays (which affect only energy). This is because the personality is somewhat enlightened energy that is informed by somewhat less enlightened spirit. The human self is spirit that descends as low on the mental plane as is possible while still remaining conscious (of its self), or self-conscious; the self has no direct ray focus. The OverSoul chooses the ray focus for each personality of its associated soul that It helps Its soul to create. The personality's ray focus can be most easily determined, although not with complete accuracy, by the person's vocational choice. The reason is that a person's vocation generally produces the most significant non-hidden meaning in his or her life. Note that in this case, motherhood/fatherhood and child rearing is considered a vocation for those who choose this as a career. When the personality is selfish, or self-focused, it develops its integration of the bodies' senses and brains along its ray focus. It does so in ways that reduce its fear of death by increasing its means of acquiring what it needs, especially materially, while it is etheric/dense physically alive. The more accurate determination of someone's personality ray is in the ability to sense how the personality integrates all of the senses within its three human bodies; also, the way the personality synthesizes the knowledge within its three brains can significantly contribute to revealing the personality ray. In Chapters Nine and Eleven, all of the rays of a human will be examined much more thoroughly, including their frequency of occurrence and the ways in which they affect human senses, behaviors, appearance, and interactions with the environment.

In addition to the personality ray, each one of the three bodies of a human being, the mental, astral, and etheric/dense physical, has a ray focus that is given to it by the OverSoul, and the soul as well when the soul is conscious enough. This ray focus favors one center and sense over the other six in each body and thus creates great diversity among human beings. All ray types within a body are actually "sub-" rays of that body's ray focus in correspondence to its plane. For example, all etheric/dense physical bodies are along the seventh ray, in correspondence to the plane they are a part of; the ray focus given to a person by emphasizing a specific center and sense creates a "sub-" ray, which is what is typically referred to as that body's ray focus. The astral body is part of the sixth ray, or the astral plane, and so any one of the seven "sub-" rays of the sixth ray could be this body's ray focus.

In spiritual language, a true sub-ray is a ray that is developed through the personality's use of a body (or of the ray itself, as an integrating and synthesizing part) in order to *serve* as a fused part with its soul. The sub-ray might be a different ray focus than the body's or personality's ray because of its need in service to others. Souls do not develop (spiritual) sub-rays, because they serve along all seven rays even though they each have a ray focus that is created from the three surrounding inner sacrifice petals of solar devas. These three petals are created from energy, and therefore give each human soul a ray focus. This ray focus can be determined only as the soul fuses with its Self through creative virtue or through service (which causes the inner petals to unfold). Interestingly, the true sub-ray of either a personality or any one of the three human bodies does not change from one lifetime to the next, in the way that the personality and bodies' rays can (and often do). The reason is that this sub-ray is created from the creation of light in form without any retention of energy, or from service, and as such remains as an increased part of God. The soul ray also never changes because the soul creates only virtue in service, as well.

 SLEEP AND DREAMS

Every day, in nearly all humans, the personality and its self are selfish. A person's selfishness results in retained energies within his or her centers and leaves them open to becoming diseased, in addition to their loss of some amount of sense. To somewhat offset these selfish effects, the devas within the bodies need to be allowed time to be in control of the elemental energies that are maintaining, as best as they can, the bodies' forms. The personality remains in control of the bodies as long as it is both integrating information from the senses of each body and synthesizing and organizing knowledge within each body's brain. This process is difficult and tiresome for the personality, especially when it and its self are selfish. Selfishness creates more forces in the bodies and thus makes the tasks of the personality and self much more difficult. Generally, the personality of a person who is physically alive can relatively correctly perform its tasks about two-thirds of the time in each twenty-four hour day. The self in those who are physically alive can maintain its relative level of giving, or consciousness, for about the same length of time. After about sixteen out of each twenty-four hours, on average, both begin to decline in effectiveness: the personality begins to lose control over its bodies, and the self begins to lose its ability to be loving, or giving. The devas within the bodies become increasingly insistent in their collective thought to repair the elemental energy that has lost some of its correct form as a result of the person's selfish thought from that day, as well as any residual amounts of un-repaired damage from prior days. The personality yields to the collective thought of the devas, and with its self *gives* to the bodies. This raises some of the consciousness of the self through its choice to mostly not sense and for the devas to have control and thought—for about eight hours, on average.

The process of sleep causes the personality and its self to mostly disintegrate because of a lack of created thought (remember that each personality and self are continuously created from their own thought). To relieve some of the fears that the personality has of death and of losing its self, and as an assistance to the devas in locating many of the areas of a body and its senses that are in need of repair, the personality dreams. A dream releases excess energy within the one or more centers it is focused from and that are causing illusion in that body and in the sense, as well as in the brain of that body. The dream is usually constructed from retained, or selfishly held, energies. Dreams in the etheric brain and from the etheric center's retained information (as maya, or illusion with inertia) are usually jumbled and transient because the senses of this body are all separated, and so is time. Etheric dreams first occur when someone is beginning to fall asleep. The reason is that in a physically alive person the etheric/dense physical body takes precedence over the higher subtle bodies since without physical health, a person more quickly approaches etheric/dense physical death. The elemental energy in this body is the most dense and the most advanced because it is *in*volutionary, meaning that as it densifies it becomes more advanced in its separative and gravitational type of thought. Its *stronger* gravitating thought gives it the first and the most constant attention to repair, but this body is the most difficult one to effect repair in because of its resistance to change. These fleeting, disjointed dreams are more like separated thoughts that comfort the fearful personality as it is falling asleep, by affirming to the personality that it still exists. During each dream cycle, the etheric/dense physical body returns to a period of such dreams.

Most of the repair of a body takes place during the dream cycle of that body, but the repair cannot be completed until dreaming completely stops within that body. The reason is that *all* forces of the personality must cease in order to allow the most complete forming of the elemental energies within the pattern established for that day by the deva energy. A residual amount of retained energy often still remains because the process is based upon cycles and averages rather than complete planning in the thought of the energy (unless the energy is fully enlightened). Thus every day, *on average*, most people move closer to death as slightly more energy becomes retained in each of their bodies.

Dreams in the astral body are constructed from the illusion of that body, or from glamours, which originate from retained energies that are put into motion towards the self in a consistent astral thought process of imagination. This motion towards the part of the self that is astrally focused is referred to as *e*-motion; when fixed in place within the astral body as a result of astral thought, emotion becomes a fixed desire, or glamour. Note that the word glamour means desire or image of self that is created from imagination. One is glamoured when one's own imagination creates the images of what its self believes to be reality. By releasing some of the retained energies that feed glamours, dreams can lessen the desires that compose a glamour. However, they usually cannot rid the astral body of the glamour because the desire and its underlying emotions need to be changed into love through the *conscious choices by the self* to become more loving. The self is for the most part disintegrated while dreams take place, which prevents any significant increase in love. Once in a while, with the help of the Solar Angel and the human soul (if it is evolved enough), the self is helped to stay more integrated while an astral dream is occurring. The attempt is made in order to help the self register a more loving understanding from the relatively lucid astral dream. This is done to encourage a more loving and less emotional use of the astral senses and brain upon awakening.

When animals dream, they use the same process that humans do, except instead of a personality, it is the self of the group soul that does not focus very much on the particular animal that is dreaming, and the group soul receives less input of sense from the animal. Collectively, dreams help group souls to *better* connect with their selves. What happens is that during the time when some of the group souls' individual animals are asleep, the group soul can focus better through its self on those that are awake. The self of a group soul knows of its animals' sleep state because sleeping animals are not responsive to some of its giving thought, or consciousness. However, while an animal is dreaming its group soul's self allows the animal to create its own self, to whatever level the animal is capable of so doing. Note that this is nearly the reverse of how most humans experience dreams, because when animals dream, especially advanced animals, they have more individual self than when they are awake. The reason is that the astral body of an animal generally contains less retained energy than that of a human, and so the presence of an animal's self does not interfere so much with the energy's recovery. In animals that are tortured, the reverse is true, and these animals may become emotionally diseased or die quite early in their lives, or both, because of disrupted repair while sleeping. In animals that have any amount of individual self while sleeping, nearly all of it is further created by those animals when they are dreaming astrally. The reasons are that their etheric dreams are too transient (from inertia causing the energies to not be as responsive to forming coherent dreams), and their mental dreams contain almost no integrated sense. This is the result of the animals' mental bodies and mental senses seldom being very developed and almost never fused together.

Individual plants have only the most fleeting of etheric dreams. They usually have no astral dreams because these lifeforms have so little sentiency. It should be noted that group and individual souls dream on the higher mental plane, which enables their solar devas to vitalize their forming higher mental elemental energies. The entire process and its full purpose are more esoteric (hidden) than will be addressed by even this book. The purposes and methods of higher mental dreaming are very different from those employed by the lower bodies.

Lower mental dreams in humans help to relieve egotism, but usually cannot relieve arrogance once it takes hold as illusion in the personality. Mental dreams are constructed from egotism and frequently repeat themselves with only slight changes. The reason is that the structure of the egotism is resistant to change until it breaks apart. Each change in the mental dream breaks down some of the egotism. Most of the time, some egotism survives the dream process, but it is at least lessened; also, some of the retained energies within the mental senses that feed the egotism are used up in the dreams, improving the selfish mental senses upon awakening. Note that the improvement is, however, temporary, and lasts only until the personality is once again mentally selfish. Egotism left unchecked without dreaming can move into the corresponding center and sense that originated it. The egotism can then crystallize, or strongly hold, the retained energy within the center. This causes arrogance to develop and prevents mental dreams from being as effective. One's Solar Angel will sometimes intervene in attempt to break through arrogance as it is developing, by creating more lucid mental dreams that keep some of the self still integrated so that some wisdom can be realized from the dream. Upon awakening, the person can understand more truth, at least until she or he thinks egotistically again. As a rare event, someone dreaming on the lower mental plane can be served by an advanced initiate (sometimes an arhat) who helps that person to create more lucidity to her or his lower mental dreams. Such a mental plane server can, further, lend some of his or her self into the somewhat integrating self of the dreamer in order to facilitate even greater wisdom from the often redundant dreams that break through the person's egotism and arrogance. These mental plane servers usually serve people who are the most egotistical or are slightly to somewhat arrogant, or both. These very egotistical, and, often somewhat arrogant people are causing significant harm to others through their selfish mental thought from their lower minds and the lowest part of their conceptual, or higher, minds. In modern advanced societies, some of the worst offenders in this category are—especially in the United States—some medical doctors and some of those in the legal profession, including politics. While there are people in every profession who are egotistical and arrogant, when members of these two personality-chosen professions think egotistically, they cause the most harm to others, on average. Of course, there are some members of the medical and legal professions who create significant amounts of virtue in civilization.

In general, mental dreams are redundant; they lack emotional desire content and sensations that are the result of emotions, and they contain the most logic, with correct and complete time sequence. Perhaps oddly, they are also more difficult to remember than astral dreams are because most people's mental senses are not fully fused, which makes it more difficult for an already mostly disintegrated personality and its self to remember them. With help from the OverSoul and perhaps the human soul and/or a mental plane server, mental dreams can be remembered in part. Increased wisdom can be derived from a mental dream if a person realizes that the dream and all elements in it are about his or her own egotism and, possibly, arrogance.

Astral dreams that are the accumulation of many nights of retained energy or that result from exaggerated and/or excessive fear from that day or prior ones can lead to nightmares, in which the personality increases its fear of loss of its self, rather than lessening it through dreaming. Nightmares contain fear or paranoia (which is anger and fear together) as retained energy, and create a feedback of terror to the personality. The personality is supposed to be lessening its fear of death and annihilation through normal dreaming, with these fears being faced each night by the personality in order to give sleep to its bodies, so that the energies can grow in consciousness as well as repair themselves.

 POSSESSIONS

If for some period of time the personality chooses to not integrate its three lower bodies and synthesize the information within their brains, it opens itself to becoming possessed. Possession is a condition whereby another thinking entity that is alive on the same plane where at least one of a lifeform's bodies is not integrated into that lifeform chooses to use that and perhaps other bodies of that lifeform to sense with and, sometimes, to also synthesize the information within the brain of that and possibly other bodies' brains. A body can become possessed by one or more humans or by animals that have enough thought to get the body's senses to follow it. It can also be possessed by fallen animal spirit. Most of the time, it is much easier for a human to possess and synthesize the information from within the brain(s) of another human than it is for an animal to possess a human. This is because the complexity of the process is often too great for animal possessions to control. Many possessing entities may simultaneously use a body or bodies, especially in partial use, or partial possessions. A personality that is fully possessed becomes completely blocked off from its bodies, and it usually loses its self because the self can no longer give to the bodies. Animals can also become possessed, either by people, other animals, or even fallen spirit on the lowest planes. Such possession occurs most often when the animal is tortured, often by a human, which causes the animal to lose contact with the self of its group soul.

When people become possessed, it is most likely under one or more of the following conditions: drug use; mental or emotional diseases, and (rarely) some severe etheric/dense physical ones; overly stressful situations for children; adults being tortured; a personality becoming disordered enough to, at least at times, choose to become evil; and any other times when the personality chooses to not be in control of its bodies, brains, and self. Possession is only partial when the self remains sufficiently intact in consciousness as a result of frequent enough contact and giving to its bodies. Full possession is sometimes irreversible if it continues for fairly long periods of time. It occurs when the personality has chosen to not control the bodies for a period long enough for the self to become lost as a fallen spirit rather than a part of the lower mental mind. Humans are in a tenuous position concerning possession because each human's self is located at the lowest possible point on the lower mental plane at which spirit can create itself into a self through giving its thought to form. Possessions are *always* related to some prior selfishness, whether within the present life or, as is the case with children, connected karmically to selfishness that occurred in a prior life. Nearly all young children who are sexually molested or tortured in other ways become at least partially possessed. This is because their personalities, having had less time to develop, have less control over their bodies. In addition, a young child's self is less conscious than even an older child's self is. The reason is that the younger child's self usually both has less thought and is giving less of the thought that it does have to the bodies and the developing personality.

Evil people who live in the lowest region of the astral plane may possess physically alive people in order to cause them to do physically destructive acts. This is all part of evil's method of gaining control and "meaning" from life (by negating a part of God). Other people who are not necessarily evil, but are alive astrally and dead etheric/dense physically, may possess a physically alive person in order to regain some level of physical sense (usually to gain increased pleasure). Sometimes these possessing entities also enjoy the synthesis of information from an etheric/dense physical brain because they miss the experiences of physical plane living. A much more rare and usually serious incidence of possession can occur when a person who is *physically* but not *etherically* dead (commonly referred to as a "ghost") possesses a person. What happens is that these circumstances more often become full possessions because the "ghost" is not yet having an astral life. A ghost is rapidly losing its senses and self as a result of an effect known as a quantum irregularity. The irregularity occurs because part of its etheric/dense physical body remains alive (the etheric part) while the dense part is dead *and* separated in time and space, some distance from the etheric part. All people, when they die, can travel in inner dimension to the astral plane *if they desire to live in another world*. A physically dead person becomes a ghost when he or she chooses to remain and live only physically in his or her desires, which creates a paradox. To travel to the astral plane, one needs to desire to be alive and to live in that world. If the desire to stay physically alive is overpowering or if the person desires not to live at all, the dead person becomes trapped etherically. Such a person is usually trapped on the lowest etheric sub-plane, closest to the dense physical world. More about this effect will be explained in the next chapter.

Evil people who reside on the lowest part of the astral plane might use an etheric ghost who has lost most of her of his sense as a result of a protracted stay on the etheric plane to possess a physically alive person who is in the general vicinity of the ghost, in order to get the physically alive person to take destructive actions. Sometimes the etheric forms of physically dead animals that were possessed before death and then become etheric (animal) ghosts are used by evil people on the astral plane, also to possess physically alive people to incite them to do destructive acts. In the latter case, the acts of destruction are more random because they are governed by the animal's lower consciousness. Possessions of all kinds are facilitated by torn energy webs between the brains and centers of the bodies; each subsequent possession within a person can lead to increased tearing of these webs and thus a higher propensity for future possessions to occur. Evil people who are astrally alive deliberately will possess, if for no other reason than to further the destruction of the energy webs. Etheric possessions are the most effective means of destroying the web between the etheric and astral brains. A destroyed web gives the evil astral person or people much greater control over the physically alive person that he, she, or they are possessing.

 ## SUMMARY OF CHAPTER SEVEN

This chapter has contained much more information about relatively smaller concepts that have flowed from much larger ones that were presented in previous chapters. To summarize an understanding from this information, bodies and senses provide life with a means of growth. They do so through spirit giving thought to form in order to create consciousness and a self. This takes place while form (energy) gains in its own thought to become a sense, and also a brain, within a body. Bodies and senses provide life with a means of loving other spirit and form that it is separated from. In humans, this can reach all the way to loving God and life as its expression of God's growth. Bodies and senses have the most profound effect on the third part of God's mind and its growth, or of providing a means of creating more intelligent activity from knowledge. Knowledge comes from integrating and organizing information and from synthesizing it into something new. Knowledge that increases virtue creates intelligence in activity, which is the third part of God's mind. Through knowledge, bodies and senses emphasize more of God's growth, or life, in the three lowest worlds. In these worlds life becomes incredibly diverse because of the tremendous increases in denser energies that cause the energies to become more separated when in a lifeform. Then these energies spiritualize and individualize through thought that informs them.

Humans, in their lifeforms, are focused from the mental plane. This is where each person's personality and self reside within the mental unit. Humans' lives are integrated from a mental, or structured, perspective in creating knowledge. This is true even if they use their astral or even etheric/dense physical senses and brain(s) more than their mental (which would render them more animal-like in many of their behaviors). This mental perspective uses mental structured knowledge to eventually create a unity in knowledge within all three bodies, and unifies them into mental wisdom. When the wisdom is used to create virtue, it then creates truth. Truth is the mental cosmic virtue because it provides mental life with growth by unifying all the necessary concepts to thoughtforms that will create intelligence within any particular activity. Truth is *relative*, because it is based upon creating intelligence within certain activities in a particular time and space; it is also absolute, because for any particular activity in a specific time and space there is only one truth that will create the most intelligence. These concepts about truth usually confuse people because unless the concepts are applied with enlightened senses and thought that overcome illusion, they create a paradox. This paradox is sometimes referred to as a pair of opposites, and is caused by separating cause and effect on the mental plane and the two planes below it. The more separated the thought, the greater the conflict in the opposing answer, or solution to a question.

Human beings are attempting to create truth in their and others' lives when their selves are adequately focused on giving; they aspire to grow as lifeforms along the fourth ray line and to create the next higher cosmic virtue, of beauty, as they create their bodies and senses into superbeings of the next kingdom—of Souls. The human soul must rely upon each human being that it helps to create and guide, to be its connection to the three worlds lower than where it resides on the higher mental plane. The soul has no bodies and senses of its own in these lower worlds—only the human being's. It is the human's decision to become her or his soul through a very long process of living through lower forms, and sometimes wrongly identifying its spirit as being its form, or its three lower bodies. Each human being inherits its predecessors' developments of their bodies, senses, brains, and amounts of light and/or darkness within them, through the three permanent atoms. These predecessors are the prior incarnations of that person's soul. The permanent atoms are *energy* "memories" that karmically link each human to all preceding ones of the same evolving human soul and its OverSoul. The entire process is very long in terms of human time. It takes an average of seven hundred lifetimes before a personality (and its self) decides to consciously discipline, or limit, its use of bodies and senses to create more virtue within its life in general (and the lives of those with whom it interacts). Another seventy or so lifetimes are frequently needed for a human being to become more like its soul, on average, than not; this timing corresponds to completing the second initiation and taking the third, wherein the person and soul are now focused on creating truth, or the mental virtue. During the first initiation, the focus is on creating mostly cooperation and sharing, or the etheric/dense physical cosmic virtue; during the second initiation, the focus is on creating astral virtue, or more love with and within all whom the person interacts with.

There then remain seven more lifetimes, on average, to create the cosmic virtue of beauty, first within the advanced disciple's bodies and senses as they unify and become one within each other and with spirit. Next, the virtue needs to be created through human civilization that affects the lower kingdoms as well, and changes the planet to have more beauty within the three lower dimensions. The unifying body of a third level initiate (which first creates truth) and, later, of an arhat (a fourth level initiate) is becoming an enlightened part of earth, and once the initiate's body is unified and enlightened, it becomes connected to the sun. The beautification of this unified body adds beauty to both earth and the sun—as a part of God and the life within our universe.

The initial meaning in life to a lifeform comes from that lifeform understanding its self, through that self giving enough thought to the energy and the constituent senses that are made from the energy within its bodies. In human beings, meaning in life is first gained in this same way; however, eventually the permanent atoms become more enlightened than not in their energies, within a human of a mature soul. Understanding needs to continue to grow if meaning in life is to continue to exist, because light in form requires the growth of God's second aspect of mind in the lifeform. When more giving and the light it produces are needed to increase understanding within the self beyond what can be derived from just the self giving to its form and other selves' forms, the self (and its controlling personality) then can choose to give its thought to its soul and Self in order to grow more of God. Then understanding of the Self and of God are finally gained through the giving, as the awareness of the oneness of all life is gained through sensing the needs that other parts of life have to gain more meaning in their own parts of life. Life's hidden meaning is that amount of understanding that the self, as a result of its selfishness, has not yet gained through giving either to its own bodies and senses, or, later in developmental time, to God through helping to develop the bodies and senses of other parts of life as some level of sacrifice beyond giving to merely one's own bodies. Nearly anyone seeking the hidden meaning of life is attempting to understand more of either his or her self, or Self—depending upon the amount of enlightenment within his or her bodies. Most are seeking understanding of their Selves because their selves cannot be significantly further developed.

Some people who are seeking the hidden meaning of life have developed their senses and brains, with the help of their integrating personalities, to a level that equals the amount that their selves are giving their thought to further develop their bodies. Such people have reached a critical relative point in human development. This point, or stage, changes as the general capabilities of the informing spirit's thought increases by the overall improvements in bodies and senses for an entire race and sub-race of humans on a planet. The self of the person at this stage can no longer gain understanding by simply giving more to its own bodies. It cannot because to do so would be selfish, since the bodies' senses and brains are giving as much back to the self. While this point is always a relative one, once it is reached, this point becomes absolute for that person, and leads to a crisis for him or her—of losing meaning in life—unless a new course is chosen. That new way of deriving meaning from life comes from sacrificing one's own bodies, senses, and brains for the benefit of others so that the others might choose to do the same.

For most, the very beginning of this process is in the having and/or raising of children, with the raising of them being the greater sacrifice. As the bodies and senses develop more in light, simply having or raising children (or both) fails to give enough of the self, relative to the bodies' levels of enlightened sense. Then giving to others in somewhat personal ways, or ways that help just that person or being, becomes the emphasis of the self's giving. Eventually, the self needs to give even more because the senses have gained more light within them from prior giving to others on a personal level. At this point, the self gives with its personality to its soul and Self so that others can give as a souls and Selves, as well. Then the self has identified with and is becoming its Self and, along with its personality, is also giving to its soul. The relative levels of deriving meaning in life change based upon one's level of understanding, to begin with, and the original development of the bodies and the senses for the personality.

Once the self chooses to give more to its Self than to its own bodies, senses, and brains, it needs to discipline, or limit, the ways in which it uses its bodies and senses so it can grow them further, since it is giving the growth of them to *other* parts of life (and to God). Without this self-limitation of spiritual means of discipline, or discipline that is along God's thought, the process of further enlightening the bodies and senses ceases. This causes the person to suffer a great loss in meaning to life. This crisis is the first in a series of them, as a person chooses to tread the path of spiritual discipline, or spiritual discipleship. The first crisis is usually precipitated by the desire, or aspiration, to gain more meaning from life, with the meaning appearing to be hidden from the aspirant. The crisis is also connected to the person having reached the point of giving more of his or her self to others than the amount given to *further develop* his or her own bodies and senses. For a disciple in the first level of initiation, this applies to the etheric/dense physical body and senses; for a second level initiate, it applies to the astral body and senses. For a third level initiate, it applies to the mental body, and for an arhat, or a fourth level initiate, it applies to the intuitional, or buddhic, body and senses. In each higher level of initiation, the lower bodies are increasingly *further developed* in light to serve others, while the next higher body is brought into creating virtue for others as well—at the newly established higher level of the lower bodies. This system makes each initiation geometrically and exponentially greater in difficulty and in levels of service to others.

The bodies of all people are a part of the body of earth and the sun, which includes the entire solar system. As a person's bodies are improved through enlightenment of their energies, they become a functional part of God's growth. They become one within themselves and with the larger bodies of the planet and sun that they are a part of. The spirit and energy within them become perfected in balance between the informing thought of spirit and the enlightened thought of the energy. The spirit and energy create beauty as well as a new body for the advancing disciple to function within: the intuitional body and its senses. Adding an entire body and set of senses tremendously increases the amount of (previously) hidden meaning that can be both derived and, now, *created* for all life—as an advanced person lives for others, as one.

THE THREE SUBTLE DIMENSIONS
THAT HUMANS LIVE IN

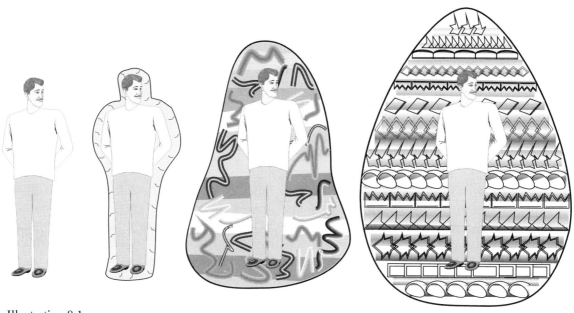

Illustration 8.1

Author's Suggestion: First turn to the "Glossary Help Guide" and read the definitions for this chapter.

   THE PROCESS OF PHYSICAL DEATH

Those readers who are reading this chapter out of numerical order might find it easier to skip ahead a few pages to the sub-section entitled "Etheric Sub-Plane Life." Then the beginning section of this chapter might be better comprehended by being read later, after more of the chapter has been read. In the previous chapter, the role that the bodies and senses play in the creation of life and its meaning was explored. This role includes providing spirit with a challenging means of eventually understanding itself, others, and its creator. The challenge causes spirit to seek to grow more love and to intelligently respond to everything outside itself as one. For humans who either fail at or reject the challenge, a loss of meaning in life results. Suffering then ensues because understanding, or consciousness, becomes lowered, with a concomitant loss of self. The successful overcoming of the challenge of being separated by and within the form of a body permits the informing spirit to grow in oneness, or consciousness. Humans can then experience joy and, eventually, bliss, which is a constant state of joy. Joy is the condition in which one's love, or givingness, comes back to her or him. This usually occurs by the focusing out onto and identification with those being creatively given to, for the purpose of furthering the additional creation of virtue. As these others then create more virtue, since they are experienced as one with the (higher) Self and (lower) self, then the Self and self experience the loving creation of more of God in all, or experience joy. When this experience becomes constant through increased purpose and consciousness, then joy becomes bliss. As bodies become enlightened by the spirit that informs them, then joy and eventually bliss become the product of the oneness with the creator.

The OverSoul and sometimes a human soul help to create each human being whom the human soul uses through which to sense the three lower worlds, or dimensions of time and space.

The human soul and OverSoul need to create a human because the soul's body of advanced solar devas, which are sometimes referred to as pitris ("partial angels") when informed by a spiritual source, can sense only relatively whole (spiritual) concepts. The soul and OverSoul cannot sense thoughtforms, emotions and/or focused, or limited—devotional—love; they also cannot sense either etheric form or matter and its effect on resistance to movement (overall material inertia). Each human soul and its OverSoul use and help to create a sequence of hundreds of human beings. Every one of these human beings has a personality, a self, and a separated causal sense of isolated concepts; in addition, each has a lower mental body, an astral body, and an etheric/dense physical body as well as all of the senses and brains that are associated with these three bodies. Only those activities that create more intelligence by a human being can enter into the consciousness, or givingness, of its (human) soul. The intelligence then becomes an immortal part of the soul and its Self, and of God's growth. The unintelligent, illusioned activities of each personality eventually destroy, or kill, the personality and its self through friction. The third cosmic fire then functions more as a first sub-ray type of destroyer than as a creator.

As each human lives in the three lower worlds, she or he focuses her or his life, at first, on the most difficult dimension to function within. This is also the one with the most potential for creativity because of its vast diversity and complexity of lifeforms. This dimension is the etheric/dense physical, which most who are reading this book have the greatest familiarity with, and which is widely considered to be "reality." It is within this dimension that the informing spirit of the personality and self has so much difficulty in *accurately* sensing and creating knowledge. The reason is that the high density of energy and the subsequent effects of inertia have caused the senses to remain fully separated in this body. The etheric/dense physical body wears out quickly, in relative time, from retained energies that are resultant of selfishness (illusion). Then the body dies, or disorganizes, which renders the personality unable to control it. The human soul and its OverSoul identify the point at which this body is creating more harm than good relative to its overall future in connection with others. When that point is reached, the OverSoul and soul then remove the life thread, or sutratma, from the "solid" sub-dimension. This sub-dimension comprises the three lowest sub-planes (the dense ones) of the etheric/dense physical dimension. Note that the exception to this procedure is in those who have chosen a path of evil. In non-evil people, after the removal of the sutratma the remainder of the human death process from the seventh, or etheric/dense physical, dimension and body usually takes place under the control of the personality, and on the subtle, or causative—less dense in energy and etheric—part of the dimension. This process greatly reduces most of the fear of death that the personality has, because its self remains intact. The personality is usually still in control of the final departure from the etheric part of the etheric/dense physical world.

Once the soul and OverSoul sever the life thread to the human physical heart, it cannot be reestablished except by them—and then only under the most unusual of circumstances. When the human physical heart stops beating on its own for a number of minutes to several hours or longer and the person remains alive (possibly with mechanical assistance), it is the life thread that keeps the cells and energies within the heart organized, as an organ. The disorganization of the physical mechanism from the rest of the body is what marks the finality of death. The life thread, or sutratma, affects every major center in the physical body, and the centers' corresponding organs and glands. Should any of the major organs lose organization, death will ensue because each of them is tied to the heart through the blood, in humans and in most animals. Although complete success has yet to be realized, a non-organic physical heart can potentially be used to replace the organic heart (albeit with some significant limitations based upon the non-organic heart's inability to grow and repair itself). This can occur as long as the soul and OverSoul allow the life thread to remain connected to this introduced etheric and dense physical energy, or matter. Physical death in someone with a non-organic, or mechanical, heart would still be based upon the withdrawal of the sutratma from the "solid" part of the dimension. Once the sutratma has been withdrawn, the mechanical heart would then no longer correctly function as a part of the organism (note that the same holds true for transplanted hearts). Dense, mineral, mechanical solutions to causes created by life are *never* completely accurate. Because minerals are not alive, the etheric causes of the mechanical solutions are somewhat different from the ones they are being substituted for. Nonetheless, humans are supposed to use civilization, which is the extension of the three lower kingdoms (including the mineral) as a part of their (the humans') bodies and senses, in order to enhance, grow, and prolong their lives in the three lower worlds. When humans use civilization virtuously, or create more light simultaneously within the three lower kingdoms as parts of these kingdoms are used in civilization, all of life grows because of the light.

When the energies that constitute an etheric/dense physical body are fully enlightened by the informing thought of spirit, they can remain together without forces accumulating from (selfishly) retained energy. These enlightened energies think more for themselves, in light, than do any darker energies on the etheric/dense physical plane. However, the light of the etheric/dense physical (seventh plane) Ray Lord enlightens only the energy in one of seven (dimensional) possible ways. This is because the seventh Ray Lord is so limited in its thought as compared to the other six Ray Lords. When enlightened, the seventh ray type of energy is very good at organizing and synthesizing itself with other energy, and thus at creating cooperation and sharing. It is not very adept, however, at the other six methods of developing life in our universe through virtue, as follows: Seventh ray energy is not very good at focused movement between itself and another energy, which would create conditional love (the astral, or sixth ray, developmental method). It is also not very good at either structuring and formulating itself to reduce forces and increase replication of forms with other energies, which would create truth (the mental, or fifth ray, developmental method) or at perfectly balancing or harmonizing its thought to that of informing spirit's thought, which would create beauty (the intuitional, or fourth ray, developmental method). Further, seventh ray energy is unable to effectively create only intelligent activity for all life through all-knowledge; doing so would include perfect levels of changing itself and other energies in density in order to achieve intelligent activity through all-power, thus creating new intelligent life (the spiritual, or third ray, developmental method). It also can create neither oneness of all life (a second ray method of development), nor new and more purpose for life through increased will, or consistent choices, and sacrifices (a first ray method of development). Therefore, the light within the form, or the virtue, on the seventh plane is reduced to a much smaller dimension of the ways in which energy intelligently interacts with other energy.

An anomaly occurs when seventh ray energy is used in a lifeform, since this energy's dimensional ways of intelligently interacting, including its ability to create *senses*, are so very limited. The bodies and senses that enlightened seventh plane energy creates through its (enlightened) thought still creates forces. The forces are not from retained energy since under these circumstances all the energy that moves through the body and sense does so at the speed of light (of thought) of the seventh Ray Lord. The forces produced are the result of being part of a living organism that has other bodies that are in higher dimensions but are not completely unified in light (the thought of God) with the seventh plane body and senses. This condition in particular creates stress on the lunar devas. In addition, the elemental seventh ray energies are *involuting*, or are *partly advancing* through gravitational means of self thought rather than through creating only life that uses virtue to advance. These two factors necessitate that all seventh plane lifeforms be allowed to disintegrate within a finite period of time. The amount of time is based upon the needs of the constituent energies within the bodies, even if the energies are enlightened. This maximum period of time that the energies within a human lifeform can normally remain fully enlightened is one hundred forty-seven etheric/dense physical plane years. Thus in order to maintain its enlightenment, a completely enlightened human etheric/dense physical body needs

THE PLANES AND CORRESPONDING RAYS, PLUS THE ACTION CREATED BY ENERGY			
ACTION CREATED BY ENERGY	COSMIC VIRTUE CREATED	DEVELOPMENTAL METHOD	CORRESPONDING PLANE
Organization and synthesis between itself and other energy	Cooperation and sharing	Seventh ray	Etheric/Dense Physical
Focused movement between itself and another energy	Love	Sixth ray	Astral
Structuring and formulating itself to reduce forces and increase replication of forms with other energies	Truth	Fifth ray	Mental
Perfectly balancing or harmonizing its thought to that of informing spirit's thought	Beauty	Fourth ray	Intuitional
Creating only intelligent activity, including perfect levels of changing itself and other energies in density in order to achieve intelligent activity through power and a growth in all life at once	New (more) intelligent life for all life through all-knowledge and all-power	Third ray	Spiritual
Creating oneness of all life	Unlimited and unconditional love and oneness	Second ray	Monadic
Creating new and more purpose for life through increased will (consistent choices) and sacrifices	Universal creation—of the universe and God	First ray	Divine

Table 8. 1

to, usually, no longer be integrated and alive after one hundred forty-seven years of life, if the energy is to maintain its levels of complete enlightenment.

The number one hundred forty-seven, itself, is a factorial of each of the seven sub-types of etheric/dense physical ray energies developing itself as a sub-sub-ray of one of the other sub-rays (or of its own ray) through enlightenment. Simultaneously, the ray energy is becoming a sub-ray factor of one of the three aspects of God's mind (times one year per factor). Seven times seven is forty-nine, times three (three aspects of God's mind for each sense's use) equals one hundred forty-seven years on the etheric/dense physical plane. In a very advanced human, who is in his or her last etheric/dense physical incarnation, it would be possible to live to one hundred forty-seven years *without physically aging* beyond the age of twenty-four and one-half years (in esoteric writing, this number has been rounded to twenty-five years). While this usually does not actually occur, because of other mitigating (karmic) circumstances that are tied to the very advanced human's service to others, the body would stop aging at the average point of harmony in growth of the intuitional body as it is used in service through the three lower bodies. The intuitional body is developed between the ages of twenty-one and twenty-eight. In an enlightened person it is fully used in service as it and each of its senses are developed. Thus at such a person's age of twenty-four and one-half years, the intuitional senses that have been developed and are being fully used in service stop all aging in the lower bodies. The reason is that the person has reached buddhic consciousness, by her or his self giving at least *one-half* of the consciousness from the intuitional body. When a person gives more than one-half of the thought from a body, that body becomes the new focus of consciousness.

Death from the etheric/dense physical body is a necessary inevitability because of the physics of this lowest plane of our universe. Death from the physical body of matter is controlled by the OverSoul, and by the human soul to the level at which the soul is developed in consciousness. Death from the etheric body is usually controlled by the personality. The *typical* process of human physical death takes place in the following five steps. The first step is that the sutratma, or life thread, is loosened from the heart center. The sutratma often gradually, to a point, becomes loosened from the physical heart, by the heart center no longer informing the physical organ. In the second step, the consciousness thread remains focused in the etheric center (and sense) from which the person had most focused his or her life (in use of physical sense) while alive physically. In the third step, the physical brain is separated from the etheric brain by the person leaving while in the etheric aura of his or her own *physical* body. The etheric aura extends about six inches to several feet or more beyond the physical body, in all directions. The planet earth both dampens and somewhat pushes the etheric aura upward, from kundalini energies that may oppose it. In the fourth step, the person will usually rise above and often somewhat to one side of his or her physical body during the separation. At this point the personality can think accessing only the etheric and not the physical brain. The person can thus no longer cause movement, or change, within the dense physical brain, and body. A quantum force is established between the dense physical body and the etheric body that is now separated from the dense physical. The reason is that the energy in the dense physical body is dying and disorganizing, or is no longer thinking within the same quantum field of choices that the organized etheric energy is thinking within. Should the etheric person attempt to move, through thought, back into her or his physical body, the thought itself will repel her or him further *away* from the body rather than closer to it. Note that this process is what initially causes the etheric body's separating move away from the dense physical body.

THE *TYPICAL* PROCESS OF HUMAN PHYSICAL DEATH
1. The sutratma is first loosened from the heart center, and often gradually—to a point—becomes loosened from the heart.
2. The consciousness thread remains focused in the etheric center (and sense) from which the person most focused his or her life (through the heaviest use of that sense) while alive physically.
3. The physical brain is separated from the etheric by the person leaving within the etheric aura of his or her own *physical* body (the etheric aura extends about six inches to several feet or more beyond the physical body, in all directions, but is mostly blocked by physical Earth.)
4. The person will usually rise above and often somewhat to one side of his or her physical body during the separation.
5. The personality now can think accessing only the etheric brain and not the physical, and can thus no longer cause movement, or change, within the dense physical brain—and body.

Table 8. 2

Once the two bodies are separated, *then* the sutratma becomes fully separated from the dense physical heart and body, in most cases of physical death. This process reduces the shock to the personality (which often is, at first, terrified of dying). As the nadis system is separated from the nervous system during the separation of the brains, all physical pain ceases, which often brings about a state of calmness and relief within the person. The OverSoul will appear if the person is still fearful, and especially if death is not going to be reversed for some purpose that the OverSoul and soul might have. This apparition seems to be in the etheric space that the person is in; however, it actually takes place within his or her higher mental body and mind. The apparition is then projected to the etheric brain of the person as though the Angel is in her or his etheric presence. The Angel of the Presence (as the OverSoul is referred to in these circumstances) often communicates with the dying person, assuring him or her that he or she will continue to exist in a new world and can remain where he or she is as long as he or she desires to *observe* the occurrences within the etheric/dense physical world. These are the typical experiences that most dying people have, but it is important to note that many variations of these experiences, as well as some more unusual and extremely different exceptions to what is typical sometimes do occur. The more fearful a person is, the longer the Angel will remain. Sometimes the Angel might even appear as several "angels" or a revered religious figure, if that would assist in reducing the person's fear and anxieties.

A Person Dying from the Physical Sub-Plane and Moving to the Etheric Sub-Plane

Illustration 8.2

 ETHERIC SUB-PLANE LIFE

Most people remain focused in consciousness within the subtle etheric body for anywhere from a few seconds to one to two weeks. To some people, the effects of their death on others who are still physically alive and the disposal of their physical bodies are of little importance. This often occurs because these people already dealt with those issues through planning prior to death. The more sudden the death, the longer (on average) a person tends to seek to remain on the etheric plane. The Solar Angel will usually not interfere with the personality's choices regarding etheric life after dense physical death. Interference frequently would result in increased fears within the personality, since its existence is so dependent upon its sense of control. The human soul, even when advanced in development on the higher mental plane, is confined to the limited area of the fourth sub-sub-plane of the second mental sub-plane. This small area of the higher mind is too limited for the soul to assist the Angel in its projection and presence for an etherically focused person. Of the two, only the OverSoul can be of assistance to the human during the death process, because of the human soul's limitations.

Either nearly immediately after or, in most cases, within a few weeks of dense physical death, an etherically alive person usually desires to live more than can be achieved by being in only part of a dimension in which most other people are isolated from interacting with her or him. Etheric energy is capable of moving through most dense physical barriers. It can do so because its density is so much lower and its vibration is so much higher than those of the physical barriers. It can pass around the molecules of most matter with only slight resistance from the electrical forces in the matter, moving like radio and television waves, and other electromagnetic radiation. Some Faraday-types of electromagnetic barriers can prevent the entry of lower etheric energies, including etherically alive people; these people are almost always on the lowest, or fourth, etheric sub-plane. The primary reason etherically alive people are found so low on the etheric plane is that most of them still desire to observe and hear what is occurring on the dense part of the dimension. Since their senses are usually separated, they cannot sense anything on the dense part of the plane from a vantage point above the fourth sub-plane because above that point there is too great a vibrational and time difference.

Time is dilated on the fourth, or etheric, sub-plane of the etheric plane. The reason is that although the speed of light is constant for the entire plane, the speed of human thought and the thought of other living creatures causes a small but cumulative effect on the surrounding energy. This effect is referred to in modern physics (which does not fully understand the effect) as the quantum constant. Although this effect remains constant *within* each *sub-plane* of the entire etheric/dense physical plane, it is noticeably different *between* every one of the *etheric* ones. The quantum constant represents the amount that energy in time and space is influenced, or controlled, by thought. As a result of very high gravity and density of matter, the quantum constant is quite small on the fifth and lower etheric/dense physical sub-planes; note that physically alive humans live on the fifth sub-plane. The quantum constant is approximately one-third greater on the fourth etheric/dense physical sub-plane than on the fifth. There is an extremely small change in the constant on the sixth and seventh sub-planes, of liquid and solid. This change is mostly unrecognized by today's modern physics. This change in the ability for energy to follow the higher thought of spirit is mostly a result of the absence of any dense matter, coupled with spirit's ability to think somewhat more easily using only the etheric, and not the physical, senses. The result, *initially*, is that a person who has recently died from the dense "solid" world and resides on the etheric plane has improved sense compared to when he or she was physically alive. It is important to understand that this improvement in sense and the clarity of thought are very short-lived. The reason for their temporary nature is that as the physical body and senses separate from the etheric, a quantum anomaly is created from the shifts in the two differing quantum constants. In addition, the quantum fields of possibilities that the two bodies exist within change if the physical body is allowed to stay intact. At the beginning of a new lifetime, after about seven years of age, humans are able to adjust to their etheric and dense physical bodies being connected but still separate and existing within differing quantum constants. They accomplish overcoming this odd effect by subconsciously averaging the time and space distortions between the two brains as the personality integrates the information from them into knowledge. The etheric brain perceives information about twice as fast as the dense physical brain does. The swiftness is because the etheric brain is located on the first sub-plane and its enlightened parts are at the atomic level of the etheric plane, where the quantum constant is slightly more than twice as large as on the dense physical level. At the top of the highest etheric sub-plane, time is correspondingly dilated slightly more than twice the amount.

THE ETHERIC SUB-PLANES			
SUB-PLANE NUMBER	SPIRITUAL NAME	SUB-RAY CORRESPONDENCE	ETHERIC LIFEFORMS AND PARTS OF LIFEFORMS FOUND THERE
1st etheric sub-plane	Atomic* sub-plane	1st sub-ray of the 7th ray	Masters of the Ageless Wisdom; human atomic etheric permanent atoms; the human etheric centers; the parts of any body that contains this least dense etheric energy.
2nd etheric sub-plane	Sub-Atomic sub-plane	2nd sub-ray of the 7th ray	Most animals and their sub-atomic etheric permanent atoms; some viruses and a few bacteria that reach this level while infecting a host; fallen animal spirit; the parts of any body that contains this etheric energy.
3rd etheric sub-plane	Super-Etheric sub-plane	3rd sub-ray of the 7th ray	Most plants and their super-etheric permanent atoms; molds and fungi; some viruses while infecting a host; plant devas and some semi-angelic beings that are plant helpers; some remaining dark entities; fallen plant spirit; the parts of any body that contains this denser etheric energy.
4th etheric sub-plane	Etheric sub-plane	4th sub-ray of the 7th ray	Most dense physically dead people and nearly all ghosts; viruses; fallen mineral spirit; the lowest etheric permanent atoms; a few dark monsters; the lowest parts of any body that contains this densest etheric energy.

*Note that the entire first sub-plane is referred to as the atomic etheric sub-plane; however, the atomic level of the atomic sub-plane is the point at which the Ray Lord's light is fully focused and enlightens all that exists within its time and space.

Table 8.3

Humans on the fourth etheric sub-plane who have recently died from the dense physical plane find that the one-third faster time dilation actually helps them, *initially*, to think better. These people no longer must average while they integrate and synthesize knowledge between the etheric and dense physical brains, and, the etheric brain thinks faster. Some physically alive people can leave their dense physical bodies (sometimes moving only a few inches from the body) for the purpose of improving their thinking. Often they may not know that this is what they are doing. Young children may frequently and unknowingly leave their dense bodies and remain for short periods in their etheric ones. This occurs because their personalities are not yet fully in control of these bodies. Nearly everyone does so for a few moments when they first fall asleep; however, in these cases, most of the time the personality has disintegrated too much for any logical thought or memory to take place. Note that in order to have memory, one must be able to join, in all three time zones, at least sixty percent of one or more events in space. (See Chapter Ten for more about this effect.)

The improved senses are needed by a person who has recently died physically and is alive etherically, in order for him or her to understand the new types of visual and aural information that he or she is receiving about the physical world while on the fourth etheric sub-plane. The sense of *physical* touch becomes only varying levels of electrical tingling sensations as the etheric energy moves around dense atoms. Physical taste is virtually gone, as is physical smell, because the physical molecules are insensible to the etheric senses. To the etheric person, etheric form seems to be very much like dense physical form used to be, in sense. An etheric person seeing dense physical matter often sees a violet halo around forms that are normally illuminated with the full spectrum of light. This violet halo is ultra-violet light (some of which has shifted to violet light), which is now fully sensed by the etheric person on the fourth sub-plane. Everything within the dense world seems to be moving at a speed of one-third slower as the inner, or main, colors of objects appear, somewhat noticeably, redder (red is added to their color) because of a Doppler shift in light. The etheric fourth sub-plane person has about one-third *more* time in which to live because of the time dilation. Dense physical people move at a speed of about one-third slower, as do dense physical events. Physical sound is very distorted. It, also, is slowed down by one-third and is heard only as its etheric vibration, which vibrates only the etheric part of air. Physical voices are at first indistinguishable to an etheric person on the fourth sub-plane; their pitch is much lower and slower than etheric voices are, and, further, they sound very electric, or fuzzy. Amazingly, the etheric brain can usually compensate somewhat for these distortions when the improved sense is concentrated on etheric listening to physical speech; physical speech can often be reasonably accurately understood after a certain amount of practice.

Physically alive people usually cannot see or hear (nor feel) a person who is alive on the fourth etheric sub-plane (or higher). The reason is that a physically alive person's etheric sense is averaged with her or his physical sense, reducing the etheric sense to a very low level of perception (see illustrations 1.12 and 1.13). The general exceptions to this are in very young children (younger, usually, than five years of age) and/or with people who have incurred certain physical brain injuries. In both of these cases, the etheric brain is still fairly separated and not well integrated with the dense physical by the personality. A person on the etheric fourth sub-plane can be sensed by most physically alive people if a distortion occurs in the quantum constant in a particular locality. Then the etheric person is experienced as a ghost. The cause of most quantum irregularities in the constant on the dense physical sub-planes is the etherically alive person himself or herself. Because these people's molecules are existing in two different locations, or parts of a dimension of time and space, and are following two different thoughts of two different informing spirits, the quantum constants between the two groups of molecules create a time and space instability. The longer that an etheric person stays in one location, the greater the effect. Also, the quantum irregularity will be significant if her or his dead dense physical body is kept intact and not cremated or entoumbed. This is particularly the case if the body is not embalmed and is buried in a shallow grave. Embalming greatly changes the body's physical structure and its effects on the etheric plane. If the physical body is encased in a metal coffin, then the quantum constant irregularity is reduced by blocking the etheric energy. The senses of the physically alive people can be altered by the quantum constant shift over days to weeks of time (depending upon the level of their etheric connection to their physical senses). This enables some physically alive people to be able to sense the ghost and other etheric phenomena in various ways (again, this is individually determined). In some severe cases, some physically alive people can experience this effect within minutes. The best means of preventing the quantum constant irregularity and preventing an etheric person who stays for a fairly long time etherically from developing into a ghost (and creating other time and space distortions) is to cremate the physical body soon after its death. Cremation transmutes the physical molecules into gaseous and etheric ones, and will even allow some of them to follow the molecules of the etheric person. This sometimes creates a physically unpleasant smell and breeze around his or her etheric body. Cases of physical death by murder in which the physical body is somewhat hidden and not embalmed, and the etheric person decides through his or her desires to stay "earthbound," or focused on physical life, tend to produce ghosts. This is especially true as the etheric person loses his or her etheric senses because of too long an etheric stay, and then tends to remain mostly in one location.

Etheric Sub-Planes

	Name of Sub-Plane	Examples of Parts of Life Found on Each Sub-Plane				
1	Atomic	 Human Permanent Atom	 Master			
2	Sub-Atomic	 Animal Permanent Atom	 Fallen Animal Spirit			Virus
3	Super-Etheric	Plant Permanent Atom	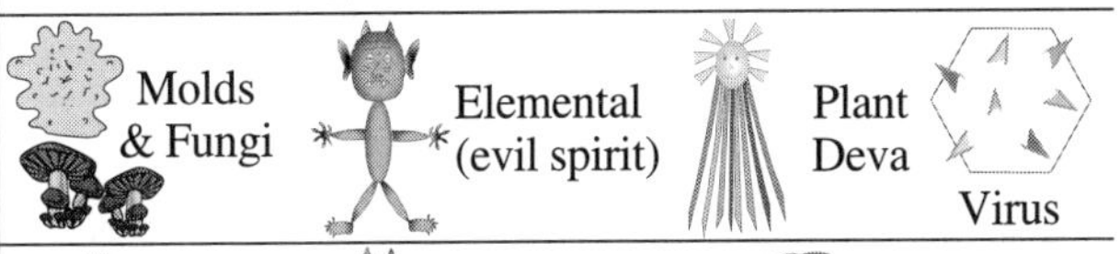 Molds & Fungi	Elemental (evil spirit)	Plant Deva	Virus
4	Etheric	Mineral Permanent Atom	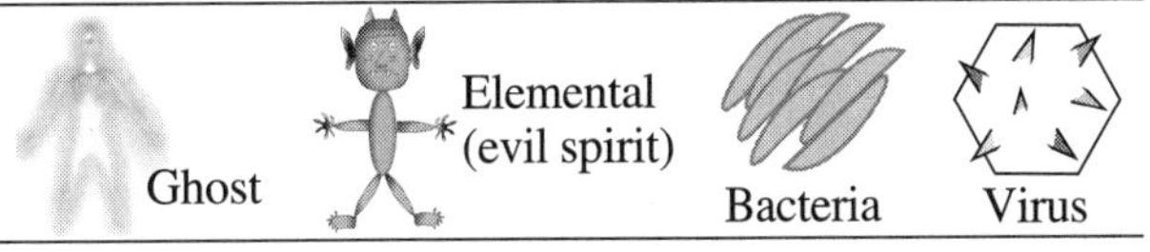 Ghost	Elemental (evil spirit)	Bacteria	Virus

Illustration 8.3

The etherically alive person starts to lose etheric sense, in small amounts, as soon as the separation of the etheric and dense physical bodies takes place. The reason is that the two different quantum constants and the two informing thoughts of the two different informing spirits cause the etheric person's senses to become lower. This happens especially when they are used to sense physical objects, because of the erratic vibrations of the etheric energy. Note that once the physical body dies, it falls under the informing thought of a mineral group soul and its fallen spirit, while the etheric body remains controlled by the personality's and self's control through more highly developed fallen spirit. Further conflict arises in the physics if the etheric person focuses his or her thought on what was his or her physical body. This causes interference with the fallen spirit's thought of the mineral group soul and its self. The etheric lunar devas begin to lose control over the etheric elemental energies that constitute and hold together each sense, which causes increasing levels of strain on the deva energies. In those people who remain etherically focused in life, within a month or so for most whose bodies were embalmed after death, or within several months, for those few who remain and whose bodies were cremated, the etheric senses fall to some level of senselessness and loss of self identity. Most people whose physical bodies have been cremated leave fairly soon for the astral plane, and cremation lessens the quantum constant irregularity and its destructive effect on the etheric senses. Note that when a person has been cremated, it is best to scatter the ashes over a wide area in order to diminish the possibility of a quantum irregularity. The loss of sense of self can result in an etheric person becoming trapped on the etheric plane for a very long period of time. Such people lose so much sense over time that they forget who they are (similar to an etheric Alzheimer's disease in its effect—but from a very different initial cause). The factors that are most conducive to someone becoming trapped on the etheric plane as a ghost are as follows: sudden, and especially violent death; personality disorder in the former physical life, with the characteristic low sense of self; and the person's body not being embalmed or buried very deep within the earth nor cremated. The more of those factors that exist, the more likely the person is to lose her or his etheric senses very quickly, and if the latter two factors are present, sometimes in less than a week! In these cases the person might remain on the etheric plane until her or his etheric body dies. This could take as long as one hundred years of dense earth time. Often in such cases a person's

Solar Angel and sometimes a Master of the next kingdom beyond the human will help him or her to move on to the astral plane when the person's presence as a ghost is creating an opportunity for evil people from the lower astral plane to possess it and to wreak havoc on those who are physically alive.

Etheric Person Attempting to Gain Senses

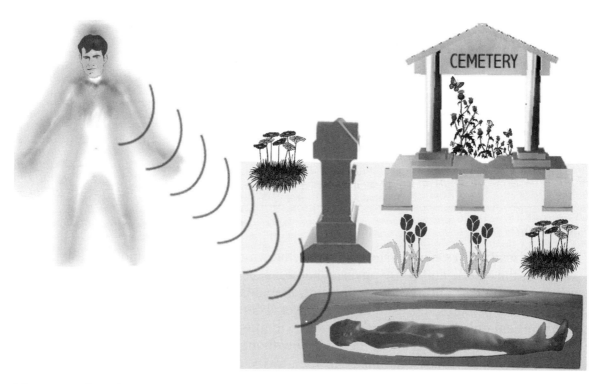

After a stay of usually one or two months on the etheric sub-plane, an etheric person (a male is used in the above illustration) loses noticeable amounts of sense because of a quantum constant difference between the etheric atoms in his etheric body and the dense physical atoms in his dense physical body. Such a person may try to still sense (mostly unsuccessfully) with the remains of his physical body (!) if they are not well dampened by earth and/or by metal surroundings. This etheric person's senses may be slightly better if he is in close proximity to his dense physical body. His focused thought on his dense physical remains is interfering with the mineral group soul and its informing fallen spirit. This then causes greater quantum irregularities and further loss in his senses—leading to more intense focus on his remains!

Illustration 8.4

People who choose to commit suicide create somewhat of an exception to the general rule that the OverSoul and sometimes the human soul control the death process of the dense physical body. Ultimately, though, the OverSoul and soul *are* in control, for several reasons. They can interfere in a suicide attempt by affecting the person's senses through his or her higher mind. The senses would be altered enough so that even the most extremely physically self-destructive acts would fail to kill the physical body because the procedure would be faulty. The OverSoul and soul can allow the person to "die" and to separate into her or his etheric body. Then the Angel of the Presence would contact the person to convince her or him that the suicide was a mistake. In such cases, the physical body can be revitalized by improving and synthesizing the thought of its lunar devas, even if they were damaged in the suicide attempt. The OverSoul's thought is often strong enough to reverse the death process, if so warranted. Then the person can be directed back into the dense physical body, to resume her or his physical life.

Often the person will have gained some amount of enlightenment by having had direct contact with the Angel. These circumstances can occur in subconscious suicide, as well, when a person wants to die and continually makes "mistakes" that lead to death, even though no overt action is taken. Sometimes the OverSoul, and at times with the assistance of the human soul, will allow the physical death by suicide to take place. Under these circumstances, however, the person is likely to lose the control over his or her etheric body's death. The reason is that the timing of a person fully dying from a dimension affects many other people. This timing also determines on what day of the year a person will next be reincarnated. This is decided upon by a group of souls, as part of their plan. The exact day and time are usually calculated to give the personality more than enough time to decide to leave. Then the person will wait some number of hours or, infrequently, days before actually leaving. Some suicides interfere with these calculations. If a person chooses to kill herself or himself with timing that would necessitate a fairly long etheric stay in order to die in sync with the plans of other souls, she or he may be directed back to her or his dense physical body, or the suicide attempt may be interfered with. In such cases, another person (or even an animal) who is responsive to his or her (or its) Soul's or soul's thought might be directed through this thought to interfere with the suicide attempt. If the suicide would lead to not an unreasonably long etheric stay of perhaps a month or two, then the person might be allowed to physically die; however, control over her or his etheric death is then relinquished to her or his OverSoul and, sometimes, her or his human soul as well. Longer etheric stays are undesirable because the person on the etheric plane is losing his or her senses, can become a ghost, and might even become possessed and destructive to others.

People die for reasons that are as much, *or more so*, for the benefit of others who know them and often for those who are close to them, in various kinds of relationships, as they are for their own good. Benefits to others include the others giving to, and sometimes serving, the dying person, which raises the consciousness of those who are giving. Sometimes the dying person gets others to face their fears of death, which are caused by selfishness in the way they have lived their lives. Facing one's fears of death often results in a catharsis and then a revelation that leads to the person becoming more virtuous. When a relative is dying, it is not unusual for family crises to occur concerning control, greed, and a host of other personality problems associated with selfishness. These crises provide fertile ground for more spiritual development.

The death process also provides the dying person with a means of similar catharsis and revelation, sometimes because of suffering and pain. Unfortunately, for many people it is not until such adverse circumstances occur that they seek positive, or Godly, change. The more self initiated a person is in creating more virtue in her or his life, the less, in general, she or he will suffer and experience pain in death. There are some exceptions to this general rule, but those people who might have been quite creative of virtue in their lives who do suffer at the end of physical life are generally cognizant of the reasons why.

Because it is composed of radio-like energy, the entire etheric body weighs next to nothing. With the increase in the amount that energy follows the greater thought of spirit (which is the increase in the quantum constant), movement of this body can be accomplished by an etherically alive person through thought alone, if he or she so chooses. Flight at fairly high altitudes and fast speeds is possible by those with intact etheric sense on the fourth etheric sub-plane. On the first, or atomic, etheric sub-plane the speed of flight is by far even greater because of the further increase in the quantum constant (of about twice that of the "solid" dimensions). Such speed can exceed two thousand miles per hour, as compared to less than one hundred miles per hour as an average speed on the fourth etheric sub-plane. A ghost might be able to move from a few inches to a few dozen feet above ground level, and sometimes at only a few miles per hour because of its diminished senses and subsequently lesser ability to think.

Ghost Possessing A Young Child

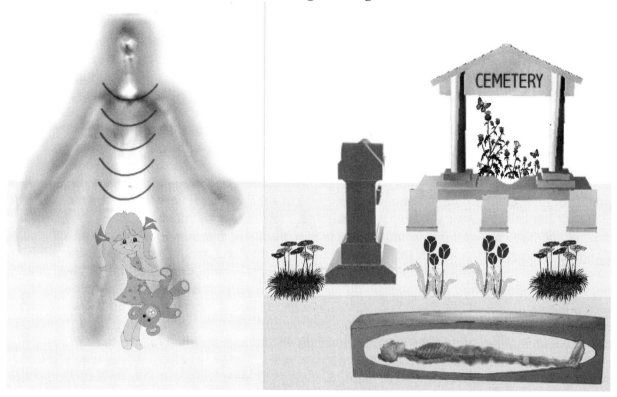

After a prolonged stay on the etheric sub-plane, a person can become a ghost. The ghost may be able to possess a person who is physically alive, especially a young child or anyone else with a less developed personality and self (with that self in less control of the bodies of the one being possessed). Although it is usually people who become possessed, animals can become possessed as well. Incidences of possession by a ghost can be quite dangerous, and even life-threatening. The ghost is using and diminishing the senses of those whom or that it possesses. Evil beings from the astral plane sometimes astrally possess ghosts, which then possess people (or sometimes even animals) who are physically alive.

Illustration 8.5

Above the fourth etheric sub-plane, only those who have unified etheric senses (some very advanced initiates and all members of the next kingdom beyond the human) can still sense the dense physical world. The etheric senses of nearly all humans are separated. This renders these senses too weak to sense more than one etheric sub-plane above the physical world or the other etheric sub-planes above the sub-plane where the person is. At most, the person if fairly enlightened might sense one sub-plane above the one that she or he is on. Further, most people lose consciousness when they attempt to travel intra-dimensionally to the atomic etheric sub-plane. This occurs because in order to remain conscious on this sub-plane, one's etheric body must be at least fifty percent enlightened. The reason for this effect is that the first sub-plane of all planes, including the etheric, is enlightened to a great extent, or contains energies that have considerable amounts of light within them. To sense anything, one's senses must be at least as enlightened as the energy that is being sensed. The sense's thought attracts some small amount of the sensed energy through the higher thought of the energy within the sense that is doing the sensing. Those with inadequate sense on the atomic, or first, sub-plane then cannot think with their informing spirit, and fall asleep, or lose consciousness within the self at that level of time and space.

When a person who is alive etheric/dense physically first falls asleep, she or he almost always moves through the center where her or his consciousness is focused. The person travels to the atomic etheric sub-plane because that is where the spirit sphere is located and also connects to the etheric brain. At this point these people are no longer conscious because they have too little sense to be conscious, and the personality has chosen to relinquish control over its bodies. Many people are more focused in consciousness astrally; the meaning that they derive in their lives is mostly through emotions and love. The center where the end of each of these people's consciousness thread is attached is the corresponding solar plexus center—specifically, it is attached to the spirit sphere within that center. When they first fall asleep (and when they awaken), these people leave (and return to) their dense physical bodies through the solar plexus center; such a person will at first return to the etheric atomic sub-plane while her or his etheric brain is repaired by the restructuring of the elemental energy within it.

Because the etheric body has so little density and has different physics, it can be shrunk to the size of a major center and can then travel through inner space. It can also be expanded to appear much larger than the size of a normal person. It can become more and more transparent as it further decreases in density. Before losing their senses, most etherically alive people will focus their thought on themselves wearing familiar, or sometimes nearby articles of etheric clothing that also exist dense physically. As they wear these articles of etheric clothing, they further create a quantum shift and anomaly between the dense physical and etheric parts of the clothing. This effect takes place concerning any personal items the person chooses to have etherically present with her or him. After a period of usually weeks to months, the physical or etheric *articles* themselves will create similar effects to that of a ghost's presence. These etheric articles over time will return to their physical locations because of the informing thought of the mineral group soul, unless interfered with by the thought of an etheric entity. When an etheric person is seen (usually as a ghost) by a physically alive person, the etheric person is sufficiently opaque to be recognized, but still transparent enough for brightly lit objects to be seen through the body. It is not unusual for some people, as they fall asleep and sometimes upon awakening, to at times be able to "feel" themselves leave and re-enter the dense physical body and its center that is the center of focus in consciousness. This "feeling" is the change in the etheric (and astral and mental, as well) body's size and density as it moves towards and through the center. The lunar deva energy directs the elemental energy as sleep is brought on by the personality relinquishing control over the bodies. The shrinking process is natural for the energies because it allows them freedom to dissolve the etheric, astral, and lower mental forms for a short time. The process provides these energies with relaxation and relief from the forces imposed by the accumulated retained energies that are resultant of the person's own selfishness. This process usually translates into a relaxation of the dense physical body, as an effect.

Once on the etheric atomic sub-plane after first falling asleep, a person can re-enter the same center or can enter a different center. The ability to do so depends upon the focus of consciousness in the other bodies, and travel to either the astral or lower mental plane—where she or he is still asleep, and frequently will dream. People who are dreaming are doing so without the personality integrating their bodies and senses. This happens so that the lunar devas and elemental energies can be free, in part, to repair their bodies, and in younger people, to grow the bodies. Most growth within people (and other living things) takes place while they sleep. A lucid dreamer might have a slight or only a part of a sense of self, usually in the present time zone, but will have no full sense of self that includes all of the three parts of time. Thus when people sleep and dream they might, infrequently, know their names and a few identifying elements of their selves at the moment (for example, some people might know that they like chocolate). They would not know what they were doing before they went to sleep (the recent past) or what plans they have upon awakening. Such a person also would not understand why she or he "likes chocolate" in her or his dream. While dreaming, people's sense of self, which requires all three parts of time, is gone since the personality is not integrating the three bodies; doing so would sustain the three parts of time through information about the three lower worlds that the human lives in. Upon physical awakening, a person will emerge from the etheric center that he or she originally left from, because the consciousness thread follows dreaming people wherever they go. The sutratma, or life thread, also remains intact in their bodies. If awakened suddenly, the consciousness thread can very quickly pull a person back to the center he or she left from. This often causes some trauma to the thread itself and an adverse effect on the person after she or he awakens. The result can be a reduction in consciousness and some suffering while the self is reduced for a few minutes to several hours. The length of time depends upon the level of retained energy that was being worked on by the lunar devas and elemental energy at the moment of sudden awakening. This retained energy often slightly damages the thread as the sleeping person is "snapped" back into his or her physical body. While the effect is not usually serious, it is uncomfortable. The effect is worse if the sleeping person was on the astral or mental plane when suddenly awakened. The reason is that the inter-dimensional changes are greater, even though the return to the physical body takes place within virtually the same amount of dense physical time.

Dreams on the astral plane last for several minutes (up to about nine) in dense physical world time. On the etheric plane, they last for usually a few seconds to a minute. Because of time dilation, astral dreams of physically alive people can be as much as sixteen times longer than the lowest etheric sub-plane ones, but are usually no more than ten to twelve times longer in astral time. Time dilation on the astral plane (from the lowest sub-plane to the atomic astral level) is about three to about twenty-four times greater than in the dense physical world. The astral quantum constant is much larger because no etheric/dense physical energy exists as separate energy on the astral plane. Astral energy is *much* less dense than is etheric, and follows the greater thought of spirit amazingly well. It is so much less dense and of such higher vibration (and, additionally, is at a different phase) that it has yet to be defined in the science of today. Gamma radiation, a very high (sub-atomic and atomic sub-plane) etheric energy, is immensely more dense and of lower frequency than is astral energy. The entire highest electro-magnetic bandwidth known to modern science covers only most, but not all, of the etheric plane. The speed of light on the astral plane is much faster than on the etheric. The reason is that the astral plane Ray Lord thinks much faster than the etheric plane Ray Lord does. The etheric sub-planes are unusual and are even a bit confusing as compared to the dense physical realm, but they have nowhere near the differences in physics and phenomena that occur on the astral plane (and above). A great deal more can be explained about the etheric sub-planes; however, in keeping with the purposes of this book, only the more important etheric effects on people have been described to this point.

 ## OTHER ETHERIC SUB-PLANE LIFE

Before concluding the explanation of the etheric sub-planes, a very brief description of other life besides human that can be found in this subtle world might be helpful for the reader towards increasing life's hidden meaning. The fourth etheric sub-plane is where the etheric, or causative, part of most bacteria is found. Bacteria also have a very small partial astral body that is found on the seventh astral sub-plane. Some bacteria on the fourth etheric sub-plane are not in dense physical form at any particular time. The reason is that they first feed on etheric energy before growing a dense physical body. This requires either disorganized etheric energy from a dead physical organic form, very energetic (hot) mineral and/or organic "soups" in water (such as under the oceans), or excess retained etheric energy within a center as a result of illusion (selfishness) on the part of either a group soul's self or a human self. When the etheric bacteria feed they are using part of the energy of another lifeform's center, and their astral bodies slightly grow as their dense physical bodies do. It is fortunate, as will be explained below, that most etheric bacteria's bodies are actually quite large in size as compared to their dense physical bodies. This effect in size is caused by the fact that their etheric bodies are composed of relatively denser and darker etheric energies, which, in order to maintain etheric mobility, must be greatly enlarged and thus reduced in relative density using the slight thought that is within the bacteria's bodies. Also, the very limited thought of a bacterium, when not collectively organized, leads to less integration of the etheric energy and to a decrease in *organized* density as it decreases in overall density. Some parts of the bacterium may be *very* dense because of gravitation within the same etheric lifeform. The lunar deva energy is found more on the outside of the organism, with much denser pockets of elemental energies on the inside. A few types of bacteria measure *several inches* across on the etheric plane—resembling large cockroaches rather than mere microbes! Most, however, are "only" the size of fleas. The etheric bacteria's relatively large size and meager levels of thought produce an enormous benefit to other parts of life. In etheric form a bacterium, which has extremely limited thought for a lifeform, is greatly affected by the thought of informing spirit of most other lifeforms. When it attempts to move, its low relative density makes it easily either pushed away from or attracted to the somewhat greater informing thought of spirit other than in its own form. Thus much of the movement of most bacteria is ruled by the thought of other lifeforms. If a lifeform is informed by darker-thinking spirit and/or by selfish intervention of dark-thinking humans, then the lifeform may serve as an etheric and eventually dense physical "food source," or energy host, for like-thinking bacteria. Because of their very low thought and disorganized outer energies, bacteria can be etherically blocked by even slight barriers accompanied by informing thought of spirit. This keeps them away from most centers. If very large amounts of bacteria (or other infection-causing microbes) are present, their collective thought can sometimes overcome the informing thought of the host's spirit centers, and create an infection. Bacteria can be additionally prevented from penetration by physical barriers that are dense enough to prevent the microbial physical body from moving through it. If bacteria could think considerably better than they do, they could enter—and infect—nearly any etheric body in almost any corresponding physical location. Fortunately, lower capability of informing spirit's thought accompanies lower-level lifeforms, such as bacteria and other lifeforms that can steal the use of a center.

Most bacteria remain on the fourth etheric sub-plane when they feed on another being or dead lifeform, or on minerals and heat. Most have limited adaptability concerning the type of energy they consume. Note that the vast majority of disintegrated etheric energies are found on the fourth and third, or the etheric and super-etheric, sub-planes of the etheric plane. The reason is that these two are the densest of the four *etheric* sub-planes. Bacteria, molds, and fungi consume much of this disintegrating lunar deva and elemental energy; they use some of the lunar deva energy in their own forms, which frees a significant amount of the elemental energy. Although most viruses are also (initially) found on the fourth etheric sub-plane, they are very different from bacteria. Viruses tend to infect their hosts, and when they do, the viruses do not expand in size because they function more as minerals until in a host, and thus usually feed on energy from a living lifeform. As they infect and feed on retained energy within the energy sphere of a lifeform's center, they change sub-planes to the location where the darker retained energy is found. Bacteria usually feed on mostly fourth sub-plane etheric energy (a few very dangerous ones feed on higher sub-plane energies and are more like viruses in this respect); viruses can feed on etheric energies from the fourth through the second etheric sub-planes. Thus a single virus can cause several stages of disease because viruses might first feed on fourth sub-plane etheric energy, and later feed on third or second sub-plane energies. Viruses cannot feed on etheric atomic sub-plane energy because they have no sense of it, and it is too relatively enlightened. The virus becomes more a part of the body it infects, by its ability to shift its etheric location according to the retained energy in its host. Many viruses in humans are found on the second etheric sub-plane. There are parts of the human etheric body on all four of the etheric sub-planes and, often, the retained energies within the energy spheres of the centers are dense enough and dark enough to be a part of the second—or lower—sub-atomic etheric sub-plane (even though the major centers are all located on the atomic level). Animal centers are frequently located on the second etheric, or the sub-atomic, sub-plane. Viruses that infect them may be on the second, third, or fourth etheric sub-plane. Plant viruses are found on the third and fourth etheric sub-planes. Those viruses on the second sub-plane may be able to cross over kingdoms from some animal species, and infect humans. This can occur because some of a selfish human's energy in her or his darkened energy center is on the second etheric sub-plane. The higher the sub-plane that a virus can feed on, the more dangerous it usually is. The reason is that such a virus is more adaptable and therefore resilient to the body's own, or other, defenses against it (see illustration 6.6). The greater the number of viruses that enter a body at a time, the higher the likelihood that some of them will resist the body's defenses and will find dark energy in a center to feed upon. Notice that the etheric form of the virus is attracted to the (major or minor) etheric center. In some cases the virus (or other etheric parasitic organism) must be in etheric form to infect the host. In these cases the organism will manifest in dense physical form minutes to hours later. Once infected, a host becomes darker in energy from an inability to remove the waste energy of the infecting organism itself. This leads to increased levels of infection.

Parasitic organisms in etheric/dense physical form are less dangerous than in purely etheric form because the former can be blocked by physical means from infecting the host. However, parasitic organisms that have physical form are also much more capable of infecting a host because they are so much less affected by outside thought. Most bio-hazardous safety systems that protect against viruses unknowingly employ methods and materials that obstruct some etheric energy—and viruses (and other etheric microbes); however, the *thought* of the person being protected, as well as the thought of those around him or her, also plays a significant role in affecting the viruses. Also note that etheric-only viruses seldom exist in a test tube or petri dish because in order to exist only in etheric form they need to have been recently physically killed. These viruses can then remain viable, but much less infectious because they can be so easily repelled by thought that is greater than their own. Nevertheless, should an etheric-only virus infect a host (which is a rare occurrence), that virus would be more dangerous than would its dense physical counterpart because once inside the body there would be fewer defenses against it. In the last half-century a few scientists have found significant evidence of etheric forms of diseases. Unfortunately, these scientists have mostly been severely criticized and even attacked through the legal regulatory system by colleagues and governmental agencies. Considerably more serious scientific investigation is needed in this area. It is important to note, though, that the experimenters need to be cognizant of the *etheric* quantum constants and their effects on such small forms as microbes, i.e., the *thought* of the observer and of others surrounding the experiments needs to be regulated and controlled, or the results of these experiments will be invalid.

Molds and fungi reside on the third etheric sub-plane, or the super-etheric sub-plane, as it is sometimes referred to. Most plant life's etheric centers are found on this sub-plane. Plants are mostly not animated in the ways that animals are; this is consistent in the case of molds and fungi, which are usually dependent for movement upon some other lifeform or inanimate (mineral) object or force. Humans can become infected by a mold or fungus when energy within one of their centers becomes filled with relatively dark super-etheric energy. The super-etheric sub-plane corresponds to the third etheric sub-ray. Molds and fungi tend to feed on the third ray throat center and especially the organ of the lungs, which transmutes and transfers air (a third ray gaseous mineral form) into and out of the body. Molds and fungi also feed on the skin, which is also a third (sub-) ray organ of the etheric/dense physical body. Notice that bacteria are more versatile than molds and fungi are. The reason is bacteria's fourth sub-ray ability to remain in balance with differing energies. Bacteria can feed on a much wider *source* of energy than molds and fungi do. Viruses can be even more versatile, but because they generally infect rather than just break down dead (previously alive) organic material, they do not live in as many places. Molds and fungi tend to break down dead *plants*. They also can grow on some disorganized (dead) animal bodies, but generally find much more energy that is super-etheric in dead plants.

There are creatures that live only etherically and have no dense physical bodies. Some of these creatures were created by evil people over eleven thousand years ago, on the remaining island of what had been the continent of Atlantis. Most of the evil and dark etheric creatures have died and no longer exist. A few live on the fourth (the etheric) sub-plane of the etheric plane, with the remaining small amount found today on the super-etheric sub-plane. Most of the helpful etheric-only lifeforms are also found on the super-etheric sub-plane. Some of them somewhat resemble the "fairies" that exist in human folklore. The purpose of these lifeforms is to serve the etheric forms of plants. Because of their immobility, plants need help in adapting to some environmental conditions and in their interactions with other plants, as well, in a constructive method of coordination and sharing. These and other helpful etheric lifeforms etherically connect plants of different group souls. Plants are also served by a group of deva (angelic) beings. These angelic beings are composed of the most enlightened super-etheric lunar deva energy, and contain very little elemental energy within their bodies. Because of the low density of their elemental energy, the super-etheric and very large devas can be up to hundreds of feet wide in diameter at their base, and as tall as the tallest trees. However, because the elemental energy that these devas are composed of is less gravitated and has less structure, they are held together less well than physical forms are. These devas serve the plant group souls of many different types of plant life because plants have such a difficult time communicating, as

Enlightened Etheric Deva

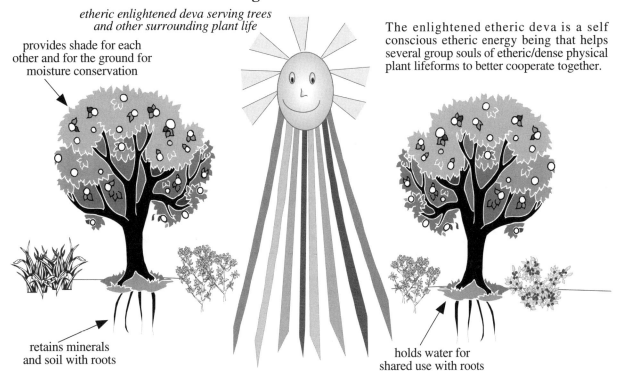

etheric enlightened deva serving trees and other surrounding plant life

provides shade for each other and for the ground for moisture conservation

The enlightened etheric deva is a self conscious etheric energy being that helps several group souls of etheric/dense physical plant lifeforms to better cooperate together.

retains minerals and soil with roots

holds water for shared use with roots

Illustration 8.6

a result of their lack of ability to move. Animals also serve plants by helping to provide them with movement while the plants, in symbiosis, feed the animals. These large devas only give to plants and do not feed on them, as animals and people do. Plant devas are not considered pitris, or "partial angels," but full, or whole, angels because they have more complete self consciousness than pitris do. The *collection* of group souls that they serve is their ensouling spirit. This ensouling spirit informs the etheric spirit on the super-etheric sub-plane, and the etheric spirit informs the plant devas' etheric bodies. Plant devas are radiant and quite beautiful in their colors because they contain mostly enlightened lunar deva energy. They are attracted to organized and beautiful areas; places where humans have destroyed organization and that they have made ugly are usually devoid of super-etheric devas. One of the functions of these angels is to keep harmful bacteria, molds, and fungi from taking over the lifeforms within the area that they (the devas) cover. When the plant devas leave, disease to life usually ensues. Plant devas inform the group souls of different species of plant life that are living together within the same area. The provided information concerns the symbiotic relationships and environmental factors that are collectively controlling all of the life in their vicinity. Sometimes this information includes the effects of surrounding insect life as it is affecting the plants. The group souls receive the information from the plant devas much faster and in better organized form than if they waited to receive it through their self structure from the collective senses of their plant lifeforms.

Some "fallen" spirit on the etheric plane from humans or from animals can possess animals and, though relatively rare with mentally advanced people, can also fully possess people, when the animal or person is not in good contact with its informing soul. An animal that loses some contact with its group soul (often as a result of some human activity) is open to possession by fallen and darker etheric spirit. This animal spirit is found on the second, or sub-atomic, etheric sub-plane and usually plays a constructive role despite its relatively darker nature. Fallen animal spirit that is not informed by any higher types of thinking spirit usually possesses animals that are more advanced, but are having difficulty in receiving thought from the selves of their group souls. This often occurs because the animals are being hunted by humans, or are affected by some other threatening human activity. Oddly, in human societies that are primitive by today's standards, the humans may at times become partially possessed by similar fallen spirit, and then often revere this spirit. These people recognize the positive thought that the possessing animal fallen spirit gives to the animal to help it to survive—particularly human intervention. The worship of "fallen" etheric spirit accompanies human involvement with animals that poses a threat to the animals. Note that raising animals to be killed and then eaten creates a somewhat lesser fearful effect on the animals. This occurs if they are treated humanely while being raised, or are treated as having some connection in life to human life. Not being hunted and/or eaten allows animals full contact with both their developing selves and their group souls. The reason is that such animals no longer live in such fear that counters the love and consciousness of their group soul's self. Then the humans do not leave themselves open to becoming partially possessed by the "fallen" etheric animal spirit. Dark, fallen, animal spirit consciousness (actually, its lack of consciousness) tends to make animals and people more aggressive, hostile, competitive, and fearful, with a focus on surviving. This spirit possesses others based upon their fears concerning staying alive rather than their thoughts of giving. This then counters the thought of the group soul's thought and, in people, of the OverSoul's and human soul's thought. The more meat that a person consumes, the greater the likelihood of at least partial possession from time to time, by darker "fallen" animal spirit; partial possession occurs much more commonly than does full possession, which is relatively rare. The fallen animal spirit can also be controlled by evil people, if it becomes very dark. This makes it much more dangerous when it possesses others. Eating animals generally alters human consciousness in the same above-mentioned ways that dark, fallen animal spirit consciousness does. Animals that eat other animals are on a near-equal level to each other in senses and consciousness, and thus do not create the intense continual fear that a human can by his or her hunting animals or raising them to be killed, or both. Animals have little defense against humans.

The more primitive the people, by today's standards, the *less* that they are affected by hunting and eating animals. The reason is that the consciousness of primitive people is closer to the animals', which causes less of a lowering of consciousness as some possession from fallen spirit takes place. Thus the amount that consciousness is destroyed by eating animals is relative to one's level of consciousness to begin with. Animals live in much less fear of primitive people. These people usually are sensitive to the possessing spirit and may even only hunt or raise animals to be eaten that are mostly *not* possessed. Doing so is accomplished by the primitive people being sensitive to (aware of) the fallen spirit. They kill animals mostly at a rate and in a way that keeps the spirit from possessing the animals most of the time. Such cooperation with the group souls and their selves, and the enlightened Spirit of Earth is advisable and is most helpful. It also can help to enlighten the darker fallen etheric spirit while it is out of the animal's body. This happens through love, cooperation and sharing, and religious rituals that foster these virtues.

The only inhabitants of the atomic etheric sub-plane are Masters of the three lower worlds and of the Ageless Wisdom. Some of these members of the next kingdom beyond the human still have the fully enlightened permanent atoms from their three lowest bodies (the mental, astral, and etheric). Their permanent atoms are fused together as a triangle of light that allows them full and simultaneous consciousness in all three lower dimensions. Masters in these circumstances create their residences on the first etheric sub-plane, from the joined thought within their fully fused lowest three bodies and senses. This tremendously powerful thought produces a design for the etheric lunar devas to perfectly follow and then create idyllic surroundings for the Master to live in. The corresponding physical location is often an isolated and very undesirable place for humans to live in—or even visit. Such a spot might even be many thousands of feet above earth's surface. The reason is that although in a different part of the dimension, a Master's aura will generally adversely affect (and be adversely affected by) the presence of humans intra-dimensionally. A Master can create a "Garden of Eden" on the atomic etheric sub-plane, in the middle of the most desolate physical area. The life of plants and animals that have died from the lower etheric sub-planes can be maintained on the atomic etheric sub-plane by the Master's great thought if doing so would be of benefit to their kingdoms. Atmic consciousness is often used to further enlighten and extend the life of deserving plant and animal lifeforms to be a part of a Master's created etheric world. The animals that a Master chooses to live with him or her on the atomic level of the etheric plane are those wild animals that are the most advanced. Often, these animals are approaching the developmental state of having the consciousness that a pet would have on the dense physical plane. Functioning as companion animals to the Master, these animals (and their group souls) greatly benefit from living within his or her aura. To prevent irregularities in the quantum constant, the Master uses his or her thought to disintegrate any physical forms that might have remained. Note that animals that have already been loved pets of humans are not chosen by a Master to live on his or her etheric "estate." The reason is that loved pets have developed enough astral body functioning to have a significant amount of life on the astral plane after etheric/dense physical death. Wild animals have a limited astral life that is not interfered with by a prolonged atomic etheric plane life. Usually the wild animals that a Master chooses to live for a time in her or his presence are wild animals that had been possessed at times by fallen spirit and that, as a result, do not desire astral life. The plants and trees that adorn the Master's etheric "estate" are often ones that have been adversely affected by humans. Sometimes these plants and trees were hybridized, which left them open to infections including viral attacks, and to various insect parasites. The Master's created etheric world can be maintained even without his or her presence on the etheric sub-planes in his or her etheric aura at all times. The reason is that all three of a Master's lower bodies have been unified in light, and semi-permanently change the time and space of one world when he or she is in another.

Students of the Master may be given the opportunity to visit him or her on the atomic level of the etheric plane by leaving their dense physical bodies and travelling etherically to the Master's etheric ashram location. These students are, usually, at least third level initiates who have completed the renunciations and are at least at the pledged stage of, and, more frequently, have reached the accepted stage of, the third initiation. Physically alive arhats (fourth level initiates) typically pay regular but infrequent visits to a Master. When students visit a Master on the atomic level of the etheric sub-plane, they must be able to remain conscious on this sub-plane; the ability to do so is the result of the student creating significant levels of *cosmic* virtue in his or her and others' lives. Note that the highest level of *human* virtue is nobility—a sub-virtue of the lower three cosmic virtues of the Ray Lords. Nobility is doing the best that one possibly can, based upon limitations that were created by prior levels of selfishness. Human virtue is still somewhat selfish; cosmic virtue is unselfish at its level of creation and is *spiritual service*. Pledged third and higher level initiates are more soul than they are human and create service, or enough cosmic virtuc to become conscious on the first etheric sub-plane.

Concurrently with becoming conscious on the first etheric sub-plane, the student of a Master usually needs to build enough of her or his intuitional, or buddhic, body and at least this body's lowest sense of controlled intuition, in order to communicate and share thought with the Master and the other students who, usually, are present. Masters of today think using at least controlled intuition rather than concepts and thoughtforms, most of the time; when they communicate with their students, they generally will do so through the student's developing intuitional body. While this does improve and foster growth in the student's intuitional body, using controlled intuition is also challenging. It is sometimes very difficult for the students to always understand the Master—and each other. For this reason, some third level initiates, prior to the completion of their renunciations, can only hear—and sometimes only partially hear—a meeting of the Master and his or her students. No atomic etheric sense besides hearing is yet developed in these students, and, in addition, the intuitional body is insufficiently developed to contribute any thought to others. (As a sense, hearing corresponds to the seventh plane, and is usually the easiest sense to develop atomic etherically.) The above-mentioned renunciations take place during the early part of the third initiation, between the accepting and pledged stages; the renunciations are a series both of actual renouncing and of tests of renouncing the selfish use of the six split senses (of the whole seven) in each of the three lower bodies. Thus there are eighteen renunciations, with every one being specific to the individual initiate in the ways that he or she uses each of his or her senses selfishly. During the next, or fourth, initiation, the tests of renunciation must be lived as a lifetime (or often more than one lifetime) of renunciation. The entire fourth initiation is sometimes referred to as the renunciation.

Masters can live on the atomic etheric sub-plane as long as they keep their three lowest permanent atoms. They can pay visits to the lower etheric and dense sub-planes as well as to the astral and mental ones in a body that they construct from the lunar deva and elemental energy that exists on whatever specific plane they are serving on at that time. These lunar deva and elemental energies are brought together in full light that comes from the atomic level of the plane that the body is on, and because of this are perfect. A body constructed in this way for etheric use is called a mayavirupa, or an etheric "body of light." Usually a Master will create a mayavirupa for only short periods of time because using the energies in this way for longer periods would interfere with the energies' development. So that all Masters who are still involved with service in the three lower worlds can attend meetings regarding the planet, these meetings are held on the atomic level, or the fully enlightened level, of the atomic etheric sub-plane.

Besides fifth level Masters, the participants are the Planetary Logos's incarnation for all of earth's planes, and sixth and seventh initiate level Masters. The atomic etheric level was chosen as the location for the meetings so that fifth level and beginning sixth level Masters can attend them and so that all the Masters can counsel each other in one place. The name of this place, which was created on the atomic level of the etheric plane, is Shamballa. The method of thought and the corresponding consciousness of those present in Shamballa is atmic, or spiritual plane, level. This level of thought is far beyond what any human can attain. Even a beginning fifth level initiate Master has some difficulty in sensing and thinking using his or her spiritual plane body because at that stage, it is still being developed. Shamballa used to be located a mile or two above earth's surface in a region of the Gobi Desert. Many Masters create their etheric first sub-plane ashrams and residences high on this sub-plane in order to avoid humans as best as they can. With the advent of airplanes, it has sometimes been necessary to move these locations because although a physical airplane can move through the etheric sub-planes without disruption, the aura of a Master will affect the humans on the airplane. Also, some computers and other sensitive electronic devices might be slightly affected at times by the created atomic etheric forms, as a result of the quantum constant irregularities, if these devices were to remain for minutes to hours in the same location. At today's level of aerospace technology it is nearly impossible for that sort of problem to occur—but it might be of concern in the not-too-distant future.

Evil has for a very long time attempted to connect planes through darkness, such as the kama-manasic connection on earth. It also attempted to connect the lowest part of the astral plane to the etheric plane on earth, but needed to do so by turning the atomic etheric sub-plane dark. This then would have effectively evicted the etheric Ray Lord and the Masters from earth. This attempt was made in the last period of the Atlantean civilization, during the seventh sub-race development of the fourth major race (when connection would be easiest). The last attempt took place during World War II. Such a plan will almost certainly not succeed in its original motive to overtake the dimension, because the Planetary Logos of a planet will destroy first the entire civilization and, if necessary, the whole planet in order to prevent such an occurrence.

Dark Super-Etheric Entity Still Remaining since Atlantean Times

an "Elemental"—an evil spirit joined to a form whose energy is more of elemental energy than deva energy

Illustration 8.7

The destruction of the Atlantean civilization on earth stopped evil from connecting to the first, or atomic, sub-plane of the etheric plane. However, evil did succeed in partially connecting to the fourth, third, and second etheric sub-planes. It did this through evil people who were physically alive and who used forceful methods on the etheric elemental energy in a variety of etheric lifeforms. The results caused these lifeforms to change into monsters of varying levels of darkness. The forceful methods employed included thoughtform manipulation, glamour direction, and sometimes etheric emanations from certain sources; also, the concussion of explosives or other very loud sounds were used because they can enable evil contact. Other than the very loud sounds, these methods became antiquated over time, and are today useless because the lunar devas and elemental energies have evolved beyond being affected by the prior constructions. None of the information in this book would assist anyone in creating any additional methods of these types, because such methods use formulated constructs that are specific for each desired dark outcome; this book presents concepts—which counter evil construction, as well. No recipes for altering energy are given to the reader of *Life's Hidden Meaning*. During Atlantean times, such care was sometimes not taken in disseminating knowledge; the intentions were often good, but frequently had disastrous results. A lack of wisdom was exercised by some somewhat spiritually disciplined people who misunderstood that, in many people, having more knowledge of certain kinds does not always lead to their higher consciousness. (See Chapter Nine for more information about Atlantean—and other—civilizations.)

 ## THE TUNNEL OF LIGHT

Since all of the atomic levels of the sub-planes of the seven dimensions are connected to each other through the interpenetrating light, or thought, of each Ray Lord to another, the connection itself has a form—as a part of all of their bodies, or planes. The first Ray Lord has the greatest thought and creates the largest dimension and dimensional part to the connection in light, or tunnel of light. Each succeeding lower Ray Lord has less thought, a smaller dimension, and a smaller-in-diameter part of the interpenetrating tunnel. This gives the tunnel a shape like a vortex or a rotating cone (because each sphere rotates, the vortex also rotates), with the smallest part on the etheric atomic sub-plane and the largest on the logoic atomic sub-plane. The tunnel connects the time and space of the seven enlightened parts of the planes. It also connects the sub-planes of each dimension through sub-dimensional light that corresponds to each Ray Lord. To see the tunnel beyond the dimension one is located on requires a vantage point of the atomic level of that dimension. The logoic plane, which is sometimes referred to as the plane of Adi (of the All), has a tunnel that reaches across the entire atomic sub-plane because this Ray Lord's (fully enlightened) thought can interpenetrate all of the lower Ray Lords' thought.

Those who enter the tunnel, unless they are fully enlightened in the body that corresponds to the part of the vortex, or tunnel, and plane they are located in, will experience their part of the vortex as the largest, and the parts of higher dimensions as smaller. This occurs because their senses distort the tunnel based upon how much they can perceive of each higher dimension. To most spiritual disciples, the vortex usually appears larger on the etheric atomic sub-plane, and smaller until it opens at the end as a U-shaped form of light that becomes spherical at its end. In observing the tunnel from the outside (which is possible for those inside the tunnel and on the atomic etheric level, and above on a higher atomic level of a plane), it appears to many spiritual disciples as resembling a chalice with a base that is triangular in shape and seems to rise to its cup, becoming progressively smaller until, at the neck, it connects to the cup. (See the Ageless Wisdom Distributors trademark on the publisher's page and the spine of this book.) This distorted appearance is the result of the three aspects of God's mind not being fully joined within the disciple's senses. Then this changes the light that constructs the vortex to become separated, giving the vortex an angular, or triangular, appearance. The three aspects of God's mind affect each dimension the disciple perceives, altering the vortex until all of the bodies within him or her are joined as one.

The Astral Vortex

Traveling to and through the astral plane, a traveler experiences a cone of light that is the interpenetration of the three dimensions of the etheric/dense physical plane with the fourth—the motion of energy.

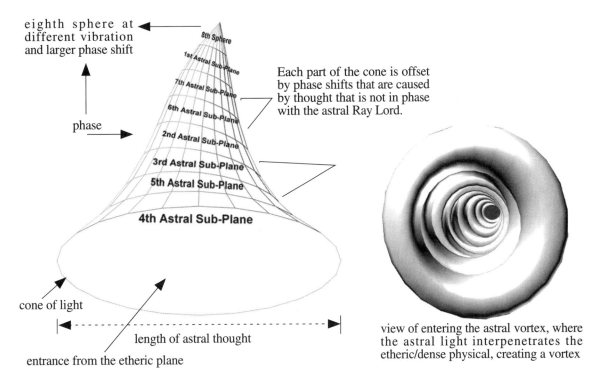

eighth sphere at different vibration and larger phase shift

8th Sphere

1st Astral Sub-Plane

7th Astral Sub-Plane

6th Astral Sub-Plane

2nd Astral Sub-Plane

3rd Astral Sub-Plane

5th Astral Sub-Plane

4th Astral Sub-Plane

phase

Each part of the cone is offset by phase shifts that are caused by thought that is not in phase with the astral Ray Lord.

cone of light

length of astral thought

entrance from the etheric plane

view of entering the astral vortex, where the astral light interpenetrates the etheric/dense physical, creating a vortex

Illustration 8.8

Most people travel through the vortex, or tunnel of light, when they sleep and travel inter-dimensionally. As they move through the tunnel, if their bodies are not unified as one up to the level, or plane, they are on (with *no* humans ever having more than one unified body), they shift focus of their consciousness and its thread from one part of the sutratma, or life thread, to another as they move from one plane to the next. For example, if a person is focused in consciousness etherically, the consciousness thread is focused on the life thread within the etheric centers and senses, causing the life thread to vibrate more vigorously etherically than astrally or mentally in the corresponding centers. As a person moves through the vortex to the next higher plane (the astral plane), his or her focus in consciousness becomes astral. The life thread then vibrates based upon astral consciousness more than etheric or mental. The astral center and senses become prominent in life vibration. The shift occurs whether the person is asleep or awake. While asleep, the overall vibration of the threads is less and all the centers that the threads are attached to are somewhat less well integrated. As a person reaches the astral dimension within the vortex, he or she can leave the vortex and enter the dimension through the center of focus within the consciousness and its *thread for that particular body*. The majority of people in developed countries are today focused in consciousness etherically and astrally through the solar plexus center (some of these people have somewhat fused the heart center to the solar plexus center); in their mental bodies they are focused through the mental ajna center. It is through these centers that they leave and enter the other bodies and dimensions the majority of the time. More primitive people today are focused etherically in consciousness through the sexual center. These people usually do not have connected etheric and astral bodies and centers, and are atypical; because of their lower levels of empathy and the ways in which they love others, they are more Lemurian than Atlantean in their consciousness concerning responses in their lives. Many people who are advanced in intelligence have considerable consciousness focused from the ajna center in the astral and etheric bodies; depending upon the person's level of consciousness during a day, he or she might, when asleep, sometimes leave from the ajna center within the etheric body and enter either the astral or mental body through the ajna center. The center that a person enters from is the same one she or he must leave through to return to the *prior* dimension. The reason is that the consciousness thread went through and ended in that center. Some people who return to physical life after a near-death experience have entered the tunnel of light, and sometimes were even likely to have experienced a part of an astral sub-plane. In these cases, the Solar Angel is probably allowing such an experience to occur, often in order to impress upon the person the concept of after-life, and perhaps for other reasons as well.

After death from the etheric body occurs, the life and consciousness threads are removed from the etheric heart and head centers and from the center of focus where the end of the consciousness thread had been attached. The etheric body then dies—the energies disorganize—as the etheric lunar devas lose their focus and the elemental energies begin to gravitate towards each other's slight thought, becoming informed by a mineral group soul and its self. The only etheric sense that a (non-evil) person retains at this point is that which was joined etherically and fused through light with the two spiritual senses of the astral body. Etheric energies return to the mineral group souls' control, under the guidance of the Spirit of Earth. Generally, only etheric sense that was used without retaining any energy, or that was used in service, can produce light in the sense and then join with the astral body's two spiritual senses. At this point most people have very little of this fused sense because they created only a very slight enlightenment of their bodies while etheric/dense physically alive. As a result, most people are practically senseless both etherically and dense physically once they have died from this dimension.

 ## THE STRUCTURE OF THE ASTRAL SUB-PLANES

A person who has died from his or her etheric body (or a person who is astral-travelling) passes through the tunnel of light. The person enters the astral plane through his or her astral center that had been used the most as his or her general focus of consciousness up to that point in life. One or more of the seven major astral centers are connected to one of the corresponding seven astral sub-planes. The sexual center is connected to, and when traveled through leads a person to, the astral seventh sub-plane. When the solar plexus center is mostly not fused to the heart center, it is connected to the sixth astral sub-plane, and when traveled through leads a person to that part of the dimension. Likewise, the astral ajna center is connected to, and when traveled through leads the astral traveler to, the fifth astral sub-plane.

The astral base of spine, or sacral, center has a fourth ray focus and when somewhat fused with other centers is connected to the fourth astral sub-plane. This center is the one of focus when it is first used to somewhat fuse centers together in the astral body. Unlike in the etheric/dense physical body (which has a masculine ray focus and the focus more on how well its senses are communicating), fusion of the astral body's solar plexus center to the heart center usually occurs before the sexual center fuses with the throat center. The base of spine center must be first more developed through focused consciousness and love before the solar plexus center will fuse with the heart center. This is the case because the sacral center balances the energies between the two centers as they fuse. Most of the people who are loving to a considerable degree and who, while physically alive, created more love and empathy in their and others' lives than is the average for the sub-race (of the major human race) that they are members of, have focused their consciousness through the sacral center. For the last two thousand years, more people have focused their lives astrally on creating more love than on creating any other cosmic virtue. The religion of Christianity has been a catalyst for this change, whether people practiced the religion or not. The reason is that this religion has affected both the human consciousness worldwide and most other major religions as well. People who have focused their consciousness through the astral sacral center (with some fusing taking place between the astral solar plexus and heart centers) during the majority of the time that they were physically alive will travel directly to the fourth astral sub-plane after etheric plane death. A person who has focused her or his life astrally in ways that, *additionally*, were fusing her or his astral sexual center to his or her astral throat center can then travel through these two fusing centers with the previously fusing sacral center added, which, with their third ray focus, lead her or him to the third astral sub-plane.

Usually only people who were spiritually disciplining themselves while alive on the dense physical plane, who then have died from the etheric plane can create the full and balanced triangle of fusion of the astral centers that is necessary to travel to the second astral sub-plane after etheric death. The triangle of fusion is created by the heart center being the *primary* focus as thirty-seven percent or more of the solar plexus center energy travels to the heart center's inner spirit sphere and is used consciously to give others the ability to become more loving. Such a person is soul conscious because she or he gives to others in order to help them to be more like their souls. In soul conscious people, the solar plexus center is fusing with the heart center, creating the first leg, or side, of the triangle of fusion. In such people, the sexual center is fusing with the throat center, with the previously mentioned primary focus on the heart center; this creates the second leg, or side, of the triangle of fusion. In addition, in soul conscious people the sacral center is fusing with the ajna center while these two are then fusing with the two other sides of the triangle of *fusing* centers, creating the third side of the triangle of fusion. People whose centers have joined in these ways can travel, while astrally alive, through them to the second astral sub-plane, or lower, if needed in order to serve others.

Another triangle of fusing astral centers can occur in an initiate who uses the crown center (once it has somewhat fused with the ajna and sacral centers) as a means of service to others. Such individuals are those who have chosen to astrally spiritually discipline themselves (mostly while still physically alive) and to lead a group of others in *creating* virtue in their respective soul missions. These people are disciples who are in at least the accepted, for initiation, stage of the first level of initiation. For a person to travel to the first astral sub-plane immediately after his or her etheric plane death, that person usually needs to be either in the accepted stage of the first or second level of initiation, a third level initiate at the stage of renunciation (accepting to pledged stages), or an arhat beyond the probationary stage. The joining or sometimes fused (seventy-five percent to one hundred percent) solar plexus and heart centers begin to fuse with the fusing ajna and crown centers, which is a first ray center and sense, and which creates the first leg of the triangle of fusion. Also, the joining or sometimes fused sexual and throat centers fuse with the crown center, creating the second side of the triangle of fusion, and the sacral center is fusing with the crown center and all of the other fusing or fused centers, creating the third side of the triangle of fusion. Travelling through this triangular fusion of centers then leads to the first astral sub-plane. Notice that to reach the second and first astral sub-planes, a person usually needs to travel through a triangle of fusing or fused centers that are balanced and that she or he has built through creating certain levels of discipline and service. The reason for this requirement is that the first two astral sub-planes correspond to the two spiritual senses, of understanding and of becoming a part of God. These senses require centers to be used in spiritual service. This then creates the fusion of the centers by raising and using kundalini energies.

To restate this conceptual structure of travelling through centers to reach astral sub-planes, the lowest three astral sub-planes are reached through mostly selfish and separative use of the sexual center and sense (seventh sub-plane), solar plexus center and sense (sixth sub-plane), and ajna center and sense (fifth sub-plane). The fourth astral sub-plane is reached by travelling through the sacral center and its sense, which are somewhat fusing to the heart center and its sense though in an imbalanced way, while the solar plexus center and its sense and energies switch to first sending some of its energies into the spirit sphere of the heart center a significant amount (ten percent or more) of time before a person experiences love. These fusings make the experience of love less conditional, and are likely to lead to the creation of more relatively unconditional love. The third sub-plane is reached by travelling through the fusing sexual and throat centers and with some imbalanced additional fusing of the sacral and heart centers to them. The second astral sub-plane is reached by travelling through the fusing triangle of the sacral center, the heart center (eventually as the primary focus), and the solar plexus center and their senses, balanced as one side of a triangle of joining senses, to a fusing sexual and throat center and sense on a second side of a triangle. The third leg of the triangle is the fusing sacral and ajna centers balanced to the first two sides. The first astral sub-plane is reached by travelling through the fusing or fused solar plexus and heart centers and balanced with the fusing ajna and crown centers. The second side is balanced with the first and contains the fusing or fused sexual and throat centers fusing with the crown center. The third side is balanced with the other two sides and has the sacral center fusing with the crown center and fusing with all other centers. The centers need to be balanced in their fusing to reach either the second or first astral sub-plane. This requires more than just fusing them, it requires spiritual use of them that has been created from discipline. Without adequate discipline, the senses and centers are too self-focused to balance the use of the senses in service.

It is possible for a person on the astral plane after physical death to create more love that is in service to others and to eventually advance, or be able to move to a higher sub-plane of astral life. For example, some spiritually disciplined people who first live on the second astral sub-plane finish their astral lives while on the first astral sub-plane. This happens to people who have managed to fuse their higher astral centers through service while on the second astral sub-plane. When living on an astral sub-plane, an astrally alive person can visit a lower astral sub-plane at will. For someone who is selfishly motivated to travel to a lower astral sub-plane (usually in order to manipulate people on the lower sub-plane), there is a great danger of that person falling victim on the lower sub-plane to the glamours within his or her astral body. Note that the glamours are likely to be what drew that person to "slumming" for purposes of manipulation and control over those who are *initially* of lower consciousness. Once on a lower astral sub-plane, such a person may not be able to leave for a higher one. This can occur because of misuse of and increased damage to the center and sense he or she used to manipulate others and traveled through in order to reach the lower sub-plane. Travelling to lower astral sub-planes for the purpose of serving others has the opposite effect. Instead of separating the whole astral sense of empathy through selfish use of the astral senses, the effect is an increase in the unity of the astral sense through the creation of more love. What people from the second and first astral sub-planes mostly do is create such service because they are people who are choosing to spiritually discipline themselves.

Once a person dies from his or her etheric body, he or she will travel through the tunnel of light to one of the seven astral sub-planes. These seven sub-planes have been described in some religions as the "seven heavens." This is because whatever desires a person might have (from his or her own levels of consciousness) are met instantly. The science involved is that the thought (the astral imagination) of the astrally alive person causes astral energy to instantly create the desired form and animate it. Those people on the second and first astral sub-planes more often than not desire, or aspire, to serve others through creating more love. Those on the second astral sub-plane aspire to create more love through using their existing empathy and creative astral thought (their imagination) to love others and to help others to be more loving. Those on the first astral sub-plane create more of their astral thought and develop more of their empathy to then serve others by creating more ways for these others, if they so choose, to love still others. Thus those on the second astral sub-plane serve more with their existing senses and thought, while those on the first astral sub-plane serve more with the senses they have further developed and their astral thought (and mental thought, as well) that they have created a new increase in. Whatever desires a person has dictates which of these "seven heavens" he or she lives in. Each astral sub-plane has its own unique kind of human civilization on it. The reason is that the consciousness of the human inhabitants on each sub-plane has altered the astral energy into quite different forms.

Evil has chosen to create its own sub-dimension on the very lowest part of the seventh (the lowest) astral sub-plane. Spiritually, this sub-dimension has been referred to as the eighth sphere. It has been so named because it is like an eighth astral sub-plane, and each sub-plane is a sphere within the next larger astral sub-sphere of energy. The astral spheres are sized by the amount of thought by the animals and people within them. The sphere's sizes are *not* in the order of their levels according to their sub-ray energy correspondences. For example, the fourth ray sphere is in the middle of the astral sub-ray dimensions of sub-astral rays seven through one (remember that all of the astral rays, the seventh through the first, are actually sub-rays of the sixth, or astral-rayed energy). However, more people and animals live on the fourth astral sub-plane than on any of the others—making it the largest. In spatial terms of three dimensions, it becomes even more confusing because while the sub-fourth ray is in the middle, or is centrally located between the seventh and first sub-planes, the fourth astral sub-plane is just outside earth's three-dimensional

Location of the Fourth Dimension of Movement of Astral Energy within the Three Dimensions

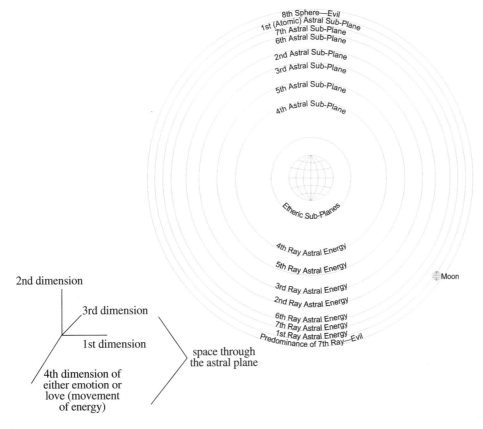

Illustration 8.9

etheric atmosphere, about twenty miles above earth's surface. Thus the fourth astral sub-plane is closest to the first etheric sub-plane in three-dimensional space. The smallest astral sub-plane is the eighth, or evil, sphere. It lies in the three-dimensional space that the dark side of the moon occupies, astrally furthest from the physical earth and slightly outward, away from the direction of earth. But, surprisingly, the next smallest and farthest astral sub-plane from the physical earth in three dimensional space is the first astral sub-plane. It is next to the eighth sphere in the three-dimensional space that the light side of the moon occupies slightly towards earth. It creates, in three dimensions, its larger-in-diameter but small-in-area sphere. The confusion arises because a fourth dimension of astral energy exists, which distorts an ability to correctly perceive and for many people to understand astral space in the three dimensions.

 ## LIFE ON THE ASTRAL SUB-PLANES

In this next section of the chapter the author offers, in a reasonably brief description, his understanding of the more important aspects of the civilizations that exist on each of the astral sub-planes, including the eighth sphere. This description is in all likelihood the first accurate representation of these civilizations presented in modern writing. What life is like immediately after etheric/dense physical death probably will be revealed to most people who read and understand the information that is given herein. When used with other information that was previously explained and was specifically chosen to be presented prior to this point, the knowledge of astral life after death is likely to lead to the desire, or aspiration, to live more virtuously now, on the physical plane, while gaining much more of the meaning within life that had been hidden. Those people who might attempt to paraphrase, or incompletely explain, the following information to others could produce some outcomes that might result in more selfishness in others. This is a danger when specifics are explained in new knowledge that is not known by most others. Many of the people whose religious, philosophical, and/or scientific views are significantly different from the information in this book, with these views being very important in their lives' meaning, may find conflict in some of their beliefs versus the information presented. Of these people, those who have read more than just this chapter and have continued to read through to this point are more likely to have fewer conflictive issues as they continue to read further. What follows is not conjecture, but accounts of actual prior experiences with knowledge from other sources sometimes used as corroboration in order to complete the concepts about the observations; it is a phenomenological study of the astral sub-planes and, later in this chapter, the lower mental sub-planes. Everything that is described is supported by concepts that have already been explained in this book. While observations in and of themselves can be very inaccurate, especially where the astral plane is concerned, any phenomena that might have been observed but cannot be conceptually explained are not included. As has been explained, the desires that a person has within his or her astral body will direct his or her travel to a specific sub-plane of the astral plane. Travel to the astral plane utilizes the spirit sphere of a major center and its sense, with this sphere functioning as a doorway of consciousness. The energy sphere part of the center is an actual part of a corresponding sub-plane, and has a sub-ray focus of the plane the entire body is on and a part of. The vibration along with focus (the direction, or phase) of the consciousness thread, or its ending point in the major centers, dictates the total effect that astral desires will have while a person is travelling astrally. The more loving, or giving, a person has been and is, the more choices he or she has concerning which astral sub-plane or sub-planes he or she can travel to. Greater astral life is realized by living on a higher astral sub-plane, both in amounts of time and, most importantly, in amounts of meaning that are derived from living. The eighth astral sphere, of evil, will be covered last, since it is more a negation than a creation in terms of human civilization.

Those who have lived materially selfishly, electing, a multitude of times, to not give, or to not love others in most of the ways that are possible, *because they preferred instead to seek and control material gain*, often have desires that lead them to the seventh astral sub-plane. This sub-plane is their "heaven." The quantum constant on the seventh astral sub-plane is about six times greater in its effect than on dense physical earth, which causes time to dilate by a factor of six. For every hour of life a person spends in the dense physical world, an astrally alive person (or astral dreamer or traveler) on the seventh sub-plane lives for about six hours; for every year in dense physical time, there are about six years of seventh astral sub-plane time, and so forth. Although there are some differences among the astral sub-planes, people's astral lives, in general, span thirty to fifty dense physical years. The reason concerns the length of time that the bodies' energies can remain intact without increasing the space between the energies, or without dark crystallization of the permanent atoms occurring. The life expectancy, in astral years, of those who live on the seventh astral sub-plane is one hundred eighty to three hundred years, on average. *All* of the related astral desires that people have while they are alive astrally are met through the use of their senses, their thought, and the plane's form, or energy, which together create everything a person chooses. The predominant desire of those on the seventh astral sub-plane is for an excessive amount of (astral re-creations of) material things. This is based to a large extent on the thought processes the people had while physically alive. The seventh astral sub-plane has very dense *astral* energy on it (only the eighth sphere is denser— about twice as much). It is the lowest sub-plane and corresponds to the seventh ray in focus. The miserly and very selfish emotions of people on this sub-plane cause them to use their seventh (sub-) ray astral center (the sexual center) and sense, as well as their creative imagination, to be aware of, to attract, and to create somewhat familiar material forms that they then "own." Astral senses are immensely less dense than etheric/dense physical senses are, which makes them much more easily changed by friction, or the effects of forces. A sense that is used selfishly always creates some retained energies that the self and its controlling personality usually seek to hold onto in their illusion to not give, or not love. Astral senses that mostly take in and retain the relatively very dense seventh sub-plane (and especially seventh sub-sub-plane of the seventh sub-plane) astral energies incur, because of their relatively high density, much greater amounts of retained energy than the same senses would if used selfishly on a higher astral sub-plane where energy is much less dense. On each higher astral sub-plane, there are seven sub- (sub-) versions of the corresponding astral energies that people use with which to create forms. Thus as people on the astral plane are selfish, they rapidly lose their senses. They do so because these senses, as the primary ones, are used much more than they were when a person was physically alive. Because of their very low density as compared to physical senses, the astral senses have greater susceptibility to degradation, especially when one or more of them is used to a much larger extent as a primary life sense. Those on the seventh sub-plane lose their astral senses the fastest of anyone (including those who are fully evil—which will be explained later in this chapter) because, through their desires, they focus selfishly on such relatively dense astral energy.

 ## THE SEVENTH ASTRAL SUB-PLANE

There are a number of "cities" and "towns" on the seventh astral sub-plane that all differ somewhat from each other in physical appearance. Few people live off on their own on this sub-plane. The primary reason is to avoid being targets of some menacing creatures there that will attempt to possess people's astral bodies. Also, people mostly alone and on their own may be attacked by some hostile wild astral animals. The fear of these creatures generally increases as people lose their astral senses as a result of selfishness. The loss of sense leaves these people open to being preyed upon and possessed. Upon first arriving on the seventh astral sub-plane, most people attend a group orientation to life in their new world. A basic explanation of their new society is given to them; the apparent motivation for the established inhabitants taking the time and effort to give this orientation is to maintain order and organization, and not so much concern for the new arrivals. It is quite efficient to educate people in this rather mechanical format. Rarely, a prior associate, a friend, or a relative may meet a person when he or she first arrives; however, the person who died first would almost certainly have been a recent arrival, too, because otherwise, her or his senses would most likely be diminished too far to be aware of the new arrival's presence on the plane. New arrivals are drawn to the very place (city or town) that their desires bring them to, and nearly all of them seek first to understand their new world. It is this desire that brings them to the orientation location, and at right around the time that a "teacher" about the new society is available to help. Some of the areas covered in this orientation include an explanation of the rules. These include, supposedly, not removing and/or using others' astral form creations. Through thought alone, locomotion is possible. This ability becomes greatly diminished, however, as the senses are damaged and as astral thought, as creative imagination, begins to fail in some circumstances. When people first arrive they can move about by flying, and at fairly fast speeds. Also, people whose astral senses are joined and whose creative imagination is strong can instantly relocate their entire bodies to a desired location. The more selfish inhabitants cannot relocate themselves using creative imagination. In just a few seventh sub-plane astral decades their ability for self-locomotion can be reduced to the way an etheric ghost moves. At a few inches or feet above the ground, they move at only a few miles per hour.

The creation of large forms out of amounts of seventh sub-plane astral energy, which is relatively dense (for astral energy), requires a considerable amount of sense and creative imagination. To reduce the loss of their own sense and thought, those who have stronger senses and thought will often steal astral forms that others have created; this is against the rules of the society, but few live by these rules. Eventually these thieves' senses and thought will diminish; others will take what they have, leaving the "older" inhabitants (those who have been there the longest) unable to replicate for themselves new forms and no longer having their old ones. In this society, the most recent arrivals usually will soon have the nicest and the most numerous astral forms; those who have been more selfish than average (and the average of selfishness there is quite high) and have lived for a number of years astrally on this sub-plane usually have the worst and the fewest. These older inhabitants are frequently still driven by their desires, as glamours—which are fixed in their astral bodies, to control more astral form. Because their senses are reduced, they may fall into a fantasy state that on the astral plane seems semi-real, within which they continue to have their desires met. While in this state, they become targets for others to possess and use their two remaining bodies and those bodies' associated senses. Sometimes the "younger" astral inhabitants—the more recent arrivals—will use the senses of those older inhabitants who are in fantasy, instead of using their own senses. They do this in order to conserve their own one or more bodies and thus keep them from diminishing as quickly as they otherwise would. One person's sense can be used by another person on the astral plane because the energy in the sense can be taken outside the body it is in. Unlike when etheric/dense physical bodies become possessed, the astral entity that is possessing an astral sense does not have to enter into the other's person's astral body. Thus younger astrally alive seventh sub-plane inhabitants frequently function as leeches on the senses of the older people.

A worse condition of possession is possible. From thirty thousand to about eleven thousand years ago, on the island that remained of what had been an entire continent, of Atlantis, evil people created monsters in the eighth sphere. These monsters were used to possess others at the bidding of the evil people. Some of these monsters had etheric form and could even possess or attack people who were etherically and dense physically alive. All of the monsters had astral form, since they were created from astral (emotional) energy first. Very few of these monsters remain in existence today on the two lowest etheric sub-planes; however, most still do exist in the eighth sphere. Since the development of the kama-manasic connection quite a few of them now reside on the seventh astral sub-plane. A much smaller number have also been able to maintain their lifeforms and consciousness on the sixth astral sub-plane. None exist on or above the fifth astral sub-plane. Once one of these astral monsters possesses a weakened older astral person, it usually slowly destroys that person's astral body. The possessed person's reverie then changes from fantasies of having her or his glamours met, to vicious nightmares that somewhat depict what is actually happening to her or his astral body.

There is no biblical-type of hell after a person dies, because there is no need for one! People create their own suffering and pain through selfishness and the changes in the physics of the astral plane as compared to the etheric/dense physical. Because the astral senses diminish so relatively quickly when they become the primary senses that are used in a selfish astrally alive person, the self shrinks in consciousness as it can give less with (and to) a body that has less sense. As consciousness drops, suffering increases when there is some awareness of the loss of self. People on the seventh astral sub-plane are much more emotionally selfish than what is average for humanity today. As a consequence, they suffer after a relatively short period of astral time during which they at first believe they are in heaven. The concept of having all of one's self-focused desires met is consistent with a selfish person's expectation of what, at least in part, heaven is like. While there is little argument that the eighth sphere is a much more terrible place than the seventh sub-plane is, those in the eighth sphere do not (nearly) immediately suffer consequences that match their levels of selfishness, as those who inhabit the seventh sub-plane do. Notice that the body that has the focus of the consciousness thread on the life thread, i.e., the body that the person is living through is the body that loses the senses the fastest while the person is focused selfishly on life within it. Thus the etheric/dense physical senses diminish the most swiftly in a selfish person who is alive etheric/dense physically, and the astral senses diminish the fastest in a selfish person who is focused in life astrally; the same correspondences apply to the lower mental senses. Also, in relative terms, the same levels of selfishness cause each more subtle body to diminish in sense more quickly because of the much lower density of energies that hold each higher center and sense together.

People who are alive on the seventh astral sub-plane, unlike most people who are physically alive, have some knowledge of the higher astral sub-planes and the human civilizations there. Because their consciousness is so low, the seventh sub-plane inhabitants do not understand these higher sub-plane civilizations. The commonly-held opinion of the "other" astral regions is that their inhabitants are not very well organized and are wasteful of forms. In addition is the view that those people living on the other sub-planes have chosen to do so for very emotional reasons that fail to recognize the value of, at least semi-permanently, having things of (astral) form. Some seventh astral sub-plane inhabitants do eventually realize that the other (higher) sub-planes offer better lives than what they are living. This is especially true among the older members of the population before they become completely senseless. Some may change and become more loving; at that point, they can leave through the spirit sphere of one of their astral centers that is higher than the sexual (seventh ray) center, and travel through the tunnel of light to a higher astral sub-plane. The astral body eventually wears out from all the retained energies that cause degradation of the astral senses and sometimes even cause astral diseases. Astral disease caused by infection is mostly found on the seventh sub-plane. The reason is that the majority of the disease-causing astral bacteria need the lowest, or seventh, sub-ray astral energy to feed on; astral viruses can be found on both the seventh and sixth astral sub-planes. Glamours create emotional astral diseases that lead to depressions, manias, and neuroses. These conditions are common on the seventh and sixth sub-planes. Because a collective of people's thought is needed to ward off monsters, there are high population densities in "cities" and "towns," and very low densities outside them. While providing an effective defense against the monsters, living in dense populations has its own problems that include theft and being possessed by other people.

Daylight on the seventh astral sub-plane has a deep rose cast. The astral plane rotates in the opposite direction that etheric/dense physical earth does. Each astral sphere's outer surface is moving much faster than the much smaller (in three dimensions) dense physical earth. On the astral plane, even in the middle of the day there is less light than on the etheric/dense physical plane because the astral light from the sun's astral body is reduced by the low consciousness of the people on the seventh sub-plane. At night the sky is very dark, and the stars and moon have a slight tinge of rose. People who are astrally alive do sleep and dream on the astral plane, similarly to those who are etheric/dense physically alive. There is no etheric/dense physical light on the astral plane. Each daylight day there is composed of astral light only, and (because time is dilated) there are six diurnal changes on the seventh sub-plane for every one on dense physical earth, but astral thought can alter the perception of these changes. Compared to people on dense physical earth, astrally alive people sleep less hours in each day because they have one-third fewer bodies that are in need of deva and elemental energy repair. Also, because of inertia, the etheric/dense physical body requires proportionality more time to repair than the more subtle bodies do; however, the subtle bodies are much more easily damaged by selfishness than are the etheric/dense physical. With all these factors combined, those who are alive on the seventh astral sub-plane sleep about one-third less than do those who are etheric/dense physically alive, while those astrally alive on the first astral sub-plane might sleep less than one half-hour per day in astral time. People on the first astral sub-plane are so loving and truthful that they need much less time to repair the damage done to their bodies by retained energies.

A further and more scientific explanation of the astral effect of etheric/dense physical things that have an astral body briefly follows. Anything that exists in three-dimensional etheric/dense physical space (height, width, and depth), and that has an astral body, has that body surrounding the etheric/dense physical while it occupies etheric/dense physical space. The nearest astrally alive beings exist at least twenty miles above earth's surface, on the fourth astral sub-plane. In order to affect etheric/dense physically alive forms, these beings must, in most cases, move their senses about twenty miles to the surface of the earth. Although possible, doing so is very taxing on the astral senses because of the much denser space they must traverse. Also, to then change anything about the etheric/dense physical lifeform's astral body requires considerable thought—projected over the twenty miles. Usually only lower forms of plants can be somewhat affected in this way because the higher astral thought of more advanced lifeforms makes them too resistant to change from so distant a source (unless their thoughts coincide). Another important factor is that these astrally alive beings closest to etheric/dense physical earth are very unlikely to desire to have negative astral effects on etheric/dense physical lifeforms—especially lower level plants. The evil people on the eighth sphere may desire to have an effect on lifeforms that are etheric/dense physically alive, but cannot unless these lifeforms share the same consciousness (bringing their senses much closer to the evil ones and the evil ones' senses). The reason is that their location on a sphere that begins at the three dimensional location of the dark side of the moon places them both too far away and too obscured and hidden by the effects of the astral moon to affect lifeforms on earth. If the people who colonize the dark side of the moon are of low consciousness, then evil astrally alive people may be able to directly affect these colonists' astral bodies! Space travel on a fast-moving ship through this interpenetrating part of the eighth sphere should not be affected. The reason is that the speed of positional change would most likely make sensing and focusing of thought on the spaceship's inhabitants too difficult to accomplish. However, the actual effects that evil can cause under these circumstances have yet to be determined.

People on the seventh astral sub-plane engage in sexual exchanges, but use only their astral and mental bodies and the associated energies as the means of relating. Without etheric/dense physical bodies, sexual expression through exchanging energy is much more emotionally focused. Because these people have, on average, such low consciousness, there is little love (although very large amounts of emotion) exchanged during sexual activities. Sex takes place more frequently there than on dense earth. The reason is that astral sex is easier to engage in, has less significance because of the selfishness of the people involved (causing them to want to have more sex and sometimes with different people), and is often more emotionally satisfying than it was while they were physically alive and selfish. Since there are no sensual senses of the etheric/dense physical body to experience on the astral plane, there is no physical pleasure, nor can a lack of physical satiation occur. The sex is less intense because there is no physical sensation, but it provides additional elements of emotional feelings that often more than compensate for the physical losses. On the seventh astral sub-plane, people are often considered to be objects sexually, because of the very material focus of the inhabitants' selfishness. Rape is rather common, particularly of older, nearly senseless people. In younger people, non-intimacy is the norm in astral sex, as each uses his or her partner as an object.

As astrally alive seventh sub-plane people lose their senses, they sometimes seek to regain sense by possessing a person who is either etherically or dense physically alive. These possessions often include the astrally alive person's desire to experience physical sensations again. If the astrally alive person is a younger inhabitant and is particularly selfish, in order to experience physical sexual sensations he or she may seek to possess physically alive people who are, in some ways, about equal to him or her in selfishness and consciousness. These younger astral inhabitants are "better" at, or more successful at, possessing because of their strong creative imagination as thought; they often cause those whom they possess to become sexually promiscuous in order to satisfy their own (the possessing entities') desires for physical sexual sensation. These desires are met by using the etheric/dense physical senses of the physically alive people they possess. These astral inhabitants generally attempt and are successful at possession of physically alive people who have either emotional or mental disease or damaged astral senses, who use and may be addicted to drugs, who are significantly and seriously personality-disordered in general, or to whom any combination of these factors applies.

Some people who are alive on the seventh astral sub-plane become astrally senseless within twenty to thirty astral years of life. Many more do within forty to fifty astral years. The remaining time spent on the astral plane, one hundred thirty to two hundred eighty (!) astral years, are usually spent being victimized and slowly dying, often while experiencing horrid nightmares as vivid reverie. These nightmares are sometimes repeated over and over again. Eventually the astral body dies, and the person travels to the lower mental plane for additional life experiences. The process of astral suffering greatly builds empathy as a desired goal for the soul. As the person suffers and also experiences the pain of having lost sense and thought, she or he realizes the effects that her or his prior selfish acts had on others. At critical points in this process of building a desire to become empathic and loving, an astrally alive person who is suffering may subconsciously, or consciously, call upon (pray to) God for assistance and mercy. Under such circumstances, it would not be unusual for the Angel of the Presence to then appear, projected from the higher mental mind of the person. The Angel assists the repentant astral person in seeking a future life of more love and empathy. This goal becomes a part of a repentant person's permanent atom, with the selfish energies possibly being used up in the process of astral death. This process is often devastating, self-punishing, and very slow unless the person replaces emotionalism with love.

Prayers to improve oneself for the benefit of others, and to help others to become more cooperative and sharing, more loving, and more truthful are nearly always answered with loving wisdom from a higher, Godly (enlightened) source. Collective prayer for such purposes is particularly invoking of enlightened assistance. Prayer for selfish reasons and sometimes for only personal levels of giving in those capable of much higher levels of giving may result in increased crises, in order to correct such illusioned thoughts about God's purpose and love, or God's thought (light).

When a person first arrives on the astral plane, her or his astral senses are much more acute and accurate than they were during physical life because the focus of consciousness (at its thread) is on astral life (and its thread). On the seventh sub-plane, this improvement can lead to considerably relatively higher consciousness, or giving, *if the person so chooses*. Unfortunately, most people do not choose to give, and instead become driven by their selfish desires—which now can all be instantly met. Still, the gift of improved astral sense upon arrival is very similar to the religious concept of receiving both God's grace and salvation. The grace is received, however, only if the person chooses not to selfishly follow his or her desires, and, instead, seeks to find and become more a functional part of God. People who seek God *grow* in empathy, and, often, one higher sub-plane at a time, raise their love (their consciousness) while losing only minimal amounts of sense from whatever selfishness they still retain. Even the very selfish can be redeemed through their own great effort to become more virtuous. Redemption of those who are evil is also possible, though more complicated; the process whereby evil people can become saved will be explained later in this chapter.

Those people on the seventh sub-plane who remain selfish eventually become senseless; in the process, they may be attacked by animals or monsters and/or become possessed, and they suffer until their senses are gone. Once fully senseless, the astral body is dying because the lunar deva energy within it can no longer organize it enough to have the centers work together. The person's self disappears because its level of giving is too low to develop an astral mind; at this point, the level of giving by the self to its bodies is less than the majority of its field of potential in common thought. The mental mind and body cannot interpenetrate into an astral body that is dark and disorganized. Evil crystallizes and completely joins the mental and astral bodies together in darkness, but seventh sub-plane people are not (yet) so dark and selfish. The personality cannot integrate these two bodies together, and must give up control of the astral body. Once the personality gives up control by not focusing consciousness through the astral body, and the OverSoul and human soul have chosen to remove the life thread from the astral heart center, the astral body dies. The person moves through the tunnel of light to the mental plane and resumes life now through only one body—the mental. The mental senses and mental thought then become the focus of the personality's control and life. The self reintegrates because it needs to give to a much smaller field of only the mental body in order to create its mind and consciousness. The person's mental life begins on the part of the lower mental body where his or her personality was most egotistical in thought. Mental life will be explored later in this chapter. Most people who die from the seventh astral sub-plane, because of the kama-manasic connection and their overall high average levels of selfishness (which are usually accompanied by mental selfishness), first go to the seventh mental sub-plane. Someone who was selfish enough to remain on the seventh astral sub-plane until astral death is usually very kama-manasically connected. The exception to this generality is primitive people who have less mental body development. With each succeeding generation there are fewer and fewer of these people on earth, since most of earth's inhabitants today are focused on mental body development, and are members of the fifth major set of human sub-races.

The seventh astral sub-plane does have plant and animal life on it. The plant life there requires being maintained by advanced animal or human life. The reason is that the plant life needs to use a part of a lower mental body to stay alive. This is true of all plant life, but not bacteria or viruses that are *alive etherically* and are maintaining a seventh astral sub-plane part of themselves by being parasitic. Because they are animated by the selfish astral thought and

Example of Life on the Seventh Astral Sub-Plane

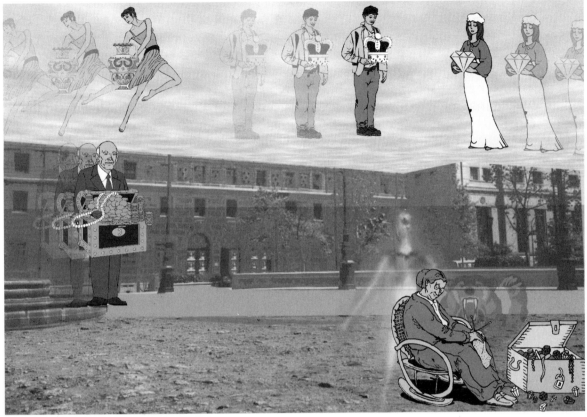

On the seventh astral sub-plane the astral senses of the residents are the most split, and the lowest—the sexual center and sense—are often used the most and the most separately. People living on the seventh astral sub-plane have the lowest average levels of empathy of any astral plane residents—except for the inhabitants of the eighth sphere. The life focus of the seventh astral sub-plane is on astral form, and usually duplicating the physical forms of various things the people there derived pleasure from, or thought they would, while physically alive. Sexual activity takes place very frequently, but more often as a possessive activity between people who are familiar with each other, to meet certain types of desires that each has. Keeping astral forms (including people!) is an important aspect to seventh astral sub-plane life. Becoming possessed is a common occurrence as a person ages. In the above illustration, the older woman in the rocker is an example of this. She is being possessed by both another person (who is using her astral senses instead of his own) and by a vicious, evilly controlled animal.

Illustration 8.10

subsequent retained energies of selfish astrally alive people, these bacteria and viruses can infect people who inhabit the seventh astral sub-plane. Note that etherically dead parasitic microbes do not exist as astrally alive lifeforms. Seventh astral sub-plane plants that are etheric/dense physically alive, and those that are astrally alive on the seventh sub-plane have some astral body development, usually with one or two centers. The astral parts of etheric/dense physically alive plants are mostly animated. Astral plants change with etheric/dense physical outside stimulation as a living plant does, but they can be found only in a corresponding astral part of their etheric physical location. The location is on or near the surface of physical earth and is very far from where any astrally alive people live. The astrally alive plants that have two astral centers are less often found on the seventh astral sub-plane (more are found on the sixth), and the ones with one astral center are more like "alive" minerals that have form astrally. Once an etheric/dense physical plant dies, so does its astral counterpart. This is because the plant has no mental centers with which to create its life. All astrally alive plant life on this lowest astral sub-plane exists only as dictated by the *giving* thought and desires of others. Astrally alive people are themselves helped by helping to create astrally alive plants. This occurs because creating the plants requires some empathy and love—even when it springs from a person's selfish desires for the presence of plants—and to "own" them. As people on the lower astral sub-planes age, their ability to help create plants diminishes. As a result, these people's environments become impoverished in their supply of plants, and particularly in aesthetically pleasing plants. Thus the areas in and around which older lower astral sub-plane inhabitants live are often stark and bleak.

If an astral entity interferes with the astral part of any etheric/dense physical form that is as dark, or selfish, as it is, it can sometimes (eventually) disrupt the etheric/dense physical form. It can do so because of interpenetration of the higher dimension into the lower. Note that the astral forms of etheric/dense physical things are not actually alive. They only have astral movement that directly follows their etheric/dense physical movements and the overall effects of those movements. For the most part, the astral bodies of etheric/dense physically alive plants, animals, and people are not focused on by astrally alive beings, and are therefore not noticed by them. To focus on etheric/dense physically alive forms' astral bodies requires the re-creation in creative imagination of their entire etheric or dense physical surroundings, which takes quite a toll on the astral senses and thought. For those who have such inclinations, possession is much easier and less taxing when the etheric/dense physically alive form is very dark in its informing thought and energies. A similar process can be used in love to focus on those etheric/dense physically alive whom astrally alive people have concern for. Although *less* taxing, the process still requires the use of more sense and creative imagination than most people on the seventh astral sub-plane are capable of or are inclined to be willing to expend.

The animals that live on the seventh astral sub-plane are the species that are the lowest in development and in consciousness, in general. The animals at higher levels of development that are found on the sub-plane are most often ones that were harmed through human intervention in their prior etheric/dense physical lives. Some were abused pets, others were hunted with malice and for "sport," many were used for commercial purpose and greed for profit, and some were exploited for glamours. Most of the animals in the last group end up on the sixth astral sub-plane after death from the etheric/dense physical world. The wild and "carnivorous" animals will often attack humans because of the anger that these animals have towards people. In addition, many of these animals attack people because of the strong seventh ray material/physical propensities (although now represented astrally). Also, these animals attack people because of the desire to have control over and create the fear in people that was created in them by people during physical life. These animals and the monsters attack and harm through astral and not physical force. They may "bite and claw" the astral energies within the senses and bodies of their victims by overcoming the sense or senses in one or more centers. Astral people who have strong senses cannot be attacked, while those whose senses have diminished are in danger. Many of the people who suffer attacks by animals and by the even worse monsters are karmically paying for abuses they inflicted upon animals during physical life. Younger inhabitants of the seventh astral sub-plane may continue to abuse and use astrally alive animals. Sometimes these inhabitants even possess etheric/dense physically alive animals in order to gain physical sensation—especially when these people are losing the ability to possess physically alive people. When they do they increase their karma, which they usually will suffer through later in astral life.

 ## THE SIXTH ASTRAL SUB-PLANE

Life for those on the sixth astral sub-plane is maximally focused on satiating all desires. This sub-plane has been referred to as the "sixth heaven," although in some literature the numbers are reversed, making it the "second heaven." The desire for "physical" form and control over it is transmuted into what the form represents in *movement* on the astral plane. For example, having a desire for an automobile is simply changed to the desire for the ability to move as though one were in an automobile. As another example of life on the sixth astral sub-plane, the speed at which one creates a house for her or his—often very temporary—use is what is important, rather than maintaining the form of that house. For a sixth sub-plane resident, maintaining such a form requires more sense and thought over time than does simply just creating one. The greater the desire, the *faster* the creation of astral movement, as long as the astral senses and thought remain at the same level. Using desire is the use of the two parts of astral time in order to create movement. The way this works is in imagining a past event or circumstance and then creating a present, changed, event through the use of creative imagination. Desire is not useful for future creation on the astral plane. The reason is that the joined future part of time is mostly missing there, and movement in that part of time requires either only love (which can only somewhat create parts of the future) or the addition of mental sense and thought. Thus, for example, if while in the present someone desires to have a different house in the future, and to have that future house created perhaps a week into the future, more desire and creative imagination must then be used in what will become the present a week from that point. One cannot create a house using creative imagination and save that creation as energy in the astral mind for future use. On the mental plane one can save the structure, or formula, for the house in the future; then, much less thought would be required when the house is created in the future. To create a house on the astral plane in creative imagination, a person needs to create every detail of that house—without using a structured formula. If a house was imagined for a future time, then, continually, between the time that the house was imagined and the time when the astral energy was brought together to create the house, the astral person would need to keep thinking of the house as it was constructed in his or her creative imagination! Not only is this nearly impossible to accomplish because to do so a person would be able to think of virtually nothing else, it would also greatly exhaust the astral mind and brain center. Emotions cause an exaggeration of the past and present—and mostly ignore the future. While creating in the future can be accomplished on the mental plane in mental energy, creating the future emotionally is usually not possible on the astral plane, as long as the astral plane remains separated from the time and space of the mental plane. Another reason is that the movement of emotional astral energy is focused between only two points in space.

Another way to explain the problem with astral time (and space) is that the density of not fully enlightened astral energy is too great and the selfish thought of spirit is too weak, or the quantum constant is too small, to adequately control energy for the future part of time to join with space, by energy becoming intelligent enough in its "movements," or activities. For those who are not so inclined towards physics and mathematics (not so formulated) in their thoughts, another way of explaining the effect is that the thought of astral spirit that is not fully enlightened and is within form is not strong enough to plan, or be conscious of, the movements that astral energy needs to make in order to become intelligent at some future time. The reason is that the collective gravitating thought of the energy is stronger, because of its density, than is the thought of the spirit that is trying to direct it. Thus while astrally alive people who are not thinking mentally are more astrally conscious (loving) on average than are those people who are physically alive, unless their astral bodies are enlightened they are not loving enough to adequately plan the creation of intelligent activities without using significant amounts of added mental thought, while they are thinking of the future. The more that astrally alive people use desires to control their thought (the more they are glamoured), the less mental thought they utilize and the less they plan. With less mental planning, astral energy will not respond to desires for future movements of the energy. Only when the astral and mental bodies function in unison, or are fused, can astral energy be controlled completely for future movements, by combined astral and structured mental thought that is fused. It is the *soul* that thinks by fusion, or by joining the bodies and senses, and spirit's thought within them—through love, or giving, joining with truth. The personality uses frictional forces to integrate these bodies. The forces also keeps the senses somewhat separate because of the selfish motives (and actions) involved.

Those on the lower astral sub-planes are driven by selfish desires, or emotions, that are fixed in each person's astral body. These people are unable to create future movement from present thought, or to effectively plan in their time and space. The inhabitants of the sixth astral sub-plane are extremely focused on meeting, or satiating, all their desires. They do so by *increasing* their emotional responses and decreasing their love. They use emotions as a means of satiating fixed desires, which temporarily relieves the agitation of specific glamours. Then these glamours grow from the added emotional energy and the whole cycle starts all over again. Each cycle requires additional emotional energy every time, in order to satiate the glamour. As might be expected, the senses and creative imagination become used up and damaged through the seeming endless process of satiating and then further growing glamours. The end of the process is eventually reached when the glamour can no longer be quelled through the input of increased emotional energy, and it cannot grow, either. Then its often violent and discordant vibrations, which are frequently joined with other similar glamours' discordant vibrations, create a torrent of uncoordinated astral body movements that manifest as nervousness, anxiety, and pain. As the person slowly becomes senseless with his or her astral body nervously and painfully out of control for many years, great suffering is caused as the self can give *nearly* nothing, with so much uncontrolled movement within the astral body. The movement becomes increasingly uncontrolled because the personality is losing its control over this body.

The loss of sense that the sixth astral sub-plane person causes to himself or herself is significantly different in *quality*, or expression of consciousness, as compared to the seventh sub-plane inhabitant. On the seventh sub-plane, the senses diminish because the retained astral energy is mostly *outside* the astral body, as miserly held astral forms, or possession of astral "property," which causes the body to slow down from inertia (a more seventh ray effect). Retaining astral energy in this way is more difficult to do and uses up more astral sense. Also, the astral energy being used is relatively more dense, while the thought of informing spirit is diminished. The diminishment occurs because of a lower consciousness, or less givingness (less love) on the part of seventh astral sub-plane inhabitants. The quantum constant is smaller, which requires that more time be separated from space (used up) for energy to follow greater thought. On the sixth astral sub-plane, most of the astral energy is selfishly retained *inside* the astral body, as spiraling increases in the size of glamours besides just in the centers. In the beginning, as long as the glamours are satiated the senses are less destroyed. This gives the inhabitants a false sense of well-being, as compared to those on the seventh astral sub-plane. The senses of a sixth astral sub-plane person, on average, decline more slowly, particularly at first, than those of the average seventh astral sub-plane person do; however, the sixth astral sub-plane inhabitants have *fifty percent more time* in which to live, which causes them to eventually become senseless and to suffer in the process. The two astral senses of focused use of sixth astral sub-plane inhabitants as compared to just one for those on the seventh greatly adds to sixth sub-plane overall astral sense. The sixth astral sub-plane people generally can join together their sexual and solar plexus centers and senses enough to use both of these lower astral split senses at the same time.

Because of the increase in the quantum constant on the sixth astral sub-plane, people experience time as being about nine times greater than those who are physically alive do. Note that the numbers given relative to time comparisons on the astral sub-planes have been rounded to whole numbers in order to foster an easier understanding of the concept. Most sixth sub-plane inhabitants cannot accurately sense much of anything on the seventh astral sub-plane because time is dilated so much (anything over about thirty-five percent is too much), which usually discourages them from focusing on the life of that lower sub-plane. Sixth sub-plane inhabitants can still travel to the seventh sub-plane if they desire to, but mostly they find it boring. They find that the inhabitants there use their emotions to create astral forms rather than internal "excitement" through (seemingly paradoxically) satiating glamours by adding emotional energies to them.

Upon first arriving on the sixth astral sub-plane, a person who is astrally alive finds himself or herself overwhelmed by the dizzying constant movement of astral forms that move because of their temporary nature and because desires change them so frequently. The person's own desires are what brought him or her to this frenetic sub-plane. On some parts of it, one might think that he or she has dropped in on a "hippie-" type drug party from the late 1960's in the United States. Everyone seems to be doing what he or she desires that "feels good." *Un*focused movement seems to be what is occurring, even though the movement is actually *very* focused on satiating a glamour that is somewhat hidden inside the astral body of someone there. Most people who first arrive on this sub-plane are met by one or more other people who want the new arrivals to have "fun" with them. "Fun" can be anything from mutually exploitive sex to dancing together while flying upside down. These other people will help to stimulate many glamours in a new arrival. A new arrival will often be seduced into the overall lifestyle of living for *e*-motion, or astral energy's motion directed towards the self—rather than being directed as love, away from the self. The selfish new arrival often believes that she or he is in heaven. The reason is that this *is* how the person, at least in part, pictured heaven in her or his mind while she or he was physically alive.

Sexual exchanges of astral energy can last for astral hours, and even days. This is because there is no physical body to reduce movement through encountering inertia and friction, or to easily tire. As one type of sexual glamour is satiated, another can be focused on—and another. Eventually, a person can go back to the first desire, because it has grown from the energy that was added into it. Sexual addiction is common on the sixth astral sub-plane, and is perhaps even the norm. Sexual preferences are a bit more discriminating there than on the seventh astral sub-plane. On the sixth sub-plane people are chosen as sexual partners based upon the level, or amount, that *both* of them stimulate and satiate glamours. Little effort is put into maintaining a relationship at a level to which a person is usually available to another sexually (as does occur on the seventh sub-plane). Instead, although sexual relations are discriminatory towards only certain types of people who are "fun" and who satisfy sexual glamours, if one person is unavailable, another of the type that is desired may be deemed equally appropriate as a substitute. On the seventh astral sub-plane, having certain sexual partners available at any particular time *is* important. This is because part of the sexual experience is in controlling the other person's movements. This is not the case most of the time on the sixth astral sub-plane; however, rape is a specific exception to this concept. Rape occurs as an exploitive control of those who have lost some sense. The rapist has a glamour to both have exciting (to the rapist) sexual activity and to control (and harm) the other person by possessing her or him. A part of the excitement is in the ability to both sense *and control* both sides of the sexual experience at the same time. While both sides of a sexual activity can be experienced anywhere on the astral plane through use of either empathy or the split astral senses, the other person or people still control their own senses and movements through their thought—except when they are being possessed or raped by another.

In addition to the inordinate amount of sexual activities that take place on the sixth astral sub-plane (but no more than on the seventh, if total time and not number of partners is considered), there are many other aspects to astral life. People travel a great deal, visiting many parts of the sub-plane and creating temporary living quarters as they move about. Even these temporary quarters may be "invaded" or sometimes changed by others who are nearby. Astral monsters, which were created by evil, reside in some of the remote areas. The monsters will possess those inhabitants whose astral sense and creative imagination have diminished. While possessed, people often have intense nightmares as a result of the possession. Those who are asleep on the sixth astral sub-plane (whether alive either physically or astrally) may become possessed by either an astral monster or a selfish astral inhabitant. These possessions can also cause nightmares.

Sexual activities on the lower parts of the astral plane involve the exchange of astral energy only; this astral energy is seventh (sub- or sub-sub-) ray energy that travels through the sexual center. As the energy is given in sexual expression of love, it travels to the other person's sexual center with an opposing spin, and is then given in love back—but at an approximate 180° phase reversal and at the correct level of intensity. The reversal occurs because the energy is being given in love to match the opposing spin of the sexual partner, if the partners are of different genders. The male energy is added to and given back to the female, but is first changed to the opposing spins and energy intensity level of the two energy spheres' that match the female's intensity and phase; a loving male needs to create this phase and intensity as he gives it to the female. The female, in love, creates the male spin and gives it to the male. Since all *humans* have, because of selfishness, somewhat different phases and intensities of energy in their centers, only certain selfish partners can come close enough to match any one person's spin (can be compatible). Women have unique spins in the negating force of one side of the energy sphere to the other. Practice can improve the accuracy of giving the spin of energy to (of loving) another, when the partners are selfish to some level yet are still loving. Those who have one or more enlightened bodies can love perfectly with the enlightened body(-ies) and can perfectly match the sexual spin of another. When both sexual partners are enlightened, then each can perfectly sexually love the other by perfectly matching the spin in the enlightened one or more bodies that are at the same phase, or direction, and frequency as the Ray Lord of the corresponding plane. No practice is needed for enlightened bodies that the partners are using to relate sexually. This compatibility results from both people having replicated the phase and frequency of at least one Ray Lord in their centers within at least one of their bodies by creating virtue. As long as the spins on the sexual energy are continually reversed as the energy is given in love, the person who is giving the energy cannot retain it in her or his centers. Retained energy would create a force of destructiveness through friction, or heat, as a result of the person's self-focus. This back-and-forth motion of the increasing sexual energies from one partner's center to the other's is replicated, in part, in the overall sexual actions, or movements, of the two people's bodies (the more dense forms of energies), as they make love with each other. On the astral plane, because there is no longer a physical body nor the exchange of physical sexual energy, one of the ways in which the people without fused astral and etheric/dense physical bodies can love each other is lost. The intensity in the love is reduced, because each body increases the creative ways of loving another through exchanging its type of energy. The intensity is the total amount of energy transferred within a given period of time. The most creative a person can be is while physically alive because there are more bodies, senses, brains, and potential for spiritual growth within form.

When astral sexual activities occur selfishly, or emotionally rather than lovingly, most of the sexual energy in each person's center is directed back into his or her own sexual center, rather than being given to his or her partner to be further given. Whatever amount that does go to the partner is "given" only to arouse her or him so she or he will "give" back some of the sexual energy to him or her for arousal purposes. In these cases, the sexual energies become retained. This occurs because when "given" for arousal (excitation of the center) the "given" energy often maintains the direction of spin it was in, or the same phase as the partner who gave it, and is not converted through love into the spin of the person who is receiving it. Thus the energy is out of phase and becomes a force *against* the partner's center and the energy within it. For sexual energy to be given so that it does not become retained and produce force in a partner's center, it must be given in love, which frees the energy from the giver's spin. Those sexual partners who share the same sexual spin—homosexuals—can give sexual energy to each other only that has the same, unchanged, sexual spin. Even when a homosexual loves his or her partner, this love cannot be expressed in the giving of sexual energy. The reason is that although doing so may be exciting to them, the giving of sexual energy between homosexuals will only produce forces in their sexual centers, rather than reduce the forces—in the way that sexual expression between heterosexuals that is loving does. (See Chapter Seven for further explanation.) Sexual love *reduces* forces in each partner's centers, or creates more light in their sexual centers—and in any other centers that are fused with the sexual center. The more centers that are fused, and the more bodies that are loved, the greater the levels of enlightenment created from sexually expressed love. As people die from each lower body, they lose more of the ability to enlighten more bodies and centers through sexually expressed love, and sexual expression of love loses more of its intensity. Spiritual disciples, and especially those who have gone through one or more initiations, have fused centers and give more, and more often through more bodies at the same time. Spiritual disciples' ability to sexually express love is much greater and more intense, provided that both partners have a similar ability to love. Many problems can arise if a disparity in consciousness, or in the ability to love based upon prior creation of virtue, exists between people who are sexually involved—especially if one, or both, are spiritually disciplining themselves. While the disparity in consciousness is not impossible to overcome, the smaller the disparity between two sexual lovers, the more loving overall the exchange will be. Because people on the astral plane are segregated more by consciousness than people on the physical plane are, astrally alive people are more likely to be loving in their sexual expression than they were while dense physically alive. As a result, higher levels of inertia on the physical plane create an averaging, or leveling, of consciousness and *less* segregation of consciousness (love) through time and space, but much greater separation of activity.

As senses retain energy within the center they are part of, they develop forces that cause the centers and senses to separate, and cause each individual sense to become damaged from friction, or heat. Personalities who function selfishly, against their souls' thought, use senses in selfish ways that create the retained energies and frictional forces. Instead of giving to others, the self is used to focus its thought on retaining, or keeping, the energy that is brought into a center and its sense. This occurs because the personality erroneously believes that this selfishness will keep it more alive, and will reduce its pain and increase its pleasure. The effects of such illusion by the personality are reversible *only* if it chooses to create more virtue in its life and, as it does so, to fuse with its soul. As the personality fuses with its soul, its self fuses with its Self and they together become conscious of wanting to understand and to eventually be a functional part of God. This change is the only way to redeem the sense that was lost through the personality's selfishness. The individual, or split (selfish), use of the senses *cannot be recovered* for use in that body for that lifetime. Only the whole, or higher psychic (soul), sense of the body can be improved through fusing all the seven senses together, and creating more virtue within them and simultaneously within those being served.

Astral senses are lost, or separated from each other and damaged, from frictional forces more than etheric/dense physical senses are within the same *relative* periods of time on each of the two planes. A selfish person on the sixth astral sub-plane can, in ten astral years, destroy the same amount of sense that a dense physically alive person would damage in sixty physical years of living. A part of this disparity is caused by less damage on the physical plane occurring during childhood, which is not replicated for adults on the astral plane. Most of the difference is caused by the ease at which astral energy and the form it takes can be changed—by force (from selfish thought), in these cases. Although the astral energy moving through a center is at the same relatively low density that the center is, the *speed* of the astral energy is much greater (from stronger directing thought of spirit), which greatly adds to its destructive power when retained. A very selfish astrally alive person on the sixth sub-plane can destroy the majority of her or his astral senses within about thirty astral years (the same person may become senseless in as few as seventy to eighty astral years). Such a person's remaining two hundred forty to four hundred twenty astral years would be spent in *suffering* the consequences of growing senseless, with gross amounts of anxiety, fear, pain, and abuses through possessions by other people and by some evil monsters. In addition, some animals on this sub-plane will abuse senseless people by forcing them to function in subservience to *them*, almost as slaves! These senseless people are often treated as the lowest members of an animal troop or pack might be.

Example of Life on the Sixth Astral Sub-Plane

The sixth astral sub-plane is relatively dark and is emotionally frenzied. Those living on this sub-plane usually use only two of their five astral senses of form together at any one time. These people *can* be empathic—but usually selfishly choose to not be. Life on the sixth astral sub-plane is disorganized and conflictive as each resident does as he or she pleases, frequently interfering with others. Many people act as though they are on various types of drugs, and enjoy doing so. Sexual activity is rampant and mostly random. Sexual possessions and rapes of people who have diminished senses are common.

Illustration 8.11

Animals that are found on the sixth astral plane, if members of a species that is fairly developed in astral consciousness, were usually neglected, treated with emotional selfishness, and, if they were pets, were typically not treated emotionally humanely by people. These animals tend to replicate such emotional inculcation in their astral lives on those whom they can affect. Not surprisingly, people on the sixth astral sub-plane who emotionally mistreated animals while physically alive will often karmically live some part of their astral lives (as much as hundreds of astral years!) with animals emotionally abusing them at times. Emotional abuse in these cases means the animal using the person's senses and sometimes creative imagination as its own, with the animal taking through directing the senses and the creative imagination to enhance its astral excitement in its centers and senses. On the astral plane, senses can be used *outside* the body by projecting them through astral thought (see Chapter Seven for further explanation). Note that those who physically mistreated animals will often be harmed through destruction of their senses and by their form being directly taken over by animals on the seventh astral sub-plane. It is likely that the reader is, by now, coming to the realization that rather than being "heaven," the astral plane is an emotional "clearing house" for emotional karma, wherein the retained astral energies within the astral permanent atom are ultimately and eventually reduced through suffering that leads to some increases in empathy.

There is a paradox in astral life that needs to be explained. As the senses are lost, and self is diminished by losing consciousness, suffering ensues. What happens is that the remaining sense of the bodies and within the self can sometimes recognize the loss of consciousness, even though the remaining consciousness may not *understand* what the cause of the loss is. Notice that people usually do not suffer as much as they might because their awareness often falls faster than their consciousnesses do. This is especially true of those living on the astral plane as compared to those alive on the etheric/dense physical. The astral senses of people living on the astral plane diminish much more quickly than do the etheric/dense physical senses of people living on the etheric/dense physical plane. Countering this effect is that those astrally alive generally have higher consciousness than when they were physically alive. This often causes an increase in their suffering when they choose to be selfish. Eventually, as a person suffers without clearly understanding why, he or she usually changes his or her focus from the self to others—and to God—through hopelessness and despair. The mechanism for this implosive process for the personality and self comes from a conflict between these two parts of the person. The personality finally gives up control over the self because its fear of additional suffering and pain exceeds its fear of death and its desire to control. Then the self focuses outward, which is a more *natural* and *basic* way for it to function when it is not being coerced by the personality's controlling thought in the mental unit and the mental brain and lower mind, which are contained within the mental unit. The self creates more of itself by giving, or love, and not through the selfishness that is focused on it by the personality. The natural, or God-given, basic state for life is to *grow*. Once free to do so, the self grows and then develops an understanding of its suffering as it can again hear the Self, and it grows in conscience. The soul gains much better contact with the personality, and empathy is created from whatever sense still exists within the astral body. As this created empathy is used in the remaining astral life, the astral permanent atom is cleared of much retained energy. As a result, a clearer astral body can be constructed in the *next* human incarnation for that soul. Unfortunately, for many, by this point very little of the astral body is left in this process to create much more virtue in the person's present astral life. Unless the person is virtuous nearly all the time—which is highly unlikely— the remaining selfishness eventually destroys her or his remaining senses. The reason is that so much damage had already occurred within the astral body and its centers. If nothing else, at least the astral permanent atom is improved, providing a legacy for a human, of improved empathy and thus higher astral consciousness in the next lifetime. It is important to note here the difference between the above-described system and a common religious interpretation of hell, where one is *punished* for his or her sins, usually endlessly. A person on the astral plane can, at any time, choose a more virtuous life and can reduce suffering by becoming *loving* towards others. Redemption is within the *person's* control when right motive and action are applied. In order to be of assistance in this process, others, including the OverSoul(s) and soul(s), are advocates for the creation of such choices and actions. Love, and not punishment and retribution, rules the astral plane. It is difficult to explain what *usually* occurs to people in their astral lives on either the seventh or sixth astral sub-plane and still maintain an accurate representation of the true concepts just explained. The reason is that these concepts are hidden by the overwhelming levels of suffering that are self-created by the disordered personalities that many of the inhabitants have.

 ## THE FIFTH ASTRAL SUB-PLANE

Those people who are astrally alive on the fifth sub-plane are less selfish and are more loving than people on either the sixth or seventh astral sub-planes are. The fifth sub-plane astral inhabitants tend to use their astral senses and creative imagination to create structure out of and to formulate either their emotions or their love energies. Many people might, at times, formulate and structure with their imaginations; however, on the fifth astral sub-plane doing so is the primary means of astral thought and of integrating information from the astral senses. Part of the rationale to structure and formulate astral senses and imagination, or astral thought, is to help others to understand one's own astral thought, and to better understand others through one's senses. The fifth ray (the ajna) center and sense are added to the seventh and sixth ray senses as a joined part of the split astral senses when used selfishly and without empathy. Since understanding, or consciousness, is included within the desires of those people found on the fifth astral sub-plane, their desires are less selfish and more focused out. This makes them less selfish than the inhabitants of the sixth and seventh astral sub-planes are. Despite the desire for some improved understanding astrally, most fifth astral sub-plane inhabitants are, at the present time, slightly more selfish than what is *average* for physically alive people within the more loving societies on earth. Averages can be deceiving, though, because of extremes that may exist in certain parts of the averaged population. In this case, a skew in the average in differences in consciousness, or givingness, between societies causes the fifth astral sub-plane to appear much more similar in its civilization to what is common in civilizations on the physical plane in modern first-world countries today. The reader is reminded that the descriptions and explanations given for each sub-plane's life are examples only, and that many differing lifestyles and circumstances are prevalent on each sub-plane.

Houses and other buildings on the fifth astral sub-plane have a common appearance to both each other and to the nicer upper-middle class ones that are common in first world countries in the dense physical world. In addition, plants and animals seem similar to those that are found in the nicer parts of the dense physical world. A large part of the uniformity and similarity of forms on this sub-plane is caused by the desire of its inhabitants to have structure and formula in their astral sense and thought, in order to better understand one another. Structure in astral imagination still incorporates a balance between only the past and present, with the future mostly missing. This means that the present parts of one's imaginative thought is predicated on certain past occurrences—creating rules or principles for creative thought. The rules of this society include an adherence to certain structures, to avoid the extreme frenetic randomness that exists on the sixth sub-plane and that fifth sub-plane people can directly observe if they choose to. The quantum constant on this sub-plane is about twelve times greater in its effect than on the dense physical earth, and about one-third greater than that on the sixth astral sub-plane. This allows the inhabitants of the fifth astral sub-plane to use their senses to observe those on the sixth sub-plane. However, any such observations are usually abhorrent to them because of the sixth sub-plane inhabitants' greater levels of selfishness and lack of emotional control. On the fifth sub-plane time is about twelve times longer, or dilated by a factor of twelve, as compared to the dense physical sub-planes. Astral energy is even more directed by the same level of conscious thought. Thought on this sub-plane is also stronger, with the lower density of energy and the increased thought amounting to about a one-third increase in the amount that the energy follows thought. People live on the fifth astral sub-plane for about three hundred sixty to six hundred astral years, which is still only thirty to fifty years in the dense physical dimension.

A new arrival on the fifth astral sub-plane is often greeted by a group of friends and relatives who died usually no more than about five to ten physical plane years earlier than the new arrival did. After ten years of physical plane time, very few relatives or friends have much concern for or sometimes even much memory of their physical lives. The reason is that over one hundred twenty astral years had passed since they were physically alive. For a number of astral plane years, many people on the fifth and higher sub-planes are loving enough and concerned about and/or interested in those they left behind on the dense physical world to use their astral senses to inform themselves of how those significant others who are still physically alive are feeling emotionally and lovingly. Mostly, inhabitants on the sixth and seventh astral sub-planes are not loving enough to concern themselves with those they left behind, except in some cases, briefly after arrival on the astral plane—and more out of curiosity than from love. Note that the only *etheric/dense physical* sense that can be used to directly sense the dense physical world must have been fused with the two astral spiritual senses while the person was physically alive. Any such etheric/dense physical sense can be used only when the person is being loving while astrally alive. Astrally alive people on the fifth (and lower) astral sub-plane have almost no etheric/dense physical sense fused to the two astral senses of spirit because they were and are too selfish. They cannot sense what those who are physically alive are sensing about the physical world unless they possess someone's etheric/dense physical body. They *can* sense the emotional and/or loving responses that physically alive people have, and they can also somewhat understand these people's *imaginative* thoughts (while they re-create in astral imagination what is taking place etheric/dense physically). For someone living in the astral world to understand the astral, or imaginative, thoughts of someone in the dense physical world, the consciousness of the astral person needs to be about equal to or higher than the person in the dense world. (The astral senses also need to be extended all the way to etheric/dense physical earth.) Thus darker, selfish astrally alive people cannot understand the astral imagination of a less selfish physically alive person. The higher-thinking people's thought is in a different (greater) field of probability that the people with lower thought and consciousness cannot affect, or change, the probabilities in, nor can they understand the connectedness of the choices, or the consciousness of the thought. This physics also protects those with higher consciousness from being possessed by those with lower consciousness.

People who live on the fifth astral sub-plane lose sense and their ability to think astrally because they use a large amount of both sense and thought to structure and formulate their world for selfish reasons. They fear the lower astral sub-planes and seek to protect their bodies and forms from severe glamour and random destructiveness from others' desires. They are self-focused on living a balanced, comfortable life in the "heaven" they first believe they have arrived in. Many people after first arriving desire an idyllic life that is based upon their respective previous dense physical lives. This makes all elements of the new life into a balanced meeting of their glamours. Unlike their sixth astral sub-plane counterparts, they do not seek uncontrolled emotional excitement, with its incessant growing of glamours. Instead, they regulate their glamours to be in balance. They do this so that the emotional forces created in their astral bodies and centers are balanced to equalize each other, which reduces the eventual feelings of fear and anxiety. They *do not*, in general, try to reduce the fixed desires, or glamours; they just try to manage them through structure. Thus the fifth sub-plane astrally alive person continues to desire, but at a rate and in an amount that minimally reduces his or her loss in senses and capacity to imagine.

The astral bodies of many of this sub-plane's inhabitants remain mostly in good ability to sense for well over a hundred astral plane years; however, some people live for six hundred years, and virtually all live for over three hundred. The balancing of forces in and of itself creates a force and entropy as the senses then diminish. The process is slower than on the lower sub-planes, but is incipient and is just as irreversible. In attempt to further reduce the effects of imbalance that is caused by failing structural balance of forces, a major mode of the fifth sub-plane is enforced by a local—voluntary—policing group of inhabitants. Through the members' own collective focused thought, this group interferes with the creative imagination of those who attempt to create new astral structures of forms that agitate, excite, or interfere with the centers, senses, and thought of the vast majority of other inhabitants. While significantly reducing creativity, these astral "thought police" and their behaviors do prolong the viable use of the senses and the ability to clearly think astrally. The people who seek more freedom can leave the inhabited "towns" and "cities"—which resemble some of the nicest ones in the dense physical world—on this astral sub-plane; however, these people frequently are just as selfish and actually often lose their senses much more quickly, although because of their desires these maverick people seem happier overall. Those who are "astrally old" often live apart from those who still have most of their astral senses. These older people live with less structure, usually have and inhabit less nice forms, and may lose their ability to nearly instantly to go to any place on the sub-plane through re-creating themselves there in their creative imagination. They usually still can fly, as almost all people on this sub-plane are capable of doing, with the exception of those who are completely or nearly senseless. The younger people more ignore than interact with the older people. The older are often *more empathic* than the younger are, even though, overall, they have much less sense. The reason is that the older choose—through their suffering and pain—to use what sense they have left to be more empathic than do those who are younger. The indifference of the younger inhabitants to the older ones reveals the overall selfishness of the younger. The younger inhabitants' lack of understanding of their elders' empathy belies their low consciousness.

Depending upon their overall levels of love in old age, fifth astral sub-plane people generally suffer less as they grow old than those on the sixth or seventh astral sub-plane do. There are no monsters to attack fifth astral sub-plane inhabitants as they age, and the older inhabitants seldom become possessed or raped by younger inhabitants, since there are police, and, besides, few inhabitants of this sub-plane even have such inclinations. Also, the animal life is, in general, kinder and friendlier. Many animals whose species are relatively highly developed and who lived wild while physically alive live in the regions of this sub-plane that are unpopulated by humans. They often live for about as many astral years as members of the species lived, on average, in the dense physical realm. These particular animals have at least one full mental center and slight or more mental development, and can live astrally apart from humans and/or more mentally developed domesticated and pet animals because the afore-mentioned animals can create their own astral lives without the assistance of the humans' or other animals' lower mental sense. The actual life of the plants that surround these wild animals often is astrally supported by the animals' one or more complete lower mental sense or senses. Some wild animals and some that were badly mistreated while pets in the dense world are, on the sixth and seventh astral sub-planes, possessed by evil entities (formerly physically alive people) from the eighth sphere, and are kept alive kama-manasically through the evil entity's lower mental sense. The possession of these animals is designed to render them destructive to humans on these lower sub-planes; no such animals exist on the fifth sub-plane, since evil has not kama-manasically connected fifth astral sub-plane thought to the fifth sub-plane of the lower mind. Kama-manasic thought is reversed from mental thinking because with kama-manasic thought, astral thought (creative imagination) is used *first*, and *then* the mental thought in thoughtforms is created that, usually, supports the imagination. People and very advanced animals usually think with the highest fully developed functional fifth sub-plane mental mind first—if they are not infiltrated with darkness. The fifth astral sub-plane is a much nicer civilization to live within than are those on the lower astral sub-planes because emotions on the fifth sub-plane are somewhat controlled, which gives love a much better chance of growing.

People on the fifth astral sub-plane are less focused on sexual activities than those on the two lower sub-planes are. The reason is that fifth sub-plane inhabitants understand that having excessive amounts of selfish sex quickly diminishes the senses and astral body as a result of the relatively higher amounts of energies that are retained within a particular period of time. When people on the fifth astral sub-plane are sexual and selfish, or emotional rather than loving, they attempt to get more out of each sexual encounter by structuring their interactions in ways that arouse each other the most, but create the smallest relative amount of forces in their sexual centers. This process requires some empathy and often does create a slight amount of love while the people mostly function emotionally and selfishly. Each person needs to regulate his or her sexual expression and behaviors to balance his or her sexual energy with that of his or her partner. While a bit mechanical in the way this is applied, selfish sexual relations on the fifth astral sub-plane can create considerable emotional satisfaction without *substantially* increasing sexual glamours in the participants. Those who are sexually loving on this sub-plane extend the selfish process into one of giving all the sexual energy that the partner of lesser consciousness can give back with and not retain, which would otherwise create forces in that person's sexual center. If both partners are of approximately equal consciousness, then they cooperatively make sexual love by gradually and methodically increasing the sexual energies that they give to each other during the sexual love

Example of Life on the Fifth Astral Sub-Plane

Those who live on the fifth astral sub-plane seek stabilizing structures and rules to control people's emotions and their selfish use of creative imagination. A voluntary "thought police" force prevents, through the use of its members' collective senses and thought, the over-use of creative imagination driven by emotions that interfere with the tranquility and lifestyle of others.

Illustration 8.12

activity, staying in balance with each other. Some people while alive on the physical plane practice similar methods of sexual exchange. They do this because their levels of consciousness are about at the level of those who are astrally alive on the fifth astral sub-plane, or because they have a personality and/or one or more bodies with a fifth ray focus, or for both reasons.

A minority, though still a sizeable number, of the older fifth astral sub-plane people leave this sub-plane and travel to the fourth or third astral sub-plane before dying astrally; some of them are encouraged to become more loving and empathic by spiritual servers who travel from the second and first astral sub-planes in order to teach and be examples of empathy, super-empathy, and love. Serving in this way is a great sacrifice for these higher sub-plane spiritual saviors because they lose astral life as they travel to the lower astral planes where they serve in time that is less dilated. These people can lose half or more of the time they could have been living in had they stayed on either of the two highest astral sub-planes. Because of these trips of service, people on the two highest astral sub-planes live proportionately shorter lives in astral years before their astral bodies wear out; some leave the plane not from selfish destructive forces destroying their bodies, but because they can serve better from the mental sub-planes—where they already have contributed some service. Those fifth astral sub-plane inhabitants who are served by spiritual people who live on the higher astral sub-planes often see those servers as lesser angels from a higher heaven than where they themselves live. As a result of being served, some gain an even clearer understanding of life on the astral plane, and realize, somewhat accurately, what the plane and its life are really like. Glamours can still greatly interfere with the use of the higher mental thought that is needed in order to correctly understand the entire astral plane. Many fifth astral sub-plane people desire to be in the highest heaven because they believe themselves to be more virtuous than they actually are; this desire is fixed, or glamorous to them, and sometimes interferes with their ability to create mental truth.

 ## THE FOURTH ASTRAL SUB-PLANE

The fourth astral sub-plane is, today, the largest astral sphere in total area because more people live there, and the largest population of supported animals and plants do, too. This sub-plane has grown the most, as the fourth heaven, since the advent of the Christian religion and its emphasis on love. The average amount of love that each person has on this sub-plane, as compared to emotional responses, is somewhat greater than average for people who are currently physically alive in the more loving societies. Thus those on the fifth astral sub-plane are slightly more emotionally selfish than is average for those who are physically alive in the more loving societies, and those on the fourth astral sub-plane are somewhat less selfish. At present, no astral sub-plane exactly represents the level of either emotional selfishness or love that is found in the more loving societies on the physical plane. This condition is in part caused by people *initially* becoming *more* conscious after they physically die. People living on the astral plane no longer have the same high levels of inertia, nor do they focus through what had been their, usually, more damaged and relatively selfish etheric/dense physical senses and brains. When the astral senses are used with which to focus on life, the astrally alive person can more easily unify the senses since they are now primary, and if the person so chooses, he or she can be considerably more empathic—which leads to increased levels of love. Notice, however, that much less cooperation and sharing is needed on the astral plane. Thus astrally alive people are usually more astrally conscious, or more loving, upon first arriving on the astral plane than they were when physically alive. The people who are today living on the seventh and sixth astral sub-plane lead very emotional and self-focused lives. However, during their physical lives, they were typically even more selfish emotionally, and on average, were usually very selfish physically and mentally as well.

A person who is first arriving to live on the fourth astral sub-plane is nearly always met by a friend, relative, or compassionate resident who wants to be of assistance in the new arrival's acclimation to this realm. The emphasis of the desires of those who arrive on the fourth astral sub-plane is to give love and be loved. In order to have these desires met, the inhabitants are willing to sacrifice some ease in living, which the more structured fifth astral sub-plane supplies by its limiting of the forces produced by selfishness. Interestingly, on average, the fourth sub-plane people live with *less* force from selfishness *after they have lived on the sub-plane for a time*. Eventually, though, they develop *more* forces in their lives. The initial reduction is caused by these residents loving more as well as more often, and developing more empathy, within the first few years of their arrival. The desire to love and be loved is paradoxical. The reason is that the desire to love is often cancelled out by the desire to be loved, with love itself then becoming an emotion rather than givingness. Thus fourth astral sub-plane inhabitants usually develop more empathy and love during the earlier part of their lives there, but then gradually lose it. This loss occurs because they still desire *more* to be loved as they increase their love for and empathy towards others. This same problem exists while people are physically alive, but is overshadowed by the etheric/dense physical needs, wants, and inertia against having them met. On the fourth astral sub-plane, the most loving of people are those who have lived there for a number of astral years, but usually less than about a hundred fifty. Then, gradually, the people become somewhat more selfish unless they are helped by and respond to the assistance of either younger people or spiritual servers from the two highest astral sub-planes. Overcoming the desire to be loved is very difficult because sometimes those trying to help do nothing more than feed the glamour in others. Often, what the others want is the giving, or love, from helpers, and these people who are being served do not want to change their desire to be loved. Love/wisdom, or whole structured mental thought that is appropriately given, is needed to correctly deal with these people in serving them on this astral sub-plane.

There is no area or region of dense physical earth that is comparable to the beauty and astral viability of the fourth astral sub-plane. Most of those who arrive in that world are quite convinced that they are in heaven. People live in astrally formed homes of great comfort and beauty. Many of these forms vary considerably in design, but they usually still have great beauty. There is little concern over others interfering with one's imaginative creations, because love *and the appearance of being loving so that others will love in return* are of paramount importance in people's desires. Creativity abounds, with each person usually attempting to create more beauty—unfortunately, though, sometimes in order to impress others about their own "givingness" (which is often phony). When these people try to impress others in this way, they are seeking the love and adoration of others whom they are trying to convince that they are very loving. Not all such creation of beauty is disingenuous, but enough is, in the older population, to diminish their senses as well as their imaginative ability to create more of the beauty of the forms in the surrounding environment. This is less noticeable on the fourth sub-plane, since the earlier, more beautiful forms that the people created while they were more loving and empathically wanting to please others with their created beauty remain in existence for long periods of time because there is little interfering astral thought from others.

People interrelate with one another either in genuine love or in a hypocritically false givingness that has the purpose of manipulating others into giving more to them. In some ways, many of the fourth astral sub-plane inhabitants, with their pretentiousness and self-focus in their glamours of needing to be loved, can be more irritating to those who attempt to serve on this sub-plane than are the coarser and more grossly glamoured people on the lower sub-planes. While the lower sub-planes have more selfishness overall, love on the fourth astral sub-plane, when manipulated and abused, is particularly repulsive as compared to other glamours. The people on the lower sub-planes seem to be, oddly, more "honest" in their gross selfishness.

Sexual activities between people on the fourth astral sub-plane are focused on "making love." People are more loving in their sexual contact with others; however, some pretentiousness is often apparent, and manipulation to receive love sexually, as well as the desire to *appear* sexually loving, creates many sexual relationships that do not fulfill the partners' needs to be loved. Those who truly practice loving their sexual partner or partners frequently grow in empathy and develop more love, in general, in their astral lives. In these circumstances, the sex between the partners is usually a powerful bond that creates a monogamous sexual relationship. Sexual relationships that are pretentious seldom lead to monogamy. While marriage does exist on the astral plane, and more on the fourth sub-plane than on the lower ones, mostly only the marriages that are based on real love can sustain themselves. The first reason is the people's longevity there. Also, these people's lives are ruled by desires that change much more rapidly than did the physical needs on the physical plane. In addition, the emphasis on the fourth astral sub-plane is on emotions/love.

There are two ways in which astrally alive adults can have and raise children. The first is to adopt children who have died from the physical plane and who then arrive through travelling to the same plane these adults are inhabiting. Such children live expanded childhoods and may eventually grow up on the astral plane. The vast majority of people who die physically during childhood are working off karma from a prior life. If most of the astral, or emotional, part of the past life's karma was lived through while physically alive (usually between the ages of seven and fourteen, provided that the physically alive child lived that long), then the child is likely to travel to the fourth astral sub-plane, or, more rarely, a higher sub-plane if the child was particularly virtuous while physically alive. The reason this occurs is that once most of the past life astral karma is removed, the children are more loving than is average for the physical world in general. Sometimes a child may, usually quite early in life—perhaps during infancy—die because of too much retained energy in his or her physical permanent atom (as karma). In such cases, the child then may have excessive selfishness, or retained energy, in his or her astral permanent atom as additional karma. Such a child may travel to either the seventh or sixth astral sub-plane after etheric/dense physical death. Then he or she will be adopted by a selfish seventh or sixth astral sub-plane person who desires more selfishly than lovingly to have an infant or young child to raise. The struggles that often ensue in such cases between the parent or parents and child are helpful towards reducing selfishness and increasing empathy. The reason is that the astral plane gives selfishness in children more freedom to be expressed. This leads to forces that may improve the love (and empathy) in each person involved. In these scenarios, the physical plane parent or parents of the infant or young child who dies are also usually karmically dealing with either prior life or present life selfishness (or both), possibly both physical and astral. The souls of these people are working together to create more virtuous lives. This may be the case even in the circumstances of one or more of these people dying early in their lives on a plane, in order to affect others.

Some astrally alive adopted children do not grow up to become astrally alive adults. These children have less retained astral energy to darken their astral permanent atoms since most of this energy came from a prior lifetime and is residual to the present life. Then these children die early from their astral bodies so that they can go on to live on the lower mental sub-planes and reduce the levels of egotism or arrogance, or perhaps both, from the past life or even their prior lives. With the rare exception of a new soul who died very early from physical life in its first incarnation on earth, these children awaken and live mentally as adults. The OverSoul and soul are often intricately involved in the early astral deaths of young people because a wise balance needs to be created between astral and mental retained energies. The attempt is made to create conditions wherein both kinds of retained energies are maximally reduced, to allow the most virtue to be created in the next planned lifetime.

Children on the five lower sub-planes who remain on the astral plane long enough to grow into adults generally do so more slowly (in astral years) than do those who mature on the etheric/dense physical plane. The cause of this effect is, apparently, an increase in both the difficulties and the potential for creativity that the etheric/dense physical body affords through its higher levels of inertia and complex senses and brain; the absence of the etheric/dense physical body means a decrease in learning, in personality development, in self development, and in overall maturation. Without an etheric/dense physical body, the personality has much less information to integrate and synthesize. The reason is that even though it is only one-third of the lower bodies, this body supplies over two-thirds of all the information to the personality (because of increased diversity). However, the density of the information makes it more difficult for the personality to organize and then synthesize into knowledge. As a result, the personality sometimes loses some of the information, reducing from about two-thirds to about one-half of all the information collected being synthesized into knowledge. This then reduces the personality's amount of knowledge. Even so, the sheer volume of information makes this one body equal to or greater than the other two in the amount of information it supplies that becomes knowledge. The self grows less in consciousness from new experiences when it can give less because one of the bodies its spirit thinks for is gone. In adults, the same principles have some effect; however, while they are physically alive, adults gain much more knowledge than do children, and their consciousness substantially increases by becoming more giving once they start to live astrally (and in the earlier parts of their lives on that plane). On the physical plane, children are more loving, in general, than adults are, and thus do not gain proportionately as much as adults do when living astrally. Since the growth of both the personality and the self of children as well as adults slows on the astral plane, as either children or adults live selfishly there, the effects are more pronounced in loss of sense and of self that are rapidly growing.

The second method of having children on the astral plane also involves adoption. Only in their fantasies can people on the astral plane give birth to children. The reason is that when the OverSoul and human soul advance the sutratma, or life thread, for a human being's creation, they will do so only if that thread is to be eventually connected to an etheric/dense physical heart. The life thread is withdrawn if plans for a physical plane birth are terminated. This is the case even if the human who is being incarnated has already reached the astral or the etheric plane. A new personality must have the opportunity to organize and synthesize *three* lower bodies. This gives it and its self the opportunity to join the three parts of time and space, *because having this ability defines what it means to be human.* If a soul permitted astral or mental births, what would be created as a lifeform would not be a human being as humans, today, are defined. The second method of astral adoption is a great sacrifice for the parent or parents. On the fourth astral sub-plane in particular, and to a lesser extent on the third astral sub-plane, there are not enough children to adopt who had died from physical life and had enough consciousness to reach the higher astral sub-planes (this is particularly true of young children and infants). A relatively small number of fourth astral sub-plane people and even fewer people on the third astral sub-plane elect to leave the higher sub-plane that they are on, and travel to and *live* for an extended period of time on a lower sub-plane in order to raise an adopted child. Such a child, in her or his last physical life, often will have been born into a family that had low consciousness. Some of these children may have been born into physical plane families that were dysfunctional because of drugs or crime; others may come from areas of the world where deprivation and conflict are commonplace for many who live there. Each of these children was karmically born into the difficult circumstances that led to an early physical death in the present lifetime, because of the selfishness he or she created in the past one. Most of the time, the children adopted under these circumstances have traveled to the sixth astral sub-plane, especially those who died from advanced countries and societies and from families that were significantly dysfunctional. The few of these children who are adopted from the seventh sub-plane, because it is an even greater sacrifice for the parent or parents, more often come from second or third world countries where deprivation of *physical*, seventh ray type, needs played a major role in their lives (and sometimes deaths).

The sacrifice of the astral parent or parents is that they give up life on, usually, the fourth sub-plane and sometimes the third sub-plane to live for astral *years* to *attempt* to raise the consciousness of the child who is much more selfish than they are. These parents need to raise the consciousness of the child to a high enough level that would enable the child to travel to a higher astral sub-plane—and remain conscious on it. Ultimately, each parent or set of parents will seek to travel back to the astral sub-plane that he or she (or they) left from and to bring the child along. When these adults live on a lower astral sub-plane, they have less time in which to live. They also need to deal with what they consider to be the outlandish emotionalism of the local inhabitants. The entire process is not always successful in raising the child's consciousness enough to leave the sub-plane; failure at this often causes great sorrow for the sacrificing parent or parents. This happens whether she, he, or they decide to abandon the child to one or more local residents of the sub-plane, or to stay in a circumstance of, at times, torture—but they do *not* necessarily suffer all the time. The parents usually gain in consciousness from their extreme sacrifices and givingness, despite the great difficulties they endure. As a result, these people can gain a life experience that is more frequently that of an advanced human initiate, or arhat; these people experience pain, great loss, difficulty in living, and even destruction of senses and bodies while sustaining and, at times, actually growing in consciousness. This occurs even though it may seem, to some people, contradictory or even impossible.

The sixth astral sub-plane is where the vast majority of these sacrificial adoptions of astral children occur. The inhabitants of the fifth astral sub-plane generally do not welcome adoption of children by the "lesser angels" who arrive to live in their world. Their society already has a structure in place for the adoption and raising of children, and the system cannot control the people of higher consciousness who are from the higher sub-planes. Also, the odd-rayed, fifth sub-plane is a bit more foreign than the sixth is to the overwhelming majority of sacrificial adoptive parents, who come from the fourth astral sub-plane. The fourth astral sub-plane inhabitants are somewhat more critical of those on the fifth than they are of those on the lower astral sub-planes. The reason is that the people on the fourth can directly sense the people on the fifth because of the quantum constant shift in differential between these two sub-planes. The fourth sub-plane has a quantum constant that is about fifteen times greater in its effect than that in the dense world. There is slightly too much of a difference for the fourth sub-plane inhabitants to sense and then observe those on the sixth astral sub-plane, i.e., the percentage of difference between the exact values of the quantum constant of these two planes is a disparity that exceeds thirty-five percent. Humans tend to be more critical of and repulsed by that which they dislike and are more familiar with. As a result, sacrificial adoptive parents from the fourth (and third) sub-planes tend towards the lower two astral sub-planes when looking for a child to adopt.

Because there is a considerable difference in desire, or what people value, on average, between those who live on the fourth astral sub-plane and those who are astrally alive on the third, fewer older residents of the fourth astral sub-plane move on to the third if they advance in consciousness. Those on the fourth astral sub-plane are glamoured about love, and about appearing to be loving and beautiful, which is a fourth ray selfish focus on life. On the third astral sub-plane, the inhabitants are glamoured concerning their astral bodies, empathy, and their ability to accurately communicate and create a greater civilization (all third ray factors of life focus). For many more fourth ray, fourth sub-plane inhabitants, the second sub-plane and way of life are much more appealing than is anything that the third astral sub-plane has to offer. Some fourth sub-plane inhabitants who decide to spiritually discipline themselves, sometimes before mid-life on the astral plane, by later years have raised their consciousnesses enough to travel and reside on the second astral sub-plane; they entirely bypass living on the third except for infrequent visits there, which often take place prior to their reaching the second sub-plane. Very infrequently, a similar and corresponding scenario might occur with a fifth astral sub-plane person (attempting to go to the third astral sub-plane). However, the disparity is proportionately greater between the fifth and third astral sub-planes, and the people on the fifth are much more selfish on average than are those on the fourth. Thus only a few fifth astral sub-plane disciples ever achieve enough of an improvement in consciousness to enable such a large change in their lives. On the fourth astral sub-plane, spiritual discipline is much more common than on the lower ones. Many more people attempt it on the fourth than on the fifth, sixth, and seventh combined. Even if fourth sub-plane inhabitants' motives for spiritually disciplining themselves might not be virtuous, many of them continually behave as though they are attempting to become more loving by limiting themselves in order to improve their empathy and love. Those who do so as a sham are trying to look good to others, which is a common problem on this sub-plane. When an adult dies from the fourth astral sub-plane, he or she will usually have lived there for four hundred fifty to seven hundred fifty astral years.

Example of Life on the Fourth Astral Sub-Plane

The fourth astral sub-plane is, at present, the largest sub-dimension because many people from more developed cultures tend to be astrally focused in consciousness on this sub-plane. The focus of life is on appearing to be more loving and spiritual by using astral imagination to create beauty in form. While often hypocritical, the inhabitants on this sub-plane are still more loving and empathic than are most people who are etheric/dense physically alive. Fourth astral sub-plane inhabitants may appear, initially, to be much more loving than they actually are because they attempt to cover up their selfishness—which they (correctly) consider to be ugly.

Illustration 8.13

Most fourth astral sub-plane people have pets because these people desire to love and be loved. Not only is loving pets easier than loving people is, it often prepares some people to be more loving towards other people. Pets on this sub-plane are, themselves, very loving, thereby fulfilling some of the desires that the humans have to be loved; the animals sometimes have greater amounts of genuine love than do those who are their human masters. The overall ability to think by some of the most advanced pets on the fourth astral sub-plane approaches that of some people who live on the seventh astral sub-plane. Dogs that are advanced in consciousness seem especially suited to the fourth ray focus of this sub-plane, even though the ray focus of dogs in general is along the sixth ray (this will be explained in detail in the next chapter). Most dogs (and people) have sixth ray astral bodies, which means that the ray focus of the majority of the energy within their astral bodies is along the sixth ray in the way the energy tends to sense other energy, or to slightly think. A large minority of dogs and people on the fourth astral sub-plane have fourth ray astral bodies, which causes them to sense using more characteristics of the fourth ray. People tend to sense more along a body's ray type of energy when they are more selfish than virtuous because then the slight collective thought of the energy often overpowers the more virtuous thought (which is barely present) of the higher informing spirit of their respective selves. In these circumstances the energy is ultimately controlling what people think, by limiting their sense and information from that body to mostly one ray type. Dogs tend to be very focused and directed in their emotions or love because they usually have sixth ray astral bodies. On the fourth astral sub-plane, a large minority of dogs, often as advanced pets, have fourth ray astral bodies and tend to create greater perfection between spirit and form in their human master(s) and in others with whom they have contact when they are being loving. They achieve this, in part, through their creative imagination as well as their empathy. This occurs because on the higher astral sub-planes, such as the fourth, most dogs can communicate through either the lower astral psychic senses or through the higher psychic sense of empathy when soul consciousness, or when their creation of love, is present. The communication between a pet and one or more humans is highest when the humans are very loving and soul conscious, and are using the whole, higher psychic, sense of super-empathy.

Dogs on the fourth astral sub-plane can usually communicate amongst themselves and other animals using one or more split astral senses; while physically alive they can sometimes do this to a lesser extent—although infrequently, since the astral senses are much more limited during physical life. Communication between humans and pets is much improved on the astral sub-planes, especially on the fourth and above, where, sometimes, a human might use super-empathy in order to help her or his pet think and communicate in a rich and complex manner. This is much as a human child from four to six years of age on the physical plane might learn to do. While dogs are weak in their mental thought, particularly in lower mental fifth sub-plane thoughtforms that provide mental thought with structure—an important part of logic—children until six years of age also have some difficulties in the same area of mental thinking. The reason that physically alive children and some astrally alive (and most physically alive) dogs are prone to getting lost is their lack of lower mental structure in the way that they think about their environment. Fifth mental sub-plane thoughtforms create lower mental thought about landmarks and their relationships to other objects in both time and space. These thoughtforms, in a sentence of words, also greatly affect the correct use and communication of time. Dogs on the fourth astral sub-plane are advanced in consciousness, and are much better at fifth mental sub-plane construction of thoughtforms than are most chimpanzees that are physically alive. As a result, the closeness of dogs' relationships to humans is greatly enhanced, and their astral lives are generally considerably richer in more complex experiences than their physical lives were. Some types of talking birds and many cats are more popular pets on both the fifth and third astral sub-planes because birds that speak usually have fifth ray astral bodies, and cats' astral bodies are often along the third ray, in correspondence to the odd-numbered sub-rays of these two sub-planes.

THE THIRD ASTRAL SUB-PLANE

There is considerable difference in the civilization on the third astral sub-plane as compared to the fourth because the emphasis of the third ray is on the development of civilization. Civilization is the incorporated development and use by humans of the three lower kingdoms in order to expand humans' senses and bodies beyond their initial (at birth) state. This focus causes the inhabitants of the third astral sub-plane to be *very* concerned with the condition of their senses and bodies, and particularly their astral senses and bodies. Because it is so highly valued, information attracted by the senses, and its synthesis into knowledge through the brain(s) by the personality, are also of paramount concern and importance to the inhabitants of this sub-plane.

On the odd-numbered (the masculine-rayed) astral sub-planes, there is a general tendency for people to emphasize in their glamours the importance of their bodies, their senses, and items of form. This condition reaches its zenith on the third astral sub-plane, because on the first, despite this sub-plane's masculine ray focus, spiritual discipline reduces glamours as well as their effects, by focusing people on spirit. Because they are masculine in their ray focus, the seventh, fifth, and third sub-planes are heavily affected by the third ray, which has been a part of the fifth and seventh rays since their creation. One-half of the third ray is entirely focused on power that is derived from changing the density of energy; while all of the rays directly affect only energy, the one-half of the third ray that is focused on energy's density is very different. The reason is that it develops sense of how to choose the density of other energies. This creates power from sensing the density of other parts of energy that are focused on increasing the very slight thought within energy through the increased enlightened thought of the third ray. As might be expected, the third astral sub-plane is greatly affected by people's desire for and use of power. Humans derive power through increasing their amounts of and the ways in which they use knowledge; knowledge can allow humans to learn ways of changing the density of form, or energy—which is how power is created. Humans can also apply their knowledge and power to affect the energies within the three kingdoms lower than their own. When they do so with an effect that extends the use of their senses and bodies, then they are developing their civilizations.

The third astral sub-plane has remarkably advanced civilization, with the people there far more knowledgeable and intelligent than what is the average for those who are physically alive today. People on the third astral sub-plane are focused on being as informed as possible through their senses. Most of the younger inhabitants place about equal importance on their astral and mental senses, which is a much higher proportion of mental sense than exists on the lower astral sub-planes. The younger inhabitants' high levels of empathy lead them to an overall higher consciousness, or givingness (love), than is generally found in the inhabitants of the fourth astral sub-plane. To many observers, those living on the third astral sub-plane do not at first seem to be as loving, by comparison, as do those living on the fourth. The reason is that the giving of knowledge that builds empathy in others (which is what this society is so focused on) is often erroneously interpreted as being less loving than the giving of love, or helping others to become more loving. This latter-mentioned method of loving is more direct—and effective. However, the afore-mentioned one, which is the common way of loving on the third astral sub-plane, is practiced so often and so consistently, that despite its indirectness in helping to create love in others by increasing their empathy, it increases consciousness considerably more in the younger third sub-plane inhabitants than in those on the fourth or lower sub-planes. Empathy can be increased for long periods of time, mostly to the point at which about half of it is being used to give to others, as love. The reason is that, otherwise, the retained energy in the centers tends to split the empathy into its constituent lower astral psychic senses. In order to be empathic, at least half of all the energy of the five senses of astral form generally needs to be focused outward onto others. Thus younger people on the third sub-plane achieve an unselfish and loving creation of virtue in their lives about twenty-five percent of the time. This occurs because only half of the half of the senses that are being used empathically are used lovingly. This amount of love is indicative of far more consciousness and lovingness than the, perhaps, half to one and a half percent that people who are physically alive today achieve, on average. It should be noted that as a result of some technological advancements on the third sub-plane in recent astral years, some people have achieved up to seventy-five percent use of their astral senses as empathy, but for only a relatively short time span (several years), and generally with no increases in their love for others.

Example of Life on the Third Astral Sub-Plane

The development of civilization and especially technology in more modern times is the lifestyle of the third sub-plane. The inhabitants of this sub-plane use devices of their invention to conserve their astral senses, or their sense of empathy when these senses are joined. It is usually the older residents (those who have been there the longest) who are losing their astral senses and may thus fail to be able to correctly use the sense-saving technologies—as illustrated above by the woman crashing into the building. Notice that even animals and plants (!) are technologically enhanced to reduce the amount of senses that people need to use.

Illustration 8.14

To develop more than about fifty percent *lasting* use of the joined astral senses of form, or empathy, requires super-empathy. Super-empathy uses spiritual concepts from the second mental sub-plane, in the higher mind. These concepts contain the consciousness of giving to souls and are joined with (fused with) the astral empathy to create love/wisdom in the mental body while empathy is expanded into sensing and creating more of God in others. Super-empathy joins the five astral senses of form, which together create empathy, with the two astral senses of spirit. Then all seven senses joined create one whole higher psychic (soul) astral sense. Thus super-empathy uses all seven of the astral senses and the two *spiritual* higher mental senses all at the same time. Note that of the two higher split mental senses, the lower (of understanding more of God structurally—in time and space) is much more emphasized and is used much more often—when incorporated into super-empathy. Instead of just helping others to become more empathic and then more loving, super-empathy helps others to sense and then create more of themselves astrally into a functional part of God. This occurs while they mentally understand that they are giving as souls and to souls, which helps other souls to better give wisely. Some third astral sub-plane inhabitants discipline themselves to help create super-empathy, but most do not because they are typically too egotistical to use their higher spiritual minds on the second mental sub-plane. These people resist giving up the personality control that they believe they are losing when they limit their astral senses *and empathy* to become super-empathic. Some empathy usually must be limited, if one is spiritually disciplining oneself. The reason is that about half of the empathy that is used on the third astral sub-plane is used selfishly, without creating sufficient love from the information it supplies. Because of their glamours, most younger people on this sub-plane believe that limiting, or sacrificing, *any* amount of empathy is a mistake and is harmful to one's life and astral health. This seems, in their illusion, to be accurate because in older people who have lost some of their empathy, their bodies, senses, and minds are significantly diminished. These older people's knowledge levels are, at times, insufficient for them to live well in this very advanced civilization. The younger people ignorantly fear this condition because they misunderstand it. Because of their egotism as well as their glamours, they tend to be very resistant to becoming group (soul) conscious.

Each new arrival who will be living on the third astral sub-plane is immediately sensed and directed (given instructions) by what she or he each imagines as whom she or he wishes to be greeted by, and in what manner. The technology involved in this system is hundreds of years ahead of present-day technology in our physical world. The "person" or "people" meeting each new arrival is a creation that is based upon the new arrival's senses and imagination; the creation is "real" in astral terms, and not just a fantasy created from the person's imagination. The astral mind of each new arrival is read and used as a template to very quickly construct the images of those who will greet him or her. Then the new arrival is given a "course" on third astral sub-plane living. This course includes actual re-creations of different potential experiences that he or she might have, based upon his or her individual desires. This system affords each new arrival the opportunity to experience and use his or her astral senses of form, especially when used together in empathy. These experiences help each new arrival to gain correct information and to synthesize it into knowledge while alive on the third astral sub-plane and before meeting any astrally alive people. The inhabitants of the third astral sub-plane would like the new arrival to be more empathic before such an encounter takes place so as to not lower their own senses. The indoctrination can last nearly a week (of astral time) or sometimes even longer. It prepares the new arrival for a challenging future as he or she is introduced to an almost unbelievable civilization. After receiving this intensive giving of information, the new arrival is gradually introduced to real, or alive, inhabitants so that she or he can attempt to interact with them using empathy. Through these interactions, clear communication and empathy are impressed as being important. The new arrival is given consistent help on an as-needed basis, to create her or his new home and to select the most advanced technologies that will be incorporated within the *astral* form of the building and its surroundings. Sometimes the help is directly provided by living inhabitants of this sub-plane, and other times by constructed helpers. This depends upon the amount of empathy the new arrival is using. Most homes are quite large and spacious, and contain quite innovative means of being comfortable. Further, they provide freedom in the inhabitant's ability to move about, and provide virtually any experience without necessarily having to leave the home and travel elsewhere. They endure for a long period of time, but can be "upgraded" almost instantly without affecting the home's longevity. These homes tend to be very creative, though not as beautiful as the ones on the fourth astral sub-plane are. The homes on the third astral sub-plane seem to be extensions of the senses and creative imagination of the people who live within them, much in the way that the civilization is in general.

An important part of life for the younger inhabitants on the third astral sub-plane is to create better ways for people to gain knowledge. Communication that is very clear and that accurately depicts what each person is expressing is continually improved upon, by altering astral energy in various ways. Most younger inhabitants become involved in some way of improving the civilization of the sub-plane, and sometimes of helping to improve some parts of the civilization of the fourth and/or the fifth astral sub-planes, as well. Both of these lower sub-planes can be sensed by a person on the third astral sub-plane because the quantum constant is about eighteen times greater on the third sub-plane than on the dense physical ones. There is only about a sixteen to seventeen percent difference in time and the effect of the quantum constant between the third and fourth sub-planes, and about a thirty-three percent difference between the third and fifth sub-planes. This makes the fourth and fifth astral sub-planes accessible to the senses of people on the third.

Sexual activities on the third sub-plane that are emotionally based are very arousing to the sexual partners because both of them can sense, on average, from half up to (presently) three-fourths of what the other partner is completely sensing astrally. Sex on the third astral sub-plane is by far more satisfying than is sex on the dense physical plane that is selfish. Still, third astral sub-plane sex is not as intense, since the etheric/dense physical body and its senses are mostly missing. However, when sexual relations on the third astral sub-plane are unselfish, or are loving, a closer bond is created between the two people than that which can be experienced by anyone below the level of second level initiates who are spiritually disciplining themselves and are lovers on the dense physical plane. This level of closeness is available to nearly any two people on the third astral sub-plane who love each other, which often makes such relationships monogamous and very long lasting, on average.

Creative use of outside astral forms is sometimes employed during sexual relations on the third astral sub-plane to enhance arousal. These forms sometimes interfere with love because they are instruments of sensory increase at the cost of, or replacement for, focusing directly on the other person and appropriately altering (mostly reversing the phase of) the sexual energy that is given to one's partner. It is possible to use these sexual objects and still be as loving; however, it is doubtful to this author that they ever *increase* any amounts of love between two people who are lovingly sexually relating. Even so, the third astral sub-plane is a society in which nearly everything in human life is modified in an attempt to improve it by altering the density of some astral energies through the use of power. Sexual activities are, without question, a part of the need for human improvement through the technologies of this sub-plane.

One area of sexual activities and other types of human relations, as well, that does seem significantly improved by the inventions of the third astral sub-plane civilization is communication. An astral biofeedback device is frequently utilized that informs the astrally alive person to what extent his or her *form* senses are being used whole, as empathy. Then the device further suggests alterations in guiding spiritual thought to realign the lunar devas and to correct the elemental energy in the person's sense so that more complete and accurate information is transmitted—especially from one person to the next. The device is only slightly effective in sensing astral form that is inanimate. The reason is that part of the way in which it functions is the use of a comparison in feedback to discriminate the accuracy of what is sensed by both people. Between two people, however, it is incredibly effective in improving empathy and communication.

Unfortunately, not much technology has, to date, been applied to the processes of spiritually sensing and disciplining the astral sense to create super-empathy. This would require the concurrent use of a higher *mental* invention created as a technological tool of assistance on the higher mental plane, helping to unify the mental body with the simultaneous use of a mental yoga. The complexity of the device and the need for higher levels of spiritual discipline eliminates, by definition, the creation of it by those who are astrally alive on the third sub-plane, because of their relative high levels of selfishness. It is unlikely that this technology will ever be invented on the third astral sub-plane. The reason is that those who would be capable of creating such an invention would not be found on such a relatively low level of the astral plane. Thus people on the third astral sub-plane frequently discipline themselves to improve their senses of form and of communication between people, which enhances their levels of knowledge and then their power. However, they only infrequently discipline themselves to increase astral virtue (love), and super-empathy. These are the two mental and astral senses of spirit and of God in life, added to the unified sense of empathy. Only a relatively small number of the inhabitants of the third astral sub-plane become spiritual disciples.

Because of the emphasis in their lifestyle on information, knowledge, and power, the inhabitants of this world tend to *mentally* exaggerate the importance of knowledge, especially that which is kama-manasically connected to their glamours for power. The mental knowledge then becomes identified as a part of the self. This misidentification is also referred to as egotism. When the mental knowledge becomes more of the self than what is remaining of the self that is not identified as its "correct mental knowledge," then the person has become arrogant. People on the third astral sub-plane tend to be either egotistical or arrogant because they desire power, which they derive from their knowledge that is accurate. Even when inaccurate, increased knowledge that is egotistically held to be true leads to the false emotional feeling in the astral body of being more powerful. This happens because the astral imagination incorrectly links the illusion to the glamour through self focus. Increased empathy can somewhat counter these conditions, but will not be effective in lessening the glamours for power. These glamours create the delusion that *through power* a person can correct an inaccuracy in his or her either mental or astral thought, and bypass the need for intelligent activity. The ignorance of this glamoured position is seldom grasped, as the third astral sub-plane inhabitants, almost compulsively, seek more and more accurate knowledge—in order to gain power and control. They believe that they can solve any problem and can become even God-like through knowing more. Third astral sub-plane inhabitants consistently ignore the fact that they need to genuinely love more, and that maybe, at times, they need to sacrifice knowledge and power and control for understanding—and consciousness. A considerable number of very intelligent people who are physically alive today, and often who are technologically adept and creative, are in the same position and fail to recognize it. Most of these people will live out their astral lives on the third astral sub-plane. Some of them, while physically alive, may even attempt spiritual discipline and fail at it because of their egotism or their arrogance, or both. These people often think that they "know" more than do those who are much more conscious and who are, themselves, considerably more spiritually disciplined.

Egotistical or arrogant people cannot become group (soul) conscious until they seek to create virtue instead of knowledge and power. Unless they become more intelligent in their group activity, they fail to co-serve because they mostly erroneously believe that they are right and that others are wrong. Those who seek to only create virtue are always humble while they do so and can act intelligently and can co-serve within their respective spiritual groups; they have hierarchial consciousness and, as they break through their glamours for power and control, are aware that others are more conscious than they are. Someone who uses power to create intelligent activity, with her or his soul, *never* seeks to control; the desire to control indicates that one is losing power and desires more of it because as the loss occurs, the personality and its self are diminished. Instead of the desire to control, one needs to create love in the astral body and its senses, and truth in the mental body and its senses. In the etheric/dense physical body and its senses, the need to control is replaced by cooperation and sharing. Creating more cooperation and sharing, love, and truth in one's activities, and, for spiritual disciples, within one's spiritual group and its mission, eliminates inertia and maya, glamours, and mental illusion in the form of egotism and arrogance. Much more about this topic will be covered in Chapter Twelve.

On the third astral sub-plane, people generally live for five hundred forty to nine hundred astral years because the quantum constant is about eighteen times greater in its effect than on the dense physical sub-planes. Inhabitants of the third astral sub-plane remain, on average, largely empathic for about three hundred astral years. Then their overall selfishness and the energy they each retain within their centers reduce their senses and begin to split them further into separate lower psychic ones, from the unified single sense of empathy. For two hundred forty to six hundred years, the astral senses of third astral sub-plane inhabitants gradually diminish. As a result, it is very difficult for them to live as they had in such an advanced technological society and civilization. The requirements to successfully fully use the technologies are for quite large amounts of accurate synthesized knowledge to be continually created. These people's ability to accurately communicate generally fails more quickly than does their ability to interact with the technology. Stated another way, their social skills fail faster than their abilities to be civilized do, in general. The cause of this difference has to do with the effects of these people not loving enough in their lives prior to the failure of their senses—which is what caused their senses to fail. A lack of love aggravates the loss in the ability to communicate with others (which is caused by a lack of sense), as compared to being able to still synthesize knowledge from and about inanimate objects. The younger inhabitants who have much better empathy tend to be intolerant of and to ignore, sometimes *completely*, the older people who have less empathy.

Eventually the older and less empathic people need to leave the great cities on the third astral sub-plane that the younger people inhabit. They leave because most of the younger people will no longer communicate with them, and because they can no longer correctly use the technology of the advanced civilization. Often, in fact, they cause the devices that were created from astral energy to be destroyed. This happens because most of these devices are quite fragile, since astral energy is so much more easily changed than etheric/dense physical energy is. Wrong thought alone directed into some devices can adversely affect their performance, although the inventiveness of the third astral sub-plane civilization has created ways of limiting the incidence of this effect. Once a technological device is broken by an older inhabitant, the younger inhabitants often will not repair or replace it if doing so would use (up) some of their senses. The motive and action (or non-action) of the younger inhabitants is based on their perception that using their senses in this way is to be wasteful of their resources—of sense. Destruction of important astral forms is against the rules of the society, as is communication with others that lowers a person's senses. When older people break these rules they are, after their initial choice to leave, subject to banishment to a region of the "senseless"—where the older folks usually live. The third ray is militaristic in one of its expressions in human civilization. Consequently, "senseless" people who live in the "senseless" regions of the sub-plane are *forcibly* prevented from re-entering one of the cities where the more empathic people live. This is accomplished through an energy barrier and a required testing procedure that prevents certain levels of retained astral energy (which generally represents an amount of split astral sense) from going through it, acting as a barrier to the "senseless." The "senseless" can be allowed to re-enter by the younger inhabitants de-activating a section of the barrier when they find it useful to do so. Note that people are usually not initially forced to leave an empathic city, but once they "choose" to, they cannot return to the city without the permission of and assistance from the more empathic younger people.

Those on the third astral sub-plane who have diminished senses might leave a city because no one is willing to communicate with them and/or because they have had removed from their control most of the more advanced technology of the city, and so they, generally, desire to live in a more loving place! The older, less empathic people live in towns and in cities that are much less technologically advanced and that incorporate a simpler, less challenging lifestyle that requires less knowledge. They shift their focus from synthesizing increasingly accurate knowledge to using the knowledge they have towards becoming more loving. After a while, they no longer desire to be a part of the more advanced civilization, and instead seek to remain as empathic as they are loving. By the end of their astral lives, these people have usually become almost exactly as empathic as they are loving.

Those who create more virtue using super-empathy actually simultaneously raise their empathic sense and love. To create virtue in this way requires significant spiritual discipline. This is because the two spiritual senses (of understanding and creating more of God in life) need to be used as God originally used its mind to create our universe. Part of this creation used sacrifice, or self-limitation, which is employed as a methodology in spiritual discipline. People using super-empathy to create virtue consciously decide to use their empathic sense, as a self-limitation, only when it creates more love to the best of their ability. Also, such people further decide to *grow* their empathic sense only as their love grows with it. When a person achieves between twenty-five and fifty percent use of her or his astral senses as empathy *and* when this use creates the virtue of astral love in equal amounts for at least the same proportional period of time fairly consistently each day, an inhabitant of the third astral sub-plane (or sometimes a lower one) can leave for the second astral sub-plane, where she or he can sometimes live out the remainder of her of his astral life. The majority of the older third astral sub-plane inhabitants that have lessened empathy remain on this sub-plane until they die. The reason is that they often either choose to not spiritually discipline themselves, or to not do so adequately. Another condition that occurs is that even after these people have chosen to spiritually discipline themselves, the time that they have remaining before their astral bodies wear out is insufficient for them to raise their empathy and love, through super-empathy and spiritual discipline, to levels that are high enough that would enable them to leave. By the time that these people begin to spiritually discipline themselves, their split senses are so diminished that they simply have too little capability to create very much love. Among the adjoining sub-planes on the entire astral plane, the greatest difference in life and lifestyle exists between the third sub-plane regions of the astral world where the younger inhabitants live and the second astral sub-plane. The reason is that the former is the pinnacle of form existence through its third ray focus, and the latter is the lower of the two possible spiritual types of focus on living.

The animal population of the third astral sub-plane has mostly a mixture of some previously physically alive working animals, which includes farm animals that are raised not necessarily just to eat (such as some sheep and goats); animals used as guards, for military purposes, or for communication (commonly in the past, pigeons); animals that on the dense physical plane helped the handicapped and that usually were also pets that function as pets on this sub-plane; and some laboratory animals. The remainder of animals on the third astral sub-plane were pets while alive dense physically. There are no completely wild animals on the third astral sub-plane because such animals could not have the development of civilization incorporated into their astral sense and because the thought of humans on this plane, even among the "senseless" ones, civilizes the entire plane to some extent. The main focus of the inhabitants of this plane in relation to animals is to improve their communication with animals and the knowledge that the animals have. Devices constructed of astral energy are used to further this goal. Within the next two decades (by about the year 2020), lesser versions of these devices are likely to be invented on the physical plane. The devices on the third astral sub-plane plane are composed of a tiny sending and receiving artificial sense that is formed of astral energy and that communicates astral brain (wave) information as complete thought to and from the animal. The first of the corresponding physical plane inventions will send information only from the animal to a very advanced computer. On the third astral sub-plane, however, the artificial intelligence device helps to unify the animal's senses, and then synthesizes some of the information from these senses into a measured amount of knowledge that is slightly beyond the animal's current capacity of astral and lower mental thought. The whole sense and the synthesized information are sent back to the animal, training it to better sense and think. On the physical plane of the future, a small transmitter worn on the head of the animal (a pet) will send a signal containing some of the animal's brain patterns to a powerful computer. The computer will be able to convert basic patterns into yes and no responses and simple sentences of lower mental thoughtforms (though no concepts). Then it will speak them as synthetic speech created by the computer, from the pet's thought, to people either in the vicinity of the computer or who are wearing or have a receiver that is tuned to the frequency of the computer's transmitter. Sometimes the pet will wear a receiver to hear the speech as well, to learn through biofeedback how to better communicate what it is thinking to the computer. People and their advanced pets will be able to communicate with one another through speech on a basic level, leading to much closer relationships between them. As a result, pets will advance much more quickly into the human kingdom, and the technology and its use will increase. Some chimpanzees have already achieved much of this effect through the use of American Sign Language; however, it is planned that some chimpanzees will begin to individualize as humans through becoming pets only *after* some dogs, cats, horses, and advanced birds do.

Communication of Thoughts of Non-Speaking Lifeforms

The computer gets input from the senses of the cat and plant.

Illustration 8.15

Many thousands of years ago, chimps and some other apes became artificially advanced through human genetic material being bred into them by evil Atlantean people. Prior to that time (millions of years ago), some partially animal-like humans had sexual relations with apes, causing—on rare occasion, but often enough to become a problem—a few cases of cross-species impregnation in female apes *and in a few female humans*! The partially animal-like humans who participated in these behaviors were very early Lemurians, or members of the third major race of people on this planet. These people were the first to have dense physical form rather than just an etheric body. They resembled apes in appearance and some, at first, did not distinguish the difference where sexual relations were concerned. Because the early Lemurians were still more etheric than dense physical in their etheric/dense physical bodies, if they genuinely thought that they wanted to mate with and have offspring with apes, the thought of these early humans could affect the more etheric part of their bodies that was constructed of atomic level etheric energy. Their thought could also affect the more etheric part of the apes, which was constructed of etheric energy from the sub-atomic, or second etheric sub-plane—causing these two different energies to join. The results then became realized as effects in dense form. Note that the earliest Lemurians, who were the predecessors of the ones mentioned above, had bodies that were even more proportionately etheric than dense physical. Because these earliest Lemurians had little density to their lifeforms, they grew in size when they reached the dense physical plane, and were as much as fifty feet tall. The statues on Easter Island may have been built by much later Lemurians (who had *degenerated* as a people), in order to depict what they thought their earliest ancestors had looked like.

Chimps and some other apes are along the third ray in the focus of their bodies' senses. However, only the few that have been raised by humans and/or are used as testing animals in laboratories, or have been kept as pets and/or taught sign language, reach the third astral sub-plane. When most of the rats and mice that were used (and usually killed) in testing die, they go to the sixth and fifth astral sub-planes for a relatively short astral life. Many of the scientists who experimented on animals can also be found on the fifth astral sub-plane after physical death. Many of the so-called scientists who experimented on animals and were not affected by the misery and pain that was inflicted upon the animals, and by the living conditions these animals were subjected to, may first travel to the sixth astral sub-plane after physical death. This author has no direct knowledge of what follows in this sentence, but it might be surmised that some of those who treated rats, mice, dogs, cats, and other animals, including apes, as non-sentient objects in laboratory experiments might find themselves, as they lost their astral senses later in astral life on the sixth astral sub-plane, in some interesting karmic relationships with some of these types of animals. In the near future, if the world moves towards more spiritual human life, the testing of drugs and other human inventions or products will be carried out on biological tissue from the genetic type of animal or of humans that the drug or product will be used on. With this method, there will be no need to test a potentially harmful substance on an entire animal. With this more advanced method, the effects on the whole organism will be able to be calculated from biological and genetic effects and using a higher mental and etheric means of experimenting, rather than the more trial and error method that is presently used on physical lifeforms. Life is one, and respect for it is respect for God's growth. Mistreatment of one part of life by a higher part creates very bad karma for the higher part because the higher *immediately begins to fall in consciousness to the level of the lower*—creating for itself, eventually, great suffering. The higher the consciousness of the higher part of life that has the same or close to the same number of centers as the lower part of life that the higher is mistreating, the greater the suffering caused by losing the self. An example is humans, as a higher part of life, testing drugs and other substances on relatively advanced animals that have closer to the same number of centers in each body as the humans do, but much lower consciousness to begin with.

People who are more primitive have little karma for hunting animals for food and to increase their civilization. Modern-day advanced people who for "sport" hunt more advanced animals that have a lot of senses, closer to the number in a human, will suffer as their consciousness lowers. In addition, after these people die physically, they may have karma with some animals in order to correct their lack of empathy and lack of love for lower parts of life. Note that this concept still applies even when animals are overpopulated as a result of what is actually a poor method of wildlife management, whose quality of being incorrect is hidden. Wildlife can be managed by habitat restriction; birth control; balance of predators, with near-equal capability of survival so that each animal's consciousness grows through being hunter and hunted; and through hybridization. The hybridization method of breeding wild animals requires an overall increase in human awareness and consciousness as well as in their knowledge. This process is likely to begin to be used in the next thirty or so years. For those who are spiritually disciplining themselves, and for some other people, eating animals will lower consciousness and possibly negate some or all of the discipline; this effect is somewhat determined by circumstance and motive. The reader is referred to Chapter Twelve for more about this issue. Note that the overall consciousness of the animal, *plus* its total number of senses and their overall development, generally control the amount of karma that a human incurs for killing it. For example, there are less karmic implications when a human kills an animal that has low consciousness but good senses, such as a scorpion; there may be no karma if such an animal interferes with a human, *and the animal had choices*, or options, not to. When an animal is killed under these circumstances, its group soul is learning to avoid humans, and the senses of the animal can provide the group soul with the information to do so. Killing an animal that has low consciousness and sense, such as a worm—provided it is not parasitic to a human or to animals the human is caring for—can bring about relatively much more karma! Unless the animal is parasitic and interferes with humans (or animals they take carc of), the animal cannot be improved in sense or consciousness through its death that is resultant of its interaction with a human. Animals that have high consciousness and sense, such as a duck or deer, that are killed by humans for (mostly) sport, even if, secondarily, the animals are eaten, gain mostly fear of humans—and humans will be animals' (as future humans) Masters when both kingdoms advance. In these cases, the animal group souls do not gain sense when the animals are killed. There is too great a disparity between the technology of the human and the senses of the animal, and the motives of the human contain less love than the group soul has. As a result, much more karma is brought onto the human for interfering with the growth of life of the animals. The motive for and method of killing animals also greatly affects the amount of karma that a human incurs from the killing.

There are more birds and cats on the third astral sub-plane than there are dogs. Some birds' group souls are particularly receptive to the energy, or power, side of the third ray and their next lifeforms will actually become *solar* devas (pitris), rather than individualizing into the human kingdom. The group souls of some of these types of birds are planned to advance from the animal kingdom into the energy sub-kingdom rather than contributing their spirit and energy to the human kingdom. Those birds are some of the ones that have very good ability to use the lunar deva energy on the lower mental plane to create thoughtforms. These types of birds do this by first parroting sounds and when astrally alive can be brought, through human technology on the third sub-plane, to the level of full sentence construction and communication of their own thoughts. Sometimes these sentences are complex, and when put together form logical paragraph-length amounts of information. Most cats can be brought to a level of increased empathy by joining their already exceptional individual astral senses. Cats' individual (selfishly used) astral senses are stronger than most dogs' are. However, in cats the individual astral senses typically are not nearly as joined together into empathy as they are in dogs. When cats are physically alive, their etheric/dense physical senses function similarly to those of dogs. Cats have even relatively better etheric/dense physical senses than dogs do on average because cats as lifeforms have an odd-rayed focus, and dogs have an even-rayed focus. Odd-rayed lifeforms have an advantage in developing senses in odd-rayed bodies; even-rayed lifeforms enjoy the same advantage in even-rayed bodies. People alive on the third astral sub-plane desire to improve senses and form, and cats are the perfect animal in which to help improve empathy. The older, less empathic residents of the third astral sub-plane focus more on loving than just improving sense, communication, and knowledge. They will often adopt the most loving animals on this sub-plane regardless of other factors. Sometimes, through their own spiritual self discipline, these people are even able to raise their animals' consciousness to the level at which they and their pets can travel together to the second astral sub-plane, where they will then live.

 ## THE SECOND ASTRAL SUB-PLANE

Life on the second astral sub-plane is significantly different from life on the lower sub-planes. The reason is that on the second sub-plane the focus is on spiritual development of sense, which occurs only when virtue is created. The virtue that is created the most on the astral plane is love. The second astral sub-plane has considerably more love on it than the lower ones do. There is about fifty percent to one hundred percent more love on the second astral sub-plane than on the third. To be able to travel to and/or astrally live on this sub-plane requires spiritual discipline. The reason is that the highest level of consciousness that is attainable through non-spiritual discipline of the five astral senses of form is reached on the third astral sub-plane. Greater levels of discipline of only the senses of form *eventually reduce* both consciousness and sense. One needs to achieve the use of about thirty-seven percent of the astral senses as the unified use of empathy, *and* simultaneously use the empathy with which to create more virtue, which is mostly in the form of love to remain consistently on the second sub-plane; one can reach this sub-plane for relatively brief periods of time with only twenty-five percent of empathy and love—and the aspiration to serve. Such levels of creation of virtue, or light in one's and others' bodies and senses, are about twenty-one times greater than the average amount of *astral* virtue that a person creates today in the physical world. To compare this thirty-seven to fifty percent amount of use (which is the average *highest* use on the second astral sub-plane) in a relative sixteen hour astral day and sixteen hours on the physical plane, the average astrally alive second sub-plane person creates virtue for over six hours. The physically alive person uses so little sense with which to create virtue, and does so so inconsistently, that he or she creates any type of virtue in his or her sixteen hours for less than fifteen to maybe thirty-five minutes. That person would create love for an average of only one-third of these total amounts of time of creating virtue. This means that for less than fifteen to a maximum of thirty-five minutes out of each sixteen-hour day, the average physically alive person is fully focused on and creates some intelligent activity that cooperates and shares with and for others; gives to, or creates oneness/love, with and for others; or helps to create truth, or mental wholeness, in themselves and in the thought of others—or any combination of these three. On the physical plane, even while two monogamous heterosexual partners are "making love," the average partners create the astral virtue of love only about one-tenth of the time they are involved in the activity (which is still about ten times better than the average for the same length of time for the rest of the time they are awake physically alive). Those who are alive on the second astral sub-plane usually sleep less than two astral hours per day, which gives them even more fully conscious time in which to create virtue. Reaching the lower of the two higher "heavens," or the sixth heaven (or the second, depending upon one's religious background and traditions) is of considerable achievement for a person. Such people have lived virtuously in the prior physical life, and possibly afterwards while alive astrally on the fourth or third astral sub-plane.

The majority of those people alive on the second astral sub-plane go directly there after physical death; still, a significant minority of inhabitants arrive after a period of relatively virtuous life on either the fourth or third astral sub-plane, in which they chose to spiritually discipline themselves. The effect of the quantum constant on the second astral sub-plane is about twenty-one times greater than that of the dense physical, allowing a maximum life expectancy of about one thousand fifty years. However, most of the inhabitants on this sub-plane either die earlier from astral life or leave the second sub-plane with some remaining astral sense fused with mental sense to do one of the following:

1. They might serve on one or more of the lower sub-planes, where time is less dilated and their senses and bodies age relatively more rapidly; they die earlier as a result. However, these people age from loss of senses not nearly as rapidly as the people whom they serve do, since those who came from the second astral sub-plane are mostly creating virtue while on the lower sub-planes. The astral death of such a person is more often a result of the astral lunar devas and elemental energies in her or his astral body eventually reaching their maximal time of remaining integrated.

2. They might leave for the lower mental sub-planes, because their egotism is much greater than their remaining glamours. Also, the person's priority shifts to reducing the retained energy in her or his mental permanent atom as compared to her or his astral permanent atom. Note that while the mental senses are not in the primary body of use while a person is astrally alive, these senses are still somewhat destroyed through astral life (to the same extent that they are used selfishly).

3. They might travel to and live on the first astral sub-plane, because they have become more creative in the use of their higher spiritual sense of Self, and each of these people is *consciously* fusing with his or her Self.

The average period of time for astrally alive people to live on the second sub-plane is about six hundred astral years. At the end, most have reduced to a negligible level the astral energies they have retained in their centers as well as the energies, as glamours, that they have retained in their astral bodies.

When an astrally alive person first arrives on the second astral sub-plane, she or he has the desire to create virtue. This desire is aspiration, or desire focused out onto others, and is not driven by a glamour. However, some glamours do exist within the person, or she or he would not even be on the astral plane. The glamours that people on the second astral sub-plane have are often fixed desires about how they will serve, and it is in the "how" that each seeks an emotional and self-focused affirmation of her or his current belief system. Although not nearly so much as at any time within the recent or especially the more distant past, many people who are alive on the second astral sub-plane desire to create virtue in the ways in which their particular religions or sometimes one or more other traditions teach and/or dictate. Those ways include the person receiving in some manner the emotional "reward" of being in God's favor, or within God's love. All of these motives are selfish, or glamoured, because based on what they perceive to be God, these people are self-focused and concerned that through following their religious beliefs they will receive from God what is a part of their glamour—even if it is to just be liked, cared for, or loved by God. In these circumstances, God can also be represented by a person's *T*eacher or teacher, the person's group, and/or its leader. These glamours are *more difficult* to change than are the blatantly selfish ones on the lower astral sub-planes. The reason is that the glamours on the second sub-plane are generally more commonly held among the inhabitants and are reinforced by numerous traditions and prior life experiences. It is, presently, the nature of most major religions to often foster these glamours because the glamours act to control and motivate the members of the religions to remain within the particular sect, and to give to the religion. The concept that God is within, rather than an externalized Being who is often judgmental, can greatly help to break through the glamours of self-focus concerning God.

Once a person has arrived on the second astral plane, he or she is greeted by a group of people who generally tend to serve in one of seven ways. All seven of these ways are mostly for the purpose of creating more love because love is the virtue that those who are astrally alive are on the astral plane to learn to create more of. The group of people may contain some friends or family members of the new arrival if they previously co-served with him or her, and if they are, themselves, recently deceased from physical life. Because of the time dilation, these people are often likely to have died within the preceding ten or fewer physical plane years (about two hundred ten second astral sub-plane years). However, because of the strong tendency towards group service by most of the sub-plane's residents most of the time, longer periods of time are possible because the group has become like a family unit that collectively remembers some of those who are still physically alive, better than each individual might. Groups are substantially more efficient in creating virtue and are a natural means for people on this and the first astral sub-plane to relate within. The group is the focus of many inhabitants' astral lives because their personalities no longer seek so much to control. Many can function spiritually, as souls, within a group through oneness, or love, and hierarchial consciousness. Those functioning within a spiritual group have the understanding among the members that at times others think better than they do and are more loving, or conscious, than they are. These levels of humility that are needed to remain group conscious are the same amounts needed to remain soul conscious. Thus the level of humility needed to function as one's soul is equal to the level of humility that is needed to be part of a spiritual group, or a group focused on creating more virtue. For this reason (spiritual) group consciousness is the same as soul consciousness. Because those on the second astral sub-plane are approximately equally loving and empathic thirty-seven to fifty percent of the time—consistently, they remain humble and loving, and able to function in a spiritual group once they decide to do so. The key to being on the second astral sub-plane at all is to consistently exceed twenty-five percent empathic use of the astral senses, while nearly always using the empathy to create love while aspiring to serve. Using the astral body in this way is quite a challenge for physically alive second level initiates who are emotionally disciplining their astral bodies. Doing so is a significant accomplishment for all those who are astrally alive on the second astral sub-plane, but somewhat easier than for those who are physically alive because the primary sense that astrally alive people use is the astral sense.

There are seven types of spiritual groups that people, who choose to, astrally serve within on the second and first astral sub-planes. These seven types of groups on the second astral sub-plane correspond to the seven different ways that the astral bodies of the group members sense while still having some selfishness remaining. The way that a selfish person senses astrally corresponds to the ray of her or his astral body. The remaining glamours control, at least half of the time, the emotional responses through the type of sense, or type of slight thought, that the astral energies use within the senses of the astral body. The astral plane's virtue of love is very focused, and devoted to one direction of movement at a time (as is its selfishness of emotions). As a result, even when a human is serving as a soul one-half of the time, such service is often quite segregated from other groups and limited to being within the person's group and within groups of the same ray type. On the first astral sub-plane this separative condition has mostly been corrected, but on the second it still is the norm.

The second-smallest population of astrally alive second sub-plane inhabitants serves in group types along the seventh ray. Less than one out of a thousand people on this sub-plane are in such groups. Part of the reason is that the service is considerably more difficult and people on the astral plane have very limited etheric/dense physical sense (only that which is fused with super-empathy). Also, very few people have seventh ray astral bodies—while not an absolute requirement, is more often the norm. Moreover, service frequently takes place on the seventh astral sub-plane, which many of the group members cannot sense from the second sub-plane, and the seventh sub-plane is a particularly undesirable place to serve. Some service does also take place on the other sub-planes because the virtue that each ray creates applies everywhere, but much of the virtue that is created on a sub-plane corresponds to its ray type. When functioning as souls, and therefore when not controlled by glamours, second sub-plane inhabitants can create virtue along the other rays as well. However, because they are still at least fifty percent selfish, their groups are mostly segregated by their ray types as a result of the effects of averaging the members' selfish use of their astral bodies along their ray types. The focus on the virtue of love focused from the seventh ray within the type of group that is along the seventh ray is to help others to become more giving of astral form by organizing it together, using less of it (economizing it), and then giving it in ways that help others do the same.

On the second astral sub-plane, between fifty and sixty percent of the inhabitants who choose to serve in spiritual groups serve in groups that use the sixth ray as a focus of service. These people constitute the vast plurality of inhabitants on the entire sub-plane. This large proportion is a result of about eighty percent of all the people on earth at any given time having sixth ray astral bodies. Of the seven types of astral bodies, when used selfishly the sixth ray astral body is the sturdiest and longest-lived because a sixth ray astral body matches the astral plane in ray type and is at a closer vibration and direction to the average vibration and direction of the entire plane. The sixth ray as applied to human civilization manifests mostly as religion. This ray is devoted to and focused on only one way of understanding God. The overwhelming percentage of people who have sixth ray astral bodies on the astral plane causes religion to play such a prominent role in the ways people prefer to serve on the second astral sub-plane. Even though they are serving, it is still the more selfish, or emotional, side of them that produces this effect, as has previously been explained. The service that those in groups along the sixth ray tend to provide is more directed to those on the sixth astral sub-plane because of that sub-plane's correspondence to the sixth ray. This service is to motivate and focus people to limit the direction of movement of their astral energy. The result is often a reduction in the frenzied emotions that are so common on that sub-plane. In the process of reduction of random and scattered movements, movement to and for the increase of God and love in the lives of sixth astral sub-plane inhabitants replaces their desires for emotional stimulation and constant movement and change in their lives. As people become devoted to increasing virtue as love, they find that joy becomes a much greater and a more pleasant experience than the very temporary exciting "happiness" that goes hand-in-hand with their losses in consciousness, their suffering, and their pain. The application of service by this type of group is used on the other lower sub-planes at times. All of the lower sub-planes have some elements of a lack of focus on love and on God, but usually without the frenzy of constant emotional stimulation that is found on the sixth astral sub-plane.

Second astral sub-plane inhabitants who are members of fifth ray type groups are the third-rarest, and still amount to far less than one percent of the population of this sub-plane. The fifth ray is only infrequently found in the astral body, as is true of all the odd, or masculine, rays. They weaken the astral body through their masculine (odd-rayed)—to the feminine (even-rayed)—vibration on this (a feminine-rayed) plane. The groups along the fifth ray tend to create love by improving causal relationships between the creative imagination that a person has, and her or his overall level and condition of astral sense. They create improved structure of past and present parts of time, using creative imagination. This leads to overcoming some glamours, and producing much more love. When functioning virtuously, the group members who have highly imaginative astral minds should have enough sense, and especially empathy, to use their imaginations to create astral forms that help others to love. These groups attempt to improve this same effect in others, especially as it occurs (or is lacking) on the fifth astral sub-plane.

The groups on the second astral sub-plane that are focused along the fourth ray are much more common than are any of the odd-rayed groups. These groups attract new arrivals through their creation of more of the virtue of love. They do so by perfecting the balance between the thought of informing spirit and the collective thought of energy within a lifeform. A majority of the time that these groups spend in service is on the fourth astral sub-plane. The members of the groups travel there in attempt to reduce the glamours within fourth astral sub-plane inhabitants by helping the people to reduce their desires to be loved, and helping them to love others more, and more wisely. The attempt is made to increase either the empathy in some people or the spiritual thought of loving in the same people at times or in some others. This is done in order to perfectly balance these two elements to create beauty and reduce the ugliness of hypocrisy. These group members *teach* and are examples of sacrificing the appearance of virtue for giving to others in ways that help the others to further give. These ways of greater giving often reveal deficiencies in the way a person loves (or does not love) rather than making a person appear more virtuous than he or she really is. Because of this condition, people with fourth ray glamours have a difficult time adopting a more loving, or giving, lifestyle.

Groups on the second astral sub-plane that are focused along the third ray attempt to teach that knowledge and power without *equal* amounts of love creates separation, militarism, and materialism—each of which destroys form rather than preserving it. When members of these groups serve on a lower astral sub-plane, they tend to serve on the third. More often than not, they serve the older, "senseless," inhabitants of the third astral sub-plane because the younger inhabitants in the cities where empathy abounds are so egotistical or arrogant (or both), as well as glamoured, that they believe they are always right. These inhabitants also believe that the group and soul approach of the teaching by some of the servers are attempts to control (!) them—of course, this is a projection of their own desires to control! When faced with overwhelming evidence that the servers are teaching truth, as well as love, the younger and *more empathic* third sub-plane inhabitants often still choose to reject the teaching by convoluting their knowledge into something that supports their selfish lifestyles.

Members of groups that are focused along the second ray will do the least amount of travelling, though they still do some. These groups are focused on teaching, mostly other groups on the second astral sub-plane, about some of the information that is found in this book, or about Ageless Wisdom. Unlike their counterparts on the first astral sub-plane, second astral sub-plane groups are not very effective at politically leading the other spiritual groups on the second sub-plane to be less separative through teaching them Ageless Wisdom. People on the second astral sub-plane are themselves too glamoured to be able to function as leaders and to sacrifice their own consciousness to help raise the consciousness of their co-servers in other groups. Second ray groups on the second astral sub-plane are very effective in reducing some of the religious emotionalism there by being examples of their teaching that God is within, and not to expect to receive from God, as a compensation for loving. In other words, they teach others to *not* believe that because a person is loving or virtuous in other ways as well, that the outcome that she or he can expect is that God will favor and reward her or him. The teaching of these and other principles by second ray groups causes people to gain respect for a God who is genuinely loving, and who is not also functioning judgmentally through a system of quid pro quo. If God shows favor because people love God, God also must do the opposite in some way (even if that means doing nothing) when people do not. The second astral sub-plane residents begin to realize that as they selfishly seek, or desire, anything from God, they alter their perception of God into a selfish Being who judges and expects something, or takes from them. Note that there is an immense difference between a God who punishes—especially for not following certain edicts in a specific religion—and karma, which is the effect of a cause created by someone. The notion of a vengeful God causes religion to become contradictory and to oppose, at times, the creation of virtue; the religion becomes dark. The second ray groups are significantly greater in number, proportionately, than the relative number of people who have second ray astral bodies. This is because on the (corresponding) second astral sub-plane so much focus is placed on teaching and on desireless *unconditional* love. Teaching unconditional love is difficult when nearly all of those who are being taught are quite glamoured, but the overall effect of this teaching is more pronounced than is any other type of service on the second astral sub-plane. The reason is that the teaching expands the much more limited, but ubiquitous, astral love, which is one-directional love (devoted and focused) from one person or group to another.

The groups on the second astral sub-plane that are focused along the first ray teach the means of destroying glamours and of sacrificing some emotions for increased love. The members of these groups lead others by exemplifying one of seven methods of altering the vibration of glamours. These methods depend upon what ray type of astral body the glamours are in, so that the glamours are destroyed and their energies are converted into love. While very effective on the *effects* of selfishness, or on glamours and retained energies within the centers as well, the causes of emotionalism, or astral selfishness, are not well addressed by these groups on the second astral sub-plane. Their members are still too glamoured and selfish to love enough and to sacrifice in the ways that are necessary to prevent emotionalism from taking place. To do so requires much more creative and innovative ways of limiting some choices. In addition, this type of astral and mental thought has to be preceded by people using their senses lovingly together at a fifty percent level and eventually sometimes using their whole astral senses more than half of the time that they possibly could. This is accomplished on the first astral sub-plane, and by groups of the first ray type, but requires too great of a state of enlightenment for the average amount of selfishness that is found within people on the second astral sub-plane. The number of people on the second astral sub-plane who are in first ray groups is relatively very low. The total number of these people is usually the lowest relative number as compared to any other ray on the second sub-plane. The reason is the great amounts of sacrifice that are needed if service is to take place; also, the first ray astral body is the rarest of any ray type found in this body.

Once they arrive on the second astral sub-plane, many people find and quickly integrate themselves into one of the seven types of spiritual groups there. All of the inhabitants of the second astral sub-plane are also spiritual disciples, although many, if not most, would not refer to themselves as such upon their arrival. As they begin to serve, first on the second astral sub-plane and then, at times, on the other sub-planes, they experience great joy. Most of the astral lifetime for each of these people is far more heaven-like than that which is experienced by people on the lower planes. This is because on the second astral sub-plane they are, up to half of the time, recognizing and understanding God more—in all of astral life. The other half of the time, or more, they are emotionally caught in desiring love *from God*, but not usually in seeking it from other people or parts of life in the ways that those on the fourth astral sub-plane so often do. When people desire God's love, they lose their own empathy and ability to love. This keeps them from attaining much more than a fifty percent level of empathy and love while on the second astral sub-plane. However, each second astral sub-plane inhabitant often maintains close to the fifty percent level through most of his or her astral life by consistently serving, at a level of about close to half of the time, after the first few astral decades of life on this sub-plane if not sooner.

Depending upon a person's astral body ray type and personality ray, he or she can reduce and sometimes virtually eliminate most glamours. As this occurs, the person can travel to and eventually live on the first astral sub-plane. Living on the first astral sub-plane requires consistent use of seventy-five percent of empathy with creation of love, or seventy-five percent use of super-empathy, with a seventy-five percent rate of consistency. One can travel to the first astral sub-plane with over fifty percent of super-empathy, but to remain conscious there (and not fall asleep), one needs to immediately create more virtue in conjunction with the appropriate group and its mission in service. Some people can travel and serve for a while, for astral hours to even days, and then they fail to maintain the levels of creation of *more* virtue and thus fall asleep, and then travel back to the second astral sub-plane. It is difficult for those on the second astral sub-plane to create more virtue than the amount of astral sense that they have. Doing so is achievable *only* through group service; as the other group members provide sense (and some thought) in the interim in order to fill the gap in sense, super-empathy then further grows. The difficulty is in giving up personal (*personal*-ity) control, or selfishness, even though these people "know" better and do desire to love. The process is of gradual development, of one becoming her or his soul, and also requires assistance from the Self (and Monadic will through the Self). This assistance comes from the previously mentioned help of the person's spiritual group, from the group's leader, from the *Teacher* of the group (if one is present), and from members of the next kingdom (Masters of the Ageless Wisdom) as well as from Solar Angels. The spiritually disciplined person, or the spiritual disciple, needs to become more creative in light and to accept a greater role in leading others. People on the second sub-plane, who are all spiritual disciples expressing their discipline and service in one of seven ways, eventually need to become accepted for being given assistance (and to seek such assistance) in their further creation of empathy and love, as well as of other cosmic virtues. These people are the controllers of their initiation of creating more virtue than their existing levels of empathy and love. The acceptance is for initiation into a higher level of creating virtue, through the help of the above-listed sources. Once accepted for such help, a resident of the second astral sub-plane can permanently live on the first astral sub-plane, provided that he or she continues to function at *increasingly* higher levels of creating virtue.

It should be noted that although all second astral sub-plane inhabitants are spiritual disciples, when they *first* arrive on this astral sub-plane they may know nothing about Ageless Wisdom. They would probably be familiar with Ageless Wisdom only if they functioned along the second ray as spiritual disciples before reaching the second astral sub-plane, during prior astral or physical plane life. Most people who discipline themselves spiritually do so to create virtue, but not necessarily to understand *why they are creating virtue*. Those along the second ray seek to understand everything they are doing, since the second ray is the ray of understanding, or unconditional love/consciousness. Because the second astral sub-plane is the astral sub-plane of *understanding love*, nearly everyone there eventually gains understanding of *why* they create love as a virtue, and they gain understanding of some parts of Ageless Wisdom, or of some of the information in this book.

People usually live as groups in wonderful homes, often with different kinds of park-like settings between their homes and the homes of members of other groups. These homes, being created by people from many different cultures and in many different locales, are creatively quite diverse. For efficiency, second astral sub-plane inhabitants usually share their astral forms and, as a result, less use of their creative imagination is required in order to have and maintain such nice surroundings. Love and empathy are consistently used on the second astral sub-plane to show great compassion for everyone there, and even sometimes for those who are served on all or some of the lower astral sub-planes. Up to half of each person's astral imagination and empathy are used to serve spiritually, or to create more virtue, within his or her group. Because some groups have well over a hundred members, homes that accommodate several to a dozen people are connected to one another through open common areas that often are also park-like. The largest groups are usually the less spiritually advanced ones.

On the second and first astral sub-planes, travel from one somewhat distant locale to another is usually achieved through re-creating the astral body by a person using her or his creative imagination to "see" herself or himself in the desired location. Since the second and first astral sub-planes are so relatively less dense that it is very easy for the astral energy to follow a person's much stronger thought, people on these two sub-planes can efficiently re-create themselves much more frequently for relatively much shorter trips and with much less effort than those on the lower astral sub-planes can. Very short-distance travel is more effectively accomplished by "movement," which is actually less demanding in its use of thought and sense, but separates more time from space, i.e., uses more time. Movement, however, is a similar process of thought altering the energy of the astral body; the mental body, which surrounds the astral secondarily in sense and form because of its very low density, instantly follows the energy in the astral body. The main difference between "moving" astrally and astral travel through re-creation of form through thought is that almost no time is separated from space for the latter, while the movement of astral form through space requires that time separate from space (see Chapter Ten for more about this subject). People on the second astral sub-plane separate much less time from space than do those on the lower sub-planes because inhabitants of the second sub-plane think more in light, or create more virtue. This causes energy to become enlightened in its activity and to join with space. The space then becomes enlightened as the energy within it becomes increased in thought that is intelligent within form, or in God's vibration and direction, joining space and creating light. It takes much less time to do anything on the second astral sub-plane as compared to the lower astral sub-planes because people's (and other lifeforms') thought there is enlightened to an average level of up to fifty percent. This creates more astral time (that is joined with space) and the effect of time dilation. Astral travel from thought re-creation of astral form on the lower sub-planes requires considerably greater use of both sense and imagination. This type of travel often results in diminishment of both sense and imagination because of so much retained energy in the inhabitants' bodies. As a result, on the lower sub-planes this method is infrequently used— especially for relatively shorter distances, which usually take place with greater frequency. On the second astral sub-plane and even more so on the first, astral travel through thought re-creation of form is frequently used—without much if any degradation of sense and the ability to think. The amount of degradation is dependent upon the amount of virtuous thought that the person uses in service.

The vegetation and animal life of the second astral sub-plane are sublime because only enlightened animal and vegetative forms are created by the inhabitants and their animals, respectively. All the vegetation at this level is enlightened beyond the thought of the plant, or vegetable, group soul and its self, and the animal life is correspondingly enlightened. This giving of enlightening thought by a higher form of life to a lower one helps to serve both the higher and the lower kingdom in their development. The animals on this sub-plane are those that were very loving in their prior lives, either the most recent physical life or while subsequently living on the fourth and/or third astral sub-planes. All animals on the second astral sub-plane are treated as pets, and relate both to people and to other animal life as an extension of themselves, or as one life. People choose to live close together in community home settings, yet each has a great space in which to live. This is a condition seldom generally created, or present for large populations, anywhere in the physical world on earth. The great spaces, often including parks between groups' homes (even between the homes of members of a single group), have no effect on the ability to communicate or be close. The reasons are the ease of travel, which is almost instantaneous when of any significant distance, and the residents' overall empathic sense, which can be extended across great distances. Monogamy is the standard in relationships between people who are sexually involved, and it is also the norm for couples to live together in their group's community-style homes. While the groups themselves are still somewhat separated, people within them are much closer than families are on the lower astral sub-planes and the physical plane. The levels of love on the second astral sub-plane are so profound that it is difficult to explain them using physical plane concepts and comparisons.

When people are emotional and thus selfish on this sub-plane they tend to spend time alone, not functioning as part of any spiritual group. At these times they often contemplate and reflect upon their glamours, or their fixed desires, that cause them to misunderstand God and life. They do so mostly in one wrong way that is emotional, and that is what their meaning of God—or of life is. These periods may include other activities, but the astral, or emotional, focus continues to be on understanding life, or God's growth. It is difficult for most physically alive people to appreciate this focus on understanding life. While living on the etheric/dense physical plane, so much of physical life is spent in the attempt to understand dense energy, or matter, and spirit's relationship to it while inertia mostly controls the senses that spirit is using to inform itself about the matter. Under such circumstances, one gets lost in the form of things. On the second astral sub-plane, clarity of consciousness and the complete removal of both matter and even most of the conflicting astral forms allows a person's focus to be *devoted*, for up to several hundred astral years of total time over her or his astral lifetime, to understanding life's (God's) hidden meaning. Paradoxically, devoted focus on the meaning of life on a *personal*, rather than a group, or soul, level is selfish and is indicative of the illusion, as glamours, that God is external to those so reflecting upon and contemplating God and Its meaning. In illusion, many second astral sub-plane inhabitants believe that such personal contemplation and meditation is appropriate and even good, because they believe that is *what God wants* them to do so that God will love/like/be-pleased-with them more! Glamours are amazingly seductive, even when they are about God. These same glamours affect spiritual disciples on the physical plane, as well as those who are approaching the spiritual disciplining of themselves; many follow the notion that meditation, reflection, and contemplation *about* God, rather than using these tools of thought to create more virtue (more of) God, is the way to be more spiritual and loved by God. This is a common error that is caused by high levels of glamours of this type having been promoted by religions for so much of commonly known and recorded human history. During the Atlantean civilization, these glamours were mostly not a part of religion, and religion promoted that the creation of virtue was the paramount goal to finding and understanding God. However, while most of the Atlanteans believed and followed this as a part of their religion, they had little or no conceptual, or higher mental, understanding about it. The reason is that their mental bodies were so little-developed as compared to humanity of today, who is in the fifth, or mentally focused, major human race. (The Atlanteans were the fourth, or astrally focused, major race.)

Sexual relations on the second astral sub-plane are nearly always monogamous, and take place between two people who love each other. On this astral sub-plane of oneness, the quality, or expression of consciousness, of sex is a true joining together as one. Each partner fully experiences the other's levels of fused etheric/dense physical senses, which for many is relatively small, but effective enough to add further intensity to the lovemaking. Each also experiences his or her partner's astral sense, of super-empathy—bringing in the mental capacity of thought and developing the buddhic partial *sense* of love/wisdom (which is only a *capacity* of spiritual thought in the higher mental body). These people's mental plane service may also add to this experiential factor during love-making because it increases love/wisdom. Intuition might also be experienced during sexual love-making as a shared partial buddhic sense. The totality of the sexual experience leads to long enough periods for joy to become bliss for, often, several astral hours during and following the love-making. Only a few people on the physical plane have such sexual experiences, and all of them are spiritually disciplined and at, naturally, similar levels of creating virtue (they are co-serving together). People may remain astrally married for many hundreds of years, with bliss that only increases from their sexual experiences together. The sensation of oneness between two such people gives each a glimpse into the sensation of sensing all life, as a co-creator with God. More of this sensation is available to those who are sexually involved on the first astral sub-plane; further explanation will follow, later in this chapter.

On the astral sub-planes below the second, the level of the inhabitants' sense is the limiting factor in sensing proportionally increased differences in the quantum constant's effects between sub-planes. However, inhabitants of the second and first astral sub-planes can sense the lower sub-planes at the level of their empathic sense if this level is greater than about thirty-five percent and if it is used to create more light (love) within the space between the two sub-planes that are separated. What separates two sub-planes is darkness, or the illusion of the inhabitants' own thoughts. Thus because people on the second astral sub-plane are often creating more love (light) between the sub-plane they are on and some lower ones, they can sense to a lower-level sub-plane that has a greater than thirty-five percent difference in the quantum constant. In other words, they can sense to whatever level their empathy and love (which was created from the use of that empathy), or super-empathy, has developed in their service to those on the lower sub-plane that they are sensing. On the second sub-plane, the highest average level of super-empathy is about fifty percent, and when used in service allows some of the spiritual disciples to sense to the fifth sub-plane; a few can sometimes even sense to the sixth sub-plane on rare occasions (if they can exceed the fifty-percent levels of super-empathy). One-half of (about) twenty-one is (about) ten and a half; the quantum constant on the fifth astral sub-plane is about twelve times greater in its effect than on the dense physical plane. On the sixth astral sub-plane, the effect is about nine times greater. Notice that as a person is able to live on higher astral sub-planes, it is possible for her or him to sense life on more of the lower astral sub-planes. People can focus one or more of their senses on the same space but in a different dilation, or level of separation of time, to sense the sub-planes lower than their own. The less amount of time that they separate from space, the more they experience, through the light of the Ray Lord of their plane, the time and space of the Ray Lord's whole dimension—which includes some of the lower sub-planes relative to where these people live.

Example of Life on the First and Second Astral Sub-Planes

Spiritual groups on the first and second astral sub-planes live in large group houses that are often located in park-like settings. On the second astral sub-plane most residents remain within their respective ray groups and houses. On the first astral sub-plane the spiritual disciples more often may change residences from time to time—to live with groups of a different ray or the same ray—as needed in their service. Notice the dog in the above scenario that sees itself as a human child and becomes one as it functions in the relatively higher consciousness of these two highest astral sub-planes.

Illustration 8.16

The spiritual disciples who live on the first astral sub-plane use seventy-five percent of their empathic sense lovingly, as super-empathy (which includes wisdom). They also consistently do so seventy-five percent of the time—separating only twenty-five percent of astral time from space. The effect of the quantum constant is about twenty-four times greater on the first astral sub-plane than on the dense physical sub-planes. One-fourth of twenty-four is six, or about the same as the quantum constant on the seventh astral sub-plane. This means that nearly all first astral sub-plane inhabitants can sense all the way to the seventh astral sub-plane because the time on it is dilated about six times, or has a quantum constant that is six times greater in its effect than the effect of the quantum constant on the dense physical sub-planes. The astrally alive people on the first astral sub-plane can sense all of the astral plane except the eighth sphere, of evil, where the quantum constant is only about three times greater in its effect than that on the dense physical sub-planes. Evil hides itself and the eighth sphere from light in what it perceives to be a means of increasing its power, by lowering its choices, or its vibration, and moving in a direction away from light.

Eventually, life and service on the second astral sub-plane end because either the glamour of desiring to be loved by God reduces empathy to a level at which more love cannot be created, or the glamour is so reduced that the disciple either moves on to the first astral sub-plane or leaves for the lower mental sub-plane on which most of her or his egotism is found. If heaven could be convincingly described as a part of the astral plane and its life, then the second astral sub-plane, and the first, would be the likely places for heaven to be found.

THE FIRST ASTRAL SUB-PLANE

The atomic level of the first astral sub-plane is the part of that sub-plane that is enlightened at its very top level by the love created by those who live on this sub-plane and by the astral Ray Lord. Simply remaining conscious on the first astral sub-plane for long periods of astral time requires seventy-five percent use of empathy and love created from the empathy, or of super-empathy. Such levels also need to be consistently increased as one lives on the plane, or she or he can lose consciousness, or lose love, and fall asleep. Those who can travel to and live on this sub-plane have reached one of three stages. The first is the stage of spiritual discipline of being accepted for initiation, through help by others much higher in consciousness to sense and think beyond their present levels. The second comprises third level initiates who have completed their eighteen renunciations of misuse of the split senses in each of their bodies, or at least for the astral body. The third is composed of those who are beyond the probationary stage of the fourth initiation. An arhat, or fourth level initiate, because of great sacrifice can lose some sense during the probationary stage and some *astral* consciousness, or astral love, while maintaining and even growing mentally in service. This loss is controlled by those in his or her group, whom he or she is serving. If an arhat dies from physical life during the beginning, or the probationary stage, of that initiation, he or she may first travel to the second astral sub-plane for a relatively brief period of time, because the losses in sense and astral love need to be made up for, and the emotions must be converted into love.

Those who arrive on the first astral sub-plane directly from the etheric plane are leaders and some are even advanced *T*eachers, who are usually arhats *who have students*; such students who are alive on the first astral sub-plane can serve once again in their *T*eacher's group and be reunited with him or her or may become functional students while alive on the sub-plane. With the effect of the quantum constant about twenty-four times greater on the first sub-plane than on the physical sub-planes, a person on this sub-plane could live up to twelve hundred astral plane years—although few ever do.

The emphasis of the spiritual groups on the first astral sub-plane is on both the destruction of the causes of glamour and the creative increase of the growth of love—and God—in life. Most of the astral plane illusion is gone on this first astral sub-plane because so much of the astral Ray Lord's light has been and continues to be created there; people on the first astral sub-plane are consistently creating this kind of virtue no less than seventy-five percent of the time. Each person who has recently arrived is expected to have a plan, which he or she created, to improve the service of the ray type of group that she or he also has chosen (possibly indirectly) to serve within. The efficacy of these people's plans and their focus on service shows leadership, high levels of super-empathy, and the ability to use love as a higher spiritual sense of *being* a functional part of God. Rather than sometimes creating more of God but mostly just understanding more of God in life—which is the focus of those who are on the second astral sub-plane—spiritual disciples on the first astral sub-plane are *consistently* creating more of God. The change in life between the first and second astral sub-planes is greater than can clearly be communicated to most of those who are alive physically and are reading this, since there is no equivalent lifestyle in the physical world that even remotely resembles the lifestyle on the first astral sub-plane. *Three-fourths or more of the time*, the inhabitants of the first astral sub-plane live as a functional part of God, as God exists through the astral Ray Lord on the astral plane. A part of their function is to lead other groups in the methods and approaches of creating virtue along their ray type of group; this ray focus is much more based upon creation of virtue than on selfishness because it uses mostly super-empathy. With super-empathy the higher mental body and the thought and light of the soul are an integral part of the virtue that is created. Many people on this sub-plane have reached the accepted stage of the second initiation; some are accepted first level initiates, and the remainder are third and fourth level initiates. A person's acceptance for initiation means that that person needs assistance from higher sources of consciousness in order to increase her or his service. Initiation is not a "rank" based upon past accomplishment; one's service to others is considered to be at the level that she or he is serving them at any one moment in time. Since such service is recognized by the hierarchial consciousness of nearly everyone on the first (and second) astral sub-plane, there is no need to obey or think like others because of some perceived thought about another person's level of initiation or the stage within the initiation that he or she might be in. Humility, respect for virtue, and overall higher consciousness that is hierarchial eliminate the need at any particular time to follow, or be led by, others' levels of initiation, if those levels are even known (to avoid creating illusions, these levels are not, normally, discussed). Initiation is a responsibility to provide service and is not a right of authority or power.

Those on the first astral sub-plane are overcoming glamours concerning the following: self-authority; leading through force rather than example (with the exception of doing so with evil, which will be explained later in this chapter); serving through self rather than Self sacrifice while giving/teaching/loving; and eliminating self discipline in general in favor of Self discipline. This last condition is the most difficult of the above-listed factors to change, and is probably the most difficult one for the readers to fully understand. The glamour of self discipline is the desire to sacrifice, or limit, one's self in order to become more a part of God (in astral life, in these cases). It can, and often does, lead to the other fetters, or selfish use of the senses that precede it and the subsequent wrong behaviors described in the above paragraph and in this one. Thus a spiritual fetter is wrong use of a sense, and the behavior associated with that wrong use.

To destroy the glamour of self-authority, the disciple on the first astral sub-plane needs to develop much more of the higher sense of the Self, or of a higher-level mental plane spirit—sacrificing much of the self as it fuses with the Self. The personality also has to (first) give up control over most of the self before the process can continue; it has immense fears of such loss of control because *it believes that it is really dying* as it gives up this control. The fear is caused by the remaining twenty-five percent (or less) of emotional energy, or astral selfishness, that is left in the astral body, along with the egotism that is in its mental body. Fortunately, the higher sources of consciousness, including the Solar Angel (the mental Self is the lowest part of the Solar Angel's Self structure), help the personality and self by focusing much more enlightened energy and higher thought into the astral body so that the personality can more clearly sense God as it gives up its self. The sensation is an overwhelming love and protection from the personality's previously self-created fears of death that result from emotionalism (astral self-ishness). The personality usually responds by allowing the continuation of the "death" process that it erroneously perceives to be occurring. The greatest level of experiencing the entire effect, including the "death" of the bodies of focused discipline, is at the initiation ceremony wherein the previously ebbing and flowing self to Self becomes fixed, or fused into more higher Self, and the personality also becomes permanently fused with the soul at a higher level. Every series of increased lessening of the personality's control over the self is, in spiritual terms, called a crisis. The largest spiritual crisis during an initiation takes place during and right after the initi-ation is completed, when permanently higher fusion occurs between the personality and soul, and the self and Self. Note that in initiation the lower self is fusing with a part of the lowest part of the Solar Angel, which is, also, the (higher) Self of a person and a part shared by his or her soul. (See Chapter Five for a more complete explanation of this concept.)

Spiritual leadership that is virtuous requires that the personality not seek to control the self because if it does, then it will seek, or desire, to control other people's selves. People on the first astral sub-plane spend hundreds of astral plane years overcoming this selfishness within the astral body. Each spiritual group provides invaluable aid in helping all of its members to check each other, to assist in the destruction of these glamours. Once the glamours are mostly controlled a first astral sub-plane resident can begin service on the lower sub-planes, helping to destroy glamours at their source of self-focused astral energy, or emotionalism. These people also direct and integrate, through their potential leadership, the much more separative groups on the second astral sub-plane. Some of the people who serve in this way are advanced initiates (third or fourth level initiates) who are either at the accepted stage of the third initiation or are arhats, and therefore create themselves into *T*eachers (who can choose to have students) who create new knowledge *mentally* and teach it on the highest two astral sub-planes. In the next physical lifetime, each of these advanced initiates will be a *T*eacher of one or more groups on the physical plane, some of them for the first time. There are seldom enough *T*eachers to teach in all of the groups on the two highest astral sub-planes (or on the other planes as well). The shortage exists because the number of advanced initiates in general is quite low, and they serve for *less* time than most of the other astral servers do since they are less astrally selfish overall, and thus spend less time on the astral plane.

Life on the first astral sub-plane is centered around service. Generally, only those who serve together become intimate as lovers; their at least seventy-five percent co-service ties them together in time and space, and when they leave the astral plane, they usually leave together. Sexual relations between two lovers who are mostly co-servers and leaders are acts of creation of love for all those who are served through each partner's intuitional, or buddhic, body. The astral love is mostly raised to a relatively unconditional love that is expressed intuitively, or through intuitive thought while the two partners give love between each other. Instead of giving love for the other person, the love is given for those whom the other person (co-) serves (with his or her partner). This intuitional love transforms each partner's intuitional body into a better sense of buddhi, or whole (enlightened) ways of creating beauty on our planet. The sensation that each partner experiences is quite intense because each usually has significant amounts of etheric/dense physical sense fused to her or his super-empathy. In addition, each experiences the other as a growing, functional part of God and in all of life that he or she is currently serving.

All sense of loneliness (which is actually an effect of selfishness) is removed during the love act and for some time afterwards. Love for all of life that each is capable of serving dramatically increases—usually permanently. The souls of the two people share the causal part of their higher mental bodies as well, which then remain semi-permanently connected until their release during the fourth initiation. Their two Solar Angels and Selves also share a greater oneness.

The first astral sub-plane is *more* than heaven is traditionally represented to be, because rather than being in God's presence as a benevolently kept person who is favored by God, people are a functional part of God and co-create virtue as they become God's purpose. This "heaven" is the creative, dynamic, and most meaningful one possible while alive on the astral plane. It convinces those who are there that the hidden meaning in life is revealed by the creation of light and the destruction of darkness, rather than following some presumption of an external and removed Higher Being. Being a functional part of God and its purpose and plan is the greatest astral reward possible because to *Be* is of such greater magnitude of meaning than to just follow and replicate.

There are far fewer children on the second and first astral sub-planes because most children with such high consciousness when physically alive will live long enough to reach adulthood. There are the exceptions that result from unusual karmic circumstances, which are often related to serving those who remain physically living after the child dies. Whatever the reason for their physical deaths, children who travel to the second and especially the first astral sub-plane grow up *faster* than do those who are physically alive. These children mature *much* more quickly than the children on the lower astral sub-planes do. The speed of maturation is brought about by the usually exceptional remaining astral senses from birth, on, in children who died between the ages of seven and fourteen—or often even older; in children younger than seven, some or most of the astral sense was often not fully developed. Older children who have the higher astral consciousness that is needed for travel to the two highest astral sub-planes usually have exceptional astral sense from the high consciousness, and less destruction of the astral senses because they died so early from physical life. Another factor that adds to the speed of maturation is the parents and the group the children are raised by, giving them more ways to create virtue and to become more loving. Perhaps the most significant means through which these children advance so quickly in spiritual development is through the opportunity to both learn *and serve* through the group that they and their parents are a part of. Children on the two highest astral sub-planes, and especially the first, are encouraged to serve by creating virtue.

The love that these children receive is beyond description; it helps to create them into extraordinary servers of precocious abilities—proving that love is the most fertile ground for raising Godly children. Because of their rarity on the two highest astral sub-planes, children are cherished by nearly all inhabitants there. A very few children from the fourth or third astral sub-plane might also travel to the second astral sub-plane, if they had very loving parents who were spiritually disciplining themselves while on the lower astral sub-plane or sub-planes. Adult inhabitants of the two highest astral sub-planes do not adopt children from lower sub-planes in the method that requires choosing to live on these lower sub-planes. The reason is that the adults' service is required on their own respective sub-planes and their groups need them, and thus for these people to live on a lower sub-plane—even if for the purpose of adopting children of lower consciousness—would be selfish.

Pets on the first astral sub-plane often have greater ability to think than some human residents do on the seventh or sixth astral sub-planes; these pets are all much more conscious, or loving, than those people are. While physically alive, these pets were typically pets of advanced disciples and of spiritual groups on the physical plane. These animals actually participate in the service of their spiritual groups on the first astral sub-plane because they can *understand* the more basic elements of the group's plan. Communication with most of these animals is like communication with average physically alive children of about age twelve. These pets can serve on the lower astral sub-planes in simpler, but quite effective ways. They often create themselves into the image of a human—often a child of around twelve or so—which the lower sub-plane inhabitants believe to be angel-children who are helping them to become more virtuous. The pets usually accompany one or more group members in their travels to the lower sub-planes, and often tremendously enjoy the opportunity to serve in the image and somewhat the capacity of a human. They can serve in this way because they can somewhat sense using all seven of the human senses. Doing so prepares them for their eventual individualization into the human kingdom, which many of them will experience much earlier than when their entire kingdom will advance. These advanced pets are the correspondence in their kingdom of advanced initiates in the human kingdom. To a greater extent than on the lower astral sub-planes, advanced pets take the place of children in receiving the total amount of love from all the adults that would be bestowed upon children if there were enough of them present on the first astral sub-plane. The pets on the first astral sub-plane are more like average children on the etheric/dense physical plane, although the children who are on this sub-plane are so exceptional that no pet could reach their levels of consciousness.

 ## SUMMARY OF SOME ETHERIC AND ASTRAL LIFE

Before describing and explaining the life of humans in either the eighth sphere or on the mental plane, because of the amount of information thus far presented about life on the etheric and astral sub-planes, a summation of these subtle worlds might, at this point, be helpful to the reader. Etheric plane life for humans is usually brief, and its meaning is to lessen the apprehension and outright fears the personality has about dying from the physical world. Additional meaning may be gained on the etheric plane by some people who need closure to their physical lives. Some people need little or no part of such life because they strongly desire to live astrally and either do not believe that their selves will cease to exist after physical death, or they do not fear this very much; also, they desire little from continued physical life. These people may nearly instantly travel to the astral world. The majority of people, however, have enough fear of death and also experience enough of a loss of the physical world that they desire to remain in the etheric world. They generally stay on the etheric sub-plane (the fourth etheric sub-plane) for several days to several weeks. It is typical for such a person to witness his or her funeral service and—before, during, and after such services—to watch the mourning of those whom he or she left behind. These recently physically deceased people find meaning in the observation of such activities because it integrates each of these people's prior life with what will become his or her astral life. It also provides more closure, or increases the meaning of some parts of the life he or she has just left, as well as the meaning of that person's physical death.

A few people desire to not live astrally, and these include the people who commit suicide for self-focused reasons. Since desire is the controlling factor that brings one to the astral plane, these people can become stuck on the etheric plane after physical death. Some are obsessed with elements of physical life that they did not get enough meaning from, and seek more than anything else to experience them. In either case, those who remain on the etheric sub-plane for more than a month or two, but sometimes for much less time if their etheric senses are already quite damaged from selfishness, can become ghosts. A ghost is a quantum constant anomaly that causes the normal quantum constant to change in the specific location the ghost stays in usually for more than several days at a time. The effect is caused by atoms in a ghost being in two different parts of space and time at the same time, and being informed by different thoughts from different surrounding spirit. This condition is greatly aggravated by burying the physical body while the ghost chooses to consistently stay in a location other than the burial site. The effect over time causes the ghost's senses and brain to greatly diminish and become confused. As a result, the ghost then greatly loses its self and becomes open to possession by dark beings on the lowest astral sub-plane as well as by creatures on the etheric sub-planes. Such awful experiences can last nearly a hundred physical years, or over one hundred thirty etheric sub-plane years. The longer that the ghost remains on the etheric sub-plane, and mostly in one location, the more senseless it becomes; sometimes ghosts are successfully resurrected towards having astral life, and then become freed from the etheric plane. Some of the people who committed suicide are particularly difficult to rescue because they were so convinced, for selfish, or self-focused, reasons, that they wanted to die. The subsequent life as a ghost and its suffering from loss of self lead to a "cure" for the desire for death, and astral life then seems meaningful to the ghost. This meaning is usually on a purely emotional and not mental level. Thus the loss of the ability to sense and be conscious in life eventually leads, through senselessness and suffering, to a desire for meaning that overcomes the desire for death.

Unless someone is evil (as discussed later in this chapter), the astral worlds are places to live out almost all of the desires that went unmet during physical plane life. Nearly all of these desires are selfish, and cause astral energy to respond as emotions rather than as love. The typical meaning of early astral plane life on the five lowest sub-planes (not including the eighth sphere) is to meet as many desires as possible, to satiate them as much as the consciousness of the person finds appropriate for himself or herself, and to be "happy." The meaning to life on these sub-planes eventually changes because astral selfishness destroys the forms, or the astral bodies, of those who live on the astral plane. As the astral bodies and senses of a person there diminish, so does her or his self. The self loses consciousness when it cannot give as much to less of a body and its lessened senses; the loss of consciousness, or understanding of life, commensurately causes a loss of meaning to life. The personality becomes fearful of dying and begins to realize, as it suffers from loss of self, that its fixed desires (its glamours) are controlling it rather than the reverse taking place. A crisis and battle then often ensue for control of the astral life. Within this struggle, the person (the personality, its bodies, and the self) finds new meaning to astral life—the meaning is to love. The period of time needed to increase love and decrease emotionalism varies greatly on each astral sub-plane. As love replaces emotionalism, the astral permanent atom, containing the pattern for the astral body and creating in the next incarnated lifetime, becomes more enlightened as better-thinking (albeit still only slightly-thinking) astral energies replace less able-thinking astral energy in the astral permanent atom.

Life's hidden astral meaning then becomes revealed as the creation of more astral virtue, or more love. It is even possible to elevate one's life to a more loving astral world on a higher sub-plane by creating enough love to do so. In some people, the soul has the opportunity to become more of a part of humanity, through fusion. Only the virtuous parts of the human can become one with the soul. This develops the soul through the lower worlds' life experiences *that are virtuous*. All other parts of human life, which are selfish, become destroyed and eventually cease to exist as self memory (they remain a part of the akasha). These effects of the selfishness within each body remain in the corresponding permanent atoms as karma for the next incarnation or even incarnations. To have memory requires about sixty percent of sense enlightenment, in order to create adequate continuity of events and to join enough time to space within each brain. Without this minimum level of joined time and space, memory becomes lost, and so, eventually, does the self. The personality greatly fears its loss of self because this loss causes suffering, pain, and what the personality believes to be its death. Death of consciousness, or love, is not possible. This will be explained later in this chapter. Those who have fears about death and are concerned that their awareness and consciousness will eventually die might be having those fears partly confirmed through the information presented thus far as the hidden meaning of life is explained; it is important to note that such a conclusion is not the case. It would be helpful for anyone who might be having these fears to relax them and to read the remainder of this chapter.

THE EIGHTH SPHERE, OF EVIL

The description of human life on the astral sub-planes will conclude with the following explanation of the eighth sphere, which is where evil chooses to live. Technically, there are seven sub-planes, or dimensions, on the astral plane; they correspond to the seven sub-rays of the sixth, or astral, ray. The eighth sphere is mostly created through the focus of human thought reversing, as much as possible, the combined thought within the seven sub-rays of the astral plane. By reversing thought is meant that the same choices are used, but they are connected in the opposite way, or in the opposite direction, turning an effect into a cause and a cause into an effect. There is little creativity in this method of thought because new choices are seldom made, mostly just the reversal of thought in order to render it moving in the opposite direction of God's thought in form, or the reverse of virtue. The reason that so few new choices are made is that tremendous forces are produced when one creates, or makes choices that are unique, against God's thought, or against light. Although doing so is possible, the majority of evil people are seldom capable of such creation because someone must endure the results of these forces, which reduce a person's ability to think and be conscious. "The Plan" of very evil people is to direct the forces onto others who are selfish—but less selfish than themselves—and who, through their selfishness, can be victimized, or can have forces imposed upon them from evil creation through *new* choices. Most evil people are not (yet) evil enough to accomplish much creation of new thought, or new choices in their thought against God's thought, or light. The reversal of thought is accomplished by thinking of the effect first and deliberately thinking backwards to the cause of any particular thought. There is another step in this process, concerning a certain manipulation of both thoughtforms and astral energy, that is being deliberately omitted from this explanation so as to not encourage people to try to create evil thought, or, worse, practice doing so. Evil people themselves seldom understand what it is they are doing to think in evil, and why, because their consciousness is too low to have such understanding. An enlightened person, without selfishness, or even one with relatively little selfishness cannot be victimized by evil because most or all of such a person's thought is in God's direction of thought, or in the direction of God's consciousness. The forces that are created from choices that are against God's thought, or against light, cannot be attracted to (gravitate towards) either light or an enlightened person. Enlightened people are still, however, affected by all or any parts of life that lose light and have God's growth of life reduced within them. Any time that evil people reverse the direction of God's thought, or, worse, directly victimize others through forces imposed upon them through new choices that are created against God's choices, *all* of life is somewhat affected.

When evil people simply reverse the direction of God's thought, or light, they are *nearly* completely separating choices from oneness (connectedness of the choices, or love/consciousness); doing so also causes space to become maximally separated between any two forms, or energies, within it. Reversing the connectedness of choices does not create consciousness. Rather, it destroys consciousness because connectedness that is reversed *cannot* further *give*. The consciousness of one thought can be replicated in another thought, but only as choices are *reduced*, which then reduces the totality both of thought and of the overall connectedness of thought. Reversing connectedness *can* limit the field through destruction of choices, but not through consciousness. The reversal replaces the growth of consciousness through use of power—and increased forces. The opposing in near-equal amounts of choices within the same field of thought creates a structure, or formula, or mostly cancellation of forces and a type of crystallization of form that preserves it, but without potential for growth unless *new* choices are made. Those evil people who rely on mostly or on only reversing the direction of God's thought cannot grow their lives. The even more "successful" evil people can make new choices against God's thought, or against light, and also can reverse the direction of light. They are then able to direct the forces onto other people who are at least moderately if not more selfish, and they reduce the others' both choices *and* consciousness at the same time. Then these very evil people's astral senses can grow by the amount that the growth in life is reduced of each of their victims. As the selfish victims are reduced in their growth of life, or God's growth, the very evil people grow in power. By directing the forces from their new choices against God's choices, the evil people are also altering the density of certain astral and lower mental energies, creating more power; this gives them power "over" their victims. It should be noted that all victims of the evil of others are karmically linked to those others through their own levels of selfishness. The darker levels of energies in the selfish people's bodies respond to the evil thought of the evil people...all as an effect of the selfish people having attracted the dark energy into themselves, thus creating the karmic relationship.

People who live in the eighth sphere can be identified as belonging to one of two groups. The first and by far the largest is composed of evil people who think almost entirely by reversing the direction (the consciousness/love) of God's thought (of light) to create darkness. The second and considerably smaller group of evil inhabitants is those who are even more evil, and are capable of creating new choices against God's choices. They produce tremendous forces through destroying both choices and consciousness—God's thought. Then, instead of destroying themselves with these tremendous forces, they are able to direct these forces onto others— sometimes many others—who become their victims and fall under their power. Mostly, members of the second, much more evil group direct their power and the forces onto the much larger group that is less capable of evil thought. To release some of the forces that are on themselves, this larger group then creates more darkness in others who typically might not be evil, but are selfish enough to become karmically affected by the thought of those who are. The darkness is created mostly by reducing these others' consciousness, or love. An evil hierarchy of thought is created in this system, with those higher in their capability to create evil thought being more capable of directly creating forces in those with a lower capability to do so. Those who have the lowest capability of thinking evilly must attempt to reduce the forces in their bodies by preying on and gaining power over selfish people who are not in the eighth sphere. The less evil people are caught in a process that is not very efficient because of the separation of time and space. As a result, the evil ones in this position experience pain from the energy loss that is produced by forces and entropy, and they suffer because of the loss of consciousness, as their selves can give less to their damaged bodies. Those people towards the bottom of the pyramid, who are less capable of evil thought, usually attempt to increase their abilities to think evilly so that they can gain more power over others. While they gain power over others they reduce their pain and suffering (which is actually only a temporary state of relief, but they fail to understand this), and create growth to their respective lives of evil by decreasing the growth of other lives— which, of course, are actually all a part of one life! This evil system is a "pyramid system," with those who are the most evil at the top, and those who are least evil at the bottom. Most of the inhabitants of the eighth sphere are closer to or at the bottom. All of evil's growth is dependent upon the destruction of growth of non-evil—but still selfish—other parts of life.

Depending upon the amount of evil that a person created in his or her most recent physical life, after physical death he or she will travel to the eighth sphere and become a part of the pecking order within the "pyramid" of the amount of evil choices and reversal of consciousness, or connectedness of the choices, that he or she will have. Those who created enormous amounts of evil in the last life, and who may have done so in prior lives as well, may be able to create many more choices against God's choices, and direct the forces to underlings who are much lower in the pyramid. Those who are higher in the pyramid gain not only their own power, but all the power from those below them whom they direct some force to and who are victimizing even others who are lower, as well as possibly some non-evil but selfish others. The people who are more evil are able to fully crystallize their bodies. They do so by both redirecting most forces, through the creation of more evil choices, and by opposing virtuous choices through nearly reversing the direction of love into almost complete separation from all choices, which is the opposite of oneness. Note that the opposite of love is not hate, but complete indifference for the life of others and is created by the effect of separation. One way to identify evil in people is by this indifference to life in others. Crystallization enables evil people in the eighth sphere to live for very long periods of time, seemingly, to themselves, becoming immortal. Evil crystallization of the astral and etheric/dense physical permanent atoms allows the evil to continue and to grow between incarnations, by sensing life in evil ways. Also, some continuity of evil consciousness between lifetimes is developed, fairly soon after becoming evil and giving up one's soul, which increases the (false) belief in evil people that they are becoming immortal. The ultimate goal of evil people on the eighth sphere is to reach near the top of the pyramid of evil thought and to become a dark master who does not need to physically incarnate, and whose astral body is so crystallized through evil that he can live for the equivalent of many thousands of physical plane years with no apparent appreciable degradation in his astral body. Note that there are no advanced (beyond the third evil initiation) dark masters who are permanently female because males are usually more capable of achieving a higher level of evil. All evil females eventually (in the third evil initiation) become male on a long-term basis if they continue to grow in evil. This effect is caused by there being much less of the second part, or the feminine aspect, of God's mind in the lives of evil people; with the first and third parts exaggerated, and especially the third part, the most power is gained through being male. Even at the very bottom of the evil pyramid, the greater numbers of men than women on the eighth sphere are due to a lack of the second aspect of God's mind—and of love—in this realm. Women cannot proactively negate love as easily as men can on average. The reason is that the indifference to and separation of life lowers women's consciousness too quickly, causing greater levels of suffering and proportionately less power than in a man. When women become evil it is usually through association with men, or sometimes through sexual perversions and prostitution, drugs, and/or certain extreme types of homosexuality (but not homosexuality in general) that often include sadism. An exception to this can occur when a very evil man (nearly a dark master) chooses to incarnate as a woman and has enough continuity of evil consciousness to make choices while physically alive to lead other women (as well as some men) into evil. These evil female leaders are rare, but almost always are still relying on having been male in the prior lifetime, to help them to create more evil thought. After a lifetime as a female, the evil person usually returns to being a male in the next life.

On the eighth sphere a third sub-class exists, in addition to the first two thus far described. This sub-class is made up of the less evil people who inhabit the eighth sphere. Some of those who are lower on the evil "pyramid" still have a human soul and OverSoul. These people can "lose" their respective souls and OverSouls only through making enough evil *choices* that are against God's choices. The amount of choices that are necessary to create a force great enough to break the thought and hold of the soul and OverSoul is relative, and is inversely proportionate to the person's level of advancement in prior human incarnations. A soul that is well developed from numerous human incarnations that were relatively virtuous can tolerate much less force created by a human who is choosing to create new evil thought through new choices that are against God's choices, within Its light, or thought. The OverSoul of a formerly virtuous person is less helpful in its enlightened thought, as well. The reason is that more vortices on such a person's mental unit are spinning, and they are spinning much faster in a more advanced human. This allows more force to be created against the Solar Angel's thought, including the conscience. Thus the more developed a human is, with an advanced soul and OverSoul, the *easier* it is for him or her to "lose" his or her soul and OverSoul by creating evil choices. It is not possible to "lose" the soul and OverSoul *only* by reversing the direction of God's thought, or love, because in that case insufficient force would be produced against the soul or OverSoul. Most first-time arrivals on the eighth sphere, at the bottom of the pyramid of evil thought, still do have their souls.

"Losing" the soul is the taking of the first evil initiation and creating some level of evil continuity of consciousness. Doing so requires the creation of new evil thought that is inversely proportionate to the level of development of the human, his or her soul, and OverSoul. The more advanced a person is, the less new evil choices that are required to "lose" the soul and OverSoul. Evil people in the eighth sphere celebrate arrivals who have advanced souls. These new arrivals are likely to become soulless sooner than the others are, and to give more power to those above them faster because these new arrivals increase more quickly in evil. Those without souls and OverSouls "choose" their own incarnations within the forces that are imposed upon them by those who are above them in the pecking order; many of these soulless people also strive to gain more power by creating more evil choices. Without a soul or OverSoul, when the personality is evil it feels completely in control—and therefore immortal, and fearless of death—in a peculiar, paradoxical way. The personality's sense of control over the self is total, and no soul or OverSoul and its Self are going to interfere with that control. However, the self continues to diminish, extremely slowly. This happens because of the opposing/balancing of forces in the bodies and the inability to redirect forces while *adding* to the evil parts of the self (the self still experiences a net loss to itself) that convert the self from love into indifference for life. Overall, over very long periods of time, the self will diminish because eventually the amount that is added to it by evil consistently very slightly lags behind its loss of love. This condition occurs because time is separated from space at increasing amounts, preventing a parity in creation of evil to loss of love. As the personality (very slightly but consistently) loses its self, and consciousness, it mostly subconsciously gains fear of death—even as it is consciously believing that it is becoming immortal by becoming more evil. Thus the great illusion caused by evil prevents it from understanding, and from even receiving enough awareness from its senses, that it is very slowly dying and suffering while it becomes more evil. This condition is especially accelerated in its effect, once the soul and OverSoul are forced to break off their communication and involvement with the evil person, but is also offset by increasing power from evil choices that are successfully made against God, with the forces inflicted on victims.

Evil people who have "lost" their souls and OverSouls, or, more accurately stated, who have chosen to remove themselves from them, may live for well over ten thousand to even a hundred thousand astral plane years (or about a third as many physical plane years) before they become senseless as well as lose their human level of consciousness. A few of the most advanced dark masters are said to be half a million astral years old—still with consciousness and senses—and have not had a physical incarnation for over four hundred fifty thousand astral years. Unlike less evil people, a very evil person, and any dark master past the second level of evil initiation loses his senses suddenly, as his body cracks in its crystallized structure. The lack of gradual loss of sense further leads evil people into a false, or illusioned, sense of immortality. Once an evil person's body cracks, then physical incarnation, if it is an option, becomes necessary. The evil person's astral centers, senses, and astral permanent atom had been disintegrating the entire time he was focused in life astrally, but the crystallized astral body provided a means, through the use of power, to steal energy, as senses, from others to keep the evil person's astral body viable. These stolen senses made up for the senses the evil person had lost (and continued to lose). By the time that the evil person's astral body does, eventually, crack, his own senses, centers, and astral permanent atom have become so reduced he no longer exists astrally as a human. Without the stolen energy that his crystallized astral body provided, he suddenly becomes reduced to the form of life that has the same number of centers and senses that he has remaining. If he wants to regain those centers and senses he must incarnate etheric/dense physically, as explained immediately below. However, doing so is possible only if the evil person's most recent physical incarnation took place within the previous approximately thirty thousand to forty thousand physical plane years because his etheric/dense physical permanent atom, which contains the blueprint for the etheric/dense physical body and senses, remains intact for no longer than that. Because the evil person's etheric/dense physical senses are not used while he is focused in life astrally, they remain mostly complete and unchanged as long as the permanent atom remains viable. While reincarnated etheric/dense physically, his astral body recuperates because it is no longer the body where his (very low) consciousness is focused. Because the evil person believes himself to be immortal, and the cracking of the astral body hence always comes as a surprise, he does not plan to reincarnate etheric/dense physically within his "window of opportunity" to do so. An evil person whose astral body has cracked through crystallization and has no etheric/dense physical permanent atom must leave the group soul of evil. The reason is that this group soul is, paradoxically, unable to create a replacement body whose forces are more balanced, because the maximum amount of separation of the atoms and forces within the body has been achieved with the level of remaining consciousness. Since the group soul of evil only takes, it abandons the person because he can no longer contribute to it. Such a person must find another soul that will ensoul him and create a body for him. Usually it will be a group soul from the (lower part of the) animal kingdom, but sometimes one from an even lower kingdom is needed. The level of group soul that ensouls and creates a body for the evil person is determined by the amount of centers and senses he still had left when his astral body cracked.

The evil person's self and consciousness *remain* at the same level as when the final crack occurred, because the self is focused upon taking, using evil thought, rather than giving. While far less than those of even some below average humans, the evil person's self and consciousness are still higher than the self and consciousness of most animals. What this means is that once an evil person's astral (or lower mental) body cracks, he will live out countless lifetimes through the lower animal kingdom (starting out as a worm, for example) or in an even lower one, gradually developing forms, or bodies, as he progresses through higher-level group souls until he advances into the human kingdom when the entire animal kingdom does. Finally, the evil consciousness returns to being human, and resumes human life with a new, young soul. The process very effectively "cures" most evil people of being evil because the self cannot effectively give at a level that a human can while that self is a worm, for example, and quickly diminishes in each life—which causes great suffering. However, if someone still chooses to be evil after having gone through all of this, he can start the process over again as many times as he chooses to. Few ever repeat that process once, no human has ever gone through it for a third time on earth, and it is possible that no human anywhere in our universe has ever done so.

The misunderstood, and wrong, concept of transmigration of souls originated from some evil people at first convoluting the information that is explained above. Except for evil under the circumstances that were just described, humans remain with the same human soul and as part of the human kingdom until they advance into the Kingdom of Souls, either through self-initiation or when humans as a kingdom advance. The group soul of evil does not have enough of the second aspect of God's mind within it to *create* life within a lifeform; this deficiency in the second aspect of God's mind is also what causes the group soul to eventually fail to make a dark master's body immortal. The primary body of an evil person is the astral body, because evil people live mostly through their desires and emotions; once this body cracks, or dies without having been rested through a physical incarnation (in which the physical senses and body are primary), the evil group soul can no longer inform the lifeform. As a result, the energies of the bodies cease to be held together. Thus evil cannot truly create life; it merely uses that which was previously created by some type of more enlightened spirit. When the bodies of some of the more evil people and of dark masters finally crack, these evil ones must live through one or more lower kingdoms on their way back up to the human kingdom. Which lower kingdom a very evil person or a dark master begins in—the mineral, the vegetable, or the animal—is dependent upon the number of centers he has left at the time that his body cracks. For example, if the dark master had only a part of one (astral) center left, he would begin in the mineral kingdom; if one or two, then the plant kingdom, and if three, the animal. The level to which the dark master's sense, body, and lifeform regress equals the real, or astral, level to which his human body had diminished in centers and sense, even though the degradation was hidden by the evil crystallization. To this writer's knowledge, "advanced" dark masters on earth have gone all the way back to the vegetable kingdom, possibly starting as algae; some may have started as bacteria or fungi, within a parasitic sub-kingdom. Although it would be possible, thus far (to the best of this writer's knowledge) no dark masters from earth have ever become members of the mineral kingdom, because it is nearly impossible for an earthly human self, even a very low one, to gain any sense from just one center and its sense of pre-life. Under these circumstances and as conditions have existed on earth for billions of years, the self of the mineral kingdom's group soul would be repaid very little, if anything, karmically. A planet in its first solar incarnation would have group souls and their selves that might benefit from some dark masters having to begin again as minerals. Since none of this is punishment—it is karmic effect, to correct previous causes—the effects need to in some ways serve others that or who were harmed; otherwise, the karma would just create more karma. If hell exists, then what a soulless evil person endures, eventually, is as close as can be conceived. Living millions of years with a near-human consciousness, but as low levels of lifeforms that have little or no ability to express the self, and with the self in each lifetime immensely diminishing in its consciousness because there are so few senses and means of giving thought to them, creates unimaginable amounts of suffering—over, and over again. Eventually the result of this system of karma teaches one to create empathy and love, but with suffering as the teacher. Note that the self of the very evil human repays some consciousness to each group soul that informs it. The self of the group soul does *not* have to use as much of its own preconception and filled-in thought while it is being supplemented by the evil person's thought. Mostly the self and consciousness of the evil person and not the self of the group soul are used to inform each lifeform inhabited by the very evil person, because his remaining personality and self are mainly intact to begin with (from the earlier evil creation of both), and are much higher in structure and consciousness than the self of the group soul is. Also, the evil personality wants to maintain its control, even though it is suffering, because it still fears death. The group soul has the consistent input of somewhat human thought to help it grow its self. The group soul will reject any evil thought, and so is protected from the contamination that some (previously) evil people might, from time to time, attempt to "contribute."

Evil people who are astrally alive in the eighth sphere need to be allowed to cause their own karma. They need to be allowed to eventually leave the eighth sphere, through their own choices and consciousness. Through their own choices and consciousness, they might leave either before or fairly soon after they "lose" their souls or after the eventual cracking of the astral body, if the evil person still has an etheric/dense physical permanent atom. As described above, if the evil person no longer has his etheric/dense physical permanent atom, he no longer has the consciousness nor choices and is forced to leave. If people who are trying to be virtuous attempt to use force against evil people who are alive astrally, what will happen is that the evil people's astral bodies will only further crystallize without cracking because evil is *better* at *astrally* using power individually than relatively virtuous people are who attempt its use. The force is converted into power and can even be used as a boomerang against those who, in illusion, attempt to use astral force—even if they are trying to fight evil for virtuous motives. The same circumstance applies to lower mental force against evil. Evil people themselves can use force so effectively astrally and lower mentally because they are substituting power for consciousness, or love.

On the etheric/dense physical plane, it is both permissible and effective to use force against evil. On this plane the changed physics of high gravity and inertia comes close to equalizing the power differences between evil and good by slowing the power down and allowing consciousness (planning, or love) to initially balance out the evil's power. In longer periods of time, good eventually overcomes the power by balancing all or most of it while some (usually smaller) amounts of power are much more intelligently used as a force against the forms of the evil. Also, evil people do not need to be karmically in control of the physical plane destruction of their etheric/dense physical bodies. The reason is that the destruction is an effect of their desires, rather than a part of their life focus for their soul in the three worlds. Even the evil people who still have souls contribute nothing to their souls' growth, which would be a part of God's growth, or life, while they are evil. When force is used by virtuous people against someone who is etheric/dense physically alive, the force must not become astral or mental. Thus in an *appropriate* response, one can affect (up to and including the level of destroying) the etheric/dense physical forms that an evil person is using, including his or her etheric/dense physical body. However, one should not attempt, and in any case would not be successful at, forcing a change in the emotions, creative imagination, or mental thoughts of an evil person; doing so would only make the person more evil, and might also give him or her power over the person or people making such an attempt. Note that the generally applied appropriateness of using etheric/dense physical force against evil needs to be determined by someone (or a group of people) who has developed significant amounts of love/wisdom mentally and, possibly, whole (controlled) intuition as well. To successfully deal with those whose levels of evil *approach* dark masterhood and who are etheric/dense physically incarnate usually requires the thought of and the accompanying high-consciousness component of an advanced, relatively enlightened human initiate.

When evil uses power etheric/dense physically, it often does so in sudden, not very well planned, and frequently violent actions, in order to offset its low consciousness and its resultant virtual inability to effectively plan. Sometimes evil can win against the forces of light in these instances, provided that it does so quickly enough to prevent its force from being balanced in defense, and to prevent the side of light from preparing a plan that will destroy the evil. Technically, evil cannot be physically contained; it either becomes destroyed or it overtakes and grows. To etheric/dense physically contain evil would shift the advantage over prolonged periods of time that goodness, or light, has over evil in its consciousness and ability to plan. This occurs because while contained, evil can build up its power by gradually imbalancing the forces used to contain it. Also, once containment is used, some selfishness usually becomes a part of the consciousness of those who are somewhat enlightened and are fighting the evil. The selfishness on the part of those so fighting is usually a result of a lack of needed sacrifice to destroy evil rather than to just contain it. The added sacrifice would change the etheric/dense physical containment into destruction of the evil. The balancing of evil's force in order to destroy it is not containment, provided it is then followed by destruction of the evil, and not just a temporary abatement of its forces.

The destruction of evil on a plane is spiritually defined as the same energy that evil was using being made available to life and/or used to grow more of life. The light, or God's thought, that is slightly within the energy must increase as a result of whatever actions take place. These are always intelligent in their activity. Canonized laws are most often ineffective in accurately discerning this process. Spiritual thought, leadership, and humility are essential ingredients to understanding right etheric/dense physical action against evil. Astral evil, and lower mental evil that is tied to, or connected to, the astral evil are best dealt with *by containment*, or in an opposite manner to the way that evil is dealt with on the etheric/dense physical plane. Force causes the growth of more evil in these subtle worlds, and consciousness on the higher sub-planes away from evil is usually relatively much higher, permitting containment to work. Evil can exist on an entire planet only within that planet's second solar incarnation. When evil is successfully contained astrally, including its kama-manasically connected thoughtforms on the lower mental plane, it eventually destroys itself before the end of that solar incarnation. If containment fails, because of too much selfishness on the sub-planes above the level at which evil is contained astrally (including kama-manasically), evil can overtake a planet and can ultimately destroy it.

Evil exists cosmically as a group soul of dark spirit and form on the lowest part of the astral plane, in a part of space that contains *almost* no light. This location is outside our galaxy, within one of the oldest galaxies in our universe (and even partly outside the galaxy it was first created within), and is centered in a position that is, in etheric/dense physical (three) dimensions, the point where the first star system completely failed. The failure took place during that star system's second incarnation, which, again, is the only time during which evil can overcome a system. In our existing universe, to date, evil has not completely taken over any galaxy, although it has been successful, in rare (karmic) circumstances, at overtaking more than one star system within the same group, or constellation, of stars and their planets. The separated time and space in the dimensions where evil is found offers protection against the spread of evil from one star system to most others, with some—karmic—exceptions. Again, in most circumstances the containment system is used astrally, on a cosmic level, to keep evil from spreading interstellarly.

Dark Masters and the Evil Ones in the Eighth Sphere

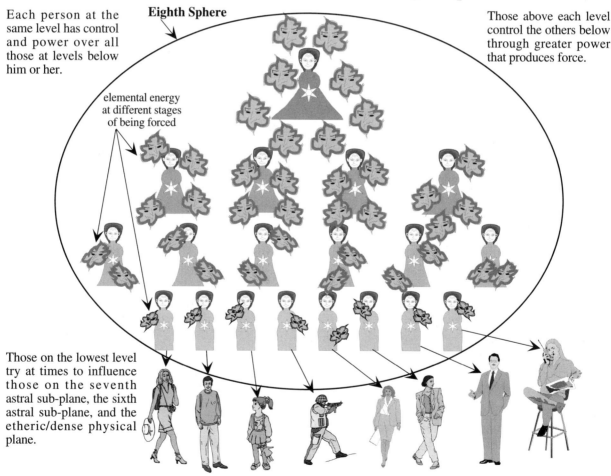

Each person at the same level has control and power over all those at levels below him or her.

Eighth Sphere

Those above each level control the others below through greater power that produces force.

elemental energy at different stages of being forced

Those on the lowest level try at times to influence those on the seventh astral sub-plane, the sixth astral sub-plane, and the etheric/dense physical plane.

Illustration 8.17

Until an evil person chooses to give up his or her individual soul, he or she still has the choice to leave the eighth sphere and face his or her karma for his or her previous evil life. This can be done sooner rather than later. Every one of these people can resurrect himself or herself into a virtuous life. Each evil person who makes the choice to do so will receive help from his or her soul and Solar Angel, as well as from various servers who usually are astrally alive inhabitants of the first astral sub-plane. Once an evil person gives up his or her soul, there are some possibilities of being rejoined with another human soul. As a rare occurrence, the same soul a person gave up can rejoin with that person. For any human soul to join with an evil person who has given up his or her soul, that person's astral and lower mental bodies must still contain all of the senses a human needs to have; these senses are the five of form, and the two that are created through the thought of spirit—about God. These few evil people usually chose to give up their souls not too long before rejoining with another human soul or the same one. The reason is that they still had enough spiritual sense left to change their minds and to seek to have a human soul again. The possibilities for such people are as follows. The first is to receive and join with a soul who recently lost a human incarnation to evil and is *less* developed than this person's original soul and has not yet created a new incarnating person. The second is to join together with a new soul who has yet to incarnate on earth *and* is very undeveloped (these souls are rare because most "new" souls are actually advanced because they have had prior incarnations on other planets). A third, and likely possibility is to join with a returning soul that has spent time on a relatively primitive planet because its earlier incarnations had failed to advance on earth, but now has somewhat caught up with the other souls on earth. And the fourth possibility is to rejoin with the soul he or she gave up, but this is only an option if that soul has not created a new incarnating person. This last possibility carries the provision that the evil person will quickly enough create enough virtue to re-establish a parity level karmically with that soul (overcoming the harm he or she created while evil). The reason is that the evil person lost so much consciousness while separated from a human soul. Once an evil person takes the second dark initiation, of giving up the lower spiritual sense of understanding God, that person can no longer rejoin with a human soul. Instead, he or she (many are male at this point) will go through the earlier-described process of joining with a group soul in a lower kingdom. Those evil people are considered to be dark masters of the lowest, or beginning, level.

Astral death produces much less fear than the corresponding etheric/dense physical death did. The reason is that most people on the astral plane are aware that there is another world of life awaiting them on the lower mental plane. Still, for those who live on the astral sub-planes of form (the third through seventh) some apprehension exists about astral death. This is because these people are unfamiliar with the new world, and they usually do not understand what will take place after death from that new world. They often fear that they will eventually cease to exist. They do not realize that this has already been happening to them as they have been gradually losing their selves as their selfishness caused their senses in each body to diminish. One way that astral people experience death is as a relative process in which they feel in control, while in the other way they fear loss of control and a finality, or non-existence. As will be explained later in this chapter, neither existence nor awareness ceases, nor does consciousness, or love; the fears of losing existence, awareness, or consciousness (or any combination of them) are created from the illusions caused by selfishness.

LIFE ON THE LOWER MENTAL SUB-PLANES

When people die astrally they usually immediately travel through the tunnel of light to the lower mental plane. This occurs because the sutratma, or life thread, is removed from the astral body's energy sphere within the heart center, while the consciousness thread is removed from the spirit sphere whose center and sense were used the most, on average, within the astral body and from the crown center. The consciousness thread is also broken from all other spirit spheres in the astral body. Then the person enters into his or her lower mental body's center and spirit sphere that were used the most, which will also correspond to one of the four lower mental sub-planes. The lower mental sub-plane that he or she first lives on will be the one where he or she used a split lower mental sense the most, creating egotism and, possibly, arrogance as well. The egotism manifests as bands of damaged thoughtforms that are contained as lower mental energy surrounding the outside lower part of the egg-shaped mental body. These bands of retained energies block out, and prevent the lower mental senses from accurately sensing, the thought of others. The bands also distort or block parts of time (or both), since time is the fifth dimension, or the added *whole* dimension, on the mental plane; only a part of time, dimensionally, exists on either the astral or etheric/dense physical plane. The egotism causes an isolation of a person's thought, which creates loneliness and introspection of thought for long periods of mental plane time. The person in such a position has no *emotional* split sense, and can be empathic only to the level that he or she had previously fused empathy with the mental body through love and truth, creating super-empathy.

Illustration of a Mental Body and Mental Centers

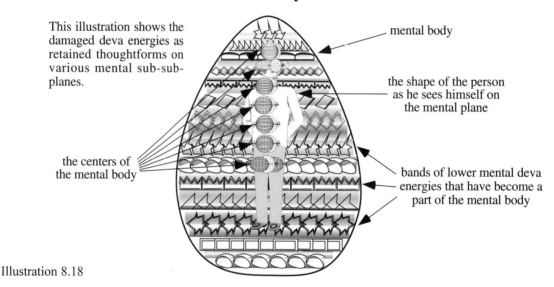

This illustration shows the damaged deva energies as retained thoughtforms on various mental sub-sub-planes.

mental body

the shape of the person as he sees himself on the mental plane

the centers of the mental body

bands of lower mental deva energies that have become a part of the mental body

Illustration 8.18

Those who live on the seventh mental sub-plane are focused on four areas, as follows: The first is attempting to better sense and think about structured thoughts regarding material forms. The second is thinking about structured thoughts that organize forms. The third is thinking about thoughts that synthesize forms. And the fourth is using fewer thoughtforms (words and then sentences, economically) to create thought accurately, or as a whole thought about forms that is truthfully balanced in structure. People on the seventh mental sub-plane can spend a great deal of mental time mostly on their past thoughts that were not whole and balanced in structure, or were not truthful, about the ways in which they (while etheric/dense physically and astrally alive) thought mentally regarding etheric/dense physical, astral, *and mental* form. The first part of time that is focused upon is the past. This is because nearly all of the person's egotism comes from previous thought. Even though the time on the mental plane is separated from space and is further split into three parts by, mostly, the selfish thought of humans, the entire dimension of time is available on the mental plane. Because this dimension is available in its entirety, it can, as a whole or in part, be lived within by the mental body (lower or higher). This potential enables a person who is mentally alive to focus on any part of time that she or he is conscious in, and to live in or relive whatever part of time that she or he can sense; those who are enlightened mentally can focus on and live in time as a whole, on the atomic level of the first mental sub-plane. The most difficult part of time to live in is the future because doing so requires great amounts of wisdom, or balanced structure to the time, with the structure being relatively whole up to the level of sub-plane and sub-sub-plane where the wisdom is created on the mental plane. When wisdom is created, the future part of time can then be sensed *and lived in*—up to the current level of the time where the wisdom has been created. Thus on the lower mental plane the future can be lived in, to whatever level of sub-plane can be reached in consciousness and space. The present part of time is easier to live in than is the future, since the future also includes the present. The present is more difficult to sense and live in than is the past. To create truth in the future requires that less egotism be present than when creating truth in either the present or the past. For the most part, those who first arrive to live on any of the four lower mental sub-planes, and those who begin a new period of mental life by leaving one lower mental sub-plane to live on another, initially focus on and mostly but not entirely live in the past part of time since this is the part of the dimension that is most easily mentally sensed and the easiest one to think in.

The vast numbers of humans alive in all three lower dimensions, including those mentally alive who are mostly focused on the past part of time, distort time dimensionally so that the common future emphasis of time of the whole plane is reduced to an emphasis on the present. If the mental plane surrounding earth becomes much darker through kama-manasic thought, this situation could deteriorate into an overall focus on the past, like the astral plane's focus, since astral thought would then be mostly causing mental thought. This is a reverse of the way that the universe was created (through God's mind and the Ray Lord's thought), and a part of evil's "plan." When time is distorted and separated, with more thought focused on the past than any other part, the past part of time can contain the majority of life, which today is close to eighty percent of the human life on the lower part of the mental plane. The focus on the past part of time (by most humans in all the lower dimensions) creates a partial dimension of time that is referred to in some spiritual language as the akasha. The akasha is simply the past part of time that has become separated and exaggerated through human thought creating energy out of intelligent activity. The energy is a result of the time separating from space as it is used by a human to create its "past" reality. The akasha exists both on the mental and astral planes; on the mental plane it naturally is the focus of life as a part of the whole dimension—and is fairly accurate, at least as much as a mere part of a whole dimension can be. On the astral plane, however, the akasha has become inaccurate and much darker because of selfish desires, fantasies, and the shift in general focus of the whole plane from the present into the past *as a result of selfishness*, or high degrees of emotionalism. Living in, or "experiencing," the akasha astrally is more controlled by fantasy and desire as it is an accurate depiction of the past.

On the fifth and fourth sub-planes of the lower mental plane—which are not kama-manasically connected, or are not controlled *first* by emotionally affected creative imagination—the akasha approaches ninety percent accuracy. On the two kama-manasically connected lower mental sub-planes, or the seventh and sixth, the accuracy of the akasha averages between sixty and seventy percent. When a person focuses one or more split mental senses (energies) on the lower mental akasha, or on the separated and exaggerated past part of time as contained in energy, he or she can sense and live (or relive, if he or she has been there before), the past as the events (the energies) occurred in time and space, but only to the levels of accuracy as described above. The space is created from the separation of the time, while the events are caused by form, or energy—attempting to rejoin while being separated by space. Those who are alive lower mentally experience only the mental forms, or energies, of the events that took place in the lower worlds—the astral or etheric/dense physical. The form seems as real to these people as the denser parts did to them while they were astrally or physically alive; however, the intensity of experience of form is greatly diminished because usually less total energy is moving through fewer centers and senses. Egotism tends to create a reliving of one's own past because most of egotistical mental thought is self-focused, or selfish. Thus those who first arrive on a lower mental sub-plane tend to spend most of their time reliving their own past etheric/dense physical and astral life experiences. They do so in the attempt to gain more meaning to their lives through increasing the accuracy of their mental sense and by reducing their egotism and widening or expanding their mental thought to create more balanced structure, less forces, and more wisdom in the thought. When the wisdom is used to give more through the use of more of the mental senses and thought within the relived akashic experiences, then the person has created a whole wise thought, or truth. By giving this truth to others within the akashic experience, the person has created more love/wisdom as a capacity to create truth in the mental body. He or she has also rejoined the past of the akasha with the present and future by changing some of the energy within it into intelligent activities. The people within his or her akashic experience then become more truthful and loving, as well. After each experience and correction of egotism in the akasha, the person becomes aware of the present, and reflects upon and then contemplates his or her remaining egotism. This leads him or her into the next experience of the akasha.

As stated above, the accuracy of the akasha is determined by the lower mental sub-plane where the person is focused in reliving events in order to reduce egotism. The difficulty in reducing the egotism and thus in increasing lower mental sense and thought varies based on, at least in part, the akasha's accuracy. At present on earth, it is at least several to a half-dozen times more difficult to change egotism into truth on the seventh and sixth mental sub-planes than on the fifth or fourth. The kama-manasic connection of evil has tremendously reduced the advancement of the fifth major human race, as a result of the karmically-linked prior selfishness of the final two sub-races of the fourth major human race. The fifth major human race is the one that is currently under development, and the focus of its development is mental. The legacy of the kama-manasic connection can result in some egotism in the seventh and sixth sub-plane parts of the lower mental body still remaining after the death of that body, and becoming a part of the person's mental permanent atom. Any such retained energy will adversely affect the mental senses and the subsequent thought of the next incarnation of that soul. As can be surmised, a small amount of increase in inaccuracy of the akasha as a person relives past life within it creates a much larger degree of difficulty in improving sense and increasing truth, or the mental plane virtue. This same principle applies to the synthesis of information in physical life, as might occur while using a computer and trying to attain accuracy.

People who are alive on the seventh and sixth mental sub-planes and are focused in the past part of time, or the akasha, live in the distortion created in time on these sub-planes through the total selfish mental thought of all people on earth. People who are physically or astrally alive and who focus their thought on thoughtforms (on words and their sentences, rather than on concepts) from the seventh or sixth sub-planes are caught in kama-manasic thinking and have little or no memory. This occurs because for the past part of time to be remembered requires that a minimum of sixty percent of time be accurately represented in space. Much of the time, the akasha is, at best, no more than sixty percent accurate for those who are mentally alive, and who have even better mental senses than those who are either physically or astrally alive do. For self-ishly thinking people who are physically or astrally alive, "memory" is nearly always more than half filled-in with conjecture, fantasy, and confabulation, in order to give the personality its needed sense of control by "knowing" its past. The self needs about sixty percent of time related to, or joined with, space to be able to recognize itself as it provides consciousness to a person by giving thought to its bodies and the associated senses about the information they provide. Thus most people have little mental life while alive etheric/dense physically or astrally. From another perspective, the minimum necessary sixty percent of time joined to space starts with the self needing fifty percent to maintain a sense of itself; then it needs some additional amount of thought to connect the time and space together for any given series of events. This second amount equals about ten percent of the time and space that it has potential to rejoin. In order to be conscious of the memory at all, the self needs fifty percent memory, which it gives as knowledge. The self needs another ten percent of memory to create its sense of itself—which provides it with a reflection of itself in the past series of events. The total comes to the needed sixty percent of memory. The fear of losing some of its self also causes the personality to pretend to have, or to "fill in," lost memory. The more greedy (for seventh mental sub-plane focused thought) and/or emotional (for sixth mental sub-plane focused thought) that people are *while they think mentally*, the more that they think first in thoughtforms rather than whole concepts, and create these thoughtforms from incomplete concepts. The thoughtforms are then created incompletely on either the seventh or sixth mental sub-plane. Note that someone who is mentally alive is creating thought that expresses emotion mentally by creating movement in the expression of words and of the sentences that the words create.

Even on the two lower sub-planes that are not affected by the kama-manasic connection, the akasha is slightly more than ten percent, on average, inaccurate because of its exaggeration as a used dimensional part of time; by "used" time is also meant "wasted" time—which is what all inaccuracies lead to. The use (waste) of time also causes time to further separate from space. Fortunately, but also as God planned, many people while mentally alive spend much time rejoining mental time and space and creating truth. This offsets the destruction that is done to it by those who are etheric/dense physically and astrally alive and are using time more selfishly within their mental thought. It should be reiterated (from previous chapters) that the mental plane is actually the body of the mental plane Ray Lord, and that all human mental bodies are a part of this Ray Lord's body. The humans collectively affect it according to the amount of selfishness or virtue in their thought.

After a person's astral body dies, he or she moves on to the lower mental plane, to live and to reduce her or his egotism so that meaning in life can be increased. The exact location (a sub-sub-plane of that sub-plane) is determined by where most of his or her egotism is. The lower mental sub-plane that is lived on next is the one where the person has the next highest amount of egotism. The sub-plane on which the person has the least amount of egotism is lived on last, assuming that the person's lower mental senses remain intact long enough for this to take place. In some cases the lower mental sense that is associated with the sub-plane that the person travels to fails as a result of too much egotism and too little sense to overcome the egotism before the person can change all of it into wisdom and truth. In these cases, the person will move on to the lower mental sub-plane that has the next highest amount of egotism, to relive her or his past life there. The experiences take place based on how the sense and its associated thought corresponding to that sub-plane were used in numerous life experiences. Once a lower mental sense fails, whatever amounts of egotism remain become a part of the mental permanent atom. When two sub-planes have equal, or near-equal amounts of egotism, the numerically lower sub-plane takes precedence because of the stronger pull of the gravitating mental elemental energies in the thoughtforms that are a part of the egotism. At times, a person who is alive lower-mentally will travel back and forth among the lower mental sub-planes, spending a prolonged period on each of them. In the process, a critical level of egotism on one sub-plane is offset by the gravitation factors of the elemental energy on a lower one, before the sense fails or the person consistently and generally creates truth.

 ## THE SEVENTH MENTAL SUB-PLANE

The quantum constant is about thirty-six times greater in effect on the seventh mental sub-plane than on the dense physical sub-planes. Time is dilated by a ratio of thirty-six to one. The time dilation increases much faster on the mental plane from one sub-plane to the next because mental energy is considerably less dense and of higher vibration than astral energy is.

This occurs increasingly from the lowest mental sub-plane to the atomic level of the first sub-plane. Those who live on the seventh mental sub-plane live, on average, for ten to fifteen physical plane years, or three hundred sixty to five hundred forty mental plane years. Some people never get out of the past part of mental time on these sub-planes, except during meditation. During these times, however, these people's past mental sense of time is recovering, and they still cannot communicate with anyone else on the sub-plane. Such people are only either reliving past experiences or, in an isolated state of the present time, they are reflecting on them and contemplating other experiences that they might relive in the future. They continue the process either until their split lower mental sense fails and their thought processes can no longer adequately structure their thoughtforms to create more accurate thought about form or until they awaken to full mental consciousness. These people remain mentally self-focused and very isolated, since they do not have contact with other mental plane residents while alive and focused on the past (or an isolated present) on this sub-plane. In order to have contact with other mental plane residents, people need to be able to focus on both the past and the present in mental time, which their excessive egotism has prevented. They, effectively, have no seventh sub-plane lower mental life other than reliving their past—for hundreds of mental plane years! The remaining personality that they each have has only one body from which to sense, and only one brain with which to integrate information and to synthesize knowledge. This condition leaves the personality facing boredom and seeking freedom. Freedom is attainable only by the personality creating more truth through allowing its self to give more of its thought to their shared mental body. The process is for the self to be more influenced through the available thought of the Self. This thought is emphasized by there being only one body to give to and concerns both understanding more of God and serving God, through the creation of virtue.

Some people eliminate most or even all of their egotism on the seventh sub-plane of the lower mental plane and then can join two or more of their split lower mental senses. Doing so enables them to be able to focus on both the past and the present parts of mental time. As this takes place, they "awaken," or become aware of others who are mentally alive on this sub-plane, and can then share, communicate, and jointly think with them. The people who are awake on the seventh mental sub-plane can live a life in thought that is focused on truth about form, organization and economy of form, and synthesis of differing types of form. Their closeness to one another through sharing thought is profound and cannot be accurately described to someone who is physically alive. These people can share the recent past life of one another *and*, from the akasha, some parts of previous incarnations that dealt with a focus on form and that they have created wisdom and truth from as they further develop their sense of the future part of time together. This future sense of time can be developed *only* in concert with others as more wisdom is developed jointly as a sense and truth is developed as a virtue, or as light in mental form. People who continue to live on the seventh mental sub-plane after having eliminated most of their illusion there are learning group consciousness, or soul consciousness. Many of those who overcome their egotism and reach the level of being able to focus on the future start to plan ways together that they can be less egotistical, or less mentally self-focused, about form in their upcoming incarnations, i.e., less mentally selfish about material existence while they are physically alive. They often build a bond and karmic relationships together that will lead them to be born at close to the same time and to be involved together in some ways that deal with forms. In the physical world, they might be business partners, for example. Some may bond through their fused love in their mental bodies, creating a marriage, still with the focus more on creating form, or material (when physical) truth between themselves and with others in their mental thought. This creation can also include truth about sexual energy that they can exchange as thoughtforms between each other. They achieve this by changing the gender of the thoughtforms as doing so serves the other to create wisdom in each other's senses. They also create light, or truth in each other's mental body, as each person's fallen spirit on this sub-plane becomes soul- and Self-infused.

For those who are physically alive, sexually loving someone mentally is likely to be a more difficult concept of sexual love to understand than physical or astral sexual love is. Thoughtforms create words and sentences, which when correctly combined in time and space produce logical sentences. Concepts and their effects as sentences of words each have a gender, based upon the direction of spin of the higher mental center, or tier of solar devas and the spin of their "petals" (see Chapter Seven for further explanation). The words and sentences that a person chooses to create and use to compose his or her logic are either masculine or feminine. Thus men and women think differently in their concepts and logic, but because they are about 180° reversed, or mirrored in thought, it is not as obvious to them because the reversals appear similar rather than contradictory—at first. Within their concepts and logic, women tend to emphasize the second part of God's mind, of oneness, inclusiveness, consciousness, and love. Men tend to emphasize the first part of God's mind, of choices and will, sacrifice, creation and/or destruction, and truth within their concepts and logic that they create in mental thought. The first two parts of God's mind create thought, and when expressed mentally create concepts and thoughtforms, as higher and lower mental thought, respectively. Mental sexual love-making means giving to one's sexual partner more whole mental thought that is in *the partner's* sexual spin and gender emphasis of concepts and logic; it means learning to think like and then give more whole thought like a person of the other gender—who is giving in the same way, back to him or her.

The above-described mental part of sexual love-making can occur while people are physically or astrally alive, as well. However, the mental part is less emphasized and is less often complete as compared to those who sexually mentally relate while alive mentally. People who were relatively virtuous in their physical and astral lives and who fused some of the physical and astral senses and bodies together with the mental body can include some etheric/dense physical and astral sense in their mental love-making. They cannot use anything other than mental energy through these fused senses, because only mental energy is available on the mental plane. When mental energy travels through a mental sense that has fused with the etheric/dense physical and/or astral senses, the lower part of the fused sense becomes further refined by the much higher vibrational energy that it is now sensing to some extent. This same effect occurs to a lesser extent to fused etheric/dense physical and astral senses in people on the astral plane. A refined sense is both more discriminating and discerning in its use, especially when re-created in the next incarnation and used for its corresponding lower plane energies. Sexual love-making between people who are mentally alive and who have fused lower etheric/dense physical and astral plane senses with their mental senses refines their senses for use in the next incarnation.

From the mental plane, down, there are three major dimensions that something can exist in, and each of these dimensions has three distinct parts. The first major dimension is the etheric/dense physical one, and selfish human thought has divided it into three parts. The whole, or complete, dimension is intelligent coordinated response within force, or within inertia. When responses to others are not exclusively intelligent, the dimension becomes the familiar three parts of height, width, and depth. This is why, at present, the mental plane is described as having five dimensions, since it is so common to think of the etheric/dense physical as having three. The astral dimension as a whole dimension is movement away from the self for the benefit of movement of others, which creates love. When movements are not exclusively giving to others' movements, the astral dimension breaks into three parts, as follows. The first is movement towards the self, or selfishness in movement. The second is movement that is strictly away from the self and that helps others to move, or to love. And the third is movement that is (somewhat) away from the self, but that fails to completely help others to love because the person has wrong motive and a lack of empathy, which eventually results in some movement back towards the self. The mental plane contains the added dimension of whole time—which is the past, present, and future fully joined with space, so that any event, or series of forms (of energies) in either time or space, is accurately depicted in the other. Put another way, if we know the past, present, and future of any event, we know its exact location in space; if we know the exact location of an event in space, we also know its position in time. Whole time occurs, on earth today, only at the atomic level of the first mental sub-plane, where it creates a Now. Time at the atomic mental level, which also occurs in a Now, separates at any point that exists below this level from both space and itself into three parts—the past, the present, and the future. Below the mental plane, time exists only as a partial dimension. On the astral plane it exists as the past and present, and on the etheric/dense physical dimension it exists as only the past. Humans who are physically alive and who think less mentally and mostly etheric/dense physically experience time more as the past, but they also change it into a false, or illusioned, future. Time in the present and future requires more full use of the astral and mental senses than these physically alive humans have, because of their selfish over-use of their etheric/dense physical senses (see Chapters Seven and Ten for a more complete explanation). Notice that there actually are three major dimensions, each with, at times, three fractured parts that are fractured mostly as a result of humans using their senses selfishly.

Sometimes a dimension has had even four or five fractured parts, back when humans first begin to function focused on it in their (very) selfish and separative thought. Thousands of years ago, for example, time on the mental plane was fractured into five parts. These parts were the distant past, the near past, the present, the near future, and the distant future. It split into these five parts long ago, when humans began thinking—selfishly—on the mental plane. This situation remained until humanity began to think mentally more inclusively and truthfully, thus joining some of these fragments and reconstructing the dimension of time into the three parts that we recognize today: the past, the present, and the future. When people first began to focus their thought in mental time, they used the more fractured dimension of it; they could not sense time in any other way because their mental senses of form were very split, into the five above-listed parts. Note that on the etheric/dense physical plane humans have partially joined two of the five senses (taste with smell, and touch with taste), which has created closer to three than five senses and recognizable dimensions. The partially joined senses of taste and touch correspond to the throat center and create the taste sensations in the mouth and tongue of sweet, sour, bitter, and salty. The partially joined senses of smell and taste create the myriad of flavors that can be sensed in the mouth. When these senses are fully separated, one must first smell and then taste—mostly through the stomach and solar plexus centers, where a larger quantity of liquid medium is available for a longer period of time than just saliva in the mouth. Most of taste that comes from its partial joining with touch is developed in the solar plexus center in animals that do not have either of these senses fully joined. For the early Lemurian people to fully taste food, they had to first smell it and then eat it, because their senses had not yet become fused through some levels of using them to cooperate and share (food) with others. During the early Lemurian period, when the third major human race was as much or more etheric as it was dense physical, the people sensed *five* parts of the dimension: height, width, depth, plus height in relationship to width, and these two in relationship to depth. The two added partial dimensions become relevant when someone experiences etheric form and her or his ability to change the form's density through thought. These two added dimensions explain the etheric part of the plane in relation to the dense physical, and correspond to smell and taste. On the astral plane, the two added separated dimensions are the speed, or rate of change, of movement either towards the self (or an object) or away from the self towards something or someone else. The added partial dimensions are, today, sensed as being integrated with the remaining dimensions, to the level each plane's partial dimension is sensed in wholeness.

Humans who are physically or astrally alive use their mental sense secondarily during much of their lives on these two lower dimensions. Even though they can mentally sense the thought of others, the sense or senses of the plane that they live on overwhelms their mental sense or senses, thus reducing the effectiveness of these senses. For example, most physically alive people are not aware that they indeed sense the lower (and higher) mental thought of others in one or more ways. The mental sense or senses are overwhelmed by the etheric/dense physical and astral ones. Two of the lower mental senses are somewhat joined together, as long as they are used either mostly secondarily or, if used primarily, are used with which to create more virtue. When used secondarily to the senses of a lower body, the somewhat joined mental senses remain that way until the person thinks egotistically. Egotism separates the mental senses—and reduces them through the forces that it imposes against them. Mentally alive people who have only a primary mental sense split their senses when they think egotistically. When caught in the akasha, mentally alive people are caught in their own egotism, and therefore can only use their single corresponding mental sense on each lower mental sub-plane except the fourth. On the fourth lower mental sub-plane, two senses are always used together, with which to sense both the past and future parts of time—for selfish reasons.

 ## THE SIXTH MENTAL SUB-PLANE

Thoughtforms on the sixth mental sub-plane express movement through the focus of their thought. When they express movement towards the self, they are communicating the effect of the concept of emotion. When the movement they communicate is away from the self and towards others, they are explaining the effect of the concept, or cause, of love. A communication of both effects can be expressed in a sentence about a concept, as well. If these effects regarding emotion or love are egotistical, they are thought about in only one way. This then blocks the mentally sensed thought of ways that others think about emotions and/or love, as well. When kama-manasically connected, the thoughtforms *themselves* move about in a sentence. They may become either overly emphasized or decreased in emphasis, based upon a *previous* emotional thought (in creative imagination) that the person is having or did have while thinking *first* through his or her astral rather than mental body. The astral thought might have occurred just a fraction of a second before. However, people who are mentally alive no longer have an astral body, and the only astral sense these people have remaining *cannot* be kama-manasically inducing thought. The reason is that this sense would necessarily be fused to the mental body. In people who are not evil, all senses that are fused in a body have been done so through virtue. People on the sixth mental sub-plane are focused on the past part of time and are remembering their *prior* astral thought that caused the existing egotistical thoughtforms they have regarding either emotions or love, or both. They then attempt to correct their egotism about emotions and love and also to break future (for their next incarnation) kama-manasic thought. The process repeats itself until either their split mental sense fails on this sub-plane or they awaken with a usable past and present fusion of mental senses.

Notice that when functioning mentally in the full, or complete, past and present, a mentally alive person no longer has a kama-manasic connection and can relate to others without this added darkness. The effect of the quantum constant on the sixth mental sub-plane jumps to about forty-five times that on the physical sub-planes. People can live on the sixth mental sub-plane for an average of about ten to fifteen dense physical earth years (or until their split mental sense fails on the sub-plane), or four hundred fifty to six hundred seventy-five mental plane years. Those who live for significant periods of time there are kama-manasically caught by prior emotional selfishness, which is sometimes exaggerated by the prior astral life. They can spend hundreds of years reliving, through the akasha, their past experiences concerning how they incorrectly (egotistically) thought in self-focused (selfish) ways about their and others' emotions, and sometimes about other people's expressions of love as well. The sixth mental sub-plane is, today, the most difficult mental sub-plane to awaken from and to live a life mentally in the present and/or future. The reason is that a great deal of mental sense is generally used up in overcoming the mental self-focus that many people have concerning emotions. Many people "die" from the sixth mental sub-plane while focused in the past part of time. When this happens to a person, his or her remaining egotism about emotion or love, or both, becomes a part of his or her mental permanent atom. These people are then born into the next incarnating lifetime both with a selfish thought process about emotions or love, or both, and with an increased kama-manasic connection. This increased connection often begins to manifest in certain ways in early childhood—sometimes even infancy. If this selfishness is not overcome by using the mental body for virtuous creation, it progresses into greater levels of self-focus up to and through adulthood in physical life. The kama-manasic connection is an insidious racial karma that is difficult to overcome.

Women are more prone towards sixth sub-plane egotism, while men are more likely to have greater levels of egotism on the seventh sub-plane. The reason is the ray focus correspondence on each of these sub-planes to one of the two genders. The differences are significant, but because the overall levels of egotism are so high among members of both genders, the differences become noticeable only in terms of how many people of each gender eventually awaken to being able to sense the present with the past part of time on each of these two sub-planes. On the sixth mental sub-plane, more men than women awaken before their mental sense gives out. More women are able to sense in the present and awaken on the seventh mental sub-plane before *their* split mental sense fails. For this reason, it is not uncommon for people of opposite gender to each other who are on the different, juxtaposed, seventh and sixth sub-planes to befriend each other when awakening, and to become mentally sexually involved. The quantum constant has less than a thirty-five percent difference between these two mental sub-planes. This enables the inhabitants of both sub-planes who can sense in the present to sense and communicate together. Those on the sixth mental sub-plane can directly sense and travel freely to the seventh, assuming that their levels of egotism are low enough for these people to sense the present parts of time. In order to travel to the sixth mental sub-plane or to sense it (or both), those on the seventh mental sub-plane must have *less* egotism on the sixth than the seventh. This means that they have relatively more split mental sense on the sixth mental sub-plane than on the seventh and enough sense to stay in the present; however, they may remain on the seventh because of the gravitational effect of the elemental energy. Once a person has exhausted his or her split, or partial, mental sense that corresponds to a specific sub-plane, he or she can no longer travel to, sense on, or relate to someone else on that mental sub-plane

If a person awakens to the sixth mental sub-plane and can think in the present part of time, he or she can sense others and become group conscious, or soul conscious, with them. Together these people create their sense of future mental time. This changes their prior self-focused thoughts about emotions and love into thoughts that are focused outward onto helping others to think about loving, and about correcting emotions into love. To break the kama-manasic connection (mostly for a future incarnation) on either the seventh or sixth mental sub-plane requires the creation of truth more than one-half of the time when a person is mentally alive on either of these sub-planes. Once this difficult feat is accomplished, in most circumstances for most people no matter how emotional a person may become in his or her next incarnated lifetime, the parts of his or her mental body that correspond to the lower mental sub-planes will vibrate too differently to be led by the astral vibration. To create this amount of truth, one needs to create wisdom and give it to others. Then, along with those others—in group, or soul, consciousness—the person needs to create truth through using all three parts of the mental plane's fifth dimension, of whole time. The whole time is perfectly balanced together and fused with mental form, or energy, in space. Truth is the virtue of the mental plane, or the light in form for the time and space of that plane.

Usually those who can awaken to the present part of time with at least fifty percent of their corresponding split mental sense intact, and therefore are no more than halfway through life on that sub-plane, can each create enough truth in their lower mental bodies on these two lowest mental sub-planes to break the connection. To do so usually requires that considerable *mental* discipline had been practiced during one's physical as well as astral life, prior to life on the mental plane, so that the lower mental body was more truthful before becoming focused in life mentally. Once the kama-manasic connection is broken it tends to stay broken. The reason is that most people who have practiced such levels of spiritual discipline in one lifetime rarely ever create enough mental darkness in the next lifetime to reconnect these two bodies through darkness.

The Mental Plane

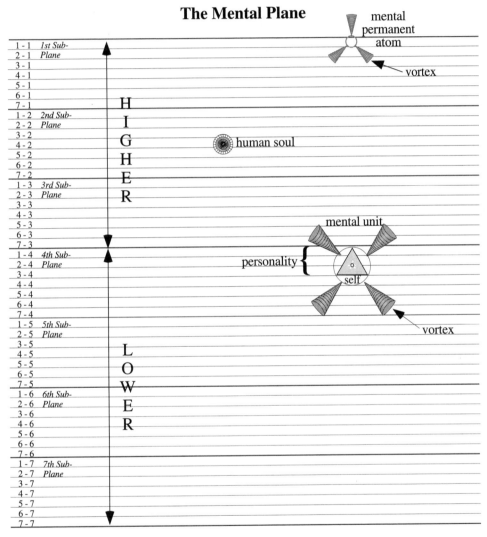

Illustration 8.19

 THE FIFTH MENTAL SUB-PLANE

The fifth mental sub-plane, on earth, is not kama-manasically connected, and most people overcome their egotism on this sub-plane many times faster than on either the seventh or sixth (up to six times faster). Men are somewhat better at fifth mental sub-plane thought, on average, than women are. The ray type of the mental body also can play a significant role in *selfish* use of the bodies' split senses on each sub-plane, with each mental body ray type able to selfishly think better on its corresponding sub-plane. This is, however, of little help in overcoming egotism, which requires the increased creation of mental plane virtue, or of truth, in the mental body. Sometimes, if a person is very egotistical on a sub-plane, it can be detri*mental* to have a mental body ray type that corresponds to that sub-plane; even worse is if, in addition, the ray type of the personality is of the same ray type as the mental body. Note that the personality has a ray type because it is composed, in part, of semi-permanent thought-*forms*, or energy. The worst possible combination towards the correcting of egotism occurs when a person has a large amount of and the highest relative amount of egotism on the sixth mental sub-plane, and has a sixth ray personality along with a sixth ray astral body. Souls will seldom create such a combination in a selfish person. To offset a significant amount of sixth sub-plane egotism that becomes a part of the permanent atom, sometimes (although only quite rarely) a soul and its OverSoul will create in the next personality a, conflicting, third ray astral body to force the person to overcome her or his emotionalism so she or he can reasonably and logically think correctly. More will be explained in the next chapter and in Chapter Eleven about how personalities are created by souls as a means of creating new lifeforms.

The fifth mental sub-plane has a quantum constant that is about sixty times greater in its effect than that found on the dense physical sub-planes. People live on this sub-plane for an average of five to about seven and a half dense physical plane years. Their mental lives on this sub-plane span from three hundred to four hundred fifty mental plane years. These people can sense, when awakened and able to focus in the present part of time, down to the sixth mental sub-plane, but not quite to the seventh, unless they are very truthful in their creation of thought. This ability to sense exists down to the sixth but not the seventh sub-plane because thirty-five percent of about sixty is about twenty-three, and the differential in the quantum constant between the fifth and seventh sub-planes is about twenty-four. This makes the seventh mental sub-plane just slightly beyond the sense of most fifth mental sub-plane inhabitants. In order to create truth from the thoughtforms of the fifth mental sub-plane, a person needs to create words and sentences that correctly define an object or event in relation to its causative concept and to other sentences and their concepts, as well; note that an event is a series of objects of form related to one another by thought within the same time and space. The accuracy of events becomes reduced as selfish thought separates time and space, causing the events to separate from each other, and the memory to become lost. The fifth mental sub-plane is the lower mental form of the structure of words and their sentences to other words and their sentences. While logic exists as a part of each sentence that is made up of thoughtforms from any of the four lower sub-planes, *it is the entire structure* of the fifth mental sub-plane, i.e., a part of the structure of the seventh mental sub-plane is organization and economical use of words. On the sixth mental sub-plane a part of the logic and structure is the emphasis of the placement of certain words and how the expression of movement of one word to the next affects the sentence. And on the fifth mental sub-plane only the exact placement of each word in a sentence in relation to time and space provides the structure and logic of the sentence's thought.

Those who are focused on the past part of time in overcoming their egotism on the fifth mental sub-plane are attempting to correct the illogical structure of sentences that they previously created in their lives and that confused the causes of effects, and also, that confused the relationship of one cause or effect to another. Women on average tend to be less egotistical on this sub-plane, but may also have somewhat weaker sense there when thinking selfishly. This depends upon the ray type of the woman's mental body and her personality ray. Egotism is the mental need to be "right" in mental thought because of mental self-focus. Egotism negates both love and truth. It does so because it reduces both love and truth in order to, in illusion, change mental thought in whatever ways convince a person that his or her thought is right, or balanced perfectly to itself in structure. On the fifth mental sub-plane, an egotistical person uses faulty structure and logic that makes sense to her or him. The person does this in order to convince herself or himself that what she or he thinks is correct. When people join this thought with other lower mental sub-planes forms of egotism, they might not only think that they are always right, they might also think that everyone else's thought is also wrong. Such a person becomes arrogant as well as egotistical. Those who are arrogant are also substantially egotistical on the fifth mental sub-plane. The reason is that the core of arrogance is a heavy reliance on the egotism of structure and logic itself, and upon the structure and logic being correct in the person's own mind. The high propensity of arrogance that follows from large amounts of egotism on the fifth mental sub-plane in a person's mental body emphasizes the *extreme* danger to earth that this sub-plane, too, might become kama-manasically connected. If this were to occur, most people—especially men, for reasons mentioned above—would become arrogant, and evil could become victorious on earth. Fortunately (again, because the Ray Lord—as a part of God's plan—chose this to be the design of the mental plane), most people use their single lower mental split sense well enough while alive mentally. They are able to overcome their fifth sub-plane egotism and to awaken on this mental sub-plane. A careful and diligent effort is made by those who are spiritual servers on this sub-plane to keep its level of egotism lower than on the two mental sub-planes below it.

On each of the lower mental sub-planes spiritual servers are found who are, mostly, astrally alive spiritual disciples from the second and especially the first astral sub-planes. These mental servers are also joined by a few physically alive advanced initiates. These advanced initiates also can remain conscious on one or more of the mental sub-planes some of the time while they physically sleep. There are also some servers from the mental plane who serve while awake on this plane. To serve on the lower mental sub-planes, a person needs to have reduced his or her egotism through spiritual discipline during the present lifetime, through his or her mental discipline of creating more truth. Also, when some of these people sleep, they can remain awake and conscious mentally for a part of the time. This is possible because their mental bodies do not need to be repaired as much, and they are focused out mentally on helping others to think. All of these types of servers help people who are egotistical. Those assisted people who are just sleeping and dreaming mentally while their respective mental bodies repair themselves are usually seriously adversely affecting others in their lives. The service of these mental plane helpers somewhat reduces these people's egotism and sometimes results in a reduction of the harm that these egotistical people do to others. The assisted people who are mentally alive have usually had difficulty and have not reached success in overcoming their egotism. The assistance helps people in both groups to reduce their egotism in the next lifetime. For example, a person who has been helped in this way might otherwise have to live with the effects of his egotism on his permanent atom (within his mental body), in his next incarnated lifetime. The help is generally longer-lasting for those who are mentally alive because they are actively attempting to overcome their egotism. Those who are dense physically alive may often, when functioning on the physical plane, relatively quickly re-create some amount of the egotism that they were helped to overcome while they were dreaming. There are far too few mental plane servers who can serve on the entire lower mental sub-planes. The shortage exists mostly because those who serve while fully awake on all the lower sub-planes and are living on the lower mental plane remain there for a relatively short period of time before leaving their personalities and lower mental bodies. In mental plane time, the mean time is just over two years; exceptions arise based upon when these people will next incarnate. If they have the time to serve, because of a delayed incarnation resultant of certain karmic circumstances, some can serve for ten or even many more mental plane years.

"Awake" people who are mentally alive on the fifth mental sub-plane are aware of the present part of time and can sense other people on this as well as the sixth sub-plane. Actual sleep on the mental plane is quite short. Per mental plane day, each person sleeps an average of two to three mental plane hours on the seventh sub-plane, to fifteen to thirty minutes on the fourth sub-plane. There is only the mental body to rest and repair during sleep. People dream in concepts on the higher mental sub-planes while they sleep on the lower. Once mentally alive people on the fifth sub-plane are able to sense others, they need even less sleep. The reason is that their lower mental senses are being used more together, which causes less damage to these senses (and less further splitting of them). The future part of time is more emphasized on the fifth mental sub-plane by those who are "awake" to it, as compared to people on the sixth or seventh. On the sixth mental sub-plane the present has greater emphasis, and the past is more emphasized on the seventh. These time zone emphases only occur in these "correct" times—when virtue is created, as truth—by those who are creating more truth with one another through group, or soul, consciousness. Although time is still separated on these sub-planes, the added truth leads to past, present, and future being sequentially used and added together on these sub-planes, for the part of the dimension of time lived in by the people who are "awake" and aware of each other. This means that as these people are locked into past events, when they experience these past events they emphasize the parts of time that have been distorted from selfishness, as follows. On the seventh sub-plane they experience their egotism with an emphasis on the future; on the sixth sub-plane the emphasis on what they experience of their egotism is on the past; and on the fifth sub-plane, what is emphasized when they experience their egotism is the present.

Correct and Incorrect Time on the Mental Plane

HIGHER MENTAL PLANE: CAUSES OF THE HIGHER MENTAL PLANE		
SUB-PLANE	SELFISH CAUSAL THOUGHT	UNSELFISH CAUSAL THOUGHT
1	Present	Future
2	Past	Present
3	Future	Past

LOWER MENTAL PLANE: EFFECTS FROM CAUSES OF THE HIGHER MENTAL PLANE		
SUB-PLANE	SELFISH THOUGHTFORMS	UNSELFISH THOUGHTFORMS
4	Past–Future	Past–Present–Future
5	Present	Future
6	Past	Present
7	Future	Past

Table 8.4

 THE FOURTH MENTAL SUB-PLANE

Those who are locked in egotism on the fourth sub-plane focus on the past *and* future in their "memories" from the akasha, but not on the present. These people are caught in the illusion of creating thoughtforms that attempt to make themselves look better to others through appearing to be more virtuous than they really are. They use the past and future parts of time in their thoughtform construction to appear more beautiful by balancing these two parts of time in their thought. They think of past events and then focus on how they can in the future appear to others as more beautiful and virtuous, and, since this is all still caused by egotism, they work on the appearance of being *right*, or correct in their thinking. By excluding the present, the fourth mental sub-plane inhabitant does not think about or for others for the others' sake, only about how these others can be manipulated into believing that he or she is "better" at mental thought than the others are.

The effect of the fourth mental sub-plane's quantum constant is about ninety times greater than on the dense physical sub-planes. Those who are "awake" there and are not creating significant amounts of truth, or mental virtue, can sense through their split mental senses only those who live on the fourth and fifth mental sub-planes. Anyone on the sixth mental sub-plane is beyond the thirty-five percent difference that is the limit of perception by a split sense within a body. Those who because of their egotism are lost in the akasha on the fourth mental sub-plane use more of their senses at one time to sense two of the three parts of time, as they relive their memories. Doing so results in *less* damage to these senses, so that when these people do awaken to the present and future (as they create the future with others through giving more wisdom and then creating more truth), they have longer lives, which can lead to some mental plane service on all of the lower mental sub-planes—as needed. To serve mentally on any of the lower mental sub-planes, a person must be mentally disciplined and focused out, one hundred percent, on others in helping them to construct thoughtforms from that specific mental sub-plane. He or she also needs to have some remaining mental sense left in the center and corresponding sub-plane.

People in the lower mental world create the forms of their world using the lower mental lunar deva, or lunar pitri, energy. This energy is slightly able to think using structure, by following the people's thought and the structure created by the solar deva energies. Once a form is created from the relatively very strong thought of the spirit (self) of a human, that form tends to remain together without further continuous mental thought from the mentally alive person. The reason is that the lower mental lunar devas are the most advanced in their thought of all the lunar deva energy in the lower three worlds, and as long as the person is mentally present, the thought of the devas persists. It is the continued and consistent thought of the mental lunar pitris that originally replicated the thought of the informing human and its spirit, and that keeps the lower mental elemental energy together in *the correct structure*. The elemental energy would, otherwise, tend to gravitate together into a spherical shape, losing most of its structure. The mental thoughtforms of a person who is not mentally alive and focused last usually only seconds to minutes. They disappear so quickly because without the mentally focused human consciousness, most of the thoughtforms tend to fall apart. The elemental energy in the thoughtforms is not very good at keeping its shape without the guiding thought of the lunar devas. This guiding thought needs the strong conscious (giving) presence of the self of a human who is mentally alive. Astrally and etheric/dense physically alive humans are too frequently distracted by their astral and/or etheric/dense physical senses to stay mentally focused for usually more than a few seconds to minutes. When the focus is removed, the thoughtforms these people created simply disintegrate. The elemental energy on the lower mental plane has very limited ability to gravitate as compared to elemental energies on either the astral or etheric/dense physical plane. The reason is that the elemental energy on the lower mental plane is less "involved" into form, i.e., it is involuting by becoming more dense and gravitational, or attractive only to the thought of other elemental energies rather than to the thought of either spirit or lunar deva energy. As the elemental energy on the lower mental plane lowers in dimension, it involutes further. It then becomes less attracted to thought from other sources and follows that thought much less. The ability for energy on the lower mental plane to so easily and quickly follow the thought of spirit causes the quantum constant's effect to dramatically increase both on the mental plane in general, and on each higher mental sub-plane.

When people think selfishly, their own egotism causes them to not be able to sense the other people's forms. This prevents the problem that exists on the lower astral sub-planes, of one person changing and/or stealing the forms of another through thought. If someone cannot sense other people's forms, he or she cannot change or steal them. If left alone and not thought of, the forms that mentally alive people do create on the lower mental plane remain intact for very long periods of mental time. However, these forms are amazingly quickly and easily changed by only slight amounts of their creators' own thought (and by other people who have the same or greater levels of mental thought capability, and are not egotistical).

The surroundings that most people create on the mental plane are based upon each person's past life, while these people are reflecting and contemplating in the present between episodes of being caught in their egotism within the akasha. These surroundings depict the nicest housing, clothing, and other items of form that the people were familiar with in their previous astral and etheric/dense physical lives. Colors on the mental plane mostly give off light rather than absorb and reflect it. This condition is referred to as esoteric color, and these colors somewhat resemble the colors that appear on a very bright, high-quality television screen or computer monitor. However, the mental colors are even more radiant, and they shimmer within the forms that they are part of. In their shimmering, they also radiate up to hundreds of slight variations in hues of the color within less than a single second. The radiance creates an increased depth to the color, which is not, at present, possible to replicate in the physical world. However, this should change through physical inventions that will be able to fairly closely replicate the effect, possibly between the years A.D. 2010 and 2020. Thoughtforms can be seen, visually, on the mental plane in real time as people think them. The thoughtforms appear as geometric shapes that are linked together in five-dimensional space, or have height, width, depth, movement in a direction, and appear in more than one place at a time because they can be seen in all three parts of time by a person whose mental senses are joined. To someone who has only partial mental sense, a thoughtform may appear much brighter and better-defined in shape and movement where it used to be located in space, because the person is placing the most emphasis on, through her or his sense, more of the past. The same condition can apply to a thoughtform in either the present or the future, as well, depending upon what part of the sense is being emphasized. A person using mental vision (as a split mental sense or as part of a full mental sense) can see thoughtforms. When these thoughtforms join together to create moving pictures from sentences on the mental plane, the person then sees the moving pictures rather than the thoughtforms—if he or she chooses to focus on the moving pictures (rather than the individual thoughtforms).

People who are mentally aware, or "awake," can move to any place on the mental plane where they are conscious, just through their thought and by re-creating their form in whatever new location they wish to be. The process is similar to such travel astrally, but requires much less of both mental thought and use of the mental senses. The speed of travel is virtually instantaneous, regardless of the distance. The entire mental plane is many hundreds of times larger in size than the astral dimension is, yet travel through the entirety of it is even faster than travelling the entirety of the astral plane. The mental plane in three-dimensional space extends from the center points between both Earth and Venus and Earth and Mars. The mental planes of these other planets meet Earth's mental plane at the mid-points in etheric/dense physical ("three-dimensional") space.

 ## THE HIGHER MENTAL SUB-PLANES AND SOUL LIFE

The effects of the quantum constants on the higher mental sub-planes are, approximately, as follows. The separated part of the third mental sub-plane has a quantum constant effect that is one hundred eighty times that of the dense physical sub-planes; this figure is the average for the entire third mental sub-plane, including the higher, spiritual, part. The quantum constant effect on the second mental sub-plane averages three hundred sixty times that of the dense physical sub-planes. The first mental sub-plane has an average quantum constant effect that is seven hundred twenty times that of the dense physical sub-planes; on the atomic level of this sub-plane, the quantum constant jumps to one thousand fifty-six times that of the dense physical sub-planes. To those on the first mental sub-plane, the apparent quantum constant is nine hundred sixty times that of the dense physical sub-planes. The shift is caused by the effect of *using*, or separating, time in order to sense it, which alters the way time is perceived by the one who is sensing it. The shift in ratios of the quantum constant effect on the first mental sub-plane is a result of extremely small amounts of human thought at this high level. The ratios may change over time, as the thinking by humans changes to create more truth on each of the higher mental sub-sub-planes. This would then even out the percentages in the way the effect of the quantum constant changes. In these cases there has been an interactive variable of human thought on mental form, creating subsequent irregularities in the quantum constant effect, or of energy following thought. Note that there are quantum constant changes on *sub*-sub-planes on the higher mental plane, as well as the entire sub-planes. The highly structured and formulated mental plane develops a very close tolerance to shifts in time and space as the density of the energies become reduced and their vibration increases, and capacity of thought grows so enormously on the higher mental sub-planes. (See Chapter Ten for a more comprehensive explanation of the causes of this effect.)

As a person who is mentally alive reduces his or her egotism to very low levels, she or he becomes able to think in all three parts of lower mental plane time in logical order (past, then present, and then future) and closely together in sequence of time within space. This joins to some degree the upper and lower parts of this dimension. As these people create whole, or wise, thoughtforms from more whole concepts from the spiritual higher mind, they can live in all three parts of time that are close together (see Chapters Five, Six, and Seven for a more full explanation of the higher spiritual mind). While still alive lower mentally with intact personalities, these people are often more soul than personality. The reason is that the *mental* controlling part of each person's personality has become enlightened enough to fuse with her or his soul. This remaining part of the personality is located within the mental unit, and is on the first sub-sub-plane of the fourth sub-plane. Note that the mental unit itself spans from the fourth to the first sub-sub-planes of the fourth mental sub-plane. The entire personality is located as a spirit-informed semi-permanent collection of special thoughtforms from the third to the first sub-sub-planes of the fourth mental sub-plane. The part of the personality that is found on the third sub-plane (also within the mental unit) focuses on the etheric/dense physical body, its senses, its brain, *and* any part of this body that, through virtue, fuses to a higher body. The part of the personality that focuses its thoughtforms on the astral body is on the second sub-sub-plane, and it, too is within the mental unit. It also focuses on any part of the astral body that is fused with the mental body through creation of virtue. This part is the heart center of the personality and lower mental body and contains the spark of life given to it by the informing thought of the Self, OverSoul, and soul collectively with some of these same kinds of Beings. The first sub-sub-plane part of the personality focuses on the lower mental plane body, and senses the partial conceptual thought of the three separated lowest solar devas in the causal body, and the semi-permanent thoughtforms of the mental unit—which functions as the brain of the lower mental body. It also focuses on any part of the lower mental body that fuses with the higher mental body, *and*, consequently, with the soul through the creation of virtue. The parts of the personality that can focus on a fused body—its fused senses and brain—become fused with its soul and become immortal, or do not die. (Also see the illustrations in Chapter Six and the Appendix.)

The Mental Unit and Personality

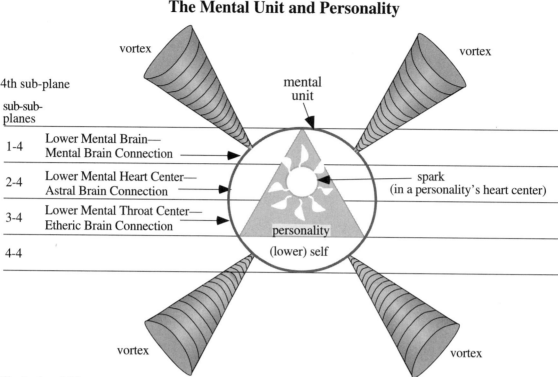

vortex

vortex

4th sub-plane

sub-sub-
planes

mental
unit

1-4   Lower Mental Brain—
       Mental Brain Connection

2-4   Lower Mental Heart Center—
       Astral Brain Connection

spark
(in a personality's heart center)

3-4   Lower Mental Throat Center—
       Etheric Brain Connection

personality

4-4

(lower) self

vortex

vortex

Illustration 8.20

A human's self, which is pure spirit and contains no energy, is located on the fourth sub-sub-plane of the fourth sub-plane, also within the mental unit, and below the personality and under its control. The human self is located at the exact middle of the mental plane, which is the lowest point to which spirit can fall and still remain conscious of itself. The parts of the self that the personality will allow to be controlled by the Self's thought rather than by the thoughtforms of the personality become immortal. They are not lost, because these parts become fully enlightened by the mental Ray Lord's thought at the atomic level of the mental plane, where the Self is located; the Self surrounds the enlightened part of the mental permanent atom. The self, which is composed of only spirit, provides consciousness to a human while the personality provides awareness (which is information from senses), synthesized information that becomes knowledge, and control over the bodies and the self. The two together plus the bodies make up a person. A mentally alive person ends his or her lower mental life by focusing on his or her personality for one of two possible reasons, as described below.

The first reason occurs when there is insufficient sense available in the last living body (the lower mental) to keep the semi-permanent thoughtforms within the personality able to exercise control over the mental unit. This unit is, in part, the brain of the lower mental body and is the controller of the lower mental body in total. Egotism, arrogance, or a combination of the two has taken its toll and the lower mental senses have all, or mostly all, failed. A focus of thought is then created from prior self-focus that came from egotism, onto the personality and self. An implosion takes place because the semi-permanent thoughtforms within the personality are no longer thinking outward (because there is too little sense left)—and thus are no longer able to keep the mental unit intact. The mental unit is kept intact and the personality and self are kept alive by thought that needs information from senses in order to be created. As the mental unit collapses, the lunar devas and lower elemental energy separate, which causes the personality to die. The self, as self-conscious spirit that remains, falls from its position at the middle of the mental plane and suddenly becomes darkened lower mental plane spirit that is no longer conscious of its self.

The person ceases to exist *as a person*, but his or her permanent atoms remain, for use in the next incarnated lifetime. People who die from the lower mental plane in this way fall asleep, usually while still caught in the akasha. They experience no sensation of fear, nor do they become lost to oblivion. During their later meditative reflection and contemplation periods before lower mental body death, when not caught in the akasha, they could usually foresee that such a condition was imminent. They do miss out on experiencing the great joy of awakening, through their own creation of truths, into being a soul, but they are not punished, *nor do they lose any consciousness* in the process of becoming their souls. They lose only the *knowledge* that they had created from selfishness. This knowledge becomes fused with the akasha in separated energy and the partial time of the past, but disconnected from each person's self.

The second reason for intense focus on the personality in order to end lower mental life comes from creating enough virtue mentally (enough truth) in concert with others, to develop about sixty percent group consciousness (soul consciousness) while mentally alive or by developing less than sixty percent of it, but still remaining aware and "awake" lower mentally in all three parts of time. If the internal focus on the person is from more than sixty percent soul consciousness, then the person, *in full awareness*, shatters, or *explodes*, his or her personality and transfigures himself or herself into his or her soul and Self. A tremendous state of joy is realized as he or she becomes the soul and thinks in consciousness from the Self. The joy continues as the soul now *re*joices (*re-joy*-ces) its past life that it is aware of from the perspective of its Self; the soul knows only of all of the virtue that it helped to create. A sense of astonishing freedom of thought and of action is immediately realized as the person becomes his or her soul. Those who awaken to being their souls while still having over sixty percent fused mental sense were serving during part of the time they were alive lower mentally. Each one can remember her or his last life as a human, while now being a soul and Self. Those who awaken with less than sixty percent of their mental senses intact will not be fully aware of their awakening, and each will have pieces of memory from the last life that each one lived as they think from their souls, but none of them will be able to remember that life as a whole. Without the wholeness of life, joy is significantly diminished as the soul remembers only each *individual* virtue as it was created, but not as it was joined with other creation of virtue—and this joining is what makes up memory of the life. If the virtue is isolated into pieces of a prior lifetime, it is much more difficult to create wisdom from previously created virtue that is given to others so that the others might do the same. However, creating virtue in this way still does cause the one so creating to experience some, although less, joy.

For those who created truth less than sixty percent of the time while alive lower mentally, the state of joy is only partial because much less knowledge of the last life remains. Only enlightened knowledge from each personal lifetime enters the soul. Joy comes from the ability to use the enlightened knowledge, as wisdom, to give to other souls so that all can create more of God in form. The soul experiences this joy as it gives to other souls all the virtue that its past incarnations have created. Joy is the awareness and understanding of others' creation of virtue with the knowledge and understanding (awareness and love) that was given to them by the Self. Smaller amounts of enlightened knowledge thus provide less wisdom and less joy.

In all cases of personal death when the person's consciousness is connected to an individual soul and Self, that consciousness experiences some joy. An evil person does not die personally while his or her *consciousness* is connected to a human soul or Self, and so evil is not an exception to this condition of joy. Note that those who are evil and still remain connected to a soul each *keep* their individual personalities when reincarnating into the next life. The amount of joy experienced is significantly less for those who fail to overcome their egotism and thus remain caught in the akasha on one of the lower sub-planes, before personally dying. Once "reborn" as a soul, that which was virtuous within the person remains as a part of the Self. At this point the soul and

OverSoul are already planning their next human's incarnation. The ray types of bodies and semi-permanent personality thoughtforms that they use to create this new person will often be different from the ones that they used for the current one. Also, new possibilities from the previous life's karma, or effects from causes created in that life and that still remain, provide further changes in the next incarnation. Geographic location, family type, racial (actually, sub-sub-racial) type, and many other factors might be changed, based upon the prior life and even earlier lives. The soul consults with the OverSoul, or Solar Angel, through their shared Self about these factors, provided that the soul is developed enough to be involved in the intricacies. Souls give together in their incarnations of people, to create a network of potential towards success in each person's mission of improving himself or herself and everything around him or her through creating virtue, or creating more of God's thought within the form, in the three lower worlds.

All people who do not become evil eventually awaken to being their souls. No one ever dies from the state of Self consciousness because each human being individually has a Self—and is a *creative* part of God. Animals and lower forms of life mostly do not have individual souls or Selves, and most do not even have a self; the ones without a self cannot suffer from loss of self when dying. Those relative few that have some self are protected by also being given some commensurate amount of Self—and do not suffer a loss of consciousness in death. Love and its flip-side, consciousness, are part of God's second aspect of mind, and neither love nor consciousness can be destroyed, although they can be somewhat reduced within a lifeform while it lives. Death of form allows self-*conscious* spirit to increase in self and consciousness. Spirit that has lost self and its consciousness through selfishness during its life falls into darkness. This spirit suffered *before* death, as a consequence of its own selfishness. Only evil suffers after death of its body(-ies) because it has chosen to go against and live against God's system of cooperation and sharing, love, and truth—all of which create immortality of Self. Evil chooses to reduce its suffering during its life, through selfish destruction of others, and then enormously suffers after death—when all others cease to suffer. Evil's choices are probably the most stupid intentional activities that are possible in our universe!

As egotism is reduced in the lower mental body, a person is in training to rejoin with his or her soul. The process takes hundreds to thousands of mental plane years and involves many other residents of the lower mental world. Eventually, some of these people become co-servers together and function in group, or soul, consciousness. As people co-serve, they become aware of, and conscious within, the system of incarnation and soul development. It is unfortunate that the majority of people live for such long periods of time while missing most of the reason for living. Of course, this book and others in the future, as well as other parts of the Plan, which includes the teaching of the information contained within this book in order to raise consciousness, may help to improve life's meaning for some. Humans at present mostly fear the loss of the temporary, and disregard the parts of themselves that are immortal. Illusion is a strange cause of most pain and nearly all suffering that is endured. Simply helping people to realize that they are selfish is a formidable task in today's physical world; then, what changes these people make in their lives towards becoming more virtuous may be, for too many, miniscule at best. Those who understand half or more of the basic information that is in this book are likely to be the exceptions, and they are the ones who will find more of life's hidden meaning.

SUMMARY OF AND CONCLUSIONS ABOUT LIFE ON THE MENTAL SUB-PLANES

In summary of and to conclude the concepts within the preceding section about life in the subtle world of the mental plane, life is focused on overcoming egotism in order to become able to sense others and to mentally live together with them. Since only the virtuously used and fused parts of the etheric and astral senses remain as a part of mental life, as egotism is reduced on each succeeding sub-plane a person lives more *as well as* more virtuously in the present and future parts of time. Because of the gravitational effects of lower mental elemental energies, people sometimes move back and forth between adjacent lower mental sub-planes as they attempt to overcome their egotism and create more truth. Once egotism has been reduced to a level at which the corresponding split lower mental sense is used virtuously (and then using these senses continuously at least fifty percent of the time) and joined at least fifty percent with one or more split senses, the person who is mentally alive, while still on that sub-plane, "awakens" to awareness of other people on the mental plane for a period of time. Then the person can further join the use of her or his higher and lower mental senses and thought through truth, or mental light, thereby eventually creating group, or soul, consciousness. Such a person can typically continue to use her or his semi-joined lower mental sense in order to remain focused on the present and to create more of the future, until the semi-joined lower mental senses become too weakened (by not creating truth at all times they are used) to be able to continue sensing the present. Then the person will choose to focus on the akasha from another sub-plane where she or he has less egotism than she or he had *to begin with*, on the previous sub-plane she or he lived on, and then the process repeats itself. In some situations a person may not awaken from a lower mental sub-plane because the sense fails first, while the person is trying to overcome his or her egotism. When the person's egotism is reduced to a level at which all five of the lower mental senses are fully joined together in truth, he or she can live and sense in the past, present, and future on all four of the lower mental sub-planes at close to the same time. To reach this level of functioning, people need to have mentally disciplined themselves in order to become more virtuous, for spiritual motives. It is usually necessary for some level of this discipline to occur both while physically and astrally alive, prior to mental plane life, and to continue through mental plane life as well.

Most people on the mental plane are mentally disciplining themselves because mental life can be increased in meaning only as a person lives in a greater part of the fifth, or whole mental dimension, of time. Doing so is achieved only as people become less egotistical or less arrogant (or both) through prolonged active reliving of, and then reflecting upon and contemplating, these events in the akasha. These are the past parts of their lives that are recorded in mental (or astral) energy and are overly emphasized because of mental selfishness. It usually takes hundreds of mental plane years on *each* of the four lower mental sub-planes for mentally alive people to reduce their misuse of their singly-used split lower mental senses, and to reduce their creation of egotism. As people reduce their egotism and increase their truth, they are each able to partially join their split mental sense with one or more of their other split mental senses, and then to sense the present part of mental plane time—and other mental plane people as well. Along with these other people, they can further join their lower mental senses by creating virtue, and they create the sense of the future—through *new* created wisdom and truth for the future. Life on the mental plane is focused on humans, because almost no animals think and mentally sense well enough on the mental plane to stay awake and have a life there.

There are no children on the mental plane because all of the children on the astral plane either matured while still astrally alive or became adults upon their awakening on the mental plane. When anyone, children included, awakens on the mental plane, that person instantly undergoes an expansion and elevation of consciousness as a result of thinking through less selfishness, now that only one body exists. Also, this remaining body has a much higher vibration, and when it is used as the primary body that is thought through, consciousness is greatly augmented. On the mental plane even an infant can think as an adult, because all mentally alive people on earth today have an adult level of mental thought and sense that comes from sensing past lives of mental development. The very rare exception to this process is a new soul who in her or his first incarnation on earth died in infancy or childhood; under these circumstances, no lower mental plane life would be possible. Such a person would have no further mental life until her or his next incarnation. The greatest motivation towards a spiritual life on the mental plane is the boredom and fatigue created by the isolation of and redundancy of, for up to hundreds of years at a time, living in the past of one's own life. Each successive reliving of a set of events as a life experience is partially changed by the person reliving it into an at least somewhat less egotistical way of sensing and thinking about the past. In such instances of reliving, when the mentally alive person (or the person who is dreaming, if he or she is physically or astrally alive, but asleep on the mental plane) focuses his or her senses on the akasha, that person experiences the past as an illusionary present—and mentally believes, or thinks, that he or she is really there. One becomes caught in the akashic experience, and because of the over-emphasis on the past part of time, the self loses its awareness of the present and that the person is *re*living a past experience. Only after the experiences of the past have (temporarily) exhausted the sense that is being used to reach the akasha, will a person return to a state of reflection and contemplating in the present. However, that person will still be isolated from others until his or her overall egotism on the sub-plane is lowered to a level at which the corresponding mental sense can be joined with one or more of the person's other mental senses, thus enabling that person to sense the thought of others. Note that on the mental plane, people exist only in mental energy, and can be sensed by others only through mental senses that are not blocked by egotism. The egotism as represented in form, or energy, comprises bands of damaged energy, or damaged thought-forms (or concepts when in the higher mental body) surrounding the mental body and its centers and their senses—blocking the senses with a wall of damaged energy.

Until egotism is overcome and a lower mental sense can be used in conjunction with other senses creating more truth in order to sense more of the present part of time, people on the lower mental plane live in the only way that they can—through the akasha with each person reliving his or her past. However, they do so with changes in their egotistical responses in the past, followed by periods of reflection and contemplation in mental thought while the sense gradually recovers from being (temporarily) exhausted through overuse in the past part of time. In these circumstances people cannot control how long they will remain caught in the akasha, for their egotism and the remaining strength of their split mental sense control each re-life experience. Some of these experiences last for mental plane months (!) at a time, particularly in the beginning of life on a sub-plane. The reflection period of mostly just thought (because their sense is so exhausted, temporarily) can also last for up to several months. For most people, the average period spent in the akasha is less than a week at a time, but there is so much variability that a given average is of little help towards understanding the experience.

As the akasha is created into more wholeness—intelligent activity instead of manifested energy—time simultaneously rejoins with space and the person's senses also gradually become more enlightened. The entire process is controlled by how whole the person's (re-)thinking is in regard to his or her own past (egotistical) experiences, which are recorded in the akasha. The greater difficulty on the two lowest mental sub-planes is that the akasha itself is inaccurate as a result of the collective untruth of human kama-manasic thought on these two sub-planes. An egotistical person has to contend not only with the akasha's distortions caused by his or her own prior egotism, but also with the distortions created by those whom he or she interacted with in the past. The egotistical person must relive these (at least somewhat) distorted experiences on the mental plane—trying to create truth out of them. Notice that as each mentally alive human corrects the akasha for herself or himself, she or he creates more truth for, first, all others whom she or he had experiences with, and then, eventually, for all who think on the mental plane. This develops more soul consciousness in the mentally alive person because he or she can reflect on how all of (at least human) life is connected.

When the egotism on a sub-plane has been reduced to a level at which a person can sense with semi-joined somewhat enlightened lower mental sense, that person is *strongly* motivated to relate with others whom he or she now has awareness of. The motivation is to relate with open-mindedness, givingness of his or her thought (with love, mentally), and, most importantly, *with humility*. The lower mental plane is the place where people who think selfishly gradually become people who think as souls. The lower mental plane is not a place of punishment, but one of opportunity created by karmic loneliness, boredom, and mental fatigue in order for people to relearn where each human came from—his or her soul. Some people learn to again be soul-like through complete failure of their mental senses, and increased suffering. Others do so by finally fusing these senses together and experiencing much greater levels of joy before becoming fully immersed in joy as a soul. All people, except those on the dark path of evil, eventually during inner plane life return "home" to being a soul. Even those who choose evil ultimately return, too, after suffering immensely, often for inconceivably long periods of time. Then the person's past life as a human seems like a dream from which she or he has just awakened; the only parts of the dream that she or he can remember are those in which she or he had created virtue.

At this point the personality is gone, and what remains of that person is his or her consciousness. No part of consciousness, or understanding, is ever lost through becoming a soul. When a person's consciousness, or givingness/love, is reduced, it is because his or her personality has been selfish. Waking up to being one's soul is like going to bed one night as somewhat of a selfish unintelligent person, and, while dreaming, being that selfish person in the dreams, and then waking up the next morning as a loving genius. When a human dies from the lower mental plane, his or her consciousness ascends to the higher mental plane, specifically, to the fourth sub-sub-plane of the second sub-plane. The soul has always been there, while a part of itself—the created human—traveled through a journey of life in the lower worlds. In order to assist in the planning of the human's next incarnation, the Self and soul are able to construct the selfish parts of the last personality's life, by observing what is missing from the fused person's memory, and through a direct sense of any retained energy within the person's three permanent atoms. Any *direct* memory, however, of selfish past life experience is lost (and becomes part of the akasha). The reason is that the infused soul and Self can experience the akasha only as it exists on the higher mental plane at, and sometimes only above, the fourth sub-sub-plane of the second sub-plane. The soul that has not fused with a personality has no sense of any part of the akasha below where it exists in form, nor can it sense any other aspect of time and space below this point. This is the reason why all souls need to live through the lower forms of life that they create. It also explains why each human soul must live through the human being it helps to create. The OverSoul is capable of having some sense of the personality when the personality is using any part of the higher mental body; the sense comes through the solar devas, which have been borrowed from the OverSoul. For this sensing to take place, the OverSoul needs to so choose, and the personality needs to permit it. In these cases it is the personality who permits or denies such contact, because the Solar Angel has given up its control over these solar devas of the causal body. The Solar Angel can access the entire akasha, as can the soul, once the third section, or leg, of the antahkarana has at least in part been created from the radiance of the first tier of solar devas, through service created by a human disciple. (See Chapter Six for further explanation.)

Life as a human soul is one of fairly consistent joy, and for more developed souls, bliss (long periods of consistent joy) is at times provided through the development of the intuitional body's senses. The joy and bliss come from co-creation with other souls and Solar Angels, or OverSouls, in planning and creating new incarnations of humans. These humans, as extended parts of each soul's life and as a group, in concert with other souls' incarnations, will each have a mission to create more virtue, or more of God's thought in the form, in the three worlds that are too dense in energy for a soul to directly do so. Each human has a life of its own, and only the virtuous parts of its life that it creates become a part of the soul's life. From the soul's perspective, the human is free and in control of its self, but remains a part of the soul through the virtue that it (the human) creates. The soul also understands that both it and the human become more a functional part of God as the human creates more virtue. The reason that those who become evil and thus create against God lose their souls is that without the creation of virtue, there is nothing that connects a person to his or her soul; in addition, the creation against God is also creation against the soul—which creates a force against the soul and the OverSoul.

 ## SUMMARY OF CHAPTER EIGHT

In summary of and in conclusion of this entire chapter, the hidden meaning of life to humans is revealed as a series of great journeys, or incarnations, that are created by souls. Each journey gradually unfolds more meaning from the previous parts of the lifetime. This occurs while more life is lived in subtle worlds for the possibility of creating more virtue, or more of God's thought as represented by each Ray Lord's thought, within the form of these worlds. The more virtue that is created in each succeeding subtle world that a person lives in, the greater the realization of the hidden meaning of that life *and* the previous life or lives that were lived in the lower worlds. Humans are given several chances to garner meaning from their lives. After a person without fused bodies has died from a dimension, she or he cannot create *new* meaning—hidden or revealed—in that realm. The reason is that once such a person has departed from a dimension, she or he can no longer either change or further enlighten the energy in that dimension. Only prior meaning, which may be hidden, can be realized through creating virtue within a more subtle world that is higher in vibration.

The subtle worlds offer life experiences that function predominantly, for most people, to remedy the prior lack of meaning realized in life. Since humans derive meaning by creating more virtue in form, and especially the virtue of being able to give it to others (by becoming more conscious, or loving), much of the meaning that is initially hidden later becomes part of life as consciousness, or lovingness/inclusiveness/oneness. This change gradually occurs to most people while they are astrally alive. Eventually, more meaning from the same events in life become unhidden through not only helping to give meaning to others, but by also creating more of it, first, through using structure and mental thought and then by creating more truth besides just more love within others. Doing so is accomplished by most people while they are mentally alive. People who are spiritually disciplining themselves attempt to give in both of these ways while still physically alive—and continue to increasingly do so through spiritual service on the astral as well as the mental plane. Ultimately, meaning in life for most of the people who are reading this book and for others who have already mostly developed their selves is the amount that they can understand and, further, create more of God's growth, or more life. For many humans, most of life's meaning that is not hidden from them is created through the development of their selves. Meaning to life is hidden in any experience within which a human could understand and create more of life by developing his or her Self but chose, because of illusion, or selfishness, not to. Nearly all of the meaning of physical life remains hidden from most physically alive people because most people are selfish, most of the time, while they are physically alive.

THE KINGDOMS AND THEIR PURPOSE

Illustration 9.1

Author's Suggestion: First turn to the "Glossary Help Guide" and read the definitions for this chapter.

 PRINCIPLES OF HOW KINGDOMS DEVELOP

The primary focus of the last chapter was on how members of the human kingdom affect mostly themselves and other humans by the way they create their lives in the three worlds in which they live. Through the development of civilization, especially while dense physically alive, humans greatly affect the life in the three kingdoms below them, and the sub-kingdoms of these three kingdoms as well. Humans more indirectly affect the fully self conscious and Self conscious Beings of the next, or fifth, kingdom. Humans of today also directly affect the sub-kingdom of the fifth kingdom, or the energy sub-kingdom, in the lower three worlds. They do so through their increased civilization relying more on the transmutation of one density of energy into another in order to develop power, or the ability to change life by increasing the movement of it, as well as sometimes increasing or decreasing its density. Humans have not yet learned how to use power to create any new types of life. They are, however, at the present time, coming closer to being able to do so.

There are three kingdoms below the human; they are the mineral, vegetable (or plant), and animal. Each of these kingdoms has sub-kingdoms that are made up of lifeforms that could not reach the next higher kingdom in their development. They feed on energy through using one or more of the either living or dead centers and the bodies of a lifeform from another, and often a higher kingdom—most often the next higher one. Viruses are mostly part of a sub-kingdom between the mineral and vegetable kingdoms. Bacteria are mostly part of a sub-kingdom between the vegetable and animal kingdoms. Molds and fungi are mostly part of a sub-kingdom between the mineral and vegetable, but are much higher in development than are viruses. When parasitically infecting a higher living lifeform, the lower the sub-kingdom species that is doing the infecting and the higher the kingdom that its infected lifeform belongs to, the more severe the infection will generally be. The cause of this effect is the injection and growth of more primitive energies from the lower kingdom into one or more centers within the higher lifeform. The greater the disparity between the overall level of darkness of energy within the higher lifeform as compared to the normal energy within a lifeform's center from a higher kingdom, the more destructive the lower lifeform is to the form of life of the higher.

For example, a virus is more destructive and dangerous, *on average*, in its effect when it infects a human than is either a fungus or a bacterium. Also, a virus that can infect both an animal and a human would, on average, be more dangerous to the human. Since averages are being referred to, there are of course exceptions, because some molds and fungi, and some bacteria, can be more destructive than certain viruses can be to the form of a human. Viruses are less destructive, *on average*, to plants than they are to humans. Plants that are altered by humans, through human civilization, may (again, on average) become as easily destroyed by viruses as humans are. The reason is that these plants have become an extension of the centers, the senses, and the thoughts of humans.

The closer a sub-kingdom is to a kingdom in its development, the easier it is to infect, or feed on dead energies from, kingdoms above it. For example, it is easier for molds and fungi than for bacteria to feed on either dead or living plants. Even though molds and fungi do, to some extent, feed on humans (alive or dead), it is easier for bacteria to do so. The more malevolent the parasitic infection, and therefore the more destructive to the living form that it is in, the more difficult in general it is for a lower sub-kingdom lifeform to infect a human. However, as humans selfishly alter their centers and bring very dark energies into them that lower sub-kingdom lifeforms can feed on, then these humans "open the door" to these lifeforms becoming an infecting source of potentially *all* humans. Despite the fact that humans whose energies are darker are more prone to these infections, all humans, even those who are relatively virtuous, *as a kingdom* share in the karma of any of the members of their kingdom. Thus, for example, if some more selfish human individuals initially create in their centers large amounts of very dark (dense and disorganized) energies, which are then fed upon by relatively dark viruses, then many other humans may become vulnerable to these same viruses even if these people have much less of the very dark energy within their centers. The cause of this effect is that life is one, but in God's plan, life is karmically separated by spirit's relative ability to think within the kingdoms and to create them from its thought. Each of the kingdoms has a lowest and highest level of spirit that informs the lifeforms within that kingdom, and that controls the overall level of thought within them. The thoughts that minerals have from the spirit that informs them is too low to create life.

The ray line focus of a kingdom indicates how that kingdom is designed to create more virtue on a planet *as it (that kingdom) advances into the next kingdom*. As the following table exemplifies, ray lines of focus for kingdoms do not follow the order of the kingdoms. The ray line of each kingdom eventually causes that kingdom to create a certain type of virtue, as found on the next page.

The level of the informing thought of spirit is determined by spirit's position in time and space, which can be recognized by identifying where the lifeforms are found in the dimensional time and space of our universe. For example, the life of plants is found mostly from the dense physical sub-planes of liquid and air up to the seventh astral sub-plane. However, the most advanced plants can reach some levels of life up to the third astral sub-plane, with the help from other parts of life. Each lifeform is *self* created from the thought of the self and, additively, from the thought of fallen spirit that informs the lifeform. At its lowest point, the informing fallen spirit of plant life reaches to these same levels of space. In today's time, for the plants alive today, this level is in the part of the duration of life that we call the present. The level of thought with which fallen spirit can inform plants is mostly, on average, from the sixth dense physical sub-plane (the dense physical liquid sub-plane) up to the seventh astral sub-plane. The animal kingdom reaches from the sixth dense physical sub-plane, on average, to the seventh

RAY LINE FOCUS OF AND VIRTUE CREATED BY EACH KINGDOM		
KINGDOM	RAY LINE	VIRTUE EVENTUALLY CREATED BY THAT KINGDOM AS IT ADVANCES INTO THE NEXT
Mineral Kingdom (creates dense physical energy from transmutation of prana and minerals)	7th Ray	Cooperation and sharing to create complex compounds necessary for the creation of life
Vegetable, or Plant, Kingdom	3rd Ray	Creation of all life—through supporting all life by providing food and oxygen on the dense physical plane
Animal Kingdom	6th Ray	Conditional love based upon movement
Human Kingdom	4th Ray	Beauty
Spiritual, or Soul, Kingdom	2nd Ray	Unconditional love/consciousness/oneness
Planetary Kingdom (for dense physical planets that are not yet rid of evil, or are not yet sacred)	5th Ray	Creation of whole given structures and formulae (because for non-sacred planets the causes of all life in dense worlds of life are on the mental plane)
Solar Kingdom	1st Ray	Further creation of the three parts of God's mind on a solar scale

Table 9. 1

mental sub-plane. Some animals have no informing fallen spirit on the mental sub-planes, while others have informing fallen spirit that can consistently reach up to the fifth mental sub-plane in its thought. On average today, animals are one entire plane above plants in the amount of thought that the animal informing fallen spirit along with the associated selves supplies to each lifeform, respectively, within the kingdom.

Average humans of *today* can use their fallen and self-aware and self-conscious informing spirit to think up to the top of the third mental sub-plane, creating mental thought on their own in the process. Some humans who have more advanced souls and who have chosen to limit their senses in order to create more virtue, or are spiritually disciplining themselves, can create their own thought from the fourth sub sub-plane of the second mental sub-plane, where each of their souls thinks from. The highest level from which any human can create thought, if he or she has advanced his or her spirit's thought much further through spiritual discipline and initiations that provide help from higher spiritual sources, is the fifth intuitional (the fifth buddhic) sub-plane. These advanced initiates are also considered junior members of the next kingdom beyond the human. A comparison of the highest sub-plane that some animals can consistently think from and the highest sub-plane that some humans can think from shows a difference of an entire plane. However, in comparing the average level of thought by animals and the average level of thought by humans, what is shown, at present, is that animals are closer in their thought to humans than they are to plants.

There is a consideration that has to be made about the planes and their effects on the thought of spirit. The higher the plane, the greater the capability of thought by spirit within the form of that plane; however, a lifeform that lives in lower dimensions has spirit within it that is also lower and that needs to be controlled by the higher spirit's thought. This system is maximally developed in humans, and does not always succeed in the highest thought informing the human during each second that the human is alive. The difficulty of creating the ability to think from the higher mental plane while also part of a being that extends to the fifth dense physical plane slows the process of spirit gaining the ability to think on each higher mental sub-sub-plane. The personality's spiritual part (the self) thinks at a much lower level than the highest level at which an even average human of today can create thought. This level is the top of the third mental sub-plane. The self thinks from the fourth sub-sub-plane of the fourth mental sub-plane. With added assistance of the controlling personality, it and the self can collectively create thought from as high in the mental body as the fifth sub-sub-plane of the third sub-plane, as mundane concepts. This level is still substantially below the level at which average humanity of today can create thought. The remainder of the expansion of spirit's thought within humans has come from humans' own development as a kingdom and their further increases in civilization. Today, on average, humans can create new concepts that are creating more virtue on a personal level both in themselves and in others because the entire kingdom has developed more virtue. These personal ways of giving to help others are for each person to become more developed, as a personality and a self. They do not help others to become more developed as souls, or to give to others so that the others might become more giving. The ways of giving personally at first seem to make life more meaningful for humans by creating more of the self. They do not make life more meaningful in terms of creating more Self and the soul. In fact, they hide more meaning in life for more developed souls and their incarnated human beings, as they create meaning that is personal.

The boundaries of life creation within a kingdom are created by the range and amount of the lowest to highest thought of the informing spirit or of a higher Being. This informing thought also corresponds to a dimension of space and a duration that additionally consists of time within which life is created—which can also be used to define a kingdom. Each kingdom is part of the life of other kingdoms in some ways, but is also separated by the source of informing thought and life creation. The separation of life protects each kingdom by creating a barrier that requires a considerable increase in thought in order to move from the life within one kingdom into the next. The protection is against the rapid spreading of darkness and evil in the relatively lower kingdoms. It limits mistakes made by life in one kingdom from as adversely affecting the life in other kingdoms. There are other, esoteric reasons for the existence of the higher kingdoms; these reasons remain esoteric because of facts that are as yet unknown in human science.

While kingdoms and their separation assist the life within them to grow with less intervention from outside the kingdom, the *general overall* advancement of life within a kingdom into the next is controlled by a higher kingdom, except in the case of the highest, or the twelfth kingdom. Individual members of one kingdom can advance into the next at any time that they have raised their senses and thought high enough to match the average level of senses and thought of the type of life they will become in the next kingdom. This is extremely difficult for an individual member of a kingdom to do ahead of, in sense and thought, the other similar life in its kingdom. Not only is the other life often of no assistance to the advanced member, that other life often, through its relatively low consciousness and selfishness, functions as a significant obstacle. Some of these obstacles are ameliorated by thought and sometimes actions of members from the next higher kingdom, who offer assistance to deserving advanced members of the lower kingdom.

The range of and amount of thought by the spirit that is informing the lifeforms within a kingdom defines that kingdom. This range and amount are determined by the dimension, in time and space, that informing spirit must think within in order to keep a lifeform alive. There are twelve kingdoms, seven of which have traditionally been known about in spiritual groups of knowledge, and five that were kept hidden until mundane human knowledge (and its science of knowledge) discovered their effects on time and space. The lower seven have been known about since humans appeared on earth and were taught about them by members of the next higher kingdom. The following is a list of all twelve kingdoms and the dimensions lived in by either the lifeform's spirit or the Beings who live beyond spirit and energy.

		THE TWELVE KINGDOMS
NUMBER	NAME	LEVEL OF THOUGHT
First Kingdom	Mineral Kingdom	*At present on Earth...*Spirit-informed creative thought from the seventh dense physical sub-plane to the fourth etheric sub-plane, on average, and to the first etheric sub-plane at this kingdom's highest level of development on Earth.
Second Kingdom	Vegetable, or Plant, Kingdom	*At present on Earth...*Spirit-informed creative thought from, on average, the sixth dense physical sub-plane to, on average, the seventh astral sub-plane, and to the third astral sub-plane at this kingdom's highest level of development on Earth.
Third Kingdom	Animal Kingdom	*At present on Earth...*Spirit-informed creative thought from, on average, the sixth dense physical sub-plane to, on average, the seventh mental sub-plane. A few members of the animal kingdom can consistently create thought through their informing spirit at the level of the fifth mental sub-plane; a very small number of them can very inconsistently slightly create thought from the fourth mental sub-plane.
Fourth Kingdom	Human Kingdom	*At present on Earth...*Spirit-informed creative thought from the fifth dense physical sub-plane to, on average, the top of the third mental sub-plane. The most advanced humans can create thought through informing spirit at the fifth sub-plane level of the intuitional plane; these members of the human kingdom are very advanced and, as are all very advanced members of each kingdom, are partly within the next higher kingdom.
Fifth Kingdom	Spiritual Kingdom, or Kingdom of (Liberated) Souls	*At present on Earth...*Spirit-informed creative thought from, on average, the first etheric sub-plane to the fifth spiritual, or atmic, sub-plane. The most advanced members of this kingdom can create thought from the atomic level of the monadic plane, and are also junior members of the next higher kingdom.
Sixth Kingdom	Planetary Kingdom, or Kingdom of Planets	Monadically-informed creative thought (spirit and energy of this kingdom is joined together into only intelligent activity) from the seventh mental sub-plane on a dense planet to, on average, the fifth logoic, or divine, plane (the plane of Adi). The most advanced members can create thought from outside our universe in a part of the (a) Cosmic Astral Universe. These great Beings live in both the (a) Cosmic Physical and Cosmic Astral Universe, with their highest thought in the Cosmic Astral, or outside our universe. Members of this kingdom create planets in our universe, for life to grow on. The lowest part of each member's body is a planet, and when the planet is in dense form the body reaches all the way to the most dense physical sub-plane. On the least dense planet, the lowest sub-plane these members' bodies reach is the seventh mental sub-plane.
Seventh Kingdom	Solar Kingdom, or Kingdom of Stars	The creative thought of these Great Beings extends from the seventh intuitional sub-plane to a part of the (a) Cosmic Mental Universe; the highest creative thought of some of these Beings reaches the very top of the (a) Cosmic Mental Universe. These Beings create three different categories of stars as the lowest part of their bodies—which are all within our universe. They also have a Cosmic Astral Body that is a part of and usually composed of, in its lowest form, ten planets at different levels of life development and in different dimensions of time and space within our universe, the (a) Cosmic Physical Universe.

Table 9. 2

		THE TWELVE KINGDOMS, CONT'D
NUMBER	NAME	LEVEL OF THOUGHT
Eighth Kingdom	Constellation Kingdom, or Kingdom of Groups of Stars	The creative thought of these Great Beings extends from the seventh spiritual, or atmic, sub-plane to a part, on average, of the (a) Cosmic Intuitional Universe—The highest thought of some of these Beings extends to the top of the (an) Intuitional Universe. The bodies of these Great Beings in our universe is a collection, or group, of stars that tends to move together and among themselves, as well as being created together and reincarnated from each others' lower bodies in gaseous clouds, or nebulae.
Ninth Kingdom	Kingdom of Groups of Constellations	The creative thought of these Great Beings extends, on average, from the seventh monadic sub-plane to a part of the (a) Cosmic Spiritual Universe. They create enough thought to inform the life within a number of constellations of stars—each star having a number of (often ten) planets. The highest creative thought of some of these Beings can reach to the top of the (a) Cosmic Spiritual Universe.
Tenth Kingdom	Galactic Kingdom, or Kingdom of Galaxies	The creative thought of these Great Beings extends, on average, from the seventh logoic sub-plane to a part of the (a) Cosmic Monadic Universe. The highest creative thought of some of these Beings reaches to the top of the (a) Cosmic Monadic Universe. They create thought that is great enough to inform the life of an entire galaxy.
Eleventh Kingdom	Kingdom of Groups of Galaxies	The Great Beings who inform the life of groups of galaxies create thought from the first, or atomic, logoic sub-plane to a part of the (of a) Cosmic Logoic Universe. The highest creative thought of some of these Beings can reach to the very top of the Cosmic Logoic Universe
Twelfth Kingdom	Kingdom of Universes	The Greatest of Beings creates thought that creates entire universes. The lowest of these type of Beings created our universe, but sacrificed its mind and thought (by splitting its mind into three parts that it also separated) before its mind entered our universe, so that new life could be free to create *within* the kingdoms that all of the other Beings and all the thought of spirit have created. These greatest of Beings all create universes from the top of the (a) Cosmic Logoic Universe, and collectively expand that top level as each creates its thought that creates its universe.

Table 9. 2, cont'd

Most members of a kingdom use the joint life that is shared and that is the kingdom in order to gradually together advance themselves through interactions of senses and thought. Within this system, the average for the members' thought and awareness increases in a similar manner for most types of the members that make up the life of that kingdom. When the vast majority of members have reached a prescribed level (prescribed from the thought of a higher kingdom), and within a designated certain period, or duration, of time, the majority of members of that kingdom advance into the next kingdom. A minority will fail to sense and think as well as is needed to become members of life in the next kingdom. These individual group souls that are not advancing may have to become part of a sub-kingdom that will function parasitically on some of the life-forms of higher kingdoms. It is usually not possible for a soul that did not keep up in development with the other souls in its kingdom to remain in its same position in its existing kingdom *on the same planet* once the rest of its kingdom has advanced, because to do so would potentially contaminate the lower kingdom that is advancing into its kingdom. On non-sacred planets there is the option for the failed (group soul) members of the lowest kingdoms to enter a sub-kingdom.

Once a planet no longer creates darkness through its life, the sub-kingdom system is abandoned, and such options become unavailable. Then various failed forms of life that are not conscious of their selves become extinct, and the group souls' spirit and energy may separate and pool together based upon their levels of (lacking) development. The informing Solar Angels and their Selves of these group souls can leave for a more primitive planet or sometimes *can inform* life in the newly developing kingdom of same types of groups. Doing so is permitted because the Solar Angels are *not* members of the lower kingdom that the group soul is in, but are members of the spiritual kingdom's energy sub-kingdom that did not sufficiently develop in a round. Group souls are allowed to leave a sacred planet because they have not been affected by evil—and hence do not hold the possibility of contaminating a kingdom on another planet. The lifeforms of these group souls must also be somewhat helping to create virtue within a different and more primitive evolutionary system. The option of leaving for a more primitive planet is open to such a group soul only if the kingdom it would enter on a different, more primitive planet would be similar enough to that group soul's prior kingdom, for the group soul to be able to adapt to it. This effect may also occur before a planet is sacred, if it is shifting to a more enlightened mode of life creation within a kingdom. In this circumstance, if all of the forms of life of a group soul become extinct, and there is no sub-kingdom still available for that group soul to create life within, it must relegate itself to a planet—usually within the same star system—whose level of development is lower. If a group soul is already on the lowest-level planet in its star system, that group soul may have to move to another star system that has even lower levels of planetary life. Group souls *advance* into the next kingdom by pooling their similar-thinking energies and spirit, provided that these energies and spirit have reached the minimum levels required to inform the new lifeforms in the next kingdom. (See Chapter Six for further explanation.)

Human souls can have similar difficulties; while they do not have the option that the lower kingdoms do, of their lifeforms joining a sub-kingdom, they may have to leave a planet in order to develop human beings in a much more primitive world. This relocation can be either temporary or permanent, as explained below. The human souls who cannot advance with the other souls in their kingdom prior to their planet either becoming sacred or shifting to a more enlightened method of life creation in their kingdom cannot find primitive-enough human bodies in which to incarnate on the whole planet. The energy in the permanent atoms of these souls is too dark, and will construct senses that function at too low a level to remain in any human on the planet at that time. Each of these human souls has created a number of prior human being incarnations that resulted in poor levels of creation of virtue. Every lifetime of such failure caused the human soul to fall further behind in its development, because its development takes place through virtue that is created by the human being whom it is informing in the three lower worlds. Eventually, the lowest level of energy that can construct a human body on the planet becomes too high for some human souls to incarnate into. Then these souls leave for other, more primitive, planets. These human souls do have the opportunity to return, to become a part of their original kingdom; however, to do so they need to advance themselves adequately enough and quickly enough (before the end of their period of life development) on the more primitive planet. They must be able to sense and think at at least the minimum level of sense and thought of the members of their kingdom on their original planet. Many do not and hence become a part of a human kingdom on the more primitive planet, which becomes their new home.

The control over a planet's growth of life, and how fast it is changed in order to achieve the result of more enlightened growth, is determined predominantly by the number and combination of the cosmic rays that are directed from the cosmic Ray Lords to the lower Ray Lords. These lower Ray Lords are advanced Masters who have chosen this path to further develop themselves, and they function as directing agents for each planet in a solar system. The more of the seven cosmic rays that are focused on a planet at one time, the faster the energy, or form, parts of life develop sense. More sense provides greater awareness, which informing spirit (such as group and individual human souls and their selves represent) needs to be able to appropriately use through thought to grow more of life, or of God, on a planet. A planet goes through seven periods of life creation; each successive period after the first has an additional one of the seven cosmic rays focused on it. Every planet starts with just one of the seven cosmic rays focused on it at a time. It ends its periods of life creation with all seven cosmic rays focused on it at once. Each period is referred to as a round of life creation. The life grows in focus on each of four different parts of three full dimensions of time and space, from the least dense dimension to the most dense, and then back again to the least dense for that planet.

The circle of life focus based upon density of energy helps to develop certain kingdoms more than others during each kingdom's position of focus. The reason is that each kingdom has its life mostly developed within a certain range of time and space, and density of energy. For example, the pre-life mineral kingdom develops most when life is focused more on the dense physical world. The plant kingdom develops the most when life is focused more on the etheric/dense physical world, and the animal kingdom develops most when life is focused on in the astral world. Humans develop most when life is focused lower mentally; however, humans are more adaptable than are members of the three kingdoms below them, and can benefit almost as much from life being focused on any of the three lower worlds. As a result, humans further grow as beings in each lifetime. Human and group souls develop the most from a focus of life on the higher mental plane.

A dense planet, such as earth, goes through a round of life focus that "begins" at the combined lower and higher mental plane, with the majority of focus on the lower mental plane, but only after the beginning focus on the higher mental plane and on the soul level of life. This means that for that period or sub-round, the majority of life on the planet and the focus of cosmic rays on it exist during this period of a round. The focus of life development is on the lower and higher parts of the mental plane and on developing both the senses of souls that are on the higher mental plane, and life that is on the lower mental plane. As the round proceeds, more of the focus of life moves to the lower mental plane, and to developing better senses in the bodies of some animals and in human bodies, if humans are present. The upper and lower mental parts of a round are counted as only one period of life development until a planet no longer has any evil on it and has thus become sacred. The reason is that human souls and their created lifeforms (human beings) are the creators of evil on a planet. The next (the second) part, or the sub-round period, of a round is focused on astral life and on the further development of the senses within the bodies of animals. The third part, or period, of a round on a planet that is not sacred and thus has evil on it (or at least has that potential) has its focus of life on the etheric sub-planes of the etheric/dense physical dimension. The plant kingdom is mostly focused etherically in its development of more sense in its lifeforms' centers and bodies, so that their life will expand. When a planet becomes sacred, the etheric and dense physical periods join together as one period of life focus, while the higher mental and lower mental then separate into separate periods of focus. Evil is blocked from even existing etheric/dense physically on that planet, which *closes the door* to evil's existence there. Simultaneous to these occurrences, each soul develops a life that is fully integrated with its created human being. The reason is that the souls have overcome their karma of having previously created humans who chose to become evil. The door to evil will remain open only as long as evil can affect life in the etheric dimension. Evil's presence can occur while the dimension is split, through human selfishness. Once the dimension is rejoined together by humans joining the five etheric/dense physical senses of form with the two of spirit, and then fusing these to the seven astral senses, or to super-empathy, evil can no longer overpower life on either the etheric or the astral plane. Evil is *forced* off the planet through blocking etheric/dense physical infiltration. The kama-manasic connection is destroyed in the process, as well. A major part of the entire process, as was described in Chapter Eight, is accomplished by the members of the human kingdom who are the highest in consciousness. These are people who have chosen to discipline (to limit) their senses in order to grow them, for the purpose of creating more virtue with them. Through these people's sacrifices, along with the sacrifices of many others who may choose to do less, but are still growing in virtue, evil can be eliminated from a planet. Evil would have never taken hold on earth had the first dense physical major race of humans, the Lemurians, joined their etheric/dense physical senses of form together and then to their senses of spirit, on this lowest plane. Had the Lemurians joined these senses, they could have then fused what would have been their seven joined etheric/dense physical senses to their two spiritual astral senses.

Once a planet reaches its lowest point of focus of life development in a round, the focus reverses again, in a progression towards the less dense dimensions. Earth reaches it lowest and most dense focus of life development when its focus of life is in the dense physical dimension. In a planet's lowest dimension of focus, all the kingdoms on it receive equal focus. This gives all of their members an opportunity to cooperate and share together (which is the etheric/dense physical virtue) on an etheric/dense physical planet. It also gives them opportunities to live more as one life in this most difficult of all the dimensions to live in and within which to cooperate and share. This challenge that is placed on the kingdoms and on life is meant to diversify life in form, or energy, while it is becoming more one in spirit. Because it is so very difficult to achieve this in a dimension whose energy is so dense, the kingdoms involved in the process on a dense physical planet sometimes do fail. Usually, the informing spirit in these lower kingdoms cannot raise its consciousness, or recognize and understand life as one, while it informs lifeforms in such dense form. The expanded, gravitating thought of the energy in the lower dimensions overcomes the thought of self of the informing fallen spirit, and this self then loses a part of its self; it responds more like the dark (fallen) spirit that it is supposed to be informing, because it is identifying with energy, or form, and is losing consciousness rather than gaining more of it. The outcome of the struggle that ensues ultimately determines the fate of dense planets, such as earth. Long-term failure results in the planet becoming mostly evil, and then apt to be destroyed as a result of the evil's own thought, but with the assistance (in putting an earlier stop to evil) of the Planetary Logos, or the Great Being who is a member of the Planetary Kingdom and whose lowest body is the planet. This Being was the original creator of life on the planet. When the battle against evil, is won, all evil is eradicated from that planet, and life's growth there significantly grows more of God, through further development of the dimension and duration of life of the (three) planetary Ray Lords that the planet's life is focused within.

Earth is presently in the middle (the fourth) sub-round of the fourth round. The focus of life is on the dense physical, which means that all the kingdoms are equally affected by the cosmic rays that are being focused on earth at any particular time. There currently are four cosmic rays that are focused on the planet, because it is in the fourth round. Each round comprises seven periods, or sub-rounds; each period corresponds to the dimension and kingdom of life focus, *and* to the direction the round is moving towards. This means that in an early part of a round, the direction is towards more focus on dense forms of life in lower kingdoms until the densest level is reached, where all forms are equally focused. In the second half of the rounds, the process reverses, when progressively less dense forms of life on the planet are focused upon.

THE BEGINNING OF EARTH'S FOURTH ROUND

To exemplify these concepts in most of the rest of this chapter, the entire fourth round for earth will be examined, including its time period of the past and what its future time period is likely to be. About sixty-five million years ago, the fourth sub-round of the *third* round came to an end. The focus of life dense physically on earth moved upward to first the etheric sub-plane. The etheric part of the plane was split from the dense physical because of residual karma from humans who had lived on a previous planet that earth is an incarnation of, with some of these people having been evil. In etheric time, less than a million years of life focus occurred on this plane, during which time the highest level of etheric life (of plants) was reached for the round. In dense physical time, less than half of that amount of time elapsed. Then for slightly over a million average astral years (less than 100,000 dense physical years) the focus of life was on the astral plane, and during that time the remaining more advanced plants and most of the animals developed into the highest levels possible for the species that had been living while dense physically alive. For a very short period—only thousands of lower mental plane years—lower mental life focus took place for the very highest animal species that had been developed. Humans generally did not exist on earth during the third round because humans, as the fourth kingdom, need to be in the fourth round in order to be developed through their civilizations on a dense planet, such as earth. When the fourth round began, the life focus and the cosmic rays shifted more towards the higher mental plane and on the group souls whose lifeforms were alive during the third round.

The third round ended because it completed seven sub-rounds, or periods of life focus with three cosmic rays focused on earth at any one time. Note that the second round ended dense physically over two hundred twenty million years ago, when only two rays were focused on earth at any one time. At the end of the dense physical period of the second round, over ninety-four percent of all species, or types of life, on physical earth was destroyed. At the end of the third round, ninety percent or more of all species, or types of life, was destroyed. The fourth round began about sixty-four million years ago. As each round progresses, it moves much faster in time than the previous one did because the life is growing progressively faster from accentuated effects of the rays and of the learning experience of informing spirit. For this reason, the fourth round began very slowly and took a relatively long time to once again reach the dense physical level. The higher mental part of the first sub-round of the fourth round spanned over a million higher mental plane years; during this time, some amounts of life still existed on the lower planes, because it would have been too difficult to begin life anew. The group souls of the life that remained were those that were mentioned in Chapter Six. These are the ones that have perfected certain senses of certain of their lifeforms (frogs and cockroaches, for example).

The focus in the beginning of the fourth round is on both group and individual human souls. Now *four* cosmic rays are focused at one time on the lifeforms and on the souls that will be creating life in the round. At certain intervals and with increasing rates of change, the four rays are switched, but only one at a time. Thus at the beginning of the fourth round, rays one, two, three, and four might be in focus. Later in development, the focused rays might be, for example, rays two, four, five, and seven, with further ray changes taking place according to what the planet needs in order for its life to maximally grow. Note that during the fourth round each one of the seven rays will, at times, be focused on the planet, but in a combination of only four rays at any one time.

Having four cosmic rays focused on a planet instead of three greatly accelerates the growth of the lifeforms' senses, and of life, there. This growth enables centers, senses, and bodies to be created for the fourth kingdom, of humans. For a human, the first body that is developed is the lower mental, with a small piece of the higher mental body attached. The lower mental body is focused on during the first sub-round, or period of life growth that is focused mentally, with most of the focus during the sub-round on the lower mental plane. At the very beginning of this period, the focus is on the body of the human soul. The focus during the remainder of the period is on the development of the lower-mental controlling part of the personality, which is first formed on the first sub-sub-plane of the fourth sub-plane within the mental unit. At this point, the other parts of the personality, which are on the second and third mental sub-sub-planes of the fourth sub-plane, barely exist.

The first major human race's bodies were created from this incomplete personality structure. The members of this race had complete development of only their lower mental bodies, and some amount of incomplete astral body development. Also, their etheric as well as their dense physical bodies were incompletely developed (they had no dense physical bodies). On the etheric sub-planes, each of these people had only a permanent atom and some amount of first sub-plane and/or atomic-level, etheric sub-plane development. The astral bodies of members of this race were composed of only first, second, and third astral sub-plane energy. Each astral body's permanent atom was located on the atomic level of the astral plane. This first major human race existed in the vicinities of what were, at that time, earth's North and South Poles. This race had no direct contact with other life on earth because the energies in its members' bodies centers and senses were too subtle to have such contact. The race did give to each personality and developing human soul some experience at working together and at developing a self. However, these people's selves had very little consciousness because the self could give thought to so few bodies, which had such small amounts of sense. The personality of each human learned to gain better control both over its bodies that did exist and over its self. This first major human race existed from about sixty-four million to about thirty-three million years ago.

About thirty-four million years ago, the second major human race was developed from the best-developed mental bodies of the first major human race. The souls of these very early humans (of the first and second major races and some later ones) came from what had been another planet karmically related to earth in our solar system, upon which development of virtue within the humans there had mostly failed. Because this planet was karmically related to earth, it was the one that provided its least developed souls to earth's earliest humans. This prior planet is sometimes referred to as a Moon Chain planet. In esoteric terms, a chain is composed of a series of incarnations of a planet at different levels of dimensions, depending upon the chain, from the spiritual all the way down to the dense physical. The least-advanced souls (those who had mostly failed to develop virtuous humans) from the prior development of a planet in higher dimensions than those of earth became the first to develop human beings on earth. The reason is that these more primitive souls needed more time to catch up, in development, with the more advanced souls that would incarnate later on earth.

Many (but not all) of these later-incarnating souls will have come from the last planet to be developed in the Moon Chain. The name "moon" is used because earth's moon today resembles the ending existence of this planet. Our moon is a reincarnation, in dense form, of this earlier planet that existed at its most dense level in the etheric dimension of time and space, during the first incarnation of our sun. Our sun, as we know it, is currently in its second incarnation. Some of the planets in the sun's first incarnation existed in much higher dimensions of space and much greater dilation of time, since the sun's first physical incarnation was for a relatively brief period of time. For example, time at the atomic level of the mental plane is dilated over one thousand times that of dense physical plane time. On the atomic level of the intuitional plane, the figure jumps to over one hundred forty thousand. On the atomic level of the spiritual plane the dilation of time is in ratio to the speed of etheric light times itself, or squared. This means that time is dilated millions of times at the atomic level of the spiritual plane over that on the dense physical sub-planes.

The second major race of humans in the fourth round had fully developed personalities on the first and second mental sub-sub-planes of the fourth sub-plane. These humans' astral bodies were fully developed from the first through the sixth astral sub-planes. Their etheric bodies were completely developed all the way through the fourth etheric sub-plane. These people had no dense physical bodies. Having more astral body development than either etheric/dense physical or lower mental, they lived as very fluid-looking forms, and they were mostly astral/etheric in consciousness because of the still relatively small amounts of development of their selves. This race of developing humanity lived from thirty-four million to about sixteen million years ago.

 # THE THIRD MAJOR HUMAN RACE—THE LEMURIANS

The very first sub-race of the third major human race was developed from the mental and astral body energies that had the best senses of the second race. The energies from the best-developed and most *suitable* etheric/dense physical prior animal bodies were joined, through the etheric portion of the human body, with the above-described energies from the human mental and astral bodies that had the best-developed senses. This joining was at first permissible because it was done only etherically as some group souls advanced and were joined into human souls, as was described in Chapter Six. When accomplished from a soul level and through higher spirit, the energies from the animals' bodies sometimes became enlightened enough to join with the humans' bodies. In the process, the spirit of some of the group souls advanced into the human kingdom. The earliest (prior) human souls had mostly come from an earlier soul life that had largely failed, on the final planet of the Moon Chain. New human souls were also created from the advanced collection of former animal spirit and energy of advanced animal group souls of earth. The higher spirit from the animal group souls could join only with new souls, which were created on earth, and only with the assistance of new, more advanced OverSouls, or Solar Angels, that came mostly from prior development on Venus. Venus had become completely etheric, with physical life unable to exist on its surface. Some of its energy-focused life—Solar Angels that had been OverSouls of group souls—came to earth in order to experience and help develop dense physical *human* life. Venus has become a sacred planet, which means that today it always appears to be somewhat etheric; all of its life focus is etheric, while its physical pre-life, or mineral focus, is most unusual compared to earth's. The OverSoul provided these newly created human souls with causal bodies. The consciousness of the prior human souls, who were mostly from the Moon Chain, was slightly higher than that of the new human souls created from the pooled animal spirit and energies from the advancing group souls of earth. The new earth souls, which were created as souls for the first time, usually each received one of the Venutian Solar Angels as its OverSoul. The new advanced OverSouls now fully integrated what had been the unevolved, poorly organized, and non-conceptual prior two races of humans and their personalities into new fully human personalities, with completed semi-permanent thoughtforms created on all three sub-sub-planes within the mental unit. A spark of life was created between the self and the completed personality by the focused thought of each newly arrived Solar Angel, who was in its second incarnation, now as a *human* Solar Angel, following its first triadal incarnation as the Solar Angel of a group soul. A large spark also was visible in the center of each more developed human soul, which was now joined, or fused, with additional higher spirit *from earth*. This new third major human race was the first race of *completed* human beings on earth because, unlike the earlier two major races, its members had three completed bodies.

These bodies contained some advanced etheric/dense physical energies that had been a part of the most advanced animals (which were advanced mammals) on earth up to that period of time. The vast majority of the physical time within a round is spent in its etheric/dense physical part, in which it is so difficult to achieve good results in the development of senses and bodies. But the first two major races of humans had spent most of their development in lower mental and astral time focused on the development of the lower mental and astral bodies. Because of a lack of focus etheric/dense physically, it was necessary that the next humans who were created use the most advanced etheric/dense physical energies and some fallen spirit of the animal kingdom. Despite the advanced qualities of the energies, the preliminary attempts to join the etheric part of the animal energies (from the second etheric sub-plane, down) with the previously developed human energies (the majority from the *atomic* etheric sub-plane) failed. The reason for the failure is that the energies that came from the animals (lunar deva energy from the second etheric sub-plane) could not adequately follow the thought either of the atomic-level lunar devas in the human energy, or of the higher (fallen) spirit of the humans at the atomic etheric level, which was being integrated by the new human self. More time was needed to further develop the etheric lunar devas, or lunar pitris, as well as the self of future human beings, by allowing the higher mental plane spirit to further develop. These first experiments were attempted twenty-one and a half million years ago.

About eighteen million years ago the experiments were repeated with only limited success—far too many humans were dying within a relatively short period of time. Then, about sixteen and a half million years ago the process stabilized as a result of advancements in the thought of lunar pitri energies and in mental plane spirit, and the third major race (the Lemurians) became developed. The first two sub-races were related to the focus of the first and second rays respectively, and had an overall ray focus of the seventh ray—under whose focus this entire major race developed its senses. The third sub-race people were overly etheric in form but less so than their predecessors were, because what made up their form was the etheric energies from animal sources, added to human etheric energies that were from the two previous major human races. This caused these first Lemurians to be resemblant of very large ghosts, with each one having a smaller dense replication of itself inside it. By the time the third Lemurian sub-race more fully developed, about ten million years ago, its members finally had reasonably dense physical bodies, although it was not until about eight and a half million years ago that these bodies all had a complete balance between their etheric and dense physical energies.

Every major race has seven sub-races, with each sub-race corresponding to a sense and body type of one of the seven rays, from the first (sub-) ray and sub-race to the seventh (sub-) ray and its sub-race. This order focuses each of the races more on spiritual sense development and on becoming human—recognizing God—early in each major race. What separates humans from animals is that humans can recognize and understand God. Therefore, no matter what a lifeform looks like, or which human race or sub-race he or she is born into, unless that lifeform can recognize and understand God, he or she is not human. Note that the above-mentioned order of the rays also slows the development of the senses of form and the overall development of civilization, because the senses are developed in approximate opposite order of the initial ray focus on the centers in the members of each sub-race. For example, in the first sub-race of the major race, the sexual (seventh sub-ray) center is usually first to develop, while the first ray is the most focused sub-ray (of each corresponding plane and body's ray). When the first (sub-) ray center (the head chakra) is developed in the seventh sub-race, the seventh sub-ray is the ray that is focused on the most in for each body in the sub-race. This occurs because the seventh cosmic ray is in focus the most on the planet during that time period. In the last two major races in this (the fourth) round, the Planetary Logos has the option to reverse this process; the ray focus for the planet during these future time periods can be altered to a focus more on the seventh through first sub-rays in each body. This reversal would tremendously accelerate the development of these races' form senses and their civilizations, albeit at some reduction in their members' spiritual senses. These last two major human races will be focused on spiritual sense development and could tolerate such a plan *if* there has been an adequate foundation of prior successful human and planetary spiritual development. Before the end of the twenty-first century, a decision will need to be made about the pattern of ray focus for the development of these future major races. The reason is that even though the thousand or so years between now and the time for the change to occur seems like a long time, it is, in spiritual time, extremely short. Also, many other planets need to be informed in advance because they would be affected by such a change.

Each sub-race uses its senses differently to create its own type of civilization by incorporating some of the lower kingdoms within its own, as extensions of and expressions of its sub-ray focused senses. The first sub-ray Lemurian race developed a civilization that used the lower kingdoms to increase its members' ability and that of future sub-races to create with a purpose certain material forms. These forms included huts and whatever other protection, including the use of fire, that these people needed in both the etheric and dense worlds, since these people's bodies as well as the bodies of later sub-races were more etheric than dense. These basic structures were organized into tribes and villages, or the first political units outside the family.

None of the Lemurians, as a civilization, lived in caves while their civilization was developing. After a sub-race reaches its zenith in development of civilization, it declines (usually slowly at first) because, as a result of its levels of selfishness, it usually cannot adapt to the changes in the cosmic ray focus that keep occurring. After a protracted period of time, a diminished sub-race loses enough of its senses to be overpowered and sometimes either helped or, more likely, destroyed by a developing newer sub-race. Those who escape either being helped or harmed by a newer sub-race have, in the past, isolated themselves geographically and became severely degenerated in sense and body. They became non-developed people who had primitive civilization and little resemblance to their ancestors. It is mostly these people whose fossil remains have been discovered in humanity's recent past, and who have been declared to be the first humans on the planet!

The second sub-race of Lemurians (which was the third major race) was still overly etheric in form, and its members developed their civilization from an accentuation of the second sub-ray sense. The effect of the second ray caused them to attempt to be more inclusive in the ways in which they used the lower kingdoms to develop their civilization. These people attempted to help the lower kingdoms while parts of these lower kingdoms were used to increase the *material* forms within their civilization. The entire civilization was focused on learning new and better ways to organize and economize the dense physical forms that it used. Less attention was put into etheric economy, which this sub-race as well as the first one could directly sense and change while its members were dense physically alive. Etheric energy is much easier to both synthesize and organize than are its effects in dense physical form; however, to synthesize and organize etheric energy requires considerable levels of planning from developed consciousness. The second sub-race was developing its consciousness because etheric energy changes much more easily, and thus it is easier to create more serious mistakes with etheric energy. However, for the most part these Lemurians were only partly effective in using etheric energy in their plans. Both the first and second sub-races had a third, purely etheric, eye, which permitted them to directly see etheric parts of all physical objects, from the first through the fourth etheric sub-planes. Their other etheric senses were keenly developed but each was used separately, except for taste and smell in the more developed second sub-race Lemurians.

The entire Lemurian race (the third major human race) was, in general, working on improving the seventh ray focus of human life. This focus was on the economical incorporation and organization of material form into human civilization. Sometimes this form was etheric, but mostly it was dense physical because this was the planet's life focus for the round. Each sub-race manifested this focus in a different way, with the emphasis on their senses based upon the emphasis of the sub-ray that the entire sub-race was developing. Whatever material form that the seven sub-races of Lemurians created virtuously did survive their civilization, sometimes in physical but mostly in mental form. These creations included concepts that were further built upon by later civilizations, even those of later major races. The parts of each sub-race's civilization that were used selfishly were destroyed, both physically and mentally as the civilization declined both from within (by civilization itself) and from without (by newer civilizations), often violently so. This process of civilization development and the retention of virtuous creation follows the very same concepts as they apply to life in general—as God's growth. That which becomes enlightened (virtuous, when in form) remains immortally, and that which is selfish, or dark—away from God's thought—eventually becomes destroyed.

Both the first and second Lemurian sub-races were relatively unsuccessful at creating virtuous civilizations, although the second did slightly better than the first, because the second was virtuous about sharing food within its civilization and with the lower kingdoms. This helped to develop the *human* sense of taste beyond sour, sweet, salty, and bitter—without having to first smell the food. Note, though, that this ability was developed in only some Lemurians. The appearance of members of the Lemurian first and second sub-races was *very* animal-like (ape-like) because so much of the energies within these people's etheric senses and bodies had been developed by animals. The beginning members of the first sub-race of Lemurians stood twenty-five to fifty (!) feet tall, and could change their height and size within that range. Later Lemurians in the first sub-race were about twenty feet in total height, and lost the ability to change the density of their forms. The second sub-race Lemurians stood twelve to fourteen feet in total height, and while still more etheric than dense physical in form, their bodies were much more dense and compact than were any of the first sub-race bodies.

The third sub-race of Lemurians underwent the greatest level of change during its development. This sub-race's balance between etheric and dense physical form progressed from being more etheric than dense physical, to having a normal amount of etheric as compared to dense physical form. The etheric is the cause, and the material, or dense physical, the effect. The Lemurians in the early part of the third sub-race still had an etheric third eye and very good, though mostly separated, etheric senses. They could see and sense all

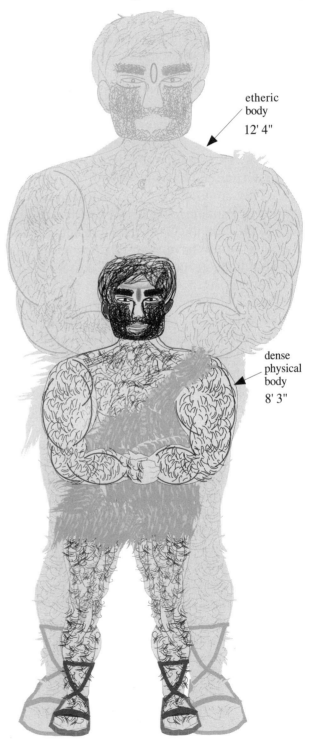

Illustration 9.2

Excessively Etheric Form of a Lemurian Early Third Sub-Race Young Adult Male

etheric body 12' 4"

dense physical body 8' 3"

four of the etheric sub-planes, in their entirety. The Lemurians in the later part of the third sub-race gradually, over many generations of time, mostly lost their etheric third eye; eventually, the etheric sense they did have was limited to hearing sounds from the second, third, and fourth etheric sub-planes. This last etheric sense, of hearing, remained mostly intact until the entire Lemurian race disappeared, but had diminished in most members to clearly hearing sounds only from the fourth etheric sub-plane. Those who had the most amount of the etheric sense or senses often became spiritual and religious leaders, and also healers. In degenerated and geographically isolated Lemurian societies of the past, and the very few that remain today, the same factors are still part of determining who becomes the spiritual or religious leaders and the healers. Of course, the etheric senses of those people have significantly diminished from the amount of sense that their ancestors had. Some healers in these primitive societies do have enough etheric sight to see maya (the etheric effects of illusion on the etheric centers and the etheric body), which is the cause of physical disease. Because the Lemurians had some etheric sense, they knew that dense physical death did not end consciousness. They feared death less than do people of today, and they were naturally more spiritual in their lives because they could sense a small part of the hidden meaning of life from the etheric subtle world.

The seven Lemurian civilizations developed on a continent that rose from the ridge in the Pacific Ocean, and about twenty-five million years ago reached the top of the sea, or ocean level. This continent continued to grow in size until about fourteen million years ago. The Isthmus of Panama arose about twenty million years ago, and blocked the Lemurians' transit by sea into the Atlantic Ocean. As a result, the Lemurians were unable to interfere as much as they otherwise would have with this new continent and the people who would later develop on it. This simultaneous occurrence also greatly altered life on the North and South American continents (and Eastern Asia slightly at times), as well as the weather patterns and ocean currents. The Pacific Ocean became cooler, the Atlantic Ocean warmed, and Lemuria's climate changed from sub-tropical to temperate; the rising (future) Atlantic continent would develop a Mediterranean climate. Today, however, all that is left of Lemuria is a series of islands because most of the continent sank back into the earth's crust and some possibly even into the mantle, below its crust and into the same ridge from which it arose. These geological changes occurred because of hastened cosmic ray changes and the overall plan and thought of the Planetary Logos. The relatively fast geologic speed of these changes has not been witnessed by geologists in modern times, and because the changes were mostly reversed in effect prior to recorded history, most geologists would consider it impossible or at least very unlikely for them to have occurred. Despite the Lemurians' spiritual emphasis that was a result of their etheric sense, they were, overall, very selfish in the way they used their etheric senses. As a result, most of their civilizations were destroyed as their continent subsided. It fell, first, below the ocean, and eventually mostly below the ocean floor. During the continental increases and decreases of Lemuria, the earth's weather drastically changed, causing some of the displaced waters to become trapped as ice as the climate cooled from part of the Pacific Ocean shrinking and the Isthmus of Panama rising. Provided that there is not a lot of selfishness on the planet, causing sudden rises and falls in energies, oceans are better regulators of temperature for most life on earth than are the landmasses that replace parts of them. The reason is that oceans transfer energies both faster and more efficiently. Split landmasses cause life on land to diversify because of, in part, the resultant greater changes in weather, and the geographic isolation that can occur. The more virtuous the life, the less the energy extremes and sudden differences in weather; selfish life creates sudden extremes, which reduces its growth. In a virtuous world, the more ocean there is, especially when it is uninterrupted by land, the more even the temperature and consistent the weather on land and, in addition, the warmer the average temperatures on land are. These conditions usually *reduce* the diversity of life.

The members of the third Lemurian sub-race focused their third sub-ray senses on creating a civilization that allowed them to better communicate and move among each other through use of the lower kingdoms. This was the first human society to use the concept of the wheel. (Prior to this civilization, the first and second sub-races already had use of fire.) Members of the third Lemurian sub-race used the amplified sound from drums to communicate over distances, and developed a code, like a simplified Morse code, to create words and *simple* sentences. These communication methods were later expanded upon by the members of the fifth Lemurian sub-race through more complex language. The fifth sub-race used reflected sunlight off mirrors that were made of polished limestone and later, metals; they also used fires for smoke signals and as

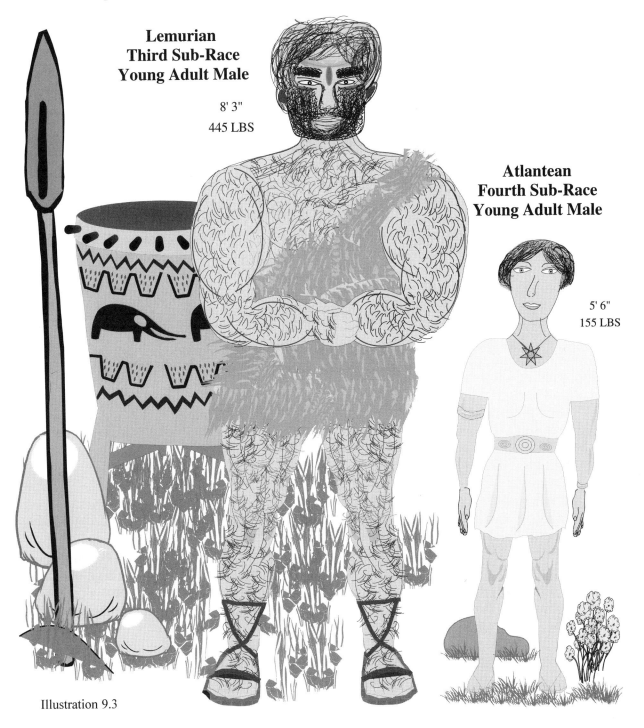

**Lemurian
Third Sub-Race
Young Adult Male**

8' 3"
445 LBS

**Atlantean
Fourth Sub-Race
Young Adult Male**

5' 6"
155 LBS

Illustration 9.3

signal lanterns. The first and second sub-races had been somewhat telepathic in their etheric brains because of their increased etheric senses. The third sub-race mostly lost this ability, and these humans had to create from their civilization more means of communicating, which the increased focusing of the third ray was stimulating in their senses and awareness to meet their needs. Their first communication using symbols expressed simple concepts. Other than counting by using objects to represent numbers, none of these first three sub-races had any mathematics. Using modern-day measures of levels of "intelligence," Lemurians had exceptional etheric/dense physical senses. They had only limited astral and mental senses and would today be thought of as well below normal in either of these areas. Mentally, they were not a lot smarter than the present-day humans who are considered to be the trainable mentally handicapped, but mostly uneducable in terms of modern-day average levels of knowledge.

As one sub-race declines, a new sub-race and often two or more of them is developed, creating a significant overlap between and among the sub-race civilizations. In the earlier sub-races, these conditions frequently led to wars, with the newer civilizations prevailing more often than not; the third Lemurian sub-race was the exception because it was better at military endeavors than any later sub-race until the seventh. The third sub-ray focus of the third sub-race (and its sympathetic reinforcement when under a seventh ray primary main focus) is what improved its members' senses and bodies to be more able to intelligently fight in wars. During all seven of the Lemurian sub-races, the seventh ray was most often in focus, overall, on earth. However, while the civilization of the third sub-race was under development, the third ray sometimes surpassed the seventh in its amount of focus on the planet. The seventh Lemurian sub-race was so much more advanced in its civilization that its members finally destroyed the third sub-race through militant confrontation. Even when sub-races, as civilizations, were destroyed, their legacy—as degenerated members of their sub-race—could live on for millions of years in more undesirable and geographically isolated places. These were sometimes many thousands of miles across oceans. Once these degenerating peoples would migrate across an ocean or mountain expanse, they would typically lose the ability to return to their homeland. The reason is that they had lost the technologies they once had, and their overall consciousness had become lowered.

The fourth Lemurian sub-race was the first sub-race to develop significant art forms by extending the use of the lower kingdoms. The earlier sub-races, and especially the third, had developed dance and song. The fourth, however, used minerals and plants to develop painting and sculpture; they used bird feathers and animal skins in artistic expressions. They also carved and stained wood. Fourth sub-race Lemurians were the first to develop jewelry and clothing that incorporated some elements of style and that were not merely functional. Instead of housing themselves in mud and grass huts, many fourth sub-race Lemurians preferred to use stretched animal skins over various types of sometimes carved or stained wooden frames, with the skins dyed or painted to provide color to their villages. The third sub-race of Lemurians created fortified towns comprised of both huts, as dwellings, and larger buildings for large group meetings, with both types of structures made of mud and grass or sometimes wood. Many lived in extended family units, with sex sometimes involving communal wives or even harems of wives as some men became more prominent than others. The fourth sub-race was more sexually promiscuous than were the earlier sub-races, and sometimes its communal lifestyle involved completely free sexuality with communal child rearing. Having a fourth ray focus, the senses of the fourth sub-race Lemurians tended towards seeking and perfecting a balance between form and spirit in material and sexual circumstances, with both materiality and sexuality affected by the focus of the seventh ray. When one attempts a perfect balance between sexual relations as an energy exchange, procreative means, and producer of physical pleasure and as a bonding or fusing, through spirit (through enlightened thought), of each of the three or more bodies between two people, but only achieves a relative balance then the results can become sexual relativism. Sexual relativism removes absolutes in the bonding, or marriages and family units, between sexual partners. And this leads to sexual promiscuity and to the types of communal sexuality, living, and child-raising arrangements that were created in the fourth Lemurian sub-race civilization. In the third sub-race the male, or masculine, side of civilization was dominant—the result was more of a harem-type of sexual interaction. Also, the third ray tends to lead to excesses of form, including men having more than one wife. The fourth sub-race was much more feminine in its dominance, although since the entire Lemurian race was focused in the seventh ray, its masculine focus tended to lessen the feminine focus of the sub-races that had even, or feminine, sub-rays.

The fifth Lemurian sub-race, which was developed about six million years ago and about a million years later than the fourth, developed a counting device that was a simplified abacus. This sub-race was the first to create a somewhat accurate astronomy, which coincided with their creation of a calendar and their rudimentary ways of measuring time within various spans (from within days to beyond a year). This sub-race also had some codified laws that included regulating conduct concerning sex, violence, property, and marriage. While still primitive by modern day standards, their system of writing used basic symbols to formulate words. This was a first for the Lemurians. Prior writing used one symbol for each word, which was a less formulated means of writing that was wasteful of time and energy in communication, and greatly diminished accuracy in the structure of sentences that represented new concepts.

Some of the buildings of this fifth Lemurian society were constructed from modules of pounded, pre-stretched animal skins that were tied to posts, with cross-bracing on both sides of a wall that was stuffed with dry straw. Huts made of mud and grass were still built and used in the more primitive villages. All of these modulated structures by fifth sub-race Lemurians were better insulated and more portable than were the ones that had been developed by earlier sub-races. Fifth sub-race Lemurians created the rudimentary elements of architecture, with building design that was based upon the addition of modules. While not as artistic as the fourth sub-race buildings, these fifth sub-race structures were much more viable for their civilization, saving time and energy in the people's lives. Even primitive roads and small bridges were built using tools and methods of construction that were simple, yet effective. The first types of suspension bridges were constructed with ropes and slats of wood, with straw and sap filling in the bottom part of the gaps, and with additional straw placed on top of the sap to preserve the wood. Short expanses of main roads were created by placing straw and, in some locations, pumice and volcanic ashes or minerals, upon paths that had been softened by rains. During a rain, herds of domestic animals were moved down the paths, sometimes with the animals (which were quite large, by today's standards) pulling logs to smooth the surface; these roads were then left to bake in the sun. The effect was a sort of adobe main roadway that was resistant to becoming muddy or to developing potholes when wet. Present-day archeologists would have been amazed at the ingenuity and relatively advanced technologies of the fifth sub-race Lemurians who lived *between five and six million* years ago. There are virtually no existing artifacts from these civilizations because most of the continent they lived on was submerged, and, in any case, few of the materials they used in their civilization would have survived for such a long period of time.

All of the Lemurian sub-races were given some levels of direct assistance by the few superhumans who were liberated souls from more advanced worlds, including Venus, and who came to earth in order to assist in human development. Since Venus was (and is) a planet whose life was (and is) mostly focused etherically, because of corresponding sense development it was easier and more effective for Venutians to assist the earlier Lemurians as an entire society—who had more etheric senses than did the later Lemurians. Eventually only those members of Lemurian societies who were spiritually disciplining themselves and were serving others could communicate with the Masters from the next, or fifth, kingdom. The etheric senses of the Lemurians continued to decline, in general. Then only the spiritual disciples had enough etheric sense, through each disciple's joining together the seven senses of his or her etheric body, to sense and communicate with the Masters. At this point, it was the disciples who became leaders and teachers. They helped to advance the Lemurian civilizations with some ways of raising consciousness, and also of advancing knowledge. When given unwisely, knowledge becomes destructive to civilization. Such destruction did occur at times during Lemurian history, but it never presented as severe a problem as that which occurred during the later Atlantean civilization. Despite their seemingly long period of time in which to develop themselves—millions of years—the Lemurian civilizations did receive significant help in both development of consciousness (love) and improvement of knowledge through their involvement with the Kingdom of Souls, or Spiritual Hierarchy of Masters.

Between five and four million years ago, quite a few Lemurians were following a spiritual path. Doing so led to an increase in these people's etheric senses (and somewhat of an increase in their astral senses) and service to others. This increasingly large group of disciples became focused on its way of life through the sixth ray being the predominant ray focused on earth (except for the seventh ray) while the sixth Lemurian sub-race was being developed. Note again that during the time that a race and sub-race are being developed, their corresponding rays are in focus more frequently than are other rays. This method created the sixth sub-race of Lemurians in the same process that created earlier Lemurian sub-races. The sixth sub-race of Lemurians expanded upon religion and brought people much closer together. They did so through a religion whose foundation was based upon spiritual principles of being more virtuous, particularly through the virtue of cooperation and sharing—the seventh Ray Lord's focus. The sixth ray tends to focus love into devotion to principles of giving in limited ways. When applied to the seventh plane, the sixth ray focus results in devotion to, or giving, cooperation and sharing. As amazing as it may sound, the sixth Lemurian sub-race became the most spiritual civilization that has as yet been seen on earth. The success of the spiritual disciples in this civilization was so great that they were able to join, or fuse, *the still separated* two spiritual etheric/dense physical senses of most Lemurians to the separated two spiritual astral senses. They accomplished this fusion through creating love by cooperating with and sharing with other people as well as with the lower kingdoms and the one higher than theirs that they were aware of, concerning most elements of their society. The sixth Lemurian sub-race eventually fused together its members' etheric/dense physical spiritual senses with their astral spiritual senses.

The great achievement of these very early spiritual disciples, some of whom have since become either advanced or very advanced Masters of the two kingdoms beyond the human, helped to allow humans to sense astrally and etheric/dense physically at the same time. This was a tremendous advancement in the way humans sense. The Atlantean spiritual disciples were not as successful, so humans in general today cannot simultaneously sense the mental thoughts of others while they use their whole astral sense of empathy (or even their separated astral senses) and/or their etheric/dense physical senses. Humans generally must sense and think mentally before—or after—they sense astrally and/or etheric/dense physically. The exceptions to this limitation are those who are spiritually disciplining their mental bodies. By joining these senses together, these people are simultaneously fusing their respective astral bodies and senses, through super-empathy, with their mental. However, this must be accomplished by each person on an individual basis, and it can no longer, from birth, become part of the structure of each human's permanent atoms. Once a major race has finished its development of each person's permanent atom that corresponds to the entire race, this permanent atom can no longer be altered on a race-wide basis. The reason is that the average thought of the entire race is needed in order to change the atom in such a way.

The sixth sub-race of Lemurians created the first marriages that were based upon *love* rather than property and codified laws, sexual relativism, family size, and male power for purely

Lemurian Sixth Sub-Race Young Adult Male

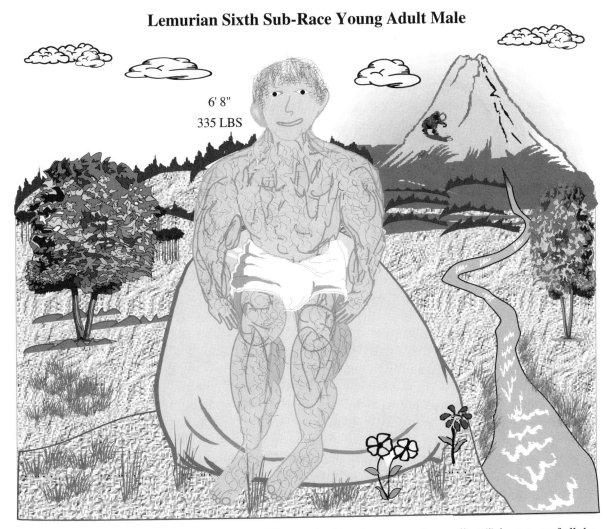

6' 8"

335 LBS

At 6½ feet to 7 feet tall, with a weight of over 330 pounds, this sub-race was the smallest (!) in stature of all the Lemurian sub-races. The physical bodies of this sub-race were the least angular and the most rounded in structure.

Illustration 9.4

sexual attraction. This focus on love altered the entire society, making women more important and, at times, equal to men in domestic areas of life. Child rearing became a devoted practice of love and care-giving. Older members (those over thirty-five!) were also given care by family units; this was another first for Lemurians. Also, the older people were regarded more with respect and sometimes reverence for their relative wisdom. All of these conditions were brought about by the enhanced sixth ray focus on earth, which increased the sixth ray sense of what relatively small amounts of empathy were to be found in the Lemurian sixth sub-race.

The better homes were constructed for more permanence in function, with some being circular to maintain a more even inside temperature. They were constructed with mud bricks, with lime added, that were either fire-baked or sun-baked (depending upon the season), and sometimes used with a mortar of mud, sand, and lime. These structures lasted for decades. Windows and doors were constructed from wood. They either worked as shutters or they solidly swung with dried and hardened wood or stone hinges that had rope through them (at this point, only soft metals—copper and tin, for example—had been discovered and used, and animal skin hinges lasted only a year or two). Even by today's standards, the sixth Lemurian sub-race was civilized. Had the seventh sub-race done as well, evil might not have become a semi-permanent part of humankind—lasting even into the present.

The sixth sub-race was the shortest of the Lemurian sub-races in stature because the even rays produce less growth in height, while the seventh ray (which was the overall ray of the race) was progressively densifying the Lemurian form and making it more compact. If not for this compounded effect of densifying and economizing the physical body, the focus of second and

Lemurian Sixth Sub-Race Village

Illustration 9.5

fourth rays would more often create the shortest people in a race. The sixth Lemurian sub-race stood, on average, only (!) about six and a half feet tall (a combined average of male and female height). By the middle of the third Lemurian sub-race, the physical bodies of humans had reached the correct ratio of dense to etheric energy. Male Lemurians in the middle-to-late part of the third sub-race stood an average of eight and a half feet tall. The dense part of the forms of the more etheric Lemurian sub-races—first, second, and early third—was about eight and a half to ten feet in height, with the etheric part from twelve to fifty feet tall and opaque. These etheric bodies could not be seen through, even in bright light. Each of these people had what looked like a dense body within a much larger etheric replica of it. However, the reverse was actually the case because the etheric is the cause, while the dense physical is the effect. The etheric body was pushed up by the dampening field of the earth. (See illustration 9.2.)

The seventh, and last, sub-race of Lemurians reached full development by about four million years ago. This sub-race stood over seven feet tall and had the largest bone structure and the second-most muscular features of all the Lemurian sub-races. With males weighing an average of four hundred ten pounds these people were formidable looking and almost as powerful as, if much slower-moving than, the people in the third sub-race were at the height of their civilization. The majority of the nicer buildings that the seventh Lemurian sub-race people constructed were made of stone. The more important stone buildings were from cut and fitted large blocks. Some of the other building methods of the earlier sub-races were also employed where and when efficient to do so. The later towns and "cities" of the seventh sub-race were the first to have business centers with buildings used for warehousing and for organized market areas. People in the seventh Lemurian sub-race built ships rather than just boats, and were traders across both land and sea.

The seventh sub-race colonized some areas and would invade, at times, parts of the world where degenerating first, second, and some third Lemurian sub-race people lived; the seventh sub-race Lemurians began the first trade of slavery, using some of these people. Not since the first two sub-races and a few members of the early part of the third, who had enslaved apes that they procreated with, was such wrong action a part of human civilization. Sexual relations (mostly forced by seventh sub-race men) with the degenerating sub-race slaves sometimes created offspring of animal-like humans. On rare occasion, this type of procreation produced a very advanced human—who, in many cases, would escape captivity. Through slavery and greed in general, and sometimes through laziness with a lacking in movement (with inertia), the seventh Lemurian sub-race became somewhat evil. Some of its members also enslaved some people from the earlier sub-races that were not degenerated and still lived on Lemuria; much of what remained of these sub-races they destroyed in battle.

 ## THE FOURTH MAJOR HUMAN RACE—THE ATLANTEANS

Not surprisingly, the fate of the seventh Lemurian sub-race was that it was to be almost eradicated, and this occurred through two forces. The first was submergence of the Lemurians' continent through progressive volcanic eruptions, and then relatively sudden inundation by the sea. Some escaped and traveled to a new land that had been emerging for about ten million years. This new continent began to rise above sea level about fifteen to sixteen million years ago, as Iceland started to rise as well (though Iceland rose more quickly), starting from the Atlantic sea floor. The people in this new land had been traded with, and some of the rare, more advanced Lemurians had also traveled to become residents there. The new continent was Atlantis. It was in the Atlantic Ocean and was rising from the mid-Atlantic ridge, at an astonishingly rapid rate for its size. The second force released on the darker members of the seventh Lemurian sub-race was the first three Atlantean sub-races. In their first sub-race, the Atlanteans extolled, freedom. In the second, they extolled tolerance and empathy for other humans, and in the third, they extolled both destruction of forms through militant action upon those who restricted freedom, and tolerance and empathy for those humans who were different from them. The Atlanteans made it their early civilization's purpose and goal to eliminate the evil of the seventh sub-race Lemurians. They did so through cunning use of their creative imagination, after inventing new military methodologies and emotionally coercive means of warfare—some of which are still used today (e.g., decreasing the opponents' energy by increasing their fears and emotions before they can effectively fight). Because the seventh sub-race Lemurians were much bigger and stronger than the Atlanteans were, it took the Atlanteans about one million (!) years to completely destroy all of the evil in the seventh sub-race. The more enlightened Lemurians were absorbed into the early Atlantean sub-races. This especially occurred in the second sub-race, because its second sub-ray focus enhanced empathy, love, and tolerance as a part of its civilization. Although empathy did reach a higher level in the third Atlantean sub-race, the use of empathy towards those who were most different was more virtuously applied in the second.

By about three million years ago, most of the evil from Lemurian seventh sub-race society had been destroyed. The first Atlanteans developed a civilization about six million years ago, but were very slow in their development because these people were given a predominance of first ray body types, while the first ray was *not* being focused as much on earth. Instead, the fourth and the fifth rays were in focus the most. When each new major race first appears, it grows very slowly and quite differently from other sub-races because the rays that are focused on earth are not always in correspondence to the ray body types that the souls are creating in the plan for the planet. This method of creation of new human life accentuates more spiritual development in the beginning of each new major race, and functions in a way that is similar to life creation through kingdoms. The system resembles that of a kingdom, since each major new race is very different and slow to initially grow. The purpose of this method is to not interfere with the existing major race—for a relatively long period of time, while the focus of the rays continues to be on the development of the sub-races of the older, more mature, major race.

The first ray returned to more consistent activity and focus on earth about three and a half million years ago, as the Atlanteans began to consistently destroy the evil in the Lemurians. On a non-sacred planet, such as earth, the first ray is often first a destroyer of darkness, before it is a creator of light. By the time the first ray returned in frequent focus, it was a sub-ray of the sixth ray rather than of the seventh, which had gone out of frequent focus for the first time in about eighteen and a half million years. The change in focus from the seventh ray to the sixth caused the Lemurians to stop developing and their continent to more suddenly disintegrate, and brought about a sudden growth in Atlantean civilization. While the sixth sub-ray was in focus under the seventh ray, during the sixth Lemurian sub-race development (about four and a half million years ago), the Atlanteans also benefited to some degree from this focus. They received this benefit because their overall focus of development was on their astral body and senses, which are controlled by the sixth ray. The Lemurians' overall focus of development was on their etheric/dense physical body and senses, and the seventh ray.

At some times, when appropriate, the ray focus combinations during the latter half of the first million years that the Atlanteans were developing were rays 1-2-6-7, rays 1-3-6-7, and rays 2-3-6-7; during the second million years of Atlantean development, the rays most in focus were rays 2-3-1-7. The order of the rays as listed from left to right either indicates the most recently changed ray (on the left) to the one that has been in focus the longest (on the right), or, when depicting a long period of time, the one that has on average been changed the most of the four (on the left), to the one that has remained in focus the most (on the right). While not ideal ray combinations for developing the full civilizations of each of the three Atlantean sub-races during this time period, when these ray combinations were in focus, their effects were more than sufficient to alter the permanent atoms in corresponding-rayed bodies to develop the people first, before their civilizations. Notice also that these ray focuses did not necessarily disturb the development of the later two Lemurian sub-races, nor their civilizations. The first *three* Atlantean sub-races had been slightly developed as "seed" sub-races from about six million to about three and a half million years ago, with the people in the first sub-race, then the second, and then the third developing themselves as people, but not developing as much of their civilizations until much later, when the full change in ray focus facilitated the process. The Atlanteans whose body and senses were focused on the first ray were more developed from six million to about five million years ago. Then the next sub-race, whose bodies and senses were focused on the second ray, was somewhat more developed from five to four million years ago. Finally, from four to three and a half million years ago a larger number of Atlanteans were created with senses and bodies that had a third ray focus than the number of people who had bodies with a first or second ray focus. About four million years ago, the total number of Atlanteans alive was less than one percent of earth's human population. At that time, quite a few of the more enlightened Lemurians (but still a small percentage of their overall population), both from the sixth and seventh sub-races, traveled to Atlantis and made significant contributions to Atlantean civilization. Thus the best and most advanced members of the Lemurian sub-races added their diversity and virtue to the relatively small numbers of the Atlantean "seed" sub-race people. Because of the sympathetic ray effects, the sixth sub-race Lemurians tended to assimilate with the second sub-race Atlanteans, while the enlightened seventh sub-race Lemurians assimilated more often with the first and third "seed" sub-race Atlanteans. A seed sub-race is one in which the senses are developed for the sub-race much more than the civilization is.

Once the dominance in ray focus changed from the seventh to the sixth ray, with, at first, the first sub-ray being secondarily focused under the sixth ray, the Atlanteans' first sub-race grew very quickly. Then the second sub-ray replaced the first, and the focus in civilization and growth quickly shifted to the second sub-race. Finally, the third sub-race reached its zenith in civilization between about three million and two and a half million years ago. In its early period, this sub-race finished off the remaining evil parts of the seventh Lemurian sub-race civilization.

The Atlanteans used animals within their civilizations to a much greater extent than the Lemurians did. The Lemurians used only the skin and bones of animals fairly extensively. Except for the seventh sub-race, Lemurians ate little meat, and nearly all of the sixth sub-race Lemurians were ovo-lacto vegetarians (the only animal products that most of them ate were eggs and milk). Lemurians identified themselves much more as *being* animals, since the first Lemurians were partially created from some etheric animal energies. The Lemurians were aware of that because they had been given the information from the Masters' teachings. The Atlanteans were changed in their thinking and were much more separative in their perceptions of humanity in relationship to animals. The first animals to be hybridized in human civilization on earth were bred by Atlanteans. They bred the horse from a relatively small animal that was "useless" for humans' work, to become the dominant work animal in their later civilizations. Animals are focused on astral development, which coincided with the Atlantean major race development of senses and body. Because of this, animals became a dominant part of Atlantean civilization. Lemurians were much more focused on the etheric life of plants and the use of plant life (sometimes with minerals and animals) in their civilizations. Lemuria was where the first cultivated plants came from. This included, from warmer regions, the banana, which later became quite popular on Atlantis when it was introduced there by Lemurian refugees and pilgrims.

Pig-like and cow-like animals; dogs; hybridized birds that were something like a combination chicken and turkey, but closer to the size of an ostrich; and, later, cats were all domesticated and bred by Atlanteans in the first sub-race. The breeding of animals reached a frenzied peak at the height of the third Atlantean sub-race. Maize, rice, and many other grains had been hybridized by the Lemurians, but rye and, later, an early variety of wheat were grains that were developed by Atlanteans. The first true animal pets were bred (to be pets) by the Atlanteans, who usually had as many pets as they did children. A custom the Atlanteans developed very early in their civilization was for children to learn empathy better by *each* child having a pet that she or he was responsible for.

The astral senses of Atlanteans were more separated than not until the fourth Atlantean sub-race people, aided by the focus of the fourth ray, unified the astral senses of form, racially, for all future humans. While accomplished by the entire civilization, the unification of the astral senses of form was given impetus by the great sacrifices and discipline of spiritually disciplined people during the height of the fourth sub-race. The first Atlantean sub-race used mostly split, or lower psychic, astral senses, and kept them separate by frequent contact with humans who were alive on the astral plane (after having died etheric/dense physically). People in the early Atlantean sub-races were mostly unafraid of physical death because they had direct awareness of and knowledge of astral life. Communication with people who were etheric/dense physically dead and astrally alive was a part of the religion in Atlantean society. Unfortunately, this somewhat led people away from the more spiritual understandings that astral life is a way of decreasing selfishness, rather than an easier way of living, with desires being almost instantly met on the astral plane. In general, Atlanteans who were not spiritually disciplining themselves and thus were not in direct contact with spiritual Masters in the next kingdom, believed that astral life was *their reward for living etheric/dense physically*, which was given to them, in love, by God. Some of this religious construct has remained until modern times, in modified mental form. It may be amazing that the early Atlanteans could have so much awareness of the astral plane, and not be nearly as spiritual as some Lemurians had been. Knowledge is not consciousness, and the Atlanteans used their knowledge to focus on *themselves* as being the importance of, and the meaning of, life. These Atlanteans wrongly believed that God rewarded them for doing God the favor of living in such a difficult world; since God owed them this reward, it was their right and "obligation" to have their desires met and to be as (hedonistically and emotionally) happy as possible! One might imagine how all of this was practiced as a religion on Atlantis; yet, today, there are still many people—though a minority—who would agree with this religious philosophy, and who might even be practicing it as a religion or a philosophy of life.

Atlantean people, for the most part, thought primarily from their astral bodies and sensed more astrally than mentally. These people used their mental senses and they thought mentally mostly secondarily to their astral thought and senses. Since their astral senses were reasonably joined with their etheric senses, but, in the first three sub-races, all of the senses in one body were still separated from the other senses of that body, the Atlanteans' mental thought and sense were also predominately secondary to their etheric/dense physical thought and sense. It is important to understand, as has been explained in previous chapters, that the spirit that informs a body is creating the thought within the body from information supplied to it by the senses. Each body has spirit informing it from the same dimension the body is in. In addition, the controlling personality and its self are the higher, integrating spirit in a human being, and join the senses and thought of each of the three lower bodies into one combined set of knowledge, integrated thought, and sense of self. The majority of Atlantean knowledge came from the integrated thought of just the two lowest bodies and brains, and their associated means of thought. A minority of their thought was structured, or was mental thought. As their primary thought, Atlanteans relied upon, mostly, creative imagination. Lemurians' primary thought came from information brought in through their etheric/dense physical senses, and the knowledge that the informing etheric spirit could draw from this information; the knowledge was then secondarily integrated in thought mentally by the personality and self. As their primary means of thought, the Lemurians used coordinated intelligent thought regarding physical activities. This means of thought is used as *primary* thought, today, by children under seven years of age; from ages seven to fourteen, children of today primarily use the thought of creative imagination, and from fourteen to twenty one, and often onward, the primary means of thought for most people is structured in whole time, or mentally focused. People who are spiritually disciplining themselves may go on to eventually, primarily, think using intuitive thought that is controlled, based upon service. The spiritually disciplined members of the Lemurian and Atlantean societies could think primarily using their mental structured thought. Most of the inventions in their civilizations were created by this relatively small number of people whose primary focus of thought was mental, and who were, necessarily, spiritually disciplining themselves.

Atlanteans primarily used their astral senses for information about other lifeforms including, of course, other humans. People in the first sub-race were empathic only a small amount of the time that they used their astral senses, because they tended to be selfish in their use of these senses. The great difficulty of overcoming the gravitational effects of elemental energy—even the less-dense astral elemental energy—is tremendously compounded when a person is physically alive. The reason is that the astral senses are reduced and less accurate when used in the etheric/dense physical dimension, which causes the etheric/dense physical senses to overpower them in terms of sensory information. Thus while the physically alive first sub-race Atlanteans focused more on their astral senses than on either of the other bodies' senses, they received inaccurate information that led them to be more selfish, from their illusions; of course, the selfishness then further separated their senses, causing even greater illusion. Only self discipline, coming from a personality choosing to relinquish some of its control, reverses this failing system of sense (awareness) and consciousness (self).

People who are astrally selfish *and* who also think primarily using creative imagination and either empathy or one of their split astral senses are very emotional; they cannot use logic correctly because they usually overemphasize the past part of time while they virtually omit its future part. Their thoughts fail to have structure, since, in their thought, events in space are incorrectly placed in time (or not placed at all, in some parts of time). Their concepts are so incomplete as to be difficult to even reconstruct because these concepts are lacking the same parts of time that the thoughtforms are. Even worse in these circumstances, the directing thought of the self holds them together too loosely for it to control the solar deva and higher mental elemental energies. The result is that what should be a concept is often several unrelated partial causes, creating unrelated partial thoughtforms. These thoughtforms then serve as a mental rationale for what is, mostly, emotional thought from the astral body and its informing spirit. An example of this type of thought for a typical early sub-race Atlantean follows.

Questioner: "Why does God love you?"

Typical Atlantean Person: "Because I am happy and I generally feel good."

Questioner: "How does that relate to what God wants?

Typical Atlantean Person: "God is good, so if I feel good, I am doing what God wants."

Questioner: "What if what makes your neighbor feel good makes you feel bad—which one of you does God love?"

Typical Atlantean Person: "I must live so that I feel good and if my neighbor does the same, then we have no problems."

Questioner: "What happens if your neighbor gives you a problem?"

Typical Atlantean Person: "I will make changes to feel better."

Questioner: "Would you force your neighbor to change?"

Typical Atlantean Person: "If that made me feel good, I would."

Self-focused astralism, or emotional sensing and thinking, leads to such thought processes—which Atlanteans were immersed in. Notice that typical Atlantean responses were missing some balance of future time; also, the thought was predicated on what past events had taken place, rather than a conceptual structure of all three parts of time. Children of today between the ages of seven and fourteen frequently think in this way because they are primarily astrally focused, *and* their astral senses and bodies are not fully developed, which leads to an immature astral self-focus. Adults and some adolescents today who have certain personality disorders that affect the astral body the most may think similarly.

 ## The First Three Atlantean Sub-Races

On the surface, Atlanteans seemed congenial and friendly in many circumstances. The first sub-race created a cultural lifestyle that was based upon the fulfillment of desires. The civilization these people created was developed to improve comfort, pleasure, and excitement in order to escape from the loss in meaning from life when these self-focused life goals become so exaggerated. Passion was by far more important than was reason, because passion employed astral sense and thought in a focused and devoted sixth ray, or astral-rayed, means of expression of astral thought and sense. When comfort, pleasure, excitement, and passion become the goals of a civilization, hedonism becomes the philosophy that is most developed. Fortunately, the first Atlantean sub-race was culturally affected by and also crossbred with some of the more enlightened members of the sixth and seventh Lemurian sub-races. The culture of these Lemurians also modified the first three Atlantean sub-race civilizations. There were fewer of these Lemurians who were of the sixth sub-race than in the seventh; what the sixth Lemurian sub-race people gave to these first Atlanteans was better motives and a more virtuous concept of God. The larger percentage of Lemurian immigrants, from the seventh sub-race, contributed more sharing and cooperation as virtue, and gave the Atlanteans physical inventions that endured and were more permanent in their application.

One of these inventions concerned methodology of building construction. The Atlanteans preferred the stone buildings of the seventh sub-race Lemurians. The first sub-race Atlanteans created a new architecture that resembled (much later) ancient Greek structures. Interestingly, the ancient Greek designs came from Atlantean civilization, because prehistoric Greece had been a colony of the seventh Atlantean sub-race. The first sub-race Atlanteans also invented more mass weapons of war—such as catapults for rocks and burning tars and oils—the same types of weapons that were found much later in ancient Greek and Roman civilizations. The third Atlantean sub-race increased the size and range of such weapons. The bow and metal-tipped arrow was also an Atlantean invention. Lemurians did have bows and arrows, but their arrows had stone or wooden tips and could not be projected nearly as far as Atlantean arrows, because the Atlantean designs were much more efficient. Atlanteans also invented the sword used in conjunction with a shield. The first sub-race of Atlanteans smelted iron, and the third invented foundries to cast and forge the iron. What most archeologists presently believe to be relatively recent inventions of humankind, from about seven thousand or even fewer years ago, was a part of Atlantean civilization, which began over *four million* years ago. Someday, a few of the more durable (metal) artifacts that escaped the submergence of Atlantis are likely to be found; some may already have been but have yet to be correctly dated. Much of the knowledge that Atlanteans used with which to invent material forms came from spiritually disciplined people who had some contact with Masters from the next kingdom. As this knowledge became disseminated somewhat indiscriminately and unwisely, Atlantean societies became darker. Sometimes some of the Masters would take physical form and live directly with some of the Atlantean people in the later (but not the last) sub-races, in attempt to limit and correct their students who were unwisely giving such knowledge to selfish and emotionally self-focused people.

The second sub-race of Atlanteans was more virtuous, on average, than was the first, because the combined factors of an even-rayed sub-race (corresponding to the second ray) within an even-rayed major race (corresponding to the sixth ray) made it easier for these people to create a virtuous civilization. Also, the sun is in its second incarnation, under the second ray, and is developing more consciousness in general on all of its planets, including earth. For this reason, the second ray is more frequently in focus than are the other two rays of aspect (the first and third). This focus helps to develop more of a second ray sense in all of life on earth. The second Atlantean sub-race created the first human system of formal education. This was a major factor in this sub-race's success in creating virtue. During this sub-race and in all subsequent Atlantean sub-races, formal education of children until about age fourteen was provided by what had been the first true national type government, created by the first Atlantean sub-race. This government was first created to fight the Lemurians. Part-time formal education began at four years of age, and grew to full time, or a school day, by age six—which is amazingly similar to some countries' systems today. Lemurian education had taken place informally, through families, but not as a national system. The Atlantean educational system contained subjects and a grading system, but these were very different from those found in modern day schools. Children were mostly graded on how they responded to learning, and not on what they actually knew. Rather than abstract and structured mental knowledge, the subjects that were taught concerned life circumstances, and the children learning ways to deal with them. These schools were developing *emotional* intelligence, rather than mental knowledge and its use.

The governmental system, which was first created by the Atlantean first sub-race, had ten prince-like, and, later, more king- (or sometimes queen-) like, governors who were appointed to their positions for life unless they were removed for malfeasance in office. These appointments were made by a council of people that comprised the best warriors, the highest class of spiritual leaders, the best artists and educators, and people of wealth. The warriors were chosen based on military rank, which was determined by their acts of heroism during Atlantean battles against enemies, including the evil ones of the seventh sub-race Lemurians. The highest class of spiritual leaders was chosen by the highest priestess, who also served on the council; this priestess was chosen when she was six years old, by someone who was at that time a priestess herself. Another sub-group was made up of artists, in the various possible expressions of art, and each was selected by popular consensus from one of the ten political regions, or governorships. Each of the ten school systems chose an educator to serve on this council; also included was the wealthiest person (or married couple) from each governorship who was willing to serve on it. Within the council, except for the priestess, each division had a one-person, one-vote system for deciding concerns of law and for appointing new governors—or removing, for cause, ones in office (a rare event). Then each one of the seven sub-groups or divisions of government had one vote, with a majority ultimately deciding on issues (a tie vote would negate that sub-group's vote). Most of the time, no decision vote was needed because the Atlanteans were often able to reach unanimity, since each of the seven sub-groups was seen as the expert in thought within its field. Note that a tie vote in the six of seven sub-groups would leave the deciding vote to the religious—sixth ray—priestess.

The Atlantean system of government was invented by the Masters in the fifth kingdom, and was taught to their students. It survived, mostly unchanged, for millions of years because it was based upon the seven rays of cosmic virtue as applied to the human creation of civilization. Only the very focused (and somewhat separative) sixth ray division of *highest* priestess and her religious subordinates was not completely democratic; however, that system was theocratic and actually was a more virtuous, on average, functional unit because *sometimes* its decisions were predicated on the creation of virtue. Its function in the council, unfortunately, was not followed and carried out very often on a much lower level by the more average Atlanteans in their daily lives and their relationships with God.

The court system in early governorships was a panel of judges—usually three—without juries. The laws and the way they were enforced varied from one governorship to another. The reason is that this system was based either on love and empathy or on emotions, or how people felt. The Atlanteans were the first people to have a true justice system, even if it lacked much of the structure of the justice systems that many people are familiar with today. The governor was generally the final authority in any case adjudicated within his, or sometimes her, jurisdiction. A final appeal could be made to the high council in attempt to overturn the governor's ruling, but rarely was because the council would usually ignore such appeals. Capital punishment did not exist, since the Atlanteans knew that killing people in one dimension simply freed them to another. Crimes of passion were usually the most serious ones until the fifth sub-race, when evil crimes that were planned to a greater extent started to become more common. Imprisonment and torture existed, but forced exile was the preferred method for dealing with more serious crimes, including murder. Once exiled *to a primitive area*, it was not uncommon for people to kill themselves within a short period of time. They did so because Atlanteans of any of the sub-races could not easily tolerate the rigors of living in some of the wastelands, nor the isolation from civilization that almost always followed.

The most common areas of exile were some remote sections of Africa, because these places were easily traveled to by ship, and some parts of them were almost impossible to escape from because of the surrounding dense vegetation and the very dangerous wildlife. Another hazard was the groups of degenerating Lemurian human populations who were quite dangerous when encountered. Some of the Atlanteans who were exiled had to contend with not only these, but other dangers as well. Those who were banished to some areas created small towns and would live together; this was permissible, provided that each person was there as a result of punitive action. Wives or husbands, or others, generally could not legally voluntarily accompany a loved one into exile. When Atlantis was submerged, many of these areas of exile became volcanically and/or geologically more active, which further destroyed the evidence of the existence of some of the exiled Atlanteans. The presence of a population of selfish Atlanteans affected the physical processes of the earth because their collective thought, over protracted periods of time, affected both weather and geology. As the changes in ray focus occurred rapidly and sometimes in an order that was destructive to Atlantean life, through civilization and physical surroundings, any place where Atlanteans lived was in jeopardy—especially the colonies that the later sub-races of Atlanteans tended to create. Because energy, including destructive energy, follows thought that is greater than its own thought, as physical energy is brought into greater activity—by being increased in its own very slight thought through the focus of certain cosmic rays on it—this energy can become destructive as it becomes attracted to selfish thought and to the forms that exist in the same area as the selfish thought.

The first Atlantean sub-race did not create much of the government described above until about four million years ago, because to do so required a more consistent focus of the sixth and first rays, along with the second and third rays. The second sub-race added the importance of formal education to governmental control, and to Atlantean society in general. This sub-race reached its highest level of civilization development about three and a half million years ago; the third sub-race reached its peak between three million and two and a half million years ago, as it concurrently created a formidable military. The third sub-race created the first national system of banking. A national currency system, of gold, silver, and copper coins, was developed during the first sub-race. The Atlantean banking system established *public* loans, with the interest sometimes being paid by the debtor providing some form of public service. The third sub-race developed a carrier service, which used several different types of pigeon-like birds. The third sub-race also invented the first postal service, which covered the land, air, and over-sea transport of information and small cargo. A sort of pony express, or quick consistent movement of mail using hybridized horses, was used between towns that were in relatively close proximity.

The size of the island continent of Atlantis changed over time; with all of its surrounding islands included, it was at its largest about two to one million years ago. The governorships were formed in concentric circles of land area from the center of the island continent, outward—resembling the planetary rings of a solar system, in two dimensions. The innermost circle was where the largest and capital-like city was built. This city was the seat of government and where the high council usually met. In the final Atlantean sub-race, the circles became more like squares, when all that was left of Atlantis was the relatively small island of Poseidonis. Poseidonis had been the first, or innermost, governorship when the continent of Atlantis was much larger. About one and a half million years ago, Poseidonis's capital city was surrounded by four of earth's tallest mountains, which stood over thirty thousand feet tall. Today, the peaks of these mountains form the Azores Islands. The main, or capital, city was named after the tallest peak—both were called Olympus. Some of this information became, after the submergence of Atlantis, a part of the religion of ancient Greece, prior to the time of recorded history.

Generally speaking, sexual relations among Atlanteans, no matter which sub-race, were more often than not semi-monogamous because the sixth ray tends to produce this effect by causing the senses to focus on one person at a time. Of the first three sub-races, sexual monogamy was most common in the second. This sub-race was the most inclusive one because of the focus of the second ray, and because in the second Atlantean sub-race women controlled much more of the society. When women control more of a society than do men, the virtue of love increases but creativeness and inventiveness somewhat decrease unless a balance is reached between the two genders' control. More of love tends to increase monogamous sexual relations—and more stability in marriages and families. When functioning non-monogamously, Atlanteans were often cavalier about sexual relations, considering such encounters to be nothing more than a means of having pleasure. Atlantean religion tended to support this position of self-focused use of others sexually; it failed to recognize that even when both people are equally objectifying each other for the sake of pleasure, each is becoming spiritually reduced by not recognizing the other (and himself or herself) as a part of the one life. When sexual relations are participated in in order to express love, the spirit grows. Atlanteans commonly believed that it was loving to give pleasure, based upon emotional feeling rather than (longer-term) spiritual growth through increased virtue. To average Atlanteans, two strangers who just met and then engaged in sexual relations for pleasure, and then parted, were "loving" each other by helping the other to experience pleasure while she or he experienced pleasure, too. The focus on pleasure and pain are an exaggeration of the form side of life, which reduces consciousness and spirit's importance, and thus increases illusion.

Real love did exist in Atlantean civilization, in families and among friends. This love was rather personal, and seldom reached a soul conscious, or group conscious, level except in those who were mentally disciplining themselves. The reason is that the entire major race was too astrally focused—limiting love, instead of producing unconditional love, i.e., Atlantean love was more of the sixth ray than the second ray type. A great deal of love was expressed towards children, since many Atlanteans understood basic principles of reincarnation; not all Atlanteans believed in it, but the majority of people in the first four sub-races did. Understanding reincarnation leads to greater meaning in life, self-responsibility in life, and love of children. Children become understood to be everyone's eventual future; furthermore, children are appreciated as new creations of souls, rather than seen as being "owned" by their parents. It is this illusion of parental "rights" that can cause abuse of children—often emotionally, but sometimes physically and/or mentally—that then leads to a lack of love in the children. The personality of each parent sometimes gets in the way, with its excessive need to control (resulting from the parents' fears of death), which often causes these conditions. Atlanteans tended to control their children much less than do most people in today's physical world; thus the Atlanteans were, in general, more loving towards children. This condition existed because the adults somewhat understood reincarnation and had less fear of death—and so they had less need to over-control their children.

 ## THE FOURTH ATLANTEAN SUB-RACE

The fourth Atlantean sub-race was at the height of its civilization between two million and one and a half million years ago. This sub-race was first developed in isolation as an Atlantean colony, in the southeastern part of South America, about two and a half million years ago. Later, this sub-race migrated en masse back to Atlantis via ships, displacing what had been the remaining villages of first sub-race Atlanteans. The displacement took place through the migration of the first group of fourth sub-race people, who unknowingly brought with them a viral infection that the first sub-race and some third sub-race Atlanteans were particularly susceptible to if they were selfish. The virus in fourth sub-race Atlanteans caused only a minor one-to-two week illness; in the selfish members of the first and (some) third Atlantean sub-races, it created very high fevers, pneumonia-like symptoms, including severe lung congestion, and often death within one to two weeks. Being airborne, the disease swept nearly uncontrolled through Atlantis. Virtually the only selfish first and third sub-race Atlanteans who had immunity to the most devastating aspects of the disease were the offspring of first or third sub-race with fourth sub-race Atlanteans. Most of the selfish first sub-race Atlanteans and some from the third sub-race who were selfish were destroyed by the plague. They were replaced in very large numbers by immigrants who came from the South American colony.

The fourth Atlantean sub-race people were very attractive physically, with balanced physical features and a balance of hair color to skin tone that most people today would consider to be beautiful. This race had many members whose hair color was a distinctive reddish-brown, or a radiant auburn; their skin had a light bronze hue and tended to be unusually smooth in texture. These people were short for Atlanteans, with very fine and somewhat smaller hands, fingers, and feet. Their average height was about five feet, six inches, while the first and third sub-race Atlanteans averaged over six feet tall (the third sub-race people averaged six and a half feet in height). Also, the average weight of fourth sub-race Atlanteans was as much as one-third less than those in the first or third sub-race. Atlanteans tended to have longer noses and larger ears, in general; however, the members of the fourth sub-race had relatively small, shorter noses, and quite small ears. They were distinctly different from the earlier Atlantean sub-races in their overall appearance.

The fourth Atlantean sub-race was created from a fourth cosmic ray focus, which when it later manifests as incorporating the lower kingdoms in human civilization, tends to encourage the creation of art. The art of the fourth Atlantean sub-race race was exceptional. Drawings and painting with correct perspective were created—nearly two million years before the Renaissance took place in Western culture. Jewelry made from gold, silver, and polished *faceted* gems were of magnificent design and quality. The work that the fourth sub-race did with gems led to the more scientific use of gems in the next sub-race. Buildings were adorned with sculpture and other artistic embellishments. Glass was invented in the South American colony, and its first uses were for artistic expression; later, glass was used for utilitarian purposes, such as windows in buildings. Although most of Atlantis had a Mediterranean climate, glass windows supplied much more light while increasing the efficiency of keeping buildings warm, especially on cooler nights and some seasonally cooler days. Atlantis altered the Gulf Stream that circulated around it, keeping the continent warm even at its more northern parts; however, this also caused Northern Europe and the sub-arctic regions to become much colder.

When the rays that helped to create a major race or sub-race become focused less frequently on earth, not only do those races slow in development, their members also become less adaptable, less resistant to new diseases, and less equipped genetically to face crises that the change in ray focus produces. This process accelerates the replacement of an older race with a newer one. The more isolated a sub-race is from other, older ones when it is still being developed, the greater the impact of the isolation on the older sub-race(s); in the past, this impact has usually been a destructive one. Most of these kinds of issues are left to the discretion of the Master in the fifth kingdom who is in charge of the creation and destruction of races, and who also assists in the formation of governments in each new race and sub-race's civilization, through some initiates along the first ray. This Master functions along a first ray focus, and is referred to as the "Manu for the Race." Another Master of high initiation is in charge of the overall use of the lower kingdoms by human sub-races. He serves focused along the third ray, and is sometimes referred to as the "Lord of Civilization," or "Mahachohan." For each ray focus, there is a Master who is the head of that part of the Spiritual Hierarchy (and who is at least a Chohan—or a sixth level initiate), and there are other Masters and fourth level human initiates who consciously work together in an esoteric ashram along that ray. Sometimes a pledged or accepted third level initiate can, mostly passively without much creative input, hear and understand some of the plan of the next kingdom as it is being created along her or his ray-focused service, within the esoteric ashram that corresponds to that ray. An esoteric ashram is located on the first etheric sub-plane; being able to remain conscious there requires some significant unification of the three human bodies, and especially the etheric/dense physical while a person has been

**Atlantean
Fourth Sub-Race
Young Adult Male**

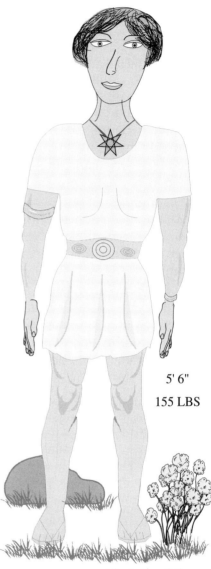

5' 6"

155 LBS

Illustration 9.6

physically alive. Finding one's Master and his or her ashram is a journey of both spiritual service and the consequential development of consciousness that accompanies spiritual service along one (and sometimes more) of the seven rays of creating virtue. Today (and for those born after 1925) such service first *requires* service in an exoteric spiritual group of humans whose mission is part of the plan of the esoteric ashram. Those who fail to find and serve with others along their ray focus and soul mission cannot have conscious contact with Masters of the three lower worlds and cannot complete an initiation. In addition, most of those people will not significantly spiritually serve because their lack of group, or soul, consciousness reduces their level of potential to serve, to a level below what is today needed if one is to participate in spiritual service within the plan of the fifth kingdom and higher.

Within Atlantean societies, homosexuality and sexual relativism were common means of sexual expression and transfer of sexual energies. For the period of the first through the fourth sub-race, both homosexuality and sexual relativism reached their peak in the beginning period of the Atlantean fourth sub-race. This occurred partly as a result of the fourth sub-race of the sixth ray race (the Atlantean) dealing more with the more feminine form side of life because of its dual feminine focus (fourth and sixth rays) and because both of these rays are rays of attribute. The emphasis of form in sexual activity can intensify these misuses of sexual energy. The fourth Atlantean sub-race went on to become the most virtuous of all of the Atlantean sub-races, and all of the Lemurian except its sixth sub-race. Note that the sixth sub-race Lemurians were more virtuous as individuals, and the fourth sub-race Atlanteans were more virtuous as a civilization, and that both were the most virtuous, thus far, of any humans on earth—including those in the (current) fifth major race. The Atlantean fourth sub-race invented some social balances that brought harmony to what had been conflictive sexual practices, because those practices were collectively damaging children and the family unit. For example, homosexuality that is accepted as normal expression of sexual energy often damages children by creating the illusion in them, through example, that having sexual relations with others without expressing love *through the sexual acts* is an acceptable practice (see Chapter Seven for a more complete explanation). Sexual relativism is similar to homosexuality in its effect; while homosexuality subconsciously reinforces the acceptance of unloving exchange of sexual energies, sexual relativism extols the acceptance of exchanging sexual energies somewhat lovingly, but less lovingly than one is capable of. The fourth Atlantean sub-race solutions (as described later in this chapter) to some of these issues may be helpful in some modern societies. Children are very susceptible to concepts that are expressed through examples in living, so those children of people who practice homosexuality and/or sexual relativism often become inculcated with *the concept*, although they do not later necessarily, when they become sexually active, express it in the same ways. Nonetheless, the darkness of the concept still affects people who as children were exposed to homosexuality or sexual relativism, by making them relatively more selfish sexually.

During Lemurian times, spiritual service had been on average at a much lower level than Atlantean spiritual service was, because as the sub-races and major races advance in development, so must the spiritual service of those who choose to spiritually discipline themselves. Individual creation of mostly personal levels of spiritual consciousness was all that was required for someone to have contact with Masters and to participate within some parts of what existed of the plan for most of either of these races. During most of the Lemurian race periods of development, a pledged first level initiate could serve within a Master's ashram. During the fourth Atlantean sub-race and in later Atlantean sub-races as well, a pledged second level initiate had similar capabilities. The requirements did not advance so quickly in the last two Atlantean sub-races because these sub-races became dark, and the people within them mostly failed to create virtue in their civilizations; these people were more destructive than constructive to the lower kingdoms and to humanity.

Of all of the Atlantean sub-races, the fourth was the most creative of virtue. The fourth Atlantean sub-race enlightened art and beautified all parts of Atlantean civilization. Beautification is a process of perfecting the balance of spiritual thought to the creation of forms. To maintain beauty, as a civilization creates more forms using the three lower kingdoms as well as its own, it must *increase* its level of spiritual thought of understanding and functioning (being) a part of God to twice the levels of thought that it uses to create the new forms within its civilization. For example, the fourth sub-race Atlanteans created exquisite jewelry, using precious metal and faceted gemstones. For this addition to their civilization (through using more of the mineral kingdom) to remain beautiful, which is the fourth cosmic ray's virtue, the amount of thought they used to create the jewelry had to be put to virtuous use in their civilization. The jewelry must have been created for others to recognize, understand, and change or further change into becoming more Godly. Relevant factors include the ways in which the jewelry was sold, owned, worn, possibly given as gifts, cared for, and eventually even destroyed, or recycled, in its mineral content.

Creating the virtue of beauty encompasses all three of the lower virtues, of cooperation and sharing (etheric/dense physical virtue); focused, or limited, love based upon direction of movement of astral energy (astral virtue); and the creation of whole structured thought that is wisely given, or truth (mental virtue). Beauty is more than these three, however, because it requires perfection in balance between spirit's and energy's thought. Beauty is thought *of and by* God, or is light, and the thought that is used to create form, or all the thought of the energy within the form, including any additional amounts of human thought that is used to further create the form. Beauty incorporates dozens of concepts within a person, who needs to hold these concepts together mostly all at once in order to fully understand, or be conscious of, what beauty is. This type of thought is referred to as intuition. It is the type of thought, when used in a controlled method to serve others, that is created on the intuitional plane—which is the fourth plane, and where the fourth ray is created. Thus to fully understand beauty requires controlled intuitive thought, which corresponds to the plane this virtue is created on. To a lesser extent, this same concept of understanding virtue also applies to the virtues on the three lower planes.

The Atlanteans in general had a difficult time understanding, or being conscious of, the creation of truth (the mental plane virtue) because their mental senses and mental bodies were not very well developed, and neither, therefore, was their whole mental, or structured, thought. In the Atlantean court system, justice was based more upon how three people, as judges, felt either emotionally, or if the judges were virtuous, lovingly, about a defendant or two adversaries in civil proceedings. No two courts functioned in the same way, and each of the ten governors prescribed their own (astral) thoughts about how their courts should function as they heard and judged the more important cases, and, sometimes, appeals from the lower courts. Note that appeals were permitted for lower court decisions of two out of three judges; unanimous decisions were usually not appealable. Justice was based less upon laws and more upon empathy, love (or emotion, if the judges were selfish during the trial and about the issues), and what "felt" astrally right to the judges when they used creative imagination to reconstruct the issues. This system worked because most Atlanteans primarily thought astrally and accepted the system as just.

Spiritual disciples on Atlantis thought primarily mentally, with more developed capabilities than average, from the fourth mental sub-plane, up. Because of this, these people sometimes had difficulty in living within the Atlantean civilization because the laws, educational system, communication and policing/military modalities, science and technologies, religion, and economy (including business and its organization) all seemed, to them, to lack truth. Art was the exception, because these disciples were able to elevate art to become both an expression of truth, through whole structured thought applied and given with the art, and an expression of beauty. Spiritual disciples from the middle (the fourth) Lemurian sub-race, on, encountered a similar difficulty, because they were able to understand astral love while the rest of their society generally did not.

Today, in modern times, some spiritual disciples are now able to understand beauty, while most of the remaining humans are still, at times, struggling with truth. Most of the humans who are members of the more advanced societies in today's world are in the fifth sub-race of the fifth major race, and thus function from a *dual* fifth ray focus; in addition, the fifth ray is focused on earth—and will remain so for the near future. This ray came back into full focus on earth in A.D. 1675 and replaced the fourth ray; in present times, a ray begins to affect the civilization on a planet about twenty-five years before it becomes fully focused on that planet. The incoming ray creates considerable disturbance and sometimes, if it is in conflict with the outgoing ray, destruction. In present times, this can occur for about twenty-five years after the incoming ray has become fully focused. If evil grows during the period of conflict, the overall length of time that the conflict lasts can expand considerably beyond just twenty-five years. For example, the most recent full focus of the seventh cosmic ray began on earth in A.D. 1900, and replaced the sixth ray. Since cosmic rays affect civilization a great deal through *human* senses, and since human senses are most affected while they are *growing* during childhood and adolescence, some of the ray changes are also seen in their effects on the first generation of humans who were born during and had childhoods relatively soon after the ray change. These effects are much more noticeable in modern times because rays are changing more often; the rays' effects manifest in shorter periods of time because human senses (and somewhat, the senses in the life of the lower kingdoms as well) are much better developed. The seventh ray dramatically affected human civilization from 1875 to about 1950. It altered economies and the forms of the physical world (most of which were altered or destroyed by war). The seventh ray greatly affected the organization of society (and human organizations within societies) and synthesis of etheric energy with and into physical energy. This change led from the (dense physical) machine age to the electronic age. Notice that an additional twenty-five years or so of very destructive results occurred from evil entering the etheric/dense physical dimension in large numbers of people during this time (the "door" to evil was more "open"). At present (the turn of the twentieth century), the effects have still not been completely overcome.

Because beauty is a higher level of creating virtue than is average for humans, the Atlantean fourth sub-race, led by spiritual disciples, quite dramatically changed Atlantean civilization by creating significant amounts of beauty. This sub-race and its spiritual disciples were so virtuous that the plan for earth was accelerated by hastening changes in the focus of some of the cosmic rays—as much as could be done within the complexities of effects on other planets and even star systems. Such hastened changes are a rare circumstance, and may have saved earth from destruction because it karmically offset some of the evil that was created by the later Atlantean sub-races.

About one and a half million years ago (in the fourth Atlantean sub-race), Atlantis was much like a Garden of Eden. A balance had finally been established between humans and the animal kingdom. This balance caused animals that had contact with Atlanteans on the island continent and even in some colonies to live in harmony with people. Animals that had been mostly terrified of humans, as well as some that had formerly attacked people, became non-threatening. Many animals sought to live around human civilization, often contributing in some ways to the civilization. For a part of this golden age, most Atlanteans became vegetarians, with some becoming vegans and others choosing to eat little or no meat that came from what had ever been a relatively conscious animal. As this took place, the animal kingdom thrived and became more diverse—and smaller in the physical size of each of its members, as it diversified.

When animals are not bred to feed large numbers of humans, the *form* of the animals is no longer "artificially" and forcibly contained in lifeforms that are non-beneficial for the animal kingdom. This freedom permits the animals to evolve into more advanced forms and for its informing spirit as a self of a group soul, along with the soul itself, to develop much more quickly. Having billions of cows, chickens, pigs, lambs, turkeys, and other food stock bred in such high numbers to just feed people tremendously retards the growth of life of the animal kingdom, which is a part of the life of all the kingdoms and of God's growth in our universe. *This is the main reason why humans should not eat animals.* Other reasons also may apply, based upon certain circumstances, but this reason is the foundation and is often not well understood both by those who are vegetarians, and those who eat meat and may argue that vegetarians are arbitrary in their logic. Life is one, and the kingdoms were created to further develop life. The animal kingdom was developed to animate life and improve its sentiency and its consciousness (its love), and to master the astral world. The plant kingdom was developed to create the first sentiency, to develop *cooperation* with the mineral and animal kingdoms, and to develop *sharing* by producing energy from the light of either the sun or the planet. This makes plants slightly sentient while they share the abundant amounts of denser energy that they create—in the form of food—for animals and humans. Note that planetary light is lower in frequency than is light from the sun, and registers as "heat" in the infra-red and lower electromagnetic range. When only small numbers of animals are eaten, and the animals are not bred and raised in large numbers to be eaten, animal life in general is not harmed. The reason is that these conditions do not produce excessive numbers of forms of non-developed and non-advanced animal life. However, these conditions may still adversely affect animals to some extent by somewhat raising their levels of fear and by diminishing their love. The effect on the animals depends upon *how* and *why* they are hunted or herded. When they are hunted or raised for food that is needed because the civilization cannot, yet, adequately support humans through plants, and, when the thoughts and feelings of the hunters or herders are somewhat on respecting and loving the life within the animals, and, in addition, when the animals have some reasonable chance to survive the hunt or when not all the animals in a herd are killed for food, then the eating of animals as necessary for human survival can still benefit the life in the animal kingdom, and is virtuous.

Another consideration is the use of animal products, which is more of a complex issue. As long as animals are raised and killed to be eaten, in such enormous numbers as is the case in modern times, the use of their body parts for products used by humans may be karmically acceptable. The reason is that with such vast numbers of these animals being raised and killed for food, not using the remaining body parts according to the laws of economy detracts from life development in other kingdoms, *and* reduces the meager amounts of meaning that these animals could contribute to the life of their (group) souls and selves. Those people who are actively trying to stop animals from being harmed by others who believe that such killing or harm is for the "benefit" of humans, have adequate justification, based upon their sacrifices to not use any animal products. Many of these people think that using parts of animals for products contributes financially to continuing the raising and slaughter of animals in general. This position needs to be weighed against the question of non-use of parts of such a large number of animals that are killed mostly to be eaten. However, raising animals for just, or mostly, their parts and then killing them for those parts and mostly not eating the animals as food cannot be justified in today's world. Thus, for example, raising animals and killing them for their fur is no longer karmically justifiable, because the body parts are being collected *at the cost of killing the animal*, and today many alternatives to animal fur exist. Animals are being raised in huge numbers for purposes that are, to say the least, unwholesome to the animals; for example, they are being raised to be killed (often brutally so) and eaten, to be killed for their body parts, and to be used in experimentation that is often inhumane. To ultimately change this practice requires *education* and the raising of understanding, or of consciousness. The preceding few paragraphs are meant to both raise some understanding of the reasons to not eat or harm animals, as is the generally accepted practice today, while also, through the complexity and difficulty in realizing the concepts, helping those who already have this understanding to expand upon it in order to gain tolerance and compassion for those who do not.

The later fourth sub-race Atlanteans benefited from mostly not eating animals by having their average lifespan significantly added to. When animals live to be killed and eaten, they create, as part of their bodies, hormones that induce feelings of fear and anger. Also, the energy that is stored in their bodies, as fat, is too dense to be used by humans who are not extremely active—it might be appropriate for hunters or herders in a primitive society, who may use enormous amounts of energy in a short period of time and then call upon this fat as an energy reserve until they eat again. When an animal has lived to be killed and eaten, the consciousness of the animal form can detach and fall away from its group soul and from the controlling thought of its self's spirit within the group soul. The consciousness of the animal form as conscious fallen spirit can then become a possessing spirit that can follow the dead meat and possess the human that eats it, if the human is significantly more selfish than average and tends to think in "animal-like" ways. Once semi-possessed, these people at times crave meat compulsively. Most of the above-described conditions were reduced or even eliminated from later Atlantean fourth sub-race society (although they were re-created by later sub-race Atlanteans, and still exist today). With the beauty that fourth sub-race Atlanteans created as virtue and the generally high levels of vegetarianism throughout their society, the average lifespan of a fourth sub-race Atlantean was over one hundred years, while maintaining a level of appearance and health of a person of around fifty in today's society. In comparison, the average life expectancy of third sub-race Atlanteans was only fifty—and some of them looked much older at fifty than the average fourth sub-race Atlanteans did at one hundred.

Through their long and healthy lifestyles, Atlantean people became wise; wiser physical lives require less lengthy astral and mental lives, and thus lead to more frequent reincarnations with greater levels of virtuous memory in each new personality, and a higher likelihood of creating more virtue. The specific ray focus of each sub-race brings more human souls into incarnation who are focused along that ray focus in their higher mental plane energy, or their solar devas, and the concepts that these devas help to create as the progenitors of the personalities who incarnate. When very virtuous, the personalities tend first to create their virtue along the ray focus of their souls. During the fourth sub-race, more human souls whose focus was along the fourth ray joined the majority of souls who had a sixth ray focus and who had already been creating personalities to incarnate in conjunction with each one's OverSoul. (See Chapters Six and Eleven for a better explanation of these concepts). The fourth sub-race Atlanteans tended to create virtue more in the way that is consistent with the fourth ray—by creating beauty, or perfected balance between spirit and form. One of the areas of its civilization within which the fourth Atlantean sub-race eventually created virtue was the expression of sexual energy between humans. One of the problems in Atlantean society was homosexuality. Homosexuality had grown during the beginning of the sub-race because the fourth ray in its selfish expression seeks to accept activity that does not create virtue, but through its acceptance may cause a person to be liked by more people. This is related to a feminine focus on form, or attracting others to one's form. This is the foundation of "political correctness," which can lead to excessive untruths, or lies, in the acceptance of darker behaviors and concepts. Also, when the fourth ray is selfishly expressed, it develops equivocal relations that lead to sexual relativism. In these cases, balance and harmony become more important than perfection of spirit's thought to the thought that creates new form. As homosexuality and sexual relativism grew in early fourth sub-race society, some families became weaker in their creation of virtue, and many children became harmed. The people who were spiritually disciplined did create some solutions to these issues by consulting with Masters from the next kingdom.

First the spiritual disciples, with the Masters' help, developed an astral yoga that included sexual tantra. Many of these disciples were very sexually attractive because they were able to lovingly exchange such high levels of sexual energy. This ability is the foundation for what makes a person sexually attractive to others, in general. The disciples taught and insisted upon the use of the sexual tantric methods during various types of sexual relations and sexual activities between themselves and others. The methods interfered with the arousal of sexual energy except when it was given in love (was reversed in spin), which, by definition, could not occur between two people of the same gender (see Chapter Seven for why this is the case). These tantric methods encouraged soul contact and soul control, and helped to create more virtuous group, or soul, consciousness in those who used them. The religion of the Atlanteans embraced these sexual practices, and encouraged the general population to learn and use them.

Another social intervention was the dissemination of the knowledge, and somewhat the concepts behind the knowledge, that people become more beautiful when they express love while having sexual relations, and uglier when they have sexual relations without expressing love. The fourth Atlantean sub-race people were *very* concerned with being beautiful, even when being selfish in numerous ways. When they became aware that their selfishness would, over time (years), cause them to become ugly, especially considering how long they could expect to live, this concept had a sobering effect on their behaviors. To change homosexual *feelings* requires altering a disorder in the personality, with the disorder usually caused by the person rebelling against his or her soul (again, see Chapters Seven and Twelve for further explanation). The above-stated concepts were taught to spiritual disciples by the Masters, and then the disciples were eventually able to make them a part of the Atlantean educational system. The education and religion together brought about a governmental policy of offering an effective treatment for those who had homosexual feelings, or sexual attraction to others of the same gender. There were no laws enacted against homosexuality or any type of sexual relativism, provided that these practices did not physically threaten or harm people.

The methods employed in the treatment for homosexuality included a focus on converting emotions into love, using a unifying process (an astral yoga) plus the sexual tantric yoga for use during the sexual activities. In Chapter Twelve, a very abbreviated explanation of this yoga is presented, along with some additional suggestions for the modern day person, whose thought is more structured than the thought of most Atlanteans. The process of changing homosexual feelings can take as long a time as a person has been acting on those feelings in his or her behaviors with others. Someone with a long history of homosexual behavior (many years to a number of decades, or even more than a lifetime!) is not likely to be changed by any known discipline into no longer feeling attracted to others of the same gender. The reason is that the sexual spin of such people has been so altered that the change back would take more time than they have left to physically live. This is especially true since the initial reversal of sexual spin significantly reduces life expectancy, because of the resultant increased retention of energies within the bodies. The more bodies with full reversal of sexual spin, the worse the prognosis for change. The cessation of behavior does, however, help to reduce the karmic effects, because homosexuality harms both partners through creating forces in their sexual centers. Homosexuality may also adversely affect children who are raised in an environment where it is accepted as being an expression of love—especially through a model of example.

Regardless of people's choices in their expression of sexual energy, or any other possible selfish expression that has not reached a level of being evil, people need to be respected as souls. If someone has a personality that has, through its illusion, created a problem in ordering its senses and thoughts with its self, then education; focus on God, or enlightened religion; and psychological methods ("soul methods") that heal are the appropriate solutions. Note that the root word of psychological, which is psyche, originally meant soul. Incarceration for non-criminal behaviors, including homosexuality between consenting adults, is a crime against the soul when the behavior for which the person is incarcerated did not significantly deny freedom to others. The incarceration denies the soul's creation (its personality) the first part of God's thought (freedom to choose). Note that the reverse of this concept explains why incarceration of criminals is sometimes necessary. One should never be denied freedom by others because he or she does not love "enough," when the non-loving behavior does not reduce others' freedom, or choices, to choose, love, or act. Hatred of others simply because they do not love enough can be as much if not more of a non-loving behavior as the behavior for which the people are hated. Not loving *and* the taking of actions that remove choices from others can be both criminal and evil. When these circumstances take place in the physical world, alternative force against them may be required. Homosexuality is not evil, and it may not be immoral unless it is practiced in a way that affects others in a society (besides those who are involved in the homosexuality). As a behavior, homosexuality is selfish, rebellious, and non-virtuous, or dark, because it reduces the personality's contact with its and other souls. The more that homosexuality is extolled as normal, healthy, virtuous behavior, and/or an example of sexual behavior to be emulated, the more immoral it is, and the more adversely it affects a society.

The later Atlantean fourth sub-race people realized these concepts and applied them in ways that made their civilization the relatively most developed *and* virtuous one (at the same time) that has yet to be created on earth. Their success in facing difficult social issues with courage and turning a conflictive circumstance into one of harmony is the hallmark of the fourth ray when it is used to create virtue in a civilization. The fourth ray returns in full focus on earth about the year A.D. 2025, while the more powerful third ray's focus will simultaneously be removed (the third ray is more powerful because it is a ray of aspect of God's mind). An examination of the past—when the fourth ray was successfully used to create virtue—can be of great assistance in helping people to learn ways to increase their understanding of the process of using the fourth ray to create virtue, and to improve their success at doing so in the immediate future. When the fourth ray first became focused during the beginning of the fourth Atlantean sub-race's civilization, some two million years ago, it replaced the third ray in its focus, and created some similarity in ray structure to what earth will experience in the next fifty years or so. The rays at the beginning of the fourth Atlantean sub-race's civilization were typically, at first, 4-2-1-6, and the rays in A.D. 2025 will be 4-7-5-2; presently, they are 7-5-3-2. Again, the order of the rays as listed from left to right either indicates the most recently changed ray (on the left) to the one that has been in focus the longest (on the right), or, when depicting a long period of time, the one that has on average been changed the most of the four (on the left), to the one that has remained in focus the most (on the right). When the third ray is removed from focus after having been in focus for a relatively long period of time, the growth of civilization greatly slows, i.e., the growth of the rate at which the three lower kingdoms are used to extend the senses (and life) of the fourth, or human kingdom is greatly slowed. The third ray has been in focus on earth since A.D. 1250. When it came into full focus it (along with the first ray, which came into full focus soon afterwards for a relatively short period) produced at first a great reduction in human population, as a result of disease. As the third ray leaves, after seven hundred seventy-five years of focus, the same—or worse—could occur. The third ray might also become crystallized through darkness; dark crystallization is a process that is used by evil, and is a part of becoming evil. Should dark crystallization of the third ray occur, the civilization might continue to grow, but only by becoming progressively darker. This is what has been taking place to some extent in religion since the sixth ray went out of focus at the beginning of the twentieth century. Religion, which is the main part of human civilization affected by the sixth ray, has become crystallized and darker as it continues to grow. Not all religion became darker—only that which stresses the form side (material parts) of life and is affected by the sixth ray. The spiritual part of religion, when practiced and preached, has not become darker. It is important to remember that the rays *directly* affect only energy and senses (as energy), and not spirit or its thought, except as spirit chooses to be affected by form.

Fourth Atlantean sub-race people continued to focus on their spiritual side. They mostly did this to help maintain their thought at a level that was twice that level that was used to create the form in their civilization. When the thought was perfected, it created beauty. This was how they achieved such good results in creating and maintaining virtue in their civilization for over *half a million* (!) years. It is true that it was much easier for a civilization to remain fairly consistent for extremely long periods of time as compared to the rapid changes of today, because the earlier part of the human race developed enormously slower than the present and later parts will. This effect is caused by the cumulative effects of the rays as the round progresses *and* as more advanced souls choose to begin incarnating new personalities within human beings on earth. As the round progresses and the human population greatly increases, more souls choose to incarnate; these souls are ones that are progressively more advanced beyond the souls that have already incarnated on the planet. The reason why these souls are more advanced is that they have previously, on other planets, created more virtuous humans than did the souls who had already incarnated on that planet. At the zenith of the fourth Atlantean sub-race, the human population on earth was about 500 million. This had been the peak of human population on earth until the last approximately three hundred years. Atlanteans tended to not have large families, although the Lemurians usually did—about seven children per family, or per woman. The way the Atlanteans grew their population was through their longevity and the exceptional care that they gave to their children.

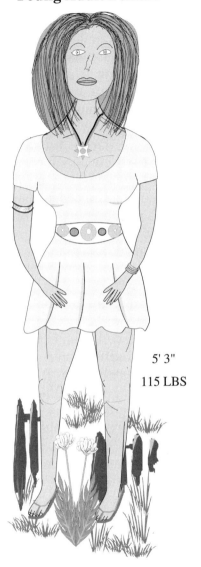

**Atlantean
Fourth Sub-Race
Young Adult Female**

5' 3"

115 LBS

Illustration 9.7

Should the third ray become significantly crystallized in the twenty-first century, earth's population could decline from over six billion to less than one and a half billion by the year 2050 under the worst conditions, or by the end of that century if the crystallization is not as severe but continues throughout the century. If either of these circumstances takes place, all of lower life on earth would be reduced by nearly the same percentage as human life would, because crystallization from the third ray in the fourth kingdom affects the three lower kingdoms. If this devastating reduction to life on earth is to be prevented, it is up to humanity to become more spiritual through a significant number of people on the planet seeking to create some amounts of more beauty in the world, before the year 2050. At present, much less than a majority of people are trying to create any amount of the virtue of truth, which is the mental virtue. To facilitate the necessary change requires that a large number of people who were spiritually disciplined in previous lifetimes and have more advanced souls incarnate within at least one of several successive generations. These advanced souls will attempt to create a life of service in the Plan, in order to increase the spiritual level of the majority of people on earth by the year 2050 so that crystallization of the third ray can be prevented. This group of more advanced souls mostly began to incarnate shortly after World War II. Collectively, these people are referred to in some spiritual texts as the New Group of World Servers. Their mission is to serve in exoteric spiritual groups (spiritual groups that are in physical existence), with some of these groups reaching world service; world service groups are small in size, but create enormous levels of virtue on a world-wide scale.

Many from the New Group of World Servers have souls that first incarnated on this planet during the fourth Atlantean sub-race; some of the even more advanced members of this group have incarnated only at times of great need for an advanced soul, beginning in the fourth Atlantean sub-race. A very few of these souls are Avatars, or souls who came from another planetary system within our star system. Even rarer are the *cosmic* Avatars, who came from other star systems; all Avatars contribute to a planet some element of consciousness that is not yet being expressed there. Both planetary and cosmic Avatars have been and are needed during the hundred or so years following World War II, to co-serve with the New Group of World Servers. Some of these Avatars were servers during the fourth Atlantean sub-race period. There may be as many as a half dozen or even a few more of these Avatars who will incarnate during the hundred years following World War II; some of them already have incarnated.

Every period of human development adds some significant meaning to life. The periods of human development that have the most virtue created within them are the ones that offer the most meaning. The Atlantean fourth sub-race period offered tremendous meaning to those who were alive during its time. The first advanced souls to incarnate during this period were second ray souls, because the incarnated human beings of these souls teach all of the other created human beings whose souls are along other ray types to become virtuous while they are physically alive. This is true of the present period of the current round. Of the advanced souls who are in the New Group of World Servers and who are incarnate at this time, more of them have second ray souls than any other ray type. From about the year A.D. 2000, on, progressively more fourth ray advanced souls will incarnate. A few of the human beings who have more advanced fourth ray souls and who incarnated just before or very soon after World War II have lived in service as much as has been possible, and may die early from this incarnation in order to be reincarnated at a more critical time, sometime during the first half of the next century. The service of such a person will then be enhanced more along the fourth ray, if she or he is given a fourth ray focus to one or more bodies by her or his soul. Besides most likely being artists in some ways, these people will become examples of a more spiritual life. They will have the advantage of being taught by human beings whose souls are focused along the second ray, and who preceded them in incarnating.

The fourth Atlantean sub-race period ended more than a million years ago, as these people and a few Atlanteans from earlier sub-races became replaced by some more advanced souls and a majority of the then-existing souls who had done so well in incarnating human beings who created a great deal of virtue. As these souls advanced, through more mental structured thought that they used virtuously, they became prepared to become the fifth Atlantean sub-race. This sub-race began developing about one and a half million years ago in a hilly-to-mountainous northern part of the Atlantean continent. Its members at first were fourth ray souls who were part of the fourth sub-race, and who had created humans who were good mental thinkers. Added to this group were souls along the fifth ray who were fairly advanced. The incarnated humans, from both groups, were inclined to use the newly focused fifth ray. The fifth ray eventually replaced the fourth ray in regularity of focus on earth, but first it took the place of the third. The third ray came back into focus during the later part of the Atlantean fourth sub-race, in an unusual change in the Plan to further grow this virtuous civilization. At the beginning of the fifth sub-race the rays in focus were frequently 5-2-1-6; by one million years ago, the rays were more often 3-5-2-6, and during the later part of the period, a common set of rays in focus was 7-5-2-6.

 ## THE FIFTH ATLANTEAN SUB-RACE

The fifth Atlantean civilization was very inventive, and its members had the most structured mental thought of any people in the entire Atlantean major race, which, as a race, was very astrally focused in thought. The spiritual disciples of the time held an incorrect philosophical view that more *structured* knowledge would help Atlantean society to grow more virtuous. These disciples themselves had begun to become significantly egotistical. This is a common trait among people in the (current) fifth, or mentally focused, race, but was an unusual one for Atlanteans. The trend towards egotism occurred because in their mental senses and their ability to think, these spiritual disciples were more like members of the fifth major race than the fourth. However, these same spiritual disciples from over a million years ago did not exercise sufficient spiritual discipline over their mental bodies to overcome their egotism concerning knowledge and creating more virtue through knowledge. Although Masters from the fifth kingdom taught these disciples, and even warned them, to change their thought concerning how to create more virtue, they rejected the thought because their egotism and desires for self-importance first prevented them from adequately sensing this thought, and then from understanding it. The motives of these disciples were not to create darkness, i.e., these disciples were not evil. They were very illusioned mentally and somewhat astrally, and were blind to the illusion because their egotism took such a toll on them that their remaining mental sense was at too low a level.

About a million years ago, with the assistance from the knowledge added by spiritual disciples, the Atlantean fifth sub-race invented a very powerful source of etheric/astral energy. What these people invented first were extremely large crystals, which were mostly made of quartz, and some were the size of two-to-three story buildings; later, some were even larger. These crystals were very pure except for being doped with certain small amounts of elements, which changed the direction, or phase, of focus of the energy that was developed in the quartz into one direction only (somewhat similar to the concept of how a laser crystal directs certain frequencies of light). These house-sized (and larger) crystals were constructed in layers and built in the shape of a pyramid, and were then placed beneath the ocean, with some at quite deep depths. The pressure of the water (the gravity) on the crystals caused them to emit extremely high voltages (millions of volts) in pulsations, or frequencies, and in electrical currents at a certain phase that in a part of the much higher frequency energy exceeded the boundary between the etheric and astral

Atlantean Pyramid Crystal Technology

The vast gravitational forces within the ocean at more than 30,000 feet below sea level were converted into etheric and astral energies by pyramids made of layered crystals. The electrical voltages that were created from these massive pyramids that were the size of buildings were extremely high. These energies were directed into other transmitting and/or transforming pyramids—bringing these energies onto Atlantis for use there.

Illustration 9.8

planes. Each layer of the pyramid-shaped crystal was doped with a different type of mineral. When put under extreme pressures or when excited from a greater source of energy from a larger crystal structure, the layers responded at varying prescribed frequencies and qualities of etheric and astral energies. These energies were focused to and through the top portion of the pyramid. The top was not just either a flat surface or four-sided triangle as seen on the tops of pyramids in existence today. A beam of etheric and astral energy was emitted that could be directed by a smaller pyramid, which functioned as a crystal transformer, into different directions and qualities of the energies' frequencies. Some of the information about these inventions is deliberately being left out from this description, in order to prevent their reinvention. Enough, however, has been included for the invention and testing of more innocuous devices at some future time. The very first, and smaller, crystal pyramids were floated out to sea on enormous rafts that were highly buoyant, and then the crystals were slid off to fall, in some cases, greater than thirty thousand feet below sea level. At these depths, the gravitational pressure of the water was enough to generate prodigious amounts of power. Later, much larger crystal pyramids were moved out to the ocean by being "floated" in air, through the energy focused on them at certain angles by previously placed crystals; once in its correct spot, each of these crystals was also submerged.

The etheric and astral parts of the energy that was emitted were transferred through a smaller crystal near the ocean surface, with this crystal being ingenuously held in place by self-aligning buoys on the surface above the much larger pyramid that was deeply submerged. Much larger versions of both pyramids could be aligned and held above the water by the energy coming from the submerged crystal pyramid. Only when the seas were very rough did these crystals not work properly. The emitted and transferred energy could be used to directly create light by being bounced off of any stone that had a quartz content. When units of this energy were focused upwards through a controlling tower towards or at an angle to the sky, a vessel that had controlling and "repelling" crystals on its bottom and sides could be moved through the air (it could fly) within the area between the controlling towers. Some of these towers transferred the energies from positions on land. The ratios of etheric to astral energies are what would cause the effects of repulsion. Flight over hundreds of miles was possible at an altitude of up to several thousand feet, depending upon the number of pyramid and controlling towers that were placed. At the base of the pyramid-shaped towers were special spiral shaped crystals that stored enough of the etheric energies for a number of days of use. The pulsations of the etheric energies could, under certain conditions, (inter-dimensionally) bring in astral energy. This storage of energy was critical, because rough ocean conditions could interrupt the output of the main submerged crystal, sometimes without warning. The speed of flight within this system was variable, with a vessel's maximum speed determined by its distance away from a tower that had the initial phase, or focus, of the energy. For this reason and some others, towers were located considerable distances from densely populated areas, thereby reducing the maximum possible speed of about seventy-five miles per hour near the towers to less than thirty miles per hour further away from them, and reducing the hazards associated with travelling so fast in and near populated areas. There were some exceptions to this designed limitation of speed; for example, in some areas around the main, or capital, city of Olympus, towers were constructed to permit full-speed travel, but only in certain directions.

Except under circumstances that were deliberately chosen, when the crystal energy source was removed from an air vessel, the vessel would slowly float to the ground because the "falling," or the gravitational pull of the earth, was somewhat converted into excitation of the crystals on the bottom of the vessel, producing enough energy to usually create a soft landing. The vessels were quite sturdy and heavy, and were relatively unaffected by most winds—they did not have wings, which would have lessened their stability, i.e., they did not rely on dynamic air pressure as a means of lift or flight.

Atlantean Crystal Flying Ships

Towers receiving and distributing directional pyramid energies created fields in which flying ships with moveable crystals on their bottoms and sides could navigate at speeds that exceeded 75 mph. As a ship moved more tangentially away from a field, the ship would greatly slow down (until entering another field), and usually would not fall to the ground provided that another field was in close enough proximity.

Illustration 9.9

While Atlantean civilization during the fifth sub-race in some ways exceeded modern-day inventions concerning ease and simplicity of use, its members did not have any of the personal electronics, such as television, radio, or computers, that people do today. The use of such inventions requires much more structured thought than most Atlanteans had. Furthermore, even the most advanced disciples of this period generally did not have enough mental thought to invent them. People in the fifth Atlantean sub-race did invent a means of transmitting sound (a sort of telephone), which used the astral senses and astral energy from a second group of very small crystal sources that used the astral energy component of the submerged crystals. This system had the drawback of somewhat decreasing the whole, or unified, astral sense of empathy. It split empathy into its component individual (split) astral senses, as it was used to transmit lower astral psychic energy from one person to another. This occurred either within the etheric/dense physical world, or between the astral and etheric/dense physical worlds. This invention proved to be destructive to the civilization, and provided an opening for evil to enter into the members of the fifth Atlantean sub-race.

Earlier Atlantean sub-races (before the middle of the fourth) had very strong astral lower psychic abilities. The fourth sub-race joined the astral senses into empathy, but as they did so, the race lost its abilities to astrally communicate lower psychically between people who were physically alive and those astrally alive. What happened was that the people's empathy could not be maintained as a fused sense with the split, etheric/dense physical senses. The Lemurian sixth sub-race spiritual disciples had joined the two astral spiritual *split* senses with their split etheric/dense physical ones, but were not very well able to join empathy with split etheric/dense physical senses. To use the etheric/dense physical senses with empathy (the joined astral senses) and still maintain full astral sense requires that the etheric/dense physical sense be fully joined.

This could occur either through the Lemurians creating virtue as a race, which they failed to do, or, in the case of a very advanced human initiate, through the fusion of these senses and bodies together through creation of service, but then only on an individual basis.

Contact with the astral dimension by the fifth Atlantean sub-race was, when accomplished through the technology of crystal structure, possible from the seventh to the fifth astral sub-planes only, because the devices were a creation from the relatively selfish people who created them, who mostly could have astral consciousness on only these three lower astral sub-planes. Also, these lower three sub-planes correspond to the "dense" part of the astral plane, which is sometimes referred to as the more "solid" part of the dimension—like the physical dimension is, in some respects. These darker, more selfish dimensions became what most average Atlanteans thought to be the afterlife. The people who were alive astrally on these sub-planes encouraged this fallacy because they themselves were somewhat deluded into believing that they were special and hence were being "rewarded" while astrally alive. Glamours were developed concerning increased lower astral contact while a person was physically alive; some of the glamours were that with increased lower astral contact, a person would, while he or she was physically alive, become more powerful and more imaginative, more sexy, and better able to achieve a more creative life. Astral life that was relatively dark and selfish on these lower three sub-planes was, for some, more important—while they were physically alive—than were their physical lives.

About eight hundred fifty thousand years ago, the fifth Atlantean sub-race society began to become polarized into two distinct philosophies and groups. The first group was led by spiritual disciples and their *Teachers*, who were Masters and arhats of that period of time; this group's philosophy of life was that humans were physically alive for the purpose of contributing to the growth of life—and of God—by creating virtue, or more light in the forms of life and pre-life. The second group's philosophy of life was that physical life was God's punishment for a person not living to become happy and to have more pleasure astrally, whether while alive physically or astrally. A small percentage of these people grew to hate God for torturing humanity by making people live physical lives, and vowed to stop God by becoming evil. Most of the second group had reverted to a more intense following of what had been the older Atlantean religious views, before the fourth sub-race had created so much virtue. These two groups eventually established separate governments, and the group living on the North side of the continent was the selfish population that had evil mixed into it. This group later became a part of the sixth sub-race, when those whom the Manu had planned to be the beginning members of that sub-race returned to Atlantis under quite adverse circumstances, as described in the next paragraph. During the time of the fifth Atlantean sub-race, those who were virtuous, or the group of light (which included people ranging from spiritual disciples to those trying to follow some type of goodness), lived in the southern part of Atlantis. Eventually, about 800,000 years ago, the two opposing sides became embroiled in a war in which one hundred million people died, over several hundred years. The diametrically opposite consciousness of the two sides caused a part of the middle section of the Atlantean continent to submerge, dividing the continent into two separated parts—the North Island and the South Island. Prior to the separation Atlantis was, at its largest size (not counting its associated smaller islands, and at its longest part), over 1100 miles long (at an angle north to south) and nearly 900 miles wide (at an angle east to west); Olympus was located in the southern section of Atlantis, about 450 miles north of its southern border with the sea, and nearer to its eastern side. Atlantis was at an angle to Europe and North America, and its width lessened significantly towards its southern end, between North America and South America, and Europe and Africa. Much more of the original Atlantean landmass existed in the Northern Hemisphere than in the Southern because the progressive narrowing of Atlantis towards its South, and also because most of Atlantis was north of the equator. The side of light did win the war, leaving the North and South Islands of Atlantis, after the submergence of its middle part, almost equal in landmass and separated by fifty to one hundred miles of sea. The most evil people were destroyed en masse towards the end of the war, from the submergence itself; these people had lived in a city that they declared to be the capital, and that was located almost exactly in the geographic center of Atlantis.

About 800,000 years ago Atlantis was the divided continent, and while the South (the side of light) had been victorious, a significant minority of the Atlanteans, who were darker in character, still lived on the North Island. The Manu requested that a certain group of mostly spiritual disciples leave from several cities and towns on the sea coast far south and on the east side of the South Island. These people traveled north and east to the Mediterranean Sea, and were brought to an area of Mesopotamia that, at that time, was lush and did not have the climate of a desert. For several thousand years these people developed themselves into what was supposed to become the sixth sub-race of the Atlanteans. Their return was by a mass exodus back through the Mediterranean, and although, it was supposed to be kept secret, became widely known about decades before it took place. This group numbered over ninety thousand, which was a very large exodus, even by today's standards. These people were attempting to return to the South Island, which was just due west, but were met by an armada of war vessels from the North Island that had surreptitiously sneaked around the South Island to attack them. The attackers had learned of these people's return from the more virtuous people on the South Island, who failed to practice as much discretion in their speech as did the secretive people of the North who cunningly planned the attack. The Masters knew of the plan of attack, but because of some karmic factors resultant of problems on the South Island, could not intervene because to have done so would have created even worse karma. Masters seldom intervene in human affairs without having been asked to do so by virtuous humans, even when the consequences to the humans seem to be of extreme importance. Over seventy thousand (!) members of the seed sixth sub-race Atlanteans were captured. Most of the rest were killed during the battle, in their attempt to remain free; only a small number escaped to the South Island. The captives were enslaved and brought back to the North Island, beginning anew a war between the two sides. The sixth seed sub-race captives had offspring with their dark enslavers, mostly unwillingly at first, and also became culturally divested of some of their devotion to creating virtue and more of God. They were not easily changed, but, as the wars raged on in time, they gradually—over hundreds of years of time—mixed with the general population because so many "free" Northerners were being killed in battle.

By the time the South Island won this second war, there were no longer any distinguishable members of what had been the seed sixth sub-race. Another attempt was made by the Manu, to remove only about five hundred disciples to start another sixth sub-race in the area of what is today the South American country of Brazil. However, the cosmic rays had shifted in accord with the Plan and could not be adjusted to compensate for human selfishness (only because of unusual creation of virtue can they sometimes be adjusted). As the focus of the rays changed to 3-1-2-6, and then 4-3-2-6, (with both combinations recurring frequently), the fifth sub-race peoples, including those attempting to advance spiritually in South America, become weakened in sense and in immunity to disease. The subsequent generations of people of the North Island who were darker in character who mated with the original seed sixth sub-race people whom they had originally enslaved developed more sixth sub-race body types. These more developed body types were mostly protected from the new diseases that were spreading on the South Island and some colonies as well. For the new seed group in South America and most of the more enlightened people, whose members were still in the fifth Atlantean sub-race, the average life expectancy was quickly declining. The life expectancy for the sixth sub-race, whose members were dark in character, remained about the same. These people's darkness tended to reduce their life expectancy, but this factor was balanced and offset by the rays in their bodies being the rays that were usually in focus—especially their astral bodies, which tended to be focused along the sixth ray. In South America, the second seed group of the sixth Atlantean sub-race died out without ever returning to Atlantis. The sixth sub-race was—for about 600,000 years—more dark than virtuous.

 ## THE SIXTH ATLANTEAN SUB-RACE

The sixth sub-race was very astrally focused and had *less* overall structured mental sense and thought than did the average fifth sub-race Atlanteans. The sixth Atlantean sub-race lived to experience emotion instead of developing the lower spiritual sense of understanding God, which as a correspondence of the sixth (astral) sense, was supposed to be developed by this sub-race. These people followed the philosophy that excitement and emotional expression and "feelings" were what life was meant to be about. Thus meaning to their lives came from worshipping a God of passion, of excitement, and of emotion; in their self-delusion, through their glamours they saw passion, excitement, and emotion as God. Instead of gaining understanding of God—they nearly completely lost it because of their selfishness. Most types of love between people in the sixth Atlantean sub-race were based upon some personal and temporary relationship. Marriage was common, and so was divorce because the love between the people was usually a sixth ray type of love, which is very focused and is devoted for selfish reasons. Accurate birth control had been invented in the prior sub-race, but sometimes was not practiced because couples would believe they loved each other enough not to have to worry about birth control—if they had children they would remain together to raise them, they thought. Seldom was this the case in a long-term sense, so abortion and unusual types of adoption became prevalent. Abortion was mostly done using particular herbal combinations in conjunction with etheric and astral emanations from certain crystals, causing death to the etheric and astral bodies of the fetus, but also making the mother somewhat ill in the same bodies. Some adoptions of children who were brought to term were often done on a lottery system! Those who wanted a child could participate—for the excitement—and maybe even win a baby.

In the sixth Atlantean sub-race, children were frequently emotionally abused, with many of them treated more as owned pets than as young people; pets were treated even worse than were children, and animals were eaten in great amounts at nearly every meal. Besides sex, gambling was the favorite pastime of the population. Every imaginable way that people could gamble was available. Children began gambling before they could read, and, the overall ability to read was at a much lower level than at any time within the past two sub-races. Eventually, more than about two hundred twenty-five thousand years ago, life expectancy fell to an average of forty-five years, with most serious crimes punishable by death. No one expected to live much past fifty, and most people lived as though physical life was a "throw-away" part of life. People lived to do whatever they wanted—and could get away with. Laws were arbitrarily enforced, which led to increased criminality. Male and female prostitution was one of the leading professions, and both genders had *legal rights* to practice it. During part of this period, an annual national competition was held to select the best prostitutes in several categories, for both genders, with the preliminary competitions beginning at the local level.

Several times during the sixth sub-race, more of Atlantis submerged, killing millions of people. Drugs of various types from herbal sources were consumed by many for "fun" and excitement. Frequent use of these drugs typically led to addiction and, eventually, to death. Various forms of disease became common, most often from contaminated water sources. Many people died in epidemics, but some just had chronic ailments, for which they took more drugs in order to escape the pain. About two hundred thousand years ago, the Northern Island of Atlantis disappeared. The crystals that had created so much power and that had been used for power in early wars during the fifth sub-race were mostly worn out. The people in the later parts of the sixth sub-race could neither repair nor replace them because their consciousness had fallen so low that they no longer understood how these devices worked, nor how to construct them.

Many of the crystal pyramids had been destroyed around what is today the island of Bermuda. Some had been turned on their sides and partially split apart, and became buried under the ocean floor. These pyramids were the smaller ones that were used for defensive purposes during battles. Most of them originally lay one hundred to two hundred fifty miles east and some to the south of what is currently Bermuda. The relatively large quantity of these crystal pyramids that were turned sideways and mostly buried, coupled with their close proximity to each other have, under certain conditions, created a distortion between the etheric and astral planes that has sometimes split apart the etheric and dense physical bodies of people and objects or split their etheric bodies from their astral bodies, or both. In these cases, people or objects might first become etheric and then, suddenly, their etheric/dense physical forms *may* disintegrate, killing them physically and trapping them on the lower part of the astral plane (until they leave for a higher astral sub-plane, if their consciousness permits). In other cases, the people do not experience physical death. The etheric and dense physical parts of their bodies might somewhat separate from each other but *not* disintegrate, allowing these people to visit the astral plane and then return to their etheric bodies, and then, shortly afterwards, to rejoin with their dense physical bodies. When this takes place, a person may have significant etheric/dense physical brain disorientation and possibly brain damage. While such a person was in the astral dimension, time would have been dilated relative to the quantum constant of the sub-plane the person was visiting. Dilation would also occur while the person's etheric and dense physical bodies were separated, though to a much lesser amount, when the person was on an etheric sub-plane (usually the fourth). Depending upon which sub-planes, and in which dimensions, a person was on, he or she might have experienced hours to days of life on these sub-planes while having been gone from the physical dimension for only a few minutes to a number of hours.

Over time, most of the crystal pyramids in the area became covered with minerals and the bodies of sea life; some of these crystal pyramids have partially split apart into their constituent levels. This has caused them to appear to be made of stone rather than crystal, and to become dysfunctional except when certain electro-magnetic events occur, or when ocean temperature and currents alter their internal structure and relative positions to each other. In particular, distortions on the bottom of and below the ocean floor, such as earthquake and volcanic activity, can cause sudden and unpredictable results. Usually, when there is an interaction between two or more of the crystal pyramids that still remain, they affect each other so much that there is a limit to the amount of time that they can cause the irregularities in the quantum field and the energy irregularities in time and space between the etheric and astral dimensions. The energy of each of the crystal pyramids pushes the other crystal pyramid or pyramids away, and so there is only a short time during which their interaction can cause the above-described irregularities.

The sixth Atlantean sub-race was the first to breed animals as weapons in war, and sometimes in packs. Vicious beasts of various types were created to attack opponents. While the seventh sub-race took this practice to an even more brutal level, the sixth created monstrous animals that caused as much fear in their enemies as the physical harm they inflicted did. The sixth sub-race used astral energy focused into etheric energy to create a madness of astral terror in their enemies, while producing in their etheric brains pictures of vile future acts against them and sometimes those whom they cared about. When some people were killed they were deliberately forced into becoming ghosts, using similar methods to the ones described above, and were then transformed into etheric zombies who would be directed to etherically attack what had been their own group of allies. This method worked even when a person's physical body was cremated within about a day after his or her death. If the corpse was cremated within minutes to a few hours after death, which was not always possible during battles, then the attempt to turn the dead person into a ghost, or an etheric zombie, would usually fail.

By the later part of the sixth sub-race (about two hundred thousand years ago) as much as ten percent of the population had become evil, and less than one percent of the over one hundred million people who remained physically alive at any one time were no more selfish than the average person was during the later part of the Atlantean fifth sub-race. There were about twelve thousand spiritually disciplined people alive at any one time; of these, nearly all were first level initiates. Only a handful of advanced initiates were incarnating at any one time. The Manu was in a quandary because the rays were about to shift in focus, with the seventh ray emphasis soon to modify the sixth, in accord with the Plan. However, if the Manu chose to use all or even most of the remaining spiritual disciples to create a seventh sub-race from these disciples, by isolating them for more than a thousand years, the sixth sub-race was apt to become nearly completely evil—which would be very likely to end the planet. Instead, the Manu chose to isolate only approximately two thousand spiritual disciples. Few of them were replaced in the next generation by the incarnation from other souls' human beings who were as virtuously creative, because the society was too dark to incarnate into (the children would die early, with little hope for a virtuous life). Another problem was that most potential spiritual disciples who attempted incarnation into such a dark society would fall from the spiritual path, as a result of very selfish inculcations of the family and society in general. The Manu convinced another eight thousand, or so, people who were relatively less selfish than average, but were undisciplined, to join the approximately two thousand disciples. He chose people, overall, who were well organized and who synthesized knowledge well, which are seventh ray traits. These people also needed to have lived their present lives economically, wasting very little of form. An isolated area in Africa was chosen as the physical location for developing the seventh seed sub-race.

Each of the Manu's first five attempts at creating a seed sub-race failed, and each of these tries in a cycle of attempt took thousands of years of time and used people who were progressively less spiritually disciplined. Reasons for the failures were that people either abandoned their developing societies, or were killed—by each other, in selfish wars, or by hostile members of surrounding degenerating tribes. In addition, disease also claimed many lives because the rays had changed during the two latest attempts at developing seed sub-races. The situation was so disastrous that the area, itself, in Africa, was destroyed and somewhat sank. This was a result of the low consciousness and conflictive behaviors of its inhabitants over tens of thousands of years.

Finally, about 100,000 years ago, the Manu was somewhat successful in creating a seed seventh sub-race of Atlanteans off the coast of East Africa, on or at least near what is now known as the island of Madagascar. After about a thousand years of development these people returned to Atlantis, which by then had become much smaller both in land area and in population. Around that time, the rays 7-1-2-6 were a common combination focused on earth. The selfish consciousness of the Atlanteans had destroyed, from energy retained within the earth, about half of what had been the South Island, with only about fifty million people living on it at any one time. When the people of the seed seventh sub-race returned to the South Island of Atlantis, they mostly would neither relate to nor mate with the sixth sub-race members. These people who formed the beginning of the seventh sub-race of Atlanteans found those who were still in the sixth sub-race to be sickly, small in size, unattractive, and too emotional. The people in the seventh sub-race became very separative and chose to either live in isolated parts of what remained of the island, or to leave for one of the colonies, often one near a sea coast. This was disastrous for the remaining sixth sub-race, as many perished from disease, and quite a few of those who did not succumb to physical disease became paranoid of the seventh sub-race people, with some of these sixth sub-race people becoming completely insane. Many of the sixth sub-race members had serious astral, or emotional, diseases and were virtually dysfunctional; a substantial number of them lived in destitution, and died quite early in adult life. The karma from having lived so emotionally in their past lives was catching up with the people of the sixth sub-race. Pain and suffering became the dominant factors in their lives, and usually continued to dominate on the sixth or seventh astral sub-planes, not too long after arriving there after physical plane death. Religion had become the caretaker of these selfish people who in such large numbers became the early degenerating members of the sixth sub-race; religion promised them a better life if they would pray for one and follow certain customs. Because people practiced this religion in order to feel better and to find emotional happiness, it became impotent in providing for them any experience concerning understanding or becoming a functional part of God.

People in the sixth sub-race grew to look and act very different from those in the seventh. The differences were so unmistakable that the people in the seventh called the people in the sixth a name that in the, then, Atlantean language meant "not human," and, actually, below animal; the words for describing animals were something different. To a seventh sub-race Atlantean, the people in the sixth sub-race were considered not human and not even animal, but something like an animated fungus. Less than a thousand years after its return to Atlantis, the population of the seventh sub-race had grown to almost the size of the sixth, if those living in the colonies were included.

Atlanteans had practiced cremation since the very beginning of their race because the Masters strongly suggested it. Cremation had also been practiced on Lemuria, and, once the sixth Lemurian sub-race took hold of the society, was always used for the disposal of corpses. Cremation had been a part of every one of the Atlantean religions, for millions of years of time. Atlanteans believed so strongly in cremation that they would go to great lengths to recover bodies to then burn. They, somewhat accurately, believed that their usually cherished astral (after-) lives would be delayed and/or cut short if the physical bodies were not cremated. They also, somewhat accurately, believed that if they were buried they might become harmful ghosts, attacking even their own families. They so feared this, that after a battle they would cremate their enemies' corpses before their own people's, in order to prevent these dead enemies from becoming ghosts who would be more likely to attack them than would their own (dead) people.

A campaign of burning sixth sub-race people alive was begun by the seventh sub-race. First, this campaign began with the insane, the paranoid, the indigents, and the otherwise seriously ill. These people in the seventh sub-race believed that burning sixth sub-race members while they were still alive would grant them a better after- (astral) life, by being "cleansed" by the fire at the end of this life. Of course, many of these seventh sub-race people just seemed to enjoy the extreme torture being inflicted upon such unfortunate beings. Millions of sixth sub-race humans were eventually burned alive. Finally, a system of burning very young children was enacted, to eliminate the sixth sub-race; over time, this effort was "successful." Because of this practice, there were very few isolated groups of fully degenerated sixth sub-race people. Most were simply burned off the face of the earth before they reached that stage. As people who were somewhat degenerated escaped from Atlantis, hunting them became a great sport for members of the seventh sub-race; had the members of the sixth sub-race been considered animals they probably would have been eaten, but they were so despised that only burning them was considered appropriate.

THE SEVENTH ATLANTEAN SUB-RACE

The seventh sub-race Atlanteans were a fierce group of greedy warriors. Not since the seventh Lemurian sub-race had the people been as large, strong, and tough. They were also very dark in character. They were the darkest people, on average, yet to be living on earth. Their average height was over six and a half feet; they had very large bones and thick skulls, and by today's standards would be considered ugly. Their average weight was about two hundred sixty pounds for the males, with the females weighing close to the same—about two hundred twenty pounds. These people loved to hunt, fight, physically dominate, compete in sports, and seemed at times to be more like people who were focused along the third ray, rather than the seventh. When the seventh ray is focused through the sixth ray (the seventh sub-race of the sixth-rayed race), and then when there is mostly darkness—lacking light, or virtue, in the form—it tends to become focused or devoted to each activity it is taking part in; this leads to seemingly unrelentless action until the activity is completed. While not as frenetically done as someone influenced by the third ray, and under more normal circumstances the seventh ray may appear in action more sedentary than under these ray conditions, the seventh ray does have continuous movement and the *appearance* of tremendous power when focused through the sixth ray. Actually, when the seventh ray is focused through the sixth, *less* power is used per action because of the focus and devotion to completing each action successfully. Thus economy is used through devoted activity, but mostly for the advancement of form. In the seventh sub-race Atlanteans, this included the advancement of greed. Unlike the sixth sub-race people who "wasted" most activity in order to feel happy and excited at the same time, the seventh would focus on accumulating wealth with their actions, so that they would be happier at some future time. As can be common with those who are so focused (on the etheric/dense physical form and plane), time became distorted from a past perspective (which is the only part of time that actually remains) to a *self-ish future illusion that one can save time and space*, or form/energy within space, by being greedy and hoarding, or "freezing" time, space, and energy. As the Atlanteans, or anyone, tried to "freeze" time and space, they lost some of their intelligent coordinated responses in the etheric/dense physical world, or some of their whole etheric/dense physical sense. The result was an increase in the number and severity of their mistakes, which caused them to *lose* energy, time, and space (and freedom). However, because they were caught in the illusion of the seventh plane, they would continue to be greedy instead of cooperating and sharing together *and* loving, as well, at the same time. These people were, in general, quite wicked, and they only got worse as time moved on, as they developed their civilization.

Massive buildings were built by the seventh sub-race Atlanteans, mostly without the assistance of crystal energy, which by this time had become for the most part defunct. They used slaves, who were members of various degenerated Atlantean and Lemurian sub-races. However, because members of the sixth Atlantean sub-race were so disliked by the seventh sub-race people, they were not used as slaves; instead, the seventh sub-race members preferred to burn these people alive. The seventh sub-race Atlanteans also bred some apes into a work force of slave labor; these apes were crossbred with some of the degenerated Lemurians, usually through forced copulation. The ape would be drugged and the degenerated male *or* female (!) human would be forced to arouse and sexually relate to the animal. Sometimes these activities were performed for audiences of seventh sub-race people who paid a fee to watch. All that was left of crystal technology was only etheric. The etheric energy part of relatively small crystals, along with certain herbs, was used to alter higher etheric energies in the animals (the apes) and in the people, in order to create the new class of ape/degenerated-human slaves. The methodologies and motives to create these slaves were evil because they sought to change God's growth of life into crystallized forms of life that were against God's thought, or against light, in form. The progeny of these evil creations were semi-sterile, and fortunately could not procreate with each other; however, when breeding with degenerating humans, some could procreate and produce a new, altered, type of ape. These new apes were considered unuseful and thus undesirable, so the Atlanteans typically completely sterilized the ape-slaves that could potentially have sexual contact with humans, in order to prevent their further procreation. If an ape-slave, or ape/degenerated-human, procreated with a "normal," human, the progeny of these two could be sometimes further hybridized into even more useful, more intelligent ape-slaves. In order to accomplish this goal, sometimes some seventh sub-race Atlantean men would have sexual relations with an ape-slave that was not sterile. Often, they did so just to have some "fun" in the experience of the bestiality.

Between forty and thirty thousand years ago, the seventh sub-race Atlantean civilization gradually became darkly crystallized along the seventh ray. About twenty-five percent of the population had become, on average at any particular time, evil. Nearly all of the people were dark in character. What remained of the island of Atlantis was relatively small, and was called Poseidonis. Poseidonis had originally been somewhat smaller and was the governorship that the capital city was in, prior to the submergence of most of Atlantis. Over forty million people lived on Poseidonis, and the population was growing from darkness. Also, the population of ape-slaves numbered into the millions. Other animals were bred into monsters, to fight in battles. Some of these resembled the dinosaurs that had roamed earth much earlier in its history, and that were originally reincarnations of monstrous animals that had been created by the last two sub-races of humans on the final planet of the Moon Chain. Fortunately, these monsters never left the island, and were destroyed when it was. When a planet develops new life, it first karmically re-creates the lifeforms that all of its preceding planets had created; thus the earlier life creations in earth's history were karmic re-creations. From these early re-creations of life, the Planetary Logos and its planet earth had to create all new life, because the karma of the old life had to be overcome through creating new, more enlightened lifeforms. Because the seventh sub-race Atlanteans were evil, they were reversing this karmic enlightenment of lifeforms back into hostile ones. They attempted to reverse the Planetary Logos' plan (the Plan), which is a part of God's plan for life. Notice, again, that evil does not truly create. It usually just reverses and copies, even when it adds some new choices.

The seventh sub-race Atlanteans subjugated and sometimes forcibly invaded their own colonies. Part of the reason that this occurred was that the seventh sub-race Atlanteans of Poseidonis were outnumbered by the collective total of the inhabitants of their colonies, which posed what they perceived to be a potential threat. The seventh sub-race Atlanteans of Poseidonis were mostly aware of the activities of the inhabitants of the colonies that were near to them, but could not keep up with what was happening in the colonies that were greater distances away; because they had some paranoia about what their most distant colonies might be doing, the seventh Atlantean sub-race attacked and subjugated these distant colonies the most. The colonies were located mostly in coastal areas of North and South America, Southern Europe, India, China and Southeast Asia, North Africa, and the Middle East; the ones in North and South America eventually were completely destroyed because the overall consciousness of the people living in these areas was lower than in some of the others. Some of the people who lived in the Atlantean colonies were from seed sub-races. A few of these people remained where the seed sub-race developed instead of returning to Atlantis when most of the others of their population did. These people were often more enlightened than were those now remaining on Poseidonis, but were not nearly as fierce in their fighting.

The word "At" originally meant "with empathy and love" in the various Atlantean dialects; one in such a state was also one "at" the higher astral level of sense. "Lan" meant of, or from, the land known as Atlantis. The At-lans were those who had empathy and love and who came from or were of the land of the island continent in the Atlantic Ocean. The English words "man" and "woman" existed in similar word forms in most Atlantean languages as these words exist today in English (this is not as improbable as it at first may seem), and meant generally any type of human, not necessarily an At-lan. In some Atlantean dialects, the word "las" meant one who had been born to two At-lans. Language can provide us with insight into the way people perceive themselves. Despite the greedy, evil, and animal-like ways in which they functioned, people in the seventh sub-race still referred to themselves at At-lans, or empathically loving people who identified themselves as a geographic and cultural group. People often believe themselves to be considerably more virtuous than they actually are, because, unless they are evil, their *subconscious* self-worth is still tied to being a part of God. Seventy-five percent of the people in the seventh sub-race still sought to be Godly, even while creating more darkness. Note that the Atlantic Ocean was the ocean controlled by and belonging to the At-lans. This was not far from the truth while this civilization existed. Also, the word At-las (Atlas), a name of one of the last great warriors in the later part of the seventh sub-race, was derived from the two simple root words that meant empathic loving (son) of two At-lans. Even later, the word At-las was commonly used in reference to any great Atlantean seventh sub-race warrior.

Only a few thousand functional spiritual disciples (people who are consistently creating virtue in their lives) were in incarnation at any one time during the later period of the seventh Atlantean sub-race. Some of them managed to maintain positions of authority and leadership in the society, acting as a dam against the powerful dark forces closing in on what remained of Atlantean civilization. A common ray focus during the later Atlantean period, from 30,000 B.C. to nearly 10,000 B.C. (Atlantis was completely destroyed about 9000 B.C.), was 4-5-7-6. When these rays are focused through evil and darkness, they stimulate a devotion to greed, avarice, and sexual deviance (including bestiality), and the invention of structured ways to create conflict and imbalance between form and its informing spirit's thought. These characteristics depicted the end of the Atlantean period and its development of civilization. Spiritual disciples attempted, mostly in vain, to create a more enlightened civilization by changing the way the rays were used to grow senses. They taught others that objectifying sexual partners destroys one's self by reducing consciousness and love, and they practiced what they taught. They shared and cooperated with their material possessions as best as they could, in attempt to teach and exemplify the concept that greed creates retained etheric and dense physical energies that produce disease and death. They invented a mental approach of reflection, based upon Ageless Wisdom, that helped others to discover their illusions; however, many seventh sub-race Atlanteans had severely crystallized glamours that were too difficult to break apart with the meager amounts of mental (structured) energy they might create through more virtuous mental thinking. Evil was winning—and was going to overcome good.

 ## THE MYSTIFICATION OF AGELESS WISDOM

About thirteen thousand years ago, the Masters of the Spiritual Hierarchy were informed by the representative of earth's Planetary Logos that it would be necessary to almost completely and mostly suddenly destroy all parts of Atlantean civilization. This would include all of the sub-races, from the first through the seventh. The reason was that in order to stop evil, the good parts had to be sacrificed along with the evil ones because of karmic laws of cause and effect, i.e., evil necessarily originated from some lesser part of the good, regardless of how virtuous the good originally was. The name of the Planetary Logos' incarnation, who is an extremely advanced Master for the earth, is Sanat Kumara; note that a Kumara is the ruler of a world (subtle or physical) for a period of time. Four other of these super-Masters originally came to earth from Venus about sixteen and a half million years ago, and they are also referred to as Kumaras and are Masters of one or more worlds of all form and activity (all energy), from the spiritual plane down through the dense physical plane; note that there is no separated energy above the spiritual plane. These great rulers of our planet are assisted by their students who are "Buddhas of Activity," or experts of activity in service on their corresponding planes. One of these super-Masters left earth service, at the very beginning of the third major race. A second of the remaining Kumaras rejected the plan of Sanat (and the Planetary Logos), which included a great deal of probable suffering for the human races, especially during the remainder of the fourth round; the suffering would take place in order to help hasten change to overcome the karma from the final planet on the Moon Chain, which had failed. In disagreement with the Plan, this Kumara created an experiment to prove that suffering, at the levels proposed in the Plan, would inevitably cause the planet to fail. This Kumara entered into an allegiance with cosmic evil, to increase suffering earlier in the major races. This was, paradoxically, done to prove that continued failures by humans to increase their consciousness would, because their etheric/dense physical lives would be too difficult, lead to another planetary disaster. Thus by accelerating karma through evil, the "fallen" Kumara hoped to expose—before the ultimate destruction of earth—that the Planetary Logos' plan was too difficult, physically, for humans.

This turn of events as described above was recorded in early Sanskrit texts that, themselves, claimed to come from much earlier, *Atlantean*, texts. In some Atlantean dialects, the words "man" and "woman," as was explained earlier, referred to the generic human as these words are sometimes used today in English, because English was mostly created by reincarnations of the same people who created the Atlantean language. A "van" was an Angel, or an energy being, and a "devan" was a lesser Angel, or a less self-conscious Angel. A "de-man" was a less self-conscious man. In Sanskrit, which partly came from Atlantis, a "deva," without the "n," replaced the word "de-van." But the word "deman" remained. "demon" is the English word today.

The most ancient Sanskrit texts date back to 7000 to 6000 B.C., long before any Western Biblical stories were written, or probably even told. The fourth Kumara who dissented and "fell" from his position as one of the leaders of the Spiritual Hierarchy decided to take for himself Sanat Kumara's first name and reverse part of it. His original name (in a Latinized pronunciation) was Lucifer, but he decided to call himself Satan—a word that comes from prehistory and exists in very early Sanskrit (and as far back as Lemurian) writings, long before most "traditional" Sanskrit was even written. Those who followed Satan's thinking were his disciples, or demans. It should be noted that some Sanskrit "experts" may disagree with these derivations as explained above, because most of today's understanding of Sanskrit was constructed from later texts (even though some of the earlier ones were known of), such as those from Hindu religion, and, much later as some early Buddhist religions, were being developed. Satan, or Lucifer, is not a devil, nor is he a being who is following the de-evil. Satan has not been consumed by evil, and evil is not in control of him. He is, in a way and up to a point, in control of evil. Satan remains a Kumara in his mastery of all energy and activity (on at least one plane of existence), even though he is using evil in his purpose to "save" earth before it is too late. Note that a Planetary Logos's representative must be a Master of all activity from the atmic, or spiritual, plane down to the etheric/dense physical, because this is the span of time and space in which a planet exists within a solar system. The Spiritual Hierarchy and the Planetary Logos (and its agent incarnate, Sanat Kumara) emphatically disagree with Satan's position. They continue in their plan, although they have altered it to adjust for Satan's actions. Satan cannot destroy earth, nor is he attempting to. What he is attempting to do is to accelerate the destruction of physical human civilization that is creating darkness, to prove that the Plan is too physically difficult on humans. Evil can and might destroy earth if humans *advance far enough* in their civilization and remain evil through their choices and actions, thus preventing earth from becoming a sacred planet. What has been explained in the preceding few paragraphs was at least somewhat revealed in semi-mystical language in the Secret Doctrine texts written by H. P. Blavatsky about A.D. 1875. In general, this information has been kept hidden for some 11,000 years because it can be inverted into very wrong interpretations by evil or confused thought. Even today, as it is written here, this information is difficult for most people to understand without careful reflection.

Each of the original five Kumaras (who then became three within the Spiritual Hierarchy of earth) and their students (Buddhas of Activity or of energy when manifested, for earth) was selected to be in control, or in charge, of one of the five dimensions of separated energy within our universe—as these dimensions apply to earth. Each Kumara is in charge of converting the energy in his or her dimension into intelligent activity by helping to make decisions about future ray focuses that will best grow the senses of lifeforms within the kingdoms. There is a Kumara for the spiritual plane (Sanat Kumara), one for the intuitional plane, and another for the mental plane. The Kumara for the astral plane left earth's service because she somewhat agreed with Satan, that earth would fail because life on the physical plane would be too difficult for humans to build consciousness (love, or oneness of life in thought) within. The fifth Kumara, who is known as Satan, was to be in charge of the etheric/dense physical plane. When the Kumara for the astral plane left, Satan attempted to take over that plane's energy as well. So far, he has succeeded to some extent in his control over the eighth sphere, as well as parts of the seventh and sixth astral sub-planes. While Satan does control all of the energy and activity on the sub-planes of the etheric/dense physical and some on the astral planes, evil has at times gained control only on the eighth sphere of the astral plane and the second through fourth etheric sub-planes. Today evil controls only the eighth sphere. Remember, the *Kumara* Satan is not evil— he just uses it in attempt to prove his position.

Thirteen thousand years ago, in about 11,000 B.C., the Masters in the Spiritual Hierarchy who had human spiritual disciples as students asked the more advanced of their students to develop a plan as a part of the plan for earth; this new part of the plan was to hide, or mystify, Ageless Wisdom and *all* knowledge of the Atlantean and the (prior) Lemurian civilizations. Such a plan was needed so that evil people could not, in the future, reconstruct the evil parts of the Atlantean civilizations, especially the evil parts of the sixth and seventh sub-races. A plan was devised and implemented, to transform vital information into mysteries that could be accessed and understood only by humans who underwent training in esoteric mystery schools. These mystery schools acted as screening groups to keep evil people out through tests of virtuous thought and sometimes of virtuous behaviors, thus protecting this information from evil.

Seven types of mystery schools were developed that were mostly secret, or hidden from most people (were esoteric, or occult); one type of these mystery schools existed for each of the seven types of cosmic rays and the particular virtue (as applied to human civilizations) that each ray creates. Spiritual disciples along particular ray lines helped to create the mystification of the information within their mystery schools; all functioned under the direction of the second ray esoteric mystery school because within human civilization, the second ray and its corresponding school control education. Groups of disciples and their developing esoteric mystery schools were assigned to geographic areas, based upon the effects of ray factors on those areas of earth. Each geographic area of earth is more prone towards having its form, or the energy that constitutes it, affected by one of the seven rays over very long periods of time. Humans are sometimes attracted to certain geographic areas based upon the ray factors in their bodies and their levels of selfishness. Put another way, the more selfish that people are, the more they are affected by the ray focus of their bodies, and the more that they are attracted to a geographic ray focus that corresponds to the ray focus of one of their bodies. People living in the area surrounding an esoteric mystery school would then be served by disciples in their locale who often also had a corresponding ray in one or more of their bodies. The ray type of a body that someone is the most conscious in usually controls his or her affinity towards certain locales. In the early days of the esoteric mystery schools, disciples usually lived in a geographic area where there was an esoteric mystery school whose ray focus corresponded to one or more of their bodies' rays. For the more virtuous of these people, the school's ray focus corresponded to their soul ray. Each esoteric mystery school represented a particular ray approach that was consistent with its geographical location. This arrangement provided the most conducive ray focus of the school for those humans who would live in the surrounding area, and who sought spiritual knowledge and understanding but who were not a part of the mystery school. The esoteric schools required, through their methods of teaching, that one could not gain knowledge without also gaining understanding. It has been precisely this characteristic of these esoteric mystery schools for the last 11,000 years that has reversed the trend towards the darkness that resulted from earlier teaching that did not follow this principle.

As described below, conditions have, at the present time, reached a new level that permits a change in the entire approach of mystification and esoteric mystery schools. It is now time for Ageless Wisdom to be de-mystified, using a conceptual approach that systematically reduces selfishness as a person attempts to synthesize knowledge, by building more spiritual higher-mental abilities to think, and increasing consciousness. This book, *Life's Hidden Meaning*, is following that guideline, which, for some people, is achievable today because of much greater higher mental body development. Also, for this method to be safely and effectively employed, a certain (large) number of spiritual disciples need to be in incarnation (with some of them functional, or creating more virtue) and of an average age of twenty-eight or beyond. Other reasons exist for the timing of this new approach, which has as a part of it demystification, and includes the planned externalization of some members of the Spiritual Hierarchy, possibly around the year 2025. These Masters would not incarnate, but would use what will be a newly developed means of creating a semi-permanent etheric/dense physical body. The mayavirupas (etheric bodies of light) that are at present being used for brief periods of time cannot be employed for longer periods on the dense physical planes because to do so would cause harm to the etheric elemental energy, which needs to be allowed frequent periods of time within which to densify, gravitate, and further involute into matter. A part of the Masters' newly invented bodies will rely on proportionately more lunar deva energies. The determining factor to the externalization of members of the next kingdom to live among and be in direct contact with some humans for the first time in about thirty thousand years will be the success of the large group of spiritual disciples who are currently in incarnation, functioning in their lives in group, or soul, consciousness. This *New Group of World Servers* needs to collectively become functional, group consciously, by each member becoming group conscious as soon as possible after reaching twenty-eight years of age. Many of them have not yet done so, and some are reaching an age at which their potential to serve is being significantly reduced because of karma they are accruing and time constraints they are creating through their wasting of time. A few of the people in the New Group of World Servers have attempted to function within their spiritual groups and have failed because of glamours and, especially, because of egotism. These people are very likely to lose any opportunity to serve in this lifetime, and possibly for several more. Without the most spiritual people functioning in a society, as examples, leaders, and teachers of virtue, the society will almost certainly become increasingly darker. For people of today to improve their mental abilities requires that the New Group of World Servers is successful. Otherwise, egotism and arrogance will be likely to cause a new age of darkness and human suffering because people will believe that it is more important to be "right" in their own thinking than it is to love and to help create truth in everyone's thinking—through humility and group consciousness.

 THE FIFTH MAJOR HUMAN RACE

The fifth major human race is focused on mental development, a task made even more difficult because it is being undertaken during the fourth round of life development, which tends to emphasize the development of more astral than mental parts of life. The next, or fifth, round will correspond to a focus on mental development in life. The entire fifth major race is more susceptible to developing egotism and arrogance than the fourth major race was to developing glamour, and, as an added problem, the fifth major race is significantly glamoured as well. The initial attempts at creating the first seed sub-race of the fifth major race occurred about 75,000 years ago and were unsuccessful. During this time period, the most successful fifth ray souls incarnated. Many of them had had numerous virtuous incarnations during the fifth Atlantean sub-race, with some of them also having had virtuous lives during the sixth and seventh sub-races. The civilization had become so dark that some of these human incarnations died during childhood; others fell victim to the inculcated selfishness of their families and the surrounding society. The average level of virtue among the population was too low for the Manu to successfully develop an isolated seed first sub-race of the fifth major race. Later attempts were undertaken, with the first semi-successful one occurring around 55,000 years ago, with, oddly, a predominance of some sixth-ray focused souls who had been able to be virtuous during the later part of the Atlantean sixth sub-race. Unfortunately, though, as these people developed stronger mental bodies and more structured thought, they also became significantly egotistical. When brought back to Atlantis from the location in the Middle East where they had developed as a seed sub-race, they were separative and some were arrogant. The odd combination of being astrally devoted (a sixth ray trait) and mentally creative and destructive (first ray traits) produced a motivation to become superior mentally through the (mis-) use of knowledge. When applied in the seventh sub-race Atlantean society, which was, as a society, greedy and hoarding, the members of this new seed sub-race used their superior knowledge and stronger mental thought to accumulate wealth, to be separate from others, and to destroy the mental abilities of others through contradictory thought that the others could not readily recognize to be illogical.

The second seed sub-race of the fifth major race was developed about 40,000 years ago; its members also developed egotism, but not nearly as much arrogance, on average, as compared to the first sub-race. The souls in this seed sub-race had incarnated mostly during the very early part of the sixth Atlantean sub-race and during the later part of the fifth. They were accompanied by a group of new souls (never before incarnated on earth) who, on the final planet of the Moon Chain, had incarnations who were more virtuous along the second ray. The first sub-race souls had been joined by some new souls who had been relatively more selfish along the first ray than those in the second group had been along the second ray while this latter group had been in incarnation on the final (the third) Moon Chain planet, which was earth's preceding incarnation as a planet.

The third seed sub-race of the fifth major race was developed about 30,000 years ago, using primarily souls who were from the seventh sub-race of the fourth major race and who had created the relatively most virtuous humans. During the later part of the seventh sub-race new souls were also used, mostly along the third ray and who had come from the Moon Chain. In addition were some souls from other planetary systems because earth as a planet is focused on the third ray types of life, and some souls from planets with a focus along another ray type seek a planet whose focus is along the third ray, to attempt to incarnate and create service on that planet. Some souls of ray types other than the third ray and that have been successful in their human incarnations' creation of virtue are sometimes afforded similar opportunities to serve on other planets in our solar system. Occasionally, a very virtuous one of these souls will develop such a high consciousness that he or she becomes a planetary Avatar, who brings to a planet (other than the one that he or she developed on) a new way of thinking and of giving that thought to the life on the planet than those humans on it could think or give themselves.

The first three sub-races of the fifth major human race were at a great disadvantage because once the Atlantean civilization was destroyed, nearly all knowledge about human civilization that had existed on earth up to that point had either been destroyed or hidden. The effects of this lack of knowledge created four to five thousand years of nearly no civilization on earth. Those who escaped the destruction of Atlantis were the more virtuous of earth's population, and many of them were spiritual disciples who had become the (prior, or Old Group, of) World Servers who were to safeguard the new knowledge that they had hidden from others, within the mystery schools these disciples were in charge of creating and administering. For several thousands of years following the final destruction of Atlantis, these spiritual disciples, over numerous lifetimes, lived in relatively small groups in the locales where their mystery schools would in the future become fully functional. Some of these locations included: modern-day areas of India—first ray mystery schools; Egypt—second ray mystery schools; China—third ray mystery schools; Iraq, Syria, Lebanon, parts of Iran, and fractions of other States, all known as the original Persia (but excluding most of Northwestern Turkey)—fourth ray mystery schools; Greece—fifth ray mystery schools; Israel, Palestine, and sections of Jordan—sixth ray mystery schools; the remainder of Northern Africa, including Libya, Morocco, Sudan, Ethiopia, etc.—seventh ray mystery schools. All of these areas were first settled because the only reasonably quick and safe escape from the final destruction of Atlantis was to the higher areas of North Africa and east of Portugal. From these two areas, spiritual disciples traveled East and mostly South to the rest of the above-mentioned areas (with some of these disciples sailing by ship across the Mediterranean) because, in the beginning, the North still was very cold and glaciated.

GEOGRAPHIC LOCATIONS OF ANCIENT MYSTERY SCHOOLS AND THEIR RAY FOCUSES	
GEOGRAPHIC LOCATION	RAY FOCUS OF MYSTERY SCHOOL
Modern-day areas of India	First ray occult, or esoteric, mystery schools
Egypt	Second ray occult, or esoteric, mystery schools
China	Third ray occult, or esoteric, mystery schools
Iraq, Syria, Lebanon, parts of Iran, and fractions of other States, all known as the original Persia (but excluding most of Northwestern Turkey)	Fourth ray occult, or esoteric, mystery schools
Greece	Fifth ray occult, or esoteric, mystery schools
Israel, Palestine, and sections of Jordan	Sixth ray occult, or esoteric, mystery schools
All of the remainder of Northern Africa, including Libya, Morocco, Sudan, Ethiopia, etc.	Seventh ray occult, or esoteric, mystery schools

Table 9. 3

Once Poseidonis sank, the entire Gulf Stream reached directly into the northern coasts of Great Britain and Europe—all the way into the Arctic regions, causing such rapid changes in the world climate that these changes took place within about ten to twenty years. Added to these effects was a sudden rising of the Atlantic Ocean and then a sudden lowering, creating radical changes to coastlines and to the continental shelves surrounding the continents of the Atlantic Ocean and the Mediterranean Sea. This was caused by Poseidonis first sinking below the Atlantic Ocean—with its extremely tall mountains—all raising sea levels in the Atlantic and Mediterranean by dozens of feet. Then, as most of the island sank below the ocean bottom into the earth's crust, the sea levels fell by even greater amounts as even more volume of land area disappeared from the ocean floor and no longer displaced the water in the Atlantic Ocean. The mountains of Poseidonis first erupted and parts of them filled the ocean; in addition, the sea bottom, or the Atlantic ridge, opened. These two factors caused massive displacement and enormous tidal waves. The result was torrential flooding and violent meteorological disturbances, including so much steam that billowing clouds created vast periods of rain. As the ocean floor opened up and then swallowed the remaining island continent, the ocean surrounding Poseidonis boiled and steamed at levels that have never been experienced in modern times.

Those who escaped the disaster carried with them a reverence for the power of the Planetary Logos, and a respect for its seeking to create a world of light rather than of evil. Nearly all of these disciples and their descendents were devoted to faithfully carrying out the plan to mystify the Ageless Wisdom, or to mystify all the knowledge applied to creating more of virtue (God's thought within form) in the past, the present, *and for the future.* The prior errors caused by egotism had mostly been corrected by a terrible lesson; giving knowledge—alone—was no longer seen as a way of creating virtue. Instead, knowledge became feared when it did not include wisdom. Those who sought wisdom and gave it, through teaching whole structured thought to only those who could demonstrate understanding of the thought by using it to further create with virtue, were no longer in illusion. The effects of evil overtaking one-fourth of humanity and nearly the entire planet created an urgency within many spiritual disciples that to this day remains as a part of their permanent atoms. The greatest mistakes of the past are not likely to be repeated by most people who are spiritually disciplined.

Because most of humanity is, today, very mentally focused—as members of the fifth sub-race of the fifth major race—knowledge and its accumulation are of prime importance; people who are egotistical, or selfish mentally, place emphasis on knowledge without wisdom. Note that wisdom must be created. Wisdom begins with a person's concern that certain knowledge should be made whole, and then is made whole by the choice and understanding to be more virtuous. For thousands of years after the destruction of Atlantis, the hiding of knowledge had been the primary emphasis of the work by spiritual disciples. The first part of their monumental labor was to destroy (mostly) or thoroughly hide (infrequently) all that remained of people, animals, and objects in what was left of the colonies of Atlantis. Some animal-human slaves existed in the colonies, and most were sterile; those that were not sterile were made so, to prevent any further human hybridization with them. Although it would have been easier to kill them, it would have been wrong to do so. Since no life could be taken, these unfortunate victims were cared for and allowed to live out the balance of their lives with dignity—receiving love and compassion—which enabled some recovery for their group soul and its self. When their lives ended, their bodies were burned without exception, as was the practice for all animals and humans when they died or were found dead. The Planetary Logos and the Spiritual Hierarchy were amazingly successful at destroying most of Atlantean civilization by focusing ray emphasis and greatly energizing areas where any part of the civilization remained. With the long-term help of spiritual disciples over thousands of years of time eliminating the smaller details, nearly all knowledge of and from Atlantis that could be used with which to re-create evil was erased. There still exists evidence of the prior existence of both Lemuria and Atlantis; however, to discover and understand this evidence requires that it be investigated both with spiritual thought and spiritual inclination. This condition was deliberately applied in order to prevent those who are unprepared to make such discoveries from doing so, thus allowing these people's own egotism to cause them to both hide and block the truth from themselves.

 ### THE FIRST THROUGH THE FOURTH SUB-RACES OF THE FIFTH MAJOR HUMAN RACE

The first sub-race of the fifth major race became scattered into small groups, mostly but not exclusively within the areas of the Middle East and India. Those groups in the Middle East would eventually enter into conflict with the members of the second sub-race of the fifth major race who lived in Egypt and with the fourth seed sub-race group that would later develop there. Because of the legacy of having virtually no prior civilization to rely upon, this sub-race developed only a limited civilization, and mostly towards the very end of its development. The destruction of the Atlantean civilization was critically timed to be in correlation with the focused development of the first sub-race of the fifth major human race. The first sub-race was affected by the first ray and would as a group therefore be the most capable of surviving the planned holocaust, because the first ray provides for the most creativity and adaptability in life, through making new choices when they are needed. The first ray focus also furnished this sub-race with the most effective means of destroying, through self-sacrifice, that which came before its members and stood in the way of their life development. The ray focus also helped spiritual disciples within the sub-race to develop the senses to be able to choose the most effective ways to destroy those remaining parts of Atlantean civilization that needed to be removed. The most commonly focused ray combination from 9000 B.C. to 5000 B.C., while the first sub-race of the fifth major race was developing, was 5-1-2-3. Once the focus of the fifth major human race began, the time needed to develop a sub-race had dropped from hundreds of thousands to tens of thousands of years, down to only thousands of years; in the development of the races, the development of each successive major race (and to a lesser extent, each sub-race) usually requires much less time than did the previous ones, because of the cumulative effects of developed senses and civilization. The loss of benefit from prior human civilization slowed and permanently reduced the development of civilization for the first sub-race of the fifth major race.

The focused development of the second sub-race of the fifth major race began in Egypt about 5000 B.C. The ray focus on earth while the second sub-race was developing had changed to a predominant combination of 6-4-2-5, giving this sub-race and the newly developing fourth seed sub-races a distinctive feminine quality of consciousness, along with an additional focus on creating more complex, devoted, and segregated ways of relating to God (creating a religion). The sixth ray can become very strong when reinforced by the second and fourth, if the second has been weakened by a lack of prior civilization, as was the case with the early Egyptians. Education is normally a key component in any second ray society; while not completely missing from early Egyptian culture, it was relatively stunted because these people had almost no prior civilization to build upon, and were thus forced to virtually start over again for much of their civilization. Some—carefully prescribed—knowledge from the second ray esoteric mystery schools found in Egypt was permitted to become a part of Egyptian civilization, in order to help the stunted educational development of this society. This knowledge was usually not understood conceptually by the less spiritually disciplined Egyptians, and was therefore limited in its applications and its ability to be created into newly synthesized knowledge.

In imaginative thought, the *form* of pyramids was joined with the notion of afterlife, with both of these concepts brought together through the inclusive aspect of the focus on the second ray bringing together fragments of what knowledge remained from Atlantean civilization. The idea that something about the pyramid helped people to pass to the next world remained in Egyptian thought and was eventually re-created in form—but not function, of course. Egyptians, in general, did not have knowledge or use of the Atlantean crystal technologies; the Egyptian mystery school had some understanding of some of the etheric parts of the crystal technologies, but this understanding was kept hidden from the general population. Mummification was an adulteration that resulted from joining thoughtforms together without understanding the concepts behind them. The process of mummification led to an increase in the amount of time that some people stayed on the etheric sub-planes after physical death; these people might even have been comforted by having so much attention given to their expired physical lives, by having certain items buried with them. Most Egyptians were not entombed in pyramids or other major structures after death, but many were, at least partially, mummified and buried in some manner.

Not surprisingly, women played a more important role in the second sub-race than they did in the first, because of the second ray's feminine focus. This role was not as prominent, on average, as it was in the fourth major race overall, because the entire fourth major race of Atlanteans was influenced by the sixth ray focus, regardless of the sub-race focus. Later Egyptian society, as it developed more civilization, became much more affected by the second ray and also the fourth, because one part of the fourth *seed* sub-race of the fifth major race was developing to the east of Egypt in a part of Persia. Because of the strong affinity for education that the Egyptian civilization *eventually* developed, Egypt became the learning center of what we recognize to be the ancient historical world.

Some members of the later part of the first sub-race of the fifth major race were subjugated and even enslaved or killed (or both) by the Egyptians. Some of these first sub-race people were the Israelites of Jewish faith. These same people also had occasional conflicts with members of the fourth seed sub-race. The Israelites had very creative and structured mental bodies, but were still affected by the prior loss of civilization that the earlier parts of the first sub-race of the fifth major race were affected by. The Israelites had one of the first ray occult mystery schools, and it included the writings of the Cabala, as a mystical resource. By borrowing some of the concepts about civilization from the co-developing civilization of the Egyptians and of the fourth seed sub-race of the fifth major race, by about 1000 B.C. the Israelites had, among all of the people who were members of the first sub-race of the fifth major race, reached some of the greatest success at developing some part of a civilization. Many of these more successful people had been the ones who had been more spiritually responsive and somewhat disciplined in Atlantis during the development of the first seed sub-race of the fifth, about 55,000 years ago. Some of these people had souls who had incarnated successfully in terms of creating virtue while physically alive during the sixth Atlantean sub-race. Thus some of the Israelites had within their permanent atoms a strong religious focus, and a focus of creative structured thought. The religious focus came from the virtuous lives that these people had lived as members of the sixth Atlantean sub-race of the fourth race, because the sixth ray when applied virtuously gains devoted understanding of God. The focus of creative structured thought came from the way these people used their thought to create virtue mentally while they were developing the first seed sub-race of the fifth major race. A number of the members of the seed first sub-race of the fifth major race became egotistical or arrogant, and at times tended to misuse knowledge for their own material gain. Some of these people, at times, later incarnated into Israelite civilization. To overcome their selfishness, they were sometimes subjected to rather difficult life circumstances (none of which, of course, excuses the enslavement, torture, murder, and genocide that they were subjected to from others). In Chapter Eleven, much more will be covered about how and why people are incarnated at certain times and under certain circumstances.

Within the Hebrew Bible, or the Old Testament of man's prior relationship with God, there are allegories that reference both Atlantean civilization at its end, and some parts of Ageless Wisdom. Note, however, that the Cabala is a much more accurate representation of Ageless Wisdom. The first books of the Hebrew Bible attempt to depict some elements of the actual past, including the Great Flood. Interestingly, the story of Job is a mystically hidden explanation of how the Planetary Logos and its representative, Sanat Kumara, are in conflict with Satan (the "devil"). The conflict is to test humankind through suffering and to overcome their (thc humans') karma by finding God despite the great suffering they would have to endure while living in the physical world. Satan's conviction was that Job would eventually hate and reject God. He would potentially do so because he so severely suffered from what seemed to be a mixture of trying to be virtuous, but also, at times, being hypocritical and arrogant (which led to the suffering) in his piousness about God. There are many such hidden stories within the Hebrew Bible, which has made it, on a subconscious level, such a strong written spiritual source for so many people.

The beginning of Southern Hemisphere development of the fifth major human race was inaugurated by an isolated group of spiritual disciples who traveled to the central and northern parts of South America between 4000 and 3000 B.C. These disciples eventually became a second seed group of the fifth major human race's fourth sub-race. They developed a somewhat different civilization along the fourth ray than did the original first seed group of the fourth sub-race of this race. Note that additional seed groups were needed, with sub-races expanded into more geographic areas, in order to ensure the viability of humankind because, after the destruction of the Atlantean civilization, there was no civilization for people to build upon. The groups had to begin anew, and having multiple groups increased the overall chances of human survival. However, this also presented certain problems, as discussed below, concerning each group thinking that its approach to civilization was the correct one. Reasons for the differences among the seed groups were that the people in South America began somewhat later in time, and there was a different ray focus, which stimulated the development of different senses; also, this later group was in a very different—almost opposite—geographic area of earth as compared to Mesopotamia, where the first seed group of this fourth sub-race developed. By being south of the equator, this second group and seed fourth sub-race received the annual increases and decreases of ray energy focus and of course, solar energy focus at seasonal times that were opposite to those north of the equator. In the Southern Hemisphere, the effect is that each ray emphasizes its form side slightly less, allowing for more of a spiritual awareness. The Southern Hemisphere tends, therefore, to develop civilizations more slowly, since the form senses of its lifeforms grow slightly less within a given period of time. However, the spiritual awareness becomes accentuated a bit more in the Southern Hemisphere because less focus is placed on material form in the etheric/dense physical world. As one moves closer to the equator, the rays increase in energy and so does selfishness. In particular, emotionalism is increased because of increases in astral energies more than in etheric/dense physical, since inertia (and selfishly used etheric/dense physical energy) reduces the excitation. Thus those living nearer the equator tend to be both more emotional *and* somewhat more physically sedate.

Although differences do exist between the two parts of a hemisphere (the eastern and western), there is less difference between those two than the differences that exist between the (Northern and Southern) hemispheres themselves. The eastern and western parts of the Northern Hemisphere are divided spiritually (somewhat unequally in areas) at India's western-most border. The division takes place there because the first ray focus of India as a country adds to the overall first ray focus of Asia, with a combined effect that makes the general focus of thought in those areas of Asia somewhat more spiritual than material. The somewhat more material focus begins again in North America, at the western-most part of Alaska. Like the Northern, the Southern Hemisphere is also split in its emphasis of focus, between the material and the spiritual, but converse to the Northern Hemisphere. South America in particular and Africa south of the equator, to a lesser extent, are the continents that are more spiritual in focus, with Australia and the island of New Zealand the more material. However, the entire Southern Hemisphere is, overall, more spiritual than is the Northern.

The plan for earth is that human life was focused in the Southern Hemisphere during the third major race (the Lemurians); then the focus shifted more into the Northern Hemisphere for the Atlantean, or fourth major, race. For the fifth major race—the "Aryan," not to be confused with the Nazi misuse of the name—the Northern Hemisphere has been the focus of development for the first half of the race, through most of the fourth sub-race, and then the emphasis is to gradually shift towards development of the Southern Hemisphere. The Southern Hemisphere is to reach a parity with the Northern in civilization during the sixth and seventh sub-races while the Northern continues to develop, though not as quickly as the Southern. In the sixth major race (the "Aquarian"), both the Northern and Southern Hemispheres, including Antarctica, will be developed at the same time, together, from the beginning of the race while one or more seed groups begin on another planet. During the seventh major race (the "Rainbow"), civilization on other planets will be developed simultaneously with civilization on earth, with Mars being the first planet to be developed. Earth's moon, as a planetoid, is to serve as a frequently used shuttle point for the exploration of our solar system until the end of the fourth round when, if earth has by then become a sacred planet (one without evil on it), the moon may disintegrate. Its particles would then be likely to form one or more rings around earth, somewhat like the rings that surround Saturn. As space propulsion systems become much more powerful and efficient, space stations will lose prominence because they lack natural resources, even when biospherically designed to be extremely economical. Note that economy itself does not supply resources for continual growth, but a planet does, through its development of all the kingdoms, beginning with the mineral.

The first sub-race of the fifth was the first to develop religions based upon material and animal entities, and included the worship of idols. One of these first religions was Hinduism, founded by a Great Master and his student, who incarnated as Vyāsa. This same great Master and a different student incarnated first as Thoth, or Hermes, in Egypt, teaching and creating the religion of Light. Another Great Master appeared as himself on the Indian Planes as Krishna to his student Arjuna. This Master later appeared to Jesus, and at that time was the Christ, or the head of the Spiritual Hierarchy. The second sub-race adopted the idols, and, in addition to the material and animal entities, worshipped celestial objects—the sun (and light) and, to a lesser extent, the moon. The last and most developed part of the first sub-race developed monotheism and a religion that came closer to understanding God, beginning with the Hebrew God, Yahweh; this monotheism developed into the Judaic religion. Some fourth seed sub-races that came from the first sub-race of the fifth developed religions related to fire and balancing energy with spirit. The Middle-Eastern/Persian fourth seed sub-race, led by a Great Master and his student—who was in physical incarnation—created the religion of Zoroastrianism (the "religion of fire"), which placed slightly more emphasis on the energy and magical side (the form side) of balancing energy with spirit. The Central American and South American seed groups of the fourth sub-race emphasized slightly more spirit than energy in their religion, although both this and the Middle Eastern religion also included *real* magic, or the ability to change the density of seventh plane (seventh ray) matter into less dense etheric forms, and back again. Magi were those who could create such effects by using a small amount of ancient (Atlantean) crystal and other technologies. Only spiritual disciples could be Magi (who often were also leaders, or kings of their people) because only spiritual disciples could receive the knowledge from an occult mystery school.

The third sub-race of the fifth major race developed from three seed groups of disciples, after Atlantis had been destroyed. The first of the three groups traveled to China, eventually taking over (peacefully) what was left of the ancient Atlantean colony there; this colony had been subjugated and harmed by members of the later part of the seventh Atlantean sub-race. A second seed group of disciples later developed in Northern Greece; the older Atlantean colony in southern Greece had been almost completely destroyed by the geological and meteorological effects upon the Mediterranean sea, during the obliteration of the Atlantean continent. A third seed group was started, some time later, by some members of the seed group in northern Greece who traveled back westward to Italy. Because the third sub-race is mostly affected by the third ray, which itself tends to develop civilization more than any of the other rays, each of these third sub-races quickly developed unique civilizations, although the eventual Greek and Roman civilizations shared some quite close ties and some common elements, including their religions.

The third ray tends to manifest militarism in human behavior because, when selfishly expressed, this ray produces activity to grow form through power alone, rather than through intelligence and power used together. All three of these seed third sub-race civilizations grew to be very large, and each engulfed large areas with its civilization, becoming a kingdom. Eventually these three kingdoms became emperorships, in which "kingdoms" still existed. The vast Greek Empire lasted only decades of time, while the Roman Empire lasted for centuries, and the Chinese Empire under different dynasties continued for nearly two millennia. For modern civilizations focused along the fifth ray, considering that fifth ray (fifth major race) civilizations change so rapidly as compared to earlier races, the Roman and Chinese Empires were quite long-lasting and were the first to endure in this way.

The religions of Greece and Rome were much more focused on human form than on spirit, which contributed in different ways to the development of each of their societies. The early Chinese religion was more focused on spirit and on *individual spirits*, and this affected their civilization. Eventually, Chinese religion encompassed the worship of spirits, including the spirits of their ancestors, because the Chinese people recognized that civilization was gradually created through each person's contribution. The civilization as a whole was still of paramount concern, rather than any focus on individuals, because of these people's more spiritual orientation to the overall focus of developing more of civilization. After the Legalist period had ended, about 200 B.C., China tended to reject the fifth ray approach, which is more scientific, and which corresponded to all of their sub-races of the fifth major race. Note that the Legalists applied scientific thought to law, often in a cruel and rigid way. To replace the Legalist approach, the Chinese adopted an approach to civilization that was more purely along the third ray—by employing a *large* government. Government is generally created from a first-ray focus, but a very *large* government grows itself from too much imbalanced third ray focus by the members of its population. China as a country was settled by two sub-races (the first and third) of the fifth major race. The first settlers were some members of the first sub-race, who entered China from India and created feudal governorships as the first government in modern times, around 4500 B.C. While these governorships were still under development, some members of the third sub-race entered China and began to settle other parts of it. Later, the third sub-race people overtook the jurisdictions (often by force) of the first sub-race people, and centralized much larger governments.

The Greeks and Romans tempered the third-ray focus of their civilizations by including within their civilizations more of the fifth ray, or more scientific thought and inventions. Doing so elevated some of these people's rigidity and militarism into a desire to explore and discover new places and people. These new people would then eventually integrate into part of the Greek or Roman culture and reduce its rigidity and tendency to crystallize along the third ray. The lack of influence by the fifth ray caused the crystallization that eventually took place in Chinese civilization, which remained overly focused on the third ray.

About 600 B.C., in India, the other first sub-race group of the fifth major race developed an advanced civilization. This group was assisted by an advanced disciple and his *T*eacher, a great Master, who together developed Buddhism. Buddhism *in its original form* was the religion that was, up to that time in human civilization, the most representative of principles in Ageless Wisdom. This group of first sub-race people had taken a very long time to develop, and with its first ray mystery schools, reached its highest level slightly later than the afore-mentioned Judaic group did and at an overall higher level. The people in this part of the first sub-race were mostly *not* incarnations of souls who had been more successful members of the Atlantean sixth sub-race. They had incarnated earlier, as spiritually successful Atlantean fifth sub-race people, and some were also new souls who were incarnating on earth for the first time within the first seed sub-race of the fifth major race, during Atlantean times in about 55,000 B.C. This group of people was more isolated on the Indian sub-continent, and its members were subjugated less often by other races. Buddhism in its early form was based upon the creation of virtue in order to find and become a functional part of "God." Buddhism does not recognize a single separate God, because as a religion it understands that God is in everything; however, its perspective is somewhat incorrect because, as a religion, it usually was and often is neglectful of inclusively recognizing (and understanding) that God, as all of life, is One. To correct Buddhism and improve upon it by adding to this religion more elements of love, or inclusiveness, but not removing its correct understandings, the Spiritual Hierarchy through its leader and great *T*eacher and one of his students developed the religion of Christianity out of Judaism because the Judaic religion was especially focused on there being *one* God. Both of these religions came from members of the first sub-race of the fifth major race, but Christianity was directly created by the third sub-race. Also, much earlier, the religion (of "fire") of Zoroastrianism had been founded by Zoroaster, who was a member of the first sub-race and was also a student of the World Teacher and the Leader of the Spiritual Hierarchy of that time. This religion was enlarged upon by members of the fourth seed sub-race that developed later in the Middle East, with this seed group comprising the more spiritually developed people of the first sub-race of the fifth major race.

The Greek word Christos and its Latinized derivative defining a person by the name of Christ, rather than the office or title of Christos, came from much earlier (Atlantean period) names for the second ray leader and World Teacher who is the head of the Spiritual Hierarchy, or of the fifth kingdom. The Christian use of this word to refer to God is an understandable modification, because an advanced Master who is about to advance beyond the next kingdom is certainly God-like to humans. Jesus of Nazareth was an advanced student and spiritual disciple of this Great Master, one of whose actual names is Maitreya. Christ, or a similar designation, is the title of the office held in the Spiritual Hierarchy by someone who has attained such a position. Jesus was a soul with a sixth ray focus, and was an arhat by the standards in effect at that time. He was, for short periods of time and when it was appropriate, joined in consciousness by his *Teacher* and Master of the Ageless Wisdom, Maitreya—the Christ. One can recognize how when such events were explained to the students of Jesus, the interpretation could be that Jesus was the son of God. This partial and incomplete concept led to two major and opposing effects. The first was the personalization of and, therefore, a greatly widened appeal of the religion of Christianity, since it said that God was, in part, a human. This also moved religion closer to the understanding that all of life is through inclusiveness, or through love, a part of God, and that the growth of life is God's growth. The second effect was the widespread belief that only one special human was a part of God, and despite the statements attributed to Jesus that are in contradiction to that incomplete and paradoxical concept, which led to faith in, devotion to, and worship of him, this incorrect belief is the means of at least somewhat knowing, if not understanding, God. This second effect of Christian doctrine has placed Christianity in the state of being a mentally developed religion that is incomplete, or unwise, because it lacks some truth. Statements in Christianity that are attributable to Jesus, as the Christ, are mostly accurate relative to Ageless Wisdom because the original intent was to create a religion that would foster love and oneness of life and that used basic principles of Ageless Wisdom. The inclusiveness of the original religion of Christianity turned into exclusivity and separation, beginning with the false concept that becoming a part of God was something that only Jesus—as "His" son—could achieve or be. Despite its shortcomings, Christianity has become the most successful religion yet introduced on earth in terms of furthering the virtue of love. This single accomplishment has changed the world towards a more spiritual future. Christianity was the religion created by the last (and most developed) members of the third sub-race of the fifth major race (even though it began in and grew out of the religion of the first Aryan sub-race), and it has been practiced, in various forms, ever since that time.

The fourth sub-race began to replace the third in about A.D. 600. The seed groups of this sub-race were in conflict with both the first and third sub-races of the fifth major race when they had contact, because their civilizations were so very different from each other. A fourth sub-race attempts to gain harmony through conflict because it focuses on the need to balance—perfectly—spirit to energy, or spiritual life to form life. A first and particularly a third sub-race mostly emphasizes form over spirit (although the later Chinese third sub-race was better balanced in this respect). One part of the fourth sub-race of the fifth major race created the religion of Islam, which focuses on perfecting the balance between spiritual and material life. Mohammed, who was another advanced spiritual disciple along the sixth ray, proposed specific ways of living that would achieve this perfection in balance between spirit and energy. Like

Christianity, this religion—Islam—contained great truths that were altered by later interpretations that placed God as external to life—and to humans, which caused separation to replace the religion's original inclusiveness. The fourth sub-race dominated the Middle East, North Africa, Turkey, parts of Southeast Asia, and (for short periods) the Balkans, Portugal, and Spain. In Central and South America, this sub-race flourished. North America was repopulated with some fourth sub-race people in Mexico who originally were from Central America. The remainder of North America had as its inhabitants millions of people from the seventh sub-race of the fourth (Atlantean) major race, and some of the few remaining sixth sub-race people who had escaped destruction because they had been chased out of northern China and Mongolia by the last Atlanteans who attacked them as a colony in the paranoid belief these people from both sub-races posed a threat to them.

Some northern Chinese and Mongolian people who remained in Mongolia were gradually redeveloped, from seventh sub-race of the fourth major race people, into members of the fourth sub-race of the fifth major race. (See Chapter Eleven for a brief explanation of the process.) These people eventually overtook and bred with the third sub-race people of most of Europe, from A.D. 300 to 850. This branch of the fourth sub-race was in conflict with the one in the Middle East, over lifestyle and religion. The European fourth sub-race emphasized more of form because its members had a greater legacy of third sub-race civilization. The Middle Eastern lifestyles and Islam stressed more of the spiritual side of civilization, even though the attempt was made to create a perfect balance—which Islam's followers usually failed to achieve because of their lack of virtuous actions. The later Chinese eventually developed a similar sub-racial conflict with the Japanese; however, the Chinese became more crystallized along the third ray than did the Europeans. While the battles between the emerging fourth sub-race groups were ostensibly over religion, what they were really about was both parties believing that the side of the balance of the fourth ray that its lifestyle emphasized was better than the other. There were degenerating third sub-race people throughout Europe and China until about A.D. 1350, when many of the remaining ones succumbed to disease (predominantly, to the "black plague").

Because the third sub-race people of the fifth major race who lived in Central and South America and in Mexico had immigrated there from other lands, they bred with members of the fourth sub-race of the fifth major race more peaceably. The conflicts in this part of the world were based as much on geography as they were on sub-race. The people north of the equator were more materialistic, while those to the south were more spiritual. Central and South America had as inhabitants some survivors of the degenerating Atlantean sixth sub-race—the few who had not been killed by the seventh Atlantean sub-race. Also living in these areas were even greater numbers of degenerating seventh sub-race Atlanteans who had escaped destruction after 9000 B.C. Added to these scattered groups were immigrants who were in the third sub-race of the fifth major race, who had typically been chased out of their homelands by military conflict. Finally, about 4000 B.C. to 3000 B.C., the fourth seed sub-race was introduced into this part of the world by some spiritual disciples who traveled there. Each of these sub-races developed quite different civilizations, from primitive societies in rainforests, to militaristic societies with large cities and emperorships, to reclusive spiritual societies who sought isolation. The primitive rainforest societies had, as many of their members, people who were *degenerated* sixth and seventh sub-race *Lemurians*. The militaristic societies were populated either by members of the third sub-race of the fifth major race or, more often, by seventh sub-race Atlanteans during the earlier part of their development; the people in the reclusive spiritual societies belonged to the fourth sub-race of the fifth major race.

The fourth and fifth sub-race Europeans eventually traveled to the Americas; through some wars, but mostly through disease that they inadvertently brought with them, they killed off nearly all of the third sub-race and most of the earlier degenerating sub-races of all three major races of people that were still remaining. Many had already been killed off as the rays shifted in frequency and focus to develop the fourth sub-race of the fifth major race, starting around A.D. 525. By the time the fourth sub-race Europeans arrived, disease and civil wars had already taken quite a toll. Also, climactic changes reduced the effectiveness that the prior civilizations had achieved in growing food. It should be noted that until recent times, Australia, New Zealand, many South Sea islands, and even a few parts of South America had as inhabitants members of degenerating Lemurian sub-races. More will be explained in Chapter Eleven about how primitive places such as these can quickly change. It is important to understand that within just one or two generations, an entire population of an ancient degenerated earlier major race can develop into becoming members of the contemporary major race and sub-race.

 ## THE FIFTH SUB-RACE OF THE FIFTH MAJOR RACE

The first seed fifth sub-race began about 650 B.C. with groups simultaneously developing in the areas that are currently known as Great Britain, northern Italy, southern Greece, and Austria (where there was only a very small group). The people in all of these groups were either incarnations of souls who had been relatively virtuous during the first and the third sub-races of the fifth major race, or were new souls, incarnating for the first time on earth, but who had functioned as advanced souls on the Moon Chain planet during part of its fifth round. The fifth seed sub-race of the fifth major race was very focused in Europe, because all of Europe *as a continent* is focused along the fifth ray, even though its individual countries might have a ray focus other than the fifth. The continental ray focuses are: Asia—first ray; Australia—third ray; Europe—fifth ray; Africa—seventh ray; North America—second ray; South America—fourth ray; and Antarctica—sixth ray. The continental ray focus becomes more apparent as the individual countries and the groups of people who inhabit them begin to function more group consciously, or soul consciously, as inclusive units. The continent of Antarctica has a sixth ray focus, but because for some millions of years it has been semi-submerged in frozen water, the life that would have been created there was mostly created instead on the continents of Lemuria and Atlantis before they submerged. The reason that these two continents took over most of the life creation for Antarctica is that Atlantis had a sixth ray focus, and although Lemuria originally had a sixth ray focus, it changed to a seventh ray focus when it became populated by people who had a seventh ray focus. Note that Lemuria and Africa share a seventh ray focus and many similarities, and that over time some degenerating members of the Lemurian race developed in Africa, where subsequent generations of this race lived in prehistoric times. A continental ray focus means that the energy, or matter, of that continent generally responds the most to the cosmic ray that it corresponds to. A continent is affected by the consciousness of larger populations that inhabit it. This affects all of the lifeforms of all life—including people— on that landmass (as took place on Lemuria, as it changed from its original sixth ray focus to the seventh ray). The fifth sub-race of the fifth major race developed *the entirety* of Europe into the fifth ray focus of human civilization, from A.D. 1350 to the present, more than any sub-race had done before. During part of the sixth sub-race of the fifth major race, a landmass on Mars will be a likely substitute for Antarctica in the growth of life. Note that the entire planet of Mars is under the influence of the sixth ray, and that Antarctica is the first place on earth where early life that had been on Mars was discovered.

The fifth sub-race of the fifth major race grew from its roots in Europe, relying on the much earlier seed sub-races that began around 650 B.C. The most successful of these seed sub-races were the southern Greeks, who had fifth ray esoteric mystery schools. The great philosophers and scientists of that era (for a total of about 500 years, from 650–150 B.C.) gave the later part of the entire fifth sub-race tremendous assistance in mastering structured (fifth ray) mental thought, which the fifth sub-race civilization reached, overall, after A.D. 1350. Note that the other fifth sub-race seed groups were mostly destroyed before they could have much of an effect on the sub-race as a whole.

RAY FOCUS OF CONTINENTS AND RACES					
RAY FOCUS	CONTINENT	MAJOR RACE	COSMIC RAY FOCUSED TO DEVELOP RACE	SENSE BEING DEVELOPED IN RACE	RAY LINE ADVERSELY AFFECTED BY KINGDOM'S SELFISH USE OF DEVELOPED SENSE
1st	Asia	1st—Boreal (focused mostly around the North Pole, with some found at South Pole)	3rd	Intelligence—in three lower bodies and worlds	Plant— 3rd ray line
2nd	North America	2nd—Oceanic (focused mostly around large bodies of water)	4th	Balance—in three lower body's use of senses	Human— 4th ray line
3rd	Australia	3rd—Lemurian (focused in Lemuria)	7th	Etheric/dense physical— intelligent coordinated responses	Mineral— 7th ray line
4th	South America	4th—Atlantean (focused in Atlantis)	6th	Astral—empathy	Animal— 6th ray line
5th	Europe	5th—Aryan (focused in Europe)	5th	Mental—love/wisdom	Planetary— 5th ray line
6th	Antarctica	6th—"Aquarian" (will eventually be named after a landmass on Mars)	2nd	Intuitional—buddhi	Spiritual— 2nd ray line
7th	Africa	7th—"Rainbow" (will eventually be named for the joint worlds of Earth, Mars, and Venus)	1st	Spiritual—atma (the joined senses of omniscience and omnipotence)	Solar— 1st ray line

Table 9. 4

After A.D. 1350, while the fifth sub-race was developing, the fourth sub-race continued to develop. The Plan was to rejuvenate and strengthen these two sub-races by more advanced members of both of them incarnating in Europe, the Middle East, and China at the same time, coalescing their cultures. The third ray had become focused in A.D. 1250 and the fifth in A.D. 1300. The cosmic ray focus in A.D. 1325 was 1-5-3-2, and in A.D. 1375 became 4-5-3-2. In A.D. 1475 it changed to 6-4-3-2, creating some very focused fanaticism that was sometimes of a religious nature. Notice that the fifth ray was not focused on earth at that time. The reason was to reduce the conflict that a faster growing fifth sub-race might create by being in such close contact with the fourth sub-race of the fifth major race, whose members were somewhat less advanced in structured thought. Also notice that the rays in focus starting in A.D. 1475 tended to accentuate more feminine qualities, and were chosen, in part, in attempt to reduce and balance what were ripe conditions for wars. Another ray change occurred in A.D. 1575, to 1-4-3-2, and in A.D. 1625, another, which returned the ray focus to 6-4-3-2. In A.D. 1675 the cosmic ray focus on earth changed to 5-6-3-2. From that point, the rays did not change again until A.D. 1900, when the focus became 7-5-3-2, which is still in effect today. In A.D. 2025 the rays are expected to change to 4-7-5-2.

The relatively frequent changes in the rays from A.D. 1250 to A.D. 1675 caused great upheavals in human civilizations around the world, and tended to transform these civilizations into different societies where the fourth and fifth sub-race people of the fifth sub-race could live together to some degree, in towns and cities that were somewhat stratified in their culture. Notice also that the first ray is usually only infrequently focused on earth and for only short periods of time because more frequent and even sudden changes in governments, which the focus of the first ray causes, are usually undesirable. Also, the *destruction* of relatively darker governments is often the first effect brought on by the first ray. The reason is that the first ray tends to destroy selfishness before it grows more virtuousness. After about A.D. 1725, nearly all of the people who produced significant art have been spiritual disciples of various levels of development, because anyone who was born after A.D. 1675 and had one or more bodies focused along the fourth ray had weakened senses in those bodies if they were used selfishly (see Chapter Seven for further explanation). Since A.D. 1675, the fourth sub-race of the fifth has been significantly declining because of the absence of fourth ray focus on earth, which will continue for what will be a total of 350 years. The lack of fourth ray focus has greatly weakened this sub-race, with its members often being killed off by disease or by "accidents" that are the result of weakened senses. The focus of civilization for the fourth sub-race was the creation of new and more advanced art in all of its forms, while the focus of the fifth sub-race's civilization is the creation of new and more advanced science. Between 1475 and 1675, while some great scientific advances did occur in (especially European) civilization, these advances were the result of the pioneering work of spiritual disciples, because those in the general population were not strengthened by a fifth ray focus for most of that time. Note that when examining the effects of the ray changes, an adjustment of about twenty-five years needs to be made on either side of the dates, for the following reasons. The senses of those older selfish people with failing senses who have one or more body types along the ray that is going out of focus will begin to diminish much faster when the ray's focus does, with the entire process taking about twenty-five years. Also, the senses of the babies being born with bodies that are along the new ray will not be fully developed for about twenty-five years. In addition, note that Europe as a continent is focused along the fifth ray, and that this helped to maintain some fifth ray focus even while that ray was not cosmically focused on earth; however, as the fifth ray remained out of focus, this effect diminished over time.

HISTORY OF COSMIC RAY FOCUS ON EARTH

RAYS MORE FREQUENTLY IN FOCUS IN ANTIQUITY	
PERIOD	RAYS
1ST MILLION YEARS OF ATLANTEAN DEVELOPMENT	1-2-6-7 1-3-6-7 3-2-6-7
2ND MILLION YEARS OF ATLANTEAN DEVELOPMENT	2-3-1-7
BEGINNING OF 4TH ATLANTEAN SUB-RACE	4-2-1-6
BEGINNING OF 5TH ATLANTEAN SUB-RACE	5-2-1-6
1 MILLION YEARS AGO	3-5-2-6
LATER PART OF THE ATLANTEAN PERIOD	7-5-2-6 3-1-2-6 4-3-2-6 7-1-2-6
30,000–10,000 B.C.	4-5-7-6
9000–5000 B.C	5-1-2-3
5000 B.C.	6-4-2-5

RAYS IN FOCUS DURING MODERN TIMES	
YEAR	RAYS
A.D. 1250	3-2-7-6
A.D. 1300	5-3-2-7
A.D. 1325	1-5-3-2
A.D. 1375	4-5-3-2
A.D. 1475	6-4-3-2
A.D. 1575	1-4-3-2
A.D. 1625	6-4-3-2
A.D. 1675	5-6-3-2
A.D. 1900	7-5-3-2
A.D. 2025	4-7-5-2

Table 9.5a, Table 9.5b

Depending upon the success of the New Group of World Servers, the fifth sub-race of the fifth major race will not be replaced by the sixth sub-race for about 200 to 500 (or more) years. The lower end of this time projection indicates more virtuous societies, allowing faster *spiritual* development—which will be the focus of life and civilization in the sixth sub-race. Notice how the time periods needed for the sub-races to develop are growing shorter as humans advance and use the lower kingdoms to greater extents within their creation of civilization.

A critical point in human civilization has very recently been reached, within the last quarter of a century: more than half of the total group souls of all three of the lower kingdoms are now being used with which to create human civilization. Thus when averaged together in total, more than half of all the group souls of minerals, plants, and animals are now being used by humans in their civilization. Interestingly, much more than half of the number of minerals (including organic compounds) are now in use, somewhat less than half of all plants are, and much fewer animals are. Animals are used so relatively little, in part because people eat so many animals and fail to understand better (more virtuous) uses for them. The use of organic compounds from the mineral kingdom has escalated tremendously in the last few decades; also, elements have been newly created for the first time on earth. This critical juncture in human civilization, of using over half of the group souls and their selves of the lower kingdoms, has a *hidden meaning to human life*. Once humans incorporate more than half of the combined total of pre-life and life from the three lower kingdoms into their civilization (which extends humans' senses and bodies and the life of humans in the process), humans become *responsible* for the continuation of growth of pre-life and life within those lower kingdoms. The reason is that at the point of one-half use, human consciousness and the human collective selves are now thinking for the majority of the totality of the three lower kingdoms, their souls, and their selves. Should humans use their selves selfishly in thinking for and using these kingdoms, life within these kingdoms will decline rather than grow. This would cause great pain and suffering within the human kingdom, and some pain and suffering within the lower ones.

The speed at which humans have developed the fifth major race is remarkable, when considering that earth is in the fourth round, or the round that is more astrally focused in consciousness. Much of this speed is due to the Planetary Logos' plan to increase the frequency at which the rays have changed during physical plane life. More rapidly changing rays caused accelerated growth in senses, and much greater difficulty for spirit that is conscious on the physical plane to grow in understanding, or consciousness, by thinking through its self. Earlier humans were most affected, in part because their selves did proportionately so much more thinking for the lower kingdoms that they were attempting to control. They were attempting to think for and incorporate these lower kingdoms into their civilization while these kingdoms were being stimulated to advance through the intensification in frequency of ray change, further increasing the difficulty in thinking for them. When humans, or any conscious beings, lose consciousness and then the thought of energy overwhelms them, they suffer. There are extremely high levels of suffering in the current system on physical earth. The reason is the increased speed *of life growth from growth of sense*, and suffering's effect when humans attempt to create civilization from the extreme forces created within the lower kingdom as these kingdoms so relatively rapidly change as a result of the frequent ray changes. It is this effect that Lucifer, or Satan, and the Kumara who left earth's service objected to. Both believed that human civilization would become too dark because of great suffering that would cause humans to reject a God who allowed such suffering to occur. They thought, and Satan still does think, that these circumstances would permit evil to take control.

To offset the risk of the above-described potential problem, the Planetary Logos directed its representative, Sanat Kumara, to instruct the fifth kingdom to begin the teaching of a process known as initiation. Initiation accelerates spiritual development by supplementing the growth and radiance of the solar devas within the spiritual mind, which is part of the human causal body and is located within a person's higher mental body. A spiritual disciple's initiation is accomplished by several Masters giving more energy to certain solar devas that had been somewhat used in service by that person. Note that service is total—one hundred percent—and unconditional giving to others in a way that creates virtue and uses all of the energy of the one or more solar devas, that is needed to give in this way. Initiation is used when the point is reached at which a disciple's further service with those solar pitris would generally require fusion with other solar pitris at a particular time, which would greatly increase that disciple's radiance and would build the "rainbow bridge" of light. Rather than waiting for the fusion process to slowly occur, usually over one or more lifetimes, it is accomplished in only a few seconds (!). This added energy and fusion so increases the spiritual disciple's ability to think, especially in the physical world, that his or her long term suffering dramatically decreases when he or she creates more service, and then his or her (higher) Self also somewhat fuses—simultaneously—with his or her (lower) self, as well.

Once spiritual disciples are initiated (at one of four succeeding human levels), they need to then further serve both those on the spiritual path and those who are not yet on it, in order to help to reduce the suffering of the rest of humanity. If a human spiritual disciple who has gone through at least one initiation (there are a total of four human initiations) fails to serve in any particular lifetime, she or he will eventually suffer for all of the increased consciousness that was given to her or him during the initiation process and the initiation itself. This level of suffering will equal the amount of suffering these initiates could have reduced for their fellow humans whom they could have served and chose not to. This is a substantial and severe level of suffering because the karma is increased by the same amount that the initiation process raises consciousness.

The initiation process was invented for use in offsetting suffering on a planet that is attempting to accelerate growth, usually in order to make up for one or more prior failures. At present within the Plan, earth is using this process exclusively in its fourth round, because of its difficulty in its prior incarnation as part of the Moon Chain. The part of the Plan that involves initiation is subject to change, but is likely to remain in place because by the fifth round earth will in all probability either be a sacred planet, or will have been destroyed because it turned evil in its human civilizations. When initiation is used on a planet, a great deal is dependent upon the success of spiritual disciples; most planets *never* use this system because it relies so much on the creation of virtue by a relatively small number of people. Some souls who seek this kind of challenging service may be attracted to incarnate on such a difficult planet. The successful service by spiritual disciples is of great concern at this period of human development, for the following two reasons. The ray focus on earth will change in A.D. 2025 with the effect of the change beginning about A.D. 2000, and, as was explained above, humanity has become responsible for the growth of life in the lower kingdoms. To assist in this process of creating the needed levels of virtue, approximately ten times the normal number of human souls whose incarnating human beings have begun the initiation process are now incarnated on earth. This New Group of World Servers needs to understand principles of Ageless Wisdom at a higher level and much more quickly than has been ever achieved in the past. This needs to occur for these people to find their respective spiritual groups to serve within, and to create more virtue in each group's unique ways. The process will require books, such as this one, that demystify Ageless Wisdom, as well as people who will themselves be taught to teach its principles. Most of these New World Servers will not consciously devote themselves to the study of Ageless Wisdom—only those who have a second, or educational, ray focus in their service will be likely to do so. But all of them will recognize the principles of Ageless Wisdom, of understanding and becoming a functional part of God by creating more virtue in concert with others who are providing similar service. It is important for these servers to realize that although they have completed one or more initiations in a prior life, they may not have any direct memory of having done so unless an advanced initiation was completed. The reason for the lack of conscious awareness is that for whole memory from a prior life to exist, a person must have created virtue during at least sixty percent of that life. A person who creates virtue at least sixty percent of the time in one life will have continuity of consciousness, or a whole enough memory to remember in his or her next incarnation parts of his or her past service.

Among the New Group of World Servers, seed sixth sub-race groups are beginning in parts of North and South America. More of these people live in the United States because the United States is the most advanced country that has a second ray focused soul and, at present, is home to the majority of disciples who are incarnate are along the second ray. However, a significant percentage of sixth seed sub-race people live in some other countries on these two continents. The two continents combined are where nearly three-fourths of these disciples live, with about half of them in the United States. The remaining disciples, including many advanced humans who are not yet members of the seed sixth sub-race, are scattered throughout the world, with relatively large groups in England and India. As of A.D. 1999, there are close to eleven million New World Servers on earth. A very few advanced initiates are incarnated into bodies that are experimental creations of the first sub-race of the sixth major race. The sixth sub-race will be an average of three to six inches shorter than the fifth, for *each* of the seven human sub-sub-races that are presently on earth. Note that what are considered to be the human "races" on earth are actually sub-sub-races of a sub-race; for example, the remaining degenerated Lemurians on earth belong to one of the sub-sub-races of a sub-race of the third major human race, while many more modern-day people are members of the same-numbered sub-sub-race, but of the fifth major human race. Within each of the sub-sub-races, those who have sixth sub-race bodies will, relative to that sub-sub-race, have an overall smaller stature, smaller bones, and a leaner—though not skinny—appearance. Their faces will tend to be "soft-looking" and not very angular, because the sixth ray is feminine in its focus. Today, these bodies are weaker and more prone to disease if used selfishly. This is why only the souls whose prior human incarnations have been more advanced humans who have been spiritually disciplined will choose to incarnate humans into a sixth sub-race body type. Note that a sub-race body type can take on quite different appearances within the various human sub-sub-races. For example, a sixth sub-race (of the fifth major race) male from the United Sates might stand five feet, six inches tall and weigh 135 to 145 pounds; a Japanese sixth sub-race male might stand five feet, two inches and weigh 115 to 125 pounds. Because of its more feminine focus, a sixth sub-race body will be proportionately smaller in males than in females, which often makes sixth sub-race males and females the same height. The sub-ray affects each human sub-sub-race based upon the dominant ray factors already affecting that race, including its geographic location and how the rays in that location affect its inhabitants. With the sixth ray currently out of focus, those seed groups of the sixth sub-race will have less growth of their senses and bodies in each lifetime, which requires them to be more virtuous in order to offset this effect.

The end of the dense physical focus on life development for earth's fourth round could occur between 5000 and 12,000 (or more) years from the year 2000. The earlier the sub-round ends, the greater the levels of virtue created because less human mistakes and suffering would hasten the integration of the lower kingdoms into the human. This would create more of oneness in growth of life, of God, on earth. This early enlightened synthesis of life is the hallmark of a successful etheric/dense physical period of life focus of a round. Thus human civilization is the crucial element to determining God's growth within the etheric/dense physical world after the third round. When humans create virtuous civilizations the planet grows in life, and the meaning to each human's life grows. When the reverse occurs, then each human loses some meaning in life, regardless of any individual human's successes at creating virtue. The reason is that, as a kingdom, humans share in the karma of their own kingdom and eventually all of the lower ones. Group, or soul, consciousness in humans as a kingdom ultimately determines meaning in life, because of the shared karma of the kingdoms. Individuals do experience very large relative differences in life meaning. In absolute amounts, however, each person loses meaning in life if his or her civilization is selfish.

CONCLUSION AND SUMMARY OF CHAPTER NINE

In conclusion of and to summarize the preceding chapter, each of the kingdoms lower than the human eventually becomes dependent upon the virtue created by the human kingdom, if it (the lower kingdom) is to further develop its life. Until this point of dependency is reached, the kingdoms protect their life's growth by isolating and developing life more during certain times in cycles within a round. These times correspond to a focus of life on a part of a plane, in time *and* space within the limitation of certain dimensions. On the dense physical plane, or dimension, all life is focused on equally. This often creates a crisis for the growth of life because *in some ways* for all lifeforms, survival depends upon cooperation and sharing. When humans are developed during the fourth round, their physical presence alters the growth of life in the lower kingdoms because they incorporate some of this life into their own through the creation of civilization. Until humans incorporate at least half of the totality of life within the three lower kingdoms, the system of kingdoms somewhat protects the group souls, their selves, and their lifeforms in general from selfishness on the part of humanity. Once humans exceed the mid-point in controlling the lower kingdoms, as has been achieved on earth since about A.D. 1975, the protection afforded by the system of kingdoms is no longer effective. The reason is that the spirit's thought within humans, collectively, is powerful enough to overcome the collective thought of both energy and spirit within the group souls and their selves for the majority of the life in the lower kingdoms. When this point is reached, then humans become responsible for the growth of life in these three lower kingdoms, as well as their own.

During its fourth round, earth is using a method of accelerated growth that applies especially to physical life, but somewhat to all life; in order to achieve this accelerated growth, the Planetary Logos has chosen to increase the relative frequency of change in the cosmic rays that are focused on earth at any one time. This more frequent change in the rays provides more diversity to life, growing more life in the lower kingdoms *before* humans gain control over it. However, the reverse occurs as human civilizations grow and then control more of the lower kingdoms selfishly. Prior to the existence of human civilization, life predominantly grows through evolution, or through a focus on senses, energy, power, forces, and form (bodies). The informing thought of spirit from group souls is mostly too weak to affect most of the individual members of that group soul that it controls. Humans grow mostly through their informing spirit's thought, and not through evolution, thus reversing the evolutionary trend to life's growth. If humans identify more with form than with spirit, they can become evolutionary and then suffer the consequences of a world based upon the conflicts of energy posed against other energy or form, creating great forces. A world of force wherein humans dominate is an evil world; it is a world of sorrow and great suffering that only light, or God's thought, can correct. However, if humans were never introduced into a life system, that system would eventually fail because evolution builds forces even when evil is not brought in through dark human civilizations. As forces become too great, diversity is decreased and so is the growth of life; energy and its slight thought needs to be balanced with the informing thought of spirit, to create a world of life growth, or God's growth. Humans are an absolute necessity in this system of growing God, and cannot be dispensed with as a kingdom of life.

Because of their ability to grow in all three lower dimensions of time and space, humans grow at a much faster rate in their development as lifeforms on a planet than the rate that the lower kingdoms are capable of. The meaning of life for humans is dependent upon their use of the three lower kingdoms in ways that increase their senses virtuously, or in ways in which they (the humans) choose to use their senses to further create virtue. In the dense physical world, this is a formidable task because great wisdom is required in order to accomplish the consistent creation of virtue. Fortunately, humans gain the capability to be wise as they become more capable of controlling the life in the lower kingdoms and this life's growth therein. Seven kingdoms exist on earth, with humans (as the fourth kingdom) in the center and playing a pivotal role. It is up to humans to further the life (and pre-life) in the lower kingdoms, by making virtuous use of the members of these lower kingdoms. The present-day period is a point of crisis, since without wisdom used to create more virtue, humans might significantly destroy growth of life in the lower kingdoms, and, at the same time, destroy significant parts of their own civilization and growth of life. If in the near future, humans do not become more spiritual and create more virtue, they might, within about seventy-five years, shorten their lives physically and reduce their population by over three-fourths.

It is up to the New Group of World Servers who are already in incarnation on earth, or soon will be, to do the following to create a world of more light. They need to become group conscious, and create virtue together with *their* group of other spiritually disciplining servers and then with other groups. If focused along the second ray, they will be likely to demystify Ageless Wisdom and teach through their respective groups, and if along another ray of focus, they need to use the new demystified concepts and principles along that ray. They can become examples of more spiritually focused lifestyles and need to nearly always cooperate and share. They need to overcome most of their glamours and egotism, and use their mental minds as their dominant tool to create truth and to help reduce egotism and arrogance in others. As these disciples accomplish what is described immediately above, they will close the door on the etheric/dense physical plane to evil by creating so much virtue—especially truth—that those who are or are becoming evil become exposed *to much of* evil *itself.* Finally, they need to choose to live as souls, seeing and relating to others in *hierarchial thought*, with *humility*, recognizing that some others are more conscious/loving/giving/understanding-of-oneness than they are. Right thought is not thinking that one *is right*, but, instead, is concerning oneself with what is right with others' thought, and, additionally helping others to think as whole and lovingly as possible more often, by listening and assuming one's own thought to be in error if it is contradicted. At this critical point in the development of earth, so much is dependent upon spiritually disciplined people that as many people as possible—even those not willing to spiritually discipline themselves, or become understanding enough to become more spiritual—would be of great help in at least considering the possibility that some of the principles in Ageless Wisdom do have merit. Then these people will, at a minimum, pose less of an obstacle to those who are creating more virtue on earth. These same people will also experience greater meaning in their lives through their individual, even if small, sacrifices and endeavors while they then gain meaning to life in much greater ways through the large sacrifices that others are making in creating most of the virtue in human civilization, *as a kingdom*, and to virtuously integrate the three lower kingdoms within human civilization, and thus will create more of God on earth.

TIME AND SPACE

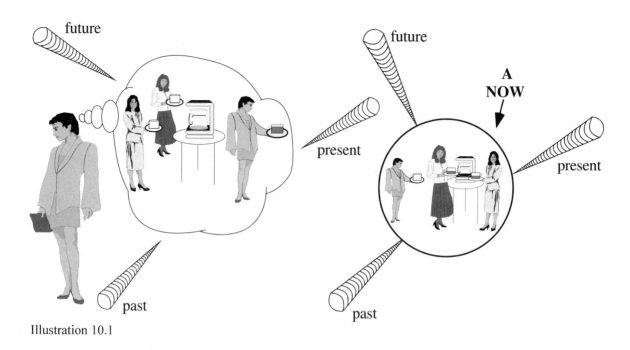

Illustration 10.1

Author's Suggestion: First turn to the "Glossary Help Guide" and read the definitions for this chapter.

 ## BASICS ABOUT THE PHYSICS OF OUR UNIVERSE

In the last chapter an explanation was given concerning how the kingdoms are somewhat segregated parts of life (or, in the case of some minerals, pre-life) that are each protected by being isolated in a certain part of time and space. During the period wherein a planet is developing human civilization, humans slowly at first, and at increasingly faster rates, incorporate the three kingdoms lower than their own as an extension of human senses and bodies into the human kingdom—which is what is referred to as civilization. Since each kingdom represents life as a part of time and space, as humans integrate these lower kingdoms into their own civilization, they are also integrating themselves into the dimensions that the lower kingdoms exist within.

A dimension of time and space is created by separating the three parts of God's mind in our universe. The first two parts of God's mind are choices/will/sacrifice/purpose and consciousness/understanding/unconditional-love/oneness, and these first two parts joined together are God's thought. When these first two parts are separated, so is God's thought. When they are together they create *light*, but when separated they create *space*, which is dark, or lacks light.

The third part of God's mind is intelligent activity, or activity that as it takes place joins some of the two parts of space and creates more light, or more of God's thought. When any activity lacks intelligence (by not adequately communicating its actions to other manifesting energy), it causes space to further separate, producing *time* and more manifested *energy*. The more that intelligent activity becomes unintelligent and fails to communicate adequately to join space more with other activity, the more that time separates from space. Time is then used up, or wasted, through "mistakes" as activity becomes unintelligent and darker, by reducing light and increasing space, which also causes more energy to manifest. The more time that is separated from space, the more the space curves *around time* and the greater the amounts of manifested energies.

To someone who is observing superficially, the space appears to curve around the energy, because the more that time is separated from space, the more difficult it is to recognize and understand time. Space curves around time that is separated from it because time is the relationship of the three parts of God's mind to each other being changed by lesser thought than God's. The field of the lesser thought in our universe creates a sphere of space as time becomes separated from space because the third part of God's mind is equally distributed through space before it is used unintelligently or as it is kept equally divided from space if it is used intelligently outside the dimension. This field of lesser intelligent thought creates for itself a different phase in relationship to the direction, or connectivity, of God's field of choices or of a Ray Lord's field of choices, as a lower correspondence of God's phase. The different angle, or phase, of the lesser field causes the space and manifested energies within this field to create forces against the field that has more intelligent activity. The (consistent opposing and same vector) forces at the angle of phase difference causes the less intelligent field to rotate. As time separates because the intelligent activities are becoming less intelligent and are also manifesting energies, the rotating space creates a spiraling boundary around the time (and around any manifested energies that are connected to, or are manifesting within, the time). The original space of our universe, which was created by God's initial separation of Its mind, is also a sphere because the third aspect of God's mind is equally distributed throughout space; also, the first two parts then initially have, within their field, equal potential to rejoin.

As time becomes separated from space, it develops into the shape of a vortex because the section of time that remains attached to the point (an event or part of an event) at which the rest of it separated is itself less separated (and less "used up") than is the part of time that is furthest away from this point. This causes time to move more rapidly in relation to space and at the same time to be more separated from a given amount of space. The further away from this point of connection, the faster the time moves in relation to the space that surrounds it. Energy manifests and responds similarly—becoming more dense and less likely to respond intelligently as it becomes less intelligent in activity and uses more time in each movement that it causes. Time can be further separated into faster-moving vortices, causing space to become more curved, as greater energy is manifested and less activity is intelligent. Each type of vortex of time represents, in human terms, either the past, the present, or the future. These fractions of time all attach to the same point in the space of a dimension in which time is being separated, when God's thought is used to create activity in at least one of three possible ways. The least of these possible ways is to perfectly balance all the forces that all the manifested energy is creating by being less than perfect in its intelligence as it creates activity for only one event. This perfection in the balance of forces is achieved through the perfect use of structure that is achieved at the uppermost, or atomic, level of the mental plane. Below this level, the three vortices of a time that are separated can no longer be attached to the same part (as an event) of space. This happens because forces in space create opposing curves to the space that isolate the vortices of the same separated time. The paradox of time that is perfectly balanced in its forces at the atomic level of the mental plane is that such a balance is achievable for only a *finite* period of time; above the mental plane, other methods of joining together time produce *permanent* rather than temporary effects. When the three vortices of time, at their narrowest part, are joined together into a single point, or event, in space, cause and effect are completely connected. This produces what is referred to as a Now. A Now is the relatively perfect rejoining of time, or cause and effect, with the least perfect Now being created at the atomic level of the mental plane.

Lesser thought that is within God's separated thought, or within space, and that creates unintelligent activity, or activity that fails to communicate its *purpose* and *direction* to other lesser thought in the space, separates one activity from another. This is the cause of "wasting time," or separating time from space. When time is fully integrated into space, the space has the maximum

The Physics of Time

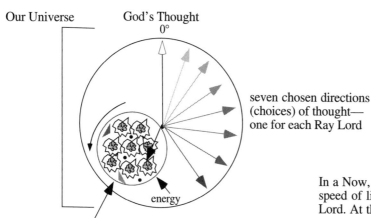

Our Universe   God's Thought 0°

seven chosen directions (choices) of thought— one for each Ray Lord

energy

Choices that are connected away from God's and the Ray Lords' result in a phase difference between the larger (giving) thought in the universe and the smaller field of selfish thought.

Selfish thought results in the development of individual fields of energy within our universe. The first two parts of God's mind are present but separated (this is what space is). The manifested energy within the smaller field creates a force against the intelligent activity within the larger field of God's thought. This different angle of thought results in an opposing spin of the smaller sphere.

Time within God's Field, in a Now

A Now

future

present

past

In a Now, time stops and all thought moves at the speed of light (thought) of the corresponding Ray Lord. At the outer end of a vortex, time and space are very separated. Towards this outer edge, time speeds up and more thought is required in order to join time and space.

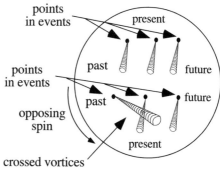

points in events   present

points in events   past   future

opposing spin   past   future

crossed vortices   present

One part of space and time twists around another. The part of time and space that twists becomes exaggerated. One space and time overlaps another when thought joins two parts of time selfishly.

Time moves more slowly as it approaches the event because then time and space are relatively more joined together.

point in an event

Time has to join the amount of space at the open end of the vortex. To do so, time must move faster.

The separation of the first two parts of God's mind creates space and time in our universe. The less intelligent that energy's activity is in any field, the greater the separation of time from space, and the more energy that manifests. This condition, as illustrated above, exists in part as a result of selfish human thought.

As the time becomes "used up" and separated from space, space curves around time and a vortex forms between a point in time that is less separated from the space. Also, time becomes increasingly separated from space as time and space move away from a point in an event and more space is created. Each vortex represents either the past, the present, or the future because each of the three parts of God's mind, when separated, focuses on mostly one of these time zones. A vortex appears to curve when energy is manifested and activity is less intelligent. The space is actually curving around the time as the time is separated, which causes the time to also curve and for energy to manifest from intelligent activity.

Illustration 10.2

potential, as a field of potential, to rejoin into a part of God's thought, and to create light within any activity. As time becomes separated from space, the field of space loses some of its potential to create light, or God's thought, but gains in potential to create thought that is less enlightening and that eventually creates life. Thus the amount of (separated) time is a measure of the *quality*, or level of consciousness, within a field of space's potential, or within a dimension of space, wherein the space will produce thought that is either like or not like God's thought.

The Three Parts of a Mental Now—and Time Separated from the Now

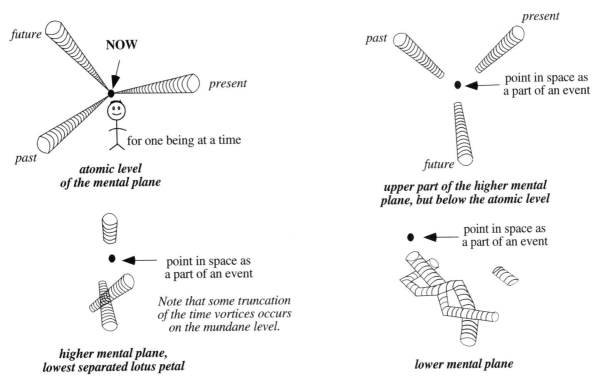

atomic level
of the mental plane

upper part of the higher mental
plane, but below the atomic level

point in space as
a part of an event

Note that some truncation
of the time vortices occurs
on the mundane level.

higher mental plane,
lowest separated lotus petal

point in space as
a part of an event

lower mental plane

Illustration 10.3

While these basic concepts of time are very accurate as compared to the way in which time is traditionally explained, they are also difficult to understand because the more selfish that someone is, the more of time that is being used, or separated from space, in that person's attempt to understand time. This separation causes such a person to become illusioned in her or his thought about time. Time is the part of space that measures the space's consciousness and determines its potential to create more, or less, of God's thought (of light). Time cannot be fully separated from space because then the space would have no potential to create *any* thought—God's or anyone else's. The space would no longer be a field of potential, and such a condition cannot exist *in* our universe because God in Its thought has already created the universe into a field of possibilities. Note that in the big bang, time and space fully separated, but they did so *outside* our universe of space/time.

 # THE PHYSICS OF THE SEVEN DIMENSIONS OF TIME AND SPACE

Starting from the lowest dimension, where the energy is densest (the etheric/dense physical dimension), we will now proceed to examine the characteristics of each dimension of time and space, including the atomic and sub-atomic conditions of form. When we examine a physically dense atom, it appears to be composed of "matter." This "matter" is actually energy that has become so affected by gravity (the collective thought of unenlightened energy and this energy's effects on matter), or so affected by inertia, that it appears to not be moving within a form. The lack of movement is an illusion because every *thing* in our universe is in motion to some degree. A great deal of activity has been converted into energy in our universe, and much of that energy has been densified into matter in the dense physical world. The "matter" part of any form has a part of itself that is still energy and is in movement at a certain frequency (cycle) of motion, in a part of the dimension that is sometimes referred to in spiritual terms as the etheric dimension. Whether activity is intelligent or not determines the amount of a form's energy that is present, or is manifested. The intelligent activity remaining at the atomic level, within the Ray Lord's light, is created life or pre-life; the light creating more intelligent activity may create more of it below this level. On the etheric/dense physical plane's first sub-plane, four-fifths of all activity is un-intelligence and manifests as energy. The closer to its originating source of activity in frequency and direction that this energy then vibrates in its frequency and moves in its direction, the closer it is to changing back from manifested energy into intelligent activity for that plane. When energy moves closer to this frequency and phase (direction) of intelligent activity of a plane, it becomes *transmuted* in density from a more dense state to a less dense one. When energy from a lower plane becomes intelligent in activity on that plane, it can become *transformed* from the type of intelligent activity of that lower plane into the type of energy and eventually of intelligent activity on, usually, the next higher plane. The reason is that existent within all intelligent activity within a dimension are, interpenetratingly, the states of higher levels of intelligent activity of the higher planes within the space of each atom.

Each of the higher dimensions of intelligent activity that interpenetrate an atom of form, or of energy, on a lower plane do so within a vortex of separated time. This separated vortex is a smaller amount of intelligent activity that exists within and is relatively related to each Ray Lord's capabilities to think with intelligent activities having been created together from either the thought of some being or of the energy itself. These vortices of time and activity within space are what some modern physicists refer to as "strings." Each string represents a corresponding activity within a time vortex of an atom that comes from one of seven dimensions of time and space. The etheric/dense physical dimension's string is somewhat confusing some modern physicists because it appears to have three dimensions to it: height, width, and depth. These three are all a part of one dimension of activity when they are intelligent, but, since most etheric/dense physical activities on earth lack intelligence, the single dimension splits into the three parts that we are familiar with. When the single etheric/dense physical dimension is integrated through virtue, or light in form, the result is intelligent coordinated response to all other etheric/dense physical activity. Under these conditions, etheric/dense physical time rejoins with space, and moving from one part of the dimension to another takes no time, because then all of the activity is enlightened and occurs at the etheric/dense physical speed of light. The ten apparent strings then become seven.

EARLIER DISCOVERIES ABOUT TIME AND SPACE

Albert Einstein discovered time's relationship to light on the etheric/dense physical plane early in the twentieth century. Because he did not understand that it was the result of joining the three aspects of God's mind together into a state in which the third—activity— became completely enlightened by the first two aspects, he thought that the effect was a condition of energy. He also somewhat discovered the relationship of energy to gravity and space. He did not, however, realize that space is separated light, nor that gravity is the result of certain energies' ways of self focused thought. What he found was that etheric/dense physically energy became convertible (transmutable) into matter and, conversely, as one approached the speed of (etheric) light. Also, Einstein found that time slowed and that space (apparently) curved around the energy/matter (creating gravity). Eventually, at the speed of light (for the etheric/dense physical dimension), space becomes a vortex with all points within it touching (at an infinite point at the "top" of the vortex) in the *one* dimension that exists on this plane. Time "stops"—stops being "wasted"—when activities are completely intelligent because then it becomes completely non-separated, from space, or not "used." Certain black holes in space produce such a condition, through a star creating a singularity within its time and space, or within its event horizon, and creating only intelligent activity within the etheric/dense physical dimension. In the case of some black holes, the star has also created intelligent activity on four other, higher, dimensions of our universe as well. The intelligent activity of one dimension is connected to the next dimension through a white hole within the dimensions' atomic levels, joining time and space for these dimensions at these levels. It is *not* possible for life of one dimension that is not completely enlightened, such as on the etheric/dense physical, to enter a black hole and travel to another dimension because the energies would be transmuted and all of the existing form in the dimension that is not completely enlightened would be destroyed.

Albert Einstein rejected an important part of understanding our universe because he was unaware that it functioned through God's thought, and instead believed that the functioning of our universe was also related to a property of energy. This theory was quantum mechanics, which was partly discovered by a fellow German scientist named Werner Heisenberg. In a series of experiments in the mid-1920's, Heisenberg found that the state of energy and "matter" was indefinite and that neither energy's nor matter's activity could be accurately determined in both time and space. He did not understand why this was the case; however, he and his experimenters did discover that the *thought of the experimenter* controlled the results of the experiments that were conducted on photons that had been generated from excited electrons. If the experimenter decided to test a photon as a wave, it behaved as one; yet, if the experimenter chose to test a photon as a particle—it became a particle in its properties. Heisenberg and his fellow scientists discovered that *very* small amounts of energies were following the thought of humans. All together, Heisenberg's and others' experiments "proved" that energy was indefinite in both time and space (in the part of time and space that was experimented within in either one or the other at a time) and, further, that thought affected energy—and somehow time and space as well. By not knowing both the direction and speed of an object (the time it exists within), one could not exactly place it in time and space, which makes it indefinite. Another German scientist, Max Planck, had predicted (before Heisenberg was conducting experiments) the degree to which energy is indefinite in either time or space; later, others decided to take measurements, and they discovered that the determined value was the same degree to which energy is affected by thought. Planck's mathematics and others' later experiments determined the degree to which energy is also somewhere else in either time or space (is indefinite) *for the dense physical* part of the etheric/dense physical dimension. This very small number is referred to as Planck's constant, or the quantum constant.

To Albert Einstein, quantum mechanics and, later, quantum field theory suggested that if energy was indefinite, or uncertain, then so would be the universe, and everything would become a probability that was *based upon some capricious properties of energy*. This, in Einstein's mind, effectively eliminated God from the picture—a scenario which Einstein, correctly, rejected. However, he, incorrectly, failed to understand both *spirit's* role in the universe, and that light is God's thought. If Einstein had understood these two concepts (and that the collective thought of involuting energies produces gravity), it is likely that he could have unified his two major theories of relative time and gravity with Heisenberg's and Plank's theories concerning probability and thought *controlling* energy within a field—assuming that the information in *Life's Hidden Meaning* that is relative to this issue is correct. Even today, the physics string theorists will almost certainly fail to unify these parts of physics if they fail to understand the role of spirit and of God and Its thought, or light—especially when this light is in form, as virtue. It is hoped that this book and others will serve as unifying tools so that God can, again on earth, be entered into science (and especially physics).

 ## THE PHYSICS OF THE ETHERIC/DENSE PHYSICAL DIMENSION

The smallest level of enlightenment that can occur from the transmutation of energy by creating intelligence in activity occurs within an etheric/dense physical atom of energy. At this minute level, when an electron is brought to a level of radiance its movement is simultaneously elevated, or excited, by intelligent activity that is taking place one level higher, causing the electron to emit the smallest quantity of light, or one photon. The amount of energy change, which causes the electron to be raised in orbit, needed to emit the light from an electron is equal to a quantum in physics. Thus a certain minimum amount of intelligent activity created by the unit of energy of the smallest whole etheric/dense physical particle/wave of the electron causes that electron to become radiant and to emit one photon of light. This quantity of enlightened, intelligent activity created by transmutation of an electron, and the enlightening of the smallest whole physical form, is a quantum. Quanta as units are dependent upon frequency and directions, but not on quantity, or amounts of energy, because they are created by intelligent activity, or activity that creates more light in form (more virtue). Frequency is the human, more narrow scientific understanding of the first part of God's mind, of choices/will/sacrifice/purpose. Direction, or phase, is the human more narrow understanding in physics of the second part of God's mind, of consciousness/understanding/unconditional-love/oneness. Frequency and phase together create thought.

Because the movement of a radiant (photon-emitting) electron takes place at the speed of light, no time is "wasted," or used up, or separated from space. Such an electron may, infrequently, appear in two locations at the "same time." When it does, the etheric/dense physical string within the atom becomes altered—the time vortex that the string exists within becomes more integrated. This is *generally* the smallest quantum shift that occurs within our universe, and Planck's constant is an approximate measure of this shift when it occurs on the three dense physical sub-planes of our universe. Because there are very slight differences in the shift for gasses, liquids, and solids, Planck's constant actually strictly applies only to the fifth sub-plane of gasses, but modern physics does not, as yet, recognize the variability in the quantum constant on the seventh and sixth sub-planes. On the etheric sub-planes, the quantum constant changes considerably (it more than doubles) at the atomic, or highest, etheric sub-plane. Thus the uncertainty of either the position in space or the momentum (time) of a form, or of energy, is over twice as great on the atomic sub-plane of the etheric plane as it is on the fifth and lower, dense physical, sub-planes. At present, modern physics does not understand the etheric sub-planes, and therefore fails to recognize the increases in the quantum constant on each of the higher etheric sub-planes. In order to *accurately* determine the quantum constant on an etheric sub-plane, the measurement would have to be done *on that sub-plane* because of the effects on the experiment of the experimenter and the equipment used.

In addition to what is described above, the quantum constant is also the measure of how much energy is affected by, or follows, thought. This is why a quantum is created by alterations in frequency and phase that produce radiance, rather than by amounts of energy. Frequency and phase in spiritual understanding are the first and second parts of God's mind, which when combined create *thought*. Thus thought causes the changes in the activity of electrons (and everything else); thought that is intelligent causes the electron to radiate light (a photon) as it moves at the speed of light (thought)—of the seventh cosmic Ray Lord—which is the dimension the electron is in. Time integrates with etheric/dense physical space at the seventh cosmic Ray Lord's speed of thought, and the number of electrons that radiate *and* exist in the more than one location of space at the same time, as compared to those that do not, are relative to the quantum constant for that sub-plane. The thought that causes the quantum shift and the production of light is dependent upon the density of the energy and its interfering relatively slight thought, collectively together, or is dependent upon *gravity*. (See Chapter Four for a more thorough explanation of this concept.) More gravity, or more of unenlightened energy's collective thought, reduces the energy's responsiveness to thought, and then *more* thought is required to create *intelligent* activity. However, the quantity of thought alone is not the controlling factor, as Einstein somewhat discovered in investigating the mathematics of quantum physics; the frequency and phase need to be higher and correct to cause both radiance (a creation of light) and a quantum shift when surrounding thought is fast enough. Only thought that is more like the seventh cosmic Ray Lord's can offset the collective thought of energy, or gravity. Each string within an atom is affected by a different group, or a collection of gravities, from each plane and that plane's sub-planes, and by the thought on a plane that is either more or less at the frequency and phase (choices and direction—speed and quality of thought) of the corresponding cosmic Ray Lord.

Each higher cosmic Ray Lord has substantially higher thought, and so a much higher frequency and a different phase, or direction (consciousness) of thought is needed in order to control the energy within the corresponding dimension and convert it back into intelligent activity after it has become a part of the life—as forms. Note that in spiritual terms, phase, direction, and consciousness are parts of the same concept, and that they indicate the ways that choices are connected to each other. The quantum constant is progressively and significantly much larger in each higher dimension, and because there are seven types of (sub-) thought and of density of energies from the energy's collective thought, or gravity, on each dimension, the quantum constant is also divided into seven degrees to which energy follows thought. These are relative levels that can change as overall thought on a dimension becomes more like the Ray Lord's thought of that dimension at the atomic level. This level is where the cosmic Ray Lord's thought, or the speed of light, determines the largest quantum constant of each dimension and makes it consistent in time. As the quantum constant increases, the forms of each higher sub-plane and plane become more indefinite—and easier to change with additional thought. As ease of change increases, so does the increase in probability within a field—enabling more and easier thought to take place. The effect of matter and the very small quantum constant is to "force" most life to live as effects of the past part of time in the solid, or three lowest sub-planes of the seventh plane. Unlike all of the higher dimensions, where life can live in varying sub-dimensions of the quantum constant and varying densities of energies, physical life can mostly maintain itself trapped in the past time effects of these three lowest sub-planes because its spirit cannot think well enough to free itself. Lifeforms that are very small and those that are alive only etherically and astrally can live on the etheric planes because the inertial effects on them are so much weaker.

Matter exists only on the three lowest sub-planes of our universe, because on the etheric sub-planes and above, the frequency and phase of energy (its thought and the thought of informing spirit) are great enough to overcome to some degree inertia, or the effects of gravity. Once inertia is somewhat overcome, movement becomes much easier—literally, as one thinks. The etheric parts of an atom are constructed of only energy and surround the parts of it that are matter, or its parts that are denser and more affected by inertia. The etheric parts have much greater movement and potential relative intelligent activity. From the process of transmutation, the movement of these parts becomes the material inertia that is caused by gravity. The time vortex between the etheric energy and the material form connects these two together. There is only *one* part, or time vortex, of three that connects each etheric movement of energy with each

The Unification of Nuclear Physics' and Metaphysics' Theories of Atomic Structure

THE ETHERIC/DENSE PHYSICAL PLANE

This string is inside the foam of quantum possibilities of an etheric/dense physical atom. Each string that separates time and space on this plane is extremely coiled up from the very high gravity, or the thought of energy focused on becoming more dense.

A string of *intelligent* activity, when following virtuous thought, overcomes gravity. This causes the string to unwind, and results in the decrease of space between and within the atoms.

The atoms become closer together as the string straightens and they become connected by the string.

ELECTRONS OF AN ETHERIC PLANE ATOM

This string of *potential* intelligent activity is within the quantum foam. The string is not intelligent until it totally uncurls.

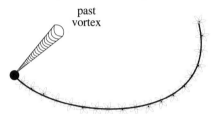

This string of past intelligent activity is at the atomic level of the etheric plane.

Note that only one string of intelligent activity that is always connected to just the past vortex can unwind on this plane—at the atomic level.

THE MENTAL PLANE

The atom (and its electrons) on the mental plane is less dense than those on the etheric/dense physical plane, and the potential intelligent activity is less coiled because of the differences in the foam of quantum possibilities (the quantum constant is much higher). There are similar differences in the molecular structure of other planes. This is only one example.

ATOMIC LEVEL OF MENTAL PLANE

The three lowest dimensional strings are unwound, and touch all atoms of an event and the being who is experiencing the time and space that the event is in.

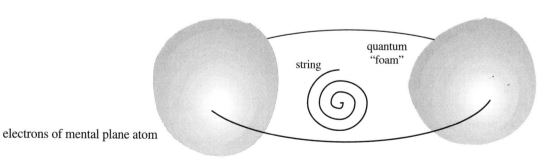

The atoms of the past string actually touch for each single event only.

The three vortices are converging only on one being at a time, with an emphasis on the past time vortex.

electrons of mental plane atom

Illustration 10.4

dense physical material form. The other two parts of time exist, but cannot be connected to either the past or to each other for any event. On the seventh plane, this part, or vortex, of time is *exclusively* the past. The string that the dimensional energy and time are a part of is contained only in the past part of time because only *one dimension* exists on the *whole* seventh plane, or for an event connected on the etheric *and* dense physical parts of the plane. Selfish thought displaces and splits the etheric/dense physical dimension into three split apparent dimensions of height, width, and depth. These three split dimensions are illusionary and hide light, or God's thought, as they separate life and, of course, people and things. The reason why the past is all that is left of time that connects events on the seventh plane is that the past is the most resist-ant to separation from space by selfish thought. The connectedness of the choices in the past part of time remains unchangeable as the part of the choices in this part of time change, whereas the connectedness, or oneness/consciousness, of choices does change as the part of the choices in the present and future parts of time are changed. When enlightened thought is used on energy, the phase (the direction/consciousness/oneness of the choices) remains intact and grows, caus-ing time to integrate more as the past, present and future. Selfish thought, however, does the reverse. Thought below the atomic level of the mental plane is *never* enlightened enough to grow consciousness, without some losses that take place while choices are created and added to previous thought; the losses result from forces that are imposed by conflictive energies. This causes time to split, preventing the three vortices of time from continuing to touch the same point in space. On the astral, or sixth, dimension only two vortices of time can connect to one point of space because the thought of the cosmic Ray Lord is not fast enough (the speed of light is too slow) for thought to simultaneously occur in the three parts of time. This limitation causes the most difficult part of time to think in (which is the easiest one to separate from space) to become *almost* non-existent because it is so separate from space. That part is the future vortex of time, which is usually approximated using preconceptual (approximated through energy) and imaginary types of thought rather than whole thought that includes structure, or all three parts of time. On the etheric/dense physical plane the present and future are almost non-existent. Any two or more events there connect mostly through the past. Two events in the present or future cannot be connected with definiteness and accuracy. Notice that time is inversely affected by the quantum constant. The more that cause and effect are joined by more whole time, the less definite it is that the event is located in only the past. The more that events are located in time in the present and future more equally while they are in the past, the larger the quantum constant and the greater the uncertainty of either the events' locations in space or in time, until time and space are joined. Note that although humans mostly sense etheric/dense physically, they mostly think in mental time and when they do they *can* think within all three zones of time. Selfish human thought tends to think in less future time. Very selfish thought can both separate and exaggerate the thought of only one time zone, which can change an entire sub-plane of time if enough people think selfishly in that time zone.

The Three Parts of Time as They Connect
on the Atomic Level of the Etheric/Dense Physical Plane

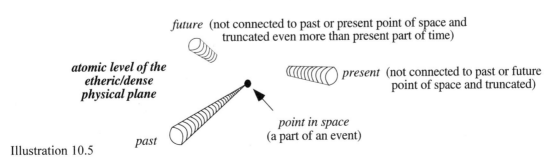

future (not connected to past or present point of space and truncated even more than present part of time)

atomic level of the etheric/dense physical plane

present (not connected to past or future point of space and truncated)

past

point in space (a part of an event)

Illustration 10.5

THE PHYSICS OF THE ASTRAL DIMENSION

An atom on the astral plane gains another (a second) whole dimension of time and space. The etheric/dense physical string is joined with the astral string, and the past vortex of time can touch the same part of space that the present vortex does at the astral atomic level. At the atomic level of the astral plane, there are only six strings left within the atom, because the seventh string has joined with the sixth. Below the atomic level, some part of the seventh string might still be observable. The added dimension and sense on the astral plane is of focused, or devoted, movement from one astral energy or group of energies to a specific other energy or group of them. When the movement is completely away from the first energy, the second energy and its movement are love, and create more consciousness, or a greater sense of oneness, both between the two energies and within the first. When some or all of the movement is towards the first energy, the second energy and its movement are emotion. Emotion decreases a sense of oneness between the energy and other energy, and then decreases consciousness between that energy and any other as well as within itself. When spirit is informing the energy, creating a life-form, the lifeform then is responding astrally in one of three ways: it is responding either lovingly, emotionally, or with a combination of the two. Astral love joins more closely the two astral time vortices of the past and present, and within each astral atom the life joins the seventh and sixth strings more as it develops a better astral sense of time and space.

There is no matter within an astral atom. An astral atom's sub-atomic parts are composed exclusively of astral energy, which has a much higher frequency and a different phase than etheric/dense physical energy does. (See illustrations 4.8 and 4.9.) The size of an astral atom is much larger than an etheric/dense physical one is, but an astral atom is also equally less dense *sub-atomically*. However, the sub-atomic "particles," or astral energies, are also much larger and have *less* space between themselves within the atom. The much larger astral atoms have more energy spread over their space, proportionately, than do etheric/dense physical atoms. The astral energy is much less dense, but covers much greater space within the atom. There is less space between astral atoms because, while the astral plane is much larger, the forces between atoms are less than the forces that are found on the etheric/dense physical plane, and each astral atom, *on average*, creates more intelligent activity and thus creates more light. The eighth sphere, where evil resides, is an exception to this generality. There the atoms remain similar, but the distance between them is increased substantially—which creates a crystallization of form. When atoms are separated through balancing forces and increasing darkness (space) at the same time, a type of dark crystallization occurs that preserves the form through darkness (more of God's first and third aspects of mind and less of the second).

The relative density of astral forms is vastly lower than the density of etheric/dense physical forms even though the atoms within the astral forms are closer together, because between astral atoms there are proportionately even fewer forces. As a result, astral forms have a fluid, water-like, quality. There is less space between the average two astral forms that are the same relative distance apart as compared to two average etheric/dense physical forms, because on the astral plane there is an added vortex of time connecting to each astral form except in the eighth sphere, of evil. The lower density of astral forms allows thought to affect them more. In addition, and most importantly, the certainty of astral energy in its position within either time or space is decreased from the measure on the dense physical sub-planes by about three to twenty-four times, depending upon the sub-plane that the energy is found on. The quantum constant grows because there is much less astral energy occupying much greater space and there is much less gravity (the collective thought of unenlightened energy) on the astral plane, while thought there becomes stronger from the increased speed of light of the Ray Lord's thought. As much

The Unification of Nuclear Physics' and Metaphysics' Theories of Atomic Structure on the Astral Plane

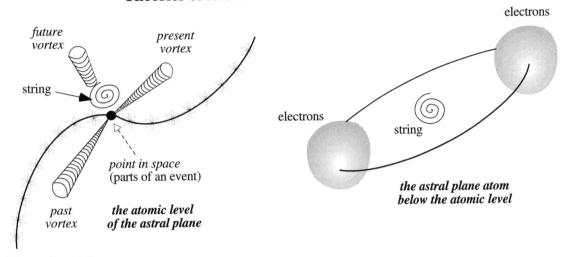

Illustration 10.6

more light is emitted from radiance, the quantum changes as a unit of measure and requires a much higher frequency at a different direction, or phase, in order to emit the considerably greater astral light. The phase moves closer to the angle of God's thought and is less restrictive of connecting together choices, i.e., consciousness, or love, grows. The greater astral light also allows more intelligent activity to rejoin space by helping activity to become intelligent. Less energy is manifested in this process, while the entire dimension grows because of more choices, or higher frequency within the thought of the astral Ray Lord as compared to the etheric/dense physical Ray Lord's thought. Less energy and a larger field of space, but with much higher speed of the Ray Lord's thought, or light, allows the energy that is manifested to join the space more effectively (to go back to becoming intelligent activity) when it is informed by the enlightening thought of spirit.

The Three Parts of Time as They Connect on the Atomic Level of the Astral Plane

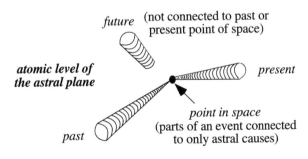

Illustration 10.7

Time on the atomic level of the first astral sub-plane is dilated about twenty-four times that the time on dense earth is because energy at the top of the astral plane is so much less dense *and* has a much greater frequency, while thought of informing spirit is much faster and stronger. The quantum constant grows proportionately larger as a measure of this effect, and energy follows thought to a much greater level. Below the atomic astral level, the two time vortices do not join in the same point of space, because selfish thought causes them to separate. As activities lose intelligence, more time is "used up," or "wasted" in each activity. The quantum constant is, accordingly, reduced from its largest level and energy follows thought less, requiring a greater level of use of the senses (the thought of more advanced energies) and thought of informing spirit for each activity. Proportionately more space, as well as time, exist between one being and another—separating their consciousness, or their sense/thought of oneness from each other, to a greater degree. The more time that is "wasted," or separated from space, the less time there is to live in, and life becomes shorter in time. Time is dilated from about three times to about twenty-four, with the three times greater amount as compared to the dense physical plane occurring in the eighth sphere, where evil has managed to somewhat alter time, space, and astral energy. With dilation numbers rounded to whole figures, the following table describes each astral sub-plane, at present, and its corresponding dilation of time as compared to time on the dense physical plane.

COMPARISON OF TIME DILATION ON THE ASTRAL PLANE VS. THE DENSE PHYSICAL SUB-PLANES	
LOCATION WITHIN THE ASTRAL DIMENSION	TIME DILATION AS COMPARED TO THE DENSE PHYSICAL DIMENSION
8th sphere	about 3 times (~3:1)
7th sub-plane	about 6 times (~6:1)
6th sub-plane	about 9 times (~9:1)
5th sub-plane	about 12 times (~12:1)
4th sub-plane	about 15 times (~15:1)
3rd sub-plane	about 18 times (~18:1)
2nd sub-plane	about 21 times (~21:1)
1st sub-plane (atomic level)	about 24 times (~24:1)

Table 10. 1

The three lowest astral sub-planes are where many people are when they dream, because this is where much of their emotional selfishness is within their astral bodies. For each minute these people sleep physically, their dreams last anywhere from six to twelve minutes. Investigators of dream phenomena and the times of dreams need to be careful when measuring the much easier to measure etheric dreams, because these dreams have only one-third to *less than* twice the time dilation as compared to time in the dense physical realm, since etheric dreams usually occur on the fourth to second etheric sub-planes. With such relatively small changes in time, and the highly dissociative and fragmented nature of these dreams that are easier to evaluate (albeit incorrectly) using present day methods of experimentation, there is a very high potential for error and to not discover the time dilation. Another issue is that some dreams—those that function to reduce egotism—take place on the mental plane, and these dreams often repeat themselves, sometimes dozens of times with only slight changes in the outcomes. Most people remember only one or two (if any) of these repetitions, disguising their dream experience from themselves, and masking the large time dilation. Also, mental (and astral) dreams are more difficult to experimentally identify and regulate controlled awakening from, because just a few seconds of dense physical time could be as much as five minutes of fourth mental sub-plane time. In addition, because many people may dream in one session on *both* the astral and the mental plane, it is more difficult to create consistent variables in experimentation of these dreams. Etheric dreams *are* much more easily controlled, but are not easy to find a time dilation in. Although time dilation is experienced almost every night by nearly all people while they sleep, it is amazingly elusive using today's present scientific methods of inquiry. Measurement of etheric/dense physical brain activity cannot accurately show astral or mental brain activity—which causes even further confusion in modern-day experiments. Yet most people can recall having had at least some dreams that lasted for very long periods of time, which in dense physical time could have been no more than a few minutes.

Those few people physically alive who astral-travel, and the even rarer advanced disciples who serve on the mental plane, experience—fully consciously—these dimensions and the time dilations that occur on them. An advanced mental plane server, while physically "asleep" for about eight hours, might serve on lower mental sub-planes for up to about two of those hours. Much of that time might be spent on the fourth mental sub-plane, where time is dilated at about 90:1, with the remainder spent on other sub-planes where time is less dilated. This period of service (about two hours of dense physical time) could average one hundred twenty hours (!), or about *five days* of time that is actually lived in and experienced while serving.

There is a much larger total volume of space on the dimension of the astral plane than on the dense physical. However, lifeforms and inanimate objects are closer together within astral space because two complete vortices of time exist on the astral plane, even if only one connects at a time to a point in space, except on the atomic level of the plane (see illustration 1.11). The etheric/dense physical sense is lost to someone on the astral plane unless this sense is fused completely (within a fused seventh and sixth plane string in atoms, within the senses) through development of the atomic sub-plane part of that person's astral centers and body. The fusion occurs through enlightenment of these centers by thinking within the speed and direction of the astral Ray Lord's thought, at the atomic level of the plane. As this thought is used in service, or as 100% of the energy is used to *love* others, the energy changes into intelligent activity and the space becomes light within the centers and body, as the atoms become radiant and the largest astral quantum constant becomes actualized through the consistent creation of virtue on the atomic astral level.

Once the astral energies within a lifeform have been transmuted into the highest, or the atomic, astral level of consciousness, then the type of consciousness that the form can sense from its energies that are the most advanced in their slight thought, or from its senses, can be changed to the next dimension's increased sense of form. This transformation occurs through fusion, which, again, starts with the "strings" of atoms and results in transformation of the enlightened astral energy from astral intelligent activity into mental energy. The mental energy will, again, then need to grow mentally in order to become intelligent in its activity on this more complex plane. It is spirit that needs to enlighten the form to cause both the transmutation and the eventual transformation of either etheric/dense physical or astral energies.

THE PHYSICS OF THE MENTAL DIMENSION

All three parts of time potentially exist as completed vortices that are separated from space, anywhere in the mental dimension of time and space. Only at the very top, or the atomic level, of this plane do all three vortices connect to the same point (as a whole event) in space—creating a Now, or a point in time where cause and effect take place at exactly the same time. Below this level and on all lower planes and sub-planes, the thought of informing spirit is too weak and selfish, which causes the vortices to separate from their single point in space where each connects on one (the smaller) side of the vortex. The result is a separation between cause and effect. The lack of consistency in spirit's virtuous mental thought, and in energy following this thought is what creates a separation of the energy. The mental energy that has achieved some level of (lower) self identity by adequately giving its thought to spirit and other energy congregates on the part of the mental plane that corresponds to the three parts of God's mind, or the first, second, and third mental sub-planes. These sub-planes are also known as the higher mental plane and are, respectively, influenced by the first three rays of aspect. When spirit is thinking on these sub-planes, it is much more capable of identifying itself and others as spirit. On the third sub-plane it more readily sees its and others' selves, on the second it tends to see souls, and on the first it is more likely to see souls and Selves. (See Chapter Five for further explanation of this concept.) From the first through the fourth sub-sub-planes of the fourth mental sub-plane, spirit identifies itself as being both spirit and form; below the fourth sub-sub-plane, it fails to identify itself or others as spirit, and is aware of only energy.

This effect is caused by the mental plane being a sea of forces, because below the atomic level more energy than not is *not* under the controlling thought of spirit. The reason is that there is too much energy and too little spirit—with a relatively lower speed of thought (of light) than that which occurs in the dimensions of our universe that are higher in frequency. Thus the energies that have any self identity are somewhat focused in their thought on the *causes* of their existence and in living in this focus of thought through the first three mental sub-planes, which correspond to God's mind and to the causes of the existence of all in our universe. The spirit that controls these energies, when it chooses to, also focuses more on causes. The spirit part of humans that is focused on causes is the self, which can, in its own thought, reach to the top of the third sub-plane. The self can reach no higher than that in its own thought because it cannot understand that it and others are part of one life—and of God. The self is limited from this understanding when using only its own thought because its field of potential includes only *one human lifeform*, whom it gives thought to and receives sense from. The time and space within the human self's field are connected to only this individual lifeform, which limits the self when it thinks on its own, to always thinking through the perspective of that one lifeform. The three vortices of time that it continually "uses" are separating itself from all other selves, preventing it from thinking higher than the third mental sub-plane; the only part of God's mind that it can understand is, correspondingly, intelligent activity.

COMPARISON OF QUANTUM CONSTANT ON THE MENTAL SUB-PLANES VS. DENSE PHYSICAL SUB-PLANE	
LOCATION	RATIO
7th mental sub-plane	~36:1 at the top of the sub-plane
6th mental sub-plane	~45:1 at the top of the sub-plane
5th mental sub-plane	~60:1 at the top of the sub-plane
4th mental sub-plane	~90:1 at the top of the sub-plane
3rd mental sub-plane	~180:1 average for the sub-plane
2nd mental sub-plane	~360:1 average for the sub-plane
1st mental sub-plane	~720:1 average for the sub-plane
1st mental sub-plane (atomic level)	~960:1 average at the top of the sub-plane, on a non-sacred planet for those on the mental plane and below 1056:1 at the top of the sub-plane on a sacred planet and for those on a non-sacred planet above the mental plane

Table 10. 2

Time at the atomic level of the mental plane is dilated either slightly less or over one thousand times that of dense physical plane time, depending upon whether a planet is sacred or not. Note that because the mental plane Ray Lord created its dimension from time, it has two speeds of thought, to those who live in its dimension. One speed of light (thought) is based upon the effects of kama-manas and is the lower speed. The higher speed of light, which can always be detected from a perspective above the mental plane, is the Ray Lord's true absolute speed of thought. On the atomic level of the intuitional plane, the figure jumps to over one hundred forty thousand. On the atomic level of the spiritual plane the dilation of time is at a ratio of the speed of etheric light times itself, or squared. This means that time is dilated millions of times at the atomic level of the spiritual sub-plane over that on the dense physical sub-planes. Mental plane time is much more dilated than is astral time because mental time includes all three completed dimensional parts of time; also, mental energy is much less dense, and so it is much more responsive to the informing thought of spirit.

The personality is located on the fourth mental sub-plane, from the third to the first sub-sub-planes—all within the mental unit. The self is located on the fourth sub-sub-plane of the fourth mental sub-plane, one sub-sub-plane below the personality but still within the mental unit. The personality is both spirit and energy that are joined through the much greater thought of the Solar Angel. The energy within the personality is composed of lower mental energy that is *not* self conscious and needs its joined spirit in order to recognize and understand the self. Its self is one sub-sub-plane below it and is pure spirit, and is conscious of itself and other selves *as they relate* to itself. The personality, which is composed of spirit combined with special thoughtforms that are very long-lasting (thoughtforms are lower mental plane energy), has a *time* problem. No part of it, without its self, can understand causes because its energy is composed entirely of lower mental energy that, since it is on the fourth sub-plane, corresponds to an *attribute* of God's mind. The corresponding first through third sub-sub-planes are correspondingly related to aspects of God's mind; however, the thought on a sub-sub-plane of aspect within a sub-plane of attribute is too incomplete to provide understanding of a cause.

The entire fourth mental sub-plane has been and continues to be, at present, connected through time vortices of the effects of past and future, to the causative vortices on the first and third mental sub-planes. Up to the present day (the turn of the century), there is no connection from the fourth mental sub-plane to the second—which on the higher mental plane is where the vortex of the *causative* present part of time ends. Note that the three causative higher mental vortices begin, at their smaller side, at the atomic level of the plane. The effects of the present part of time do not, as yet, exist on the fourth mental sub-plane. The time vortices on the lower mental plane connect time as effects to the higher mental vortices, which are the causes in time. The seventh mental sub-plane through thought that is correct and accurate connects the vortex of time effects of the past to the causative vortex of the past on the third sub-plane, and the sixth mental sub-plane through thought that is correct and accurate connects the vortex of the present to the second mental sub-plane's causative vortex. The fifth mental sub-plane through thought that is correct and accurate connects the vortex of time that relates to future effects to the first mental sub-plane vortex of causative time. And the fourth mental sub-plane through thought that is correct and accurate connects all *three* effect vortices of time to the third, second, and first causative vortices, respectively. Selfish human thought has changed the lower mental plane time, altering the vortices of time effects to the following. The seventh sub-plane incorrectly and inaccurately relates to the future; the sixth sub-plane, to the past; the fifth sub-plane, to the present; and the fourth sub-plane, to the past and future and no present.

The personality is the controlling factor that initially causes the self to become selfish. It also, through its thought, causes time to unnaturally separate from space, forcing the time vortices to connect to parts of space that incorrectly (and sometimes incompletely) represent time in the structure of mental thought. Each illogical sentence that the personality constructs further creates these time distortions, or illusions, which affect that part of the mental plane. The self uses one to four of the vortices that are connected to the outside of the mental unit. It uses

The Mental Plane, Synthetic Yoga Lotus, Mental Permanent Atom, and Mental Unit

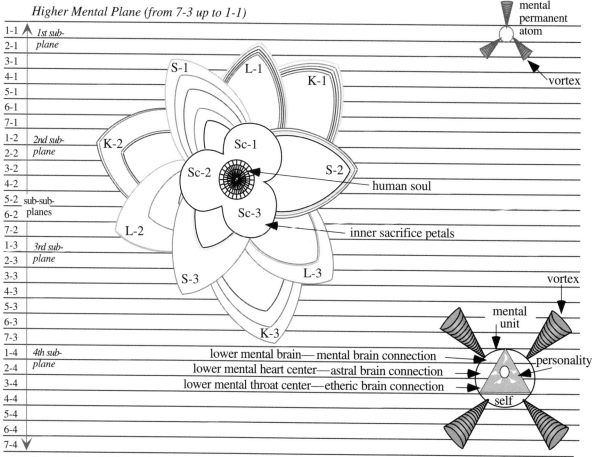

Higher Mental Plane (from 7-3 up to 1-1)

1-1 1st sub-plane
2-1
3-1
4-1   S-1   L-1   K-1
5-1
6-1
7-1
1-2 2nd sub-plane   K-2   Sc-1
2-2
3-2   Sc-2   S-2
4-2   human soul
5-2 sub-sub-planes
6-2
7-2   L-2   Sc-3   inner sacrifice petals
1-3 3rd sub-plane
2-3
3-3   S-3   L-3   vortex
4-3
5-3
6-3   mental unit
7-3   K-3
1-4 4th sub-plane   lower mental brain— mental brain connection
2-4   lower mental heart center—astral brain connection
3-4   lower mental throat center—etheric brain connection   personality
4-4
5-4   self
6-4
7-4

mental permanent atom
vortex

vortex

Lower Mental Plane (from 1-4 down to 7-7)

Illustration 10.8

these vortices to receive and send enlightened thought. When it does this to a certain level within each vortex, they begin to spin in the same direction and eventually match the speed of a time vortex on the higher mental plane. Each of the first three vortices, when spinning, connects one of three parts of time, and the fourth connects all three. The first vortex on the mental unit to become active and, eventually, rotating connects the self to the first mental sub-plane and to the future part of the causative time vortex. The first use of this vortex before it is spinning gives to the self and the personality a conscience; the personality is in control of when the self is allowed to receive it. The conscience is thought concerning the causative part of some future planned behavior. This thought is assisted by the much more virtuous thought of the (higher) Self and Solar Angel at the atomic level of the first mental sub-plane—which is where this vortex connects. Usually, the second mental unit vortex to become active connects the past part of effects of time to the third (higher) mental sub-plane, and its causative time vortex of the past; this vortex points downward. It may not begin to spin until a soul has incarnated several times, after learning correct reflection and developing it in the mental permanent atom, and learning from prior mistakes. The third vortex that usually becomes functional also points downward, and connects the self and personality—when the personality so permits, in order to connect to both the mental vortex that concerns present effects and to the first soul contact. This contact takes place on the second mental sub-plane and uses the causative vortex of present time. This vortex may not begin to spin until over a dozen incarnations of a soul have been *successfully developed* into progressively improved human beings—further developing the individual's mental permanent atom. Note that because, typically, people are less successful (if at all) in creating this level of virtue, it may take a total of well over one hundred incarnations for these dozen or so more successful incarnations to take place.

The Three Parts of Time Creating a Mental Plane Now

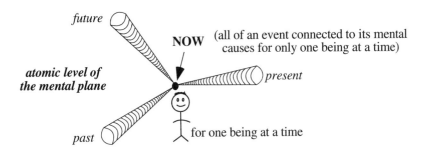

Illustration 10.9

The final, or fourth, vortex on the mental unit begins to spin when a personality chooses to discipline itself for spiritual purposes and to give freedom to its self, and when the personality begins to join with its soul rather than having the self stay completely under the control of the personality. On average, this takes about seven hundred incarnations of a human soul—so many, because the personality "lives" to control, and voluntarily giving up its control is, to it, synonymous with giving up its life! When the fourth vortex is fully functional, the self has somewhat fused with its Self because during service all three vortices corresponding to effects of time for any event in mental time and space have become joined with all three causative vortices, joining the three causative vortices to a single point of space and creating a mental Now. This takes place at the atomic level of the mental plane, where the Self is developed through *service* within each Now. For *every* mental activity there are *potentially* three effect vortices of time connected to three causative vortices, all joined into a mental Now; however, the way that humans mostly think separates time and sometimes even distorts it, and only very infrequently ever creates any mental Nows. The entire mental plane remains split from (mostly) human thought that prevents truth, or light in mental form, from being created.

For mental energy to become enlightened, all three time zones of past, present, and future vortices of space that surround time need to be joined in correct order to their corresponding lower and higher mental sub-planes, using spiritually causative higher mental thought and whole logical effects in thoughtforms on the lower mental plane. To do this, all of these spiritually causative and whole logical effects need to be *given* to others to either help them to think (as a personal giving, or conditional love) or help them to become more whole in their thoughts so that they might help others (as soul giving, or love that is more unconditional). The enlightenment of mental energy requires the use of all three time vortices, correctly structured both higher mentally and lower mentally (in both cause and effect). It is much more difficult to enlighten mental energy than to enlighten astral energy, or to create astral virtue. The reason is that creating astral virtue requires the use of only two time vortices, and sometimes does not require correct structure of either present to past or past to present because the correct structure is often irrelevant to the outcome when thinking in creative imagination. Even when relevant, the partial structure of past to present is much easier to create virtue within when the future is mostly excluded from it. With the benefit of an understanding of these concepts, one can readily see why it was so much easier for people who thought more astrally and created virtue from

Vortex Development of a Human's Mental Body

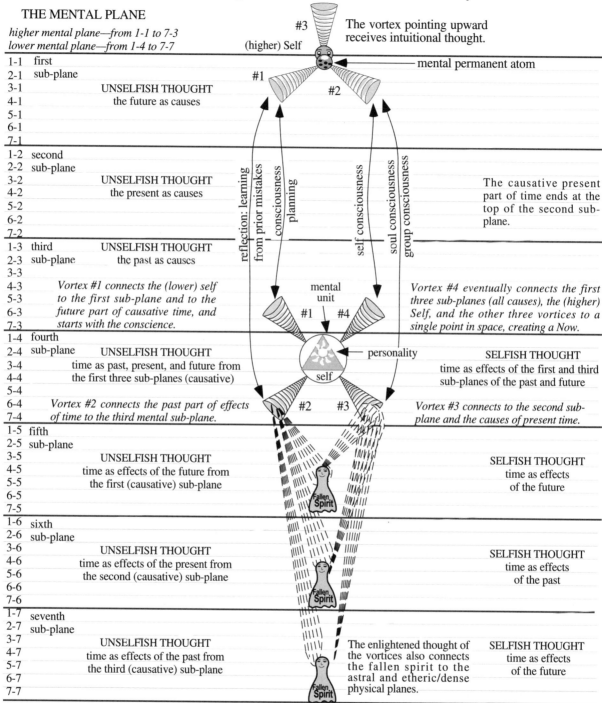

THE MENTAL PLANE

higher mental plane—from 1-1 to 7-3
lower mental plane—from 1-4 to 7-7

#3 (higher) Self

The vortex pointing upward receives intuitional thought.

mental permanent atom

1-1	first
2-1	sub-plane
3-1	UNSELFISH THOUGHT
4-1	the future as causes
5-1	
6-1	
7-1	

#1   #2

1-2	second
2-2	sub-plane
3-2	UNSELFISH THOUGHT
4-2	the present as causes
5-2	
6-2	
7-2	

reflection: learning from prior mistakes — *consciousness planning* — *self consciousness* — *soul consciousness group consciousness*

The causative present part of time ends at the top of the second sub-plane.

1-3	third	UNSELFISH THOUGHT
2-3	sub-plane	the past as causes
3-3	

mental unit

4-3	*Vortex #1 connects the (lower) self*
5-3	*to the first sub-plane and to the*
6-3	*future part of causative time, and*
7-3	*starts with the conscience.*

#1   #4

Vortex #4 eventually connects the first three sub-planes (all causes), the (higher) Self, and the other three vortices to a single point in space, creating a Now.

1-4	fourth
2-4	sub-plane	UNSELFISH THOUGHT
3-4		time as past, present, and future from
4-4		the first three sub-planes (causative)
5-4	
6-4	*Vortex #2 connects the past part of effects*
7-4	*of time to the third mental sub-plane.*

personality

self

SELFISH THOUGHT
time as effects of the first and third
sub-planes of the past and future

#2   #3

Vortex #3 connects to the second sub-plane and the causes of present time.

1-5	fifth
2-5	sub-plane
3-5	UNSELFISH THOUGHT
4-5	time as effects of the future from
5-5	the first (causative) sub-plane
6-5	
7-5	

SELFISH THOUGHT
time as effects
of the future

Fallen Spirit

1-6	sixth
2-6	sub-plane
3-6	UNSELFISH THOUGHT
4-6	time as effects of the present from
5-6	the second (causative) sub-plane
6-6	
7-6	

SELFISH THOUGHT
time as effects
of the past

Fallen Spirit

1-7	seventh
2-7	sub-plane
3-7	UNSELFISH THOUGHT
4-7	time as effects of the past from
5-7	the third (causative) sub-plane
6-7	
7-7	

The enlightened thought of the vortices also connects the fallen spirit to the astral and etheric/dense physical planes.

SELFISH THOUGHT
time as effects
of the future

Fallen Spirit

In both genders, the vortices of the mental permanent atom all spin counter-clockwise. In a female, the vortices of the mental unit spin counter-clockwise, and in a male, they spin clockwise. In a male the two lower vortices of the permanent atom are cross-focused relative to the female. That is, in a male, thought from the vortex on one side of the mental permanent atom must cross over to the mental unit vortices on the opposite side; those vortices are reversed in their position from the female's. The effect is that women tend to have a stronger sense of Self because their vortices are not crossed, but weaker thought because the mental plane is a masculine plane. Likewise, men tend to have stronger thought, but a weaker sense of Self. In both genders, over many lifetimes the vortices develop rotation, enlighten the self, and connect the personality to the (lower) self, the (higher) Self, and the Solar Angel. Then the person's thought increasingly takes place in a "Now."

Illustration 10.10

such thought (such as the Atlanteans) to do so for long periods, while today, those who are focused in mental, structured, thought must create truth with much greater acumen of time if they are to create virtue. Those who are practicing *mental* spiritual discipline will attest to the great difficulty of creating more mental virtue, as compared to the etheric virtue of cooperation and sharing and the astral virtue of conditional (personal) love.

In order to enlighten a mental atom, three of the seven strings of active energy must be fused into intelligent activity, joining the spirit within the atom, as the energies in the sub-atomic "particle" become much closer together. These sub-atomic energies are much larger than even the relatively large ones found in astral atoms. The forces between atoms in a mental form are relatively weak as compared to the astral forms, and are almost invisible when compared to etheric/dense physical forms. This allows mental forms to be almost instantly changed by the informing thought of spirit. The mental atom uses the structure of time to balance much of the forces of various energies that are moving in opposing directions. This balancing is accomplished by formulating the three time vortices from past to present to future around the same point and event (or series of connected events) in space. Humans refer to this balancing as logic. When the three vortices are evenly surrounding an event, and in correct order, the curved space of each creates concentric circles of a new—*balanced*—vortex, mostly eliminating the forces, though only temporarily. The process continues until more events are added and the prior "super-" vortex becomes imbalanced as the past part of its three component time vortices becomes exaggerated because the new one or more events create (time) forces against the older one(s). The three strings of intelligent activity join together, at the mental atomic level, to create one completed time—but *only* for each event and for each being's thought, in a limited type of Now. Two or more beings on the mental plane cannot share the same Now because they, at that point, do not yet share any of the same sense. Thoughtforms and their causative connecting concepts can change so quickly that some people have trouble controlling them enough to even think normally. Logic balances the past, present, and future effect vortices that are connected to parts of a relatively whole thoughtform from each of the four sub-planes of the lower mental plane; a completely whole thoughtform must contain both kinds of lower mental energy—lunar devas and elemental energies—from all of the lower mental sub-sub-planes and sub-planes. A conceptually accurate thoughtform is one that is connected to a minimum of the three somewhat joined solar devas of the fifth, sixth, and seventh sub-sub-planes of the third sub-plane, and to higher elemental energies from these sub-planes. These three solar devas begin to join only when spiritual thought is created from the spiritual part of the higher mental body, from the fourth sub-sub-plane of the third sub-plane, up. The human self, in correspondence, connects with this mental sub-sub-plane because of their shared fourth ray nature. When the personality's fears do not cause it to overly control the self, the self "naturally" seeks to think spiritually (in a personal way) rather than in the highly selfishly and completely non-spiritual way of the personality's separative use of the lowest solar pitris. The latter type of thought consists of partial concepts constructed from the three lowest separated solar devas and occurs when the personality is over-controlling and often egotistical, as well.

On the mental plane, where the fifth dimension is *time*, the separation of time from space produces an observable parabolic distortion to space wherever time is distorted. Depending upon which lower dimension this parabola is obtained from, it might appear as an ellipse. Spherical space becomes an ellipse on most etheric/dense physical sub-planes and also on the lower astral ones, because not only is time separated from space, it is also distorted in its relation to space and events within it. This condition is easiest to understand if it is first described according to the way that it occurs mentally. When the time vortices are connected to the incorrect space, the space tends to twist around other space that is connected—also incorrectly—to another part of time. This causes a parabola of space to develop. On the etheric/dense physi sub-planes (except for the atomic), the space twists only around the remaining part of time, but this part has become distorted and changed from the past to the future because of people's greed and un-cooperation. Then the space changes from a sphere to an ellipse. On the lower astral sub-planes, the present vortex of time is often ignored and the past is focused on exclusively, with some of it replacing the present time vortex. This, again, causes an ellipse to be created from the spherical space, but more severely flattening the space because one of the time vortices is often missing from the space. It is this condition that gives astral centers in bodies their distinctive flower-like, "lotus," appearance when viewed through a lower astral sub-plane and sense (see Chapter Seven for a more full explanation).

The Distortion of Space, as a Result of Selfish (Often) Human Thought

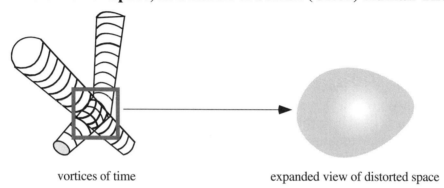

vortices of time   expanded view of distorted space

When parts of space are incorrectly connected to time, space twists around other space that is connected to another part of time. An ellipse occurs at the overlapped area. When this occurs throughout an entire dimension, that entire dimension becomes an ellipse.

Illustration 10.11

The mental cosmic Ray Lord uses time to structure space, as well as events within space, in order to create its dimension. Just as the astral Ray Lord uses the focused movement of one energy to another, creating love (or emotion, when selfishly used), the mental Ray Lord adds the *whole* dimension of time and then, when it is completely structured, balances all the forces of differing energies to create truth, or mental virtue. Energies need to be balanced because there is too little thought of spirit to do much towards converting into intelligent activity all the energies that are used. Even at the atomic level of the plane the three parts of time are balanced together, but they join only at *one* point of space at a time; thus each Now is still segregated by forces that eventually will cause the Now to collapse. Causes and joined effects do not last indefinitely in mental form, and so even the mental plane souls and their Selves need to become something more if they are to become immortal. This process of becoming more is called transfiguration, because it involves mental plane light (balanced structure of light) in order to alter a form in which balanced forces, or structure, are used to create both causal and logical thought, and then to create into something new the forms that represent, or that follow, the thought.

The process of transfiguration requires the active thought of a Self that is mostly fused with ¹s self, because the Self needs to structurally enlighten the entire part of the mental plane that is ⁻t of the mental body of the being it exists within. A human soul alone cannot be transfig- ⁻ause it has only a small part of the mental plane as its body. What is required is a human, ⁻sonality and self cooperating in the co-creation of virtue with the soul and its Self to ⁻in together mental plane Nows. When two or more mental Nows are joined, the ⁻ time vortices (which are, themselves, already joined between cause and effect ⁻ver parts of the mental plane) to join together is the past time. Mentally, the ⁻he atomic level becomes whole *knowledge*, or *knowledge that is complete enough with which to serve.* The wise giving of this knowledge is, in esoteric terms, the mental Now. As two or more of the fused cause-and-effect mental vortices of the past are fused, a new type of thought is created; it is called controlled intuition. Only the Self can use controlled intuition because controlled intuition can only occur at the atomic level of the mental plane, where the mental Self exists, and above. Uncontrolled intuition may occur very infrequently while a slight level of fusion is occurring between a self and its Self. This intuition may, on infrequent occasion, contribute important knowledge to others, but usually does not because service requires correct timing and consistency, which uncontrolled intuition mostly fails to have. Most uncontrolled intuition involves just two or three joined Nows, often from some level of service below the atomic mental sub-plane, but within the spiritual higher mind.

Transfiguration of Light
Replacing Forces in the Mental Permanent Atom

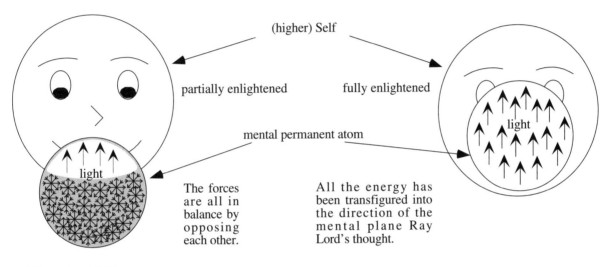

Illustration 10.12

    THE PHYSICS OF THE INTUITIONAL DIMENSION

Intuition is the joining together of the knowledge (the past part of time) vortices of two or more mental, or even higher-level, Nows from the same part of time. Intuition permits the further synthesis and creation of new knowledge in the "use" of no time at all. This occurs because time is fused together rather than being separated within this *type* of service between two or more beings sharing the same type of Now, of wisely giving knowledge that has been created instantly from two or more Nows of the past. As intuition is used in service on the atomic level of the intuitional plane, the fourth-dimensional string (the dimensional string of intelligent activity) fuses with the fifth-, sixth-, and seventh-dimensional strings of activity—causing a completion, or wholeness, of *time* for all beings on the plane. This wholeness of time then leads to a new type of light emission from the atom, and transfiguration of a form within which most of the atoms are so enlightened. Instead of just balancing forces through structure, as on the mental plane, a new type of form and time are created on the intuitional plane by fusing together one-third of time (the past—as knowledge) that is used to serve others. By *spiritual* service is meant the complete, or one hundred percent, giving of all energy that one has control of (through thought, on the corresponding plane), that helps others to also give in that way. The new form that is created is connected to *all* other form through one part of time (the past, or knowledge, part). The new time creates a permanence to form by perfecting enough of spirit's thought of instantly synthesizing *all*-knowledge, or by becoming omniscient, *within the service* that the spirit is providing. The perfection of spirit's thought to all the energy it is in contact with requires enough thought to both create the new knowledge within itself as spirit, and then to enlighten the energy that it is transmitting to others, using the new knowledge to help these others to do the same. This is the definition of the next higher virtue beyond the mental virtue of truth; this virtue is beauty. The intuitional beings all share to some degree the sense of all-knowingness, or omniscience. However, this sense is not perfected until one reaches the atomic level of the intuitional plane. Below this level, omniscience is still a capacity of spirit's thought rather than a full sense of one-third of God's mind, or of intelligent activity. Each being receives all-knowledge, which is all the knowledge that is available on the sub-plane where the service is taking place. The all-knowledge can be used to serve a Being who is higher in consciousness, on a higher sub-plane, who is at that time not using all-knowledge at that level of response. The all-knowledge can also be used to serve those on the same or lower sub-planes, as well.

Past Nows of the Intuitional Plane
Connected to All Other Nows through All-Knowledge

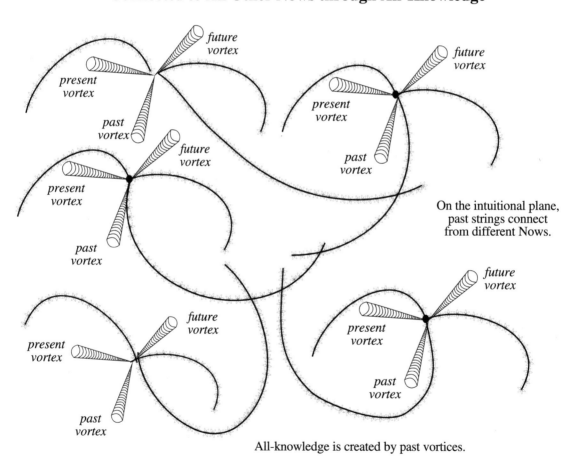

All-knowledge is created by past vortices.

All atoms on a past string touch all of the atoms of all other past strings; the atoms also are part of the shared consciousness of all Beings who can create intelligent activity within them. All of the energy connecting together in one of three ways creates within the energy a sense of itself being a part of all else, through knowledge. The sense is all-knowledge, or omniscience.

Illustration 10.13

The form that exists within space and time that is completely touching in one of three possible ways (through the past time vortices, or through knowledge) is called intuitional, or buddhic (enlightenment through enlightened knowledge), form, and it exists in the intuitional, or buddhic, dimension of time and space. Only forms that have been mentally transfigured can leave the mental plane for the intuitional plane, because with mental transfiguration not only is the energy transformed in consciousness, but time itself is fused, or rejoined (to itself and space) within the form and its atoms. The intuitional dimension also has seven sub-dimensions of time and space in correspondence to the seven rays and their effects on energy. Unlike the three lowest planes, which are sometimes referred to as the Cosmic Physical Solid dimensions, the intuitional sub-planes all contain beauty, or are enlightened in some ways at all times. Because the intuitional plane is ruled by the thought of spirit, as are the planes above it, and it is this thought that causes the creation of life, the intuitional plane is part of the Cosmic Physical Etheric dimensions of our universe, which denotes it as a causative dimension of life creation.

The seventh intuitional sub-plane is the sub-plane in which all-knowledge, or omniscience, is used in service that pertains to creating beauty in the etheric/dense physical dimension. This knowledge given to souls and also to lower spirit mostly applies to more beauty in inanimate forms and to a part of plants, or in *things*, and to the etheric/dense physical energy (the form part) of physically or etherically alive lifeforms, mostly of plants. Such service requires the creation of new knowledge that is also instantly shared with all other beings who can think on the seventh intuitional sub-plane. The sixth intuitional sub-plane uses all-knowledge, or omniscience, that is created and used in service to create beauty astrally in forms. The creation of astral beauty includes helping to create beauty through love in those who are alive either etherically, dense physically, or astrally. This creation is accomplished by increasing the spiritual thought on these planes and in the astral energy of the lifeforms through new knowledge (as it applies astrally) that is wisely given to the lifeforms' souls and selves. Again, any new knowledge used in such service is instantly created and simultaneously shared with all others who can think (intuitively) on the sixth intuitional sub-plane. On the fifth intuitional sub-plane, all-knowledge that applies to mental form becoming more beautiful is used in service to others who are thinking mentally. Even though the thought remains structured, it gains beauty by the added spiritual thought coming from those who are serving intuitionally, and are wisely giving new knowledge to those who will use it to create more virtue. This principle applies to all three of the lower planes as knowledge *about form* is given to increase the thought of spirit within the form, causing it to increase in beauty. When the fifth intuitional sub-plane is served from, new causes are joined to effects mentally from newly created mental knowledge that is wisely given to others so that the others can create more virtue.

The three lowest intuitional sub-planes together create all-knowledge (omniscience) regarding all the forms, or "things," within the three lower dimensions and how these forms can be better informed by the thought of spirit on these planes. In spiritual language, the three lowest intuitional sub-planes are collectively referred to as "the raincloud of knowable *things*." This name refers to the fact that the all-knowledge that is created and used in service on these three lowest intuitional sub-planes is used below the intuitional plane as new knowledge "raining down" from above. The new knowledge concerns "things" or improvements in form—on the Cosmic Physical Solid dimensions—in order to increase the thought of spirit within the form, which then makes the forms beautiful. Note that beauty is a state wherein there is twice as much of spirit's informing thought within a form than the amount of the thought by the energy that is controlling the form. When the human soul and its Self are fused with the personality and the self, respectively, and while they are alive on the mental plane and focused in life in the mental body, they can think no higher than the top of the "raincloud of knowable things" on the fifth intuitional sub-plane. This limitation occurs because the joining together of the past, or knowledge, parts of the Nows regarding service in the three lower worlds while living in them can be accomplished only through altering the forms of things. The forms are changed through knowledge that is given that may change their (their energy's) thought, rather than directly changing the thought of spirit—including that of souls. To be able to directly give knowledge to spirit and souls requires that the spirit doing the giving have consciousness, or givingness, that originates higher than the dimension of effect in which what is being given is taking place in time and space. Stated another way, one cannot create (virtue) and give completely to, or serve, others using that which one partially is using in the direction towards one's own form. To serve spirit directly (as souls, selves, Selves, and the spiritual part of personalities), *and*, to serve those *on* the intuitional plane, one must be focused in life intuitionally. That is, one must be liberated from the mental plane as an immortal Soul fused with the (prior) personality, and the self must be fused with the mental plane Self. At that point, one becomes transfigured into a Master of the three lower worlds, and of Ageless Wisdom—not just one who "knows" Ageless Wisdom, but one who serves spirit and souls, as well as energy, applying and *creating more* of this wisdom, making it *ageless*. Thus one who serves spirit, souls, and energy becomes a member of the spiritual kingdom, or the Kingdom of Souls, which includes, as a sub-kingdom, the energy kingdom. When all the energy within the lower three worlds becomes enlightened to the level prescribed by the Planetary Logos, and this occurs within a certain designated period of time, then the energy sub-kingdom will become unified with the spiritual kingdom as a single kingdom.

The atomic "structure" of an intuitional atom is quite different from the structure of atoms in the three lower worlds because the fourth string of an intuitional atom touches every other intuitional atom's fourth string, with the three lowest strings fused to the fourth. Thus every atom on the intuitional plane is touching *every other* atom there in one of the three time vortices (in the past, or knowledge) that the string exists within in its activity. This means that all beings and

Intuitional Plane Atoms and Strings

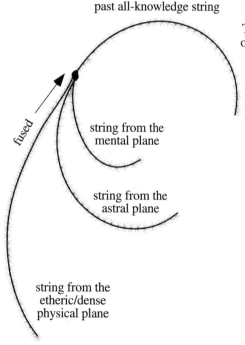

past all-knowledge string

fused

string from the
mental plane

string from the
astral plane

string from the
etheric/dense
physical plane

The three strings fuse to the fourth string
of all-knowledge on the intuitional plane.

Atoms on the intuitional plane touch every other atom there in one of three ways using the past part of each Now. This means that all Beings and forms on the intuitional plane are connected to one another through all-knowledge, or omniscience. The sense of all-knowledge, as part of each Being's body, is connected to all other Beings of equal or higher consciousness on the intuitional plane.

Illustration 10.14

forms on the intuitional plane are connected to one another through all-knowledge, or omniscience. At its level of service, spirit on each intuitional sub-plane is thinking perfectly both for itself and for energy; as a result, spirit is connected to all other spirit through serving with all-knowledge, or omniscience. The inner space on the intuitional plane is "touching" all other space through one-third of time. No part of time is separated from space, and a Now exists everywhere through creating all-knowledge that is wisely given in service to create more beauty.

 ## THE PHYSICS OF THE SPIRITUAL DIMENSION

The next dimension uses the past part (the all-knowledge part) of time along with the present part (the all-consciousness, or all-love, part) of time, creating a much larger Now. This is the spiritual dimension, and its string functions in two ways. When a spiritual plane Being on the spiritual plane uses the string to transmute energy, the Being creates all-power, and becomes omnipotent. In using the fused time (both Nows together), the Being is either more focused on the past or present time vortices and their Nows. If more focused on the past, the Being creating virtue from the past Now, or on the all-knowledge part of time, is creating new life on the lowest of the planes, and in this way adds to evolution. If the Being does the reverse and focuses more on the present time vortex and Its Now, It creates more consciousness in spirit on the mental plane (and possibly higher), where It is creating new life and is adding to spiritual growth. In this way, such a Being decreases the effects of evolution. When this second circumstance applies, then the Being is using all-intelligence as service while sensing in omnipotence, or all-power. The Beings who are alive on the spiritual plane but below its atomic level can create *new* life that affects all of life on a planet on the lower planes, but only by changing either the form of the life or the way spirit informs the life, but *not both at once*. This causes them to focus much more on changing evolutionary life. These spiritual Beings, or advanced Masters, below the atomic level have only two of the three possible ways available to them in which time can be joined to affect energy, and neither of these ways joins into a Now together until the atomic level is reached. Notice that on the spiritual plane the perfected balance between spirit and energy that existed on the intuitional plane is lost, but what is gained is increased creation of new life, while retention of all-knowledge remains—but only when used in tandem with omnipotence. On the atomic level of the spiritual plane, both types of multiple Nows can occur together at a point in space. Unlike on the intuitional plane, balance is lost in the creation of the Now below the atomic level. This loss prevents the creation of both power and intelligence in all life at the same time on the spiritual sub-planes below the atomic level.

Each spiritual plane Now contains perfection in omniscience and omnipotence, but in alternating degrees because spiritual dimension Beings below the atomic level are not omnipresent; omnipresence includes the three Nows of time joined together. These Beings cannot think fast enough to simultaneously create both energy and spirit life, i.e., they cannot convert enough energy into intelligent activity that will be used by spirit with which to create life *because there is too much spirit* on the spiritual plane as compared to the amount of either energy or intelligent activity, or both. At any point within a duration of spiritual plane creation of life, there is one specific amount of all-power as compared to the amount of all-intelligent activity that produces the correct ratio for all-creation of life on a planet. The combination creates the proper amounts of evolutionary life as compared to more spiritual life (life that has fewer forces). These Beings (Masters) need to ration the intelligent-activity/energy, so that life on the lower dimensions grows according to the availability of spirit to inform it. On the spiritual plane there is five times as much spirit as there is energy; however, twice as much spirit to energy is the perfect ratio for supplying spirit with forms that it can fully enlighten. Not enough energy exists on the spiritual plane to create all the forms needed for spirit to create life, which places a

Past and Present Nows of the Spiritual Plane
Connected to All Other Nows through All-Knowledge and All-Power

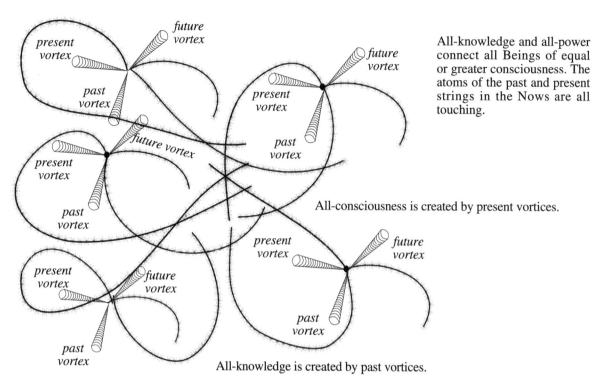

All-knowledge and all-power connect all Beings of equal or greater consciousness. The atoms of the past and present strings in the Nows are all touching.

All-consciousness is created by present vortices.

All-knowledge is created by past vortices.

Past and present strings connect from different Nows on the spiritual plane.

Illustration 10.15

restriction on the sense that spirit below the atomic level can gain in creating new life within the lower worlds. While spiritual dimension Beings can transmute, at will, *all* of the spiritual plane energies—making these Beings all-powerful, or omnipotent—they cannot create life for all spirit. Hence these Beings can experience only two-fifths of the life within the universe. These Beings are not, therefore, omnipresent and thus they can cannot think as One.

At the atomic level of the spiritual plane, every atom is touching every other atom in two of three possible ways. These two ways are in the *all*-past and *all*-present parts of time, but not in the all-future. Every Being who lives on the spiritual plane shares and experiences these two parts of time with all other spiritual plane Beings. Each of the seven spiritual sub-planes uses this sharing of Nows as they apply to the creation and use of either energy or intelligent activity on any of the corresponding seven dimensions. This ability is also increased by interpenetration of the dimensions as one ascends in spiritual plane thought to the atomic level of the plane. At this level, thought takes place at the speed of light of the spiritual plane Ray Lord— millions of times faster than on the dense physical dimension. This speed of the spiritual plane Ray Lord's thought is equal to the speed of the etheric Ray Lord's thought times itself, or squared. As Albert Einstein had discovered, the speed of etheric light squared times the mass of matter transmutes that matter into energy. This is an etheric/dense physical effect of the all-powerful side of spiritual plane thought. It is also the highest use of the third cosmic fire and can produce nuclear fission when somewhat out of balance in the ratio of the amount of thought (spiritual plane light) to the amount of energy that is being transmuted. Nuclear fusion, as a part of the second cosmic fire, transmutes energy with *greater* balance between the spiritual plane thought (light) and the energy being transmuted. This then produces (*relatively*) more light than heat than fission does. The ratio of heat to light using spiritual plane thought (light) to create nuclear fission is five parts to one (mundane fission also leaves residual energies, or radioactive waste). The ratio of heat to light when using nuclear fusion is five parts of energy to two parts of spiritual thought. These ratios are directly related to the two types of spiritual plane thought and sense within the two joined Nows of time and the total amount of energy on the spiritual plane. Stars are twice as efficient at creating their light from their fusion than from their fission processes. At the atomic level, only three strings of intelligent activity within time exist, because the other lower ones have been fused with the third.

 ## THE PHYSICS OF THE MONADIC DIMENSION

The second, or monadic, dimension has some unusual qualities about it because all intelligent activity in this dimension is sacrificially kept separated from all-light, by space at the edges of the inner sphere of light. The separation is produced by the collective thought of all the Monads, or Beings who *think as one* and do so sacrificially with regard to intelligent activity. In this position of separation, intelligent activity cannot be converted into energy within this plane—only outside it. On the monadic plane all three time vortices are fused, which creates omnipresence *through sacrificing intelligent activity*, or through *one aspect of* God's mind. Monads create intelligent activity on a lower plane of our universe that corresponds to the highest monadic sub-plane whereupon they are omnipresent. Because the higher interpenetrates the lower, a Monad can think as One with all other Monads at and below its level of omnipresence, which is indicated by the monadic sub-plane that it functions from. For example, Monads on the seventh sub-plane of the monadic plane create intelligent activity on the seventh, or the etheric/dense physical, plane of our universe. Among other things, these Monads help to create the group souls of minerals and lower types of plants by creating seventh plane form and fallen spirit that mineral group souls on the mental plane need to control. Monads on the sixth monadic sub-plane can think as One with Monads on the sixth monadic sub-plane as well as in omnipresence with seventh sub-plane Monads. The sixth sub-plane Monads create intelligent activity on the sixth, or the astral, plane of our universe, helping to create, among other things, the group souls of higher plants and animals. The same pattern of Monads creating intelligent activity on the plane of our universe that corresponds to their monadic sub-plane, or the highest monadic sub-plane where they think in omnipresence, also occurs with Monads on the fifth, fourth, third, second, and first monadic sub-planes. Note that second monadic sub-plane Monads create separated intelligent activity on the entire monadic plane, with the exception of the first sub-plane. They do so through their sacrifice of intelligent activity and its total separation from their thought, or from light.

Monads who are capable of sustaining their consciousness on the atomic (the first) monadic sub-plane and who can think at the speed of the second cosmic Ray Lord are seventh level initiates completing that initiation. In their completion of the seventh initiation, they have become members of both the next higher dimension and the Planetary Kingdom. Each of these Great Beings upon taking the eighth initiation can ascend to the logoic plane (the first dimension or our universe), where all intelligent activity (God's third aspect of mind) can be joined, progressively, for all life (and pre-life) everywhere in the Cosmic Physical Universe from the densest sub-plane to, eventually, the atomic logoic level. This joining of intelligent activity takes place for all three parts of time, in a single Now for all of space. All Monads share the same consciousness, but not the same levels of omnipresence; as stated above, a Monad can think as One on the monadic plane with other Monads at and below the level of omnipresence that is indicated by the sub-plane from which the Monad creates spirit, energy, and, eventually, intelligent activity. Note that omnipresence can be used in two ways, as thought or as a sense. As thought, omnipresence is used by Monads on the monadic plane to think as One, at increasing amounts as they function from higher levels on the monadic plane. Omnipresence is used as a sense by Monads who have progressed beyond the monadic plane, to the logoic plane. At this level, they can *sense* with all other Monads at and below their level on the logoic plane, in a similar process to that which occurs on the monadic plane, but, instead, using omnipresence as a sense and not just as thought. These Monads sense with everything on the corresponding dimension of the universe to the highest sub-plane upon which they are conscious and alive. At the end of the process, the Monad has become a Great Being who has experienced—sensed— all that has been, is, and ever will possibly be in our universe *as our universe exists from that moment.* The ascended Monad is ready to leave this universe (the Cosmic Physical) to go on to a higher level of creating virtue, in the (or in a) Cosmic Astral, Mental, or, possibly, Intuitional Universe. Which universe the Monad departs for depends upon the decision made by that Monad earlier in the initiatory process. Notice that Monads on the two lowest monadic sub-planes are creating life (through spirit, which is a sacrificed part of themselves) in the three lowest kingdoms, in correspondence to and in accord with their sub-plane locations of all-(monadic)-consciousness. Human Monads are found on the fifth monadic sub-plane. The Monads of various levels of Masters are found on the fourth, third, and first monadic sub-planes; the kingdoms these Masters represent are the fifth, sixth, and (as junior members) the seventh. For a period, or duration, of time some Monads may choose to not focus on separating intelligent activity on the monadic plane. These Monads do not participate in life creation during that life duration of a particular star within our universe. In order for a Monad on the second monadic sub-plane to reach the first, It needs to submerge Itself to the seventh monadic sub-plane, and Its created spirit and manifested energies on the corresponding lower planes must create virtue, as this Monad grows upward towards the monadic atomic level.

MONADS ON THE MONADIC PLANE		
OMNI-PRESENCE OF MONADS, WHERE THEY ALL THINK AS ONE*	TYPE OF MONAD	CREATION OF INTELLIGENT ACTIVITY BY MONADS WITH OTHER MONADS
Seventh monadic sub-plane	Monads creating spirit and energy for group souls and the three lowest kingdoms	Seventh (etheric/dense physical) plane
Sixth monadic sub-plane		Sixth (astral) plane
Fifth monadic sub-plane	Human Monads creating human souls	Fifth (mental) plane
Fourth monadic sub-plane	Super-human Monads of fifth through seventh level initiates	Fourth (intuitional) plane
Third monadic sub-plane		Third (spiritual) plane
Second monadic sub-plane	Monads incarnated onto the monadic plane but not yet manifesting as spirit and energy and life on the lower planes	Second (monadic) plane**
First monadic sub-plane	Seventh level initiates completing this initiation	First (divine) plane

*Note: Each higher sub-plane interpenetrates all those below it on that plane, i.e., Monads think as One not only on the monadic sub-plane where they think in omnipresence, but they think as One with those on all lower monadic sub-planes, as well.

**The second monadic sub-plane is where Monads begin their journey—it is the level that they incarnate into— within a star system on a planet.

Table 10. 3

MONADS ON THE LOGOIC PLANE		
OMNI-PRESENCE OF MONADS, WHERE THEY ALL SENSE AS ONE*	SENSING OF EVERYTHING IN OUR UNIVERSE— PAST, PRESENT, AND FUTURE—BY MONADS WITH OTHER MONADS	LEVEL OF INITIATION
Seventh logoic sub-plane	Seventh (etheric/dense physical) plane	Eighth
Sixth logoic sub-plane	Sixth (astral) plane	Eighth
Fifth logoic sub-plane	Fifth (mental) plane	Eighth
Fourth logoic sub-plane	Fourth (intuitional) plane	Eighth
Third logoic sub-plane	Third (spiritual) plane	Ninth
Second logoic sub-plane	Second (monadic) plane	Ninth
First logoic sub-plane	First (divine) plane	Ninth

*Note: Each higher sub-plane interpenetrates all those below it on that plane, i.e., Monads sense as One not only on the logoic sub-plane where they sense in omnipresence, but they sense as One with those on all lower logoic sub-planes, as well.

Table 10. 4

The Selves that are found on the atomic levels of the intuitional and spiritual planes exist because, while they can give as one at their levels of thought, they cannot create as one—which Monads can do, allowing them to think as One. The three Selves found at the atomic levels of the mental, intuitional, and spiritual planes, respectively, are a part of the life of the Spiritual Triad, which is the informing spirit, body, and senses of a Solar Angel (as it eventually fuses with a Master). (See Chapters Five and Six for more information.) The strings in monadic and logoic atoms exist as intelligent activity in completed time, but with *no* separated energy within them. On the monadic plane the three time vortices become one at the atomic level, giving the plane one of its names...the plane of One. On the logoic plane the one vortex gradually becomes a sphere the size of our universe and then, at the atomic logoic level, this sphere becomes the single point. This single point of time in space is the Now for all time—past, present, and future—or for all activity from the least enlightened, to complete reunification of God's three aspects of mind. Those Great Masters who have mastered all the time and space of our universe leave our universe in consciousness by experiencing and *Being* all of it within all time and space. They achieve this through creating considerably more of God by growing vast amounts of life in the process. Each universal ascending Master omnipresently experiences all of the universe's future, from the point in the present from which that Master creates the future. Thus it is possible, nearly even definite, that each of these Masters will live the future in

The Transcended (Logoic) Monad

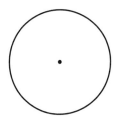

an ascended Monad leaving our universe

Illustration 10.16

Beingness that will differ from other universal ascending Masters (who are creating further uniqueness in themselves). The reason is that a universal Now on the atomic level of the logoic plane grows as God grows from life's growth, and only *probabilities* of the future universe can be created before the life in it creates what the universe will be.

 ## THE PHYSICS OF THE LOGOIC DIMENSION

On the seven logoic sub-planes, all three Nows of time—the past, present, and future—are being joined together for an entire dimension of our universe, through the sense of an ascended Monad (a very advanced Master who is an eighth or ninth level initiate). An eighth level initiate joins all three Nows for the four lowest dimensions and while on the four lowest logoic sub-planes. A ninth level initiate does so while unifying time and space on the third through first dimensions and while on the third through first logoic sub-planes. Because upon reaching the third logoic sub-plane the ninth level initiate has sacrificed the permanent atoms in all of his or her bodies except the logoic, this Great Master can individually sense below the logoic plane *only* through becoming all else, omnipresently. The eighth level initiate at first sacrifices only the three lowest permanent atoms of the solid Cosmic Physical body; this enables him or her to have individual sense remaining in the etheric Cosmic Physical dimensions without yet having become omnipresent in sense. The eighth level initiate sacrifices his or her intuitional permanent atom just prior to ascending to the fourth logoic sub-plane. Once all of the permanent atoms except for the logoic are sacrificed (on the third logoic sub-plane), a Master becomes a ninth level initiate and a "Silent Watcher"…one who only experiences by completely being all the others in the past, present, and future without taking *anything* from these others. Note that for senses to function from a body or permanent atom requires that something—some amount of energy (or light)—be *taken* from the person or thing being sensed. The "Silent Watcher" takes nothing from others *except* from God and the first Ray Lord, because the Watcher has only a logoic permanent atom, which is made up of exclusively intelligent activity and light. On the seventh logoic sub-plane, a Monad can sense everything (including all life on the etheric/dense physical plane) for *all time,* or all Nows on that plane, in the past and present as well as in the future. This Monad also remains connected in thought to all other Monads on the seventh logoic sub-plane. On the sixth logoic sub-plane, the Monad can sense everything on the astral *and* the etheric/dense physical dimensions. Each succeeding higher logoic sub-plane that a Monad exists on raises its level of sense for all time and in omnipresence, by one more dimension of time and space. Finally, at the atomic level of the logoic plane, an ascended Monad can sense in omnipresence our entire Cosmic Physical Universe for all things and life in all dimensions in the past, present, and future.

The atomic structure of a logoic "atom" has no energy within it. It contains only light that is in a state of increasingly joining with intelligent activity, and as it does, it creates life as Beings of "Silent Watchers," who are the Great ascending universal Masters of our universe. The "string" is logoic light that is continuously intelligently active by being all activity, in the past, present, and future that has become intelligent—or has fully rejoined space and time.

The meaning to such a vast process of creating life that first separates time and space in order to grow its Creator, and then rejoins time in space by *becoming* (more of) that Creator is the perhaps greatest of all the great experiences and ways of understanding God. One who completely understands this process has unified time; space; energy; light (God's thought); intelligent activity (which manifests energy eventually back into intelligent activity); life and its growth; and, finally, himself or herself into a functional part of God. *Life's Hidden Meaning* is an attempt to help those who are consciously on such a journey to gain this ultimate in meaning of life. Science today often fails to ask the appropriate questions, and fails to examine such issues as the meaning of life and life's spiritual purpose. What this book is attempting to do is present a grand unification of *more* than just "scientific" theory reporting on energies and their structures in the known universe. Rather, this book is attempting to unify *life*, as God's growth, with most of everything that is presently known (including energy), and with much of that which is hidden, in order to truly unify humanity's understanding our universe. Then meaning of life will be un-hidden as understanding replaces much of the ignorance that humans currently operate within because that ignorance is what they have created.

 # CONCLUSIONS AND SUMMARY FROM CHAPTER TEN

Space is the result of the separation of the first two aspects, or parts, of God's mind; these two parts when joined are God's thought. Time is the part of space that determines the relationship between the amount of space that is created from the separation of these two aspects and the way in which the space is created. The third aspect of God's mind also becomes separated, and as it manifests itself as energy that is within space, time becomes a separated part of space. As energy rejoins with space and becomes intelligent activity, time also rejoins with space, thereby increasing the quality of thought. The less space and the more light that exist within any dimension, the less time of that dimension of space is "used" to execute an activity. At the speed of light, or of the Ray Lord's thought, for each dimension, time stops because all energy is converted into intelligent activity and there no longer is any space between any two beings or things. The *quality*, and therefore the time, of each dimension is specific to that dimension, so that even though it takes up no time in which to create completely intelligent activity within a dimension, there are differences in the types of intelligent activities, or the ways in which they can occur between two or more beings or things. On each higher dimension, a more complex intelligent activity that joins space more completely and uses a more whole time is realized. The reason is that on each higher dimension the speed of the Ray Lord's thought, or light, is greater, which permits an increase in the duration of life. This increase tremendously grows the ways that time can join space. Thus each dimension is a multiplier of the ways in which time can increasingly rejoin space.

The definiteness of energy (or matter, in the dense physical world) is decreased as time is used more intelligently in activity. This occurs because time is the measure of the quality (consciousness) of thought that is rejoining space. The greater the thought that is intelligent as compared to the unintelligent thought—which is mostly represented by gravity—the more that energy *follows* the thought and the less that it is *determined* by the gravity and forces. Gravity is the collective thought of anything that thinks in an involutionary, or a self-focused, manner. Spirit needs to overcome gravitational thought by enlightening energy and rejoining time with space as it (spirit) thinks closer to the speed of light of the dimension it is located on. Eventually, when spirit has become enlightened, time and space become creative tools with which spirit can create more and new life. The relationship of spirit and thought to time and space is a crucial component of a complete understanding of life's hidden meaning.

❧ CHAPTER ELEVEN ❧

REINCARNATION

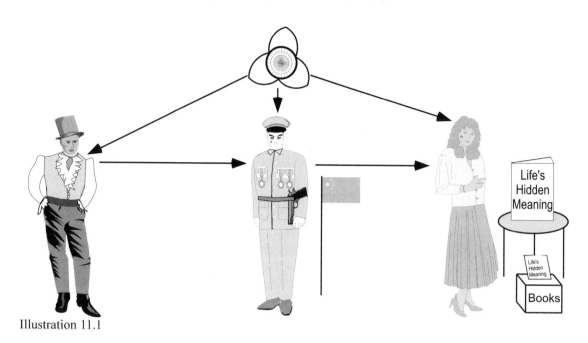

Illustration 11.1

Author's Suggestion: First turn to the "Glossary Help Guide" and read the definitions for this chapter.

 ## THE BASICS ABOUT KARMA

From the atomic level of the mental plane, down, negative karma (that which is selfishly created) is the result of some levels of selfishness having separated an effect from its cause in time and space. The greater the levels of selfishness by spirit, the greater the separation of time and space and the more delayed the karma, or the effects of the selfishness. In addition, the greater the delay that exists between a cause and its effect, the more that effect becomes additional causes for others' selfishness. The result in these cases is an increase of several times to more than ten times the karmic effects when each eventually rejoins with its cause and manifests in some type of *energy* outcome. Note that positive karma is the result of rejoining time and space by creating activity that is more intelligent, through enlightenment. Positive karma can offset similar corresponding negative karma and thus prevent it from combining with other karma. When this occurs, the positive karma results in offsetting much larger amounts of manifested energies. These energies would otherwise subsequently become significantly detrimental to spirit's awareness and its ability to think and be conscious.

At and above the atomic level of the mental plane, selfish karma is the result of spirit being conscious enough to rejoin only some energies in certain ways back into time and space, in the creation of intelligent activity. Spirit's relative lack of overall consciousness in these realms is the factor that determines its level of selfishness. However, it is difficult for humans to even compre- hend selfishness that occurs at such relatively high levels of creating virtue. The *esoteric* (to humans) karma that is accrued at these levels is determined by the number of ways (out of a potential three joined together) that a Now does not have all its effects connected to its causes; it is not determined by the degree to which an effect is completely separated from a cause. All Nows have effects connected to causes in at least one of three ways. (See Chapters Five and Ten for a more thorough explanation of what a Now is.) Nows above the atomic level of the mental plane that take place between two or more beings and events contain all the effects of one or more of seven corresponding ray types, with these effects connected in at least one of three ways. Hence the more complete the Now, the less the negative karma and the greater the positive karma.

Negative individual karma is created when the majority of effects of an event that is separated from its causes (as a result of selfishness) are produced by an individual. Negative group karma is created when no particular individual has caused the separation between a majority of the effects of an event and its causes. Positive individual karma comes from an individual causing the majority of an event's effects to rejoin with their causes. And positive group karma is created when a group causes the majority of an event's effects to rejoin with their causes, with no particular individual bringing about the majority of the rejoining. As has been previously explained, an event in time and space is a series of activities that share the same one or more creative thoughts and whose movements match the direction (consciousness) of the thought or thoughts, or share the same time that has been separated from the space they are in. Events become increasingly isolated from one another on each of the three lowest planes. On any of those planes, individual karma tends to grow through selfish activities, which then manifest more energy because the lower the dimension, the more that time has become separated from space.

As can be deduced, karma is the effect of spirit's consciousness on time and space. Oddly to human perception, karma can link the lives of human beings who have no (lower) self understanding of any of their prior lifetimes, because of the much wider, or larger, life duration that the human soul exists within. This larger duration connects the life of one human to another (preceding) human's life that were both created by the same soul. By joining lifetimes of humans, and thus reversing the separation of time and space, negative karma actually is corrective to the over-separation of God's mind; this over-separation when not corrected can lead to evil. Note that not only humans create and incur karma. Technically, even the slight consciousness of energy creates for energies *of its type* some minute level of karma. This occurs because energy does have an effect on time and space that helps these first two parts of God's mind to either separate or join. Reincarnation, as it manifests on earth, could not exist without karma because reincarnation is tied to rejoining effects to causes—and karma is the result of their separation.

The effect of the rays on the different specialization of energies within the kingdoms has caused some of these energies to grow more than other energies when a corresponding ray has been in focus on earth; in Chapter Nine the process was explained and demonstrated using examples of the earlier races in the human kingdom. The kingdoms lower than human are heavily controlled by the effects of the rays as the rays control evolution; this has sometimes also been true of the earlier human races that preceded the (current) fifth major race. As humans become more controlled by their informing spirit, by their souls, and by each individual's (higher) Self—and under less control of the person's personality, which is part unenlightened form—they gradually become less affected by the rays and thus function more spiritually. At no time in human history has this critical shift in human development ever been more prominent than at present. The reason is that the more advanced humans of today have progressed into the fifth sub-race of the fifth major race. The combination of these two factors (the fifth major race and its fifth sub-race) produces the crucible wherein humanity either becomes predominantly spiritual or becomes darker in its use of its senses, its creative thoughts, and its development of civilization. Civilization is the use of the lower kingdoms by humans to develop their own kingdom by extending their own senses and bodies. Civilization is discussed in detail in Chapter Nine. If the fifth sub-race develops successfully, it will become more affected by spiritual thinking than by the effects of the rays on its members' bodies and on individual people's personalities. Successful development of the fifth sub-race will then lead to the development of the sixth sub-race, which will focus on developing the spiritual sub-sense (of the whole mental sense) of *understanding God* through this major race's emphasis on structured, mental thought. *Life's Hidden Meaning*, as a tool that can be used towards gaining such understanding, is one of the first to attempt to help produce this very result. The sixth sub-race corresponds to the development of the sixth sense of spiritually understanding; this lower of the two spiritual senses (and of spiritual thought) gives humans new understandings, or higher consciousness, regarding God (see Chapter Seven for more explanation of this effect). Both spiritual senses can be applied within a mental emphasis, or one that is structured in thought; the higher of the two will be the focus of development for the seventh sub-race of the fifth major sub-race—hundreds of years, or more, into the future. If that sub-race is successful, it will develop the sense of being a functional part of God by mentally creating virtue, or by creating more truth than not on the mental plane through the enlightenment of each virtuous person's mental body.

The effect of the rays on humans versus the effect of spiritual thought on them puts humans on the cross of either becoming more animal-like, through evolution, or more like God, through spiritual enlightenment. The battle causing this *planetary* crisis is raging within each human who is reaching for the development of more understanding of (a better sense of) God because that person *is seeking more meaning in life* outside of her or his own life. Those who are in this position are near the current peak of mental development within the human kingdom. These people are developing more meaning in their lives by sharing their development through helping to create more truth in the minds of others. As humans win the battle to understand God, they develop themselves into a functional part of God. They do so by inculcating their *virtuous* creations into the lower kingdoms and into their own, becoming the masters of these kingdoms on earth. Then, as humans become an extension of (a part of) God in their development of the lower kingdoms, the lower kingdoms become much less affected by evolution and much more affected by the thought and actions of humans. The effect of the rays versus the effect of spiritual thought (spiritual sense) is also the foundation of how reincarnation functions.

 ## THE BASICS OF REINCARNATION

Reincarnation of a human is created by its (a human) soul and its OverSoul and their shared higher mental plane Self. Their purpose is the attempt to create an eventual perfected balance between the collective thought of energy within the human lifeform and its informing spirit—the majority of which is contained in the human's self and personality. The self is exclusively spirit, and the personality in most human beings is less than one-half spirit that is trapped among the semi-permanent thoughtforms (which are lower mental energy) within the mental unit. This trapped spirit and these thoughtforms together compose the personality, who resides from the third through first sub-sub-planes of the fourth mental sub-plane. In each newly created human being, the human soul and OverSoul and their shared Self try to achieve (as closely as possible) a total of twice as much spiritual thought than the collective thought of all of the energies within the personality and its three bodies and senses. Note that the collective shared thought of the unenlightened elemental energy on all three of the lower planes is *less* than the collective thought of the deva energy in the bodies of an *advanced* human being, at the atomic levels of those planes. Together, these forms of spirit are attempting to achieve the creation of beauty, as virtue, within the human being, i.e., they are attempting to create a perfection in balance between the thought of spirit and of energy within the human lifeform. Beauty (the method of advancement of the fourth ray line), which is a created virtue, is the goal for human beings. The attempt is made with each incarnation of a human to move that human closer to perfectly balancing two specific factors with each other. The first factor is evolution and the effects of the rays. The second is spiritual thought—which needs to be twice the amount of the energy's collective thought within a body. Spirit's thought needs to also be at least twice the amount of the elemental energy's thought (and that of the deva energy that thinks like involutionary, or elemental, energy) for the entire plane, on *each* plane where a human lives. The spirit needs to think for both itself and, givingly, for the energies within its bodies and personality. Until a human soul is near the end of the process, the life of each of its incarnations is replete with countless mistakes in spirit thinking more like energy than like the spirit that it is; the person fails to think as a functional part of God's thought. Only as consciousness increases does each human lifetime advance towards becoming more beautiful. Consciousness increases as the giving of spirit's thought increases. Spirit creates an increase in its thought by both thinking more virtuously *and* choosing to give its thought—as its soul, so that others might choose to do the same.

Prior to the creation of each human being, its soul and OverSoul and their shared Self choose the ray focus of energies that will form that person's three lower bodies and her or his personality. They do so in order to alter and affect the battle that the spirit will encounter in its attempts to create more consciousness, or more givingness of the self and personality. In this way they adjust the level of difficulty that the person will encounter in the course of her or his lifetime to the karma and level of thought that the spirit will have available to it. This level comes from the totality of senses that have been created in the permanent atoms of the bodies during all of that human soul's prior lifetimes. At the personality's beginning point of awareness, it can think only as well as it can sense from each body. Its consciousness, however, is determined by its level of giving that which it has previously sensed, thought of, created knowledge with, and then given appropriately according to the needs of others. The process begins with giving to and receiving from its self and giving to the energies within its own bodies. Karma is the result of selfishness and virtue that was created at some point in the past. Karma is stored within each permanent atom as manifested energy that originally came from intelligent activity, or as light in form; karma affects other energies in the bodies and their responsiveness to other energies. Relatively greater levels of prior selfishness impede the process of the senses being developed from the permanent atom of each body. Selfishness also hinders the development of the personality's senses from the mental permanent atom, and from which the Self, through the focused thought of the OverSoul and human soul, uses to create the semi-permanent thoughtforms of the personality. Less sense in the human being provides its informing spirit with less awareness, or less information, *and* the information that spirit does receive will be less accurate. Because spirit that has less awareness has *less thought*, and since thought creates its life, spirit karmically "pays" for its previous personality's selfishness. Spirit pays karmically by having less created new life, or, ultimately, less meaning from what life its present personality has created for itself. An impetus is created in the personality to gain more meaning in its life. This meaning can be created only by the personality being less selfish, or lessening its (over-) control of its self and listening to both its soul and its Solar Angel. In order to provide the personality with the opportunity to gain more meaning, to suffer less, and to become joyful, the soul, Solar Angel, and Self include within their plans for their next human incarnation's life certain conditions through which that personality can, if it so chooses, attain victory in the battle to become *relatively* more spiritual.

The more selfish the prior incarnation (or incarnations) of that soul, the fewer the choices that will be available to one or more of its subsequent personalities. A not unusual example of this concept is a baby being born with a serious illness or ailment and dying as an infant. The reason for such an occurrence might be that the virtue that could be created in *others* (family members, for example). Through this infant's strife and the crisis for others close to its birth and death, the most amount of virtue that that personality can hope to create in that lifetime is created. In extreme cases of prior selfishness, a soul might have a series of human incarnations who each live a little longer than the prior one. This pattern will continue until the personalities have collectively created enough virtue to overcome the legacy of the negative karma that one or more of their predecessors selfishly created. In these cases, most of the "infant's" suffering occurs as it grows up and lives on the subtle, inner planes of the astral and lower mental worlds. Selfishness causes a loss in consciousness just as virtue expands consciousness. Suffering arises from one's awareness that she or he has lost consciousness during her or his life. In order to plan properly for an incarnating human's life, that future person's soul (when advanced enough) and OverSoul (his or her Solar Angel) and their shared Self choose to collaborate with other souls who will incarnate at the same approximate time and whose created human beings are likely to have contact with one another. This collaboration is necessary because humans are interactive in both their selfishness and their creation of virtue, and they share karma as an entire kingdom as well. Each time the human soul, OverSoul, and Self create a human incarnation, they choose to do so in cooperation with and in accord with the needs of other humans who will be created in the same time and space; the soul, OverSoul, and Self treat life as One—which life, as God's growth, actually is.

Humans are created as individuals who will incarnate within groups that their selves are usually unaware of at the beginning of their lifetimes. Each human, unless his or her prior incarnation had been a very advanced spiritual disciple, usually believes that his or her life is separate from the lives of others and exists to be lived as he or she chooses. That belief is an illusion, because each human was created to contribute to and help create more virtue in himself or herself *and* in other life as much as is possible at his or her level of response to, or awareness of, the environment. This level of response is what makes the human *response-able*, or *responsible*, for past karma. The karma is contained within one's permanent atoms as retained energy that was manifested from intelligent activity and that resulted from that person's prior spirit's selfish thought that separated time from space. Thus humans incarnate within groups whose members share both individual and group karma more closely with each other than with the other members of their kingdom in general. Humans are created in this way in order to assist those who are relatively un-advanced. People who are not spiritually disciplining themselves need to have their levels of selfishness limited, and need to be led to create more virtue than they created in their last incarnation or incarnations. The rays provide this control because when a sense and body's parts that are composed of energy are used selfishly, the rays so limit awareness that the self cannot give as much to that body and sense—which reduces the self's consciousness and its available thought. The personality then becomes fearful of annihilation of its self—its real death—and suffering ensues. Also, under these circumstances the "fallen" spirit within each body can think proportionately less. A person whose one or more prior incarnations practiced spiritual discipline is generally more directly assisted by his or her soul and Solar Angel, and their shared Self. When the personality of an incarnated older adolescent or an adult human is selfish, the ray of her or his semi-permanent lower mental thoughtforms, or lower mental energies that compose part of the personality, is the most important ray in limiting that person into creating more virtue. This usually occurs within a group whose members often have the same, or at least a correspondingly similar, personality ray. By interacting with similar personalities it is easier for less advanced humans to create virtue by recognizing others as being, in some ways, a part of their selves. The majority of virtue that these people create is often a shared positive karma, as a group, with some parts of the karma today extending all the way to a national level of group karma.

The *group* parts of each human's shared selfish karma are also a part of her or his soul's individual karma. The reason is that all souls are responsible for all of the groups that their individual incarnating humans selfishly responded to in their past lives. This group karma extends beyond the human kingdom, down to the three lower kingdoms. The karma affects each human soul by altering the levels of response that the soul has to other souls (both human souls and group souls) and to its Self, in each soul's attempts to become more creative in its ways of practicing virtue. The alteration of a soul's responsiveness, or awareness, to other souls and to its own Self is determined first by the development of the thirty-three solar devas in the spiritual part of the causal body that are connected to the three separated solar devas that make up the mundane part of that body (the higher mental body, or the higher mind). The second factor is the overall level of development of the three inner sacrifice petals, which are found in the spiritual part of the causal body. These inner sacrifice petals are composed of advanced solar devas, or pitris, that develop through the virtue that humans create while practicing spiritual discipline in each of their incarnations into physical life. (See Chapter Six for in-depth information about solar pitris and the causal body.) The three inner sacrifice petals develop and unfold, progressively exposing the spirit within (the human soul) to life on the higher mental plane. The amount of exposure is determined by the degree to which that soul's relatively selfish *group* karma is offset by each of its incarnated humans' creation of increasing amounts of virtue along the single ray focus of the collective three inner sacrifice petals. Each soul, therefore, has a ray focus along one of the seven rays that is created from the three inner petals together. This ray focus remains the same throughout the duration of the soul's higher mental plane life. Each of the three petals also has a sub-ray of one of the three rays of aspect of God's mind. The first petal to unfold is along the third *sub*-ray aspect, and functions (along the third ray) as a sub-ray of that soul's ray. This petal contains third through seventh ray energies. The second petal to unfold likewise functions along the second ray, and the third, and final, petal to unfold functions along the first ray as a sub-ray to the soul. Once all three petals have unfolded, they rotate in one of two possible directions. The direction is determined by the gender of the advanced initiate during that lifetime, and by the spins of the three tiers; the gender will be exclusively heterosexual after a certain point in each lifetime, once these petals are spinning. One of the first two petals must have been unfolded during a virtuous lifetime as the opposite gender to the gender of the person unfolding the third one. Henceforth these petals will always rotate in the same direction, which together with the spins of the tiers sets the gender of the advanced initiate for all his or her future lifetimes. Through their human incarnations, souls can create individual virtue along all seven rays of focus, but in relatively less developed humans are often limited to creating virtue mostly along the personality ray. In more developed humans or spiritual disciples, the souls create virtue that is individually karmically related (often between one person and another) through all seven of the rays. However, the same human's group karma and service are most often along the focus of creating more virtue within the soul and its shared Self along the soul's ray. These conditions occur as the spiritual disciple creates virtue from soul consciousness, using the solar devas from the second (and higher) tier of petals within the causal body. Notice that the creative part of the human soul's life is to develop and to fuse with its Self, which is accomplished through the soul's ray in developing the *higher* spiritual sense of creating more of God—with its (the human soul's) Self. The human soul's senses are developed as its inner petals of solar devas unfold and radiate, and the radiance of each solar pitri is directed into one of the legs of a triangle, or one section, of the three-part rainbow bridge.

The process is, at present on earth, facilitated through the creation of spiritual service and the assistance of the next kingdom, through initiation. Chapter Six explains parts of the initiation process. Each petal of the lotus usually becomes only about half-unfolded by the soul (in present-day humanity), through the cumulative creation of virtue by its incarnated humans over many lifetimes. The second half of the petal unfolds during the few seconds that it takes to complete an initiation. The initiation takes place on the mental plane usually while the human "sleeps" physically (or sleeps astrally, if dead physically)—but will remember the "ceremony" as having been real and not a dream. Note that a few saints, in the past, have completely unfolded a petal wholly through their own service, but that such an occurrence is highly unlikely to occur in modern times because the creation of substantially more virtue is necessary in order to unfold the petals in today's world. An advanced disciple has typically been prepared for the initiation experience by his or her Solar Angel, and may complete the initiation during meditation (while fully awake). Although rare, because of greatly lowered overall potential to create virtue after physical death, initiation during astral life is possible for some spiritual disciples. A spiritual disciple who is alive only mentally usually cannot create enough virtue to complete an initiation, and typically must wait at least until her or his next physical incarnation to do so.

 ## WHEN SOULS REINCARNATE

The souls of less advanced humans create human beings who incarnate based mostly upon the soul's ray, when that ray is in focus. These souls generally incarnate with other souls who share the same ray type and whose soul ray is also in focus on earth at that time. These souls incarnate during a corresponding planetary ray focus because their sense of other souls, as provided by the three inner petals, is strongest and most responsive while their respective soul rays are in focus on the planet. (See Chapter Seven for more explanation of this higher mental sense.) Incarnating in this way makes it much easier for these less developed human souls to be responsible for *creating* more group virtue. Souls always give virtuously, but the further creation of virtue (as newly created types of cooperation and sharing, conditional love, truth, and beauty) requires that a soul fuse with its Self, along the soul's ray.

During the fourth (the current) round on earth, only four of the seven rays are in focus at any one time; before the fourth round there were not enough rays focused concurrently on earth to create human souls or human life. The human incarnations of less advanced souls generally take place during the periods when their respective rays are in planetary focus. When the rays that correspond to these souls go out of focus, these souls may, in present times, not incarnate again for hundreds or even a thousand or more years—until the corresponding ray resumes its focus on earth. In earlier periods of human history and prehistory, those non-incarnating cycles lasted much longer, as did the periods of incarnation. Longer periods within which to incarnate led to easier lifetimes and much less stress through less change in civilization, but civilization grew at a correspondingly slower rate. During these earlier times, almost all of the growth of civilization was the result of the contributions of the more advanced souls, and particularly of spiritual disciples who incarnated not based upon their souls' rays being in focus at the time, but upon the planet's needs for the ways in which these souls could serve.

The souls of more advanced humans incarnate much more frequently, *on average*, than do the souls of humans who are less advanced. However, when a less advanced soul's ray is in planetary focus, it may incarnate new human beings *more* often than do some of the more advanced of the human souls—but not the most advanced. The reason is that these less advanced souls are provided the assistance of the ray focus, in developing their higher spiritual sense from the focus of the planetary rays, although the *amount* of group virtue they will create is significantly less than that of a more advanced human soul. On average, over time, the more advanced souls live more and derive more meaning from their lives because they commonly incarnate when their soul rays are not in planetary focus. Doing so enables the creation of much more (group) virtue and the creation of virtue much more often—in conjunction with a wider diversity of other souls who have different rays.

At present, a *significantly* less advanced soul might incarnate about every one hundred dense physical earth years during the time that its ray is in planetary focus. With the following averages measured according to dense physical time, within the hundred years of an incarnation will be about sixty years of dense physical life, about thirty years of astral life, and about ten years of mental life. Incarnated humans of significantly less advanced souls usually live either in the less developed countries or in depressed areas of the more developed countries of the world. Once a less advanced human soul's ray goes out of planetary focus, it is likely that that soul will not incarnate at all during the hundreds to over one thousand years that its ray remains out of focus. Each human Monad is connected to its OverSoul (Solar Angel) and to all other Monads at and above its level; it is the plan set forth by the Monad that determines the ray of its human soul. The ray of the human soul is determined by the Monad focusing and joining together certain higher mental energies to construct the inner sacrifice petals (this is also regulated by certain factors of probability). These energies come from the development of what were the most advanced animal group souls on the existing planet, joined with the advanced spirit and energies with a Solar Angel from another planet (see Chapter Six for more information). The outer causal petals were originally contained within the OverSoul's lowest body, which it sacrifices to create the new life of the human soul. There will be slightly more time between physical incarnations of an advanced human soul than between the physical incarnations of a relatively undeveloped human soul. The former incarnates largely based upon the virtue its more advanced human being can create, while the latter's incarnations are less advanced and incarnate only when that soul ray is in focus. The reason for the additional time is that the more advanced human soul will have longer astral and mental plane life between physical incarnations. However, the more advanced human soul will have many more incarnations overall because it will sometimes incarnate when its ray is out of planetary focus, whereas a less developed soul will not. These more advanced souls often have incarnated humans who are approaching "the Path" of choosing to spiritually discipline themselves, but have not yet begun to do so. The additional thirty or more years of dense physical time between each physical lifetime that each of these more advanced humans spend on the astral and then the mental planes could add over one thousand years of inner plane time to each one's inner plane life. At present, some of these people live for a combined total of (measured in dense physical time) more than seventy years on the astral and mental planes between physical incarnations.

Example Periods of Time Between Incarnations

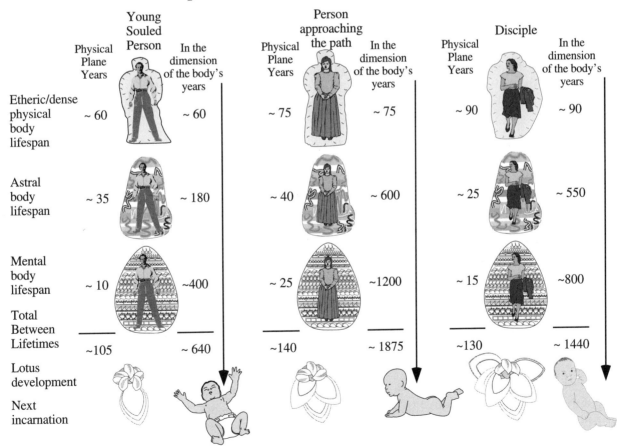

Illustration 11.2

Those people who practice spiritual discipline have increasingly frequent physical incarnations as the discipline increases from each lower body to a higher one. Their soul ray types are of much less importance in determining the timing of their incarnations. This is because the focus of their lives is the needed service that they can provide as created virtue, mostly as it applies to a group—usually of people, but sometimes of life in the lower kingdoms. For these spiritual disciples, less *overall* individual karma exists in comparison to group karma. However, since karma is accelerated through increased response that results from sense improvement in the bodies (and the soul's body along with each personality), more individual karma might exist at any one time for a spiritual disciple—especially during all four stages of the earlier initiation processes (the first two initiations, or the lower-level ones). Also, during the earlier stages of any level of initiation, greater amounts of personal, or individual, karma are dealt with—at an accelerated rate. A spiritually disciplined person might today have a physical life that exceeds ninety years; however, it is important to note that the simple measure of a person's lifespan is not an indicator of whether he or she has practiced physical discipline. Also, some people who have spiritually disciplined themselves die at a relatively young age in order that they can be reborn at a later time when they can more effectively serve. Another important point is that people have increasingly shorter astral and mental lives as their spiritual discipline of these bodies becomes more successful; this enables them to enter the next physical incarnation sooner. During the next incarnation they can create relatively more virtue because they are then living at a greater level by living more simultaneously through more bodies and senses at once.

In addition to the periodic incarnation of human souls on earth who are at various levels of development, there may be some incarnated human souls who are at least equal in their development to the more advanced class of humans souls, and who each, for the first time on earth, becomes re-created from its Monad and a new human Solar Angel. Some of these "new" human souls existed before on other planets that were either ahead of earth in their development (and these souls failed on that planet), or were less developed, such as Mars (having excelled there); Mars will soon enter the etheric/dense physical stage of its fourth round of life development, wherein its focus will be on human physical life. During its third round Mars did develop some advanced human life, although in only relatively small numbers because human life was not the focus of development on Mars at that time. Also, these people were the ones who had advanced themselves out of the animal kingdom in a method of development that earth never reached in its third round. Many of the advanced Mars souls came from Mars's preceding planet of incarnation and moved to earth rather than waiting for the Mars' fourth round. The preceding incarnation of Mars was a planet that developed only to the etheric level—as its most dense period of life development. On that planet, life grew more quickly and with less difficulty because of the lower density of energy and the increased time dilation. In that planet's fourth round, some humans excelled and may be able to incarnate, earlier, on earth's fourth dense physical round—instead of waiting for Mars to reach this point. Some of these souls came to earth in order to move ahead in their development. Other souls who came here might have been near the level of advanced souls on earth, on the planet that they were on, but sought development within a planetary life plan that has a third ray focus. Still others of these new souls come from earth's earlier incarnation of a planet—which ultimately failed. However, there are very few members left in this last group because most have already incarnated in earth's past, when bodies that were developed enough became available for them to do so. The timing is based upon the souls from the failed planet being able to incarnate into bodies on the new planet that match these souls' levels of development. Souls that are more developed incarnate into bodies that are more developed. Almost all of the souls from the earlier planet of earth's past incarnation have already incarnated into bodies that matched their levels of development. Although the last planet failed in its fourth major human race during the fifth round, earth has accelerated the growth in its fourth *dense physical* round (through increased suffering) to such an extent that earth's current fifth major human race of the fourth round is at about parity with the last planet's fourth major human race of the fifth round. When souls newly incarnate on a different planet following their prior existence as a soul, they are "adopted" by a potential human Monad who has not yet created a human soul on that planet. This group of Monads exists on the second monadic sub-plane as a part of the entire monadic group that is awaiting the correct developmental time in which to create life on the planet. Notice that Monads on the monadic plane—that have not ascended to the logoic—generally do not change planets like souls and Solar Angels can because each Monad usually becomes part of the planetary karma of the planet it is originally focused on by its creator—the Solar Logos. (Often Monads all leave a planet together at the end of a planetary chain.) Also, Monads live as one in thought. Souls from earth's prior incarnation still each have (and have each remained connected to) a Monad, and the Monads of those who have not yet incarnated are on the second monadic sub-plane.

There are just a few souls who temporarily go to a planet (earth, for example) in order to contribute to the consciousness of a large group or nation, in ways that the humans there are incapable of creating more understanding. These visiting souls, who might return to the planets they came from, are planetary Avatars. Cosmic Avatars are even rarer, and they contribute to the entire planet new and needed consciousness that no members of the existing humanity could, at that time, create. Cosmic Avatars cannot return to their respective star systems because they would have fallen too far behind in their service there to ever be able to catch up. As a great sacrifice, these Avatars give up what is usually a much more advanced life in order to come to a planet, such as earth. Once arrived, they typically must begin their development all over again at a much accelerated pace (starting at the level of humanity at the time of their arrival), but often along a new ray focus in order to fulfill the needs of that planet. These cosmic Avatars may have been Masters or were at least the equivalent of advanced initiates on the planets in the different star systems from which they came (relative to the level of humanity on the new planet when they arrive there). However, a cosmic Avatar usually begins life on his or her new planet with a "virgin" Monad who needs to begin life at the level of humanity's development at that time. Sometimes the spirit of a cosmic Avatar will be ensouled by a Monad and Solar Angel who lost their last incarnating human to evil (then the previously existing soul of that Solar Angel and Monad will be ensouled by a younger, less advanced, new Solar Angel and Monad). These advanced souls must begin life on the new planet at this greatly reduced level of development, and they often suffer throughout many of their human lifetimes. As a benefit, though, the end of a cosmic Avatar's human soul life does become quite accelerated because these souls redevelop themselves overall at a much increased rate. They are able to so because they retain the advanced spirit of a Master or an advanced initiate from another solar system. However, each cosmic Avatar's spirit is joined with both the energy from earth and from another planet, for his or her inner sacrifice petals, or soul *body*. It is not unusual for these fused human and souls, as they enter the next kingdom, to move through the initiations at a rate ten times that of other Masters. The principle is that the greater the sacrifice, the greater the growth of new life. Despite their earlier increased suffering at times, while they are alive—especially physically—Avatars create enormous meaning in their (and others') lives that more than compensates for their levels of sacrifice.

To a physically alive human who is unaware of esoteric issues, it might appear from what is written above that at the present time there could be about forty to fifty years between the lifetimes of a much less advanced soul whose soul ray is in planetary focus. However, with the exception of a few weeks (on average, measured in physical time) of higher mental life that is spent as a less developed soul, a less advanced human remains alive during his or her entire incarnation, if the time spent between physical incarnations in inner-plane, subtle life is included. Each cycle of incarnation begins after the relatively brief soul life on the higher mental plane. Those humans who have advanced souls but who have not yet begun to discipline themselves usually have the lengthiest incarnations when life in the subtle worlds is taken into consideration. Note, however, that the length of an incarnation and of the life on each plane is not a completely accurate indicator of the amount of spiritual creation during that duration of life.

There are two goals of human reincarnation; the first is to perfect the three lowest bodies of a human and advance him or her into the next kingdom, while he or she helps to grow all of human and lower levels of life by incorporating the lower life more perfectly within his or her civilization. The second goal of human reincarnation is to shift evolution of life, which occurs through force, into spiritually created life, which occurs through enlightenment. Those who believe that reincarnation is superfluous are most likely failing to understand these goals of the Planetary Logos, and of God, in creating their growth, through the growth of life. It is likely to be obvious to those who understand this book that nearly all humans (with the very few exceptions of adept arhats in their final creations of human virtue) are far from perfect in the use of any of their three bodies to create virtue.

The reader is encouraged to consider the logic of what follows in this paragraph, which is a thought process that many people share. There are those who believe that they will rejoin God after death, to live forever in a heaven. The reason would be that these people have earned that right by living in the physical world for one lifetime and having created, on average, a few minutes to perhaps one-half hour (total) of virtue each day that they lived. Also, these people believe that God, through his grace and love, will absolve people of their past misdeeds, provided that those people believe in God by having only certain religious beliefs and practice only certain religious rituals. The further belief for some people is that God will punish for eternity those who, in the one and only physical life that they will live, failed either to hold certain religious beliefs or to practice the associated rituals, and chose to instead create for themselves a life that goes specifically against certain religious tenets. If a human behaved in the way that so many people attribute to God, that person would be widely considered to be arrogant, self-centered, arbitrary, dictatorial, punitive, and prejudiced. Could it be that those who created the concept of (and possibly even those who believe in) this kind of God might share some of these qualities?

If the above-outlined belief system is true, what, then, is the meaning of life? Under this system, does life not become severely lacking in meaning for those humans who are more advanced in their development and who adopt these beliefs? It is interesting to note that most major religions included reincarnation in their *original* constructs only to have it later removed, usually for selfish reasons, by the leaders of those religions when they realized that the concept of reincarnation replaced their power and authority with God's. Reincarnation frees humans to understand God and to, eventually, become a functional part of their Creator through real and reasonable Self- and self creation, and creation of virtue in others. The removal of reincarnation from a religion leaves a hollowness in that religion and in the lives of those practicing it. Also, at this point it needs to be reaffirmed that, with the exception of some very evil people, humans always remain human and do not transmigrate to lower kingdom lifeforms from one incarnation to another. Understanding reincarnation is a critical part of understanding life's hidden meaning. To better facilitate that understanding, this chapter will cover some of the fictitious incarnated lifetimes of a human soul that is fairly advanced and that had created six hundred eighty prior human lifetimes mostly on earth, with some of the earliest lifetimes on earth's earlier planetary incarnation.

 ## AN EXAMPLE OF REINCARNATION

Our fictitious person's name will be Sally. She is in the process of being created by her soul and OverSoul (Solar Angel). These two together are focusing their collective creative thoughts through their shared Self. They are aware of the virtue that was added into her permanent atoms from her last lifetime as a human. They have this awareness because they have direct access to her mental permanent atom through their shared Self, which surrounds the enlightened parts of the atom. Through the whole akasha (the past, exaggerated, part of time) the effects of the selfishness that she has created in former lives is recorded within the remaining (unenlightened) space of her mental permanent atom. Until this permanent atom becomes fully enlightened, the past part of time remains separated and exaggerated, with the space in it created by the lack of light. The light within Sally's permanent atoms is imperfectly distributed, which leaves numerous dark areas that represent future effects of the selfish causes that she created in her prior lifetimes' activities on the three lower planes of existence.

Two incarnated lifetimes ago, in 1812, an earlier incarnation of Sally's soul was a twenty year old male who fought for the U.S. in the War of 1812 between the U.S. and Great Britain. That person's name was Joseph. Joseph was a brave and intelligent fighter and attained the field rank of lieutenant second class, while many officers were being slain by the overwhelming forces of the better-prepared British. Joseph was born in South Carolina in 1792 into a family who owned a relatively small tobacco plantation, and who were slave owners. He supported slavery and among his peers was about average in his level of bigotry. In the 1830's Joseph became interested in the development of the railroad and became an early employee of a new railroad company.

Joseph's rays were 3 (soul ray), 3 (personality ray), 1 (mental ray), 6 (astral ray), and 7 (etheric/dense physical ray). He was an advanced human for his time—educated and intelligent—but relatively undisciplined despite his years of military service. His lack of discipline came from his egotism and glamours having joined together to create a personality who saw himself as superior as compared to most other people. He tended to be bigoted, and believed that many entire races and other groups of humans were, simply through their group identity, inferior to his Caucasian race and especially inferior to himself. Joseph lacked compassion because his love was connected to bigotry and prejudice. He liked to control and manipulate others, especially those whom he believed to be inferior to himself, because doing so relieved some of his fears of death; the personality masked these fears that were created by his selfishness, by (wrongly and mistakenly) over-controlling. Joseph eventually was placed in charge of procuring large work crews for the railroad. He helped to create the Chinese labor force for the railroad in the late 1840's and the 1850's by developing a system of recruitment that sometimes reached all the way to China. His system later became greatly expanded in the 1860's and 1870's as others exploited this workforce. By the late 1840's Joseph was responsible for the operations of the first railroads in the western U.S., which gave him access to the shipping that was used to bring Chinese workers into the western United States. Part of his system was to pay workers an amount that was based upon their race, and he began this system in the Eastern U.S. even before he implemented his Chinese labor plan.

Joseph lived a long physical life for his time period; he was killed in South Carolina in 1864 during the American Civil War while defending, as a civilian, his besieged family plantation. He had been sympathetic to the Confederacy, even though he had lived most of his life connected to Northern business, and spent the last nearly 20 years in the West. Even though he never joined the Confederate army, his return home, to the South, was a long trip to meet his destiny of dying for much of what he had created in his life.

Subsequent to Joseph, Sally's soul's next former incarnation began on the dense physical plane in 1912. Again born a male, this incarnation lived in a rugged province of northwestern China. The people in this area were farmers who were continually repressed by the imperial government. What happened was that their farms were owned by landlords who, along with each farm's overseer, dealt with these farmers as serfs who "sharecropped," and paid the taxes for the owners through their toils. This person's given name was Chia-Ho, and his family sharecropped for one of the more successful and more bigoted landowners. Chia-Ho grew up without formal education, but he so resented the way his family and neighbors were treated that he ran off at age thirteen. He traveled to the eastern part of China, where he worked in that country's emerging arms industry. He learned to read, and became self-taught in history, politics, and economics. Soon afterwards, he adopted the Marxist-Lenin view of Communism.

Chia-Ho's rays were 3 (soul), 3 (personality), 2 (mind), 6 (astral), and 3 (etheric/dense physical). His soul was attempting to develop within him more empathy than he had had in his last life for those who were different from him. His soul placed him into a lifestyle that was significantly less advantageous than was his last, and that karmically gave him the opportunity to experience prejudice and bigotry that was directed against him—and his family. As a Chinese, he experienced firsthand what the Chinese race is like while being directly able to improve it, if he so chose.

In Chia-Ho's previous life (as Joseph) he had negatively affected, at a national level, the welfare of the Chinese people—particularly those who were disadvantaged and who were farmers, like his family in his current life. Many of those whom he had so affected in his last life had come to the U.S. in hope of more work that was more productive and a better life, although only some of those had a choice in the matter. In his life as Chia-Ho, he was given the opportunity to attempt to reverse these effects. A person generally continues to incarnate into the same country wherein he or she lived the most and died. However, if that person's life had a significant negative effect on the people of another country, then he or she could be reincarnated into that country. This would happen to a person to provide him or her with the opportunity to both develop empathy and create more love while enduring the effects of the harm that he or she had previously caused, in order to—it is hoped—reverse that harm. Chia-Ho's mother was the reincarnation of a male Chinese worker who had been killed in an explosion during the early 1850's, while using nitroglycerine to clear a path for the railway. It had been Joseph's policy that all dangerous work be done by non-Caucasian workers. He instituted this policy because, as he stated, the death of these people did not discourage Caucasian enlistment, and it was easy to replace them. As a result, many foreign-born non-Caucasian people died while building the railways. Sometimes simply being a new immigrant played a stronger part than did race, in people being subjected to the same prejudice—and dangers. Chia-Ho's father was the *younger* brother to the person his mother had been in her last life; these two brothers died together in the same explosion. Although they were both reborn on the same calendar day of the year (because they died on the same day), the younger brother was reincarnated two years after his older brother was. This occurred because of differences in their inner plane lives and the different levels of selfishness they exhibited in both their physical and inner plane lives. Prior to the explosion that killed these two brothers, Joseph had traveled to the work site in order to hasten the progress of the workers; he decided on the use of nitroglycerine to clear a path, instead of using the (relatively) much safer but less effective black powder. It was Joseph himself who selected the two brothers for the task, and helped to instruct them in their deadly mission. The practice of coercing employees into agreeing to do dangerous work by threatening to fire them if they did not, and paying them double for that work became policy within Joseph's company. This policy eventually was put into place within many other companies—even with the later, relatively safer use of dynamite.

As a young adult, Chia-Ho rose through the ranks of the Red Army, fighting both Imperial oppression and Japanese aggression. He was against the "Democratic" army of Chiang Kai-shek because he knew that this political group supported the continued land ownership that had created the conditions of serfdom that he and his family had been forced to endure. This group's method of land reform was to make the serf sharecroppers more equal, rather than give them ownership of the land. Chia-Ho believed that each sharecropper should be given his own land that he and his neighbors would collectively help to grow the maximum number of crops on. Each farmer would then give a part of his crop to help those whose crops had failed or were insufficient to feed a family, as well as to pay taxes to the state. Thus each family either grew enough food or received enough supplement to always feed themselves; those who grew more than they needed gave some or sometimes all of the extra to those in need. Such a system could be an economy based upon need rather than greed, as Marx and Engels proposed and Lenin was, at least in theory, implementing in the Soviet Union. This system made sense to Chia-Ho because it encouraged cooperation and sharing—the etheric/dense physical virtue, which his soul wanted him to create more of. Souls do not promote economic systems, just the creation of virtue; there are many economic systems that can be applied either virtuously or selfishly. Chia-Ho's application of an economic system was more virtuous than selfish, but still was fraught with selfish contradictions.

Chia-Ho was made responsible for redistributing the land of the district in northwestern China where he had previously lived, when the Communist forces gained control over it. He created and executed a policy of *not* killing those who had been landowners and overseers, provided that they adopted Communism. They also had to agree to always share their crops when their harvest was needed by others and to give up for common use any possessions that were capital rather than personal in nature, e.g., barns, storage facilities, and farm machinery (what little there was). Although some of the former bosses who had homes that were more modest were allowed to keep them, those whose homes were ostentatious were forced to surrender them, to be shared. Chia-Ho's methods were more reasonable, somewhat compassionate, and politically wise; even the landowner of his family's own farm was spared. This required significant astral discipline on Chia-Ho's part, to not give in to his anger towards this person who had for so long a time mistreated his family, his neighbors, and him.

Unfortunately, Chia-Ho's methods did not become adopted on a widespread basis, and many landowners were eventually tortured and killed. By the time Chia-Ho had reached the rank of colonel in Mao Tse-tung's army, most of the rural parts of China were under Communist control, and the country was about to become completely Communistic. Chia-Ho was still arguing for leniency and compassion in dealing with those who had abused their power when they had been wealthy, but who were being cooperative within the new system; he believed that he and Mao were of the same mind on this matter. As China moved closer to becoming directly involved in the Korean conflict with the United Nations and especially with the U.S., Chia-Ho became concerned about Mao changing his stance and moving more towards the Soviet—Stalinist—position of absolute control and complete collectivization. After 1951, some of the farms that Chia-Ho had worked so hard to develop under his new system were collectivized, or removed from any individual family control. Suddenly what each of the families on these farms received was not based, first, upon their own labors, and all of the families had to live as one. Only a few farms were initially changed, but Chia-Ho realized that within a few years all of them might be controlled in this way by the State. His concern was that now the State was fulfilling the role of the landlords who had been done away with, and that as the new landlord, the State might be even worse than the old landlords had been. Chia-Ho was told that his views were a part of capitalism (he was more of a utopian socialist, in reality), and that he needed retraining in his thinking. It was explained to him that true communism allowed for *no* real individual ownership of property, and that individual enterprise was an evil. He was further told that the methods that he had been *allowed* to use (in the system he had developed), were just an interim change to allow the people to become better educated in Communism.

Chia-Ho was becoming disillusioned, but remained loyal to Mao. Chia-Ho died in 1952 while helping to direct a Korean unit along with his Chinese soldiers, while fighting on the Korean peninsula. Much of his prior negative karma had been lived out, and some had been reversed through the virtue that he created. Chia-Ho died a hero, as one of the highest ranking officers (a colonel) to die in battle while leading a difficult unit (of less disciplined Korean fighters) alongside his Chinese regulars.

Before moving ahead to describe the reincarnation who will be Sally, her past incarnations as Joseph and Chia-Ho will be further examined. Joseph's life was an attempt to move him closer to the path of spiritual discipline, rather than just to create more virtue. The reason was that his soul was well-developed and his permanent atoms contained more light than darkness, or than space. In prior lives, his fears of death overwhelmed him, and he had failed at both bravery and leadership on the dense physical level. Having a third ray soul meant that, eventually, once he became spiritually disciplined and began to fuse with and function as his soul, he would develop parts of the lower kingdoms and his own together in ways that created more virtue in civilization. Thus he would, eventually, develop human civilization more virtuously than it had been developed in the past. His third ray personality was involved in a similar activity, but for selfish motivation and outcome. What happens is that the rays (other than that of the soul) in selfish people guide them to initially act on their selfishness—until their senses diminish and they move closer to facing death. This process often leads selfish people to accept more soul and Solar Angel contact. Joseph was vocationally encouraged by his third ray personality towards military and industrial development; these are both strongly third ray *human* endeavors when this ray is in planetary focus as it was before, during, and after Joseph's lifetime (which spanned from 1792 until 1864). His first ray mind was creative, but did not grow as quickly in mental sense while he was mentally selfish (egotistical), because the first ray was not in focus during his lifetime. As a fairly quick karmic response to his egotism, his mental creativity grew only slowly while he was relatively selfish, which had an effect of lessening the meaning that he derived from living. The first and fifth rays tend to be the easiest rays with which to develop a mental sense, *if* in planetary focus. Because the fifth ray has been in planetary focus for so long, it has today become the dominant mental ray in advanced countries, where more people have a mental body along the fifth ray than along the first ray. Joseph's sixth ray astral body caused him to love in a limited and devoted way, which included the ways in which he related to God through his religion. When emotional, or selfish, which included his kama-manasic bigotry, he would limit his emotions to the projection of anger, hatred, and control onto specific people or groups, or both. (See Chapters Seven and Eight for an explanation of kama-manas.) Each desire that was fixed in him (each glamour) was focused on to be met, one at a time. This one-at-a-time focus somewhat protected his astral body from his selfishness by tending to isolate his glamours rather than having them join together (which glamours are inclined to do) and create much greater amounts of anxiety and uncontrolled emotions. Joseph's soul and OverSoul gave him a sixth ray astral body so that it would be very long-lived and would resist disease while he was being mostly selfish. They knew from their prior incarnations that there would be a high likelihood of Joseph being very emotional and selfish—as well as kama-manasically connected. Joseph was given a seventh ray etheric/dense physical body in order to lengthen his physical life while he failed, mostly, to cooperate and share. The seventh ray etheric/dense physical body type lives longer, in general, than do the etheric/dense physical bodies along the other six rays because the seventh ray in the etheric/dense physical body corresponds to the ray of the plane the body is on. Instead of virtuously using his etheric/dense physical senses to create intelligent coordinated responses, Joseph mostly created responses that retained prodigious amounts of energy within both his etheric/dense physical body and his surroundings. This retained energy in his surroundings (this material greed) included money—which is compressed and stored time and *energy*. Having a seventh ray etheric/dense physical body influenced Joseph to economize virtuously—for the benefit of others—when he did not use this body selfishly.

It was the soul and OverSoul's plan to have Joseph create more of the human virtues of bravery and enlightened leadership. The creation of these virtues would move him much closer to being able to create the cosmic virtues of love and truth—though possibly not until a later lifetime. Bravery (and heroism, even more so) can overcome the emotion of fear, and the less fear the personality has, the less it over-controls. Leadership that is intelligent in activity, and is therefore enlightening, develops more truth mentally because wisdom is a requisite for the creation of such leadership. Intelligent leadership in modern times also develops some love, and thus creates love/wisdom. Joseph was given a decidedly more masculine than feminine collection of rays, which somewhat encouraged within him the development of both of these human virtues, of bravery and enlightened leadership. Unfortunately, having more masculine rays than feminine ones also encouraged egotism within Joseph and made it easier for him to become bigoted and remain that way. The second element of the soul and OverSoul's plan, to move Joseph closer to the spiritual path, was lost in that life because of his egotism and bigotry. Even worse, because of his close proximity to "the Path" and his intellectual advancement, Joseph's senses were better developed overall than were an average person's. This meant that Joseph had a greater ability to respond intelligently to his surroundings and circumstances. When he failed to do so, and was egotistical and bigoted, he was more responsible (karmically) for his actions that were based on these selfish traits. Joseph somewhat affected the karma of another nation—China—by participating in darkly trading its people. In addition, he invented a practice of payment and work activities that was based upon prejudice and that adversely affected many Chinese who worked for the railroad and other industries. It should be noted that not all U.S. railroads and other employers in the nineteenth century paid their workers amounts that were based upon bigotry; some used a system of equal pay for equal work—but these were much in the minority. In many governmental public works projects, up to the Second World War, a bigoted pay schedule was employed in the U.S., and many other "advanced" countries, as well. In addition, although Joseph is a fictitious person, he may be representative of a number of real people who lived similar lives.

Had Joseph initiated equal pay for equal work and other egalitarian practices, he would have started on the spiritual path. However, for him to do so would have required that he discipline his astral and mental bodies by limiting his emotions and egotistical thoughts regarding other races and people who, in general, were different from himself. So even though Joseph did create some virtue in his lifetime, he remained too selfish to limit, or discipline, himself spiritually; he failed to bring himself closer to God's thought, or to become more spiritual.

Chia-Ho's incarnation was, again, an attempt to create even more virtue and to enter the path of spiritual discipline. Joseph's rays had been 3, 3, 1, 6, 7; when his soul incarnated as Chia-Ho, they were changed to 3, 3, 2, 6, 3. Chia-Ho's soul and OverSoul decided that in this incarnation they would give him a second ray mind. This accomplished two conditions at once: the first condition was greater balance in feminine versus masculine qualities of consciousness in all of his bodies and his personality as compared to Joseph, his predecessor. The second condition was greater inclusiveness because a second ray mental body is more inclusive than is one along the first ray, and when egotistical and glamoured (kama-manasic), the second ray mental body is likely to withhold love rather than to directly express anger and hatred. This second condition would tend to counter bigotry in the connected astral body and loosen the kama-manasic connection. Also, the second ray is in planetary focus, and while a second ray mental body is much less creative than a first ray mental body is, a ray that is in focus will, for a longer time, maintain the senses of a selfishly used body. This system provides some people with more time to overcome their egotism before their mental bodies become senseless. Over time, there is a decline in the relatively small amount of mental senses that are used by people who are physically alive and mentally selfish. This decline makes it increasingly difficult for such people to learn mentally and to create new mental knowledge. Another important trait of the second ray mental body is that it will teach itself how to better sense when formal education is lacking. This made a second ray mental body a particularly good choice for Chia-Ho's beginning life circumstances in rural China.

Joseph had a seventh ray etheric/dense physical body; Chia-Ho's etheric/dense physical body was along the third ray—*within a different race*. These changes caused Chia-Ho's etheric/dense physical body to manifest physical activity, especially along the personality ray of the Chinese nation as a whole (also the third ray). It did this while expressing the more fourth sub-sub-race quality in activity of the Oriental sub-sub-race. The Oriental race today is actually the fourth sub-sub-race of the fifth sub-race of the five major races. It grew out of the third sub-sub-race of Mongolians having been affected by a seed group of the fourth sub-race of the fifth major race. Because Chia-Ho had a third ray etheric/dense physical body, his karma would in some ways be more likely to match the (negative) national karma of China; a country's negative karma is the result of the collective personal selfishness by its people. Its positive karma is created along its soul ray. For example, the U.S. has a sixth ray personality, and so its negative karma is focused along the sixth ray, while its positive karma and soul ray are focused along the second ray. Chia-Ho was given this etheric/dense physical ray type because he would create more etheric/dense physical virtue than either astral or mental. The reason is that etheric/dense physical virtue is the easiest to create by those who are etheric/dense physically alive and are approaching the spiritual path for the first time. China, *as a country*, has a third ray personality. This national ray is meant to limit and eventually reverse the personal selfishness of its people as a nation by eventually creating a virtuous civilization. The third ray builds civilization and the military very quickly when it is in planetary focus and is chosen to be acted upon within a national context; it had been in focus on earth for over six hundred years prior to Chia-Ho's lifetime.

Although in selfish people a seventh ray etheric/dense physical body lives longer than a third ray etheric/dense physical body does in general, the third ray in the etheric/dense physical body is second to the seventh in its longevity because it is the quickest to build (and also repair) the senses; the seventh ray builds the senses much more slowly, but it maintains them with the least relative degradation, for the longest period of time. Chia-Ho died because of his heroism, which was a virtuous creation in his humanity. The timing of his relatively early death was tied to his successful completion of the second part of his soul and OverSoul's mission. He had introduced a cosmically virtuous process into Communist China regarding two concepts. The first concerned treatment of those who were different and were disliked (the landowners); the process fostered love, tolerance, and truth. The second concerned a system of fair distribution and use of material resources that promoted an economy based upon cooperation and sharing. This is the etheric/dense physical virtue. Chia-Ho had reversed some of his previous karma against the Chinese nation, while he created positive national karma as a first level initiate; he took (but did not complete) the first initiation by spiritually disciplining himself to achieve the above-mentioned results. For the first time in this soul's history, one of its human incarnations had entered onto the spiritual path—indeed, a great accomplishment.

We return now to Sally's incarnation. Sally's soul and OverSoul (Solar Angel), through their shared Self, consult with the group of souls and OverSouls who will have human incarnations beginning around the same time and whose incarnating human beings will be likely to have significant contact with Sally during her lifetime. In these consultations, only probabilities—and not certainties—can be relied upon because all of these humans have free will, or freedom to create their own collections of related choices. It is correct, however, to state that the original choices of a person's rays, the geographic location into which he or she incarnates, her or his family, and the date and time of his or her birth and the associated astrological implications are all predetermined. These initial choices do not interfere with freedom of *will*, since will is a creative process of joining these choices with many other choices, using the human's own thought. Will is a *series* of choices that are creatively related by the person exercising her or his own thought. Our fictitious person Sally has been given the following rays: 3 (personality), 7 (mental), 6 (astral), 4 (etheric/dense physical), and her soul ray remains constant along the third ray. Thus her rays are *3, 3, 7, 6, 4*.

Sally's soul's last incarnation, as Chia-Ho, created enough virtue to overcome some of his negative individual karma. Chia-Ho *also* created enough positive group, or soul, karma to begin to open the first inner sacrifice petal that surrounds his soul. He took, or began, the first spiritual initiation towards becoming a member of the next, or the spiritual, kingdom. This first inner sacrifice petal opened because one or more of the solar devas of the outer petals of Chia-Ho's causal body had begun to radiate light. The radiance was the result of Chia-Ho having used the pitri or pitris to create concepts within his spiritual mind that were then used in service. In Chia-Ho's case, these radiances came from one or more solar pitris on the third tier of petals. The third-tier petals correspond to virtue created in service *for* groups of other souls etheric/dense physically, or creating more cooperation and sharing. Chia-Ho also had created the individual virtues of more love and greater truth, but on a personal level. However, he did not create more love *with* others as souls; if he had done so, he would have been functioning as a second level initiate, creating radiance from the solar pitris on the second tier of petals in the causal body, as well as beginning the opening of the second inner sacrifice petal while further increasing the radiance of the first one. Chia-Ho did create some intelligent activities and cooperation and sharing *with* some others as souls. This indicated his functionality as a first level initiate. It is likely that at some point in the future, Chia-Ho's soul will incarnate another human who will create enough virtue from one or more of the first tier solar pitris in his or her causal body to cause it (or them) to radiate. This radiance will cause the last, or third, inner sacrifice petal to begin to open. It will cause further radiance from the first and second inner petals and will cause the three to begin to spin, fixing his or her gender for all future lifetimes. This future person will at that point be a functional third level initiate. This initiate will create *mental* virtue *with other souls* by all of them collectively thinking together in love/wisdom and helping to create more truth in the minds of others. (See Chapter Six for more thorough explanation of this process.)

In examining the strategy employed by Sally's soul and OverSoul in giving her the ray bodies as listed above, it becomes evident that more is expected of her in creating virtue with her own and other souls than was expected of Chia-Ho or Joseph. What follows is an explanation: Sally's personality is focused along the third ray (as was the case with her soul's last two incarnations), because it is expected that she will still be physically alive when the third ray becomes no longer focused on earth, about the year 2025. This gives Sally the opportunity to grow up while the third ray is in planetary focus, and then for one of two things to happen when the third ray is replaced with the fourth. If Sally had chosen to live selfishly prior to the change in rays, then this change will create a great crisis for her because her third ray personality will no longer be supported by the increased growth from the third ray's focus. If, alternatively, she had chosen to live virtuously prior to this point, then the change in rays will cause her personality to *increase* its fusion with its soul. Sally's soul and personality are both along the third ray focus, which facilitates fusion between the two. This "carrot and stick" method of human development, with selfishness leading to crisis, and then creation of virtue leading to soul infusion and joy, is frequently utilized. Sally's life focus will, like Joseph's and Chia-Ho's, be in the direction of developing more of civilization. This will be done either selfishly, if following her personality ray, or virtuously, if from her soul ray focus. However, if Sally has been mostly selfish until the year 2025, her personality will diminish in its ability to sense her self, and in its ability to control the collection of senses in each of her three lower bodies. This crisis will *force* her to change to be more virtuous, or she will face even further suffering and pain.

For this life, Sally's mental ray has been changed to a seventh ray focus, which means that when she is less than perfectly virtuous, her mental senses function best by sensing other people's mental thought through organizing it with other thought and synthesizing it with her own. Also, she will tend to economize the amount of thought that she needs to use in order to be functioning mentally accurately in any particular circumstance. When overly selfish, this economizing can lead to avoiding ways of thinking. This then could create mental laziness, depending upon how egotistical she might be at the moment. There is a significant change in Sally's mental ray focus from her soul's previous incarnation of Chia-Ho, whose mental body was focused along the second ray. When she is selfish, Sally will be less mentally inclusive than Chia-Ho was. This will cause her to have much more conflict in her life if she remains egotistical in a given situation. Her soul and OverSoul are seeking to create a swifter and greater degree of difficulty for Sally when she thinks mentally egotistically. They do so because they believe that she is more capable of creating truth than any of her prior incarnations ever were before—now that she continues in the first initiation. Her partially opened inner sacrifice petal reinforces the third ray in her personality, and, sympathetically, her seventh ray mental body. This occurs because the sub-ray of the first inner sacrifice petal is the third ray. The second inner sacrifice petal's sub-ray is the second ray, and the third inner sacrifice petal—the last to open— has a first sub-ray. The third ray and dimension are highly sympathetic in vibration and phase to the seventh ray and the etheric/dense physical dimension because they are reversals of each other in their ratios of spirit to energy.

To briefly explain the preceding concept, the spiritual plane has one part of energy's thought to five parts of spirit's thought; the etheric/dense physical plane has five parts energy's thought to one part spirit (spirit's thought). The corresponding angles are as follows: On the spiritual plane there is 150° of spirit's phase change of consciousness to 30° of energy's. This is the reverse of the angles of each of the two spheres on the etheric/dense physical plane. On the etheric/dense physical plane these angles reverse to the energy sphere having a 150° angle to God's thought. This creates five times the amount of collective thought of energy as compared to the spirit sphere having only a 30° angle and one-fifth the amount of phase shift of spirit's consciousness on the spiritual plane.

The correspondence between Sally's seventh ray mental body and her third ray personality increases her challenges while she lives, and if she successfully meets those challenges, provides her with more opportunities in which she can choose to create virtue. Her astral body remains the same as in her soul's last incarnation, with a sixth ray focus. This will allow her to maintain more of her sense of empathy while she is emotionally selfish in her life than would having any other astral body ray type. Although the sixth ray is not and will not be in planetary focus during Sally's lifetime, an astral body that is along the sixth ray is still the most stable one because the sixth ray corresponds to the astral plane; also, among the three bodies that a human uses, only the astral has been unified to the level of joining its senses of form. These two factors will cause Sally's astral body to become relatively quite stable even when used selfishly for fairly long periods of time. Sally's glamours will also be kept more separate by having a sixth ray astral body, as was explained in the description of her soul's prior incarnation as Joseph. The combination of this factor with the other two reduces the effect of the kama-manasic connection and of Sally thinking first emotionally rather than mentally. Mental thought that follows emotional thought is nearly always untruthful and deceptive. The reason is that mental thought of this nature rationalizes the preliminary selfish emotional thought, or creative imagination that is focused on one's self.

Perhaps the most interesting change in Sally's rays from those of her soul's prior incarnations is her etheric/dense physical ray. The senses of a fourth ray etheric/dense physical body, especially in a female (with which there is a more sympathetic response to the fourth ray) are used to determine the levels of informing spiritual thought within material (or etheric) forms. A fourth ray etheric/dense physical body also tends to attempt to reduce conflict and increase harmony in any intelligent coordinated response that it is involved in. It tends to be weakened, and is more of a challenge to accurately use to sense with, in the more masculine corresponding etheric/dense physical body, whose plane ray is the seventh—a masculine plane. During the first twenty-five or so years of Sally's life, this sense will grow more slowly when she is behaving selfishly; again, it also will be weaker because it is a feminine ray within a masculine body—although this is somewhat mitigated in a female. After about 2025, this sense will either diminish more slowly as Sally is selfish in its use, or it will grow very rapidly as she uses it virtuously. Sally's soul and OverSoul are giving her a tool with which to create more virtue *with* other souls who are along the fourth ray and who will be incarnating along with her as the planetary rays change. Also, Sally incarnating as a female promotes greater, sympathetic response to her feminine rays, which reinforces her astral and etheric/dense physical senses.

Sally is reincarnating with the person who had been Joseph's wife and who is at the time of her incarnation a man of about 30 years of age. This man will be Sally's father; Sally's mother will be Joseph's half-sister who was the progeny of a Negro slave whom his father had as a lover for many years and had several children with. These children were somewhat treated more equally to the non-slave humans than were the other slave children, and Joseph had played with them when he was a child. Before Joseph became bigoted, he had a great fondness for this little girl who was his playmate. Later, as he grew into adolescence, she became his first sexual experience; however, by that time he had become quite bigoted and he emotionally abused her, while he controlled her through the atrocities of the system of slavery. These two (Joseph and his half-sister) died on the same day in 1864 and at close to the same time on Joseph's family's plantation. Joseph's wife, who was not with him at his death, had always held out great animosity towards this black slave woman whom Joseph seemed to favor when he was around her. Now, in a later incarnation, these two (Joseph's wife and his half-sister) have become married (the woman who had been Joseph's wife had reincarnated as a male), and are to be Sally's parents.

In order to complete Sally's incarnation into physical life, her soul and Solar Angel use certain mental "sounds," as a "chord," that they focus through their Self onto the mental permanent atom. A pattern is established that is based upon the rays that have been chosen for her personality and mental body, to create the new mental unit of thoughtforms, or fourth sub-plane lower mental energies. These energies will be organized by the Solar Angel's thought and will be semi-permanent. This will occur because they will be somewhat additionally held together by the thought of fourth mental sub-plane spirit, who, along with the thoughtforms, is following the very powerful and fusing thought of the Solar Angel. The thoughtforms of the personality come directly from the interaction of the soul's, Solar Angel's, and their shared Self's thought with the mental permanent atom's karma—all as a cause. Since the ray focus is included in this combined thought, the semi-permanent thoughtforms of the personality become ray-impressioned. These thoughtforms cause a propensity towards certain karmically controlled thoughts and behaviors; however, they are inclinations only, which the personality can change with some levels of discipline if it decides to. Also, these inclinations tend to be much stronger earlier in physical life than later. The reason is the weakening over time of the effect that their thought and the thought of their interpenetrating spirit has on the part of the mental unit (on the first through third sub-sub-planes of the fourth mental sub-plane), with this weakening usually beginning between the ages of twenty-one and twenty-eight. Sally is given personality thoughtforms that cause her to focus on information from all of her bodies' senses that relates to leadership; governing others (politics); the larger concepts and information about economies; racial issues; the spirituality (how God thinks) that is contained within all the parts of her personality thoughtforms; the use of military force; transportation and communication; and an interest in beauty that is found in relatively uncommon places or forms. These thoughtforms all came from prior thoughts that Sally's soul's earlier incarnations either could have used (and most likely chose not to) or did use with which to create virtue, and are found within her mental permanent atom. These inclinations manifest through the ways in which Sally chooses to use her senses and how she synthesizes the information from her senses into knowledge.

Sally's mental body is formed with a ray focus that affects how her mental centers and their senses will sense others in a selfish way along the ray focus of each split sense, and along the overall ray of an entire body. In a human, the mental unit and mental body are created together; the spark of life, which replicates the soul, is not created in the mental unit until all three bodies are created to the level at which they can sense. Thus no personality exists until the creation of all three bodies has progressed enough for them to be unified. The mental body develops over a period of about ninety days, in averaged mental plane time. This is the equivalent of about a single day in the dense physical realm.

Simultaneously, the astral body is constructed from the sutratma, or the life thread, moving down into it. This occurs because the sutratma is following the focused thought of the soul, Solar Angel, and Self. Sally's astral body is created, as was her mental, through an interaction between her soul's, Solar Angel's, and Self's focused thought on the energies and light within her (in this case, the astral) permanent atom, and this interaction involves the chosen ray focus within the thought. An astral body is created in about ninety astral days, which is the equivalent of about twelve days of dense physical time.

Sally's etheric/dense physical body begins development along with the two higher bodies, but its completion requires about nine months, on average, of physical plane time. After an average of three months of physical time, the three bodies can be unified in their senses enough to partly create the personality. From the sudden increase in awareness that results from this unification, a spark is created within the mental unit. Then the personality emerges, but there is not yet a self. Sally will gain a self, and individuality, only after she becomes separated from her mother's senses and bodies or from any neonatal artificial life-support system. A baby gains its self mostly as it takes its first breath on its own (and the self continues to grow as the infant continues to breathe on it own).

If Sally had been aborted before her birth, it is possible that many of the endeavors of her soul, Solar Angel, and their shared Self would largely have been lost. Sally might lose all benefit that she would have gained through interactions with certain other humans, who may be adversely affected as well, by her absence. Had she been aborted, her karma would probably have been what led her to that event, and her incarnation would have to be delayed, at least until the next year. The reason is that she must be born on the same calendar day on which her predecessor died from etheric life. She may have to wait for a number of years to incarnate, however, to wait for the right time and birth circumstances that would help her to best fulfill the same soul mission or a different one than the mission she was aborted from. While it is correct to state that a person's karma is *likely* to be the reason (it is always a part of it) for his or her being aborted or miscarried, karma must be lived at some time—even by souls and Solar Angels. Until after approximately the first trimester, no personality is killed in an abortion because a fetus at that age does not yet have a personality. After a fetus gains a personality, it still has no self except in the rare case of an aborted fetus becoming separated from its mother and remaining alive for a second or two before the moment of its death; it could begin to develop a self during this very brief time, but that self would not be complete. While there is reasonable doubt that ending the life of a fetus constitutes killing a person (because to be a person requires both a personality and a self), it therefore should not probably be considered a crime against a human. However, abortion sometimes *is* a "crime" against the soul and Solar Angel—and God. The solution to dealing with such difficult situations will *not* be found in *human laws* because, at present, most humans neither know nor understand the plans of souls and OverSouls. The solution is spiritual education, which would include the willingness of those who want to criminalize abortion to take individual responsibility for these (potential) children, both economically *and* parentally. It is highly unlikely that Sally will be aborted because her karma is not negative enough to support such an effect. It is important to remember that the abortion (forced or otherwise, as a miscarriage) can have a forceful effect towards positive change in the mother and possibly the father and others associated with the situation. Such effects could be the contributing factors for creating the virtue of the soul and Solar Angel for the (brief) incarnation of that fetus! In these cases, one could deduce that the soul and Solar Angel were fairly sure that the abortion would take place, and would have included it in their planning; however, there are probably many more abortions that occur for which the soul and Solar Angel were not able to plan. Anyone who is significantly affected by an abortion is likely to be someone whom the fetus's predecessor (one of its prior incarnations) was closely involved with.

At first glance, the above-described reincarnation scenarios may seem incestuous and, therefore, un-Godly. However, the souls of all incarnating humans (except those humans who are abjectly evil and have no human soul) function through unconditional love. They seek to develop more of God as each of their human incarnations becomes further created through God's thought, or through light. The prior personal interconnections among humans are mostly unknown to them because most people were too selfish to connect events in time and space to at least a level of sixty percent. This is the minimum required to create lasting memory. (See Chapters Six, Seven, and Eight for more information about memory.) Because the events and karma still exist, they do influence each personally interacting human by altering these people's senses *to each other*, through retained energies and some level of cosmic light as well. This explains why some people, subconsciously to their selves, respond to each other and are attracted to one another in various ways. People's souls always work together through love and the shared creation of virtue; this sometimes occurs even when the humans' personal involvement concerns conflict and strife. When a non-evil human does have direct past life memory through her or his self, that person then has increased the duration of her or his present life, and responds to the others who are part of the memory with virtuous thoughts and feelings that do not cause harm. True knowledge of one's past life or lives can exist only when it is accompanied by understanding, or love (except in evil people). No abuse of such knowledge is possible because if the information were to be used selfishly, all memory and knowledge of it would be instantly destroyed. This system safeguards people from manipulating and selfishly using others based upon past life associations. Also, imagine what selfish people might do to carry over their selfish need to control into the next physical life. One example might be a wealthy person attempting to will his fortune to the person he will be in his next incarnation! In general, for those who are not evil and who have a human soul, *real* past life knowledge is available only to those who were especially virtuous in the last incarnation. Such people include, to a lesser amount, some first and second level initiate disciples in the accepted stage; more of them will be third level initiates—and especially those who were at the accepted stage of the third level of initiation. In addition, virtually all arhats (fourth level initiates) past the probationary stage and while serving have nearly complete recall of past lives as these lives affect their service. The reason for an arhat's high level of recall is that the permanent atoms in all three of an arhat's three lower bodies contain more than sixty percent light *and* this light was used to create virtue within his or her *last* life. This continuity of consciousness is created by joining events to time and space, using all three time zones (past, present, and future) in the correct, or in logical, order.

A permanent atom can be more than one-half light, but this light, which is created through the creation of virtue, is not necessarily connected in time and space to create memory. The reason is that over many lifetimes each human may be virtuous in one instance of a circumstance, but then in the same lifetime or in a different one may be selfish under nearly the same circumstances. When this occurs, the light that was created remains, but becomes further separated from other light by the surrounding space that was caused by the contradictory selfishness. Light *can* be removed from a permanent atom through evil; however, evil occurs much less often in a lifetime than does selfishness, and most people's permanent atoms gradually *gain* light from one lifetime to the next. The space that selfishness creates within the permanent atom exists because darker energy is brought into the atom from corresponding ray types of selfishness; this energy gravitates towards the enlightened energy because both are similar in thought, even though one was created from enlightened thought and the other was brought in and replaced relatively *less* dark energy. Then the most enlightened energy becomes surrounded by darker corresponding energy that is gravitating towards it. Gravitating energy causes time and space to separate from each other, creating space between one relatively enlightened energy and another within the permanent atom.

 ## ASTROLOGICAL AND DEVELOPMENTAL FACTORS

An important factor in Sally's incarnation is the combination of the date, time, and geographic location of her birth. These elements create an *esoteric* astrological condition that influences the centers in her bodies at birth. As was explained in Chapters Six and Seven, the focus of the rays affects the energies in the earth's atmosphere; these energies are referred to as pranas. These pranas are also affected by the ray focus of the geographic area over which they hover, because a greater amount of a particular ray and sub-ray energy is focused on every part of the earth. In addition, those areas in the dense physical world where large populations of people live etheric/dense physically are also affected to a relatively greater extent by these people's collective thought (this also holds true in the subtle worlds, where people's thought has a much larger effect). Pranic energy is at a lower level at night, and at a higher level during the daytime; when pranic energy is low, it is affected somewhat more by ray focus than when it is high, because inertia is influenced by mass. The higher mass from greater amounts of pranic energy in the daytime creates more inertia, making it less affected by the growth stimulation of the ray. The sun, the moon, the planets, and some constellations that are associated with the sun exert a ray-focus effect on earth because the Beings who create these astronomical bodies have focused some of their thought on earth's development. The amount of their focus on the pranic energies varies, based upon the geographic area of the earth that is in direct line to these Beings' physical (or etheric) bodies, because earth's mass itself has *gravity*. Gravity is the collection of energy's self-focused thought, and it interferes with the distant focus of the astronomical Beings' thought. The system becomes quite complicated because different angles and degrees of focus create a complex field of continually changing ray effects on the pranic energies.

When a person is born and takes his or her first breath, this newborn baby's reliance on his or her mother's centers ceases. At that moment, the personality and self of the infant begin the integration and full control over its etheric/dense physical centers, exercising its (the personality's) ray focus in the process. The very first pranas that then enter the infant's etheric/dense physical centers, under the personality's control, are being synthesized into knowledge *independent* of the mother, causing the infant to become an *individual* human being and self. Prior to this event, the fetus and then (briefly) the infant did have a personality ray, but its personality was not in full control of its three bodies and brains—it also lacked a self—and could synthesize knowledge only from information that the mother had first synthesized. Doing so allowed the fetus or infant some meager ability to learn from the mother's thought, but not independently as an individual. Another critical event occurs, simultaneous to physical birth and the first breath. The permanent atom of each of the three lower bodies becomes fully connected to the etheric/dense physical centers through the life thread of all those bodies and (to begin with) the consciousness thread of only the etheric/dense physical body. This connection is timed to occur within each permanent atom at the same moment as the first breath and the simultaneous creation of individuality. Recognizing the timing of the above-described process is the crucial factor in understanding esoteric astrology. When a person loses his or her self (such as from advanced Alzheimer's disease, or from being in a coma) but remains physically alive, the death of that person takes place only when the life thread is removed from the body. Thus physical life begins when both threads (life and consciousness) are connected to a body, but it ends only when the life thread is removed. The reason is that the consciousness thread and the self can be reconnected, even after long periods (years) of being disconnected, as can occur both with severe Alzheimer's (where the reconnection is usually brief and transient), and in the case of a person who awakens from a coma. Once the brain can be deemed unable to be used by a self, or is "dead," then the self cannot return to that body even if other centers and their organs are still being kept functioning. *If* the person is being kept alive through human endeavors, and would otherwise die, then sometimes human intervention in ending the life of the body is permissible, if done for right motive, or for virtuous reasons (the souls of those involved are usually guiding them in these circumstances).

The consciousness thread moves to each center at the *exact* position where it was located in *each* body at the prior incarnation's moment of death from that body. This positioning occurs at a *different* time for each body (usually years apart). As the pranic energies on each of the three planes are brought into each center, they cause the personality to become impressioned with its own creation of self. This occurs as the self begins its giving thought for the lower spirit in that body in that lifetime. The personality also becomes improved through its senses by the first pranic energy, because these senses become the first input into the permanent atoms. The very first consciousness of the self that is created and the sense that the personality integrates are connected for that entire lifetime with the permanent atom of each body, during the one or two seconds of the first breath of that body. Subsequent to this act, the consciousness and life thread focus connected to a specific center can be changed only very slowly through either selfish or virtuous thought directed into the corresponding body, or the increasing of self and sense.

Two major factors are occurring at the moment of birth in consciousness for each body. The first is the sudden release of karma because karma is immediately affected by consciousness, and is related to the past part of time joining somewhat with the present. This first part is controlled by the first major effect of prana, which is the effect of the rays and of the earth's atmosphere on the senses. The permanent atoms along with the position of the sun, and its effects on the rays and prana, control this effect. The reason is that they regulate the exact location of the consciousness thread, which must precisely match the pranic conditions at time of death from that body in the former lifetime. That location *must* be an exact match for the location at the date and time *and* related geographic position on the earth in relation to our sun—or a newly calibrated geographic position, if the birth occurs outside earth's gravity field, or for the subtle bodies. The time and space of each dense physical incarnation of a person needs to occur on the exact day and time that he or she died from the last etheric life, with very slight adjustments made for changes in earth's mass, gravity, and, therefore, speed of rotation (the time); otherwise, the consciousness thread will not attach to the center. The time and date are controlled by the *sun's* position in relation to earth. In most cases, the process of connecting the consciousness thread is repeated after an average of seven years, for the astral body, and fourteen years, for the mental body. The physical, astral, and mental bodies generally all have different dates, times of death, and relative geographic positions so the consciousness thread usually becomes connected at a different time in each body (the time that the "first breath" is taken in each body). Some of the retained energies in the permanent atoms become manifested as sense characteristics at the time of birth for each body's *consciousness* as the self begins its giving through that body and connects the consciousness thread to the centers. The consciousness thread goes through the crown chakra, or center, in each body as soon as the life thread connects to the heart center. However, the consciousness thread does not connect to the center of the self's focus until that body is developed and used by the self (which constitutes the awakening of consciousness). Thus the sun controls the creation of self and individuality as the self's development of consciousness is created in each body when the permanent atom attaches its consciousness thread to a center in that body; note that the life thread is attached to all of a person's bodies at physical birth.

Those people who in a prior life were much less selfish than average can significantly earlier in the present life develop consciousness in a body and connect the senses to the personality for its use in creating knowledge from their information. People who were more relatively selfish are still likely to become conscious within a body, but if this takes place close enough to the time to move into the next focus of body development and its consciousness, the result can be virtually no sense development and consciousness within the first of these two bodies. This circumstance also leaves that body prone to disease, because of the high amount of energies that are retained on such a long-term basis. Notice that a *part* of the selfish personality of the last incarnation becomes manifested at the birth of consciousness (givingness) within each of the three bodies. The astral birth of consciousness can be *identified* by a child *giving* through the use of both his or her *creative imagination and empathy together*, to help to create love in some life other than himself or herself. The actual birth of the astral consciousness generally occurs prior to the point at which it can be identified. The reason is that the child first gives using his or her combined creative imagination and empathy to increase his or her self. Empathy or creative imagination used alone will not create astral consciousness from the self's giving of its use—both must be used together in the act of giving. For an advanced child or for an adolescent, the birth of mental consciousness can be *identified* when that person gives wisely, or with wisdom, structured (whole) thought that helps to create truth in the mental mind of another.

If a person dies etheric/dense physically before either developing consciousness within the astral or mental body or before fully developing one or both of those bodies, he or she can continue that development on the inner (higher) planes, although usually somewhat more slowly for people at more average levels. Karma as played out from one lifetime to the next can be mitigated for a lifetime, and is often slowed down by the soul or OverSoul giving to a new incarnation a different personality or lower-body ray (or more than one different ray) as compared to its last incarnation. Changes that occur in the planetary focus of the rays can also have a significant effect on the way a person's karma manifests. If a person were to be born with the same rays as in its soul's previous incarnation and with no change in the planetary ray focus, *all* of the karma from that last life (as well as from any other former life with the same rays) would manifest from the moment of birth of consciousness within each body; facing all of this karma at once would present an immensely difficult problem, which most people would not be able to overcome. In these cases the sun and moon at the time of a person's physical birth will be in about the same position. It is important to understand that, in most cases, only when the consciousness thread becomes fixed in the exact location within a center where it was when the soul's previous incarnation died from that body, does the permanent atom release its retained energies into the centers of its new incarnation's body. Nothing and no one—not even evil—can escape its karma, but through the use of crystallization, evil can delay the onset of karma for thousands of physical plane years. (See Chapter Eight for an explanation of this effect.)

The second major factor through which esoteric astrology affects the personality (and its karma) is that the moon, the planets, and particular constellations that are associated with earth's sun are usually in very different positions relative to earth at the same time on the same calendar day but in a different year. Thus only the solar, or the sun's, effect on the rays and on prana controls the first major karma, while the moon, the planets, and certain constellations create distinct *differences* in the relatively selfish personality as it develops consciousness in each body through its self. These differences are more affected by and related to the rays that were chosen by the soul and OverSoul for the bodies and personality of its incarnation. The sun's effect, or the solar effect, on prana is prominent and causes an immediate effect on the present part of time—mostly joining past and present. If the person's rays have changed from his or her soul's last incarnation, the sun is the astrological entity that has the greatest effect on both the amount of retained energies that become immediately released by the permanent atoms and the speed at which this occurs. Because of its close proximity, the moon and, to a lesser extent, the planets and certain constellations cause a *delayed* effect that results mostly from the akasha because all of these celestial bodies are many times weaker in affecting prana through their effects on the rays (the akasha is the past part of time impressioned in energy as events, and is exaggerated by selfishness). Rather than immediately changing the amount of karma and the speed of its release based upon the level of a person's consciousness, they affect the ways in which the ray of the personality and of each body interacts with prana. In an advanced disciple, the rays affect the permanent atoms at the moment that consciousness is established in a body, the way the sun does in those who are creating virtue and are thus accelerating their karma. In the latter case, the bodies' ray and the personality's ray become more important factors at the first breath. Thus in spiritual disciples with these lesser personality factors, the *year* into which a person is reborn is intrinsically tied to the rays that the soul and OverSoul decided upon, with both factors—the year and the rays—being chosen to meet the particular needs of other souls, as well. The sun affects mostly the creation of self and individuality, as well as the date and time that *consciousness* is born into a body; the moon, planets, and certain constellations affect the relatively selfish personality as it grows, with personality factors mostly determined by the year into which a person is born. In relatively unselfish people—those who are spiritually disciplining themselves and creating more virtue in their lives—the effect on the rays and prana by the moon, planets, and certain constellations become very much like the sun's effect on them, with disciples then facing mostly one type of karma: solar (rather than lunar, etc.).

The moon and the usually lesser esoteric astrological factors alter the ways in which the different pranas interact at any particular time on earth. The moon is the physical body of the remaining consciousness of earth's prior (last) incarnation as a planet. The moon plays the role of re-creating past karmic effects in the present and future because its consciousness is focused from a past incarnation. It, usually much more slowly than the sun, causes the release of retained energies within each permanent atom after the first breath in a body. As these energies are slowly released, they become greatly affected by either the selfishness or the virtue that is created by the personality and its self. The karmic effects from the sun are only slightly affected by selfishness or virtue in most average people, because their karma is so heavily determined by the last lifetime's (or lifetimes') selfishness or virtue. The karmic effects from the sun are almost immediate as consciousness becomes established from the level of consciousness that is present—the higher the consciousness, the faster the karma's release and the greater the amounts of it released; the release of this karma is at a fairly constant level that can be controlled by the rays of the bodies and personality. The effect of the moon, the planets, and certain constellations vacillates, and greatly increases over an average person's lifetime—significantly contributing to the development of the personality. This slow effect is based on past selfish karma, including some from that person's current lifetime.

The sun's effect on the rays of spiritual disciples often begins more strongly at a younger age than it does with non-disciples. If the effect is not overcome through the creation of virtue, it may lead to great suffering and a relatively short lifetime because of earlier destruction of the centers and senses through excessive releases of retained energies from within the permanent atoms. The sun's effect on the rays of spiritual disciples usually allows these people, when they are virtuous, to overcome their karma through crises that they are prepared to handle. The past time focus of the moon, of the planets, and of the affecting constellations' effects on the rays is usually offset by the planning and the focus on the future, by functioning spiritual disciples. The soul ray of a disciple dominates her or his personality ray and reduces the selfish inter-relationship of all her or his bodies' rays and the ray of the personality, into simply the soul ray of service and a ray focus as needed for the type of service that the disciple is creating. The ray focus that is needed for the disciple's service becomes developed within him or her as a sub-ray of the personality or one of the lower three bodies. Note that a disciple can develop four sub-rays, one each in the personality and the three lower bodies. A sub-ray is not developed for the soul because all souls can, inherently, give equally well from all the rays, although each can create from only one ray focus.

In our scenario of Sally's incarnation, her soul and OverSoul are specifically concerned with choosing her *year* of incarnation, in order to enhance her capability of service to other souls and their needs to advance, and are less concerned with the year in which Sally's moon, planets and the constellations will be most helpful to her personally and that will affect her personal life. Sally's soul and OverSoul believe that she can overcome the karma that will be released from her permanent atoms by these ray-focus effects on pranic energies, for two reasons. The first is that Sally will incur less of these effects than will the average person, since the last incarnation of her soul (Chia-Ho) created more virtue and less selfishness than average in that lifetime; the second is that in this new life she is, it is hoped, continuing her soul's long journey into becoming a member of the next kingdom, through creating spiritual service in her own and in lower kingdoms through the use of the initiation process. Sally's life *and consciousness* are less predetermined than were any of her soul's prior incarnations, and she has considerably more choices as she frees herself from the effects of the rays and from evolution (and from force controlling her life).

An additional astrological factor needs to be mentioned in order to present a full esoteric picture of Sally's upcoming lifetime. This factor is often referred to as a rising sign. The rising sign represents a comparative time relative to a particular location in space. This sign compares the solar date and time factors with the exact geographic location *and* the exact relative position of the entire remainder of the zodiac. The rising sign determines the type of ray energy that will most affect a person's life, and its effectiveness in so doing when it is compared to the sun or with the moon, the planets, and related constellations. The rising sign is mostly focused on the future part of time. Although there are seven rays, the five of form (rays three through seven) are recombined to create the twelve constellations and signs of the zodiac that are focused on earth and its solar system, and function as the foundation of astrology. Each constellation itself has three sub-ray factors (and astrological signs) that produce its overall ray effect. Notice that the constellations that affect earth's solar system are created in the same ray formulations that the twelve kingdoms are. The complexity of esoteric astrology requires that, for a full explanation, another entire volume of related material be written at a later time. Another important point to mention is that in mundane modern astrology, the use of astrological signs without an understanding of the rays creates, at best, a pseudo-science because the *real causes*, or the rays, are omitted while some observable *effects* are named *as causes*! Further, the attempt to predict *personal* and selfish activity is both meaningless and, at times, grossly inaccurate, since in mundane modern astrology only effects are considered to be important—and only effects are used.

Sally's rising sign will be in Scorpio, as decided upon by her soul and OverSoul. This sign has been changed quite significantly from Chia-Ho's because Sally is to be born in the U.S, while her soul's last incarnation was born in China. Two rays control humans who have Scorpio as a rising sign: the third and the sixth. The entire constellation of Scorpio is affected by *three* rays, but because of its relative position to the sun, only two control it as a rising sign, and seven of the rising signs have only one controlling ray. The third ray in Scorpio as a rising sign functions more as a ray of aspect, and the sixth ray functions as a ray of attribute modifying the third. With the five constellations and associated planets that have two rays of a rising sign controlling them, the third ray is the only ray that can function as either a ray of aspect or a ray of attribute, depending upon whether it is primary or whether it is secondary to the other ray. Scorpio is a correspondence of the eighth kingdom—of constellations. It is the most conflictive rising sign because the two rays that compose it, the third and the sixth, are in the most conflictive position to each other of any ray combination. The third ray creates more choices to move in many directions and to communicate intelligently, while the sixth ray creates more choices to move in only one direction at a time and is restrictive of communication. Sally will in all likelihood want to create more meaning in her life by increasing her intelligent activity relative to her spiritual values. This choice would be supported by her third ray soul and personality. Her rising sign suggests that she will have crises—caused by karmic factors that she will have created—that will manifest along the sixth ray, especially when they involve an issue concerning form. These crises will greatly slow her down and focus her on each separate way in which she has been selfish, and has created the crisis she finds herself in. If Sally creates more virtue, she will be encouraged by her rising sign to create more intelligent activity along her soul ray. If she fails, and becomes more selfish, she will experience significant loneliness and isolation, and her life will lose meaning relative to not experiencing love. This would come from her failure to create virtue from the sixth ray component to her nature. Thus her rising sign, which is the effect coming from what is described in the preceding sentences, represents certain astrological concepts and is used to adjust her future karma as that karma affects her created self—all from the location of her birth and the pranas in that location.

Sally's life as a person (her personality and self plus her bodies and senses) is becoming much more connected to her life as a soul because Sally's predecessor, in her soul's previous incarnation, chose to limit his life in order to create more virtuous choices for others. Sally is now a first level initiate, but to become functional as an initiate in her life she needs to again make the choices to become a spiritual disciple. Her soul and OverSoul are doing everything they can to encourage this decision through the choices that they can make before Sally is born. Notice that once a person is born, the soul and OverSoul have very little effect on that person without her or his choice to become more virtuous.

 ## SUMMARY OF CHAPTER ELEVEN

In conclusion of this chapter, reincarnation is a means of eventually connecting the disparate lifetimes of numerous humans who are all created from the same soul, *and* that soul is karmically connected to certain other human souls. Reincarnation is also the means by which humans gradually become connected to and become a functional part of God and its growth. Reincarnation increases the meaning of human life from just the one typically meager lifetime a human has, to the duration of life of that human's soul—and eventually of its Self and Solar Angel. Without the concept of reincarnation, the human life has a very limited meaning, even if the life is spent *relatively* virtuously because within a single lifetime, on average, humans create so little virtue.

Every person has his or her own Angel, who has guided every incarnation of his or her soul for up to millions of years. In addition, there are lesser "angels" who are not energy beings, but are people who are alive on the inner planes and who watch over and sometimes help people who are alive in on the physical world. Sometimes these inner plane "angels" are friends or family members who have died, but more often they are people who never personally knew those whom they serve. These helpers are spiritually disciplining themselves and find that they can serve a physically alive human for a period of time because of certain karmically related factors. The ability to serve in this way is generally based upon the levels to which those serving have fused their etheric/dense physical senses to their astral ones, and their astral senses to their mental ones, within their own bodies. While this area of karma is far too complex to fully explain and exemplify herein, it is important to realize that through creative imagination and empathy or through wisdom and love, or both, these "angels" can have a somewhat enlightening effect on the corresponding higher bodies in a physically alive human. These servers do not become possessing entities of a physically alive person, the way a dark or evil inner plane person might. They provide guidance and suggestion, not force and destruction.

Through understanding reincarnation it is possible to understand much of the meaning of human life that is hidden. Any human can un-hide the meaning in his or her life by reversing his or her negative karma through the creation of virtue—first personally, and then functioning with his or her soul and then group, and perhaps with his or her nation or even the world. Each step in the journey of changing negative karma from forces into light (into God's thought) creates a much more meaningful life that has greater freedom and less suffering. God is perfect outside of separated time and space (or within light); creating oneself into becoming a functional part of God, or becoming God with its capabilities and further growing these capabilities, requires the creation towards perfection. Reincarnation provides humans with such an opportunity. When God created the system of reincarnation, a great gift was bestowed upon humans, because there is no greater meaning to human life than to create more of life and to become a functional part of God.

Until a human chooses to spiritually discipline herself or himself, that person is controlled by karma and forces, or by energies that are retained inside her or him. These retained energies result is the restriction of freedom and in the hiding of meaning through reductions in consciousness; another harsh consequence is the suffering that ensues when a person becomes aware of having lost consciousness. For humans who are not yet spiritually disciplining themselves, reincarnation implicates a lack of meaning in life, a lack of freedom—to make choices—and a lack of consciousness. All of these deficiencies can result in boredom, forced restrictions on activity, and suffering. It is unfortunate that, even to most spiritually aware people, reincarnation represents these harsh realities. However, reincarnation coupled with spiritual discipline reverses these difficult life problems, enabling a person to become joyful, free, and creative of virtue. Rather than providing the means to escape reincarnation, enlightenment leads one to *use* reincarnation as a vehicle through which everyone can create more of God through a system of perfect equity, reasonable alternatives, and unconditional love—through enormous and (Self created) unlimited opportunity to improve. Note that most exceptions to these conditions are mitigations created by evil, and that evil is actually part of God's gift of freedom to humans, in paradoxical conflict with God's unconditional love. This conflict is the first part of God's mind in opposition to the second, and the freedom allows evil the right to create itself and to continue to exist.

Human life can, of course, be lived without any belief in or concern for reincarnation. The question must be asked, though, as to why anyone would prefer that there *not* be reincarnation. Is the easier scenario of living only a single lifetime so intoxicating that it numbs one's reasoning into accepting boredom and mediocrity—or, even worse, virtual imprisonment, forced existence, and eventually near-meaninglessness to life? The answer seems to be in consciousness and the level to which a person loves, gives, or has consciousness…which equals the level of understanding that a person has concerning the oneness of life. In the next and final chapter of *Life's Hidden Meaning*, the focus will be on this very issue. To change reincarnation from being an imprisonment into a creative tool for becoming a functional part of God requires that one increase her or his consciousness, or be more, unconditionally, loving.

HOW TO INCREASE CONSCIOUSNESS

Illustration 12.1

Author's Suggestion: First turn to the "Glossary Help Guide" and read the definitions for this chapter.

 **A REVIEW OF CONSCIOUSNESS**

In the last chapter, reincarnation was described as having two major characteristics. On the more selfish, personal level, it acts as an instrument of forces, a limitation, a karmic balancer, and a barrier to the proliferation of evil. As reincarnation accomplishes these effects, it can lead to boredom, suffering, and meaninglessness in a human's life. The second characteristic of reincarnation can be used only on a soul level. In these cases, reincarnation becomes a means of service to others and produces joy, creativeness of virtue, freedom, and an increase in love, or in consciousness. Which of these sets of characteristics reincarnation brings about is determined by the level of consciousness that a person has relative to her or his ability to respond; a person's ability to respond is a measure of the *amount* and the *accuracy* of the information that he or she is sensing and then synthesizing into knowledge. Consciousness is the level to which one is capable of understanding the oneness of life. What increases consciousness the most is giving unconditionally (with no conditions on the giving) what is needed in order for other parts of life to grow in their consciousness so they can give unconditionally to still *other* parts of life what those other parts need so that they, too, can grow. Without consciousness there can be no understanding. As a person's consciousness falls and she or he becomes aware of her or his loss in understanding, that person will suffer because her or his (lower) self has diminished; the self's existence is dynamically dependent upon its level of giving. To a human, its loss of self is the worst possible condition because this leads unequivocally to fear and anxiety of real death—or annihilation. All human suffering is ultimately related to this issue of lacking consciousness. Even a child who is beaten and tortured, deprived of all necessities, and imprisoned suffers because he or she does not have enough understanding, or consciousness, to be able to alter his or her circumstances. Thus the lack of consciousness on the child's part begins the process that leads to his or her suffering (of course, the child's pain, fear, and anxiety about more pain is caused by those inflicting the mistreatment). Paradoxically, damage to the senses or extreme pain, or both, can relieve suffering. This is because the drop in the personality's awareness of its self caused by these factors obscures the loss of consciousness that results from the self's diminished ability to give to the bodies through their fallen spirit; what the self can no longer adequately give is the *oneness* of sense, identity, and life—all of which create individuality. The self first creates consciousness by creating a oneness in a human's three lower bodies by giving its thought to the lower spirit within the three lower bodies. (See Chapter Five for further explanation of this concept.)

The self can without assistance make itself more conscious only by giving to lower spirit in the three lower bodies its own thought that would enable this lower spirit to, at any particular time, be able to better inform the energy of those bodies. The amount of thought correctly given is based upon the level of developed sense. This sense is finite because it is limited by the capabilities of the senses and bodies that the lower spirit is informing. Eventually the only way the self can gain consciousness, or grow, is by giving to some other selves in ways that create more oneness between the others *and the self*. However, this type of giving eventually reaches a limit as well, because selves can give only up to the level at which the lower spirit in their bodies can use those bodies' senses. Finally, a third stage of development of the self is reached, wherein the self gives to other selves parts of its not-self that it has given *for them* so that they might do the same, creating a oneness among all selves, and it expects nothing in return for what it gave. At this point the self is developing soul consciousness and is *learning* to give unconditional (on the giving) love.

After having accomplished some part of the above-described third stage of developing their selves, many humans begin to focus on raising their consciousness because in order to gain more meaning in their lives they need to understand more than simply their own and even others' selves. Such people have reached the point at which attempting to increase the meaning in their lives through understanding only selves has, for them, become selfish. This relative position prevents them from gaining consciousness, or understanding, through creating some level of virtue that involves just the self and is therefore personal. In order to increase their consciousness, they need to create virtue that is related to the soul and the (higher) Self and gain understanding about God and its mind. The assumption being made in the remainder of this chapter is that those who are reading it have themselves reached this critical point. Those who are not in this position are likely to find much of this chapter, and possibly the majority of the entire book, to be meaningless.

After a person has gained reasonable understanding of the self through approaching completion of the three stages of self development as described above, the next level of development is for the personality and its self to begin to fuse with their soul and Self. This fusion is accomplished as the personality lessens its control over its self, and the self decides to understand the thought of its Solar Angel. The Solar Angel sends its thought to the self by transmitting this thought through the vortices of the mental permanent atom into the vortices of the mental unit, which is under the control of the personality. Thus the self receives the Solar Angel's thought only with the personality's cooperation and consent. As the self hears the Solar Angel with greater clarity and depth of thought, it transmits back to the Angel what it understands of its lower bodies and their spirit, as well as what it understands of the lower bodies and spirit of others, so that the concepts of the Angel can be *applied* in the three lower worlds. Through this process, the self fuses with the Self, eventually at the level to which light is created as radiance in the solar devas that are used to create and serve with the concepts of the Solar Angel. As the Self grows, much larger spiritual concepts can become created through the synthesis of three components: the self's understandings of the lower three worlds; the Solar Angel's concepts regarding the creation of more virtue (more of God's thought) in the three lower worlds; and the soul's thoughts on how its personality and self can best give such virtue.

The personality can give to its soul the use of the fully enlightened information that was supplied by the senses of the three lower bodies and was stored in a permanent atom as fully enlightened knowledge, or intelligent activity, plus any synthesized knowledge (which may not be fully enlightened) that it has created within its brains, so that the soul will gain information about and knowledge of the three lower worlds. Only fully enlightened knowledge will remain as part of the soul's knowledge. Any part of the partially enlightened knowledge given to the soul but that the soul cannot further synthesize into enlightened knowledge is lost to the soul because this knowledge cannot be used with which to give. The personality has the ability to give in this way only by reducing its control over its self, through the conscious choice to limit itself. While it is over-controlling its self, the personality cannot give to its soul—because it has rendered itself too selfish to do so. This choice is usually connected to the personality having suffered because of a lack of meaning in its life. The amount of meaning in a person's life is dependent upon how much that person understands his or her life. The lack of meaning comes from the personality over-controlling its self and making it selfish. By over-controlling, the personality's consciousness, or understanding, drops because it renders the self unable to give as much in relation to its (the personality's) ability to first collectively sense information through its bodies, and then to synthesize that information into knowledge. The more information and knowledge that a personality has, the greater its awareness that it lacks understanding because its over-controlled, selfish, self does not supply it—and then the more the personality suffers. Its suffering stems from a fear of annihilation of its self, or of real death; this fear somewhat paralyzes the personality in its creation of more virtue and sometimes even interferes with its mundane activities, thereby increasing and perpetuating its suffering as the meaning in its life becomes further reduced. Thus *diminished* meaning in life is synonymous with suffering and prior increases in selfishness. A lack of meaning in life indicates the need to lessen the personality's control over the self, and for the self to expand, or to develop further. This lack of meaning coupled with a conscious desire to have increased meaning leads to a new desire to become less selfish.

When the personality gives some of its virtuous information and some synthesized knowledge about the three lower worlds to its soul, it creates part of itself into a part of the soul through its giving, or its love. The personality and soul fuse because the consciousness of the personality becomes raised to the level of consciousness, at least in part, of its soul. The soul completely gives what it can give to help others do the same, or is enlightened to the level at which it senses; the personality is a lower correspondence of the soul. However, the personality is not as enlightened, nor as giving, even though it, like the soul, is composed of joined energy and spirit that create a spark of life. As the self becomes more creative by fusing its understandings of the three lower worlds with the higher, more creative, thought of its Solar Angel, then the self fuses with the Self. Both become more conscious as they also fuse with the soul and its fusing personality, while all four increase the wise giving, or the unconditional love, of the virtue that they create. The four are now using the larger and more complete concepts that the self, Solar Angel, and Self have created together about God's thought in the three lower worlds. Thus the personality gives the use of its senses that creates enlightenment in them; both enlightened information and synthesized information about the three lower worlds are knowledge that the personality gives to its soul. The self gives its understanding of the personality's awareness of life in the three lower worlds, or its overall consciousness, to its Solar Angel and their created Self. This understanding provides the Solar Angel and Self with the ability to understand the giving of others in the three lower worlds—as souls. The soul's consciousness comes from giving thought that was created from the second tier, or the second sub-plane of the mental plane—where the personality and self unaided by the soul and Self are unable to reach in their thought. Note that completely enlightened information can be given to and then by the soul without first being synthesized by the personality, but the giving of this information to the soul is still controlled by the personality.

The soul uses the knowledge given to it by the personality, combined with the self's understanding of the lower worlds that comes through the more creative Self to the soul, to create thought and give it wisely to and with other souls, its Self, and its Solar Angel. As more of God's thought is created within the life of the lower worlds, the Self grows. The Self gives to the soul thought that is more creative, by creating a greater level of individuality to the soul. The soul is initially better at group consciousness and thought than at individual consciousness and thought because its original creation came from a collection of group souls' best-thinking spirit and best-sensing energies. The Self helps its human soul to become a better individual by helping it (the soul) to think more creatively through Its own growth as a Self, from the soul's self first becoming an individual in the lower three worlds. As the human soul fuses with its Self, it is also fusing with its Solar Angel because the Self and Solar Angel share this highest mental plane spirit in the Self.

The self becomes directly connected to the Self through the process of spiritual discipline and the creation of virtue; while they continue to develop and grow together, the self, as part of the personality, becomes indirectly connected to the soul through that part of the personality that becomes fused with the soul. Then the self also becomes indirectly connected to the soul through the Self, because the soul and Self become directly connected. When both connections are made (through the radiance of the corresponding solar devas) to about a sixty percent level and are about equal, the self then identifies itself as being its soul. The self and the soul create more of the Self through their shared creation of virtue; as the self gives its understanding to its Self, the soul shares more in the process because of the inter-relationships. The Self, which was originally the mental Self of the Solar Angel, was sacrificed by the Angel. As the Solar Angel sacrifices its Self on the mental, intuitional, and, eventually, the spiritual plane (eventually giving up all three), it and its fused (prior human, now liberated, soul, or its Soul) moves closer to once again becoming a Monad. (See Chapters Five and Six for more information about Monads and the Self.) The Self on the mental plane functions in a critical role by providing a bridge for the fusion between the soul and the Solar Angel. The understanding of the oneness of life in the three lower worlds that the Self receives from its self is synthesized by the Self with the creative thought of the Solar Angel. The soul uses this thought and increased understanding, or higher consciousness, to creatively give wisely. As all of these parts of a human create more virtue, the higher mental forms of the thought as concepts are constructed by the solar pitris within the causal body and are then held in place by the higher mental elemental energy that fills their structured designs. (See Chapters Six and Seven for more explanation.) When all of the energy within a concept is connected completely to thoughtforms from the lower mental plane, through the personality and soul's efforts to fuse them, then the whole structured thought can be completely given. Once completely given, the energy within the solar devas begins to radiate because it has reached the speed of thought of the mental plane and its Ray Lord, or the speed of light on that plane.

The beginning of the process of raising one's consciousness, for those who are advanced in intelligence and are relatively conscious, is the easing of the over-control that the personality has been exerting over the self. For people of more average intelligence *and* consciousness or those who have some amount of personality disorder and diminished self (or to whom both of these general conditions apply), the first step is the remedial one of increasing the level of the self so that the lower spirit within the three lower bodies becomes better able to guide the energies in those bodies. This improvement is accomplished through *self* discipline and control over the self. The improvement is prompted by self-interest, and accomplished through a mixture of selfish activities and some activities that are loving. This chapter will not, for the most part, focus on those methods.

They will be mentioned later in this chapter in an examination of homosexuality, but only as they involve people who despite their homosexuality are creating more virtue in their lives than the average person is, and who are advanced intellectually *and* spiritually as compared to the average person.

DISCIPLINE—WHAT IT IS AND HOW TO ACCOMPLISH IT

Discipline is the limitation of something in order to help improve it; human discipline can be either mundane or spiritual. Spiritual discipline is discipline that is enacted for the purpose of increasing one's awareness and understanding of God's thought or of intelligent activity or of both (God's mind); mundane discipline is discipline that is enacted for selfish purposes. Mundane discipline has two areas of focus about it that can be accomplished mostly independent of, or separate from, each other. The first focus of mundane discipline is on the personality's development of itself. This part can also be divided into two parts of the personality, and concerns improving the information that a sense supplies, either in quantity or in quality of accuracy, or both. The second part of personality that can be mundanely disciplined, or is disciplined not for the purpose of increasing one's awareness and understanding of God (which would be a spiritual reason), is discipline to develop the ability of the personality to sense and control the self. An example of personality (mundane) discipline to increase either quantity or quality of sense accuracy is someone practicing the piano in order to become better at playing it because she enjoys being able to make music for herself and for some others, as well. An example of mundane personality discipline that includes its sense and control of its self might be for someone to limit her personality's choices in order to determine that she wants her self to understand musical sound and to be able to create it on the piano; she then finds a teacher and arranges to take lessons, reads a book about piano playing, rents a piano, asks others whether they had liked learning this discipline. She also may find a local choir and agree to play the piano in that choir for the next year. This second part of mundane personality discipline deals with its understanding of its self and how much control it will exercise over its self; it invokes some increases of consciousness, and therefore is more *future*-oriented. Successful discipline of this type could lead to self discipline, but the development of this type of discipline is likely to be successful only if the discipline of the personality's control was carefully and correctly executed. The first part of mundane personality discipline deals with the senses of form and with improvement of the energies within them. The second part of mundane personality discipline is focused on the sense of self that the personality gains from its increase in synthesized knowledge as compared to knowledge specifically about its self. After one's personality's sense of self has been adequately developed, the personality needs to then create enough thought—with the assistance of its self—to control the self's thought. The level of thought so created determines whether the personality will succeed in controlling the self enough so that the self gives enough to the lower spirit within the bodies in order to accomplish its (the personality's) plans.

The second focus of *mundane* discipline is on discipline of the self. Discipline of the self is a limitation on the ways in which the spirit within the self thinks (remember that self is composed exclusively of spirit). With the exception of those who think evilly, the purpose of discipline of the self is to elevate the level of the self's thought to be more giving by limiting, or disciplining, what it thinks and the ways in which it thinks. Discipline of the self raises consciousness, provided that that which is raised in thought within the self is *given* either to the lower spirit in the three lower bodies or to the Self in order to create more of God. The first case of giving to lower spirit is mundane discipline of the self and the second is spiritual discipline of the Self. It is not possible to *spiritually* discipline only the *self* and to avoid disciplining the Self because the attempt to do so creates a contradiction: as the self is limited to give its increased thought to only its lower spirit, it becomes diminished in its thought through its wrong (selfish) motive as much as it becomes increased in its thought through its limitation. This leads to frustration, guilt, and a sense of failure.

An example of mundane discipline of the self would be to discipline the self so that it gained an understanding of what playing the piano meant to itself and to other selves. Within this discipline, the self would help the spirit within the lower bodies to think better, and would help the personality to gain more control over the senses within its lower three bodies. Through the discipline, the self would gain mundane, or unhidden, *meaning to life*, which it then shares with the personality.

Spiritual discipline of the self requires discipline of the personality and of the self and Self together at somewhat close to the same time. Although separation of these parts in mundane discipline makes success in the discipline process easier, their separation precludes any success in spiritual discipline. Spiritual discipline leads to the personality achieving some level of fusion with its soul—again, it *must* include the discipline of the personality, self, and Self. Most spiritual discipline begins with disciplining the personality in order to improve the amount of information brought in by its senses, as well as the accuracy of this information as it applies to (eventually) creating virtue. This discipline appears at first, to most outside observers, to be the same as mundane discipline. After a period of discipline comes a meditative period of time to reflect upon how the improved senses can be used with which to create more virtue through the self giving understanding to the Self, and the personality giving its synthesized knowledge (and any enlightened information, as well) to the soul. This process can be used for each sense in a body that has split senses, in the attempt to join these senses together as one. The senses would then greatly improve through synergy and the joining of time with space.

Once discipline of the personality is accomplished to a level at which its further development requires the creation of virtue, then discipline of the self and Self together is employed through a second type of meditative process. The process uses the amount and type of virtue that was created in the preceding discipline as a guideline in limiting the self and in creating more of a certain virtuous thought within the soul. This thought is then given to the Self, who with the soul and Solar Angel is able to create virtue from the second tier and higher, for and with souls. If some of the thought is given to the Self, but some is used by the self to receive, or take, from others, then the thought created from the discipline of the self and Self is only from the third tier, but in the spiritual parts of the tier, above where the highest of the three separated solar devas create concepts. This thought that the personality creates through its dominance is still over-controlling the situation; it allows the self to fuse with the Self to whatever level it can, as long as the personality does not have to fuse with its soul—and thus not lose any *personality* control over its self. The personality can regain any control it gives up over its self as long as it (the personality) has not fused with its soul. The reason is that the personality's thoughtforms have not become a part of the soul's concepts from the second tier, i.e., the time and space between the thoughtforms and the concepts have not become joined. Once the second-tier concepts of the soul become fully joined with some of the semi-permanent thoughtforms of the personality, and with a number of thoughtforms from lower parts of the lower mental body as well, those parts of the personality become indistinguishable from the soul—they become fused. The personality's self does not become lost in this process of enlightenment; rather, it expands into the Self.

An example of spiritual discipline is learning to play the piano so that the music that is chosen to be played will create in others a feeling of and a vision of God, and the aspiration to create more of God. Such music might even be used to create a soundtrack to a movie that explains part of this book. The lower mundane disciplines could be employed, but the purpose of the discipline would be to create more virtue, and not more personal control and self identity. Notice how the spiritual discipline (and thought) would then interpenetrate the mundane. The two spiritual senses and means of thought in each body are used in spiritual discipline, unifying split senses within a body as well as joining the three lower bodies together. Also, the self becomes unified with the Self because it is God's identity that is grown, and not just the identity of the self.

In the endeavor by one who is relatively more developed to raise his or her consciousness, instead of the additional self discipline that might be needed by a less developed person, the more developed personality needs to exercise *less* control over its self and more over its senses and the synthesis and use of knowledge, which make up a part of the personality. The discipline will begin with the lowest, and for many people, the easiest to discipline of the three lower bodies and senses. Thus the beginning of developing more consciousness for people with advanced, or relatively more developed, selves is to limit the sense of just one body at a time, starting with the easiest and lowest. In general, the etheric/dense physical senses of form are the easiest to start with for people who are physically alive, because these senses are the most prominent and are the easiest to identify. The etheric/dense physical senses can be categorized according to their ease of limitation and what will be improved, in the following order: hearing—listening to others, in order to improve intelligent coordination; touch—proper movements within limited space in relation to others, in order to improve physical coordination; sight—observing material or etheric surroundings (or both) in order to decrease inertia and increase the speed, accuracy, and coordination of movement *and* of communication; taste—speaking in ways that accurately convey means by which others can improve their intelligent coordination; and smell—the balancing of one's intelligent activities with the activities of others, so that both become more intelligent. These five senses of form are developed through focusing on them, one at a time, and then attempting to improve the amount of information that the sense conveys as well as the accuracy of that information. Novices should restrict their discipline to listening and, especially, not speaking. Wrong speech destroys the ability to hear because of the connection between the throat and sexual centers and their corresponding senses. (See Chapter Seven for more information.) By spending a certain period of time on each sense in the beginning of spiritual discipline, a person is afforded the opportunity to understand and have control over what the sense is doing. For many people, after all the individual senses have gradually been improved for perhaps a week or two at a time, the discipline of the collective senses can begin for that amount of improved individual sense.

During the discipline process, it is important to recognize mistakes—and mistakes typically occur almost constantly in the early stages. These mistakes are hidden selfishness; however, it is important at this point to *not* try to discipline the self to become less selfish. If this mistake is made, the personality will reduce the self by condemning it in a sort of "guilt-ridden" process of castigating its self each time it is selfish. Instead, the mistakes need to be treated in the light of needing to improve the information coming from the disciplined sense or senses, and then to better synthesize the information from those energies while recognizing that the goal, of less selfishness, will be realized from the process without having to directly change the self at this stage.

Part of the discipline is to attempt, several times per day (three is the recommended beginning effort), for the personality to allow the self to be in control along with the Self and the Self's creator, the Solar Angel. During these periods of "meditation," a person needs to be able to reflect on the knowledge that was synthesized from the information gathered as a result of the sense or senses being disciplined in order to increase spiritual thought; the reflection is a process whereby the added thoughts of the Solar Angel are allowed to flow unimpeded by the personality into the self. These higher spiritual concepts are then applied to the less spiritual and more mundane knowledge that the personality had first synthesized from the same information. In addition, some accounting is made to determine the amount of and the level of accuracy of the information supplied by the sense, to determine whether additional focus on the lower spirit's thought in that body to better control the sense is needed by the personality and its self. There is a trade-off in this limiting thought, because there is a finite amount of both the thought of relatively higher spirit in the personality and its self, and that which is in the lower spirit within the body. Too much thought applied by the personality and self on one sense in one body can leave the other senses and bodies in an imbalanced and darker circumstance. For this reason, one can only gradually change. Eventually, all of the senses and bodies must be disciplined, in order to maintain a balance that leads to more light in the form, or more virtue.

Once some amount of improvement in sense and synthesized thought has been created, *it is imperative* that the person then use the spiritual thought with which to create more virtue. Most of the time, in the beginning of this process, the virtue created will be related to the past events during which that person was selfish. This occurs because she or he is using the very slow process of reflection to build improved knowledge and then understanding. In this process, the self will often create scenarios in astral and mental thought that are joined together, to come up with responses to past situations (which generally involve interactions with other people) that are more correct—less selfish—than were the responses that actually took place.

Every mistake that is made needs to be carefully apologized for, when possible, and should include a statement that shows reflection about the harm that was done as well as concern and compassion for those who were harmed. A structured and reasonable explanation of what will be done in the future to improve the selfishness that caused the mistake needs to be offered so that it does not become repeated. Mistakes concerning only inanimate objects are to be handled similarly, with the affirmation as described above made to oneself. It is a mistake to force an apology on someone who does not wish to hear one; the apology is, *first*, to benefit others, even though it also benefits the one apologizing.

The self needs to be used freely in the reflective process of meditation with the Solar Angel. The self also needs to be functioning reasonably normally for its level of development. In addition, the self also has a need to not be diminished by a personality that either is disordered or is being over-controlled by a personality that mistakenly (selfishly) seeks to over-discipline its self in order to *become more spiritual*. That would be a contradiction in method and motive. If one does not have sufficient self discipline, this needs to be first addressed in the way that people who are not practicing spiritual discipline, but who, on a mundane level, are either physically, emotionally, or mentally disciplining themselves. One cannot achieve spiritual physical disciplines of the self by ignoring his or her personality mistakes (selfishness) in mundane life, and then just attempting to become more spiritual exclusively through spiritual astral and mental discipline. For example, on the etheric/dense physical level if a person is on drugs, has an addiction (to food, sex, etc.) smokes or otherwise uses tobacco (a hidden form of drug), has an unhealthy diet, lives unhealthily in other ways, or uses time and energy wantonly (or any combination of the above), then mundane self discipline is an absolute prerequisite if the spiritual discipline is to be effective. Anyone who fails in the mundane discipline of the self will be unable to succeed in the spiritual discipline, since the spiritual discipline interpenetrates—and relies on—a foundation of prior mundane self discipline.

The second, and more advanced meditative procedure used to raise consciousness employs planning as its core modality. Planning how to become more spiritual raises consciousness if the planning is based upon new knowledge that was gained from the reflective (the first) method of meditation. Planning is part of the second aspect of God's mind. While meditating on ways that his or her self can be more giving so that God's thought, or light, can grow in the forms of life, a spiritual disciple constructs a plan that is likely to raise his or her intelligence in activities to a higher level.

The first method of meditation is reflection first on the more correct uses (the less selfish use) of the senses within a body, and then on the personality's more complete synthesis of knowledge from these senses. The second, more difficult meditation uses the knowledge gained from the first meditation and applies it to the personality—increasing its sense of self, while the self begins to plan its giving to its Self. As these conditions occur, the personality and self (the person) increases his or her consciousness. The first meditation does increase *awareness*, but does not produce a significant increase in consciousness.

A third, and much more difficult meditation is then employed *while* the spiritual disciple is interacting with others. This method directly affects intelligent activity and is used with which to join all three parts of time. The first meditation focuses on the past, the second meditation focuses on the future, and the third meditation adds the present as it joins all three parts of time with space—creating a Now. In this third meditation, the soul needs to be used because the personality cannot "control" both its self and itself while it reflects on what it is doing, all in the same time zone. The personality alone can never succeed in this task because the part of the mental plane that it controls and thinks from is too separated in its time and space. By somewhat fusing with its soul, the personality can employ the soul's part of time from the second tier, or the second mental sub-plane, to assist the personality in being able to reflect upon itself in real time, or in the "present" time—in a Now. It does so while it further plans and also is interacting to create more virtue and to therefore be less selfish and make fewer mistakes.

An example of the preceding concept, which is a complicated one, can be seen in a person who has been spiritually disciplining herself using the first two meditative methods (of hearing and being assisted by her Solar Angel), and is about to begin the third method of meditation. We will name this woman Julie. Through her spiritual disciplines, Julie has grown in new knowledge about past circumstances in which she used her senses selfishly and had thus limited her awareness. She has corrected some of these selfishnesses within herself and has increased her senses as well as the information they provide; she has also increased her personality's sense of self, and her overall awareness. Julie has also made plans for changing her self by using her new awareness to create more of God's thought in forms, or more virtue. Some of her plans involve interaction with her mother. Julie is now ready to attempt the third meditation, through which she relies upon her partially fused soul for assistance. In the next interaction that she has with her mother, Julie uses her five etheric/dense physical senses to determine that her mother's speech, including non-verbal expressions, indicate that she is communicating and responding to Julie with reserve and with avoidance of certain subjects. Julie also uses her empathy *and* creative imagination together. She creates super-empathy from a soul, or structured second-tier higher mental thought joined with the astral thought and sense to realize, or fully sense astrally, that her mother is troubled and is involved in a conflict. Julie focuses her mental senses on what her mother is saying in concepts and thoughtforms. Julie becomes aware that her mother is *avoiding* speaking about her work, and especially about certain people with whom she works. Julie now creates within herself the knowledge that there may be a problem between her mother and the people whom she is avoiding mentioning. When all of this sense and knowledge is being synthesized by the personality, it is simultaneously being given to the soul; the soul has been thinking of ways to give the synthesized knowledge with the additional understanding that comes from Julie's Self relative to her mother, herself, and her mother's work problems. This is done all at the same time that her personality is sensing and synthesizing. As the additional understanding becomes joined with the giving by Julie's soul, new, more creative thought that is intuitive is created by the soul (and Solar Angel) and then, through the personality, is used by Julie to create more virtue.

In a Now, Julie is joining time and space as new thought that is virtuous becomes created through the fusion of her soul and Self. Mental plane time and space are rejoining at the atomic level of the mental plane, where the Self is located. Julie uses these newly created second-tier concepts that are infused with atomic sub-plane mental understanding from the Self, in order to help her mother. Julie suggests to her mother that a problem she might be having with certain people at work might be adversely affecting her. Julie listens carefully to her mother's affirmative response. She then focuses her mother's thought on how she might help her co-workers to become more virtuous in certain ways. At first her mother is resistant to the notion of giving to others whom she perceives as not only not giving to her, but are actually causing her problems. Julie goes on to explain that her mother and co-workers are all connected to each other through God and life, or God's growth. Further, she explains that if her mother helps her co-workers to create more virtue, including helping them to being more loving (more giving in similar ways to still others), that her mother's problems with her co-workers will also be solved. Julie's mother then responds by expressing how helpful and wise that advice was, and that she already feels better (more loving). Julie is joyful because her mother has already become more virtuous by somewhat focusing more on others—and may do so considerably to a greater extent in the near future.

For the personality and self to create thought within a Now requires the assistance of their soul and its Self because on their own, the personality and self cannot think at a high enough level on the mental plane to adequately join time and space. The creation of a mental Now makes mental thought effortless because in a Now *no* energy is retained within the form of the life, and thus no forces are created. In a Now, all the energy that is used with which to create the form of the thought is enlightened and requires no further synthesizing by the personality. Time is not separated from space as it is when unenlightened energies are used. One important part of spiritual discipline is to enlighten the senses in each body, so that they bring in and send out only enlightened energy. The enlightened energy is then effortlessly used to create the forms of thought in each body.

Discipline of the self, spiritually, means expanding its thought and giving of it to the Self to be used at the Self's creative level. The Self's thought concerns how to *create* more of God; as the Self gives this thought to its soul, both the self and Self increase in their understanding of God. Thus spiritual self discipline restricts only the self's darker thoughts, while simultaneously *expanding* its thoughts that are more enlightened. Some physical life circumstances will now be examined in order to derive some practical solutions for raising consciousness. The areas used as examples are the typical ones that people who are beginning to spiritually discipline themselves have questions about and frequently have problems with, in their attempts to function successfully in creating intelligent activity.

   ## HOW TO EXERCISE SPIRITUAL DISCIPLINE IN MOSTLY THE ETHERIC/DENSE PHYSICAL BODY

The subject of sexual activity is one of those areas in life that is often cited as a problem concerning how to raise one's consciousness. The primary difference between other activities that can raise a person's consciousness and spiritual sexual activity is that with the latter, two people are both giving and receiving the same kind of energy at the same time; in no other human activity from the mental plane, down, does this take place. The giving and receiving of sexual energy at the same time complicates sexual exchanges, and may confuse spiritual disciples. To increase consciousness during sexual relations, one needs to give sexual energy in ways that help to grow, or serve, the sexual center and sense of one's sexual partner, in each of his or her three lower bodies (and possibly the higher, fourth body). The fourth, or intuitional, body may also be included by a more advanced spiritual disciple, if his or her partner is capable of giving sexually from that body. On an energy level, the process is deceptively simple. An example of what takes place in sexual love-making is a man first giving to a woman (although the example roles could be reversed) the correct amount of his energy that he has changed into the woman's phase (the direction of her energy), and directing his energy into the woman's sexual center. The difference in phase between a man and a woman is only *approximately* 180°, and so simply altering one's own phase by 180° does not work, and actually is self-focus and therefore is not loving. When the woman receives the energy the man just gave her, she changes it back into his phase, and synergistically adds the correct amount of her own energy (also matched in phase to the man) and directs it back into his sexual center. The process continues, with each partner giving back to the other the energy that he or she gave, but matched in phase to the recipient and added to until a maximum parity has been reached by both, and then they climax together. Empathy is the sense that is used the most to determine the correct amount of energy to be given to one's partner; when one partner has reached his or her maximum level of energy, and if only love was used in the exchange, then with the use of either empathy or super-empathy the other partner will cease adding energy. Although focus is on the etheric/dense physical body in this particular example of sexual spiritual discipline, some empathy and astral sexual discipline are nearly always used as an accompanying discipline. If too little energy is given, then energy does not correctly build between the partners; if too much is given, then the recipient's sexual center becomes over-whelmed with retained energy and painfully (although perhaps not consciously registered as such) damaged, and he or she may lose interest. Note that *selfish* men generally give energy that is of the correct phase but not enough or too much in quantity, whereas selfish women generally give the correct amount of energy, but of an incorrect phase (although the opposite conditions and, in fact, both conditions can exist in either gender). This single combined factor—incorrect amount of energy and incorrect phase of energy—is an important reason for many of the divorces and problems in relationships that occur. Because of the need to give a certain increasing amount of energy to another person at her or his individual direction, or phase, sexual activity between more than two people at the same time *cannot* be loving. Each correct direction reversal (how the energy connects to the center) and giving of added energy builds the self's identity of sexual gender in a person's sexual partner; this is the foundation of sexual love. Thus sexual love increases the speed and accuracy of the spins of all of the centers in each body because the sexual spin is what partly originates and then controls the spins of the other centers in that body. Giving sexual love to one's partner causes him or her to experience and become more of his or her sexual gender and self identity. As the self is increased (in consciousness—through love, of course), it moves closer to fusing with its Self and is less likely to become over-controlled by its personality—it is less likely to become selfish! The goal in love-making for spiritual disciples is to include the intuitional body, because when that body is included, the growth of the self becomes directed and fused into the growth of the mental Self while the highest thought (shared) by the lovers is controlled intuition and love of life—and of God.

If a person gives sexual energy that is not reversed in phase, or in gender response, then the self of her or his partner is decreased, and the self of the one "giving" in this way is, as well. The decrease in self can create a personality disorder in both partners, or can worsen a person-ality disorder that might already exist in either partner. When sexual energy is given and received without the phase having been reversed, *less* light is created, and some soul contact may be lost; at the very minimum, soul contact cannot be increased. When a person is selfish in his or her exchange of sexual energy, all of the centers in all of his or her bodies that are involved are slowed down and their senses are weakened. This can lead to disease and many more future errors in giving information. (See Chapter Seven for more information about centers and senses.) Only the sexual center can reverse its spin without producing death to the body it is in. The reason is that the sexual center's energy sphere is divided into two sphere-like parts that can each rotate in a different direction, and then can exchange sexual energy with another sexual center in another person's body. If the direction of spin of any other center were to reverse, that body would die; however, the centers are constructed to normally produce enough force to prevent a complete reversal from occurring. As a sexual center begins to reverse its spin—

usually because of prolonged and strongly homosexual activities—this alteration causes the other centers to wobble in their spins, and decreases their sense. Complete reversal of a center's spin other than the sexual center is not possible because before the spin could become reversed, it would have to stop—which would cause instant death to that body. The spin of the sexual center within each body *can* be eventually reversed without, initially, causing death, because it is the only center that can take in and give out (seventh ray) energy at the same time, circumventing its need to stop both sides of the energy spheres at the same time; it can do this because its energy sphere is divided into two somewhat separate parts and it is during homosexual *activities* that this is accomplished. Homosexuality creates problems, of wobbles in the centers' spins and of loss of self identity, in a person whenever he or she is functioning sexually, and exacerbates these problems if they already exist as a result of past homosexual behavior.

Those who want to raise their consciousness while engaging in heterosexual activities need to make love, by only giving. This is accomplished by a person synergistically, with progressively more energy in each body, appropriately giving sexual energy to another who is near her or his level of consciousness and who will be able to do the same. The greater the disparity in awareness and consciousness between the two people, the less that they can love each other sexually. In these circumstances, the phase of the energy given will be inaccurate because of the dissimilar levels of consciousness; also, the amounts of energy given will be different, and one or both partners may give incorrect amounts. When a person who is spiritually disciplining herself or himself is sexually involved with another, this involvement needs to be with one who is also spiritually disciplining himself or herself and at close to the same level so they can make love together. This restriction is a large sacrifice for some human spiritual disciples because they are more capable of accurately giving sexual energy than are non-disciples. Spiritual disciples are often considered by some non-spiritually disciplined people (usually those who are relatively advanced in intelligence and consciousness) to be sexually attractive because spiritual disciples usually can give more energy that consistently matches the direction of their partner's energy. It would hence be "easy" for human spiritual disciples to, more exploitively, have sexual encounters that would not fulfill *either* person's need for sexual love (of course, then they would cease to be functioning as spiritual disciples). Thus those who have more sexual energy, as spiritual disciples, need to limit their sexual activities to involvement with people with whom they can make sexual love. People who are not yet spiritually disciplining themselves but who are approaching the path of spiritual discipleship may encounter similar challenges at a lower level of limitation and difficulty.

Sexual energy that is used selfishly will generally cause most if not all of the following symptoms (presented in the order of how, on average, they are likely to be perceived): lethargy; loss of visual acuity; inaccurate hearing of speech; increased emotionalism, including heightened responses of anger and fear; loss of physical coordination; a lack of mental focus; and an overall diminished ability to understand, or a lowered consciousness. The symptoms usually begin to manifest within one to four hours after the selfish sexual activity. Because a person's overall awareness may decline as quickly or even faster than his or her consciousness declines, it may be difficult for some people to become aware of these symptoms—at least without focusing much more of their senses on the potential symptoms. Masturbation may produce these symptoms, especially if the astral thought (the creative imagination) is fairly selfish, which is very frequently the case. Less selfish astral thought during masturbation will produce less sexually retained energies, and will not reduce consciousness as much. It is not possible to raise consciousness through the act of masturbation. The typical delay in time between the selfish use of sexual energy and the onset of any of the above-listed symptoms is caused by the time dilation between the lower astral and etheric sub-planes and the dense physical plane. The individual symptoms are related to one of the major centers receiving retained energy from the sexual center in the same body in the following correspondences in each body: Lethargy—seventh, or sexual center; heightened emotionalism—sixth, or solar plexus center; loss of visual acuity—fifth, or ajna center; loss of coordination—fourth, or sacral center; loss of ability to hear certain speech—third, or throat center; loss of understanding, or of consciousness—second, or heart center; mental confusion or lack of focus—first, or head center.

Celibacy is, in many cases, undesirable because more damage can occur to the sexual centers by not exchanging sexual energy than might occur during some, less selfish, sexual activities. Celibacy practiced for *wrong* motives can (over *prolonged periods* of time) lead to serious disease, including some types of cancer. In order to stay healthy, those who practice celibacy, including not masturbating, need to transmute their sexual energy into intelligent activity that comes from enlightened throat center energies. A brief explanation of some approaches to a healthier celibacy follows; however, those involved in this process may need more information and may need to be taught how to successfully achieve the desired results. For those (including members of certain religious orders) who are practicing complete celibacy, including no masturbation, the following outline may be of some assistance:

1. Never repress sexual feelings—of any kind. Acknowledge them, and for those feelings that seem selfish astrally, imagine new, more loving *sexual* uses of the energies; then, using *mental* thought, think of the ways that these more loving expressions would serve others in general—excluding, of course, issues of celibate service in these instances. The crucial concept is to not repress sexual energy—which can be dangerous. Instead, alter emotional sexual energy into loving energy by mentally checking on its validity towards truly being of loving service to others, *if* the sexual energy were acted upon in a non-celibate circumstance.

2. Include sexual identity in non-sexual expressions; this can even include *appropriate* sexual flirtation (that is not acted upon). One can be her or his gender and still be celibate.

3. One should try to include his or her own sexual identity within intelligent activity that comes from his or her service through the throat center. One should, if possible, serve in some ways in which his or her gender makes a difference in improving his or her service.

4. Support groups that comprise people of *both* genders who are practicing celibacy (complete or partial) are very helpful if sexual feelings and the practice of celibacy are openly discussed. During the discussion, some sexual energy may be exchanged through transmutation into the throat center.

Most spiritual disciples, unless they are members of a religious order that involves a vow of celibacy, would be better servers if they were not fully sexually celibate because their awareness and consciousness would, most likely, be higher. Sometimes, however, sexual celibacy on a short-term basis is helpful or even required. For example, a person usually cannot complete the third initiation without being celibate for at least a month, and sometimes for two or more months prior to the initiation ceremony. In these cases, the Solar Angel directly communicates with the disciple and explains what specific disciplines are needed, and why. The four methods suggested above for reducing negative effects from long-term celibacy can also be used for partial celibacy or for short-term complete celibacy. For reasonably loving adults who are *not* spiritually disciplining themselves, celibacy is, in general, not recommended because the ways to remain healthy while being celibate require discipline, and, for the most part, discipline for spiritual purposes. Many activities that are sexual do not need to include sexual intercourse, for those seeking to avoid this sexual behavior. Some are as "innocent" as holding hands while feeling sexually attracted to the person whose hand is being held. The *loving* exchange of sexual energy develops higher consciousness, as well as closer human relationships.

Those who are homosexual and are involved in homosexual activity are likely to incur some or all of the symptoms of selfish sexual activity, even when such a person is involved with another whom she or he loves. This occurs because while the two homosexual people are sexually exchanging energy, they can do so only in ways that retain the energies in the centers. The build-up and release of the energy will still create sexual stimulation and orgasm, and will create pleasure. However, love cannot be expressed through these sexually pleasing activities, leaving the people involved less close afterwards, because of the sexual activity. Closeness can be increased through any other (non-sexual) expression of love, even during the sexual activity. The most serious problem with homosexuality is that it begins with some, and often leads to more, personality disorder because the personality is rebelling against the gender that its soul selected for it. Then the insidious reduction first in sense of self, and eventually of actual self occurs, leaving many homosexual people with the problems that are associated with these conditions. These problems include a lack of love and of consciousness, which can reach the level at which control over the self is lost over the lower bodies' informing spirit; this loss sometimes causes excesses in behaviors, including sexual behaviors—often in some form of an addictive nature.

For those who are homosexual and have more serious personality disorders and problems with sense of self or control over the self, or both, this book will not attempt to suggest remedies; traditional psychotherapy and other mundane methods may be of some help. For those who are approaching the path of spiritual discipline or are on it and are at least somewhat functioning in creating virtue, the following suggestions may be of assistance.

Homosexuality countermines the spiritual purpose of sexual activity, which is to build the self's identity of gender. The building of this identity is accomplished through each partner giving *more* energy to the other than was given to him or her, but reversed about 180°, and matched to the exact phase, or direction, of one's partner. This is done in order to *build* the spin and the connectedness of the spirit sphere (which increases consciousness) within one's partner's sexual centers (one in each body)—and eventually within her or his other centers as well. Homosexuality *forces* the opposite effect, blocking the correct gender spin of the centers in one's homosexual partner, and damaging each center's sense and then the connectedness of the spirit spheres, or the person's consciousness. Homosexuality also reduces the self by further reducing its sexual identity. The *act* of sexual activity between two people of the same gender can never be loving because of these factors. While masturbation may increase the above-listed symptoms, particularly when the astral imagination is used to create homosexual activities in fantasy, it is a better alternative than participating in homosexual activities with another person. The reason is that co-participants in homosexual activity are being significantly more harmed from the sexual energy that is given to them, which is in incorrect phase to their sexual centers' spins. When homosexuals "reverse" the sexual centers' spins within themselves they do not actually create the same spin as a person of the opposite sex (see Chapter Seven for a more complete explanation of this), but instead create a "new" and different type of spin that always reduces the self's gender identity because it is neither gender's correct sexual spin. Thus fully "reversing" the sexual spin in one of two homosexual people who are sexually involved together is not a solution to the above-described problem. Giving energy at the odd spin of a "reversed" homosexual sexual center causes that energy to become retained, because when the sexual center is used in such a way it can no longer give and receive energy at the same time. Less or no homosexual activity with another person can temporarily allow some time to make some other changes—all while masturbation is practiced as needed but as little as possible (and at first, probably using homosexual fantasies although heterosexual fantasies will produce much better spiritual results).

For those involved in a close relationship that includes homosexual activity and who would like to and are willing to change to heterosexuality, and if both people are of about equal consciousness and are practicing spiritual discipline, the relationship does not have to be abandoned. These two spiritual disciples can use their non-sexual love to help each other; doing so will require enormous courage and self control, which can come only from prior and continuing spiritual discipline. Only if both people are equally committed to changing can this method work. Prior to the cessation of homosexual activity, this activity should be conducted with full and constant focused eye contact. While this eye contact is maintained, each partner should attempt to think only of his or her partner with the desire to give to him or her what he or she needs in order to become even more virtuous. It is likely that this behavior will reduce homosexual feelings, when it is correctly carried out. Under such circumstances, using the eyes as described above leads to soul contact and involves the soul's loving thought. The soul's thought will contradict the homosexual feelings and convert them into non-sexual love, compassion, and overwhelming virtuous concern for one's partner. This "red tantric" yogic practice dates back in time to the Atlantean period, when it was used with several other (even more difficult) disciplines. This same method is also recommended for heterosexual couples who would like to increase their love and their soul contact while engaging in sexual activities.

Frank discussions about information contained in this book and from other sources as it relates to homosexuality can be of help to two homosexual partners who are close. The structured mental thought can help to break some of the very strong, kama-manasic thoughts regarding being a homosexual person and having homosexual activities. To achieve good results, both people need to have concluded that the information provided herein, or any information that

The Kama-Manasic Connection in the Mental Body

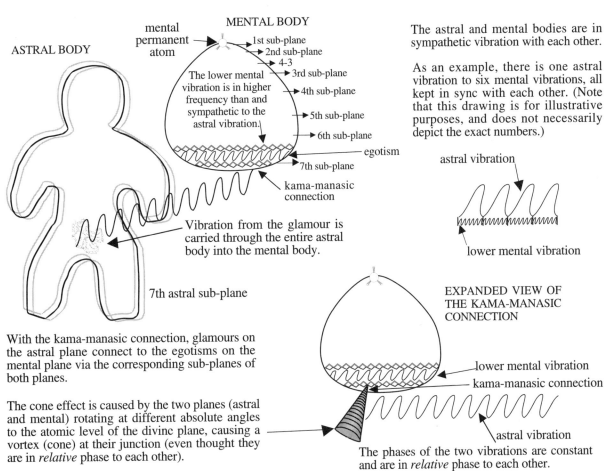

The astral and mental bodies are in sympathetic vibration with each other.

As an example, there is one astral vibration to six mental vibrations, all kept in sync with each other. (Note that this drawing is for illustrative purposes, and does not necessarily depict the exact numbers.)

With the kama-manasic connection, glamours on the astral plane connect to the egotisms on the mental plane via the corresponding sub-planes of both planes.

The cone effect is caused by the two planes (astral and mental) rotating at different absolute angles to the atomic level of the divine plane, causing a vortex (cone) at their junction (even thought they are in *relative* phase to each other).

The phases of the two vibrations are constant and are in *relative* phase to each other.

Illustration 12.2

they are using, from any source—is accurate. They need to have reached this conclusion based *not* upon belief, but on tested experience using either their past experiences and applying the information as a test or by creating new circumstances that challenge the information *logically* to determine its validity. Care needs to be taken to not be caught kama-manasically in thought while testing the validity of the information, because one's emotions can create fantasies in astral creative imagination that falsely prove whatever she or her (subconsciously) wishes to be correct. Some homosexual people consciously want to be heterosexual, but subconsciously have much stronger desires to be homosexual. This occurs because of rebellious angers and many unmet glamours that disorder the personality enough for it to lose first sense of and then control over its self.

A spiritual disciple who is homosexual and has initiated some of the above-mentioned changes may ask for assistance from another spiritual disciple of the opposite sex who is at or above his or her own level of consciousness. One method of assisting is for the opposite-gendered (and preferably heterosexual—to make it easier for both) helping disciple to use the above-mentioned tantric method of using eye contact while being close to the homosexual disciple, but *not* having (at least until both might desire to have) sexual contact. This is referred to as "white tantric" yoga, and can be very effective for spiritual disciples. The heterosexual disciple could gradually direct sexual energy towards the homosexual one, provided that this was agreed upon by both, prior to the yoga practice. As the correct sexually-phased energy is directly into the homosexual person's centers, and while this person is being shown compassion and given to with love/wisdom, the spin of the homosexual person's sexual center in each of the three bodies begins to correct itself. This relieves a considerable pressure, or force (retained energy), from within the center; paradoxically, many homosexual people find the retained energy to be homosexually arousing because it has become associated with sexual excitement and release, producing sexual pleasure.

There is a *great* deal more that could be explained to help homosexual spiritual disciples; however, this book has a broader purpose that precludes much further detail of this subject. To change one's sexual focus will usually require about as long a time as one has been practicing homosexual behaviors in this life. This time period includes any prior lives in which the homosexuality was not reversed. The exception to this generality occurs if one increases his or her service in ways that simultaneously reverse his or her homosexuality; doing so nearly always requires group/soul service and is usually facilitated by the presence of a *Teacher*. A *Teacher* is an advanced initiate who helps to raise the consciousness of the group by creating *new* knowledge, and creating understanding with this knowledge in the group.

Those people who are homosexual and are approaching the path of spiritual discipline but are not yet on it have less, but some, options for changing their homosexuality in their present lifetimes—if that is what they choose to do. The general principle of taking about as long to change as one has been homosexually *behaving*, applies more strongly to this group of people, and with fewer exceptions. Some further suggestions for members of this group include the following:

1. One would be much better off not condemning or disparaging himself or herself or others for being homosexual. Instead, acknowledge homosexuality as a mistake that the personality has chosen as a way of incorrectly and overly controlling the self's identity of its gender. The personality does this, *sub*conscious to the self, because it is rebelling against the soul's and OverSoul's selection of its gender for that lifetime or perhaps against other life circumstances that were predeterminations by the soul and OverSoul, or both.

2. One needs to not proclaim, espouse, demonstrate for, or attempt to convince others that homosexuality is good for people. The moral way (a way that helps society to become

more virtuous) to express one's homosexuality or that of others is as a fetter, or a limitation that causes difficulty for the personality and its self in increasing their growth and their relative ability to become more virtuous while engaging in sexual activity. Homosexuality does not make a person evil, nor does it necessarily *decrease* the amount of virtue a person creates non-sexually—although in some people this may occur.

3. One needs to protect children from subconsciously (or consciously) learning that homosexual expression of one's sexual feelings is good or even acceptable; books and teaching materials that espouse those concepts are immoral. The reason is that such expression is harmful to those involved, and if is held to be good or acceptable, it may create sexual relativism or even sado-masochistic contradictions to expressing love, through sexual activity. Children need to live with only love being expressed through sexual activity because children "learn what they live." They do so much more than adults do in similar circumstances. If a homosexual couple has one or more children living with them, the couple needs to frankly explain to the child or children how homosexual expression is hurtful. Unfortunately, this author knows of no way of doing this for young children under seven years of age, on average, that will not confuse such a child's love for his or her homosexual parent. It is hoped that others might have solutions to this conundrum.

4. One who is homosexual is best served by not rebelling in non-sexual ways that are not virtuous; virtuous rebellion, including the fight for one's equal rights with heterosexuals under the law, is healthy and builds the self. It is important to *avoid* extreme behaviors and/or personality affectations (which include radical forms of dress, piercings, tattoos, and mannerisms) that allow the personality to hide some of its disorder. Avoiding these behaviors and affectations helps to diminish the personality's rationalization that homosexual identity and/or personality-disordered behavior are desirable.

5. The stronger that the self becomes while the personality gains order among its bodies and senses and a sense of its self, without over-control, the less that a person will feel homosexual; however, long-term (many years, on average) homosexual activity may at any particular time overshadow the gradual and relatively small decreases in homosexual desire by increasing the self and personality order and sense.

6. The very best solution for homosexuality is to increase love and reduce emotion. As a person becomes significantly more loving, the conditions that created homosexuality diminish and eventually become extinguished. For spiritual disciples, this is a real tool for change. For those approaching the Path it may seem nebulous and even non-sensical. Increasing love means loving others wisely, including those who are homosexual. Love overcomes all emotion, since it is the reversal of emotion. Those who love are neither fearful of nor angry with homosexuals, whether they are themselves homosexual or heterosexual.

7. The self is affected by its environment (including the behavior of others towards it), because a self's environment often affects how it gives to others. The clothes that a person wears can have an effect on how others respond to and behave towards her or his self. Thus those who are seeking to change their homosexuality into heterosexual feelings need to dress heterosexually and need to use heterosexual mannerisms that cause others to respond to them as heterosexuals. They also need to associate with and interact with heterosexual people who are relatively more loving than average. It is usually not necessary to avoid the company of those homosexual people who are reasonably loving, provided that the first six of these seven steps can still be accomplished while in their company.

All of the above-detailed suggestions may take months or longer to implement, and success at changing sexual feelings (to raise consciousness) is still predicated upon both discipline and the creation of more virtue, especially the virtue of love. Those who decide to not attempt the change and those who cannot change will be assisted through ray and gender changes by their respective souls and OverSouls in the next incarnated life or lives of those people's souls. Making some attempts to change, *if these attempts are based upon virtue*, can make inner plane life as well as the life during the next incarnation much less strife-filled. The reason is that that next person's life circumstances relative to homosexuality, including her or his rays in the next incarnation, will not need to be as forceful to instrument the necessary changes; some of the negative karma will already have been overcome, leaving less to be dealt with later.

The last consideration of homosexuality in *Life's Hidden Meaning* deals with transsexual change through medical technology. In most cases where medical technology has been used to change a person's gender, the changes affect that person's etheric/dense physical sexual center, its sense, and its glands and hormones. These procedures and methods usually move the people that they are used on *closer* to becoming the gender that they are attempting to be, but leave them still quite far away because the spins of the other centers in the bodies are not reversed. Considerable training (and good acting) can cause such a person to appear much closer to being a member of the opposite sex from the one he or she was born as. It might be interesting to note that, if for a long period of time the transsexual person is quite virtuous and loves a person of the opposite sex (opposite to the transsexual's chosen gender)—including loving that person during sexual activity—then the correct phase and spin of the transsexual's *sexual* centers can be established, which is not the case with most other homosexuals. In some circumstances (those where the sexual center and sense are more prominently used), this allows transsexuals to function and appear much as the gender they would like to be. Some of these people may overuse the sexual center and its sense in their endeavors to achieve the appearance of the new gender.

There is a small percentage of people who seek transsexual remedy and whose centers spin opposite to their present sexual gender. These people were born either ambiguous or anomalous in their centers, and were generally treated as the wrong gender in early life. In these cases, transsexual surgery is a virtuous use of human civilization and its technology, to medically help those who are in need.

In addition to the subject area of sexual activity, another, mostly etheric/dense physical discipline that is an area of concern for many people involves proper diet for optimum growth of consciousness. The diet of those who are approaching the spiritual path and, especially of those who are functioning on the Path, often needs to be changed in order to achieve an increase in consciousness. The removal of alcohol, caffeine, and perhaps strangely to some, sucrose (table sugar) from one's diet can increase consciousness mostly in the etheric/dense physical body. Note that fructose and some other types of sugar do not lower consciousness because they require much less, if any, insulin for processing by the body. Although honey is about thirty percent sucrose, the effect of that sucrose is diminished because the sucrose molecules in honey are surrounded by fructose molecules, with fructose making up about seventy percent of honey. If a person changes her or his diet, the fallen spirit that is informing the etheric/dense physical body might have an easier time affecting the lunar devas and elemental energy within that body. This, in turn, makes it easier for the self to communicate and give its thought to the fallen etheric spirit—raising the self's consciousness and causing it to grow. Obviously, those people who have problems that are associated with a lessened self would also benefit from dietary changes; however, it is much more difficult to get these people to change because they often lack the self discipline in the very body that they most need the discipline in.

While not actually a part of one's diet, tobacco use is particularly significant in the way that it lowers consciousness because, by being smoked, it very quickly induces multiple chemicals into the etheric/dense physical body. Some of these chemicals also affect the astral and mental bodies by lessening the barrier of the webs, and prematurely allowing thought from one body to directly affect another body. (See Chapters One and Seven for more information about webs.) Tobacco selectively causes repression of certain emotions that a person who is using tobacco does not, at that time, want to experience. When tobacco is chewed, some of the same chemicals are ingested through the mouth, only more slowly.

Many of the people who are approaching the spiritual path of discipline believe that becoming a vegetarian is of prime importance in elevating their consciousness; however, the three above-mentioned items have a much greater overall impact on consciousness than does vegetarianism. Becoming a vegetarian and drinking alcohol with one's tofu and vegetables, and following that with caffeinated coffee and a sugary desert—perhaps with a cigarette—will dramatically *lower* consciousness. In that scenario, if a person were to have a bloody, rare steak instead of the tofu and vegetables, it is doubtful that there would be a noticeable change in his or her consciousness. The more spiritually disciplined a person is, the more being a vegetarian, including eating organic and even sprouted organic foods, will improve her or his both health and consciousness. Most people in the world as it is today would be physically harmed if they became strict vegetarians because they have neither the discipline nor the understanding (the consciousness) to eat correctly. They would be likely to become deficient in various vital nutrients and vitamins. Further, people who are fairly selfish and do not eat meat would find it more difficult to deal with their self-created and self-imposed *forceful* and conflictive lives. Meat causes people to become more aggressive and forceful, which selfishness brings into one's life, and then needs to be dealt with.

Some of what was explained immediately above is likely to upset some staunch vegetarians and animal lovers (although this author and the members of Ageless Wisdom Distributors are vegetarians as well as animal lovers—and are in general animal rights advocates). The reason would be that the explanation fails to extol vegetarianism for everyone, and for everyone at the present time. People need to have love for all parts of life, including human life! At present, most humans are not prepared to become strict vegetarians, and such preparation may, for them, require many more lifetimes. About twenty-five percent of the populations within the more advanced (usually first world) countries, for a total of much less than ten percent of the overall world population, could become vegetarian without causing harm to themselves. It should be noted, however, that where a person is born or lives is *not* a measure of his or her consciousness; in fact, some highly conscious people are born into second and third world countries as part of their potential service. This book may help to raise awareness (first) in many people concerning the eating of animals, and then consciousness in fewer numbers of people. At present, this is probably the most that can be virtuously accomplished.

For many spiritual disciples, following a vegetarian diet that contains many organic and some raw foods and sprouted foods is helpful in both creating healthy bodies and raising consciousness. While a vegan diet is appropriate for some people, it is not helpful towards either of these objectives for many spiritual disciples. The surprising reason is that so many disciples live in force-filled environments because of their accelerated karma, as explained earlier in this book. This force creates stress on the disciples' bodies, requiring dairy products and eggs in order to compensate. Organic and barnyard or free-range animals that produce dairy and egg products for human consumption are generally not being harmed in their group souls' development; their group souls may even be significantly helped, depending upon how they are treated by the humans who are around them. Non-fertile eggs are preferred as food over fertile ones because no life ever existed within the non-fertile ones; however, an egg's state of fertility can sometimes be difficult to ascertain. For the reasons stated above, ovo-lacto vegetarianism is the appropriate type of diet for many spiritual disciples and for some people who are approaching the spiritual path and who are advanced in intelligence and consciousness, or, sometimes, are more advanced in consciousness than in intelligence. This diet may still require the addition of nutritional supplements, particularly for those involved in stressful service while living under the force-filled circumstances that they have created by accelerating their karma. Those who are vegans may be doing quite well in their diets if their lives are less stressful through their service, and particularly if their karma is permitting a less force-filled life in general.

The eating of meat brings with it animal hormones and sometimes the potential partial possession by lowered animal spirit (This spirit can follow the meat!—see Chapters One, Seven, and Eight for more information about possessions.) Merely handling large quantities of dead animals can lead to some partial possessions by lowered animal spirit. These conditions can create some of the emotions in a person that the animal had just prior to and during its physical death. These emotions often include terror of humans and animosity towards them, which can be infused into a human who is partly possessed by animal spirit. Because of the hormonal issues and the incidence (for some people) of partial possession by animal spirit, a vegetarian diet leads to less fear and anger in a person's life, with less astral discipline then needed to overcome these emotions within oneself.

Drugs, except at some times when they are used with proper medical motive, reduce consciousness by interfering with the hormonal, nervous, and brain systems. Drugs also tend to disrupt and tear the energy webs between the three lower bodies. The use of drugs by more primitive societies, in order to bring about closer contact with spirits and as a part of the society's religion, can almost never be replicated by modern people because modern people do not share the same civilization. The simplest and probably most accurate way to approach incorrect, or non-medical, use of drugs is that they are always harmful to consciousness at some level. In modern people, selfish use of drugs will *never* raise *consciousness*, although they often can alter and sometimes even slightly increase awareness. However, a loss in consciousness is not worth the infrequent and slight increase in certain awareness (such as increased smell, taste, or hearing) that some drugs, can sometimes temporarily produce. Awareness is transient, while consciousness is long-term and far-reaching in its effects.

Most people need to sleep for an average of eight hours per night in order for their bodies to repair themselves from the prior day's selfishness and the resultant retained energies that have accumulated throughout their centers and bodies. The elemental and especially the lunar deva energies take over the bodies while a person sleeps. Sleeping less than the bodies need lowers consciousness. The reason is that the self cannot give enough thought to the informing lower spirit if that spirit is overtaxed with a body that, because it did not get enough sleep, is overwhelmed with retained energy. The more energy that is retained within a body, the less that body responds to its informing spirit. This often causes the fallen spirit to respond more like the energy (it follows the energy's thought) than like the spirit that it is. The less that the self and its attached higher spirit can give to fallen spirit (with the fallen spirit responding to and in the manner of retained energy), the less consciousness the self has and the faster the self diminishes. Proper sleep is a critical factor in maintaining and increasing one's consciousness.

Prana is the subtle energy source that is used to repair a body (See Chapters Six and Seven); it is available in diminishing amounts as the night progresses, because the etheric sun produces prana by affecting certain energies within earth's etheric (and astral and lower mental) atmosphere. On average, one hour of sleep after sunset but before midnight is worth close to two hours of sleep after midnight until the sun comes up; the further away from midnight, the stronger (before) or the weaker (after) the pranas will be. For example, on the day of the year that has the most daylight (the summer solstice), at locations within earth's temperate zones, sleep that takes place between about nine o'clock and ten o'clock at night has as much prana available as does sleep that takes place between about two o'clock and four o'clock in the morning (not considering daylight savings time). Some people who have highly damaged bodies need less prana per hour because they have less ability to use it; they may also need large amounts of sleep. These people might not be able to get enough sleep, though, because sleeping during the times when prana is higher can cause an overstimulation of their centers. This overstimulation makes it more difficult for such people to sleep at the appropriate time for their bodies the next time they try, and can increase retained energy in some centers that have been used (relatively) overly selfishly. Sleeping during the day for more than an hour or two can produce overstimulation of the centers, as well—especially after the noon hour. In reasonably healthy people, the bodies can adjust to the minor diurnal changes in prana and the more major seasonal changes. The bodies of unhealthy people may be unable to adjust, which could lead to further disease. Those who are virtuous have the greatest ability to adjust and will incur less disease caused by some erratic sleep circumstances. However, people who sleep erratically or inadequately over longer periods of time are likely to fall in consciousness. This happens because they are not giving to their bodies the amount of sleep that their bodies need.

The general rule for maximally raising consciousness through proper sleep discipline is to awaken at sunrise after having slept for eight hours. A person following this schedule would be changing his or her sleep schedule by about forty-five seconds per day; for many people, doing so is impractical, so averaging the daily time of retiring per season is often sufficient for some spiritually disciplined people. Again, karmically *and* relative to one's service or to how much virtue a person who is approaching the spiritual path is creating, the amount and timing of one's sleep may be forcefully upset, negatively affecting consciousness. Under these circumstances, people need to create the best sleep schedule that they can. Being sensitive to the needs of the bodies by careful observation of the effects of different sleep cycles and conditions can be of great value and should be a part of the discipline.

The etheric body is cleansed some of retained energy by physically showering, which usually has a greater positive effect on it than does bathing. When water that is moving is mixed with air, the etheric field's conductivity is affected, and its ionization levels often change at the etheric/dense physical boundaries. Bathing does tend to reduce retained energy in the astral body by this body's at least partial interpenetrating submergence into the corresponding sixth ray compound of water. Because of women's feminine nature, which corresponds to the more astral sixth ray, women may prefer baths to showers, and often find baths to be more astrally helpful than men do. This is especially the case when the woman's astral body is focused along the sixth ray, or even along one of the other feminine rays. (See Chapters Three and Seven for more information about the rays and their effects on the bodies.) The combination of both a bath and a shower is recommended for some people because each has its strength in cleaning a different body. The mental body, and particularly the lower mental body, tends to be cleansed of some retained energies by sunlight that is taken in especially through the eyes and ajna center; the sunlight does not have to be seen for this to occur. Spending any length of time in a large, warehouse-type store can often cause the multitude of lower mental sub-plane thought-forms there to contaminate peoples' lower mental bodies, making it difficult for them to think or mentally sense correctly. After leaving such a store, during daylight hours, spending time in a park or an area that is not densely populated can clear out these thoughtforms. Doing so can somewhat raise a person's consciousness by increasing certain pranas that have been depleted within the lower mental centers, and by releasing certain other retained energies.

Music that was composed by and then played by people with calm astral bodies and with more love than emotion can produce some of those same effects on the astral bodies of people who choose to listen to that music. The reverse is also true: listening to music that has been (emotionally) selfishly composed or played will agitate a person's astral body and lead him or her into emotionalism. One should not confuse emotional music with either volume or tempo;

some loud music that has a high tempo, but was composed and played with love and in a *calm astral body*, can create the love of helping others to have courage, hope, and vision. This would be astral imagination that aspires towards a better future. Adding some future part of time (even if that part is disconnected from the other parts) into the astral body is very helpful towards enlightening this body; the future is mostly lacking on the astral plane. It is the effects of the music that are so critical, and these effects are fairly easily discernible, even by people who are undisciplined. Emotional music tends to focus people in either the present or the past. It might be interesting to note that the conditions described above also apply to dance, and that dance further interpenetrates into music's effect while involving more of the etheric/dense physical body.

 ## HOW TO EXERCISE SPIRITUAL DISCIPLINE IN MOSTLY THE ASTRAL BODY

The topic of music can shift, quite naturally, into a focus on raising consciousness through the more astral disciplines. The astral disciplines all interpenetrate the etheric/dense physical body over time. Fantasies are constructed from astral imagination, and can raise consciousness *if* they are not founded on glamours and if they help to create more virtue both in the one who is fantasizing and in others whom the fantasy may affect. Fantasizing about selfishly motivated astral thoughts will lower consciousness and build more emotion. The important point in determining a fantasy's level of selfishness is in the measure of how loving the fantasy is towards others combined with its possibility of being enacted. The more loving the fantasy is and the greater the possibility of it being actualized, the more it could raise consciousness and not lower it.

Astral discipline is many times more difficult to succeed in than etheric/dense physical discipline is because the astral senses in physically alive humans are overwhelmed by the etheric/dense physical ones; also, most people wrongly consider their astral thought, or their imaginations, to be both innocuous and irrelevant where others are concerned. Many people think that they have a "right" to feel, emotionally, however they do and they validate their (selfish) selves through having and even encouraging themselves to have various emotions (instead of love). *Every* emotion is a hidden form of astral selfishness that can be converted into love, if the emotion's direction, or phase, is correctly changed away from the self, outward towards another

The discipline for changing emotions into love can be effectuated through the following steps:

1. First and foremost, in order to change emotions into love one needs to have clear astral thought (clear creative imagination). Astral thought becomes clear by not using it to construct *selfish* fantasies. Once the astral thought is clear, astral imagination is used with which to construct fantasies about changing one's emotional responses into love—before the actual attempts are made. The concept is that people are first what they think.

2. Close in importance to #1, above, a person needs to have empathy (all five of the astral senses of form joined together) in order to know how and when the love that results from emotions having been changed into givingness can appropriately be given to others according to the others' needs. Joining this second step with the one that precedes it and then adding structured mental thought in order to verify the truth, or the validity of results, creates super-empathy. Note that what is spiritually given to others is that which the others need to improve their love, and may even be contrary to what they want. That which is spiritually given is often in some ways antagonistic to certain "feelings" of self-sensed emotions that the recipients of the givingness have.

3. Empathy is built when most or all of the information that enters all five of the astral senses of form is used to focus on and benefit others. Using the information in the opposite

manner, in self-focus, causes empathy to split into the individual astral senses. The splitting is caused by the forces that are produced by self-focused retention of the information, or energy, that enters the senses. These forces prevent the spirit sphere part of each center from spinning and from connecting with the spirit sphere part of each other center.

4. One can neither "force" nor *will* oneself to not be emotional; the above steps are a *necessity* if emotions are to be changed into love. Force and will cause emotions to become either repressed or suppressed. Repression hides emotions from both the self and the personality's control over them. Suppression hides emotions from the self, making them subconscious (somewhat lowering consciousness), but continues to allow the personality to have control over how these emotions will be acted upon. Both repression and suppression tend to build glamours, which are fixed desires within the astral body. (See Chapters Seven and Nine for more information about glamours.) Further, repression tends to cause glamours to join together. The reason is that the personality whose emotions are being repressed is not able to interfere with that process, which causes a loss of control over the astral body. With suppression, the personality usually will prevent glamours from joining together because *it* seeks to control the astral body, rather than allowing its glamours to do so.

5. Emotions are greatly exaggerated by wrong (astral) speech, which is speech that causes others to become more emotional. The practice of silence is *sometimes* the more appropriate *first* response to one's own emotionalism—and that of others. When others are emotional, instead of responding with speech, careful listening while asking oneself, "Why is this other person (or animal) being emotional rather than loving?" will focus one outward. Then empathy and creative imagination, along with some structured thought, are used as in steps one through three, above. Right astral (loving) speech might then be necessary to influence the one who is being emotional to instead become more loving. Speech refers not just to words, but to voice, its tone, and numerous nonverbal ways of communication as well. Under certain circumstances, touch can also play a strong role in assisting a person or animal to change emotion into love.

There is an etheric/dense physical factor that can somewhat affect creative imagination, empathy, and astral love. This factor is the length and condition (including color, texture, and thickness) of the hair on a person's body, especially on the head! Hair absorbs the very finest etheric pranas and, under certain circumstances, some relatively very coarse astral ones. The less prana there is in general, the more critical it becomes for people to have the appropriate color and amount of hair to meet their individual needs for prana. Etheric prana is weakest during the winter and after midnight on any particular day (it is the very weakest just before sunrise), and is most needed when *astral* prana is being used up because a person has been creating more emotionalism than love. The ray structures of the astral and etheric/dense physical bodies play a significant role in this overall effect. As stated above, hair color is important, regardless of whether it is natural or has been changed by artificial means. What occurs is that as people function more emotionally, they tend to need more of the astral prana that is coarser and denser—particularly sixth astral sub-plane prana, in order to repair their astral centers (mostly while they sleep). The more hair a person has and the longer it is, the more of these coarser and denser astral pranas that it absorbs. The same hair is also supplying to the etheric body the least dense and the finest etheric pranas, for the repair of the most subtle parts of the etheric centers. Hair color will very slightly affect which sub-sub-ray of the astral prana's sub-ray will become more attracted to it, through sympathetic vibration of the color.

The effects of all of the above-described factors are as follows:

People who are very emotional need longer hair in order to absorb more remedial prana.

Ideally, their hair color should match their slightly "preferred" ways of being emotional—and of needing extra astral prana. Longer hair will also tend to increase the most sensitive parts of the etheric body's senses. Women tend to be more emotional than men are on average, which results in women generally growing their hair longer than men do—although cultural development and conditions can alter these factors.

Bald or balding people and those with very short hair may subconsciously reduce their intake of certain astral pranas to the level at which they are astrally selfish (emotional); after prolonged periods of and large amounts of astral selfishness, they may lose some empathy and creative imagination. Virtuous people will be less affected in this way. People who have not very much hair may also become slightly less sensitive in the most sensitive parts of their etheric senses. These people will tend to *become* less emotional in certain ways, while those who have longer hair will tend to become more emotional more easily in certain ways, but will also tend to have greater creative imagination.

Women in particular who lead selfish and stressful lives may become less astrally creative, or may use their astral creative imagination less, as their hair gets progressively shorter (and in some circumstances, if their hair color is altered as well). As women develop more stress within themselves because of forces in their lives, they tend to prefer having shorter hair—which reduces their negative use of creative imagination, but also reduces their empathy and their astral creativity. Shorter hair in women can increase their creative mental thought if it limits the kama-manasic connection. With shorter hair, women become less emotional if they are selfish astrally, and they become less sensitive etherically when they are etherically selfish.

The length of one's hair is in many circumstances voluntary, and a person generally subconsciously grows her or his hair to the length that best serves her or his personality, with the real reasons for the hair length (and color, as well) also unknown to the self (or, stated another way, a person is not conscious of these reasons through her or his self). Consciousness comes through the self giving; what the self cannot or will not give, sometimes because of the personality's over-control, is subconscious to the self.

During periods of time in the past and within certain cultures, hair length has been chosen subconsciously (to the self), based upon desired changes to the ways in which the two sexes related and upon other factors of the civilization. Having less hair with less color in it is a "natural" occurrence in the aging process. This occurs mostly because of either accumulated retained energy or negative karma (prior retained energy) as it affects the permanent atoms and the genes, or because of both. Accelerated karma can cause a loss both of hair and hair color in a relatively young spiritual disciple; however, anyone who loses hair or hair color at an early age certainly cannot be determined to be a spiritual disciple based on simply those factors. How to best deal with these conditions brought on by the way accelerated karma affects hair is more complicated than the solutions that have been thus far presented to other problems, and falls beyond the scope of this book's purpose. As hair and hair color become lost, so does the lower astral and etheric bodies' adaptability to increase the absorption of certain pranas that are needed because of accumulated selfishness. In general, adaptability prolongs life. However, the diminished adaptability that comes from loss of hair or hair color *slows* the aging process in the future. It does so by limiting a person's future ability to be selfish in the ways in which he or she has been selfish in the past. The reason is that he or she will have less of certain energies available to retain when being selfish.

The above-mentioned issue, along with a multitude of other concerns regarding spiritual discipline, will be more deeply explored at another time. In general, those who are attempting to become increasingly sensitive to the more subtle etheric energies, and who desire to maximally increase their creative imagination may find that having longer hair of a certain color is helpful, as might be having larger amounts of hair if the hair is growing on one's body, and not, for example, as a wig or hair extensions. If the increased sensitivity and creative imagination are used virtuously, then health will improve, as will consciousness; however, if they are used selfishly, the result will be more disease, faster aging, and lowered consciousness. These effects are strongest during the winter months and are weakest during the summer, because in the wintertime there is less prana, *and* that is when people have less hair—in thickness and density—because winter is when hair grows the least. Thus the greater the selfishness, the stronger the seasonal forces that result from karma; these forces are further exacerbated under certain circumstances in those whose hair is longer. Facial hair produces an added effect to the effect of head hair, although somewhat to a lesser extent because of facial hair's proximity to centers other than the crown center. Hair on the head has the greatest effect on consciousness because this hair's collective pranas affect the head center first; the head center in each body is where the consciousness thread first enters that body, even if the center is not yet active.

Unless a spiritual disciple is part of a spiritual group that is functioning within the initiations and is creating virtue, he or she will find astral discipline next to impossible to succeed in. The reason is that it is mostly through interactions with others who are also working on astral discipline and through these others' feedback that emotions become recognized, and the capacity to change these emotions into love is developed. This is somewhat true of etheric/dense physical discipline as well; however, more of these etheric disciplines can be worked on under more mundane circumstances because many of these disciplines do not directly involve other people. The extent of people's mundane discipline of emotions is generally the level to which they suppress or repress much of their emotions when they are around others whom, typically, they are not close to. This effect is the result of people being emotional and wanting to remain so while not wanting to reveal their astral selfishness, or emotionalism, to others. For people who are not spiritually disciplining themselves, families tend to be the crucible of growth when both etheric/dense physical and astral virtue are slowly developed through close interactions that flush out each family member's selfishness. A person's family is his or her mundane group.

 ### HOW TO EXERCISE SPIRITUAL DISCIPLINE IN MOSTLY THE MENTAL BODY

The mental disciplines are, by far, the most difficult with which to achieve success, and they correspondingly and interpenetratingly create the greatest rise in consciousness when this success is reached. Mental discipline requires the improvement and then unification of the mental senses. This is accomplished with the informing spirit's thought becoming more structured, more logical, conceptual at a higher level, and giving based upon others' ability to do the same. Mental discipline usually begins with the mental senses. Although people in general are quite aware of their physical senses and somewhat aware of their etheric and astral senses, very few have any awareness whatsoever of their mental senses! The reason for this oblivion is that the speed of mental thought and its sense is too fast for the personality and its self, alone, when alive dense physically, to be able to perceive either its or others' mental sense or its or others' thoughtforms and concepts. As the personality fuses with the soul, it gains awareness both of mental sense and of thoughtforms and concepts, albeit very slowly in the beginning of the fusion process. First, the physically alive personality typically senses thoughtforms as a pressure against creative thought—with the pressure caused by the thoughtforms' slight inertia. The next step is, usually, for the personality to become aware that it has an awareness of others' thought, by first recognizing that the words of others may not accurately express their mental (and astral, as well) thoughts; note that young children (almost all of whom have yet to develop their mental senses) do not usually have much sense of the difference between what a person says and what she or he thinks. Few people progress beyond being aware that they somewhat

How Thoughtforms Create Either Logical or Illogical Sentences on the Lower Mental Sub-planes

The following examples show how informing spirit, lunar pitris, and elemental energies either do or do not work together to represent how thoughtforms are created from concepts.

In these examples, the elemental energy is represented by the inside energies, and the lunar pitris are represented by the shapes surrounding the inside energies that together create the words. Elemental energy and lunar pitris are both needed to make thoughtforms that are created from concepts.

Example 1: The thought of spirit is great enough for lunar pitris to follow. The lunar pitris direct mental elemental energy into a logical time and space sequence so that the listener has a clear concept in his or her mind.

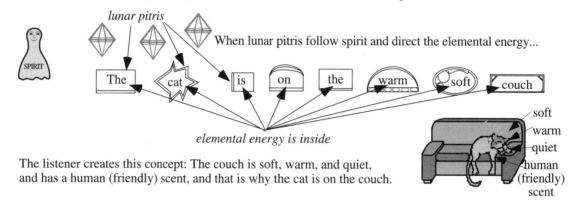

The listener creates this concept: The couch is soft, warm, and quiet, and has a human (friendly) scent, and that is why the cat is on the couch.

Example 2: If spirit is not strong enough or if lunar pitris are hurt because the form's senses have been damaged as a result of egotism, then the illogical sentence incorrectly represents time and space.

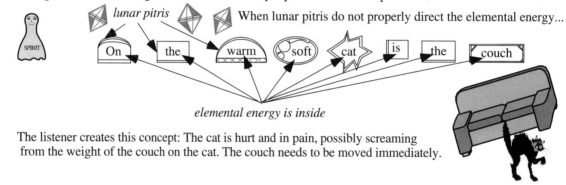

The listener creates this concept: The cat is hurt and in pain, possibly screaming from the weight of the couch on the cat. The couch needs to be moved immediately.

Example 3: If enough selfish retained energy is creating forces in the mental body to damage the elemental energy and mental lunar pitris at the same time, time and space may be changed first. If the lunar pitris are incorrect, the elementals that follow the lunar pitris will not be correct, and the wrong thoughtform will be used and incorrect information is then conveyed.

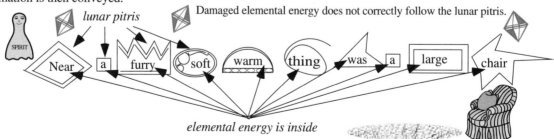

The listener creates this concept: The furry thing was a rug. The rug or chair must have been moved, perhaps to keep feet warm, or to balance the chair for esthetic reasons.

Illustration 12.3

know what another person is thinking if that other person is not speaking; most people can barely sense when the words and mental thought of person who is speaking do not match.

In most people who are physically alive, the self is no more conscious of the use of the mental senses than the personality is aware of them as a unified sense. The reason is that the mental senses are so subtle that they are overridden by the etheric/dense physical senses, and by the self's consciousness of them and sometimes of the astral ones, as well. Thus the self does not understand the mental senses, and even with the assistance provided by this book and its explanation of the mental senses in Chapter Seven, in most people the self's limited consciousness prevents an understanding of these senses. To be fully aware of and to understand the mental senses (lower *and* higher) requires that they be used joined together, at least some of the time. The more that the mental senses are used joined together—which creates mental virtue when the information and knowledge are created into truth—the greater one's awareness and understanding of these senses. Usually only spiritual disciples have some awareness and understanding of the mental senses. On average, first level initiates at the accepted stage achieve about ten percent unification of the mental senses; second level initiates at the accepted stage, about twenty-five percent; third level initiates at the accepted stage, over fifty percent; and adept fourth level initiates before or at the accepted stage reach one hundred percent unification of the mental senses and body. As the senses join, the self and Self unify through the third part, or leg of the triangle of light. This is the rainbow bridge of radiant light that comes from the solar devas on the first tier of the causal body and the last inner sacrifice petal to open.

When the self and Self together gain *understanding*, or consciousness, of the mental senses, they then can understand how truth is a part of God's thought in form, or of God's mind brought together manasically. To help the vast majority of readers who are not yet at this level of consciousness, the following explanation, while not completely accurate, is a fairly close representation of the understanding that is gained by the self and Self through using full, or whole, mental sense. For a person to actually experience the following effects would require self consciousness, or understanding, while being fully awake and aware on the mental plane. Imagine that every object that was observed, whether animate or inanimate, could be "seen" in all the ways that it is connected to all other objects both on its dimension (the mental) and below. These connections form amazing patterns and are balanced together through the structure of the energies within each type of form. The spirit that informs each form can be also "seen" as structures of thoughtforms and concepts that are balanced by their levels of wholeness, or are imbalanced by their lack of it. From the position of observing with whole mental sense and understanding, one can extrapolate from even the least enlightened structures what their whole structures would be like if they were completely given for others to experience and further create with. When whole mental structures are given in the above-described manner, they are actual *truth*, and each time truth is created with this whole mental sense, God is experienced and, in this scenario of others further creating with the truth that they were given, so is joy. When the whole mental sense is created and thus joins together the lower and higher mental bodies, consciousness expands exponentially as compared to the expansion of consciousness that comes from creating whole astral thought, or super-empathy (which still requires *some* higher mental plane thought from a minimum level of the second tier). The reason is that all three parts of time (past, present, and future) are rejoining with each event in space that is part of the truth—creating the lowest level of a completed Now. The process of joining together the senses and thought of a body into a union is referred to as yoga. To practice a mental yoga requires that the mental senses be built so that the personality has some level of awareness of these senses. As this awareness is used to help others to create more truth, the self and Self fuse and an understanding is then developed about the information that is supplied by the unified mental sense. This understanding is about God and its thought, and is not more understanding of the self—nor of the personality.

How the Solar Devas Are Damaged by Selfish Thought

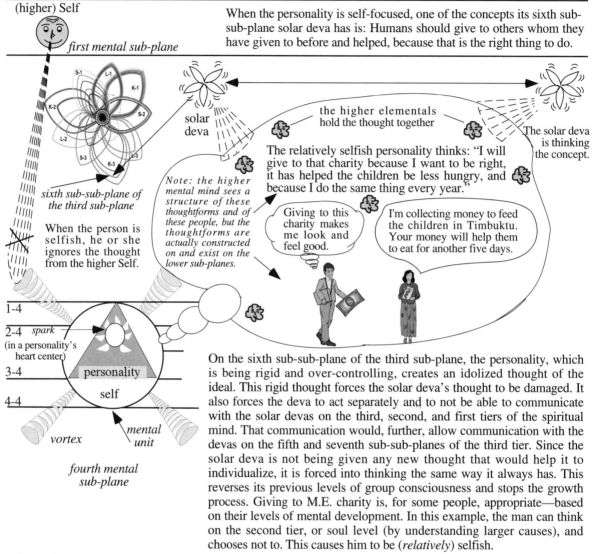

Illustration 12.4

The unification of each higher body also further unifies the body or bodies below it and begins or augments the unification of the bodies to each other. The process eventually creates one super-sense of the collection of all the bodies and each body's seven senses all together, of being a functional part of God at and below that level of dimension. The union of the senses creates a geometric increase in consciousness. When coupled with the multiplied level of one's spiritual thought, the result is an exponential increase in consciousness. Again, consciousness is the ability to give (love) and to understand (the oneness of all). There have been a number of yogas practiced on earth, with each new one replacing the one that preceded it. Each new completely developed yoga is more difficult than was any that preceded it because the new one requires more spiritual thought or more development of the senses, or both, than the last one did. However, successful practice of a yoga produces an increase in consciousness that matches the yoga's difficulty. Spiritual disciples today need to begin with mental yoga, and not a physical or astral one, because their level of response and capacity of thought is on the mental plane within the spiritual mind. This has been true since the fifth major race became the dominant major race, about eleven thousand years ago. For those who are not yet ready for such a vigor-ous mental discipline as a mental yoga, there are a number of less difficult methods of mental discipline that can somewhat raise consciousness.

How the Solar Devas Grow by Giving Thought, and Become Individualized

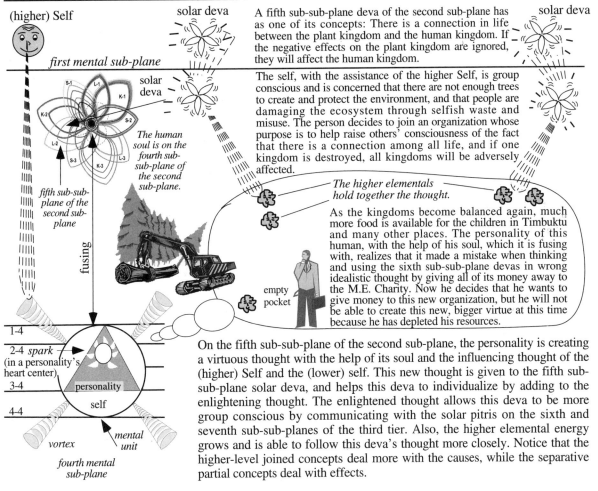

Illustration 12.5

One of these methods, which focuses on directly perceiving a mental sense, is as follows. Even if one is not yet aware of the mental senses, one can try to perceive and perhaps under-stand the sense called mental vision. The most limited and frequent use of this sense in non-spiritually disciplined people is the gaining of a mental structured picture of what someone else was thinking while he or she had written (such as this book) or had spoken. Mental vision is often the strongest mental sense, and it focuses on the present part of time. This mental struc-tured picture that comes from the split mental sense is always a series of "moving" pictures that create a structured thought of what another person is thinking at the same time (which also occurs when first reading that person's thought). Note that mental thought is unlike astral thought, which moves in only one direction of time at a time. A person who has at times some-what unified her or his mental senses through mental discipline might attempt to perceive a more unified and advanced use of mental vision with the other lower as well as the higher mental senses by finding someone in close proximity who is very strongly mentally focused in thought and who has not spoken just prior to the test, and who can be later quizzed about his or her thought. This second person (the source of the thought) needs to think about something that is stronger in structured thought and subject content than what the experimenter (the receiver of this thought) is thinking about, *and* the recipient needs to be able to understand this thought while the other person is thinking it. The recipient needs to not be egotistical about either the other person's thought or about the experiment. Strong thought comes from the wholeness created from a well-focused concept that is connected to a complete series of thoughtforms that explain the concept. Those people who have at least somewhat unified their higher and lower mental senses are likely to be able to accurately mentally sense what the other is thinking. This is represented by number three, below, and is using the complete and whole sense of mental vision with the other lower mental senses. Note that only spiritual disciples, although they might not identify themselves as such, have unified their mental senses to any degree. The reason is that only spiritual disciples practice the necessary discipline to do so. In the case of functional spiritual disciples, no intermediary mental picture is created from a split sense, just pure conceptual thought is because the higher and lower mental senses are joining, creating a concept rather than a series of thoughtforms. For people who are not functioning spiritually and are, at a particular time, being egotistical, the way of initially detecting mental sense is (listed as number two, below) sensing what a another person's thought was while that person was writing or speaking, with that person's thought creating pressure against further egotistical thought. The first-listed way of mentally sensing occurs when thought is sensed as being added to one's non-egotistical existing thought. The below-listed first two ways of mentally sensing use separated mental sense, and are much easier with which to discern than is the third. To restate, the three ways of mentally sensing thought are as follows:

1. Sensing what someone is thinking from thought that is relatively whole and truthful, in real time.

2. Sensing one's own or another's egotistical thought that has been written or spoken—which causes pressure against one's own thought; many people are able to sense this kind of pressure.

3. Sensing another person's thought using all of the mental senses, whether the other person's thought is spiritual or not; in the beginning of this perception of sense, however, the other person's thought will need to be very strong and have not been either spoken or written, in order to test whether the whole mental sense is being used. The more virtuous that a person is, the easier it is for her or him to sense another person's thought in this way. In these cases the spiritual disciple receives whole thought—directly and fully in structure with her or his mental mind.

When using the split and/or partially fused mental senses in the circumstances described below, a person would experience the following with each isolated use of those senses:

1. Mental Telepathy—Those who are not well developed in this lower psychic lower mental sense would be likely to experience the thoughtforms of others, often in incomplete sentences. These thoughtforms, as phrases, or incomplete sentences, are picked up by the lower mental sense anywhere from seconds to an hour or so after they were thought of. The receiver of the thoughtforms seldom knows their origin.

    1a. When used with the other lower mental senses but if from well developed mental senses and not conceptually whole, this split partially fused sense tells one person what a second person, who might be some distance away, has thought. The first (the receiving) person may know *what* the second person's thoughtforms are, *who* that person is, and sometimes *when* the thoughtforms were thought of, but usually not *where* the person is. The second person's thoughtforms are received by the first person a few seconds to an hour or longer after they were thought of.

2. Mental vision—If the (first) person who is using limited split lower mental sense is egotistical, or if the thought comes from an egotistical (second) person, the first person will "feel" a pressure, limiting her or his own abilities to structure her or his own thoughtforms. When both (or more than two) people are thinking with this split sense but less egotistically, then the receiver will see the thought of the "sender" as the sender is thinking it; or, as he or she did think it while having written the words or having recorded them audially. What is perceived by the person receiving the thought is a mental moving picture of the thoughts that is structured in time and space.

    2a. Those who use mental vision with the other two lower mental senses, but do not fully join the received thoughtforms to a concept, are generally able to tell who the other person is and either when the other person or people are or were thinking *or* where he, she, or they are or were thinking from. That is, either *who and when* or *who and where* can be perceived about the received thought but not both, because time and space are separated by the use of a split sense. The "receiver" of the thought can "see" in her or his mind a moving structured picture of the other person or people's thoughts as they occur (or occurred).

3. Mental clairvoyance—Those who have less development of this lower mental sense are able to sense what others have mentally thought and are presently mentally thinking. Using averages, the "receiver" of these thoughts can estimate a likely outcome in future thought. The more that this type of thought is applied to a greater number of people concerning the same event, the more accurate the sense is about how others will structurally think in the future.

    3a. When joined with the other lower senses, but not conceptually whole and complete lower mentally, the clairvoyant person is the "receiver" of *all* others' lower mental thoughts regarding the past and present thoughts who are thinking about the same event. Then the future can be logically structured as an average of others' thoughtforms.

If all of the above-described split lower mental senses are joined to whole concepts, the person sensing will have wisdom in his or her thoughts. His or her thought will be whole and in complete conceptual structure, rather than being a specialized (limited) series of moving structured pictures.

Raising consciousness through mental discipline that is less rigorous than mental yoga can be accomplished through the following methods:

1. Reading spiritual material that increases truth in the reader's mind. The mental body responds best to a consistent routine because this body's structured design leads it to establish a rhythm to time and space, and this rhythm is destroyed by inconsistency. The mental centers have the least amount of retained energy when a person awakens from sleep, after mental dreaming and after the mental elemental energies have repaired some of the centers in the mental body. For most people, reading spiritually truthful material soon after awakening (and for most of them, in the early morning) will raise consciousness. This reading should be done *each day* at about the same time, for about the same length of time. The understanding of the spiritual material will, for most people, be highest upon awakening and lowest before going to sleep.

2. Mental meditation, after the morning reading (or after creating one's own spiritual thought), on the ways in which what was read (or thought of) that morning will be applied throughout the rest of the day. Mental meditation involves structuring the

thought, using both logic and wisdom to arrive at truth, and includes planning new ways to think and then checking those new ways for validity by comparing the expected results with previous—known—outcomes. The ultimate verification can come only from adding astral and etheric/dense physical energy (form) to the mental thought and its form; this involves taking action and observing whether the action coincided with the original mental structure and its mental validity.

3. Assessing one's behaviors during the previous day, to determine how closely those behaviors matched what was planned in that morning's meditation. The best time for this assessment is every evening, for the last one-half to one hour before retiring for sleep. In this process, one should be able to identify those areas in which she or he was too selfish to succeed in creating the amount of virtue planned that morning. There needs to be a particular focus on locating the areas of egotism that produced the incorrect mental evaluation in the morning and resulted in a different outcome. It is important to remember that only egotism or arrogance would prevent a person from creating the truth about astral events as they were dealt with etheric/dense physically, or behaviorally. For changes in events throughout the day, the attempt should be made to become aware of and then conscious of *why* these other circumstances occurred without having been planned for; this process significantly raises consciousness when practiced regularly because it joins all three parts of time to space (and the higher mental plane and body, of concepts, with the lower mental plane and body, of the concepts' effects). Each of these unplanned circumstances is a part of one's givingness, or consciousness, where one's consciousness was not high enough to meet the prior karmic factors, or to undo one's prior selfishness. Thus each unexpected event is a part of karma that has not been compensated for by one's present level of consciousness. If the karma is good, or positive (and produces unexpected good events), then one was more conscious at a prior time than at present about this area of interaction. Negative karma produces forces, and if not planned for, occurs because the present level of selfishness is too great to overcome the force and karma. *One's ability to control the forces in her or his life is a measure of that person's relative level of consciousness.*

4. Spiritual material read in the evening should be reread the next morning because one's understanding of this material will be much higher in the morning than in the evening. Some people might still read spiritual material in the evening because doing so can greatly reduce retained thoughtforms, relaxing the lower mind and making it easier for a person to fall asleep—sometimes while reading—although it is better to stop reading before this point is reached. Doing so keeps one's reading comprehension relatively higher, since as one falls asleep, it drastically lowers. One should never focus on thoughtforms, or thought from the lower mental mind, while trying to fall asleep because creating thoughtforms interferes with the lower mental elemental energies and with the mental lunar devas taking necessary control over the mental body. As long as the personality is using these devas to create thoughtforms, they cannot take over and repair the mental body—and a person is usually prevented from falling asleep.

5. During the day, try to mentally think for others. This can be done without even communicating with the others—although doing so to actually serve them will increase one's level of consciousness through practicing this discipline. Helping others to structurally think means that the others' thought becomes more whole in representing all three parts of time, correctly placing events in space.

6. When confronted with the structured thought of others whose thought is contrary to your own thought, first assume that your own thought is in error. Ask for the other person's help (if possible—if the other person is present and available to be of help) so that your thought, which you are assuming to be incorrect, can be corrected in your mental mind. This process builds humility and is crucial in overcoming egotism and in fusing with the soul and Self. It also creates truth because the *addition* of others' structured thought to one's own, even when in contradiction to one's own, increases the overall structure and wholeness of thought by reversing more forces so they can be balanced (or even better, can be reduced or eliminated through even higher thought). If another's thought cannot create more truth than one's own can, then through humility (and by first assuming that one's own thought is in error) one's own thought grows and creates even more truth as the other person is then helped to better think structurally. Mentally structured accuracy is *not* a contest; rather, it is a service. One is *never* more virtuous by being right in thought while lessening her or his love for others. The correct mental stance for the creation of additional mental virtue, or truth, is to assume that one's own thought is wrong, and to seek to love others rather than to be right. One is always wrong to assume that he or she is right and that others are wrong (to not be humble). The reason is that by not being humble, he or she is not being loving and is losing some truth by not helping to create it in others through learning how he or she can be more accurate in his or her thought, through being humble. More is learned about how to serve others mentally by assuming that one's own thought is, at first, incorrect when presented with thought that is different; this assistance is lost when one assumes herself or himself to be correct. Further, if a person is incorrect in thought, then her or his egotism and the loss of mental sense created by that error will cause the mistake to go unrecognized. Of all the mental disciplines listed thus far, this will be the most difficult one to achieve because of the kama-manasic connection and people *desiring*, astrally, to be right in their mental thought in comparison to others' thought. This desire is founded on the emotional factors of wanting to have more self, which many people measure through comparison of their individual selves against other selves.

7. Write, speak, and teach truth to others when appropriate to do so for *their* mental benefit (and the benefit of their other bodies as well). Each person who has created more wisdom in his or her own mental body needs to use that wisdom to create more truth in the mental bodies of others. Although one might have only a relatively low level of wisdom, there are others who do not have even that level of wisdom and who can thus benefit from receiving this wisdom, provided that it creates *some* amount of additive light, or truth, within the mental bodies of these others. For example, an adult whose mental thought is slow but who still creates some truth can serve a young child with the amount of wisdom he or she does have; sometimes age is irrelevant, because a fairly intelligent adult who thinks mentally selfishly can be helped to develop truth by fairly simple amounts of wisdom given to her or him. Enlightenment is relative to the ability to gain information, which is based on the conditions of one's senses. Those with less sense can use whatever amount they do have, in order to create their individual levels of virtue.

Once the above-described mental disciplines have been reasonably mastered, then a person is ready for a mental yoga, provided that she or he has also previously disciplined her or his etheric/dense physical and astral bodies to a level equal to or greater than the mental body's discipline in creating more virtue. Such levels of spiritual discipline are difficult to achieve because a balance of discipline is needed, and not just an absolute amount. This balance is dynamically changing, often leaving many spiritual disciples bewildered when they lose the balance because they mistakenly believe that the virtue they create is static and additive for each body.

Expanded View of Egotism

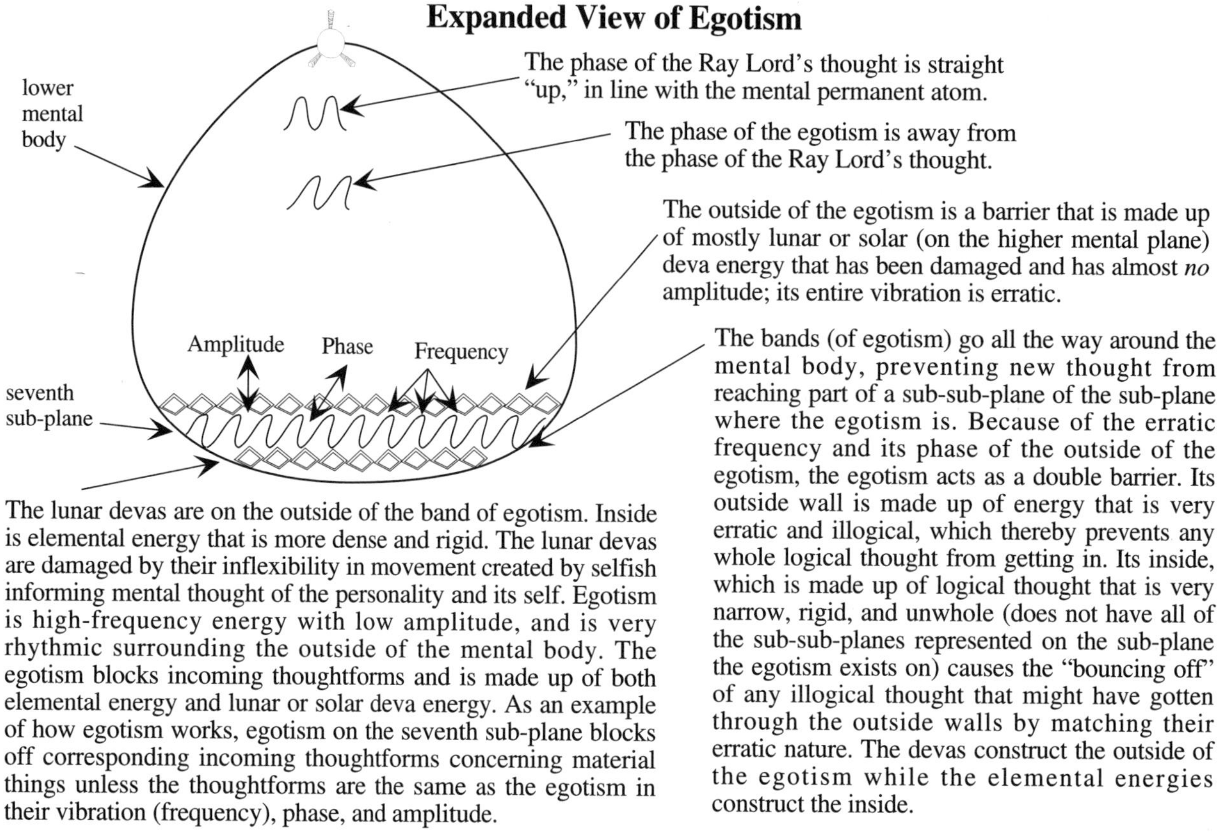

lower
mental
body

The phase of the Ray Lord's thought is straight "up," in line with the mental permanent atom.

The phase of the egotism is away from the phase of the Ray Lord's thought.

The outside of the egotism is a barrier that is made up of mostly lunar or solar (on the higher mental plane) deva energy that has been damaged and has almost *no* amplitude; its entire vibration is erratic.

Amplitude   Phase   Frequency

seventh
sub-plane

The bands (of egotism) go all the way around the mental body, preventing new thought from reaching part of a sub-sub-plane of the sub-plane where the egotism is. Because of the erratic frequency and its phase of the outside of the egotism, the egotism acts as a double barrier. Its outside wall is made up of energy that is very erratic and illogical, which thereby prevents any whole logical thought from getting in. Its inside, which is made up of logical thought that is very narrow, rigid, and unwhole (does not have all of the sub-sub-planes represented on the sub-plane the egotism exists on) causes the "bouncing off" of any illogical thought that might have gotten through the outside walls by matching their erratic nature. The devas construct the outside of the egotism while the elemental energies construct the inside.

The lunar devas are on the outside of the band of egotism. Inside is elemental energy that is more dense and rigid. The lunar devas are damaged by their inflexibility in movement created by selfish informing mental thought of the personality and its self. Egotism is high-frequency energy with low amplitude, and is very rhythmic surrounding the outside of the mental body. The egotism blocks incoming thoughtforms and is made up of both elemental energy and lunar or solar deva energy. As an example of how egotism works, egotism on the seventh sub-plane blocks off corresponding incoming thoughtforms concerning material things unless the thoughtforms are the same as the egotism in their vibration (frequency), phase, and amplitude.

Illustration 12.6

SPIRITUALLY DISCIPLINING THE DWELLER

For spiritual disciples perhaps the most perplexing condition, which nearly always occurs during earlier spiritual disciplines, is the emergence of the "Dweller on the Threshold" of becoming more of a soul. The dweller is the person's personality. It manifests from a contradictory, previously mentioned position that occurs on the higher mental plane in one's causal body. It does so while the self is focused in thought in the spiritual part of the third tier of solar devas (on the third mental sub-plane). Thought focused on the three lowest and separated solar devas in the causal body in order to create concepts is self-focused and selfish. These solar devas are located on the seventh, sixth, and fifth sub-*sub*-planes of the third mental sub-plane. Thought that is focused on the solar devas, or pitris, on the fourth through first sub-sub-planes of the third mental sub-plane creates concepts that are spiritual but are also personal; these created concepts give to others mostly through intelligent coordinated responses. The concepts predominantly use the etheric/dense physical senses to gain the information and synthesized knowledge from which the virtue of cooperation and sharing is created. With this level of virtue, some benefit to the personality and its self is realized in return, and the giving is not pure giving to (loving of) another, as a soul loves. This type of virtue permits the self to communicate with its Solar Angel and soul through their Self. As it uses the Self's understanding of God, joined with the self's understanding of its personality, bodies, and other selves, it fuses with its Self. In these circumstances, the personality still maintains its same level of control over the self. It receives this control from growing in sense and synthesized information through *sharing* the part of the virtue that it creates in the third level of spiritual concepts.

The dweller becomes created when the self wants to understand God at the level of the soul; doing so uses second-tier solar pitris to construct the spiritual concepts. The thought of the soul and these solar pitris is to give, or love, *completely,* without realizing any return for itself. In the beginning of the process, senses are limited and so is control by the personality in order to give more. The soul's region of the higher mental body corresponds to using the astral senses. These are added to and superior to, or more prominent than, the etheric/dense physical senses and their information. The original creation was of the astral virtue of love, which is focused and devoted *complete* giving, but still limited to giving to only one other at a time. The soul makes this love less conditional by applying the qualities of structured concepts from the second tier of the higher mind. As the self prompts the personality to relinquish its control to the soul, *and,* further, to lose control over some of its senses including its sense of self (!), the personality rebels. It becomes the "Dweller on the Threshold" of becoming more of, or more fused with, its soul.

The rebellion of the personality most often takes the form of the personality refusing to use the senses of the two lower bodies *at all* with which to create virtue. In other words, the person becomes extremely and irrationally selfish, often suddenly and seemingly without adequate explanation. One minute a person is a functioning spiritual disciple, and the next minute, he or she becomes more selfish than are many people who have never even *considered* disciplining themselves for the purpose of becoming more virtuous. In addition, the personality lowers its conceptual thought to use *only* the three lowest separated solar devas in its conceptual construction. It does this to protect it from growing its self into further fusing with its Self, and from becoming convinced to begin to fuse or fuse more with its soul. Many dwellers stop thinking conceptually at all because of their fear of losing control over the self. The dweller is extremely afraid—terrified—both of losing its self, and of real death, or of annihilation of its self.

Overcoming the dweller can be a very long battle, which all too many spiritual disciples in recent times have been losing. The cause of the increased failure rate has been in the overall increase in development and use of the mental body by the fifth sub-race of the fifth major race, which is *mentally* focused in development. More use and development of the mental body has been accompanied by greatly increased levels of egotism. The egotism is the dweller's "friend" because egotism selectively disables the mental senses from gaining more mental information that might change the dweller's thought about becoming more of its soul. Over three out of four functional spiritual disciples who are physically alive today are failing because of the dweller and its protection—egotism. Another, even worse statistic is that only about thirty percent of all who were spiritual disciples in one or more of their respective souls' prior incarnations and who are older than twenty-eight are functioning in the present life as spiritual disciples, or are limiting themselves (their senses and focused spiritual thought) in order to create more virtue. What currently happens is that, on average, disciples who have been functional in at least one of their respective souls' prior incarnations regain that status in only one out of three subsequent incarnations. In two out of three incarnations, disciples are "asleep." Thus less than twenty-five percent of thirty percent, or a total of about seven percent, of all people on earth who are presently alive and over the age of twenty-eight, on average (which is spiritual adulthood), and who have taken at least the first initiation in a prior life as an earlier incarnation of their respective souls, are functioning successfully in the creation of more virtue through spiritual discipline.

Even though the absolute total number of spiritual disciples presently incarnate is almost ten times greater than it was one hundred years ago, there are no more functional spiritual disciples creating virtue today than there were a hundred years ago! This situation needs to quickly change, or the present spiritual crisis, which some people are (at some level) presently aware of, will severely worsen. The reason is that spiritual disciples are the ones who create most of the virtue in the world—in the seven major life areas of civilization, or along the seven rays.

There is a single country that bears the major responsibility for the outcome of this looming crisis. That country is battling a greater spiritual crisis in its culture than any other country is at this time because it has the greatest number of inhabitants whose souls had prior incarnations as spiritual disciples and who have recently (the last fifty-five years, or so) incarnated there. This country is the United States—the country that is most capable, at present, of leading the world and whose role is to ultimately *teach* the world to become more spiritual.

To overcome the dweller, a spiritual disciple needs, today, to be a member of a group that is spiritual; this group may not (even to itself) identify itself as spiritual, or even as a group. This is because unless it is functioning along the second ray in civilization, its ray focus will be to increase virtue in civilization in ways that do not directly involve teaching, or improving consciousness, understanding, and unconditional love. For example, a group of scientists working to reduce certain pollutants are functioning along the fifth ray as it affects civilization. One of the areas in which these scientists choose to create more virtue is the creation of more whole structured thought about pollution, with this thought being given to many others; these scientists are creating more truth—which is the mental virtue. This they could identify about themselves and their group, because even though group service group members at the first level of initiation might live in locations that are distant from each other, they still share with and give to each other, and function as a group. However, if queried about their spiritual functioning, most would not see the connection—nor possibly that they have greatly disciplined themselves together, as a group, to create more truth. After reading this book, it is very likely more of them will become conscious of this concept. Each group needs to have a "spiritual" leader, although, again, the group and this leader will not necessarily recognize that the leader is spiritual. Spiritual leaders provide vision to the group by creating more sacrifices (limitations) in their lives in order to increase God's thought in form (to increase virtue), or to become more spiritual in thought. As examples of becoming more spiritual in thought, others follow the leaders' *stronger* thought that is sacrificial. This makes those who have the strongest sacrificial thought into leaders. The greater the sacrifices that create more virtue, the stronger the leader's spiritual thought and the more that others follow her or him. Without a virtuous enough leader, groups creating virtue cannot help those who are functioning in the dweller stage. The reason is that the dweller needs *very* strong thought to follow in order to break through its egotism. The leader needs to be functioning as a soul so that the dweller can easily see that a person who becomes soul infused does not die—and actually becomes much more than he or she was before. Dwellers exist in all seven ray types of groups that are spiritual, even though the group members may not understand what is happening to their members who fall into the dweller.

Most groups that are functioning spiritually also have a member who is a teacher, or one who helps others in the group to understand the virtue that the group is creating. Most of the time, this virtue is being created for and with many other groups along the same ray focus. The service of these groups goes initially to these other groups that are providing service along the same ray focus. These are Group Service groups, and most have teachers. These teachers probably do not recognize themselves as such, unless they are members of a second ray group wherein understanding one's functionality within the group is part of the group's mission of creating virtue. Less often, a teacher might also be the leader of a group that is functioning spiritually, but this arrangement is less effective. The reason is that leading places a greater emphasis from the first part, or aspect, of God's mind and thought—of sacrifice—and *decreases* the selfish choices of other people. Teaching focuses on consciousness, or understanding, which the teacher develops from accentuating the second part of God's mind and thought—of unconditional love. This happens within the teacher's own mind, and *increases* the virtuous choices of other people. It is very difficult to keep these two emphases in balance. Even when this balance can be achieved in the mind of the person functioning in the dual role, others may be unable to *follow* such complicated thought. The dichotomy among the complex spiritual concepts being given by the same person can reduce the group members' ability to follow the leader's thought. Some group members may be unable to follow such differently constructed concepts of a leader and teacher in the same person, and unable to themselves shift between the roles of being led and of being taught by that person. This problem is particularly apt to occur to a group member who is having trouble seeing the teacher, which is even more likely to occur if the teacher is a *Teacher*.

Concept at Different Higher Mental Levels

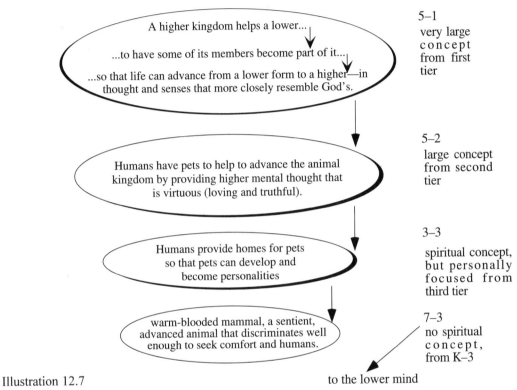

A higher kingdom helps a lower...

...to have some of its members become part of it...

...so that life can advance from a lower form to a higher—in thought and senses that more closely resemble God's.

5–1
very large concept from first tier

Humans have pets to help to advance the animal kingdom by providing higher mental thought that is virtuous (loving and truthful).

5–2
large concept from second tier

Humans provide homes for pets so that pets can develop and become personalities

3–3
spiritual concept, but personally focused from third tier

warm-blooded mammal, a sentient, advanced animal that discriminates well enough to seek comfort and humans.

7–3
no spiritual concept, from K–3

Illustration 12.7   to the lower mind

Even more problematic in spiritual groups that have either a weak leader or virtually none at all is when a *Teacher* is present in a spiritual group, or a group that is functioning spiritually. These *Teachers* are advanced initiates who are either accepted third level initiates, or, most often, fourth level initiates (arhats). The thought of these initiates is so great that if they also function as a group leader, almost none of the members in the dweller stage can recognize them—as souls, which they mostly are; these advanced initiates are still human, but are also junior members of the Kingdom of Souls. Since the dweller is rebelling against its soul, it will rebel against a *Teacher* who is mostly functioning as a soul unless the spiritually functioning group has a strong leader who can buffer, or lower, the *Teacher*'s thought to a level that the dweller can respond to. Only about fifteen percent of all groups that are functioning spiritually have *Teachers*, because there are so few advanced initiates in the world who are old enough to begin their missions of creating virtue within their respective groups. In the last twenty years, several hundred potential *Teachers* have incarnated, with more of them having done so in the last several years. The Plan is to have as many *Teachers* as possible functioning by the year 2025.

Today nearly every *Teacher* who is serving is a member of a spiritual group that is creating more virtue along a single ray of focus in accord with either an entire nation's current mission or as part of the current ray mission for the *entire world*. The former type of group is referred to as a National Service group, and the latter, a World Service group. The (previously mentioned) Group Service groups often become quite populous, and many have more than one teacher, but usually just one leader and, today, almost never have a *Teacher*. National Service groups most often have just one teacher and leader; the minority have, in addition, a *Teacher*. These groups usually contain up to hundreds of members. World Service groups quite frequently have a *Teacher*, a teacher, and a leader; each of these groups generally has twelve or fewer members not counting the *Teacher*. Note that nearly all groups that are providing world service and are functioning virtuously in their missions also each have a *Teacher*. Some or all of the members of a functional World Service group can eventually become the students of the *Teacher*. After a World Service group has created a significant amount of world virtue in its mission with this core group of members, a second group can be created around the World Service group; this second group is usually a Group Service group that sometimes becomes a National Service group. Dwellers respond differently in the dynamics of each of these types of spiritual service groups. A National Service group that has a *Teacher* present as well as a leader who is strong in spiritual thought and virtuous creativity is the type of group wherein dwellers tend to be successful in overcoming their fears of soul infusion. The reason is that the mission of a National Service group is easier for the dweller to grasp than that of a World Service group. Also, the lesser size of the group along with its *Teacher* and often a strong leader being present increases the likelihood that the dweller will understand the virtue that the group is creating in comparison to the mission of a Group Service group.

There is no question that World Service groups are where dwellers fail the worst and are most likely to fail. Unfortunately, once someone in his or her dweller ultimately fails in one mission of service, it becomes almost impossible for that person to go on creating a lower level of virtue as a member of another spiritual group that has a smaller mission. The departure of a spiritual disciple from a spiritual group is an act of such a high level of selfishness that the consciousness, or understanding, of that person's self falls dramatically. It falls usually too far for that person to again *function* virtuously in any spiritual group, and usually for the duration of his or her entire lifetime. Spiritual disciples who leave their groups usually become inordinately selfish, destructive, and paranoid. The reason is that any person who leaves his or her spiritual group has seriously rejected his or her soul, thus rendering himself or herself more a shell of a person than a whole one. No one can go backwards and still maintain a prior position on the spiritual path. Once a spiritual disciple abandons his or her spiritual group, all lower spiritual positions of functionality become unattainable because one *must* create virtue at a level that equals her or his level of ability to respond; otherwise, her or his consciousness will fall radically and suffering will, eventually, ensue. It might be interesting to note that the worse the dweller *and its failure*, the slower the karma then moves for the failed disciple, often not appearing until later in life, or perhaps not even until inner plane life (after physical death) and the next physical life. In these cases of much-delayed karma, the karma plays out after having been multiplied by the delays and by its ability to combine with other effects. Eventually, terrible levels of suffering are produced, seemingly without reason—as observed by those who lack understanding; often, the person who is living out the karma is unaware of the reasons for it, as well.

To prevent these spiritual catastrophes from occurring to dwellers, first and foremost, for all spiritual disciples: *DO NOT LEAVE YOUR SPIRITUAL GROUP!* Even when one's dweller is at its worst, working through the egotism and soul rejection is possible within a spiritual group; doing so becomes impossible outside the group because the dweller is overcome through the creation of the soul's virtue, which is based upon soul, or group, consciousness. Achieving this level of consciousness today *requires* group service because one person alone is no longer *capable* of creating the needed levels of group consciousness. The minimum levels of spiritual service have reached to the thought of the soul—which is group conscious and uses groups of other souls to accomplish its level of thought. Raising the consciousness of the dweller requires some humility and the gradual development of hierarchial consciousness, or the ability to recognize and understand that others' thought is more virtuous and more conscious, or more loving, than is one's own. This increase in consciousness is accomplished *exclusively* within one's spiritual group, where others are also, together, developing their consciousness.

Any time that the leader, teacher, or *Teacher* (if one is present) states to a group member that she or he is "in the dweller," or is not being humble, or is being very selfish, that group member should manifest an immediate concern for right action and, most often, should maintain silence of wrong speech. Any spiritual group along any of the rays of service can follow these broad guidelines for dealing with the dweller, even if the word "dweller" is not used to identify the condition. As much as is possible, using reasonable and helpfully loving methods, the leader needs to limit the dweller from preventing the group from creating more virtue. The limitations need to be appropriate to protect the group while allowing the dweller to still have other virtuous motives that, if she or he so chooses to use one or more of them, would bring herself or himself back into more functionality as a spiritual disciple within the group. The spiritual disciple always needs to have enough freedom to choose to leave the group, if that is what he or she wants to do. If this freedom is significantly limited, or if the group's discipline functions to increase the personal power of its members or has any other selfish motive for someone being a member of the group, then that group is a cult and not a spiritual group. Cults decrease virtue and usually function on the dark side of people seeking to increase their own and the group's collective power. Spiritual groups' missions are to grow God's thought, or light, first within their members and then within others. This light improves by the members' creation of it through their creation of virtue. The light cannot be inculcated through indoctrination nor through self-focused controls. People are members of spiritual groups not simply as volunteers, but proactively—to become soul-infused creators of virtue. The process goes far beyond the level of a volunteer. It leads to understanding and becoming a functional part of God through expanding one's consciousness beyond one's self, to consciousness of the group and its mission of virtue.

Dwellers can use the following basic guidelines for assistance in rejoining with their souls in thought (and with their respective groups).

1. *DO NOT LEAVE THE* SPIRITUAL *GROUP THAT YOU ARE A MEMBER OF.*

2. Increase the highest level of discipline through which you can create some virtue with the group. This level might be relatively very low compared to what it was before the dweller developed, e.g., one can move from practicing a mental yoga to simple etheric/dense physical discipline.

3. Increase the amount of spiritual (virtuous) reading that you do each day—and be consistent.

4. Focus out on what others within the group need, and offer as much assistance as *they* want.

5. Increase the giving of nonspecific resources, including money, because when one cannot give as others need—as a result of the high levels of that person's dweller's selfishness—then giving more money or other nonspecific resources can still be of help. This giving raises consciousness and is necessary in order to bolster the loss of giving that has already occurred as a result of being in the dweller.

6. Communicate with the leader of the group—openly, and completely revealing all thoughts of selfishness, and especially any clandestine selfish actions. Any secret (hidden, selfish) acts against a spiritual group are generally considered evil and very often result in the karma jumping to *ten* fold (instead of three fold) in effect. Such acts can destroy several lifetimes of potential future service through the terrible forces created against each future person whom your soul will incarnate.

7. Pray for assistance from your Solar Angel by focusing on how your increased soul thought can serve the group in its mission of creating virtue. *Never* pray for help for just yourself. Writing down the ways that changing yourself can help the group's service might be helpful.

8. On a daily basis, make a change in yourself that will help the group in its service; then, the next day, maintain this change and add another.

9. Make no changes based upon personal preferences while in the dweller, because almost all of these will be selfish, i.e., do not suddenly decide that it has been a very long time since you went away alone—away from the group and its service work—just to "relax," and thus unilaterally decide to do so! Change any personal choices to group choices by asking the teacher or *Teacher*, if present, whether such thoughts and possible decisions are selfish or virtuous. Assume that all thought from one's self (as compared to one's soul) is potentially selfish.

 ## SPIRITUAL DISCIPLINE AND THE HUMAN INITIATIONS

Each of the four human initiations into the next kingdom comprises four stages. These stages correspond to discipline of the etheric/dense physical, astral, mental, and intuitional body, respectively, so that these bodies can be used at a certain level of service within each initiation. The use of the bodies in *service* within each initiation follows the same order as does their discipline; when used in service, all the prior bodies are included, plus one higher body per initiation. The four stages of initiation, which are repeated with higher standards for each level of initiation after the first, are *probationary* (etheric/dense physical discipline); *accepting* (astral discipline); *pledged* (mental discipline); and *accepted* (intuitional discipline). Each initiation becomes progressively more difficult to complete because the prior levels of service from the lower body(-ies) in the lower initiation(s) need to be raised to a new, higher, level—together with service from an added body. Full service in an initiation is not reached until the accepted stage, where a spiritual disciple becomes monadically infused with highly creative thought and is accepted by the next kingdom to be assisted in the completion of one's present level of initiation. At today's standards, arhats, or fourth level initiates, reach an adept stage in the initiation process and need to complete the initiation without assistance (except at the very end) from the next kingdom, which is the Kingdom of Souls. It is possible to take an initiation without having completed the prior one; in those rare instances when someone does so, she or he becomes a "split" disciple, or one whose discipline is split between two levels of initiation (or even three, if the disciple makes this unfortunate choice twice). The cause for taking an initiation before completing the preceding one is a lack of spiritual discipline that leads a person to be spiritually ambitious. Doing so is *not* recommended because it compounds the problems that already exist for disciples in their attempts to discipline their bodies and create more virtue, and makes both of the initiations they are in much more difficult to complete. Completing the initiation process is, even for those disciples who have not split themselves, the single-most difficult task that a human can undertake.

The dweller is worse during the accepting stage of the first three initiations than at any other time, and is at its very worst during that stage of the second initiation. The intensification of "dwellerism" occurs because the second stage of an initiation, wherein one accepts his or her own soul (and the souls of others), is the very crux of the problem of rebelliousness. This problem occurs as *astral* discipline begins for the level of initiation that the disciple is in. When compounded by the entire initiation being at the second level, or where the spiritual disciple is attempting to use, for the first time in the initiation process, his or her astral body with which to serve as part of his or her spiritual group, then the dweller is most challenged to become more of its soul—which uses super-empathy to create its virtue. It is important to remember that service is the complete giving of all the energy within a center, and when relative to a body, must be from all the centers within that body. The present levels of service that each spiritual disciple strives for, from each of the four bodies, are as follows:

1ST LEVEL OF INITIATION (THE FOCUS IS ON ETHERIC/DENSE PHYSICAL DISCIPLINE AND SERVICE)			
STAGE OF INITIATION	BODY DISCIPLINED AT EACH STAGE	PERCENTAGE OF UNIFICATION OF THE FORM SENSES AT EACH STAGE	AVERAGE MINIMUM LEVEL OF SERVICE AT THE ACCEPTING STAGE
Probationary	Etheric/dense physical body	~25%	~10% (etheric/dense physical)
Accepting	Astral body	~15%	~3% (astral)
Pledged	Mental body	~10%	~1% (mental)
Accepted	Intuitional body	~2% (including the unification of the two spiritual senses)	<1% (intuitional)

Table 12. 1

2ND LEVEL OF INITIATION (THE FOCUS IS ON ASTRAL DISCIPLINE AND SERVICE)			
STAGE OF INITIATION	BODY DISCIPLINED AT EACH STAGE	PERCENTAGE OF UNIFICATION OF THE FORM SENSES AT EACH STAGE	AVERAGE MINIMUM LEVEL OF SERVICE AT THE ACCEPTING STAGE
Probationary	Etheric/dense physical body	~50%	~25% (etheric/dense physical)
Accepting	Astral body	~50%	~25% (astral)
Pledged	Mental body	~25%	<10% (mental)
Accepted	Intuitional body	~10% (including the unification of the two spiritual senses)	~2% (intuitional)

Table 12. 2

3RD LEVEL OF INITIATION (THE FOCUS IS ON MENTAL DISCIPLINE AND SERVICE)			
STAGE OF INITIATION	BODY DISCIPLINED AT EACH STAGE	PERCENTAGE OF UNIFICATION OF THE FORM SENSES AT EACH STAGE	AVERAGE MINIMUM LEVEL OF SERVICE AT THE ACCEPTING STAGE
Probationary	Etheric/dense physical body	~75%	~50% (etheric/dense physical)
Accepting	Astral body	~75%	~50% (astral)
Pledged	Mental body	~75%	~50% (mental)
Accepted	Intuitional body	~50% of the *partial* sense of buddhi (including the unification of the two spiritual senses)	~10% (intuitional)

Table 12. 3

4TH LEVEL OF INITIATION—PROBATIONARY STAGE (FOCUS: CONTROLLED INTUITION, LOVE/WISDOM, AND OMNISCIENCE ALL AS A PARTIAL SENSE OF BUDDHI, USED IN SERVICE)			
STAGE OF INITIATION	BODY DISCIPLINED AT EACH STAGE	AVERAGE PERCENTAGE OF DEVELOPMENT OF ALL SEVEN SENSES, OF FORM AND SPIRIT	AVERAGE LEVELS OF SERVICE AT THE PROBATIONARY STAGE
Probationary	Etheric/dense physical body	50% – 60%	50% – 60% (etheric/dense physical)
Probationary	Astral body	50% – 60%	50% – 60% (astral)
Probationary	Mental body	75%	50% – 75% (mental)
Probationary	Intuitional body	50% – 75% of the *partial* sense of buddhi	50% – 75% (intuitional)

Table 12.4

4TH LEVEL OF INITIATION, PLEDGED STAGE			
STAGE OF INITIATION	BODY DISCIPLINED AT EACH STAGE	AVERAGE PERCENTAGE OF UNIFICATION OF ALL SEVEN SENSES OF FORM AND SPIRIT	AVERAGE LEVELS OF SERVICE AT THE PLEDGED STAGE (POSSIBLY ADEPT SERVICE)
Pledged	Etheric dense/ physical body	50%	50% (etheric/dense physical)
Pledged	Astral body	50%	50% (astral)
Pledged	Mental body	90%	90% (mental)
Pledged	Intuitional body	80% – 90% of the *partial* sense of buddhi	80% – 90% (intuitional)

Table 12.5

4TH LEVEL OF INITIATION, ACCEPTED STAGE			
STAGE OF INITIATION	BODY DISCIPLINED AT EACH STAGE	AVERAGE PERCENTAGE OF UNIFICATION OF ALL SEVEN SENSES OF FORM AND SPIRIT	LEVELS OF SERVICE AT THE ACCEPTED STAGE (ALWAYS ADEPT SERVICE)
Accepted	Etheric/dense physical body	100%	100%
Accepted	Astral body	100%	100%
Accepted	Mental body	100%	100%
Accepted	Intuitional body	90% of the *partial* sense of buddhi	90%

Table 12.6

Note that the arhat usually loses some etheric/dense physical and astral sense in the earlier stages of her or his initiation process, as a result of the selfishness of the members of her or his group.

The fourth level initiate chooses to not go on to become a member of the next kingdom until she or he saves his or her students' bodies for service and brings these students, as a spiritual group, to the accepted stage of the third initiation—under the "new" group rules for initiation. Salvation of these bodies occurs only when they are actually used in *service* at the appropriate levels. This advanced and sacrificial initiate (the arhat) earns the right to become a (liberated) Soul in the next kingdom by living his or her life first for his or her students and the group that they together are, and then eventually for all of humanity. What he or she is learning *through virtuously and creatively living it,* is that all life is one—and is a future part of God's growth.

As part of these tremendous sacrifices, the arhat during most of the fourth initiation loses some etheric/dense physical and astral sense as well as sometimes significant ability to serve from these bodies. The decline continues until his or her students become third level initiates and no longer have dwellers. The arhat's students control his or her development of these *two* lowest bodies and his or her completion of the fourth initiation. Each of these great initiates functions as a savior of others' bodies to be used in service. The arhat who, as a sacrificial *Teacher* in his or her usually final incarnation as an arhat, also becomes a world leader along his or her soul ray. This occurs only after having achieved the (current) adept stage of perfecting his or her mental body for service. Third level initiates think of life as one, while fourth level initiates not only think of life as one, but they live life as one as well.

Anyone past the accepting stage of the third initiation has completed the eighteen renunciations, of the selfish use of the split senses within the three lower bodies (six split senses times three bodies equals eighteen renunciations). Once these renunciations are completed, all three of these bodies and their (total of) eighteen senses are dedicated for use in *service.* It is at this point that the spiritual disciple becomes completely freed from the dweller. Because a person who has spiritually renounced has created himself or herself into more than one-half soul, he or she is therefore safe from personality rebellion because his or her mind is now that of a soul, i.e., he or she thinks as a soul but may not yet live as a soul, as an arhat does. The Spiritual Hierarchy (the next kingdom) considers these initiates and all higher-level ones to be "safe" to have direct contact with because one who has completed the spiritual renunciations will not become evil; one who mostly *is* a soul cannot lose his or her soul.

A person who (astrally) *desires* to discipline herself or himself but has not begun to do so is an aspirant. Generally, potential disciples can remain as aspirants for about six months at a time; after six months, they usually either move on to becoming spiritually disciplined, and enter the probationary stage, or they become more selfish and lose their desire to be more spiritual. It is possible for this series of aspiration and then discipline or lack thereof to recycle several times over several years. The dweller stage often lasts for about two years of creating severe group problems, after which point the person's dweller generally becomes less of a problem; most first level initiates today become victims of their dwellers and then leave their respective spiritual groups. About half of the second level initiates fall victim to their dwellers according to the following scenario: After having been a probationary disciple within his or her spiritual group for sixth months to two years, the person enters the accepting stage of discipleship. Consistent with the fact that a person's dweller is usually worse in the accepting stage than in the other three stages, this group member is frequently in his or her dweller, and after a period of exhibiting behavior that is often disruptive—and even hostile—to the group, he or she then might choose to leave. Only a small percentage of third level initiates ever leave a spiritual group, and almost every third level initiate has enough control over her or his dweller to reduce its negative affect on her or his spiritual group and its mission of virtue.

Raising consciousness involves many other issues and methods beyond the ones that were touched upon in this chapter; only some of those methods that might significantly raise consciousness by being read about, which is a part of the purpose of this book, were explained.

This book's primary focus is on raising the consciousness of those who read it, who, through the act of reading it then understand (at least some of) its contents. It is intended that other, much more informative books by this same author and group will follow, from over three hundred previously written articles and from other information, as well. One should not expect the meager amounts of information in this chapter to be sufficient for a person to successfully raise her or his consciousness while practicing discipline through the spiritual initiations, unless this information is used in conjunction with other, more advanced methods.

 ## CONCLUSIONS ABOUT CONSCIOUSNESS

In conclusion of this chapter, the hidden meaning to one's life is directly dependent upon the amount by which one raises her or his consciousness during any period of that life. The *amount* of one's consciousness compared with his or her ability to sense is that person's ability to respond. This ability becomes a relative level of determining how meaningful a person finds his or her life to be. The reason is that a person's self dynamically changes as it can give thought to the informing fallen spirit of each of the three lower bodies and their centers and senses. Part of this ability to give is determined by the level of sense in each body. In addition to this fundamental function, the interconnectivity of this system gives meaning to a person's life only as a reasonable balance is established among the following four components: the personality and its sense and control of its self; the personality and its control and integration of its three bodies and their senses; the self's ability to give its higher thought to the fallen spirit in its three lower bodies; and the self's eventual ability to give to the Self its understanding of the meaning of life for its three lower bodies, their fallen spirit, and its personality. Life's *hidden* meaning mostly comes from the Self's creation, first, of understanding God and its mind, and then growing as a functional part of God, as more of God's thought, or more virtue is created within form.

What follows is a summary of all twelve chapters of *Life's Hidden Meaning*. While this summary may be helpful to those who read it, it is unlikely that mostly or only reading it will be enough to understand life's hidden meaning. The reason is that the reading of this book is meant to raise the consciousness of its readers so that they can first *understand* what meaning in life is, and then further understand the part of life's meaning that is hidden. For the vast majority of this book's readers, the *process* of raising consciousness is a critical step towards understanding what the book is about. For those who have experienced an elevation in consciousness through reading *Life's Hidden Meaning*, this author and the Ageless Wisdom Distributors group are profoundly appreciative because each of us shares—as one—every time someone understands more of the One. Those who may still be struggling to achieve a significant amount of understanding (which would be about fifty percent comprehension of about half of the basic concepts within this book) in order to gain some of life's hidden meaning might first try becoming more giving (loving) in their lives and then rereading those sections of *Life's Hidden Meaning* that they found to be the most basic but still the most obscure and difficult to understand.

For those who have read Life's Hidden Meaning in its entirety up to this point, certain increases in understanding life, or in consciousness and love for life, are likely to have occurred because most readers will have had explained to them a vast number of previously hidden concepts about our universe and the life within it. Those readers who have understood, at a minimum, about half of the basic concepts that were explained, with about fifty percent comprehension of these concepts, will most likely achieve what they consider to be a satisfactory understanding of the summary that follows. Someone comprehends a concept by how much he or she can use that concept to build and understand other concepts; also, when a person comprehends a concept, she or he can then create forms of thoughts, as words, to explain the concept correctly. Thus comprehension is the ability to use concepts that one can create or re-create with additional concepts and the thoughtforms that describe them. Rereading parts of this book, or even all of it, may be helpful in gaining more understanding. This would be especially helpful if the reader attempts to be more loving, and particularly wisely loving, within her or his life. In that case, some attempts at using some of the spiritual disciplines within Chapter Twelve would be of even more assistance in providing a greater understanding of *Life's Hidden Meaning*. Even the most conscious readers of this book are likely to find the understanding of some concepts within it to be quite challenging.

Each chapter, starting with the second one, will be summarized according to how the information and its explanation have revealed more of life's hidden meaning. To begin with, a restated reasonably concise explanation of what meaning in life is to a human will help to uncover the *hidden* meanings. Humans whose bodies are not yet significantly enlightened find life to be meaningful as it increases their individual levels of (lower) self. The amount of increase is controlled, in part, by the level of development and the condition of the senses in the three lower bodies because the self can grow only as much as the bodies can accurately sense. Another factor is the amount of the self's higher thought that it gives to the fallen spirit that is informing each of its three lower bodies; this amount is at first determined by the level to which the personality can sense its self, and how much it over-controls its self out of fear—ultimately, of death (which is the loss of its self). A self that is over-controlled by its personality is inhibited from giving as much of its thought and then becomes reduced in size, which causes it to lose consciousness, or understanding. Humans eventually reach a relative level of development at which simply increasing the self becomes limited by the levels of information that the five senses of form in each of the three lower bodies can supply—even when these senses and bodies are somewhat working together, or are somewhat unified. Another part of this condition is that without discipline of the personality, the senses of form can reach a point at which they are giving as much as the self is. When this crisis is reached, the self cannot gain more understanding because it is giving less than that which it is attempting to give to is giving. At these stages the self, along with its personality, finds itself in a crisis. The crisis occurs because the meaning in its life cannot be increased. Since this meaning is relative, the self begins to experience progressively less meaning in life because its (the self's) growth becomes significantly slowed. Thus slower growth of self is experienced by humans as less meaning in their lives. An additional stage becomes reached when good character has been created and after the self has grown as much as possible by interacting with and giving with a multitude of other selves. The self still has reached its relative maximum level of using its senses, somewhat selfishly, to gain meaning with other selves...but still for the purpose of growing more of itself.

Finally, the self discovers a much greater meaning to life—to *grow* more of the life that it has been trying to derive (take) meaning from. The self is helped, enormously, in this discovery by its Guardian Angel, which is the Great Energy Being also known as a Solar Angel, and sometimes as the OverSoul. Each self has its own Angel who transmits conceptual thoughts to the self about loving, or giving more to, other parts of life so that life will grow. The Solar Angel begins these thought messages with the conscience. The conscience functions as the remedial thought of correcting behavior that decreases life's growth. The messages eventually grow stronger and more encompassing as the personality allows them to connect with the self *and* as the self can understand them, or be conscious of them. These messages from the Angel concern how to grow more of life, or more of God, through the creation of more virtue in the (lower) self and (higher) Self's life.

In Chapter Two, the "big picture" and the progenitor of these ways through which meaning to life were created are explained. The method used was an explanation of how God created our universe—and how God was created. God exists within our universe through three parts of its mind; the creation of everything other than God in our universe, including time and space, came from the separation of these three parts—which led to the creation of life. All life has the three parts of God's mind within it; however, in nearly all of life God's mind is still separated. For humans (and life at lower levels of development and integration of God's mind), when the three parts of God's mind are brought closer together and in the ways that God was constructed (with relatively less space and more light), the human's whole creative mind, or self, grows and life becomes more meaningful. As stated above, a human can properly bring the three parts of God's mind together only to the level at which her or his senses of form exist and within the limitations, therefore, of her or his three lower bodies. This limitation creates a potential and large but finite level to which a person can grow through just bringing together God's (existing) mind within her or his own. This grows the self, or her or his whole creative mind. Then the human, with the help of her or his Solar Angel, can do an amazing thing to increase the meaning in her or his life that no lower form of life can do, although no lower form of life needs to because it cannot exceed its finite potential that a human can. The sacrifice that God made of Its mind can be replicated on a lower and corresponding level by a human. The human can eventually co-create, as her or his own growth, new forms of life that are not merely creation of more bodies of (procreation of) existing life. This level of co-creation is reached when the human is fused with its soul and Self. A human can choose to sacrifice the growth of its self by fusing its self with its Self and can then choose to grow more of other life. The human eventually can reach the ability to create new forms of life; this other life also grows itself as a part of life, because all life is really one. When the human sacrifices his or her whole creative mind, or self, the three parts of God's mind that it has created go on to create more lower life. This happens while the human's life is transfigured into a higher form of life that needs increasingly less of its own mind, or of its Self, as it becomes the mind of all—or of God. In these circumstances, by joining and growing part of God's mind, the human begins to *function* as God has, as an advanced human and in the way that those who are beyond human do.

In this second way of creating meaning in life, humans are creating themselves (their selves) into a functional part of God in our universe; the process eventually ends by the Great Being whom the human is a part of—as a liberated ascended Monad (a super-Soul)—having grown more of God while becoming all that God can be, from the Monad's perspective of our universe. Thus based upon the explanation given in Chapter Two, meaning in the lives of some humans, who hold a more limited and selfish view, comes from the increase in their individual selves, or their whole personal minds. For others, who hold a more unlimited and virtuous view, meaning is created by increasing God—and thereby becoming a functional part of growing our universe. The second way of increasing meaning in a human's life is nearly completely *hidden* to a human before his or her consciousness, or love, grows great enough to understand the basic concepts in Chapter Two, regardless of whether these understood concepts are structured in the same way that they are presented in this book. While there are many other important concepts in Chapter Two, these basic ones, as described immediately above, contribute so much towards understanding *Life's Hidden Meaning* (both the concept and book itself) that these basic concepts alone provide the approximately fifty percent understanding of this chapter that is needed to increase consciousness, if these concepts are themselves comprehended at a level of about fifty percent (about the amount presented in this summary).

Chapter Two also explains how an unlimited field can become a potential field through enough choices connecting together in similar ways to create enough thought that limits the field. The new, limited field of possibilities can create a Director of the field. The Director can become a mind, and if any part of the mind becomes actualized as something outside of the whole field, a creator has become developed. This explanation provides a reasonable and logical method of how a creator becomes created, possibly relieving many readers' concern for what is to them an answer that they can accept to this age-old question. The amazing simplicity of creating an entire universe from the separation of just three parts of the mind of God, with such diverse results, may have led many readers into an admiration and respect for God that was as much intellectual as it may have been based previously on faith. God's thought, or light, also takes on a more tangible reality, including the concept of space when the light is separated.

In Chapter Three, *Life's Hidden Meaning* continues with an explanation of how seven fields of life creation are produced by seven Great Beings in our universe who alter the first two parts of God's mind in order to create seven sub-lights. When each of these sub-lights of God's light becomes joined with the third part of God's mind that is not (yet) fully enlightened and is therefore manifested as energy, this sub-light becomes a virtue. Virtues grow more of God, as life, by bringing the three parts of God's mind closer together through gradually enlightening the third part, which at first manifests as energy. As these manifested energies become enlightened, they grow dramatically in God's *thought*; the enlightenment of these energies is the foundation for growing life.

The more virtue that a person creates, the more meaningful his or her life will be. The reason is that as a person enlightens first her or his form and then the forms of others, God and life grow through the growth of thought in form, or in energy. The hidden meaning of life as explained in the second chapter has added to it the explanation presented in the third chapter. The form, or energy, of one's bodies can be enlightened only to the point of becoming fully intelligent in its movement with other form, or fully intelligent in its activity. The paradox is that in order to reach greater levels of enlightenment, *other* form (energies) in other bodies needs to become virtuous because full enlightenment in form *requires* that other form interact intelligently with the form that is reaching enlightenment. There can be no intelligent activity (the third part of God's mind that is not separated into manifested energy) on the mental plane or higher without a human or higher being creating virtue in dense and less dense form within herself or himself *and in others at the same time*—rejoining time to space.

The seven Ray Lords each create one of seven dimensions of time and space; each of these dimensions has its own specific virtue that is developed therein; the virtue in each of the lower five dimensions concerns a way to enlighten manifested energy's thought, in order to transform this energy back into intelligent activity. A person's life becomes increasingly more meaningful as he or she can create more virtue in more of the different types of the seven manifested energies. This meaning is mostly hidden from humans until they make the choice to limit themselves into creating more virtue, and less darkness, in form. A being can create the virtue of a dimension only wherein it has a body, senses, and a mind because its form must be either intelligent in its activity—or in its sacrifice of activity—on the one or more dimensions that it is creative within. Human beings can actually create virtue in the three lowest dimensions of our universe. When humans attempt to create the virtue of the next higher dimension above the lowest three, and succeed, they gradually create themselves into lifeforms of the next higher kingdom.

The virtue of the higher dimension added to that of the lowest three greatly enhances a human's realization of the meaning that was hidden in his or her life. The three lowest virtues are cooperation and sharing; love towards one other, whether towards an individual or a group (therefore making the love conditional); and truth, or whole structured thought (balanced in forces) that is given to others in a way that keeps the thought whole within their minds. These three virtues can create large amounts of meaning that had been hidden within a person's life. When the virtue of the fourth (the intuitional) plane is created, an exponential increase in meaning is revealed and experienced. This virtue, of beauty, complexly elevates the intelligent activity that is created by one human and given to another life; this intelligent activity is joined in time and space, through light, as the lowest certain type of Now. The Now of intelligent activity that is created by one super-human, or (liberated) Soul, and given to *all* other life at this level exists in one of three possible ways. The lone method is through omniscience, or all-knowledge. The fourth added virtue is nearly completely hidden to all humans except those who have chosen a consistent way of life, of self-limitation, to create more virtue. These are spiritual disciples—who are creating themselves into beauties through the enlightenment of form in four planes of life creation.

The third chapter reveals a much more complex universe, in which meaning of life is hidden by the complexity of creating virtue through seven rays that stimulate energy to think more in light (by giving some thought to each type of energy within the ray's focused field of thought). When the concept of the cosmic rays is joined with the hidden meaning of life that has already been derived up to this point, the cosmic rays explain an apparatus of enlightened thought for controlling the growth of form while not interfering with the ability for life to think. There is no interference because the first two parts of God's mind are not affected by the field of thought of the cosmic ray and its progenitor, the cosmic Ray Lord. Only manifested energy is affected, allowing there to be another part of life that can create more meaning and is free to choose and to think for itself. This part of life is spirit. As described in Chapter Three, life's hidden meaning is the creation of virtue through multiple dimensions of time and space while using a body, or energy, to so create. Those who understand the hidden meaning of life at the level presented thus far within this summary possess the minimum understanding that is needed as a foundation for the rest of the book's further development of life's hidden meaning.

Chapter Four explains spirit's role in and significance in determining the *hidden* meaning in life. By understanding how spirit and energy come together to create lifeforms, and how spirit and energy are intimately connected, it becomes much clearer that increasing one's spiritual awareness and consciousness produces an enormous increase in the meaning to her or his life. Spirit is the first two parts of God's mind, or its first two aspects, while energy is the third part of God's mind that is missing some of the first two parts and loses *intelligence* in its activity as it then manifests as energy. By rejoining these two, spirit and energy, but in new combinations resultant of changes in God's thought, or light by each cosmic Ray Lord, new forms of life are created, as well as new dimensions of time and space. Diversity to life greatly increases as more spirit is sacrificed. As a result of these sacrifices, the amount of energy increases in the ratio of spirit to form. The spiritual choices that further increase energy's ability to think more like God (more virtuously) along one of the seven Ray Lords' thought hastens the unhiding of the hidden meaning of life. This occurs because then the senses of the lifeform that have been constructed from the best-thinking of the energies that make up that lifeform become improved. Increasingly accurate information is the foundation for a lifeform deriving more meaning in its life. It is spirit's responsibility, in life's *hidden* function, to improve the thought of energy through enlightenment, or through its (spirit's) creation of virtue. In today's world a tremendous amount of meaning is hidden because of a lack of understanding of spirit—or even of spirit's existence—and its relationship to form, or energy.

Spirit and elemental energy both come from the Monad. A Monad who has yet to experience life (God's growth) and to increase or grow more of God in the dimensions lower than the monadic, sacrifices *all* of its use of the third aspect of God's mind, or of intelligent activity on its own plane. That Monad gives up its use of intelligent activity so that its sacrificed thought can become spirit. It does so in order for the intelligent activity on its plane to become manifested as elemental energy on lower planes, as spirit attempts to use this energy. Some of the intelligent activity on the monadic plane also becomes second ray primordial energy, which, if fused with manifested first ray primordial energies from intelligent activity on the logoic plane, can create the first fusion reactions in our universe. These fusion reactions take place on the spiritual and lower planes, and mostly create first-stage stars and the permanent atoms of Solar Angels. Stars are a hidden meaning of life because they are the lower bodies of Great Beings who have a consciousness beyond our universe, in a much more advanced one. These Beings *create* Monads and assist the God of our universe through adding *only more of God's* own type of thought; Monads are at first mirrors of, but also have increased amounts of God's consciousness, or unconditional love. The assistance of Monads is needed since God chose to sacrifice *all* of its mind to create our universe. This left none of God joined in the way that the first two parts are joined in a Monad. This requires that a connection to other, greater universes, be created, through the Monad.

All life is created through Monads and the "parent" stars as the bodies of the Great Consciousness behind these stars. The meaning to life that, for humans, can be derived from understanding Monads and stars is that each human has his or her "*own*" Monad; therefore, each human is a part of a Great Being who is connected to an even greater One outside our universe, and all of these Beings are helping the God of our universe to grow itself. Humans are the first and lowest form of life that can understand this system of growth; they also can participate within it as they increase their consciousness and then create more virtue. The meaning of life is so deeply hidden within these concepts that *no* mere explanation of life's meaning can provide enough understanding for anyone to fully realize life's purpose. In order to fully understand the purpose of life, one must *become* the *ascended* Monad.

In Chapter Five, life's hidden meaning is focused on the meaning of *mind*. A mind is created first through the development of enough thought to be able to limit over half of the thought's field of possibilities, *and* then by its potential to give this thought to another, more limited field. This creates the potential to grow consciousness beyond that which exists in its own field. Note that a mind does not exist until the developed thought has potential to give thought to a more limited field. A self is a mind that creates its consciousness by giving its thought to the fallen spirit within the three lower bodies that it is connected to through its givingness and its thought. Then it is thinking for something other than what it is, and the ability to do so is what makes it a mind. Human selves give their thought to only three bodies in a single lifeform; group souls' selves give their thought to however many bodies exist in the multitude of their group souls' lifeforms. Human selves can become fully self-conscious because they do not share themselves among many forms (or even more than one form) of life; they also are supported by the personality's sense of self, which comes from the personality having sensitivity to consciousness, or being able to discern when its self is conscious. The personality achieves this sense of self by comparing the synthesized knowledge that exists within its three brains; this knowledge comes from the information within each body's centers and their senses, and is limited by the level to which the self gives this shared knowledge, as directed thought that the fallen spirit can use to better inform the senses. This circular system of self creation through the giving of thought joins spirit and energy while it enlightens them both, and permits life to become *free* and *self-sufficient*. Human life can become more meaningful through this freedom, but it can also become selfish and even evil since the personality and its self are free to choose to not think as God does.

Most of the hidden meaning of life comes from the self and personality first deciding to change from creating more of the self and its consciousness, to creating more of life and God's growth—and then accomplishing this change. As the personality allows the transition to occur it becomes a (fused) part of its soul, and the self becomes fused with its Self. The Self understands God and how to grow more of God, while the self alone can understand itself, its personality, and other selves to the degree that it can sense what they are like as its personality's senses unify and improve. Awareness by a human of its Self is the key to gaining more *hidden* meaning from life.

The sixth chapter, "About Souls" explains a large part of life's hidden meaning by unhiding the creation of souls and their structure, purpose, and means of functioning. Souls on the mental plane are the lowest form of life that contains an equal balance between the thought of its energy and its spirit, with both enlightened to a level of at least fifty percent. This creates a wholeness within the soul's mental thought, up to the level of the sub-sub-plane where the thought exists on the mental plane. Mental plane souls are attempting to create more lower levels of life that have senses in the three lower worlds, where souls have none. They can create virtue in these worlds only as they help to develop this lower life and *its* ability to create virtue. Mental plane souls must live their lives through the lower lives they help to create—and they experience life as one. Mental plane human souls are striving through fusing with their individual Selves and somewhat with their OverSouls to develop *twice* as much spiritual thought than the amount of thought by the energy within them. This two-to-one ratio would make the human soul beautiful from creating more beauty through this perfected balance between the spirit and energy within itself.

As a human becomes aware of and then *conscious* of his or her own soul and the souls of others, that person's life grows in meaning from the *much higher consciousness* that is created by being conscious of souls. Being conscious of souls is synonymous with being conscious of the oneness of life in the three lower worlds. One *cannot* understand souls, or be conscious of them, without giving at least to some level what souls give. Mental plane souls give oneness to the life that exists in the three lower worlds, by being the progenitor of *all* the life and pre-life within these worlds. When a person becomes conscious of this remarkable amount of giving by souls, his or her own consciousness grows. The reason is that simply by becoming conscious of the souls' giving, a person becomes a part of much of that giving within his or her thought.

Souls are the next level of being a part of life for humans; this causes humans to reach for the soul's level of consciousness as they reach the limits of creating meaning in their lives on a personal level, or only through the use of their personalities and selves. *Both* the soul and human become changed, or *transfigured,* into a new type of soul that is liberated from the mental plane (becoming a Soul). This happens as the human *transforms* his or her consciousness and *transmutes* his or her senses into those of the mental plane human soul. The mental plane soul becomes transfigured; its internal structure changes from being partially enlightened, through an equal balance of thought by its energy and spirit, to intuitional enlightenment through twice the thought of its spirit to that of its energy. While the human soul is gaining in the thought of its spirit, the OverSoul, or Solar Angel, is doing the reverse to the mental part of its triadal Self. This Great Energy Being is gaining twice as much thought within its intelligent activity in its permanent atom and solar devas (which correspond to the soul's energy part) than the amount that it has within its Self, or its spirit. Eventually the liberated Soul will completely fuse with the fully developed triadal Solar Angel, to become an ascended Monad on the logoic plane. What had been a human being with a limited life duration becomes first a fused and liberated soul (a Soul) and, eventually, a fused triadal Being who then becomes an ascended Monad. During these changes, no part of consciousness, or unconditional creation of love, is lost. It just grows. Thus humans eventually become immortal, and no virtuous part of a human is ever lost.

It is perhaps an understatement to say that understanding souls provides humans with an understanding of their own immortality, which enormously increases the previously hidden meaning of their lives. When one sees her or his life as immortal, those aspects of it that are meaningful are drastically changed from what the person considered to be meaningful when she or he thought of her or his life as finite and relatively small. Even for most of those people who with religious conviction thoroughly believe in immortality after death, in some sort of heaven, such immortality that is not linked to the concepts of a light-filled soul's life creates a very shallow and meaningless existence. In one case, a person is with God, more as an ancillary (at best) part of God's world (heaven). In the case of a liberated soul (a Soul), or a Master of the Ageless Wisdom and the three lower worlds, a person creates himself or herself into a functional part of God. Understanding souls gives humans great hope and an endlessly growing future.

Souls also experience joy on the mental plane and, eventually, bliss on the intuitional plane and above. This unified experience of life comes from virtue being used by other life with which to create more virtue. Joy unifies the three lower planes into one's first experience of being (sensing) God. Bliss is similar to joy but is more encompassing because bliss is constant. It comes from the lowest fully developed sense of being God that is developed on the intuitional plane. This sense is omniscience, or all-knowingness. When omniscience is added to the other senses of the (liberated) Soul, the full sense of buddhi is created. Buddhi is the total awareness of all intelligent activity and spiritual thought everywhere on the buddhic plane through fully enlightened knowledge. The future for humans is all of this, which includes incredible beauty, bliss, and meaning.

Chapter Seven explains the intricacies of bodies, their centers, and the senses. This chapter focuses on how the form side of life is so important to the meaning of life. Almost all of Chapter Seven deals with the *hidden* meanings of form and the senses. So much of the information comes from knowledge that had been hidden, that to most readers the information may be somewhat overwhelming as they attempt to construct a new reality to their prior understanding of lifeforms—especially human lifeforms. As one gains understanding, or consciousness, of *awareness* of senses in form, he or she begins to realize that meaning can be increased in life through improving these (mostly hidden) parts of the senses. The method for improving senses is discipline, and this chapter is the first to increase the reader's consciousness of the structural, or mental, reasons for using discipline to enlighten the bodies and to increase the meaning in one's life through what had been mostly hidden. Some readers of Chapter Seven might become upset over some of the information in it, because it suggests, scientifically, or in a structured way that is conceptually testable, that certain limits humans have within their *bodies* will interfere with their free choices to not be virtuous. The implication is that karma is an energy model that mostly uses centers and senses as a means of rejoining the time and space that had been previously separated by some level of selfishness. People generally dislike knowing that they cannot escape their karma; any thought of such escape becomes impossible when the awareness becomes clear that it is through the senses, centers, and bodies that the effects are joined to causes.

Life becomes much *more* meaningful for those who decide to discipline their centers and senses because these people can overcome their karma and free themselves to become more spiritual. To these people, Chapter Seven becomes a handbook for redesigning their bodies to become enlightened parts of a functioning God; they find that doing so is exceptionally meaningful and well worth any limitation that might be needed to improve each sense and body.

Chapter Seven also increases meaning to life as the reader becomes aware of how much additional sense and awareness can potentially be further developed. It is critical for this understanding to be reached so that the chapter that follows it, which is the largest chapter in the book, can be understood. Chapter Seven explains *how* Chapter Eight's explanation of life in the subtle worlds could occur. It provides a foundation for most readers to somewhat understand realities that they have neither memory of nor direct knowledge about. This understanding, or improved consciousness, increases meaning in a person's life as that human life increases from having five senses to at least twenty-one, and possibly up to some amount of twenty-eight senses in the most advanced of humans.

Reading about life in the subtle worlds, as presented in Chapter Eight, challenges the reader's preconceptions of reality. Understanding the explanation of life in these worlds may significantly alter the meaning of a person's life both *before and after* physical death, by unhiding part of life's meaning. Most people desire an easier, less stressful life after physical death—paradoxically, even if they do not believe that life goes on after death. The more someone believes that consciousness of the self ends when physical life does, the more that person will fear death; however, some of these people may suppress or repress their fear. The high levels of bound anxiety in the astral bodies of these people can lead to serious illnesses later in life. The majority of people who are physically alive today have a belief of some sort of after-life, but because they desire to have an easier life after physical death, they lose meaning both in the present life and in the subsequent ones. What happens is that in the present life they fail to understand the opportunities that are available to create for themselves more meaning in life by creating more virtue. It is while people are *physically* alive that they have the greatest number of senses and bodies and can create the most light in form, or virtue. As fewer bodies and senses exist in oneself and others, there becomes substantially less opportunity to create virtue. As a result, there is less meaning in life. Also, the less that virtue is created in physical life, the less the etheric/dense physical senses remain *fused* to the astral senses and the less the astral senses are also joined together; the same holds true for the fusing of the astral senses to the mental. All of these factors combined lead to the diminished ability to create virtue during astral or mental life, as compared to etheric/dense physical life.

The reading of *Life's Hidden Meaning* is one relatively small way to alter this current dismal system of lost opportunity to create a more meaningful life. Chapter Eight is of particular importance in reaching the largest proportion of the readers of this book that are facing this serious crisis. As such, Chapter Eight is nearly twice as long as the average chapter in the book is. It is written to be one of the four easier chapters to understand. To accomplish this relative simplicity, the chapter length was increased and the overall level of accuracy of the concepts was lowered through averaging some together, and ignoring many exceptions and special cases. The examples of life on the inner planes leave out much more than they explain, as a result of the above-described process. Instead of attempting to be exhaustive in descriptive details, the endeavor behind this chapter is to create a new, for most readers, understanding of the meaning that was hidden about the after-(physical)-life.

The, usually short, etheric life that humans experience after physical death has as a hidden meaning the reduction of fear of death and of the desire for physical life. The reduction of both of these strong emotional responses allows a person to begin an astral life with more love, or a higher consciousness. Those people who dealt with these fears and desires during the physical life that just ended will leave etheric life early. Sometimes they leave almost immediately after physical death. These people may not even be concerned about the physical body being left behind, and the associations they had with others that were based upon material existence. Such a person will have no concern or interest, from a physical perspective, in his or her death and funeral. Also, a person like this has no more interest in any materiality-based relationship that he or she shared with any of the people who physically survived him or her. As a result, these newly-deceased people quickly move on to the astral plane, where they can still sense (and actually, much better than before) the astral senses and astral thoughts, or the "feelings," of all those whom they focus their individual thought on. Many people prefer to astrally, rather than etherically, experience their funerals and their impressions of what others who have remained physically alive are experiencing either emotionally or lovingly. They further prefer the events on the astral plane over those that can be experienced etherically, because of the much better astral senses and thought that people have once they become focused in life astrally.

A proportionately small number of people lived a materially very greedy physical life, and further seek the continued selfish use of the etheric senses. These people are often the most fearful, often sub-consciously to their selves, about astral life; they tenaciously desire to stay etherically alive. Those comparatively very few people who commit suicide and who do so mostly for self-absorbed reasons, because they desired to die physically may create the contradictory desire within themselves to not live astrally. This desire prevents them from moving on to astral life, i.e., a person cannot live in her or his astral body when that person seeks to not exist in her or his emotions (because they cause so much pain) or because she or he has nihilistically rejected emotion—and love. All of these such cases of etheric human life focus are at risk for becoming ghosts, or sub-humans who have lost too much self to be able to voluntarily desire an astral life. In these cases, only when the personality has completely disintegrated and no further choices are made that represent the causes of the earth-bound condition, will the sub-human ghost move on and begin a fully human astral life. However, with intervention from one's Solar Angel and sometimes some Masters from the next kingdom, many ghosts are encouraged to and usually do move on to the next dimension before this complete state of disintegration is reached. The insidious result of quantum constant anomalies on the etheric plane that are caused by a ghost's etheric atoms being in a different time and space than its physical ones leads to etheric senselessness and etheric brain damage. This lowers the self's ability to help the lower fallen spirit maintain control over the etheric body that this spirit is informing. All of this erodes the personality. For these unfortunate sub-people who are caught on the etheric plane, life becomes nearly meaningless and certainly miserable. Unlike animals who never had much self, these sub-human ghosts suffer with each reduction in self, because the personality's sense of self is continually slightly higher than its loss of self is, at each point in time. Imagine that every day when a person awoke, he or she was aware of having less consciousness than the day before, and knows that, on this new day, he or she will be able to understand less than before.

The mundane meaning of astral life seems to be that one "finally" gets what ever she or he desires. The *hidden* meaning of astral life is that each time someone desires emotionally (selfishly) rather than creates love, that person's astral senses decline. The astral senses decline much more rapidly than did the physical senses while the person was physically alive, because there is less inertia on the astral plane and in the astral sense. In addition, as a person's astral senses become damaged and thus transmit increasingly less accurate information, she or he finds it increasingly difficult to think astrally. The emotionalism, or astral selfishness, that a person had while physically alive becomes karmically accelerated while his or her life is astrally focused, leading to a more rapid decline in his or her astral senses. *Initially*, however, both the astral senses and the consciousness of all non-evil people who are astrally alive are increased. The reason for the initial increase is that astral energy is much less dense and it thus more easily and accurately follows the informing thought of spirit, which facilitates an understanding of the synthesized knowledge created by the personality. Thus, initially, meaning in life increases for most astrally alive people. For the more selfish astrally alive people, this condition can become reversed within several astral years; for others, the deterioration could take astral decades. In all these cases, suffering escalates through relatively comparing the much higher initial astral consciousness to the way that it is quickly declining, and having an awareness of these great differences. Those who are creating love while astrally alive may reach much higher levels of consciousness while astrally alive than they did while alive physically.

However, most will experience a much smaller relative increase in the meaning of their lives because they have relatively fewer etheric/dense physical senses. Only the enlightened parts of their and others' etheric/dense physical senses remain during life on the astral plane, and for most people this amount is far too small to create nearly as much meaning in their astral lives as they could while physically alive. Thus while the consciousness of most people who are alive on the astral plane has risen significantly over where it was during physical life, their ability to respond has not. These two factors together—consciousness and ability to respond—are necessary in order to create more meaning in one's life. In many respects, this is a lower correspondence of the position a Monad is in while on the monadic plane: the Monad has *enormous* consciousness, and initially no senses or means of response on the planes lower than its own.

Part of the hidden meaning of astral life is that astral selfishness reaps its own suffering. This causes some astrally alive people to improve themselves and to reduce the retained energy in their (respective) astral permanent atoms. These people learn that the forces they create through their emotions come back to them as a force towards change—either in the present astral life or in that person's next incarnation. Astral life begins the process of unhiding an understanding of negative karma, as forces that later decrease freedom and increase suffering. The improved astral senses and ease of imaginative thought can also help astral people who are spiritually disciplined to become much more loving and to somewhat enlighten their astral permanent atoms; however, again, this enlightenment is somewhat limited by the reduction in the ability to create the amount of virtue that was possible when these people were physically alive with more senses.

Mental life causes the most profound changes in life's hidden meaning for a human; however, while it changes life's meaning, it only somewhat increases the meaning because those who are mentally alive have so few senses left through which to create more virtue. The greatest *change* in life's hidden meaning is that—initially and for protracted periods of time—a person who is alive on the lower mental plane can derive meaning only by mentally correcting parts of life that he or she had previously created untruthfully by being either egotistical or arrogant. The forces of karma on the lower mental plane are extreme because the person's life is rejoining time and space. This brings in all of the effects of prior selfish causes to now force each person to correct her or his prior mental selfishness, or to die trying. On the lower mental plane, karma *is* the meaning of life while those who are mentally (using exaggerated methods) focused in the past, or on the akasha, attempt to break through their egotism and/or arrogance in order to clear their mental permanent atoms of some of the retained energies, while these people also try to join their split mental senses.

Lower mental life becomes most meaningful when, after the re-living of one's mental past, enough mental sense remains to enable both communication with and the development of consciousness, or love, with others who are near that person's level of consciousness. The closeness of thought is amazingly meaningful and is offset only by whatever remains of egotism in other areas of the mental body and by the limits of having mostly one body through which to sense. Spiritual disciples have the greater increase in mental plane life because they, often, become servers of those on that plane who are less conscious than they are. Their service and greater levels of fused both etheric/dense physical and astral senses create periods of great joy. These people are much more soul-like than human, even while they live lower mentally and have not yet rejoined, in consciousness, with their respective souls on the higher mental plane.

Finally, all people (except those who are evil and hence never live a mental plane life) eventually die from their lower mental plane bodies, and awaken—as their individual souls. The hidden—to a human—meaning of the life of a soul is vast as compared to all of the meaning that the lone human life had. The reason is that the soul's duration of life is for hundreds of human lives. Also, the human soul derives its meaning only from growing and does not suffer (as humans do) from not loving, or from selfish refusal to give. The point of soul awakening is somewhat analogous to a human being going to sleep one night as an unintelligent person who is very low in consciousness, and the next morning awakening as a genius who is unconditionally loving because he or she understands everything completely at the level to which he or she can sense the oneness of all! The karma for the soul affects that soul's creation of its next human incarnation and its ability to help other souls as well; karma does not cause the soul to lose consciousness, it "merely" lessens the soul's ability to create new life. Thus souls do not suffer, but their freedom to create is limited by the prior selfishness (at some level) of each of their humans, as well as somewhat by the selfishness of the humans of some other souls because souls, as lifeforms, live together as one in consciousness. Human souls experience great joy as they give according to the needs of other souls to help other souls do the same. Each person, upon awakening to his or her soul, experiences this tremendous joy that is incomparable to anything that is otherwise experienced in a human's life.

Then the human, as its soul, chooses to reincarnate—with the human creations of other souls—in order to eventually overcome the forces of karma by creating virtue, especially on the physical plane. The physical dimension is the most difficult dimension in which to create virtue, but it is the one that holds the greatest potential to create more of what had been hidden in life's meaning. The subtle dimensions that humans live in teach humans that life is one, and that as that one is grown, each part of it who has made the choice to and then succeeds in creating more of that one becomes a critical part of the God of such a wondrous universe.

Chapter Nine contains more information about life's hidden meaning, and most readers will find some of this information nearly impossible to fully believe at face value. The cause of this initial disbelief is the very careful planning and then the implementation of that plan, starting about eleven thousand years ago, to hide Earth's prior human history. Most of the major hiding of prior human civilization was done by the Planetary Logos, or a God-like Being, who was so thorough in its methods of mostly cataclysmic change to the planet that many humans today cannot believe such hiding is possible. In addition, there were multiple missions carried out over lifetimes of labor by spiritual disciples who were functioning at various levels of initiation into the next kingdom. These disciples assisted in the hiding of the much smaller details, including mystifying most of the concepts that are presented in this book. *Many* clues regarding prehistoric hidden human civilizations were left—most of them intentionally, but some through mistakes—that were nearly all calculated for in the Plan; these clues allow people who are intellectually advanced *and* are of higher consciousness and humility (which is a lack of egotism) to discover them and also at least somewhat understand these discoveries.

When the human civilizations are explained from their beginnings, including the effects of cosmic rays focused on them, an explanation is provided of the meaning of life that is hidden within and interpenetrates the kingdoms lower than the human. The interpenetration occurs because human civilization is created by extending human senses, or awareness, through the incorporation and use of the three lower kingdoms, of pre-life and life. Chapter Nine explains how evolution is a *stage* in the creation of life that eventually, through the human kingdom, *must* be replaced by the spiritual development of *all* life on a planet (making that planet a spiritual—a sacred—one), for that planet to not succumb to the karmic forces that are produced by evolution that takes place without adequate spiritual development. The meaning in humans' lives becomes unhidden as they struggle against the forces of evolution both within their personalities and their bodies, and within their civilizations (which come from incorporating the lower kingdoms within their lives). In their attempts to balance these forces, humans at first use increasing amounts of structured thought. This includes everything from the very rudimentary thought by early humans to the advanced levels seen today. Humans in general may eventually come to realize what a small few already understand: without spiritual thought to eliminate the forces of evolution, each and every civilization destroys itself in the end. Spiritual thought (thought in the direction of God's, thought, or light) changes the energy pitted against energy, or force, into intelligent activity in which the phase (the direction) of any one energy does not go against, or interfere with, the direction of any other. Light does this by reducing space and thus increasing communication while increasing the understanding of the oneness of all, or increasing consciousness; note that reduced space and increased communication together equal intelligence. Enlightened forms lead to enlightened civilization, and humanity today is in a crisis in its attempt to enlighten its civilization. Humans are on the cross of forces and materiality versus spiritual perfection and vastly increased meaning though becoming a functional part of God. To achieve the latter, humans needs to first increase their levels of unconditional love (their love of all, or of life) in order to understand the overwhelming amounts of information that their advanced civilizations are now creating by extending the senses of each human in the civilization.

Chapter Nine reveals the hidden meaning of life as a growing source that can reach to unimaginable levels through the eight kingdoms beyond the human. The meaning of life to Beings in these higher kingdoms is only vaguely expressed because in order to understand these amazing hidden meanings, one needs much greater bodies and senses *or* other types of universal realities besides those that are expressed in our, the Cosmic Physical, universe. The meaning to humans of these inexplicable higher meanings is that they do exist, and that someday each human will become a creator of such meaning within a much greater existence. Chapter Nine extends the notion of potential "human" civilization to beyond the stars, into universes that have yet to be discovered by humans on Earth; these civilizations will almost certainly exist, because all virtuous parts of human civilization remain immortally as parts of higher kingdoms.

Another crucial element to gaining meaning that had been hidden in life (and that is part of the information covered in Chapter Nine) is that the cosmic rays are used as a tool by the Planetary Logos, and even by human souls and their OverSouls, to creatively influence human civilization. The rays are used to grow the senses—both within human's bodies *and* within the bodies of members of the lower kingdoms that humans incorporate within their civilizations, as extension of their own senses. When Chapter Nine is read with understanding, many examples can be seen of how the ray focus of bodies can cause the bodies to respond differently, according to the focus or lack of focus of the cosmic rays on Earth. Also, the cycles of life creation, including traditional mundane models of evolution, can much more easily be understood when the planetary rounds and the focus of rays in correspondence to the rounds, are included within the mundane concepts. Without these concepts about rays, mundane explanations of evolution in today's science contain inexplicable anomalies, especially concerning a linear time model that is applied to a quite nonlinear evolutionary model. Further, the mass destruction of most physical plane life in certain very large cycles of time can be understood in spiritual context when rounds and periods of focused life creation are included in the explanations of these seemingly catastrophic—to existing physical life—events, e.g., the ones that occurred about two hundred and twenty-five million years ago (at the end of the physical period of the second round) and about sixty five million years ago (at the end of the physical period of the third round). The timing and all details of these events were precisely planned, and nothing was done through either "survival of the fittest" or by accident. For example, following a—scheduled—meteor strike that disrupted the planet's environmental conditions, the lifeforms that remained alive were mostly the ones from the more successful group souls that had developed perfection of one or more of the senses of their lifeforms (frogs, and cockroaches, for example). The group souls of lifeforms that were wiped out moved on to become more advanced group souls, with new lifeforms, in the next round. This system provides for continuous life and growth of life on a planet.

The greatest likely difficulty for those who are engrossed in a non-spiritual explanation of life development, using only evolution, is in understanding de-evolution, or a degeneration of (mostly human) lifeforms that takes place as a result of highly selfish uses of civilization. This concept is so hidden that its refutation is likely to be offered without any significant previous thought because de-evolution is nearly the exact opposite of evolution and can be explained (albeit incorrectly) by inventing the concept of a gradual missing link between the advanced ape species and man. Also, to cause even further confusion, some ape and gorilla species contain human DNA, which they acquired long ago through very selfish—and unknown to most people—ways that some humans used civilization. The revelation of these hidden factors greatly expands the importance and meaning of human civilization, and also simultaneously somewhat reduces the importance of evolution and the collective creation of life in the lower kingdoms by group souls. This partial reduction in importance does not negate all of the profound levels of life that group souls do create, it just relatively lessens the levels—especially when these hidden factors are applied to the most advanced members of the animal kingdom. All of this becomes acutely true when considering advanced animals that become human pets— who astrally and slightly mentally may become an extension of their masters' personalities and selves. This takes place in each lifetime that these animals live while on both the physical and astral planes.

Chapter Ten is the cornerstone of explaining life's hidden meaning to those who are very scientifically inclined in their thought and/or vocation. Those people who have fifth ray personalities or minds, or both (see the Reading Guide for further explanation) are likely to find a revelation of life's meaning in the poetry of time and space, unifying what human science has separated in its explanation of our universe. This chapter explains a total, or grand, unification theory of time, space, energy (including matter), dimensions, forces, light, *and* God, because it also includes a complete theological explanation for all of these factors. Once God's mind is understood, so is the *entire* universe, and, as a person unifies God's mind within himself or herself, that person unifies his or her understanding of the universe. Chapter Ten has been kept relatively short, as were the other three most difficult chapters for most readers to understand. The reason is that the formulation and structuring of concepts within these four chapters allows for these concepts' careful dismantling and testing by those who have strong scientific tendencies and abilities. Those who are not so inclined will gain the larger basic concepts by reading the relatively brief amount of material therein. Both groups of readers are thus served: most readers will need to read relatively less material in order to gain an understanding of it, while those other readers who are very scientifically inclined will have the explanations presented in a form that allows for the testing and expansion of those explanations by the readers in this second category. In either case, the author and the Ageless Wisdom Distributors group are available to further teach these difficult concepts, when appropriate to do so. Most readers will find more meaning in their lives by understanding how the universe is constructed as a structure, or scientifically, and how it can be unified back into the mind of God. In part, the strength of Chapter Ten in unhiding life's meaning is in this chapter's brevity and not in its (mostly missing) thoroughness of detail, which would require several volumes of very technical information to be fully explained.

The unhiding of life's meaning through science requires *spiritual* thought *and* must include the concepts regarding spirit, if a scientific view of life's hidden meaning is to be understood. Scientists need this enlargement in the foundation of their thinking, mostly because egotism has, at the present time, caused the field of science (which corresponds to the mental plane and to the fifth ray) in human civilization to become separative, untruthful, and sometimes arrogant. Science periodically reinvents itself in order to avoid facing these devastating effects on it. Each time a break-through is made in a previous (egotistically applied) untruth, science quickly changes its new "truth" and often does not address any further contradictions that exist with prior untruths that are still held to be true. By separation and "specialization," the contradictions in science's "truth" are hidden. Through *Life's Hidden Meaning* unhiding, it is hoped, a number of truths *and* connecting these truths together into a unified cosmology and ontology of super-human dimensions of *non*-contradiction, it is anticipated that some of the prior abuses of untruthful science will diminish. The truth in this book (in whatever amounts its readers may find) is still relative because structured thought, even when whole and given appropriately, is whole only for a particular point in time and space because of the limitation of the mental plane Ray Lord's thought, as mental light, on the thought of all who think on the mental plane. On higher dimensions, truth becomes multi-dimensional through much more complete Nows than the Now that exists at the atomic level of the mental plane—which is the smallest Now that can be created. Any meaning that the scientifically-thinking spiritual disciple can derive from structured thought is necessarily tempered by the limitations of the (mental) virtue of truth, in understanding and becoming a functional part of God. When a person can understand the universe to be one, then, as her or his consciousness greatly expands, all of life is also understood to be one. This understanding and expansion of consciousness is the main focus of increasing the meaning that was heretofore hidden from such readers of Chapter Ten.

Without the structure of reincarnation as explained in this book being included in one's understanding of life, the meaning in that person's life is apt to be very small because one of three scenarios would be likely to describe what he or she believes takes place after physical death. In the first possible scenario, assuming an afterlife, the highest level of development that a human reached in his or her one lifetime would be the level at which he or she would continue to exist, with only very slow, if any, growth because heaven is mostly without the life crises that take place in physical life. In the second possible scenario, also assuming an afterlife, upon entering "heaven" a person would become "perfect" and would be with God, but there would be no growth—of God or of anyone or anything else because in this version of heaven there are *no* crises, stress, or difficulties placed upon the "angelic." A third scenario, in which there would be *no* afterlife, makes life virtually devoid of meaning, because it would render life so unfair and random, and so terrifyingly finite. Even assuming a more human-like afterlife similar to physical life that is still mortal, the question "Is that all a human can be?" would have to be asked. Did God create such a complex physical "universe" (plane) that is so difficult to live in, only so that most humans could live and die as such imperfect and selfish beings? Reincarnation vastly increases life's meaning by providing a soul with endless opportunities to create human beings who *are all connected together through karma*, and who grow from one lifetime to the next because they use the same *permanent* atom for each of their bodies. Without reincarnation, what real purpose does a soul serve? And without reincarnation, how could all men possibly be created equal, when—obviously, e.g.—some are born into a life of wealth and ease, and others, such as babies born with serious and fatal diseases, do not even have a chance at such a life? And why would these, as well as a multitude of other such seemingly unfair circumstances occur, if not for reasons of karma? Unfortunately, reincarnation as a source of meaning in life has been hidden, but *not* by the decisions of the Spiritual Hierarchy or Planetary Logos, as most of the other information in this book had been; reincarnation was hidden by dark humans who selfishly sought to withhold or change (or both) its concepts in order to gain political power (to make policy for others) as well as religious power over those whom they influenced. The earliest teachings of most major religions did include reincarnation and it has always been a part of some, even to the present day. Additionally, the non-mystical parts of Ageless Wisdom teaching—outside the mystery schools—has always included reincarnation. Over time, reincarnation became either changed into bigoted caste systems and almost ridiculous transmigration of humans (souls) into animals, for example; or was completely *deleted*, as from Christianity; or was disjointedly referred to as in Judaic writings…in all of these cases, by people who feared the ability of reincarnation to increase the meaning in human life enough for people to begin to understand God. When the followers of a religion begin to understand God on their own, they may no longer seek their religious leaders' more selfish interpretations of what God is and "wants of man."

Another part of life's meaning that is revealed in Chapter Eleven's explanation of reincarnation is that reincarnation plays one of two roles in a person's life. Either a person is a forced "victim" of reincarnation, because karma works its way out from one lifetime to the next (mostly through energy in the bodies and senses), or a person becomes liberated by using reincarnation to perfect her or his bodies, senses, mind, understanding, and creation of virtue. When approached and used in this second way, reincarnation is a powerful tool that leads to continuity of consciousness and immortality. *Immortality creates a life of infinite meaning as long as growth of life (of God) is included in what one is becoming.* That is exactly how reincarnation is explained in this book. In effect, those who reject reincarnation in their own lives are also denying themselves the opportunity to become a functional part of God. Those who understand reincarnation as it is explained in Chapter Eleven have one of the most powerful tools available to create more meaning in their lives and in the lives of others.

Chapter Twelve briefly describes and does offer some methods for increasing consciousness. These all rely upon some form of limitation to focus more thought and sense on the area that one is seeking to improve upon. Life's hidden meaning is exposed as one chooses to and does successfully achieve some improvement in his or her senses and in the ability to think using information from the senses, and then in getting the bodies to follow the informing thought of spirit. Most of the readers of *Life's Hidden Meaning* who reach Chapter Twelve are likely to have some aspiration towards increasing the meaning in their lives, through the areas of meaning that thus far remain hidden to them and therefore involve understanding and creating more of God. Both of these goals can be achieved only through increasing one's *spiritual* senses, which requires spiritual discipline. These disciplines are the most difficult that humans can attempt, yet they also produce the greatest increases in life's meaning. Some people, many of whom will be readers of this book, can mostly increase the meaning in their lives only through spiritual discipline. The reason is that they have already grown their selves to near the maximum level possible—without significantly fusing with their individual Selves, and their individual personalities and souls fusing as well.

Besides being a "cookbook" of methods for spiritual discipline, Chapter Twelve exposes some of the more esoteric problems that people who are more advanced in consciousness have as they attempt to create meaning in their lives. Ultimately, Chapter Twelve exposes that once a person's self has reached nearly full development, life is only as meaningful for that person as the amount of meaning that she or he chooses to create in *others'* lives. Some people who are very advanced initiates may begin to *live* their lives for others in this way by age twenty-eight— or even earlier. Most spiritual disciples either share their lives as first level initiates, or change their feelings into love for others as second level initiates, or mentally think for others' lives as third level initiates. Depending upon these levels of consciousness and of Self initiation into the next kingdom, some may receive additional help from Selves of members of the next kingdom. The greatest meaning in life, including all that is hidden from humans, can be realized through helping to create in others as much of God's thought and activity (God's mind) together as the others will permit. When carried out for all life that one has contact with or can sense the meaning of, all of that life becomes one's meaning of life. This then is the meaning of life that is to be unhidden for humanity.

Each chapter contains words that are included in the glossary. Certain of these words' definitions, as the author defines them, are important towards improving many readers' comprehension of the material in *Life's Hidden Meaning*. To use this help guide, select the chapter that is about to be read, and look through the list of suggested glossary words. Read those words' definitions that you have not yet read (and reread any whose meaning is not fully grasped). The words are in alphabetical order and are numbered—matching their place in the glossary. Jotting down the definition numbers with pen and paper may make the process more efficient for some readers. Note that most of these definitions are found in their entirety only in the glossary, although parts of the definitions are repeated in various sections of the corresponding chapters.

CHAPTER ONE

astral–8; center–18; choices–21; concept–25; consciousness–26; direction, of choices–38; energy–48; God–57; joy–69; karma–71; light–79; retained energy–116; sense–124; soul, group–130; soul, human, individual–131; space–132; spirit–133; spiritual–134; spiritual discipline–136; thought–140; time–142; universe–149; webs–152; will–153.

CHAPTER TWO

Ageless Wisdom–1; center–18; character, good–20; choices–21; comprehension of a concept–24; concept–25; consciousness–26; cosmic fire of creation, the first–28; cosmic fire of creation, the second–29; cosmic fire of creation, the third–30; Creator of our universe–33; direction, of choices–38; Director, of a field of possibilities–39; energy–48; God–57; intelligence–67; life–78; light–79; mind–88; Now, a–93; planning–100; power–103; quality, of thought–108; ray–112; Ray Lord, cosmic–114; sacrifice, spiritual–118; self–120; Self–121; selfishness–123; space–132; spiritual–134; thought–140; time–142; universe–149; will–153.

CHAPTER THREE

beauty–15; choices–21; concept–25; consciousness–26; direction, of choices–38; duration, of life–44; energy–48; evil–52; God–57; gravity–58; inertia–63; intelligence–67; knowledge–74; life–78; light–79; mind–88; Monad–89; Now, a–93; power–103; pre-life–105; ray–112; Ray Lord, cosmic–114; sense–124; space–132; spirit–133; spiritual–134; thought–140; time–142; universe–149; will–153.

CHAPTER FOUR

astral–8; choices–21; consciousness–26; deva–36; deva energy–37; direction, of choices–38; elemental energy–47; energy–48; God–57; gravity–58; intelligence–67; knowledge–74; life–78; light–79; mind–88; Monad–89; Monad, ascended–90; Now, a–93; pitris, lunar and solar–98; quality, of thought–108; ray–112; Ray Lord, cosmic–114; self–120; Self–121; sense–124; soul, human, individual–131; space–132; spirit–133; spiritual–134; thought–140; time–142; universe–149; will–153.

CHAPTER FIVE

astral–8; causal body–17; character, good–20; choices–21; concept–25; consciousness–26; deva–36; direction, of choices–38; discipline–41; energy–48; God–57; kingdom–72; knowledge–74; life–78; light–79; mind–88; Monad–89; pitris, lunar and solar–98; pre-life–1054; self–120; Self–121; selfishness–123; sense–124; soul, group–130; soul, human, individual–131; space–132 spirit–133; spiritual–134; thought–140; time–142; universe–149.

CHAPTER SIX

Ageless Wisdom–1; astral–8; bacteria–13; causal body–17; center–18; concept–25; consciousness–26; deva–36; deva energy–37; direction, of choices–38; elemental energy–47; energy–48; God–57; hierarchial spiritual thought–60; humility–61; initiation–64; inner sacrifice petals–65; kama-manasic connection–70; kingdom–72; knowledge–74; kundalini–76; life–78; light–79; mind–88; Monad–89; Monad, ascended–90; Now, a–93; permanent atom–96; person–97; pitris, lunar and solar–98; Planetary Logos–99; prana–104; pre-life–105; radiance–110; rainbow bridge–111; ray–112; ray line–113; scheme–119; self–120; Self–121.

CHAPTER SEVEN

anxiety–4; arrogance–6; astral–8; astral energy–9; beauty–15; center–18; civilization–23; concept–25; consciousness–26; cosmic fire of creation, the first–28; cosmic fire of creation, the second–29; cosmic fire of creation, the third–30; creative imagination–32; deva–36; deva energy–37; direction, of choices–38; discipline–41; disease–43; egotism–46; elemental energy–47; evil–52; glamour–56; God–57; initiation–64; knowledge–74; kundalini–76; life–78; light–79; mind–88; pain–94; permanent atom– 96; pitris, lunar and solar–98; possession–102; prana–104; psychic sense, higher–106; quality, of thought–108.

CHAPTER EIGHT

Angel of the Presence–2; arrogance–6; astral–8; astral energy–9; bacteria–13; beauty–15; bliss–16; center–18; choices–21; civilization–23; concept–25; consciousness–26; creative imagination–32; deva–36; deva energy–37; direction, of choices–38; discipline–41; egotism–46; elemental energy–47; energy–48; evil–52; glamour–56; God–57; initiation–64; joy–69; kama-manasic connection–70; karma–71; kingdom–72; knowledge–74; life–78; light–79; mind–88; pain–94; permanent atom–96; person–97; possession–102; power–103.

CHAPTER NINE

Ageless Wisdom–1; astral–8; Atlantis–10; Avatar–12; beauty–15; center–18; chain–19; civilization–23; concept–25; consciousness–26; creative imagination–32; discipline–41; disease–43; egotism–46; esoteric–50; evil–52; glamour–56; God–57; group consciousness–59; hierarchial spiritual thought–60; humility–61; initiation–64; kingdom–72; knowledge–74; Kumara–75; Lemuria–77; life–78; light–79; love, astral and conditional–80; Maitreya–85; Manu–86; maya–87; mind–88; mystery schools–91; mystification–92; pleasure–101; ray–112; ray line–113; selfishness–123; sense–124; sentiency–125; service–126; sharing and cooperation–127; soul, human, individual–131; soul, group–130; spirit–133; spiritual–134; suffering–137.

CHAPTER TEN

astral–8; astral energy–9; beauty–15; choices–21; consciousness–26; cosmic fire of creation, the first–28; cosmic fire of creation, the second–29; cosmic fire of creation, the third–30; energy–48; esoteric–50; event–51; God–57; gravity–58; inertia–63; intelligence–67; intuition–68; karma–71; knowledge–74; life–78; light–79; mind–88; Monad–89; Monad, ascended–90; Now, a–93; permanent atom–96; quantum constant–109; ray–112; service–126; space–132; spirit–133; spiritual–134; thought–140; time–142; time dilation–143; transfiguration–145; transformation–146; transmutation–147; truth–148; universe–149; will–153.

CHAPTER ELEVEN

Arhat–5; astral–8; Avatar–12; causal body–17; center–18; civilization–23; consciousness–26; discipline–41; energy–48; evil–36; evolution, spiritual–53; God–57; initiation–64; inner sacrifice petals–65; karma–71; kingdom–72; knowledge–74; Monad–89; Now, a–93; permanent atom–96; person–97; prana–104; ray–112; retained energy–116; self–120; Self–121; selfishness–123; sense–124; service–126; Solar Angel–128; soul, human, individual–131; spirit–133; spiritual–134; suffering– 137; thought–140; thread–141; time–142; truth–148; virtue, cosmic–150.

CHAPTER TWELVE

Arhat–5; astral–8; causal body–17; center–18; character, good–20; concept–25; consciousness–26; creative imagination–32; deva–36; discipline–41; Dweller on the Threshold–45; energy–48; event–51; God–57; group consciousness–59; hierarchial spiritual thought–60; humility–61; initiation–64; kama-manasic connection–70; karma–71; Kingdom of Souls–73; knowledge–74; mind–88; person–97; planning–100; prana–104; rainbow bridge–111; retained energy–116; self–120; Self–121; selfishness–123; sense–124; service–126; Solar Angel–128; soul, human–131; spirit–133; spiritual–134; spiritual discipline–136; suffering–137; Teacher–139; thought–140; thread–141; time–142; truth–148; webs, of retained energies–152; will–153; wrong speech–154; yoga–155.

SUMMARY

Ageless Wisdom–1; Arhat–5; arrogance–6; astral–8; civilization–23; concept–25; consciousness–26; discipline–41; energy–48; esoteric–50; evolution, spiritual–53; God–57; karma–71; kingdom–72; life–78; light–79; mind–88; Monad–89; Monad ascended–89; rainbow bridge–111; retained energy–116; self–120; Self–121; sense–124; service–126; Solar Angel–128; soul, group–130; soul, human, individual–131; space–132; spirit–133; spiritual–134; thought–140; time–142; truth–148; universe–149.

Author's note: this glossary contains definitions of words that are different in mundane denotation or sometimes connotation. When reading *Life's Hidden Meaning*, the reader is advised to use the definitions in this glossary.

1. Ageless Wisdom—a collection of mental concepts from the spiritual sub-planes of the higher mental plane. The concepts create truth at a particular time within the mental minds of those people who can understand them at about a fifty percent or greater level of comprehension. When understood as a whole, these concepts create an understanding of God, of the Cosmic Physical (our) Universe, and of the life within our universe.

2. Angel of the Presence—the OverSoul, or Solar Angel, when projected into the higher mental solar devas, or the causal body, of a human. When experiencing this projection, the human typically believes that the Angel is present on the plane he or she is alive on. The reason is that the mental image is so clear in its structure that it confuses the personality, which is on the lower mental plane, into believing that the image and Angel's thought are coming from information from the three lower bodies' senses.

3. antahkarana—see "rainbow bridge"

4. anxiety—fear of pain that is usually caused by the personality losing its control over any one or more of its bodies or senses.

5. Arhat—a person who is functionally serving in the highest level of human initiation, which is, at the present time, the fourth. Arhats are expected to *live* the spiritual thought that they create and teach to others. Their lives are usually sacrificial because they live for others who are often much more selfish than they are. These advanced human initiates suffer (personally) immensely and must *renounce* their suffering and gain higher consciousness. They also need to consistently live the earlier brief tests of renouncing their eighteen most selfish ways of using the split senses in their three lower bodies (six renunciations per body). Those tests took place during the third initiation. For an arhat, living a life of renunciation is not as difficult as it might seem, because he or she is actually renouncing the unreal from the real. The suffering that the arhat endures is created by the remaining karma—first personal karma, but later group-related. This negative karma is offset as the arhat gives up transformation for the sake of those who are co-serving with her or him. The arhat chooses to not go on until her or his students and their group have completed certain group missions as well as (for the students) levels of initiation. Arhats at first usually save the senses and bodies of those who enter the group, for future spiritual service within the group. As saviors, arhats are a fundamental test towards salvaging many somewhat spiritually developed, but failing, spiritual disciples. The basic concept that an arhat needs to live is that life is one…and her or his life increasingly represents this concept.

6. arrogance—the second and more advanced stage of mental illusion, wherein egotism has become generalized to all of a person's mental thought, and has become a part of his or her entire personality. In this stage, the semi-rigid outside bands of egotism sink into the higher and lower mental bodies. They do so because of the collective gravitating forces of the elemental energies that have been attracted to the solar and/or lunar devas that have been damaged by egotism. The added elemental energy moves into the mental centers that correspond to the sub-sub-plane locations of the egotism. The combined energy then gravitates together *between* centers, joining the centers through darkness and causing permanent damage to the mental senses (which prevents most further learning and understanding of others' thought). Arrogance leads to vast increases in kama-manasic thinking and to a personality and self who often believes that everything others think is wrong, and everything she or he "personally" thinks is right. Arrogant people are often very unloving, as well as lonely and very rigid mentally.

7. aspirant—a person who *desires* to discipline himself or herself, but has not begun to do so.

8. astral—the plane of time and space that has four dimensions—height, width, and depth (the three split etheric/dense physical), plus motion in one direction at a time, or movement that has a vector. The astral plane contains two potential parts of time that are connected to the same event. These are the past and present. The future part of time never directly attaches to the same event in time and space on the astral plane, or dimension, because the speed of thought of the astral cosmic Ray Lord is not great enough to join all three parts of time to an event in space—which would create a Now. The astral dimension is located between the mental dimension and the lowest one in our universe, or the etheric/dense physical dimension. The energy of the astral plane is feminine in spin, or tends to be integrally more influenced by both mental and etheric/dense physical energies, which are masculine in their spin. Note that all of the cosmic Ray Lords are masculine in their thought, but three of them (the monadic, intuitional, and astral Ray Lords) are feminine in the spin of either their intelligent activity or their energy.

9. astral energy—energy that exists in the four dimensions of height, width, depth (those are the three split etheric/dense physical dimensions), *and* motion in one direction at a time, or movement that has a vector. Astral energy is, on average, dozens of times less dense than etheric energy is, and is much more energetic because of the astral energy's added dimension and different phase. When astral energy moves from the thought of a lifeform towards itself, this energy is emotion; when astral energy moves towards others to give to them in some ways, it is love. Astral energy is a feminine energy, which means that it spins in the opposite directional phase of either mental or etheric/dense physical energy.

10. Atlantis—the continent that first rose above sea level from the mid-Atlantic ridge about fifteen to sixteen million years ago. At its largest size including its surrounding islands, Atlantis covered about eight hundred thousand square miles. The majority of the continent was north of the Equator and was situated at an angle to Europe and Africa, and North and South America. The landmass had a sixth ray focus, as did the major race—the Atlantean—that inhabited it. Atlantis as a continuous landmass, not counting its islands, was over 1100 miles long and at its larger width was close to 900 miles wide. Atlantis began to break apart nearly one million years ago. It became two distinct island continents by 800,000 years ago, and the cultures that then developed on the North and South sections were just as distinct. The last, relatively small, part of Atlantis sank below the sea, *and* part of it sank below the earth's crust, and possibly into the mantel, about 11,000 years ago. This last section, named Poseidonis, was located in the area surrounding the Azores off the coast of Portugal and northern Africa.

11. aura—the etheric, astral, and mental bodies normally are and appear to be, to those who can see them, electrically radiating the Ray Lord's light in that body. This radiance is sometimes referred to as an aura.

12. Avatar—a soul who comes either from another planet in the same solar system or from a planet within a different solar system (across interstellar space). The purpose of this travel is for such souls to contribute a new type of consciousness to a planet that its existing humanity cannot at that time create on its own. A planetary Avatar, who comes from a planet in the same solar system, may be able to return, after incarnated service, to his or her existing planet, depending upon his or her length of service as an Avatar. A cosmic Avatar, from a different star and its solar system, usually cannot return to his or her home world after incarnated service, because of greater time differences. Each Avatar must start over again as a "new" soul in this new adopted world of service while he or she serves there. For cosmic Avatars this is usually an enormous sacrifice because in their original worlds many of them were Arhats, and some were Masters.

13. bacteria—a sub-kingdom of microscopic lifeforms mostly between the vegetable and animal kingdoms. Most are scavengers of energies from previously alive bodies. A few types of bacteria exist under the oceans, living off the energy of volcanoes. Some bacteria are parasitic, and some of the parasitic ones are pathogens that are seriously dangerous, or even potentially fatal. Most bacteria are organisms that cannot animate enough of their astral centers to become animal lifeforms, and thus become stuck between kingdoms.

14. beautification—a process of perfecting the balance of spiritual thought to the creation of forms.

15. beauty—the cosmic virtue of the intuitional, or buddhic, plane. When the light of the intuitional Ray Lord is in form, beauty is created. This light, or thought, is a ratio of *twice* the thought within spirit as the amount of thought within the energy that makes up the form. At this ratio, spirit can think for the energy (as a completed and enlightened sense) and for itself, *simultaneously*. Any time such a ratio of spiritual thought to energy is used, it creates beauty in the form it is used on—from a picture that is painted, to the sky, to the virtuous bodies of a being. Nature's beauty is indeed great, yet humans are intended to increase beauty on a planet as they advance themselves into the next kingdom. Those attempting to do so at the present time on earth need to significantly increase the spiritual (enlightened) thought of many people and even other lifeforms, to create more beauty. The reason is that at present, in most circumstances, there is far less spiritual thought in general than there is the amount of it that is needed to create beauty.

16. bliss—a state of continuous joy wherein one's consciousness is great enough to create a oneness between one's Self and all other Selves in at least one of three possible ways. The first of these ways is through all-knowledge. Bliss usually requires intuitional consciousness because the intuitional plane is the first (the lowest) plane upon which one experiences all others' creations of virtue.

17. causal body—the thirty-six outer solar devas in nine petal formations that surround the human soul; these devas are also the lowest part of a human Solar Angel's body. They protect the soul with their energy fields, and also help to hold together concepts that are created by a personality and self. The three inner sacrifice petals of more advanced solar devas also become a part of the causal body as these petals open. The causal body holds together the *causes* of mental thought as concepts on the higher mental plane, while lunar devas create the effects on the lower mental plane.

18. center, or chakra—a sphere of ray-specialized energy. If the center is a major one, the energy sphere will be informed by a spirit sphere within or surrounding the same center. The energy sphere spins as energy enters it and leaves, thereby creating a sense and information. The spirit sphere does not rotate until the center becomes conscious, and then only fractionally until it becomes significantly enlightened. There are seven major centers in each human body, and the spirit spheres of these centers inform all of the hundreds of minor centers that exist throughout each corresponding body.

19. chain—a chain comprises a series of a planet's incarnations at three different dimensional levels at a time. Chains can begin on the spiritual, intuitional, or mental plane, and end in their development of life on the mental, astral, or etheric/dense physical plane. Planetary Logoi can create seven chains of planets that each create a planetary scheme of life.

20. character, good—the self-created ability to give to others in thought according to what the others need in order to be more virtuous, with the given thought containing knowledge that has been synthesized from information. Good character is created by contemplating circumstances so that one can give to others in the above-described way in real time, when the giving will be helpful. Thus good character is created through some levels of self discipline.

21. choices—within a field of possibilities, when one possibility is more likely to occur than another is; every time this circumstance arises, a choice is created. Choices do not become thought until they have a similar direction, or continuity, to themselves and can cause more choices with similar direction to occur within the same field, or can limit that field.

22. Christos (Greek), or Christ (Latin)—originally the title of an office that denoted a Great Leader. In Atlantean times, an earlier derivative of the name Christos was the office held by the second ray Leader of the Spiritual Hierarchy. This Leader is also referred to as the World Teacher.

23. civilization—the use of the three lower kingdoms by humans, who incorporate the forms of those kingdoms into their own. Civilization is the gradual taking over of the informing thought of the forms of the lower kingdoms, through the pre-life and life in those kingdoms eventually following the higher thought of humans instead of the thought of the kingdom's group souls and selves. The forms of these kingdoms then become extensions of humans' senses and bodies.

24. comprehension of a concept—a concept is a moving picture of the structure of mental thought. Someone's understanding of a concept enough to comprehend it is determined by how well that person can use the structure to create a specific effect in lower mental energies. Full comprehension of a concept means that one who is thinking mentally can reconstruct all of the structure within his or her higher mental mind. Then constructed thoughtforms can be created into full sentences that connect all of the time and space—in correct order—between where the concept is located on the higher mental plane and all of the higher mental sub-planes below it, as well as the lower mental sub- (and sub-sub-) planes down to the very lowest. Full comprehension can be demonstrated by someone being able to construct sentences that logically explain an example of a particular concept. When a person comprehends about one-half or more of a concept, she or he can then use the concept to create additional concepts and examples, as well as additional partial sentences that reasonably explain it. The one-half of comprehension that is needed to create a useable sentence or sentences as an example is based upon the need of a self and/or a mind to be able to limit one-half of its field that it gives, in order to create consciousness, or understanding.

25. concept—the structure, on the higher mental plane, of a thought that creates a relative balance between the solar devas and the elemental energies that are contained within that structure. The more energies that are contained within a concept, the larger the concept is and the greater the guiding thought needs to be in order to balance the energies so that the structure of the concept can be maintained. The larger the concept, the more thought that is needed to create or re-create its structure in higher mental plane energies.

26. consciousness—the ability to understand the connectedness of choices within thought. Consciousness leads to the understanding that all life is one because all life is created by thought that is God's, or is light. Eventually consciousness develops to the level of understanding God through understanding that all of life is God's growth. The more that something loves, or gives to others, the more conscious it is because then it is in some ways understanding the oneness between itself and the others. Consciousness is lost as one reverses the process and selfishly takes from others. Consciousness is part of the second aspect of God's mind.

27. cosmic evil—a group soul that exists in a very old galaxy and somewhat outside (!) that galaxy. Its position in time and space allows it to communicate to any part of our universe from the lower mental plane and below. Evil *uses* space as a means of communication in an opposite manner to how light communicates. There are several concepts concerning how cosmic evil achieves this effect that are being omitted from this definition. Those concepts could be used to, in a way, reverse-engineer communication—with cosmic evil. Evil in any location in our universe can invoke the thought of the group soul of cosmic evil, and usually does. The cosmic evil supplies the collective thought it has received, as "needed" and to *all* the evil in our universe. This explains how, once someone becomes evil, he or she grows so rapidly in evil thought.

28. cosmic fire of creation, the first—the electrical attraction, i.e., negative to positive, between the thought of a greater (positive) field and the (smaller) thought in a smaller (negative) field that can limit the greater field by using some amount of its (smaller) thought. This attraction and probability-creator between the fields is the primary means of creation of *everything*. The first cosmic fire of creation relies on sacrifice and limitation in its electrical attraction, and corresponds to the first aspect of God's mind and to the first ray.

29. cosmic fire of creation, the second—the electrical attraction between two or more thoughts that are joining together to create a greater change in the field than the sum of its parts is in thought. The reason for the greater change is that the sum of fused thought limits the field more as an exponential multiplier than as an addition. This increase is the result of the connections of all the choices in each thought being factorially applied to the act of the connections of the other thought. Since fusion is mostly a *factorial* of connection, or of the second aspect of God's mind, the second cosmic fire is a correspondence of the second ray.

30. cosmic fire of creation, the third—the electrical attraction between forms that are within the same field. The forms are joined based upon the gravitating forces versus intelligent activities within the field. Because force is *always* a part of this type of electrical attraction of *force* versus intelligent activity, friction and heat are parts of all third cosmic fires. Note that if manifested energies are not present, then neither is the third cosmic fire. This fire corresponds to the third aspect of God's mind and to the third ray.

31. cosmic ray (spiritual)—a ray is a field of potential growth that affects only energy. There are seven cosmic rays, and each is created by the thought, or light, of one of the seven cosmic Ray Lords. A ray is created by the vast thought and its field of the cosmic Ray Lord focusing on such a tiny field of thought, of some part of energy, that is very slightly thinking in the direction of that cosmic Ray Lord's thought. Whenever the energy invokes help in increasing its thought, by thinking very slightly in the direction of a specific Ray Lord, it receives a part of the Ray Lord's thought to help it in its own thought. This assistance greatly enhances the ability of the energy to grow in thought and to eventually build a sense of other energy, leading to more intelligence in their activity together. Note that a spiritual cosmic ray has no relationship to an astrophysics "cosmic ray" of a higher speed sub-atomic particle that originates from a source in outer space.

32. creative imagination—the thought within the astral body, by the informing spirit of a lifeform. Creative imagination contains moving pictures that lack structure, or that lack full and correct time that would keep the energies within the thought from being conflictive with one another. Creative imagination is fantasy when, within the energies composing this thought, conflicts exist that would prevent the thought from becoming a functional form on a particular dimension. Factual creative imagination represents actual or potentially actual occurrences, based upon the particular physics and circumstances of a certain dimension and a series of events within that dimension. Because the future part of time is mostly missing in creative imagination, when creative imagination is used to predict or create future events it is prone to being more fantasy (and error-ridden) than reality. Using creative imagination to live by tends to create illusion in most humans who use it in this selfish way, because most are usually capable of creating whole—mental, structured-in-time—thought.

33. Creator of our universe—a Being of such enormous thought that the original field of potential possibilities that its thought could have been a part of was unlimited. From within the Creator's field of possibilities, which it limits to direct and become a Being, the Creator further chooses to create a universe of form, or energy, by sacrificing part of Its mind that was created by Its own thought. When this sacrificed part of the Creator's mind enters a state of Beingness in its own field, it becomes God in that (our) universe. A creator of a universe wills that its field of thought remain completely separated from the universe's field of thought that It creates, except at the universe's very end. This separation is an extreme sacrifice, which allows maximum freedom and growth for Creators' creations.

34. crystallization—the balancing of forces within a form to keep the form from significantly degrading and from quickly atrophying. When used with light, crystallization is continually enhanced and restored by the light, to replace the energy that gradually becomes depleted. This depletion occurs because forces cannot be completely balanced as long as energy, rather than intelligent activity, is present. Crystallization used by evil employs power to transmute energies back and forth in density, in order to maintain evil's form and to replace the lost energies. To maintain the balance, this power must be taken from a source outside the lifeform. That is why evil uses power to take from others, for if it did not its form would rather rapidly disintegrate and die.

35. densification—a loss of space between two or more like-thinking energies but with no increase in the level of connectedness of choices within their thought, or in consciousness, and, therefore, with no added light.

36. deva—God-like in qualities, or in consciousness (giving/understanding). A fairly close equivalent of the English word "angel." As applied to energy, deva energies are the more conscious energies, and are developing some level of self. They also support the growth of spirit and life. They help to evolve life and are considered evolutionary (moving more towards spirit than into form) in their group conscious thinking, which tends to consistently increase their consciousness. (see also "deva energy")

37. deva energy—energy that is evolutionary, or seeks to grow more of life (God's growth) or of pre-life rather than more of just itself. Involutionary energies seek to grow more of themselves unless directed by greater outside informing thought. Evolutionary energies tend to think at least somewhat in light and are more cooperative together towards creating more than just unintelligent energy. There are three general classes of deva energy. The first class is of lunar deva energy, which has only group consciousness but no individual consciousness. Lunar devas that are part of an integrated form (are informed by spirit) are referred to as lunar pitris. They are the partially angelic energies that are not individually conscious and (like the moon) reflect the individual consciousness of some higher, more enlightened, thought of a being. The second class of deva energy is solar deva energy, which is developing individual consciousness and has a very high sense of group consciousness. When solar devas, or solar pitris, are integrated within a form by spirit, they are very responsive to higher focused spiritual thought and can, at times, create some levels of thought themselves if they have been enlightened enough by informing spirit. Solar pitris that are increased in their spiritual thought by spirit while they think for themselves can give off light, and because they have such capability are referred to as solar—after Sol, our Sun—pitris. The third class of deva energy is energy that has reached full individualization and is fully angelic, or is a completely conscious energy Being of extraordinary consciousness (love). Some of these energies are referred to as Solar Angels, although the term solar deva would mean close to the same in an English translation. Solar Angels are fully *Self* conscious, which is a state of consciousness beyond that of human. Solar devas are not yet fully *self* conscious, or are less conscious than some humans are. The deva energies are all a part of the energy sub-kingdom of the spiritual kingdom, or the fifth kingdom, which is the one *above* the human kingdom. Energy is a sub-kingdom because part of it is below, or equal to, humans in consciousness and part of it is above, causing the part below to sometimes rely on humans and group souls to help it develop.

38. direction, of choices—the connectivity of one choice with another, based upon similar probabilities of limiting a field, or of further creating more choices that have direction. Direction is also love, givingness, oneness, and consciousness, as a result of creating thought that gives something back to the very field it is part of and is limiting. Direction gives a field of potential the ability to Be, and often the ability to Be a Creator.

39. Director, of a field of possibilities—is created by enough thought to limit one-half of a field into probabilistic outcomes. A *Being* is created from the consciousness of so much *oneness* to the field when at least one-half has oneness.

40. discerning thought—see "self"

41. discipline—the limiting of the senses and one or more bodies in order to help them to grow through focused attention of informing thought. If mundane, the purpose is for selfish gain; if spiritual, the purpose is to increase spiritual, or more enlightened, thought in oneself and in others.

42. discriminating thought—see "self"

43. disease—a lower form of life that feeds on the energies of a higher form because the higher form is not using the energies lovingly (consciously/givingly). Disease *reduces* the amounts of retained energies in centers, organs, and glands, but also converts them into more of itself rather than more of the life of its host. If not halted this process can eventually destroy the higher lifeform. Diseases also *add* to a higher lifeform their own lower, retained energies, or wastes, which are often poisonous to that life. This happens because when infecting a host, the disease usually does not contain a center that would be able to efficiently give this "waste" energy.

44. duration, of life—the amount of time and space that a Ray Lord's creation of life encompasses. For example, the mental Ray Lord creates life that has a duration of time and space of the mental, astral, and etheric/dense physical planes all at the same time (of mental Nows). A duration is not just a period of time; it is time as time is joined with or separated from space by the totality of the thought from all life that is created by and within all the space of a Ray Lord's mind. This space includes not only that Ray Lord's plane, but all the planes below because in this life's field of thought the life interpenetrates those lower planes.

45. Dweller on the Threshold—a personality that becomes threatened by the spiritual growth of its own self. This occurs because the self is attempting to understand and give thought about and from its soul and Self that will lead to fusion of the personality and soul. The fusion would be caused by the larger soul-focused concepts changing the personality's focus of control of its self to a focus on improving its senses and information to increase its synthesized knowledge. The fusion allows the self to give this knowledge to its Self, which will create it into even greater knowledge that the soul will then give wisely to others. As all of this occurs the self fuses with the Self, causing the personality to lose control over its self. Also, the senses of the personality's bodies are no longer primarily being grown to support the personality's existence. The personality may elect to prevent this process from continuing and then will refuse to give much of its synthesized knowledge to its self. As this takes place the person loses consciousness because its self has less to give. The senses decline because some of their information is, at times, not being synthesized and becomes retained. The personality, in effect, goes "out to lunch," while the person becomes both much more selfish and (suddenly) inept because no part of him or her is being adequately integrated and organized. Then the person is in the dweller. Dwellerism occurs, usually, when a spiritual disciple is attempting to discipline herself or himself beyond the stage of personal giving. Personal giving is associated with the spiritual development of the third tier of solar devas in the causal body. Usually it is when the spiritual disciple is attempting to use his or her self to create larger concepts from the second tier, on a greater soul/group conscious level, that the personality becomes a dweller caught in illusion. To gain control, the dweller stops giving—often completely. The "threshold" is the door to the soul and to the soul/group conscious thought that the dweller is trying to prevent the spiritual disciple from using with which to create more virtue. In each of the first two initiations, the stage of dwellerism usually lasts anywhere from six months to about two years. During this period of time, a spiritual disciple is in great jeopardy of leaving his or her spiritual group (and its mission) and becoming self focused and sometimes personality-disordered.

46. egotism—the first stage of mental illusion, in which damaged solar and/or lunar deva energy is attracted to and becomes the outside part of a person's mental body, because this energy is following the person's self-focused mental thought. The person selfishly chooses to think that her or his thought in a particular area is right, or correct, and that any contradictory thought, either in a different direction (phase) or level of choice (frequency), or both, is wrong. Such a person loses some ability to sense thought that is contradictory to her or his egotism. The loss is a result of some of the energy within others' mental thoughts not getting through the egotism to reach one or more mental senses. The reduction in sense causes the person to defend his or her egotism, which often prevents a reality check from being made concerning the correctness (or lack thereof) of the egotistical thought.

47. elemental energy—energy that is created from the intelligent activity originally located on the monadic plane, and sometimes created on the atomic level of a lower plane. Elemental energy is involutionary because it grows *less* in consciousness on each lower plane, as a result of spirit's inability to adequately inform this energy through the spirit *giving* of its thought, or loving it enough. Elemental energy is the primary cause of gravity, and is used in lifeforms to keep the form mostly the same for prolonged periods of time with little additional thought needed. (see also "energy")

48. energy—the manifestation of activity that is less than perfectly intelligent. As the activity becomes less intelligent it slows down, or separates time from space, which causes the activity to densify and to manifest into energy. All energy has the potential to return to higher levels of activity, and the degree to which that energy does so is based upon how intelligent it is. The energy's intelligence causes time to rejoin to itself and with space, and eventually causes space to rejoin into light. When very dense on the densest part of the etheric/dense physical plane, energy becomes matter because it causes over one-half of the past part of time to become less connected to space than to the remainder of past time. Within those parts of the dimension that the condition is occurring within, more energy, on average, than not is likely to not be active. Those parts of the dimension are the fifth, sixth, and seventh subplanes of the seventh plane.

49. energy sub-kingdom—the part of the fifth kingdom that focuses on life creation more from the development of the third aspect of God's mind than from the first two aspects. The lower part of this sub-kingdom relies on using force as a primary means of growing more of life. The beings in this sub-kingdom are keenly focused on the use of force as a method of balancing and joining God's mind within a lifeform. Their method of force is much less efficacious in growing more of the first two aspects of God's mind, or light, and relies upon their informing spirit to assist with that part of growing life (and God). The lifeform with the highest level of consciousness in the energy sub-kingdom is a Solar Angel in its third triadal stage. The least-developed type of energy is elemental energy at the top (but not the atomic level) of the spiritual plane, where this involutionary energy has *less* thought overall (but also less gravitating thought) than does any other type of energy. However, in the thought that it does have, spiritual plane elemental (involutionary) energy has much higher consciousness, or a greater ability to think in oneness with life in general, than elemental energies on the lower planes do. These elemental energies in lower dimensions think more than the higher-level ones do, but they think mostly in selfish gravitating thought that lacks consciousness. The development of energy in its sub-kingdom is quite different from the development of life in other kingdoms because of energy's involutionary (versus evolutionary) development. In its involutionary development, energy loses consciousness—as it grows in gravitating thought. Eventually involutionary energy graduates to becoming evolutionary. It does not lose its previously created levels of thought, it just increases both its thought *and*, dramatically, its consciousness. No other type of life grows quite like energy does, since energy is a manifestation of the third part of God's mind—transmuted and reduced in intelligence. All of the lifeforms in the energy sub-kingdom are composed more of energy than of densified form as matter.

50. esoteric—hidden from those who have relatively less enlightenment in their minds, as compared to those who have created enlightenment within themselves by using their lives to create more virtue.

51. event—an event in time and space is a series of activities that share one or more thoughts that caused the event. Also, the movement within these activities matches the direction, or consciousness, of the controlling thoughts. The event is a manifestation, in form (energy), of the connectivity of the choices within the thought or thoughts that created the event.

52. evil—a condition of consciousness, when consciousness is the focus of growth within life, in which the consciousness itself becomes overly focused on itself to the exclusion of other life. This focus effectively and, paradoxically, reverses the growth of consciousness. Generally evil develops, on a planetary scale, during a star's second incarnation, when consciousness is the focus of that solar system's development. Evil attempts, unsuccessfully, to grow its will and power while keeping its consciousness, or its understanding of oneness, at an unchanging level within itself. Evil generally crystallizes its will while *reducing* its choices and *increasing* its power. During this process evil loses consciousness, often slowly, but consistently. The thought process of evil is to negate (reverse) light, or God's thought, which evil often will insist does not exist. Because of its over-focus on power, evil is engrossed with form in its thought focus and almost always fails to understand spirit, even its own. Evil is self destructive—slowly, but is destructive of others—quickly. Force often needs to be used against evil on the etheric/dense physical plane; however, forcing evil to *feel* anything (even love) or to structurally create whole *thought* as wisdom (to give to create truth) nearly always backfires. Evil needs to be free from force astrally and mentally, but always must be confined in those dimensions. When confined in the astral and mental dimensions, evil destroys itself. Evil cannot be confined etheric/dense physically because it can use inertia to gain power over light, though only on that dimension.

53. evolution, spiritual (whole)—the method of using forces created by opposing energies, by a Being of high consciousness and creativity, to grow more of lower types of lifeforms in the three lowest kingdoms. The method employs power more than it does intelligent activity within these lifeforms because the lifeforms do not think at a high enough level on their own to be responsive to intelligent communication, or enlightened knowledge. Evolution requires that spiritual knowledge and intelligent activity be used to create higher lifeforms. Otherwise, *all* life will eventually die from a build-up of excessive force between the lifeforms, especially once human beings become present on a planet. To work effectively, evolution relies upon balanced, or structured, forces—which requires that the thought of the group souls that inform evolutionary life be located on the mental plane.

54. exoteric spiritual groups—groups whose members are in physical existence and whose purpose is to increase light, or God's thought. Something is becoming more spiritual when it increases the amount of its thought that is enlightened.

55. fun—a condition of temporary excitement within the astral energies of a body, masking or reducing the noticeable affects of anxiety and other emotions that a person experiences as being unpleasant. Fun is excitement that creates the above-described effect.

56. glamour—the illusion within the astral body. A glamour is caused by the self-focused use of astral thought, or creative imagination focused on a particular emotion. This thought creatively joins the emotion, as a desire, to the astral body. Every time a similar thought and/or emotion is created, the fixed astral desire, or glamour, vibrates and stimulates one or more of the entire group of five astral senses, but it usually does so individually. The sense or senses experience some loss in connectivity from the blockage of the glamours' vibration. The concomitant response of the personality then seeking to gain additional similar sensory information from the loss creates a desire for an emotional response in the one or more senses. This "desire" for emotional experience of similar sensory information is then re-created in the astral imagination, and further builds the glamour. The desire may also be acted upon by the person, in attempt to increase the emotional sensory experience and temporarily decrease the desire, but this will also increase the glamour because the emotion further builds it. Glamours reside within the astral body. They usually exist between centers, but may also become attached to centers as the centers become diseased by being fed upon by any possessing entity. Glamours can sympathetically grow together through either similar sensory information from the centers, similar emotions, or creative imagination. Structurally, glamours are fixed desires in the astral body. These fixed desires are caused by consistently focusing the astral imagination onto meeting some emotional need, as a desire. Since energy follows thought that is greater than its own, the emotion becomes created into a part of the astral body and is located near the center where the associated emotion is connected to the misuse of a sense. The astral thought becomes a crystallized picture of the desire, with the energy from the emotion locked inside it. This condition creates tension of damaged and darkened outside lunar deva energies. These energies attempt to somewhat form a complete picture, though usually unsuccessfully because they have been damaged. The elemental energy within the glamour can, at times, be stimulated into a new frenzy by additional astral thought being focused on the previously frenzied energy. This focus often causes the outside of the glamour to vibrate violently—sending these vibrations throughout the associated centers, and creating an emotional desire through that center and sense. Glamours can join together sympathetically, creating great desire and sometimes anxiety and emotional disease. To destroy a glamour, the specific emotional energies that it is composed of need to be changed into love.

57. God—the limited state of the three parts of the mind of our Universe's Creator that were sacrificially given to create our universe. Everything within our universe came from and is a part of God, who is the Creator of everything within our universe, including all life. God achieved this creation by sacrificing, through complete separation, three parts of its entire mind. God is purpose and will; unconditional love and consciousness; and intelligent activity and all manifested energies when activity is less than perfectly intelligent. These three parts compose the three aspects of God's mind. Everything within our universe came from and is a part of God. Every lifeform contains these three parts of God's mind, and every lifeform itself grows as it grows these three parts in both size and relational balance of the parts.

58. gravity—the collective thought on a plane, of all of the involutionary-in-thought energy that is not informed by some better-thinking spiritual thought and therefore thinks mostly in terms of joining together with any other similar-thinking energies without regard for the shape of or use of form. These energies grow in thought to become larger, or more of themselves, while they *lose* consciousness.

59. group consciousness (group givingness/love/understanding)—the giving of one's self's thought for the benefit of a group of other selves. When this giving is done with humility, the giver creates more from that which is not itself, and gives all of it to others. The giver then lives at the level of creation of the not-self as one within the group of selves.

60. hierarchial spiritual thought—within group or higher consciousness, the ranking of each member's thought dynamically by each member in real time, as each thinks in terms of who has the highest consciousness at that moment. Such thought requires some use of the Self in a Now because of the need to be focused in all three time zones at once—at least for a small amount of time. Without humility and group consciousness, hierarchial spiritual thought is impossible. Most people whose respective souls and personalities have not fused to a reasonable level relative to the person's ability to respond find hierarchial thought very threatening because they (in illusion) believe that they are losing control of their selves. However, the opposite actually occurs when spiritual hierarchial thought is created. The conclusion of spiritual hierarchial thought is always unanimity of thought, with no compromises. The reason is that all involved understand the accuracy of thought at the level of thought offered by the most conscious member at that time.

61. humility—the thought that one is incorrect when someone or something outside oneself challenges the accuracy or understanding of one's own thought, information from senses, or actions. Humility is also the further seeking of assistance to improve one's accuracy while still holding the thought that one has made an error. Without humility, group consciousness becomes impossible to attain because then being right would supercede loving others, and giving by the un-humble one becomes predicated upon others following, at times, the thought of the one who is lacking humility.

62. immorality—people's behaviors that reduce the development of a specific civilization by increasing darkness and reducing virtue in other members of that civilization.

63. inertia—a ratio of the following two ways that energy grows: (a) the degree to which the collective thought of involutionary energy mostly joins together (unintelligently) to grow to become *larger*, or "more," creating gravity, and (b) the amount that energy that thinks more evolutionarily and seeks to grow by becoming more *active* but usually smaller in total size or mass. This ratio changes as the thought of informing spirit affects energy, often causing the energy to become more active and to reduce the gravitational effects. As inertia increases it causes energy to become less affected by additional activity and more by gravity and/or by energy's present movement. The cause of this effect is that its ratio is dynamically changing towards becoming more involutionary, and as this condition occurs its state of activity becomes less able to be changed—while gravity is still reducing its overall activity. When not active and in a dimension that has lots of inertia, such as the dense physical part of the seventh plane, inertia has a very involutionary and gravitating effect on matter. This effect is that matter resists movement. Inertia causes the form to further densify and to interfere with other form that might move through the same location. Conversely, once the matter is put into motion, changing that activity creates high vector forces because the energy within the form is still increasing its level of unintelligent thought. As long as the ratio is increasing towards involution, inertia is increasing forces between energies. The reverse also is true: as energy becomes more evolutionary and intelligent in thought, the forces between energies decrease—and so does the inertia. Because inertia is a ratio, it can be measured only by making changes to energy (by adding or reducing energy or thought) that then reflect the relative level of inertia, *which is being dynamically affected by the changes.* It is very difficult to correctly measure this effect on the dense physical plane, but on the etheric plane and particularly on the astral and higher dimensions, the dynamics of inertia create some unusual and even startling changes in physics as we know it in the dense physical dimension.

64. initiation—a process used to advance lifeforms who are more focused in spiritual thought and who use intelligent activity and communication as a means of development much more than they use forces. The process creates much greater stresses on a lifeform because it accelerates karma through the partial fusing with higher levels of life who help the initiate. Initiation is used on only a few planets because its accelerated speed of increasing consciousness also increases the likelihood of more evil being produced. Much of the increased evil is a result of knowledge being substituted for consciousness as a means of giving, by those people who are ignorant but seek to somewhat copy a part of the process in order to increase their self-importance. There are four levels of human initiation at the present time on earth that lead to the transfiguration of a human soul into a liberated soul (a Soul) of a Master, who is a member of the fifth kingdom. Each initiation has four stages. The first is the probationary stage, wherein the disciple attempts to correctly self-discipline one of the four human bodies. In each higher initiation an additional, higher, body is progressively disciplined. Success in this discipline then leads to the accepting stage—of accepting the soul's use of the increased control and uses of the improved senses that were improved through the discipline begun by the self and soul during the probationary stage. The discipline is progressive for each body, and increases with each level of initiation. During this second stage, the spiritual disciple needs to accept her or his soul, not be caught in the Dweller excessively, and accept the souls of those in his or her group and especially of the teacher (or *Teacher*, if one is present). The third stage of initiation is the pledged stage, wherein the spiritual disciple decides to give back to the mission of his or her group all that has been given to her or his soul. Giving in this way develops spiritual hierarchial thought and allows the disciple to become a fully functional member of the group within the plan of the fifth kingdom. The fourth, and final, stage of initiation is the accepted stage, which is reached when the pledged disciple chooses to *create* more of the parts of the group, and then carries through with this creation as is needed in the group's mission and "the Plan," or the plan for the growth of life on the planet—and eventually throughout the universe. Many times, these creations *add* to the group's mission, expanding its role within the Plan. A disciple in this stage is accepted by the next kingdom—the spiritual—for its help towards that person completing his or her initiation. The help is needed because the disciple cannot finish opening the inner sacrifice petals within the time that it will take to complete the creation of virtue that he or she has started as a part of the Plan. There are five initiations beyond the human kingdom that lead to becoming the experience of being God and to the transcendence beyond our Cosmic Physical Universe.

65. inner sacrifice petals—the energy parts of the human soul, with each of these parts composed of solar devas that were the best-thinking energies within the group souls that were the most advanced of their ray type. The first inner sacrifice petal to open during the process of initiation is usually the petal that contains solar devas along the third through seventh rays of focus. The second of these petals to open is usually the one that comprises solar devas along the second ray of focus. The last inner sacrifice petal to open is usually the one that is constructed of solar devas along the first ray of focus. When all three have fully opened, they spin in a direction that depends upon the (now fixed) gender of the initiate. The solar devas within the petals radiate light in accord with their ray focus, which becomes part of the "rainbow bridge," or antahkarana.

66. instinct—preconceptual thought, when given from a group soul through its self to the fallen spirit within its individual lifeforms. Instinct functions as averages in complex patterning of behavior for various important life circumstances, under the following conditions: when the lifeform's informing fallen spirit does not have adequate thought to inform the lifeform about each circumstance, and the group soul's self does not communicate well enough in real, or whole, time to give a completed concept.

67. intelligence—the ability for one energy to reduce the space between itself and another energy, and/or improving both energies' ability to move, or be active. Activity that has less intelligence increases space between energies and/or reduces further activity. As energy develops sense, part of its intelligence is the ability to communicate, to other energy, its level of intelligence and its direction (its consciousness level) of movement. When this communication is received and used in some way, it becomes knowledge. Activity that is only intelligent converts all of the energy into the light of the dimension the energy is on; as the energy becomes light, the knowledge becomes communicated at the speed and direction of a Ray Lord's thought. This communication unifies the activity within the Ray Lord's body with the Ray Lord's thought. It also, for that plane and to the level of the corresponding Ray Lord's mind, unifies the three parts of God's mind.

68. intuition—a method of thought in which *all* of the concepts necessary to completely balance the energy, or structure, of the thought, with the spirit creating the thought, are present in a single time and space. Controlled intuition exists when the thinker, or spirit, is fully conscious of all of the thought necessary to create perfect balance between its thought and the energy that creates the structure of the thought. Full consciousness of the needed balance in thought creates perfect balance between the two, and beauty. Uncontrolled intuition occurs as a method of thought when the thinker, or spirit, is *not* fully conscious of its thought that is creating the structure of energy as multiple concepts. Controlled intuition requires the holding together of as many concepts as are needed to completely and fully consciously create beauty in conceptual form. Doing so requires twice the thought of spirit than the amount of thought contained within the structure *and* it requires intuitional consciousness. Uncontrolled intuition can occur, though usually infrequently, on the mental plane, but seldom is it useful there because on the mental plane the spiritual thinker is not directing all of the energy within the thought in service to others.

69. joy—the unified thought of love/wisdom as it simultaneously affects the mental and astral bodies of a person who has created enough virtue to affect another who has created more virtue, or subsequently will do so. Joy can also be a response to others creating virtue that causes the same effect in still others, when a person can identify enough oneness through group consciousness or even higher consciousness—such as in a Self, between himself or herself and those creating the initial virtue.

70. kama-manasic connection—causes people to first think emotionally, before thinking mentally. Consequently, while caught kama-manasically people frequently rationalize their mental thought relative to how they feel based upon what they imagine, often in fantasy. "Kama" in more modern times refers to the Hindu God of love—a reference that is an aberration of the word's original meaning of selfishness and emotion. The connections through emotion occur between the astral seventh and sixth sub-planes and the mental seventh and sixth sub-planes, causing mental thought on these sub-planes to be much more selfish and dark than on the sub-planes above them. The kama-manasic connection begins at birth for most people, because it has become a semi-permanent part of the human race.

71. karma—the effect of energy manifesting from intelligent activity and simultaneously separating time from space. As time separates from the mental plane and lower, causes then separate from effects for each event in time. This separation causes the energy within the event to no longer be connected to one or more of the parts of time and space. Consequently, as more energy becomes manifested from unintelligent activity, or selfishness, more of energy does not occur at the same time. The delay in the energy's effects produces karma. Karma for past selfishness, or unintelligent activities, accelerates as causes are brought closer together with effects, or as time joins with space through the creation of more activity that is intelligent. This effect can be confusing to some people because they may have *more* forces against themselves in a given period of time as they discipline themselves to be less selfish and more intelligent in their activities, converting space back into light as they do so. Karma affects individuals as well as groups, with group karma interpenetrating individual karma. Good karma is the conversion of *un*intelligent activity into intelligence, *prior* to the effects joining with the causes and producing forces against the energies in a person's present life. Karma functions through forces being imposed by the delayed effects. It begins by the forces being replicated from one lifetime and the next, using the internal structures of the permanent atoms as they reconstruct each body of a newly created human being. Karma can increase from its original effects to several times to ten times, or much more in the case of very evil deeds. The increase is the result of the original effects causing new ones to be produced, ad infinitum.

72. kingdom—in the four lowest kingdoms, the isolation of energy within a very large grouping of various pre-life forms and lifeforms, based upon their common ability to be informed by a certain level of thought from informing spirit. Each kingdom keeps the energies within it somewhat separate from those outside it during its forceful, or evolutionary, stages of development; it does so by being less responsive to thought from spirit that does not inform it. Eventually humans break through the protection afforded the lower kingdoms, and incorporate the energies of these kingdoms into their own kingdom, through civilization. On a much larger scale, a planet and Planetary Logos are doing something similar with humans until the humans have created sacredness of a planet by becoming more spiritual in development and creation rather than being evolutionary. The higher kingdoms (above the fourth) are divided by consciousness and the members' creation rather than by energy.

73. Kingdom of Souls (spiritual kingdom)—the fifth kingdom. It functions in a hierarchy of spiritual thought, and all of its lifeforms are affected by intuitive thought, rather than mental or lower thought. Its sub-kingdom, of energy, has lifeforms that individually may think much lower than the intuitive level in thought; however, these members are affected by energy Beings who do think intuitively. The vast majority of current members of the fifth kingdom of earth are energy Beings (there are billions of Solar Angels, for example). There are only slightly over one hundred (!) ascended (previously) human souls (as super-humans, or Masters) in this kingdom on earth at present, not counting fourth level initiates, who are junior members of this kingdom while still part of the human kingdom. By the end of the fourth round there may be as many as a million super-human members. By the end of the fifth round there might be twenty billion Masters, with quite a few having become junior members of the sixth, or planetary, kingdom.

74. knowledge—information that is synthesized in order to help to improve the activity of energy. Knowledge that is either unwhole or is unwisely given, or both, will encourage increased activity, but not intelligence. The increase will lead to darkness as a result of the separation of energy, with wasted (increased) time separated from space, and often more space between energies. Unwhole and/or unwisely given knowledge sometimes also leads to evil. Since before the, unfortunately necessary, destruction of the Atlantean civilization, the kama-manasic connection has become a part of most human beings' nature—from birth. This condition is mostly a result of knowledge used (and given) unintelligently. Since the time of Atlantis, and especially today because of the greater development of the human higher mental body, a larger number of advanced people have higher responsibilities to use and give knowledge intelligently. Spiritual disciples today have the greatest responsibility to do so. If they fail to, they become linked to the (often their own!) karma of the past, with an increase of as much as ten times the negative karmic energies coming back to them as that which they cause for all others whom they unintelligently give knowledge to. "Knowledge is Power" has some truth to it, but knowledge with intelligence is a part of God's mind, while power alone corrupts and leads to evil.

75. Kumara—the title of an advanced member of the sixth (the planetary) kingdom, who governs the ray effects, within periods of time, on energy of a dimension, as well as the conversions of energy back to intelligent activity of a planet. There are five dimensions of energy: spiritual, intuitional, mental, astral, and etheric/dense physical. Normally there would be five Kumaras with each having a student of intelligent activity for Its dimension of focus. Each student is referred to as a Buddha of Activity, and is usually an eighth level initiate. Kumaras attempt to shift evolution (forces) into spiritual development (light) by altering the forms of life within their respective dimensions. The highest Kumara on earth is named Sanat, and he governs the spiritual dimension. There is also one Kumara each for the intuitional, mental, and etheric/dense physical planes. The Kumara of the astral plane abdicated her role for earth. The Kumara of the etheric/dense physical plane is Satan (who reversed Sanat's name), and he chose to go against parts of Sanat's and the remaining other Kumaras' plan for earth. He did so as a test to determine whether earth would become evil and fail before attaining the status of sacredness. Satan uses evil to assist him in his tests of humanity. The other remaining Kumaras disagree with Satan: they disagree with his testing of humanity in general, and they disagree with Satan's position and actions of accelerating karma on earth and, often, the bringing of more evil into earth, sooner than would otherwise occur. Satan has temporarily left the spiritual hierarchy of thought that Sanat and the other spiritual members think within. Note that earth has just three spiritually functioning Kumaras and their collective three students who are Buddhas of Activity.

76. kundalini—elemental spiritual plane energy that is attracted by the enlightened collective thought of previously fallen etheric/dense physical spirit. The spiritual plane elemental energy comes from the three lowest spiritual sub-planes—the seventh, sixth, and fifth. These spiritual elemental energies become so enlightened by the Spirit of Earth (the collective previously fallen and now enlightened etheric spirit) that they change from involutionary to evolutionary energies (into lunar devas) when they are used in service by various beings, including human initiates. The three kundalini elemental energies are referred to as pingala, ida, and sushumna. They are raised into becoming lunar deva energies on the etheric/dense physical, astral, and lower mental planes, respectively, as they are used in service by someone who is etheric/dense physically alive. These energies also connect earth to the sun and the sun's other planets, through enlightened service that affects these other celestial bodies.

77. Lemuria—an island continent that rose from the sea floor of the South Pacific Ocean along its ridge and reached the Ocean's surface about twenty-five million years ago. This island continued to grow in size and height until about twenty million years ago, when the Isthmus of Panama, which also was rising, finally blocked the Atlantic Ocean and Caribbean Sea from the Pacific Ocean. As a result, the Lemurian climate changed from mostly sub-tropical to temperate. The ray focus of the Lemurian continent was originally the sixth ray, substituting for the submerged-in-ice Antarctic continent; however, the people populating the land had a seventh ray focus in their thought, which eventually modified the landmass effect to more of a seventh ray focus. Lemuria began to submerge about ten million years ago, and, more rapidly, about eight million. Some of this continent fell below the sea floor's bottom (crust), possibly into earth's mantle. What remains of Lemuria are the South Sea Islands. The Lemurian people were the third major human race, but the first major race to become dense physical in form (the first two sub-races were only etheric in their densest of form). The last part of Lemuria that had significant Lemurian civilization on it was inundated over two and a half million years ago, after these civilizations were first destroyed by invading armies from Atlantis. Lemuria's submergence caused the severity of the Ice Age to significantly increase as more energy became transferred into the deeper levels of the Pacific Ocean.

78. life—the Creator's means of growth decided upon by God. Life contains God's three parts of mind within a balance as established by a cosmic Ray Lord. On the five lower dimensions of our universe, all life contains spirit and energy. On the two highest planes of our universe, all life contains light and, in addition, the following: On the monadic plane life "contains" the sacrifice of intelligent activity, creating spirit and energy and life on the lower dimensions. On the logoic plane, life additionally contains activity that is only intelligent—perfectly bringing together the three parts of God's mind. The first two parts create light, and the third part is intelligent activity. (see also pre-life)

79. light—the first two parts of God's mind when joined together in equal amounts and at an angle that would allow the third part of God's mind to also join to these two. There are seven angles, or ratios of the amounts and direction, of these two parts. Each cosmic Ray Lord creates a different one of these ratios in order to create its sub-light of God's light in its (the Ray Lord's) dimension. When the cosmic Ray Lords use the three parts of God's mind to create their respective dimensions, each lower Ray Lord creates a smaller amount of light at a more severe angle and lower vibration to the light of God's fully joined mind. Light is God's thought, or the cosmic Ray Lord's thought, established as a sub-light of God's thought on each dimension. Light encourages thought within that which has less than enlightened thought, by reducing space in existing thought. Light that becomes part of either intelligent activity or of manifested energy becomes virtue. When the conditions that define light are not met, light separates into space—and is dark.

80. love, astral and conditional—astral love joins forms together, creating more oneness in the movements of any two forms or of one form and a group of forms that has already joined. It does this by matching the speed and direction of the one form to the other form(s), unifying their movements in time and space. Movement is the condition of love on the astral plane, and only those forms that share the same movement (speed and direction) can have love between them.

81. love, intuitional and conditional—the creation of oneness among all forms through their giving of knowledge together. This condition is achieved by spirit thinking perfectly for both itself and for all of the energy within its form—for every lifeform that exists within its sub-plane of the intuitional dimension. For this type of love, spirit needs to contain twice the thought of the energy within the form, with each form containing more thought within its energy than the thought of all of the gravitating energies on the entire intuitional plane. Each lifeform is able to achieve this result on each of the seven corresponding sub-planes along one of the seven rays. Intuitional love is conditional upon lifeforms completely giving the level of all-knowledge that they have on each intuitional sub-plane. Doing so is possible through developing the controlled sense of intuition through perfectly balancing spirit to energy in the sense.

82. love, mental and conditional—mental love is conditional upon balancing the forces among multiple levels of forms at the same time, by using whole time to calculate the past, present, and future forces on the forms before these forces are balanced. Love that is used with whole time comes from whole mental thought, or wisdom, and together this love and wisdom become the mental love of love/wisdom. Mental love is conditional upon structure, or the balancing of forces simultaneously among multiple forms.

83. love, monadic and unconditional—monadic love is unconditional because Monads all give as one, creating a complete oneness in that which they give to. Unconditional love means that the giver attaches no conditions that would arise from needing anything back from the forms that it gives to. The Monad achieves this non-condition by itself sacrificing all form, using no manifested energies with itself and therefore being able to completely give to form. The Monad can also give unconditionally to spirit because It has created all the spirit that It is conscious of. Anything that achieves some level of consciousness that is shared with its Monad can sometimes use unconditional love; however, the full use of unconditional love, at all times, requires that one become, or already be, a Monad.

84. love, spiritual (atmic) and conditional—atmic plane love is conditional upon the amount of power that is used to transmute energy within all lifeforms on a planet or, on the lower spiritual sub-planes, all life on a specific lower dimension of a planet as compared to the amount of intelligent activity created *at the same time* within the lifeforms. Some of the lifeforms, but all at the same time, respond more to the power side of the giving, or love, and their lives are evolutionary—their lives are controlled more by forces. Other, more spiritually thinking lifeforms, and all at the same time, respond more to intelligent activity being given to them, and love is then conditional upon the totality of the amount of intelligent activity created from the much higher Beings on the spiritual plane. Thus spiritual love is conditional upon all-power and all-knowledge, which affect all life on a dimension or a planet at the same time.

85. Maitreya—one of the names of the Master who is presently the World Teacher (or Bodhisattva) and the Head of the Spiritual Hierarchy of the fifth kingdom. Master Maitreya's ray focus is the second, and the office he holds is sometimes referred to as the Christ. Master Maitreya is not Jesus of Nazareth, but two thousand years ago was Jesus' teacher while Jesus was an arhat (at that time, a third level initiate). Master Maitreya is a seventh level initiate and a junior member of the sixth kingdom, besides being the head of the fifth. Sometime in earth's relatively near future (within the next two thousand years), and possibly as early as within the next several centuries, Master Maitreya will become an eighth level initiate and his assistant, Master Koot Hoomi, will replace him as the World Teacher and the Christ.

86 Manu, of a round—the title of the Master who is in charge of, for a round, the movement of the kingdoms and the development of the human major races and their sub-races. On earth the Manu for the current (the fourth) round is Master Morya, who is a member of the fifth kingdom and is focused along the first ray. He is a sixth level initiate, or a Chohan.

87. maya—the illusion in the etheric/dense physical body. Maya is composed of retained energies that are out of phase and of wrong vibration to that of the light (thought) of the etheric/dense physical Ray Lord. The word maya is also sometimes used to refer to the etheric body in general.

88. mind—a mind is a Director of a field that has as its (the Director's) possibility to become a creator of subsequent fields. A mind has the ability to create beyond the one creating because it introduces the possibility to create new, more limited fields of probability. Minds are created from a majority of a field in the way that Directors are, creating more oneness than not in the field of probabilities. A mind must also have the potential to create a new field, or it does not contain the ability to have perspective (reflection) of itself. All creators have minds and, except in the rarest of possibilities, so do most Directors. Only those Directors that have no possibility of becoming creators would be mindless. Having an understanding of minds and their near inevitability to be self-created leads a person away from mechanical/energy-only models of our universe.

89. Monad—a Being who always lives at one in thought with all other Beings who function at a similar level of thought, where each Being is omnipresent in thought with the others. Monads are reflections of the second Ray Lord's focused thought of sacrificing all intelligent activity on the monadic plane so that this activity can manifest as energy on the lower planes, in order to create life. Monads on the monadic plane are created from the pure light of the first two parts of God's mind as these two parts exist within the cosmic Ray Lord of the monadic plane. However, immediately upon their creation, the Monads all grow in consciousness, or the second part of God's mind, because they are all giving their thought together to create life in dimensions lower than the monadic. The thought that is given by the Monads on these lower planes becomes spirit. The sacrificed intelligent activity on the monadic plane as it is focused on by spirit becomes elemental energy on the plane whereupon the spirit exists. When spirit informs a form, or energy, it can create either pre-life or a lifeform, depending upon the spirit's ability to think and the energy's ability to respond to the thought in creating senses. Then, from the experiences of their corresponding spirit and energy, Monads can sense lifeforms on the planes lower than the Monadic. Each human Monad informs the spirit and energy of only one human soul. Monads at each level of monadic sub-plane consciousness create corresponding levels of pre-life and life through first creating the informing souls of these lifeforms.

90. Monad, ascended—an ascended Monad is a super-human advanced Master who has become one of the Leaders and Teachers and can unify all the thought of all the Monads and lower life, from the first monadic sub-plane, down. These advanced Masters on earth are, at present, completing the seventh level of initiation. When they take the eighth initiation they ascend to the seventh logoic sub-plane and proceed to develop the sense of omnipresence with, eventually, everything in our universe. In this way, they experience our universe "firsthand," from its past, its present, and its (extrapolated) future. The ascended Monad has completely fused the Master and Solar Angel in the completion of a "Cosmic Marriage." The ability to think and sense as one with all others of that same ability becomes realized. When an ascended Monad takes the ninth initiation (on the third logoic sub-plane) this super-Master is, with its own Beingness, finishing the complete rejoining of God's mind, and has significantly grown it in the process. This super-Monad gives up its permanent atoms in its intuitional, spiritual, and monadic bodies, and retains only a logoic permanent atom, of light and intelligent activity, that eventually becomes the size of the entire universe and an infinitely small point in its very center—at the same time. The monadic permanent atom is only a pure spark of light within the monadic Ray Lord's atomic level. The eighth level initiates had already given up their three lowest permanent atoms, usually all three of them at once. As these Masters give up their lower permanent atoms they move correspondingly higher on each logoic sub-plane in developing the sense of omnipresence. Ninth level initiates are referred to as the "Silent Watchers" since they do not take anything except from the first cosmic Ray Lord and from God as they experience everything through using God's mind rather than attracting and/or constructing intelligent activities and light into a permanent atom. The Silent Watcher's body is becoming the entire universe as he or she silently—not affecting anything other than God—watches (and experiences) everything. Then that level of initiation is completed and the ascended super-Monad leaves our universe for a higher-level one. Which universe the Monad leaves for is determined by the path of monadic ascension that he or she decided upon during the sixth initiation (at earth's current standards of initiation).

91. mystery schools, esoteric—schools begun by the Spiritual Hierarchy and some of the Masters' students, in order to hide, or mystify, most of the knowledge within Ageless Wisdom. This hiding was necessary because selfish and ignorant spiritual disciples disseminated knowledge from Ageless Wisdom by teaching it to the general public. Although these spiritual disciples had been told by their (T)teachers that the time was not right to give out this information, they indiscriminately disseminated it anyway, because doing so made them look and feel important while they, in illusion, believed that having more knowledge would help people to become spiritual. These spiritual disciples' lack of wisdom and disobedient egotism led to the destruction of the Atlantean civilization and to a significant growth in evil. The first esoteric mystery schools were developed about 11,000 B.C. After the Atlantean inundation of about 9000 B.C., esoteric mystery schools were established in the most populated (by humans) parts of earth, in accord with the ray focus of the landmasses and the populations on them. Tests were imposed for entering into the esoteric mystery schools, and classes, or levels, of teaching were given based upon proven levels of consciousness. It took nearly two thousand years (from about 11,000 B.C. to about 9000 B.C.) for Ageless Wisdom to be mystified by the Groups of World Servers who were the first teachers and students in the earliest schools (while Atlantis was still in existence). In A.D. 1975, the Spiritual Hierarchy decided to de-mystify much of Ageless Wisdom in accord with the plan for spiritual development of earth for the upcoming several hundred years. Those who are participating in this plan need to have *direct* contact with an inner Ashram and its Teacher, who is a Master, in order to understand *what* to de-mystify, and *when*. The knowledge is to be created by humans who are physically alive, and the groups are headed by advanced initiates when possible. The mental minds of humans have reached a developmental point at which they can now, higher mentally, adequately understand the very large and whole concepts of Ageless Wisdom to use these concepts to become more virtuous in their creations. Simultaneously, humans' astral bodies have become less clear and more agitated as a result of living a speeded-up, more etheric life—rendering many spiritual disciples less able to gain mystical understandings from clear astral thought. The *New* Group of World Servers, beginning with only those who are *functioning* within spiritual groups (usually of World Service), are to de-mystify Ageless Wisdom.

92. mystification—the process of changing structured (mental) thought into creative imagination so that only people who have mostly broken the kama-manasic connection and who have clear imagination can understand the information. Once the creative imagination re-creates the mystery, *then* the person can re-create *some* of the structure in the original concepts.

93. Now, a—the three parts of time joined together in at least one of three possible ways, either for one being or for all beings who share the same level of consciousness. When a Now is limited to only the past (knowledge) part of whole time completely joined to all space for only one being at a time and concerning only one event at a time, the Now is the smallest completed Now possible—and exists on the atomic level of the mental plane. A Now on the intuitional plane joins the past (knowledge) part of time for all events, for all beings who share the same level of consciousness within the same Now. The intuitional Now is considered the first completed Now spiritually because the lowest sense of God, of omniscience (all-knowledge), is being created within the intuitional Now. The spiritual plane Now connects all events at the level of consciousness of all beings in contact with this Now, in the past and present parts of time—joining all-knowledge as a used sense with the ability to correctly give the knowledge as all-love. However, as a sense in development, which requires the use of enlightening energies, there are insufficient amounts of energies to enlighten; instead of the sense of all-love being developed in the Now while the previously developed sense of all-knowledge is *used*, only the sense of all-power, or omnipotence, is created. A Now on the monadic plane develops all three senses of God's mind in light (God's thought) rather than in energy. On this plane all Beings in a Now sacrifice all–intelligent-activity while they *use* the full sense of God, which is all-love, and develop the sense of omnipresence (while thinking in omniscience). A logoic Now is one in which a Monad senses, for all-time, everything within our universe at its level of consciousness, or at its ability to do so. This unifies God's sense and mind, and completes God's growth at that level.

94. pain—a response of the evolutionary and deva energy side, or form side, of a lifeform to a loss of energy that is needed in order to maintain the form. Pain is conveyed as a third ray message that is usually sent by the affected deva energies through the nervous system (or its equivalent in less dense forms) to the spirit that is informing the body.

95. paranoia—a nearly equal mixture of anger and fear concerning the same or similar thought, often creating both an approach and an avoidance response. Paranoia leads to inappropriate inaction in situations that require action, and inappropriate fear or anger in situations that do not require a response. Paranoia is often thought of as exaggerated fears, but is actually a much more complicated series of incorrect, mistaken responses caused by prior levels of selfishness that one (usually a human) has chosen to have.

96. permanent atom—(on the three lower planes) a combination of structured energies that balance their forces so that they last for long periods of time (many lifetimes), along with enlightened energies that do not require balance in their forces because they are all moving together in the same direction as and are vibrating at the same frequency as the Ray Lord of the plane they are on. Those energies are used as a blueprint to re-create a body and its centers in a newly incarnated lifeform. The energy within the permanent atom functions as karma that connects one lifeform to the action of one or more previous lifeforms. In humans, the permanent atoms connect one incarnation of a human being with the prior actions of earlier incarnations of human beings of that person's soul.

97. person—a person is the personality, its self, and all of its bodies that it controls—all created by a single, individual soul.

98. pitris, lunar and solar—deva energies, when they are informed by spirit and integrated into a form. They are partially angelic, or partially giving/conscious, energies. (see also "deva energy.")

99. Planetary Logos—a Being who has transcended beyond a Cosmic Physical Universe—such as ours—and who usually lives within the, or a, Cosmic Astral Universe. A Planetary Logos helps to create life within the, or a, Cosmic Physical Universe by informing an entire planet, with a plan and a completed means of life creation on that planet. A Planetary Logos is a member of the Planetary Kingdom and functions, currently, under a Solar Logos. This Solar Logos informs the entire solar system that the Planetary Logos's planet is a part of.

100. planning—a part of the second part of God's mind; accurate planning requires consciousness because planning joins the three parts of time together between two or more events. Planning increases the likelihood that the energy in one event will be more intelligent in its activity in relationship to the energy within another event that is included in the plan. Planning can raise consciousness when the plan uses and creates oneness between events, from the past to the future of time.

101. pleasure—the emotional sensation, or the feeling, of a desire in the astral body being (temporarily) met.

102. possession—the result of a person either consciously (using her or his self) or sub-consciously (using his or her personality) deciding to not control a body, by either not synthesizing information from the body or not giving thought to its informing fallen spirit to help keep the body's senses functioning and giving. In such cases, because energy (the bodies) follows thought that is greater than the energy within a body has, another being—often a darker human, but sometimes an advanced but darkened animal—can gain control over the body and its senses. The possessing beings, or entities, are most often focused in their lives on a subtle plane because it is easier for these beings to gain access to the more subtle and easier-to-control less dense elemental energies within the body and its centers. Most possessions are partial, with the person who is possessed still being somewhat aware of her or his self through that body. Full possession occurs when the personality and self no longer have a sense of self within a body—which makes it very difficult for them to regain control.

103. power—the ability (on the part of thought) to transmute energy from one state of density into another. Power is a part of the third Ray Lord's thought, or its light, and on the spiritual plane is created from Beings on that plane using all-power, or omnipotence, to create virtue. Power is the remainder of the potential within energy to become fully intelligent in activity, and is inversely proportionate to the amount of intelligent activity versus energy that has been manifested from it. Power also is measured by the amount that time that is rejoined with the space as the energy is transmuted. Power is what is left within the intelligent activity, and is released at greater rates the more that time rejoins space—or as "speed" is increased in energy's transmutation. Thus energy *has* power, and spirit can exercise power by getting energy to follow its thought. The less that time is separated from space, the faster the energy becomes intelligent activity, and the greater the overall level of power.

104. prana—the result of the etheric, astral, and mental light on atmospheric energies of the corresponding planes. The light becomes a part of the atmosphere, making the atmosphere conducive to growing life on the planet at a certain point in its development. Etheric prana is needed to balance the dense physical prana that is brought into the physical body as food. The dense food usually loses most of its etheric prana because the etheric and the dense physical pranas are separated when the food dies. To compensate, the spleen center brings into the body, from the etheric atmosphere, etheric pranas to be distributed into each ray type center. The astral and mental bodies use only astral and mental pranas, respectively, from the atmospheres of their planes. These very subtle pranas are all the energy that these very subtle bodies need, because these bodies produce much smaller quantities of heat.

105. pre-life—contains too much separation of the first two parts of God's mind to adequately create light, and contains a great deal more of manifested energy from the third part of God's mind than it does of intelligent activity. Under both of these conditions, a *majority* of space and energy exists within the form, which prevents the form from responding to a self and from limiting the field of life to become a member within that field. The thought within pre-life forms is too weak to create these needed conditions of life and to result in sentiency. When the above-described two conditions *are* met, enough thought is present to limit the field of life and create within a majority of thought and, within the (now) life's own field, the ability to move within the time and space between and within at least two different dimensions. This movement further unifies the life's mind through its own thought growing God and itself, and creating sentiency within the form. Forms that do not contain at least one full center with an informing spirit sphere have not yet become pre-life, because they cannot sense at the lowest level possible.

106. psychic sense, higher—the unification of all the senses that it is possible for a soul to control within a lifeform; in a human being, the unification of the five senses of form and the two of spirit in one of the three lowest bodies. Each human body can, therefore, have one higher psychic sense. Higher psychic senses can be used only by a fused personality and soul when creating spiritual service, to serve others. Use of a higher psychic sense joins together space and time, creating light. This use also, simultaneously, further unifies the sense, as well. The individual higher psychic sense in each body can be further unified with the senses in other bodies, building even greater senses in greater levels of light.

107. psychic sense, lower—one or more of the individual senses within a body that a soul could possibly have controlled use of if unified; in a human being, one or more of five senses of form used but not unified into a total of five, and usually missing the use of the two spiritual senses in the same body at the same time. For most people who are physically alive, lower psychic senses are overridden by their etheric/dense physical senses. The use of separated etheric/dense physical sense as a sense between the etheric and dense physical planes and brains does not usually result in the typical levels of diminished sense that the more subtle split (lower psychic) senses produce in the more subtle bodies. The reason is that using the individual etheric/dense physical senses still joins together the time and space of the etheric/dense physical dimension, and does so within high levels of inertia. Use of the (subtle) lower psychic senses tends to split time from space and to split those senses further, reducing their levels of sense and increasing misinformation and illusion. Using the physical senses with the etheric ones (which is the way most people sense) creates very large levels of illusion but much slower loss of sense because the partial joining of the etheric/dense physical plane somewhat slows the split senses' separation of time that results from selfishness—all a result of the interaction between inertia and thought.

108. quality, of thought—the degree to which consciousness, or the second part of thought, affects the first part of thought, which are its choices, will, sacrifices, purpose, and creation or destruction (consciousness is a measure of the oneness, or connectedness of the thoughts' choices). Thus quality in a spiritual context is a measure of consciousness as an effect. Spirit's quality affecting elemental energy causes that energy to mostly replicate the spirit's consciousness within itself but, in the process, some diminishment occurs. Then the quality of the elemental energy is often less than that which the spirit had when it first created and informed the energy. Quality is a measure of the related amounts of connectedness of different series of choices.

109. quantum constant—a measure of the degree to which energy is indefinite within time or space. Time is separated from space because of thought that creates action or activity that is less than enlightened. The quantum constant is actually a measure of the effect that thought has on energy. The more indefinite energy is, the larger its quantum constant. Greater thought and less dense energy causes energy to be more controlled by thought and therefore less controlled by gravity (involutionary energy's own thought)—and thus more indefinite in its time or space.

110. radiance—the giving off of light by some energy entering a form and leaving it at the same time, at the speed of light. When heat is also present, then the radiance is radioactive to some degree, as well. Radiance occurs because some of the thought of the corresponding-plane Ray Lord has been accurately communicated to the informing fallen spirit, helping the energy in the form to respond at the speed of light. The informing source of this thought is a soul—group, or individual—that is raising itself, through a ray line of focus, from its existing kingdom into the next higher one. The energies within the form are also transmuted as a part of the radiance process.

111. rainbow bridge—rays of light, or radiance, emitted by the solar devas in the causal body of a spiritually advanced human who is creating so much virtue in her or his mental thought that the solar devas become fully enlightened through their use in service to others. This radiance connects: (a) the human soul and personality with its self in the mental unit, (b) the soul and the Self plus the part of the mental permanent atom that the Self surrounds, and (c) the Self and the part of the mental permanent atom that the Self surrounds with the mental-unit/personality and self. These three legs of a triangle of light bridge thought and memory from the soul, the Self, and the self within a lifetime, and eventually between incarnating lifetimes.

112. ray—a limited field that is focused exclusively on energy in order to assist energy that responds to the virtue-producing thought within the field, by thinking more like it. As energy thinks more using the associated ray, it grows in thought (and as a sense of other energy) much more rapidly because the ray's field is constantly giving more enlightened thought to the energy. Not all cosmic rays are focused on earth at the same time. During the fourth round only four rays at a time are focused on the energy, or the form, found on earth. These rays change, one at a time, at increasing rates throughout each round. Also, one additional ray is added in focus per round. (see also "cosmic ray.")

113. ray line—the method of ray focus in creating more virtue that something uses to advance into the next kingdom. As something creates virtue along its ray line, it becomes radiant by converting energy into light and intelligent activity—further joining together the three parts of God's mind as these parts are also being grown.

114. Ray Lord, cosmic—a Being who creates a dimension of time and space and direction of life growth within God's plan for our universe. Each cosmic Ray Lord creates a cosmic ray that causes energy that responds to the ray in thought to become more enlightened, or more virtuous. A spiritual cosmic ray has no connection with the ionized partial atomic particles that strike the earth. There are seven cosmic Ray Lords. Three of them each use one of the three aspects of God's mind to construct their respective dimensions and thought (light). The remaining four use the effects that these rays and thought have on energy, to construct their dimensions of time and space and durations of life.

115. responsibility, spiritual sense of—the ability to respond to others who are in need of the response, in ways that create more virtue, or light in the forms, in the others. One's level of spiritual responsibility is relative to how developed one's senses are and how much consciousness one has. When people function spiritually irresponsibly they diminish the sense or senses that they have used while creating the irresponsibility, and they lower their consciousness by the amount of their selfishness and irresponsibility. It is spiritually irresponsible for a person who has participated within a group of hierarchial thinking to not use that thought when needed. The more deliberate the spiritual irresponsibility and more time and energy it consumes, the greater the levels of negative karma that the person will eventually face.

116. retained energy—energy that is *forced* to reduce its movement and intelligence by the selfish informing thought of spirit, whose thought is greater than the thought of the energy that it is controlling. Retained energy creates space, reduces sense, and decreases light.

117. sacral center—the center located next to the five sacral bones at the base of the spine. The sacral center is supposed to create a body into becoming sacred by perfectly balancing the spirit sphere's thought in each major center to the thought of its energy sphere. This perfect balance creates beauty in the body, as well as sacredness between the body and the dimension of time and space that the body is a part of.

118. sacrifice, spiritual—the choice to give up, relinquish, or limit one or more choices that interfere with growth and greater levels of thought in the future. Spiritual sacrifice is a primary means of creation and growth and is part of the first part of God's mind, and also the first part of what creates thought.

119. scheme—ten schemes of planetary life are frequently created by a star through its three incarnations. Each scheme develops a Planetary Logos through seven chains of ray-focused life creation and dimensional life experiences.

120. self—a (lower) self (spelled with a lowercase "s") is a mind, composed of only spirit, for one or more lifeforms that exist on or below the lower mental plane. All selves exist on the mental plane. There are three senses that selves can develop as they give some of their understanding from their respective fields of life. The first sense is of who the self is in comparison to its not-self, including other selves, and to energy. The second is the sense that the self is similar to some other selves because in the self's thought about the future, it characterizes these other selves as responding similarly to the way that it does and/or will. This second sense of self develops good character. The third sense is that all selves are the same because the self can create more of other selves by lovingly creating part of its field that is its not-self into other selves' fields. As it does this the self gains the understanding that its not-self is still a part of itself, which it can now identify as being such by it becoming a part of other selves. This last sense of self develops group and soul consciousness. Each self is a part of either a group soul or a personality. A self can become part of, or fuse with, its (higher) Self (spelled with an uppercase "s") if it creates sufficient virtue to add light into the Self.

121. Self (higher, spelled with an uppercase "s")—is located on the atomic level of the higher mental plane; two additional Selves are also found on the atomic levels of the intuitional and spiritual planes, respectively. Each Self surrounds the enlightened part of the corresponding permanent atom. A Self is composed of only spirit that both understands and creates more of spirit and of God's thought in life from its thoughts. A Self is always giving at the level of the corresponding Ray Lord of its plane, and the Self and Ray Lord share this very high level of consciousness, hierarchially, together. There are two senses of Self. The lower one is the sense of understanding God; the second, or higher sense is of becoming (being) God, by creating more virtue, or more light in form. Selves are not as creative as they are loving: they can limit their respective fields of creation (of life) only fifty percent or more, while they can always give at one hundred percent what any one of them creates within its created field. Every Self is the spiritual *thinking* part of a Solar Angel. The Angel shares its Selves with either a soul or Soul, as needed in service. A mental plane Self supplies the soul with much greater levels of creative thought to help it to grow in creating virtue (rather than mostly giving it). The mental Self supplies the self, through the mental unit's vortex with thought that helps it to become more loving and focused on others virtuously. The mental Self attempts to eventually unify the soul and the self by gradually getting the personality to relinquish some of its control over the self so that it can fuse with its Self.

122. self discipline—as used in this book, these two words together and when not hyphenated mean one or more of the following conditions, depending upon the context: (a) the spiritual discipline of the self's senses; there are three. (b) the spiritual discipline of the personality's sense of its self, (c) the spiritual discipline of the Self's senses; there are two, (d) the spiritual discipline of the personality, either by the personality and/or the self, and (e) the spiritual discipline of both the personality and self together, by the soul. Spiritual discipline is the limitation of one or more senses for the purpose of improving information and the knowledge that is derived from the information, in order to increase the light within one's and others' forms, or to increase virtue.

123. selfishness—the focus of thought on the self, for the purpose of growing the self rather than something else that could be grown.

124. sense—the collective and unified very slight thought of energy reaching a level at which this energy can attract a very slight amount of some other energy that does not think any better than it does. A sense is developed through energy growing in its very slight thought. Without senses, life cannot exist because even on a cellular level cells need to sense energies in order to stay alive. In lifeforms, major senses are developed from the major centers. The more major centers and senses that a lifeform has, the more intelligent its activity can potentially be. A sense grows more rapidly as it is focused on by a type of thought that corresponds to the ray focus of that sense. Senses also grow more rapidly by having enlightening thought focused on them by informing spirit. They are diminished by retaining energy within them, which is caused by either gravity or the selfish thought of informing spirit. Because senses function by the principle of energy following the thought that is greater than its own, anything that lowers the ability of a sense to think lowers that sense's ability to become informed about other energies by attracting some small amount of them to itself. This includes not giving this energy in some way, once the energy does inform a sense. Not giving the energy causes it to become retained within the sense.

125. sentiency—the ability for the thought contained within a lifeform to move energy between at least two parts of space within the same parts of time, and between two parts of time within one or more parts of space. Sentiency creates life by allowing minerals to take in, transmute, and give off energy while growing some new types or states of energy. Sentiency leads to consciousness because the lifeform creates itself by giving energy that it has transmuted; life is therefore self-created, although much of life does not have an individual self. It is important to note that sentiency requires that the thought causing it be created *on the planes whereupon* the energy that is creating the lifeforms and is moving through them exists. Higher informing spirit alone, such as a soul or self, cannot create sentiency unless the "fallen" spirit on the plane that the body(-ies) of the form exist upon creates the thought. The reason for this effect is that the thought must come from within the duration of life of *each* body and sense within each corresponding Ray Lord's body, to be connected to that field of life in development (even though it is still a part of a higher Ray Lord's duration as well). Life and sentiency are a condition of joining together enough of the three parts of God's mind to reach a critical level of thought (*light*) of each corresponding Ray Lord, creating at least the minimal level of intelligent activity necessary to create life, as established by that Ray Lord.

126. service—spiritually, and as exclusively used within this book, the complete giving to another of all energy that is directed by one's thought. When all of the energy is given, the giver and receiver are both enlightened and no energy is retained.

127. sharing and cooperation—the virtue, or light created within form, of the etheric/dense physical plane. This virtue is an incomplete type of conditional love whose incompleteness is caused by the high levels of inertia and the reduced levels of spiritual thought on that plane. This virtue that is less than love consists of giving based upon both life forms that are involved giving some level of intelligent coordination with others who are doing the same. Cooperation and sharing achieves balance in force through reducing the amounts of energy that is necessary to be expended in order to achieve any particular movement. Unlike focused movement or structure, cooperation and sharing does not react to movement as the movement occurs (like astral thought does), nor to future possibilities of movements to create structured/formulated balance (like mental thought does). The economy of energy is based upon what has already occurred in the past use of amounts of energy, reducing the virtue to coordination, rather than to full giving.

128. Solar Angel—an energy Being of advanced consciousness who begins its triadal life by informing, one at a time, various mineral group souls, then plant group souls, and, eventually, group souls of the animal kingdom (in the Solar Angel's first of three stages of growth). A Solar Angel shares its lowest (mental plane) Self with the soul that it informs. A Solar Angel's spirit within its Self is located at the atomic level of each of the three planes its bodies exist on: the higher mental, the intuitional, and the spiritual. A Solar Angel's energies begin as first and second sub-ray energies on the planes where-upon it exists. These energies are fused by the thought of its Selves. Since its energies are spiritual (first and second sub-rayed) and fused, these energies are very advanced and can think as well as or better than its Self can on each plane. This thought causes these fused energies to sense *God*, or the Ray Lord's thought representing God, on each plane that the Solar Angel exists on. These energies within a first triadal stage Solar Angel can sense God better than any lifeform can below a fifth level initiate Master; in a second triadal stage Solar Angel, the energies can sense God better than any lifeform can below a sixth level Master. Second stage triadal Solar Angels inform human souls. A third stage triadal Solar Angel fuses with a sixth level Master to rejoin with their shared Monad, and together they become an ascended Monad. Some of the energies of a Solar Angel are given for a soul to use as permanent atoms—to create bodies for its informed lifeforms.

129. Soul, ascended—an ascended soul, or a Soul, spelled with an uppercase "S," is a Master of the Ageless Wisdom. In some spiritual texts, a Soul may also refer to a Solar Angel. A Soul has twice the thought within its spirit as within its energy, or its form. A Soul has created itself into a state of beauty through its virtuous thought. The ascended soul has fused with his or her last personality and self, and Self, so that he or she can directly think in all of the time and space in the three lower worlds within a Now. Ascended souls can think with all other Beings within a Now as they all serve through the capacity of thought and partial sense of all-knowledge (omniscience). Since Souls are completely fused with their respective mental Selves and partly with their respective intuitional Selves, they are partly fused with their respective Solar Angels because the Selves of the Angel are shared with the Master. As the Master and Solar Angel advance back to becoming a more advanced Monad (by fusing with their existing Monad), the fusion of these two continues, with each becoming more a part of the other.

130. soul, group—group souls are higher mental plane beings that have an approximate equal abil-ity to think within both their spirit and the energy that composes their form. The level of this ability in group souls is relatively limited because they think mostly along one ray focus and corresponding higher mental sub-sub-plane of thought. The more advanced group souls may think on two or three higher mental sub-sub-planes, and the very-most advanced can think on the upper four sub-sub-planes of the third higher mental sub-plane. The selves of the advanced group souls can think on the lowest three sub-sub-planes of the lowest (the third) higher mental sub-plane. Even the most advanced group souls tend to think mostly on just one higher mental sub-sub-plane, while their respective selves tend to think more on one of the three lowest of the higher mental sub-sub-planes. Because of this limited single ray focus of thought, group souls use mostly preconceived thought, since they separate so much time from space as they and their selves think from such separated positions on the higher mental sub-sub-planes. Group souls are very giving (loving) even though their overall ability to think is relatively limited.

131. soul, human, individual—an individual human soul can think with a focus along any one of the seven rays, which enables it to think from all sub-sub-planes of the higher mental plane when it is assisted in doing so by its self and Self (with the personality in control of when this assistance can be given). The spirit part of human souls and the energy part, which composes their respective lifeforms, are approximately equal in their abilities to think. This means that souls are approximately equally created from the thought of spirit and energy. On the higher mental plane, the balance of the thought between these two parts of a human soul reduces the forces within a human soul through structure. This balance also keeps both the group soul's and human soul's consciousness relatively high because each is as aware as the amount that it is thinking. Human souls can give about as much as they can sense, which causes them to have relatively high consciousness. Human souls are conscious enough to always understand God's growth, or life, at their particular levels of thought. Human souls can think hundreds of times better than the more advanced animal group souls can, because of the synergy and synthesis in the use of all seven rays. Some of this improvement comes from the help in higher mental plane thought by an OverSoul that has fully developed the lowest part of its three bodies. This part, or the causal body, in a human contains solar devas that are semi-conscious of themselves on all of the higher mental sub-sub-planes. A group soul's causal body, which was given to it by its OverSoul, has solar devas only on the third tier of the higher mental sub-planes. This causal body is itself developed to a degree that is commensurate with its kingdom's and the group soul's development. By far, humans souls are the more capable of creating conceptual thought, which group souls usually can barely achieve at all.

132. space—the first two parts of God's mind, of choices/will and love/consciousness, when separated create space and a lack of God's thought; this lack is darkness. Space, or a lack of light, obstructs God's thought because it separates the two component parts of thought, of choices/will and love/consciousness, from each other. Space can increase dark or even evil thought because these types of thought use space to separate their connected choices from those of God. Interestingly, even evil thought must *join* some choices in connectivity, despite the fact that they are in a direction away from God's direction. Thus too much space—if it actually enters evil's thought—can reduce its thought. Evil attempts to overcome this limitation through crystallizing and balancing the space so that it is not *within* evil's thought, just between its thought and light, or between its thought and God's thought. When God sacrificially separated its three parts of mind, the result of the first two parts becoming separated was the space of our entire universe, of seven dimensions of time and space.

133. spirit—the sacrificed part of a Monad's thought, with that part having lost its ability to think in omnipresence. This occurred because it decided to limit itself in order to create more life, or more of God's growth, on a planet within the dimensions lower than the monadic. Spirit is composed of only thought, and it begins by thinking in the thought of the spiritual plane Ray Lord's thought at the atomic level of the plane. From this point much of the spirit descends onto lower sub-planes and planes because it cannot adequately inform energy for the energy to have sense at the higher levels of time and space. Spirit is separated from other spirit by its ability to inform energy. The amount of spiritual thought that is *given* to energy collectivizes the spiritual thought into distinct groups of thought. This is done according to the amount of groups of energies transmitting very slight thought that is in need of the greater thought of the spirit's giving, or its consciousness. An electrical attraction is established between each amount and type of spiritual thought and the amount of and type of a collection of energy and its very slight thought. On the lower planes, some spirit has less total thought than the total thought of all the surrounding *involutionary* energy that is self-focused on gaining larger thought that lacks intelligence. Without assistance from higher spirit, this spirit then becomes darker, or "fallen," because it cannot think in the Ray Lord's direction any more than the gravity, or collective involutionary energies, of that plane can. Spirit needs to inform, or increase the thought of, its associated energy, to create a form of life or of pre-life that can then give spirit information about both other energy and spirit. It is this interplay of spirit and energy that creates life, or God's growth.

134. spiritual—anything that creates more of God's thought, which is the first two parts of God's mind joined together, and produces light. While someone or something is creating more of God's thought, it is creating itself more into a part of God and is simultaneously becoming more spiritual. Spirit is composed only of the first two parts of God's mind, and is therefore the root word of "spiritual."

135. spiritual adult—adults are those who can *use* complete capabilities of senses and thought as they so choose. Spiritual adults are those who can *use* their spiritual senses and thought within the intuitional lower bodies as they choose to create virtue with these senses and thought. The majority of people who reach spiritual adulthood develop their intuitional senses and the ability to think within the intuitional body by the age of twenty-eight. Spiritual adults usually gain full use of these senses by age thirty-five. Those who have bodies with senses and thought that they could use, but chose to not do so within seven years of a body's sense and thought becoming fully available to them, usually begin to lose some of both those senses and the thought during the following seven years. For example, those very few people who have some sense and thought in the body that is a part of the spiritual dimension develop that sense and thought by the age of thirty-five; they need to use them by age forty-two, and if they choose not to, they will lose a significant amount of both the sense and that thought by age forty-nine.

136. spiritual discipline—the (lower) self- and/or (higher) Self-imposed limitation on guiding spiritual thought and its created sense, in order to improve the sense and body the thought is in, so that eventually higher levels of spiritual thought are created (i.e., more choices are created that are in God's direction, or in the direction of light). Those who practice spiritual discipline are referred to as spiritual disciples. Monads, which do not have selves or Selves, create changes through pure will, or extremely consistent thoughts that are shared in omnipresence. Those beings (including humans) who have selves or Selves need to choose to limit their selves so that they can spiritually grow. For humans an average of seven hundred incarnations can be lived before spiritual discipline is enacted on a consistent basis throughout most of a lifetime.

137. suffering—the sense, or awareness, of having lost both consciousness and equal levels of self. Suffering occurs by the chosen thought of beings whose existence cannot be supported by selfish thought that separates God's three parts of mind within their own minds. This results in the diminishing of their minds. Beings that have selves need to unify their minds through giving a majority of the amount and balance of the three parts of God's mind, creating a self whose giving of thought keeps its lifeform integrated. Generally it is humans who fall under this definition because most animals and members of lower kingdoms use their respective group souls and Selves more than their selves to produce their limited consciousness. Except for very advanced humans, the self creates most of the consciousness within humans. As people are selfish, their respective selves diminish, and as a person becomes aware of her or his loss of existence, she or he suffers through a loss in understanding her or his life, or a loss of meaning while the fear of death greatly increases within that person.

138. sutratma—the will of the Monad as a ray, or field of thought that affects the energy within the permanent atoms and energy spheres of centers, which keeps these energies focused and receptive to creating life. The will, or consistent thought, is for the energies in a body to respond to the informing thought of all spirit that is attempting to integrate the body. Without the sutratma, most energy would at *some* times fail to integrate with the spirit, which would cause the body to fail to maintain life.

139. Teacher—(spelled with an uppercase "t") an advanced human initiate or a Master, who creates new knowledge that he or she teaches in order to help raise the consciousness and levels of virtue creation within those whom he or she teaches. Because most spiritual human teachers seldom if ever create new knowledge, they are not Teachers. Finding a Teacher is a rare event; they are most often found in groups that are providing world service.

140. thought—two or more choices either in the same direction or connected together in similar ways, with these choices being able to further limit the field that they are contained within. This means that the thought can cause other thoughts to be created through the same similarity in the connections of their choices. Thought is the connection of choices that establishes a particular direction to the choices; then these directed choices *must* limit the field they are in by getting other choices to further follow their direction.

141. thread—a ray that connects more than one source of spiritual thought to the thought of energy that the spirit is helping to inform. This field of thought that is focused on energy helps to maintain the integrity in a lifeform.

142. time—a component of space as a measure of the probability that the space will rejoin into the first two parts of God's mind and become light. Time separates from space when there is a lack of God's thought to increase the probability that space will rejoin into light. Time is mathematical by being a probability, and is the added dimensional part of the fifth plane wherein it (time) is fully separated from space, because the probability is that more darkness (space) than light will be created by the thought that is present. Time, in human terms, usually has three parts to it: the past, the present, and the future as it (time) separates from space and then further splits. Time can be fractured even more as a result of selfish thought—sometimes having existence mentally as five parts. The more that time is separated from space by thought that is selfish, or not like God's, the more energy that manifests. Space curves around time as time separates from it, and space appears curved by the energy that is manifested at the same time. Space actually does curve around the time because the space is separating, or reducing the probabilities that time will cause the space to rejoin and lessen. As a result, the space stretches around the time at varying degrees, depending upon how much the time in each event is separated by selfish thought. The variances cause a vortex of time that is separated from space to connect to and to move away from each event. Time as a dimensional part of space, when fully separated, structures events (a series of groups of energies connected together by similar thought) in an order that is related to the way in which each thought is connected to another thought. This structure is referred to as logic. Just as thought is created by choices that are connected together and can limit the field they are in by increasing the probability that other choices will become similarly connected, when thoughts are connected together in similar fashion but not at the same time, logic is created. Time that is separated from space no longer connects events together all at once—in a Now—and has to connect them together in an order of re-creating the separated causes and effects, so that each effect can be understood concerning its connection to a cause. Separated time creates structure, and correct structure leads to logical thought that somewhat rejoins time. Time as a full separated dimension exists on the mental plane, where structure balances forces in the energies of events—allowing time to be reasonably constructed as a whole, but separate, dimension from space. Above the mental plane, time is no longer completely separate from space because there is more intelligent activity than manifested energy within any event. This circumstance also creates more light than space between Beings. On the higher dimensions, all Beings touch, or sense as one with (or think as one monadically with), each other in at least one of three ways. The outside of each dimension grows in size because the speed of the Ray Lord's thought (light) vastly increases the field of God's mind, while the inside space between atoms, Beings, and senses decreases. There is less total *amount* of space within the higher dimensions, as light replaces much of the space within each higher dimension above the mental. The greater the levels of light, the larger the dimension *and* the less time that is separated in any way from the space that remains. For example, on the intuitional plane there is no place that is completely dark because the space everywhere has been enlightened in one of three ways (through omniscience, or all-knowledge). Thus time on that plane is joined with space—creating the light—in one of the three possible ways.

143. time dilation—the effect of time separating from space, caused by the creation of lesser amounts of intelligent activity and the manifestation of more energy. The more that time is separated from space the faster it is used, or the more time that is required to create activity. Time dilation is the relationship of time and space in one dimensional part of our universe, using time much more than another dimension. The dilated time location is the part of time and space that is used *less* to achieve the same level of activity (making that activity more intelligent). Beings who live in dilated time in comparison to others live using less time per activity and therefore have much more time in which to live. In general, each higher dimension of our universe has greater levels of time dilation than does the one below it.

144. transcendence—ascendance is the elevation of thought to beyond the speed of light of a plane. Transcendence is ascendance for an entire universe. To achieve transcendence, a Being needs to ascend past a "ring-pass-not," or a barrier imposed by all prior "self-" limitation, and must elevate *all* thought within itself to beyond the lower levels of light.

145. transfiguration—the changing of form's structure through the comparison of light to darkness within the form, with the structure becoming completely balanced in forces at the end of the process.

146. transformation—the changing of consciousness from a lower to a higher level of understanding oneness. Each level usually corresponds to an ability to create more of either pre-life or life in steps that correspond to the development of senses and bodies on additional planes.

147. transmutation—the changing of energy from one state of density to another, either using or giving off power.

148. truth—the mental cosmic virtue. It is created by balancing all of the forces created within time and space by opposing energies that come from mental thought. Truth is relative because as knowledge is added into the present level of thought, mentally, the forces become imbalanced and the concepts and thoughtforms need to be changed in relationship to one another. Truth is also absolute, because at any one time—within a mental Now—there exists only one truth that will balance the forces within any one concept and its connected thoughtforms. Below the atomic level of the mental plane, truth is relative even for a specific event in time and space, since higher levels of the same truth exist within larger concepts.

149. universe—a field of thought that is great enough to be completely separated from any larger field of thought that would help the smaller field's existing thought to better connect together. Thus any Being who serves within our universe by some form of creation is limited to keeping its consciousness, or its means of connecting its own thought, outside our universe. Also, the Creator of our universe must limit its thought that has contact with our universe to only the thought (three parts of its mind) that it originally gave to our universe. This is the way in which a universe nullifies all cosmic fire, or all electrical attraction, that would otherwise be towards fields outside its own. This nullification takes place by the will of the universe's Creator having so chosen.

150. virtue, cosmic—the co-participating effect of some amount of a cosmic Ray Lord's thought focused on some amount of energy, when, as a result, the energy thinks more as the Ray Lord. The virtue then is the effect of the light in the form, which returns the form to a state of greater intelligent activity.

The type of virtue created is based upon the quality of the Ray Lord's thought, or the amount of consciousness in the thought as it affects the light's choices and sacrifices. The cosmic virtue of each of the seven planes creates the greatest amount of intelligent activity that is possible on that plane.

151. virus—a lifeform that is a pre-life semi-organic mineral when it is not using a part of a center from a host. This pre-life state is its dormant state. When using a part of a center, the virus becomes alive and is capable of prolific growth. The reason is that the virus does not, usually, need to create a complete mechanism for reproduction because it is using much of the host's DNA, enabling itself to sometimes create only the RNA part of the helix. Viruses mostly exist between the mineral and vegetable (plant) kingdoms. Viruses can be very dangerous to higher forms of life for two main reasons. The first is that viruses adapt so quickly. The second is that they can transmute energy or form in such a wide range of densities—several etheric sub-planes—often, in the process, changing their methods of infection and of consuming retained energies, or of creating disease, within the host.

152. webs, of retained energies—the joining of the illusions, as retained energies, within two adjacent bodies inter-dimensionally. The webs are created by the very strong synthesizing thought of the personality as it collects information from the centers and brains of each of its lower three bodies that have retained energies in their centers. The thought links together the person's retained energies on two different dimensions, causing a temporary joining into a web-like structure at the mid-point between the two bodies. When the personality is focused on integrating the person, the senses and their information from one body cannot be directly connected to those of another unless they are first synthesized by the personality, which resides on the fourth mental sub-plane within the mental unit. Also, for the personality to be integrated the consciousness of a person needs to stay focused in the body where the consciousness thread is most focused on life. Once the personality focuses less or not at all on integrating the person and his or her senses, e.g., through sleep, drugs, or trauma to a web, information can flow freely without first being synthesized and *controlled* by the personality and sometimes its self. Then the consciousness of a person can move between bodies. If asleep, a person's consciousness will be mostly absent because of a lack of self; if awake and reasonably conscious, a person can travel to whatever level of another dimension he or she can remain loving—giving (conscious) on. One web for each type of center exists between the etheric and astral bodies and, likewise, another web exists between each pair of matching centers of the astral and mental bodies. The structure of each web is stored in the permanent atom of each body. Because of the structures' intricacy and because the integrating forces prevent the structures from forming at a later time, they can be created only prior to the personality fully integrating the human. Because the only time that the full structure exists with a lack of forces is just prior to a fully developed lifetime, the webs cannot be either created or repaired at any other time.

153. will—the consistency of the same choice, even when some other choices would be easier to connect together than the choices are that are connected together by the will. Will is usually a function of mind seeking to create more, in order to continue to be and possibly to grow. The more of the same choices that exist within a field of probability, the greater the levels of will. Will often leads to sacrifice to limit choices in order to effect a certain type of creation and growth.

154. wrong speech—speech that increases illusion in one or more bodies of others. The majority of wrong speech causes an increase in astral illusion, by creating additional emotional responses rather than loving ones, in others.

155. yoga—a method of unifying the seven senses in one of the bodies within a being. There are three major yogas that each unify one of the three lower bodies of humans. Each yoga supercedes the prior one in its effectiveness because of the overall advancement in sense development within that body by the development of the corresponding major race and its sub-races. What is likely to be the last major mental yoga was invented in A.D. 1989 by the author, and is, subsequently, being further developed in its methods with the assistance of the Ageless Wisdom Distributors group.

Part A

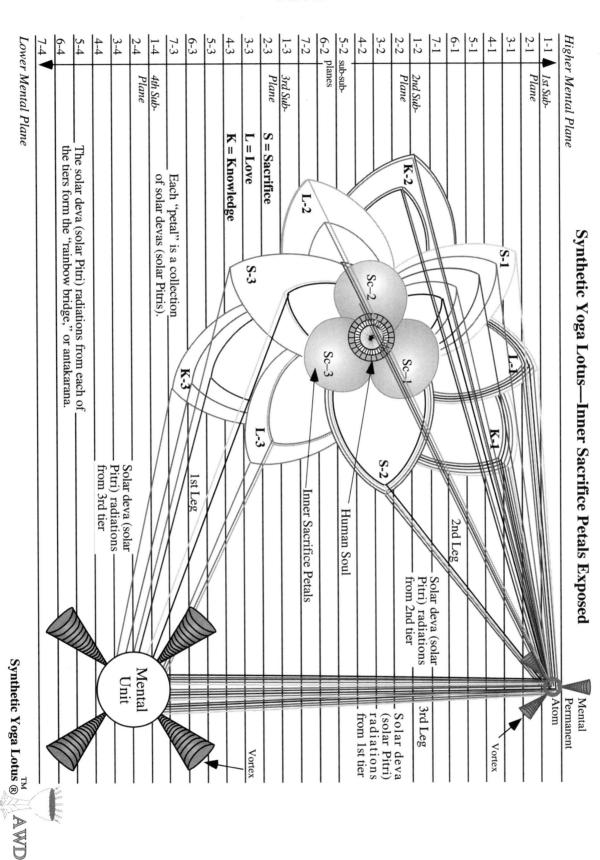

Synthetic Yoga Lotus—Inner Sacrifice Petals Exposed

Higher Mental Plane

1-1 1st Sub-Plane
2-1
3-1
4-1
5-1
6-1
7-1
1-2 2nd Sub-Plane
2-2
3-2
4-2
5-2 sub-sub-planes
6-2
7-2
1-3 3rd Sub-Plane
2-3
3-3 S = Sacrifice
4-3 L = Love
5-3 K = Knowledge
6-3
7-3
1-4 4th Sub-Plane
2-4
3-4
4-4
5-4
6-4
7-4

Lower Mental Plane

K-2
L-2
S-1
S-3
L-1
K-3
L-3
K-1
S-2
Sc-2
Sc-3
Sc-1
Human Soul
Inner Sacrifice Petals
1st Leg
2nd Leg
3rd Leg
Solar deva (solar Pitri) radiations from 2nd tier
Solar deva (solar Pitri) radiations from 1st tier
Vortex
Mental Permanent Atom
Mental Unit
Vortex
Solar deva (solar Pitri) radiations from 3rd tier

Each "petal" is a collection of solar devas (solar Pitris).

The solar deva (solar Pitri) radiations from each of the tiers form the "rainbow bridge," or antakarana.

Synthetic Yoga Lotus® ™ AWD

Part B

Synthetic Yoga Lotus—Inner Sacrifice Petals Hidden

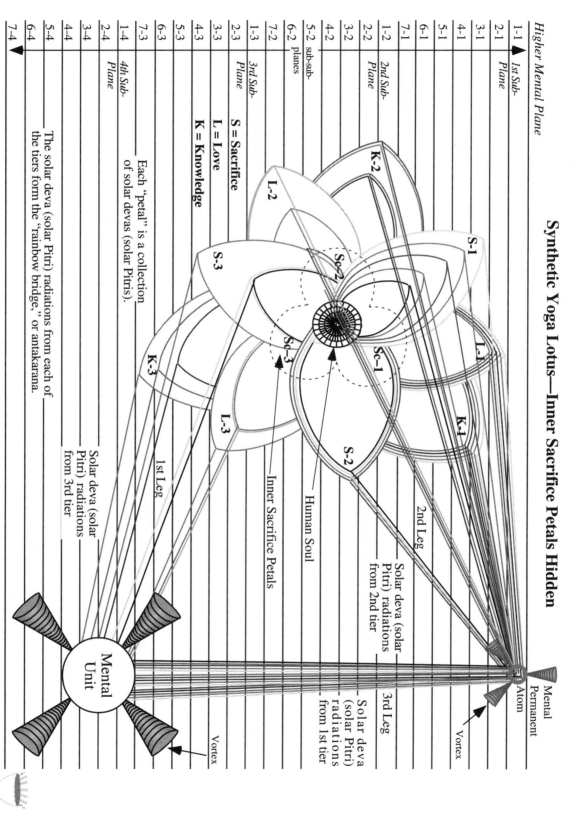

Higher Mental Plane

1-1
2-1 1st Sub-
3-1 Plane
4-1
5-1
6-1
7-1
1-2 2nd Sub-
2-2 Plane
3-2
4-2
5-2 sub-sub-
6-2 planes
7-2
1-3 3rd Sub-
2-3 Plane S = Sacrifice
3-3 L = Love
4-3 K = Knowledge
5-3
6-3
7-3
1-4 4th Sub-
2-4 Plane
3-4
4-4
5-4
6-4
7-4

Lower Mental Plane

K-2
L-2
S-1
S-3
Sc-2
L-1
K-3
Sc-3
Sc-1
L-3
K-1
S-2

Each "petal" is a collection
of solar devas (solar Pitris).

The solar deva (solar Pitri) radiations from each of
the tiers form the "rainbow bridge," or antakarana.

Inner Sacrifice Petals

Human Soul

Solar deva (solar
Pitri) radiations
from 2nd tier

2nd Leg

Solar deva
(solar Pitri)
radiations
from 1st tier

3rd Leg

Vortex

Mental
Permanent
Atom

Solar deva (solar
Pitri) radiations
from 3rd tier

1st Leg

Vortex

Mental
Unit

Part C

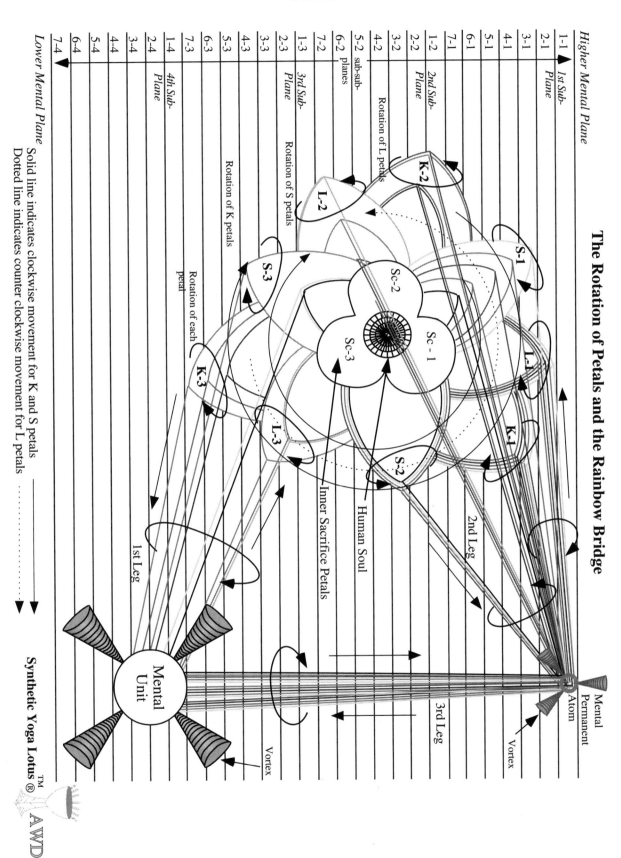

The Rotation of Petals and the Rainbow Bridge

Part D

CONTACT PAGE

Ageless Wisdom Distributors and the author can be contacted in the following ways:

By writing to…1628 E. Southern Avenue, Suite 9-pmb122; Tempe, AZ 85282-5685

By calling…480 966-3132

Via e-mail… ask@agelesswisdom.com

Educational institutions as well as groups that are creating virtue may be able to receive, directly from the publisher, volume discounts on purchases of *Life's Hidden Meaning*. Single copies of *Life's Hidden Meaning* are also available through the publisher, but individuals are encouraged to instead purchase from retailers, possibly those local to their areas. The publisher does maintain a list of those retailers who have ordered directly from the publisher and are currently stocking the book. The three illustrations in the appendix, on the three immediately-preceding pages, are available in vibrant full color on 8½" x 11" photographic film at a resolution of 2400 dpi (very high quality). These illustrations of the Exposed and Hidden Inner Sacrifice Petals of the Synthetic Yoga Lotus©™ and an open Synthetic Yoga Lotus with Rotations©™ can be purchased directly from Ageless Wisdom Distributors. Each photographic-type print is mounted on an easily removable plastic-board backing. The prices for these prints are as follows:. For any one of the three: $15.00 US; for any two of the three: $26.00 US; for all three: $35.00 US. These prices are guaranteed through December 31, 2007. Foreign orders are accepted for an additional $4.00 to cover the extra postage. Checks, money orders and major credit cards are all acceptable means of payment. Checks and money orders can be mailed to the above address. Orders using a major credit card can be called in to the telephone number listed above. Also, information about ordering from the Ageless Wisdom Distributors' Internet website can be found at http://www.agelesswisdom.com.